Ali Kazerani
COURTESY OF ALI KAZERANI

Nina Kostenko
COURTESY OF NINA KOSTENKO

Joseph Kurtz
COURTESY OF MOSHE RAPPS

Ulfat Farah Matin
COURTESY OF ULFAT FARAH MATIN

Joshua Mok
COURTESY OF JOSHUA MOK

Janice Mumberson
COURTESY OF JANICE MUMBERSON

Miguel Rolo
COURTESY OF MIGUEL ROLO

Tracy Singh
COURTESY OF TRACY SINGH

Stephanie Stone
COURTESY OF STEPHANIE STONE

Michael Strasser
COURTESY OF MICHAEL STRASSER

Dave J. Thibault
COURTESY OF DAVE J. THIBAULT

Tracy Yee
COURTESY OF TRACY YEE

Stephanie Yu Foon Moi
COURTESY OF VANESSA YU FOON MOI

Christina Zarandi
COURTESY OF CHRISTINA ZARANDI

Absent

Anton Allen, Michelle Alliston, Abbas Basravi, Arun Chetram, Sandy Chohan, Patrick Choo, Aniesha Coach, Linda Cooke, Luca Corrente, Candace DeBarros, Cassandra De Santis, Lorenzo Di Nino, Shaan Dubey, Anges Gendelman, Ridah Ghoari, Phoebe Hanna, Mumbi Kamau, Henry Ly, Cassie Ma, Pia Marino, Miriam Martin, Deniz Melen, Nihit Narang, Vivian Ng, Steven Park, Peter Pavlovic, Stephanie Guglietta Petrelli, Nadia Pulla, Riannon Raskin, Sara Rezafard, Rehan Shaikh, Sujitha Suntharalingam, Salman Vajid

CENGAGE Learning™

CENGAGENOW

Just What You Need to Know and Do NOW!

CengageNOW is an online teaching and learning resource that provides you more control in less time and delivers better student outcomes—NOW!

What instructors are saying...

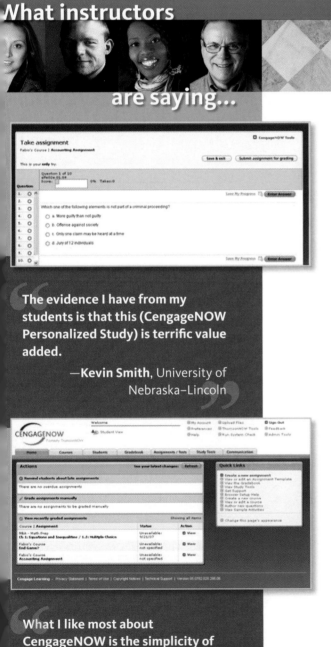

> The evidence I have from my students is that this (CengageNOW Personalized Study) is terrific value added.
>
> —**Kevin Smith**, University of Nebraska–Lincoln

> What I like most about CengageNOW is the simplicity of using it...
>
> —**Mina Yavari**, Hancock College

CENGAGENOW IS AN ONLINE TEACHING AND LEARNING RESOURCE.

CengageNOW offers all of your teaching and learning resources in one intuitive program organized around the essential activities you perform for class - lecturing, creating assignments, grading, quizzing, and tracking student progress and performance. CengageNOW's intuitive "tabbed" design allows you to navigate to all key functions with a single click and a unique homepage tell you just what needs to be done and when. CengageNOW, in most cases, provides students access to an integrated eBook, interactive tutorials, videos, animations, games, and other multimedia tools to help them get the most out of your course.

CENGAGENOW PROVIDES MORE CONTROL IN LESS TIME

CengageNOW's flexible assignment and grade book options provides you more control while saving you valuable time in planning and managing your course assignments. With CengageNOW, you can automatically grade all assignments, weigh grades, choose points or percentages and set the number of attempts and due dates per problem to best suit your overall course plan.

CENGAGENOW DELIVERS BETTER STUDENT OUTCOMES

CengageNOW Personalized Study; a diagnostic tool (featuring a chapter specific Pre-test, Study Plan, and Post-test) empowers students to master concepts, prepare for exams, and be more involved in class. It's easy to assign and if you want, results will automatically post to your grade book. Results to Personalize Study provide immediate and ongoing feedback regarding what students are mastering and why they're not - to both you and the student. In most cases, Personalized Study links to an integrated eBook so students can easily review topics.

academic.cengage.com/now

CengageNOW MAKES IT EASIER TO DO WHAT YOU ALREADY DO.

Designed by instructors for instructors, CengageNOW mirrors your natural workflow and provides time-saving, performance-enhancing tools for you and your students—all in one program!

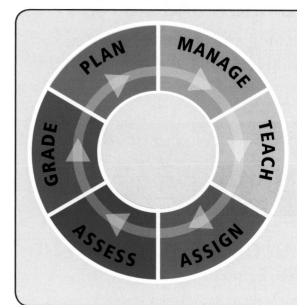

YOU CAN USE CENGAGENOW TO...

- ▶ **Plan** your curriculum;
- ▶ **Manage** your course and communicate with students;
- ▶ **Teach** with more freedom;
- ▶ **Assign** practice or homework to reinforce key concepts;
- ▶ **Assess** student performance outcomes;
- ▶ **Grade** with efficiency and control to get the results you want.

STUDENTS CAN USE CENGAGENOW TO...

- ▶ **Manage** their time;
- ▶ **Prepare** for class;
- ▶ **Practice & Reinforce** key concepts learned in class;
- ▶ **Study** for exams more effectively;
- ▶ **Get the Grade** they want.

The flexibility of CengageNOW allows you to use a single aspect of the program, or for maximum power and effectiveness, to use all of the teaching and learning resources to create and customize your own material to match your course objectives.

CENGAGENOW SEAMLESSLY INTEGRATES WITH POPULAR COURSE MANAGEMENT PROGRAMS

CengageNOW on Blackboard, WebCT, and eCollege provides students with seamless single sign-on access to CengageNOW through the school's course management system (CMS). After entering a simple access code just once at the beginning of the term, students get seamless access to both their CMS and CengageNOW textbook specific assignments and activities, with results flowing to your Blackboard, WebCT, or eCollege gradebook. Rich content, seamless integration with CengageNOW functionality, and only one gradebook to manage.

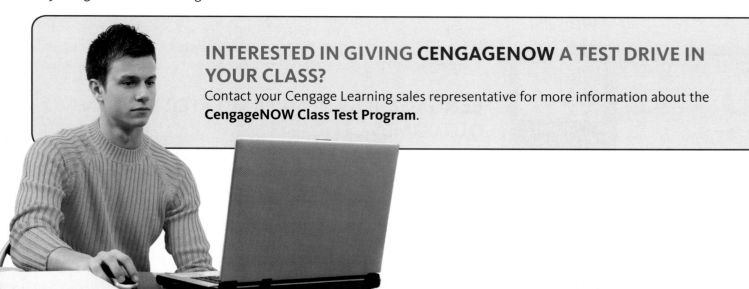

INTERESTED IN GIVING CENGAGENOW A TEST DRIVE IN YOUR CLASS?

Contact your Cengage Learning sales representative for more information about the **CengageNOW Class Test Program**.

CONTEMPORARY MARKETING

CONTEMPORARY MARKETING

SECOND CANADIAN EDITION

DAVID L. KURTZ
University of Arkansas

H.F. (HERB) MACKENZIE
Brock University

KIM SNOW
York University

NELSON / EDUCATION

NELSON / E D U C A T I O N

Contemporary Marketing, Second Canadian Edition

by Louis E. Boone, David E. Kurtz, H.F. (Herb) Mackenzie, and Kim Snow

Associate Vice President, Editorial Director:
Evelyn Veitch

Editor-in-Chief, Higher Education:
Anne Williams

Executive Editor:
Jackie Wood/Amie Plourde

Marketing Manager:
Kathaleen McCormick

Developmental Editor:
Lesley Mann

Photo Researcher and Permissions Coordinator:
David Strand

Content Production Manager:
Susan Wong

Production Service:
Pre-Press PMG

Copy Editor:
Wendy Thomas

Proofreader:
Nicole Ferraro

Indexer:
Rebecca Francescatti

Manufacturing Manager:
Joanne McNeil

Design Director:
Ken Phipps

Managing Designer:
Katherine Strain

Interior Design:
Liz Harasymczuk Design

Cover Design:
Martyn Schmoll

Cover Image:
Carsten Reisinger/Shutterstock

Compositor:
Pre-Press PMG

Printer:
Courier

Library and Archives Canada Cataloguing in Publication

Kurtz, David L. Contemporary marketing / David L. Kurtz, H.F. MacKenzie, Kim Snow. — 2nd Canadian ed.

Includes bibliographical references and index. ISBN 978-0-17-650003-0

1. Marketing—Textbooks. I. MacKenzie, H. F. II. Snow, Kim, 1956- III. Title.

HF5415.K88 2009 658.8
C2009-900027-X 302.23'0971
C2001-903232-3

ISBN-13: 978-0-17-650003-0
ISBN-10: 0-17-650003-0

Additional reoccurring photo credits:

Page 17: Ugnutina/Shutterstock; Page 19: Merve Poray/Shutterstock; Page 23: Bruce Parrott/Shutterstock; Page 31: Bocos Benedict/Shutterstock; Page 36: maxstockphoto/Shutterstock; Page 41: iStockphoto/Wendell Franks, mashe/Shutterstock; Page 47: iDesign/Shutterstock; Page 74: Merve Poray/Shutterstock; Page 124: Logo used with permission of Second City
Part Opener blue background; Opening vignette orange banner; Assessment Checkmark; Etiquette Tips for Marketing Professionals box banner; Go Green box banner; Scales of Justice icon; Solving an Ethical Controversy box banner; Video Case reel icon; Appendix orange banner; Second City logo

This edition is dedicated to Louis E. "Gene" Boone.

Dear Principles of Marketing Student:

Contemporary Marketing, Second Canadian Edition, was written for you. Our goal is to provide you with a truly "contemporary" resource containing the most current and relevant marketing information available.

An important theme of this book is connecting with the customer. We've done this by writing with you in mind. From student focus groups we learned what features work and what needed improvement. New **Go Green** boxes in every chapter reflect your concern for environmental awareness in marketing, from "Job Opportunities Are Greening" to "The Economics of Green." Chapter-opening features examine a successful product or organization and conclude with a short **connecting with customers** summary that helps you evaluate how this success was achieved. The popular **Marketing Success** and **Marketing Failure** boxes were retained and updated, since nothing teaches like examples. We've even made it easier for you to connect with what you've studied by providing answers to the chapter self-assessment questions—a perfect way to verify you've understood all the key concepts.

In addition, we've included many features in the book that will not only help you to excel in this course, but will teach you how to market your skills to prospective employers.

A special prologue to the text, **"Planning a Career in Marketing,"** provides you with a look at the trends and opportunities available for future marketers in an increasingly diversified professional field. It describes essential elements of an effective résumé and discusses the latest trends in electronic job searches. The prologue also provides answers to many of the questions typically asked by applicants.

Marketer's Minute end-of-part interviews get one-on-one with marketing professionals, who share with you how their background and education have contributed to their career achievements. They offer practical tips and advice on starting a career in marketing.

Etiquette Tips for Marketing Professionals in each chapter equip you with a winning playbook for business and social settings. Topics include "How to Deal with Rude People," "How to Conduct Phone Surveys," "Preparing an Effective Direct-Mail Piece," and many more.

Solving an Ethical Controversy features integrated in each chapter provide you with a thorough treatment of many of the ethical issues affecting marketing. They list the pros and cons of real-world ethics quandaries such as "Too Much Data, Not Enough Protection?" and "How Should Buying Firms Deal with Vendors?" The end-of-chapter **Ethics Exercises** give you additional hands-on experience with ethical decisions.

Contemporary Marketing, Second Canadian Edition, is truly student-focused. Why are we so certain that you will find the text easy-to-understand, lively, and engaging? Because a dedicated group of marketing students at York University worked with us on the text to help achieve this goal. They generously donated their time to conduct research and contribute many of the examples in the text. We're convinced that this book truly connects with our customers. We hope you agree.

H. F. (Herb) MacKenzie

Kim Snow

Contemporary Marketing, Second Canadian Edition, helps you connect with your customers!

Contemporary Marketing, Second Canadian Edition, covers all the hot issues and latest developments, immersing students in the excitement of the dynamic marketing arena:

OPENING VIGNETTES

Opening vignettes reflect the exciting theme of the Second Canadian Edition and set the stage for each chapter as they turn the spotlight on how real-life companies rise to the marketing challenge of connecting with their customers!

GO GREEN

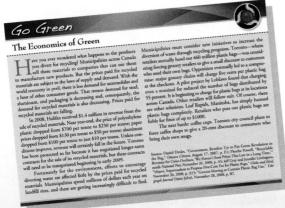

Go Green boxes help students understand how environmental awareness can make a difference in marketing.

ETHICS EXERCISES

End-of-chapter **Ethics Exercises** give students hands-on experience grappling with ethical decisions.

ETHICS EXERCISE

As mentioned in the chapter, some analysts predict that bar codes may soon be replaced by a wireless technology called *radio frequency identification (RFID)*. RFID is a system of installing tags containing tiny computer chips on, say, supermarket items. These chips automatically radio the location of the item to a computer network where inventory data are stored, letting store managers know not only where the item is at all times but also when and where it was made and its colour and size. Proponents of the idea believe RFID will cut costs and simplify inventory tracking and reordering. It may also allow marketers to respond quickly to shifts in demand, avoid under- and overstocking, and reduce spoilage by automatically removing outdated perishables from the shelves. Privacy advocates, however, think the chips provide too much product-preference information that might be identified with individual consumers. In the meantime, Wal-Mart is asking its top suppliers to begin using the new technology on products stocked by the giant retailer.

1. Do you think RFID poses a threat to consumer privacy? Why or why not?
2. Do you think the technology's possible benefits to marketers outweigh the potential privacy concerns? Are there also potential benefits to consumers, and if so, what are they?
3. How can marketers reassure consumers about privacy concerns if RFID comes into widespread use?

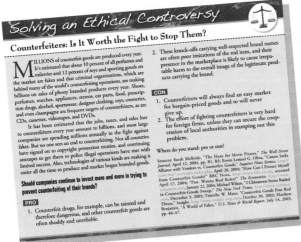

APPLYING ETHICS

Solving an Ethical Controversy features integrated in each chapter spark lively class discussions as they list the pros and cons to real-world ethics quandaries, such as "Kids, Parents, and Violent Video Games," "Energy from Ethanol: Hope or Hype?", "Too Much Data, Not Enough Protection?", and much more.

MARKETER'S MINUTE

Marketer's Minute end-of-part interviews were written and conducted by York University marketing students. They get one-on-one with marketing professionals, who share how their education and background have contributed to their career achievements as well as the success of their organizations.

assessment check 1

1.1 Define target market.

1.2 Distinguish between a consumer product and a business product.

ASSESSMENT CHECKS

Assessment Checks are brief two- or three-question checkpoints following coverage of major topics to ensure students understand core concepts before moving on to the next major topic. Suggested answers are available at the end of the chapter for self-checking.

assessment check answers

1.1 Define target market.
A target market is the specific segment of consumers most likely to purchase a particular product.

1.2 Distinguish between a consumer product and a business product.
A consumer product is purchased by the ultimate buyer for personal use. A business product is purchased for use directly or indirectly in the production of other goods and services.

State-of-the-art support readies *Contemporary Marketing,* Second Canadian Edition, students to make the connections they need!

Contemporary Marketing, Second Canadian Edition, delivers the best. Innovative supplements give students hands-on experience with real-world marketing issues and a first-hand view of the excitement in the powerfully charged marketing arena.

STUDENT SUPPLEMENTS

CengageNOW™ for *Contemporary Marketing,* Second Canadian Edition, is an online assessment-driven and student-centred tutorial that provides students with a personalized learning plan. Based on a diagnostic Pre-Test, a customized learning path is generated for each student that targets his or her study needs and helps the student to visualize, organize, practise, and master the material in the text. Media resources enhance problem-solving skills and improve conceptual understanding. An access code to CengageNOW can be bundled with any new *Contemporary Marketing,* Second Canadian Edition textbook.

Contemporary Marketing website (http://www .contemporarymarketing2.nelson.com) offers additional learning resources for students. The website, designed specifically for *Contemporary Marketing,* Second Canadian Edition, includes a Student Resources section with study aids, career information, interactive quizzes, flashcards, PowerPoint slides, CBC and Marketing Minute videos, and more.

Technically superior, *Contemporary Marketing,* Second Canadian Edition, is unrivaled!

The Second Canadian Edition of *Contemporary Marketing* offers the most technologically advanced package available. *Contemporary Marketing* takes advantage of the latest technology to bring more innovation, flexibility, and excitement to your classroom.

CengageNow for *Contemporary Marketing,* Second Canadian Edition, is an online assessment-driven and student-centred tutorial that provides students with a personalized learning plan. Based on a diagnostic Pre-Test, a customized learning path is generated for each student's personalized study needs, helping them to visualize, organize, practise, and master the material from the text. Media resources enhance problem-solving skills and improve conceptual understanding. An access code to CengageNOW for *Contemporary Marketing,* Second Canadian Edition, can be bundled with new textbooks.

The End-of-Chapter Video Package includes 18 videos to accompany the cases at the end of each chapter, enabling students to see how real companies—like Organic Valley Farms, American Apparel, and Lonely Planet—deal with various marketing scenarios.

The Second City Theater, Inc., Continuing Case Video shows how the famous comedy organization combined a creative and entrepreneurial spirit with successful marketing and business strategies. Entertaining and enlightening, these videos examine the history of the theatre company as well as the successful business practices that have allowed for its expansion and growth.

End-of-Part CBC Video Exercises will add visual impact and current, real-world examples to your lectures. The video segments from CBC programs are used as the basis for the CBC Video Exercises on the website at **http://www.contemporarymarketing2.nelson.com**.

CBC

When it comes to instructor resources, *Contemporary Marketing, Second Canadian Edition,* has no competition.

Behind every effective leader is a solid support system. *Contemporary Marketing,* Second Canadian Edition, equips instructors with the most thorough teaching tools available—bringing innovation to their fingertips.

NELSON EDUCATION TESTING ADVANTAGE

Nelson Education Ltd. believes that a good quality multiple-choice test bank can test not just what students remember, but higher-level thinking skills as well. Recognizing the importance of multiple choice testing in today's classroom, Nelson has created the Nelson Education Testing Advantage program (NETA) to ensure the high quality of our test banks. NETA was created in partnership with David DiBattista, a 3M National Teaching Fellow and professor of psychology at Brock University. NETA ensures that test bank authors have had training in two areas: developing clear multiple choice test questions while avoiding common errors in construction, and creating multiple choice test questions that "get beyond remembering" to assess higher-level thinking. The aim of our partnership is to bring you an unprecedented level of support for multiple choice assessment. The **Test Bank** and **ExamView Computerized Test Bank** for *Contemporary Marketing* were developed under the NETA program. We're sure you'll be impressed with the results!

INSTRUCTOR'S MANUAL & MEDIA GUIDE

The Instructor's Manual with Collaborative Learning Exercises, Media Guide, and Nelson Education Testing Advantage (NETA) Support provides an excellent resource for instructors at every stage of the game—from its guidelines for first-year instructors to its fresh ideas for veteran marketing professors. Each chapter of the IM begins with a complete set of teaching tools, including Annotated Chapter Objectives, Lecture Outlines, and guidelines for incorporating PowerPoint slides into your lectures. In addition, the *Instructor's Manual* includes complete solutions to all the end-of-chapter questions, exercises, and cases. At the end of the IM is a media guide that includes information for the media elements of the text, including all 18 chapter video cases and the Second City Theater running video case. The IM also includes guidelines to writing effective multiple choice questions—part of our Nelson Education Testing Advantage (NETA) support.

POWERPOINT® PRESENTATION SLIDES

PowerPoint® Presentation Slides provide a complete teaching experience for instructors and a memorable learning experience for students. The *Expanded* presentation includes 40 to 50 slides per chapter. It outlines and explains the main chapter concepts and includes figures from the text to enhance student learning. The *Basic* version covers key chapter contents for students.

VIDEO PACKAGE

The **18 End-of-Chapter Video Cases** highlight marketers as small as The Little Guys Home Electronics and as large as BP. Each gives students a glimpse into how marketers actually work, strategize, and meet challenges in the real world. The written cases appear at the end of the book, and the video segments are available on DVD.

The Second City Theater, Inc., Continuing Case Video is a seven-part running case. The video and accompanying written cases, which appear at the end of each part of the text, enable students to build on their knowledge as they follow the famous comedy organization through its development into a successful business enterprise. The video segments are available on DVD.

Marketer's Minute interviews and CBC videos have been created for use at the end of each part of the text. The video segments are available on the *Contemporary Marketing* website, and CBC vidio teaching notes are included in the *Instructor's Manual & Media Guide.*

SUPPORT WEBSITE

The *Contemporary Marketing* website (**http://www.contemporarymarketing2.nelson.com**) contains a complete array of useful resources for both instructors and students, including:

- **Instructor Resource Centre,** where the text supplements are available in electronic format for viewing or downloading.

- **Student Resource Centre,** featuring career information, interactive quizzes, flashcards, PowerPoint slides, CBC and Marketer's Minute videos, and more.

Because the business world moves at an unprecedented pace today, the Principles of Marketing course must race to keep up. Trends, strategies, and practices are constantly changing, though a few things remain the same—the need for excellence and the necessity to evolve and innovate.

You've come to trust *Contemporary Marketing* to cover every aspect of marketing with a critical but fair eye. A hallmark of the book is its focus on how marketing concepts apply to today's business issues. But *Contemporary Marketing,* Second Canadian Edition, goes far beyond ensuring overall accuracy and quality. Instructors have come to expect additional qualities from an introductory marketing text: complete, easy-to-understand coverage of all relevant topics in a lively, engaging writing style that makes students forget that they are reading a postsecondary-level textbook. You'll find this and so much more in *Contemporary Marketing*.

FEATURES OF THE SECOND CANADIAN EDITION

Here are just a few of the important themes, trends, and practices we've focused on for this edition:

- *Connecting with customers*: Every opening vignette in the text now concludes with a short summary entitled "Connecting with the Customer." This enhances the discussion of whatever organization or product was discussed in that opening scenario and asks students to think critically about what they have done and continue to do to remain at the top of their markets. Understanding this connection can be a student's best help in understanding how marketing is conducted every day.

- *Planning a Career in Marketing*: Career planning and awareness begin on page 1 of the text with the prologue Planning a Career in Marketing, adapted by Stéfan Danis, CEO and Chief Talent Officer, and his team of experts at Mandrake Executive Search. (Mandrake is Canada's largest executive search firm with a specialty in the marketing field.) This popular feature ensures that students in Principles of Marketing courses keep up with the newest trends and shifts in career fields and offers practical insights to help students prepare for a successful business career.

- *Concise Coverage*: A common complaint among both instructors and students is that principles of marketing texts are much too long to be covered in a single term. At the same time, they quickly state that they do not want a watered-down version of a text in the form of an "essentials" edition. The authors have worked diligently to streamline the Second Canadian Edition. By eliminating the now familiar subject matter of the e-commerce chapter (Chapter 4 in the first edition) and redistributing any topics that are still required into other chapters, the overall length of the book has been reduced from 19 to 18 chapters. At the same time, wording and examples in the chapters have been tightened to reduce the overall chapter length. Opening vignettes have been pared down to one page instead of two. The result is a text that provides the rigour and comprehensiveness instructors expect but is still short enough to cover.

- *Strategic Focus*: In response to instructors who dislike the overly descriptive nature of the typical Principles of Marketing text, the Second Canadian Edition of *Contemporary Marketing* continues to place the marketing planning chapter near the beginning of the text so that it can be assigned much earlier in the term, helping to equip students with a solid foundation of strategic thinking. The appendix "Creating an Effective Marketing Plan," which immediately follows the discussion of strategic marketing planning in Chapter 2, has been streamlined for easier reading. However, it continues to provide detailed, real-life planning material and includes a planning case that illustrates the strategic marketing planning concepts discussed in the chapter. Each chapter closes with a special section assessing strategic implications of chapter concepts on marketing. Finally, an end-of-book appendix, "Financial Analysis in Marketing," provides additional strategic and analytic tools for the reader.

- *Environmental Awareness*: The ethical focus of the first edition is extended through the introduction of new Go Green boxes. Unique to the Canadian edition, these boxes describe issues in environmentally aware marketing today. How businesses respond to the issue of global warming is becoming more and more pervasive, so these Go Green boxes are sure to appeal to students by demonstrating the connection between their marketing careers and opportunities for social responsibility. Our reviewers recognized these boxes as a major strength of the text.

- *Marketoids*: Also unique to the Canadian edition are Marketoids, a trivia element in chapter margins that replaces the old "Briefly Speaking" quotations. This feature introduces Canadian content in a fun yet informative way.

- *More Cases*: Many instructors requested alternative cases to provide more flexibility for different assignments from one academic term to the next. In the Second Canadian Edition, one more case has been added to every chapter. This provides the instructor with flexibility to adjust to time constraints and multiple sections or to use different case assignments for different terms. The end-of-case questions have been fine-tuned to require more critical thinking. Overall, 60 percent of the cases are new, while 20 percent have been updated and revised.

- *End-of-Chapter Video Cases*: To provide a third case option in our end-of-chapter cases, we've produced a new video case for each and every chapter, designed to exceed your every expectation. Students need to know the basics about life in the real world of marketing and how businesses succeed and grow—but they don't need a bunch of talking heads putting them to sleep. So although we admit that you will indeed see a few talking heads, they're just there because they really do know what they're talking about, and they have something important for students to hear. But do trust us . . . the videos we've created for this new edition of *Contemporary Marketing* contain so much more! A complete set of written cases accompanies these chapter videos and can be found in the end-of-book video case appendix. The written segments contain discussion questions. As with the Second City cases, answers to the questions can be found in the *Instructor's Manual*, as can a complete video synopsis, a list of text concepts covered in the videos, and even more critical-thinking exercises. The video cases are as follows:

Chapter 1: Harley-Davidson Keeps Riders Coming Back
Chapter 2: Timbuk2's Success Is in the Bag
Chapter 3: Organic Valley Farms: Producing Food That's Good for People and the Earth
Chapter 4: Nielsen Media Research Watches the TV Watchers
Chapter 5: High Sierra Sport Company Excels in B2B
Chapter 6: Lonely Planet Brings You the World
Chapter 7: Nielsen Media Research Plays the Rating Game
Chapter 8: Harley-Davidson Rules the Road by Understanding Its Customers
Chapter 9: The Little Guys Home Electronics: Big on Customer Relationships
Chapter 10: Wild Oats Natural Marketplace: Offering Products at Their Peak
Chapter 11: Rebranding at JPMorgan Chase
Chapter 12: American Apparel: Supply Fits the Demand
Chapter 13: BP Connects with Drivers
Chapter 14: The Toledo Mud Hens: Family Fun = A Winning Strategy
Chapter 15: BP: Beyond Petroleum
Chapter 16: Harley-Davidson: Selling the Thrill
Chapter 17: Washburn Guitars: How Much Is the Maya Worth?
Chapter 18: Whirlpool: Innovation for Every Price Point

- *End-of-Part Continuing Video Case*: You've come to expect only the best from us in choosing our continuing video case company, and we've taken it one step further with our new choice. No other company combines Second City Theater's unique brand of social and political satire with successful and proven business and marketing practices. These unique practices have helped The Second City grow from a small but successful comedy troupe into a large international business. With several theatres in two countries, troupes performing every day all over the world, and performances on international cruise lines, The Second City has found a way to turn comedy into business—and in the process they've had fun! Students and instructors alike know and love many of the famous faces that started performing at Second City—Dan Aykroyd, John Candy, Martin Short, Eugene Levy, Tina Fey, Gilda Radner, John Belushi, and the list goes on and on. But how many students realize just how important good business and marketing strategies are in keeping a comedy business that started in 1959 thriving and growing all the way into 2009 and beyond? We've focused on all the aspects of The Second City Theater's marketing strategy so that students can learn—in a way that's interesting and fun. So sit back, get some popcorn, and enjoy the show! Written case segments at the end of each part of the text contain critical-thinking questions designed to provoke discussion and interaction in the classroom setting. Answers to the questions can be found in the *Instructor's Manual*, as can a complete video synopsis, a list of text concepts covered in the videos, and even more critical-thinking exercises.

KEY CHAPTER CHANGES

Here is an outline of the key changes and new features of the Second Canadian Edition.

CHAPTER 1 MARKETING: THE ART AND SCIENCE OF SATISFYING CUSTOMERS

- A new opening vignette has been added on "CV Technologies: The Ups, and Downs, and Ups, and…" This vignette was specifically written to demonstrate the importance of marketing to a firm. Instructors can discuss marketing expenses as a percentage of sales, as well as how traditional and more modern marketing techniques can be used together.

- The debate as to whether marketing is an art or a science has been introduced to this chapter.

- Go Green boxes are a new feature in every chapter of the second edition. "Job Opportunities Are Greening" is the Go Green box for Chapter 1.

- A new Etiquette Tips box has been included on "Forms of Address: Which One Do You Use, and When?"

- A new Marketing Success box entitled "A Google?" has been included.

- A new case, "Golfers Are Joining the Hybrid Club," has been added, while the second case, "How the Rolling Stones Keep Rolling," has been updated.

CHAPTER 2 STRATEGIC PLANNING AND THE MARKETING PROCESS

- The new opening vignette, "Loblaw: The Search for a Winning Strategy," is an engaging profile that everyone across Canada can relate to.

- The Go Green box explains that "Green Is a Socially Responsible Strategy."

- The new Etiquette Tips box examines "How to Handle Interruptions."

- A new Solving an Ethical Controversy box asks, "Should Retailers Ban the Salvation Army from Their Sidewalks?"

CHAPTER 3 THE MARKETING ENVIRONMENT, ETHICS, AND SOCIAL RESPONSIBILITY

- The new opening vignette focuses on "AIDS Niagara: Part of Canada's Answer to a World Problem."
- The discussion of technology has been significantly updated, with new material on Wi-Fi, RFID tags, VoIP, IPMS, etc.
- The new Etiquette Tips explores the question "To Give or Not to Give at the Office."
- "T&T Supermarket: Haw Gao Hit" is the subject of the new Marketing Success box.
- The new Solving an Ethical Controversy box queries, "Amazon: Helpful or Intrusive?"
- The Go Green box, "When It's Time to Go, Go Green," looks at really going green with natural funerals.
- Both cases in this chapter are new and timely: "General Motors: Here Today. Where Tomorrow?" and "iTunes and the Future of Music."

CHAPTER 4 CONSUMER BEHAVIOUR

- The new opening vignette asks, "Who Buys Hybrid Cars—and Why?"
- The discussion of the decision-making process is introduced at an earlier point than in the first edition, giving students an easy-to-relate-to introduction to the challenging concepts of the chapter.
- The new Solving an Ethical Controversy box examines "Kids, Parents, and Violent Video Games."
- The new Marketing Failure box focuses on "Social Media: Marketers Struggle to Get It Right."
- "Smart Cars" are the topic of this chapter's Go Green box.
- The new Etiquette Tips box looks at "Handling Angry Customers."
- A new case for Chapter 4 considers "Burger King's Whopper-Sized Portions."

CHAPTER 5 BUSINESS-TO-BUSINESS (B2B) MARKETING

- The discussion of offshoring and outsourcing has been improved, with new material included on nearshoring.
- The new Marketing Success box explores how "Boeing Soars to New Heights."
- The Go Green box topic is "From Consumer Markets to Business Markets."
- The new Solving an Ethical Controversy box asks, "How Should Buying Firms Deal with Vendors?"
- "Keeping Customers out of Voice Response Hell" is the topic of the new Etiquette Tips box.
- New cases for this chapter include "Chip Wars: Intel vs. AMD in the B2B Market" and "Windsor Factory Supply."

CHAPTER 6 SERVING GLOBAL MARKETS

- "Finland and Nokia: Hot Competitors in a Cold Climate" is the subject of the new opening vignette.
- The new Marketing Success box explores how "Nike Sells Status in China."

- The new Etiquette Tips box gives tips on "Entertaining Foreign Guests."
- "ISO 14000" is the topic of the Chapter 6 Go Green box.
- The new Solving an Ethical Controversy box examines "Fair-Trade Pricing for Coffee Growers: Is It Fair to Everyone?"
- One existing case has been updated ("Harlequin—Canada's Global Publishing Company"), and a new case has been added ("Hyundai Gets a Second Chance").

CHAPTER 7 MARKETING RESEARCH, DECISION SUPPORT SYSTEMS, AND SALES FORECASTING

- The new opening vignette "Points Cards or Market Research" looks at loyalty cards.
- The Chapter 7 Go Green box analyzes how "Shell Did the Research."
- A recent consumer alarm is the focus of the new Marketing Failure box: "Winners and HomeSense Customer Data Hacked."
- The new Etiquette Tips box explores "How to Conduct Phone Surveys."
- The new Solving an Ethical Controversy box queries, "Did Microsoft Control the Supply of Xbox 360s or Just Forecast Too Low?"
- A new case on "Forecasting Pitfalls for SUV Makers" has been added to this chapter.

CHAPTER 8 MARKET SEGMENTATION, TARGETING, AND POSITIONING

- The new opening vignette profiles how "American Idol Is a Hit with Canadian Teens."
- The new Marketing Success box explores how "Campbell's Segments Its Soups."
- "How to Say (and Do) the Right Thing" is the topic of the new Etiquette Tips box.
- The Go Green box for this chapter focuses on "Households and the Environment."
- The "I Am Canadian" case has been updated, and a new case, "Beauty at Every Age," has been added.

CHAPTER 9 RELATIONSHIP MARKETING AND CUSTOMER RELATIONSHIP MANAGEMENT (CRM)

- The new opening vignette shows how "Best Buy Bets on Customers."
- "Toyota's Customer One Program" is the topic of the Go Green box.
- The new Solving an Ethical Controversy box asks, "Too Much Data, Not Enough Protection?"
- The new Etiquette Tips box explores "How to Deal with Rude People."
- The new Marketing Failure box looks at "The Perils of Big Partners" (LookSmart and Microsoft).
- The case "Hilton Is OnQ with Customers" has been updated, and a new case, "The True Cost of Customer Service," has been added.

CHAPTER 10 PRODUCT AND SERVICE STRATEGIES

- The new opening vignette focuses on "Satellite: The New Sound of Radio."
- The new Etiquette Tips box offers suggestions on "Giving the Right Gift."

- The Go Green box topic is "Cotton Ginny Launches Eco-Ganic Clothing."
- The new Marketing Success box asks, "Is iZ the Next Big Thing?"
- "Silencing Cell Phones in Movie Theatres" is the hotly debated topic profiled in the new Solving an Ethical Controversy box.
- The case on "The Canadian Word for Coffee—Tims" has been updated, and a new case, "Pampering Pets: Lavishing Our Friends with Love" has been added.

CHAPTER 11   DEVELOPING AND MANAGING BRAND AND PRODUCT CATEGORIES

- "Conquering Floors with P&G's Swiffer" is the topic of the new opening vignette.
- The new Marketing Success box explores how "Bell Builds on Its Brand."
- Suggestions for "Avoiding Technical Jargon" are offered in the new Etiquette Tips box.
- "Eco-Friendly Packages" are discussed in the Go Green box.
- The new Solving an Ethical controversy box asks, Counterfeiters: Is It Worth the Fight to Stop Them?
- The case "What Will Become of the Box?" has been updated and a new case has been added on "Worm Poop: New Product?"

CHAPTER 12   MARKETING CHANNELS AND SUPPLY CHAIN MANAGEMENT

- The new opening vignette explores how Zappos.com delivers "Shoes to Your Door."
- Material on electronic storefronts has been moved to this chapter from the old (first edition) Chapter 4, which has been deleted in the second edition.
- The new Etiquette Tips looks at "Preparing an Effective Direct-Mail Piece."
- The new Marketing Success explores "Skipping the Box Office Rush."
- "RFID: Do You Want Chips in Your Wallet or on Your Shopping Cart?" is the topic addressed in the new Solving an Ethical Controversy box.
- The new Go Green box explores "Greening the Supply Chain."
- A new case, "Heavy Metal at Hyundai," has been added to this chapter, while the case "BAX to the Future: How a Logistics Firm Has Survived and Grown" has been updated.

CHAPTER 13   RETAILERS, WHOLESALERS AND DIRECT MARKETERS

- The opening vignette "Forzani: Focused Growth" has been updated.
- Nearly all of the sources have been changed and updated, reflecting the rapid change that is taking place in the Canadian retail environment.
- The new Go Green box explores "Buying Green—Get Bamboozled."
- The new Solving an Ethical Controversy box queries, "Are Gift Cards Truly a Gift?"
- "Providing the Personal Touch to Retail Transactions" is the topic of the new Etiquette Tips box. This is a subject that the many students who have part-time retail jobs can relate to.

- The new Marketing Success box explores how "Pete's Frootique Wins One Customer at a Time."
- The new case, "Let's Have a Party—Bring Your Wallet," deals with topics from both Chapters 12 and 13. It is included here as it is an important example of retailing that should draw student interest.

CHAPTER 14 INTEGRATED MARKETING COMMUNICATIONS

- The new opening vignette box covers how "Gillette Fuses Its Marketing Communications."
- "Greenwashing" is the subject of the Chapter 14 Go Green box.
- The new Etiquette Tips box explores "Cultural Considerations in Marketing Messages."
- The new Marketing Success box discusses how "Beer Grows Up."
- "Scotiabank—You Are Richer than You Think" has been added as a new case.

CHAPTER 15 ADVERTISING AND PUBLIC RELATIONS

- New material on the disadvantages of comparative advertisements has been added to this chapter.
- The new Etiquette Tips box provides "Advertising Do's and Don'ts."
- The Go Green box considers "The End of Plastic Bags?"
- The new Solving an Ethical Controversy box explores "Using Sex to Sell."
- "HDTV and Super Bowl Advertising" are featured in the new Marketing Success box.
- New cases focus on "Lululemon" and "Mobile Media."

CHAPTER 16 PERSONAL SELLING AND SALES PROMOTION

- The new opening vignette deals with "Selling Food Equipment Solutions" at a Canadian company, TFI Food Equipment Solutions.
- The section on the sales process has been substantially rewritten, with clear examples and instructions.
- The section on telemarketing describes efforts behind the creation of the Do Not Call List in Canada and reviews new developments in call centre outsourcing.
- The new Marketing Success box examines how "Star Salesman Lifts Boeing's Profits."
- The Go Green box looks at "Wind Power—Catch the Wind."
- The new Solving an Ethical Controversy box asks, "Sales Quotas—Are They Fair?"
- "Sears Ties Up with Ty Pennington" is the subject of a new case for this chapter.

CHAPTER 17 PRICE CONCEPTS

- The new opening vignette, "Pricing a Home: A 'Lot' to Consider," offers a good discussion of setting price in the housing market and features a unique property for sale.
- Many examples in this chapter have been updated, reflecting more current marketing issues.
- The new Marketing Success box, "Good for the Sole," looks at Canadian shoe distributor Solemates.

- The new Solving an Ethical Controversy box deals with "Energy from Ethanol: Hope or Hype?" It provides a very timely look at the effect of alternative fuels on food costs.

- New cases include "Value Menus Fill Customer Cravings" and "Cinema Prices: Back to the Future."

CHAPTER 18 PRICING STRATEGIES

- The new opening vignette, "VANOC: Setting a Price for Everyone," examines the pricing strategy used for tickets for the 2010 Vancouver Olympics.

- The new Marketing Failure box is "The Joy of Ripping You Off: Priceless!"—a look at controversies over hidden fees charged by credit card companies.

- The Go Green box, "Paying the Price," looks at cost issues for energy-efficient cars.

- The new Etiquette Tips box offers hints on "Making Your Complaint—Effectively."

- New cases include "Air Canada: Everyone Takes a Shot" and "Can You Squeeze Blood from a Fan?"

PEDAGOGY

As with the first edition of *Contemporary Marketing*, the Second Canadian Edition is packed with new pedagogical features to keep students interested and bring the text topics to life:

- *Assessment, Assessment, Assessment*: In every marketing department in the country, assessment and assurance of learning among students has become increasingly important. As a result, we've provided students with assessment checks after every main head in every chapter. Answers at the back of the chapter help students self-review to ensure they've understood the chapter's contents.

- *Assurance of Learning Review*: Assurance of learning is further enhanced by new end-of-chapter self-quizzes. In addition to ensuring that students are learning throughout the chapter, we've taken assessment one step further by incorporating new end-of-chapter self-quizzes called Assurance of Learning Review. These questions are designed to quickly assess whether students understand the basic concepts covered in the chapter.

- *Critical Thinking*: In response to our reviewers, and reflecting the importance of analysis and independent thought in today's classrooms, Critical Thinking Exercises have been added at the end of each chapter, replacing "Applying Chapter Concepts" from the first edition.

- *Business Etiquette*: Schools realize that it has become increasingly important to understand proper business etiquette when entering the business world, so more and more schools are adding business etiquette to their curriculums. Every chapter of *Contemporary Marketing* contains an Etiquette Tips for Marketing Professionals box, addressing all aspects of proper behaviour, including communications etiquette, business dinners, and even the most effective way to create customer relationships. Student focus groups for the Second Canadian Edition revealed that this box is, perhaps surprisingly, one of the most-read and popular features of *Contemporary Marketing*!

- *Success and Failure*: Marketing Success and Marketing Failure boxes provide an informative glimpse into the stories behind triumphs and disasters in the world of marketing.

- *Ethical Awareness*: Every chapter includes a special experiential feature called Solving an Ethical Controversy. This feature is designed to facilitate class debates of current ethical issues. Each begins with a brief background and is followed by a series of pro and con points designed to elicit class discussion of the issues. To keep the discussion vigorous, we've removed the Summary from the end of the box (as presented in the first edition). In additional, an Ethics

Exercises section appears at the end of each chapter. These are short case scenarios that can be used as homework assignments or as a basis for classroom discussion.

- *Marketer's Minute*: Students often have an amazing ability to grasp chapter concepts and intellectually understand marketing and what a marketing career entails. However, they often do not understand how careers are created and maintained and fail to understand in a real-life sense what a career in marketing may involve on a day-to-day basis. Every part in the text ends with an interview of an actual marketing professional and includes information about his or her education, career path, and day-to-day responsibilities. Participants include global marketing manager for IBM Deborah McKenzie, Grace Mistry of BMO Bank of Montreal, Amanda Herold of Bell Canada, and Domenic Vivolo of Astral Media. The traits all of them have in common are their hard work, dedication, professionalism, and success. This feature gives students a true understanding of how to make the most of their marketing courses and launch a real marketing career for themselves.

- *Additional Pedagogical Features*: The authors conducted a thorough review of *Contemporary Marketing*'s instructional elements. In addition to the pedagogy described above, the Second Canadian Edition continues to offer these user-friendly features.

  1. *Review of Chapter Objectives.* In addition to a review of each chapter learning objective, a series of review questions is included as part of the chapter review.
  2. *Marketing Terms You Need to Know.* Page numbers are included.
  3. *Projects and Teamwork Exercises.* This section includes discussion questions.
  4. *Internet Exercises.* Several content-related Internet exercises are included for each chapter.

THE CONTEMPORARY MARKETING RESOURCE PACKAGE

With its precedent-setting learning materials, *Contemporary Marketing* has continued to improve on its signature package features—equipping students and instructors with the most comprehensive collection of learning tools, teaching materials, and innovative resources available. As expected, the Second Canadian Edition continues to serve as the industry benchmark by delivering the most extensive, technologically advanced, user-friendly package on the market.

FOR THE INSTRUCTOR

CengageNOW (ISBN 0-17-647512-5)

Designed by instructors and students for instructors and students, CengageNOW gives you what you want to do, how you want to do it. CengageNOW is an integrated online suite of services and resources with proven ease of use and efficient paths to success, delivering the results you want—NOW! CengageNOW includes self-assessments that generate a personalized study plan, auto-graded homework assignments, a gradebook, an e-book, and more. CengageNOW also includes content that is tagged to the core marketing outcomes. Instructors can track students' progress toward the core outcomes in their class. Students will find this product fun, and instructors will find it extremely useful. CengageNOW also includes seamless integration with WebCT and Blackboard. Full descriptions of CengageNOW are included in the *Instructor's Manual* on the Instructor's Resource CD (see below).

Instructor's Resource CD-ROM (ISBN 0-17-647416-1)

Key instructor ancillaries are provided on CD-ROM, giving instructors the ultimate tool for customizing lectures and presentations. These ancillaries include the following:

- *Instructor's Manual with Collaborative Learning Exercises, Media Guide, and NETA Support.* Adapted for the Second Canadian Edition by H. F. (Herb) MacKenzie and Kim Snow, the Canadian text authors, the *Instructor's Manual* contains both chapter-related and book-related materials. The chapter-related content includes chapter overviews, a summary of changes in the second edition, and lecture outlines (organized by learning objective and correlated to

PowerPoint slides). You'll also find answers to all of the end-of-chapter materials and various critical-thinking exercises. Collaborative learning exercises are included for each chapter, which give students a completely different way to apply chapter concepts to their own lives. Book-related materials include support for the Nelson Education Testing Advantage (NETA) Test Bank (see details below) and a Media Guide. NETA support consists of a guide to creating effective tests, "Multiple Choice Tests: Getting Beyond Remembering," by David DiBattista of Brock University. The Media Guide offers full descriptions of CengageNOW, along with complete video synopses for the end-of-chapter videos, the part-ending Second City videos, the Marketing Minute videos, and the web-based CBC videos.

Nelson Education
Testing Advantage

- *Introducing the Nelson Education Testing Advantage (NETA) Test Banks.* In most college and university courses, a large percentage of student assessment is based on multiple choice testing. But many instructors use multiple choice reluctantly, believing that it is a methodology best used for teaching what a student remembers rather than what she or he has learned. Furthermore, the quality of publisher-supplied test banks can vary.

    Nelson Education Ltd. believes that a good-quality multiple choice test bank can test not just what students remember, but higher-level thinking skills as well. Recognizing the importance of multiple choice testing in today's classroom, Nelson has created the Nelson Education Testing Advantage program to ensure the high quality of our test banks.

    The test bank for *Contemporary Marketing* was developed under the Nelson Education Testing Advantage. NETA was created in partnership with David DiBattista, a 3M National Teaching Fellow and professor of psychology at Brock University. NETA ensures that test bank authors have had training in two areas: developing clear multiple choice test questions while avoiding common errors in construction, and creating multiple choice test questions that "get beyond remembering" to assess higher-level thinking.

    The outcome of NETA development is that as you select multiple choice questions from your Nelson test bank for inclusion in tests, you can easily identify whether items are memory-based or require your students to engage in higher-level thinking. By making your selections appropriately, you can construct tests that contain the proportion of recall and higher-level questions that reflects your personal instructional goals.

    All NETA test banks are accompanied by David DiBattista's guide for instructors, "Multiple Choice Tests: Getting Beyond Remembering." This guide has been designed to assist you in using Nelson test banks to achieve your desired outcomes in the classroom.

    The NETA test materials are presented in two formats:

    1. *Test Bank.* Containing more than 4000 questions, this is a new adaptation of the U.S. Test Bank by Theresa Champion of Niagara College. Every question and answer in the U.S. version was read and reviewed for accuracy by multiple sources. A Canadian proofreader checked all questions, including the new or revised questions created for the Second Canadian Edition. Each chapter of the test bank is organized by chapter objective, and each question categorized by difficulty level, type of question, and text page reference. About 1800 multiple choice, 1400 true/false, 300 matching, and 300 essay questions are included in the Test Bank. Files are provided in rich text format for easy editing and printing with all common word-processing formats.

    2. *ExamView.* All Test Bank questions are included in the ExamView computerized version. The easy-to-use software is compatible with Microsoft Windows and Mac. Create tests by selecting questions from the question bank, modifying these questions as desired, and adding new questions you write yourself. You can administer quizzes online and export tests to WebCT, Blackboard, and other formats.

- *Basic and Expanded PowerPoint Presentations.* After reviewing competitive offerings, we are convinced that our PowerPoint presentations are the best you'll find. We offer two separate collections. The Basic PowerPoint collection contains 10 to 20 slides per chapter. This collection is a basic outline of the chapter. The Expanded PowerPoint collection includes 20 to 40 slides per chapter and provides a more complete overview of the chapter. The Expanded collection includes figures and tables from the chapter, Web links, and video links. Power-Points are easily printed to create customized transparency masters. H. F. (Herb) MacKenzie and Kim Snow, the Canadian textbook authors, also adapted the PowerPoint presentations, ensuring consistency with the content of the book.

- *Image Library.* Many of the figures and illustrations from the book are provided in jpeg format so that you can incorporate them into PowerPoint Presentations you create yourself. (Note: Some graphics may not be available due to copyright restrictions.)

- *Resource Integration Guide (RIG).* The RIG is written to provide the instructor with a clear and concise guide to all of the ancillaries that accompany the text as well as how best to use these items in teaching a Principles of Marketing course. Not only are all of the book's ancillaries organized clearly for you, but we also provide planning suggestions, lecture ideas, and help in creating assignments. This guide will help instructors prepare for teaching the course, execute teaching plans, and evaluate student performance.

- *Day One.* Day One—Prof InClass is a PowerPoint presentation that you can customize to orient your students to the class and their text at the beginning of the course. (See the description below.)

Turning Point: JoinIn on TurningPoint®

Now you can author, deliver, show, access, and grade, all in PowerPoint… with no toggling back and forth between screens! JoinIn on Turning Point is the only classroom response software tool that gives you true PowerPoint integration. With JoinIn, you are no longer tied to your computer. You can walk about your classroom as you lecture, showing slides and collecting and displaying responses with ease. There is simply no easier or more effective way to turn your lecture hall into a personal, fully interactive experience for your students. If you can use PowerPoint, you can use JoinIn on TurningPoint!

Chapter Video Cases on DVD (0-3245-3652-6)

Brand-new end-of-chapter video cases for every chapter of the text focus on successful real companies' processes, strategies, and procedures. Real employees explain real marketing situations with which they have been faced, bringing key concepts from the chapter to life. Contact your Nelson Education sales representative for details.

The Second City Theater, Inc., Continuing Case Video on DVD (ISBN 0-3245-3652-6)

This brand-new continuing video case combines the entrepreneurial and creative spirit with which Second City was founded with the reality of successful marketing and business strategies. Rarely has a creative enterprise so uniquely brought real business savvy to its success. In these videos we examine the history of the theatre company as well as the successful business practices that have allowed for its expansion and growth. The written and video cases are divided into seven sections and are created to be used at the end of each part of the text.

CBC Video Cases and Marketer's Minute Interviews (ISBN 0-17-647418-8)

CBC Video Cases and Marketer's Minute interviews are previewed at the end of each part of the text. These videos will add visual impact and current, real-world examples to your lectures. Teaching notes are included in the Instructor's Manual & Media Guide, and the video segments are available on the *Contemporary Marketing* website.

Contemporary Marketing, Second Canadian Edition, Website

Our text website (**http://www.contemporarymarketing2.nelson.com**) is filled with a whole set of useful tools. Instructors will find all the key instructor resources in electronic format: PowerPoint collections, Instructor's Manual & Media Guide, the Resource Integration Guide, and Day One—Prof InClass presentations. Students will also find a host of valuable resources, including interactive quizzes, CBC Video Cases, and Marketer's Minute interviews.

FOR THE STUDENT

CengageNOW (ISBN 0-17-647512-5)

Designed by instructors and students for instructors and students, CengageNOW gives you what you want to do, how you want to do it. CengageNOW is an integrated online suite of services and resources with proven ease of use and efficient paths to success, delivering the results you want—NOW! CengageNOW includes self-assessments that generate a personalized study plan, auto-graded homework assignments, a gradebook, an e-book, and more. Instructors can track students' progress to the core outcomes in their class. Students will find this product fun and instructors will find it extremely useful.

Contemporary Marketing, Second Canadian Edition, Website

Our text website (**http://www.contemporarymarketing2.nelson.com**) is filled with a whole set of useful tools. Students will find a host of valuable resources, including interactive quizzes, vocabulary flashcards, CBC and Marketing Minute videos, and more.

ACKNOWLEDGMENTS TO THE SECOND CANADIAN EDITION

Your authors have benefited immensely from the comments and suggestions of many reviewers and colleagues. This input has come via focus groups, publisher reviews, contributions to supplementary text materials, e-mailed suggestions, conference networking, classroom visits, and coffee shop chats. Regardless of the format, all these ideas have helped shape the Second Canadian Edition of *Contemporary Marketing* into a text that serves as the benchmark for other texts.

We'd like to thank the outstanding reviewers whose diligent and thoughtful comments were instrumental in our revisions:

Peter Burgess, George Brown College
Theresa Champion, Niagara College
Mark Cleveland, University of Western Ontario
Tanya Drollinger, University of Lethbridge
Craig Dyer, Red River College
Daniel F. Gardiner, University of British Columbia
Kent Hudson, University of Prince Edward Island
Melanie Lang, University of Guelph
Shirley Lichti, Wilfrid Laurier University
Kelley Main, University of Manitoba
Sherry McEvoy, Fanshawe College
Leighann Neilson, Carleton University
G. Elizabeth Pett, Niagara College
Donald Shiner, Mount St. Vincent University

Thanks to all the students at Red River College and Algonquin College who participated in our marketing focus groups. We learned a lot from you!

Every project of this nature involves many hours of work but this project was made easier because of the assistance of many dedicated students mostly from York University who juggled their lecture, personal, and work schedules to help out. We are grateful for their many hours of research and suggestions on how to make the book student friendly. Our sincere thanks go to:

Anton Allen
Michelle Alliston
Abbas Basravi
Alisha Birkett
David Bit-Yunan
Aliza Chagpar

Arun Chetram
Sandy Chohan
Patrick Choo
Aniesha Coach
Linda Cooke
Luca Corrente

Candace DeBarros
Cassandra De Santis
Lorenzo Di Nino
Shaan Dubey
Papia Dutta
Anges Gendelman

Ridah Ghoari
Lilian Hanna
Phoebe Hanna
Jonathan Hutchison
Rajiv Joshi
Mary Junne
Mumbi Kamau
Ali Kazerani
Nina Kostenko
Joseph Kurtz
Henry Ly
Cassie Ma
Pia Marino

Miriam Martin
Ulfat Farah Matin
Deniz Melen
Joshua Mok
Nihit Narang
Vivian Ng
Steven Park
Peter Pavlovic
Stephanie Guglietta Petrelli
Nadia Pulla
Riannon Raskin
Sara Rezafard
Miguel Rolo

Rehan Shaikh
Tracy Singh
Stephanie Stone
Michael Strasser
Sujitha Suntharalingam
Dave Thibault
Salman Vajid
Tracy Yee
Stephanie Yu
Christina Zaradi
and Janice Mumberson
(Queen's University)

We appreciate the help of the marketing professionals who contributed to the Marketer's Minutes: Stéfan Danis, Deborah McKenzie, Charles Hendriks, Grace Mistry, Amanda Herold, Domenic Vivolo, and Victoria McManus. We also thank those who contributed to the Prologue: Stéfan Danis and his colleagues at Mandrake Executive Search, including Daniela Ionescu, Daphne Bykerk, Louise Daigneault, Michael Gates, Janine Turner, Stephen Miliç, Donna Pearl, and Tina Santos, as well as Cindy Fruitman, Vice President at NEXCareer.

Finally, this new edition would never have become a reality without our highly competent editorial, production, and marketing teams at Nelson Education. Sincere thanks go to Evelyn Veitch, Associate Vice President and Editorial Director; Amie Plourde and Jackie Wood, Acquisitions Editors; Lesley Mann, Managing Developmental Editor; Susan Wong, Content Production Manager; Kristiina Bowering, Project Manager, Asset Management Services, Media Production Services; Liz Harasymczuk, Designer; Kathaleen McCormick, Marketing Manager; and Joanne McNeil, Manufacturing Buyer. Special thanks also go to freelancers for their dedicated and diligent work: David Strand, Photo and Permissions Researcher; and Wendy Thomas, Copy Editor.

We are grateful for the many suggestions and contributions of dozens of people who teach the introductory marketing course on a regular basis and are in the best position to comment on what works best—and what doesn't work at all. Every recommendation made a difference in the creation of the Second Canadian Edition. We welcome any comments, suggestions, or constructive criticisms you wish to provide.

H. F. (Herb) MacKenzie & Kim Snow

H. F. (HERB) MACKENZIE

Dr. H. F. (Herb) MacKenzie is Chair, Marketing, International Business, and Strategy, and an associate professor of marketing at Brock University, St. Catharines, Ontario. He has taught in the undergraduate, graduate, and executive education programs at universities in Canada, Europe, and the Middle East, and has been consulting to both private- and public-sector businesses since 1985. He has over 15 years of industrial sales and sales management experience and has published many cases, conference proceedings, and articles in the areas of sales management, buyer–seller relationships, and distribution channel management. He has co-authored Canadian editions of textbooks on selling, sales management, and marketing and has edited three Canadian marketing casebooks. He has received numerous awards from his students, including Professor of the Year, Marketing Professor of the Year, and Faculty of Business Faculty Award of Excellence (twice).

Dr. Kim Snow is an associate professor of marketing at York University in Toronto. Dr. Snow received her Diploma in Business Administration from Wilfrid Laurier University, and her MBA and PhD from the University of Bradford, U. K. She has been a member of the faculty at York University since 1992. She has published numerous articles in the area of service marketing, service quality, customer satisfaction, and marketing research. She is faculty advisor for the American Marketing Association Student Chapter at York University and has been a member of the Executive Advisory Board for the Professional Chapter of the American Marketing Association in Toronto. She has been a member of the Editorial Advisory Board and Internet Editor for the *Managing Service Quality Journal*. Prior to joining York University, Kim spent 17 years working in the financial services industry.

KIM SNOW

Dave Kurtz would never have been mistaken for a scholar during his high school days in Salisbury, Maryland. In fact, he was a mediocre student, so bad that his father steered him toward higher education by finding him a succession of backbreaking summer jobs. Thankfully, most of them have been erased from his memory, but a few linger, including picking peaches, loading watermelons on trucks headed for market, and working as a pipe fitter's helper. Unfortunately, these jobs had zero impact on his academic standing. Worse yet for Dave's ego, he was no better than average as a high-school athlete in football and track.

But four years at Davis & Elkins College in Elkins, West Virginia, turned him around. Excellent teachers helped get Dave on a sound academic footing. His grade point average soared—enough to get him accepted by the graduate business school at the University of Arkansas, where he met Gene Boone. After graduate school, the two became career co-authors, with over 50 books between them. Gene and Dave also got involved in several entrepreneurial ventures.

Today, Dave Kurtz is back teaching at the University of Arkansas after duty tours in Ypsilanti, Michigan; Seattle; and Melbourne, Australia. He is the proud grandfather of five "perfect" kids and a sportsman with a golfing handicap too high to mention. Dave, his wife, Diane, and four demanding canine companions (Daisy, Lucy, Molly, and Sally) live in Rogers, Arkansas. Dave holds a distinguished professorship at the Sam M. Walton College of Business in nearby Fayetteville, home of the Arkansas Razorbacks.

contents in brief

contents in brief

contents

Opening Vignette
Cv Technologies: The Ups, And Downs, And Ups, And...   19

Etiquette Tips for Marketing Professionals
Forms of Address: Which One Do You Use, and When?   31

Marketing Success
A Google?   34

Go Green
Job Opportunities Are Greening   36

Solving an Ethical Controversy
Identity Theft: Is Privacy Also Stolen?   41

part 2
UNDERSTANDING BUYERS AND MARKETS 127

chapter 4
CONSUMER BEHAVIOUR 128

part 3

chapter 7

MARKETING RESEARCH, DECISION SUPPORT SYSTEMS, AND SALES FORECASTING 228

Opening Vignette
Points Cards or Market
Research 229

Go Green
Shell Did the Research 231

Marketing Failure
Winners and HomeSense
Customer Data
Hacked 238

**Etiquette Tips for Marketing
Professionals**
How to Conduct Phone
Surveys 241

**Solving an Ethical
Controversy**
Did Microsoft Control the
Supply of Xbox 360s or Just
Forecast Too Low? 248

part 4
PRODUCT DECISIONS 321

chapter 10
PRODUCT AND SERVICE STRATEGIES 322

chapter 11

DEVELOPING AND MANAGING BRAND AND PRODUCT CATEGORIES   352

Opening Vignette
Conquering Floors With
P&G's Swiffer   353

Solving an Ethical Controversy
Counterfeiters: Is It Worth the
Fight to Stop Them?   356

Marketing Success
Bell Builds on Its
Brand   359

Etiquette Tips for Marketing Professionals
Avoiding Technical
Jargon   362

Go Green
Eco-Friendly Packages   364

part 5

DISTRIBUTION DECISIONS   387

chapter 12

MARKETING CHANNELS AND SUPPLY CHAIN MANAGEMENT   388

chapter 13

RETAILERS, WHOLESALERS, AND DIRECT MARKETERS   424

part 6
PROMOTIONAL DECISIONS   461

chapter 14
INTEGRATED MARKETING COMMUNICATIONS   462

chapter 15
ADVERTISING AND PUBLIC RELATIONS 500

Opening Vignette
Celebrity
Endorsements 501

Etiquette Tips for Marketing Professionals
Advertising Do's and
Don'ts 504

Go Green
The End of Plastic
Bags? 505

Solving an Ethical Controversy
Using Sex to Sell 510

Marketing Success
HDTV and Super Bowl
Advertising 514

chapter 18
PRICING STRATEGIES   608

Planning a Career in Marketing

Adapted by Stéfan Danis, CEO and Chief Talent Officer at Mandrake Executive Search

STUDY OF MARKETING EXPANDS INTO OTHER ACADEMIC PROGRAMS

As you meet more and more of your marketing classmates during the months ahead, you are likely to be amazed at the diversity of interests—to say nothing of career interests—of your fellow students. Many of them will be taking this course as a requirement for one of the different majors in your school's business program. But you are also likely to find more academic diversity than ever before. These students come from majors ranging from the fine arts and interior design to leisure services, hospitality management, and sports marketing and management. But each of them is as interested as you to learn about marketing and how to apply it to his or her chosen field.

Today, marketing is recognized as an invaluable tool in all kinds of industries, not just in the traditional areas involving consumer products such as fashion accessories, autos, and flat-screen TVs, or services such as banking. More and more frequently marketing concepts and strategies are put to use in marketing:

- people (such as celebrities and political candidates)

- organizations (such as nonprofits, schools, and even hospitals and medical practices)

- places (such as cities vying to host conventions and sports tournaments, attract new businesses, and entice tourists to visit and permanent residents)

- causes (such as environmental protection and gay rights)

- events (such as concerts, rallies, and sporting events)

In the 1960s and 1970s, the consumer packaged goods and advertising industries were essentially where the majority of marketers could be found. They are affectionately referred to as old economy marketers. Times have changed; industries that once sought out the classically trained talent found in these two legacy sectors have now started to train their own marketing talent.

Marketing-driven sectors will continue to use the traditional recruiting grounds of agencies and businesses that specialize in consumer goods, but many other industries are rapidly developing their own marketing strengths. Today, a graduating marketing student can expect to rise to the top of his or her profession not only by considering consumer goods businesses, but also by entering many different robust sectors such as banking, telecom, leisure and tourism, broadcasting, or retail. Acquiring solid marketing experience in Canada is also a great ticket to an international marketing role abroad. Canadians are seen as the most exportable marketing workers in the world based on their strong work habits, multicultural makeup, and liberal moral values.

Overview

Congratulations on your decision to take this course. After all, marketing is a pervasive element in our lives. In one form or another, it reaches every person. As you begin this course, you should be aware of three important facts about marketing.

MARKETING COSTS ARE A BIG COMPONENT OF YOUR TOTAL BUDGET

Approximately 50 percent of the total costs of products you buy are marketing costs. In short, half of the $20 you pay for that chart-topping CD goes, not for the plastic disc, but for marketing costs. The same is true of the price of a new flat-screen monitor for your desktop, your DVD player, and the $34 000 Toyota Prius you want so badly.

But costs alone do not indicate the value of marketing. The high living standard that you, your family, and your friends enjoy is in large part a function of our country's efficient marketing systems. When considered from this perspective, the costs of marketing seem more reasonable. For example, effective marketing can expand overall sales, thereby spreading fixed production costs over more units of output and reducing total output costs.

MARKETING PROVIDES AN OPPORTUNITY TO CONTRIBUTE TO SOCIETY AS WELL AS TO AN INDIVIDUAL COMPANY

Marketing decisions affect everyone's welfare. How much quality should be built into a product? Will people buy a safer product if it costs twice as much as the current version? Should every community adopt recycling programs? Because ethics and social responsibilities are critical factors for marketers in a business environment tarnished by both ethical and legal failings of a number of well-known companies and their leaders, it is essential that marketers strive to exceed customer and government expectations of behaviour. Reading the "Solving an Ethical Controversy" feature included in every chapter will increase your awareness of the role of high ethical standards in every dimension of marketing and allow you to examine the not always black-and-white ethical issues such as prescription drug pricing, online privacy, advertising to children, and invasive practices such as spam, pop-up ads, and telemarketing.

Not only does marketing influence numerous facets of our daily lives, but decisions regarding marketing activities also affect everyone's welfare. Opportunities to advance to more responsible decision-making positions come sooner in marketing than in most occupations. This combination of challenges and opportunities has made marketing one of the most popular fields of academic study.

A recent survey by executive recruiter Korn/Ferry International revealed that the best route to the top of the corporate ladder begins in a company's marketing team. The growing global economy demands proven market leaders in winning the fight to increase a firm's worldwide market shares—part of the reason that three of every eight CEOs have marketing backgrounds. Finance, which had long dominated as the top career path for senior executives, fell to third place, and executives who had completed international assignments—many of the assignments being marketing related—came in second.

YOU MAY CHOOSE A CAREER IN MARKETING

When asked about their conception of an ideal entry-level job following graduation, most students mention salary and opportunity for professional growth and advancement. While compensation is almost always an issue, the 21st-century job seeker also wants to feel recognized for his or her achievements, be assigned new responsibilities, and work in continuous-learning environments. Many will also include as an important issue working for a family-friendly organization that offers a high quality of life.

Of the many career paths chosen by business graduates, the marketing category is the single largest employment grouping in the Canadian labour force, and job growth in the field is expected to accelerate. It is estimated that the number of jobs in marketing, advertising, communications, sales, and customer management will grow much faster than the average for all occupations. Every successful organization—profit-seeking or not-for-profit—recognizes the necessity of effective marketing in accomplishing its goal of providing customer satisfaction by hiring highly motivated, professionally educated marketing specialists to design and implement these customer-driven programs.

Marketing-related occupations account for 25 to 30 percent of jobs in the typical highly industrialized nation. History has shown that the demand for effective customer-centric marketers is not as affected by cyclical economic fluctuations.

It should be noted that the sales function is marketing's Trojan horse. In other words, many sales positions also fulfill the function of marketing. Sales positions are expected to represent half of the marketing jobs in Canada. Sales roles in the area of key account management (the ones focused on the largest retailers) have morphed into marketing/sales roles as the consolidating few but increasingly powerful large retailers in Canada demand marketing plans from all their vendors. Such plans were really only developed for consumers in the past and now need to be developed for both consumers and customers (retailers). Separately, the marketing roles at multinationals with a Canadian office are shifting. This large employer segment is increasingly relying on global campaigns to market products to consumers. Because only few of these products are developed in Canada, the marketing teams focus more on local area tactics or sales-based communication.

A typical example of a recruitment ad

YOUR QUEST FOR A SUCCESSFUL, REWARDING CAREER

Selecting a career may be the most important decision you will ever make. That's why *Contemporary Marketing* begins by discussing the best way to approach career decisions and how to prepare for an *entry-level position*—your first permanent employment after leaving school. We then look at a range of marketing careers and discuss employment opportunities in fields related to each major part of the text.

Until recently, entry-level positions had been more difficult to find. As the economy suffered after September 11, 2001, so did the job market. Today, economic conditions are improving, and job prospects are brighter for students. Still, you need to do everything you can to enhance your career opportunities as getting into the industry is the greatest challenge. You've already taken an important first step by enrolling in a class using this textbook. You will need to continue to be creative in your job search. But as you know, creativity has never been in short supply on the country's campuses.

During the next few months, you will be introduced to all the key functional areas of marketing. As you learn about marketing concepts, you will also be able to identify areas of employment that you may wish to pursue.

THE JOB YOU LOVE IS HERE.

- workopolis.com has **four times more jobs than its nearest competitor***
- **More companies hire** through workopolis.com than any other job site in Canada
- **46 of the 50 Best Employers** in Canada have posted on workopolis.com

Visit workopolis.com to find the job you love.

workopolis.com
CANADA'S BIGGEST JOB SITE

COURTESY OF WORKOPOLIS

The tone and presentation of a recruitment ad help organizations convey their corporate brand and values to help them attract graduates who are a good fit.

Education will improve your prospects of finding and keeping the right job. In a recent year, the average full-time employee 18 or older with a high school diploma earned just under $20 000. By contrast, the average employee with a bachelor's degree earned $30 000-plus annually—one and a half times more than the pay of the high school grad. Better educated graduates also found jobs more quickly than others. Applying yourself in class, expanding your experiences through career-directed volunteer efforts, part-time and summer jobs, and high-quality internships—and selecting the right major—will put you well on your way to improving these salary statistics when you launch your career.

In addition to taking classes, try to gain related experience either through a job or by participating in campus organizations or both. Internships, carefully selected summer and part-time jobs, and volunteer activities on campus and in your community can also give you invaluable hands-on experience while you pursue your education. During the recent tight job markets when youth unemployment soared above 10 percent, work experience often set people apart from other job seekers in the eyes of recruiters. Work-related experience—including internships—is often invaluable for traditional students who entered college or university immediately following graduation from high school and who possess little or no work experience.

Think of the job market as very fluid and competitive, requiring you to start planning now. Accumulating the experiences that will distinguish you from your colleagues is critical, as employers may be hiring on campus two semesters before your graduation, or they may offer annual internship opportunities.

As you learn the art and science of marketing brands, services, and causes, use these insights to market the most important brand of all: yourself. Ask employers what they are looking for and start acquiring the skills, competencies, and experiences that will make you stand out when you look for summer employment or when you graduate. Remember that marketing is not only about having a great product; it is about standing out in the crowd.

The reality of the business world is that putting out the effort, achieving good marks, acquiring student government experience, and landing good summer jobs will not necessarily be the clincher when you apply for a job. It's still true that who you know can play an important part in your access to good jobs. Today, many jobs are not advertised or posted. A substantial percentage are hidden and accessible only through networking. Learn to network early to ensure you can reach this vast pool of opportunities. In addition, focus on understanding what your unique qualities are so that you can compellingly convey what makes you different when the time comes.

This career-focused Prologue provides you with a brief look at the trends and opportunities available for future marketers in an increasingly diversified professional field. It describes essential elements of an effective résumé and discusses the latest trends in electronic job searches. Finally, it provides a listing of primary marketing information sources that contain answers to many of the questions typically asked by applicants. This information will provide valuable career-planning assistance in this and other future courses, whether your career plans involve marketing or you decide to major in another field.

Many of the marketing positions you read about throughout the text are described here. Specifically, the job summaries describe the job and the responsibilities and duties that are typically required as well as the usual career path for each of these marketing-related positions.

Marketing your skills to a prospective employer is much the same as marketing a product to a consumer. Increasingly, job seekers are selling their skills online, bypassing intermediaries such as employment agencies, and levelling the playing field between applicant and potential employer. The greatest challenge for online job seekers is learning how to market themselves.

Despite the vast databases and fancy tools of the giant career sites such as Workopolis.com, Monster.ca, and Career-Builder, which may receive hundreds of thousands of visits each day, savvy job seekers often augment their coverage by zeroing in on niche boards offering more focused listings. For example, sales applicants can check out Salesgiant.com; aspiring bankers can go to baystreetworks.com; and cause marketing types to charityvillage.ca.

In many instances, students desiring interviews with specific employers or in certain geographic locations will go directly to the employer's or region's website to learn of available positions. Most employers include an employment site as part of their home page. Some offer virtual tours of what it is like to work for the firm. For example, the Enterprise Rent-a-Car website features profiles of young assistant managers as they perform daily work activities.

As you begin your career, you will apply many of the principles and concepts discussed in the text, including how to do the following: target a market, capitalize on brand equity, position a product, and use marketing research techniques. Even in jobs that seem remote from the marketing discipline, this knowledge will help you stay focused on the most important aspect of business: the consumer.

COURTESY OF MAX TREMBLAY, WORKOPOLIS

Workopolis.com is only one of the 3000 sites for job seekers. Graduates may find niche sites just as useful as larger ones.

STANDING OUT FROM THE CROWD OF JOB SEEKERS

Edited by Cindy Fruitman, Vice President at NEXCareer

COURTESY OF CINDY FRUITMAN

In a tight job market, employers can afford to be choosy in deciding which applicants will make the cut, be interviewed, and, possibly, be offered a position. And often the applicant's accumulated job and leadership experiences will be key decision criteria in determining whether he or she is given serious consideration as a potential employee.

Students often choose to continue their studies following graduation and pursue an MBA degree or enter a master's program specially suited to their career goals. For example, students interested in a marketing research career may decide to study for a specialized master's degree in this field offered by a growing number of universities. A student who wishes to extend formal education in a specialized degree program should seek advice on specific programs from instructors who teach in that area. For example, a marketing research professor is likely to have information on master's programs in that field at different universities.

Other activities that enhance your personal worth are internships and volunteering. Internships have been described as a critical link in bridging the theory–practice educational gap. They help to carry students between the academic present and the professional future. They provide students with an opportunity for learning how classroom theory is applied in real-world business environments.

An internship is a partnership between the student, the academic institution, and the agency or internship site. All these parties assume definite responsibilities, perform specific functions, and achieve benefits as a result of their involvement. In addition, internships can serve as critical networking and

figure 1
Résumé Blunders

The following is a list of errors that have appeared in résumés, job applications, and cover letters received by Monster.com and CareerBuilder.com:

- "Here are my qualifications for you to overlook."

- "Accomplishments: Completed 11 years of high school."

- "Qualifications: No education or experience."

- "Fired because I fought for lower pay."

- "I am a rabid typist."

- "I am relatively intelligent, obedient, and loyal as a puppy."

- "My objective is simple: I want your job."

- "Please remember dear Sir/Madam, that I have failed in a few subjects in my diploma in computer engineering, and that I have no degree."

- "Reason for leaving: it had to do with the IRS, FBI, and SEC."

- "Reason for leaving: my boss said the end of the world is near."

Sources: "Résumé Faux Pas," Monster.com, http://content.monster.com, accessed August 16, 2006; "Résumés from Hell and Their Lessons," CNN.com, March 1, 2006, http://www.cnn.com.

job-hunting tools. In some instances, internships are precursors of specific employment opportunities, allowing students to demonstrate technical proficiency while providing cost-effective employee training for the company or not-for-profit organization.

YOUR RÉSUMÉ

A résumé is the number-one marketing tool for convincing prospective employers you possess the qualifications required for the position they are seeking to fill. After reading your résumé, the employer should have a clear understanding of who you are and the skills you possess. A good résumé is your vehicle to a job interview so it is worthwhile investing the time to create a powerful document.

Writing a résumé is your first opportunity to showcase who you are and what you can bring to an organization. Your résumé should be focused, tailored, and representative of you. With help from your faculty advisor and career counsellor and a number of reference materials in both hard and soft copy, you can put together a document that sells your strengths.

A good résumé summarizes academic, professional, and personal accomplishments while making focused statements about yourself. It is often the only written record of credentials on which an evaluation and selection can be made. Don't procrastinate—a well-written résumé takes time to prepare. It separates you from the crowd. And unlike an interview or a test, you have complete control over how you present the information!

Think of your résumé as a print advertisement of your personal brand. The fundamentals of print advertising are that your main message should be easily remembered—think of a 30-second TV ad, a billboard or a one-page magazine ad (ideally a résumé would be on one page too!). Like any ad, the fundamentals of branding are that your message should be distinct, memorable, and consistent. Your résumé should demonstrate that you have what buyers want; customize your résumé to the audience. To start the process, focus on brevity by trying to put the essentials on one page, which is often called an executive summary. It details who, what, when, where, how, and why: who you are as a person, who will provide a testimonial for you, what your objective is, what your skills are, what your experience is, when and where you went to school, how to contact you, and why you are a good candidate. You can then expand on these fundamentals on further pages, but you have managed to condense all that matters to a prospective—and busy—employer on one page. Business summary recommendations are typically written on one page to provide focus; so should the résumé.

Three basic formats can be used to prepare the résumé, which follows the executive summary. A *chronological résumé* arranges information in reverse chronological order, emphasizing job titles and organizations and describing responsibilities held and duties performed. The *chronological résumé* is the most common and most preferred among hiring managers and recruiters. This format is easy to read as it highlights continuity and career growth. A *functional résumé* accents transferable skills, accomplishments, and strengths while placing less emphasis on job titles and work history. A *functional résumé* is often used when changing careers or industries or when there are gaps between jobs. Some individuals use a *combined résumé* format, which emphasizes skills first, followed by employment history. This format highlights a candidate's potential and suits students who have little experience directly related to their desired positions. A *combined résumé* is shown in Figure 2.

Most executive summaries include full names as well as mail and e-mail addresses. If the username of your e-mail address is something like "MachoDude" or "SnowBunny," replace it with one related to your real name or location to convince employers to take you seriously. Your contact information should appear on every page of your résumé.

A career profile or objective typically follows the contact information. Academic information is provided next, followed by work experience. Education remains at the top of your résumé for your first few years of employment. The general rule is to move it to the end of your résumé once you have had at least five years of work experience. Applicants with limited work history and no internship experience typically focus on relevant personal activities and interests. Any and all professional and extracurricular activities as well as academic work and internship experiences should be included on your résumé. Although employers will usually not contact references until they have met you and deem you an appropriate candidate, you are well advised to include them on the résumé. It's preferable to put their names, titles, and companies without their contact information, with a note "Please advise before calling." Including references at this stage indicates that you have thought ahead and that you have references at a senior executive level who will vouch for you, even though you are not inviting the reader to contact them yet. An ideal reference for a student is a professor, an internship boss, or a supervisor for an unpaid role you have held. As you progress in your career, references will become increasingly valuable.

The most important point to remember in creating an effective résumé is to present the most relevant information in a clear, concise manner that emphasizes your best attributes. And always check the spelling, especially company names!

figure 2

Combined Résumé

Julie Smith
56 Yonge Street
Toronto, ON M4E R7K
416.475.3821 jsmith@rogers.com

Objective
Joining a growth-oriented merchandising company that values creativity and a highly productive employee.

Competencies

Reliable	Intelligent	Hard Working
Creative	Persuasive Presenter	Team Player

Experience
Administration
Management responsibilities in a major retail buying office, supervised assistant buyer

Category Management
Experience in buying home improvement and sport, fitness categories

Planning
Leader of a team charged with reviewing the company's annual vendor evaluation

Problem Solving
Successfully developed a program to improve margins in the tennis and golf categories

Work Experience

Northern Canada Stores	Senior Buyer	2005-Present
Noram Department Stores	Merchandiser	2003-2005
	Sales Assistant	2002-2003

Education
Bachelor of Arts   York University 1998-2002
Double major in marketing and retailing

Personal
Sports. Actively competed in squash (A level) and represented the club at various meets
Music. Grade 8 piano
Languages. English and French (strong comprehension)
Travel. Has backpacked through Europe and visited Australia on exchange program
Gardening. Avid gardener who maintains a small English garden
Reading. Voracious reader; I prefer biographies and non-fiction
Computer. Familiar with Adobe, Excel, Word, PageMaker and Macintosh

References (Please advise before calling)

Joe Stein	VP	Noram Department Stores
Peter Henkell	Director of Marketing	Northern Stores
Liza Hume	Assistant Professor	York University

COVER LETTER

All résumés should be accompanied by a cover letter. A cover letter sets the stage for the résumé, highlights critical job skills, and demonstrates communication skills. There are three types of cover letters: solicited, unsolicited, and referral.

A solicited letter is sent in application to an open position. In other words, you have been asked or invited to submit your résumé. An unsolicited letter is sent when there doesn't appear to be a job opening or advertised position available. Finally, a referral letter is sent to the contact person to whom you have been referred and usually makes mention of the person who put you in touch with the contact.

Like gift-wrapping on a present, a cover letter should attract the attention and interest of the reader and should be addressed to a specific person. The letter should be tailored to the industry and state the role for which you are applying, how you learned of the position, and why you are a good candidate. The cover letter states what you can do for the employer and is written in a positive manner.

Additionally, your cover letter should address next steps and thank the reader for his or her time. You should specifically state when you will follow up and close with an appreciation for being considered for the position. Double-check the cover letter for grammar and spelling accuracy, since employers often use it to evaluate written communication skills, while also confirming the spelling of the recipient's name.

Mark your calendar and follow up on the date you indicated in your cover letter. If you indicated you would call, use the opportunity to ask questions and set a date for an interview.

EMPLOYMENT DECISIONS

Employers considering you to be a viable job candidate now know a lot about you. You should also know a lot about the company. The primary purpose of further interviews is to determine whether you can work effectively within the organization.

If you continue to create a positive impression during subsequent interviews, you may be offered a position with the firm. Again, your decision to accept the offer should depend on how well the opportunity matches your career objectives. Make the best entry-level job decision you can and learn from it. Learn your job responsibilities as quickly and thoroughly as possible; then start looking for ways to improve your performance and that of your employer.

LETTERS OF RECOMMENDATION

Although most reference checks are conducted via telephone, and letters of recommendation are less common today, it is still good to have them on file. References may be obtained from former or current employers, supervisors from volunteer experiences, and professors and others who can attest to your academic and professional competencies. Letters of recommendation serve as testimonials to your performance in academic and work settings. The best references provide information relevant to the industry and specific marketing specialty as well as opinions on your skills, abilities, and character.

An effective letter of recommendation does the following:

1. States the length and nature of the relationship between the job candidate and the person providing the reference.

2. Describes the candidate's academic and career growth potential.

3. Reviews important achievements.

4. Outlines personal characteristics about the type of colleague the candidate will likely make.

5. Summarizes the candidate's strengths and abilities.

Because letters of recommendation take time and effort, it helps to provide a résumé and any other information relevant to the recommendation, along with a stamped, addressed envelope. When requesting letters of recommendation, you should allow ample time for your references to compose them—as long as a month is not unusual.

In addition to including a cover letter, résumé, and letters of recommendation, candidates should include photocopies of transcripts, writing samples, or other examples of work completed. For example, if you are applying for a position in public relations, advertising, or sports marketing, you may want to include examples of professional writing, graphics, and audio-visual tapes and DVDs to support written evidence of your credentials. Research and service projects that resulted in published or unpublished articles may also enhance your portfolio.

figure 3

Tips for Preparing an Electronic Résumé

Tips for Preparing an Electronic Résumé

- Use a plain font. Use a standard serif typeface, such as Courier, Times, Arial, Univers, or Futura. Simplicity is key.
- Use 11- to 14-point type sizes.
- Keep your line length to no more than 65 characters (letters, spaces, and punctuation).
- Do not use graphics, bullets, lines, bold, italics, underlines, or shading.
- Use capital letters for your headings.
- Justify your text to the left.
- Use vertical and horizontal lines sparingly. Lines may blur your type.
- Omit parentheses and brackets, even around telephone numbers. These can blur and leave the number unreadable.
- Use white paper and black type.
- Use a laser-quality printer.
- Print on one side of the paper only.
- Don't compress space between letters. Use a second page rather than pack everything into one page and have it scan unclearly.
- Do not staple pages of a résumé together.
- Use industry buzzwords. Keyword searches often look for industry jargon.
- Place your name as the first text on the résumé. Do not put anything else on that line.
- Fax résumés on the *fine mode* setting. It is much easier to read than the *standard mode* setting.
- Do not fold your résumé. A crease makes scanning—and retrieving—difficult.
- If you are sending your résumé in the body of an e-mail transmission, do not distinguish between pages, as the full e-mail will download into the database as one sheet.
- Don't send a résumé as an e-mail attachment unless you are specifically instructed to do so. Many employers discard unsolicited attachments.

REPRINTED FROM JOBWEB (WWW.JOBWEB.COM) WITH PERMISSION OF THE NATIONAL ASSOCIATION OF COLLEGES AND EMPLOYERS, COPYRIGHT HOLDER.

Source: Mary Lebeau, "Tips for Electronic Resumes," JobWeb Career Library, http://www.jobweb.com, accessed September 8, 2006. Reprinted from JobWeb (www.jobweb.com) with permission of the National Association of Colleges and Employers, copyright holder.

DEALING WITH AUTOMATED SYSTEMS

The Internet has significantly affected the entire recruiting and hiring process. Many employers have applicant tracking systems or automated résumé-processing capabilities. As a result, you should prepare a technology-compatible résumé or e-résumé and cover letter. Figure 3 contains a number of tips for creating an effective electronic résumé. The information contained on e-résumés is transferred to a company's database. The information may be entered into the database manually—from a printed or electronic copy, scanned or copied from the electronic version.

Employers who review electronic résumés and those posted on some of the 3000 websites currently carrying job postings frequently save time by using computers to search for keywords in job titles, job descriptions, or résumés to narrow the search. In fact, *manager* is the number-one word for which companies search. Regardless of the position you seek, the key to an effective electronic résumé is to use exact words and phrases, emphasizing nouns rather than the action verbs you are likely to use in a printed résumé. For example, a company looking for a marketing account manager with experience in Lotus 1-2-3, Microsoft Word, and Microsoft Excel programs is likely to conduct computer searches for only those résumés that include the job title and the three software programs.

LEARNING MORE ABOUT JOB OPPORTUNITIES

You should carefully study the various employment opportunities you have identified. Obviously, you will like some more than others, but you should examine a number of factors when evaluating each job possibility:

1. Actual job responsibilities, position title, to whom the position reports, opportunities for advancement

2. Industry characteristics, growing or shrinking market, typical career path, length of time in roles before promotion, average salary, hours expected in a work week

3. Company information—size, scope, public, private, national, international, reputation in the marketplace, company values, culture

4. Location, travel expectations

5. Compensation, base salary, bonuses, vacation entitlement, hours, benefits

6. How/If this position contributes to your long-term career vision and strategy

Too many job applicants consider only the most striking features of a job, such as tier-one company, location, or salary. However, a comprehensive review of the opportunity should provide a balanced perspective of the overall employment opportunity, including both long-term and short-term factors.

JOB INTERVIEWS

According to Tim Cork, president at NEXCareer, a corporate outplacement and human resources consulting firm, "Employers make hiring decisions within the first few minutes of the job interview." The decision is based on three criteria: attitude, aptitude, and action. This is the foundation for Tim's national best-selling book *Tapping the Iceberg*. Your aptitude has landed you the interview and now you need to convince the interviewer you have the right attitude and the ability to "get the job done."

The interview demands considerable planning and preparation on your part. You need to enter the interview equipped with a good understanding of the company, its industry, and its competition. Prepare yourself for the interview by learning as much as you can about the company and, if possible, the person interviewing you.

1. When was the company founded?

2. What is its current position in the industry?

3. What is its financial status?

4. In which markets does it compete?

5. How is the firm organized?

6. Who are its competitors?

7. How many employees does it have?

8. Where are its other locations?

9. What are its values?

10. What is its culture?

Having this information is extremely useful. First, knowing so much about the firm should give you a feeling of confidence and should contribute to your positive attitude. Second, it demonstrates knowledge and an interest in the organization. You can make a more informed decision about joining the organization and you can make a solid impression on the interviewers as they try to determine how much you know about the company. A job applicant who fails to make an effort to obtain information risks being eliminated from the process early on.

Train for your career like it's the most important race of your life.

Plan ahead to get ahead.   DestinyME™

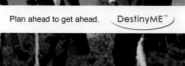

DestinyMe provides career counselling through customized programs that will help you to develop:

• Your career strategy
• An immediate action plan
• Comprehensive tools for every step of the way
• Strategies to get the job you want

The 4-phase Career Consultation

Career Mapping
↓
Personal Marketing
↓
Networking
↓
Closing

For more information or to book an appointment
416-927-6843

www.destinyme.ca   DestinyME™

COURTESY OF NEXCAREER

Live and online services such as DestinyME complement the services of your school's career centre. Their aim is to help job seekers be well prepared and positioned for entry into the job market.

To find information on a particular company, start with its website. Then search the Internet to see what has been in the news or online about the organization. Additionally, you can find directories online. Industry Canada's website is one source that provides information on Canadian public companies. The reference librarian at your college or university can direct you to sources to use in investigating a firm. Talk to your business professors as they may also provide information, or ask friends and relatives if they have any input or sources for you to contact. Either they or people they know may have had experience with the company.

Interviewers usually cite poor communication, lack of preparation, and lack of confidence as the main reasons for an unsuccessful job interview. Remember that the interviewer will make a determination about whether you communicate well based on your responses and reactions to the questions posed. You will need to be specific in answering and asking questions. A general rule of thumb is to answer with an example of a situation, action, and result (SAR). Basically, provide context to your answer, outline the specific behaviour you took to address the situation, and describe what happened as a result. The most common questions asked in an interview are these:

• Tell me about yourself.

• What are your strengths?

• What are your weaknesses?

• Why should I hire you?

It is important to know the name of the person (or persons) interviewing you, his or her regular job responsibilities, and who will make the final hiring decision. In many cases, the people who conduct initial job interviews work in the human resources department. These interviewers typically make recommendations to line managers about which applicants appear most suitable for the vacancy. Line managers get involved later in the hiring process. Some hiring decisions result from joint interviews conducted by both a human resources representative and the immediate supervisor of the prospective employee. Most often, immediate supervisors make the decision alone or in combination with input from senior employees in the department who will be colleagues of the new hire. Rarely does human resources have sole hiring authority for professional marketing positions. As you did for the company, consider doing an Internet check on the individuals who will interview you; you may discover a community leader, an active board member, or a former tennis champion. Insert your findings in the interview as a way to break the ice to demonstrate you have done your homework.

Preparing for an interview doesn't end here. You need to make a strong first impression so you'll need to dress for the occasion, as the "Etiquette Tips for Marketing Professionals" feature explains.

In a typical format, the interviewer talks very little during the interview. The interviewer will ask open-ended, behaviourally based questions. This approach forces you to talk about yourself while providing examples of past behaviour. Because past behaviour is the best predictor of future behaviour, the interviewer wants to see how you respond and react in different situations. Be sure to answer the question directly, express your thoughts clearly, and keep the conversation on target. Usually, you will be given the opportunity to ask questions. Come prepared. Listen carefully to the responses. Remember that if you prepare, it will become a mutual exchange of information. It is advisable to write down all the typical questions you are expected to be asked and think through ahead of time how you will answer them. Practise makes perfect, and rehearsing until the answers are natural is a sound strategy.

A successful first interview will probably result in an invitation to return for a second interview. In some cases, this invitation will include a request to take a battery of tests. Most students do very well on these tests because they have had plenty of practise in the classroom!

MARKETING POSITIONS

The basic objective of any firm is to market its goods or services. Marketing responsibilities vary among organizations and industries. In a small firm, the owner or president may assume many of the company's marketing responsibilities. A large firm needs a staff of experienced sales, marketing, and advertising managers to coordinate these activities. The "Career Path" features that follow outline major marketing positions, providing job descriptions and projected career paths for each. Each position is also cross-referenced to the chapter in this text that discusses the marketing area in detail.

ETIQUETTE TIPS FOR MARKETING PROFESSIONALS

How to Dress for Your Job Interview

LANDING a job interview is a big step on the road to starting your career. Making the most of the opportunity to create a good impression—and to learn something about the company you might work for—begins with presenting yourself well. This means being prepared; projecting confidence, eagerness, and dependability; and looking the part. Here are some tips for dressing for the interview. Unless you are applying for a very unusual job, in which case you can actually call ahead and find out what attire is appropriate, these suggestions will serve you well.

1. Dress conservatively. A dark two-piece suit in a current style is best for men and women, with a conservative long-sleeved shirt or blouse. Men should choose a conservatively patterned tie. Keep conventional jewellery and makeup to a minimum.
2. Make sure your clothes are clean and well-pressed and that there are no runs in stockings or holes in socks.
3. Wear clean, well-polished shoes.
4. Make sure your nails are clean and short. If you wear polish, use a conservative colour.
5. Use a minimum of cologne or perfume.
6. Keep your pockets free of noisy coins and keys or bulging items like phones or pagers.
7. Leave nose rings, eyebrow rings, and other unusual body ornaments at home.
8. Keep your hair neat, groomed, and short (for men) or off your face (for women). Men should be clean-shaven.
9. Carry a portfolio or briefcase (women might carry one instead of a purse to avoid clutter).

Looking professional is the first step to conducting a successful interview—and landing a job. So think first what the interviewer would like to see in a job candidate and dress accordingly. Then both you and the interviewer will be more at ease.

Sources: "Dress for Interview Success," http://www.collegegrad.com/jobsearch/, accessed June 30, 2004; Randall S. Hansen, "When Job-Hunting: Dress for Success," *Quintessential Careers*, http://www.quint careers.com, accessed June 30, 2004; Joann S. Lublin, "Dated Suit, Dirty Nails Can Tip the Balance If You're Job Hunting," *The Wall Street Journal*, June 1, 2004, p. B1.

Career Path 1: Marketing, Advertising, Product, and Public Relations Managers
Related Chapters: Chapters 1–2 (marketing); Chapters 10–11 (product); Chapters 14–15 (advertising and public relations)

Edited by Daphne Bykerk, Partner and Marketing Practice Leader at Mandrake Executive Search

Marketing management spans a range of positions, including from most senior to junior, chief marketing officer (CMO) or vice president of marketing, director of marketing, marketing manager, sales manager, product manager, advertising manager, promotion manager, and public relations manager. The CMO or vice president directs the firm's overall marketing policy, and all other marketers report through channels to this person. Sales managers direct the efforts of sales professionals by assigning territories, establishing goals, developing training programs, and supervising local sales managers and their personnel. Advertising managers oversee account services, creative services, and media services departments. Promotions managers direct promotional programs that combine advertising with purchase incentives designed to increase the sales of the firm's goods or services. Public relations managers are responsible for communicating with the firm's various publics, conducting publicity programs, and supervising the specialists who implement these programs.

Job Description
As with senior management positions in production, finance, and other areas, top marketing management positions often involve long hours and extensive travel. Work under pressure is also common. For sales managers, job transfers between headquarters and regional offices may disrupt one's personal life.

Career Path
A degree in business administration, preferably with a concentration in marketing, is usually required for these positions. In highly technical industries, such as computers, pharmaceuticals, chemicals, and electronics, employers typically prefer bachelor's degrees in science or engineering combined with master's degrees in business administration. Liberal arts students can also find many opportunities, especially if they have business minors. Most managers are promoted from positions such as sales representatives, product or brand specialists, and advertising specialists within their organizations. Skills or traits that are most desirable for these jobs include high motivation levels, maturity, creativity, resistance to stress, flexibility, and the ability to communicate persuasively.

Career Path 2: Sales Representatives and Sales Managers
Related Chapter: Chapter 16

Edited by Louise Daigneault, Sales Practice Leader at Mandrake Executive Search

Millions of items are bought and sold every day. The people in the firm who carry out this activity may have a variety of titles—sales representative, account manager, account executive, manufacturer's representative, sales engineer, sales agent, retail salesperson, wholesale sales representative, and inside sales or service sales representative. In addition, many organizations require that all marketing professionals spend some time in the field to experience the market firsthand and to understand the challenges faced by front-line personnel.

Job Description
Salespeople are usually responsible for developing prospective client lists, meeting with current and prospective customers to discuss the firm's products, and then following up to answer questions and supply additional information. By knowing the business needs of each customer, the sales representative can identify products that best satisfy these needs. Following a customer purchase, they are likely to revisit their customers to ensure that the products are meeting the customers' needs and to explore further business opportunities or referrals provided by satisfied buyers. Some sales of technical products involve lengthy interactions. In these cases, a salesperson may work with several clients simultaneously over a large geographic area. Those responsible for large territories may spend most of their workdays on the phone, receiving and sending e-mail messages, or on the sales floor.

Depending on the industry, sales professionals are often focused on either finding new clients or maintaining the account base through organic growth. The business-to-business environment, where sales professionals are often rewarded and compensated on how much new business they can generate, requires individuals with strong skills in relationship building, research, planning, and presentation. The business-to-consumer environment often requires sales professionals to be skilled in planning, as well as being strong in negotiation, analytics, and problem solving.

Career Path

The background needed for a sales position varies according to the product line and market. Most professional sales jobs require a college or university degree, and many companies run their own formal training programs that can last up to two years for sales representatives in technical industries. This training may take place in a classroom, in the field with a mentor, or most often using a combination of both methods. Sales managers are usually promoted from the field; they are likely to include successful sales representatives who exhibit managerial skills and promise. Sales management positions begin at a local or district level, then advance to positions of increased authority and responsibility such as area, key accounts, regional, national, and international sales manager.

Career Path 3: Marketing Communications Specialists
Related text: Chapters 14–15

Edited by Michael Gates, Marcomm Practice Leader at Mandrake Executive Search

Marketing communications is an area that provides many career options. The area can be subdivided into advertising, direct marketing, interactive marketing, sales promotions, and design (public relations is covered separately in this prologue).

There are two distinct streams that one can pursue to build a career in marketing communications; one is to work for an agency, and the second is to work in a company, often referred to as a client role.

Of the agency opportunities, advertising is the largest industry and it has three main departments: client service, media, and creative. The client service role is to manage the relationship with the client, develop strategy, brief the creative teams, and lead the process. The media department plans and buys the advertising working with television, radio, print, and out-of-home (billboard) media companies. The creative department is responsible for the look and content that the consumer ultimately sees, hears, touches, smells, or feels; the two main disciplines are copy writing and art direction. The work of the creative department can be high profile, and many award shows in the industry recognize the best ads and campaigns.

Direct marketing (also called database marketing and customer relationship marketing—CRM) is a large and growing field. Those working in this area could use databases to learn more about their customers in order to design promotional material aimed specifically at them.

Interactive marketing includes website design, e-commerce solutions, and e-mail marketing. There is a growing convergence of direct and interactive marketing as the lines between the functions blur.

Sales promotion agencies develop programs such as contests, in-store promotions, games, and give-aways. The programs may launch a new product or support a product or business in a competitive or seasonal situation.

Design agencies specialize in helping companies develop their visual identity and brand. They may provide services such packaging design, logo and identity design, company naming, and brand architecture plans. The key departments are client service and creative.

Job Description

The marketing communications jobs call on you to develop communications to help your company or your agency's customers reach their customer. The role needs solid business acumen combined with an understanding of how to build a brand and a business. Marketing communications offers a wide variety of career options, from creative services (developing and producing ads) to direct marketing.

Career Path

An entry-level position is usually as an account executive, and strong performers usually move to the next level in three to five years. Marketing communications attracts people from a wide variety of backgrounds and education as great value is placed on on-the-job learning. Marketing communications roles within a company are available as well at the entry level. In the creative area, degrees or diplomas in art and design are usually expected. Specialized educational programs provide specific training in advertising, direct marketing, and e-commerce and can be taken full-time, post-graduate, or through an industry program. Migration between agency and company roles is quite common after four to eight years. The agency roles offer the chance to work with many clients and industries in a creative environment.

Career Path 4: Public Relations Specialists
Related Chapters: Chapters 14 and 15

Edited by Janine Turner, PR Practice Leader at Mandrake Executive Search

Specialists in public relations strive to engender and nurture positive relationships with various publics in order to meet organizational goals or to mitigate issues or crises. Traditionally, public relations specialists would assist in arranging media interviews, overseeing company archives, responding to information requests, and handling special events. Today, they play a more strategic role in both protecting and promoting an organization's or product's reputation, supporting marketing goals, and affecting the legislative landscape. Specialized areas in which public relations professionals operate include crisis management, investor relations, media skill training, and government relations.

Job Description

While public relations specialists work a normal work week, they must be "on guard" 24 hours a day for events that may have an impact on their organization. Occasionally, they are required to be on the job or on call around the clock to respond to an emergency or crisis. Approximately 10 000 public relations specialists are currently employed in Canada, with about 10 percent in service industries. Public relations positions tend to be concentrated in large cities where corporate or organizational head offices are based. Most public relations consulting firms are concentrated in Toronto, Vancouver, Calgary, Montreal, and Ottawa.

Essential characteristics for public relations specialists include the ability to express thoughts clearly and simply—both verbally and in writing; strong presentation skills; a keen interest in current events, social trends, and business; strategic thinking and creativity.

Career Path

A university degree combined with public relations experience, usually gained through one or more internships, is considered excellent preparation for a career in public relations. A few Canadian universities and many community colleges offer public relations or communications degrees or diplomas. New employees in larger organizations are likely to participate in formal training programs; those who begin their careers at smaller firms typically work under the guidance of experienced members. Entry-level positions carry such titles as coordinator or account assistant. A potential career path in a public relations firm includes a promotion to account executive, account supervisor, vice president, and senior vice president.

Career Path 5: Purchasing Agents and Managers
Related Chapter: Chapter 5

Edited by Stephen Milič, Logistics Practice Leader at Mandrake Executive Search

In the 21st-century business world, the two key marketing functions of buying and selling are performed by trained specialists. Just as every organization is involved in selling its output to meet the needs of customers, so too must all companies make purchases of goods and services required to operate their businesses and turn out items for sale.

Modern technology has transformed the role of the purchasing agent. The transfer of routine tasks to computers now allows contract specialists, or procurement officers, to focus on products, suppliers, and contract negotiations. The primary function of this position is to purchase the goods, materials, component parts, supplies, and services required by the organization. These agents ensure that suppliers deliver quality and quantity levels that match the firm's needs; they also secure these inputs at reasonable prices and make them available when needed.

Purchasing agents must develop good working relationships both with colleagues in their own organizations and with suppliers. As the popularity of outsourcing has increased, the selection and management of suppliers have become critical functions of the purchasing department. In the government sector, this role is dominated by strict laws, statutes, and regulations that change frequently. The most significant trend in the last few years has been the implementation of Supplier Certification: suppliers must meet strict guidelines relating to product specs (most often of concern is quality).

Job Description

Purchasing agents can expect a standard work week with some travel to suppliers' sites, seminars, and trade shows.

Career Path

Organizations prefer university- or college-educated candidates for entry-level jobs in purchasing. Strong analytical and communication skills are required for any purchasing position. New hires often begin their careers by enrolling in extensive company training programs in which they learn procedures and operations. Training may include assignments dealing with production planning. Professional certification is becoming an essential criterion for advancement in both the private and the public sectors. A variety of associations serving the different categories of purchasing confer certifications on agents, including Certified Purchasing Manager, Professional Public Buyer, Certified Public Purchasing Officer, Certified Associate Contract Manager, and Certified Professional Contract Manager.

Career Path 6: Retail and Wholesale Buyers and Merchandise Managers
Related Chapter: Chapter 13

COURTESY OF DONNA PEARL/ MANDRAKE

Edited by Donna Pearl, Retail Practice Leader at Mandrake Executive Search

Buyers working for retailers and wholesale businesses purchase goods for resale. Their goal is to find the best possible merchandise at the lowest prices. They also influence the distribution and marketing of this merchandise. Successful buyers must understand what appeals to consumers and what their establishments can sell. Product bar codes and point-of-purchase terminals allow organizations to accurately track goods that are selling and those that are not; buyers frequently analyze this data to improve their understanding of consumer demand. Buyers also check competitors' prices and sales activities and watch general economic conditions to anticipate consumer buying patterns.

Job Description

Jobs as retail and wholesale buyers and merchandise managers often require substantial travel, as many orders are placed on buying trips to shows and exhibitions. Effective planning and decision-making skills are strong assets in this career. In addition, the job involves anticipating consumer preferences and ensuring that the firm keeps needed goods in stock. Consequently, the people filling these positions must possess such qualities as resourcefulness, intuitiveness, and self-confidence.

Career Path

Most retail and wholesale buyers begin their careers as assistant buyers or trainees. Large retailers seek university- or college-educated candidates, and extensive training includes job experience in a variety of positions. Advancement often comes when buyers move to departments or new locations with larger volumes—or become merchandise managers to coordinate or oversee the work of several buyers.

Career Path 7: Marketing Research Analysts
Related Chapter: Chapter 7

COURTESY OF TINA SANTOS/ MANDRAKE

Edited by Tina Santos, Research Practice Leader at Mandrake Executive Search

These marketing specialists assist marketers in identifying and defining opportunities in a variety of areas from product innovation to advertising. They generate, refine, and evaluate marketing actions and monitor marketing performance. Marketing research analysts devise methods and procedures for obtaining needed, decision-oriented data. Once they compile data, analysts evaluate it and then make recommendations to marketing management.

Job Description

Firms that specialize in marketing research and management consulting employ the majority of the nation's marketing research analysts. These positions are often concentrated in larger cities, such as Toronto, Montreal, and Vancouver. Those who pursue careers in marketing research must be capable of working accurately with detail, display patience and persistence, work effectively both independently and with others, and operate objectively and systematically. Significant analytical and computer skills are essential for success in this field.

Career Path

A bachelor's degree with an emphasis in marketing provides sufficient qualifications for most entry-level jobs in marketing research. Because of the importance of quantitative skills and the need for competence in using analytical software packages, this education should include courses in statistics, calculus, and survey design. Courses in psychology would contribute to understanding people, cultures, and behaviour patterns. Experience in conducting interviews or surveys while in school can be an asset.

Career Path 8: Logistics: Material Receiving, Scheduling, Dispatching, and Distributing Occupations
Related Chapter: Chapter 12

COURTESY OF STEPHEN MILIC/ MANDRAKE

Edited by Stephen Milic, Logistics Practice Leader at Mandrake Executive Search

Logistics offers a myriad of career positions. Job titles under this broad heading include material receiving, scheduling, dispatching, materials management executive, distribution operations coordinator, distribution centre manager, and transportation manager. The logistics function includes responsibilities for production and inventory planning and control, distribution, and transportation.

Job Description

These positions demand good communication skills and the ability to work effectively under pressure.

Career Path

Computer skills are highly valued in these jobs. Employers look for candidates with degrees in logistics and transportation. However, graduates in marketing and other business disciplines may succeed in this field.

ADDITIONAL INFORMATION SOURCES

Helpful career information is available for you at the *Contemporary Marketing* website: **http://www.contemporarymarketing.nelson.com**. The site provides a vast number of career resources, such as links to job sites, career guidance sites, newspaper job ads, and company information.

Marketer's Minute: Talking about Marketing Careers, a feature at the end of each of the seven parts of this text, consists of an interview with a marketing executive in a major organization. By reading about a marketing executive's typical day, learning what keeps each of them motivated, and hearing their views on industry trends, you'll have a glimpse into today's marketing industry. You'll also hear what they have to say about the most important skills for new grads, from general advice to tips on giving presentations.

part 1

DESIGNING CUSTOMER-ORIENTED MARKETING STRATEGIES

chapter 1

Marketing: The Art and Science of Satisfying Customers

CHAPTER OBJECTIVES

1. Define *marketing*, explain how it creates utility, and describe its role in the global marketplace.

2. Contrast marketing activities during the four eras in the history of marketing.

3. Explain the importance of avoiding marketing myopia.

4. Describe the characteristics of not-for-profit marketing.

5. Identify and briefly explain each of the five types of nontraditional marketing.

6. Outline the importance of creativity, critical thinking, and the technology revolution in marketing.

7. Explain the shift from transaction-based marketing to relationship marketing.

8. Identify the universal functions of marketing.

9. Demonstrate the relationship between ethical business practices, social responsibility, and marketplace success.

CV TECHNOLOGIES: THE UPS, AND DOWNS, AND UPS, AND... .

From barely known in 2002, to *Marketing* magazine's 2005 Marketer-of-the-Year, to fighting its way back in 2008, CV Technologies (CVT) is one of Canada's most exciting marketing stories.

In 1996, when CVT went public, it had a virtually unknown product: COLD-fX, a ginseng-based remedy for the common cold and flu. The product was sold in only a few health food stores until CVT heard that the Edmonton Oilers were using it. CVT agreed to supply the team with COLD-fX in exchange for participation in a research study of the product's effectiveness. Unfortunately, the company continued to lose money and, by early 2003, bankruptcy threatened. CVT had to lay off 25 scientists, sell its equipment, and vacate its operating location. Revenue for the year was only $1.5 million, while the company recorded a loss of $1.8 million. Things looked bleak.

Almost immediately after CVT hired a public relations professional, the *National Post* ran a front-page article on COLD-fX, and hundreds of newspaper and magazine articles soon followed. Sales grew rapidly, and the company had to outsource some manufacturing to meet demand. In July 2004, Don Cherry of *Hockey Night in Canada* fame agreed to become a celebrity spokesperson for the company and to forgo fees in exchange for a percentage of CVT's future earnings that were to be contributed to Rose Cherry's Home for Kids. Cherry appeared in radio, television, and print ads and was prominently shown in point-of-purchase displays at retail locations where COLD-fX was sold. Comedian Rick Mercer gave the product a plug on *Rick Mercer's Monday Report* on CBC-TV. During the year, CVT developed strong trade relations, increasing participating retail merchants from about 1000 to more than 4000 outlets. Sales grew to $6.4 million; marketing expenses were $1.3 million. CV Technologies made a small profit: $150 918. The company described 2004 as its "breakout year."

Throughout 2005, favourable publicity continued. CVT was selected as the best-performing company from among nearly 2000 companies on the TSX Venture Exchange. It won the Ernst & Young Entrepreneur of the Year Award in Health Sciences. The Deloitte Tech Fast 50 selected it as one of the 50 fastest-growing companies in Canada. Stories appeared in *Maclean's, Profit* magazine, and *Globe and Mail*'s Report on (Small) Business. CVT opened a Toronto sales and marketing office, and it entered the Quebec market, where it gained credibility through its association with the Montreal Canadiens. Distribution continued to grow to 6000 retail outlets, including health food stores and Costco, Loblaws, and Shoppers Drug Mart locations. Sales quintupled to $31.9 million; profit increased nearly 70 times to $10.1 million. Marketing expenses were $5.2 million.

During 2006, sales continued to increase to $41.4 million, and marketing costs grew to $8.3 million, but profit dropped to only $639 016. CVT started to focus on the U.S. market, building distribution through the country's largest pharmacies in preparation for the 2006 cold and flu season. It hoped for strong U.S. sales in 2007. Overall sales grew only marginally to $42 million as sales in the U.S. were very disappointing. Many U.S. retailers returned unsold inventory. CVT had increased its marketing expenses to $16.4 million ($10.5 million to support the U.S. launch). The end result was a loss of $9.8 million.

Going into 2008, the company is optimistic. CVT has tapped into "Brand Power" ads in which a female spokesperson describes four product benefits to mothers, the company's new target market. First-quarter profits were a record $6.8 million on sales of $21.3 million. But only $400 000 of those sales were in the U.S. CVT plans to continue in the U.S. market, but it will focus on the northeastern states and will manage its marketing costs to be in line with sales. COLD-fX is the company's core product, but it also has a portfolio of other products that are in various stages of market development: Remember-fX, Cell-fX, Ad-fX, Menta-fX, and Pressure-fX.[1]

connecting with customers

CVT connects with customers by effectively combining traditional marketing media—radio and television ads, and point-of-purchase displays—with newer promotion techniques: public relations, celebrity endorsements, and word-of-mouth promotion. Its strong endorsements have created awareness and credibility in each market where it was successful: the Edmonton Oilers (Alberta), Don Cherry (Ontario), and the Montreal Canadiens (Quebec).

Chapter Overview

- "I only drink Tim Hortons coffee."
- "I buy all my electronics at Future Shop."
- "My next car will be a Toyota Prius."
- "I go to all the Vancouver Canucks games at General Motors Place."

THESE words are music to a marketer's ears. They may echo the click of an online purchase, the *ping* of a cash register, the cheers of fans at a stadium. Customer loyalty is the watchword of 21st-century marketing. Individual consumers and business purchasers have so many goods and services from which to choose—and so many different ways to purchase them—that marketers must continually seek out new and better ways to attract and keep customers. Sometimes they miss the boat, allowing other companies to make the most of opportunities. Amazon.com, which recently cleared $1 billion in quarterly sales, lags far behind Apple in one area of e-business—the digital delivery of music and movies. Completely trounced by Apple's iTunes, Amazon has scurried to come up with a better way to serve music customers. When Apple signed with major label EMI to deliver online music without digital rights management (DRM) software, it announced plans to have 50 percent of its music DRM-free by the end of 2007. Now Amazon has signed with competing major labels—Warner, Sony/ BMG, and Universal—and has 4.5 million DRM-free songs in its catalogue,

compared to only 2 million available through Apple.[2]

The technology revolution continues to change the rules of marketing during this first decade of the 21st century and will continue to do so in years beyond. The combined power of telecommunications and computer technology creates inexpensive global networks that transfer voice messages, text, graphics, and data within seconds. These sophisticated technologies create new types of products, and they also demand new approaches to marketing existing products. Media mogul Rupert Murdoch, chairman of News Corp.—parent company of Fox and MySpace.com—takes a hard line on the news and information industry and the importance of developing new ways to communicate with consumers. "Most newspaper companies still have their heads in the sand, but other media companies are aggressive," he says. "And there are completely new start-up companies. There is a great pace of development, which is very exciting. At News Corp., we have been developing online extensions of traditional media for the last few years."[3]

Communications technology contributes as well to the globalization of today's marketplace, where businesses manufacture, buy, and sell across national borders. You can bid at eBay on a potential bargain or eat a Big Mac or drink Coca-Cola almost anywhere in the world; your DVD or CD player was probably manufactured in China or South Korea. Both

Honda and Toyota manufacture cars in Canada, while some Volkswagens are imported from Mexico. Finished products and components routinely cross international borders, but successful global marketing also requires knowledge to tailor products to regional tastes. Restaurants in Newfoundland and Labrador, for example, often have cod tongues on their menu. This delicacy is seldom found elsewhere in Canada.

Rapidly changing business landscapes create new challenges for companies, whether they are giant multinational firms or small boutiques, profit-oriented or not-for-profit. Organizations must react quickly to shifts in consumer tastes, competitive offerings, and other market dynamics. Fortunately, information technologies give organizations fast new ways to interact and develop long-term relationships with their customers and suppliers. In fact, such links have become a core element of marketing today.

Every company must serve customer needs—create customer satisfaction—to succeed. We call customer satisfaction an art because it requires imagination and creativity and a science because it requires technical knowledge, skill, and experience. Marketing strategies are the tools by which businesspeople identify and analyze customers' needs and then inform these customers about how the company can meet those needs. Tomorrow's market leaders will be companies that can make the most of these strategies to create satisfied customers.

This new Canadian edition of *Contemporary Marketing* focuses on the strategies that allow companies to succeed in today's interactive marketplace. This chapter sets the stage for the entire text, examining the importance of creating satisfaction through customer relationships. Initial sections describe the historical development of marketing and its contributions to society. Later sections introduce the technology revolution, the universal functions of marketing, and the relationship between ethical business practices and marketplace success. Throughout the chapter—and the entire book—there will be discussions of customer loyalty and the lifetime value of a customer. ◆◆◆

WHAT IS MARKETING?

Production and marketing of goods and services—whether it's a new crop of organically grown vegetables or digital cable service—are the essence of economic life in any society. All organizations perform these two basic functions to satisfy their commitments to society, their customers, and their owners. They create a benefit that economists call **utility**—the want-satisfying power of a good or service. Table 1.1 describes the four basic kinds of utility: form, time, place, and ownership.

Form utility is created when the firm converts raw materials and component inputs into finished goods and services. By combining glass, plastic, metals, circuit boards, and other components, Canon makes a digital camera and Pioneer produces a plasma television. With fabric and leather, Prada manufactures its high-fashion line of handbags. With a ship and the ocean, a captain and staff, and food and entertainment, Royal Caribbean creates a cruise. Although the marketing function focuses on influencing consumer and audience preferences, the organization's production function creates form utility.

Marketing creates time, place, and ownership utilities. *Time and place utility* occur when consumers find goods and services available when and where they want to purchase them. Vending machines and convenience stores focus on providing place utility for people buying newspapers, snacks, and soft drinks. The owners of Golf Without Limits created time and place utility when they opened their indoor golf centre in Waterloo, Ontario. Customers can play a round of simulated golf at any of 30 world-class courses, regardless of season, weather, or time of day.[4]

The transfer of title to goods or services at the time of purchase creates ownership utility. Purchasing a new DVD, signing up for the Royal Caribbean cruise, or visiting Golf Without Limits creates ownership utility.

All organizations must create utility to survive. Designing and marketing want-satisfying goods, services, and ideas are the foundation for the creation of utility. Organizations recently have begun to elevate the function of marketing in their hierarchies; top marketing executives may be promoted to senior vice presidential positions. But where does the process start? In the toy industry, manufacturers try to come up with items that children will want to play with—creating utility. But that's not as simple as it sounds. At the Toy Fair held each February in New York, Canadian and U.S. retailers sift through goods at the different booths of manufacturers and suppliers, looking for the next Bratz dolls or Lego building blocks—trends that turn into classics and generate millions of dollars in revenues over the years.

In the area of entertainment, podcasts are creating a buzz. Podcasts—recorded audio files that are distributed through Internet download—create utility through their ability to be stored on computers or digital music devices and played back whenever the consumer wants. Start-up firms such as Odeo.com are scrambling to tap this market as quickly as possible. Odeo.com creates utility by organizing its shows according to topic—users can click on headings such as food and technology. To further help its listeners, Odeo employees scan the site for the best shows and post their "Staff Picks" on the Featured Channels page.[5]

① Define *marketing,* explain how it creates utility, and describe its role in the global marketplace.

utility Want-satisfying power of a good or service.

Marketoid

Fifty thousand golfers participate in corporate golf tournaments each year at Angus Glen in Markham, Ontario, one of Canada's best courses.

COURTESY SYNERGEX CORPORATION

Synergex promises to get your product "on the right shelf, at the right time." It helps provide place and time utility.

table 1.1   *Four Types of Utility*

TYPE	DESCRIPTION	EXAMPLES	ORGANIZATIONAL FUNCTION RESPONSIBLE
Form	Conversion of raw materials and components into finished goods and services	Dinner at Swiss Chalet; iPod; shirt from Mark's Work Wearhouse	Production*
Time	Availability of goods and services when consumers want them	Dental appointment; digital photographs; LensCrafters eyeglass guarantee; Canada Post Xpresspost	Marketing
Place	Availability of goods and services at convenient locations	Soft-drink machines outside gas stations; on-site day care; banks in grocery stores	Marketing
Ownership (possession)	Ability to transfer title to goods or services from marketer to buyer	Retail sales (in exchange for currency or credit-card payment)	Marketing

*Marketing provides inputs related to consumer preferences, but the actual creation of form utility is the responsibility of the production function.

But how does an organization create a customer? Most take a three-step approach: identifying needs in the marketplace, finding out which needs the organization can profitably serve, and developing goods and services to convert potential buyers into customers. Marketing specialists are responsible for most of the activities necessary to create the customers the organization wants. These activities include

- identifying customer needs

- designing products that meet those needs

- communicating information about those goods and services to prospective buyers

- making the items available at times and places that meet customers' needs

- pricing the merchandise and services to reflect costs, competition, and customers' ability to buy

- providing the necessary service and follow-up to ensure customer satisfaction after the purchase[6]

A DEFINITION OF MARKETING

The word *marketing* encompasses such a broad scope of activities and ideas that settling on one definition is often difficult. Ask three people to define marketing, and three different definitions are likely to follow. We are exposed to so much advertising and personal selling that most people link marketing only to those activities. But marketing begins long before a product hits the shelf. It involves analyzing customer needs, obtaining the information necessary to design and produce goods or services that match buyer expectations, satisfying customer preferences, and creating and maintaining relationships with customers and suppliers. Marketing activities apply to profit-oriented businesses such as Canadian Tire and Amazon. ca as well as not-for-profit organizations such as Mothers Against Drunk Driving and the Canadian Red Cross. Even towns, cities, and provinces of Canada engage in marketing activities. Today's definition takes all these factors into account. **Marketing** is an organizational function and a set of processes for creating, communicating, and delivering value to customers and for managing customer relationships in ways that benefit the organization and its stakeholders.[7]

YOU WANT TO KEEP YOUR QUALITY OF LIFE.

WE HAVE LIFESTYLE INSURANCE.

With Desjardins Financial Security's leading-edge Lifestyle Insurance, we protect your quality of life in the event of illness or loss of independence. Lifestyle Insurance provides tax-free funds that allow you to select the healthcare you need, when and where you need it.

As the life and health insurance arm of Desjardins Group, Canada's largest integrated financial cooperative with more than $144 billion in assets, we support more than five million Canadians with tailor-made lifestyle insurance through independent representatives.

Support and guidance... that's what we are all about!

Secure your lifestyle today!
1-877-438-7656
desjardinsfinancialsecurity.com/lifestyle

Desjardins
Financial Security®

Money working for people

Life, health, retirement

COURTESY DESJARDINS FINANCIAL SECURITY

To build strong client relationships, companies such as Desjardins Financial Security must be able to establish trust. It is part of Desjardins Group—Canada's largest integrated financial cooperative with more than $144 billion in assets.

The expanded concept of marketing activities permeates all organizational functions in businesses and not-for-profit organizations. It assumes that organizations conduct their marketing efforts ethically and that these efforts serve the best interests of both society and the organization. The concept also identifies the marketing variables—product, price, promotion, and distribution—that combine to provide customer satisfaction. In addition, it assumes that the organization begins by identifying and analyzing who its potential customers are and what they need. At all points, the concept emphasizes creating and maintaining long-term relationships with customers and suppliers.

marketing Organizational function and a set of processes for creating, communicating, and delivering value to customers and for managing customer relationships in ways that benefit the organization and its stakeholders.

TODAY'S GLOBAL MARKETPLACE

Several factors have forced marketers—and entire nations—to extend their economic views to events outside their own national borders. First, international agreements are being negotiated in attempts to expand trade among nations. Second, the growth of electronic commerce and related computer technologies is bringing previously isolated countries into the marketplace for buyers and sellers around the globe. Third, the interdependence of the world's economies is a reality because no nation produces all the raw materials and finished goods its citizens need or consumes all its output without exporting some to other countries. Evidence of this interdependence is illustrated by the introduction of the euro as a common currency to facilitate trade among the nations of the European Union and the creation of trade agreements such as the North American Free Trade Agreement (NAFTA) and the World Trade Organization. As a result of NAFTA, Canada enjoys access to a market totalling approximately 425 million people.

Marketoid

Canadian Tire is Canada's most-shopped retailer, attracting approximately 88 percent of Canadian consumers annually.

Rising oil prices affect the price that Canadian consumers pay for just about everything—not just gasoline at the pump. Consider the fuel surcharge on airline tickets. While these charges are visible, many increases that are due to higher oil prices are not so visible. However, when companies pay more to send and receive shipments, these increased costs get passed on to consumers as price increases. If the winter is mild, it might not cost so much to heat a house or apartment—but when temperatures drop and more oil and natural gas are used, costs to individual consumers can skyrocket. Threatened or real disruptions in the supply of oil also have dramatic economic impacts. Tribal disputes in Nigeria caused a cutback in oil production there. Hurricane Katrina caused drilling rigs and refineries to shut down temporarily along the U.S. Gulf Coast. Recent fires at refineries in Ontario and Alberta resulted in gasoline shortages in many areas of Canada. All these factors affect oil prices.

To remain competitive, companies must continually search for the most efficient manufacturing sites and most lucrative markets for their products. Canadian marketers now find tremendous opportunities serving customers not only in traditional industrialized nations but also in Latin America and emerging economies in Eastern Europe, the Middle East, Asia, and Africa, where rising standards of living create increased customer demand for the latest goods and services. Expanding operations beyond the Canadian market gives domestic companies access to more than 6.5 billion international customers. In addition, companies based in these emerging economies are beginning to compete as well. Since its acceptance into the World Trade Organization, China's exports have risen tremendously. Between 1997 and 2006, Canada's imports from China increased five-fold, while Canada's exports to that country tripled. China surpassed the United Kingdom and Japan to become Canada's second-largest trading partner.[8] China has become a manufacturing centre for many firms based in other countries as well. Japan's Fuji Photo Film recently announced that it would shift production of its digital cameras to China.[9]

Service firms also play a major role in today's global marketplace. Although the Toronto Stock Exchange is based in Toronto, investors from around the world trade several billion dollars every day over the exchange. Executive search firm Sterling-Hoffman Management Consultants employs 50 people in Canada, but 200 in India. This has allowed the company to improve its competitiveness through reduced staffing costs for activities such as basic accounting work, collections, graphic design, and market research.[10] India is an attractive supplier of many outsourced services as it has a large, English-fluent population of young workers. As many as 2.9 million students graduate each year in India with post-secondary degrees.[11]

Canada is also an attractive market for foreign competitors because of its size, proximity to the United States, and the high standard of living that Canadian consumers enjoy. The United States has made more investment in Canada than in any other country. Companies such as Avon, Wal-Mart,

assessment check 1

1.1 Define *marketing* and explain how it creates utility.

1.2 What three factors have forced marketers to embrace a global marketplace?

Home Depot, Procter & Gamble, General Electric, and Dell are actively targeting Canadian consumers. Among them, they perform such activities as production, assembly, distribution, service, and selling in Canada. In fact, several of them use their Canadian operations as major global suppliers for some of their product lines, frequently exporting their goods and services to the United States as well as to other countries. Approximately 85 percent of all Canadian exports go to the United States, while about 20 percent of U.S. exports come to Canada. Over $1 billion in trade crosses the Canada–U.S. border every day.

Although many global marketing strategies are almost identical to those used in domestic markets, more and more companies are tailoring their marketing efforts to the needs and preferences of consumers in foreign markets. It is often difficult to standardize a brand name on a global basis. The Japanese, for example, like the names of flowers or girls for their automobiles, names such as Bluebird, Bluebonnet, Violet, and Gloria. Canadians, on the other hand, prefer rugged outdoorsy names such as Challenger, Mustang, Mountaineer, and Cherokee.

② Contrast marketing activities during the four eras in the history of marketing.

exchange process
Activity in which two or more parties give something of value to each other to satisfy perceived needs.

FOUR ERAS IN THE HISTORY OF MARKETING

The essence of marketing is the **exchange process**, in which two or more parties give something of value to each other to satisfy perceived needs. Often people exchange money for tangible goods, such as video games, clothes, or groceries. In other situations, they exchange money for intangible services, such as a haircut or an education. Many exchanges involve a combination of goods and services, such as dinner in a restaurant where dinner represents the good and the wait staff represents the service. People also make exchanges when they donate money or time to a charitable cause, such as Habitat for Humanity.

Although marketing has always been a part of business, its importance has varied greatly. Figure 1.1 identifies four eras in the history of marketing: (1) the production era, (2) the sales era, (3) the marketing era, and (4) the relationship era.

THE PRODUCTION ERA

Prior to 1925, most firms—even those operating in highly developed economies in Western Europe and North America—focused narrowly on production. Manufacturers stressed production of quality products and then looked for people to purchase them. The prevailing attitude of this era held that a high-quality product would sell itself. This **production orientation** dominated business philosophy for decades; in fact, business success was often defined solely in terms of production successes.

The production era reached its peak during the early part of the 20th century. Henry Ford's mass-production line exemplifies this orientation. Ford's slogan, "They [customers] can have any colour they want, as long as it's black," reflected the prevalent attitude toward marketing. Production shortages and intense consumer demand ruled the day. It is easy to understand how production activities took precedence.

However, building a new product is no guarantee of success, and marketing history is cluttered with the bones of miserable product failures despite major innovations. In fact, more than 80 percent of new products fail. Inventing an outstanding new product is not enough. That product must also fill a perceived marketplace need. Otherwise, even the best-engineered, highest-quality product will fail. Even Henry Ford's horseless carriage took awhile to catch on. People were afraid of motor vehicles, which spat out exhaust, stirred up dust on dirt roads, got stuck in mud, and tied up horse traffic. Besides, at the speed of seven miles per hour, they caused all kinds of accidents and disruption. It took savvy marketing by some early salespeople—and eventually a widespread perceived need—to change people's minds about the product. Today, most of us could not imagine life without a car and have refined that need to preferences for certain types of vehicles, including SUVs, convertibles, trucks, and hybrids.

THE SALES ERA

As production techniques in North America and Europe became more sophisticated, output grew during the period from the 1920s into the early 1950s. As a result, manufacturers began to increase their emphasis on effective sales forces to find customers for their output. In this era, firms attempted to match their output to the potential number of customers who would want it. Companies with a

figure 1.1

Four Eras of Marketing History

ERA	Production	Sales	Marketing	Relationship
PREVAILING ATTITUDE	"A good product will sell itself."	"Creative advertising and selling will overcome consumers' resistance and persuade them to buy."	"The consumer rules! Find a need and fill it."	"Long-term relationships with customers and other partners lead to success."
APPROXIMATE TIME PERIOD*	Prior to 1920s	Prior to 1950s	Since 1950s	Since 1990s

FROM BOONE/KURTZ. CONTEMPORARY MARKETING, 13E. © 2008 SOUTH-WESTERN, A PART OF CENGAGE LEARNING, INC. REPRODUCED BY PERMISSION. WWW.CENGAGE.COM/PERMISSIONS

*In Canada and other highly industrialized economies.

sales orientation assume that customers will resist purchasing nonessential goods and services and that the task of personal selling and advertising is to persuade them to buy.

Although marketing departments began to emerge from the shadows of production and engineering during the sales era, they tended to remain in subordinate positions. Many chief marketing executives held the title of sales manager. But selling is only one component of marketing. As marketing scholar Theodore Levitt once pointed out, "Marketing is as different from selling as chemistry is from alchemy, astronomy from astrology, chess from checkers."

THE MARKETING ERA

Personal incomes and consumer demand for goods and services dropped rapidly during the Great Depression of the 1930s, thrusting marketing into a more important role. Organizational survival dictated that managers pay close attention to the markets for their goods and services. This trend ended with the outbreak of World War II, when rationing and shortages of consumer goods became commonplace. The war years, however, created only a pause in an emerging trend in business: a shift in the focus from products and sales to satisfying customer needs.

EMERGENCE OF THE MARKETING CONCEPT

The marketing concept, a crucial change in management philosophy, can be linked to the shift from a **seller's market**—one in which there were more buyers for fewer goods and services—to a **buyer's market**—one in which there were more goods and services than people willing to buy them. When World War II ended, factories stopped manufacturing war supplies and started turning out consumer products again, an activity that had, for all practical purposes, stopped during the war.

The advent of a strong buyer's market created the need for **consumer orientation** by businesses. Companies had to market goods and services, not just produce and sell them. This realization has been identified as the emergence of the marketing concept. Marketing would no longer be regarded as a supplemental activity performed after completion of the production process. Instead, the marketer would play a leading role in product planning. *Marketing* and *selling* would no longer be synonymous terms.

seller's market Market in which there are more buyers for fewer goods and services.

buyer's market Market in which there are more goods and services than people willing to buy them.

consumer orientation Business philosophy incorporating the marketing concept that emphasizes first determining unmet consumer needs and then designing a system for satisfying them.

marketing concept
Company-wide consumer orientation with the objective of achieving long-run success.

Today's fully developed **marketing concept** is a *companywide consumer orientation* with the objective of achieving long-run success. All facets—and all levels, from top to bottom—of the organization must contribute first to assessing and then to satisfying customer wants and needs. From marketing manager to accountant to product designer, every employee plays a role in reaching potential customers. Even during tough economic times, when companies tend to emphasize cutting costs and boosting revenues, the marketing concept focuses on the objective of achieving long-run success instead of short-term profits. Because the firm's survival and growth are built into the marketing concept, company-wide consumer orientation should lead to greater long-run profits.

Consider Apple Computer. Named first in a list of the top 20 innovative companies worldwide in a poll by Boston Consulting Group, respondents said Apple "delivers great consumer experiences with outstanding design."[12] Apple's popularity has surged with the introduction of its iPod line. Every teen wants one. Every college student wants one. Even baby boomers, who are close to retirement, want one. And where do they download songs? Apple's iTunes Music Store. In a deal with Disney, Apple now offers ABC shows such as *Lost* and *Grey's Anatomy* on its video iPod. And Disney's purchase of Pixar Animation Studios should increase the offerings. Many industry watchers credit Apple's co-founder and CEO Steven Jobs. Jobs, who left the company for 12 years, came back in a big way. Jobs has always been viewed as an innovator, and even his critics concede that he knows how to make what consumers want. And he won't compromise on quality. "I'm as proud of what we don't do as I am of what we do," says Jobs.[13]

A strong market orientation—the extent to which a company adopts the marketing concept—generally improves market success and overall performance. It also has a positive effect on new-product development and the introduction of innovative products. Companies that implement market-driven strategies are better able to understand their customers' experiences, buying habits, and needs. Like Apple, these companies can, therefore, design products with advantages and levels of quality compatible with customer requirements.

THE RELATIONSHIP ERA

relationship marketing
Development and maintenance of long-term, cost-effective relationships with individual customers, suppliers, employees, and other partners for mutual benefit.

The fourth era in the history of marketing emerged during the final decade of the 20th century and continues to grow in importance. Organizations now build on the marketing era's customer orientation by focusing on establishing and maintaining relationships with both customers and suppliers. **Relationship marketing** involves long-term, value-added relationships developed over time with customers and suppliers. Strategic alliances and partnerships among manufacturers, retailers, and suppliers often benefit everyone. It took a decade and more than $13 billion from four countries to launch the world's largest passenger plane, the Airbus 380. To develop the new aircraft, Airbus merged its partner companies into one large firm. Then it worked with more than 60 airports during the design phase to make sure that they could accommodate the aircraft. By the time Singapore Airlines conducted the first test flight, 13 other airlines had already placed orders for the Airbus 380.[14] The concept of relationship marketing, which is the current state of customer-driven marketing, is discussed in detail later in this chapter and in Chapter 9.

CONVERTING NEEDS TO WANTS

Every consumer must acquire goods and services on a continuing basis to fill certain needs. Everyone must satisfy the fundamental needs for food, clothing, shelter, and transportation by purchasing things or, in some instances, temporarily using rented property and hired or leased transportation. By focusing on the benefits resulting from these goods and services, effective marketing converts needs to wants. A need for a pair of pants may be converted to a desire for jeans—and further, a desire for jeans from Abercrombie & Fitch or American Eagle Outfitters. The need for food may be converted to a desire for a taco from Taco Bell or groceries from Sobeys or Real Canadian Superstore. But if the need for transportation isn't converted to a desire for a Honda Odyssey or a Ford Mustang, extra vehicles may sit unsold on a dealer's lot.

Consumers need to communicate. But converting that need to the desire for certain types of communication requires skill. It also requires listening to what consumers want. Consumers' demand for more cell

assessment check 2

2.1 What is the major distinction between the production era and the sales era?

2.2 What is the marketing concept?

2.3 Describe the relationship era of marketing.

phone and wireless services seems nearly unlimited—providing tremendous opportunities for companies. New products appear continually to feed that demand. The number of Wi-Fi Internet users has been increasing in recent years, laying the groundwork for the next generation of technology—WiMax—which allows even faster Internet access over greater areas. Infonetics Research is forecasting an annual increase in sales of 87 percent for WiMax products through 2010. Canada's Nortel Networks is investing heavily in WiMax and other fourth-generation wireless gear.[15]

AVOIDING MARKETING MYOPIA

③ Explain the importance of avoiding marketing myopia.

The emergence of the marketing concept has not been devoid of setbacks. One troublesome problem led marketing scholar Theodore Levitt to coin the term **marketing myopia.** According to Levitt, marketing myopia is management's failure to recognize the scope of its business. Product-oriented rather than customer-oriented management endangers future growth. Levitt cites many service industries—such as dry cleaning and electric utilities—as examples of marketing myopia. But many firms have found innovative ways to reach new markets and develop long-term relationships. Table 1.2 illustrates how firms in a number of industries have overcome myopic thinking by developing broader marketing-oriented business ideas that focus on consumer need satisfaction.

marketing myopia Management's failure to recognize the scope of its business.

When Miraz Manji opened The Learning Achievement Centre near the University of Toronto in 2005, his vision was to own a successful business providing tutoring services to students. Business was poor, and he quickly ran out of money. With the assistance of the Canadian Youth Business Foundation, Manji decided to supplement his business by providing printing and copier services to students. When Manji broadened his vision to provide services to students, his business became a success. By 2008, the business was a leader in printing services and was also achieving success mentoring rather than simply tutoring students.[16] Another firm, Renewable Environmental Solutions, converts remains from a Butterball turkey-processing plant into barrels of crude oil. Experts anticipate a huge wave of similar innovative products and marketing in the energy industry over the next few years.[17]

assessment check 3

3.1 What is marketing myopia?

3.2 Give an example of how a firm can avoid marketing myopia.

EXTENDING THE TRADITIONAL BOUNDARIES OF MARKETING

Today's organizations—both profit-oriented and not-for-profit—recognize universal needs for marketing and its importance to their success. During a television commercial break, viewers might be exposed to an advertisement for a Nissan Altima, an appeal to help feed children in foreign countries, a message by a political candidate, and a commercial for Tim Hortons—all in the space of about two minutes. Two of these ads are paid for by firms attempting to achieve profitability and other objectives. The appeal for funds to feed children and the political ad are examples of communications by not-for-profit organizations and individuals.

table 1.2   *Avoiding Marketing Myopia*

COMPANY	MYOPIC DESCRIPTION	COMPANY MOTTO—AVOIDING MYOPIA
Nokia	A cell phone manufacturer	Connecting People
Visa	A credit card company	Life Takes Visa
Purolator	A courier company	Where Business Is Going
Corporate Express Canada	An office supplies company	Productivity in Your Hands
Michelin	A tire manufacturer	A Better Way Forward
Xerox	A photocopier manufacturer	The Document Company
La-Z-Boy	A furniture manufacturer	Comfort. It's What We Do.

Marketing helps raise money to support social causes. The Canadian Cancer Society is a not-for-profit organization that supports research on cancer to improve the lives of Canadians.

COURTESY CANADIAN CANCER SOCIETY

MARKETING IN NOT-FOR-PROFIT ORGANIZATIONS

There are more than 160 000 not-for-profit and volunteer organizations in Canada, contributing over $60 billion annually to Canadian GDP. This is more than is contributed by accommodation and food services, agriculture, mining and oil and gas extraction, motor vehicle manufacturing, or retailing. That makes not-for-profit organizations big business.

Not-for-profit organizations operate in both public and private sectors. Federal, provincial, and municipal government units and agencies pursue service objectives that are not keyed to profitability targets. The Canada Border Services Agency is a federal government agency that provides border security services and helps facilitate the flow of people and goods across the Canadian border; individual provincial government departments regulate labour safety, environmental conservation and natural resources, and alcohol control; municipal school boards are responsible for overseeing educational and curriculum standards for their district. The private sector contains an even greater array of not-for-profit organizations, including zoos, hospitals, universities and colleges, ethnic and religious associations, and charities, such as the Make-a-Wish Foundation of Canada. Regardless of their size or location, all these organizations need funds to operate. Adopting the marketing concept can make a great difference in their ability to meet their service objectives.

Some not-for-profits form partnerships with business firms that promote the organization's cause or message. Home Depot has partnered with the National Wildlife Federation to offer environmentally friendly products. These items are marked with National Wildlife Federation stickers and sold in Home Depot retail outlets. Generally, the alliances formed between not-for-profit organizations and commercial firms benefit both. The reality of operating with multimillion-dollar budgets requires not-for-profit organizations to maintain a focused business approach. Consider some current examples:

- U2 band founder Bono recently launched a line of clothing called Red in an effort to raise money for the Global Fund to Fight AIDS, Tuberculosis, and Malaria. American Express, Converse, Giorgio Armani, and The Gap have pledged to sell the Red-themed products and donate some of the proceeds to the fund. American Express offers a Red credit card, and Armani sells a stylish pair of Red sunglasses.[18]

- Petro-Canada, Bell Canada, Royal Bank of Canada, Hudson's Bay Company, General Motors of Canada, and Rona are all national partners who have contributed millions of dollars to support the 2010 Olympic and Paralympic Winter Games to be held in Vancouver.

- M & M Meat Shops encourages its franchisees across Canada to support community-based charities and programs. Since 1989, at the corporate level, it has raised more than $12.5 million in support of the Crohn's and Colitis Foundation of Canada.

The diversity of not-for-profit organizations suggests the presence of numerous organizational objectives other than profitability. In addition to their organizational goals, not-for-profit organizations differ from profit-seeking firms in several other ways.

④ Describe the characteristics of not-for-profit marketing.

CHARACTERISTICS OF NOT-FOR-PROFIT MARKETING

The most obvious distinction between not-for-profit organizations and for-profit—commercial—firms is the financial **bottom line**, business jargon that refers to the overall profitability of an organization. For-profit organizations measure profitability by sales and revenues, and their goal is to generate revenues above and beyond their costs to make money for all stakeholders involved, including employees, shareholders, and the organization itself. Not-for-profit organizations hope to generate as much revenue as possible to support their causes, whether it is feeding children, preserving wilderness, or helping single mothers find work. Historically, not-for-profits have had less exact goals and marketing objectives than for-profit firms, but in recent years, many of these groups have recognized that, to succeed, they must develop more cost-effective ways to provide services, and they must compete with other organizations for donors' dollars. Marketing can help them accomplish these tasks.

Other distinctions exist between the two types of organizations as well, each of which influences marketing activities. Like profit-seeking firms, not-for-profit organizations may market tangible goods and/or intangible services. The Royal Ontario Museum sells individual passes and memberships, provides educational programs for adults and special Saturday morning programs for children (intangible services), and sells reproductions and adaptations of many of its pieces (tangible goods). But profit-seeking businesses tend to focus their marketing on just one public—their customers. Not-for-profit organizations, however, must often market to multiple publics, which complicates decision making about the correct markets to target. Many deal with at least two major publics—their clients and their sponsors—and often many other publics as well. Political candidates, for example, target both voters and campaign contributors. A college or university targets prospective students as clients of its marketing program, but it also markets to current students, parents of students, alumni, faculty, staff, local businesses, and local government agencies.

A customer or service user of a not-for-profit organization may wield less control over the organization's destiny than would be true for customers of a profit-seeking firm. Not-for-profit organizations also often possess some degree of monopoly power in a given geographic area. An individual contributor might object to United Way's inclusion of a particular local agency, but that agency will still receive a portion of that donor's contribution.

In another potential problem, a resource contributor—whether a cash donor, a volunteer, or someone who provides office space—may try to interfere with the marketing program in order to promote the message that he or she feels is relevant.

assessment check 4

4.1 What is the most obvious distinction between a not-for-profit organization and a commercial organization?

4.2 Why do for-profit and not-for-profit organizations sometimes form alliances?

NONTRADITIONAL MARKETING

5 Identify and briefly explain each of the five types of nontraditional

As marketing evolved into an organization-wide activity, its application has broadened far beyond its traditional boundaries of for-profit organizations engaged in the creation and distribution of tangible goods and intangible services. In many cases, broader appeals focus on causes, events, individuals, organizations, and places in the not-for-profit sector. In other instances, they encompass diverse groups of profit-seeking individuals, activities, and organizations. Table 1.3 lists and describes five major categories of nontraditional marketing: person marketing, place marketing, cause marketing, event marketing, and organization marketing. These categories can overlap—promotion for an organization may also encompass a cause; a promotional campaign may focus on both an event and a place.

PERSON MARKETING

Person marketing involves efforts designed to cultivate the attention, interest, and preferences of a target market toward a celebrity or authority figure. Celebrities can be real people, such as a local television news or sports announcer, or local radio personality. These people are often promoted in magazine ads or on billboards in an attempt to increase viewership or listenership. Celebrities can be fictional characters, such as SpongeBob SquarePants, who has appeared on boxes of Kraft Macaroni & Cheese. Or they can be widely recognized authority figures. Campaigns for political candidates and the marketing of celebrities are examples of person marketing. In political marketing, candidates target two markets: They attempt to gain the recognition and preference of voters and the financial support of donors. Oprah Winfrey uses person marketing to promote her *O* magazine, where she appears on every cover. The "Etiquette Tips for Marketing Professionals" feature provides guidelines for putting your best foot forward in business situations.

person marketing Marketing efforts designed to cultivate the attention, interest, and preference of a target market toward a person (typically a political candidate or celebrity).

table 1.3   *Categories of Nontraditional Marketing*

TYPE	BRIEF DESCRIPTION	EXAMPLES
Person marketing	Marketing efforts designed to cultivate the attention and preference of a target market toward a person	Athlete Steve Nash Political leader Stephen Harper Celebrity Nelly Furtado
Place marketing	Marketing efforts designed to attract visitors to a particular area; improve consumer images of a city, province, or nation; and/or attract new business	Saskatchewan: Land of Living Skies Nova Scotia: Canada's Ocean Playground Manitoba: Friendly Manitoba
Cause marketing	Identification and marketing of a social issue, cause, or idea to selected target markets	"Reading Is Fundamental." "Friends don't let friends drive drunk." "Be a mentor."
Event marketing	Marketing of sporting, cultural, and charitable activities to selected target markets	Grey Cup 2010 Vancouver Winter Olympics Calgary Stampede
Organization marketing	Marketing efforts of mutual-benefit organizations, service organizations, and government organizations that seek to influence others to accept their goals, receive their services, or contribute to them in some way.	United Way: Without you, there would be no way. Canadian Red Cross: Anywhere. Anytime. Sierra Club: Explore, enjoy, and protect the planet.

An extension of person marketing involves *celebrity endorsements*, in which well-known athletes, entertainers, and experts or authority figures promote products for companies or social causes for not-for-profit organizations. Golfer Tiger Woods and tennis player Maria Sharapova can be seen in ads for TAG Heuer watches. Actor William Shatner can be seen in ads for Priceline.com. Wines endorsed by celebrities are currently hot. Two of the top 10 best-selling wines at the Ontario Liquor Control Board stores in 2007 were endorsed by Dan Aykroyd and Wayne Gretzky. The LCBO projects annual sales of 11 000 cases of the former and 18 000 cases of the latter. Other new wines on the market are only *quasi-endorsed*: for example, Jailhouse Red and Marilyn Merlot from the "Elvis Presley" and "Marilyn Monroe" collections. Perhaps they can be described as "a heavy bouquet of kitsch with a nose of profit, and only a hint of exploitation."[19]

PLACE MARKETING

place marketing
Marketing efforts to attract people and organizations to a particular geographic area.

Another category of nontraditional marketing is **place marketing,** which attempts to attract customers to particular areas. Cities, provinces, regions, and countries publicize their tourist attractions to lure vacation travellers. They also promote themselves as good locations for businesses. Place marketing has become more important in the world economy—not only for tourism but also to recruit business and workers. As they rebuild, cities or regions that have suffered war or natural disasters may advertise reopening attractions to tourists alongside opportunities to businesses. The reopening of a zoo in postwar Afghanistan received worldwide attention, as did the first Mardi Gras celebration in New Orleans after Hurricane Katrina.

While tourism is not the only aspect of place marketing, tourism is a $56-billion industry in Canada. Every year, more than 35 million people visit Canada, and the majority of them are tourists. The Canadian Tourism Commission (CTC) is a Crown corporation that helps promote Canada to the world as an all-season tourism destination. In recent years, tourism has been suffering in Canada due to SARS, West Nile virus, mad cow disease, and a very competitive marketplace where many countries have been aggressively promoting tourism as well. Michele McKenzie, president and CEO of the CTC says, "To realize our potential, we had to find a way to define Canada's vast and diverse country, with one simple yet compelling brand promise—one that had universal appeal to translate across the world's many languages and cultures.[20] After much consultation and consumer research, the CTC decided on "Canada. Keep Exploring" as a tagline. Canada's 188 000 tourism businesses will use it to help build a consistent and memorable brand impression of Canada while allowing each district or region to promote its own uniqueness and allow visitors to create one-of-a-kind experiences.

ETIQUETTE TIPS FOR MARKETING PROFESSIONALS

Forms of Address: Which One Do You Use, and When?

WHEN you meet someone new in a professional situation, do you say "Mr.," "Dr.," or "Ms.," and hope you've got it right? Most people have experienced this confusion at one time or another. Whether you're interviewing for a job or making a sales call, you are marketing yourself to the other person—and you want to make sure you address that person with the correct title. Here are a few guidelines to help you navigate the maze successfully:

1. Always use a title and last name until you are asked to use a person's first name. Even if you are introduced to someone by first name—such as Patricia Graham—continue to address her as "Ms. Graham" until she specifically invites you to do otherwise. In many cultures, first names are never used in business situations.

2. Listen. If someone else makes an introduction for you, pay attention to the way the introduction is made. Make a mental note of which form of address is used.

3. Introduce a lower-ranking person to a higher-ranking person. For example, you might introduce your new assistant to a department manager by saying, "Ms. Lopez, this is my new assistant, Jeremy Morgan."

4. If you aren't certain which title to use, at least make an attempt by saying "Mr." or "Ms." Through conversation—or the help of someone else who is present—you will be able to refine the title to "Dr.," "Judge," "Chief," or "Mrs.," if appropriate.

Sources: Susan Bryant, "Business Etiquette You Should Know," Monster.com, http://wlb.monster.com, accessed February 2, 2006; Hilka Klinkenberg, "Manners Mom Never Taught You," Novatrain, http://www.novatrain.com, accessed February 2, 2006; Lydia Ramsay, "Minding Your Global Manners," Business Know-How, http://www.businessknowhow.com, accessed February 2, 2006.

CAUSE MARKETING

A third category of nontraditional marketing, **cause marketing,** refers to the identification and marketing of a social issue, cause, or idea to selected target markets. Cause marketing covers a wide range of issues, including literacy, physical fitness, gun control, family planning, prison reform, control of overeating, environmental protection, elimination of birth defects, child-abuse prevention, and punishment of convicted drunk drivers.

cause marketing
Identification and marketing of a social issue, cause, or idea to selected target markets.

An increasingly common marketing practice is for profit-seeking firms to link their products to social causes. Canadian companies now spend millions of dollars per year on cause marketing, a practice that essentially began only 20 years ago. Mars Inc.'s M&Ms division donates 50 cents to the Special Olympics for each specially marked candy wrapper mailed back to the company by consumers. Kendall-Jackson Wine Estates of California donates 50 cents per bottle to the Make-A-Wish Foundation of Canada for every bottle of wine it sells in Canada. Avon has long been recognized for its commitment to fighting breast cancer; in one decade, the company raised $250 million (U.S.) for the cause while also creating greater awareness of Avon products. Recently, the nonprofit organization Cause Marketing Forum began issuing the Cause Marketing Halo Awards to organizations for "leadership and outstanding achievements in the field of cause marketing."

Surveys show strong support for cause-related marketing by both consumers and company employees. In one recent survey, 92 percent of consumers had a more positive image of companies that support important social causes, and four of five respondents said that they would change brands to support a cause if the price and quality of the two brands remained equal. "Consumers look for relationships with brands, not just transactions," notes a cause marketing expert.[21] Cause marketing can help build these relationships.

EVENT MARKETING

event marketing
Marketing of sporting, cultural, and charitable activities to selected target markets.

Event marketing refers to the marketing of sporting, cultural, and charitable activities to selected target markets. It also includes the sponsorship of such events by firms seeking to increase public awareness and bolster their images by linking themselves and their products to the events. Sports sponsorships have gained effectiveness in increasing brand recognition, enhancing image, boosting purchase volume, and increasing popularity with sports fans in demographic segments corresponding to the sponsors' business goals.

Some people might say that the premier sporting event is baseball's World Series. Others might argue that it's the Super Bowl, which many consumers claim they watch only to see the debut of innovative new commercials. Those commercials are expensive and can run as much as $2.5 million (U.S.) for 30 seconds of airtime, or $83,333 a second. But they reach an estimated 90 million viewers. Companies now also feed their commercials to websites and make them available for downloading to personal computers and video iPods. Experienced marketers caution that firms planning such a big expenditure should make it part of a larger marketing plan, not just a single shot at fame.[22]

For those who prefer the international pageantry of the Olympics, marketers have plenty of plans. The promotion of upcoming Olympics—both summer and winter—begins years in advance. Before the end of each Olympics, hosts of the next games unveil their logo and the marketing takes off from there. Corporate sponsors such as Adidas and Nike try to target the next Olympic gold medal winners, draping them in clothing and gear with company logos. The 2008 Olympics in Beijing, China, were particularly important because of the huge consumer market there. Sales of premium sportswear topped $350 million (U.S.) for Nike and $300 million (U.S.) for Adidas, two years before the event. Adidas paid between $80 million (U.S.) and $100 million (U.S.) in cash and uniforms to be an official sponsor of the Beijing Olympics, but the company believes the investment will pay off in sales and long-term relationships with Chinese consumers.[23]

ORGANIZATION MARKETING

organization marketing
Marketing by mutual-benefit organizations, service organizations, and government organizations intended to influence others to accept their goals, receive their services, or contribute to them in some way.

Organization marketing attempts to influence others to accept the goals of, receive the services of, or contribute in some way to an organization. Organization marketing includes mutual-benefit organizations (conservation groups, labour unions, and political parties), service and cultural organizations (colleges and universities, hospitals, and museums), and government organizations. Colleges and universities use organizational marketing to help raise funds. The University of Alberta, in anticipation of its centenary, launched its Campaign 2008 in September 2000. Doug Nelson, associate vice president and chief development officer, called the $500-million fundraising campaign the largest in the history of Western Canada.[24]

In an effort to improve its public image and to recruit new members, the Canadian Forces recently launched its Operation Connection program. Military personnel have been making public appearances at many of the largest crowd-drawing events across Canada, including the Grey Cup, the Calgary Stampede, the Maritime Tattoo Festival, and the Pacific National Exhibition. Referring to the Grey Cup, Captain Holly Brown, public affairs officer for the Canadian Forces Recruiting Group, says, "Football fans are people who enjoy outdoors adventure and sports and those are the people who might enjoy the Forces." The Forces also supports its marketing efforts with a new Forces.ca website that features flash graphics and a "cool section" where visitors can find a media gallery of video clips, screen savers, and games.[25]

Marketoid

Canadian universities award more than 200 000 degrees, diplomas, and certificates each year; nearly 60 percent are awarded to women.

assessment check 5 ✓

5.1 Identify the five major categories of nontraditional marketing.

5.2 Give an example of a way in which two or more of these categories might overlap.

CREATIVITY AND CRITICAL THINKING

The challenges presented by today's complex and technologically sophisticated marketing environment require creativity and critical-thinking skills from marketing professionals. **Creativity** is a human activity that produces original ideas or knowledge, frequently by testing combinations of ideas or data to produce unique results. It is an extremely valuable skill for marketers. Creativity helps them develop novel solutions to perceived marketing problems. It has been a part of the human endeavour since the beginning of time. Leonardo da Vinci conceived his idea for a helicopter after watching leaves twirl in the wind. Swiss engineer George de Mestral, noticing that burrs stuck to his wool socks because of their tiny hooks, invented Velcro. Companies rely on creativity at all levels. After spending years in the shadow of Coca-Cola, Pepsi has emerged in its own spotlight. The firm still sells less cola than Coke, but creative marketing has placed it squarely in the forefront of a broadened soft drink and snack-food industry. Instead of focusing on one type of drink, Pepsi began to develop sports drinks and flavoured water, which more and more consumers wanted. Pepsi's Aquafina is now the number one water brand, and the firm's Gatorade boasts 80 percent of the sports drink market.[26]

Critical thinking refers to the process of determining the authenticity, accuracy, and worth of information, knowledge, claims, and arguments. Critical thinkers do not take information at face value and simply assume that it is accurate; they analyze the data themselves and develop their own opinions and conclusions. Critical thinking requires discipline and sometimes a cooling-off period after the creative fire of a new idea. In many instances, it requires analyzing what went wrong with an idea or a process and figuring out how to make it right. PepsiCo, just mentioned, certainly relied on critical thinking to support its new product strategy. Microsoft has joined its MSN Internet product group and its research unit to form an Internet research lab to develop and evaluate new products. "Its goal is to hit the sweet spot in the middle between science and engineering, where each is . . . better together," explains Microsoft's Gary William Flake, who heads up the new project.[27]

THE CANADIAN PRESS (LARRY MACDOUGAL)

Organization marketing: The Canadian Forces connect with the public at the Calgary Stampede.

THE TECHNOLOGY REVOLUTION IN MARKETING

As we move through the opening decade of the 21st century, we also enter a new era in communication, considered by some as unique as the 15th-century invention of the printing press or the first radio and television broadcasts early in the 20th century. **Technology** is the business application of knowledge based on scientific discoveries, inventions, and innovations. Interactive multimedia technologies ranging from computer networks to Internet services to wireless devices have revolutionized the way people store, distribute, retrieve, and present information. These technologies link employees, suppliers, and customers throughout the world. Technological advances continuously revolutionize marketing. Now that more than half of all Canadian homes and apartments contain at least one personal computer, online services and the Internet offer a new medium over which companies can market products and offer customer service. Because Canadian consumers place approximately 70 million orders online annually, worth about $12.8 billion, marketers are doing their best to make the most of this medium.[28] The "Marketing Hit" feature discusses one company that helped revolutionize online marketing.

Marketers can develop targeted marketing campaigns and zoned advertising programs for consumers located within a certain distance from a store and even within specific city blocks. RedFlagDeals.com searches online stores and store flyers for the best prices, Canadian coupons, and free stuff and, for customers who subscribe to its Bargains Newsletter, there is a weekly e-mail of hot deals. To encourage visitors to its website, Home Depot Canada offers a "Hammer Drop" special each day at 8 a.m. The sale lasts for one day only, unless the product sells out.

Technology can also open up entirely new markets. Cell phones have helped bring the entire continent of Africa into the world marketplace. With a cell phone in hand, farmers no longer have to trek miles to a pay phone to negotiate prices for their goods. Wildlife researchers use cell phone signals to track endangered animals, and fishermen can call ahead to the mainland to find out where to take their catch.[29]

(6) Outline the importance of creativity, critical thinking, and the technology revolution in marketing.

Marketoid

Canadians sent approximately 1.5 billion text messages in 2005, 4.3 billion in 2006, and 9.5 billion in 2007.

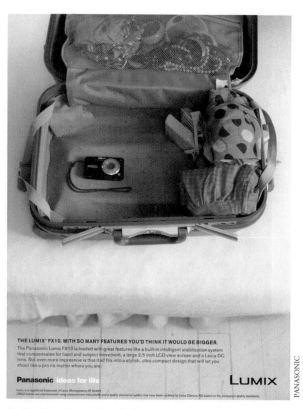

THE LUMIX® FX10. WITH SO MANY FEATURES YOU'D THINK IT WOULD BE BIGGER.

The Panasonic Lumix FX10 is loaded with great features like a built-in intelligent stabilization system that compensates for hand and subject movement, a large 2.5 inch LCD view screen and a Leica DC lens. But even more impressive is that it all fits into a stylish, ultra compact design that will let you shoot like a pro no matter where you are.

Panasonic ideas for life   **LUMIX**

Leica is a registered trademark of Leica Microsystems IR GmbH.
LEICA lenses are manufactured using measurement instruments and a quality assurance system that have been certified by Leica Camera AG based on the company's quality standards.

PANASONIC

Technology is continually bringing new and improved products to meet changing customer needs.

INTERACTIVE MARKETING

Interactive media technologies combine computers and telecommunications resources to create software that users can direct themselves. They allow people to digitize reports and drawings and transmit them, quickly and inexpensively, over phone lines, coaxial cables, or fibre-optic cables. People can subscribe to personalized news services that deliver article summaries on specified topics directly to their fax machines or computers. They can communicate via e-mail, voice mail, fax, video-conferencing, and computer networks; pay bills using online banking services; and use online resources to get information about everything from theatre events to a local car dealer's special sale. People can make phone calls via the Internet using voice over Internet protocol (VoIP). Many calls are now transmitted via VoIP because it is cheaper than conventional phone lines—presenting a potentially important interactive medium for marketers.

The World Wide Web provides marketers with tremendous interactive technologies. Compared with traditional media, the hypermedia resources of the Web offer a number of advantages. Data move in seconds, and interactive control gives users quick access to other information resources through related pages, at either the same or other sites, and easy navigation through documents. Because the medium is dynamic, website sponsors can easily keep information current. Multimedia capacities increase the attractiveness of documents and sites.

Interactive marketing refers to buyer-seller communications in which the customer controls the amount and type of information

---

marketing success   A Google?

Background. When Sergey Brin and Larry Page founded Internet search engine Google just over a decade ago, most people had never heard the mathematical term *googol*, which refers to the number 1 followed by 100 zeros. But the name fit the new software company, whose "mission is to organize the world's information and make it universally accessible and useful."

The Challenge. Brin and Page had created a service that would change the way people communicate and conduct business—but to be successful, they had to make the product easy for people to find and use.

The Strategy. The Google website has a clean, clear design with simple prompts that are easy for anyone to follow. The Google search engine returns its results in less than half a second. More important, it delivers accurately the type of information a user is looking for. Google provides features such as a spell checker, translation of foreign language web pages, and a calculator. All these features are free to the user. As a business, Google generates much of its revenue through advertising that is clearly separated from search results, so users do not become confused or frustrated by unwanted advertising images.

The Outcome. Google continues to grow and move into new markets such as China, new relationships such as a partnership with Sun Microsystems to develop new software to protect computers against harmful programs such as spyware, and new products such as the geographical search and view feature Google Earth. The firm has also started selling video content such as CBS TV programs and professional basketball games. Still, Google's marketers and executives remain focused on delivering information and services in ways that improve people's lives. "We believe strongly that in the long term, we will be better served . . . by a company that does good things for the world even if we forgo some short-term gains," wrote Brin and Page in a founders' letter that accompanied the firm's initial public offering of stock. "We aspire to make Google an institution that makes the world a better place."

Sources: Adi Ignatius, "In Search of the Real Google," *Time,* February 20, 2006, pp. 36–49; Steven Levy, "Google and the China Syndrome," *Newsweek,* February 13, 2006, p. 14; Mike Langberg, "In China, Google Founders Wake up to the Real World," *Seattle Times,* January 30, 2006, http://seattletimes.nwsource.com; Google website, http://www.google.com, accessed January 27, 2006; "Google, Sun & Harvard vs. Spyware and AdWare," *Search Engine Journal,* January 25, 2006, http://www.searchenginejournal.com; Nicholas Hoover, "Google Secrets," *Optimize,* January 2006, http://www.optimizemagazine.com.

received from a marketer. This technique provides immediate access to key product information when the consumer wants it. Interactive marketing allows marketers and consumers to customize their communication. Customers may come to companies for information, creating opportunities for **one-to-one marketing.** The Vancouver Organizing Committee for the 2010 Olympic and Paralympic Winter Games has created an interactive website, Vancouver2010.com, to meet the needs of many stakeholders: employees and potential employees; volunteers and participants; sponsors and partners; students and teachers; suppliers who are looking for procurement opportunities; and interested visitors who might like to shop at the online store, play games or take quizzes, meet the mascots, or simply get information on event schedules and ticketing.

Interactive marketing can also allow larger exchanges, in which consumers can communicate with one another using e-mail or electronic bulletin boards. These electronic conversations establish innovative relationships between users and the technology, providing customized information based on users' interests and levels of understanding. Marketers can also use web logs (blogs) and wireless phones to foster these communications. Yahoo! has been testing Shoposphere, a networking site within its own shopping site that lists reviews, blogs, and shopping lists posted by members. For example, a card game enthusiast can post a "Poker Night" shopping list telling new players where to find the essentials—including table, strategy books, and accessories.[30]

Internet protocol television (IPTV) is another interactive technology for marketers and consumers alike to embrace. IPTV allows a two-way digital broadcast signal to be sent through a telephone or cable network by way of a broadband connection. AT&T and Verizon Communications both plan to offer a full range of IPTV services soon. Services in the works include Caller ID, e-mail, and voice mail on television; the ability to program a digital video recorder from a cell phone; the capability to pull up sports statistics during a game; and the possibility of viewing events from multiple camera angles.[31] A number of movie studios and television networks now make it possible for Microsoft Xbox 360 users to download to own or rent hundreds of full-length TV shows and movies.

Interactive promotions put the customer in control. Consumers can easily get tips on product usage and answers to customer service questions. They can also tell the company what they like or dislike about a product, and they can just as easily click the exit button and move on to another area. As interactive promotions grow in number and popularity, the challenge will be attracting and holding consumer attention.

BROADBAND

Broadband technology—an always-on Internet connection—can deliver large amounts of data at once, making online marketing even faster and easier than it was a few years ago. Consumers can access web pages, and websites can process credit card purchases much more quickly via broadband. The number of households with broadband connections is increasing rapidly because of this speed advantage. However, Canada's position in the wired world has been steadily falling. While we were once the best-connected Internet users in the world, we were recently ranked tenth in the industrial world with about 50 percent of households having broadband connection. South Korea ranked first, with approximately a 95 percent household adoption rate. Download speeds are also much slower in Canada than in many other industrialized countries.[32] Broadband is growing in the United Kingdom, Europe, and China as well.

WIRELESS

More and more consumers now have Internet connections via **wireless technology** for their laptop and handheld computers, which is both a challenge and an opportunity for marketers. The number of Canadian consumers with these connections is rapidly increasing, which means they use wireless devices such as cell phones or notebook computers to access the Web and check their e-mail. As this percentage increases, the stage is set for **mobile marketing**—marketing messages transmitted via wireless technology.

interactive marketing Buyer-seller communications in which the customer controls the amount and type of information received from a marketer through such channels as the Internet, CD-ROMs, interactive toll-free telephone numbers, and virtual reality kiosks.

one-to-one marketing Customized marketing program designed to build long-term relationships with individual customers.

broadband technology Extremely high-speed, always-on Internet connection.

Go Green

Job Opportunities Are Greening

Traditionally, the colour green was described as dark, light, or bright. Today, we are more likely to describe green as army, asparagus, emerald, forest, hunter, jade, jungle, lime, moss, olive, pine, or sea green. Traditionally, "green" jobs were largely science-based positions: contaminant and waste management, environmental engineering, water conservation and quality management, soil testing, forest conservation, agronomy, etc. Today, green jobs are more likely to be cross-functional or cross-disciplinary, and many require only a marginal understanding of science. That's great news for many people, including want-to-be marketers. Green job opportunities are hot.

Todd Latham, publisher of two Toronto-based environmental magazines, sees opportunities for people who are simply passionate about the environment. This could include—among others—lawyers, accountants, builders, economists, journalists, and marketers. This may help explain why enrollments are declining in the majority of university-level degree programs that are focused on environmental careers, but green jobs are growing much faster than jobs in the overall economy. In Canada, 530 414 people are employed in environmental jobs—3.2 percent of working-age Canadians.

There are increasing opportunities for green entrepreneurs, people who want to start green businesses. As green products become more popular, there will be opportunities for green manufacturers, and they will employ green salespeople and green marketers. There will be opportunities for new green service firms, such as Carbonzero, a Toronto-based firm that uses recognized international carbon accounting standards to measure greenhouse gas emissions for clients and then helps them reduce or neutralize their impact on the environment.

Many green jobs will continue to require technical or scientific backgrounds, and entry standards for some jobs are very high—either a master's degree or a Ph.D. However, a major task for many organizations within the environmental industry will be their ability to "sell" green science and gain popular acceptance. There will be key positions for those who can work with teams of people from various stakeholder groups—company technical people and senior-level management, government agencies, public interest groups—and communicate effectively with them. Many people in the industry—such as Michael Gerbis, president of Ottawa-based Delphi Group, an environmental consulting firm that has worked with many of Canada's Fortune 100 companies—see education and technical expertise as necessary but not sufficient qualities for new employees. Enthusiasm and communications skills are what differentiates the best green job applicants from the rest.

Source: Derek Sankey, "Staffing the Green Machine," *Ottawa Citizen,* March 17, 2007, p. D10; Diana McLaren, "Green Jobs Take Root and Proliferate," *Globe and Mail,* February 14, 2008, http://www.globeandmail.com, accessed February 14, 2008; Delphi Group website, www.delphi.ca, accessed April 14, 2008; Carbonzero website, www.carbonzero.ca, accessed April 14, 2008.

Wireless ads offer tremendous potential to target certain audiences. And because these ads appear by themselves on a handheld user's screen, they command more attention than a traditional banner ad on a computer screen would. Although 70 percent of consumers say they would prefer to download ad-free content to their handheld devices, 20 percent say they would still download ad-supported content.[33] And many consumers are interested in watching live television programs on the go—another opportunity for mobile marketing. Bell Mobility, Telus, and Rogers all offer MobiTV content to their cell phone customers. Companies such as Motorola, Intel, Nokia, and Texas Instruments are joining together to enable live broadcasts. And the Mobile Marketing Association (MMA), along with a number of major firms, is exploring the best ways to engage in mobile video advertising. "We all believe that it is going to be a significantly large opportunity," predicts Laura Marriott of the MMA.[34] One research firm predicts that the global mobile commerce market—mobile entertainment downloads, ticket purchases, and other transactions—will soon reach $88 billion.[35] Denmark-based Mobintech believes it has solved the problem of small screen size. It has developed "personal display glasses" that, when connected to a mobile phone, give the viewer the impression of watching a 30-inch television from a distance of about two metres.[36]

assessment check 6

6.1 Define creativity and critical thinking.

6.2 Why are both of these attributes important for marketers?

6.3 Why is interactive marketing an important tool for marketers?

FROM TRANSACTION-BASED MARKETING TO RELATIONSHIP MARKETING

As marketing progresses through the 21st century, a significant change is taking place in the way companies interact with customers. The traditional view of marketing as a simple exchange process, or **transaction-based marketing**, is being replaced by a different, longer-term approach that emphasizes building relationships one customer at a time. Traditional marketing strategies focused on attracting customers and closing deals. Today's marketers realize that, although it's important to attract new customers, it's even more important to establish and maintain a relationship with them so they become loyal repeat customers. These efforts must expand to include suppliers and employees as well. Over the long term, this relationship may be translated to the **lifetime value of a customer**—the revenues and intangible benefits that a customer brings to an organization over an average lifetime, minus the investment the firm has made to attract and keep the customer.

Marketers realize that consumers are getting more and more sophisticated. They quickly recognize marketing messages and may turn away from them if the messages don't contain information that consumers want and need. So marketers need to develop new techniques to establish and build trusting relationships between companies and their customers.[37] As defined earlier in this chapter, relationship marketing refers to the development, growth, and maintenance of long-term, cost-effective exchange relationships with individual customers, suppliers, employees, and other partners for mutual benefit. It broadens the scope of external marketing relationships to include suppliers, customers, and referral sources. In relationship marketing, the term *customer* takes on a new meaning. Employees serve customers within an organization as well as outside it; individual employees and their departments are customers of and suppliers to one another. They must apply the same high standards of customer satisfaction to intradepartmental relationships as they do to external customer relationships. Relationship marketing recognizes the critical importance of internal marketing to the success of external marketing plans. Programs that improve customer service inside a company also raise productivity and staff morale, resulting in better customer relationships outside the firm.

Relationship marketing gives a company new opportunities to gain a competitive edge by moving customers up a loyalty ladder—from new customers to regular purchasers, then to loyal supporters of the firm and its goods and services, and finally to advocates who not only buy its products but recommend them to others, as shown in Figure 1.2.

Relationship building begins early in marketing. It starts with determining what customers need and want, then developing high-quality products to meet those needs. It continues with excellent customer service during and after purchase. It also includes programs that encourage repeat purchases and foster customer loyalty. Marketers may try to rebuild damaged relationships or rejuvenate unprofitable customers with these practices as well. Sometimes modifying a product or tailoring customer service to meet the needs of these customers can go a long way toward rebuilding a relationship.

By converting indifferent customers into loyal ones, companies generate repeat sales. The cost of maintaining existing customers is far below the cost of finding new ones, and these loyal customers are profitable. Some of the best repeat customers are those who are also willing to spread the word—create a buzz—about a product. **Buzz marketing** can be very effective in attracting new customers by bridging the gap between a company and its products. Companies as diverse as Microsoft and Build-a-Bear Workshop have tapped customers to create buzz about their products. Toronto-based Agent Wildfire describes itself as "marketing firestarters dedicated to the idea that today's consumers trust, pay more attention to, and act on the opinions of their social networks more than any other source of influence."[38] The company helps clients manage buzz and create customer relationships and has its own official blog—Buzz Canuck (buzzcanuck.typepad.com)—dedicated to all aspects of social network marketing. Companies are increasingly establishing their own blogs as a way of communicating with their customers. Maggie Fox, CEO of Social Media Group of Dundas, Ontario, says, "It's all about business intelligence. You can find out what the marketplace thinks of your products, unvarnished and in real time, and it's through comments from people who use your products and care enough to let you know."[39]

Effective relationship marketing often relies heavily on information technologies such as computer databases that record customers' tastes, price preferences, and lifestyles. This technology helps companies become one-to-one marketers who gather customer-specific information and provide individually

7 Explain the shift from transaction-based marketing to relationship marketing.

lifetime value of a customer Revenues and intangible benefits that a customer brings to an organization over an average lifetime, minus the investment the firm has made to attract and keep the customer.

figure 1.2

Converting New Customers to Advocates

customized goods and services. The firms target their marketing programs to appropriate groups rather than relying on mass-marketing campaigns. Companies who study customer preferences and react accordingly gain distinct competitive advantages.

DEVELOPING PARTNERSHIPS AND STRATEGIC ALLIANCES

Relationship marketing does not apply just to individual consumers and employees. It also affects a wide range of other markets, including business-to-business relationships with the firm's suppliers and distributors as well as other types of corporate partnerships. In the past, companies have often viewed their suppliers as adversaries against whom they must fiercely negotiate prices, playing one off against the other. But this attitude has changed radically, as both marketers and their suppliers discover the benefits of collaborative relationships.

strategic alliances
Partnerships in which two or more companies combine resources and capital to create competitive advantages in a new market.

The formation of **strategic alliances**—partnerships that create competitive advantages—is also on the rise. Alliances take many forms, from product-development partnerships that involve shared costs for research and development and marketing to vertical alliances in which one company provides a product or component to another firm, which then distributes or sells it in agreed territories or markets. Vancouver-based Xenon Pharmaceuticals and Takeda Pharmaceutical of Japan formed a strategic alliance to develop and commercialize oral formulations of Xenon's pain product, XEN401, for Japan and certain other Asian countries. Once Takeda commercializes the product, it will pay royalties on all sales to Xenon.[40] Jenex Corporation of Burlington, Ontario, formed a strategic alliance with U.S.-based Competitive Technologies, giving that company the right to sell Jenex's Thermapik in specified geographic territories around the world. The product is designed to relieve itch and pain caused by insect bites and stings. To maintain exclusive rights to distribute the product, Competitive Technologies must guarantee a specified sales volume.[41]

Not-for-profit organizations often make use of strategic alliances to raise awareness and funds for their causes, or to achieve their goals. *National Geographic* teamed up with Oriental Weavers to create a line of rugs inspired by world cultures. The National Geographic Society's proceeds from this collection go to its World Cultures Fund, which supports the study and a preservation of world cultures. Imagine Canada, through its Caring Company program, annually recognizes winning partnerships between not-for-profit and for-profit businesses. Recent winners of a Business and Community Partnership Award included Alberta Conservation Association and Suncor Energy Foundation for their boreal habitat conservation initiative. Among other things, these two companies have combined resources to preserve and protect one of the last great blue heron rookeries in northern Alberta.[42]

assessment check 7

7.1 How does relationship marketing give companies a competitive edge?

7.2 What is a strategic alliance?

(8) Identify the universal functions of marketing.

COSTS AND FUNCTIONS OF MARKETING

Firms must spend money to create time, place, and ownership utilities. Numerous attempts have been made to measure marketing costs in relation to overall product costs, and most estimates have ranged between 40 and 60 percent of total costs. On average, one-half of the costs involved in a product, such as a Subway sandwich, a Ford Fusion, or a trip to Australia, can be traced directly to marketing. These costs are not associated with wheat, metal, or other raw materials. Nor are they associated with baking, welding, or any of the other production functions necessary for creating form utility. What functions does marketing perform, and why are they important in creating customer satisfaction?

As Figure 1.3 reveals, marketing is responsible for the performance of eight universal functions: buying, selling, transporting, storing, standardizing and grading, financing, risk taking, and securing marketing information. Some functions are performed by manufacturers, others by marketing intermediaries such as retailers or wholesalers.

Buying and selling, the first two functions shown in Figure 1.3, represent **exchange functions.** Buying is important to marketing on several levels. Marketers must determine how and why consumers buy certain goods and services. To be successful, they must try to understand consumer behaviour.

figure 1.3

Eight Universal Marketing Functions

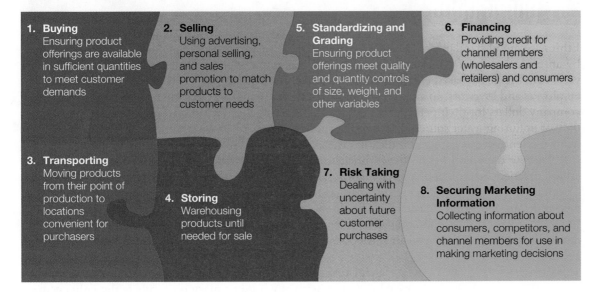

In addition, retailers and other intermediaries must seek out products that will appeal to their customers. Because they generate time, place, and ownership utilities through these purchases, marketers must anticipate consumer preferences for purchases to be made several months later. Selling is the second half of the exchange process. It involves advertising, personal selling, and sales promotion in an attempt to match the firm's goods and services to consumer needs.

Transporting and storing are **physical distribution functions**. Transporting involves the physical movement of goods from the seller to the purchaser. Storing involves warehousing goods until they are needed for sale. Manufacturers, wholesalers, and retailers all typically perform these functions.

The final four marketing functions—standardizing and grading, financing, risk taking, and securing marketing information—are often called **facilitating functions** because they assist the marketer in performing the exchange and physical distribution functions. Quality and quantity control standards and grades, frequently set by federal or provincial and territorial governments, reduce the need for purchasers to inspect each item. For example, if you request a certain size tire for your automobile, you expect to get it.

Financing is another marketing function because buyers often need access to funds to finance inventories prior to sales. Manufacturers often provide financing for their wholesale and retail customers. Some types of wholesalers perform similar functions for their markets. Finally, retailers frequently allow their customers to buy on credit, with either store charge cards or major credit cards.

The seventh function, risk taking, is part of most ventures. Manufacturers create goods and services based on research and their belief that consumers need them. Wholesalers and retailers acquire inventory based on similar expectations of future consumer demand. Entrepreneurial risk takers accommodate these uncertainties about future consumer behaviour when they market goods and services.

The final marketing function involves securing marketing information. Marketers gather information about potential customers—who they are, what they buy, where they buy, and how they buy. By collecting and analyzing marketing information, marketers can understand why consumers purchase some products while passing others by. This information also helps determine what consumers want and need—and how to offer goods and services to satisfy them. So marketing is the direct connection between a firm and its customers, the link that helps build and maintain lasting relationships.

assessment check 8

8.1 Which two marketing functions represent exchange functions?

8.2 Which two functions represent physical distribution functions?

8.3 Which four functions are facilitating functions?

(9) Demonstrate the relationship between ethical business practices, social responsibility, and marketplace success.

ETHICS AND SOCIAL RESPONSIBILITY: DOING WELL BY DOING GOOD

Ethics are moral standards of behaviour expected by a society. Most companies do their best to abide by an ethical code of conduct, but sometimes organizations and their leaders fall short. Several years ago, the Texas-based energy giant Enron collapsed, taking with it the retirement savings of its employees and investors. In another scandal, executives from Tyco were convicted of using millions of company dollars for their personal benefit. And chemical manufacturer Monsanto was convicted not only of polluting water sources and soil in a rural Alabama area for decades but of ignoring evidence its own scientists had gathered indicating the extent and severity of the pollution.

Despite these and other alleged breaches of ethical standards, most businesspeople do follow ethical practices. Over half of all major corporations now offer ethics training to employees, and most corporate mission statements include pledges to protect the environment, contribute to communities, and improve workers' lives. This book encourages you to follow the highest ethical standards throughout your business and marketing career. Because ethics and social responsibility are so important to marketers, each chapter in this book contains a critical-thinking feature entitled "Solving an Ethical Controversy."

Social responsibility involves marketing philosophies, policies, procedures, and actions whose primary objective is the enhancement of society. Social responsibility often takes the form of philanthropy, which involves making gifts of money or time to humanitarian causes. Many firms—both large and small—include social responsibility programs as part of their overall mission. These programs often produce such benefits as improved customer relationships, increased employee loyalty, marketplace success, and improved financial performance. Timberland Co., manufacturer of boots, outdoor clothing, and accessories, is well known for its high ethical standards and socially responsible programs. The company donates large sums of money to charities each year, and its employees are given paid time off to volunteer for their favourite organizations—from the animal shelter to the local preschool. Approximately 30 Timberland Canada employees recently spent a day—starting at 6 a.m.—involved in a park rejuvenation project. They repaired park benches, painted over graffiti-tagged walls, repainted chess tables, remounted backboards and basketball nets, and cleaned the grounds throughout the park.[43]

Many Canadian companies are committed to improving their communities through corporate philanthropy. HP Canada invites educational institutions to submit proposals designed to improve teaching technology in their classrooms. In 2007, the company awarded 10 grants valued at $35 000 each to elementary and high schools, and four grants valued at $90 000 to higher education institutions.[44] Pfizer Canada has a matching gift program. When a Pfizer Canada employee donates or raises funds for a worthy cause of his or her choice, the company contributes a matching amount.[45]

Marketoid

Approximately 75 percent of leading Canadian companies are engaged in corporate social responsibility activities.

assessment check 9

9.1 Define *ethics*.

9.2 What is *social responsibility*?

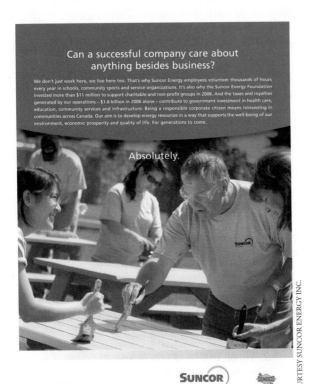

COURTESY SUNCOR ENERGY INC.

Suncor Energy asks, "Can a successful company care about anything besides business?" It does.

Solving an Ethical Controversy

Identity Theft: Is Privacy Also Stolen?

Most of us who own or use computers and use them to shop online, surf the Web for information, or even e-mail our friends harbour at least a tiny fear that somehow our personal information will be stolen without our knowing it. That fear is justified. Approximately one in 10 Canadians has been a victim of identity theft. More than three-quarters of Canadians are concerned about becoming victims according to an Ipsos-Reid survey conducted for Capital One Canada. The Canadian Council of Better Business Bureaus estimates that identity theft costs Canadian companies and consumers $2 billion annually. The problem is now so prevalent that security measures have become a marketable service. Some financial institutions have begun to offer free protection against identity theft to credit-card holders. Everyone agrees that computer technology has revolutionized the way we live our lives and conduct our business. But has it also compromised our right to privacy?

Has computer technology created the means for invading our privacy and made us more vulnerable to crime?

PRO

1. Identity theft is one of the easiest crimes to commit—and one of the hardest to catch. Despite billions of dollars lost to identity theft, few criminals are caught and charged. Credit card numbers are sold for as little as 50 cents; bank account information sells for $30 to $400.
2. The Internet provides a gateway to thousands of databases, credit reports, Social Insurance Numbers, and similar information needed for identity theft. Experts predict that the number of these identity thefts will soar in the next few years. PhoneBusters, an anti-fraud agency managed by the Competition Bureau Canada and the Ontario Provincial Police, reports that consumer losses due to identity theft were approximately $6.5 million in 2007. That amount was exceeded by September 2008.

CON

1. Consumers have many ways to protect themselves from identity theft. Financial institutions are increasingly taking actions to protect customers from identity theft. As well, consumers should take more action on their own to protect their own identity. Visa offers a toll-free hotline through Call for Action and posts fraud-prevention tips on the Web (**http://www.callforaction.org**).
2. Nearly 50 percent of identity thefts still occur through low-tech means such as digging through trash or peeking over someone's shoulder at an ATM machine. Consumers can go a long way toward protecting themselves by investing in a paper shredder.

Where do you stand: pro or con?

Sources: Chris Atchison, "Stop, Thief?" *Profit*, October 2008, pp. 49–54; Pierre Julien, "Canadian Very Vulnerable to Identity Theft, Survey Shows," itbusiness.ca, available http://www.directioninformatique.com, accessed October 2, 2008; Ipsos North America, press release, November 22, 2005, available http://www.ipsos-na.com, accessed October 5, 2008; Marc Saltzman, "Identity Thieves 'Phishing' the Internet," *Star-Phoenix* (Saskatoon), September 20, 2008, p. E14.

Strategic Implications

UNPRECEDENTED opportunities have emerged out of electronic commerce and computer technologies in business today. These advances and innovations have allowed organizations to reach new markets, reduce selling and marketing costs, and enhance their relationships with customers and suppliers. Thanks to the Internet, commerce has grown into a global market.

As a new universe for consumers and organizations is created, marketers must learn to be creative and think critically about their environment. Profit-seeking and not-for-profit organizations must broaden the scope of their activities to prevent myopic results in their enterprises.

Marketers must constantly look for ways to create loyal customers and build long-term relationships with those customers, often on a one-to-one basis. They must be able to anticipate customer needs and satisfy them with innovative goods and services. They must be able to do this faster and better than the competition. And they must conduct their business according to the highest ethical standards. ◆◆◆

REVIEW OF CHAPTER OBJECTIVES

(1) Define *marketing*, explain how it creates utility, and describe its role in the global marketplace.

Marketing is an organizational function and a set of processes for creating, communicating, and delivering value to customers and for managing customer relationships in ways that benefit the organization and its stakeholders. Utility is the want-satisfying power of a good or service. Four basic kinds of utility exist: form, time, place, and ownership. Marketing creates time, place, and ownership utilities. Three factors have forced marketers to embrace a global marketplace: expanded international trade agreements; new technologies that have brought previously isolated nations to the marketplace; and greater interdependence of the world's economies.

(2) Contrast marketing activities during the four eras in the history of marketing.

During the production era, businesspeople believed that quality products would sell themselves. The sales era emphasized convincing people to buy. The marketing concept emerged during the marketing era, in which there was a company-wide focus on consumer orientation with the objective of achieving long-term success. The relationship era focuses on establishing and maintaining relationships with customers and suppliers. Relationship marketing involves long-term, value-added relationships.

(3) Explain the importance of avoiding marketing myopia.

Marketing myopia is management's failure to recognize a company's scope of business. It focuses marketers too narrowly on products and thus misses potential opportunities to satisfy customers. To avoid it, companies must broadly define their goals so they focus on fulfilling consumer needs.

(4) Describe the characteristics of not-for-profit marketing.

Not-for-profit organizations operate in both public and private sectors. The biggest distinction between not-for-profits and commercial firms is the bottom line—whether the firm is judged by its profitability levels. Not-for-profit organizations may market to multiple publics. A customer or service user of a not-for-profit organization may have less control over the organization's destiny than do customers of a profit-seeking firm. In addition, resource contributors to not-for-profits may try to exert influence over the organization's activities. Not-for-profits and for-profits may form alliances that effectively promote each other's causes and services.

(5) Identify and briefly explain each of the five types of nontraditional marketing.

Person marketing focuses on efforts to cultivate the attention, interest, and preferences of a target market toward a celebrity or noted figure. Place marketing attempts to attract visitors, potential residents, and businesses to a particular destination. Cause marketing identifies and markets a social issue, cause, or idea. Event marketing promotes sporting, cultural, charitable, or political activities. Organization marketing attempts to influence others to accept the organization's goals or services and contribute to it in some way.

(6) Outline the importance of creativity, critical thinking, and the technology revolution in marketing.

Creativity produces original ideas, while critical thinking determines the authenticity, accuracy, and worth of any information, knowledge, claims, or arguments. These two processes combine to develop innovation and analyze the best course of action for a firm. Technology is the business application of knowledge based on scientific discoveries, inventions, and innovations. Interactive technologies allow marketers direct communication with customers, permit more meaningful exchanges, and put the customer in control.

(7) Explain the shift from transaction-based marketing to relationship marketing.

Relationship marketing represents a dramatic change in the way companies interact with customers. The focus on relationships gives a firm new opportunities to gain a competitive edge by moving customers up a loyalty ladder from new customers to regular purchasers and then to loyal supporters and advocates. Over the long term, this relationship may be translated to the lifetime value of a customer. Organizations may form partnerships—called *strategic alliances*—to create a competitive advantage. These alliances may involve product development, raising awareness, and other activities.

⑧ Identify the universal functions of marketing.

Marketing is responsible for eight universal functions, divided into three categories: (1) exchange functions (buying and selling); (2) physical distribution (transporting and storing); and (3) facilitating functions (standardization and grading, financing, risk taking, and securing market information).

⑨ Demonstrate the relationship between ethical business practices, social responsibility, and marketplace success.

Ethics are moral standards of behaviour expected by a society. Companies that promote ethical behaviour and social responsibility usually produce increased employee loyalty and a better public image. This image often pays off in customer growth, since many buyers want to associate themselves with—and be customers of—such firms. Social responsibility involves marketing philosophies, policies, procedures, and actions whose primary objective is the enhancement of society. These actions also generally promote a firm's public image.

assessment check answers

1.1 Define *marketing* and explain how it creates utility.
Marketing is an organizational function and a set of processes for creating, communicating, and delivering value to customers and for managing customer relationships in ways that benefit the organization and its stakeholders. It creates time, place, and ownership utilities.

1.2 What three factors have forced marketers to embrace a global marketplace?
International agreements are being negotiated in attempts to expand trade among nations. The growth of technology is bringing previously isolated countries into the marketplace. The interdependence of the world's economies is now a reality.

2.1 What is the major distinction between the production era and the sales era?
During the production era, businesspeople believed that quality products would sell themselves. But during the sales era, emphasis was placed on selling—persuading people to buy.

2.2 What is the marketing concept?
The marketing concept is a company-wide consumer orientation with the objective of achieving long-term success.

2.3 Describe the relationship era of marketing.
The relationship era focuses on building long-term, value-added relationships over time with customers and suppliers.

3.1 What is marketing myopia?
Marketing myopia is management's failure to recognize the scope of a company's business.

3.2 Give an example of how a firm can avoid marketing myopia.
A firm can find innovative ways to reach new markets with existing goods and services.

4.1 What is the most obvious distinction between a not-for-profit organization and a commercial organization?
The biggest distinction between for-profit and not-for-profit organizations is the bottom line—whether an organization is judged by its profitability.

4.2 Why do for-profit and not-for-profit organizations sometimes form alliances?
For-profits and not-for-profits may form alliances to promote each other's causes and services. For-profits may do so as part of their social responsibility programs.

5.1 Identify the five major categories of nontraditional marketing.
The five categories of nontraditional marketing are person, place, cause, event, and organization marketing.

5.2 Give an example of a way in which two or more of these categories might overlap.
Overlap can occur in many ways. An organization might use a person to promote its cause or event. Two organizations might use one marketing effort to promote an event and a place—for example, NBC Sports and the National Thoroughbred Racing Association combining to promote the Kentucky Derby at Churchill Downs.

6.1 Define creativity and critical thinking.
Creativity produces original ideas or knowledge. Critical thinking is the process of determining the authenticity, accuracy, and worth of information, knowledge, claims, or arguments.

6.2 Why are both of these attributes important for marketers?
Creativity and critical thinking are important for marketers because they generate new ideas and then use discipline to analyze the best course of action.

6.3 Why is interactive marketing an important tool for marketers?

Interactive marketing technologies create direct communication with customers, allow larger exchanges, and put the customer in control.

7.1 How does relationship marketing give companies a competitive edge?

Relationship marketing can move customers up a loyalty ladder, generating repeat sales and long-term relationships.

7.2 What is a strategic alliance?

A strategic alliance is a partnership formed between two organizations to create a competitive advantage.

8.1 Which two marketing functions represent exchange functions?

Buying and selling are exchange functions.

8.2 Which two functions represent physical distribution functions?

Transporting and storing are physical distribution functions.

8.3 Which four functions are facilitating functions?

The facilitating functions are standardization and grading, financing, risk taking, and securing market information.

9.1 Define *ethics.*

Ethics are moral standards of behaviour expected by a society.

9.2 What is social responsibility?

Social responsibility involves marketing philosophies, policies, procedures, and actions whose primary objective is the enhancement of society.

MARKETING TERMS YOU NEED TO KNOW

These terms are printed in red in the text. They are defined in the margins of the chapter and in the Glossary that begins on p. G-1. Other important terms are printed in bold black type in the chapter but not included in this list. Their definitions can be found in the Glossary.

utility 21	relationship marketing 26	interactive marketing 34
marketing 22	marketing myopia 27	one-to-one marketing 35
exchange process 24	person marketing 29	broadband technology 35
seller's market 25	place marketing 30	lifetime value of a customer 37
buyer's market 25	cause marketing 31	strategic alliances 38
consumer orientation 25	event marketing 32	
marketing concept 26	organization marketing 32	

ASSURANCE OF LEARNING REVIEW

1. Identify the four types of utility, and give an example of each.
2. What condition in the marketplace gave rise to the need for a consumer orientation by businesses after World War II?
3. Define *relationship marketing* and describe how it fits into the marketing concept.
4. Why do not-for-profit organizations need to engage in marketing efforts?
5. Give an example of how Big Apple Bagels could use one or more of the nontraditional marketing techniques to promote the opening of a new franchise.
6. What might be some of the benefits of mobile marketing for firms that use it to reach out to consumers?
7. Describe the significance of the shift from transaction-based marketing to relationship marketing. When does relationship building begin?
8. Identify the two exchange functions of marketing and explain why they are important to the overall marketing program.
9. How does the physical distribution function create utility?
10. How do ethics and social responsibility help a firm achieve marketplace success?

PROJECTS AND TEAMWORK EXERCISES

1. Consider each of the following firms and describe how the firm's goods and/or services can create different types of utility. If necessary, go online to the company's website to learn more about it. You can do this alone or in a team.
   a. Swiss Chalet, Wendy's, Red Lobster, or another restaurant chain
   b. Costco, Vistek, or another company that provides online digital photo service
   c. Calgary Stampede
   d. eBay
   e. Sobeys, Real Canadian Superstore, Overwaitea, or another grocery store chain

2. With a classmate, choose a Canadian-based company whose products you think will do well in certain markets overseas. The company can be anything from a music group to a clothing retailer—anything that interests you. Then write a plan for how you would target and communicate with overseas markets.

3. Choose a company that interests you from the following list, or select one of your own. Research the company online, through business magazines, or through other sources to learn what seems to be the scope of its business. Write a brief description of the company's scope of business as it is now. Then describe strategies for avoiding marketing myopia and expanding the company's scope of business over the next 10 years. Use your creativity and critical-thinking skills to come up with ideas.
   a. E*Trade Canada
   b. TD Canada Trust
   c. Delta Hotels and Resorts
   d. Research in Motion (RIM)
   e. Canadian Tire

4. With a classmate, choose one of the following not-for-profit organizations. Then come up with a for-profit firm with which you think your organization could form a strategic alliance. Create a presentation—an ad, a poster, or the like—illustrating and promoting the partnership.
   a. Canadian Cancer Society
   b. Make-A-Wish Foundation of Canada
   c. Habitat for Humanity Canada
   d. Save the Children Canada
   e. Canadian Kennel Club

5. With a classmate, choose one of the following for-profit organizations. Then create a presentation using person, place, cause, event, or organization marketing to promote its products.
   a. MasterCard (or VISA)
   b. L'Oréal Paris
   c. Honda Canada
   d. Swiss Chalet
   e. Future Shop

CRITICAL-THINKING EXERCISES

1. How does an organization create a customer?
2. How can marketers use interactive marketing to convert needs to wants and ultimately build long-term relationships with customers?
3. Why is utility such an important feature of marketing?
4. What benefits—monetary and nonmonetary—do social responsibility programs bring to a business?
5. Why is determining the lifetime value of a customer an important analysis for a company to make?
6. Why is it important for a firm to establish high ethical standards for its business practices? What role do you think marketers play in implementing these high standards?

ETHICS EXERCISE

While you are being interviewed for a job as a marketer for a large company that manufactures boxed prepared meals—such as macaroni and cheese or chicken with biscuits—the interviewer steps outside the office. From where you are sitting, you can see a stack of papers on the interviewer's desk that contain advertisements by a competitor who makes similar products. You have an interview scheduled with the competitor for the following week.

1. Would you take a quick look at the ads—and any accompanying marketing notes—while the interviewer is out of the office? Why or why not?
2. In your next interview, would you tell the competitor that you saw the ads? Why or why not?
3. When the interviewer returns, would you mention the ads and offer your own commentary on them? Why or why not?

INTERNET EXERCISES

1. **Exploring the CMA's website.** The Canadian Marketing Association's website contains lots of useful and interesting information for students and others. One section is devoted to careers. Visit the CMA's website (http://www.the-cma .org). Answer the following questions:
   a. Describe the Canadian Marketing Association. What is its purpose?
   b. Click on *Marketing-Jobs.ca*. Select three marketing jobs you think you would like. What makes these jobs attractive to you?
   c. Click on *Student Membership*. (See Membership Centre on right side of page.) What are the benefits of having a student membership?

2. **Not-for-profit marketing.** Virtually all not-for-profit organizations have websites. Two examples are the Canadian Salvation Army (http://www.salvationarmy.ca) and Save the Children Canada (http://www.savethechildren.ca). Visit the websites of at least two not-for-profit organizations. Compare and contrast how each uses the Web to support its mission and the role played by marketing. Which site did you find to be the most effective? Defend your answer.

Note: Internet web addresses change frequently. If you don't find the exact sites listed, you may need to access the organization's or company's home page and search from there or use a search engine such as Google.

Case 1.1

Golfers Are Joining the Hybrid Club

If you're a golfer, you know the difference between a wood and an iron. They're both clubs, but a fairway wood is the club you normally use to hit the ball long distances. An iron is used for greater accuracy. Golfers have their favourite clubs—those they feel confident will blast them out of sand traps or pitch them onto the green or just know they can hit straight when the pressure is on. Over the years, they may exchange a putter or replace a worn driver, but they remain loyal to clubs that fit their swing and particular brand of game. The only way they'll change is if they know with certainty that a new club will significantly improve their game.

Recently, some golf club manufacturers have begun to stir this devotion up. Companies such as Calloway, TaylorMade, Ping, and Nike Golf have introduced hybrid clubs—clubs designed to capture the best features of both fairway wood and iron. Manufacturers have shifted the centre of gravity in the hybrid to the back and bottom of the club. This helps launch the ball high into the air. The flat face gives the ball a spin, allowing it to stop faster and with greater accuracy. But figuring out the technology was just the first challenge for these firms. Getting golfers to switch is another game altogether. Marketers have found ways to use different types of marketing to get their message across to golfers.

Celebrities can do a lot to spark the popularity of a new golf product. So manufacturers have tapped celebrity golfers from around the world to promote the hybrid clubs. Eight-time LPGA champion Rachel Hetherington of Australia touts the benefits of her Hogan Edge CFT hybrid club in an interview for *Golf for Women* magazine. "My hybrid has transformed the long-iron shots I used to hate," she says. Events that feature charitable causes and golf stars have been a hit as well. At a recent benefit golf tournament sponsored by the Children's Aid Foundation—which raised nearly a quarter of a million dollars—women had the opportunity to try out some of the hybrid clubs under the eye of LPGA golf star Sandra

Post. One Canadian firm held nearly six months' worth of weekly sweepstakes in which it gave away hybrid clubs. Magazines such as *Golf Digest* and websites such as PGATOUR.com give constant reviews and updates on the new equipment as well.

As hybrids move on to their next generation, manufacturers are always listening to what their customers want. In developing its Slingshot Tour Hybrid, the Nike Golf design team incorporated suggestions from the players themselves. "The mandate from the players was that it would need to have clean lines, compact shape, and minimal offset," stated Nike Golf. The firm listened—and then staff members went out on the links with the new clubs and played the PGA Tour season.

Marketers are hoping that amateurs will follow the pros' lead and try the hybrids. "Hybrid clubs have helped make the game more enjoyable and playable for many more golfers," says Dan Murphy, director of marketing for Precept Golf. "And that goes both for average players and better players." More enjoyment may mean more players and more games played, and ultimately more hybrid clubs sold.

Questions for Critical Thinking

1. Describe the role of relationship marketing in making the hybrid clubs successful in the marketplace.
2. What type of strategic alliances could golf equipment manufacturers use to promote their hybrids?

Sources: "Golf Equipment," Golf Equipment Source, http://www.golfequipmentsource .com, accessed February 2, 2006; "Adams IDEA Hybrid Irons Sweepstakes," The Golf Channel, http://www.thegolfchannel.com, accessed February 2, 2006; "Women's Golf Classic Scores a Great Day for a Great Cause," Children's Aid Foundation, http://www.cafdn.org, accessed February 2, 2006; Chuck Stogel, "Companies Expanding Lineups to Suit Hybrid Club Buzz," PGATOUR.com, http://www.pgatour .com, accessed February 2, 2006; "Nike Golf's Slingshot Franchise," Golf Business Wire, January 11, 2006, http://www.golfbusinesswire.com; E. Michael Johnson, "Help Is on the Way," Golf Digest, March/April 2005, http://www.golfdigest.com; Rachel Hetherington with Stina Sternberg, "5 Ways to Use Your Hybrid Club," Golf Digest, March/April 2005, http://www.golfdigest.com.

Case 1.2

How the Rolling Stones Keep Rolling

The Rolling Stones have been singing about relationships for 40 years. And that's the point: not whether you like the British rock group's songs and not whether you think Mick Jagger is too old to be doing what he keeps doing. However, Jagger has been knighted by the queen of England, which is unusual for any CEO. The Rolling Stones are a highly successful company because they have built relationships over the years with thousands of fans who listen to their music and buy tickets to their concerts, with concert promoters and music industry professionals, and with various business partners. Mick Jagger is an excellent marketer. After all, few bands last for four years, and Mick, Keith, and Charlie have been at it for more than four decades! (The fourth member, Ronnie Wood, joined the band in 1974.) In fact, the Stones have made many of the most successful rock tours of all time. The Voodoo Lounge tour in 1994 set a record when it grossed $121.2 million (U.S.). After U2's 2005–06 Vertigo tour topped out at $389 million (U.S.), the Stones came back with the Bigger Bang tour. By the time the tour ended in the summer of 2007, it had grossed over $558 million (U.S.). Since 1989, the band has generated more than $2 billion (U.S.) in gross revenues.

Forming collaborative relationships with other businesses has been an important part of the Stones' marketing strategy. The group has sponsorship deals with companies such as Anheuser-Busch, Microsoft, Sprint, and E*Trade. Then there are the merchandisers, promoters, venue owners, and others who have business relationships with the band.

But most important of all are the fans—consumers who have been buying the group's records, tapes, CDs, and concert tickets for decades. By now, the group has developed hundreds of thousands of fans, mostly baby boomers—yet each Rolling Stones song is like a one-to-one marketing message to a fan. An entire generation grew up, graduated from school, began careers, and has lived their adult lives to tunes like "Jumping Jack Flash," "Shattered," "Under My Thumb," and "Stealing My Heart." Marketing can't get any more personal than that.

Technology has helped the Stones' empire grow over the years, yet the band is one of the last big-name rock 'n' roll acts to go online. That's because much of the group's music was recorded more than 30 years ago, before music was being distributed via the Internet. But Jagger has been a fan of the Internet as an entertainment and communications medium for a number of years. He financed a firm called Jagged Internetworks, a video streaming service. Making the Stones' music available online is a marketing manoeuvre that should reach both old fans and new ones. In addition to the various promotion and financial managers, the Rolling Stones actually have their own information technology (IT) specialist, Todd Griffith. Griffith is in charge of the band's website, **http://www.rollingstones.com**, which handles everything from e-mail for individual band members to computer-aided design drawings of concert venues that are used by the technical crew. Griffith even figured out how to reduce the number of plugs and cables required at a concert venue by making use of wireless networks—no small feat.

The Rolling Stones have proven that they are more than just a rock band. "The thing that we all had to learn is what to do when the passion starts to generate money," explains guitarist Keith Richards. "You don't just start to play your guitar thinking you're going to be running an organization that will maybe generate millions." But generate millions they have. When asked how long they plan to go on playing, Richards answers definitively: "Forever." Richards and the Stones may even get to play again in Blackpool, England, where a 44-year ban on the band was lifted in 2008.

Questions for Critical Thinking

1. How important is customer loyalty to the success of the Rolling Stones? Explain your answer.
2. In what ways can you see technology helping or hurting the group's marketing efforts over the next few years?
3. Has the group avoided marketing myopia? Why or why not? How can it do so in the future?

Sources: Company website, http://www.rollingstones.com, accessed March 28, 2008; "Rolling Stones Smash Records with Tour," *Calgary Herald,* October 4, 2007, p. E3; Tom Chivers, "Rolling Stones' 44-year Blackpool Ban Lifted, *Telegraph.co.uk,* http://www.telegraph.co.uk, March 28, 2008, accessed March 28, 2008; Chris Gaither, "Stones to Open Vaults to Net Downloads," The Boston Globe, August 18, 2003, http://www.boston.com; Ryan Naraine, "Real Gets Rolling Stones; Best Buy Deal," *Internetnews.com,* August 18, 2003, http://www.internetnews.com; Rebecca Reid, "Rolling Stones Marry Hi-Fi and Wi-Fi for Concert Shows," *ComputerWorld,* July 30, 2003, http://www.computerworld.com; Boby Kurian, "UB to Sponsor Rolling Stones' Indian Summer," *The Hindu Business Line,* February 17, 2003, http://www.blonnet.com; Andy Serwer, "Inside the Rolling Stones Inc.," *Fortune,* September 30, 2002, pp. 58–72.

Video Case 1.3

Harley-Davidson Keeps Riders Coming Back

The written case on Harley-Davidson appears on page VC-2. The recently filmed Harley-Davidson video is designed to expand and highlight the concepts in this chapter and the concepts and questions covered in the written video case.

chapter 2

Strategic Planning and the Marketing Process

CHAPTER OBJECTIVES

1. Distinguish between strategic planning and tactical planning.

2. Explain how marketing plans differ at various levels in an organization.

3. Identify the steps in the marketing planning process.

4. Describe successful planning tools and techniques, including Porter's Five Forces model, first and second mover strategies, SWOT analysis, and the strategic window.

5. Identify the basic elements of a marketing strategy.

6. Describe the environmental characteristics that influence strategic decisions.

7. Describe the methods for marketing planning, including business portfolio analysis and the BCG matrix.

LOBLAW: THE SEARCH FOR A WINNING STRATEGY

In 2006, Loblaw—Canada's largest food distributor with more than 134 000 full- and part-time employees and more than 1000 corporate and franchised locations—reported its first annual loss in 19 years. It has since returned to profitability, but almost everyone agrees it will be a challenge to develop and implement a sustainable winning strategy for the future.

A decade ago, Loblaw was the clear leader in the Canadian grocery market. Its retail brand, President's Choice (PC), was an innovative initiative. While other retailers had started to establish store brands, Loblaw promoted its PC brand better than many manufacturers promoted their well-known national brands. Estimates were that PC branded products accounted for between 30 and 35 percent of Loblaw sales—good for Loblaw and good for its customers. Generally, the margin on store brands is about 10 percentage points higher than on manufacturers' brands, and consumers save between 20 and 40 percent by purchasing these brands. It is likely that Loblaw made higher margins than normal with its PC brand as these products were promoted and sold as equivalent to or better than many national brands in quality, and many customers shopped at Loblaw simply because it had their favourite PC products. Canadian consumers fell in love with Decadent Chocolate Chip Cookies, Memories of Szechwan Peanut Sauce, and other PC product introductions. Loblaw has since let its first mover advantage in this area slide. It now has 25 percent of its sales from private labels while, across the industry, grocery chains average about 24 percent sales from store brands. How did Loblaw lose its dominance?

There are many opinions concerning what went wrong at Loblaw. Some analysts—and former president Richard Currie—believe problems started with its loss of competitive focus. It began to compete with two very different groups of competitors: other grocery retailers, and mass merchandisers such as Wal-Mart, Shoppers Drug Mart, and Canadian Tire. However, Loblaw may have had few options. With its dominant market share, growth in Canada would be very difficult to achieve if it stayed focused only on the grocery business. The cost of gaining each percentage point of market share would be very high. At the same time, it was clear that Wal-Mart, the world's largest retailer, was about to enter the Canadian grocery market, and that would mean that Loblaw's market share would decline. The most likely option for growth was to add a broad assortment of general merchandise, and this is what it did. The problem is that it has not seen the cross-over traffic from the food area to the merchandise sections of its stores.

Things may be changing, however. In less than two years, its Joe Fresh line of clothing has grown in popularity, with sales in 2007 of more than $400 000. The new executive chairman, Galen Weston, Jr., (shown in photo) has a goal of $1 billion in sales of Joe Fresh products by 2010. As well as a stronger push on its Joe Fresh clothing line, other elements of the company's turnaround strategy include more competitive pricing, improved customer service, better promotion for its President's Choice and No Name brands, a broader assortment of quality, value-added grocery products, and added emphasis on health and beauty products. While Loblaw searches for the right strategy, Wal-Mart has turned up the competitive pressure with its addition of a number of new supercentres with expanded grocery aisles.

connecting with customers

While it certainly has its challenges, Loblaw is still fighting from a position of strength. It has a number of banners targeting many different customer segments: Real Canadian Superstores, Zehr's, Extra, No Frills, Loblaws, Fortinos, Provigo, and Maxi. It has its PC brand of quality products and has added promising new store brands, including Blue Menu and PC Organics. The company is trying to make a broad appeal to Canadians with its latest ads featuring Galen Weston, Jr., and customers seem to be responding.[1]

Chapter Overview

- "Gas prices are rising. Should we redesign our cars and trucks to be more fuel efficient?"

- "We have fewer customers eating at our restaurant on weekends. Should we revamp our menu? Lower our prices? Use special promotions? Update the dining room decor?"

- "Recent marketing research shows we are not reaching our customer target—consumers in their early to mid-20s. Should we consider another advertising agency?"

MARKETERS face strategic questions every day—planning strategy is a critical part of the job. The marketplace changes continually in response to changes in consumer tastes and expectations, technological developments, competitors' actions, economic trends, and political and legal events, as well as product innovations and pressures from suppliers and distributors. Although the causes of these changes often lie outside a marketer's control, effective planning can anticipate many of the changes. Loblaw has been struggling in recent years as it tries to find a winning growth strategy, and this requires constant planning, constant monitoring, and constant adjustment because the competitive environment where it operates is a very dynamic one.

This chapter provides an important foundation for analyzing all aspects of marketing by demonstrating the importance of gathering reliable information to create an effective plan. These activities provide a structure for a firm to use its unique strengths. Marketing planning identifies the markets a company can best serve as well as the most appropriate mix of approaches to satisfy the customers in those markets. While this chapter focuses on planning, we will examine in greater detail the task of marketing research and decision making in Chapter 8. ◆◆◆

MARKETING PLANNING: THE BASIS FOR STRATEGY AND TACTICS

planning Process of anticipating future events and conditions and of determining the best way to achieve organizational goals.

Everyone plans. We plan which courses we want to take, which movie we want to see, and which outfit to wear to a party. We plan where we want to live and what career we want to pursue. Marketers engage in planning as well. **Planning** is the process of anticipating future events and conditions and of determining the best way to achieve organizational objectives. Of course, before marketing planning can even begin, an organization must define its objectives. Planning is a continuous process that includes identifying objectives and then determining the actions through which a firm can attain those objectives. The planning process creates a blueprint for marketers, executives, production staff, and everyone else in the organization to follow for achieving organizational objectives. It also defines checkpoints so that people within the organization can compare actual performance with expectations to indicate whether current activities are moving the organization toward its objectives.

Planning is important for both large and small companies. Microsoft CEO Steve Ballmer recently announced the company's biggest reorganization in several years, with a plan to help the company respond faster to the never-ending changes in the technology marketplace. Its seven divisions have been forged into three new groups—Platform Products & Services, which includes Windows; the Business Group, which includes Office and Microsoft Business Solutions; and the Entertainment & Devices division, which includes Xbox. "Our goal in making these changes," Ballmer told employees, "is to enable Microsoft to achieve greater agility in managing the incredible growth ahead and executing our software-based services strategy."[2]

At the other end of the size spectrum, newlyweds Jennifer Melton and Brennan Johnson started their business, called Cloud Star, with a simple plan. Jennifer began making her German shepherd's food at home when she realized that the pet, adopted from a shelter, had severe allergies to commercial dog foods. After getting an overwhelmingly positive response to their home-baked treats at animal shelter bake sales, Melton and Johnson began to market their own line of bake-at-home dog treats that were free of many of the ingredients often found in commercial foods. Within a few years, they added dog shampoos and conditioners to their product line. They base much of their planning on feedback from customers. "Most of our growth and our decisions for which area we wanted to go into have been from listening to our customers and what they want from us," explains Melton.[3]

Marketing planning—implementing planning activities devoted to achieving marketing objectives—establishes the basis for any marketing strategy. Product lines, pricing decisions, selection of appropriate distribution channels, and decisions relating to promotional campaigns all depend on plans formulated within the marketing organization.

An important trend in marketing planning centres on relationship marketing, which is a firm's effort at developing long-term, cost-effective links with individual customers and suppliers for mutual benefit. Good relationships with customers can arm a firm with vital strategic weapons, as home improvement retailers such as Home Depot and Lowe's have become aware.

Many companies now include relationship-building goals and strategies in their plans. Relationship marketers frequently maintain databases to track customer preferences. These marketers may also manipulate product spreadsheets to answer what-if questions related to prices and marketing performance. In the business-to-business marketplace, software giant Oracle hopes to save its customers tens of millions of dollars every year on expensive consulting services. By acquiring Siebel Systems, a maker of customer-relationship-management software, Oracle closed a gap in its product line and hopes to become the top one-stop supplier of business software applications in accounting, sales, and human resources departments. With Siebel's software and Oracle's databases and applications servers, "existing Oracle customers are going to get much better CRM software out of this," says one industry expert.[4]

STRATEGIC PLANNING VERSUS TACTICAL PLANNING

Planning is often classified on the basis of its scope or breadth. Some extremely broad plans focus on long-range organizational objectives that will significantly affect the firm for five or more years. Other more targeted plans cover the objectives of individual business units over shorter periods.

Strategic planning can be defined as the process of determining an organization's primary objectives and then adopting courses of action that will eventually achieve these objectives. This process includes, of course, allocation of necessary resources. The word *strategy* dates back to a Greek term meaning "the general's art." Strategic planning has a critical impact on a firm's destiny because it provides long-term direction for its decision makers.

Strategic planning is complemented by **tactical planning**, which guides the implementation of activities specified in the strategic plan. Unlike strategic plans, tactical plans typically address shorter-term actions that focus on current and near-future activities that a firm must complete to implement its larger strategies. As Eastman Kodak's traditional camera and film business continues its sharp decline, CEO Antonio Perez faces the challenge of getting through a few difficult years of plummeting sales, cutbacks, and layoffs while implementing a new strategy, focusing on the company's core strength in digital imaging. "Digital imaging . . . is the DNA of the company and what we really do well—better than anyone else in the world," says Perez. "We eliminated any other business where we didn't think we could be No. 1 or 2." Tactics that support the new strategy include developing the first Wi-Fi camera and the first dual-lens digital camera, and partnering with Motorola to build better camera phones. As for traditional photography, says Perez, "We will always sell film as long as there are customers to buy it."[5]

PLANNING AT DIFFERENT ORGANIZATIONAL LEVELS

Planning is a major responsibility for every manager, so managers at all organizational levels devote portions of their workdays to planning. However, the amount of time spent on planning activities and the types of planning typically vary. Interruptions, such as all managers face every

Sidebar

Marketoid

According to Statistics Canada, there are approximately 4.5 million cats and 3.5 million dogs in Canada.

marketing planning
Implementing planning activities devoted to achieving marketing objectives.

(1) Distinguish between strategic planning and tactical planning.

strategic planning
Process of determining an organization's primary objectives and adopting courses of action that will achieve these objectives.

tactical planning
Planning that guides the implementation of activities specified in the strategic plan.

assessment check 1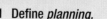

1.1 Define *planning*.

1.2 Give an example of strategic planning and tactical planning.

(2) Explain how marketing plans differ at various levels in an organization.

ETIQUETTE TIPS FOR MARKETING PROFESSIONALS

How to Handle Interruptions

MANAGERS at all levels of an organization are interrupted every few minutes, every day. Interruptions are part of a manager's day that can't be avoided. Because they're estimated to use up more than one-fourth of every employee's workday, however, interruptions can make planning very difficult. Here are some suggestions for dealing with them tactfully.

1. If someone stops by just to chat, say something friendly but unmistakable such as "I'm sorry I don't have time to talk right now. Can we catch up later?"
2. If your office is located near the copier or water cooler where people gather, try turning your desk away from the doorway or getting a partition, a file cabinet, or even a large plant to shield you from view.
3. Remove extra chairs from your office or cubicle to make it a less inviting place for others to kill time.
4. Discourage visitors who linger too long by getting up and moving away from your desk, by picking up some work or positioning yourself in front of your computer, or even by excusing yourself to go to the restroom.
5. If someone who reports to you asks to see you and you must make time, but you can't do it immediately, acknowledge the person's request and its importance to both of you. Then suggest a time that works for you. For instance, "Chris, I agree it's important for us to discuss this. I really have to finish this e-mail before noon. Let's meet in your office at one o'clock."

6. If your boss asks to see you and you're in the middle of something, use a similar strategy but let him or her choose the time. "Janet, I know that's a critical discussion we need to have. I'm trying to finish the e-mail you asked me to send to the sales staff by the noon deadline. Would you like me to finish that up, or should I put it off so we can meet now?"
7. If you really need a block of time without interruptions, ask your staff and co-workers to respect that time, forward phone calls, turn off your cell phone and pager, and if you have a door, close it.
8. If you must answer the phone, do it promptly, thank the person for calling, and get a callback number. Say, "I'm meeting with someone now, but I'll get back to you right after the meeting," and be sure to do so.
9. Avoid creating interruptions for others by asking yourself before phoning them whether they really need to hear from you right now. If not, call later.

Sources: "Controlling Office Interruptions," Life Organizers.com, http://www.lifeorganizers.com, accessed February 9, 2006; "10 Easy-to-Learn Tips on Handling Interruptions," Performance.com, http://www.superperformance.com, accessed February 9, 2006; "Business Etiquette," Newspaper Association of America, http://www.naa.org, accessed October 7, 2005; Bob Lang, "Proper Business Etiquette for Using Electronic Communicating Devices," http://www.baltimoremd.com, accessed October 7, 2005; "Interruptions Cost $588B," *Red Herring*, September 8, 2005, http://www.redherring.com; "Peter Post," *Boston Globe*, July 31, 2005, http://www.boston.com.

day, are one of the great impediments to planning. Check the "Etiquette Tips for Marketing Professionals" feature for some tactful ways to minimize interruptions in your workday.

Top management—boards of directors, chief executive officers (CEOs), chief operating officers (COOs), and functional vice presidents, such as chief marketing officers—spend greater proportions of their time engaged in planning than do middle-level and supervisory-level managers. Also, top managers usually focus their planning on long-range strategic issues. In contrast, middle-level managers—such as advertising executives, regional sales managers, and marketing research directors—tend to focus on operational planning, which includes creating and implementing tactical plans for their own units. Supervisors often develop specific programs to meet goals in their areas of responsibility. Table 2.1 summarizes the types of planning undertaken at various organizational levels.

When it is most effective, the planning process includes input from a wide range of sources: employees, suppliers, and customers. Some marketing experts advocate developing a network of "influencers"—people who have influence over other people's opinions through authority, visibility, or expertise—to provide input and spread the word about company plans and products. Valuable input can come from almost anywhere. When De Beers, the diamond company, opened its first retail store, it held a huge opening party with nearly 1000 celebrity guests. But before the party, a gathering of

assessment check 2

2.1 How do marketing plans differ at different levels of the organization?

2.2 Why is it important to get input from others when planning?

Go Green

Green Is a Socially Responsible Strategy

In 2005, Hewlett-Packard (Canada) commissioned Globe Scan to survey Canadians concerning their views on corporate social responsibility. Among the important findings was that 40 percent of the more than 1500 respondents reported that they had punished a company within the previous 12 months by not purchasing its products or by spreading negative word-of-mouth because the company did not act in a socially responsible manner. If this isn't enough to convince companies to have greater environmental concern, perhaps Wal-Mart—with its own green strategy—will force changes, at least among its suppliers. The company plans to reduce packaging on the products it sells by 5 percent by 2013. If successful, this would be equivalent to removing 213 000 trucks from the highways and would save approximately 324 000 tonnes of coal and 254 million litrs of diesel fuel per year. The company reported that by simply reducing the size of a cardboard box by one square inch on a line of toys it sold across North America, it saved $3 million. Those savings, of course, allow Wal-Mart to support its low-price strategy to consumers.

Among manufacturers, Procter & Gamble has been researching green products. It recently introduced Tide Coldwater, which contains a proprietary surfactant that makes oily stains soluble in cold water and new enzymes that can break down proteins and starches at low temperatures. The company claims that if everyone in New York City washed their laundry in cold water for one day, the energy saved could light the Empire State Building for a month. Japanese automobile manufacturer Subaru has North America's first "zero-landfill" assembly plant. Its entire plant out-performs the best Canadian household: 99.8 percent of its waste gets recycled and 0.2 percent gets incinerated. Subaru is promoting its green manufacturing in its advertising and in 2009 is expected to sell some automobile models as PZEVs—Partially Zero Emission Vehicles, not ZEVs, but the closest thing on the market. Increasingly, companies can be expected to make a green strategy part of their marketing strategy.

Sources: Hewlett-Packard, "Expectations for Corporate Social Responsibility Rising with Clear Consequences for Not Measuring Up," news release, April 20, 2006, available http://h41131.www4.hp.com/ca/en/pr/04202006a.html, accessed October 25, 2008; Joe Schwarcz, "Wal-Mart Wades into the Green Waters," *Gazette* (Montreal), March 3, 2007, p. J11; Donna Nebenzahl, "Green Firms 'Win Customers,'" *Vancouver Sun*, March 31, 2007, p. E7; Daniel Drolet, "Government, Retailers Try to Put Green Revolution in the Bag," *Ottawa Citizen*, April 17, 2007, p. E1; Michael Vaughan, "Subaru Looks to Green for Its Identity, *Globe and Mail*, September 18, 2008, p. G2.

COURTESY OF LA-Z-BOY INCORPORATED

La-Z-Boy defines itself as a company that sells comfort.

less than 150 very special and influential guests was held. "Some of the richest people in the world are in these rooms," said a De Beers jewellery expert who attended the party. "There are women here who would buy a $10 000 ring and forget about it in a week."[6]

STEPS IN THE MARKETING PLANNING PROCESS

The marketing planning process begins at the corporate level with the definition of a firm's mission. It then determines its objectives, assesses its resources, and evaluates environmental risks and opportunities. Guided by this information, marketers within each business unit then formulate a marketing strategy, implement the strategy through operating plans, and gather feedback to monitor and adapt strategies when necessary. Figure 2.1 shows the basic steps in the process.

DEFINING THE ORGANIZATION'S MISSION AND OBJECTIVES

The planning process begins with activities to define the firm's **mission**, the essential purpose that differentiates the company from

table 2.1   *Planning at Different Managerial Levels*

	MANAGEMENT LEVEL	TYPES OF PLANNING EMPHASIZED AT THIS LEVEL	EXAMPLES
Top Management	Board of directors	Strategic planning	Organization-wide objectives; fundamental strategies; long-term plans; total budget
	Chief executive officer (CEO)		
	Chief operating officer (COO)		
	Divisional vice presidents		
Middle Management	General sales manager	Tactical planning	Quarterly and semi-annual plans; divisional budgets; divisional policies and procedures
	Business unit manager		
	Director of marketing research		
Supervisory Management	District sales manager	Operational planning	Daily and weekly plans; unit budgets; departmental rules and procedures
	Supervisor—telemarketing office		

Marketoid

In 2008, the largest ever Canadian diamond was found in the Northwest Territories; it weighs 25.13 carats and has been independently valued at $440 000.

(3) Identify the steps in the marketing planning process.

mission Essential purpose that differentiates one company from others.

others. The mission statement specifies the organization's overall goals and operational scope and provides general guidelines for future management actions. Adjustments in this statement reflect changing business environments and management philosophies.

Although business writer Peter Drucker cautioned that an effective mission statement should be brief enough "to fit on a T-shirt," organizations typically define themselves with slightly longer statements. A statement may be lengthy and formal or brief and informal. Here are several examples:

- 3M: "To solve unsolved problems innovatively."
- Mary Kay Cosmetics: "To give unlimited opportunity to women."
- Merck: "To preserve and improve human life."
- Wal-Mart: "Always low prices."
- Intel: "To delight our customers, employees, and shareholders by relentlessly delivering the platform and technology advancements that become essential to the way we work and live."
- Retail Council of Canada: "To be the Voice of Retail in Canada by providing advocacy, research, education and services that enhance opportunities for retail success, and increase awareness of retail's contribution to the communities and customers it serves."
- Google: "To organize the world's information and make it universally accessible and useful."

figure 2.1

The Marketing Planning Process

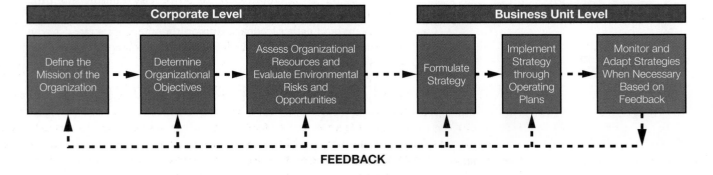

An organization lays out its basic objectives, or goals, in its complete mission statement. These objectives in turn guide development of supporting marketing objectives and plans. Soundly conceived objectives should state specific intentions such as the following:

- Generate a 10 percent profit over the next 12 months.
- Attain a 20 percent share of the market by 2012.
- Add 50 new stores within the next year.
- Develop 12 new products in 24 months.
- Expand operations to China by 2012.
- Cut operating costs by 5 percent.

ASSESSING ORGANIZATIONAL RESOURCES AND EVALUATING ENVIRONMENTAL RISKS AND OPPORTUNITIES

The third step of the marketing planning process involves an assessment of an organization's strengths, weaknesses, and available opportunities. Organizational resources include the capabilities of the firm's production, marketing, finance, technology, and employees. An organization's planners pinpoint its strengths and weaknesses. Strengths help them to set objectives, develop plans for meeting those objectives, and take advantage of marketing opportunities.

Chapter 3 will discuss environmental factors that affect marketing opportunities. Environmental effects can emerge both from within the organization and from the external environment. For example, the technological advances provided by the Internet have transformed the way people communicate and do business around the world. In fact, the Internet itself has created entirely new categories of business.

FORMULATING, IMPLEMENTING, AND MONITORING A MARKETING STRATEGY

Once a firm's marketers figure out their company's best opportunities, they can develop a marketing plan designed to meet the overall objectives. A good marketing plan revolves around an efficient, flexible, and adaptable marketing strategy.

A **marketing strategy** is an overall, company-wide program for selecting a particular target market and then satisfying consumers in that market through a careful blending of the elements of the marketing mix—product, distribution, promotion, and price—each of which is a subset of the overall marketing strategy.

In the two final steps of the planning process, marketers put the marketing strategy into action; then they monitor performance to ensure that objectives are being achieved. Sometimes strategies need to be modified if the product's or company's actual performance is not in line with expected results. When the Canadian Tulip Festival was formally launched in Ottawa in 1953, it attracted flower enthusiasts from around the world. Over the years, the venue grew to include a parade, craft show, regatta, fireworks displays, and outdoor concerts featuring high-priced performers. The festival's budget reached $2 million by 2004, but several years of poor weather and an increase in competing events eventually led to the festival declaring bankruptcy in 2006. Under the direction of a local business executive, David Luxton, the festival was refocused to reflect its origins in international friendship. The craft fair and outdoor concerts were cancelled. Local embassies were invited to present their national cuisine and promote their culture at booths set up in an International Pavilion. Music and dance were accommodated on a small stage, and a number of activities were centred on families and children. More than 125 000 people—an increase of approximately 40 percent over the festival's best attendance, achieved in 2001—visited

marketing strategy
Overall company-wide program for selecting a particular target market and then satisfying consumers in that market through the marketing mix.

assessment check 3

3.1 Distinguish between an organization's mission and its objectives.

3.2 What is the importance of the final step in the marketing planning process?

④ Describe successful planning tools and techniques, including Porter's Five Forces model, first and second mover strategies, SWOT analysis, and the strategic window.

the International Pavilion in 2007. The festival received 20 to 25 percent of the revenues from each booth. The large attendance has captured the attention of potential corporate sponsors, and the festival has regained its financial viability.[7]

SUCCESSFUL STRATEGIES: TOOLS AND TECHNIQUES

We can identify a number of successful marketing planning tools and techniques. This section discusses four of them: Porter's Five Forces model, first and second mover strategies, SWOT analysis, and the strategic window. All planning strategies have the goal of creating a **sustainable competitive advantage** for a firm, in which other companies simply cannot provide the same value to their customers that the firm does—no matter how hard they try.

Porter's Five Forces
Model developed by strategy expert Michael Porter, which identifies five competitive forces that influence planning strategies: the threat of new entrants, the threat of substitute products, rivalry among competitors, the bargaining power of buyers, and the bargaining power of suppliers.

PORTER'S FIVE FORCES MODEL

A number of years ago, the renowned business strategist and one of the world's best-known business academics Michael E. Porter identified five competitive forces that influence planning strategies in a model called **Porter's Five Forces.** Recently, Porter updated his model to include the impact of the Internet on the strategies that businesses use. As illustrated by Figure 2.2, the five forces are potential new entrants; bargaining power of buyers; bargaining power of suppliers; threat of substitute products; and rivalry among competitors.

Potential new entrants are sometimes blocked by the cost or difficulty of entering a market. It is a lot more costly and complicated to begin building aircraft than it is to start up an Internet résumé service. In fact, the Internet has reduced the barriers to market entry in many industries.

figure 2.2

Porter's Five Forces Model

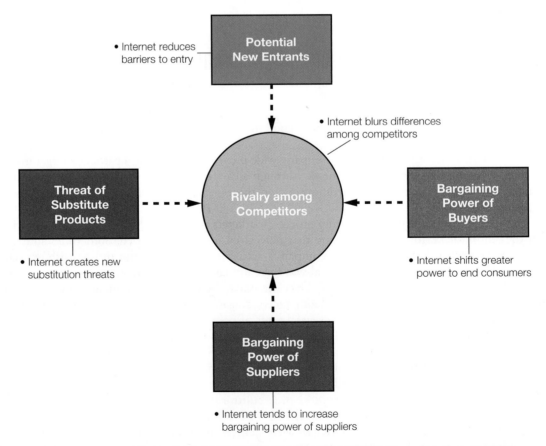

If customers have considerable bargaining power, they can greatly influence a firm's strategy. The Internet can increase a customer's buying power by providing information that might not otherwise be easily accessible, such as supplier alternatives and price comparisons. Before going to the showroom, for instance, Canadian car buyers can check out the true value of a trade-in on the Internet at websites such as CanadianBlackBook.com and research new car costs at carquotes.ca.

The number of available suppliers to a manufacturer or retailer affects their bargaining power. If a seafood restaurant in Manitoba has only one supplier of Nova Scotia lobsters, that supplier has significant bargaining power. But seafood restaurants located throughout Nova Scotia have many lobster suppliers available, which gives their suppliers less bargaining power.

If customers have the opportunity to replace a company's products with the goods or services from a competing firm or industry, the company's marketers may have to take steps to find a new market, change prices, or compete in other ways to maintain an advantage. Sometimes substitute products drive companies out of business altogether. The increasing ease of downloading free music from online peer-to-peer networks is hurting everyone in the music industry. Consumers bought just 25 million copies of the 10 top-selling CDs in 2006, down from 60 million copies of the 10 best-selling CDs in 2000. Calgary-based Melodiya Records sold 75 copies of Arcade Fire's 2004 debut CD, *Funeral,* but only 25 copies of its 2007 follow-up CD, *Neon Bible.* Although this independent retailer continues to survive, nearly 3000 have gone out of business across North America in one recent four-year period.[8]

The four previous forces influence the rivalry among competitors. In addition, issues such as cost and differentiation or lack of differentiation of products—along with the Internet—influence the strategies that companies use to stand out from their competitors. With increased availability of information, which tends to level the playing field, rivalry heats up among competitors, who try to differentiate themselves from the crowd.

It's always nice to be remembered when you're not sick during cold and flu season. This year, boost your immune system with COLD-fX® and reduce the frequency, severity and duration of cold and flu symptoms. COLD-fX® is Canada's #1 selling cold remedy.

cold-fx.ca

BE WELL.

COLD-fX continues to promote its position as Canada's cold remedy market leader. It is attempting to exploit its first-mover advantage.

FIRST MOVER AND SECOND MOVER STRATEGIES

Some firms like to adopt a **first mover strategy**—attempting to capture the greatest market share and develop long-term relationships by being the first to enter the market with a product or service. Being first may also refer to entering new markets with existing products or creating significant innovations that effectively turn an old product into a new one. Naturally, this strategy has its risks—companies that follow can learn from mistakes by first movers.[9] Apple has held firmly to the lead it established with its iTunes online music store, recently passing the 1 billion mark in downloads purchased. That success grew directly from Apple's leading the way in the market for digital music players, in which the iPod still dominates, with about 78 percent market share in its domestic market and about 50 percent market share worldwide. "With each passing year since [iTunes] was introduced," says an industry authority, "Apple has continued to expand its lead both on the hardware side and the service side. It's certainly become more difficult for its competitors."[10]

On the other hand, Apple failed terribly with another first mover introduction, its Newton handheld computer, while others overtook the lead in the market. Businesses often thrive on a **second mover strategy,** observing closely the innovations of first movers and then improving on them to gain advantage in the marketplace. Charles Stack is credited with making the first sales transaction on the Internet, but few people will remember his Books.com. Jeff Bezos was a "fast follower" and opened his online bookstore, Amazon.com, in July 1995. In 2007, Amazon sales exceeded $14.8 billion.[11]

first mover strategy
Theory advocating that the company that is first to offer a product in a marketplace will be the long-term market winner.

second mover strategy
Theory that advocates observing closely the innovations of first movers and then introducing new products that improve on the original offering to gain advantage in the marketplace.

SWOT ANALYSIS

SWOT analysis Analysis that helps planners compare internal organizational strengths and weaknesses with external opportunities and threats.

An important strategic planning tool, **SWOT analysis,** helps planners compare internal organizational strengths and weaknesses with external opportunities and threats. (SWOT is an acronym for *strengths, weaknesses, opportunities,* and *threats.*) This form of analysis provides managers with a critical view of the organization's internal and external environments and helps them evaluate the firm's fulfillment of its basic mission. A careful SWOT analysis would be an important first step to turning around an underperforming business, as described in the "Marketing Hit" feature.

A company's strengths reflect its **core competencies**—what it does well. Core competencies are capabilities that customers value and competitors find difficult to duplicate. As Figure 2.3 shows, matching an internal strength with an external opportunity produces a situation known as *leverage.* Marketers face a problem when environmental threats attack their organization's weaknesses. Planners anticipate constraints when internal weaknesses or limitations prevent their organization from taking advantage of opportunities. These internal weaknesses can create vulnerabilities for a company—environmental threats to its organizational strength.

Vancouver-based Coastal Contacts illustrates how a company can leverage its strengths to take advantage of market opportunities. Roger Hardy started the company in 2000 with little more than a computer, a phone, and a Ping Pong table. By 2008, his company had sold more than 100 million contact lenses online, to more than 1.5 million customers in over 150 countries. The opportunity Hardy saw was the eyeglasses market—10 times the size of the contact-lens market. The company's strengths included a base of loyal customers (many of whom used both contact

figure 2.3
SWOT Analysis

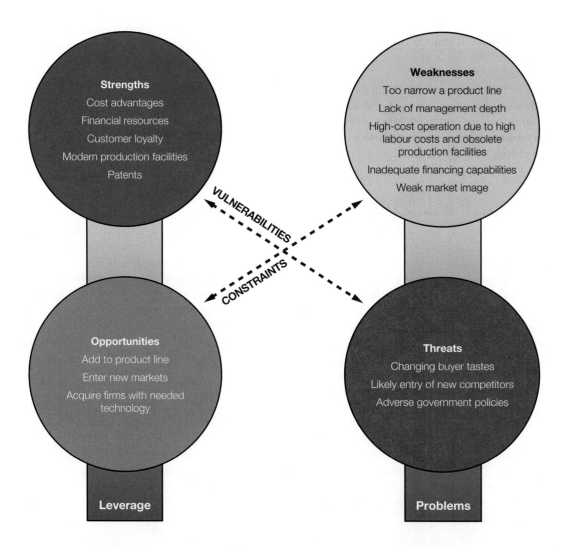

lenses and eyeglasses), and the knowledge and processes it developed selling online and shipping lightweight overnight shipments around the world. When the company added eyeglasses to its product mix, it differentiated itself on both selection and price. Where most retailers carried a few hundred styles of frames, Coastal Contacts carried many thousands of styles; where most retailers had to have high margins as they sold only a few pairs of eyeglasses per day, Coastal Contacts could succeed with much smaller margins. Within three months, Coastal Contacts was selling 500 pairs of eyeglasses per day or more. Roger Hardy has a goal for Coastal Contacts: to be a $1-billion business by 2015.[12]

THE STRATEGIC WINDOW

The success of products is also influenced by conditions in the market. Professor Derek Abell has suggested the term **strategic window** to define the limited periods during which the key requirements of a market and the particular competencies of a firm best fit together.[13] The view through a strategic window shows planners a way to relate potential opportunities to company capabilities. Such a view requires a thorough analysis of (1) current and projected external environmental conditions, (2) current and projected internal company capabilities, and (3) how, whether, and when the firm can feasibly reconcile environmental conditions and company capabilities by implementing one or more marketing strategies.

"China has begun to enter the age of mass car consumption. This is a great and historic advance," says China's state-run news agency, Xinhua. In just a few years, demand for cars has soared in China, and the government has funnelled the equivalent of billions of dollars into building highways. Carmakers at home and abroad are watching this strategic window carefully. "China is going to become the second-largest market in the world sometime over the next two or three years," says the head of China distribution for Ford. After that, he believes, it could be the world's largest market.[14]

strategic window
Limited periods during which the key requirements of a market and the particular competencies of a firm best fit together.

assessment check 4

4.1 Briefly explain each of Porter's Five Forces.

4.2 What are the benefits and drawbacks of a first mover strategy?

4.3 What are the four components of the SWOT analysis? What is a strategic window?

marketing success — Cleaning Up

Background. Concord, Ontario-based KIK Corp. was a one-plant, 100-employee manufacturer of household bleach operating on a day-by-day basis in 1995 when David Cynamon was recruited on a 90-day contract to assess the ongoing viability of the operation. Gerry Pencer, Cynamon's father-in-law and the founder of private-label soft-drink manufacturer Cott Corp., recruited Cynamon for the position. At the time, Cynamon recalls, "KIK had no brand. It was one product, and one plant."

The Challenge. A serious weakness that Cynamon identified was the size of KIK Corp., a small company operating in a highly fragmented industry. Cynamon says, "If I have 35 competitors and they're not all on the same page, this market, this industry will never develop."

The Strategy. Cynamon saw a tremendous opportunity here: private-label manufacturing. It had made Cott Corp. extremely successful. Why would it not work for household bleach? His strategy became two-pronged: first, consolidate the industry by buying competition; second, promote private-label bleach.

The Outcome. Today, KIK Custom Products operates 23 manufacturing facilities and four distribution centers, and employs more than 4000 people. Its product line includes bleach, fabric softeners, dish detergents, liquid laundry detergents, and many other items that it sells to about 86 percent of the largest retailers in North America. It is also a contract manufacturer for companies such as Johnson & Johnson and Procter & Gamble, making such well-known consumer brands as Windex, Shout, Fantastik, Javex, and Fleecy. Sales recently exceeded $1 billion.

Sources: KIK Corp. website, http://www.kikcorp.com, accessed May 4, 2008; Boyd Erman, "KCP a Lesson in M & A Froth," *Globe and Mail,* February 14, 2008, p. B4; Jennifer Myers, "The Man with the Midas Touch," *Profit,* May 2005, pp. 46–52.

⑤ Identify the basic
elements of a
marketing strategy.

ELEMENTS OF A MARKETING STRATEGY

Success for a product in the marketplace—whether it is a tangible good, a service, a cause, a person, a place, or an organization—depends on an effective marketing strategy. It's one thing to develop a great product, but if customers don't get the message about it, the product will die. An effective marketing strategy reaches the right buyers at the right time, persuades them to try the product, and develops a strong relationship with them over time. The basic elements of a marketing strategy consist of (1) the target market and (2) the marketing mix variables of product, distribution, promotion, and price that combine to satisfy the needs of the target market. The outer circle in Figure 2.4 lists environmental characteristics that provide the framework within which marketing strategies are planned.

THE TARGET MARKET

A customer-driven organization begins its overall strategy with a detailed description of its **target market**: the group of people toward whom the firm decides to direct its marketing efforts and ultimately its merchandise. Zellers stores serve a target market consisting of consumers purchasing for themselves and their families. Other companies, such as Bombardier, market most of their products to business buyers such as Air Canada and government purchasers. Still other firms provide goods and services to retail and wholesale buyers. In every instance, however, marketers pinpoint their target markets as accurately as possible. Although the concept of dividing markets into specific segments is discussed in more detail in Chapter 9, it's important to understand the idea of targeting a market from the outset. In 2006, Marissa McTasney—a Brooklin, Ontario, "mompreneur"—started Tomboy Trades (now called Moxie Trades). She specifically targeted women construction workers and do-it-yourselfers. When she was looking for work boots for herself and was dissatisfied with the choices she found, Marissa decided to investigate further. When she found a company in China that was willing to manufacture pink work boots, she ordered 30 pair. From there, she added more colours—baby blue, red, and green—more products—hard hats, tool belts, safety glasses, and form-fitting T-shirts, all styled for women—and more distribution options— from direct distribution, to online selling through Home Depot Canada, then through all 281 Zellers locations in Canada. Marissa is now considering other outlets in Canada and the United States and a line of tools to complement the company's other products.[15]

Diversity plays an ever-increasing role in targeting markets. By 2017, Canada is expected to include 1.8 million Chinese and another 1.8 million South Asians—combined, they will make up approximately half of all visible minorities. Canada's banks are certainly paying attention. The Royal Bank of Canada advertises in Punjabi, Hindi, Mandarin, and Cantonese. Scotiabank advertises during festivals such as Eid, Diwali, and Chinese New Year. TD Canada Trust employs ethnic, bi- or multi-lingual staff and makes sure there is promotional material at its branches in languages that ethnic Canadians prefer. It has 43 percent of the South Asian-Canadian market, higher than RBC, Scotiabank, and CIBC combined. It is the leader among Chinese Canadians, too, with 29 percent of the market. Gavin Barrett of Toronto agency Rao, Barrett and Welsh says that winning banks must build relationships with these groups, and that will require that they "provide experiences that have cultural relevance." The typical Canadian, for example, may be attracted by haggle-free mortgages, but many Asians prefer to haggle. "For Asians, finding the best deal is a way to build relationships... and a way to brag to their families."[16]

Marketoid

The 1901 Canadian Census recorded about 25 different ethnic groups; the 2006 Canadian Census recorded members from more than 200 different ethnic origins.

figure 2.4

Elements of a Marketing Strategy and Its Environmental Framework

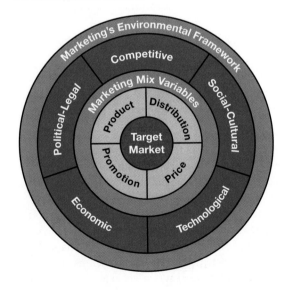

MARKETING MIX VARIABLES

marketing mix Blending of the four strategy elements—product, distribution, promotion, and pricing—to fit the needs and preferences of a specific target market.

After marketers select a target market, they direct their company's activities toward profitably satisfying that segment. Although they must manipulate thousands of variables to reach this goal, marketing decision making can be divided into four strategies: product, distribution, promotion, and pricing strategies. The total package forms the **marketing mix**—the blending of the four strategic elements to fit the needs and preferences of a specific target market. While the fourfold classification is useful to study and analyze, remember that the marketing mix can—and should—be an ever-changing combination of variables to achieve success.

Figure 2.4 illustrates the focus of the marketing mix variables on the central choice of the target market. In addition, decisions about product, distribution, promotion, and price are affected by the environmental factors in the outer circle of the figure. The environmental variables may play a major role in the success of a marketing program, and marketers must consider their probable effects.

Product Strategy

In marketing, the word *product* means more than a good, service, or idea. Product is a broad concept that also encompasses the satisfaction of all consumer needs in relation to a good, service, or idea. So **product strategy** involves more than just deciding what goods or services the firm should offer to a group of consumers. It also includes decisions about customer service, package design, brand names, trademarks, patents, warranties, the life cycle of a product, positioning the product in the marketplace, and new product development. Xerox Canada offers many innovative document solutions, services, and systems. The company continually improves its product offerings to help customers improve their work processes and business solutions. Hewlett-Packard (HP), a manufacturer of digital photo printers, among other products, is moving into retail photo printing with the introduction of its Photosmart Express self-service photo kiosk. The kiosk printer is the first to use ink-jet technology in this market. It includes an easy-to-use touch screen to guide customers through the process of producing 4-by-6-inch prints in as little as five seconds. HP faces stiff competition from Fuji and Kodak, but the kiosk printer is "basically closing a loop," says an analyst in the digital imaging market. "They can generate revenue from home printing, online printing, and now, retail printing."[17]

Wells Fargo Foothill Canada has a clear target market: middle-market companies. After more than 35 years in the U.S. market, it has entered the Canadian marketplace.

product strategy
Decisions about what goods or services a firm will offer its customers; also includes decisions about customer service, packaging, brand names, and the like.

Distribution Strategy

Marketers develop **distribution strategies** to ensure that consumers find their products in the proper quantities at the right times and places. Distribution decisions involve modes of transportation, warehousing, inventory control, order processing, and selection of marketing channels. Marketing channels are made up of institutions such as retailers and wholesalers—intermediaries that may be involved in a product's movement from producer to final consumer.

Technology is opening new channels of distribution in many industries. Computer software, a product made of digital data files, is ideally suited to electronic distribution. But all kinds of other products are now bought and sold over the Internet as well. By affecting everything from warehousing to order processing, technology has made the success of Amazon.com and eBay possible. Although these firms operate differently, both rely on technology for various distribution tasks.

Distribution is the perfect place for many companies to form alliances. Sony's music division formed an agreement with Universal Music Group to form Duet, an online music service that will make thousands of songs available to consumers legally over the Internet. Rogers Communications signed a deal with Apple to bring the iPhone to Canada in 2008. Rogers was Apple's logical choice to distribute the iPhone in Canada as it is the only carrier that has a GSM network, the technology required to run the iPhone. Being the only carrier to distribute the product in Canada will also be beneficial for Rogers, which is expected to add as many as 100 000 new customers as a result. Solutions Research Group predicts that 22 percent of iPhone customers will be former Bell Canada customers, and another 9 percent will come from Telus.[18]

distribution strategy
Planning that ensures that consumers find their products in the proper quantities at the right times and places.

Promotional Strategy

Promotion is the communications link between sellers and buyers. Organizations use varied ways to send messages about their goods, services, and ideas. They may communicate messages directly

promotion Communications link between buyers and sellers. Function of informing, persuading, and influencing a consumer's purchase decision.

As part of its marketing strategy, Xerox continually introduces new products that add value for its customers.

pricing strategy
Methods of setting profitable and justifiable prices.

Marketoid

In 2007, approximately 19.2 million passenger cars and light vehicles were registered in Canada.

assessment check 5 ✓

5.1 What are the two components of every marketing strategy?

5.2 Identify the four strategic elements of the marketing mix.

⑥ Describe the environmental characteristics that influence strategic decisions.

through salespeople or indirectly through advertisements and promotions. When it unveiled the new Eclipse Spyder, Mitsubishi acted on marketing research indicating that North Americans are intrigued by Japanese culture, including its art, fashion, and food. So the carmaker celebrated its new-product introduction to the strains of pounding Japanese rock and a performance by Japanese drummers in native dress.[19]

In developing a promotional strategy, marketers blend the various elements of promotion to communicate most effectively with their target market. Many companies use an approach called **integrated marketing communications (IMC)** to coordinate all promotional activities so that the consumer receives a unified and consistent message. Consumers might receive newsletters, e-mail updates, discount coupons, catalogues, invitations to company-sponsored events, and any number of other types of marketing communications about a product. Toyota dealers mail maintenance and service reminders to their customers. A political candidate may send volunteer workers through a neighbourhood to invite voters to a special reception.

Pricing Strategy

Pricing strategy deals with the methods of setting profitable and justifiable prices. It is closely regulated and subject to considerable public scrutiny. One of the many factors that influence a marketer's pricing strategy is competition. The computer industry has become all too familiar with price cuts by both current competitors and new market entrants. After years of steady growth, the market has become saturated with low-cost computers, driving down profit margins even farther. There's plenty of competition in the air travel and automobile manufacturing industries as well. Canada's auto dealers have seen a 17 percent growth in sales of subcompact cars in 2007. Among the top-five sellers, only Hyundai saw a decrease. To fight back, Hyundai dropped its price of its Accent model to $9995 across Canada. Richard Cooper of J.D. Power & Associates says, "That psychological (four digit) barrier is quite important for consumers, particularly younger consumers, and those are probably the people they have in their sights right now."[20] A good pricing strategy should create value for customers, building and strengthening their relationship with a firm and its products.

THE MARKETING ENVIRONMENT

Marketers do not make decisions about target markets and marketing mix variables in a vacuum. They must take into account the dynamic nature of the five dimensions of the marketing environment shown back in Figure 2.4: competitive, political-legal, economic, technological, and social-cultural factors.

Concerns about the natural environment have led to new regulations concerning air and water pollution. Automobile engineers, for instance, have turned public concerns and legal issues into opportunities by developing hybrid cars. These new models are fuelled by dual energy: a gasoline engine and an electric motor. Toyota was the first to enter the market with its Prius, which depends on both an electric motor and a backup gasoline engine. Note that the marketing environment is fertile ground for innovators and entrepreneurs.

Businesses are increasingly looking to foreign shores for new growth markets. China-based Lenovo Group, the third-largest computer maker in the world, is taking its first steps in North America and other foreign markets with low-priced desktops and notebooks designed for consumers and small businesses. The company recently purchased IBM's stagnant personal computer business. "Lenovo will offer the new PCs as the smart choice for today's most savvy entrepreneurs, priced to fit the budgets and computer needs of even the smallest firms," says its chief marketing officer.[21]

Technology has changed the marketing environment as well, partly with the advent of the Internet. Throughout this text, you will encounter examples of the ways the Internet and other technological developments are continuously altering how firms do business. And as technology forces these changes, other aspects of the environment must respond. Sometimes legal disputes arise over who owns which innovations. A long-running patent infringement suit brought against Waterloo-based Research In Motion (RIM), the maker of the BlackBerry handheld device, was recently settled for a one-time payment of $612.5 million days before an injunction was expected to shut down the popular wireless e-mail service. In return for the settlement, NTP, which brought the suit, issued Research In Motion a licence to use its patented technology in the future. The end of the case followed several setbacks for both sides and was a particular relief to corporate BlackBerry customers. "It was going to be a nightmare because we have 3000 BlackBerry users," said a UPS spokesperson.[22] Amazon.com founder and chief executive Jeff Bezos has suggested that software and Internet patents should have a shorter lifespan than other patents—perhaps because of the rapid changes in technology—and that they should be open to public comment before being issued.

Competition is never far from the marketer's mind. Among the companies finding themselves increasingly vulnerable to competition from the Internet, for instance, are Canada's major newspaper publishers, major TV networks, and magazine and book publishers. Digital and online business entrepreneurs are looking for versatile ways to offer competing content and services to users everywhere, faster and more cheaply than ever before. Google and Yahoo! are posting record earnings. Microsoft is shifting more and more resources to the Internet. Torstar is one company that is fighting back. Through its flagship daily newspaper, *Toronto Star*, it launched three new websites in early 2008: parentcentral.ca, healthzone.ca, and yourhome.ca. Targeting such niche audiences could be good for advertising sales on these websites.[23]

Some experts have coined the phrase **rule of three**, meaning that, in any industry, the three strongest, most efficient companies dominate between 70 and 90 percent of the market. Here are a few examples—all of which are household names:

- *Fast-food restaurants:* McDonald's, Burger King, Wendy's
- *Cereal manufacturers:* General Mills, Kellogg's, Post
- *Running shoes:* Nike, Adidas, Reebok
- *Airlines:* Air Canada, WestJet, Porter Airlines
- *Pharmaceuticals:* Merck, Pfizer, Bristol-Myers Squibb[24]

While it may seem like an uphill battle for the remaining hundreds of companies in any given industry, each of these firms can find a strategy for gaining competitive ground.

In the highly competitive airline industry, for example, Calgary-based Corporate Jet Air chose a niche strategy for its 2008 market entry. It offers three flights daily between Calgary and Toronto, and only business-class service. Customers must purchase a package of 10 one-way trips that must be taken within one year and must pay in advance. Although the $16 000 price may seem high, it is competitive with Air Canada's executive-class fares. Also,

CIBC targets small businesses with customized advice in its *Professional Edge®* service.

WWF-Canada helps Canadians fight climate change and reduce their footprint on the planet.

Solving an Ethical Controversy

Should Retailers Ban the Salvation Army from Their Sidewalks?

DURING a recent Christmas season, U.S. retailer Target banned the Salvation Army's traditional bell ringers and red collection kettles from its stores, angering many consumers. The company said it was simply enforcing its existing rules against solicitation on store premises, but the venerable Christian charity claimed that the snub could cost it $9 million in donations, with repercussions not only at Christmas but throughout the year. The move hurt Target, too. "I don't plan to buy another thing at Target until they change their policy toward the Salvation Army," said one clergy member who, like many others, urged churchgoers to boycott the store. Meanwhile, at Wal-Mart and Sam's Club locations, the Salvation Army's traditional red kettle and bell-ringing season was extended to allow the charity to raise extra money for disaster relief and other humanitarian causes.

Is it ethical for retailers to ban charitable groups from their stores?

PRO

1. Many other big retailers such Best Buy, Home Depot, and others also prohibit solicitations. It is not an unusual policy and is not aimed directly at any one charity.

2. Target already donates more than $100 million a year to charities, including the Salvation Army. The firm just doesn't want charities to pressure customers on their sidewalks.

CON

1. With so many disasters in recent years, the Salvation Army deserves as many opportunities as it can get to help people by collecting donations.
2. With sidewalk donations, customers are afforded an easy way to contribute to the charity's many efforts for those in need, increasing goodwill to the store.

Where do you stand: pro or con?

Sources: Target website, http://www.target.com/, accessed January 25, 2006; "Churches and Wal-Mart Help Rescue Salvation Army from Target's Snub," NewsMax.com, December 16, 2004, http://www.newsmax.com, accessed January 25, 2006; Don Teague, "Target Bans Salvation Army Solicitations," MSNBC, December 13, 2004, http://www.msnbc.com, accessed January 25, 2006.

the new airline picks up and drops off passengers by limousine service, and check-in time is allowed up to 20 minutes before departure.[25]

The social-cultural environment includes a variety of factors, including prevailing cultural norms. Sometimes a company policy can have unintended consequences when store customers feel that it betrays their cultural norms, as U.S. retailer Target found out when it banned charity solicitations on its premises (see the "Solving an Ethical Controversy" feature).

The marketing environment provides a framework for all marketing activity. Marketers consider environmental dimensions when they develop strategies for segmenting and targeting markets and when they study consumer and organizational buying behaviour.

assessment check 6

6.1 What are the five dimensions of the marketing environment?

6.2 How does technology influence the marketing environment?

⑦ Describe the methods for marketing planning, including business portfolio analysis and the BCG matrix.

METHODS FOR MARKETING PLANNING

As growing numbers of companies have discovered the benefits of effective marketing planning, they have developed planning methods to assist in this important function. This section discusses two useful methods: the strategic business unit concept and the market share/market growth matrix.

BUSINESS PORTFOLIO ANALYSIS

Although a small company may offer only a few items to its customers, a larger organization frequently offers and markets many products to widely diverse markets. CIBC and BMO offer a wide range of financial products to businesses and consumers; Kraft Foods stocks supermarket shelves with everything from macaroni and cheese to mayonnaise. Top managers at these larger firms need a method for spotting product lines that deserve more investment as well as lines that aren't living up to expectations. So they conduct a **portfolio analysis**, in which they evaluate their company's products and divisions to determine which are strongest and which are weakest. Much like securities analysts review their portfolios of stocks and bonds, deciding which to retain and which to discard, marketing planners must perform the same assessment of their products, the regions in which they operate, and other marketing mix variables. This is where the concept of an SBU comes in.

Strategic business units (SBUs) are key business units within diversified firms. Each SBU has its own managers, resources, objectives, and competitors. A division, product line, or single product may define the boundaries of an SBU. Each SBU pursues its own distinct mission, and each develops its own plans independently of other units in the organization.

Strategic business units focus the attention of company managers so that they can respond effectively to changing consumer demand within limited markets. Companies may have to redefine their SBUs as market conditions dictate. Hewlett-Packard recently created a separate new company unit for its iPaq handheld computer, splitting handhelds from its operations for laptops, desktops, and workstations.[26]

strategic business units (SBUs) Key business units within diversified firms.

THE BCG MATRIX

To evaluate each of their organization's strategic business units, marketers need some type of portfolio performance framework. A widely used framework was developed by the Boston Consulting Group. This **market share/market growth matrix** places SBUs in a four-quadrant chart that plots market share—the percentage of a market that a firm controls—against market growth potential. The position of an SBU along the horizontal axis indicates its market share relative to those of competitors in the industry. Its position along the vertical axis indicates the annual growth rate of the market. After plotting all of a firm's business units, planners divide them according to the matrix's four quadrants. Figure 2.5 illustrates this matrix by labelling the four quadrants stars, cash cows, question marks, and dogs. Firms in each quadrant require a unique marketing strategy.

Stars represent units with high market shares in high-growth markets. These products or businesses are high-growth market leaders. Although they generate considerable income, they need inflows of even more cash to finance further growth. Apple's popular iPod is the No. 1 selling portable digital music player in the world, but because of rapidly changing technology, Apple will have to continue to invest in ways to update and upgrade the player. The introduction of new models that can store and play video content such as music videos and television reruns is one example of Apple's market growth strategy.[27]

Cash cows command high market shares in low-growth markets. Marketers for such an SBU want to maintain this status for as long as possible. The business produces strong cash flows, but instead of investing heavily in the unit's own promotions and production capacity, the firm can use this cash to finance the growth of other SBUs with higher growth potentials. For instance, Microsoft might use the

figure 2.5

BCG Market Share/Market Growth Matrix

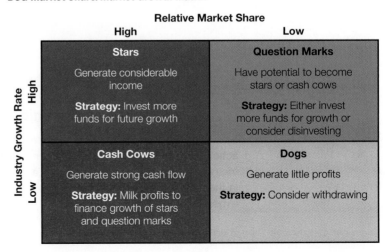

profits from sales of its Windows operating system to finance research and development for new Internet-based technologies.

Question marks—sometimes called *problem children*—achieve low market shares in high-growth markets. Many new product introductions begin life as question marks. Marketers must decide whether to continue supporting these products or businesses since question marks typically require considerably more cash than they generate. If a question mark cannot become a star, the firm should pull out of the market and target other markets with greater potential. With a new CEO, Six Flags is looking for ways to bring new customers to its 29 theme parks throughout Canada, the United States, and Mexico. The shareholders have been promised change, and everything is up for grabs, including the ad campaign, the rides, and the parks themselves. "This industry relies too much on big rides," says CEO Mark Shapiro. "We have to diversify. We have to focus on more concerts and more themed attractions." Industry experts agree, saying that renewed ties with Hollywood—film producer Harvey Weinstein has recently joined the Six Flags board—could help make the parks a family destination again.[28]

Dogs manage only low market shares in low-growth markets. SBUs in this category promise poor future prospects, and marketers should seriously consider withdrawing from these businesses or product lines. In some cases, these products can be sold to other firms, where they are a better fit. As mentioned previously, IBM sold its PC business to Lenovo so that it could concentrate on its business services.

assessment check 7

7.1 What are SBUs?

7.2 Identify the four quadrants in the BCG matrix.

Strategic Implications of Marketing

NEVER before has planning been as important to marketers as the 21st century speeds ahead with technological advances. Marketers need to plan carefully, accurately, and quickly if their companies are to gain a competitive advantage in today's global marketplace. They need to define their organization's mission and understand the different methods for formulating a successful marketing strategy. They must consider a changing, diverse population and the boundaryless business environment created by the Internet. They must be able to evaluate when it's best to be first to get into a market and when it's best to wait. They need to recognize when they've got a star and when they've got a dog—when to hang on and when to let go. As daunting as this seems, planning can reduce the risk and worry of bringing new goods and services to the marketplace. ◆◆◆

REVIEW OF CHAPTER OBJECTIVES

① Distinguish between strategic planning and tactical planning.

Strategic planning is the process of identifying an organization's primary objectives and adopting courses of action toward these objectives. In other words, strategic planning focuses on the big picture of which industries are central to a firm's business. Tactical planning guides the implementation of the activities specified in the strategic plan. Once a strategy is set, operational managers devise methods (tactics) to achieve the larger goals.

(2) **Explain how marketing plans differ at various levels in an organization.**

Top management spends more time engaged in strategic planning than do middle- and supervisory-level managers, who tend to focus on narrower, tactical plans for their units. Supervisory managers are more likely to engage in developing specific plans designed to meet the goals assigned to them—for example, streamlining production processes so that they operate more efficiently.

(3) **Identify the steps in the marketing planning process.**

The basic steps in the marketing planning process are defining the organization's mission and objectives; assessing organizational resources and evaluating environmental risk and opportunities; and formulating, implementing, and monitoring the marketing strategy.

(4) **Describe successful planning tools and techniques, including Porter's Five Forces model, first and second mover strategies, SWOT analysis, and the strategic window.**

Porter's Five Forces are identified as the five competitive factors that influence planning strategies: potential new entrants, bargaining power of buyers, bargaining power of suppliers, threat of substitute products, and rivalry among competitors. With a first mover strategy, a firm attempts to capture the greatest market share by being first to enter the market; with a second mover strategy, a firm observes the innovations of first movers and then improves on them to gain advantage. SWOT analysis (strengths, weaknesses, opportunities, and threats) helps planners compare internal organizational strengths and weaknesses with external opportunities and threats. The strategic window identifies the limited periods during which the key requirements of a market and the competencies of a firm best fit together.

(5) **Identify the basic elements of a marketing strategy.**

Development of a marketing strategy is a two-step process: (1) selecting a target market and (2) designing an effective marketing mix to satisfy the chosen target. The target market is the group of people toward whom a company decides to direct its marketing efforts. The marketing mix blends four strategy elements to fit the needs and preferences of a specific target market. These elements are product strategy, distribution strategy, promotional strategy, and pricing strategy.

(6) **Describe the environmental characteristics that influence strategic decisions.**

The five dimensions of the marketing environment are competitive, political-legal, economic, technological, and social-cultural. Marketers must be aware of growing cultural diversity in the global marketplace.

(7) **Describe the methods for marketing planning, including business portfolio analysis and the BCG matrix.**

The business portfolio analysis evaluates a company's products and divisions, including strategic business units (SBUs). The SBU focuses the attention of company managers so they can respond effectively to changing consumer demand within certain markets. The BCG matrix places SBUs in a four-quadrant chart that plots market share against market growth potential. The four quadrants are stars, cash cows, question marks, and dogs.

assessment check answers

1.1 Define *planning*.

Planning is the process of anticipating future events and conditions and of determining the best way to achieve organizational objectives.

1.2 Give an example of strategic planning and tactical planning.

Eastman Kodak's strategic plans include focusing on the company's core strength in digital imaging. The company's tactical plans include developing the first Wi-Fi camera and the first dual-lens digital camera, and partnering with Motorola to build better camera phones.

2.1 How do marketing plans differ at different levels of the organization?

Top managers usually focus their planning activities on long-range strategic issues. In contrast, middle-level managers focus on operational planning, which includes creating and implementing tactical plans for their own units. Supervisors develop specific programs to meet the goals in their areas of responsibility.

2.2 Why is it important to get input from others when planning?

Input from a variety of sources—other employees, suppliers, or customers—helps ensure that many ideas are considered. Involving those people in planning can also turn them into advocates for the plan.

3.1 Distinguish between an organization's mission and its objectives.

The firm's mission is the essential purpose that differentiates the company from others. Its objectives guide development of supporting marketing objectives and plans.

3.2 What is the importance of the final step in the marketing planning process?

In the final step of the marketing planning process, managers monitor performance to ensure that objectives are being achieved.

4.1 Briefly explain each of Porter's Five Forces.

Porter's Five Forces are the threats of potential new entrants, which increases competition in a market; bargaining power of buyers, which can depress prices; bargaining power of suppliers, which can increase cost or reduce selection; threat of substitute products, which can lure customers to other products; and rivalry among competitors, which can bring about price wars or divert companies from their main goals.

4.2 What are the benefits and drawbacks of a first mover strategy?

The benefits of a first mover strategy include being able to capture the greatest market share and develop long-term relationships with customers. Disadvantages include the possibility that companies that follow can learn from mistakes by first movers.

4.3 What are the four components of the SWOT analysis? What is a strategic window?

SWOT analysis helps planners compare internal organizational strengths and weaknesses with external opportunities and threats. SWOT is an acronym for *strengths, weaknesses, opportunities, and threats*. A strategic window defines the limited periods during which the key requirements of a market and the particular competencies of a firm best fit together.

5.1 What are the two components of every marketing strategy?

The basic elements of a marketing strategy are (1) the target market and (2) the marketing mix variables.

5.2 Identify the four strategic elements of the marketing mix.

The marketing mix consists of product, distribution, promotion, and price strategies.

6.1 What are the five dimensions of the marketing environment?

The five dimensions of the marketing environment are competitive, political-legal, economic, technological, and social-cultural factors.

6.2 How does technology influence the marketing environment?

The Internet and other technological developments continuously alter how firms do business. As technology forces these changes, other aspects of the environment must respond.

7.1 What are SBUs?

Strategic business units (SBUs) are key business units within diversified firms. Each SBU has its own managers, resources, objectives, and competitors.

7.2 Identify the four quadrants in the BCG matrix.

The BCG matrix labels SBUs stars, cash cows, question marks, and dogs.

MARKETING TERMS YOU NEED TO KNOW

These terms are printed in red in the text. They are defined in the margins of the chapter and Marketing Plan appendix and in the Glossary that begins on p. G-1. Other important terms are printed in bold black type in the chapter but not included in this list. Their definitions can be found in the Glossary.

ASSURANCE OF LEARNING REVIEW

1. State whether each of the following illustrates strategic or tactical planning:
   a. Wal-Mart decides to enter the Japanese market.
   b. A local bakery decides to add coffee to its list of offerings.
2. Summarize in one or two sentences a strategic plan that a top manager in a business unit might be involved with. Now state in a sentence or two a tactical plan that a middle-level manager might focus on.
3. What is the difference between a firm's mission and its objectives?
4. Define marketing strategy.
5. Over which of Porter's Five Forces do consumers have the greatest influence?
6. Cite examples of firms that have succeeded with first and second mover strategies.
7. When using the strategic window, what three factors must marketers analyze?
8. Why is identifying a target market so important to a company?
9. Give an example of each of the four strategies in the marketing mix.
10. Identify a major way in which technology has changed the marketing environment in the last five years.
11. What is another name for SBUs?
12. Describe the characteristics of each of the four quadrants in the BCG matrix.

PROJECTS AND TEAMWORK EXERCISES

1. Choose a company whose goods and services are familiar to you. With at least one other classmate, formulate a mission statement for that company.
2. Once you have formulated the mission statement for your firm, identify at least five objectives.
3. Create a SWOT analysis for yourself, listing your own personal strengths, weaknesses, opportunities, and threats.
4. ABC has made some of its TV shows (such as *Lost* and *Desperate Housewives*) available for download to iPods and to PCs. Discuss how this strategy demonstrates a strategic window for the company.
5. Use your library resources or an Internet search engine to collect information on one of the following companies (or select one of your own). Identify the firm's target market(s). Note that a large company might have more than one target market. Write a brief proposal for a marketing strategy to reach that market.
   a. MasterCard
   b. Costco
   c. Volkswagen
   d. Old Navy
6. With a classmate, choose a company whose products you have purchased in the past. Create two ads for one of the company's products (or product lines). One ad should focus on the product itself—its features, packaging, or brand name.

The second ad should focus on pricing. Present your ads to the class for discussion. Which ad is more effective for the product and why?

7. On your own or with a classmate, research a firm that has been around for a long time, such as Ford, General Electric, or DuPont. Use your research to determine the ways that technology has changed the marketing environment for your firm. Present your findings in class.
8. Suppose you are a marketer for a large Canadian toy manufacturer. Top executives at the company have determined that growth overseas is an essential objective, and they want you to look at the Indian market's potential in the next five years. Write a memo to your manager explaining how you think the social-cultural environment may affect your firm's marketing strategy overseas.
9. Team up with one or more classmates to research companies on the Web, looking for firms that have created successful SBUs such as L.L. Bean's outdoor and fitness department, which is aimed at women. Then create an advertisement for one of those SBUs.
10. Go back to the firm you selected in Question 5 (or choose a different firm). Further research the company's products so you can create a hypothetical BCG matrix for some of the company's products. Which products are the stars? Which are the cash cows and question marks? Are there any dogs?

CRITICAL THINKING EXERCISES

1. Why is it important from a marketing standpoint for an organization to define its goals and objectives?
2. What are the potential benefits and drawbacks if a firm strays from its core competencies?
3. Describe a consumer product that you think is particularly vulnerable to substitution. If you were a marketer for that product, what steps might you take to defend your product's position?
4. Suppose you were a marketer for a luxury skincare line. What factors in the marketing environment might affect your marketing strategy and why?
5. Suppose you were a marketer for a small firm trying to enter one of the dominant industries illustrating the rule of three. Which marketing strategy might you select and why?

ETHICS EXERCISE

Suppose you work for a company that makes snowboards. As part of the marketing team, you have assisted in creating a SWOT analysis for the company and have discovered some good and not-so-good things about your employer. Strengths include customer loyalty, a patented design, and competitive prices. The company has been based on the West Coast, but the owner sees an opportunity to enter the Ontario market. But you are concerned about the firm's weaknesses—the product line is narrow, you suspect the company doesn't have the financial resources to expand right now, and the owner keeps a tight rein on everything.

1. Should you speak to your manager about your concerns or keep quiet? Why?
2. Would you look for a job at another firm or remain loyal to the one you work for? Why?

INTERNET EXERCISES

1. **Strategic versus tactical planning.** Review the chapter material on the differences between strategic and tactical planning. Visit the company websites listed here and, by searching news and announcements, determine whether the decisions listed were the result of strategic planning, tactical planning, or a combination of the two. Be prepared to defend your conclusions.

   a. The decision by Airbus (http://www.airbus.com) to proceed with the launch of the A380, the world's largest commercial airliner

   b. Wal-Mart Stores' (http://www.walmartstores.com) international expansion plans

   c. The recent decision by Eastman Kodak (http://www.kodak.com) to discontinue the manufacture and distribution of most film cameras

2. **Marketing planning methods.** Two marketing planning methods described in Chapter 2 were business portfolio analysis and the BCG matrix. Review the material and then perform the following exercises:

   a. Go to the website of 3M (http://www.mmm.com). Based on the information you find, divide 3M into its main strategic business units.

   b. Philips is a large Dutch-based diversified company specializing in consumer electronics and products. Go to the firm's website (http://www.philipsusa.com). Select five product lines, such as televisions and electric shavers. Classify each product in the BCG matrix. Justify your classifications.

   c. It is not uncommon for companies to sell individual products, or even complete product lines, to other companies. Using Google or another Internet search engine, identify a recent product sale. Using business portfolio analysis or the BCG matrix, prepare a brief report discussing why the seller sold the product and why the buyer purchased it.

Note: Internet web addresses change frequently. If you don't find the exact sites listed, you may need to access the organization's home page and search from there or use a search engine such as Google.

Case 2.1

A Farewell to Regional Jets?

Not too long ago, small regional jets, which carry 50 passengers in a single class, were the craft of choice among airlines, who ordered the $24-million planes by the dozen. With business travel booming, regional jets seemed to be an ideal solution for service to midsize cities. The two biggest manufacturers of the planes, Montreal-based Bombardier and Embraer of Brazil, considered them the stars of their product lineup and couldn't make them fast enough. Soon there were about 1,600 regional jets in the air, carrying about 20 percent of all domestic passengers.

Then the marketing environment changed as low-priced competitors moved into the business travel market, and business slumped generally following the September 11, 2001, terrorist attacks. To bring back passengers, many carriers flying regional jets reconsidered their pricing strategies and lowered fares, making the jets, which aren't very fuel-efficient, even more costly to fly. Delta Air Lines and Northwest, which both used regional jets on many flights, filed for bankruptcy. Delta returned 30 of its leased jets, and Northwest put an order for 13 on hold. Independence Air sold or returned 29 jets and took 28 more out of service, then ceased all flights. Industry experts predict that as many as 200 regional jets will soon end up in storage.

"The day of the regional jet is over, in terms of demand," said one airline industry consultant. "They can't make money." In a few short years, the market for regional jets had dried up.

Bombardier and Embraer were ready, however, with revised strategic plans. Soon they began rolling out a new breed of regional jet. Carrying between 70 and 100 passengers, the new craft are economical and roomy enough to have separate first-class sections, an amenity that business travellers crave. While most observers believe that the smaller jets won't disappear altogether, there's little doubt that they have seen their day. Because they were cramped and uncomfortable, frequent travellers probably won't miss them. But Bombardier, which guaranteed its airline customers that regional jets would have resale value, might face a $2.6-billion bill when the 50-seaters hit the used-airplane market.

Questions for Critical Thinking

1. What are some of the strengths, weaknesses, opportunities, and threats that face the aircraft manufacturing industry, as represented by Bombardier and Embraer?

2. Which elements of the marketing mix have airlines emphasized in their battle to retain their business passengers? Do you think they have chosen the most effective strategies? Why or why not?

Sources: "United One-Ups Small Regional Jets," USA Today, *February 6, 2006,* http://www.usatoday.com; Joe Sharkey, "No Room for the Passengers, Never Mind the Carry-Ons," *The New York Times,* January 31, 2006, http://www.nytimes.com; Marilyn Adams, "Regional Jets Appear on Endangered Species List," *USA Today,* November 2, 2005, p. 1B; "The Rise and Fall of Regional Jets," Marginal Revolution, November 2005, http://www.marginalrevolution.com.

Case 2.2

Starbucks' Strategy: It's a Small World After All

If your strategy is growth, you might as well go for the whole cuppa joe. That's what Starbucks is doing—expanding into international markets as if it were the most natural thing to do. To some experts, it is the best plan for a company that has been called by Wall Street analysts "the last great growth story." Others are a bit more skeptical. Why, for instance, would an American coffee maker try to pitch its brew against world-famous French dark espresso? "American coffee, it's only water. We call it *jus des chausettes*," sniffs Bertrand Abadie, a documentary filmmaker. (In case you don't speak fluent French, he called your favourite Starbucks flavour "sock juice.") Then there's China—a nation of about 1 billion tea drinkers. How does Starbucks intend to convert a nation whose favourite drink for the past 4500 years has been tea? Other countries are in the picture as well, such as Japan and Spain. "We're taking the long view that opportunities are so large and that these are the early days," explains Starbucks CEO Howard Schultz.

Starbucks has a plan. Currently, the company has about 6500 stores worldwide, with about one-fourth of those located in 29 countries outside the United States and Canada. According to Schultz, in the next few years, Starbucks intends to increase that number to 25 000 stores around the world, with 15 000 outside North America. "We're building a brand, not a fad," he explains. The Starbucks brand includes everything from its special flavors to its logo—a mermaid on a green background—which is already one of the most famous product images in North America.

Part of the company's strategy is to target younger consumers around the world. Austria's 20-something coffee drinkers already view Starbucks as something new and tasty. "The coffeehouses in Vienna are nice, but they are old. Starbucks is hip," says one newspaper editor. In Spain, the new Starbucks stores are teeming with teens, young adults, and tourists. "We're not going to capture everybody, but I see a younger generation of Spaniards and people of all sorts," observes CEO Schultz. The company is also selling a little bit of luxury in many of these countries, where the average income is lower than in the United States and Canada. A medium-size latte sells for 20 yuan, or about $2.65 in Shanghai, China—a luxury for a household whose monthly income might be around $143 (U.S.). But Chinese consumers view it as an affordable treat.

Scouting the right locations for international shops is also part of Starbucks' planning. In China, local marketers literally stand outside potential locations with handheld clickers, tallying every possible customer who walks by. Young fashionable couples get enthusiastic clicks. These consumers represent the emerging middle class in China—people with a bit of extra cash to spend and a desire for consumer goods. Starbucks analyzes pedestrian traffic through a location and researches where the newer, trendy areas will be in the next few years. Then marketers figure out where consumers live, work, and play. Finally, they put together a plan for a new store.

Strategic alliances may be a vital factor in Starbucks' ultimate success around the world. In Japan, the firm has partnered with a local handbag manufacturer, Sazaby Inc. In Spain, Starbucks has joined forces with Grupo Vips, the second-largest family-owned restaurant operator in the country. And in France, Starbucks executives have talked with several companies, although Schultz denies he is looking for an outright partner. "Many of those conversations were not so much about partnering but learning about doing business in France and sharing information about their experience," he insists.

Growth is not easy or simple, and Starbucks will have to persevere in an uncertain marketing environment around the world. Some experts accuse Starbucks and other companies of trying to "sell American culture" to international consumers and predict that the novelty will wear off soon. The company has been caught in political turmoil as well. Consumers boycotted a Starbucks store in Lebanon in protest against the war in Iraq, and Starbucks was forced to close its stores in Tel Aviv because of the violent conflict between Israelis and Palestinians. Then there are the skeptics in France. "The first café was founded in Paris over 300 years ago," claims one French scholar. "Starbucks is not going to compete with the French café. The café isn't just somewhere to drink coffee, it's a place where people go for social contact. In a big place with hundreds of customers, that's difficult."

But Schultz remains optimistic. "Perhaps we can be a great example of something that is American, that is very respectful of the French culture, and we want to bridge that gap." Perhaps Starbucks can get the whole world to sit down and drink a cup of American coffee.

Questions for Critical Thinking

1. Create a brief SWOT analysis of Starbucks focusing on its plans for international growth. Do you think this strategy is a good one for the company? Why or why not?
2. Identify the dimensions of the marketing environment that are mostly likely to affect Starbucks' strategy for global growth and explain why.

Sources: Andy Serwer, "Hot Starbucks to Go," *Fortune,* January 26, 2004, pp. 61–74; Noelle Knox, "Paris Starbucks Hopes to Prove U.S. Coffee Isn't Sock Juice," *USA Today*, January 16, 2004, p. B3; Laurent Rebours, "Starbucks Opens First French Shop to American Joe," *USA Today,* January 15, 2004, http://www.usatoday.com; Geoffrey A. Fowler, "Starbucks' Road to China," *The Wall Street Journal,* July 14, 2003, pp. B1, B3; Jason Singer and Martin Fackler, "In Japan, Adding Beer, Wine to Latté List," *The Wall Street Journal,* July 14, 2003, pp. B1, B3; Amy Wu, "Starbucks' World Won't Be Built in a Day," *Forbes.com,* June 27, 2003, http://www.forbes.com; Gavin Edwards, "The Logo," *Rolling Stone,* May 15, 2003, p. 110; Helen Jung, "Lattés for All: Starbucks Plans Global Expansion," *The News Tribune*, April 20, 2003, http://www.globalexchange.org.

Video Case 2.3

Timbuk2's Success Is in the Bag

The written case on Timbuk2 appears on page VC-3. The recently filmed Timbuk2 video is designed to expand and highlight the concepts in this chapter and the concepts and questions covered in the written video case.

Creating an Effective Marketing Plan

Overview

"What are our mission and goals?"
"Who are our customers?"
"What types of products do we offer?"
"How can we provide superior customer service?"

THESE are some of the questions addressed by a **marketing plan**—a detailed description of the resources and actions needed to achieve stated marketing objectives. Chapter 2 discussed **strategic planning**—the process of anticipating events and market conditions and deciding how a firm can best achieve its organizational objectives. Marketing planning encompasses all the activities devoted to achieving marketing objectives, establishing a basis for designing a marketing strategy. This appendix deals in depth with the formal marketing plan, which is part of an organization's overall business plan. At the end of this appendix, you'll see what an actual marketing plan looks like. Each plan component for a hypothetical firm called Wild Canada Clothing is presented. ◆◆◆

marketing plan Detailed description of the resources and actions needed to achieve stated marketing objectives.

strategic planning Process of determining an organization's primary objectives and adopting courses of action that will achieve these objectives.

business plan Formal document that outlines a company's objectives, how they will be met, how the business will achieve financing, and how much money the firm expects to earn.

COMPONENTS OF A BUSINESS PLAN

A company's **business plan** is one of its most important documents. The business plan puts in writing all the company's objectives, how they will be achieved, how the business will obtain financing, and how much money the company expects to earn over a specified time period. Although business plans vary in length and format, most contain at least some form of the following components:

- An *executive summary* briefly answers the who, what, when, where, how, and why questions for the plan. Although the summary appears early in the plan, it is typically written last, after the firm's executives have worked out the details of all the other sections.

- A *competitive analysis* section focuses on the environment in which the marketing plan is to be implemented. Although this section is more closely associated with the comprehensive business plan, factors specifically influencing marketing are likely to be included here.

- The *mission statement* summarizes the organization's purpose, vision, and overall goals. This statement provides the foundation upon which further planning is based.

- The overall business plan includes a series of *component* plans that present goals and strategies for each functional area of the enterprise. They typically include the following:

  The *marketing* plan, which describes strategies for informing potential customers about the goods and services offered by the firm as well as strategies for developing long-term relationships. At the end of this appendix, a sample marketing plan for Wild Canada Clothing is presented.

  The *financing* plan, which presents a realistic approach for securing needed funds and managing debt and cash flows.

The *production plan*, which describes how the organization will develop its products in the most efficient, cost-effective manner possible.

The *facilities plan*, which describes the physical environment and equipment required to implement the production plan.

The *human resources plan*, which estimates the firm's employment needs and the skills necessary to achieve organizational goals, including a comparison of current employees with the needs of the firm, and which establishes processes for securing adequately trained personnel if a gap exists between current employee skills and future needs.

This basic format encompasses the planning process used by nearly every successful organization. Whether a company operates in the manufacturing, wholesaling, retailing, or service sector (or a combination), the components described here are likely to appear in its overall business plan. Regardless of the size or longevity of a company, a business plan is an essential tool for a firm's owners because it helps them focus on the key elements of their business. Even small firms that are just starting out need a business plan to obtain financing. Figure 1 shows the outline of a business plan for Wild Canada Clothing.

figure 1

Outline of a Business Plan

The Wild Canada Clothing Business Plan

I. Executive Summary
- Who, What, When, Where, How, and Why

II. Table of Contents

III. Introduction
- Mission Statement
- Concept and Company
- Management Team
- Product

IV. Marketing Strategy
- Demographics
- Trends
- Market Penetration
- Potential Sales Revenue

V. Financing the Business
- Cash Flow Analysis
- Pro Forma Balance Sheet
- Income Statement

VI. Facilities Plan
- Physical Environment
- Equipment

VII. Human Resource Plan
- Employment Needs and Skills
- Current Employees

VIII. Résumés of Principals

CREATING A MARKETING PLAN

Keep in mind that a marketing plan should be created in conjunction with the other elements of a firm's business plan. In addition, a marketing plan often draws from the business plan, restating the executive summary, competitive analysis, and mission statement to give its readers an overall view of the firm. The marketing plan is needed for a variety of reasons:

- To obtain financing because banks and most private investors require a detailed business plan—including a marketing plan component—before they will even consider a loan application or a venture capital investment.

- To provide direction for the firm's overall business and marketing strategies.

- To support the development of long-term and short-term organizational objectives.

- To guide employees in achieving these objectives.

- To serve as a standard against which the firm's progress can be measured and evaluated.

In addition, the marketing plan is where a firm puts into writing its commitment to its customers and to building long-lasting relationships. After creating and implementing the plan, marketers must re-evaluate it periodically to gauge its success in moving the organization toward its goals. If changes are needed, they should be made as soon as possible.

FORMULATING AN OVERALL MARKETING STRATEGY

Before creating a marketing plan, a firm's marketers formulate an overall marketing strategy. A firm may use a number of tools in marketing planning, including business portfolio analysis and the BCG matrix. Its executives may conduct a SWOT analysis, take advantage of a strategic window, study Porter's Five Forces model as it relates to their business, or consider adopting a first mover or second mover strategy, all of which are described in Chapter 2.

spreadsheet analysis Grid that organizes information in a standardized, easily understood format.

In addition to the planning strategies discussed in Chapter 2, marketers are likely to use **spreadsheet analysis,** which lays out a grid of columns and rows that organize numerical information in a standardized, easily understood format. Spreadsheet analysis helps planners answer various "what if" questions related to the firm's financing and operations. The most popular spreadsheet software is Microsoft Excel. A spreadsheet analysis helps planners anticipate marketing performance given specified sets of circumstances. For example, a spreadsheet might project the outcomes of different pricing decisions for a new product, as shown in Figure 2.

Once general planning strategies are determined, marketers begin to flesh out the details of the marketing strategy. The elements of a marketing strategy include identifying the target market, studying the marketing environment, and creating a marketing mix.

When marketers have identified the target market, they can develop the optimal marketing mix to reach their potential customers:

- *Product strategy.* Which goods and services should the company offer to meet its customers' needs?

- *Distribution strategy.* Through which channel(s) and physical facilities will the firm distribute its products?

- *Promotional strategy.* What mix of advertising, sales promotion, and personal selling activities will the firm use to reach its customers initially and then develop long-term relationships?

- *Pricing strategy.* At what level should the company set its prices?

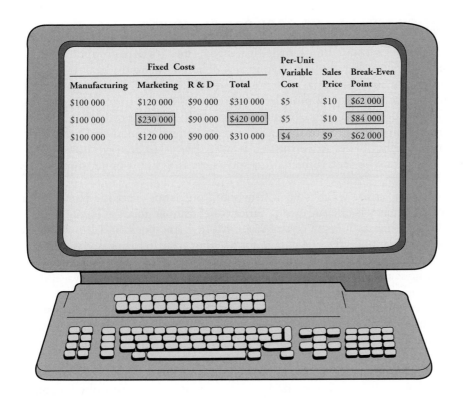

figure 2

*How Spreadsheet
Analysis Works*

Fixed Costs				Per-Unit Variable Cost	Sales Price	Break-Even Point
Manufacturing	Marketing	R & D	Total			
$100 000	$120 000	$90 000	$310 000	$5	$10	$62 000
$100 000	$230 000	$90 000	$420 000	$5	$10	$84 000
$100 000	$120 000	$90 000	$310 000	$4	$9	$62 000

THE EXECUTIVE SUMMARY, COMPETITIVE ANALYSIS, AND MISSION STATEMENT

Because these three elements of the business plan often reappear in the marketing plan, it is useful to describe them here. Recall that the executive summary answers the who, what, when, where, how, and why questions for the business. The executive summary for Google would include references to its current strategic planning process for its search services, which relies on developing new "ways in which technology can improve upon existing ways of doing business."[1] It would go on to answer questions such as who is involved (key people and organizations), what length of time the plan represents, and how the goals will be met.

The competitive analysis focuses on the environment in which the marketing plan is to be implemented. For Travel Alberta, the strengthening of the Canadian dollar creates a major challenge. It becomes more difficult to convince international tourists that Alberta still provides value, at the same time that Albertans see that their own dollar goes further when they decide to take foreign vacations.[2] Alberta does have one advantage over other Canadian provinces: it does not charge provincial sales tax. This helps make Alberta an attractive vacation destination for Canadians from other provinces.

The mission statement puts into words an organization's overall purpose and reason for being: what it does, whom it serves, and how it will be successful. The mission statement of Quebec-based Uniboard Canada is "to be the leading integrated supplier of engineered wood products in the furniture, store fixtures, millwork, kitchen cabinets, and flooring industries in North America." Uniboard differentiates itself by developing, expanding, and promoting value-added branded products more quickly and efficiently than its competitors. Its products are manufactured in 10 plants in Quebec, Ontario, and Ohio.[3]

DESCRIPTION OF THE COMPANY

Near the beginning of the marketing plan—typically following the executive summary and before the mission statement—a description of the company is included. The company description may include a brief history or background of the firm, the types of products it offers or plans to introduce, recent successes or achievements—in short, it consists of a few paragraphs containing the kind of information often found on the home page of a company's website.

STATEMENT OF GO'ALS AND CORE COMPETENCIES

The plan then includes a statement of the firm's goals and its core competencies—those things it does extremely well or better than anyone else. The goals should be specific and measurable and may be divided into financial and nonfinancial aims. A financial goal might be to add 75 new franchises in the next 12 months or to reach $10 million in revenues. A nonfinancial goal might be to enter the European market or to add a new product line every other year. Travel Alberta, mentioned previously, has a stated financial objective of achieving $6.5 billion in tourism revenue by 2011. A nonfinancial objective is to achieve 80 percent satisfaction among industry users who seek information and marketing knowledge from the Travel Alberta website.[4]

Core competencies are what make a firm stand out from everyone else in the marketplace. Costco's core competency is offering a wide variety of consumer goods at low prices, including some luxury-brand items such as Lilaque crystal vases, Mont Blanc pens, and Royal Doulton figurines. Jim Sinegal, co-founder and CEO, is known for keeping costs low, but not wages and benefits. He believes strongly in the value of his company's nearly 119 000 employees and rewards them well. "Our attitude," he says, "is that if you hire good people and pay them a fair wage, then good things will happen for the company."[5]

Small businesses often begin with a single core competency and build their business and reputation on it. It is important for a new firm to identify its core competency in the marketing plan so that investors or banks understand why they should lend the firm money to get started or to grow to the next stage. Leslie Blesius successfully fended off competitors such as Pottery Barn and Restoration Hardware when she was establishing her upscale home furnishings shop. She focused on what she did better than the chains, offering personalized services such as in-home consultations and installations, more selection, and more custom options. "It's all about how much we can help," Blesius says. Her strategy was so successful that she was able to survive and even expand, offering new furniture lines and opening a bed-and-bath section."[6]

OUTLINE OF THE MARKETING ENVIRONMENT (SITUATION ANALYSIS)

Every successful marketing plan takes into consideration the marketing environment—the competitive, economic, political-legal, technological, and social-cultural factors that affect the way a firm formulates and implements its marketing strategy. Marketing plans may address these issues in different ways, but the goal is to present information that describes the company's position or situation within the marketing environment. J. Crew, for instance, has a well-known brand name and a CEO with an impressive track record: Mickey Drexler, who previously headed The Gap. Says one industry watcher, "It's very much a merchant-driven company, dealing with an upper-income demographic that is spot-on to the current environment." So a marketing plan for J. Crew would include an evaluation of competing stores such as The Gap and Urban Outfitters, any technological advances that would affect such factors as merchandise distribution or inventory, social-cultural issues such as fashion preferences and spending habits of customers, and economic issues affecting a pricing strategy.

One such method for outlining the marketing environment in the marketing plan is to include a SWOT analysis, described in Chapter 2. A SWOT analysis identifies the firm's strengths, weaknesses, opportunities, and threats within the marketing environment. A SWOT analysis for J. Crew might include strengths such as its corporate leadership, brand name, and upscale target market. Weaknesses might include the risks inherent in the business of correctly spotting fashion trends. A major opportunity lies in the fact that J. Crew can expand almost anywhere—in fact, it plans to add between 25 and 35 new stores every year—and it will also expand its offerings to include a line of children's wear, a lower-priced casual line, and wedding attire. Threats include competition from other trendy stores, sudden changes in customer preferences, and economic dips that affect spending.[7] A SWOT analysis can be presented in chart format so it is easy to read as part of the marketing plan. The sample marketing plan in this appendix includes a SWOT analysis for Wild Canada Clothing.

THE TARGET MARKET AND MARKETING MIX

The marketing plan identifies the target market for the firm's products. The target market for Whirlpool's pedestal-mounted washing machine and Moen's sleek shower grab bar is baby boomers, the oldest of whom are entering their 60s.[8] For another target market, Toyota's planned spin-off series of the hit TV drama *Prison Break* consists of two-minute episodes for mobile phones. The target market is young consumers.[9] And marketers promoting bands such as Girl Authority, a squeaky-clean nine-girl band with a new album, are aiming at both preteen girls and parents looking for wholesome entertainment for their kids.[10]

The marketing plan also discusses the marketing mix that the firm has selected for its products. When Nokia launched its N-Gage, a handset that plays games, the company used a marketing mix that included product, distribution, promotion, and pricing strategies. By expanding its well-known communications product line to include a new handheld game device, Nokia set its new product in direct competition with game machines made by Nintendo and Sony but expanded the social aspect of its system by offering simplified game development based on the Internet's Java technology. This feature allows players to communicate with friends while in the game. The company negotiated deals with major wireless service providers to distribute N-Gage. And the product's distribution expanded when the company began offering trials, purchase, and downloads of popular games from its website, **http://www.n-gage.com**. Nokia spent an estimated $100 million promoting the initial handset. Drawing on the success of a well-known software marketer, Nokia announced a new partnership with leading international video game developer Gameloft. N-Gage had an initial retail price of $200, but Nokia dropped its base price to $99 for customers who prepay for wireless service. Also, wireless carriers offer special discounted prices for N-Gage, depending on the service contract customers select.[11]

BUDGET, SCHEDULE, AND MONITORING

Every marketing plan requires a budget, a time schedule for implementation, and a system for monitoring the plan's success or failure. Typically, a budget includes a breakdown of the costs incurred as the marketing program is implemented, offset by projected sales, profits, and losses over the time period of the program.

Most long-range marketing plans encompass a two- to five-year period, although companies that do business in industries such as auto manufacturing, pharmaceuticals, or lumber may extend their marketing plans further into the future because it typically takes longer to develop these products. However, marketers in most industries will have difficulty making estimates and predictions beyond five years because of the many uncertainties in the marketplace. Firms also may opt to develop short-term plans to cover marketing activities for a single year.

The marketing plan, whether it is long term or short term, predicts how long it will take to achieve the goals set out by the plan. A goal may be opening a certain number of new stores, market share growth, or achieving an expansion of the product line. Finally, the marketing program is monitored and evaluated for its performance. Monthly, quarterly, and annual sales targets are usually tracked; the efficiency with which certain tasks are completed is determined; customer satisfaction is measured and so forth. All of these factors contribute to the overall review of the program.

At some point, a firm may opt to implement an *exit strategy*, a contingency plan for the firm leaving the market. A common way for a large company to do this is to sell off a business unit. An example is Wal-Mart's decision to leave South Korea, selling its stores there after failing to make a success of its 16 South Korean outlets. The stores were sold to Shinsegae, a local retailer, for nearly $900 million. Wal-Mart was following in the backtracking footsteps of several other multinationals, including Nokia, Nestlé, Carrefour, and Google, all of which have exited the demanding South Korean market.[12]

An exit strategy is equally important for a small business. There are 2.5 million small business owners in Canada. About 90 percent have sales under $1 million. A common growth strategy among such businesses is to open a second location. Deloitte partner Richard Carson says, "Many people don't think about the degree to which that second location will have synergy or cannibalization with the first."[13] Not having a good exit strategy when a second location is failing could result in bankruptcy.

SAMPLE MARKETING PLAN

The following pages contain an annotated sample marketing plan for Wild Canada Clothing. At some point in your career, you will likely be involved in writing—or at least contributing to—a marketing plan. And you'll certainly read many marketing plans throughout your business career. Keep in mind that the plan for Wild Canada is a single example; no one format is used by all companies. Also, the Wild Canada plan has been somewhat condensed to make it easier to annotate and illustrate the most vital features. The important point to remember is that the marketing plan is a document designed to present concise, cohesive information about a company's marketing objectives to managers, lending institutions, and others who are involved in creating and carrying out the firm's overall business strategy.

FIVE-YEAR MARKETING PLAN
WILD CANADA CLOTHING, INC.

TABLE OF CONTENTS

EXECUTIVE SUMMARY

This five-year marketing plan for Wild Canada Clothing has been created by its two founders to secure additional funding for growth and to inform employees of the company's current status and direction. Although Wild Canada was launched only three years ago, the firm has experienced greater-than-anticipated demand for its products, and research has shown that the target market of sports-minded consumers and sports retailers would like to buy more casual clothing than Wild Canada currently offers. The company is also interested in extending its product line as well as adding new product lines. In addition, Wild Canada plans to explore opportunities for online sales. The marketing environment has been very receptive to the firm's high-quality goods—casual clothing in trendy colours with logos and slogans that reflect the interests of outdoor enthusiasts around the country. Over the next five years, Wild Canada can increase its distribution, offer new products, and win new customers.

COMPANY DESCRIPTION

Wild Canada Clothing was founded three years ago by entrepreneurs Lucy Neuman and Nick Russell. Neuman has an undergraduate degree in marketing and worked for several years in the retail clothing industry. Russell operated an adventure business called Go West! which arranges group trips to locations in Manitoba, Saskatchewan, Alberta, and British Columbia before selling the enterprise to a partner. Neuman and Russell, who have been friends since college, decided to develop and market a line of clothing with a unique—yet universal—appeal to outdoor enthusiasts.

Wild Canada Clothing reflects Neuman's and Russell's passion for the outdoors. The company's original cotton T-shirts, baseball caps, and fleece jackets and vests bear logos of different sports—such as kayaking, mountain climbing, bicycling, skating, surfing, and horseback riding. But every item shows off the company's slogan: "Go Play Outside." Wild Canada sells clothing for both men and women, in the hottest colours with the coolest names—such as sunrise pink, sunset red, twilight purple, desert rose, cactus green, ocean blue, mountaintop white, and river rock grey.

Wild Canada attire is currently carried by small retail stores that specialize in outdoor clothing and gear. Most of these stores are concentrated in British Columbia, Alberta, Ontario, and Quebec. The high quality, trendy colours, and unique message of the clothing have gained Wild Canada a following among consumers between the ages of 25 and 45. Sales have tripled in the last year alone, and Wild Canada is currently working to expand its manufacturing capabilities.

Wild Canada is also committed to giving back to the community by contributing to local conservation programs. Ultimately, the company would like to develop and fund its own environmental programs. This plan will outline how Wild Canada intends to introduce new products, expand its distribution, enter new markets, and give back to the community.

The executive summary outlines the who, what, where, when, how, and why of the marketing plan. Wild Canada is only three years old and is successful enough that it now needs a formal marketing plan to obtain additional financing from a bank or private investors for expansion and the launch of new products.

The company description summarizes the history of Wild Canada—how it was founded and by whom, what its products are, and why they are unique. It begins to "sell" the reader on the growth possibilities for Wild Canada.

It is important to state a firm's mission and goals, including financial and nonfinancial goals. Wild Canada's goals include growth and profits for the company as well as the ability to contribute to society through conservation programs.

WILD CANADA'S MISSION AND GOALS

Wild Canada's mission is to be the leading producer and marketer of personalized, casual clothing for consumers who love the outdoors. Wild Canada wants to inspire people to get outdoors more often and enjoy family and friends while doing so. In addition, Wild Canada strives to design programs for preserving the natural environment.

During the next five years, Wild Canada seeks to achieve the following financial and nonfinancial goals:

- *Financial goals*

  1. Obtain financing to expand manufacturing capabilities, increase distribution, and introduce two new product lines.

  2. Increase revenues by at least 50 percent each year.

  3. Donate at least $25 000 a year to conservation organizations.

- *Nonfinancial goals*

  4. Introduce two new product lines—customized logo clothing and lightweight luggage.

  5. Enter new geographic markets, including the Atlantic Provinces.

  6. Develop a successful Internet site, while maintaining strong relationships with retailers.

  7. Develop its own conservation program aimed at helping communities raise money to purchase open space.

This section reminds employees as well as those outside the company (such as potential lenders) exactly what Wild Canada does so well and how it plans to achieve a sustainable competitive advantage over rivals. Note that here and throughout the plan, Wild Canada focuses on relationships.

CORE COMPETENCIES

Wild Canada seeks to use its core competencies to achieve a sustainable competitive advantage, in which competitors cannot provide the same value to consumers that Wild Canada does. Already, Wild Canada has developed core competencies in (1) offering a high-quality, branded product whose image is recognizable among consumers; (2) creating a sense of community among consumers who purchase the products; and (3) developing a reputation among retailers as a reliable manufacturer, delivering the requested number of products on schedule. The firm intends to build on these competencies through marketing efforts that increase the number of products offered as well as distribution outlets.

By forming strong relationships with consumers, retailers, and suppliers of fabric and other goods and services, Wild Canada believes it can create a sustainable competitive advantage over its rivals. No other clothing company can say to its customers with as much conviction "Go Play Outside"!

The situation analysis provides an outline of the marketing environment. A SWOT analysis helps marketers and others identify clearly a firm's strengths, weaknesses, opportunities, and threats. Again, relationships are a focus. Wild Canada has also conducted research on the outdoor clothing market, competitors, and consumers to determine how best to attract and keep customers.

SITUATION ANALYSIS

The marketing environment for Wild Canada represents overwhelming opportunities. It also contains some challenges that the firm believes it can meet successfully. Figure A illustrates a SWOT analysis of the company conducted by marketers to highlight Wild Canada's strengths, weaknesses, opportunities, and threats.

The SWOT analysis presents a thumbnail sketch of the company's position in the marketplace. In just three years, Wild Canada has built some impressive strengths while looking forward to new opportunities. Its dedicated founders, the growing number of brand-loyal customers, and sound financial management place the company in a good position to grow. However, as Wild Canada considers expansion of its product line and entrance into new markets, the firm will have to guard against marketing myopia (the failure to recognize the scope of its business) and quality slippages. As the company finalizes plans for new products

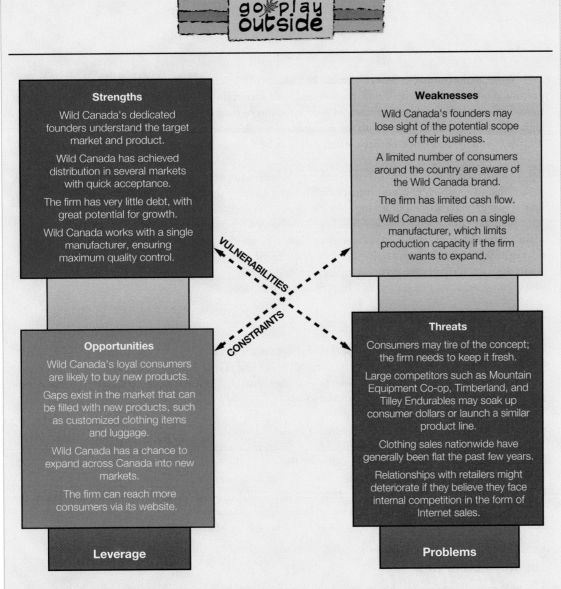

figure A

SWOT Analysis for Wild Canada Clothing, Inc.

and expanded Internet sales, its management will also have to guard against competitors who attempt to duplicate the products. However, building strong relationships with consumers, retailers, and suppliers should help thwart competitors.

COMPETITORS IN THE OUTDOOR CLOTHING MARKET

The outdoor retail sales industry sells more than $500 million worth of goods annually, ranging from clothing to equipment. The outdoor apparel market has many entries. L.L. Bean, Timberland, Bass Pro Shops, Patagonia, Tilley Endurables, and Mountain Equipment Co-op are among the most recognizable companies that offer these products. Smaller competitors such as Title IX, which offers athletic clothing for women, and Ragged Mountain, which sells fleece clothing for skiers and hikers, also grab some of the market. The outlook for the industry in general—and Wild Canada in particular—is positive for several reasons. First, consumers are participating in and investing in recreational activities that are near their homes. Second, consumers are looking for ways to enjoy their leisure time with friends and family without overspending. Third, consumers are gaining more confidence in the economy and are willing and able to spend more.

While all the companies listed earlier can be considered competitors, none offers the kind of trendy, yet practical products provided by Wild Canada—and none carries the customized logos and slogans that Wild Canada plans to offer in the near future. In addition, most of these competitors sell performance apparel in high-tech manufactured fabrics. With the exception of the fleece vests and jackets, Wild Canada's clothing is made of strictly the highest quality cotton, so it may be worn both on the hiking trail and around town. Finally, Wild Canada products are offered at moderate prices, making them affordable in multiple quantities. For instance, a Wild Canada T-shirt sells for $15.99, compared with a competing high-performance T-shirt that sells for $29.99. Consumers can easily replace a set of shirts from one season to the next, picking up the newest colours, without having to think about the purchase.

A survey conducted by Wild Canada revealed that 67 percent of responding consumers prefer to replace their casual and active wear more often than other clothing, so they are attracted by the moderate pricing of Wild Canada products. In addition, as the trend toward health-conscious activities and concerns about the natural environment continue, consumers increasingly relate to the Wild Canada philosophy as well as the firm's contributions to socially responsible programs.

THE TARGET MARKET

> Wild Canada has identified its customers as active people between the ages of 25 and 45. However, that doesn't mean someone who is 62 and prefers to read about the outdoors isn't a potential customer as well. By pinpointing where existing customers live, Wild Canada can make plans for growth into new outlets.

The target market for Wild Canada products is active consumers between the ages of 25 and 45—people who like to hike, rock climb, bicycle, surf, figure skate, in-line skate, ride horses, snowboard or ski, kayak, and other such activities. In short, they like to "Go Play Outside." They might not be experts at the sports they engage in, but they enjoy themselves outdoors.

These active consumers represent a demographic group of well-educated and successful individuals; they are single or married and raising families. Household incomes generally range between $60 000 and $120 000 annually. Despite their comfortable incomes, these consumers are price conscious and consistently seek value in their purchases. Regardless of their age (whether they fall at the upper or lower end of the target range), they lead active lifestyles. They are somewhat status oriented but not overly so. They like to be associated with high-quality products but are not willing to pay a premium price for a certain brand. Current Wild Canada customers tend to live in British Columbia, Alberta, Ontario, and Quebec. However, one future goal is to target consumers in the Atlantic Provinces, Manitoba, and Saskatchewan.

THE MARKETING MIX

> The strongest part of the marketing mix for Wild Canada involves sales promotions, public relations, and nontraditional marketing strategies such as attending outdoor events and organizing activities like day hikes and bike rides.

The following discussion outlines some of the details of the proposed marketing mix for Wild Canada products.

PRODUCT STRATEGY. Wild Canada currently offers a line of high-quality outdoor apparel items including cotton T-shirts, baseball caps, and fleece vests and jackets. All bear the company logo and slogan, "Go Play Outside." The firm has researched the most popular colours for its items and given them names that consumers enjoy—sunset red, sunrise pink, cactus green, desert rose, and river rock gray, among others. Over the next five years, Wild Canada plans to expand the product line to include customized clothing items. Customers may select a logo that represents their sport—say, rock climbing. Then they can add a slogan to match the logo, such as "Get Over It." A baseball cap with a bicyclist might bear the slogan "Take a Spin." At the beginning, there would be 10 new logos and five new slogans; more would be added later. Eventually, some slogans and logos would be retired, and new ones introduced. This strategy will keep the concept fresh and prevent it from becoming diluted with too many variations.

The second way in which Wild Canada plans to expand its product line is to offer items of lightweight luggage—two sizes of duffel bags, two sizes of tote bags, and a daypack. These items would also come in trendy and basic colours, with a choice of logos and slogans. In addition, every product would bear the Wild Canada logo.

DISTRIBUTION STRATEGY. Currently, Wild Canada is marketed through regional and local specialty shops scattered throughout British Columbia, Alberta, Ontario, and Quebec. So far, Wild Canada has not been distributed through national sporting goods and apparel chains. Climate and season tend to dictate the sales at specialty shops, which sell more T-shirts and baseball caps during warm weather and more fleece vests and jackets during colder months. Wild Canada obtains much of its information about overall industry trends in different geographic areas and at different types of retail outlets from its trade organization, the Canadian Outdoor Industry Association.

Over the next three years, Wild Canada seeks to expand distribution to retail specialty shops throughout the nation, focusing next on the Atlantic Provinces. The firm has not yet determined whether it would be beneficial to sell through a major national chain such as Bass Pro Shops, Mountain Equipment Co-op, or Sports Experts as these outlets could be considered competitors.

In addition, Wild Canada plans to expand online sales by offering the customized product line via Internet only, thus distinguishing between Internet offerings and specialty shop offerings. Eventually, we may be able to place Internet kiosks at some of the more profitable store outlets so consumers could order customized products from the stores. Regardless of its expansion plans, Wild Canada fully intends to monitor and maintain strong relationships with distribution channel members.

PROMOTIONAL STRATEGY. Wild Canada communicates with consumers and retailers about its products in a variety of ways. Information about Wild Canada—the company as well as its products—is available via the Internet, direct mailings, and in person. The firm's promotional efforts also seek to differentiate its products from those of its competitors.

The company relies on personal contact with retailers to establish the products in their stores. This contact, whether in-person or by phone, helps convey the Wild Canada message, demonstrate the products' unique qualities, and build relationships. Wild Canada sales representatives visit each store two or three times a year and offer in-store training on the features of the products for new retailers or for those who want a refresher. As distribution expands, Wild Canada will adjust to meet greater demand by increasing sales staff to make sure its stores are visited more frequently.

Sales promotions and public relations currently make up the bulk of Wild Canada's promotional strategy. Wild Canada staff works with retailers to offer short-term sales promotions tied to events and contests. In addition, Nick Russell is currently working with several trip outfitters to offer Wild Canada items on a promotional basis. Because Wild Canada also engages in cause marketing through its contribution to environmental programs, good public relations have followed.

Nontraditional marketing methods that require little cash and a lot of creativity also lend themselves perfectly to Wild Canada. Because Wild Canada is a small, flexible organization, the firm can easily implement ideas such as distributing free water, stickers, and discount coupons at outdoor sporting events. During the next year, the company plans to engage in the following marketing efforts:

- Create a Wild Canada Tour, in which several employees take turns driving around the country to campgrounds to distribute promotional items such as Wild Canada stickers and discount coupons.

- Attend canoe and kayak races, bicycling events, and rock climbing competitions with our Wild Canada truck to distribute free water, stickers, and discount coupons for Wild Canada shirts or hats.

- Organize Wild Canada hikes departing from participating retailers.

- Hold a Wild Canada design contest, selecting a winning slogan and logo to be added to the customized line.

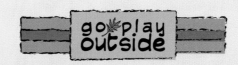

An actual plan will include more specific financial details, which will be folded into the overall business plan. For more information, see the "Financial Analysis in Marketing" appendix on page A-1 of this book. In addition, Wild Canada states that, at this stage, it does not have plans to exit the market by merging with another firm or making a public stock offering.

PRICING STRATEGY. As discussed earlier in this plan, Wild Canada products are priced with the competition in mind. The firm is not concerned with setting high prices to signal luxury or prestige, nor is it attempting to achieve the goals of offsetting low prices by selling high quantities of products. Instead, value pricing is practiced so that customers feel comfortable purchasing new clothing to replace the old, even if it is just because they like the new colours. The pricing strategy also makes Wild Canada products good gifts—for birthdays, graduations, or "just because." The customized clothing will sell for $2 to $4 more than the regular Wild Canada logo clothing. The luggage will be priced competitively, offering a good value against its competition.

BUDGET, SCHEDULE, AND MONITORING

Though its history is short, Wild Canada has enjoyed a steady increase in sales since its introduction three years ago. Figure B shows these three years, plus projected sales for the next three years, including the introduction of the two new product lines. Additional financial data are included in the overall business plan for the company.

figure B

Annual Sales for Wild Canada Clothing: 2008–2013

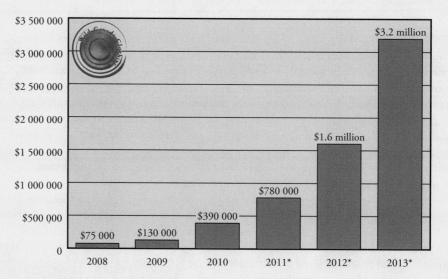

*Projected sales

The timeline for expansion of outlets and introduction of the two new product lines is shown in Figure C. The implementation of each of these tasks will be monitored closely and evaluated for its performance.

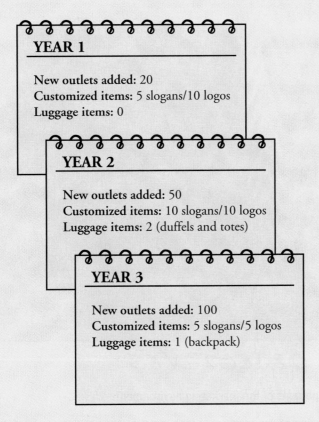

YEAR 1

New outlets added: 20
Customized items: 5 slogans/10 logos
Luggage items: 0

YEAR 2

New outlets added: 50
Customized items: 10 slogans/10 logos
Luggage items: 2 (duffels and totes)

YEAR 3

New outlets added: 100
Customized items: 5 slogans/5 logos
Luggage items: 1 (backpack)

figure C

**Timeline for First Three
Years of Marketing Plan**

Wild Canada anticipates continuing operations into the foreseeable future, with no plans to exit this market. Instead, as discussed throughout this plan, the firm plans to increase its presence in the market. At present, there are no plans to merge with another company or to make a public stock offering.

The Marketing Environment, Ethics, and Social Responsibility

CHAPTER OBJECTIVES

1. Identify the five components of the marketing environment.

2. Explain the types of competition marketers face and the steps necessary for developing a competitive strategy.

3. Describe how marketing activities are regulated and how marketers can influence the political-legal environment.

4. Outline the economic factors that affect marketing decisions and consumer buying power.

5. Discuss the impact of the technological environment on a firm's marketing activities.

6. Explain how the social-cultural environment influences marketing.

7. Describe the ethical issues in marketing.

8. Identify the four levels of the social responsibility pyramid.

AIDS NIAGARA: PART OF CANADA'S ANSWER TO A WORLD PROBLEM

MORE than 2 million people die each year from AIDS and an equal number become infected with HIV. The problem is particularly acute in Africa. In Swaziland, for example, over 40 percent of the adult population has HIV. In Rwanda, 280 000 people have HIV/AIDS and life expectancy is now 44 years. In Botswana, life expectancy will soon reach the mid-20s. One prediction is that by 2015, one in six Africans will die from AIDS. Most AIDS in Africa is spread by unsafe sex practices. Ukraine, by contrast, has been seeing AIDS spread more rapidly through unsafe drug injection practices. It now reports more annual AIDS deaths than any other European country. HIV/AIDS can have a devastating effect on the political, legal, economic, social, and cultural environments of countries where it is a problem.

Canada is not immune. Currently more than 58 000 Canadians are living with AIDS and, while help is better here than anywhere in the world, Canadians with AIDS still must live, not only with the disease, but with discrimination caused by fear and ignorance concerning its risks to the general population.

In 2008, an Ontario restaurant owner fired a waitress whose husband had HIV. An Ontario judge refused to hear evidence until an HIV-infected witness was masked or moved to a larger courtroom. In British Columbia, a security guard delayed a scheduled takeoff when he allegedly recognized someone in a group of travellers and ordered a wipe-down of the aircraft because he had concerns about "diseases."

Fortunately, there are groups across Canada, such as AIDS Niagara, that provide services to help people living with HIV or AIDS; to their friends, colleagues, and families who may be directly affected; and to the general public, who can benefit from greater HIV/AIDS awareness and knowledge. AIDS Niagara is a member of the Ontario AIDS Network (OAN) and the Canadian AIDS Society (CAS). It also has access to the resources of AIDS Service Organizations (ASOs) across Canada. AIDS Niagara became a registered not-for-profit charity in 1990. Its programs are funded by various levels of government, including the Public Health Agency of Canada, the Ontario Ministry of Health and Long-Term

Care, and the Niagara Region's Public Health Department. It also receives funding through association with a local bingo, through proceeds from the sale of "break-open" tickets at two local businesses, and by organizing an annual AIDS Walk for Life fundraising event. Some funding also is provided by GlaxoSmithKline, a private, for-profit organization, and by three nearby United Ways. Volunteers contribute to the organization by serving on its board of directors, providing reception and office services, performing fundraising activities, staffing community information displays, and helping provide a variety of services to its client groups.

Some Canadian for-profit organizations are also involved with AIDS. Ontario-based Apotex was the first company to successfully sell its low-cost AIDS drug to Rwanda's government, following legislation passed by the Government of Canada that was designed to force manufacturers of patented, brand-name drugs to license generic drug manufacturers to produce lower-priced generic versions for sale to developing countries.[1]

connecting with customers

How does AIDS Niagara connect with its clients? It provides a host of services for people with HIV/AIDS, including the Friendly Visiting program, which matches a client with a compatible volunteer "buddy"; Newcomer Support Services, focused on migrant workers and various newcomer groups; StreetWorks, a harm reduction program that provides needle exchanges, condoms, and safer sex and needle-use information; a Supportive Housing program with assisted living services; various peer support programs; and caregiver programs to assist those who work with and care for people with HIV/AIDS.

Chapter Overview

CHANGE is a fact of life for all people, including marketers. Adapting to change in an environment as complex and unpredictable as the one dealing with HIV/AIDS provides challenges but also opportunities.

Although some change may be the result of crises, more often it is the result of a gradual trend in lifestyle, income, population, and other factors. General Motors has finally lost its spot as the world's largest automaker to Toyota. With the recent rapid gasoline price increase, consumers have turned away from trucks and SUVs, and indications are that Toyota will increase its lead considerably. Due to its declining sales, General Motors has announced the closing of several of its North American plants, including its truck plant in Oshawa, Ontario, and its engine plant in Windsor, Ontario, resulting in the loss of thousands of manufacturing jobs.[2] Technology can trigger a sudden change in the marketplace: in one fell swoop, it appeared that Internet music downloads had replaced traditional CDs. And within mere months of offering its first iPod, Apple introduced the video iPod.

Marketers must anticipate and plan for change. They must set goals to meet the concerns of customers, employees, shareholders, and members of the general public. Industry competition, legal constraints, the impact of technology on product designs, and social concerns are some of the many important factors that shape the business environment. All potentially have an impact on a firm's goods and services. Although external forces frequently are outside the marketing manager's control, decision makers must still consider those influences together with the variables of the marketing mix in developing—and occasionally modifying—marketing plans and strategies that take these environmental factors into consideration.

This chapter begins by describing five forces in marketing's external environment—competitive, political-legal, economic, technological, and social-cultural. Figure 3.1 identifies them as the foundation for making decisions that involve the four marketing mix elements and the target market. These forces provide the frame of reference within which all marketing decisions are made. The second focus of this chapter is marketing ethics and social responsibility. This section describes the nature of marketers' responsibilities both to business and to society at large. ◆◆◆

ENVIRONMENTAL SCANNING AND ENVIRONMENTAL MANAGEMENT

environmental scanning Process of collecting information about the external marketing environment to identify and interpret potential trends.

Marketers must carefully and continually monitor crucial trends and developments in the business environment. **Environmental scanning** is the process of collecting information about the external marketing environment to identify and interpret potential trends. The goal of this process is to analyze the information and decide whether these trends represent significant opportunities or pose major threats to the company. The firm can then determine the best response to a particular environmental change.

We are currently seeing unprecedented rising fuel and energy costs in Canada and an increasing concern about greenhouse gas emissions. Toronto-based Pollution Probe and Calgary-based Canadian Association for Wind Power see alternative sources of energy and technologies to reduce energy costs providing attractive opportunities for Canadian businesses, and *Profit* magazine says "green power" provides among the best business opportunities for Canadian entrepreneurs.[3] RenewABILITY Energy Inc., based in Waterloo, Ontario, has developed a Power-Pipe, which reclaims and recycles hot water that would otherwise go down the drain. This provides users with considerable cost savings as reduced energy is needed to reheat the water and, along with reduced energy needs, there is a decrease in greenhouse gas emissions. This new product has application in university residences, health clubs, apartment buildings, food processing plants, pulp and paper mills, as well as in private homes.[4]

Marketoid

Canada—which has approximately 0.5 percent of the world's population—accounts for approximately 2 percent of the world's greenhouse gas emissions.

Environmental scanning is a vital component of effective **environmental management.** Environmental management involves marketers' efforts to achieve organizational objectives by predicting and influencing the competitive, political-legal, economic, technological, and social-cultural environments. In the political-legal environment, managers who are seeking modifications of regulations, laws, or tariff restrictions may lobby legislators or contribute to the campaigns of sympathetic politicians. In an about-face, global tobacco giant Altria, which recently changed its corporate name from Philip Morris, is gathering support among tobacco growers to lobby in favour of a bill to bring the tobacco industry under government regulatory power in the United States. Company management now favours the move because of the need to create uniform manufacturing and marketing standards that would apply for all tobacco companies.[5]

For many domestic and international firms, competing with established industry leaders frequently involves *strategic alliances*—partnerships with other firms in which the partners combine resources and capital to create competitive advantages in a new market. Strategic alliances are especially common in international marketing, where partnerships with local firms provide regional expertise for a company expanding its operations abroad. According to one study, about 35 percent of all corporate revenues worldwide are the result of some kind of strategic alliance.[6] Members of such alliances share risks and profits. Alliances are considered essential in a country such as China, where laws require foreign firms doing business there to work with local companies. Through successful research and development efforts, firms may influence changes in their own technological environments. A research breakthrough may lead to reduced pro-

duction costs or a technologically superior new product. While changes in the marketing environment may be beyond the control of individual marketers, managers continually seek to predict their impact on marketing decisions and to modify operations to meet changing market needs. Even modest environmental shifts can alter the results of those decisions.

figure 3.1

Elements of the Marketing Mix within an Environmental Framework

environmental management Attainment of organizational objectives by predicting and influencing the competitive, political-legal, economic, technological, and social-cultural environments.

> ### assessment check 1
>
> **1.1** Define environmental scanning.
>
> **1.2** How does environmental scanning contribute to environmental management?

THE COMPETITIVE ENVIRONMENT

As organizations vie to satisfy customers, the interactive exchange creates the **competitive environment.** Marketing decisions by individual firms influence consumer responses in the marketplace. They also affect the marketing strategies of competitors. As a consequence, decision makers must continually monitor competitors' marketing activities—their products, channels, prices, and promotional efforts.

Few organizations have **monopoly** positions as the sole supplier of a good or service in the marketplace. Utilities, such as natural gas, electricity, water, and cable TV service, have traditionally accepted considerable regulation from local authorities who controlled such marketing-related factors as rates, service levels, and geographic coverage. In exchange, the utilities gained exclusive rights to serve a particular group of consumers. But the **deregulation movement** of the past three decades has ended total monopoly protection for most utilities. Many shoppers can choose from alternative cable TV and Internet providers, cell phone and traditional telephone carriers, and even gas and electric utilities. Some firms, such as pharmaceutical giants Merck and Pfizer, have temporary monopolies from patents on new drugs. When Health Canada approves a new drug for lowering cholesterol or improving sleep, its manufacturer is typically granted exclusive rights to produce and

① Identify the five components of the marketing environment.

competitive environment Interactive process that occurs in the marketplace among marketers of directly competitive products, marketers of products that can be substituted for one another, and marketers competing for the consumer's purchasing power.

One more reason to ♥ your Country Harvest.

100% OF THE HARVEST NOW WITH 25% LESS SODIUM

100% whole grain. A source of omega-3 polyunsaturates. The same great taste of Country Harvest now with 25% less sodium.*

www.countryharvest.com

COURTESY WESTON BAKERIES LTD

Capitalizing on society's concern for healthier food alternatives, Weston Bakeries offers whole-grain bread with omega-3 added and sodium reduced.

② Explain the types of competition marketers face and the steps necessary for developing a competitive strategy.

Marketoid

Costco sales in 2007 were $63.1 billion.

market the product during the life of the patent. Theoretically, this gives the manufacturer a chance to recoup the millions spent on developing and launching the drug. Once the patent expires, all bets are off—and competitors can flood the market with generic versions of the drug.

Through industry megamergers, often on a global scale, some companies seek to dominate markets without ceding the controls that regulated monopolies forfeit. As a result of mergers, the auto, tobacco, accounting, and telecommunications industries are all dominated by three or four giants. Rather than seeking sole dominance of a market, corporations increasingly prefer to share the pie with just a few rivals. Referred to by economists as an **oligopoly**, this structure of a limited number of sellers in an industry where high start-up costs form barriers to keep out new competitors deters newcomers from breaking into markets, while ensuring that corporations remain innovative. In one of the numerous ongoing legal actions being pursued against Microsoft, the European Committee for Interoperable Systems (ECIS)—which includes firms such as IBM, Oracle, Nokia, RealNetworks, and Sun Microsystems—has filed a complaint alleging that Microsoft does not make its Office program compatible with competing programs and continues to engage in unethical bundling of certain products. So far, the European Commission has imposed fines totalling $1.68 billion against Microsoft, but the latest—a $1.39-billion fine in 2008—is under appeal.[7]

TYPES OF COMPETITION

Marketers face three types of competition. The most *direct* form occurs among marketers of similar products, such as when a Petro-Canada station opens across the street from a Shell retail outlet. The cell phone market provides consumers with such alternative suppliers as Bell, Rogers, Fido, and Telus.

Costco—which sells everything from home generators to birthday cakes—also takes direct aim at luxury retailers. Costco offers diamond jewellery, cashmere sweaters, and Coach and Kate Spade handbags. And in a new venture with Synergy Brands, the retailer will sell Synergy's line of designer luxury goods, including handbags, wallets, briefcases, and other goods. "The new line fits with Costco's history of success with luxury products, which contribute to the treasure hunt atmosphere the company tries to deliver to its clubs," writes one industry watcher.[8]

A second type of competition is *indirect* and involves products that are easily substituted. In the fast-food industry, pizza competes with chicken, hamburgers, and tacos. In entertainment, a movie could be substituted for a concert or a night at the bowling alley.

Canada's Wonderland, Six Flags La Ronde, and Vancouver's Playland—traditional hot spots for family vacations—now compete with outdoor adventure trips. Approximately one-half of Canadian adults will decide not to make this year's vacation a tranquil week at the beach or a trip to an amusement park. Instead, they'll choose to do something more adventurous—thrill-filled experiences such as skydiving, whitewater rafting, participating in an archaeological dig, or rock climbing. So marketers have to find ways to attract consumers to their specific brand as well as to their type of product.

A change such as a price increase or an improvement in a product's attributes can also affect demand for substitute products. A major drop in the cost of solar energy would not only increase the demand for solar power but also adversely affect the demand for such energy sources as heating oil, electricity, and natural gas. In Canada, the Green Budget Coalition, made up of 20 leading environmental and conservation organizations, is lobbying the federal government to establish a

100 000-unit solar roof program, providing cost incentives until 2015 when it expects solar panels will be more cost competitive.[9] In Japan, more than 168 000 solar roof panels have already been installed.[10] And Japanese scientists have announced that they can extract gasoline from cattle dung. "The new technology will be a boon for livestock breeders," who have to struggle to find ways to dispose of nearly half a million tons of waste per year, notes a Japanese agricultural engineering professor.[11]

One substitute, the Internet access known as wireless fidelity, or Wi-Fi, has experienced a rocky start. While industry observers project that every laptop and handheld computer will soon be able to receive Wi-Fi, it's difficult to predict how many people will use it. A wireless network allows computers, printers, and other devices to be connected without the inconvenience of stringing cables in offices or homes. Wi-Fi connects various devices and allows them to communicate with one another through radio waves. Any PC with a Wi-Fi receptor can connect with the Internet at so-called hot spots—locations with a wireless router and a high-speed Internet modem. By one estimate, the number of registered hot spots worldwide now exceeds 70 000.[12] They are found in a variety of places, including airports, libraries, and coffee shops. For instance, most Starbucks shops are Wi-Fi hot spots. More and more coffee shops, bookstores, and even cities are offering free Wi-Fi hot spots for at least a few hours at a time. Many hotels, though, still charge their guests a daily fee for wireless access.

Many believe that the successor to Wi-Fi will be WiMax, a new wireless standard. WiMax recently got a huge boost when Intel announced that it would begin producing computer chips incorporating this new wireless standard.[13] Unlike Wi-Fi's relatively limited geographic coverage area—generally around 100 metres—a single WiMax access point can provide coverage over many kilometres. Hundreds of cities across North America have announced plans to build WiMax networks that will, in essence, turn these cities into giant hot spots. WiMax also has the potential to bring high-speed Internet access to rural areas where traditional forms of broadband are too expensive or impractical. WiMax is the only practical and cost-effective way to provide broadband access to sparsely populated regions.

The final type of competition occurs among all organizations that compete for consumers' purchases. Traditional economic analysis views competition as a battle among companies in the same industry (direct competition) or among substitutable goods and services (indirect competition). But marketers know that all firms compete for a limited number of dollars that consumers can or will spend. In this broader sense, competition means that purchase of a Honda Accord might compete with a vacation in Europe.

Because the competitive environment often determines the success or failure of a product, marketers must continually assess competitors' marketing strategies. New products, updated features or technology, increased service, and lower prices are all variations that marketers look for. When changes occur in the competition, marketers must decide how to respond.

Guzzles people, not gas.

The Pilot, as its name might suggest, has nothing to do with flying, but has everything to do with moving large numbers of people safely and efficiently. As with all five Honda trucks, the Pilot is built on a unibody frame. Along with being stronger, smoother and quieter-riding than traditional truck frames, a unibody truck is also lighter, resulting in lower overall vehicle weight, making the Pilot one of the most fuel efficient 8-passenger SUVs. It's also helped earn the Pilot Top Safety Pick for 2007 by the Insurance Institute for Highway Safety. To learn more about the safe and efficient Pilot, visit honda.ca.

TOP SAFETY PICK 2007
INSURANCE INSTITUTE
FOR HIGHWAY SAFETY

HONDA

Competition among auto manufacturers will increasingly focus on fuel efficiency as environmental regulations and gas prices increase.

AGENCY: GRIP LIMITED/PHOTOGRAPHER: CHRIS WOODS, COURTESY HONDA CANADA

DEVELOPING A COMPETITIVE STRATEGY

Marketers at every successful firm must develop an effective strategy for dealing with the competitive environment. One company may compete in a broad range of markets in many areas of the world. Another may specialize in particular market segments, such as those determined by customers' geographic location, age, or income characteristics. Determining a **competitive strategy** involves answering the following three questions:

1. Should we compete?

2. If so, in what markets should we compete?

3. How should we compete?

The answer to the first question depends on the firm's resources, objectives, and expected profit potential. A firm may decide not to pursue or continue operating a potentially successful venture that does not mesh with its resources, objectives, or profit expectations. Semiconductor manufacturer Texas Instruments shed its defense electronics business unit, which makes missile sensors and radar and night-vision systems, to an aircraft company where this unit was a better fit. When pharmaceutical giant Merck spun off Medco, its profitable pharmacy-benefits-management subsidiary, it cited a decision to concentrate on its core business—developing breakthrough medicines.

Answering the second question requires marketers to acknowledge their firm's limited resources—sales personnel, advertising budgets, product development capability, and the like. They must accept responsibility for allocating these resources to the areas of greatest opportunity. Some companies gain access to new technologies or markets through acquisitions and mergers. However, problems can arise when political or legal issues interfere. When the Bank of America purchased Regina-based CUETS Financial, problems resulted since Cuba is the second most popular sun destination, after Mexico, for Canadian tourists. Unfortunately, it is illegal for U.S. companies to do business in Cuba, so CUETS Financial credit cards cannot be used when Canadian cardholders travel there.[14]

Answering the third question requires marketers to make product, distribution, promotion, and pricing decisions that give the firm a competitive advantage in the marketplace. Firms can compete on a variety of bases, including product quality, price, and customer service. Tim Hortons, Starbucks, and McDonald's all sell coffee. But after looking at the competition, McDonald's brought a premium coffee supplier on board. It is now selling richer, more flavourful coffee—priced lower than that of competing coffee brands Tim Hortons and Starbucks. Starbucks, however, continues with its competitive strategy of offering premium coffee in a setting where customers like to relax and linger. Tim Hortons, along with its free-standing locations, has been focusing its nontraditional restaurant development in convenient locations for its customers. It has recently partnered with Wal-Mart Canada to offer coffee at all Wal-Mart Canada Supercentres.[15]

time-based competition Strategy of developing and distributing goods and services more quickly than competitors.

TIME-BASED COMPETITION

With increased international competition and rapid changes in technology, a steadily growing number of firms are using time as a strategic competitive weapon. **Time-based competition** is the strategy of developing and distributing goods and services more quickly than competitors. Although a video option on cell phones came late to the Canadian market, the new feature was a big hit, attracting new customers to cell phone providers. The flexibility and responsiveness of time-based competitors enable them to improve product quality, reduce costs, and expand product offerings to satisfy new market segments and enhance customer satisfaction.

Your retirement is about more than numbers.

At RBC, we don't start with the numbers, we start with you. Our advisors ask unexpected questions that get right to the heart of what's really important to you. A mobile financial planner can meet with you to understand your vision of retirement, and help you create a financial strategy that gets you there. After all, your retirement is about so much more than numbers.

Call now to have an RBC mobile financial planner come to your home.
📞 1-866-335-4055   🖳 rbc.com/yourfuture

FIRST ＞ FOR YOU

Competition among businesses that offer financial planning services is increasing as baby boomers plan for retirement. RBC will send a mobile financial planner to your home.

assessment check 2

2.1 Distinguish between direct and indirect competition and give an example of each.

2.2 What is time-based competition?

In rapidly changing markets—particularly those that involve technology—time-based competition is critical to a firm's success. Google and CBS both offer their own news to mobile phone users. In addition, several other firms—Motorola, T-Mobile, and Sony Ericsson—have announced partnerships with Google that position a Google search bar on mobile phones. In the race for digital entertainment customers, Apple launched a new minicomputer designed as a "hub" for consumers' digital entertainment, as well as a home stereo system linked to the iPod.[16]

THE POLITICAL-LEGAL ENVIRONMENT

Before you play the game, learn the rules! It is a bad idea to start playing a new game without first understanding the rules, yet some businesspeople exhibit a lack of knowledge about marketing's **political-legal environment**—the laws and their interpretations that require firms to operate under certain competitive conditions and to protect consumer rights. Ignorance of laws, ordinances, and regulations, or noncompliance with them, can result in fines, negative publicity, and expensive civil damage suits.

The existing Canadian legal framework was constructed on a piecemeal basis, often in response to issues that were important at the time individual laws were enacted. Businesspeople need considerable diligence to understand its relationship to their marketing decisions. Numerous laws and regulations affect those decisions, many of them vaguely stated and inconsistently enforced by a multitude of different authorities.

Regulations enacted at the federal, provincial, and municipal levels affect marketing practices, as do the actions of independent regulatory agencies. These requirements and prohibitions touch on all aspects of marketing decision making: designing, labelling, packaging, distributing, advertising, and promoting goods and services. To cope with the vast, complex, and changing political-legal environment, many large firms maintain in-house legal departments; small firms often seek professional advice from outside lawyers. All marketers, however, should be aware of the major regulations that affect their activities.

GOVERNMENT REGULATION

Marketing decisions are influenced by many laws and regulations—federal, provincial and territorial, and municipal. Table 3.1 lists many of the most important federal laws that affect marketing decisions in Canada. These laws have been enacted to ensure fair and competitive trade practices and to protect Canadian consumers.

The **Competition Act** is the most comprehensive legislation in Canada, and you will continue to see references to it in several later chapters. It replaced earlier pro-competition legislation, the 1923 Combines Investigation Act, which proved to be largely ineffective, partly because all violations under the Act had to be treated as criminal acts and guilt was almost impossible to prove, and partly because competition had to be virtually eliminated before legal action would be taken. Dissatisfaction with this Act eventually led to the passing of the Competition Act in 1975, later amended in 1986 when additional changes dealing primarily with mergers and acquisitions were made. The Competition Act is administered by Industry Canada, whose mission is to "foster a growing competitive, knowledge-based Canadian economy." Among the many program areas of Industry Canada is "setting rules and services that support the effective operation of the marketplace." The Competition Act assists in this effort by fostering competition and by protecting consumers, both of which are necessary to have a

political-legal environment Component of the marketing environment consisting of laws and interpretations of laws that require firms to operate under competitive conditions and to protect consumer rights.

table 3.1   *Selected Federal Legislation of Interest to Canadian Marketers*

Agreement on Internal Trade Implementation Act

Bills of Exchange Act

Boards of Trade Act

Broadcasting Act

Canadian Tourism Commission Act

Competition Act

Competition Tribunal Act

Consumer Packaging and Labelling Act

Copyright Act

Food and Drugs Act

Hazardous Products Act

Industrial Design Act

Interest Act

Official Languages Act

Patent Act

Personal Information Protection and Electronic Documents Act

Precious Metals Marking Act

Radiocommunication Act

Standards Council of Canada Act

Telecommunications Act

Textile Labelling Act

Timber Marking Act

Trade-marks Act

Weights and Measures Act

③ Describe how marketing activities are regulated and how marketers can influence the political-legal environment.

Competition Act The most comprehensive legislation in Canada, designed to help both consumers and businesses by promoting a healthy competitive environment.

healthy marketplace. Many of the laws and regulations within the Competition Act can be roughly categorized within three specific marketing areas: pricing, promotion, or distribution.

Among the pricing practices that are covered by the Competition Act are price fixing, bid rigging, price discrimination, predatory pricing, double ticketing, and resale price maintenance. Promotion issues include misleading advertising (or even verbal product misrepresentation), referral selling, and bait-and-switch selling. Distribution issues include refusal to deal, exclusive dealing, and pyramid selling. Table 3.2 summarizes these practices. Many of these topics are discussed in greater detail in later chapters that deal with these specific marketing areas.

Many of these practices, such as price fixing, bid rigging, price discrimination, predatory pricing, and misleading advertising, are criminal offences. Others such as tied selling, refusal to deal, and exclusive dealing are noncriminal offenses where actions are taken based on how each particular situation reduces or interferes with competition or otherwise affects consumers in the marketplace.

Provincial and territorial consumer protection legislation in Canada is generally focused on the rights of buyers and sellers with respect to direct sales contracts. These sales include direct mail or telemarketing sales, door-to-door sales, or seminar sales where customers are enticed to a hotel, convention centre, or some other venue where the intention is to sell a product or service to them. This legislation is commonly referred to as the Consumer Protection Act or the Direct Seller's Act in most provinces or territories. These laws are also called "cooling-off" laws because an important aspect they have in common is the right of the buyer to reconsider a buying decision that was made under the persuasive influence of a salesperson. The cooling-off period may vary depending on the provincial or territorial legislation. A notice that informs the customer of the cooling-off period must be part of the contract. If a buyer demands that a contract be cancelled, the seller must return the purchase price and any trade-in that was taken (or a sum of money equal to the value of the trade-in) within a specified period of time. Companies should know what legislation covers each territory where they sell.

As you can see with federal legislation and with varied provincial and territorial legislation, there is a need to harmonize laws, regulations, and practices in order to raise awareness and to improve the

t a b l e   3 . 2   *Some Marketing Practices Covered by the Competition Act*

Price Issues:

Price fixing	Sellers collude to set prices higher than they would be in a free market
Bid rigging	Sellers collude to set prices with respect to one or more bids or quotations
Price discrimination	A seller charges different prices for the same quantity and quality of products to two customers who are in competition with each other
Predatory pricing	Sellers set prices so low they deter competition from entering a market, or with the intention to drive competition from the market
Double ticketing	An item has been ticketed with two prices (the lowest price must prevail although there are now limits to protect sellers)
Resale price maintenance	Manufacturers or other channel members try to influence the price at which products are sold to subsequent buyers

Promotion Issues:

Misleading advertising	Representations, in print or made orally, concerning a product are false or misleading
Referral selling	Price reductions or other inducements are offered to a customer for the names of other potential customers
Bait-and-switch selling	Sellers attract customers with low prices but then offer another product at a higher price because they are unable to provide the originally promoted item
Tied selling	A seller requires a buyer to purchase another product or to refrain from purchasing a product from a specific manufacturer as a condition to getting the product they want

Distribution Issues:

Refusal to deal	Sellers refuse to sell to legitimate buyers
Exclusive dealing	A seller refuses to sell to another channel member unless that customer agrees to buy only from that seller
Pyramid selling	Salespeople are paid to recruit additional salespeople, and each new salesperson pays to "invest" in the scheme, with some of that investment going to earlier participants in the scheme—not to be confused with genuine multi-level marketing plans

marketplace for Canadian consumers. The Consumer Measures Committee, created under the Agreement on Internal Trade, is a joint federal, provincial, and territorial committee that focuses attention on common issues. In the areas of direct selling, cost of credit disclosure, and the manufacture and selling of upholstered and stuffed articles, harmonization is now complete. The committee is now focused on harmonizing consumer protection legislation in the area of electronic commerce and the rules governing debt collection through collection agencies.[17]

GOVERNMENT REGULATORY AGENCIES

Governments at all levels have established regulatory agencies that influence marketing decisions and practices, including those related to product development and commercialization, packaging, pricing, advertising, personal selling, and distribution. Federal agencies may provide advice and assistance to Canadian businesses or may have responsibility to regulate specific industries. Those that regulate industries usually have well-defined responsibilities. The National Energy Board, for example, regulates the construction and operation of interprovincial and international pipelines and power lines; pipeline traffic, tolls, and tariffs; the export and import of natural gas; and the export of oil and electricity, among other things. It also conducts studies into specific energy matters, holds public inquiries, monitors Canada's energy supplies, and provides energy advice to the Minister of Natural Resources in areas where it has expertise derived from its regulatory functions.[18]

One agency that is particularly important to marketers is the Canadian Radio-television and Telecommunications Commission (CRTC), which has the authority to regulate and supervise all aspects of the Canadian broadcasting system. The CRTC works closely with the broadcasting and telecommunications industry to establish standards relating to television violence, gender portrayal, ethnic and minority representation, advertising to children, quality and accessibility of service, and customer billing practices. The CRTC also regulates the companies that supply industry-related technology, including cable television, mobile telephones, satellite television and radio, and direct-to-home television. Some examples of other Canadian federal regulatory agencies and their major areas of responsibility are provided in Table 3.3.

OTHER REGULATORY FORCES

Public and private consumer interest groups and self-regulatory organizations are also part of the legal environment. Consumer interest organizations have mushroomed in the past 25 years, and today, hundreds of groups operate at national, provincial and territorial, and municipal levels. People for the Ethical Treatment of Animals (PETA), which operates in Canada, the United States, India, Germany, and many other countries, opposes the use of animals for product testing. The Humane Society of Canada tries to "protect animals and the earth." It has been calling for a boycott of the rodeo and chuckwagon events at the Calgary Stampede since the death of nine horses travelling to the Calgary Stampede. Other groups attempt to advance the rights of minorities, Canadian seniors, the homeless, and other special-interest causes. The power of these groups has also grown. Pressure from anti-alcohol groups such as Mothers Against Drunk Driving has had an impact on criminal laws and offender sentencing in Canada. Anti-tobacco groups have had a similar impact on legislation and regulations concerning the sale and use of tobacco products in Canada.

Self-regulatory groups represent industries' attempts to set guidelines for responsible business conduct. Advertising Standards Canada (ASC) is the advertising industry's self-regulatory body. Its mission is to ensure the integrity and viability of advertising in Canada. ASC administers the Canadian Code of Advertising Standards, the principal instrument of self-regulation. ASC tries to promote truth and accuracy in advertising and to ensure that advertising is not offensive to viewers, listeners, or readers. It provides consumers with a mechanism to complain about any particular advertisement. It reviews and advocates voluntary resolution of advertising-related complaints between consumers and businesses. ASC also provides industry with a mechanism to resolve competitive disputes about advertising, and with a clearance service that is a fee-based review of advertising copy to help ensure that advertising complies with current laws and regulations.[19] In addition to ASC, many individual trade associations set business guidelines and codes of conduct and encourage members' voluntary compliance.

The Canadian Marketing Association (CMA) has over 800 members who include the country's largest financial institutions, insurance companies, retailers, publishers, charitable organizations,

Marketoid

Without Canada's $91.6 billion of energy-sector exports in 2007—19.7 percent of the total value of Canadian exports—Canada would be in a trade deficit position with the world.

Marketoid

In 2007, Advertising Standards Canada received 1445 complaints from consumers, a 40 percent increase over 2006.

table 3.3 Some Examples of Canadian Federal Regulatory Agencies

FEDERAL AGENCY	MAJOR AREAS OF RESPONSIBILITY
Canada Border Services Agency	To ensure the security and prosperity of Canada by managing the access of people and goods to and from Canada.
Canadian Environmental Assessment Agency	To provide Canadians with high-quality environmental assessments that contribute to informed decision making in support of sustainable development.
Canadian Intellectual Property Office	To accelerate Canada's economic development by fostering the use of intellectual property systems and the exploitation of intellectual property information; encouraging invention, innovation, and creativity in Canada; administering the intellectual property systems in Canada (patents, trademarks, copyrights, industrial designs, and integrated circuit topographies); promoting Canada's international intellectual property interests.
Canadian Space Agency	To promote the peaceful use and development of space, to advance the knowledge of space through science, and to ensure that space science and technology provide social and economic benefits for Canadians.
Communications Research Centre Canada	To be the federal government's centre of excellence for communications R&D, ensuring an independent source of advice for public policy purposes. To help identify and close the innovation gaps in Canada's communications sector by engaging in industry partnerships, building technical intelligence, and supporting small and medium-sized high-technology enterprises.
Measurement Canada	To ensure equity and accuracy where goods and services are bought and sold on the basis of measurement, in order to contribute to a fair and competitive marketplace for Canadians.
Technology Partnerships Canada	To provide funding support for strategic research and development, and demonstration projects that will produce economic, social, and environmental benefits to Canadians.

assessment check 3

3.1 What are the purposes of the Competition Act?

3.2 Name a self-regulatory group and describe its mission.

relationship marketers, and others. It is the Canadian marketing industry's leading advocate on legislative matters and has participated in a variety of government-led initiatives on such issues as privacy, electronic commerce, consumer protection, and the prevention of telemarketing fraud. The CMA has a number of internal task forces that develop self-regulatory standards and policies on ethics, privacy, and marketing to children and teenagers and has developed the Code of Ethics and Standards of Practice to which its members must adhere. In an effort to protect consumer privacy and curb unwanted mail or phone solicitation, the CMA provides a Do Not Contact service, which its members honour.

④ Outline the economic factors that affect marketing decisions and consumer buying power.

THE ECONOMIC ENVIRONMENT

The overall health of the economy influences how much consumers spend and what they buy. This relationship also works the other way. Consumer buying plays an important role in the economy's health; in fact, consumer outlays perennially make up some two-thirds of overall economic activity. Because marketing activities are directed toward satisfying consumer wants and needs, marketers must understand how economic conditions influence the purchasing decisions consumers make.

Marketing's **economic environment** consists of forces that influence consumer buying power and marketing strategies. They include the stage of the business cycle, inflation and deflation, unemployment, income, and resource availability.

economic environment Factors that influence consumer buying power and marketing strategies, including stage of the business cycle, inflation, unemployment, income, and resource availability.

STAGES IN THE BUSINESS CYCLE

Historically, the economy has tended to follow a cyclical pattern consisting of four stages: prosperity, recession, depression, and recovery. Consumer buying differs in each stage of the **business cycle**, and marketers must adjust their strategies accordingly. In times of prosperity, consumer spending maintains a brisk pace, and buyers are willing to spend more for premium versions of well-known brands. Growth in services such as banking and restaurants usually indicates a strong economy. When economists predict such conditions as low inflation and low unemployment, marketers respond by offering new products, increasing their promotional efforts, and expanding distribution. They might even raise prices to widen profit margins. But high prices for some items—such as energy—can affect businesses and consumers alike. When costs increase, businesses have three alternatives: pass the costs on to customers through higher prices, increase the number of customers, or up-sell customers on new or more expensive products. Ontario-based Pizza Pizza chose the last option when it recently added higher-priced and more exotic toppings, such as mango and mesquite chicken, to its pizzas.[20]

During the most recent economic downturn, consumers focused on more basic, functional products that carried lower price tags. They limited travel, restaurant meals, and entertainment. They skipped expensive vacations and cooked their own meals. But they did one surprising thing—they invested in improving their homes. Instead of buying larger homes or vacation properties, they spruced up what they had—which kept the home improvement industry going. During a recession, marketers consider lowering prices and increasing promotions that include special offers to stimulate demand. They may also launch value-priced products likely to appeal to cost-conscious buyers.

Consumer spending sinks to its lowest level during a depression. The last true depression in Canada occurred during the 1930s. Although a severe depression could occur again, most experts see it as a slim possibility. Through its monetary and fiscal policies, the federal government attempts to control extreme fluctuations in the business cycle that lead to depression.

In the recovery stage, the economy emerges from recession and consumer purchasing power increases. But while consumers have money to spend, caution often restrains their willingness to buy. A family might buy a new car if no-interest financing is available. A couple might decide to book a trip through a discount travel firm such as Expedia.ca or Travelocity.ca. Companies like these can make the most of an opportunity and develop loyal customers by offering superior service at lower prices. Recovery still remains a difficult stage for businesses just climbing out of a recession because they must earn profits while trying to gauge uncertain consumer demand. Many cope by holding down costs. Some trim payrolls and close branch offices. Others cut back on business travel budgets, substituting teleconferencing and videoconferencing.

Business cycles, like other aspects of the economy, are complex phenomena that, despite the efforts of government, businesspeople, and others to control them, sometimes have a life of their own. Unforeseen natural disasters such as Hurricane Katrina, major tragedies such as the attacks of September 11, 2001, and the effects of war or peace all have an impact on business and the economy as a whole. The most effective marketers know how to recognize ways to serve their customers during the best of times—and the worst of times.

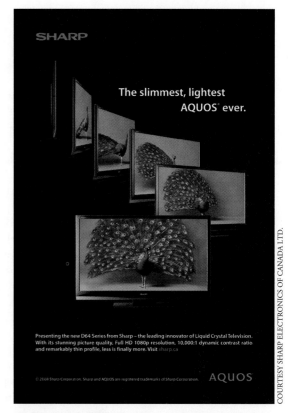

During an economic recovery, consumers feel more comfortable spending money on high-quality, luxury items such as big-screen televisions.

INFLATION AND DEFLATION

A major constraint on consumer spending, which can occur during any stage of the business cycle, is **inflation**—rising prices caused by some combination of excess demand and increases in the costs of raw materials, component parts, human resources, or other factors of production. Inflation devalues money by reducing the products it can buy through persistent price increases. These rising prices increase marketers' costs, such as expenditures for wages and raw materials, and the resulting higher prices may therefore negatively affect sales. Canadian inflation hit a heart-stopping high in 1981 of 12.6 percent, and a low in 2008 of 1.4 percent, well below the 3.4 percent average inflation rate among industrial countries where there has been pressure from rising energy and food prices.[21]

During a recession or during periods of high inflation, consumers look for ways to curb their spending.

If inflation is so bad, is its opposite, *deflation*, better? At first, it might seem so. Falling prices mean that products are more affordable. But deflation can be a long and damaging downward spiral, causing a freefall in business profits, lower returns on most investments, and widespread job layoffs. The last time that Canada experienced significant deflation was in the Great Depression of the 1930s. During the recent recession, economists worried about deflation, as interest rates declined and some product prices declined. But rates and prices stabilized.

UNEMPLOYMENT

Unemployment is defined as the proportion of people in the economy who are actively seeking work but do not have jobs. Unemployment rises during recessions and declines in the recovery and prosperity stages of the business cycle. Like inflation, unemployment affects the ways consumers behave. Unless unemployment insurance, personal savings, and union benefits effectively offset lost earnings, unemployed people have relatively little income to spend—they buy food, pay the rent or mortgage, and try to keep up with utility bills.

Currently unemployment hovers around 6 percent nationally, which indicates that the economy is growing.[22] Not surprisingly, when jobs are created, consumer confidence rises, and consumer spending increases.

INCOME

Income is another important determinant of marketing's economic environment because it influences consumer buying power. By studying income statistics and trends, marketers can estimate market potential and develop plans for targeting specific market segments. For example, Canadian household incomes have grown in recent years. Coupled with a low rate of inflation, this increase has boosted purchasing power for millions of consumers. A rise in income represents a potential for increasing overall sales. However, marketers are most interested in **discretionary income**, the amount of money people have to spend after buying necessities such as food, clothing, and housing. Those whose industry involves the necessities seek to turn those needs into preferences for their goods and services.

Changes in average earnings powerfully affect discretionary income. Historically, periods of major innovation have been accompanied by dramatic increases in living standards and rising incomes. Automobiles, televisions, telephones, and computers are just a few of the innovations that have changed consumers' lives—and standards of living. Statistics Canada tracks personal income and discretionary income, then determines how much of that income is spent on personal consumption. Marketers can use these figures to plan their approaches to everything from product development to the promotion of their goods and services.

Income also affects how much money individuals can and will donate to not-for-profit organizations. The "Etiquette Tips for Marketing Professionals" feature can steer you through the maze of decisions involved in making such donations at work.

RESOURCE AVAILABILITY

Resources are not unlimited. Shortages—temporary or permanent—can result from several causes, including lack of raw materials, component parts, energy, or labour. Canadians are concerned very much by rising world oil prices, influenced of course by supply and demand. As talks between the European Union and leaders in Iran about Iran's nuclear capabilities broke down, economists worried that Iran—the second-largest oil producer in the Organization of the Petroleum Exporting Countries (OPEC)—could withhold its supply. Also, attacks by Nigerian militants on oil production facilities have slowed production there. Nigeria is the largest oil producer in Africa, and the eleventh-largest in the world. In addition, terrorist threats to Saudi Arabia's oil industry infrastructure—including an attempted attack on one of its major oil-exporting terminals—have caused worldwide concern.[23]

One reaction to a shortage is **demarketing,** the process of reducing consumer demand for a product to a level that the firm can reasonably supply. Oil companies publicize tips on how to cut gasoline consumption, and utility companies encourage homeowners to install more insulation to reduce heating costs. Many cities promote mass transit and carpooling for consumers. A shortage presents marketers with a unique set of challenges. They may have to allocate limited supplies, a sharply different activity

Marketoid

The unemployment rate for women in Canada is lower than that for men.

demarketing Process of reducing consumer demand for a good or service to a level that the firm can supply.

ETIQUETTE TIPS FOR MARKETING PROFESSIONALS

To Give or Not to Give—at the Office

JUST about everyone wants to support a good cause. Most of us have our favourites, depending on where we live and which issues strike us close to the heart. At the workplace, on occasion you might be asked to donate to a certain charity or nonprofit organization. Here are a few tips for sorting through these requests and deciding whether to participate:

1. If you are unfamiliar with the organization, ask for information about whom it serves, where, and in what ways. Ask how donations are used.
2. Consider whether the organization is consistent with your own views. Would you support it outside the workplace?
3. If you decide to contribute, do so within your own means. Don't feel obligated to make a donation that you cannot afford. Be sure that donations are collected anonymously, and ask for a receipt for your tax records.
4. If you prefer to decline, do so politely. You might have several reasons for deciding not to contribute—your own

expenses, other charitable obligations, or a different point of view from that of the organization. You do not have to give an elaborate explanation. Simply say, "I'm sorry, but I'm not able to contribute at this time."

5. If you feel pressure after declining, recognize that charitable donations—even if they are supported by your manager or the company as a whole—are not required of you. You cannot be fired for declining to contribute.
6. If you want to support the mission of the organization but cannot make a financial donation at the moment, offer to volunteer in some way. You may be asked to help in the fundraising effort.
7. Try to keep your decision private instead of discussing it with others.

Sources: "Letting Shareholders Choose Their Own Charities," Warren Buffett Secrets, http://www.buffettsecrets.com, accessed May 24, 2008; United Way website, http://www.unitedway.org, accessed May 24, 2008; Caren Chesler, "Buttonholed!" *Investment Dealers' Digest,* February 27, 2006.

from marketing's traditional objective of expanding sales volume. Shortages may require marketers to decide whether to spread limited supplies over all customers or limit purchases by some customers so that the firm can completely satisfy others.

Marketers today have also devised ways to deal with increased demand for fixed amounts of resources. Reynolds Metal Co. addresses the dwindling supply of aluminum through its recycling programs, including cash-paying vending machines. This reverse vending system not only addresses the shortage issue but also deals with potential waste in a socially responsible way. And it creates time and place utility for consumers who want to recycle, thereby increasing recycle rates.[24]

THE INTERNATIONAL ECONOMIC ENVIRONMENT

In today's global economy, marketers must also monitor the economic environment of other nations. Just as in Canada, a recession in the United States, Europe, or Japan changes buying habits. Changes in foreign currency rates compared with the Canadian dollar also affect marketing decisions. The high value of the Canadian dollar has made it more expensive to ship Canadian goods to the United States and has made it less attractive for U.S. companies to operate manufacturing plants here. Houston-based Men's Wearhouse owns 116 Moores retail stores in Canada, but it recently decided to close its manufacturing plant—Golden Brand Clothing (Canada)—in Montreal, due to intense foreign competition and the Canadian dollar's value. Labour costs and other factors affect Canadian firms' decisions to shift manufacturing operations overseas, decisions that have resulted in the loss of thousands of manufacturing jobs across the country, but most particularly in Ontario and Quebec.[25]

As China exports more and more goods to the world, including Canada, some people voice concern over the widening trade gap. Only recently have broad economic reforms allowed China to play in the global marketplace. Today the currency reserves in China's central bank surpass those of Japan. The world's largest shopping mall is located in Beijing, and two-thirds of all DVD players and other electronic equipment are produced in China. Some economists believe that it is only a matter of time before China's economy is the largest in the world.[26]

assessment check 4

4.1 Identify and describe briefly the four stages of the business cycle.

4.2 Explain how inflation and income affect consumer buying decisions.

Politics in other countries affect the international economic environment, as well. Elections in countries such as Brazil and Mexico could result in a shift away from free-market policies. Turmoil in Venezuela could affect the oil industry.

But some valuable lessons have been learned. Whereas developing nations often relied on private funds from industries and organizations to jump-start their economies a decade ago, they now look to establish and build strong export industries. Global demand for certain commodities has helped these nations—such as Argentina, which exports soybeans—strengthen their economies.[27]

⑤ Discuss the impact of the technological environment on a firm's marketing activities.

technological environment Applications to marketing of knowledge based on discoveries in science, inventions, and innovations.

THE TECHNOLOGICAL ENVIRONMENT

The **technological environment** represents the application to marketing of knowledge based on discoveries in science, inventions, and innovations. Technology leads to new goods and services for consumers; it also improves existing products, offers better customer service, and often reduces prices through new, cost-efficient production and distribution methods. Technology can quickly make products obsolete—e-mail, for example, quickly eroded both letter writing and the market for fax machines—but it can just as quickly open new marketing opportunities, in entirely new industries.

Pets have been wearing RFID—radio-frequency identification—transmitters for years, in case they got lost. Now RFID tags are used in many industries to locate everything from library books to laundry detergent. An RFID tag contains a computer chip with an antenna. A reader scans the tag and transmits the data from the tag to a computer. This innovation means that retailers, manufacturers, and others can locate and track inventory without opening packages. One medical centre is even considering using RFID microchips to help locate wandering Alzheimer's patients. Critics warn that improper use of RFID technology could lead to loss of privacy because products or people could be tracked without their knowledge.[28]

Technology can sometimes address social concerns. In response to pressure from the World Trade Organization, Japanese automakers were first to use technology to develop more fuel-efficient vehicles and reduce dangerous emissions with offerings like the Toyota Prius and a hybrid version of the Honda Civic. Both vehicles run on a combination of gasoline and electricity. Biotech firms have been researching ways to reduce the cost of making ethanol fuel out of cellulose materials—crop waste, weeds, forest underbrush, garbage, anything organic. Bill Gates, founder of Microsoft, has invested $84 million in another ethanol firm. Cellulose biomass energy made from waste, grass, and other materials could account for about half of current transportation petroleum in as little as 40 years.[29]

Industry and government—as well as educational and other not-for-profit institutions—all play roles in the development of new technology. But improvements often come at a price. Research and development efforts by private industry represent a major source of technological innovation. Pfizer, a global pharmaceutical company, discovers, develops, manufactures, and markets innovative medicines. Among its most publicized breakthroughs are the cholesterol-lowering drug Lipitor, which ranks as the biggest-selling prescription drug in North America; Viagra, a revolutionary treatment for erectile dysfunction; and Trovan, one of the most prescribed antibiotics in North America. The cost of bringing a new drug to market can run as high as $1.7 billion (U.S.).[30] Canadian companies may have a competitive advantage in the future as they continue to recruit visible minorities and immigrants from around the world. Beng Ong, a Singapore native and scientist at the Xerox Research Centre in Mississauga, has captured more than 100 patents. Beng Ong says, "Typically, in research, you do not want someone from the same school or background. You want diversity in training...."[31] Beng Ong and his multinational team have recently developed an inexpensive synthetic compound that may provide an easy-to-make alternative to the silicon chip.

Another major source of technology is the government, including the military. Air bags originated from airplane ejection seats, digital computers were first designed to calculate artillery trajectories, and the microwave oven is a derivative of military radar systems. Even the Internet was first developed by the U.S. Department of Defense as a secure military communications system.

APPLYING TECHNOLOGY

Marketers monitor the technological environment for a number of reasons. Creative applications of new technologies not only give a firm a definite competitive edge but can also benefit society. Vancouver-based Angiotech Pharmaceuticals developed a drug-coated medical device called Taxus. Simply, it is a stent that is implanted in heart patients to keep blood vessels open and enhance blood flow, but it is coated with drugs that inhibit the growth of scar tissue, previously a common problem. Marketers who monitor new technology and successfully apply it may also enhance customer service. Boeing is equipping its aircraft with Wi-Fi access so that passengers with laptops can log onto the Internet while in flight. This service is particularly helpful to business travellers who want to make the most of their workday in flight. Boeing predicts that the move will pay off. "Wi-Fi is on an explosive growth path," says Boeing's president, Scott E. Carson.[32]

VoIP—which stands for voice-over Internet protocol—is an alternative to traditional telecommunications services provided by companies such as Rogers Communications. The telephone is not connected to a traditional phone jack but instead is connected to a personal computer with any type of broadband Internet connection. Special software transmits phone conversations over the Internet, rather than through telephone lines. A VoIP user dials the phone as usual. Recipients can receive calls made using VoIP through regular telephone connections—land or wireless. Moreover, you can call another person who has VoIP using a regular landline or cell phone. A growing number of consumers and businesses have embraced VoIP, mainly because of the cost savings and the extra features offered by VoIP.

the **Office Affair**   EPISODE #5 … **When performance and privacy get together**

The Protector
Job Erase feature automatically deletes any trace of data. It's like nothing ever happened.

Mr. Endurance
Handles up to 6,650 sheets of paper — keeps going and going.

Unparalleled functionality. Features to get excited about. And styling that turns heads. No wonder so many businesses have fallen in love with bizhub from Konica Minolta. Experience bizhub for yourself at **konicaminolta.ca** or call **1-877-958-5627**. It will leave your office talking. **All you need is Hub.**

KONICA MINOLTA

The essentials of imaging

bizhub

COURTESY KONICA MINOLTA BUSINESS SOLUTIONS (CANADA) LTD.

The Konica Minolta bizhub allows users to print, copy, e-mail, manage network jobs, transfer digital documents, and send jobs remotely. It also uses state-of-the-art biometric security.

As convenient as the Internet, cell phones, and Wi-Fi are for businesspeople and consumers, the networks that facilitate these connections aren't yet compatible with each other. So engineers are working on a new standard that would enable these networks to connect with each other—paving the way for melded services such as video exchanges between a cell phone and a computer. Called the Internet Protocol Multimedia Subsystem (IPMS), the new standard will attempt to create a common interface so that data can be carried across networks between different devices.[33] The implications for various communications providers are enormous—not only will they find new ways to cooperate but they will also find new ways to compete. Subsequent chapters discuss in more detail how companies apply technologies—such as databases, blogs, and interactive promotional techniques—to create a competitive advantage.

assessment check 5

5.1 What are some of the consumer benefits of technology?

5.2 Why must marketers monitor the technological environment?

THE SOCIAL-CULTURAL ENVIRONMENT

⑥ Explain how the social-cultural environment influences marketing.

As a nation, Canada is becoming older, more affluent, and more culturally diverse. The birthrate is falling, and **microculture** populations are rising. People express concerns about the environment, buying ecologically friendly products that reduce pollution. They value the time at home with family and friends, cooking meals at home and exchanging vacation photos over the Internet. Marketers need to track these trends to be sure they are in tune with consumers' needs and desires. These aspects of consumer lifestyles help shape marketing's **social-cultural environment**—the relationship between marketing, society, and culture.

social-cultural environment Component of the marketing environment consisting of the relationship between the marketer and society and its culture.

To remain competitive, marketers must be sensitive to society's demographic shifts and changing values. These variables affect consumers' reactions to different products and marketing practices. As the baby boom generation—those born between 1946 and 1965—reaches middle age and retirement, marketers are scrambling to identify this generation's needs and wants. Fuelled by hopes of a long life with plenty of time and money to spend, the baby boom generation views retirement much differently than their predecessors did. Marketers already know that boomers want to travel and enjoy their leisure time. But they aren't playing shuffleboard—they are taking up fly fishing, yoga, and boating. They are also spending money on vacation homes and in craft stores. Some are even starting a second career, establishing their own small businesses. Aging boomers also need health care goods and services—as they live longer, they may need everything from physical therapy for a repaired knee to a motorized scooter to get around.[34]

Another social-cultural consideration is the increasing importance of cultural diversity. Canada is a mixed society composed of various micromarkets, each with its unique values, cultural characteristics, consumer preferences, and purchasing behaviours. Rogers Communications has been actively targeting these important micromarkets and now offers the most multicultural programming in Canada with more than 65 channels, broadcasting in more than 20 languages.[35] Vice chairman Phil Lind says, "The multicultural market is relatively untapped compared to where it's going to be in the next five or 10 years. This thing is going to be really big."[36] T&T Supermarket is another company that has targeted some of Canada's important micromarkets as described in the "Marketing Success" box.

Marketers also need to learn about cultural and societal differences among countries abroad, particularly as business becomes more and more global. Marketing strategies that work in Canada often fail when directly applied in other countries and vice versa. In many cases, marketers must redesign packages and modify products and advertising messages to suit the tastes and preferences of different cultures. Chapter 7 explores the social-cultural aspects of international marketing.

consumerism Social force within the environment designed to aid and protect the consumer by exerting legal, moral, and economic pressures on business and government.

CONSUMERISM

Changing societal values have led to **consumerism**, defined as a social force within the environment that aids and protects the buyer by exerting legal, moral, and economic pressures on business. Today, everyone—marketers, industry, government, and the public—is acutely aware of the impact of consumerism on the nation's economy and general well-being.

marketing success   T&T Supermarket: Haw Gao Hit

Background. StatsCan predicts that the Chinese and South Asian minorities in Canada will each number approximately 1.8 million people by 2017. While they will become increasingly important market segments in the future, both groups currently offer tremendous opportunities to marketers who can identify and cater to their unique needs.

The Challenge. T&T Supermarket wanted to cater to Asian Canadian consumers with uniquely Asian foods, including, for example, sauces from Hong Kong, noodles from Taiwan, fruit from the Philippines, snacks from Japan, spices from Thailand, and many other items that appeal to Asian tastes. Other items include fresh sushi, prepared deli products, in-house bakery products, and fresh seafood, such as live giant prawns, tilapia, lobster, conch, and elephant clams.

The Strategy. T&T Supermarket has focused on "quality, innovation and on-going improvement in product selection, customer service, and shopping convenience to ensure a high degree of customer satisfaction." It advertises weekly specials in ethnic media, on its website, and through e-mail to customers who wish to receive them. Stores typically are 35 000 to 55 000 square feet, and all are bright and clean. Store employees are bilingual and need to be familiar with the products they sell and how they are prepared and used in cooking. The company also offers promotions during important festivals, such as Chinese New Year and the Dragon Boat Festival. In one six-week promotion, T&T gave away 96 airline tickets to winners' Asian destinations of choice.

The Outcome. T&T Supermarket now has 16 stores in Canada: eight in Greater Vancouver, two in Calgary, one in Edmonton, and five in Greater Toronto. Every location is busy as customers shop for their favourite foods. Caucasian customers now account for as many as 40 percent of shoppers at some locations, testament to the growing popularity of Asian foods, but also to the marketing strategy of this growing Canadian retailer.

Sources: Company website, http://www.tnt-supermarket.com, accessed June 11, 2008; Eve Lazarus, "Eastern Star," *Marketing*, September 24, 2007, pp. 49–52.

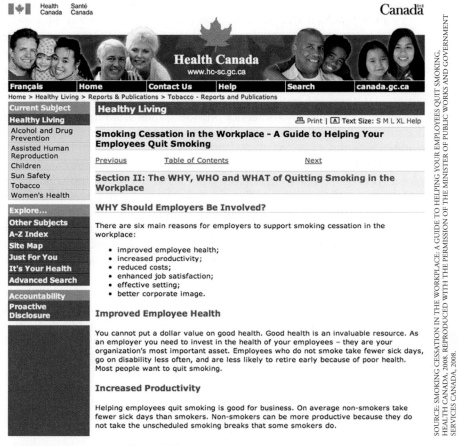

SOURCE: SMOKING CESSATION IN THE WORKPLACE: A GUIDE TO HELPING YOUR EMPLOYEES QUIT SMOKING, HEALTH CANADA, 2008. REPRODUCED WITH THE PERMISSION OF THE MINISTER OF PUBLIC WORKS AND GOVERNMENT SERVICES CANADA, 2008.

The changing social-cultural environment is making it less acceptable to be a smoker. Health Canada provides six reasons that employers should support smoking cessation programs.

In recent years, marketers have witnessed increasing consumer activism. There have been calls to ban Canadian seal product imports in the United Kingdom. Nestlé was targeted in Italy following the launch of its Partners' Blend fair-trade coffee. Adidas was focused on for using kangaroo leather in its sports shoes. Ryanair was criticized for its policy of having a quota on the number of disabled people it will allow on each flight. In India, Coca-Cola was blamed for creating water shortages and pollution. Pepsi was targeted for using a performing chimpanzee in its advertising.[37] No organization, industry, or country is immune.

But firms cannot always adjust to meet the demands of consumer groups. The choice between pleasing all consumers and remaining profitable—thus surviving—defines one of the most difficult dilemmas facing business. Given these constraints, what do consumers have the right to expect from the companies from which they buy goods and services? The most frequently quoted answer came from a speech made by U.S. president John F. Kennedy more than four decades ago. Although this list does not amount to a definitive statement, it offers good rules of thumb that explain basic **consumer rights:**

1. *The right to choose freely.* Consumers should be able to choose from among a range of goods and services.

2. *The right to be informed.* Consumers should be provided with enough education and product information to enable them to be responsible buyers.

3. *The right to be heard.* Consumers should be able to express their legitimate displeasure to appropriate parties—that is, sellers, consumer assistance groups, and consumer affairs offices.

4. *The right to be safe.* Consumers should be assured that the goods and services they purchase are not injurious with normal use. Goods and services should be designed in such a way that the average consumer can use them safely.

consumer rights In their most basic form, these rights include a person's right to choose goods and services freely, to be informed about these products and services, to be heard, and to be safe.

These rights have formed the conceptual framework of much of the legislation enacted in Canada and the United States during the first 40 years of the consumer rights movement. However, the question of how best to guarantee them remains unanswered. In Canada, different classes of consumer products fall under the jurisdiction of different government agencies. Regulations concerning food are administered by the Canadian Food Inspection Agency. Food labelling regulations force disclosure of such details as expiration date, ingredients, and nutritional values on packaged foods. Vehicles fall under the jurisdiction of Transport Canada. Provincial governments may regulate the marketing of farm products, such as eggs and milk, and of service providers, such as homeopathic and chiropractic practitioners and insurance agents and brokers. They, and sometimes municipal governments, may regulate pesticide use.

Consumers' right to safety encompasses a vast range of products, from automobiles to children's toys. Sometimes it seems as though safety recalls are reported in the media too regularly. You might even receive a letter in the mail from a manufacturer informing you of a recall for a part on your refrigerator or car. Many Canadian retailers—including Mountain Equipment Co-op, Zellers, and Canada's largest sporting goods retailer, Forzani Group—pulled plastic bottles containing bisphenol A (BPA) from their shelves and have replaced them with BPA-free products. They and other retailers took this action even before Health Canada became the first regulatory body in the world to determine that BPA is a dangerous substance.[38]

Consumerism, along with the rest of the social-cultural environment for marketing decisions at home and abroad, is expanding in scope and importance. Today, no marketer can initiate a strategic decision without considering the society's norms, values, culture, and demographics. Understanding how these variables affect decisions is so important that some firms have created a new position—typically, manager of public policy research—to study the future impact on their organizations of a changing societal environment.

assessment check 6

6.1 Define consumerism.

6.2 Identify the four consumer rights.

---

(7) Describe the ethical issues in marketing.

ETHICAL ISSUES IN MARKETING

The five environments described so far in this chapter do not completely capture the role that marketing plays in society and the consequent effects and responsibilities of marketing activities. Because marketing is closely connected with various public issues, it invites constant scrutiny. Moreover, since marketing acts as an interface between an organization and the society in which it operates, marketers often carry much of the responsibility for dealing with social issues that affect their firms.

Marketing operates outside the firm. It responds to that outside environment, and in turn is acted on by environmental influences. Relationships with employees, suppliers, the government, consumers, and society as a whole frame the social issues that marketers must address. The way that marketers deal with these social issues has a significant effect on their firm's eventual success. The diverse social issues that marketers face can be divided into two major categories: marketing ethics and social responsibility. While these two categories certainly overlap, this simple classification system provides a method for studying these issues.

The wave of corporate fraud and conflicts of interest in big business during the past decade is still being addressed in the form of court trials and guilty pleas by wrongdoers. Cases against senior executives at Enron and Tyco International brought jail sentences for those who were convicted. Other companies have responded proactively, by tightening their own ethical codes and even hiring managers whose role is specifically to enforce them. Hundreds of Canadian and U.S. companies now have such managers, including Dun & Bradstreet, Dow Corning, Nortel Networks, Wal-Mart, and even the Government of Canada, which now has an ethics commission for the House of Commons and a Senate ethics officer.

marketing ethics
Marketers' standards of conduct and moral values.

Environmental influences have directed increased attention toward **marketing ethics,** defined as the marketer's standards of conduct and moral values. Ethics concern matters of right and wrong: the responsibility of individuals and firms to do what is morally right. As Figure 3.2 shows, each element of the marketing mix raises its own set of ethical questions. Before any improvements to a firm's marketing program can be made, each of them must be evaluated.

Creating an ethics program may be complicated and time consuming, but it is worthwhile. A code of ethics may mitigate some responsibility and help reduce some fines and sentences, but responsibility for its implementation ultimately rests with senior executives. If management doesn't openly support it, communicate its value internally, reward ethical behaviour, and punish unethical behaviour, its value becomes questionable. A step-by-step framework for building an effective program is shown in Figure 3.3. Cynics, of course, can always question the value of an ethics officer and a code of ethics. While Nortel Networks has an ethics officer and a 44-page *Code of Business Conduct,* it also had a senior ethics advisor and a code of ethics when it was involved in its most unethical business practices.[39]

figure 3.2

Ethical Questions in Marketing

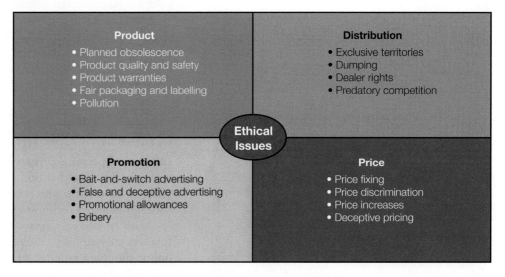

Ensuring ethical practices means promising customers and business partners not to sacrifice quality and fairness for profit. In exchange, organizations hope for increased customer loyalty toward their brands. Yet issues involving marketing ethics are not always clear-cut. The issue of cigarette advertising, for example, has divided the ranks of advertising executives. Is it right for advertisers to promote a product that, while legal, has known health hazards?

For years, charges of unethical conduct have plagued the tobacco industry. In the largest civil settlement in history, tobacco manufacturers agreed to pay $206 billion (U.S.) to 46 U.S. states. Four other states—Florida, Minnesota, Mississippi, and Texas—had separate settlements totalling another $40 billion (U.S.). The settlement frees tobacco companies from claims for the cost of treating sick smokers. In Canada, British Columbia passed its Tobacco Damages and Health Care Cost Recovery Act and sued for $10 billion to recover past health care costs from tobacco companies. The tobacco companies filed an appeal, but it was rejected by the Supreme Court in 2008, paving the way for the province's lawsuit to proceed.[40] New Brunswick became the second Canadian province to file a similar lawsuit. Speculation is that the payoff in Canada will be higher per capita than in the United States because of Canada's public health care system, where health care costs are borne entirely by government. In the United States, most health care costs are borne by private insurers.[41]

People develop standards of ethical behaviour based on their own systems of values, which help them deal with ethical questions in their personal lives. However, the workplace may generate serious conflicts when individuals discover that their ethical beliefs are not necessarily in line with those of their employer. For example, employees may think that shopping online during a lunch break using a work computer is fine, but the company may decide otherwise. The quiz in Figure 3.4 highlights other everyday ethical dilemmas.

How can these conflicts be resolved? In addition to individual and organizational ethics, individuals may be influenced by a third basis

Marketoid

Canada's two largest tobacco manufacturers were fined a total of $1.1 billion in 2008—the largest criminal fines and civil settlements in Canadian history—after pleading guilty to aiding and abetting the smuggling of cigarettes.

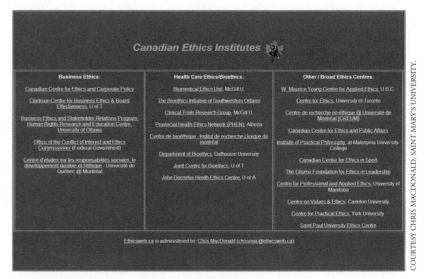

Concern with ethics in business, health care, sports, and other areas has led to the growth of ethics institutes across Canada.

figure 3.3

Ten Steps for Corporations to Improve Standards of Business Ethics

1. Appoint a senior-level ethics compliance officer.

2. Set up an ethics code capable of detecting and preventing misconduct.

3. Distribute a written code of ethics to employees, subsidiaries, and associated companies and require all business partners to abide by it.

4. Conduct regular ethics training programs to communicate standards and procedures.

5. Establish systems to monitor misconduct and report grievances.

6. Establish consistent punishment guidelines to enforce standards and codes.

7. Encourage an open-door policy, allowing employees to report cases of misconduct without fear of retaliation.

8. Prohibit employees with a track record of misconduct from holding positions with substantial discretionary authority.

9. Promote ethically aware and responsible managers.

10. Continually monitor effectiveness of all ethics-related programs.

Source: O.C. Ferrell and John Fraedrich, *Business Ethics: Ethical Decision Making and Cases*, Sixth Edition. Copyright © 2005 by Houghton Mifflin Company. Adapted with permission of Houghton Mifflin Harcourt Publishing Company.

Marketoid

There are 38 million phone numbers, including cell phones, in Canada.

of ethical authority—a professional code of ethics that transcends both organizational and individual value systems. A professional peer association can exercise collective oversight to limit a marketer's individual behaviour. Any code of ethics must anticipate the variety of problems that marketers are likely to encounter. Promotional matters tend to receive the greatest attention, but ethical considerations also influence marketing research, product strategy, distribution strategy, and pricing.

ETHICS IN MARKETING RESEARCH

Invasion of personal privacy has become a critical issue in marketing research. The proliferation of databases, the selling of address lists, and the ease with which consumer information can be gathered through Internet technology have all increased public concern. The "Solving an Ethical Controversy" feature raises the issue of whether retailers are helpful or intrusive as they try to personalize customers' online shopping experiences. From an ethical standpoint, a marketing research practice that is particularly problematic is the promise of cash rewards or free offers in return for marketing information that can then be sold to direct marketers. Consumers commonly disclose their demographic information in return for an e-mail newsletter or a favourite magazine.

Privacy issues have mushroomed with the growth of the Internet, with huge consequences to both consumers and marketers. CardSystems, a credit card processor, mistakenly released financial data on 40 million consumers to a hacker. CitiGroup lost data on 3.9 million customers when unencrypted backup tapes it had shipped disappeared.[42]

Canadians concerned about Internet privacy can get a lot of information from the Electronic Commerce Branch of Industry Canada at **http://www.ic.gc.ca/epic/site/ecic-ceac.nsf/en/home**, and by exploring its various programs and services. The Canadian Marketing Association also provides valuable services for Canadian consumers at **http://www.the-cma.org**. There are tips for protecting your privacy, dealing with spam, identifying fraudulent offers, and resolving complaints. You may also register online for its Do Not Contact service. This will reduce the number of contacts you receive because members of the Canadian Marketing Association agree to not contact registered users. The Canadian Radio-television and Telecommunications Commission recently awarded a five-year contract to Bell Canada to establish and maintain a national do-not-call registry. This list will greatly reduce the number of unwanted calls to people who have registered.

ETHICS IN PRODUCT STRATEGY

Product quality, planned obsolescence, brand similarity, and packaging questions all raise ethical issues. Feeling the competition, some marketers have tried packaging practices that might be considered misleading, deceptive, or unethical. Larger packages take up more shelf space, and consumers notice them. An odd-sized package makes price comparisons difficult. Bottles with concave bottoms give the impression that they contain more liquid than they actually do. Are these packaging practices justified in the name of competition, or are they deceptive? Growing regulatory mandates appear to be narrowing the range of discretion in this area.

How do you evaluate the quality of a product like a soft drink? By flavour or by ingredients? Citing several studies, some consumer advocates say that the ingredients in soft drinks—mainly the high sugar content—can be linked to obesity in consumers, particularly children. Not surprisingly, the beverage

figure 3.4

Test Your Workplace Ethics

Workplace Ethics Quiz

The spread of technology into the workplace has raised a variety of new ethical questions, and many old ones still linger. Compare your answers with those of others surveyed on page 119.

Office Technology

1. Is it wrong to use company e-mail for personal reasons?
   ❑ Yes ❑ No

2. Is it wrong to use office equipment to help your children or spouse do schoolwork?
   ❑ Yes ❑ No

3. Is it wrong to play computer games on office equipment during the workday?
   ❑ Yes ❑ No

4. Is it wrong to use office equipment to do Internet shopping?
   ❑ Yes ❑ No

5. Is it unethical to blame an error you made on a technological glitch?
   ❑ Yes ❑ No

6. Is it unethical to visit pornographic websites using office equipment?
   ❑ Yes ❑ No

Gifts and Entertainment

7. What's the value at which a gift from a supplier or client becomes troubling?
   ❑ $25 ❑ $50 ❑ $100

8. Is a $50 gift to a boss unacceptable?
   ❑ Yes ❑ No

9. Is a $50 gift from the boss unacceptable?
   ❑ Yes ❑ No

10. Of gifts from suppliers: Is it OK to take a $200 pair of football tickets?
    ❑ Yes ❑ No

11. Is it OK to take a $120 pair of theatre tickets?
    ❑ Yes ❑ No

12. Is it OK to take a $100 holiday food basket?
    ❑ Yes ❑ No

13. Is it OK to take a $25 gift certificate?
    ❑ Yes ❑ No

14. Can you accept a $75 prize won at a raffle at a supplier's conference?
    ❑ Yes ❑ No

Truth and Lies

15. Due to on-the-job pressure, have you ever abused or lied about sick days?
    ❑ Yes ❑ No

16. Due to on-the-job pressure, have you ever taken credit for someone else's work or idea?
    ❑ Yes ❑ No

Source: Ethics Officer Association, Belmont, Massachusetts; Leadership Group, Wilmette, Illinois; surveys sampled a cross-section of workers at large companies and nationwide; used with permission from Ethics Officer Association.

industry disagrees, arguing that lack of exercise and a poor diet in general are greater contributors to weight gain than regular consumption of soft drinks. But at least one leading epidemiologist, the American Cancer Society's Dr. Michael Thun, wants to see new labels on soft drink cans. "I think it would be a good candidate for a warning," he observes.[43]

ETHICS IN DISTRIBUTION

Two ethical issues influence a firm's decisions regarding distribution strategy:

1. What is the appropriate degree of control over the distribution channel?

2. Should a company distribute its products in marginally profitable outlets that have no alternative source of supply?

The question of channel control typically arises in relationships between manufacturers and franchise dealers. For example, should an automobile dealership, a gas station, or a fast-food outlet be forced to purchase parts, materials, and supplementary services from the parent organization?

The second question concerns marketers' responsibility to serve unsatisfied market segments even if the profit potential is slight. Should marketers serve retail stores in low-income areas, serve users of limited amounts of the firm's product, or serve a declining rural

Companies are beginning to develop products for consumers who are concerned about ethics, social responsibility, and the environment.

Solving an Ethical Controversy

Amazon: Helpful or Intrusive?

AMAZON is one of the premier Internet retailers, with annual sales of approximately $7 billion in books, music, DVDs, electronics, and thousands of other products through its websites Amazon.ca and Amazon.com. Amazon even competes against eBay, with nearly a million third-party sellers accounting for a quarter of its sales. The site has "developed an extremely loyal customer base, and they've cultivated that by continually lowering prices and adding features to their website," said an industry expert.

Many of those features are designed to make shopping a personalized experience. Software tools help Amazon suggest new products when customers log on, narrow their site searches, track favourite authors and topics, read recommended blogs, and even avoid buying stuff they have already purchased. Privacy advocates, however, fear that by storing the vast amounts of personal information about buying habits that allow this kind of "relationship building," Amazon might be getting a little too personal, particularly if the data become vulnerable to theft or misuse. One objection is that the company doesn't request customer permission to collect the data or offer a way to erase the information.

Should Online Retailers Such as Amazon Continue to Collect Personal Information about Customers without Permission?

PRO

1. The benefits of personalized Internet shopping outweigh the possible risks for those who choose to use it.
2. Online retailers collect little more information than consumers already make available when they bank online or use a credit card in a store.

CON

1. Customers should be offered a chance to opt out of the data collection process if they choose.
2. Retailers cannot guarantee the security of the information.

Where do you stand: pro or con?

Sources: Elinor Mills, "A9 Searches for Purpose," C/Net News, February 10, 2006, http://insight.zdnet.co.uk; Antone Gonsalves, "Amazon.com A9 Search Engine Adds Zoom People Search," TechWeb, January 17, 2006, http://www.techweb.com; Elizabeth M. Gillespie, "Amazon.com Sitting Pretty 10 Years Later," Associated Press, July 5, 2005, http://news.yahoo.com.

market? These problems are difficult to resolve because they often involve individuals rather than broad segments of the general public. An important first step is to ensure that the firm consistently enforces its channel policies.

ETHICS IN PROMOTION

Promotion raises many ethical questions, because it is the most direct link between a firm and its customers. Personal selling has always been a target of criticism—and jokes about untrustworthiness. Used-car dealers, horse traders, and purveyors of quick remedies have been the targets of such barbs. But promotion covers many areas, ranging from advertising to direct marketing—and it is vital for marketers to monitor their ethics in all marketing communications. Truth in advertising—representing accurately a product's benefits and drawbacks, warranties, price, and availability—is the bedrock of ethics in promotion.

Marketing to children has been under close scrutiny for many years because children have not yet developed the skills to receive marketing messages critically. They simply believe everything they see and hear. For example, snack foods, candy, soft drinks, and other junk foods are for sale in abundant quantities in many schools throughout the country, where children are a captive audience. Organizations now pay to advertise at participating schools. While these schools argue that the advertising revenues actually help students through funded programs, critics disagree. "It teaches children that . . . they're for sale," warns Gary Ruskin, executive director of the consumer group Commercial Alert.[44]

Some companies are taking a stance against promoting certain products to children. Kraft Foods recently announced plans to cut back on advertising fatty and sugary foods to children, adding new logos to its food and drinks that highlight its more nutritional offerings. Competitors such as Quaker Oats and General Mills soon followed suit. "This is a great step by Kraft," said Margo Wootan, nutrition policy director for the Center for Science in the Public Interest. "This will help support parents' efforts to get their kids to eat better. I think we are going to see more of these changes."[45]

Promoting certain products to post-secondary students can raise ethical questions as well. These students are a prime market for firms that sell everything from electronics to beer. And it's the beer that has people worried, particularly because laws prohibit the sale of alcohol to students who are under the legal drinking age. Even if they don't drink illegally, students can collect and wear promotional hats, shirts, duffle bags, and other items that display popular alcohol names and logos. According to researcher Dr. James D. Sargent, "Promotional items are related to early onset drinking, and I think the responsible thing to do would be for these industries to quit distributing them."[46]

ETHICS IN PRICING

Pricing is probably the most regulated aspect of a firm's marketing strategy. As a result, most unethical price behaviour is also illegal. Some aspects of pricing, however, are still open to ethics abuses. For example, should some customers pay more for merchandise if distribution costs are higher in their areas? Do marketers have an obligation to warn vendors and customers of impending price, discount, or return policy changes?

Credit card companies often walk a fine line between ethical and unethical pricing practices. While consumers are almost always informed of credit card terms on their agreements, the print is usually tiny and the language hard to understand. For instance, a credit card issuer might advertise the benefits of its premium card. But the fine print explains that the firm is allowed to substitute a different plan—with a higher interest rate—if the applicant doesn't qualify for the premium card. In addition, certain laws allow companies to levy charges that consumers might not be aware of. For example, under a provision called universal default, a company can legally raise its interest rate on a card if the customer is late paying other bills—even if that credit card is paid on time.[47]

All these concerns must be dealt with in developing a professional ethic for pricing products. The ethical issues involved in pricing for today's highly competitive and increasingly computerized markets are discussed in greater detail in Chapters 18 and 19.

> **assessment check 7**
>
> **7.1** Define marketing ethics.
>
> **7.2** Identify the five areas in which ethics can be a problem.

SOCIAL RESPONSIBILITY IN MARKETING

Companies can do business in such a way that everyone benefits—customers, the companies themselves, and society as a whole. While ethical business practices are vital to a firm's long-term survival and growth, **social responsibility** raises the bar even higher. In marketing, social responsibility involves accepting an obligation to give equal weight to profits, consumer satisfaction, and social well-being in evaluating a firm's performance. In addition to measuring sales, revenues, and profits, a firm must also consider ways in which it has contributed to the overall well-being of its customers and society.

Social responsibility allows a wide range of opportunities for companies to shine. If they are reluctant at first, government legislation can mandate socially responsible actions. Government may require firms to take socially responsible actions in matters of environmental policy, deceptive product claims, and other areas. Also, consumers, through their power to repeat or withhold purchases, may force marketers to provide honest and relevant information and fair prices. The four dimensions of social responsibility—economic, legal, ethical, and philanthropic—are shown in Figure 3.5. The first two dimensions have long been recognized, but ethical obligations and the need for marketers to be good corporate citizens have increased in importance in recent years.

(8) Identify the four levels of the social responsibility pyramid.

social responsibility Marketing philosophies, policies, procedures, and actions that have the enhancement of society's welfare as a primary objective.

figure 3.5

The Four-Step Pyramid of Corporate Social Responsibility

Philanthropic
*Be a good
corporate citizen*

▶ Contribute resources to the
community; improve quality of life

Ethical
Be ethical

▶ Obligation to do what is right, just, and fair
▶ Avoid harm

Legal
Obey the law

▶ Law is society's codification of right and wrong
▶ Play by the rules of the game

Economic
Be profitable

▶ The foundation upon which all others rest

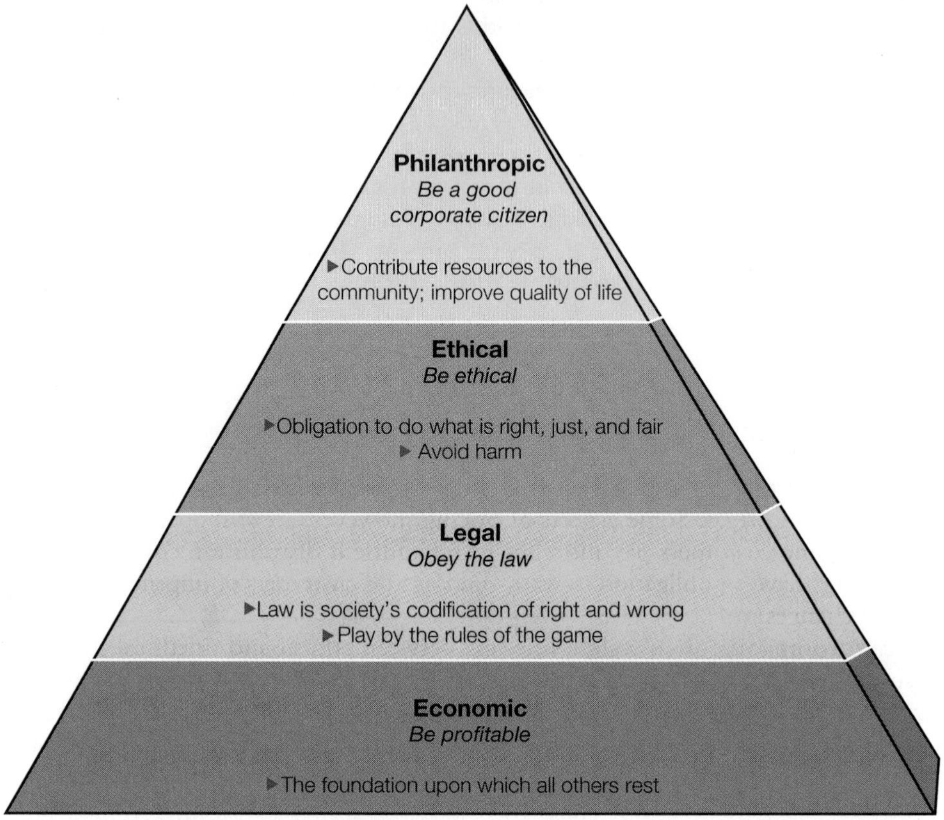

Source: Archie B. Carroll, "The Pyramid of Corporate Social Responsibility: Toward the Moral Management of Organizational
Stakeholders," *Business Horizons* 34, July–August, 1991. Used with permission.

The locus for socially responsible decisions in organizations has always been an important issue. But who should accept specific accountability for the social effects of marketing decisions? Responses include the district sales manager, the marketing vice president, the firm's CEO, and even the board of directors. Probably the most valid assessment holds that all marketers, regardless of their stations in the organization, remain accountable for the social aspects of their decisions.

MARKETING'S RESPONSIBILITIES

The concept of business's social responsibility traditionally has concerned managers' relationships with customers, employees, and shareholders. In general, managers traditionally have felt responsible for providing quality products at reasonable prices for customers, adequate wages and decent working environments for employees, and acceptable profits for shareholders. Only occasionally did the concept extend to relations with the government and rarely with the general public.

Today, corporate responsibility has expanded to cover the entire societal framework. A decision to temporarily delay the installation of a pollution-control device may satisfy the traditional sense of responsibility. Customers would continue to receive an uninterrupted supply of the plant's products, employees would not face layoffs, and shareholders would still receive reasonable returns on their investments. Contemporary business ethics, however, would not accept this choice as socially responsible.

Contemporary marketing decisions must consider their global effect. Some clothing manufacturers and retailers have come under fire for buying from foreign suppliers who force employees to work in dangerous conditions or pay less than a living wage. Giant pharmaceutical companies, for example, that refuse to allow the development of low-cost versions of their patented drugs to combat epidemics in Africa of diseases such as AIDS, malaria, or tuberculosis have been accused of ignoring the global reach of corporate responsibility. Marketers must also take into account the long-term effects of their decisions and the well-being of future generations. Manufacturing processes that damage the environment or that use up natural energy resources are easy targets for criticism.

Marketers can use several methods to help their companies behave in socially responsible ways. Chapter 1 discussed cause marketing as one channel through which companies can promote social causes—and at the same time benefit by linking their people and products to worthy undertakings. Socially responsible marketing involves campaigns that encourage people to adopt socially beneficial behaviours, whether they be safe driving, eating more nutritious food, or improving the working conditions of people half a world away. And organizations that sponsor socially responsible programs not only help society but also develop goodwill for an organization, which could help the bottom line in the long run.

MARKETING AND ECOLOGY

Ecology—the relationship between organisms and their natural environments—has become a driving force in influencing the ways in which businesses operate. Many industry and government leaders rank the protection of the environment as the biggest challenge facing today's corporations. Environmental issues such as water pollution, waste disposal, acid rain, depletion of the ozone layer, and global warming affect everyone. They influence all areas of marketing decision making, including product planning and public relations, spanning such topics as planned obsolescence, pollution control, recycling waste materials, and resource conservation.

In creating new-product offerings that respond to consumer demands for convenience by offering extremely short-lived products, such as disposable diapers, ballpoint pens, razors, and cameras, marketers occasionally find themselves accused of intentionally offering products with limited durability—in other words, of practicing **planned obsolescence**. In addition to convenience-oriented items, other products become obsolete when rapid changes in technology create superior alternatives. In the computer industry, upgrades that make products obsolete are the name of the game. The Saskatchewan Waste Electronic Equipment Program (SWEEP) has been launched in response to the mounting piles of obsolete electronic equipment in that province. Director of operations Ken Homenick estimates that Saskatchewan's 71 SARCAN Recycling locations will recycle 1050 tonnes of electronic hardware waste every year. SWEEP was established by Electronic Products Stewardship Canada (EPSC), a not-for-profit organization founded by 16 leading electronics manufacturers. The organization works with government to establish standardized legislation that will make it easier for its members to meet legal requirements for "end-of-life" electronic products throughout Canada.[48]

Public concern about pollution of such natural resources as water and air affects some industries, such as pharmaceuticals or heavy-goods manufacturing, more than others. Still, the marketing system annually generates billions of tons of packaging materials such as glass, metal, paper, and plastics that add to the world's growing piles of trash and waste. Recycling such materials is another important aspect of ecology. HP uses recycled plastic from HP inkjet cartridges to make new inkjet cartridges. Since it patented the technology to recycle Laserjet and inkjet cartridges, it has recycled millions of pounds of used cartridges.[49] Recycling can benefit society by saving natural resources and energy as well as by alleviating a major factor in environmental pollution—waste disposal.

Marketoid

It is estimated that 1 million plastic bags are handed out worldwide every minute.

green marketing
Production, promotion, and reclamation of environmentally sensitive products.

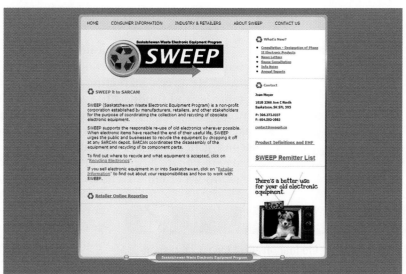

COURTESY OF SWEEP

Saskatchewan Waste Electronic Equipment Program (SWEEP) was established by manufacturers, retailers, and other stakeholders for the purpose of coordinating the collection and recycling of obsolete electronic equipment.

Go Green

When It's Time to Go, Go Green

Joel Makower, founder of Greenbiz.com, says, "Green has gone from a movement to a market." Canadian businesses are beginning to recognize that there is a market for green products. A survey of 1000 Canadians by *Marketing* and Ipsos Reid found that 57 percent of respondents were willing to spend more for environmentally friendly products. Still, Canadians are slow to accept the idea of going green when it's finally time to go, however. The concept of going green—natural burial—started in the United Kingdom in 1993 and there are now approximately two dozen natural burial sites there. In the United States, there are 10 sites, but more are under development.

In Canada, Royal Oak Burial Park in Victoria, British Columbia, is scheduled to open what it hopes will be Canada's first natural burial site. One-third of an acre—called the Woodlands—will be initially dedicated to natural burials, but there are plans for future expansion. There are some rules for those who wish to have a natural burial here:

- Remains may not be embalmed.
- Remains must be in a biodegradable shroud, container, or casket.
- Families may plant indigenous plants and trees on the gravesite.
- Individual markers will be replaced by a common memorial cairn—with the names inscribed on it—at the entrance to the site.

The Guelph, Ontario-based Natural Burial Co-operative was incorporated in 2006 and is currently in negotiations to secure a natural burial site northwest of Toronto. The company plans to open its first site in early 2009. President Mike Salisbury hopes to follow the U.S. model: a burial ground and a conservation area. He says, "Green burial doesn't necessarily mean people want to bury their loved ones more cheaply; they want meaningful memorials."

If there is a societal shift to natural burials, it won't be because of price. Among the new products on the market are eco-friendly caskets. Imperial Evergreen Casket of Burnaby, British Columbia, manufactures a biodegradable basket-weave casket in a variety of colours, some adorned with wildflowers. Northern Caskets of Ontario manufactures its EnviroCasket, made from sustainably harvested poplar wood and containing no dyes, chemicals, varnishes or stains, or metal hinges in its construction. Both products are competitively priced with more traditional caskets.

Sources: Rebecca Harris, "Turning Green," *Marketing*, June 11, 2007, pp. 18–20, 24, 29–31; Barbara Righton, "Going Most Gently into the Night," *Maclean's*, February 18, 2008, p. 73; "Natural Burial at Royal Oak Burial Park," available http://www.robp.ca/burial.shtml, accessed June 22, 2008; Graeme Stemp-Morlock, "Green Burial Options are Here," *Green Living Magazine*, available http://www.naturalburial.coop/2008/05/29/green-burial-options-are-here/#more-487, accessed June 22, 2008; Natural Burial Co-operative website, http://www.naturalburial.coop, accessed June 22, 2008.

Marketoid

Nearly half of Canada's 2462 farms that reported growing certified organic field crops and hay in 2006 were in Saskatchewan.

Many companies respond to consumers' growing concern about ecological issues through **green marketing**—production, promotion, and reclamation of environmentally sensitive products. In the green marketing revolution of the early 1990s, marketers were quick to tie their companies and products to ecological themes. Consumers have responded by purchasing more and more of these goods, providing profits and opportunities for growth to the companies that make and sell them. Auto manufacturers such as Toyota and Honda are already making second-generation hybrid autos. Starbucks offers its own Ethos bottled water, along with a pledge to donate 5 cents from every bottle toward a $10-million program that will help improve drinking-water conditions around the world. Wal-Mart has built a 206 000-square-foot store that is designed to be sustainable. General Electric has announced a corporate initiative called Ecomagination, backed by a $1.5-billion yearly investment in research on cleaner technologies. GE has also launched an ad campaign that highlights the environmental benefits of specific products and services.[50]

One area of green marketing that is growing increasingly popular is the organic food industry. In 2006, certified organic products accounted for less than 1 percent of the $46.5 billion that Canadians spent in national grocery stores. However, much of Canada's organic produce is exported.[51]

assessment check 8

8.1 Identify the four levels of the social responsibility pyramid.

8.2 What are the benefits of green marketing?

Strategic Implications

ARKETING decisions that businesses make are influenced by changes in the competitive, political-legal, economic, technological, and social-cultural environments. Marketing ethics and social responsibility will continue to play important roles in business transactions in your hometown and around the globe.

As the Internet and the rapid changes in technology that it represents are fully absorbed into the competitive environment, competition will become even more intense than it is today. Much of the competition will result from innovations in technology and scientific discoveries. Business in the future will be propelled by information technologies, but sustained by creative thinking and the willingness of marketers to meet challenges. Marketers will face new regulations as the political and legal environment responds to changes in Canada and abroad. As the population ages and the social-cultural environment evolves, marketers will seek to meet the demands for new goods and services for consumers, such as increased health care. As always, they will try to anticipate and make the most of every opportunity afforded by the business cycle.

Ethics and social responsibility must underlie everything that marketers do in the 21st century—those who find ways to "do well by doing good" will succeed. ◆◆◆

REVIEW OF CHAPTER OBJECTIVES

① Identify the five components of the marketing environment.

The five components of the marketing environment are (1) *the competitive environment*—the interactive process that occurs in the marketplace as competing organizations seek to satisfy markets; (2) *the political-legal environment*—the laws and interpretations of laws that require firms to operate under competitive conditions and to protect consumer rights; (3) *the economic environment*—environmental factors resulting from business fluctuations and resulting variations in inflation rates and employment levels; (4) *the technological environment*—applications to marketing of knowledge based on discoveries in science, inventions, and innovations; and (5) *the social-cultural environment*—the component of the marketing environment consisting of the relationship between the marketer and society and its culture.

② Explain the types of competition marketers face and the steps necessary for developing a competitive strategy.

Three types of competition exist: (1) direct competition among marketers of similar products; (2) competition among goods or services that can be substituted for one another; and (3) competition among all organizations that vie for the consumer's purchasing power. To develop a competitive strategy, marketers must answer the following questions: (1) Should we compete? The answer depends on the firm's available resources and objectives as well as its expected profit potential. (2) If so, in what markets should we compete? This question requires marketers to make product, pricing, distribution, and promotional decisions that give their firm a competitive advantage. (3) How should we compete? This question requires marketers to make the technical decisions involved in setting a comprehensive marketing strategy.

③ Describe how marketing activities are regulated and how marketers can influence the political-legal environment.

Marketing activities are influenced by federal, provincial and territorial, and municipal laws that require firms to operate under competitive conditions and to protect consumer rights. The Competition Act, administered by Industry Canada, is the most comprehensive legislation in Canada. Government regulatory agencies can provide advice and assistance to Canadian businesses or, like the National Energy Board, can have responsibility to regulate specific industries. Public and private consumer interest groups and industry self-regulatory groups also affect marketing activities. Marketers can seek to influence public opinion and legislative actions through advertising, political action committees, and political lobbying.

④ Outline the economic factors that affect marketing decisions and consumer buying power.

The primary economic factors are (1) the stage in the business cycle, (2) inflation and deflation, (3) unemployment, (4) income, and (5) resource availability. All are vitally important to marketers because of their effects on consumers' willingness to buy and consumers' perceptions regarding changes in the marketing mix variables.

⑤ Discuss the impact of the technological environment on a firm's marketing activities.

The technological environment consists of applications to marketing of knowledge based on discoveries in science, inventions, and innovations. This knowledge can provide marketing opportunities. It results in new products and improves existing ones, and it is a frequent source of price reductions through new production methods or materials. Technological applications also pose a threat because they can make existing products obsolete overnight. The technological environment demands that marketers continually adapt to change, since its scope of influence reaches into consumers' lifestyles, competitors' products, and industrial users' demands.

⑥ Explain how the social-cultural environment influences marketing.

The social-cultural environment is the relationship between marketing, society, and culture. To remain competitive, marketers must be sensitive to society's demographic shifts and changing values, which affect consumers' reactions to different products and marketing practices. Marketers must consider the increasing importance of cultural diversity, both in Canada and abroad. Changing societal values have led to consumerism. Consumerism is the social force within the environment designed to aid and protect the consumer by exerting legal, moral, and economic pressures on business. Consumer rights include the following: (1) the right to choose freely, (2) the right to be informed, (3) the right to be heard, and (4) the right to be safe.

⑦ Describe the ethical issues in marketing.

Marketing ethics encompass the marketer's standards of conduct and moral values. Each element of the marketing mix raises its own set of ethical questions. Ethics in product strategy may involve quality and safety, packaging and labelling, and pollution. Ethics in distribution may involve territorial decisions. In promotion, ethical issues include honesty in advertising and promotion to children. Pricing may raise questions about price fixing and discrimination, price increases, and deceptive pricing.

⑧ Identify the four levels of the social responsibility pyramid.

The four dimensions of social responsibility are (1) *economic*—to be profitable, the foundation upon which the other three levels of the pyramid rest; (2) *legal*—to obey the law, society's codification of right and wrong; (3) *ethical*—to do what is right, just, and fair and to avoid wrongdoing; (4) *philanthropic*—to be a good corporate citizen, contributing to the community and improving quality of life.

 assessment check answers

1.1 Define environmental scanning.

Environmental scanning is the process of collecting information about the external marketing environment to identify and interpret potential trends.

1.2 How does environmental scanning contribute to environmental management?

Environmental scanning contributes to environmental management by providing current information about the five different environments so marketers can predict and influence changes.

2.1 Distinguish between direct and indirect competition and give an example of each.

Direct competition occurs among marketers of similar products, such as auto manufacturers or gas stations. Indirect competition involves products that are easily substituted. Pizza could compete with fried chicken or tacos. A trip to Canada's Wonderland could compete with a trip to a Toronto Blue Jays game.

2.2 What is time-based competition?

Time-based competition is the strategy of developing and distributing goods and services more quickly than competitors.

3.1   What are the purposes of the Competition Act?

The purposes of the Competition Act are to foster competition and protect consumers, both of which are necessary to have a healthy marketplace.

3.2   Name a self-regulatory group and describe its mission.

Advertising Standards Canada is the advertising industry's self-regulatory body. Its mission is to ensure the integrity and viability of advertising in Canada.

4.1   Identify and describe briefly the four stages of the business cycle.

The four stages of the business cycle are prosperity, recession, depression, and recovery.

4.2   Explain how inflation and income affect consumer buying decisions.

Inflation devalues money and therefore may restrict some purchasing, particularly goods and services that are not considered necessary. Income also influences consumer buying power—the more discretionary income a household has, the more goods and services can be purchased.

5.1   What are some of the consumer benefits of technology?

Technology can lead to new or improved goods and services, offer better customer service, and reduce prices. It can also address social concerns.

5.2   Why must marketers monitor the technological environment?

Marketers need to monitor the technological environment in order to stay current with—and possibly ahead of—competitors. If they don't, they may wind up with obsolete offerings.

6.1   Define consumerism.

Consumerism is a social force within the environment that aids and protects the buyer by exerting legal, moral, and economic pressures on business.

6.2   Identify the four consumer rights.

The four consumer rights are as follows: the right to choose freely, the right to be informed, the right to be heard, and the right to be safe.

7.1   Define marketing ethics.

Marketing ethics refers to the marketer's standards of conduct and moral values.

7.2   Identify the five areas in which ethics can be a problem.

The five areas of ethical concern for marketers are marketing research, product strategy, distribution, promotion, and pricing.

8.1   Identify the four levels of the social responsibility pyramid.

The four levels of social responsibility are economic, legal, ethical, and philanthropic.

8.2   What are the benefits of green marketing?

Green marketing, which responds to consumers' growing concerns about ecological issues, offers consumers high-quality products without health risks or damage to the environment. Marketers who engage in green marketing may find themselves in a booming industry such as organic foods.

MARKETING TERMS YOU NEED TO KNOW

These terms are printed in red in the text. They are defined in the margins of the chapter and in the Glossary that begins on p. G-1. Other important terms are printed in bold black type in the chapter but not included in this list. Their definitions can be found in the Glossary.

environmental scanning 90	Competition Act 96	consumerism 104
environmental management 91	economic environment 98	consumer rights 105
competitive environment 91	demarketing 100	marketing ethics 106
time-based competition 94	technological environment 102	social responsibility 111
political-legal environment 95	social-cultural environment 104	green marketing 113

ASSURANCE OF LEARNING REVIEW

1. Why is environmental scanning an important activity for marketers?
2. What are the three different types of competition? Give an example of each.
3. What are the three questions marketers must ask before deciding on a competitive strategy?
4. What is the purpose of the Competition Act? The Canadian Radio-television and Telecommunications Commission (CRTC)?
5. Describe an industry or firm that you think might be able to weather an economic downturn and explain why.
6. Why do marketers monitor the technological environment?
7. How might marketers make the most of shifts in the social–cultural environment?
8. Describe the importance of consumer rights in today's marketing activities.
9. Why is it worthwhile for a firm to create an ethics program?
10. How can social responsibility benefit a firm as well as the society in which it operates?

PROJECTS AND TEAMWORK EXERCISES

1. With a classmate, choose two firms that compete directly with each other. Select two of the following or choose your own. Then develop a competitive strategy for your firm while your partner develops a strategy for his or hers. Present the two strategies to the class. How are they similar? How are they different?
   a. Home Depot and Rona or Lowe's
   b. Apple and Dell
   c. Paramount Canada's Wonderland and Six Flags La Ronde or Vancouver's Playland
   d. VISA and MasterCard
   e. Honda and Ford
   f. Tim Hortons and Starbucks

2. Track your own consumer purchasing decisions as they relate to your income. Compare your decisions during the academic year and the summer. Do you have a summer job that increases your income? How does that affect your decisions?

3. Canada Post essentially enjoys a monopoly on the delivery of most mail. With a classmate, develop a strategy for a business that would compete with Canada Post in areas that firms such as Purolator, UPS, FedEx, and DHL do not already address.

4. Choose one of the following products. Working in pairs or small groups, present arguments for and against having Canada impose certain regulations on the advertising of your product. (Note that some products already do have regulations—you can argue for or against them.)
   a. alcoholic beverages
   b. tobacco
   c. casinos
   d. prescription medications

5. With a classmate, research one of the recent large cases involving unethical and illegal activities by executives for companies such as Enron, Tyco, MCI, Nortel Networks, Martha Stewart Living Omnimedia, and Hollinger International. Describe the charges made against these executives and the outcome. Do you think they were fairly charged and punished? Why or why not?

CRITICAL THINKING EXERCISES

1. Environmental scanning is important for any business wanting to identify important trends that may affect its future marketing actions. Identify five current trends that are predicted to have a major influence on Canadian businesses in the next decade. Explain how or if each of these trends will affect you personally as a consumer.

2. Suppose you and a friend want to start a company that markets frozen fish dinners. What are some of the questions about the competitive environment that you would like to have answered before you begin production? How will you determine whom your customers are likely to be? How will you reach them?

3. The social-cultural environment can have a strong influence on the decisions marketers must make. In recent years, animal rights groups have targeted the manufacture and sale of foie gras, a European food delicacy made from goose and duck liver. Activists cite the cruel treatment of these birds, while chefs and restaurant owners claim otherwise. Animal rights groups are pressuring restaurants to stop serving foie gras. Others argue that consumers should be allowed a choice. What aspects of the social-cultural environment are affecting the marketing of foie gras? Which of the other components of the marketing environment may come into play, and how?

4. Approximately 400 million rebates—worth about $6 billion—are offered to Canadian and U.S. consumers by marketers every year. But do consumers like them? Often rebates require more effort than a consumer is willing to make to receive the cash back. Critics of the promotional effort say that marketers know this—and are banking on consumers' not redeeming them. One expert estimates that this translates to about $2 billion of extra income in the pockets of retailers and manufacturers.[52] Do you think rebate programs are ethical? Why or why not?

5. The disposal of nuclear waste has been an ongoing public safety issue, one with which marketers who work for nuclear power companies must deal. Most of Canada's nuclear waste is stored in Ontario. Smaller amounts exist in Quebec and New Brunswick.[53] The Ontario government has been trying to negotiate nuclear storage at several Ontario towns but has met considerable resistance. Supporters argue that this is important to building Ontario's nuclear power capacity, while critics are skeptical of its safety and usefulness. As a marketer, how would you approach this issue?

ETHICS EXERCISE

Some retail firms protect their inventory against theft by locking their premises after hours even though maintenance and other workers are inside the stores working all night. Employees have charged that they are forbidden to leave the premises during work hours and that during an emergency, such as illness or injury, precious time is lost waiting for a manager to arrive who is authorized to unlock the doors. Although workers could open an emergency exit, in some cases they claim that they will be fired for doing so.

Employers assert that managers with keys are on the premises (or minutes away) and that locking employees in ensures their own safety as well as cutting down on costly "shrinkage."

1. Under what circumstances, if any, do you think locking employees in at night is appropriate?
2. If you feel this practice is appropriate, what safeguards do you think should be put into effect? What responsibilities do employers and employees have in such circumstances?

INTERNET EXERCISES

1. **Developing a competitive strategy.** Review the material in the chapter on how companies develop a competitive strategy, including the key questions that must be answered.
   a. Visit the website of a company such as Procter & Gamble (http://www.pg.com) or Colgate (http://www.colgate.com). Pick one of the company's products and analyze how the firm answered each of the key questions when it developed a competitive strategy for the product you selected.
   b. Gatorade (http://www.gatorade.com) and Powerade (http://www.powerade.com) are the two leading brands in the growing market for sports drinks. Gatorade is a Pepsi brand and Powerade is a Coke brand. Visit each product's website and compare and contrast the competitive strategies used by both companies to build their respective brands.
   c. Companies discontinue products from time to time. Using Google or another search engine, identify a product that has recently been discontinued. Research the product and the company that produced it, and write a brief report summarizing the reasons behind the decision.

2. **Ethics and social responsibility.** Many companies use the Web to highlight their ethical standards and social responsibility. Visit each of the following websites and prepare a brief summary of what you found.
   a. Green marketing and environmentalism: Ford Motor Company (http://www.ford.com/innovation/environmentally-friendly)
   b. Coffee producers and fair trade: Starbucks (http://www.starbucks.com/aboutus/default.asp)
   c. Ethical standards and credo: Johnson & Johnson (http://www.jnj.com/our_company/our_credo/index.htm)

Note: Internet web addresses change frequently. If you don't find the exact sites listed, you may need to access the organization's or company's home page and search from there or use a search engine such as Google.

ETHICS QUIZ ANSWERS

Here is how others have responded to the quiz on page 109.

1. 34% said personal e-mail on company computers is wrong.
2. 37% said using office equipment for schoolwork is wrong.
3. 49% said playing computer games at work is wrong.
4. 54% said Internet shopping at work is wrong.
5. 61% said it is unethical to blame your error on technology.
6. 87% said it's unethical to visit pornographic sites at work.
7. 33% said $25 is the amount at which a gift from a supplier or client becomes troubling, while 33% said $50, and 33% said $100.
8. 35% said a $50 gift to the boss is unacceptable.
9. 12% said a $50 gift from the boss is unacceptable.
10. 70% said it's unacceptable to take the $200 football tickets.
11. 70% said it's unacceptable to take the $120 theatre tickets.
12. 35% said it's unacceptable to take the $100 food basket.
13. 45% said it's unacceptable to take the $25 gift certificate.
14. 40% said it's unacceptable to take the $75 raffle prize.
15. 11% reported they lied about sick days.
16. 4% reported they have taken credit for the work or ideas of others.

Case 3.1

General Motors: Here Today. Where Tomorrow?

Few people were surprised when it was announced in 2007 that Toyota had passed General Motors (GM) as the world leader in automobile market share. Toyota had been creeping toward first place for years. In Canada, however, GM still has the lead. But, following a major shift in consumer preferences in early 2008, many people question how long it will be before Toyota becomes Canada's market share leader as well.

At least some of GM's current problems can be traced back to 2003 when it decided to abandon its EV1 experimental electric car. GM had leased a small number of EV1 cars to select customers, but then decided to withdraw them and discontinue its development. At that time, both Toyota and Honda were offering gas-electric hybrid cars. In 2007, GM announced it would again begin to develop an electric car—the Chevrolet Volt—for introduction in 2010. While this in itself will provide considerable challenge and will cost billions of dollars, GM needs to improve its technology—as do all competing car manufacturers—to meet greatly improved fuel economy standards that will come into place in 2017.

How are competitors preparing for the future—Toyota already sells six hybrid models in North America and plans to introduce a new generation hybrid in 2010. It is also planning to lease a limited number of electric cars by then also. Honda—which already offers among the best fuel economy in the world—is developing more hybrids as well, but it also plans to introduce diesel engines in its larger models. Ford is planning to introduce two new hybrid models and is continuing to promote its Eco Boost engines. Nissan has already introduced the Toyota hybrid system in its Altima and plans to have its own hybrid system by 2010. It also plans to offer electric cars similar to GM's technology.

While there may be several technologies that ultimately are introduced, there is certainly an advantage to developing an improved technology early. Consulting firm 2953 Analytics, for example, suggests that Toyota now has its cost down to $4000 for each hybrid system. GM vice chairman Bob Lutz estimates that GM will be fortunate if it can get its cost per vehicle down to $10 000 by 2010.

Car cost will be an important criterion in future car purchases. Much of the change in consumer preference now has been driven by rapidly rising fuel prices in Canada. May 2008 was a very volatile month in the Canadian automotive market. Total sales were down marginally from the same month in the previous year, but there was a large shift among both manufacturers and vehicle types. GM truck sales dropped 32.9 percent to 16 011 units while Toyota truck sales increased by 14.4 percent to 6776 units. GM car sales dropped 5.8 percent to 20 266 units while Toyota car sales—not including Lexus—increased 15.8 percent to 19 888 units.

The largest U.S. truck dealership noted the change in U.S. consumer preference. It had considerable success selling GM's Silverado pickup in the past, but by May 2008, even at discounts one-third off the sticker price, customers were walking away. Ken Thompson, manager of fleet sales, describes the problem as "pump paralysis," as the cost for a fill-up exceeds $100. Industry analyst John Casesa says that pickups and larger SUVs have been generating nearly all of the industries' operating income. He says, "For the last 20 years, pickups and sport utilities have more than made up for losses on all of Detroit's other vehicles." GM chief executive officer Rick Wagoner describes the consumer shift as "a structural change, not just a cyclical change."

How does the current GM situation affect Canada? With almost no warning, GM announced in June 2008 that it would be closing its truck plant in Oshawa, Ontario, putting 2500 people out of work. While many Canadians are upset, David Cole, who heads the Center for Automotive Research, says it should have been very predictable. The U.S. housing crisis and increasing gas prices are only part of the story. The increase in the value of the Canadian dollar has also wiped out Canada's advantage in vehicle manufacturing.

GM's decision may be unpopular in Canada, but the company has many tough decisions that will determine its future success or failure. Here today. Where tomorrow?

Questions for Critical Thinking

1. Which of the five forces in marketing's external environment—competitive, political-legal, economic, technological, and social-cultural—has contributed to GM's current situation?
2. What are the advantages and disadvantages of being the first mover in the "green" car market? Of being the second mover?

Sources: Greg Keenan, John Partridge, and Karen Howlett, "Truck Plant Cuts Could Force GM to Repay Government Incentives," globeandmail.com, http://www.globeandmail.com, accessed June 3, 2008; Greg Keenan, "How a Stunning Sales Drop Changed It All," globeandmail.com, http://www.globeandmail.com, accessed June 5, 2008; "GM Canada Sales Plunge 20%," The Canadian Press, http://www.globeandmail.com, accessed June 3, 2008; Doron Levin, "As Pickups Gather Dust, An Industry Scrambles," Bloomberg News, http://www.globeandmail.com, accessed June 5, 2008; David Welch, "GM: Live Green or Die," *Business Week*, May 26, 2008, pp. 36–41.

Case 3.2

iTunes and the Future of Music

By any measure, Apple dominates the world of legal music downloads. Its iTunes Music Store, pumped by the company's sales of more than 42 million iPod players, has grown in just a few years to account for 83 percent of the downloadable music sold on the Internet. Selling songs for 99 cents at a rate of 3 million a day—or 1 billion a year—the iTunes operation just breaks even financially, after royalties and operating costs are taken out. But iTunes and the iPod go hand in hand, and the highly profitable little iPod now accounts for half of Apple's revenues. As one industry observer said of iTunes, the iPod, and Apple's proprietary music software, "It's really very difficult to separate any of those elements" in accounting for their market power.

But there's room for competition in the $13-billion worldwide retail music business, and competitors won't be the only problem iTunes faces in the near future. Music piracy is still a threat, and Apple has used the availability of free (though illegal) downloads to argue against variable pricing in its recent contract renewal negotiations with the four biggest recording companies—Sony BMG, Universal, Warner Music, and EMI. "Music labels would much rather have variable prices, so they can charge more for hits and perhaps less for older tracks," said an industry expert. "Apple likes the $0.99 price because it is simple, uniform, not too high to discourage buyers, and very easy to administer and merchandise." In addition, as CEO Steve Jobs told a press conference, the price for legal downloading must compete with the free cost of illegal networks. Apple won its point and will continue to sell songs for 99 cents.

So will Microsoft. Microsoft is offering an online music service, in partnership with MTV, to compete directly against iTunes with 2 million songs, compared with iTunes's 3 million. For a subscription fee of about $10 a month, it also offers access to 130 radio stations of all genres and 500 different playlists. Called URGE, the new service uses Microsoft's Media Player software and comes with a 14-day free trial.

Another challenge to iTunes's dominance may come from Samsung's new Helix, a tiny radio and music player that can pick up XM Satellite Radio's 70 commercial-free stations and play up to 750 downloaded songs. Users can store songs they hear on the radio by simply pressing Record to capture the track from the beginning for instant music portability—no computer required.

And legal challenges looming from France may spread internationally. Legislation is working its way through the French National Assembly to compel iTunes and other online music stores with proprietary music management software to open their code to others. If passed, the law will support a push to standardize formats across the industry so that songs from any vendor could be played on any digital player. An iTunes download, say, could then be used on the Linux operating system, just as any music CD can play on any CD device. Savvy users of music downloads can already work around the compatibility problem, and with Apple's market domination, it hasn't hampered many music fans. But some observers think that whatever the outcome in France, other countries will follow France's example. Still, they'll have to get there before the hackers do.

Questions for Critical Thinking

1. Apple has said that if the French legislation passes, it will consider giving up the French share of its business by pulling iTunes from the French market. Could such a strategy succeed? Do you think it would be wise from a marketing standpoint? Why or why not?

2. iTunes now carries music videos and short films for downloading, as well as hit TV shows including *24, Prison Break,* and *SpongeBob SquarePants.* What type of marketing strategy is behind these additions to the iTunes library? How successful do you think it will be?

Sources: David Pogue, "XM Radio Fans Can Record It if They Hear It," *The New York Times,* May 25, 2006, http://www.nytimes.com; Matthieu Demeestere, "Microsoft, MTV Challenge Apple iTunes," Agence-France Presse, May 17, 2006, http://www.afp.com; Brian Holmes, "Fox Shows to Debut on iTunes," *Earth Times,* May 10, 2006, http://www.earthtimes.org; Walaika K. Haskins, "Apple Wins iTunes Price Battle," Newsfactor Network, May 2, 2006, http://www.newsfactor.com; Rob Pegoraro, "France Takes a Shot at iTunes," *Washington Post,* March 26, 2006, http://www.washingtonpost.com; Doreen Carvajal, "Paris Acts to Open up Online Sales of Music," *International Herald Tribune,* March 22, 2006, http://www.iht.com; Matthew Yi, "One Billion Songs Sold on iTunes in 3 Years," *San Francisco Chronicle,* February 24, 2006, http://www.sfgate.com; Mike Musgrove, "Big Hit of the Holidays: 14 Million iPods Sold," *Washington Post,* January 11, 2006, http://www.washingtonpost.com.

Video Case 3.3

Organic Valley Farms: Producing Food That's Good for People and the Earth

The written case on Organic Valley Farms appears on page VC-4. The recently filmed Organic Valley Farms video is designed to expand and highlight the concepts in this chapter and the concepts and questions covered in the written video case.

STÉFAN DANIS

COURTESY OF STÉFAN DANIS

Over my dead body will I under-whelm a customer.

Talking About Marketing Careers

Here are highlights of our interview with Stéfan Danis, CEO and Chief Talent Officer at Mandrake Executive Search. For the complete video interview and transcript, go to http://www.contemporarymarketing2.nelson.com

Q3: What do you enjoy most about your job?
SD: The opportunity to connect with people and play an important consultative role with them. The job facilitates becoming the career mentor to executives. I can change the course of their life by moving them to jobs better aligned with their strengths and values and interests. And I have a chance to alter the course of an organization by bringing in an executive who can lead them to a new level.

I also enjoy the fact that you can build a fairly pure personal brand for yourself, and your reputation can be monetized as a result. Our firm has a brand reputation, but so do all the individuals who work here. You do good work; soon enough, everyone wants a piece of you. You can then make entrepreneurial choices about what to work on, for whom, when, at what price, [choices that] are rarely afforded to corporate executives. Although I exist at work to serve customers, I choose how I deliver it and at the end of the day, I feel 100 percent in control over my work destiny.

Q4: What are some things that keep you motivated and focused?
SD: Over my dead body will I under-whelm a customer.

I have built my personal brand and will do what I have to do to get the job done. I have had a hand in building a good-sized enterprise and my paranoia is that it could disappear tomorrow, so I worry enough to be very focused. Earning good praise from customers is a great motivator for me; I aim to delight clients; I'm a suck for good feedback.

Q7: Any tips or advice you can give us about time management?
SD: You have total control over your choices if you do the following.

1. Determine what your time is worth and outsource the stuff that someone else can do cheaper than you.
2. Determine what your values are and make promises to yourself that align with them. I've broken down all the key stakeholders in my life into 16 categories. For example, I want to have my customers say I am invaluable to them. This means I have to be visible and add value to them. This translates into a number of projects or initiatives I will do personally to achieve that status with all of them. This equals a certain number of hours. Put the hours in the calendar before the year starts. Then I want my two young daughters to say I am devoted, caring, loving, inspiring, and fun. This translates into projects and initiatives and promises, which convert into hours. I have my whole life mapped out with respect to the commitments I make to friends, my community, my health, my parents, etc.

If you only do what you are committed to, in time the fluff will disappear, and the activities will yield higher ROT (Return on Time).

Q8: What is the biggest misconception of individuals working within the field of marketing?
SD: Time and time again people get surprised in life. More than 50 percent of the individuals I meet who are terminated never saw it coming. Same with customer management; many surveys are sent, but few direct questions are asked of the customer. Marketers assume too much and at times don't practise listening. In a world where there are consumers and customers, customers aren't partnered with in the way they should be, and marketers put too much emphasis on the consumer, ahead of the customer.

Q12: What are the most important skills a graduate should possess?

SD: The focus today is more about EQ, being a self-starter, commitment, and a positive attitude. Work provides many opportunities to work in teams; one needs collaborative skills like communication and leadership. For the projects one self-manages, industriousness and being a self-starter are key as there is now so little training and companies are not great at on-boarding—you need to find your own way and cannot wait for input. Finally, commitment is my last favourite ingredient; having drive and stamina is the difference between B and A players of equal skill.

Q13: What advice would you give to a new grad?

SD: Be clear on what your values are and see if they align with the organization's. Intersect your skills with your interest, and confirm you can make money at it before you embark on a venture that will not maximize your financial opportunity.

Laughter's Part of the Plan

The Second City (SC) cultivates a unique relationship with its customer when its actors step on stage and confidently ask the audience for "a suggestion of anything at all." This bold request, which launches the actors into a series of hilarious improvisations, has been with the company since its beginning. On December 16, 1959, a group of University of Chicago students began performing sketch and improvisational comedy in a local coffee shop. Soon playing to sold-out crowds, The Second City found its name, identity, and first marketing move all in one place. Journalist A. J. Leibling had lambasted Chicago in a series of articles dubbing the town "The Second City" as he saw it subpar to cities such as New York and Paris. The cast of Second City proceeded to use headlines and cutting-edge comedy to reclaim the put-down and produce a nonstop series of compelling comedy revues. Training some of the greatest names in comedy, SC has developed a theatre company that has captured the hearts of the entertainment industry for decades.

The Second City has expanded from its theatrical roots in the "Windy City" to become a brand recognized throughout the world. On the television screen; on stages in Toronto, Detroit, Las Vegas, and Denver; at college assemblies, in corporate events; across the Internet; and even on the high seas with performances for Norwegian Cruise Lines, Second City operates a marketing plan as bold and captivating as its comedy.

Its long lists of famous alumni are a cherished legacy for the company. As actors such as John Candy, Mike Myers, and Tina Fey have ascended to stardom, they have become the faces of The Second City, leading the customer right to the very stage whence these stars first shone. The Second City has formulated its marketing concept around the talent and exposure of its comedic success stories throughout the last 50 years.

Kelly Leonard, Second City's vice president, recognizes how SC's continued growth has fostered its target market.

"We keep a presence in promoting ourselves to concierges, convention bureaus, and other visitor/tourist related groups. We are a strong tourist destination, so we like to keep our face in front of that market." Their product, their talent, has been seen around the world. So when tourists visit Chicago, a stop at The Second City makes for a fun night of entertainment. This is the most significant relationship for the company. It treats the audience to a night of sketch comedy based on current headlines and cultural issues, followed by a free set of improvisational comedy, the company's signature art form. The audience sits just feet away from Second City's product, its actors, who could jump into the lights of Hollywood in the blink of an eye.

The Second City performs new comedy revues around the globe to turn its recognizable brand into an accessible product. Its first international move was in 1973 when founder Bernie Sahlins and Andrew Alexander, the company's chief executive officer, launched a new SC theatre in Toronto. The stage has cultivated the talents of actors such as Martin Short, Rick Moranis, and Dan Aykroyd. It also provided Alexander with the cast of SC's first move onto the television medium, *Second City Television*. SCTV became the biggest promotional agent for the company to date and developed a relationship with SC's audience across international lines.

Today, The Second City keeps focused on its core initiative: to find, cultivate, and produce great comedic talent. For the consumer, this means ground-breaking talent from the early generations of Alan Arkin and Barbara Harris to more recent graduates such as Horatio Sanz and Steven Colbert.

The Second City has theatres in Chicago, Toronto, Detroit, Las Vegas, and Denver. Each of these operates with SC's concentration on current events and improvisation to orient shows around the creative tradition of the company. It also provides a convenient frame of reference for its consumer. To reach their respective audiences, the theatres employ distinctive marketing strategies. In Detroit, shows are tailored to the local audience. In Las Vegas, The Second City stands out as a comparatively less-glamorized venue in an overglamorized city; in Detroit and Denver, the two newer establishments, shows and promotion are building a core audience in the community; and in Chicago, the theatre supplements its flagship Mainstage with additional, more eclectic shows to re-attract the local crowd.

Understanding its tourist appeal and the tourist industry helped Second City's top management find a new market. VP Kelly Leonard noticed an opportunity with Norwegian Cruise Lines to produce Second City revues for vacationing travellers, a move that resulted in an exclusive deal with the company. Aboard ship, SC performs for a demographic similar to its tourist market. Consequently, Second City Theatricals distributes SC comedy around the globe and has an exciting strategic alliance with the cruise line.

Marketers at The Second City appreciate the fact that awareness of their company is spread primarily by word of mouth. The Second City works to enrich this initial relationship by expanding the mix of services offered by the company. Kelly Leonard attributes Second City's success in forming long-term relationships with consumers through "our expanded services . . . We offer workshops and shows in the high schools; we play the colleges; we provide corporate entertainment—basically, we're creating a series of in's that cross over a variety of ages and experiences. The more stuff that we can create that is pure to what we do, the better we are positioning ourselves for the future."

The Second City has always been an intensely creative business environment. Since it first began as a daring start-up theatre company, it has attracted innovators both on and off its stage. It has also attracted an audience wanting to think, interact, and, most of all, laugh about whatever it is that they've been thinking about and that suddenly became their "suggestion" for the night.

Questions

1. What is Second City's target market? What decisions has it made based on this knowledge?
2. How do you think Second City chooses where to put its theatres?
3. Explain the short- and long-term aspects of Second City's relationship with its customer.
4. How does The Second City vary its product to account for varying locations?

Part I CBC Video Case

CBC

Visit the website for Contemporary Marketing at http://www.contemporarymarketing2e.nelson.com to view the CBC video and video case summary for Part I.

UNDERSTANDING BUYERS AND MARKETS

chapter 4

Consumer Behaviour

CHAPTER OBJECTIVES

① Define *consumer behaviour* and describe the role it plays in marketing decisions.

② Describe the interpersonal determinants of consumer behaviour: cultural, social, and family influences.

③ Explain each of the personal determinants of consumer behaviour: needs and motives, perceptions, attitudes, learning, and self-concept theory.

④ Distinguish between high-involvement and low-involvement purchase decisions.

⑤ Outline the steps in the consumer decision process.

⑥ Differentiate among routinized response behaviour, limited problem solving, and extended problem solving by consumers.

WHO BUYS HYBRID CARS—AND WHY?

If you could buy a new car today, what would it be? Maybe you'd choose a pickup truck for power and durability. Or what about that sleek sports car? Or you might be practical—as long as you turn the ignition key and the car starts, you're happy. Have you ever thought about a hybrid? Many people today are.

Gas/electric hybrid vehicles are fuelled by a combination of gasoline and battery-powered electricity. As a result, they are more fuel efficient than gas-only vehicles, and they produce fewer emissions. But although a few years ago hybrids were considered the domain of quirky auto engineers and consumers whose primary concern was saving the planet, they are now increasingly cruising the streets and highways across the country. Consumers have stopped just looking and are driving them off the dealers' lots. And more and more auto manufacturers are paying attention.

Toyota and Honda were two of the first major auto manufacturers to put a hybrid model on the market. The Toyota Prius and Honda Civic hybrid have now been through several model years. Both companies are also producing hybrid versions of their most popular cars. Toyota offers a hybrid Highlander SUV and Camry, along with the luxury Lexus RX400h. Honda offers a hybrid Accord in addition to its Civic. As more consumers are taking the hybrids for a test-drive, other manufacturers have begun rolling out their own versions. Chevrolet has introduced a hybrid Malibu, and Ford a hybrid Fusion and Five Hundred.

But what about consumers who can't let go of the wheel of their SUV or pickup? Many drivers wouldn't consider downsizing to a sedan, no matter how much gas they might save. No need to worry—automakers haven't forgotten those consumers. Soon hybrid versions of the Chevy Silverado and Tahoe, the Saturn Vue, the GMC Sierra, and others will be rolling off the assembly line. Sweden's AB Volvo—one of the world's biggest truck manufacturers—has unveiled its own new technology for cutting fuel consumption in heavy vehicles. The company plans to launch hybrid vehicles powered by diesel engines backed by electric batteries charged with the energy released from the brakes.

Why are consumers gravitating toward hybrids? Reducing fuel consumption is one issue. Each gallon of gasoline *not* burned by a vehicle prevents the release of emissions that combine to create 7.5 kilograms of carbon dioxide in the atmosphere. But preventing pollution is not the whole story. With fluctuating—sometimes soaring—gas prices, cars and trucks that use less gas simply make sense. Critics argue that the high purchase price of many hybrid vehicles, which can run several thousand dollars above their gas-only counterparts, offset gasoline savings. But *Consumer Reports* recently reported that the Toyota Prius and Honda Civic Hybrid recovered their initial costs in the first five years or 120 000 kilometres of ownership, actually saving owners $300 to $400. Other models still lag in savings.

Finally, customer satisfaction is high for hybrids. Current owners typically score them well on surveys of reliability and performance. "These benefits add up to an inviting package for many car buyers who are willing to pay a premium for a hybrid," concludes *Consumer Reports*.[1]

---

connecting with customers

The car companies are connecting with customers by providing the types of vehicles their customers are asking for. This is evident by the increase in sales of hybrid cars and trucks, roughly doubling every year. Still, hybrids make up a small fraction of total car sales. But industry experts think the percentage of hybrid vehicles sold will grow rapidly in coming years.

Chapter Overview

WHY does your best friend drive five kilometres out of the way for Tim Hortons coffee—when the local coffee shop is much closer? Why do people prefer one brand of pop over another? The answers to these questions aren't obvious but they directly affect every aspect of the marketing strategy, from product development to pricing and promotion, and finding them is the goal of every marketer. Developing a marketing strategy requires an understanding of customer behaviour, the process by which consumers make purchase decisions. **Customer behaviour** includes both individual consumers who buy goods and services for their own use and organizational buyers who purchase business products.

A variety of influences affect both individuals buying items for themselves

customer behaviour Mental and physical activities that occur during selection and purchase of a product.

and personnel purchasing products for their firms. This chapter focuses on individual purchasing behaviour, which applies to all of us. **Consumer behaviour** is the process through which the ultimate buyer makes purchase decisions for everything from toothbrushes to autos to vacations. Chapter 5 will shift the focus to business buying decisions.

consumer behaviour Mental and physical activities of individuals who actually use the purchased goods and services.

The study of consumer behaviour builds on an understanding of human behaviour in general. In their efforts to understand why and how consumers make buying decisions, marketers borrow extensively from the sciences of psychology and sociology. The work of psychologist Kurt Lewin, for example, provides a useful classification scheme for influences on buying behaviour. Lewin's work determined that behaviour is a function of the interactions

① Define *consumer behaviour* and describe the role it plays marketing decisions.

of personal influences and pressures exerted by outside environmental forces.

Consumer behaviour is influenced by the interactions of interpersonal influences—such as culture, friends, classmates, co-workers, and relatives—and personal factors—such as attitudes, learning, and perception. In other words, inputs from others and an individual's psychological makeup affect his or her purchasing behaviour. Before looking at how consumers make purchase decisions, we first consider how both interpersonal and personal factors affect consumers. ◆◆◆

Marketoid

As of April 2007 the estimated population of Canada was 32,852,849; therefore there are 32,852,849 consumers in Canada or individuals who influence consumer purchases.

---

② Describe the interpersonal determinants of consumer behaviour: cultural, social, and family influence.

INTERPERSONAL DETERMINANTS OF CONSUMER BEHAVIOUR

You don't make purchase decisions in a vacuum. You might not be aware of it, but every buying decision you make is influenced by a variety of external and internal factors. Consumers often decide to buy goods and services based on what they believe others expect of them. They may want to project positive images to peers or to satisfy the unspoken desires of family members. Marketers recognize three broad categories of interpersonal influences on consumer behaviour: cultural, social, and family influences.

CULTURAL INFLUENCES

culture Values, beliefs, preferences, and tastes handed down from one generation to the next in a society.

Culture can be defined as the values, beliefs, preferences, and tastes handed down from one generation to the next. Culture is the broadest environmental determinant of consumer behaviour. Marketers need to understand its role in consumer decision making, both in Canada and abroad. They must also monitor trends in cultural values as well as recognize changes in these values.

figure 4.1

Integrated Model of the Consumer Decision Process

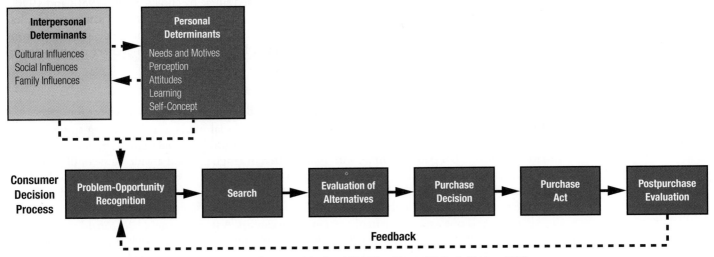

Source: Roger Blackwell, Paul W. Miniard, and James F. Engel, *Consumer Behaviour,* 10th Edition (Mason, OH: South-Western, 2004).

Marketing strategies and business practises that work in one country may be offensive or ineffective in another. Strategies may even have to be varied from one area of a country to another. Nowhere is that more true than in Canada, where the population continues to diversify at a rapid pace. As a result, companies like Wal-Mart are tailoring their marketing campaigns to different cultural groups. Wal-Mart's marketing strategy revolves around a theme called Store of the Community. This strategy includes having products on the shelves for different cultural groups, as well as hiring policies and communications that attract these groups. They even produce specific television ads aimed at the Italian, Portuguese, Cantonese, and South Asian communities that air on cultural stations in the appropriate language. The Canadian population is also moving rapidly away from the two original cultural groups; only 11 percent of Canadians identify themselves as of British ethnic origin and 9 percent claim a French background.[2]

assessment check 1

1.1   Why is the study of consumer behaviour important to marketers?

1.2   Describe the work of Kurt Lewin.

Core Values in Canadian Culture

Some cultural values change over time, but basic core values do not. **Core values** are underlying motivations that move society forward and are shaped by the people one grows up with. The core values of peace and order have been consistent for many years but other core values have changed. These changes have been confirmed by Michael Adams, president of the research company Environics, who has studied the social values of the Canadian population for over 20 years. His extensive work in studying changing social values has covered not only the Canadian population but how we compare to our U.S. neighbours.[3]

One needs only to look at the changing form of the family to see how slowly core values change. In the 1950s, the standard picture of the Canadian family was made up of a father, a mother who stayed at home to look after the

The importance of family is a core value in Canadian culture. This ad promotes family life with special family moments.

children, and children. A controversial marriage at that time might be one of mixed religious faiths. By the 1960s, interfaith marriages were no longer unusual, but the marital landscape was being changed by common-law marriages, divorce, and those who remained single by choice. By the 1980s and 1990s, the Canadian population accepted interracial marriages and relationships between same-sex couples. Even as today's population grows older and "family values"—those important beliefs passed on from one's relatives—appear to have increased in importance. It is unlikely we will ever see a return to the 1950s view of the family.[4]

International Perspective on Cultural Influences

Cultural differences are particularly important for international marketers. Marketing strategies that prove successful in one country often cannot extend to other international markets because of cultural variations. Europe is a good example, with many different languages and a wide range of lifestyles and product preferences. Even though the continent is becoming a single economic unit as a result of the expansion of the European Union and the widespread use of the euro as currency, cultural divisions continue to define various markets.

Packaging is one area where marketers must be careful. A few years ago, McDonald's announced that all 30 000 of its restaurants in 100 countries would feature the same packaging for its food and beverages. Wrappers would feature photos of real consumers enjoying themselves by playing sports, listening to music, or reading to children. Two years later, the firm dropped the idea, adopting instead localized packaging, including nutritional labels. Why did McDonald's do such a turnabout? People in different countries value different activities. They also want different information on package labels.[5]

Microcultures

Cultures are not homogeneous entities with universal values. Each culture includes numerous **microcultures**—groups with their own distinct modes of behaviour. Understanding the differences among microcultures can help marketers develop more effective marketing strategies.

Canada, like many nations, is composed of significant microcultures that differ by ethnicity, nationality, age, social class, rural versus urban location, and geographic distribution. There are many examples of our various microcultures. Canada's wealthy, who tend to live in established urban neighbourhoods, could be considered a microculture, but within that microculture could be found further microcultures. For example, the Quebec market has 15 different lifestyle types that have been identified as having significantly different product and activity preferences compared to the populations in other provinces. Another example of a microculture is Orthodox Jews, who purchase and consume only kosher foods. Understanding these and other differences among microcultures contributes to successful marketing of goods and services.[6]

Canada's racial mix continues to change. According to Statistics Canada, by 2017, roughly one in every five Canadians will belong to a group that classifies itself as a visible minority. This would be the highest proportion of the population ever and represents a remarkable increase from the 2001 census when only 13 percent of the population classified themselves in this group. Marketers need to be sensitive to these changes and to the differences in shopping patterns and buying habits among ethnic segments of the population. Businesses can no longer succeed by selling one-size-fits-all products; they must consider consumer needs, interests, and concerns when developing their marketing strategies.[7]

Other changes predicted for these microculture segments of the population will affect what products companies market and how they market them. For example, the composition of microculture segments is likely to change. By 2017, it is expected that the group identifying themselves as South Asian is likely to be as large as the Chinese group, making these the two largest ethnic groups in Canada. Blacks are predicted to remain as the third-largest group but the fastest-growing group will be made up of those who are of West Asian, Korean, and Arab heritage. The visible minority population is younger than the rest of the population and is predicted to remain so. Ontario and British Columbia will be home to most of these visible minorities, as is the case today, but they will represent an increasing percentage of the populations in these provinces.[8]

Marketing concepts may not always cross cultural boundaries without changes. For example, new immigrants may not be familiar with cents-off coupons and contests. Marketers may need to provide specific instructions when targeting such promotions to these groups.

Figure 4.2 shows the proportion of the Canadian population made up of minority groups. One group, the French Canadians, are more often viewed as one of Canada's two main cultural groups. Although no racial or ethnic microculture is entirely homogeneous, researchers have found that each of these ethnic segments has identifiable consumer behaviour profiles.

French-Canadian Consumers

From a marketing point of view, it doesn't make a difference whether you treat the French-Canadian market as a microculture or one of Canada's two main cultural groups. What does matter is that this group is very large and significantly different from the rest of Canada in many ways. However, like other cultural groups, the 6 million French-speaking inhabitants of Quebec and the pockets of French-speaking communities across the rest of Canada are not a homogeneous group. Quebec is the largest French-speaking area in North America but there are also about 600 000 English-speaking residents in the province and as many other nationalities in the province as there are in the rest of Canada.[9]

Almost half of the population of Quebec lives in Montreal, and 60 percent of those are French speaking. French Canadians are more likely to live in cities than in rural areas, with 80 percent of the population living in urban communities.[10]

The population of Quebec, like many areas of Canada, is getting older. Currently, Quebec ranks as one of the youngest populations, but a variety of factors, such as a drastic decrease in birth rates and increasing life expectancy, will give Quebec one of the oldest populations by the year 2031. One of the fastest-growing segments of the population is women 80 years of age and older.[11]

Consumer behaviour depends on psychological and social factors. Recently, Jacques Bouchard, founder of a Quebec advertising agency and the father of made-in-Quebec advertising, duplicated a study he did in the 1970s to determine what psychological and social factors were important to Quebecers. The results of his study indicate that while Quebecers are looking more and more like the rest of Canada, strong differences still exist in many areas, and there are lasting influences from the days when the differences were much greater. For example, the Roman Catholic Church has very strong roots in Quebec. In the past, the church was a key influence in family decisions and a centre for social activities. Today, 22 percent of Quebecers, more than any other region in Canada, state their belief in God has declined over the years. Quebec has moved from having a high birth rate to having one of the lowest birth rates in the world. What has not changed is their love for children—78 percent of Quebecers said having a child is an experience every woman should have as opposed to 58 percent for the rest of Canada. Quebecers are planners, which is why they are more likely to prepare a shopping list than other Canadians. They top the rest of Canada in their use of perfumes, bath products, and other beauty products. They also have the highest consumption rates per capita for beer and wine. With all the changes occurring in their lives, 66 percent of Quebecers feel the need to sustain and demonstrate their traditions; this compares with only 47 percent for the rest of Canada.[12]

Marketing to the Quebec population has moved through several distinct phases and seems to be on the brink of moving into yet another. Up to the 1970s, marketers used the same marketing

SOURCE: ADAPTED FROM THE STATISTICS CANADA WEBSITE ARTICLE "VISIBLE MINORITY GROUPS, 2006 COUNTS, FOR CANADA, PROVINCES AND TERRITORIES - 20% SAMPLE DATA" AT HTTP://WWW12.STATCAN.CA, ACCESSED JUNE 30, 2008."

figure 4.2

Cultural Groups as a Percentage of the Total Population

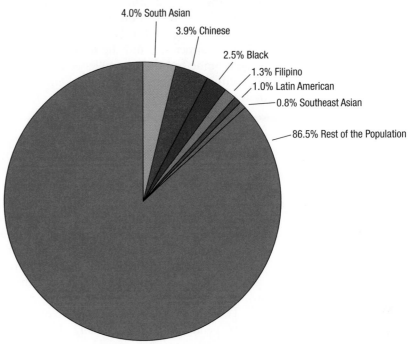

4.0% South Asian
3.9% Chinese
2.5% Black
1.3% Filipino
1.0% Latin American
0.8% Southeast Asian
86.5% Rest of the Population

strategies for Quebec as they used for the rest of Canada and merely translated advertising copy into French. Then along came Jacques Bouchard. He put forward the "twin beds" theory: where advertising was concerned, Quebec and the rest of Canada shared the same bedroom but slept in different beds. He demonstrated that marketing campaigns would be more successful if they were designed specifically for the Quebec market. Today, with the distinctions that have made Quebec unique disappearing and the move toward global markets, the "twin beds" theory is being challenged. Some feel that the Quebec identity has become so strong and established that Quebecers are feeling less threatened by marketing that is more Canadian or global rather than specific to their market.[13]

Chinese Canadians

Chinese immigrants have been coming to Canada since 1788 when they first landed on Vancouver Island. This group didn't represent a significant number until the 1980s, a decade that saw a large insurgence of Hong Kong Chinese before the colony was repatriated by China in 1997. Along with the Hong Kong group came their wealth, talents, education, and an entrepreneurial spirit to invest in Canada. They established themselves in four major centres across the country, representing nearly 11 percent of the population in Vancouver, nearly 6 percent in Toronto, 3.5 percent in Calgary, and nearly 3 percent in Edmonton. These relatively large clusters mean that their cultural influence will be maintained for some time. The influx of people from Asian countries is expected to slow in the coming years but this group will maintain a large influence on Canadian society.[14]

The impact of this cultural group on marketing strategies is significant. Chinese-Canadian consumers spend $30 billion annually. The average Chinese household spends $63 500 a year, $5000 above the country's average. This group is generally young, is made up of early adopters, and likes high-end brands, particularly if they perceive they are getting the products at a good price. They relate best to advertising and packaging in their own language, feeling that it shows respect. They like to shop in Chinese malls and supermarkets such as T&T Supermarkets that carry imported products.[15]

It might have been the company or it might have been the lobster. All I know is I've never laughed that hard before or since.

Whether retracing the footsteps of ancestors along the walls of a centuries-old fortress or choosing an excursion based on our world-renowned food and wine, you will enjoy every minute of your Nova Scotia holiday.

Direct flights daily to Halifax from most major cities.
1 800 565 0000
Go online to novascotia.com for more information.

NOVASCOTIA.COM

NOVA SCOTIA DEPARTMENT OF TOURISM, CULTURE & HERITAGE.

People from microcultures are often used in ads to enhance the effect of the message.

South-Asian Canadians

Like the Chinese Canadians, the South-Asian Canadian group comes from several cultures, including Punjabi, Urdu, and Tamil. This is the second-largest cultural group in Canada, representing about 2.5 percent of the population. Roughly 30 percent of this group was born in Canada. The largest number lives in Toronto and surrounding communities but significant numbers can be found in all the larger centres across the country. A smaller number of this group is elderly, suggesting that parents and grandparents did not accompany the family when they moved to Canada. South Asians tend to associate more with their own sub-ethnic group rather than the South-Asian community as a whole, a feature that fragments the segment into even smaller groups who maintain strong links with the communities they left.[16]

Some companies, Telus being a notable example, have started to develop marketing campaigns aimed at the South-Asian market. Telus, partnering with India's largest telecom provider, has developed a service called "Apna Des," meaning "my country." With this service Telus's South-Asian consumers have access to Bollywood music, cricket scores, and news from home. Using a picture of a peacock and a headline "Apna Des de rang only at Telus," meaning "The colours of my country only at Telus," the company ran ads in South-Asian newspapers aimed at older consumers and banner ads on websites aimed at younger consumers.[17]

Other Cultural Groups

More than 80 ethnic groups live in Canada. Many of these groups live in clusters or pockets across the country. For example, both Kitchener, Ontario, and Abbotsford, British Columbia, have large German populations. Communities where these population clusters live have developed cultural infrastructures that include newspapers, social clubs, and even radio stations. In order to effectively market to specific cultural groups, both an understanding of these infrastructures and access to them are helpful. In Canada, as in most multicultural nations, marketing too is becoming more multicultural so it is important to understand which aspects of a marketing strategy will be affected by cultural influences and which won't.[18]

SOCIAL INFLUENCES

Every consumer belongs to a number of social groups. A child's earliest group experience comes from membership in a family. As children grow older, they join other groups such as friendship groups, neighbourhood groups, school groups, and organizations such as Girl Guides and neighbourhood sports teams. Adults are also members of various groups at work and in the community.

Group membership influences an individual's purchase decisions and behaviour in both overt and subtle ways. Every group establishes certain norms of behaviour. **Norms** are the values, attitudes, and behaviours that a group deems appropriate for its members. Group members are expected to comply with these norms. Members of the Alberta Fish and Game Association, the Canadian Medical Association, and any local social or cultural club tend to adopt their organization's norms of behaviour. Norms can even affect non-members. Individuals who aspire to membership in a group may adopt its standards of behaviour and values.

Differences in group status and roles can also affect buying behaviour. **Status** is the relative position of any individual member in a group; **roles** define behaviour that members of a group expect of individuals who hold specific positions within that group. Some groups (such as Rotary Club or Lion's Club) define formal roles, and others (such as friendship groups) impose informal expectations. Both types of groups supply each member with both status and roles; in doing so, they influence that person's activities—including his or her purchase behaviour.

The Internet provides an opportunity for individuals to form and be influenced by new types of groups. Mailing lists and chat rooms allow groups to form around common interests. Some of these online virtual communities can develop norms and membership roles similar to those found in real-world groups. For example, to avoid criticism, members must observe rules for proper protocol in posting messages and participating in chats.

Groups often influence an individual's purchase decisions more than is realized. Most people tend to adhere in varying degrees to the general expectations of any group that they consider important, often without conscious awareness of this motivation. The surprising impact of groups and group norms on individual behaviour has been called the **Asch phenomenon,** named after social psychologist S. E. Asch, who through his research first documented characteristics of individual behaviour.

Asch found that individuals would conform to majority rule, even if that majority rule went against their beliefs. The Asch phenomenon can be a big factor in many purchase decisions, from major choices such as buying a house or car to deciding whether to buy a pair of shoes on sale.

Reference Groups

Discussion of the Asch phenomenon raises the subject of **reference groups**—groups whose value structures and standards influence a person's behaviour. Consumers usually try to coordinate their purchase behaviour with their perceptions of the values of their reference groups. The extent of reference-group influence varies widely among individuals. Strong influence by a group on a member's purchase requires two conditions:

reference groups People or institutions whose opinions are valued and to whom a person looks for guidance in his or her own behaviour, values, and conduct, such as family, friends, or celebrities.

1. The purchased product must be one that others can see and identify.

2. The purchased item must be conspicuous; it must stand out as something unusual, a brand or product that not everyone owns.

Reference-group influence would significantly affect the decision to buy a Jaguar, for example, but it would have little or no impact on the decision to purchase a loaf of bread. The status of the individual within a group produces three subcategories of reference groups: a membership group to

Marketoid

The fourth-largest cultural group in Canada is Scottish, which has grown from 550 000 in 1871 to over 4 million today.

which the person actually belongs, such as a political party; an aspirational group with which the person desires to associate; and a dissociative group with which the individual does not want to be identified.

Children are especially vulnerable to the influence of reference groups. They often base their buying decisions on outside forces such as what they see on television, opinions of friends, and fashionable products among adults. Advertising, especially endorsements by celebrities, can have much bigger impacts on children than on adults, in part because children want so badly to belong to aspirational groups.[19]

Social Classes

opinion leaders Trend-setters who purchase new products before others in a group and then influence others in their purchases.

Research has identified six classes within the social structures of both small and large North American cities: the upper-upper, lower-upper, upper-middle, and lower-middle classes, followed by the working class and lower class. Class rankings are determined by occupation, income, education, family background, and residence location. Note, however, that income is not always a primary determinant; pipe fitters paid at union scale earn more than many university professors, but their purchase behaviour may be quite different.

Family characteristics, such as the occupations and incomes of one or both parents, have been the primary influences on social class. As women's careers and earning power have increased over the past few decades, marketers have begun to pay more attention to their position as influential buyers.

People in one social class may aspire to a higher class and therefore exhibit buying behaviour common to that class rather than to their own. For example, middle-class consumers often buy items they associate with the upper classes. Although the upper classes themselves account for a very small percentage of the population, many more consumers treat themselves to prestigious products, such as antique carpets or luxury cars.

Opinion Leaders

In nearly every reference group, a few members act as **opinion leaders.** These trendsetters are likely to purchase new products before others in the group and then share their experiences and opinions via word of mouth. As others in the group decide whether to try the same products, they are influenced by the reports of opinion leaders.

Generalized opinion leaders are rare; instead, individuals tend to act as opinion leaders for specific goods or services based on their knowledge of and interest in those products. Their interest motivates them to seek out information from mass media, manufacturers, and other sources and, in turn, transmit this information to associates through interpersonal communications. Opinion leaders are found within all segments of the population.

KOHLER: As I See It, #1 in a series

ARTIST: Sanjay Kothari

SUITE: Escale

Destination: Guilin, China. Transportation provided by Kohler.

1-800-4-KOHLER
kohler.com/escale

THE BOLD LOOK
OF **KOHLER**

COURTESY OF THE KOHLER COMPANY

A product for those aspiring to a higher social class.

Information about goods and services sometimes flows from the Internet, radio, television, and other mass media to opinion leaders and then from opinion leaders to others. In other instances, information flows directly from media sources to all consumers. In still other instances, a multi-step flow carries information from mass media to opinion leaders and then on to other opinion leaders before dissemination to the general public. Figure 4.3 illustrates these three types of communication flow.

Some opinion leaders influence purchases by others merely through their own actions, which is particularly true in the case of fashion decisions. Tour de France winner Lance Armstrong has influenced different types of purchases, ranging from bicycles to the yellow stretch bracelets sold to raise money for cancer research. Consumers who purchase new bikes are opting for road bikes instead of the previously popular mountain bikes—often because of Armstrong's influence.[20]

FAMILY INFLUENCES

Most people are members of at least two families during their lifetimes—the ones they are born into and those they eventually form later in life. The family group is perhaps the most important determinant of consumer behaviour because of the close, continuing interactions among family members. Like other groups, each family typically has norms of expected behaviour, different roles, and status relationships for its members. These influences may mean that what is considered appropriate in one family may be

---

Solving an Ethical Controversy

Kids, Parents, and Violent Video Games

WHO buys and plays video games? Teenage boys are probably the biggest group of video game consumers. But adults—including the parents of children and teenagers—account for 35 percent of video game players. Eighty percent of these parents view video gaming as family entertainment instead of watching a movie or playing a round of Monopoly. But there is a darker side to video gaming. While many games are harmless, others contain violence and sexually explicit material. Some psychologists worry that prolonged exposure to images in these games can result in more violent, aggressive behaviour by children and teens. Although there is a rating system, some game manufacturers allegedly circumvent it by embedding hidden images in their games. And children or teens have easy access to games that are intended for an adult audience.

Should there be stricter laws limiting the sale of video games?

PRO

1. Children are a vulnerable audience. "Generally, the research shows that violence in video games increases children's aggressive behaviour and decreases their helpful behaviour," notes psychologist Elizabeth Carli.

2. Playing a violent video game is more harmful than watching a violent television show. "If you are actively involved in learning, you remember things better," says Carli. "So in a game you do things over and over again, whereas in the movies or on television you watch it once. And in the game there is reinforcement for it. So if it is killing people that you're doing, you get a reward for that."

CON

1. Critics of the studies linking video games to aggressive behaviour cite numerous flaws in the research. They claim that violence is part of mainstream entertainment, and other media should be examined just as closely.

2. Two-thirds of parents in one survey said that it is not the role of government to shield children from violent games—parents should take that responsibility.

Where do you stand: pro or con?

Sources: "Attorney Sues 'Grand Theft Auto' Makers," *Associated Press,* January 27, 2006, http://news.yahoo.com; May Wong, "Survey: More Parents Playing Video Games," Associated Press, January 26, 2006, http://news.yahoo.com; Benjamin Radford, "Reality Check on Video Game Violence," Live Science, December 2005, http://www.livescience.com; Daniel DeNoon, "Psychologists Attack Violent Video Games," WebMD, August 19, 2005, http://www.webmd.com.

figure 4.3

Alternative Channels for Communications Flow

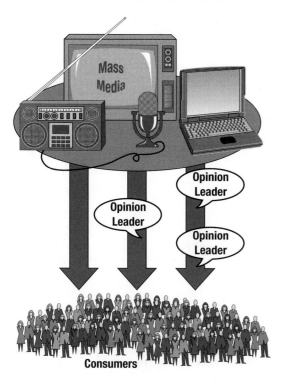

inappropriate in another, as in the case of violent video games described in the "Solving an Ethical Controversy" feature.

The traditional family structure consists of a husband, wife, and children. However, according to Statistics Canada, this structure has been steadily changing over the last century. A number of demographic factors have contributed to this change. The birth rate has declined to 1.52 children per woman in Canada. An increase in the number of childless couples and higher divorce and separation rates have all contributed to smaller households. The most recent census shows there were as many single-person households in Canada as there were households with four or more people, each group representing 25 percent of the population. There has also been a trend for young adults aged 20 to 29 to remain at home longer.[21] These statistics have important implications for marketers because they indicate a change in who makes buying decisions. Still, marketers describe the role of each spouse using these four categories:

1. *Autonomic role* is seen when the partners independently make equal numbers of decisions. Personal-care items would fall into the category of purchase decisions each would make for him- or herself.

2. *Husband-dominant role* occurs when the husband usually makes certain purchase decisions. Buying a life insurance policy is a typical example.

3. *Wife-dominant role* has the wife making most of the buying decisions. Children's clothing is a typical wife-dominant purchase.

4. *Syncratic role* refers to joint decisions. The purchase of a house follows a syncratic pattern.

The increasing occurrence of the two-income family means that women have a greater role in making family purchase decisions. Today, women have more say in large-ticket family purchases such as automobiles. And studies show that women take the lead in choosing entertainment such as movies and restaurants.[22] Studies of family decision making have also shown that households with two wage earners are more likely than others to make joint purchasing decisions. Members of two-income households often do their shopping in the evening and on weekends because of the number of hours spent at the workplace, as mentioned earlier. Shifting family roles have created new markets for a variety of products. Goods and services that save time, promote family togetherness, emphasize safety, or encourage health and fitness appeal to the family values and influences of today.

Children and Teenagers in Family Purchases

As parents have become busier, they have delegated some family purchase decisions to children, specifically teenagers. Children learn about the latest products and trends because they watch so much television and cruise the Internet, often becoming the family experts on what to buy. As a result, children have gained sophistication and assumed new roles in family purchasing behaviour.[23]

The purchase of a new car is often influenced by family structure.

Children and teenagers represent a huge market, and they influence what their parents buy, from cereal to automobiles. Marketers are so aware of the impact this market segment has on household spending that companies such as Kellogg have developed marketing strategies aimed at children. The company developed a standard for any product that they market to children. This standard includes the amount of fat, calories, sodium, and sugar acceptable per serving and they print these facts on the front of the box. Products not meeting this standard will either be changed or not advertised to children.[24]

Even after they grow up, children continue to play roles in family consumer behaviour, often by recommending products to their parents. Advertisers try to influence these relationships by showing adult children interacting with their parents.

assessment check 2

2.1 List the interpersonal determinants of consumer behaviour.

2.2 What is a microculture?

2.3 Describe the Asch phenomenon.

PERSONAL DETERMINANTS OF CONSUMER BEHAVIOUR

Marketoid

As of July 1, 2006, the median age of the population in Canada was the highest ever at 38.8 years up from 38.5 in 2005.

Consumer behaviour is affected by a number of internal, personal factors in addition to interpersonal ones. Each individual brings unique needs, motives, perceptions, attitudes, learned responses, and self-concepts to buying decisions. This section looks at how these factors influence consumer behaviour.

NEEDS AND MOTIVES

Individual purchase behaviour is driven by the motivation to fill a perceived need. A **need** is an imbalance between the consumer's actual and desired states. A person who recognizes or feels a significant or urgent need will then seek to correct the imbalance. Marketers attempt to arouse this sense of urgency by making a need "felt" and then influencing consumers' motivation to satisfy their needs by purchasing specific products.

Motives are inner states that direct a person toward the goal of satisfying a felt need. The individual takes action to reduce the state of tension and return to a condition of equilibrium.

Maslow's Hierarchy of Needs

Psychologist Abraham H. Maslow developed a theory that characterized needs and arranged them into a hierarchy. Maslow identified five levels of needs, beginning with physiological needs and progressing to the need for self-actualization. A person must at least partially satisfy lower-level needs, according to Maslow, before higher needs can affect behaviour. In developed countries, where relatively large per-capita incomes allow most people to satisfy the basic needs on the hierarchy, higher-order needs may be more important to consumer behaviour. Table 4.1 illustrates products and marketing themes designed to satisfy needs at each level.

Children often influence what their parents buy.

Explain each
of the personal
determinants of
consumer behaviour:
needs and motives,
perceptions,
attitudes, learning,
and self-concept
theory.

need Imbalance between
a consumer's actual and
desired states.

motive Inner state that
directs a person toward
the goal of satisfying a
need.

Physiological Needs

Needs at the most basic level concern essential requirements for survival, such as food, water, shelter, and clothing. The Coca-Cola Co. promotes its Dasani bottled water with the slogan "Pure Refreshment," emphasizing that it satisfies physiological needs.

Safety Needs

Second-level needs include security, protection from physical harm, and avoidance of the unexpected. To gratify these needs, consumers may buy insurance or security devices. The Co-operators Insurance appeals to these needs by saying, "A Better Place for You."

Social/Belongingness Needs

Satisfaction of physiological and safety needs leads a person to attend to third-level needs—the desire to be accepted by people and groups important to that individual. To satisfy this need, people may join organizations and buy goods or services that make them feel part of a group. American Express advertises its Membership Rewards program, which features the ability to use its frequent-flyer points on almost any airline, as if it is an exclusive club.

Esteem Needs

People have a universal desire for a sense of accomplishment and achievement. They also wish to gain the respect of others and even to exceed others' performance once lower-order needs are satisfied. Lexus automobiles reinforce their drivers' esteem needs with their advertising, which touts the company's "pursuit of perfection."

Self-Actualization Needs

At the top rung of Maslow's ladder of human needs is people's desire to realize their full potential and to find fulfillment by expressing their unique talents and capabilities. Companies specializing in exotic adventure vacations aim to satisfy consumers' needs for self-actualization. Other travel providers offer specialized educational trips that appeal to consumers' desires for a meaningful experience as well as a vacation. Some of these packages are aimed at the baby boomer or senior markets and usually involve an informal course of study—whether it's cooking, history, anthropology, or golf.

Maslow noted that a satisfied need no longer motivates a person to act. Once the physiological needs are met, the individual moves on to pursue satisfaction of higher-order needs. Consumers are periodically motivated by the need to relieve thirst and hunger, but their interests soon return to focus on satisfaction of safety, social, and other needs in the hierarchy. People may not always progress through

table 4.1   **Marketing Strategies Based on Maslow's Hierarchy of Needs**

PHYSIOLOGICAL NEEDS	Products	Vitamins, medicines, food, exercise equipment, bottled water
	Marketing Themes	Bayer—"Science for a better life"; Puffs facial tissues—"A nose in need deserves Puffs indeed"; Ocean Spray cranberry juice—"Crave the wave"
SAFETY NEEDS	Products	Car air bags, burglar alarm systems, retirement investments, insurance, smoke and carbon-monoxide detectors, medicines
	Marketing Themes	Volvo—"Protect the body. Ignite the soul"; Blue Cross—"Enjoy the Benefits of Good Health"
BELONGINGNESS NEEDS	Products	Beauty aids, entertainment, clothing, cars
	Marketing Themes	Old Navy clothing—"Spring Break from Coast to Coast"; Ford – "Built for Life in Canada"
ESTEEM NEEDS	Products	Clothing, cars, jewellery, hobbies, beauty spa services
	Marketing Themes	Lexus automobiles—"The Pursuit of Perfection"; Jenn-Air kitchen appliances—"For the Love of Cooking"
SELF-ACTUALIZATION NEEDS	Products	Education, cultural events, sports, hobbies, luxury goods, technology, travel
	Marketing Themes	Gatorade—"Is It in You?"; Dodge cars and truck—"Grab Life by the Horns"

the hierarchy; they may fixate on a certain level. For example, some people who lived through the Great Depression were continually worried about money afterward.

Critics have pointed out a variety of flaws in Maslow's reasoning. For example, some needs can be related to more than one level, and not every individual progresses through the needs hierarchy in the same order; some bypass social and esteem needs and are motivated by self-actualization needs. However, the hierarchy of needs continues to occupy a secure place in the study of consumer behaviour.

PERCEPTIONS

Perception is the meaning that a person attributes to incoming stimuli gathered through the five senses— sight, hearing, touch, taste, and smell. Certainly, a buyer's behaviour is influenced by his or her perceptions of a good or service. Only recently have researchers come to recognize that people's perceptions depend as much on what they want to perceive as on the actual stimuli. It is for this reason that Holt Renfrew and Godiva chocolates are perceived so differently from Wal-Mart and Hershey, respectively.

A person's perception of an object or event results from the interaction of two types of factors:

1. Stimulus factors—characteristics of the physical object such as size, colour, weight, and shape

2. Individual factors—unique characteristics of the individual, including not only sensory processes but also experiences with similar inputs and basic motivations and expectations

perception Meaning that a person attributes to incoming stimuli gathered through the five senses.

Jackson-Triggs: Appealing to self-actualization needs.

Perceptual Screens

The average North American is constantly bombarded by marketing messages. According to industry experts, a typical supermarket now carries 30 000 different packages, each serving as a miniature billboard vying to attract consumers' attention. Over 6000 commercials a week are aired on network TV. Prime-time TV shows carry more than 15 minutes of advertising every hour.[25] Thousands of businesses have set up websites to tout their offerings. Marketers have also stamped their messages on everything from popcorn bags in movie theatres to airsickness bags on planes.

Marketing clutter has caused consumers to ignore many promotional messages. People respond selectively to messages that manage to break through their **perceptual screens**—the mental filtering processes through which all inputs must pass.

All marketers struggle to determine which stimuli evoke responses from consumers. They must learn how to capture a customer's attention long enough to read an advertisement, listen to a sales representative, or react to a point-of-purchase display. In general, marketers seek to make a message stand out and gain the attention of prospective customers.

One way to break through clutter is to run large ads. Doubling the size of an ad in printed media increases its attention value by about 50 percent. Advertisers use colour to make newspaper ads contrast with the usual black-and-white graphics, providing another effective way to penetrate the reader's perceptual screen. Other methods for enhancing contrast include arranging a large amount of white space around a printed area or placing white type on a dark background. Vivid illustrations and photos can also help to break through clutter in print ads.

Consumers' perceptions that they should steer clear of certain products to avoid chemicals that could hurt the environment have led to the creation of ads promoting the benefits of safer alternatives.

The psychological concept of closure also helps marketers create a message that stands out. *Closure* is the human tendency to perceive a complete picture from an incomplete stimulus. Advertisements that allow consumers to do this often succeed in breaking through perceptual screens. General Mills uses this technique with their Cheerios brand of breakfast cereal. They use a cheerio to dot the "I" on the package and replace the "o" in some of their promotional material.

Word-of-mouth marketing can be a highly effective way of breaking through consumers' perceptual screens. Take the early Harry Potter books. Although the series featuring the orphaned English schoolboy who is sent to wizardry school is now a huge international success, early popularity of the first two books was based on word of mouth. Before North American marketers even got wind of the bespectacled young wizard from England, kids were requesting the books at their local bookstores, reading them, and passing them along to friends.

A new tool that marketers are exploring is the use of virtual reality. Some companies have created presentations based on virtual reality that display marketing messages and information in a three-dimensional format. Eventually, experts predict, consumers will be able to tour resort areas via virtual reality before booking their trips or walk through the interiors of homes they are considering buying via virtual reality. Virtual reality

marketing failure   Social Media: Marketers Struggle to Get It Right

Background. Websites like MySpace and Facebook along with blogs and podcasts all fit into the wide range of online communications referred to by marketers as social media. Marketers see social media as an effective way to get information about products and services out to a large number of consumers without seeming to be doing marketing.

The Challenge. Marketers face two challenges in dealing with social media. The first is to seamlessly interface with the users who have the uncanny ability to spot fakes. The second challenge is to educate other marketers on how to use social media. Avoiding early mistakes, such as experienced by Sony, who was exposed for launching a "flog"—a fake blog—is important in developing these communications tools.

The Strategy. Marketers have tackled the challenge by researching the social media world and by sharing successful techniques with others trying to develop social media communications. Advertising

agencies have turned to public relations experts for help in developing more subtle promotional messages.

The Outcome. While the large advertising agencies are still struggling to get social media campaigns right, smaller marketing companies who have already developed the blend of advertising and public relations skills are more successful. One such company, the Social Media Group, based in the small town of Dundas, Ontario, is landing some big clients such as the Ford Motor Company. The Social Media Group had worked with other large companies such as Yamaha and Harlequin to develop their social media communications but the Ford account meant a doubling of staff from four to eight. Social media is such an important new communication channel that marketing companies will continue to find ways to reach the over 8 million Canadians who currently visit sites such as Facebook on a daily basis.

Sources: Chris Powell, "Marketers Lack Social Media Grace," *Marketing,* April 8, 2008; Jeromy Lloyd, "The Society of Social Media," *Marketing,* October 29, 2007, pp. 16–18.

technology may allow marketers to penetrate consumer perceptual filters in a way not currently possible with other forms of media.

With selective perception at work screening competing messages, it is easy to see the importance of marketers' efforts in developing brand loyalty. Satisfied customers are less likely to seek information about competing products. Even when competitive advertising is forced on them, they are less apt than others to look beyond their perceptual filters at those appeals. Loyal customers simply tune out information that does not agree with their existing beliefs and expectations.

ATTITUDES

Our perception of incoming stimuli is greatly affected by our attitudes. In fact, a consumer's decision to purchase an item is strongly based on his or her attitudes about the product, store, or salesperson.

Attitudes are a person's enduring favourable or unfavourable evaluations, emotions, or action tendencies toward some object or data. As they form over time through individual experiences and group contacts, attitudes become highly resistant to change. Sometimes it takes a possible threat, such as global warming, to change consumers' attitudes. Many people have discovered the benefits of owning a smaller car as outlined in the "Go Green" feature.

Because favourable attitudes likely affect brand preferences, marketers are interested in determining consumer attitudes toward their offerings. Numerous attitude-scaling devices have been developed for this purpose.

attitudes A person's enduring favourable or unfavourable evaluations, emotions, or action tendencies toward some object or idea.

Attitude Components

An attitude has cognitive, affective, and behavioural components. The *cognitive* component refers to the individual's information and knowledge about an object or concept. The *affective* component deals with feelings or emotional reactions. The *behavioural* component involves tendencies to act in a certain manner. For example, in deciding whether to shop at a warehouse-type food store, a consumer might obtain information about what the store offers from advertising, trial visits, and input from family, friends, and associates (cognitive component). The consumer might also receive affective input by listening to others about their shopping experiences at this type of store. Other affective information might lead the person to make a judgment about the type of people who seem to shop there—whether they represent a group with which he or she would like to be associated. The consumer may ultimately decide to buy some canned goods, cereal, and bakery products there but continue to rely on a regular supermarket for major food purchases (behavioural component). All three components maintain a

PETERBOROUGH EXAMINER/THE CANADIAN PRESS (CLIFFORD SKARSTEDT)

Word-of-mouth marketing helped the **Harry Potter** *books leap to success. Fans gather at a Peterborough, Ontario, bookstore for the release of the final instalment.*

Go Green

Smart Cars

© OLARU RADIAN-ALEXANDRU/SHUTTERSTOCK

The hybrid cars described at the beginning of the chapter are not the only trend in vehicle sales influenced by the move toward more environmentally friendly modes of transportation and major changes in consumer attitudes. Smaller cars are another, and most notable of these is the Smart car, now produced by Mercedes-Benz.

The Smart car, first introduced into Canada in the fall of 2004, is a perky little two-seater that sells for less than $20 000. Canada was used as the North American test market and the car proved to be a success here. The original 800 units were sold as soon as they were unloaded. Thousands of cars have been sold through dealerships across the country since then. In some cases, purchasers waited up to six months for their cars.

Purchasers of Smart cars can boast about how environmentally friendly their cars are on several fronts. These cars require less material to make and can go 100 kilometres on roughly four litres of diesel fuel. The car was designed with the environment in mind: its module construction makes it easier to recycle parts. The raw materials used in the car are all environmentally friendly, with no lead, chromium, mercury, or cadmium.

The success of the Smart car is not solely because it is environmentally friendly or the owners want to flaunt the downsizing of their ecological footprint. The car meets the needs of a large number of urban Canadians, many of whom are often the only person in their vehicle. Most Canadians tend to see their vehicle as just an appliance that gets them from one place to another and these people are willing to purchase smaller vehicles to do so. While the bright "look at me" colours are likely to attract younger drivers, the older segment of Smart owners prefers the practical, understated simplicity of the car.

Source: Michael Adams, "Smarter Than You Think," *Marketing*, August 14, 2006, p. 20; www.thesmart.ca, accessed August 23, 2007.

relatively stable and balanced relationship to one another. Together, they form an overall attitude about an object or idea.

Changing Consumer Attitudes

Since a favourable consumer attitude provides a vital condition for marketing success, how can a firm lead prospective buyers to adopt such an attitude toward its products? Marketers have two choices: (1) attempt to produce consumer attitudes that will motivate purchase of a particular product, or (2) evaluate existing consumer attitudes and then make the product features appeal to them.

If consumers view an existing good or service unfavourably, the seller may redesign it, offer new options, or try to change attitudes through promotional communications. Several advertising companies have decided to change the way they bring their messages to young consumers on sites such as Facebook, since they have had varying degrees of success, as described in the "Marketing Failure" feature.

Or an attitude may not be unfavourable—just one that does not motivate the consumer toward a purchase. Wal-Mart marketers discovered that upscale consumers view the deals they get on peanut butter, paper towels, and laundry detergent at Wal-Mart as good, but they go elsewhere to purchase fine wine, jewellery, and high-end electronics. So in an effort to change these consumers' attitudes, Wal-Mart recently built a new U.S. store that caters specifically to them. This chic Wal-Mart Supercentre offers premium foods, clothing, electronics, housewares, and fitness products—along with a café wired for Wi-Fi Internet access, wider aisles, and restrooms decorated in faux marble. If the store succeeds, Wal-Mart will begin to add those items in existing stores in more affluent neighbourhoods and may even build more stores for its wealthy customers.[26]

Modifying the Components of Attitude

Attitudes frequently change in response to inconsistencies among the three components. The most common inconsistencies result when new information changes the cognitive or affective components of an attitude. Marketers can modify attitudes by providing evidence of product benefits and by correcting misconceptions. Marketers may also attempt to change attitudes by engaging buyers in new behaviour. Free samples, for instance, can change attitudes by getting consumers to try a product.

Sometimes new technologies can encourage consumers to modify their attitudes. Some people, for example, are reluctant to make purchases online. According to recent research, more Canadians are shopping (browsing or collecting information about products) online—in fact, 81 percent are doing so—however, only 56 percent are actually making online purchases. To address online shopping concerns and encourage more online purchases, companies are adding more user participation items, such as personal blogs for customers, to their websites. E-tailing experts suggest the next steps to encourage more online purchases are to make websites more like in-store shopping experiences. For example, make it easier for customers to return items. By making these changes more retailers can be as successful online as Canadian Tire and the Future Shop, who both have large online sales.[27]

LEARNING

Marketing is concerned as seriously with the process by which consumer decisions change over time as with the current status of those decisions. **Learning,** in a marketing context, refers to immediate or expected changes in consumer behaviour as a result of experience. The learning process includes the component of **drive,** which is any strong stimulus that impels action. Fear, pride, desire for money, thirst, pain avoidance, and rivalry are examples of drives. Learning also relies on a **cue**—that is, any object in the environment that determines the nature of the consumer's response to a drive. Examples of cues are a newspaper advertisement for a new Thai restaurant—a cue for a hungry person—and a Shell sign near a highway—a cue for a motorist who needs gasoline.

A **response** is an individual's reaction to a set of cues and drives. Responses might include reactions such as purchasing Frontline flea and tick prevention for pets, dining at Pizza Hut, or deciding to enroll at a particular community college or university.

Reinforcement is the reduction in drive that results from a proper response. As a response becomes more rewarding, it creates a stronger bond between the drive and the purchase of the product, likely increasing future purchases by the consumer. Reinforcement is the rationale that underlies frequent-buyer programs, which reward repeat purchasers for their loyalty. These programs may offer points for premiums, frequent-flyer miles, and the like. WestJet, like many airlines, offers incentives for booking online and for frequent fliers.

learning Knowledge or skill that is acquired as a result of experience, which changes consumer behaviour.

Marketoid

In 2006, baby boomers—Canadians born between 1946 and 1965—started turning 60. That year, more than 400 000 or 1100 a day reached that age.

Applying Learning Theory to Marketing Decisions

Learning theory has some important implications for marketing strategists, particularly those involved with consumer packaged goods. Marketers must find a way to develop a desired outcome such as repeat purchase behaviour gradually over time. **Shaping** is the process of applying a series of rewards and reinforcements to permit more complex behaviour to evolve.

Both promotional strategy and the product itself play a role in the shaping process. Marketers want to motivate consumers to become regular buyers of certain merchandise. Their first step in getting consumers to try the product might be to offer a free sample package that includes a substantial discount coupon for the next purchase. This example uses a cue as a shaping procedure. If the item performs well, the purchase response is reinforced and followed by another inducement—the coupon.

The second step is to entice the consumer to buy the item with little financial risk. The discount coupon enclosed with the free sample prompts this action. Suppose the package that the consumer purchases has still another, smaller discount coupon enclosed. Again, satisfactory product performance and the second coupon provide reinforcement.

The third step is to motivate the person to buy the item again at a moderate cost. A discount coupon accomplishes this objective, but this time the purchased package includes no additional coupon. The only reinforcement comes from satisfactory product performance.

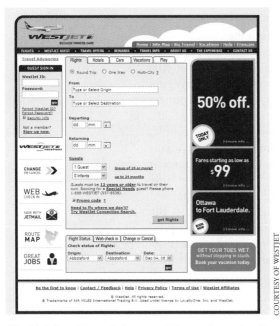

WestJet: Providing reinforcement for customer loyalty

self-concept A person's multifaceted picture of himself or herself.

assessment check 3

3.1 Identify the personal determinants of consumer behaviour.

3.2 What are the human needs categorized by Abraham Maslow?

3.3 How do perception and learning differ?

The final test comes when the consumer decides whether to buy the item at its true price without a discount coupon. Satisfaction with product performance provides the only continuing reinforcement. Repeat purchase behaviour is shaped by effective application of learning theory within a marketing strategy context.

SELF-CONCEPT THEORY

The consumer's **self-concept**—a person's multifaceted picture of himself or herself—plays an important role in consumer behaviour. Say a young woman views herself as bright, ambitious, and headed for a successful marketing career. She'll want to buy attractive clothes and jewellery to reflect that image of herself. Say an older man views himself as young for his age; he may purchase a sports car and stylish clothes to reflect his self-concept.

The concept of self emerges from an interaction of many of the influences—both personal and interpersonal—that affect buying behaviour. The individual's needs, motives, perceptions, attitudes, and learning lie at the core of his or her conception of self. In addition, family, social, and cultural influences affect self-concept.

A person's self-concept has four components: real self, self-image, looking-glass self, and ideal self. The *real self* is an objective view of the total person. The *self-image*—the way an individual views himself or herself—may distort the objective view. The *looking-glass self*—the way an individual thinks others see him or her—may also differ substantially from self-image because people often choose to project different images to others than their perceptions of their real selves. The *ideal self* serves as a personal set of objectives, since it is the image to which the individual aspires. In purchasing goods and services, people are likely to choose products that move them closer to their ideal self-images.

4 Distinguish between high-involvement and low-involvement purchase decisions.

THE CONSUMER DECISION PROCESS

Although they might not be aware of it, consumers complete a step-by-step process in making purchasing decisions. The time and effort devoted to a particular purchasing decision depend on how important it is.

Purchases with high levels of potential social or economic consequences are said to be **high-involvement purchase decisions.** Buying a car or deciding where to go to university or college are two examples of high-involvement decisions. Routine purchases that pose little risk to the consumer are **low-involvement decisions.** Purchasing a candy bar from a vending machine is a good example.

Consumers generally invest more time and effort in buying decisions for high-involvement products than in those for low-involvement products. A home buyer will visit a number of listings, compare asking prices, apply for a mortgage, have the selected house inspected, and even have friends or family members visit the home before signing the final papers. Few buyers invest that much effort in choosing between Nestlé's and Hershey's candy bars. Believe it or not, though, they will still go through the steps of the consumer decision process—but on a more compressed scale.

Figure 4.1, on page 131, shows the six steps in the consumer decision process. First, the consumer recognizes a problem or unmet need, searches for goods or services, and evaluates the alternatives before making a purchase decision. The next step is the actual purchase act. After buying the item, the consumer evaluates whether he or she made the right choice. Much of marketing involves steering consumers through the decision process in the direction of a specific product.

Consumers apply the decision process in solving problems and taking advantage of opportunities. Such decisions permit them to correct differences between their actual and desired states. Feedback from each decision serves as additional experience in helping guide subsequent decisions.

assessment check 4

4.1 Differentiate between high-involvement decisions and low-involvement decisions.

4.2 Categorize each of the following as a high- or low-involvement product: shampoo, computer, popcorn, apartment, cell phone service.

PROBLEM OR OPPORTUNITY RECOGNITION

During the first stage in the decision process, the consumer becomes aware of a significant discrepancy between the existing situation and a desired situation. Perhaps the consumer realizes that there is little food in the refrigerator. By identifying the problem—an empty refrigerator—the consumer can resolve it with a trip to the grocery store. Sometimes the problem is more specific. The consumer might have a full refrigerator but no mustard or mayonnaise with which to make sandwiches. This problem requires a solution as well.

⑤ Outline the steps in the consumer decision process.

Suppose the consumer is unhappy with a particular purchase—say, a brand of cereal. Or maybe he or she wants a change from the same old cereal every morning. This is the recognition of another type of problem or opportunity—the desire for change.

What if our consumer just got a raise at work? He or she might want to try some of the prepared gourmet take-home dinners offered by the local supermarket. These dinners are more expensive than the groceries our consumer has purchased in the past, but now they are within financial reach. The marketer's main task during this phase of the decision-making process is to help prospective buyers identify and recognize potential problems or needs. This task may take the form of advertising, promotions, or personal sales assistance. A supermarket employee might suggest appetizers or desserts to accompany our grocery shopper's gourmet take-home dinner.

SEARCH

During the second step in the decision process, the consumer gathers information about the attainment of a desired state of affairs. This search identifies alternative means of problem solution. A high-involvement purchase might mean conducting an extensive information search, whereas low-involvement purchases require much less research.

House remodelling requires considerable expense and time for homeowners. Kitchens, which are packed from floor to ceiling and wall to wall with cabinets and fixtures, are one of the most expensive rooms to remodel, so they require many high-involvement purchase decisions.

The search may cover internal or external sources of information. An internal search is simply a mental review: Is there past experience with the product? Was it good or bad? An external search involves gathering information from all kinds of outside sources—for instance, family, friends, co-workers or classmates, advertisements or salespeople, online reviews, and consumer magazines. Because conducting an external search requires time and effort, it is usually done for high-involvement purchases.

The search identifies alternative brands for consideration and possible purchase. The number of alternatives that a consumer actually considers in making a purchase decision is known in marketing as the **evoked set.** In some searches, consumers already know of the brands that merit further consideration; in others, their external searches develop such information. The number of brands included in the evoked set vary depending on both the situation and the person. For example, an immediate need might limit the evoked set, while someone who has more time to make a decision might expand the evoked set to choose from a broader range of options.

Consumers now choose among more alternative products than ever before. This variety can confuse and complicate the analysis necessary to narrow the range of choices. Instead of comparing one or two brands, a consumer often faces a dizzying array of brands and sub-brands. Products that once included only one or two categories—regular coffee versus decaffeinated—are now available in many different forms—cappuccino, latte, tall skinny latte, flavoured coffee, espresso, and iced coffee, just to name a few possibilities.

Marketers try to influence buying decisions during the search process by providing persuasive information about their offerings in a format useful to consumers. The marketer must find creative ways to penetrate a consumer's evoked set of alternatives.

evoked set Number of alternatives that a consumer actually considers in making a purchase decision.

Marketoid

The fertility rate, the average number of children each Canadian woman has, is 1.54.

EVALUATION OF ALTERNATIVES

The third step in the consumer decision process is to evaluate the evoked set of options. Actually, it is difficult to completely separate the second and third steps because some evaluation takes place as the search progresses; consumers accept, discount, distort, or reject information as they receive it.

The outcome of the evaluation stage is the choice of a brand or product in the evoked set or possibly a decision to keep looking for alternatives. To complete this analysis, the consumer must develop a set of evaluative criteria to guide the selection. **Evaluative criteria** are the features that a consumer considers in choosing among alternatives. These criteria can either be objective facts (government tests of an automobile's mileage) or subjective impressions (a favourable view of a brand of clothing). Common criteria include price, brand name, and country of origin. Evaluative criteria can vary with the consumer's age, income level, social class, and culture. If you were in the market for a flat panel TV, your criteria might include price and brand name. A Samsung 50-inch HDTV sells for as much as $2500 retail. But an LG TV sells for much less. You must decide which is most important to you—the known brand name of Samsung or the lower price offered by LG.

Marketers attempt to influence the outcome of this stage in three ways. First, they try to educate consumers about attributes that they view as important in evaluating a particular class of goods. They also identify which evaluative criteria are important to an individual and attempt to show why a specific brand fulfills those criteria. Finally, they try to induce a customer to expand the evoked set to include the product being marketed.

evaluative criteria Features that a consumer considers in choosing among alternatives.

PURCHASE DECISION AND PURCHASE ACT

The search and alternative evaluation stages of the decision process result in the eventual purchase decision and the act of making the purchase. At this stage, the consumer has evaluated each alternative in the evoked set based on his or her personal set of evaluative criteria and narrowed the alternatives down to one.

The consumer then decides where—or from whom—to make the purchase. Sometimes this decision is part of the evaluation; perhaps one seller is offering a better price or better warranty than another. The purchase may be made online or in person at a retail store. The delivery options might also influence

ETIQUETTE TIPS FOR MARKETING PROFESSIONALS

Handling Angry Customers

PART of building healthy, long-lasting relationships with customers is learning how to deal with them when they are dissatisfied or downright irate about the quality of goods and services they have received. Regardless of what kind of business you are in, at some point you will probably encounter someone who is upset. If you take a deep breath and follow these tips, you may find that you can handle the situation better than you thought you could. If all goes well, you may even strengthen your firm's relationship with that particular customer.

1. *Remain calm.* This is the most important rule for handling just about any interaction. Keep in mind that the customer isn't upset at you, personally—just frustrated with a product or your company. If you respond to someone's anger by getting angry yourself, the situation will only get worse. So keep cool, and the other person may cool down more quickly as well.

2. *Be respectful.* Be polite and respectful of the other person's feelings and state of mind. If you remain calm and considerate, you can help the customer focus specifically on the problem at hand.

3. *Listen carefully.* Everyone wants to be heard. Ask the customer to describe the problem to you. Listen carefully, and take notes if possible. As the person talks, he or she may begin to calm down.

4. *Confirm the problem.* When you think the customer has finished describing the complaint, repeat it back so you are sure you understand completely. Simply say, "Let me make sure I have understood you correctly," and restate the problem.

5. *Take responsibility for the next step.* If you have the authority to solve the problem, tell the customer exactly what you are going to do and when. If you do not have the authority, say so—and then explain what the next step will be. If at all possible, promise to follow the problem through to its solution, even if you are not able to make the correction yourself. A follow-up call to make sure the problem is resolved—and the customer is satisfied—is one more step toward building a lifelong relationship.

Sources: "Telephone Etiquette Guide," California State University–Fullerton, http://www.fullerton.edu, accessed March 14, 2006; Gene Mage, "How to Deal with an Enraged Customer," Making It Work, http://www.makingitwork.com, accessed March 14, 2006; Nancy Friedman, "Strategies for Handling Irate Callers," Networking Today, http://www.networkingtoday.ca, accessed March 14, 2006.

the decision of where to purchase an item. For example, a local electronics store might deliver your flat panel TV for free, whereas an online retailer might charge $50 for delivery.

POST-PURCHASE EVALUATION

The purchase act produces one of two results. The buyer feels either satisfaction at the removal of the discrepancy between the existing and desired states or dissatisfaction with the purchase. Consumers are generally satisfied if purchases meet their expectations.

Sometimes, however, consumers experience some post-purchase anxieties called **cognitive dissonance.** This anxiety results from an imbalance among a person's knowledge, beliefs, and attitudes. A consumer may experience dissonance after choosing a particular automobile over several other models when some of the rejected models have desired features that the chosen one does not provide.

Dissonance is likely to increase (1) as the dollar values of purchases increase, (2) when the rejected alternatives have desirable features that the chosen alternatives do not provide, and (3) when the purchase decision has a major effect on the buyer. In other words, dissonance is more likely with high-involvement purchases than with those that require low involvement. The

cognitive dissonance Imbalance between beliefs and attitudes that occurs after an action or decision is taken, such as a purchase.

assessment check 5

5.1   List the steps in the consumer decision process.

5.2   What is meant by the term *evoked set*?

5.3   What are evaluative criteria?

⑥ **Differentiate among routinized response behaviour, limited problem solving, and extended problem solving by consumers.**

routinized response behaviour Rapid consumer problem solving in which no new information is considered; the consumer has already set evaluative criteria and identified available options.

limited problem solving Situation in which the consumer invests some small amount of time and energy in searching for and evaluating alternatives.

extended problem solving Situation that involves lengthy external searches and long deliberation; results when brands are difficult to categorize or evaluate.

consumer may attempt to reduce dissonance by looking for advertisements or other information to support the chosen alternative or by seeking reassurance from acquaintances who are satisfied purchasers of the product. The individual may also avoid information that favours a rejected alternative. Someone who buys a Toyota is likely to read Toyota advertisements and avoid Nissan and Honda ads.

Marketers can help buyers reduce cognitive dissonance by providing information that supports the chosen alternative. Automobile dealers recognize the possibility of buyer's remorse and often follow up purchases with letters or telephone calls from dealership personnel offering personal attention to any customer problems. Advertisements that stress customer satisfaction also help reduce cognitive dissonance.

A final method of dealing with cognitive dissonance is to change products. The consumer may ultimately decide that one of the rejected alternatives would have been the best choice and vows to purchase that item in the future. Marketers may capitalize on this with advertising campaigns that focus on the benefits of their products or with tag lines that say something like "If you're unhappy with them, try us."

CLASSIFYING CONSUMER PROBLEM-SOLVING PROCESSES

As mentioned earlier, the consumer decision processes for different products require varying amounts of problem-solving efforts. Marketers recognize three categories of problem-solving behaviour: routinized response, limited problem solving, and extended problem solving. Some marketers base this problem-solving behaviour on the following: price, the level of involvement of the purchaser, the number of brands to choose from, frequency of purchases, and the customer's perceived risk.[28] Table 4.2 provides a summary. The classification of a particular purchase within this framework clearly influences the consumer decision process.

Routinized Response Behaviour

Consumers make many purchases routinely by choosing a preferred brand or one of a limited group of acceptable brands. This type of rapid consumer problem solving is referred to as **routinized response behaviour.** A routine purchase of a regular brand of soft drink is an example. The consumer has already set evaluative criteria and identified available options. External search is limited in such cases, which characterize extremely low-involvement products.

Limited Problem Solving

Consider the situation in which the consumer has previously set evaluative criteria for a particular kind of purchase but then encounters a new, unknown brand. The introduction of a new shampoo is an example of a **limited problem solving** situation. The consumer knows the evaluative criteria for the product, but has not applied these criteria to assess the new brand. Such situations demand moderate amounts of time and effort for external searches. Limited problem solving is affected by the number of evaluative criteria and brands, the extent of external search, and the process for determining preferences. Consumers making purchase decisions in this product category are likely to feel involvement in the middle of the range.

assessment check 6

6.1   What is routinized response behaviour?

6.2   What does limited problem solving require?

6.3   Give an example of an extended problem-solving situation.

Extended Problem Solving

Extended problem solving results when brands are difficult to categorize or evaluate. The first step is to compare one item with similar ones. The consumer needs to understand the product features before evaluating alternatives. Most extended problem-solving efforts involve lengthy external searches. High-involvement purchase decisions usually require extended problem solving.

table 4.2 **Consumer Problem Solving**

	ROUTINIZED RESPONSE BEHAVIOUR	LIMITED PROBLEM SOLVING	EXTENSIVE PROBLEM SOLVING
Price	Low	Moderate	High
Level of involvement of the purchaser	Low	Moderate	High
The number of brands considered	Few	Moderate	Several
Frequency of purchases	High	Moderate	Low
Customer's perceived risk	Low	Moderate	High
Sometimes called	Habitual Buying Behaviour	Variety-Seeking or Dissonance-Reducing Buying Behaviour	Complex Buying Behaviour

Strategic Implications

MARKETERS who plan to succeed with today's consumers will understand how their potential market behaves. Cultural influences will play a big role in marketers' relationships with consumers, particularly as firms conduct business on a global scale but also as they try to reach diverse populations in Canada. In addition, family characteristics are changing—more women are in the workforce—which forecasts a change in the way families make purchasing decisions. Perhaps the most surprising shift in family spending is the amount of power—and money—children and teenagers now wield in the marketplace. These young consumers are becoming more and more involved, and in some cases know more about certain products, such as electronics, than their parents do and very often influence purchase decisions. This holds true even with high-involvement purchases like the family auto.

Marketers constantly work toward changing or modifying components of consumers' attitudes about their products to gain a favourable attitude and purchase decision. Finally, they will refine their understanding of the consumer decision process and use their knowledge to design effective marketing strategies. ◆◆◆

REVIEW OF CHAPTER OBJECTIVES

① **Define *consumer behaviour* and describe the role it plays in marketing decisions.**

Consumer behaviour refers to the buyer behaviour of individual consumers. Consumer behaviour plays a huge role in marketing decisions, including what goods and services to offer, to whom, and where. If marketers can understand the factors that influence consumers, they can develop and offer the right products to those consumers.

② **Describe the interpersonal determinants of consumer behaviour: cultural, social, and family influences.**

Cultural influences, such as the general work ethic or the desire to accumulate wealth, come from society. Core values may vary from culture to culture. Social or group influences include social class, opinion leaders, and reference groups with which consumers may want to be affiliated. Family influences may come from parents, grandparents, or children.

③ **Explain each of the personal determinants of consumer behaviour: needs and motives, perceptions, attitudes, learning, and self-concept theory.**

A need is an imbalance between a consumer's actual and desired states. A motive is the inner state that directs a person toward the goal of satisfying a need. Perception is the meaning that a person attributes to incoming stimuli gathered through the five senses. Attitudes are a person's enduring favourable or unfavourable evaluations, emotions, or action tendencies toward something. Learning refers to the immediate or expected changes in consumer behaviour as a result of experience. In self-concept theory, a person's view of himself or herself plays a role in purchasing behaviour. In purchasing goods and services, people are likely to choose products that move them closer to their ideal self-images.

④ **Distinguish between high-involvement and low-involvement purchase decisions.**

Purchases with high levels of potential social or economic consequences are called high-involvement purchase decisions. Examples include buying a new car or home. Routine purchases that pose little risk to the consumer are called low-involvement purchase decisions. Choosing a candy bar or a newspaper are examples.

⑤ **Outline the steps in the consumer decision process.**

The consumer decision process consists of six steps: problem or opportunity recognition, search, alternative evaluation, purchase decision, purchase act, and post-purchase evaluation. The time involved in each stage of the decision process is determined by the nature of the individual purchases.

⑥ **Differentiate among routinized response behaviour, limited problem solving, and extended problem solving by consumers.**

Routinized response behaviour refers to repeat purchases made of the same brand or limited group of items. Limited problem solving occurs when a consumer has previously set criteria for a purchase but then encounters a new brand or model. Extended problem solving results when brands are difficult to categorize or evaluate. High-involvement purchase decisions usually require extended problem solving.

assessment check answers

1.1 Why is the study of consumer behaviour important to marketers?

If marketers can understand the behaviour of consumers, they can offer the right products to consumers who want them.

1.2 Describe the work of Kurt Lewin.

Kurt Lewin proposed that behaviour is the function of the interactions of personal influences and pressures exerted by outside environmental forces.

2.1 List the interpersonal determinants of consumer behaviour.

The interpersonal determinants of consumer behaviour are cultural, social, and family influences.

2.2 What is a microculture?

A microculture is a group within a culture that has its own distinct mode of behaviour.

2.3 Describe the Asch phenomenon.

The Asch phenomenon is the impact of groups and group norms on individual behaviour.

3.1 Identify the personal determinants of consumer behaviour.

The personal determinants of consumer behaviour are needs and motives, perceptions, attitudes, learning, and self-concept theory.

3.2 What are the human needs categorized by Abraham Maslow?

The human needs categorized by Abraham Maslow are physiological, safety, social/belongingness, esteem, and self-actualization.

3.3 How do perception and learning differ?

Perception is the meaning that a person attributes to incoming stimuli. Learning refers to immediate or expected changes in behaviour as a result of experience.

4.1 Differentiate between high-involvement decisions and low-involvement decisions.

High-involvement decisions have high levels of potential social or economic consequences, such as selecting an Internet service provider. Low-involvement decisions pose little financial, social, or emotional risk to the buyer, such as a newspaper or litre of milk.

4.2 Categorize each of the following as a high- or low-involvement product: shampoo, computer, popcorn, apartment, cell phone service.

High-involvement products are the computer, apartment, and cell phone service. Low-involvement products are the shampoo and popcorn.

5.1 List the steps in the consumer decision process.
The steps in the consumer decision process are problem or opportunity recognition, search, alternative evaluation, purchase decision, purchase act, and post-purchase evaluation.

5.2 What is meant by the term *evoked set*?
The evoked set is the number of alternatives that a consumer actually considers in making a purchase decision.

5.3 What are evaluative criteria?
Evaluative criteria are the features that a consumer considers in choosing among alternatives.

6.1 What is routinized response behaviour?
Routinized response behaviour is the repeated purchase of the same brand or limited group of products.

6.2 What does limited problem solving require?
Limited problem solving requires a moderate amount of a consumer's time and effort.

6.3 Give an example of an extended problem-solving situation.
An extended problem-solving situation might involve the purchase of a car or a college education.

MARKETING TERMS YOU NEED TO KNOW

These terms are printed in red in the text. They are defined in the margins of the chapter and in the Glossary that begins on p. G-1. Other important terms are printed in bold black type in the chapter but not included in this list. Their definitions can be found in the Glossary.

customer behaviour 130	motive 140	evaluative criteria 148
consumer behaviour 130	perception 141	cognitive dissonance 149
culture 130	attitudes 143	routinized response behaviour 150
reference groups 135	learning 145	limited problem solving 150
opinion leaders 136	self-concept 146	extended problem solving 150
need 140	evoked set 148	

ASSURANCE OF LEARNING REVIEW

1. Why is it important for marketers to understand cultural influences in the countries where they plan to market their goods and services?
2. Describe a microculture with which you are familiar.
3. Choose a group that you identify with or are a member of. Identify the norms of that group. What is your status in the group? What is your role?
4. Identify and describe the four categories of roles that spouses can play in making purchase decisions.
5. Describe the two factors that interact to create a person's perception of an object. How is this important for marketers?
6. What is shaping? How would you use shaping to motivate consumers toward a new type of skin care product made with vitamins and minerals?
7. Describe the problem or opportunity recognition stage of a recent purchase you made. How did it lead you to the next step?
8. Suppose you were going to look for a new place to live next year. What would be your evaluative criteria?
9. Why is it important for marketers to recognize into which category of problem solving their goods and services fall?

PROJECTS AND TEAMWORK EXERCISES

1. Choose a partner. Each of you should think about your participation in family purchases. How much influence do you have on your family's decisions? Has this influence changed over time? Why or why not? Compare your answers with those of your partner.
2. With a classmate, watch a half hour of television or go to a place on the Internet where you can find advertisements. Of all the advertisements you see in that time period, note which one made the greatest impression on you, and describe why it did. (Did you remember the product? The slogan? The background music? The spokesperson?) Compare your response with your classmate's.
3. With a classmate, select a good or service that has suffered from a poor image recently—it may have performed poorly in the public eye or simply gone out of style. Think about how you would go about changing consumers' attitudes toward the product, and present your plan to the class.
4. On your own or with a classmate, select a print advertisement and identify its cognitive, affective, and behavioural components as well as your attitude toward the advertisement. Discuss the advertisement with your class.
5. Choose a partner and select a low-involvement, routinized consumer product such as toothpaste or detergent. Create an ad that you think could stimulate consumers to change their preferred brand to yours.

CRITICAL THINKING EXERCISES

1. Describe what you think the core values of Canadian culture are. Do you share all of those values? Why or why not?

2. Describe a good or service toward which you have changed your attitude. What influences caused you to make the change? If you haven't experienced a change, describe a good or service toward which you have a strong attitude—and how marketers might be able to change your attitude.

3. Describe a recent high-involvement purchase that you made. What and who influenced the purchase? On Maslow's hier- archy, what needs did you think the purchase would satisfy? Were those needs actually satisfied? Why or why not?

4. Outline three of the four components of your self-concept: self-image, looking-glass self, and ideal self. How close do you think these are to your real self?

5. Think about a purchase that created cognitive dissonance within you after the purchase was made. How did you resolve the anxiety created by the purchase?

ETHICS EXERCISE

Marketing directly to children has become a controversial strategy, particularly on television, because so many programs are aimed at the very young. Some critics think that many ads directed at children mislead and take advantage of children's inability to distinguish fantasy from reality. Marketers say that parents whose children ask for what they see advertised can still say no if they don't wish to buy. Research some articles that illustrate both sides of this issue. Then select a specific children's product (a toy, game, movie, food or candy, for instance) and observe the seller's marketing strategy (ads, commercials, coupons, contests, and so on).

1. Do any characteristics of the campaign support the idea that advertising to children should be carefully regulated?

2. Write a report about your observations, explain why you came to the conclusion you did, and cite your research.

INTERNET EXERCISES

1. **Consumer decision process.** Assume you're in the market for each of the following products. Follow the first three steps in the consumer decision process model shown in the text (problem-opportunity recognition, search, and evaluation of alternatives). Use the Web to aid in your decision process. For which of the three products did you find the Web the most helpful? The least helpful?

   a. A new or used vehicle.

   b. A notebook computer.

   c. A vacation.

2. **Targeting the ethnic consumer.** Chinese and Asians make up a growing percentage of Canadian consumers. Procter & Gamble is one of many companies that are aggressively targeting ethnic consumers. Visit the P&G website **(http://www.pg.com)** and others like it and prepare a report summarizing P&G's efforts to target these important consumer segments.

Note: Internet Web addresses change frequently. If you don't find the exact sites listed, you may need to access the organization's or company's home page and search from there or use a search engine such as Google.

Case 4.1

What Will Consumers Read?

You have just been handed the challenge of developing a new magazine for the Canadian market. You were hired as the market development manager for the publishing company a year ago and have spent most of your time until now working with the research department preparing a recommendation for the project. The time has come for you to prepare your final report, and you still can't decide which project to recommend. You review the options, hoping that one will finally stand out.

Your first thought was to aim the magazine at the one-third of the population who are baby boomers. You know that the first wave of the boomers have turned 60. At first this seemed like the way to go but the research suggested that even though there are a large number of boomers there are significant differences within this group. You know that this demographic group has disposable income—their net worth is double the country's average. You know they spend their money, about $35 billion a year. This group is expected to live until age 76 for males and 83 for females. They have been setting new trends their entire lives, and moving into their 60s has not changed that. In the past, people getting ready to retire have downsized their homes, but this group is upsizing and buying second homes. They are buying luxury cars and are signing on to the Internet in record numbers.

Your research also shows that getting advertising that appeals to this group may be more difficult than for other groups. The people working in the ad industry tend to be much younger and really have not tried to understand this aging group of the population. They are therefore designing ads to attract a younger audience and buying ad space in magazines aimed at the younger segment.

There's already a magazine on the market that aims at the group you're interested in—*50Plus* has been published by CARP (Canada's Association for the Fifty-Plus, formerly Canadian Association of Retired Persons) for several years and has a circulation of over 200 000 with 60 percent female readership.

Another major decision is whether to aim the magazine at men, women, or both. Your research indicates that men and women have totally different consumer behaviour patterns. For example, both men and women felt that advertising didn't connect with them; however, women felt that it was important to them. Women were significantly less satisfied with the treatment they received from companies, and their number one complaint was that they are not taken as seriously as men. When asked to name a company that actually does look after its female customers, most women were unable to name even one. This information seemed to suggest there was a market for a magazine aimed at women that provided information about products and services for them. It also suggested that it would be more difficult to have a magazine that attracted both men and women. A review of current readership statistics for other magazines confirmed this. Most magazines were aimed at one gender but not both. The exceptions to this trend were the publications of television listings and *Reader's Digest*.

Your research looked at environmental factors that were affecting consumer behaviour in all segments. Most research indicated that the effects of a tight economy, globalization, and terrorist attacks had the most impact shown in trends that include a reluctance to travel, less tolerance for risk, a return of family values, increased television viewing, an increase in home improvements, and higher concern for safety.

After reviewing your research again, you feel you have enough information to make some recommendations in your report.

Questions for Critical Thinking

1. Do you think it is possible to publish a magazine aimed at both men and women? Provide your rationale.
2. What type of topics can be covered in a magazine aimed at the baby boomer market?
3. How do current trends affect magazine publications?

Sources: Shirley Roberts, "Hunkering Down for a Long Winter," *Marketing*, October 8, 2001, p. 25; Chris Powell, "Manly Magazines," *Marketing*, July 12, 2004, p. 11; Joanne Thomas Yaccato, "Through the Gender Lens," *Marketing*, June 3, 2003, p. 14; Thelma Beam, "It's All About Sex, Right?", *Marketing*, September 27, 2004, p. 21; "Consumer Magazines: Circulation, Page Rates and Readership," *Marketing*, September 24, 2001, p. 40; Sarah Dobson, "Online Oldster Boom," *Marketing*, October 4, 2004, p. 4; Rebecca Harris, "The Boomers' Golden Age," *Marketing*, July 12, 2004, p. 14; David Chilton, "50 Plus Readies Name Change," *Marketing*, January 5, 2006.

Case 4.2

Burger King's Whopper-Sized Portions

Burger King is bucking a trend. While other chain restaurants are catering to health- and fitness-conscious diners, Burger King is serving up meals to those who want their food filled with the flavours that only fat and salt can provide. Under pressure from the media and consumer advocacy groups, the biggest fast-food restaurant, McDonald's is trying to appease critics with more healthful menu offerings. Other restaurants have joined forces with organizations like Weight Watchers to offer meals for consumers who want to trim their waistlines. But Burger King feels no such pressure. Instead, the company has figured out who eats at Burger King and what they want. And it intends to serve it to them.

Choosing where and what to eat may not seem like a huge decision, but it involves a number of factors. Consumers may be influenced by cost, by their friends and family, by the location of the restaurant and how much time the meal will take, and by their perception of or attitude toward the restaurant and its food. Thinking that its customers wanted a low-fat menu, Burger King struggled to sell several such items before changing course altogether. A marketing survey revealed that although only 18 percent of the population called themselves regular fast-food eaters, these customers accounted for 49 percent of Burger King's business. Company executives call them Super Fans—men aged 18 to 34 who are avid sports fans and whose "grey collar" jobs aren't the most important aspect of their lives. These guys like their food to come in large portions with lots of meat and spicy sauces. And they are downing the 760-calorie Enormous Omelet Sandwich—no less than two omelets and cheese slices, three strips of bacon, and a sausage patty in a bun—in record numbers. "It's designed for people who like to start the day with a hearty breakfast," remarks the chief product officer for Burger King. The new omelet sandwich has helped increase breakfast sales 20 percent.

Along with the new menu items clearly aimed at the Super Fan market, Burger King took a new direction in promoting its products to this market. Burger King was ready to take a risk with its promotional strategy after a 21-month slide in sales. The risk paid off. Faced with the challenge of having a smaller promotional budget than most of its competitors, the decision was made to focus all its resources on young adult males. The result was a series of promotions with attitude. The first all-Canadian campaign showed young men trying to make room for a Whopper by having their teeth pulled, jaws widened, and hands enlarged. Next was the "Subservient Chicken" promotion, where visitors to the Burger King website could get a man dressed in chicken suit to perform silly stunts. These campaigns resulted in a sales increases of more than 18 percent compared to McDonald's, who experienced about an 11 percent increase.

The new strategy was working so well Burger King continued with another round of television commercials and website ads. One new television commercial was called "Manthem," in which a young man sitting in a fine-dining restaurant with a petite portion of food in front of him jumps up and shouts, "I am man, hear me roar." At this point he takes off to the nearest Burger King where he can get a meaty sandwich, singing as he goes, "Way too hungry to settle for chick food." The other means of getting its message out to this market was placing ads on mobile websites, designed to be seen on a cell phone screen. When these ads are placed on mobile sites such as CBS Sportsline they reach a large audience who fit their Super Fan profile.

Despite nutrition-centred criticism from some groups, consumers like what they are being served at Burger King. Burger King has figured out who its customers are, what they like to eat, and how to get the message out them.

Questions for Critical Thinking

1. What factors are involved in your own decisions about where and what to eat? Is this usually a high-involvement or low-involvement decision? Where do you eat most often? Why?

2. Do you think Burger King is making a good marketing decision to focus essentially on one group of consumers—the Super Fans? Why or why not?

Sources: Bruce Horovitz, "Burger King Gets New CEO as IPO Nears," *USA Today*, April 10, 2006, p. 7B; Michael S. Rosenwald, "Why America Has to Be Fat," *Washington Post*, January 22, 2006, http://www. washingtonpost.com; "Burger King Launches King-Size Meal," AllBusiness, January 3, 2006, http://www.allbusiness.com; "Triple Whopper: Portion Fit for King Kong," Diet-Blog, December 30, 2005, http://www .diet-blog.com; Amy Johannes, "Burger King Launches Gorilla-Sized Burger for King Kong Tie-In," *Promo*, December 15, 2005, http://promomagazine.com; Bruce Horovitz, "Marketers Cash in as Nation Bellies Up to Snack Bar," *USA Today*, June 8, 2005, http://www.usatoday.com; Bret Beun, "A Really Big Idea," *Newsweek*, May 23, 2005, p. 48; "A BIG Breakfast at Burger King," CNN Money.com, March 29, 2005, http://money.cnn.com; Chris Daniels, "Beyond Text," Marketing, *May 28, 2007*; Michelle Halpern, "Love It / Loathe It," *Marketing*, May 22, 2006; "Secrets of a Hot Agency's Success," Marketing, March 21, 2005; Isabelle Raymond, "Bold About the Burger," *Marketing*, December 12, 2005.

Video Case 4.3

Nielsen Media Research Watches the TV Watchers

The written video case on Nielsen Media Research appears on page VC-5. The recently filmed Nielsen Media Research video is designed to expand and highlight the concepts in this chapter and the concepts and questions covered in the written video case.

chapter 5

Business-to-Business (B2B) Marketing

CHAPTER OBJECTIVES

1. Explain each of the components of the business-to-business (B2B) market.

2. Describe the major approaches to segmenting business-to-business (B2B) markets.

3. Identify the major characteristics of the business market and its demand.

4. Discuss the decision to make, buy, or lease.

5. Describe the major influences on business buying behaviour.

6. Outline the steps in the organizational buying process.

7. Classify organizational buying situations.

8. Explain the buying centre concept.

9. Discuss the challenges of and strategies for marketing to government, institutional, and international buyers.

SAM BATS SCORE A HOMER WITH MAJOR LEAGUE BASEBALL

Most Canadians, when they think of Major League Baseball, think of the Toronto Blue Jays. A few may think of Canadians Jason Bay of the Pittsburgh Pirates or Adam Loewen of the Baltimore Orioles. True baseball enthusiasts may remember former Canadian baseball players such as Hall of Fame pitcher Ferguson Jenkins and former National League MVP Larry Walker (five all-star game appearances, seven Gold Glove awards, 367 home runs, and lifetime batting average of .314). But there is another Major League Baseball story that Canadians should know—the story of Sam Holman and the Sam Bat.

Sam Holman is the founder of Ottawa-based The Original Maple Bat Corp., a major supplier of bats to Major League teams. It all started when Bill MacKenzie, a scout for the Colorado Rockies and drinking buddy of Sam's, complained to him in a bar one night that baseball teams were regularly breaking baseball bats and were spending lots of money for replacement ones. Sam immediately began to research baseball bats and soon built his first "Rideau Crusher" prototype. The bat was tested by members of the Ottawa Lynx Triple A team with positive reviews, but it was a trip to a Toronto Blue Jays batting practise in 1997 that was the real beginning for Sam's bats, now called Sam Bats. Centre fielder Joe Carter tried the bat and hit a homer on his first try. Since then, hundreds of Major League players have adopted Sam Bats. Barry Bonds set the single-season Major League home run record in 2001 (73) and holds the all-time home run record (762). Following his 2001 season, he was quoted in *The Ottawa Record:* "Sam wants to give me the credit. But it took both of us to do it. I give thanks to God for my ability, and I give thanks to Sam for producing something that gives me a lot of confidence." *Sports Illustrated* called the Sam Bat a "21st-century Excalibur." What makes the Sam Bat different? It's made of maple instead of ash, the traditional wood used for baseball bats. The maple bats are stronger and lighter than other wooden bats, making their swing speed faster and increasing their durability.

Sam Bats are expensive when you look at the initial price, and Sam Holman cannot afford to heavily discount the price when he has only one major product and 80 percent of his business is done with one group of customers. His business is built on product superiority. The bat improves the performance of individual players, and the durability of the bat means that overall cost savings can result due to the reduced need for replacement bats.

As you will see in this chapter, in business-to-business marketing, sellers must frequently appeal to more than one person. The success of Sam Bats is because both the Major League teams and the players who use the bats see them as superior to competitors' bats. Price is one purchase criterion but seldom the deciding one; it is more often performance or the value that arises over the life of the product. Many business-to-business customers realize that "the lowest price is not always the lowest price."[1]

connecting with customers

The company describes its bat as "one of the prettiest and yet meanest bats in the world." It welcomes current professional players to provide a current bat—even if cracked—and it will produce a Sam Bat to demonstrate its superiority. Each bat has the distinctive Sam Bat logo, which can be seen from the furthest bleachers, and as batters improve their batting performance, their teams increase their win-loss records, and fan satisfaction increases. This is often an important advantage for business-to-business marketers—to be able to increase a customer's satisfaction.

Chapter Overview

W E are all aware of the consumer marketplace. As consumers, we're involved in purchasing needed items almost every day of our lives. In addition, we can't help noticing the barrage of marketing messages aimed at us through a variety of media. But the business-to-business marketplace is, in fact, significantly larger. The Government of Canada purchases more than $20 billion annually.[2] For example, it spends an estimated $2 million just for remanufactured toner cartridges.[3] Worldwide business-to-business commerce conducted over the Internet now totals more than $2 trillion (U.S.).[4] Whether conducted through face-to-face transactions, via telephone, or over the Internet, business marketers each day deal with complex purchasing decisions involving multiple decision makers. They range from simple reorders of previously purchased items to complex buys for which materials are sourced from all over the world. As illustrated by the opening vignette, they involve the steady building of relationships between organizations such as The Original Maple Bat Co. and Major League Baseball teams and players. Customer satisfaction and customer loyalty are major factors in the development of these long-term relationships and are often determined by factors other than price.

This chapter discusses buying behaviour in the business or organizational market. **Business-to-business,** or **B2B marketing** deals with organizational purchases of goods and services to support production of other products, to facilitate daily company operations, or for resale. But you ask, "How do I go about distinguishing between consumer purchases and B2B transactions?" Actually, it's pretty simple. Just ask yourself two questions:

1. Who is buying the good or service?
2. Why is the purchase being made?

Consumer buying involves purchases made by people like you and me. We purchase items for our own use and enjoyment—and not for resale. By contrast, B2B purchases are made by businesses, government, and marketing intermediaries to be resold, combined with other items to create a finished product for resale, or used up in the day-to-day operations of the organization. So answer the two questions— "Who is buying?" and "Why?"—and you have the answer. ◆◆◆

> **business-to-business (B2B) marketing**
> Organizational sales and purchases of goods and services to support production of other products, for daily company operations, or for resale.

NATURE OF THE BUSINESS MARKET

Firms usually sell fewer standardized products to organizational buyers than to ultimate consumers. Whereas you might purchase a cell phone for your personal use, a company generally has to purchase an entire communications system from a supplier such as Nortel, whose Meridian Communications Portfolio offers digital voice and Internet technology in a single network.[5] Purchases such as this require greater customization, more decision making, and usually more decision makers. So the buying and selling process becomes more complex, often involving teams of decision makers and taking an average of 6 to 36 months to complete.[6] Because of the complexity of the purchases, customer service is extremely important to B2B buyers. Advertising plays a much smaller role in the business market than in the consumer market, although advertisements placed in business magazines or trade publications are common. Business marketers advertise primarily to announce new products, to enhance their company image and presence, and to attract potential customers who would then deal directly with a salesperson. Personal selling plays a much bigger role in business markets than in consumer markets, distribution channels are shorter, customer relationships tend to last longer, and purchase decisions can involve multiple decision makers. Table 5.1 compares the marketing practises commonly used in both B2B and consumer marketing.

table 5.1 *Comparing Business-to-Business Marketing and Consumer Marketing*

	BUSINESS-TO-BUSINESS MARKETING	CONSUMER MARKETING
Product	Relatively technical in nature, exact form often variable, accompanying services very important	Standardized form, service important but less than for business products
Promotion	Emphasis on personal selling	Emphasis on advertising
Distribution	Relatively short, direct channels to market	Product passes through a number of intermediate links en route to consumer
Customer relations	Relatively enduring and complex	Comparatively infrequent contact, relationship of relatively short duration
Decision-making process	Diverse group of organization members makes decision	Individual or household unit makes decision
Price	Competitive bidding for unique items, list prices for standard items	List prices

Like final consumers, an organization purchases products to fill needs. However, its primary need—meeting the demands of its own customers—is similar from firm to firm. A manufacturer buys raw materials such as wood pulp, fabric, or grain to create the company's product. A wholesaler or retailer buys the manufactured products—paper, clothing, or cereal—to resell. Mattel buys everything from plastic to paints to produce its toys, Canadian Tire buys finished toys to sell to the public, and passenger airlines buy and lease aircraft from manufacturers such as Boeing and Airbus. The "Marketing Success" feature discusses how these two companies compete for orders. Institutional purchasers such as government agencies and nonprofit organizations also buy products to meet the needs of their constituents, whether it is global positioning system (GPS) mapping devices or meals ready to eat (MRE) for troops in the field.

Companies also buy services from other businesses. A firm may purchase law and accounting services, an office cleaning service, a call centre service, or a recruiting service. Jan-Pro, a commercial cleaning service company that has been in business since 1991, is one such service company. The chain has more than 87 master franchise offices throughout Canada and the United States, along with almost 7000 individual franchise operations.[7]

Environmental, organizational, and interpersonal factors are among the many influences in B2B markets. Budget, cost, and profit considerations all play parts in business buying decisions. In addition, the business buying process typically involves complex interactions among many people. An organization's goals must also be considered in the B2B buying process. Later sections of the chapter will explore these topics in greater detail.

Some firms focus entirely on business markets. For instance, DuPont sells materials such as polymers, coatings, and colour technologies to manufacturers that use them in a variety of products. Caterpillar makes construction and mining equipment, diesel and natural gas engines, and industrial gas turbines. SAP provides collaborative business software that lets companies work with customers and business partners using databases and other applications from every major software vendor. Other firms sell to both consumer and business

Earn
DOUBLE
TD Points

Turn your business expenses into travel.
The TD Canada Trust Business *Visa* Card with Travel Rewards.

You can spend a lot of money running your business. Now it can pay you back. By applying for a new Business *Visa* Card with Travel Rewards, or adding Travel Rewards to your existing Business *Visa* Card, before May 25, 2007, your business purchases will help you earn TD Points you can redeem towards travel. You'll earn one TD Point for every dollar you spend on purchases with your card. Especially right now, since you'll earn double TD Points on purchases until July 31, 2007. Plus, to help you travel sooner, we'll start you off with 10,000 Bonus TD Points upon enrolment. That's a $150 value in travel savings. So apply for a new Business *Visa* Card with Travel Rewards or add Travel Rewards to your existing Business *Visa* Card today and get your business expenses working for you.

EARN DOUBLE TD POINTS PLUS GET 10,000 BONUS POINTS UPON ENROLMENT.[1]
APPLY BY MAY 25, 2007

Call 1-866-827-3757 or visit a TD Canada Trust branch.
For more information visit tdcanadatrust.com/businessrewards

1. Offer applies only to new TD Canada Trust Business Visa Cardholders that enrol in the Travel Rewards Program (the "Program") before May 25, 2007 or existing Business Visa Cardholders that enrol in the Program before May 25, 2007. Existing Program members are not eligible for this offer. Bonus Points will be awarded to the new Program member upon enrolment. On or before July 31, 2007, you will receive two TD Points instead of the standard one for every $1 on purchases posted to your Account or six TD Points instead of the standard five for every $1 posted to your Account for travel arrangements purchased at the TD Canada Trust Visa Travel Rewards Centre. TD Points are earned on purchases less refunds, rebates and other similar credits and excluding fees, cash advances, TD Canada Trust Visa Cheques, balance transfers, interest charges or optional services. For standard Program terms and conditions, see the "Travel Rewards Program Terms and Conditions" in your Business Visa Cardholder Agreement or visit www.tdcanadatrust.com/tdvisa/agreements.jsp for an online copy of the Business Visa Cardholder Agreement. Offer may be changed, extended or withdrawn at any time without notice and cannot be combined with any other offer. Some conditions apply. *Visa International Service Association/Used under license.

COURTESY OF TD BANK FINANCIAL GROUP

TD Canada Trust promotes its Business VISA Card to businesses that wish to receive travel rewards on their business expenses.

markets. Intel's digital and wireless computer technology is found in business computing systems and personal computers. Bell Canada, Rogers Communications, and Telus sell Internet and phone service to both consumers and businesses. Note also that marketing strategies developed in consumer marketing are often appropriate for the business sector, too. Final consumers are often the end users of products sold into the business market and, as explained later in the chapter, can influence the buying decision.

The B2B market is diverse. Transactions can range from orders as small as a box of paper clips or copy-machine toner for a home-based business to transactions as large as thousands of parts for an automobile manufacturer or massive turbine generators for an electric power plant. As mentioned earlier, businesses are also big purchasers of services, such as telecommunications, computer consulting, and transportation services. Four major categories define the business market: (1) the commercial market, (2) trade industries, (3) government organizations, and (4) institutions.

COMPONENTS OF THE BUSINESS MARKET

commercial market Individuals and firms that acquire products to support, directly or indirectly, production of other goods and services.

The **commercial market** is the largest segment of the business market. It includes all individuals and firms that acquire products to support, directly or indirectly, the production of other goods and services. When Hewlett-Packard buys computer chips from Intel, when Sara Lee purchases wheat to mill into flour for an ingredient in its breads, and when a plant supervisor orders light bulbs and cleaning supplies for a factory in Saskatchewan, these transactions all take place in the commercial market. Some products aid in the production of other items (the computer chips). Others are physically used up in the production of a good or service (the wheat). Still others contribute to the firm's day-to-day operations (the maintenance supplies). The commercial market includes manufacturers, farmers, and other members of resource-producing industries, construction contractors, and providers of such services as transportation, public utilities, financing, insurance, and real estate brokerage.

trade industries Retailers or wholesalers that purchase products for resale to others.

resellers Marketing intermediaries that operate in the trade sector.

The second segment of the organizational market, **trade industries,** includes retailers and wholesalers, known as **resellers,** who operate in this sector. Most resale products, such as clothing, appliances, sports equipment, and automobile parts, are finished goods that the buyers sell to final consumers. In other cases, the buyers may complete some processing or repackaging before reselling the products. A retail meat market may purchase a side of beef and then cut individual pieces for its customers. Lumber dealers and carpet retailers may purchase in bulk and then provide quantities and sizes to

---

marketing success — Boeing Soars to New Heights

Background. After years of head-to-head competition in the market for commercial and military aircraft, it seemed as though Boeing would finally take a back seat to its long-time rival Airbus. Boeing's profits were slowing, orders were down, its stock price had dropped, and it hadn't launched a new model in more than a dozen years.

The Challenge. Boeing needed to figure out what its customers—major air carriers such as Air Canada and various governments—would want to buy in the coming years. Airbus was counting on passengers wanting cheaper flights to hub cities, which airlines would provide via Airbus's own big planes. Travellers then would transfer to connecting flights on smaller planes.

The Strategy. Boeing bet on passengers wanting to fly directly to their destinations, bypassing hubs and connecting flights for the convenience of one takeoff and landing. Its fuel-efficient, midsized 777 wide-body plane recently shattered the distance record for

commercial flight, covering nearly 22 000 kilometres in a single flight. And the company is introducing its new 787 Dreamliner jet, with high-tech features to save even more fuel, a significant operating cost.

The Outcome. Boeing was right. The aircraft maker's order book is full. Air Canada is scheduled to take the first of its 37 Dreamliners in 2012. Boeing's stock price has tripled in the last couple of years. Although industry analysts say Boeing and Airbus are both so good at what they do that neither eclipses the other for long, at the moment, Boeing has come out on top.

Sources: "Boeing Poised for Supremacy over Airbus: Barron's," Reuters, March 12, 2006, http://news.yahoo.com; Steve Gelsi, "Boeing Gaining Altitude, Barron's Says," *MarketWatch,* March 11, 2006, http://www.marketwatch.com; Andrew Romano, "Boeing's New Tailwind," *Newsweek,* December 5, 2005, p. 45; Scott Deveau, "Air Canada Stung by Delays at Boeing," *Calgary Herald,* May 9, 2008, p. D3.

meet customers' specifications. In addition to resale products, trade industries buy computers, display shelves, and other products needed to operate their businesses. These goods, as well as maintenance items and specialized services, such as scanner installation, newspaper inserts, and radio advertising, all represent organizational purchases. Wendy Almquist founded Beans Wax Candle Co., a wholesale soy candle business. The company supplies candles for customers such as Carlson Marketing Group, Almquist's former employer, which offers the candles as incentive gifts, and to Smith & Hawken, a garden retailer that sells the candles under its private label.[8]

The government category of the business market includes domestic units of government—federal, provincial or territorial, and municipal—as well as foreign governments. This important market segment makes a wide variety of purchases, ranging from highways to social services. The primary motivation of government purchasing is to provide some form of public benefit, such as national defence or pollution control. But government agencies have also become creative when it comes to selling—local police departments and federal and provincial agencies are selling unclaimed shipments, seized assets, and surplus goods through public sales, public tenders, and auctions. Public Works and Government Services Canada operates eight Crown Assets Distribution Centres across Canada where it disposes of everything from vehicles, boats, household appliances, and jewellery to tools and agricultural equipment, and many other items.

Institutions, both public and private, are the fourth component of the business market. This category includes a wide range of organizations, such as hospitals, churches, skilled care and rehabilitation centres, colleges and universities, museums, and not-for-profit agencies. Some institutions—such as in higher education—must rigidly follow standardized purchasing procedures, but others have less formal buying practises. Business-to-business marketers often benefit by setting up separate divisions to sell to institutional buyers.

Business markets include computer chips, such as Intel's Xeon, which is used in HP's BladeSystem c3000 server.

Marketoid

The Crown Assets Distribution website, http:// crownassets.pwgsc.gc.ca, **receives 50 000 visitors per month.**

① Explain each of the components of the business-to-business (B2B) market.

B2B MARKETS: THE INTERNET CONNECTION

Although consumers' use of Internet markets receives the bulk of public attention, more than 94 percent of all Internet sales are B2B transactions.[9] Many business-to-business marketers have set up private portals that allow their customers to buy needed items. Service and customized pages are accessed through passwords provided by B2B marketers. Online auctions and virtual marketplaces offer other ways for buyers and vendors to connect with each other over the Internet.

During the early Internet boom, start-up companies rushed to connect buyers and sellers without considering basic marketing principles such as targeting their market and making sure to fulfill customers' needs. As a result, many of these companies failed. But the companies that survived—and new firms that have learned lessons from the mistakes of the old—have established a much stronger marketing presence. For instance, they recognize that their business customers have a lot at stake and expect greater value and utility from the goods and services they purchase.[10]

The Internet also opens up foreign markets to sellers. One such firm, a cotton exchange called The Seam, survived the Internet boom and bust and now connects U.S. cotton traders instantaneously with textile mills from countries that include Turkey, Brazil, and China. The Seam is expanding its services into the wholesale peanut market worldwide.[11]

Go Green

From Consumer Markets to Business Markets

PAUL Jenkins and Miriam Goldberger started Wildflower Farm (www.wildflowerfarm.com) just over 20 years ago as a wholesale dried flower business. It quickly expanded to become a pick-your-own flower farm. Approximately 10 years ago, Paul and Miriam noticed clumps of rich green grass growing in shaded areas around trees near their farm and decided to see if this grass could provide natural grass pathways through their wildflower meadows. Some experimentation eventually led to the development of a drought-tolerant, low-maintenance turf grass, which they named Eco-Lawn.

Eco-Lawn is a blend of seven fine fescue grasses. It creates a deep root system so it can naturally find the nutrients it needs from the soil, eliminating the need for water, fertilizers, and chemicals. Slow-growing, Eco-Lawn needs mowing about once per month, although some people prefer to simply leave it to grow. The reduced need for water provides another benefit: Eco-Lawn is grub resistant.

Eco-Lawn grass seeds are grown in Oregon, where many of the world's best grass seed is grown. The seeds are shipped to Wisconsin, where they are cleaned and packaged for Wildflower Farm, and are then shipped to a warehouse in Buffalo, New York, where the packages are stored. From this warehouse, Wildflower Farm ships to customers throughout the United States. Large shipments are brought to the company's location in Coldwater, Ontario, where they are sold from the company-owned retail location or shipped to retailers or consumers across Canada. In 2008, Wildflower Farm sold more than 100 000 kilograms of grass seed, much of it for orders of one or two 2.25-kilogram bags. The company has started to focus on business markets, where order sizes are much larger. Miriam Goldberger has been travelling to cities such as San Francisco and Toronto, making "lunch and learn" presentations to landscape architects who are increasingly designing "green buildings," and to municipalities who want to reduce their lawn water and maintenance costs. Wildflower Farm—and Eco-Lawn—is changing "lawnscaping" for homeowners and businesses across North America.

Sources: Wildflower Farm website, www.wildflowerfarm.com, accessed October 26, 2008; Personal interviews with Paul Jenkins and Miriam Goldberger, October 3–4, 2008.

DIFFERENCES IN FOREIGN BUSINESS MARKETS

Companies that sell to businesses in foreign markets must consider the possibility of variations in government regulations and cultural practises. Some business products need modifications to succeed in foreign markets. In Australia, Japan, and Great Britain, for instance, motorists drive on the left side of the road. Automobiles must be modified to accommodate such differences.

Business marketers must be willing to adapt to local customs and business practises when operating abroad. They should also research cultural preferences. A company even needs to consider what ink colours to use for documents because colours can have different meanings in different countries. Factors as deceptively simple as the time of a meeting and methods of address for associates can make a difference. When Toronto-based Samco Machinery got a $3-million contract to supply roll-forming machinery to a subsidiary of India's car manufacturer Tata, it discovered doing business in India involves considerable red tape, and a need to accommodate a more casual Indian attitude about the meaning of a signed contract.[11]

assessment check 1 ✓

1.1 Define B2B marketing.

1.2 What is the commercial market?

② Describe the major approaches to segmenting business-to-business (B2B) markets.

SEGMENTING B2B MARKETS

Business-to-business markets include wide varieties of customers. So marketers must identify the different market segments they serve. By applying market segmentation concepts to groups of business customers, a firm's marketers can develop a strategy that best suits a particular segment's needs. The overall process of segmenting business markets divides markets based on different criteria, usually organizational characteristics and product applications. Among the major ways to segment business markets are demographics (size), customer type, end-use application, and purchasing situation.

SEGMENTATION BY DEMOGRAPHIC CHARACTERISTICS

As with consumer markets, demographic characteristics define useful segmentation criteria for business markets. For example, firms can be grouped by size or based on sales revenues or number of employees. Marketers may develop one strategy to reach Fortune 500 corporations with complex purchasing procedures and another strategy for small firms where decisions are made by one or two people. Small businesses and consumers accounted for more than half of the 1.45 million new BlackBerry subscribers in North America in one recent quarter. As a result, Research In Motion introduced new software starting at $499 per company to specifically target small businesses with 30 or fewer potential users. The software was given free as a promotion to companies that bought five new BlackBerrys.[12]

SEGMENTATION BY CUSTOMER TYPE

Another useful segmentation approach groups prospects according to type of customer. Marketers can apply this concept in several ways. They can group customers by broad categories—manufacturer, service provider, government agency, not-for-profit organization, wholesaler, or retailer—and also by industry. These groups may be further divided using other segmentation approaches discussed in this section.

 Customer-based segmentation is a related approach often used in the business-to-business marketplace. Organizational buyers tend to have much more precise—and complex—requirements for goods and services than ultimate consumers do. As a result, business products often fit narrower market segments than consumer products do. This fact leads some firms to design business goods and services to meet detailed buyer specifications. Tetra Tech FW, Inc., provides a variety of environmental services, including technology development, design, engineering, and remediation for organizations around the world. Because the company's customers include government agencies as well as private firms—and because customers' needs are different—Tetra Tech FW offers a range of programs to suit each type of customer. For instance, the firm provides consulting services for utilities, helps communities clean up polluted water sources, and even conducts missions to clear public and private sites of unexploded ordnance. It is currently working with mines in Canada, Mongolia, Romania, Bulgaria, Australia, Peru, Chile, Argentina, Brazil, and most Central American countries.[13]

customer-based segmentation Dividing a business-to-business market into homogeneous groups based on buyers' product specifications.

North American Industrial Classification System (NAICS)

For many years, North American B2B marketers have used numerical classification systems as tools for segmenting markets and identifying new customers. However, with implementation of the North American Free Trade Agreement (NAFTA), members needed a joint classification system that would allow marketers to compare business sectors among the member nations. In effect, marketers required a segmentation tool they could use across borders. The **North American Industrial Classification System (NAICS)** was developed for that purpose. It provides considerably more detail than was previously available with earlier classification systems. NAICS created new service sectors to better reflect the economy of the 21st century. They include information; health care and social assistance; and professional, scientific, and technical services.

 Table 5.2 demonstrates the NAICS system for wine manufacturers. NAICS uses six digits. The first five digits are fixed among the members of NAFTA. The sixth digit can vary among Canadian, U.S., and Mexican data. In short, the sixth digit accounts for specific data needs of each nation.[14] Excelcorc sells corks to Canadian wineries from Newfoundland to British Columbia. Knowing that Canadian wine manufacturers are classified under NAICS classification 312130 allows Excelcorc to quickly identify and get valuable information on the customers in its target market.

North American Industrial Classification System (NAICS) Classification used by NAFTA countries to categorize the business marketplace into detailed market segments.

Marketoid

NAICS Canada 2002 consists of 20 sectors, 103 subsectors, 328 industry groups, 728 industries, and 928 national industries.

table 5.2   *NAICS Classifications for Wine Manufacturers*

31	Manufacturing
312	Beverage and Tobacco Product Manufacturing
3121	Beverage Manufacturing
31213	Wineries
312130	Canadian Wineries

Source: NAICS, U.S. Census Bureau, http://www.census.gov/epcd/www/naics.html.

SEGMENTATION BY END-USE APPLICATION

end-use application segmentation
Segmenting a business-to-business market based on how industrial purchasers will use the product.

A third basis for segmentation, **end-use application segmentation,** focuses on the precise way in which a business purchaser will use a product. For example, a printing equipment manufacturer may serve markets ranging from a local utility to a bicycle manufacturer to the Department of National Defence. Each end use of the equipment may dictate unique specifications for performance, design, and price. Praxair, a supplier of industrial gases, for example, might segment its markets according to user. Steel and glass manufacturers might buy hydrogen and oxygen, while food and beverage manufacturers need carbon dioxide. Praxair also sells krypton, a rare gas, to companies that produce lasers, lighting, and thermal windows. Many small- and medium-sized companies also segment markets according to end-use application. Instead of competing in markets dominated by large firms, they concentrate on specific end-use market segments.

SEGMENTATION BY PURCHASE CATEGORIES

Firms have different structures for their purchasing functions, and B2B marketers must adapt their strategies according to those organizational buyer characteristics. Some companies designate centralized purchasing departments to serve the entire firm, and others allow each unit to handle its own buying. A supplier may deal with one purchasing agent or several decision makers at various levels. Each of these structures results in different buying behaviour.

When the buying situation is important to marketers, they typically consider whether the customer has made previous purchases or if this is the customer's first order. Toronto-based Akuni Adventures, for instance, offers discounts for repeat customers and for large groups.[15]

Increasingly, businesses that have developed customer relationship management (CRM) systems—strategies and tools that reorient an entire organization to focus on satisfying customers—are able to segment customers by the stage of the relationship between the business and the customer. A B2B company, for example, might develop different strategies for newly acquired customers than it would for existing customers to which it hopes to cross-sell new products. Similarly, building loyalty among satisfied customers requires a different approach than developing programs to "save" at-risk customer relationships. CRM will be covered in more depth in Chapter 9.

assessment check 2

2.1 What are the four major ways marketers segment business markets?

2.2 What is the NAICS?

(3) Identify the major characteristics of the business market and its demand.

CHARACTERISTICS OF THE B2B MARKET

Businesses that serve both B2B and consumer markets must understand the needs of their customers. However, several characteristics distinguish the business market from the consumer market: (1) geographic market concentration, (2) the sizes and numbers of buyers, (3) purchase decision procedures, and (4) buyer–seller relationships. The next sections consider how these traits influence business-to-business marketing.

GEOGRAPHIC MARKET CONCENTRATION

The Canadian business market is more geographically concentrated than the consumer market. Manufacturers converge in certain regions of the country, making these areas prime targets for business marketers. For example, the Canadian chemical industry is largely concentrated in Alberta, Ontario, and Quebec. The oil and gas industry is largely concentrated in Alberta and Newfoundland. Jet manufacturing in Canada is dominated by Bombardier Inc. of Montreal. When the company decided to build a new plant to manufacture its proposed C-series aircraft, it chose Montreal over sites in Toronto, New Mexico, and Northern Ireland. Montreal had been viewed as the favoured site because the company already did so much of its jet assembly there.

Certain industries locate in particular areas to be close to customers. Firms may choose to locate sales offices and distribution centres in these areas to provide more attentive service. It makes sense that the Ottawa area is favoured by companies that sell to the federal government. Satyam Computer Services Ltd., an India-based company with offices in 45 countries, recently opened a new office in Mississauga, Ontario. Sanjay Tugnait, the Canadian manager, says, "Many of our clients in the banking, pharmaceuticals, and manufacturing verticals [industries] have their offices in Mississauga."[16]

The Canadian automobile assembly industry is concentrated in southwestern Ontario, due primarily to its proximity to Michigan, the centre of North American automobile manufacturing. There is no surprise that so many automobile parts manufacturers are located in this area as well. As the suppliers to the industry concentrate near their customers, they then make the area more attractive for industry expansion. As Internet-based technology continues to improve, allowing companies to transact business even with distant suppliers, business markets may become less geographically concentrated. Much of government spending, for example, is now directed through the Internet.

YOU NAME IT

We'll Customize A Supply Chain Solution For It

Wherever you manufacture, however you store inventory and distribute products, Ryder designs and operates end-to-end supply chain solutions that deliver a competitive advantage for businesses like yours. Unmatched experience, flexibility, and expertise make Ryder the company that other companies rely on around the globe. So, if you want to maximize efficiency, enhance visibility, and improve customer satisfaction, just name it, and we'll get it done.
Call 1-888-88-RYDER or visit www.ryder.com.

Ryder

SUPPLY CHAIN, WAREHOUSING & TRANSPORTATION SOLUTIONS

©2005 Ryder System, Inc. All rights reserved.

COURTESY OF RYDER SYSTEMS, INC.

Ryder offers its customers warehousing, transportation, and fleet management services "wherever you manufacture, however you store inventory and distribute products." By serving the needs of different types of firms, Ryder segments its customers by type.

SIZES AND NUMBERS OF BUYERS

In addition to geographic concentration, the business market features a limited number of buyers. Marketers can draw on a wealth of statistical information to estimate the sizes and characteristics of business markets. The federal government is the largest single source of such statistics. Information can be accessed from several important sources: Statistics Canada (**http://www.statcan.ca**), Industry Canada (**http://www.ic.gc.ca**), and Strategis (**http://www.strategis.ic.gc.ca**). Many government units and trade organizations also operate websites that contain helpful information.

Many buyers in limited-buyer markets are large organizations. The international market for jet engines is dominated by three manufacturers: United Technology's Pratt & Whitney unit, General Electric, and Rolls-Royce. These firms sell engines to Boeing, Bombardier, and the European consortium, Airbus Industrie. These aircraft manufacturers compete for business from passenger carriers such as Air Canada, Northwest Airlines, British Airways, KLM, and Singapore Airlines, along with cargo carriers such as Purolator, DHL, Federal Express, and United Parcel Service.

Trade associations and business publications provide additional information on the business market. Private firms such as Dun & Bradstreet publish detailed reports on individual companies. These data serve as a useful starting point for analyzing a business market. Finding data in such a source requires an understanding of the NAICS, which identifies much of the available statistical information.

THE PURCHASE DECISION PROCESS

To market effectively to other organizations, businesses must understand the dynamics of the organizational purchase process. Suppliers who serve business-to-business markets must work with multiple buyers, especially when selling to larger customers. Decision makers at several levels may influence final orders, and the overall process is more formal and professional than the consumer purchasing process. Purchasers typically require a longer time frame because B2B involves more complex decisions. Suppliers must evaluate customer needs and develop proposals that meet technical requirements and specifications. Also, buyers need time to analyze competing proposals. Often, decisions require more than one round of bidding and negotiation, especially for complicated purchases.

BUYER–SELLER RELATIONSHIPS

An especially important characteristic of B2B marketing is the relationship between buyers and sellers. These relationships are often more complex than consumer relationships, and they require superior communications among the organizations' personnel. Satisfying one major customer may mean the difference of millions of dollars to a firm. The "Solving an Ethical Controversy" feature discusses an important question many buyers and sellers face.

Relationship marketing involves developing long-term, value-added customer relationships. A primary goal of business-to-business relationships is to provide advantages that no other vendor can provide—for instance, lower price, quicker delivery, better quality and reliability, customized product features, or more favourable financing terms. For the business marketer, providing these advantages means expanding the company's external relationships to include suppliers, distributors, and other organizational partners. It also includes managing internal relationships between departments. North

---

Solving an Ethical Controversy

How Should Buying Firms Deal with Vendors?

IT'S not unusual for vendors to give their valued customers gifts of various types, but many companies have strict rules about what buyers can accept. At Canada Post, for instance, conflict of interest guidelines state, "Do not accept gifts from customers, competitors, contractors, or suppliers that could be considered to obligate you or the corporation in any way; gifts of nominal value are permitted (approximately $100)." Petro-Canada's guidelines provide several criteria: an accepted benefit must be of token and non-material value; the exchange must create no obligation, and the gift or entertainment must occur infrequently. The conflict of interest guidelines state, "As a rough guide, we should not accept entertainment that could not be justified on a Petro-Canada expense statement were we offering it rather than receiving it."

Is it acceptable for buyers to receive gifts or gratuities from vendors?

PRO

1. Most buyers can be trusted to make the right decision about vendors based on criteria such as price and quality rather than gifts.

2. Gifts of nominal value are simply a way of thanking important customers and do not influence sales.

CON

1. It's too difficult to make impartial decisions about which vendors to use if you accept anything of material value from them.

2. Such gifts merely drive up the cost of doing business, which hurts customers and shareholders in the long run.

Where do you stand: pro or con?

Source: Canada Post, "Living Our Values," available http://www.canadapost.ca/corporate/about/conduct_vision_values/pdf/code_conduct-e.pdf, accessed May 19, 2008; Petro-Canada, "The Way We Do Business," available http://www.petro-canada.ca/pdfs/ir-code_of_conduct-04-000-f-e.pdf, accessed May 19, 2008.

Hill News promotes internal relationships through a number of employee benefits programs, including profit sharing, tuition and books for training programs, interest-free loans for computer equipment, and matching programs for fundraising and donations. For more than 20 years, the company has hosted a breakfast for suppliers, customers, and employees and their families on the Thursday before the Calgary Stampede. Such programs and promotions foster strong relationships with all of the company's stakeholders.[17]

Close cooperation, whether through informal contacts or under terms specified in contractual partnerships and strategic alliances, enables companies to meet buyers' needs for quality products and customer service. This holds true both during and after the purchase process. Tetra Tech FW, mentioned earlier, has formal Client Service Quality and Shared Vision programs, which are designed to engage customers in continuous communication leading to customer satisfaction.

Relationships between for-profit and not-for-profit organizations are just as important as those between two commercial organizations. Wal-Mart is a longtime corporate sponsor of Children's Miracle Network, an international organization that helps improve children's health and welfare by raising funds for state-of-the-art care, cutting-edge research, and education. Between 1987 and 2007, Wal-Mart raised and donated more than $430 million to 170 children's hospitals in the network.[18]

EVALUATING INTERNATIONAL BUSINESS MARKETS

Business purchasing patterns differ from one country to the next. Researching these markets poses a particular problem for B2B marketers. Of course, as explained earlier, NAICS is correcting this problem in the NAFTA countries.

In addition to quantitative data such as the size of the potential market, companies must also carefully weigh its qualitative features. This process involves considering cultural values, work styles, and the best ways to enter overseas markets in general. LG Electronics, a $38-billion global appliance and electronics maker based in South Korea, focuses on understanding the particulars of important local markets in all its new-product introductions. LG conducts in-country research and opens local manufacturing and marketing facilities. The company's Middle East marketing director says, "Gone are the days where you could just roll out one product for the global market. We speak to consumers individually." Some of the company's products include a programmable Russian karaoke phone, a kimchi fridge to isolate the strong odour of South Korea's national dish and keep it away from other foods, a microwave with a skewer rack and special heat setting for kebabs that is marketed in Iran, and a fridge for Saudi Arabia that includes a special bin to hold dates at their ideal temperature.[19]

In today's international marketplace, companies often practise **global sourcing**, which involves contracting to purchase goods and services from suppliers worldwide. This practise can result in

BECAUSE THE WAITING SHOULD END WHEN THE WINNING BEGINS...

BUSINESS OWNERS ARE BANKING AT CANADA'S CREDIT UNIONS

Because good news comes with its own set of challenges, questions soon follow. How do you finance that new opportunity, how do you seize the day? Waiting for the breakthrough was tough enough - waiting for answers from a bank doesn't cut it. And that's why business owners are turning to credit unions. **Because trust turns opportunities into action,** credit union Account Managers take the time to know you and your business before challenges arise. We use more than formulas and ratios - our people stay with you for the long run so the trust grows naturally. **Because the person who serves you is empowered to help you.** Responsive, professional, way more personal. That's business banking without a bank. Are you open to a stress-free comparison?

visit
www.CanadasCreditUnions.com
Ask questions, meet other business owners, find the credit union team nearest you and book your comparison today.

Commercial loans and mortgages | Operating lines | Current accounts On-line banking | Smart people who make time for you

business banking @ CANADA'S CREDIT UNIONS
it's **WHO** you know.

Canada's credit unions are seeing an increase in business banking as their account managers take the time to develop closer relationships with their business customers: "Because the person who serves you is empowered to help you."

® HANDS & GLOBE Design is a registered certification mark owned by the World Council of Credit Unions, used under license.

COURTESY CREDIT UNION CENTRAL OF CANADA

assessment check 3a

3.1 Why is geographic segmentation important in the B2B market?

3.2 In what ways is the buyer–seller relationship important in B2B marketing?

3.3 What is global sourcing?

substantial cost savings. Office Depot plans to expand its wood-fibre purchases from northern Canada, but also from Russia and the Far East.[20] Clothing maker Coldwater Creek uses suppliers in Hong Kong and New Delhi.[21] Mexico is now outsourcing its social-security services to India, and Canadian bankers and dealers have started commissioning investor reports and research from there as well.[22]

Global sourcing requires companies to adopt a new mind-set; some must even reorganize their operations. Among other considerations, businesses sourcing from multiple multinational locations should streamline the purchase process and minimize price differences due to labour costs, tariffs, taxes, and currency fluctuations.

Marketoid

On average, Koreans eat nearly 20 kilograms of kimchi each year. The Korean Food Academy has categorized more than 100 different types.

global sourcing
Purchasing goods and services from suppliers worldwide.

derived demand
Demand for a resource that results from demand for the goods and services that are produced by that resource.

BUSINESS MARKET DEMAND

The previous section's discussion of business market characteristics demonstrated considerable differences between marketing techniques for consumer and business products. Demand characteristics also differ in these markets. In business markets, the major categories of demand include derived demand, joint demand, inelastic demand, volatile demand, and inventory adjustments. Figure 5.1 summarizes these different categories of business market demand.

DERIVED DEMAND

The term **derived demand** refers to the linkage between demand for a company's output and its purchases of resources such as machinery, components, supplies, and raw materials. The demand for computer microprocessor chips is *derived* from the demand for personal computers. If more businesses and individuals buy new computers, the demand for chips increases; if fewer computers are sold, the demand for chips decreases. In recent years, worldwide slowdowns in sales of personal computers reduced demand for chips. But STATS ChipPAC, Southeast Asia's biggest packager of semiconductors, expects to make its first profit in several years. The company runs tests of specialized chips used in products such as the iPod and LCD televisions, and these electronic products are enjoying a big resurgence in demand.[23]

Organizational buyers purchase two general categories of business products: capital items and expense items. Derived demand ultimately affects both. Capital items are long-lived business assets that must be depreciated over time. *Depreciation* is an accounting term that refers to charging a portion of a capital item's cost as a deduction against the company's annual revenue for purposes of determining its net income. Examples of capital items include major installations such as new manufacturing plants, office buildings, and computer systems.

Expense items, in contrast, are items consumed within short time periods. Accountants charge the cost of such products against income in the year of purchase. Examples of expense items include the supplies necessary to operate the business, ranging from paper clips to machine lubricants.

figure 5.1

Categories of Business Market Demand

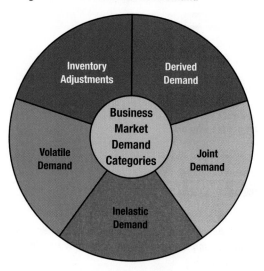

VOLATILE DEMAND

Derived demand creates volatility in business market demand. Assume that the sales volume for a gasoline retailer is increasing at an annual rate of 5 percent. Now suppose that the demand for this gasoline brand slows to a 3 percent annual increase. This slowdown might convince the firm to keep its current gasoline pumps and replace them only when market conditions improve. In this way, even modest shifts in consumer demand for a gasoline brand would greatly affect the pump manufacturer.

JOINT DEMAND

Another important influence on business market demand is **joint demand,** which results when the demand for one business product is related to the demand for another business product used in combination with the first item. Both lumber and concrete are required to build most homes. If the lumber supply falls, the drop in housing construction will most likely affect the demand for concrete. Another example is the joint demand for electrical power and large turbine engines. If consumers decide to conserve power, demand for new power plants drops, as does the demand for components and replacement parts for turbines.

joint demand Demand for a product that depends on the demand for another product used in combination with it.

INELASTIC DEMAND

Inelastic demand means that demand throughout an industry will not change significantly due to a price change. If the price of lumber drops, a construction firm will not necessarily buy more lumber from its suppliers unless another factor—such as lowered mortgage interest rates—causes more consumers to purchase new homes.

inelastic demand Demand that, throughout an industry, will not change significantly due to a price change.

INVENTORY ADJUSTMENTS

Adjustments in inventory and inventory policies can also affect business demand. Assume that manufacturers in a particular industry consider a 60-day supply of raw materials the optimal inventory level. Now suppose that economic conditions or other factors induce these firms to increase their inventories to a 90-day supply. The change will bombard the raw-materials supplier with new orders.

Further, **just-in-time (JIT)** inventory policies seek to boost efficiency by cutting inventories to absolute minimum levels and by requiring vendors to deliver inputs as the production process needs them. JIT allows companies to better predict which supplies they will require and the timing for when they will need them, markedly reducing their costs for production and storage. Widespread implementation of JIT has had a substantial impact on organizations' purchasing behaviour. Firms that practise JIT tend to order from relatively few suppliers. In some cases, JIT may lead to **sole sourcing** for some items—in other words, buying a firm's entire stock of a product from just one supplier. Electronic data interchange (EDI) and quick-response inventory policies have produced

Marketoid

When Wal-Mart decided to cut back the shelf space it devotes to Sam's Club cola, Cott Corp., the manufacturer of the cola, lost half of its stock market value. Analysts estimate that just losing four feet of shelf space will reduce Cott Corp.'s sales by $100 million.

H.F. (HERB) MACKENZIE

Derived demand also applies to expense items. When demand for a manufacturer's product declines, its production decreases, and its demand for operating supplies such as drill bits and other cutting tools also declines.

similar results in the trade industries. The latest inventory trend, **JIT II,** leads suppliers to place representatives at the customer's facility to work as part of an integrated, on-site customer–supplier team. Suppliers plan and order in consultation with the customer. This streamlining of the inventory process improves control of the flow of goods.

Although inventory adjustments are critical in manufacturing processes, they are equally vital to wholesalers and retailers. Perhaps nowhere is inventory management more complex than at Wal-Mart, the largest retailer in the world, with sales of $375 billion (U.S.). With no signs of slowing down, suppliers such as Procter & Gamble and Unilever—giants themselves—work closely with Wal-Mart to monitor and adjust inventory as necessary. "One of the reasons why P&G and Wal-Mart have had such a positive relationship is that they both are strongly data-driven," explains one former senior P&G executive. Other suppliers, such as Remington, Revlon, and Hershey Foods, generate at least 20 percent of their total income from Wal-Mart, so inventory management is critical for those companies as well.[24]

---

assessment check 3b ✓

3.4 How does derived demand create volatile demand?

3.5 Give an example of joint demand.

3.6 How might JIT II strengthen marketing relationships?

---

(4) Discuss the decision to make, buy, or lease.

THE MAKE, BUY, OR LEASE DECISION

Before a company can decide what to buy, it should decide whether to buy at all. Organizational buyers must figure out the best way to acquire needed products. In fact, a firm considering the acquisition of a finished good, component part, or service has three basic options:

1. Make the good or provide the service in-house.

2. Purchase it from another organization.

3. Lease it from another organization.

Manufacturing the product itself, if the company has the capability to do so, may be the best route. It may save a great deal of money if its own manufacturing division does not incur costs for overhead that an outside vendor would otherwise charge.

On the other hand, most firms cannot make all the business goods they need. Often, it would be too costly to maintain the necessary equipment, staff, and supplies. Therefore, purchasing from an outside vendor is the most common choice. Xerox manufactures more than 18 different types of colour printers to meet nearly any business need—from affordable colour laser printers to high-performance ink-jet printers. Its wide array of products, coupled with its track record of a century of supplying businesses, has made it a leader in the B2B printer market.[25] Companies can also look outside their own plants for goods and services that they formerly produced in-house, a practise called *outsourcing* that the next section will describe in more detail.

In some cases, however, a company may choose to lease inputs. This option spreads out costs compared with lump-sum costs for up-front purchases. The company pays for the use of equipment for a certain time period. A small business may lease a copier for a few years and make monthly payments. At the end of the lease term, the firm can buy the machine at a prearranged price or replace it with a different model under a new lease. This option can provide useful flexibility for a growing business, allowing it to easily upgrade as its needs change.

Companies can also lease sophisticated computer systems and heavy equipment. For example, some airlines prefer to lease airplanes rather than buy them outright because short-term leases allow them to adapt quickly to changes in passenger demand.

THE RISE OF OUTSOURCING AND OFFSHORING

offshoring Movement of high-wage jobs from Canada to lower-cost overseas locations.

Chances are, if you dial a call centre for a firm such as Dell, GE, or Bell Canada, your call will be answered by someone in India.[26] Microsoft recently nearly doubled its workforce in India to 7000, and IBM employs nearly 50 000 Indians.[27] In recent years, there has been a growing concern related to the movement of jobs to lower-cost overseas locations, a business practise referred to as **offshoring.** This relocation of business processes to a lower-cost location can involve production offshoring or services offshoring. China has emerged as the preferred destination for production offshoring, while India has emerged as the dominant player in services offshoring.

China still leads the way in offshore manufacturing, making two-thirds of the world's copiers, microwaves, DVD players, and shoes, and virtually all of the world's toys. It is expected to become a source of service outsourcing for many, although most of its 8000-plus software services providers are tiny firms with fewer than 2000 employees each. Such small firms are seen as risky business partners, with less ability to hang on to their key players and fewer financial resources to survive long term. Fragmented Chinese firms hoping to do business with firms that need such services face another obstacle—the possibility that Indian companies may buy them up and consolidate them to expand their own operations.[28]

Some U.S.-based firms want to remain closer to home but take advantage of the benefits of locating some of their operations overseas. Canada and Mexico are attractive locations for these **nearshoring** operations. Russian outsourcing firm Luxoft recently opened an office in Vancouver and now has two specialists already at work for Boeing in nearby Seattle, Washington. It costs 20 to 30 percent less to have the work done in Canada.[29] In today's highly competitive marketplace, firms are looking to improve efficiency and cut costs on just about everything, including customer service, human resources, accounting, information technology, manufacturing, and distribution. **Outsourcing,** using outside vendors to produce goods and services formerly produced in-house or in-country, is a trend that continues to rise. Businesses outsource for several reasons: (1) they need to reduce costs to remain competitive; (2) they need to improve the quality and speed of software maintenance and development; (3) outsourcing has begun to offer greater value than ever before. There is an increasing trend to outsource professional, value-added services. Purolator Courier outsources some of its legal work to India.[30] Toronto-based chartered accounting firm Horwath Orenstein outsources work to India, where Datamatics now processes more than 1000 tax returns annually for it. There are more than 140 000 practising CAs in India, and another 350 000 people are currently pursuing the CA designation.[31]

Outsourcing allows firms to concentrate their resources on their core business. It also allows access to specialized talent or expertise that does not exist within the firm. The most frequently outsourced business functions include information technology (IT) and human resources, with other white-collar service jobs such as accounting, drug research, technical R&D, and film animation increasingly being outsourced as well.[32] Software is now a $200 billion-a-year industry in Canada and the United States. But many firms are now outsourcing their business to other countries, particularly India. One reason is the cost of labour—a starting call centre operator or a programmer with a college degree earns around $10 000 a year. Another reason is the large pool of highly educated, English-speaking workers. In a new twist on outsourcing, some Indian firms may soon be hiring increasing numbers of North Americans, as they aim higher and look to form full-fledged business partners with their North American customers. The numbers are still small, but because higher-level consulting services are based on close customer relationships, it makes sense to hire more North Americans.[33]

Eastern Europe is becoming an increasingly popular outsourcing location thanks to its multilingual population. Giants such as Boeing, BMW, General Motors, Siemens, and Nortel contract with small programming firms in Bulgaria, while IBM, Hewlett-Packard, Oracle, and Alcatel have support centres or software labs in Romania. German software powerhouse SAP AG has a Bulgarian research lab with 180 engineers who write Java software for SAP's innovative products around the world. "There is an exceptionally high level of talent in Eastern Europe," says Kasper Rorsted, managing director for Europe, Middle East, and Africa at Hewlett-Packard.[34]

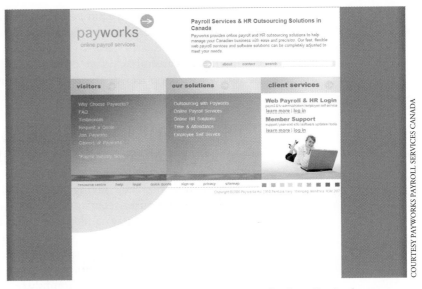

Payworks offers payroll and HR outsourcing services for Canadian businesses.

nearshoring Moving jobs to vendors in countries close to the business's home country.

outsourcing Using outside vendors to produce goods and services formerly produced in-house.

Outsourcing can be a smart strategy if a company chooses a vendor that can provide high-quality products and perhaps at a lower cost than could be achieved on the company's own. This priority allows the outsourcer to focus on its core competencies. Successful outsourcing requires companies to carefully oversee contracts and manage relationships. Some vendors now provide performance guarantees to assure their customers that they will receive high-quality services that meet their needs.

PROBLEMS WITH OUTSOURCING AND OFFSHORING

Outsourcing and offshoring are not without their downsides. Many companies discover that their cost savings are less than vendors sometimes promise. Also, companies that sign multi-year contracts may find that their savings drop after a year or two. When proprietary technology is an issue, outsourcing raises security concerns. Similarly, companies that are protective of customer data and relationships may think twice about entrusting functions like customer service to outside sources.

In some cases, outsourcing and offshoring can reduce a company's ability to respond quickly to the marketplace, or they can slow efforts in bringing new products to market. Suppliers who fail to deliver goods promptly or provide required services can adversely affect a company's reputation with its customers.

Outsourcing and offshoring are controversial topics with unions, especially in the auto industry, as the percentage of component parts made in-house has steadily dropped. These practises can create conflicts between non-union outside workers and in-house union employees, who fear job loss. Management initiatives to outsource jobs can lead to strikes and plant shutdowns. Even if they do not lead to disruption in the workplace, outsourcing and offshoring can have a negative impact on employee morale and loyalty.

assessment check 4

4.1 Identify two potential benefits of outsourcing.

4.2 Identify two potential problems with outsourcing.

---

(5) Describe the major influences on business buying behaviour.

THE BUSINESS BUYING PROCESS

Suppose that CableBox, Inc., a hypothetical manufacturer of television decoder boxes for cable TV service providers, decides to upgrade its manufacturing facility with $1 million in new automated assembly equipment. Before approaching equipment suppliers, the company must analyze its needs, determine goals that the project should accomplish, develop technical specifications for the equipment, and set a budget. Once it receives vendors' proposals, it must evaluate them and select the best one. But what does *best* mean in this context? The lowest price or the best warranty and service contract? Who in the company is responsible for such decisions?

The business buying process is more complex than the consumer decision process. Business buying takes place within a formal organization's budget, cost, and profit considerations. Furthermore, B2B and institutional buying decisions usually involve many people with complex interactions among individuals and organizational goals. For instance, purchasing agents for Healthcare Materials Management Services, the procurement arm of St. Joseph's Health Care London (SJHC) in London, Ontario, must verify the signature on each procurement request before processing it, to be sure it is that of an authorized SJHC representative.[35] To understand organizational buying behaviour, business marketers require knowledge of influences on the purchase decision process, the stages in the organizational buying model, types of business buying situations, and techniques for purchase decision analysis.

INFLUENCES ON PURCHASE DECISIONS

B2B buying decisions react to various influences, some external to the firm and others related to internal structure and personnel. In addition to product-specific factors such as purchase price, installation, operating and maintenance costs, and vendor service, companies must consider broader environmental, organizational, and interpersonal influences.

Environmental Factors

Environmental conditions such as economic, political, regulatory, competitive, and techno-logical considerations influence business buying decisions. CableBox may wish to defer pur-chases of the new equipment in times of slowing economic activity. During a recession, sales to cable companies might drop because households hesitate to spend money on cable service. The company would look at the derived demand for its products, possible changes in its sources of materials, employment trends, and similar factors before committing to such a large capital expenditure.

Political, regulatory, and competitive factors also come into play in influencing purchase decisions. Passage of a law freezing cable rates would affect demand, as would an introduction of a less expensive decoder box by a competitor. Finally, technology plays a role in purchase decisions. A few years ago, cable-ready televisions decreased demand for set-top boxes, and smaller, more powerful satellite dishes have cut into the market for cable TV, reducing derived demand. But customers still need the boxes to access premium channels and movies, even with digital service. CableBox can benefit from technological advances, too. As more homes want fast Internet connections, adding cable modems to its product line may present a growth opportunity.

Organizational Factors

Successful business-to-business marketers understand their customers' organizational structures, poli-cies, and purchasing systems. A company with a centralized procurement function operates differently from one that delegates purchasing decisions to divisional or geographic units. Trying to sell to the local store when head office merchandisers make all the decisions would clearly waste salespeople's time. Buying behaviour also differs among firms. For example, centralized buying tends to emphasize long-term relationships, whereas decentralized buying focuses more on short-term results. Personal selling skills and user preferences carry more weight in decentralized purchasing situations than in centralized buying.

How many suppliers should a company patronize? Because purchasing operations spend over half of each dollar their companies earn, consolidating vendor relationships can lead to large cost savings. However, a fine line separates maximizing buying power from relying too heavily on a few suppliers. Many companies engage in **multiple sourcing**—purchasing from several vendors. Spreading orders ensures against shortages if one vendor cannot deliver on schedule. However, dealing with many sellers can be counterproductive and take too much time. Each company must set its own criteria for this decision.

Interpersonal Influences

Many people may influence B2B purchases, and considerable time may be spent obtaining the input and approval of various organization members. Both group and individual forces are at work here. When committees handle buying, they must spend time to gain majority or unanimous approval. Also, each individual buyer brings to the decision process individual preferences, experiences, and biases.

Business marketers should know who will influence buying decisions in an organization for their products and should know each of their priorities. To choose a supplier for an industrial press, for example, a purchasing manager and representatives of the company's production, engineering, and quality control departments may jointly decide on a supplier. Each of these principals may have a dif-ferent point of view that the vendor's marketers must understand.

To effectively address the concerns of all people involved in the buying decision, sales personnel must be well versed in the technical features of their products. They must also interact well with employees of the various departments involved in the purchase decision. Sales representatives for medical products—traditionally called detailers—frequently visit hospitals and doctors' offices to discuss the advantages of their new products and leave samples with clinical staff. Representatives for IBM would most likely try to talk with staff who would potentially use its Linux application. See the "Etiquette Tips for Marketing Professionals" feature for some ideas about how to manage telephone communications if your company has an automated voice-response system to answer calls from customers.

ETIQUETTE TIPS FOR MARKETING PROFESSIONALS

Keeping Customers out of Voice Response Hell

YOU'VE probably been on the receiving end of a company's customer service operation that consists entirely of recorded menus and messages. Though they can save nearly 80 percent of the cost of having a human operator take a service call, 14 of 15 automated response systems failed in a recent survey of customers. Here are some ways to help your own customers avoid the frustrations that many feel during such phone calls.

1. Tailor your menus to suit different kinds of customers. New voice response systems can provide you with information about incoming callers based only on the originating phone number, so you can offer each caller the right menu from the start.
2. Because you can identify incoming callers, route important ones immediately to live operators in relevant departments such as collections, account management, or marketing, instead of putting them on hold.
3. Make sure your system can route calls to employees who are working at home or on the road. If they're the right people for your customers to talk to, keep them accessible to your callers.
4. Don't set the system up to automatically cross-sell products to customers who must wait on hold. Cross-selling is a major complaint among half of customers surveyed about voice response systems.
5. Ensure that your system answers calls promptly, minimizes the time on hold, and doesn't force callers to repeat information or continually identify themselves.
6. Make it easy to reach a human voice. Remember that most of your competitors will let most of their customers get trapped in voice-response systems. Be the one who doesn't.

Sources: "When to Take the Call and When to Use Voicemail," Earnware Corporation, http://www.earnware.com, accessed March 7, 2006; David H. Freedman, "Service with a Smile. Really," *Inc.,* October 2005, pp. 75–76; Alexandra DeFelice, "A Business Imperative: Improve Service Now," Destination CRM.com, July 26, 2005, http://www.destinationcrm.com.

The Role of the Professional Buyer

Many large organizations attempt to make their purchases through systematic procedures employing professional buyers. In the trade industries, these buyers, often referred to as **merchandisers,** are responsible for securing needed products at the best possible prices. Wal-Mart has buyers for shoes and clothing that will ultimately be sold to consumers. Ford has buyers for components that will be incorporated into its cars and trucks. A firm's purchasing or merchandising unit devotes all its time and effort in determining needs, locating and evaluating alternative suppliers, and making purchase decisions.

Purchase decisions for capital items vary significantly from those for expense items. Firms often buy expense items routinely with little delay. Capital items, however, involve major fund commitments and usually undergo considerable review.

One way in which a firm may attempt to streamline the buying process is through **systems integration,** or centralization of the procurement function. One company may designate a lead division to handle all purchasing. Another firm may choose to designate a major supplier as the systems integrator. This vendor then assumes responsibility for dealing with all the suppliers for a project and for presenting the entire package to the buyer. In trade industries, this vendor is sometimes called a **category captain.**

A business marketer may set up a sales organization to serve national accounts that deals solely with buyers at geographically concentrated corporate headquarters. A separate field sales organization may serve buyers at regional production facilities.

Corporate buyers often use the Internet to identify sources of supply. They view online catalogues and websites to compare vendors' offerings and to obtain product information. Some use Internet exchanges to extend their supplier networks.

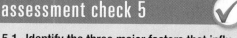

assessment check 5

5.1 Identify the three major factors that influence purchase decisions.

5.2 What are the advantages and disadvantages of multiple sourcing?

Purchasing managers like Chuck MacLean, pictured above, are increasingly earning the Certified Purchasing Professional (CPP) accreditation through the Purchasing Management Association of Canada.

MODEL OF THE ORGANIZATIONAL BUYING PROCESS

6 Outline the steps in the organizational buying process.

An organizational buying situation takes place through a sequence of activities. Figure 5.2 illustrates an eight-stage model of an organizational buying process. The additional steps arise because business purchasing introduces new complexities that do not affect consumers. Although not every buying situation will require all these steps, this figure provides a good overview of the whole process.

Stage 1: Anticipate or Recognize a Problem/Need/Opportunity and a General Solution

Both consumer and business purchase decisions begin when the recognition of problems, needs, or opportunities triggers the buying process. Perhaps a firm's computer system has become outdated or an account representative demonstrates a new service that could improve the company's performance. Companies may decide to hire an outside marketing specialist when their sales stagnate.

The problem may be as simple as replacing standard operating supplies that a company has depleted from its inventory, or as complex as buying major information technology hardware and systems that the company is purchasing for the first time. Brock University, for example, purchased two communications switches for a planned upgrade to a student residence telephone system. Once the need for the upgrade was determined, the switches were included in an upcoming budget, and a time for the upgrade was decided. This all happened long before a purchase order was issued.

Stage 2: Determine the Characteristics and Quantity of a Needed Good or Service

In some instances, this part of the process may involve technical experts; in other instances, decisions concerning both characteristics and quantity are simple.

figure 5.2

Stages in the B2B Buying Process

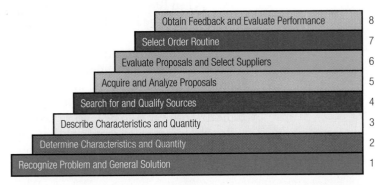

Obtain Feedback and Evaluate Performance	8
Select Order Routine	7
Evaluate Proposals and Select Suppliers	6
Acquire and Analyze Proposals	5
Search for and Qualify Sources	4
Describe Characteristics and Quantity	3
Determine Characteristics and Quantity	2
Recognize Problem and General Solution	1

Source: Based on Michael D. Hutt and Thomas W. Speh, *Business Marketing Management: A Strategic View of Industrial and Organizational Markets*, 8th edition (Mason, OH: South-Western, 2004).

In the example of the communications switches, the characteristics and quantity were determined by the communications capacity that the upgrade was required to handle, and by the existing communications equipment in place at the university. Adding components made by the same manufacturer as the main communications system helps ensure compatibility and decide responsibility if future problems arise.

Stage 3: Describe Characteristics and the Quantity of a Needed Good or Service

After determining the characteristics and quantity of needed products, B2B buyers must translate these ideas into detailed specifications. Sometimes this simply requires using the manufacturer's model or part numbers from its catalogues. The purpose of this stage is to ensure that competing suppliers all have a clear understanding of what is requested and that their subsequent quotations can be compared.

Stage 4: Search for and Qualify Potential Sources

Both consumers and businesses search for good suppliers of desired products. Sometimes a public call for proposals is made, particularly when the purchasing is being done by a public sector organization. In such instances, the potential sources find the purchasing organization. In many instances, organizations maintain a list of approved, or qualified, suppliers to which they send requests for proposals. In the example of the communications switches, the manufacturer and model of the switches were decided before requests for proposals were sent out. Brock University asked for a quotation from the manufacturer and from six authorized Canadian distributors of the manufacturer.

Stage 5: Acquire and Analyze Proposals

The next step is to acquire and analyze suppliers' proposals, which are often submitted in writing. If the buyer is a government or institutional purchasing unit, this stage of the purchase process almost always involves competitive bidding. During this process, each marketer must develop its bid, including a price, that will satisfy the criteria determined by the customer's problem, need, or opportunity. While competitive bidding is less common in the business sector, a company may follow the practise to purchase nonstandard materials, complex products, or products that are made to its own specifications.

Stage 6: Evaluate Proposals and Select Suppliers

Next in the buying process, buyers must compare vendors' proposals and choose the one that seems best suited to their needs. Proposals for sophisticated equipment, such as a large computer networking system, can include considerable differences among product offerings, and the final choice may involve trade-offs.

Price is not the only criterion for the selection of a vendor. Relationship factors like communications and trust may also be important to the buyer. Other issues include reliability, delivery record, time from order to delivery, quality, and order accuracy.

When Brock University opened the quotations it received for the two communications switches, it found that the manufacturer declined to offer a price as it sold component equipment only through authorized dealers, a practise common in business-to-business marketing. Four of the six quotations were for approximately $35 000. One quotation was for approximately $59 000 as the company would not offer the equipment without a service contract even though it was clearly stated that the proposal should be for the supply of equipment only. The final quotation was for approximately $21 000. At first glance, this might appear to be the clear winner but, in such an instance, the reason for the low price should be investigated. When the potential supplier was contacted to recheck its price, Brock University determined the company was offering refurbished equipment by mistake. The company voluntarily retracted its proposal.[36]

Stage 7: Select an Order Routine

Once a supplier has been chosen, buyer and vendor must work out the best way to process the purchase order. Ordering routines can vary considerably. Most orders will, however, include product descriptions,

H.F. (HERB) MACKENZIE

In business-to-business markets, price is often much less important than quality. Product failure for an inexpensive item can have tremendous financial consequences for a company.

quantities, prices, delivery terms, and payment terms. Today, companies have a variety of options for submitting orders: written documents, phone calls, faxes, or electronic data interchange.

Stage 8: Obtain Feedback and Evaluate Performance

At the final stage, buyers measure vendors' performances. Sometimes this judgment will involve a formal evaluation of each supplier's product quality, delivery performance, prices, technical knowledge, and overall responsiveness to customer needs. At other times, vendors are measured according to whether they have lowered the customer's costs or reduced its employees' workloads. In general, bigger firms are more likely to use formal evaluation procedures, while smaller companies lean toward informal evaluations. Regardless of the method used, buyers should tell vendors how they will be evaluated.

Sometimes firms rely on independent organizations to gather quality feedback and summarize results. J.D. Power and Associates conducts research and provides information to a variety of firms so that they can improve the quality of their goods and services.

assessment check 6

6.1 Why does the organizational buying process contain more steps than the consumer buying process?

6.2 List the steps in the organizational buying process.

CLASSIFYING BUSINESS BUYING SITUATIONS

⑦ Classify organizational buying situations.

As discussed earlier, business buying behaviour responds to many purchasing influences, such as environmental, organizational, and interpersonal factors. This buying behaviour also involves the degree of effort that the purchase decision demands and the levels within the organization where it is made. Like consumer behaviour, marketers can classify B2B buying situations into three general categories, ranging from least to most complex: (1) straight rebuying, (2) modified rebuying, and (3) new-task buying. Business buying situations may also involve reciprocity. The following sections look at each type of purchase.

The most complex category of business buying is new-task buying. It is common for a number of people to be involved in this type of buying decision.

Straight Rebuying

The simplest buying situation is a **straight rebuy,** a recurring purchase decision in which a customer reorders a product that has satisfied needs in the past. The buyer already likes the product and terms of sale, so the purchase requires no new information. The buyer sees little reason to assess competing options and so follows a routine repurchase format. A straight rebuy is the business market equivalent of routinized response behaviour in the consumer market. Purchases of low-cost items such as paper clips and pencils for an office are typical examples of straight rebuys. Marketers who maintain good relationships with customers by providing high-quality products, superior service, and prompt delivery can go a long way toward ensuring straight rebuys.

Modified Rebuying

In a **modified rebuy,** a purchaser is willing to re-evaluate available options. Buyers may see some advantage in looking at alternative offerings within their established purchasing guidelines. They might take this step if their current supplier has let a rebuy situation deteriorate because of poor service or delivery performance. Price, quality, and innovation differences can also provoke modified rebuys. Modified rebuys resemble limited problem solving in consumer markets.

B2B marketers want to induce current customers to make straight rebuys by responding to all their needs. Competitors, on the other hand, try to lure those buyers away by raising issues that will convince them to reconsider their decisions.

New-Task Buying

The most complex category of business buying is **new-task buying**—first-time or unique purchase situations that require considerable effort by the decision makers. The consumer market equivalent of new-task buying is extended problem solving. PPG Industries operated a range of legacy and new software programs and packages in its 16 business units. When it was ready to construct a network to allow it to integrate information with its customers, suppliers, and other partners, PPG knew that both the benefits and the investment in the network would be high, making the choice of platform of the highest importance. "In selecting a platform," says the company's vice president of information technology, "we had to be able to communicate and establish relationships with a single individual all the way up to the largest companies in the world." In the end, the company chose Microsoft's. NET platform.[37]

A new-task buy often requires a purchaser to carefully consider alternative offerings and vendors. A company entering a new field must seek suppliers of component parts that it has never before purchased. This new-task buying would require several stages, each yielding a decision of some sort. These decisions would include developing product requirements, searching out potential suppliers, and evaluating proposals. Information requirements and decision makers can complete the entire buying process, or they may change from stage to stage.

Marketoid

Many buyers are among the 40 000 members and program participants of the Purchasing Management Association of Canada.

Reciprocity

Reciprocity—a practise of buying from suppliers that are also customers—is a controversial practise in a number of procurement situations. An office equipment manufacturer may favour a particular supplier of component parts if the supplier has recently made a major purchase of the manufacturer's products. Reciprocal arrangements traditionally have been common in industries featuring homogeneous products with similar prices, such as the chemical, paint, petroleum, rubber, and steel industries.

Reciprocity suggests close links among participants in the organizational marketplace. It can add to the complexity of B2B buying behaviour for new suppliers who are trying to compete with preferred vendors. Business-to-business buyers in Canada see it as a positive, widespread practise. In Japan, close ties between suppliers and customers are common. Although buyers and sellers enter into reciprocal agreements in the United States, both the Department of Justice and the Federal Trade Commission view them as attempts to reduce competition.

ANALYSIS TOOLS

Two tools that help professional buyers improve purchase decisions are value analysis and vendor analysis. **Value analysis** examines each component of a purchase in an attempt to either delete the item or replace it with a more cost-effective substitute. Airplane designers have long recognized the need to make planes as light as possible. Value analysis supports using DuPont's synthetic material Kevlar in airplane construction because it weighs less than the metals it replaces. The resulting fuel savings are significant for the buyers in this marketplace.

Vendor analysis carries out an ongoing evaluation of a supplier's performance in categories such as price, EDI capability, back orders, delivery times, liability insurance, and attention to special requests. In some cases, vendor analysis is a formal process. Some buyers use a checklist to assess a vendor's performance. A checklist quickly highlights vendors and potential vendors that do not satisfy the purchaser's buying requirements.

> **value analysis**
> Systematic study of the components of a purchase to determine the most cost-effective approach.
>
> **vendor analysis**
> Assessment of supplier performance in areas such as price, back orders, timely delivery, and attention to special requests.

assessment check 7

7.1 What are the four classifications of business buying situations?

7.2 Differentiate between value analysis and vendor analysis.

THE BUYING CENTRE CONCEPT

> **8** Explain the buying centre concept.

The buying centre concept provides a vital model for understanding B2B buying behaviour. A company's **buying centre** encompasses everyone who is involved in any aspect of its buying activity. A buying centre may include the architect who designs a new research laboratory, the scientist who works in the facility, the purchasing manager who screens contractor proposals, the chief executive officer who makes the final decision, and the vice president for research who signs the formal contracts for the project. Buying centre participants in any purchase seek to satisfy personal needs, such as participation or status, as well as organizational needs. A buying centre is not part of a firm's formal organizational structure. It is an informal group whose composition and size vary among purchase situations and firms.

> **buying centre**
> Participants in an organizational buying decision.

BUYING CENTRE ROLES

Buying centre participants play different roles in the purchasing decision process, which are summarized in Figure 5.3. **Users** are the people who will actually use the good or service. Their influence on the purchase decision may range from negligible to extremely important. Users sometimes initiate purchase actions by requesting products, and they may also help develop product specifications. Users often influence the purchase of office equipment. Office Depot knows this. Recently, the company redesigned its office supply stores to make them more attractive to shoppers. The new layout includes a fresh colour scheme and graphics, and a "pod" structure that displays related or complementary items, such as binding and filing products, in horseshoe-shaped pods along the walls where customers can find them easily. The modular fixtures can be adapted to Office Depot stores of any size and shape, and they are lower in height to allow salespeople to more easily find customers and offer assistance.[38]

Gatekeepers control the information that all buying centre members will review. They may exert this control by distributing printed product data or advertisements or by deciding which salespeople will speak to which individuals in the buying centre. A purchasing agent might allow some salespeople to see the engineers responsible for developing specifications but deny others the same privilege. The

figure 5.3

Buying Centre Participants and Their Roles

Source: From BOONE/KURTZ. *Contemporary Marketing, 13th edition.* © 2008 South-Western, a part of Cengage Learning, Inc. Reproduced by permission. www.cengage.com/permissions

office manager for a medical group may decide whether to accept and pass along sales literature from a pharmaceutical detailer or sales representative.

Influencers affect the buying decision by supplying information to guide evaluation of alternatives or by setting buying specifications. Influencers are typically technical staff such as engineers or quality control specialists. Sometimes a buying organization hires outside consultants, such as architects, who influence its buying decisions.

The **decider** chooses a good or service, although another person may have the formal authority to do so. The identity of the decider is the most difficult role for salespeople to pinpoint. A firm's buyer may have the formal authority to buy, but the firm's chief executive officer may actually make the buying decision. Alternatively, a decider might be a design engineer who develops specifications that only one vendor can meet.

The **buyer** has the formal authority to select a supplier and to implement the procedures for securing the good or service. The buyer often surrenders this power to more influential members of the organization, though. The purchasing manager often fills the buyer's role and executes the details associated with a purchase order.

B2B marketers face the task of determining the specific role and the relative decision-making influence of each buying centre participant. Salespeople can then tailor their presentations and information to the precise role that an individual plays at each step of the purchase process. Business marketers have found that their initial—and in many cases, most extensive—contacts with a firm's purchasing department often fail to reach the buying centre participants who have the greatest influence, since these people may not work in that department at all.

Consider the selection of meeting and convention sites for trade or professional associations. The primary decision maker could be an association board or an executive committee, usually with input from the executive director or a meeting planner; the meeting planner or association executive might choose meeting locations, sometimes with input from members; finally, the association's annual-meeting committee or program committee might make the meeting location selection. Because officers change annually, centres of control may change from year to year. As a result, destination marketers and hotel operators are constantly assessing how an association makes its decisions on conferences.

Sometimes, firms must be creative to reach all of the people who may be involved in making purchase decisions for a company. Sony of Canada holds lunch-hour product demonstrations in the spring and fall at 15 of Canada's largest business towers in Toronto, Vancouver, Calgary, Montreal, and Ottawa. This way, it reaches both consumers and business decision makers who may purchase anything from a Sony camera to a $50 000 projector screen.[39]

INTERNATIONAL BUYING CENTRES

Two distinct characteristics differentiate international buying centres from domestic ones. First, marketers may have trouble identifying members of foreign buying centres. In addition to cultural differences in decision-making methods, some foreign companies lack staff personnel. In less developed countries, line managers may make most purchase decisions.

Second, a buying centre in a foreign company often includes more participants than Canadian companies involve. International buying centres employ from 1 to 50 people, with 15 to 20 participants being commonplace. Global B2B marketers must recognize and accommodate this greater diversity of decision makers.

International buying centres can change in response to political and economic trends. Many European firms once maintained separate facilities in each European nation to avoid tariffs and customs delays. When the European Union lowered trade barriers between member nations, however, many companies closed distant branches and consolidated their buying centres. The Netherlands has been one of the beneficiaries of this trend.

Still, marketers who are flexible and quick to respond to change can get a jump on the competition in foreign markets if they can readily identify the decision maker in the process. When China's computer maker, Lenovo Group, purchased IBM's personal computer business, it decided to sidestep some of the cultural hurdles of doing business abroad when language, customer needs, and management styles all differ from those of the home country. Lenovo retained many of IBM's key executives from the PC division when it finalized the purchase of the company.[40]

TEAM SELLING

To sell effectively to all members of a firm's buying centre, many vendors use **team selling,** combining several sales associates or other staff to assist the lead account representative in reaching all those who influence the purchase decision. Team selling may be extended to include members of the seller firm's own supply network into the sales situation. Consider the case of small resellers of specialized computer applications whose clients require high levels of product knowledge and access to training. By working with its supply network—for example, by forming alliances with suppliers to provide training or ongoing service to end clients—resellers are able to offer a higher degree of support.

> ### assessment check 8
>
> **8.1** Identify the five roles of people in a buying centre decision.
>
> **8.2** What are some of the problems that Canadian marketers face in dealing with international buying centres?

DEVELOPING EFFECTIVE BUSINESS-TO-BUSINESS MARKETING STRATEGIES

A business marketer must develop a marketing strategy based on a particular organization's buying behaviour and on the buying situation. Clearly, many variables affect organizational purchasing decisions. This section examines three market segments whose decisions present unique challenges to B2B marketers: units of government, institutions, and international markets. Finally, it summarizes key differences between consumer and business marketing strategies.

⑨ Discuss the challenges of and strategies for marketing to government, institutional, and international buyers.

Marketoid

The City of Toronto issued a 131-page request for proposal (RFP) involving 21 000 pieces—more or less—of street furniture, hoping to find a single successful bidder to ensure coordination of advertising throughout the city.

CHALLENGES OF GOVERNMENT MARKETS

Government markets include the federal government, provincial and territorial governments, and municipal governments. These markets are large and are extremely important to many business marketers in Canada. Purchasing authorities for the various levels and units involved in these markets purchase a wide variety of products, including computers and office supplies; aircraft and component parts; vehicles and automotive supplies; safety clothing and equipment; concrete and lumber; fasteners, fittings, and repair supplies; and many other items.

The federal government purchases approximately $20 billion worth of goods and services annually.[41] To compete effectively, business marketers must understand the unique challenges of selling to federal government units. One challenge results because government purchases typically involve dozens of interested parties who specify, evaluate, or use the purchased goods and services. These parties may or may not work within the government agency that officially handles a purchase. For example, much of the purchasing for the federal government is done through Public Works and Government Services Canada (PWGSC). This department purchases more than 17 000 types of goods and services from business marketers.[42]

Contractual guidelines create another important influence in selling to government markets. The government buys products under two basic types of contracts: fixed-price contracts, in which seller and buyer agree to a set price before finalizing the contract, and cost-reimbursement contracts, in which the government pays the vendor for allowable costs, including profits, incurred during performance of the contract. Each type of contract has advantages and disadvantages for B2B marketers. Although the fixed-price contract offers more profit potential than the alternative, it also carries greater risks from unforeseen expenses, price hikes, and changing political and economic conditions.

While there is some variability between departments, purchasing procedures are largely determined by the size of the individual purchase. For purchases below $5000, most departments use acquisition cards (credit cards), local purchase orders, or releases against standing offers. A standing offer is not a formal contract. PWGSC issues standing offers for a variety of regularly purchased goods and services that are often needed by several government units. Business marketers agree to provide these goods and services at specific prices for a particular period of time and under a predetermined set of terms and conditions. Once a standing offer has been issued by PWGSC, government units must generally use the standing offer for any purchases of items that are included in the standing offer and that meet the buying unit's requirements. The government saves money from increasing the volume it purchases from holders of standing offers, and the business marketers who hold the standing offers benefit from increased sales.

For purchases over $5000, most federal government units use the services of PWGSC, which then asks for proposals from qualified suppliers. Business marketers may register online with the federal government so that they are considered when the need for their products or services arises. More commonly, business marketers access MERX, a privately owned e-tendering service used by the federal government as well as by many provincial, territorial, and municipal governments, and by other public sector purchasing authorities. Approximately 1000 new tendering opportunities are posted on MERX each week. There are usually 1500 open tendering opportunities online at any one time.[43] Since public sector purchasing authorities have different thresholds at which purchasing procedures come into effect, business marketers need to know the particular policies used by each of the units to which they wish to sell.

While provincial and territorial governments individually purchase much less than the federal government, collectively they are more important. Purchasing procedures for provincial and territorial government purchasing units are generally similar to those used by the federal government; however, there is even more variability between them. Alberta, for example, uses the Alberta Purchasing Connection for its e-tendering requirements, while most provinces use MERX. The Province of Nova Scotia has been using the reverse trade show concept for several years. These shows are held at various locations around the province. Public sector units manage display booths, and representatives from private sector businesses visit them to access information on their purchasing needs and to explore whether these units might benefit from the products and services that these private businesses sell. Business marketers need to be aware of any unique conditions that exist in each province or territory where they sell.

CHALLENGES OF INSTITUTIONAL MARKETS

Institutions constitute another important market. Institutional buyers include a wide variety of organizations, such as schools, colleges, universities, hospitals, libraries, churches, and not-for-profit agencies.

Institutional markets are characterized by widely diverse buying practises. Some institutional purchasers behave like government purchasers because laws and political considerations determine their buying procedures. Many of these institutions, such as hospitals and prisons, may even be managed by government units.

Buying practises can differ between institutions of the same type. In a small hospital, the chief dietician may approve all food purchases, while in a larger medical facility, food purchases may go through a committee consisting of the dietician and a business manager, purchasing agent, and cook. Other hospitals may belong to buying groups, perhaps health maintenance organizations or local hospital cooperatives. Still others may contract with outside firms to prepare and serve all meals.

Within a single institution, multiple buying influences may affect decisions. Many institutions, staffed by professionals, such as physicians, nurses, researchers, and instructors, may also employ purchasing managers or even entire purchasing departments. Conflicts can arise among these decision makers. Professional employees may prefer to make their own purchase decisions and resent giving up control to the purchasing staff. This conflict can force a business marketer to cultivate both professionals and purchasers. A salesperson for a pharmaceutical firm must convince physicians of the value to patients of a certain drug while simultaneously convincing the hospital's purchasing department that the firm offers competitive prices, good delivery schedules, and prompt service. The pharmaceuticals industry spends between $8000 and $15 000 per physician on marketing every year.[44] Some observers see a new trend among some doctors to reject free gifts and samples often offered by drug company representatives, which might create additional conflicts in the purchasing process.[45]

Group purchasing is an important factor in institutional markets because many organizations join cooperative associations to pool purchases for quantity discounts. For example, the Niagara Public Purchasing Committee was formed to purchase common supplies for the regional municipality of Niagara; the cities of Niagara Falls, Port Colborne, St. Catharines, Thorold, and Welland; Niagara College and Brock University; and a number of transit commissions, public libraries, hospitals, electric utilities, and school boards. Each purchasing authority can decide when and if it would like to participate in the tendering for any particular product or service. Responsibility for calling tenders and negotiating prices is shared among them, but control of ordering, scheduling, receiving, and payment remains with individual purchasing authorities.[46]

Diverse practises in institutional markets pose special challenges for B2B marketers. They must maintain flexibility in developing strategies for dealing with a range of customers, from large cooperative associations and chains to midsized purchasing departments and institutions to individuals. Buying centres can work with varying members, priorities, and levels of expertise. Discounts and effective distribution functions play important roles in obtaining—and keeping—institutions as customers.

MERX is Canada's leading e-tendering service—connecting sellers with public sector buyers.

CHALLENGES OF INTERNATIONAL MARKETS

To sell successfully in international markets, business marketers must consider buyers' attitudes and cultural patterns within areas where they operate. In Asian markets, a firm must maintain a local presence to sell products. Personal relationships are also important to business deals in Asia. Companies that want to expand globally often need to establish joint ventures with local partners. International marketers must also be poised to respond to shifts in cultural values.

Local industries, economic conditions, geographic characteristics, and legal restrictions must also be considered in international marketing. Many local industries in Spain specialize in food and wine; therefore, a maker of forklift trucks might market smaller vehicles to Spanish companies than to German firms, which require bigger, heavier trucks to serve the needs of that nation's large automobile industry.

Remanufacturing—production to restore worn-out products to like-new condition—can be an important marketing strategy in a nation that cannot afford to buy new products. Developing countries often purchase remanufactured factory machinery, which costs 35 to 60 percent less than new equipment.

Foreign governments represent another important business market. In many countries, the government or state-owned companies dominate certain industries, such as construction and other infrastructure sales. Additional examples include airport and highway construction, telephone system equipment, and computer networking equipment. Sales to a foreign government can involve an array of regulations. Many governments, like that of Canada, limit foreign participation in their defence programs. Joint ventures and countertrade are common, as are local content laws, which mandate domestic production of a certain percentage of a business product's components.

assessment check 9

9.1 What are some influences on government purchases?

9.2 Why is group purchasing important in institutional purchases?

9.3 What special factors influence international buying decisions?

Strategic Implications

TO develop marketing strategies for the B2B sector, marketers must first understand the buying practises that govern the segment they are targeting, whether it is the commercial market, trade industries, government, or institutions. Similarly, when selling to a specific organization, strategies must take into account the many factors that influence purchasing. B2B marketers must identify people who play the various roles in the buying decision. They must also understand how these members interact with one another, other members of their own organizations, and outside vendors. Marketers must be careful to direct their marketing efforts to their organization, to broader environmental influences, and to individuals who operate within the constraints of the firm's buying centre. ◆◆◆

REVIEW OF CHAPTER OBJECTIVES

① Explain each of the components of the business-to-business (B2B) market.

The B2B market is divided into four segments: the commercial market, trade industries, governments, and institutions. The commercial market consists of individuals and firms that acquire products to be used, directly or indirectly, to produce other goods and services. Trade industries are organizations, such as retailers and wholesalers, that purchase for resale to others. The primary purpose of government purchasing, all levels, is to provide some form of public benefit. The fourth segment, institutions, includes a diverse array of organizations, such as hospitals, schools, museums, and not-for-profit agencies.

② Describe the major approaches to segmenting business-to-business (B2B) markets.

Business markets can be segmented by (1) demographics, (2) customer type, (3) end-use application, and (4) purchasing situation. The North American Industrial Classification System (NAICS), instituted after the passage of NAFTA, helps further classify types of customers by the use of six digits.

③ Identify the major characteristics of the business market and its demand.

The major characteristics of the business market are geographic concentration, size and number of buyers, purchase decision procedures, and buyer–seller relationships. The major categories of demand are derived demand, volatile demand, joint demand, inelastic demand, and inventory adjustments.

④ Discuss the decision to make, buy, or lease.

Before a company can decide what to buy, it must decide whether to buy at all. A firm has three options: (1) make the good or service in-house; (2) purchase it from another organization; or (3) lease it from another organization. Companies may outsource goods or services formerly produced in-house to other companies either within their own home country or to firms in other countries. The shift of high-wage jobs from the home country to lower-wage locations is known as offshoring. If a company moves production to a country close to its own borders, it uses a nearshoring strategy. Each option has its benefits and drawbacks, including cost and quality control.

⑤ Describe the major influences on business buying behaviour.

B2B buying behaviour tends to be more complex than individual consumer behaviour. More people and time are involved, and buyers often seek several alternative supply sources. The systematic nature of organizational buying is reflected in the use of purchasing managers to direct such efforts. Major organizational purchases may require elaborate and lengthy decision-making processes involving many people. Purchase decisions typically depend on combinations of such factors as price, service, certainty of supply, and product efficiency.

⑥ **Outline the steps in the organizational buying process.**

The organizational buying process consists of eight general stages: (1) anticipate or recognize a problem/need/opportunity and a general solution; (2) determine characteristics and quantity of needed good or service; (3) describe characteristics and quantity of needed good or service; (4) search for and qualify potential sources; (5) acquire and analyze proposals; (6) evaluate proposals and select supplier(s); (7) select an order routine; and (8) obtain feedback and evaluate performance.

⑦ **Classify organizational buying situations.**

Organizational buying situations differ. A straight rebuy is a recurring purchase decision in which a customer stays with an item that has performed satisfactorily. In a modified rebuy, a purchaser is willing to re-evaluate available options. New-task buying refers to first-time or unique purchase situations that require considerable effort on the part of the decision makers. Reciprocity involves buying from suppliers that are also customers.

⑧ **Explain the buying centre concept.**

The buying centre includes everyone who is involved in some fashion in an organizational buying action. There are five buying centre roles: users, gatekeepers, influencers, deciders, and buyers.

⑨ **Discuss the challenges of and strategies for marketing to government, institutional, and international buyers.**

A government purchase typically involves dozens of interested parties. Social goals and programs influence government purchases. Many Canadian government purchases involve complex contractual guidelines and often require detailed specifications and a bidding process. Institutional markets are challenging because of their diverse buying influences and practises. Group purchasing is an important factor, since many institutions join cooperative associations to get quantity discounts. An institutional marketer must be flexible enough to develop strategies for dealing with a range of customers. Discounts and effective distribution play an important role. An effective international business marketer must be aware of foreign attitudes and cultural patterns. Other important factors include economic conditions, geographic characteristics, legal restrictions, and local industries.

 assessment check answers

1.1 Define B2B marketing.
Business-to-business, or B2B, marketing deals with organizational purchases of goods and services to support production of other products, to facilitate daily company operations, or for resale.

1.2 What is the commercial market?
The commercial market consists of individuals and firms that acquire products to be used, directly or indirectly, to produce other goods and services.

2.1 What are the four major ways marketers segment business markets?
Business markets can be segmented by (1) demographics, (2) customer type, (3) end-use application, and (4) purchasing situation.

2.2 What is the NAICS?
The North American Industry Classification System (NAICS) is a unified system for Canada, Mexico, and the United States to classify customers and ease trade.

3.1 Why is geographic segmentation important in the B2B market?
Certain industries locate in particular areas to be close to customers. Firms may choose to locate sales offices and distribu-

tion centres in these areas to provide more attentive service. For example, the Ottawa area is favoured by companies that sell to the federal government.

3.2 In what ways is the buyer–seller relationship important in B2B marketing?
Buyer–seller relationships are often more complex than consumer relationships, and they require superior communication among the organizations' personnel. Satisfying one major customer may mean the difference of millions of dollars to a firm.

3.3 What is global sourcing?
Global sourcing involves contracting to purchase goods and services from suppliers worldwide.

3.4 How does derived demand create volatile demand?
Assume that the sales volume for a gasoline retailer is increasing at an annual rate of 5 percent. Now suppose that the demand for this gasoline brand slows to a 3 percent annual increase. This slowdown might persuade the firm to keep its current gasoline pumps and replace them only when market conditions improve. In this way, even modest shifts in consumer demand for a gasoline brand would greatly affect the pump manufacturer.

3.5 Give an example of joint demand.

Both lumber and concrete are required to build most homes. If the lumber supply falls, the drop in housing construction will most likely affect the demand for concrete.

3.6 How might JIT II strengthen marketing relationships?

JIT II leads suppliers to place representatives at the customer's facility to work as part of an integrated, on-site customer–supplier team. Suppliers plan and order in consultation with the customer. This streamlining of the inventory process improves control of the flow of goods.

4.1 Identify two potential benefits of outsourcing.

Outsourcing allows firms to concentrate their resources on their core business. It also allows access to specialized talent or expertise that does not exist within the firm.

4.2 Identify two potential problems with outsourcing.

Many companies discover that their cost savings are less than vendors sometimes promise. Also, companies that sign multi-year contracts may find that their savings drop after a year or two.

5.1 Identify the three major factors that influence purchase decisions.

In addition to product-specific factors such as purchase price, installation, operating and maintenance costs, and vendor service, companies must consider broader environmental, organizational, and interpersonal influences.

5.2 What are the advantages and disadvantages of multiple sourcing?

Spreading orders ensures against shortages if one vendor cannot deliver on schedule. However, dealing with many sellers can be counterproductive and take too much time.

6.1 Why does the organizational buying process contain more steps than the consumer buying process?

The additional steps arise because business purchasing introduces new complexities that do not affect consumers.

6.2 List the steps in the organizational buying process.

The steps in organizational buying are (1) anticipate or recognize a problem/need/opportunity and a general solution; (2) determine characteristics and quantity of needed good or service; (3) describe characteristics and quantity of needed good or service; (4) search for and qualify potential sources; (5) acquire and analyze proposals; (6) evaluate proposals and select supplier(s); (7) select an order routine; and (8) obtain feedback and evaluate performance.

7.1 What are the four classifications of business buying situations?

The four classifications of business buying are (1) straight rebuying, (2) modified rebuying, (3) new-task buying, and (4) reciprocity.

7.2 Differentiate between value analysis and vendor analysis.

Value analysis examines each component of a purchase in an attempt to either delete the item or replace it with a more cost-effective substitute. Vendor analysis carries out an ongoing evaluation of a supplier's performance in categories such as price, EDI capability, back orders, delivery times, liability insurance, and attention to special requests.

8.1 Identify the five roles of people in a buying centre decision.

There are five buying centre roles: users (those who use the product), gatekeepers (those who control the flow of information), influencers (those who provide technical information or specifications), deciders (those who actually choose the product), and buyers (those who have the formal authority to purchase).

8.2 What are some of the problems that Canadian marketers face in dealing with international buying centres?

International buying centres pose several problems. In addition to cultural differences in decision-making methods, some foreign companies lack staff personnel, so in less developed countries, line managers may make most purchase decisions. A buying centre in a foreign company often includes more participants than Canadian companies involve. Also, international buying centres can change in response to political and economic trends.

9.1 What are some influences on government purchases?

Social goals and programs often influence government purchases.

9.2 Why is group purchasing important in institutional purchases?

Group purchasing is an important factor because many institutions join cooperative associations to get quantity discounts.

9.3 What special factors influence international buying decisions?

An effective international business marketer must be aware of foreign attitudes and cultural patterns. Other important factors include economic conditions, geographic characteristics, legal restrictions, and local industries.

MARKETING TERMS YOU NEED TO KNOW

These terms are printed in red in the text. They are defined in the margins of the chapter and in the Glossary that begins on p. G-1. Other important terms are printed in bold black type in the chapter but not included in this list. Their definitions can be found in the Glossary.

business-to-business (B2B) marketing 160
commercial market 162
trade industries 162
resellers 162
customer-based segmentation 165
North American Industrial Classification System (NAICS) 165

end-use application segmentation 166
global sourcing 170
derived demand 170
joint demand 171
inelastic demand 171
offshoring 172
nearsourcing 173

outsourcing 173
value analysis 181
vendor analysis 181
buying centre 181

ASSURANCE OF LEARNING REVIEW

1. Which is the largest segment of the business market? What role does the Internet play in the B2B market? What role do resellers play in the B2B market?
2. How is customer-based segmentation beneficial to B2B marketers? Describe segmentation by purchasing situation.
3. How do the sizes and numbers of buyers affect B2B marketers? Why are buyer–seller relationships so important in B2B marketing?
4. Give an example of each type of demand.
5. For what reasons might a firm choose an option other than making a good or service in-house? Why is outsourcing on the rise? How is offshoring different from outsourcing?
6. What are some of the environmental factors that may influence buying decisions? Identify organizational factors that

may influence buying decisions. Describe the role of the professional buyer.
7. Why are there more steps in the organizational buying process than in the consumer buying process? Explain why feedback between buyers and sellers is important to the marketing relationship.
8. Give an example of a straight rebuy and a modified rebuy. Why is new-task buying more complex than the first two buying situations?
9. In the buying centre, who is a marketer likely to encounter first? In the buying centre, who has the formal authority to make a purchase? What is the purpose of team selling?
10. Describe some of the factors that direct Canadian government purchases. Why are institutional markets particularly challenging?

PROJECTS AND TEAMWORK EXERCISES

1. In small teams, research the buying process through which your school purchases the following products:
   a. lab equipment for one of the science labs
   b. the school's telecommunications system
   c. food for the cafeteria
   d. classroom furniture
   Does the buying process differ for any of these products? If so, how?
2. As a team or individually, choose a commercial product, such as computer chips, flour for baking, paint, or equipment, and research and analyze its foreign market potential. Report your findings to the class.
3. In pairs or individually, select a firm in your area and ask to interview the person who is in charge of purchasing. In particular, ask the person about the importance of buyer–seller relationships in his or her industry. Report your findings to the class.
4. In pairs, select a business product in one of two categories— capital or expense—and determine how derived demand will affect the sales of the product. Create a chart showing your findings.
5. As a team, research a firm such as Nortel, Bombardier, or General Motors to learn how it is using outsourcing and/or offshoring. Then report on what you think the benefits and drawbacks to the firm might be.

6. Imagine that you and your teammates are buyers for a firm such as Tim Hortons, Canadian Tire, Delta Hotels & Resorts, or another firm you like. Map out a logical buying process for a new-task purchase for your organization.
7. Form a team to conduct a hypothetical team selling effort for the packaging of products manufactured by a food or beverage company such as Kraft or Labatt Breweries. Have each team member cover a certain concern, such as package design, delivery, or payment schedules. Present your marketing effort to the class.
8. Conduct further research into provincial or territorial government purchasing. Which provinces use MERX Canadian Public Tenders? What are the advantages of using MERX? Why might a provincial or territorial government decide to not use MERX?
9. Find an advertisement with marketing messages targeted for an institutional market. Analyze the ad to determine how the marketer has segmented the market, who in the buying centre might be the target of the ad, and what other marketing strategies might be apparent.
10. In teams, research the practise of remanufacturing of business products such as factory machinery for foreign markets. What challenges do marketers of such products face?

CRITICAL THINKING EXERCISES

1. Imagine that you are a wholesaler for dairy products such as yogurt and cheese, which are produced by a cooperative of small farmers. Describe what steps you would take to build relationships with both the producers—farmers—and retailers, such as supermarkets.
2. Describe an industry that might be segmented by geographic concentration. Then identify some of the types of firms that might be involved in that industry. Keep in mind that these companies could be involved in other industries as well.

3. Imagine that you are in charge of making the decision to lease or buy a fleet of automobiles for the limousine service for which you work. What factors would influence your decision and why?
4. Do you think online selling to the federal government benefits marketers? What might be some of the drawbacks to this type of selling?

Suppose you work for a well-known local restaurant, and a friend of yours is an account representative for a supplier of restaurant equipment. You know that the restaurant owner is considering upgrading some of the kitchen equipment. Although you have no purchasing authority, your friend has asked you to arrange a meeting with the restaurant owner. You have heard unflattering rumours about this supplier's customer service.

1. Would you arrange the meeting between your friend and your boss?
2. Would you mention the customer-service rumours either to your friend or your boss?
3. Would you try to influence the purchase decision in either direction?

1. **Bombardier Inc.** Bombardier is a global company headquartered in Canada and is a world-class supplier of transportation machinery and equipment, such as aircraft and rail systems. Visit the Bombardier website. What are Bombardier's core businesses? Search this website to find information on Bombardier's suppliers and its customers. How does Bombardier use its website to manage its business relationships with them? http://www.bombardier.com

2. **Selling to national retailers.** A high percentage of B2B marketing consists of manufacturers selling products to national retailers. Each retailer establishes standards for vendors. Visit each of the following websites to learn more about what it takes to sell products to that retailer. Prepare a report on your findings.

   a. Hudson's Bay Company: http://www.hbc.com/hbc (click on *Vendors*)
   b. Home Depot: http://corporate.homedepot.com/wps/portal (click on *For Suppliers*)
   c. Wal-Mart Stores: http://www.walmartstores.com (click on *Suppliers*)

Note: Internet Web addresses change frequently. If you don't find the exact sites listed, you may need to access the organization's or company's home page and search from there or use a search engine such as Google.

Case 5.1

Chip Wars: Intel vs. AMD in the B2B Market

Do you know what kind of microprocessor chip powers your computer or laptop? Do you care? Not long ago, consumers were happy to buy computers with Intel chips inside, and Intel was happy to count on orders from Dell and other manufacturers who were eager to give consumers what they wanted. But in the last few years, that situation has changed.

Fewer consumers are paying attention to what's inside their computers today, partly because microchip technology is becoming more complex and more confusing to the average computer user. But an even more threatening development to Intel is the rise of a small but feisty competitor called Advanced Micro Devices (AMD), which is battling Intel on several levels.

Not only is AMD producing a chip that some observers say is a better product than Intel markets, but the company is also mounting a legal challenge. Intel holds an 80 percent market share (by unit volume), which AMD calls an unlawful monopoly. AMD claims that Intel has also forced computer makers and retailers to use or carry its products. AMD filed charges that Intel used these illegal sales tactics on three continents. None of the legal dust has settled yet, but in the meantime AMD finally overtook Intel in the North American retail market for personal computers.

Intel is fighting back, and AMD's hard-won lead may not last for long. Both companies are hard at work trying to produce faster, more powerful chips at lower cost. Intel's CEO Paul Otellini says its most important competitive asset is the firm's sheer scale of manufacturing capacity and its newer, faster chips to replace its Pentium 4 processor. The company already has four factories making the new chips and is shifting other factories over. In addition to faster processing, the new chips require less power. Intel also inked a deal to put its chips in Apple computers for the first time, starting with a laptop bearing the new Napa chip. And Dell, one of Intel's largest customers, is showing no signs of disloyalty.

Intel's senior vice president for digital enterprise sums up its strategy: "We're going to ramp it like crazy and deliver it in volume. . . It's a better product, and people buy better products."

Questions for Critical Thinking

1. In what ways do Intel and AMD create value for their business customers?

2. How important is it for a chip manufacturer to market its B2B products (microprocessor chips) to end users in the personal computer market who aren't particularly tech-savvy? What advantages or disadvantages does such a strategy offer?

Sources: Michael Kanellos, "Intel CEO Throws Down Gauntlet to AMD," CNet News. com, March 10, 2006, http://news.com.com; Frank Mitchell Russell, "Chip Giant Intel Ramps Up Microprocessor War with AMD," *San Jose Mercury News,* March 7, 2006, http://www.mercurynews.com; Mark LaPedus, "Intel vs. AMD Becomes an Epic," *InformationWeek,* December 16, 2005, http://www.informationweek.com; Megan Barnett, "A Chip on His Shoulder," *U.S. News & World Report,* October 17, 2005, pp. EE12–EE16.

Case 5.2

Windsor Factory Supply

Windsor Factory Supply (WFS) is a 100-percent employee-owned, full-line industrial distributor and, as such, all of its sales are B2B sales. It sells thousands of industrial products—mainly to manufacturers, but also to government and institutional accounts. (It does for many business customers what Wal-Mart and Canadian Tire do for consumers.) The company started in Windsor, Ontario, in 1955 as a two-man operation. Sales the first year were approximately $50 000.

The company was fortunate in many ways. First, it was strategically located close to the centre of automotive manufacturing in Canada, and the three large North American automobile manufacturers all became important customers. Second, it was close to the Canada–United States border. Many U.S. manufacturers who sold through Canadian distributors selected ones located in or near Toronto. That meant customers in Windsor who wanted to buy these products would have to place orders with a distributor located some distance away, wait for the distributor to order the material from the United States, and then wait for delivery of the material from the U.S. manufacturer—sometimes physically routed through their Canadian distributor. Deliveries could take days or even weeks. Windsor Factory Supply would send two trucks across the border into Detroit each morning, one to each end of the city. When Canadian customers wanted important material from the United States, WFS would find a Detroit-area distributor, negotiate a discount as it would act as a sub-distributor, and bring the material into Canada, often the same day that their customer requested it.

Such willingness to provide outstanding service for its major customers helped Windsor Factory Supply quickly grow. By the 1990s, the company had five additional locations: Leamington, Sarnia, Wallaceburg, London, and Mississauga. In early 2008, WFS acquired Keep Industrial Supply, adding three new locations, although it will continue to operate under the respected Keep Industrial name in those locations. In late 2008, WFS opened a branch in South Carolina to support one of its major customers there. WFS has always been willing to negotiate supply contracts with important customers. It operates what is referred to as commodity management programs, whereby it will carry inventory and manage the supply of a large number of specific items, guaranteeing their availability when and where the customer needs them. Sometimes, these programs result in on-site inventory agreements.

WFS has a strong internal culture and a healthy business philosophy. Sales in 2008 are approaching $100 million. The company's foundation is built on quality, satisfaction, and dependability. President Rick Thurston describes the company philosophy: "Our business is built on relationships. Of course, we are always looking for opportunities, but we know that sometimes it is important to curb growth so that quality service to existing accounts is not compromised."

Questions for Critical Thinking

1. Describe how environmental factors, organizational factors, and interpersonal influences will affect sales for Windsor Factory Supply.

2. How important is the buying centre concept to Windsor Factory Supply? Explain.

3. How can commodity management programs and other special inventory management programs be used to add value for Windsor Factory Supply's customers? How can such programs contribute to the company's long-term success?

Sources: Windsor Factory Supply website, http://www.wfsltd.com, accessed August 8, 2008; Rick Thurston, person interview and correspondence, August 5, 2008.

Video Case 5.3

High Sierra Sport Company Excels in B2B

The written case on High Sierra appears on page VC-8. The recently filmed High Sierra video is designed to expand and highlight the concepts in this chapter and the concepts and questions covered in the written video case.

Serving Global Markets

CHAPTER OBJECTIVES

1. Describe the importance of global marketing from the perspectives of the individual firm and the nation.

2. Identify the major components of the environment for global marketing.

3. Outline the basic functions of GATT, WTO, NAFTA, FTAA, and the European Union.

4. Identify the alternative strategies for entering international markets.

5. Differentiate between a global marketing strategy and a multi-domestic marketing strategy.

6. Describe the alternative marketing mix strategies used in global marketing.

7. Explain the attractiveness of Canada as a target market for international marketers.

FINLAND AND NOKIA: HOT COMPETITORS IN A COLD CLIMATE

Winters are cold and dark in Finland. They linger for months across all the Scandinavian countries. But Finland is a hot competitor in the global economy. According to the World Economic Forum, Nordic countries in general are more competitive than many other regions in the world. And Finland tops all the charts, while the United States—the world's largest economy—ranks second. What makes Finland so important in the world marketplace? Economic experts say that Finland has a well-educated workforce, a population that knows how to use technology, and a well-managed economy.

Nokia, the world's leading cell phone maker, is one of Finland's best-known companies. Famous for its phone design, Nokia introduced the first digital portable GSM phone, the first handset with changeable colours, and the first wireless application protocol (WAP) phone. But Nokia is really known for the aesthetics of its phones—designs that have turned phones into fashion accessories or even jewellery. Design chief Frank Nuovo likens his company's phones to a person's watch. "If you buy a watch you wear it all the time," he explains. "It's on your person, and so it has a higher emotional purchase level—it has to fit your body, and yourself, as you are projecting yourself. Of all the technological products that have been developed, the mobile phone has the potential to be on the same level as the watch or the purse." With fashion in mind, Nokia began offering consumers phones in different colours, with changeable covers, and with slight shape variations that differentiated its phones from those of its competitors. Then the firm went a step farther by hiring photographer and director David LaChapelle, who helped produce a marketing campaign called "Distinctly Bold." Consumers who visit the company website today can find all kinds of tips for coordinating a fashionable wardrobe—with a cell phone, of course.

But competitors such as Samsung and Motorola were closing in on Nokia. Nuovo likes to say that these firms were merely imitating Nokia's successes, but the fact was that they were gaining ground rapidly. "What happened is everybody had targeted the number one player and all of our successes," he argues. "They copied so many of our successes, they took our successes and innovated on top, and it's a natural evolution of the market for the gap to close." But instead of allowing the competition to roll over them, Nokia designers surged ahead once again with new designs that integrated beauty and function. A recent ad for its new 8800 model calls the phone "a perfect moment when aesthetics and functionality meet in perfect harmony."

Industry experts agree that one reason Nokia is so successful is that it creates universal designs—they are useful and appealing to consumers from many cultures. Frank Nuovo calls it Nokia DNA. "It is a physical characteristic and a usability style," he tries to explain. His designers draw from every aspect of life. They study men and women to learn what each wants in a product. And perhaps most important, the design team is made up of employees from 30 different countries. But there is no question that Nokia's philosophy is rooted in Finland and the Finnish values of performance, utility, and simplicity—not to mention the country's focus on technology. Economists suggest that other nations, particularly those in Europe, might benefit from examining this small nation's way of life.[1]

---

connecting with customers

Nokia connects with its customers by designing phones to be fashion statements. They do this by designing models, styles, and colours their customers want.

Chapter Overview

CANADIAN and foreign companies are crossing national boundaries in unprecedented numbers in search of new markets and profits.

Global trade can be divided into two categories: **exporting**, marketing domestically produced goods and services abroad, and **importing**, purchasing foreign goods and services. Figure 6.1 shows the nations with which Canada trades. The United States accounts for 66.5 percent of our imported products and 79 percent of our exported products. Japan, the United Kingdom, and the European Union countries account for another 9.5 percent of exports.[2] Global trade is vital to a nation and its marketers for several reasons. It expands markets, makes production and distribution economies possible, allows companies to explore growth opportunities in other nations, and makes them less dependent on economic conditions in their home nations. Many also find that global marketing and trade can help them meet customer demand, reduce costs, and provide valuable

information on potential markets around the world.

For North American marketers, global trade is especially important because the Canadian and U.S. economies represent a mature market for many products. Outside North America, however, it is a different story. Economies in many parts of sub-Saharan Africa, Asia, Latin America, Europe, and the Middle East are growing rapidly. This opens up new markets for Canadian products as consumers in these areas have more money to spend and as the need for goods and services by foreign companies expands. Exports of machinery and industrial products each represent 21 percent of all Canadian products sold to other countries, with energy products accounting for another 19 percent.[3] Global trade also builds employment. The United Nations estimates that 65 000 transnational corporations are operating today, employing more than 54 million workers directly and through subsidiaries.[4]

Global marketers carefully evaluate the marketing concepts described in earlier chapters. However, transactions that cross national borders involve additional considerations. For example, different laws, varying levels of technological

capability, economic conditions, cultural and business norms, and consumer preferences often require new strategies. Companies that want to market their products worldwide must reconsider each of the marketing variables (product, distribution, promotion, and price) in terms of the global marketplace. To succeed in global marketing, today's marketers answer questions such as these:

- How do our products fit into a foreign market?
- How can we turn potential threats into opportunities?
- Which strategic alternatives will work in global markets?

Many of the answers to these questions can be found by studying techniques used by successful global marketers. This chapter first considers the importance and characteristics of foreign markets. It then examines the international marketing environment, the trend toward multinational economic integration, and the steps that most firms take to enter the global marketplace. Next, the importance of developing a global marketing mix is discussed. The chapter closes with a look at Canada as a target market for foreign marketers. ◆◆◆

exporting Marketing domestically produced goods and services in foreign countries.

importing Purchasing foreign goods, services, and raw materials.

---

① Describe the importance of global marketing from the perspectives of the individual firm and the nation.

THE IMPORTANCE OF GLOBAL MARKETING

As the list of Canada's and the world's largest companies shown in Table 6.1 reveals, most if not all are in global markets. For most companies—large and small—global marketing is rapidly becoming a necessity. The demand for foreign products in the fast-growing economies of Pacific Rim and other Asian nations offers one example of the benefits of thinking globally. Companies with a strong brand image such as Nike are finding some success in these markets, as described in the "Marketing Success"

table 6.1 *Largest Companies in the World and in Canada*

WORLD'S LARGEST COMPANIES			CANADA'S LARGEST COMPANIES	
RANK	COMPANY	COUNTRY OF ORIGIN	BY ASSETS	BY EMPLOYEES
1	Exxon Mobil	United States	EnCana Corp.	Onex Corp.
2	Wal-Mart Stores	United States	Royal Bank of Canada	George Weston Ltd.
3	Royal Dutch/Shell Group	Netherlands	Toronto-Dominion Bank	Magna International
4	British Petroleum (BP)	United Kingdom	Manulife Financial	Royal Bank of Canada
5	General Motors	United States	Bank of Nova Scotia	Metro Inc.
6	Chevron	United States	Imperial Oil	Alcan Inc.
7	Ford Motor Co.	United States	Suncor Energy	Canadian Tire
8	DaimlerChrysler	Germany	Manufacturers Life Insurance	Bombardier Inc.
9	Toyota Motor Corp.	Japan	Husky Energy	BCE Inc.
10	ConocoPhillips	United States	Bank of Montreal	Bank of Nova Scotia

Sources: Data from Scott DeCarlo, "The Forbes Global 2000: Ranked by Annual Sales," *Forbes*, March 30, 2006, http://www.forbes.com; "Top 1000 Publicly Traded Companies, 2007, Edition," *Globe and Mail*, http://www.globeandmail.com, accessed September 8, 2007; "50 Biggest Employers, 2007 Edition," *Globe and Mail*, http://www.globeandmail.com, accessed September 8, 2007.

feature. Canada is often viewed as an exporter of natural resources such as lumber, wheat, and energy products, but other products such as machinery and industrial products are equally important to our economy. In a recent year, Canada exported $86.7 billion of energy products, $94.6 billion in equipment, and another $82.5 billion in automotive products. Both the value and volume of imports and exports reached record levels in 2006.[5]

The United States is by far our largest trading partner, as shown in Figure 6.1. The North American Free Trade Agreement and the improved pipeline infrastructure that allows more natural gas and crude oil to move across the border are contributing factors to the success of this relationship.

marketing success Nike Sells Status in China

Background. Nike is a company with a strong brand, and its logo—the swoosh—is recognized almost anywhere. Founded in the mid-1960s by Phil Knight, the company established itself in the minds of consumers with ads for its running shoes featuring Michael Jordan and other athletes. Today, Nike includes brands such as Converse, Starter, Cole Haan, and Bauer. To continue its success, the firm needs to grow globally.

The Challenge. How does a firm crack the enormous potential market in China? Nike is determined to outfit millions of Chinese consumers with shoes bearing the swoosh—and is well on the road to doing so.

The Strategy. As soon as the Chinese government began to allow foreign products to be marketed to its citizens, Nike was there. Many of its shoes were already manufactured in Asia, so the leap seemed to be a natural one. Nike launched a TV commercial in China featuring track and field star Liu Xiang becoming his nation's

first Olympic gold medallist in hurdling at the Athens Olympics. Instead of focusing on running shoes, however, the ad focused on Chinese pride. The commercial was a hit. Positioning itself for the 2008 Beijing Olympics, Nike is driving hard in China, opening an average of 1.5 new stores each day, using marketing messages that emphasize status and pride rather than the benefits of its products.

The Outcome. According to one survey, Chinese consumers now view Nike as the "coolest brand." Sales increased 66 percent in one year, an indication that Chinese consumers continue to be hungry for Western goods. The new Chinese middle class "seeks Western culture," says social scientist Zhang Wanli. "Nike was smart because it didn't enter China selling usefulness, but selling status."

Sources: Matthew Forney, "How Nike Figured Out China," *Time*, http://www.time.com, accessed March 24, 2006; Jon Birger and David Stires, "CEO on the Hot Seat," CNN Money.com, February 6, 2006, http://money.cnn.com; Andrew Patterson, "Phil Knight's Not Diversified," Motley Fool, February 3, 2006, http://www.fool.com.

figure 6.1

Top Canadian Trading Partners

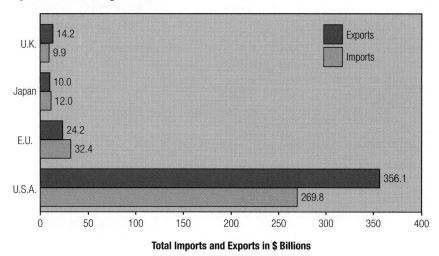

Total Imports and Exports in $ Billions

Country	Exports	Imports
U.K.	14.2	9.9
Japan	10.0	12.0
E.U.	24.2	32.4
U.S.A.	356.1	269.8

Source: "Adapted from the Statistics Canada website article "Imports, Exports, and Trade Balance of Goods on a Balance of Payment Basis, by Country or Country Grouping, 2007," at http://www40.statcan.ca/l01/cst01/gblec02a.htm, accessed June 24, 2008."

Marketoid

Exports of metal ores and alloys hit a record high of $45.2 billion in 2006, up 25.5% from the previous year, mainly due to increased demand from China.

Our next largest trading partner is the European Union, which has purchased over $20 billion worth of goods from us in one year. Japan and the United Kingdom also play an important role in our international trade, each purchasing around $10 billion a year.[6]

Wal-Mart currently ranks as the world's largest private employer (1.5 million people) and largest retailer (annual sales are 50 percent greater than its four largest competitors combined). The retail giant is currently devoting billions of dollars in expansion efforts in Great Britain, the European mainland, Japan, Central America, and South America. After some early stumbles with foreign languages, customs, and regulations, the company is beginning to gain its stride overseas. Propelled by its highly sophisticated global inventory management and a passion for offering consumers a widening choice of products at the lowest possible price, the retail giant accounts for a significant percentage of imports from China.[7]

The rapid globalization of business and the boundless nature of the Internet have made it possible for every marketer to become an international marketer. However, becoming an Internet global marketer is not necessarily easy. While larger firms have the advantage of more resources and wider distribution systems, smaller companies can build websites for as little as a few hundred dollars and can bring products to market quickly. PayPal, the online payment service owned by eBay, helps such firms complete transactions with their customers. Many small online companies have turned to PayPal to collect customer payments from anywhere in the world.[8]

Just as some firms depend on foreign and Internet sales, others rely on purchasing raw materials abroad as input for their domestic manufacturing operations. A furniture manufacturer may depend on purchases of South American mahogany, while furniture retailers are taking advantage of increased Chinese-made styling and quality and their traditionally low prices.

SERVICE EXPORTS

Manufacturing no longer accounts for the lion's share of annual production output in Canada. Today, more than seven of every 10 dollars included in the nation's gross domestic product (GDP) comes from services—banking, entertainment, business and technical services, retailing, and communications. Services also account for more than 75 percent of all employment in Canada. This profound shift from a largely manufacturing to a largely service economy is also reflected in the nation's exports.[9]

The importance of service exports to all nations and the difficulty in measuring service transactions has prompted the International Monetary Fund (IMF) to classify and define service categories and transactions, assisting government statistical agencies to collect and compare data. Service categories include travel, transportation, government services, and other (such as business services). A service transaction is included in a country's export numbers when a client, the service, or the supplier crosses a border or a commerce presence is set up abroad. A major contributing factor in services being exported and measured is technology. Information technology has allowed services that once were considered nontransferable or storable to travel long distances quickly and easily from where they are produced through sophisticated telecommunications networks. This trend is likely to continue as technological advancements reach developing countries, allowing services such as health, education, and banking to grow in these markets.[10]

The amount spent on tourism represents roughly 2 percent of the GDP. A significant portion of this amount was spent by foreign visitors on Canadian-produced goods and services, considered to be a tourism export. If a traveller purchased an airplane ticket on an Air Canada flight from anywhere in the world to Canada, it would be included as a tourism export, along with the money spent on hotels, travel, meals, and entertainment while staying in Canada. The popularity of Canada as a tourist destination has been declining in recent years. Canada still receives $60 billion of the total tourist dollars spent annually worldwide but a decline in Americans visitors has hurt the industry. The lower number of American visitors has been blamed on security concerns, potential passport issues, and a stronger Canadian dollar. The reduction in American visitors has been partially offset by the increase in visitors from China, Mexico, France, Germany, and South Korea. The non-American visitors, although fewer in number, stay longer and spend more.[11]

Several groups across the country are responsible for marketing Canada. Organizations such as the Canadian Tourism Commission (CTC) were established to promote Canadian companies to international markets. The Canadian Tourism Commission is the federal body, but each province and even different regions within the provinces vie for the tourist dollar in order to keep the roughly 510 000 Canadians working in the tourist trade employed. Federal and provincial agencies promoting Canada often team up with industry organizations such as the Hotel Association of Canada and corporations such as Xerox Canada in order to increase the effectiveness of promotional campaigns. Tourism British Columbia has been particularly successful in marketing British Columbia as a travel destination. Not only have its campaigns been recognized with several awards but it has a high response rate to its lead-generating mail campaigns. Tourism is so important to the Canadian economy that millions are spent on marketing. For example, Tourism British Columbia spends a total of $58 million annually, $4 million of it going to its direct mail campaign.[12]

BENEFITS OF GOING GLOBAL

Besides generating additional revenue, firms expand their operations outside their home country to gain other benefits, including new insights into consumer behaviour, alternative distribution strategies, and advance notice of new products. By setting up foreign offices and production facilities, marketers may encounter new products, new approaches to distribution, or clever new promotions that they may be able to apply successfully in their domestic market or in other international markets.

Global marketers are typically well positioned to compete effectively with foreign competitors. A major key to achieving success in foreign markets is a firm's ability to adapt its products to local preferences and culture. To satisfy China's large and diverse population, Samsung offers a variety of models and price ranges on its appliances and electronics. Samsung marketers know that people who live in the hot and muggy climate of Guangdong province need larger refrigerators than those who

The global coverage and international reputation of the Hilton name combine to generate additional sales revenues around the world as both business and vacation travellers select accommodations for their stays.

Leveraging Canada's Games:
2008-2012 Olympic Games tourism strategy

Canada

The Canadian Tourism Commission provides international travellers easy access to information about Canadian companies and events.

Efficient transportation systems are an important component of a nation's infrastructure, as shown in this aerial view of Montreal.

assessment check 1

1.1 Define *importing* and *exporting*.

1.2 What is the largest category of exports from Canada?

1.3 What must global marketers be able to do effectively to reach international markets?

live in the north. And Procter & Gamble knows that rural Chinese consumers need a lower-priced Tide than those who live in the city. So P&G sells Tide Clean White throughout the countryside while city dwellers can pick up Tide Triple Action.[13]

Since firms must perform the marketing functions of buying, selling, transporting, storing, standardizing and grading, financing, risk taking, and obtaining market information in both domestic and global markets, some may question the wisdom of treating global marketing as a distinct subject. As the chapter will explain, however, both similarities and differences influence strategies for global and domestic marketing.

② Identify the major components of the environment for global marketing.

THE INTERNATIONAL MARKETING ENVIRONMENT

As in domestic markets, the environmental factors discussed in Chapter 3 have a powerful influence on the development of a firm's global marketing strategies. Marketers must pay close attention to changing demand patterns as well as competitive, economic, social-cultural, political-legal, and technological influences when they venture abroad.

Marketoid

Tourism spending reached $66.9 billion in Canada in 2006 with Canadians accounting for 75 percent of the total.

INTERNATIONAL ECONOMIC ENVIRONMENT

A nation's size, per-capita income, and stage of economic development determine its prospects as a host for international business expansion. Nations with low per-capita incomes may be poor markets for expensive industrial machinery but good ones for agricultural hand tools. These nations cannot afford the technical equipment that powers an industrialized society. Wealthier countries may offer prime markets for many industries, particularly those producing consumer goods and services and advanced industrial products.

But some less-industrialized countries are growing fast. India and China, for example, may rival the United States in world economic importance in a generation or two. Although per-capita income in the United States is almost seven times that of China and about twelve times that of India, those countries have larger populations and thus more human capital to develop in the future.[14] Their ability to import technology and foreign capital, as well as to train scientists and engineers and invest in research and development, ensures that their growth will be rapid and their income gaps with the developed countries will close quickly.[15]

Infrastructure, the underlying foundation for modern life and efficient marketing that includes transportation, communications, banking, utilities, and public services, is another important economic factor to consider when planning to enter a foreign market. An inadequate infrastructure may constrain marketers' plans to manufacture, promote, and distribute goods and services in a particular country. People living in countries blessed by navigable waters often rely on them as inexpensive, relatively efficient alternatives to highways, rail lines, and air transportation. Thai farmers use their nation's rivers to transport their crops. Their boats even become retail outlets in so-called floating markets such as the one located outside the capital city of Bangkok.

Marketers expect developing economies to have substandard utility and communications networks. China encountered numerous problems in establishing a modern communications industry infrastructure. The Chinese government's answer was to bypass the need for landline telephone connections by leapfrogging technologies and moving directly to cell phones.[16]

Changes in exchange rates can also complicate international marketing. An **exchange rate** is the price of one nation's currency in terms of another country's currency. Fluctuations in exchange rates can make a nation's currency more valuable or less valuable compared with those of other nations. In today's global economy, imbalances in trade, dependence on fossil fuels, and other conditions affect the currencies of many countries, not just one or two.[17]

exchange rate Price of one nation's currency in terms of another country's currency.

At the beginning of this century, most members of the European Union switched to the euro as the replacement to their traditional francs and liras. The long-range idea behind the new currency is that switching to a single currency will strengthen Europe's competitiveness in the global marketplace.[18] Russian and many Eastern European currencies are considered *soft currencies* that cannot be readily converted into such hard currencies as the dollar, euro, or Japanese yen.

INTERNATIONAL SOCIAL-CULTURAL ENVIRONMENT

Before entering a foreign market, marketers should study all aspects of that nation's culture, including language, education, religious attitudes, and social values. The French love to debate and are comfortable with frequent eye contact. In China, humility is a prized virtue, colours have special significance, and it is insulting to be late. Swedes value consensus and do not use humour in negotiations.[19] The "Etiquette Tips for Marketing Professionals" feature offers some examples that will help you deal with cultural differences that arise in business dealings with foreign guests.

Language plays an important role in international marketing. Table 6.2 lists the world's 10 most frequently spoken languages. Marketers must make sure not only to use the appropriate language (or languages) for a country but also ensure that the message is correctly translated and conveys the intended meaning. Abbreviations and slang words and phrases may also cause misunderstandings when marketing abroad. Among the most humourous—and disastrous—language faux pas by marketers are product slogans that are carelessly translated, such as Kentucky Fried Chicken's "Finger lickin' good," which was translated into Chinese as "Eat your fingers off," and the slogan of an American chicken producer, Perdue Farms, Inc., "It takes a tough man to make tender chicken," when translated into Spanish became "It takes a sexually excited man to make a chicken affectionate."[20]

Export Development Canada helps Canadian companies who export their products and services to developing countries.

ETIQUETTE TIPS FOR MARKETING PROFESSIONALS

Entertaining Foreign Guests

IN today's global marketplace, you have a good chance of attending—or even hosting—a function at which foreign customers or colleagues are your firm's guests. Although you may feel nervous about the event, knowing how to act correctly will help you and your guests relax and feel comfortable. The best thing you can do is plan ahead and learn what you can about the culture that your guests represent. Keep in mind that different cultures have different norms of behaviour—being on time is very important to Europeans, whereas being late is acceptable to Latin Americans. Here are some hints that should help make the gathering a success.

1. Many business discussions—and deals—take place over a meal. So brush up on your table manners. Even if your guests have slightly different customs, they will recognize your good etiquette. "What turns foreigners off the most is the lack of protocol and table manners that North American businesspeople have. I constantly hear complaints about it," warns Samantha von Sperling of Polished Social Image Consultants.

2. Treat your guests with more formality than you might think is necessary. Foreign businesspeople expect more formality than North Americans do. For example, men should stand to greet women.

3. If you are at a restaurant, assist your guests if they appear to need help with the menu. If they are uncertain, recommend something that is easy to eat—pass by the lobster or ribs. Try to ascertain ahead of time whether they will expect multiple courses, and help them order accordingly.

4. Take the time to establish a relationship, particularly with Chinese or South American guests. Don't jump into business discussions over appetizers. Instead, chat about non-business issues, but don't ask overly personal questions or talk too much about yourself. If English is a second language for your guests, be sure to speak clearly and try to avoid slang or other expressions that are difficult to interpret.

5. Above all, treat your guests with respect, and remember that the ultimate goal of good manners is to make everyone at the gathering feel comfortable—regardless of the business outcome. "Treating people with respect, consideration and honesty . . . that's really the key," says Peter Post of the Emily Post Institute. "And sincerity is an important part of it, that the things you are doing are coming from the heart."

Sources: Business English Training, http://www.business-english-training.com/chinawork.htm, accessed March 24, 2006; "Hosting Foreign Visitors," U.S. Department of Energy Chicago Operations Office, http://www.ch.doe.gov, accessed March 14, 2006; Mary K. Pratt, "Sensitivity, Planning Key to Hosting Foreign Clients," *Boston Business Journal*, August 15, 2005, http://boston.bizjournals.com.

table 6.2   *The World's Most Frequently Spoken Languages*

RANK	LANGUAGE	NUMBER OF SPEAKERS
1	Mandarin (Chinese)	1 billion
2	English	514 million
3	Hindustani	496 million
4	Spanish	425 million
5	Russian	275 million
6	Arabic	256 million
7	Bengali	215 million
8	Portuguese	194 million
9	Malay-Indonesian	176 million
10	French	129 million

Source: Data from "Most Widely Spoken Languages in the World," http://www.infoplease.com, accessed March 27, 2006.

INTERNATIONAL TECHNOLOGICAL ENVIRONMENT

More than any innovation since the telephone, Internet technology has made it possible for both large and small firms to be connected to the entire world. The Internet transcends political, economic, and cultural barriers, reaching to every corner of the globe. It has made it possible for traditional brick-and-mortar retailers to add new business channels. It also helps developing nations in becoming competitive with industrialized nations. However, a huge gap still exists between the regions with the greatest Internet usage and those with the least. Asia, Europe, and North America together account for nearly 87 percent of the world's total Internet usage, Latin America and the Caribbean follow with almost 8 percent, while Africa accounts for less than 3 percent, Oceania/Australia just below 2 percent, and the Middle East also below 2 percent. Despite those numbers, Africa's usage grew 430 percent in just one year, and the Middle East jumped nearly 400 percent.[21]

Technology presents challenges for global marketers that extend beyond the Internet and other telecommunications innovations. A major issue involving food marketers competing in Europe is genetic re-engineering. Although Canadian grocery shelves are filled with foods grown with genetically modified organisms (GMOs), most Canadians are unaware they are eating GMO foods because no labelling disclosures are required. However, in Europe, several organizations have moved to ban these foods. Local and regional authorities have declared themselves "GMO-free," but the European Court of Justice has yet to issue a ruling that would ban GMOs throughout the European Union.[22] This complex issue affects almost every marketer in the global food industry.

Marketoid

Environmental concerns are causing countries to look at nuclear power with renewed interest. Nuclear power requires uranium. Canada is the world's largest producer of uranium, supplying 30 percent of the world demand.

INTERNATIONAL POLITICAL-LEGAL ENVIRONMENT

Global marketers must continually stay abreast of laws and trade regulations in each country in which they compete. Political conditions often influence international marketing as well. Political unrest in places such as the Middle East, Afghanistan, Africa, Eastern Europe, Spain, and South America sometimes results in acts of violence, such as destruction of a firm's property or even deaths from bombings or other terrorist acts. As a result, many Western firms have set up internal **political risk assessment (PRA)** units or turned to outside consulting services to evaluate the political risks of the marketplaces in which they operate.

The political environment also involves labour conditions in different countries. In Europe, dockworkers went on strike and demonstrators fought police and smashed windows in the European Parliament building to protest legislation that would liberalize cargo handling at ports. Unions worried that the bill would eliminate jobs and reduce wages, while cargo-handling firms worried that they would lose contracts to competitors.[23]

The legal environment for firms operating abroad results from three forces: (1) international law, (2) Canadian law, and (3) legal requirements of host nations. International law emerges from the treaties, conventions, and agreements that exist among nations. Canada has several agreements or treaties with other governments. These agreements set terms for various aspects of commercial relations with other countries, such as the right to conduct business in the treaty partner's domestic market. Other international business agreements concern worldwide standards for various products, patents, trademarks, reciprocal tax treaties, export control, international air travel, and international communications.

Since the 1990s, Europe has pushed for mandatory **ISO (International Organization for Standardization) certification**—internationally recognized standards that ensure a company's goods, services, and operations meet established quality levels. The organization has two sets of standards: the ISO 9000 series of standards sets requirements for quality in goods and services; the ISO 14000 series sets standards for operations that minimize harm to the environment. Today, many companies follow these certification standards as well. Currently, about 760 900 organizations in 154 countries participate in both series.[24] The International Monetary Fund, another major player in the international legal environment, lends foreign exchange to nations that require it to conduct international trade. These agreements facilitate the entire process of world marketing. However, there are no international laws for corporations—only for governments. So marketers include special provisions in contracts, such as which country's courts have jurisdiction.

The second dimension of the international legal environment, Canadian law, includes various trade regulations, tax laws, and import/export requirements that affect international marketing. The

CHRIS HARRIS ©ALLCANADAPHOTOS.COM

Many Europeans view the protests against foods grown with genetically modified organisms (GMOs) as an extension of the growing demand for organic foods—both in Europe and North America. Although more expensive to produce because they require more intensive use of human resources, organic foods grown without synthetic pesticides or chemicals are one of the fastest-growing segments of both the North American and European grocery industries. In 2002, organic food sales were only 2 percent of the Canadian grocery market but sales are increasing at a rate of 20 percent per year.

laws regarding international trade are administered by several different government agencies. For example, Agriculture and Agri-Food Canada has the responsibility for the agri-food (agriculture and food) trade policy. Other regulations such as the Export and Import Permit Act (EIPA) fall under the Department of Foreign Affairs and International Trade. The EIPA controls the flow of certain types of goods, including lumber, textiles, clothing, steel, and military items. Several government agencies, including International Trade Canada and exportsource.ca, a federal government website, are set up to assist companies to work through the various legal requirements. Exportsource. ca (http://exportsource.ca) is a comprehensive site covering customs requirements, standards and permits, requirements under international trade agreements, international law sources, and intellectual property. The federal government provides individual assistance to large and small companies wanting to enter foreign markets through its Trade Commissioner Service. It not only provides advice on doing business in certain markets but will identify barriers, regulations, and certifications required based on the specific company, products, and markets, help to identify key contacts around the world, and even help companies work through all the required paperwork.[25]

Finally, legal requirements of host nations affect foreign marketers. Global marketers generally recognize the importance of obeying these legal requirements since even the slightest violation could set back the future of global trade.

TRADE BARRIERS

tariff Tax levied against imported goods.

Assorted trade barriers also affect global marketing. These barriers fall into two major categories: **tariffs**—taxes levied on imported products—and administrative, or non-tariff, barriers. Some tariffs impose set taxes per kilogram, litre, or unit; others are calculated according to the value of the imported item. Administrative barriers are more subtle than tariffs and take a variety of forms such as customs barriers, quotas on imports, unnecessarily restrictive standards for imports, and export subsidies. Because the GATT and WTO agreements (discussed later in the chapter) eliminated tariffs on many products, countries frequently use non-tariff barriers to boost exports and control the flows of imported products.

Canada and other nations are constantly negotiating tariffs and other trade agreements. Two significant agreements are the North American Free Trade Agreement (NAFTA) and the Free Trade Area of the Americas (FTAA). NAFTA involves Canada, the United States, and Mexico. The FTAA involves Canada and 34 other countries within North, South, and Central America, including large countries like the United States, Argentina, and Brazil, and smaller ones like Bahamas and Haiti.[26]

Tariffs

Canada's stated objectives with regard to negotiations relating to tariffs is "to improve access for Canadian exports through the elimination of tariffs abroad while at the same time, taking into account domestic industry realities." In other words, we are trying to reduce the amount of tariffs we pay to enter other markets while at the same time protecting our industries by imposing tariffs on some goods entering our country. But moves designed to protect businesses at home are often a double-edged sword. They frequently end up penalizing domestic consumers because prices typically rise

Go Green

ISO 14000

ISO stands for International Organization for Standardization, a non-governmental body that establishes management systems standards and certification processes used throughout the world. In fact, almost 800 000 organizations, both private and public, in 154 countries have implemented ISO best practises. The ISO has two families of standards: the 9000 series, which addresses "quality management," was first established in 1992, and in 1994 the 14000 series was developed to address "environmental management."

The 14000 series of standards has two goals: to help organizations "minimize harmful effects on the environment caused by their activities, and to achieve continual improvement of its environmental performance." This set of standards was developed to apply to any organization, anywhere in the world regardless of size, culture, or social conditions. As with all such standards, there are those who criticize them and those who really like them.

The critics have argued that the standards are aimed mainly at large organizations. In order to address this concern, the ISO produced a separate set of standards in the 14000 series for smaller operations. Other smaller firms believe their environmental issues are not large enough to warrant the work and expense to incorporate such an extensive set of standards. Other factors limiting companies from jumping on the ISO bandwagon include the lack of expertise within the company, the large amount of paperwork involved, and no clear cost savings.

Judging by the number of organizations that have adopted the standards, there are many fans of the program. Those companies supporting the standards have cited enhanced environmental awareness and accountability throughout the organization as the primary benefits. Other positive outcomes from incorporating the standards within a firm include improved operational controls and procedures, a reduction in environmental emissions and waste products, improved communication within and between companies, and an implementation of systems that constantly review and improve environmental procedures.

One thing is for sure, whether the environmental standards an organization implements are the ISO ones or not, all organizations are going to be pressured to address environmental issues in future.

Sources: International Organization for Standardization, www.iso.org, accessed October 29, 2007; Frederic Marimon Viadiu, Marti Casadesus Fa, Inaki Heras Saizarbitoria, "ISO 9000 and ISO 14000 Standards: An International Diffusion Model," *International Journal of Operations and Production Management*, Vol. 26, Nos. 1/2, 2006, pp. 141–166; Nicole Darnell, "Why Firms Mandate ISO 14001 Certification," *Business and Society*, Vol. 45, No. 3, 2006, pp. 354–82; Susan L. K. Biggs, "ISO 14001 Hits 10-Year Mark," *Quality Progress*, Vol. 40, No. 8 (August 2007), pp. 67–69; "ISO 9000 and ISO 14000—in Brief," International Organization for Standardization, http://www.iso.org, accessed March 27, 2006.

under protectionist measures for both domestic products and imported products. It is also questionable whether tariffs are an effective means of improving the competitive environment for our products either domestically or abroad. The end result would seem to be higher prices for the consumer with little benefit for the companies involved.[27]

Tariffs can be classified as either revenue or protective tariffs. **Revenue tariffs** are designed to raise funds for the importing government. Most early government revenue came from this source. **Protective tariffs**, which are usually higher than revenue tariffs, are designed to raise the retail price of an imported product to match or exceed that of a similar domestic product. Some countries use tariffs in a selective manner to encourage or discourage certain consumption practises and thereby reduce access to their local markets. For example, Canada has a policy called General Preferential Tariff (GPT) in which we give preferential treatment to imports from developing countries. Introduced in 1974, this policy was intended to stimulate growth in areas of the world that are less economically advanced. The policy was initially implemented for a 10-year period but has been extended several times and currently applies to more than 100 countries. The policy is constantly monitored, and changes have been implemented from time to time. For example, on August 1, 2007, GPT status was removed from Bulgaria and Romania.[28]

Tariffs also can be used to gain bargaining clout with other countries, but they risk adversely affecting the fortunes of domestic companies. One industry that causes great debate between countries is agriculture. Currently, there is a disagreement over the high tariffs imposed by the EU on agricultural products from developing nations.[29]

INTRODUCING
SINGAPORE AIRLINES SUITES
A CLASS BEYOND FIRST

COURTESY OF SINGAPORE AIRLINES

Some industries, such as airlines, need special approvals from government agencies in order to do business in Canada.

import quotas Trade restrictions that limit the number of units of certain goods that can enter a country for resale.

Other Trade Barriers

In addition to direct taxes on imported products, governments may erect a number of other barriers ranging from special permits and detailed inspection requirements to quotas on foreign-made items in an effort to stem the flow of imported goods—or halt them altogether. European shoppers pay about twice the price for bananas that North Americans pay. The reason for these high prices? Through a series of import licence controls, Europe allows fewer bananas to be imported than people want to buy. In addition, the European countries set up a system of quotas designed to support banana growing in former colonies in Africa and Asia, which restricts imports from Latin American and Caribbean countries. Although the EU tried to modify the system, the World Trade Organization (WTO) rejected the new proposal, saying it did not do enough to provide market access.[30]

Other forms of trade restrictions include import quotas and embargoes. **Import quotas** limit the number of units of products in certain categories that can cross a country's border for resale. The quota is supposed to protect domestic industry and employment and to preserve foreign exchange, but it doesn't always work that way.

The ultimate quota is the **embargo**—a complete ban on the import of a product. Since 1960, the United States has maintained an embargo against Cuba in protest of Fidel Castro's dictatorship and policies such as expropriation of property and disregard for human rights. Not only do the sanctions prohibit Cuban exports—cigars and sugar are the island's best-known products—to enter the country, but they also apply to companies that profit from property that Cuba's communist government expropriated from Americans following the Cuban revolution.[31]

Other trade barriers include **subsidies.** Airbus, the European aircraft consortium, often comes under attack from trade officials because it is so heavily subsidized. The Europeans, on the other hand, argue that Boeing and Lockheed Martin benefit from research done by NASA and other organizations.[32] Some nations also limit foreign ownership in the businesses. And still another way to block international trade is to create so many regulatory barriers that it is almost impossible to reach target markets. China presents a maze of regulations controlling trade. However, one barrier that was recently lifted was the requirement that a foreign firm enter into a joint venture with a Chinese firm. But most experienced businesspeople agree that it is still easier to navigate all the regulations with a Chinese partner than to try to go it alone.[33]

Foreign trade can also be regulated by exchange control through a central bank or government agency. **Exchange control** means that firms that gain foreign exchange by exporting must sell foreign currencies to the central bank or other foreign agency, and importers must buy foreign currencies from the same organization. The exchange control authority can then allocate, expand, or restrict foreign exchange according to existing national policy.

DUMPING

The practise of selling a product in a foreign market at a price lower than it commands in the producer's domestic market is called **dumping.** Critics of free trade often argue that foreign governments give substantial support to their own exporting companies. Government support may permit these firms to extend their export markets by offering lower prices abroad. In retaliation for this kind of interference with free trade, some governments add import tariffs to products that foreign firms are dumping on their markets to bring prices in line with their domestically produced goods. As part of the softwood dispute, the United States imposed a tariff, charging that Canadians were dumping the product into its markets.[34]

In a move against the dumping of cheap leather shoes into the European market by Chinese and Vietnamese manufacturers, the EU applied

assessment check 2

2.1 What are the three criteria that determine a nation's prospects as a host for international business expansion?

2.2 What are the two major categories of trade barriers?

import duties starting at 4 percent and increasing to 19.4 percent on the Chinese shoes and 16.8 percent on the Vietnamese shoes. According to EU officials, more than 1.2 billion pairs of Chinese shoes had been sold at cheap prices in Europe the previous year. The duties would last for six months while the EU investigated the dumping allegations but could continue for as long as five years.[35]

MULTINATIONAL ECONOMIC INTEGRATION

A noticeable trend toward multinational economic integration has developed over the six decades since the end of World War II. Multinational economic integration can be set up in several ways. The simplest approach is to establish a **free trade area** in which participating nations agree to the free trade of goods among themselves, abolishing all tariffs and trade restrictions. A **customs union** establishes a free trade area plus a uniform tariff for trade with non-member nations. A **common market** extends a customs union by seeking to reconcile all government regulations affecting trade. Despite the many factors in its favour, not everyone is enthusiastic about free trade, particularly Canadians who hear news reports of Canadian jobs being outsourced to lower-wage nations such as Bangladesh, China, and India and worry that their jobs may be affected. So it is important to consider both sides of the issue. Although productivity and innovation are said to grow more quickly with free trade, Canadian workers may face pay-cut demands and potential job loss as more companies move their operations overseas.[36]

GATT AND THE WORLD TRADE ORGANIZATION

The **General Agreement on Tariffs and Trade (GATT)**, a trade accord that has sponsored several rounds of major tariff negotiations, substantially reducing worldwide tariff levels, has existed for six decades. In 1994, a seven-year series of GATT conferences, called the Uruguay Round, culminated in one of the biggest victories for free trade in decades.

The Uruguay Round reduced average tariffs by one-third, or more than $700 billion (U.S.). Among its major victories were:

- reduction of farm subsidies, which opened vast new markets for exports

- increased protection for patents, copyrights, and trademarks

- inclusion of services under international trading rules, creating opportunities for financial, legal, and accounting firms

- phasing out of import quotas on textiles and clothing from developing nations, a move that cost textile workers thousands of jobs when their employers moved many of these domestic jobs to lower-wage countries, but benefited retailers and consumers

A key outcome of the GATT talks was establishment of the **World Trade Organization (WTO)**, a 149-member organization that succeeds GATT. The WTO oversees GATT agreements, mediates disputes, and continues the effort to reduce trade barriers throughout the world. Unlike GATT, WTO decisions are binding. Countries that seek to become members of the WTO must participate in rigorous rounds of negotiations. China, the world's largest nation, is one of the newest members of the WTO, and its entrance into the organization has not been without disagreements. As a market, China holds enormous potential for exporters, but the nation's government has traditionally made it very difficult for foreign firms to operate there. But as China relaxed some of its trade barriers, it was admitted to the WTO.

To date, the WTO has made only slow progress toward its major policy initiatives—liberalizing world financial services, telecommunications, and maritime markets. Trade officials have not agreed on the direction for the WTO. Its activities have focused more on complaint resolution than on removing global trade barriers. Big differences between developed and developing areas create a major roadblock to WTO progress. These conflicts became apparent at the first WTO meeting in Singapore in the late 1990s. Asian nations want trade barriers lifted on their manufactured goods, but they also want to protect their own telecommunications companies. In

free trade area Region in which participating nations agree to the free trade of goods among themselves, abolishing tariffs and trade restrictions.

Marketoid

In 2006 aluminum exports rose almost 26 percent to $9.6 billion. Most of Canada's aluminum is exported from Quebec to the United States.

(3) Outline the basic functions of GATT, WTO, NAFTA, FTAA, and the European Union.

General Agreement on Tariffs and Trade (GATT) International trade accord that has helped reduce world tariffs.

World Trade Organization (WTO) Organization that replaces GATT, overseeing GATT agreements, making binding decisions in mediating disputes, and reducing trade barriers.

addition, they oppose monitoring of corruption and labour practises by outsiders. North Americans want free trade for telecommunications, more controls on corruption, and establishment of international labour standards. Europe wants standard rules on foreign investments and removal of profit repatriation restrictions but is not as concerned with worker rights. Currently, six major players in the WTO—the EU, the United States, Japan, Australia, Brazil, and India—are trying to negotiate more liberalized farm trade and the opening of markets for industrial products, but no major agreement has been reached.[37]

North American Free Trade Agreement (NAFTA) Accord removing trade barriers among Canada, Mexico, and the United States.

Free Trade Area of the Americas (FTAA) Proposed free trade area stretching the length of the entire Western Hemisphere and designed to extend free trade benefits to additional nations in North, Central, and South America.

THE NAFTA ACCORD

More than a decade after the passage of the **North American Free Trade Agreement (NAFTA)**, an agreement between Canada, the United States, and Mexico that removes trade restrictions among the three nations over a period, negotiations among the nations continue. The three nations insist that they will not create a trade bloc similar to the European Union—that is, they will not focus on political integration but instead on economic cooperation.[38] NAFTA is particularly important to Canadian marketers because the United States is this country's largest trading partner. Proponents of NAFTA claim that the treaty has been good for the economy, citing an increase in service exports and direct investment, among other benefits. Critics charge that U.S. and Canadian workers have lost jobs to cheap Mexican labour. However, NAFTA supporters point out that the availability of cheap labour has allowed the prices of some goods to drop, leaving Canadians with more money to spend and stimulating the economy. Every day, NAFTA countries conduct nearly $2.2 billion in trade with each other, with a GDP growth of 49 percent for Canada, 48 percent for the United States, and 40 percent for Mexico since the passage of the agreement.[39]

figure 6.2

The 27 Members of the European Union

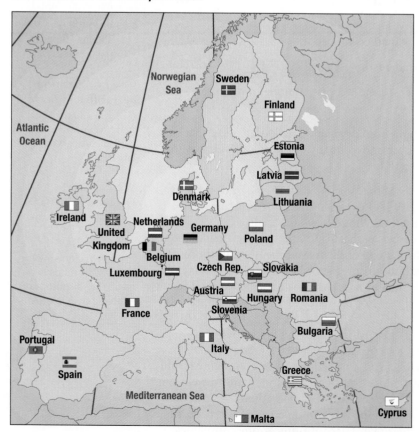

THE FREE TRADE AREA OF THE AMERICAS

NAFTA was the first step toward creating a **Free Trade Area of the Americas (FTAA)**, stretching the length of the entire Western Hemisphere, from Alaska's Bering Strait to Cape Horn at South America's southern tip, encompassing 34 countries, a population of 800 million, and a combined gross domestic product of more than $11 trillion (U.S.). The FTAA would be the largest free trade zone on earth and would offer low or nonexistent tariffs, streamlined customs, and no quotas, subsidies, or other barriers to trade. In addition to Canada, the United States, and Mexico, countries expected to be members of the proposed FTAA include Argentina, Brazil, Chile, Colombia, Ecuador, Guatemala, Jamaica, Peru, Trinidad and Tobago, Uruguay, and Venezuela. The FTAA still has many hurdles to overcome as countries wrangle for conditions that are most favourable to them.[40]

THE EUROPEAN UNION

The best-known example of a multinational economic community is the **European Union (EU)**. As Figure 6.2 shows, 27 countries make up the EU: Finland, Sweden, Denmark, the United

Kingdom, Ireland, the Netherlands, Belgium, Germany, Luxembourg, France, Austria, Italy, Greece, Spain, Portugal, Hungary, Poland, the Czech Republic, Slovakia, Slovenia, Estonia, Latvia, Lithuania, Malta, Bulgaria, Romania, and Cyprus. The European members represent 7 percent of the world's population.[41]

The goal of the EU is to eventually remove all barriers to free trade among its members, making it as simple and painless to ship products between England and Spain as it is between Newfoundland and British Columbia. Also involved is the standardization of regulations and currencies that businesses must meet. Instead of having to comply with multiple currencies and laws, companies will be able to streamline their efforts. In addition to simplifying transactions among members, the EU seeks to strengthen its position in the world as a political and economic power.[42]

In some ways, the EU is making definite progress toward its economic goals. It is drafting standardized eco-labels to certify that products are manufactured according to certain environmental standards as well as creating guidelines governing marketers' uses of customer information. Marketers can also protect some trademarks throughout the entire EU with a single application and registration process through the Community Trade Mark (CTM), which simplifies doing business and eliminates having to register with each member country. It is, however, sometimes difficult to obtain approval for trademark protection. Yet marketers still face challenges when selling their products in the EU. Customs taxes differ, and no uniform postal system exists. Using one toll-free number for several countries will not work, either, because each country has its own telephone system for codes and numbers.

Mexico has successfully negotiated a trade agreement with the EU that makes it easier for European companies to set up their operations in Mexico, which benefits EU companies by giving them the same privileges enjoyed by Canada and the United States, and brings new investors to Mexico.

European Union (EU) Customs union that is moving in the direction of an economic union by adopting a common currency, removing trade restrictions, and permitting free flow of goods and workers throughout the member nations.

Marketoid

Canada's merchandise trade with the United States and Mexico has increased 122 percent since 1993.

assessment check 3

3.1 What is the World Trade Organization (WTO)?

3.2 What countries are parties to the NAFTA accord?

3.3 What is the goal of the European Union (EU)?

GOING GLOBAL

(4) Identify the alternative strategies for entering international markets.

Globalization affects almost every industry and every individual throughout the world. Traditional marketers who decide to take their firms global may do so because they already have strong domestic market shares or their target market is too saturated to offer any substantial growth. Sometimes, by evaluating key indicators of the marketing environment, marketers can move toward globalization at an optimal time. The Canadian wine industry went global not only to increase international sales but to increase domestic sales. It seems Canadian wine drinkers are more likely to drink Canadian wine if it is accepted by the European market. Winemakers in Ontario and British Columbia banded together to enter the fiercely competitive European wine market by promoting icewine from Canada as a country rather than from individual wineries. Canadian wine, long thought to be inferior to wines from other areas of the world, has improved considerably from the 1960s, when the industry was starting to expand, and icewine is one product in which Canada has a competitive advantage because of our climate. Canadian icewine, considered to be a premium product, caught the attention of the sophisticated European market when it started winning awards at prestigious competitions. Marketers worked at keeping the upmarket image by premium pricing, distributing through high-end retailers, promoting taste-testing events, and partnering with airlines such as British Airways and Virgin Airlines to serve icewine to their first-class passengers.[43]

Most large firms—and many smaller businesses—already participate in global commerce, and virtually every domestic marketer, large or small, recognizes the need to investigate whether to market its products overseas. It is not an easy step to take, requiring careful evaluation and preparation of a strategy. Common reasons that marketers cite for going global include globalization of customers, new customers in emerging markets, globalization of competitors, reduced trade barriers, advances in technology, and enhanced customer responsiveness.[44]

FIRST STEPS IN DECIDING TO MARKET GLOBALLY

Successful global marketing starts at the top. Without the enthusiasm and support of senior managers, export efforts are likely to fail. But before a firm even begins to formulate a strategy, marketers must ask themselves:

- Will our product sell well in the new target culture?

- Is our target market familiar yet with our product or our name?

- Do we feel comfortable doing business in this particular country and culture? Will it be a good fit?

- How well developed is the infrastructure? Can we deliver our product successfully to the marketplace?[45]

Once these questions are answered, a firm can take the following steps:

1. *Prepare an international business plan.* The plan should include an evaluation of the firm's needs and goals.

2. *Conduct research into foreign markets.* The federal government departments of Industry Canada and Foreign Affairs and International Trade provide information and assistance to companies wanting to move into foreign markets.

3. *Evaluate distribution possibilities.* Should this be a joint venture with a local firm?

4. *Evaluate methods for financing the expansion.*

5. *Learn all the rules and regulations for bringing the product to market in the new country.*[46]

STRATEGIES FOR ENTERING INTERNATIONAL MARKETS

Once marketers have completed their research, they may choose from among three basic strategies for entering international markets: importing and exporting; contractual agreements such as franchising, licensing, and subcontracting; and international direct investment. As Figure 6.3 shows, the level of risk and the firm's degree of control over global marketing increase with greater involvement. Firms often use more than one of these entry strategies.

A firm that brings in goods produced abroad to sell domestically or to be used as components in its products is an importer. In making import decisions, the marketer must assess local demand for the product, taking into consideration factors such as the following:

- ability of the supplier to maintain agreed-to quality levels

- flexibility in filling orders that might vary considerably from one order to the next

- response time in filling orders

- total costs—including import fees, packaging, and transportation—in comparison with costs of domestic suppliers

figure 6.3

Levels of Involvement in International Marketing

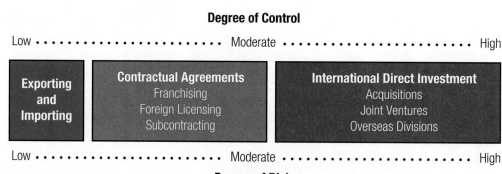

Exporting, another basic form of global marketing, involves a continuous effort in marketing a firm's merchandise to customers in other countries. Many firms export their products as the first step in reaching international markets. Furniture retailer IKEA has built an entire exporting strategy around what it does best: selling modular furniture. Because IKEA's furniture is lightweight and comes in components—customer assembly required—the firm can ship its goods almost anywhere in the world at a low cost, unlike traditional furniture.[47]

First-time exporters can reach foreign customers through one or more of three alternatives: export-trading companies, export-management companies, or offset agreements. An export-trading company (ETC) buys products from domestic producers and resells them abroad. While manufacturers lose control over marketing and distribution to the ETC, it helps them export through a relatively simple and inexpensive channel, in the process providing feedback about the overseas market potential of their products.

The second option, an export-management company (EMC), provides the first-time exporter with expertise in locating international buyers, handling necessary paperwork, and ensuring that its goods meet local labelling and testing laws. However, the manufacturer retains more control over the export process when it deals with an EMC than if it were to sell the goods outright to an export-trading company. Smaller firms can get assistance with administrative needs such as financing and preparation of proposals and contracts from large EMC contractors.

The final option, entering a foreign market under an offset agreement, teams a small firm with a major international company. The smaller firm essentially serves as a subcontractor on a large foreign project. This entry strategy provides new exporters with international experience, supported by the assistance of the primary contractor in such areas as international transaction documentation and financing.

CONTRACTUAL AGREEMENTS

As a firm gains sophistication in global marketing, it may enter contractual agreements that provide several flexible alternatives to exporting. Both large and small firms can benefit from these methods. Franchising and foreign licensing, for example, are good ways to take services abroad. Subcontracting agreements may involve either production facilities or services.

Franchising

A **franchise** is a contractual arrangement in which a wholesaler or retailer (the franchisee) agrees to meet the operating requirements of a manufacturer or other franchiser. The franchisee receives the right to sell the products and use the franchiser's name as well as a variety of marketing, management, and other services. Fast-food companies such as McDonald's have been active franchisers around the world.

One advantage of franchising is risk reduction by offering a proven concept. Standardized operations typically reduce costs, increase operating efficiencies, and provide greater international recognition. However, the success of an international franchise depends on its willingness to balance standard practises with local customer preferences. McDonald's and Pizza Hut are expanding into India with special menus that feature lamb, chicken, and vegetarian items, in deference to Hindu and Muslim customers who do not eat beef and pork.

franchise Contractual arrangement in which a wholesaler or retailer agrees to meet the operating requirements of a manufacturer or other franchiser.

Foreign Licensing

A second method of going global through the use of contractual agreements is **foreign licensing.** Such an agreement grants foreign marketers the right to distribute a firm's merchandise or use its trademark, patent, or process in a specified geographic area. These arrangements usually set certain time limits, after which agreements are revised or renewed.

Licensing offers several advantages over exporting, including access to local partners' marketing information and distribution channels and protection from various legal barriers. Because licensing does not require capital outlays, many firms, both small and large, regard it as an attractive entry strategy. Like franchising, licensing allows a firm to quickly enter a foreign market with a known product. The arrangement also may provide entry into a market that government restrictions close to imports or international direct investment. The World Poker Tour

foreign licensing Agreement that grants foreign marketers the right to distribute a firm's merchandise or to use its trademark, patent, or process in a specified geographic area.

USED WITH PERMISSION FROM McDONALD'S CORPORATION

As every international traveller knows, McDonald's has expanded its franchised fast-food operations around the globe. The restaurant chain focuses on providing all of its customers with menu choices and variety.

has grown tremendously, partly due to foreign licensing agreements. Following the model of golf's PGA Tour, Steve Lipscomb, founder of the poker tournament TV show, created a way for individual poker enthusiasts to sign up and play in tournaments around the world. By licensing the show in different countries such as France and Italy, Lipscomb maintains a company standard that can be translated—literally—to different markets. The televised tournaments on the World Poker Tour have become extremely popular, having already awarded players around the globe a total of $100 million in prize money.[48]

Subcontracting

A third strategy for going global through contractual agreements is **subcontracting,** in which the production of goods or services is assigned to local companies. Using local subcontractors can prevent mistakes involving local culture and regulations. Manufacturers might subcontract with a local company to produce their goods or use a foreign distributor to handle their products abroad or provide customer service. Manufacturing within the country can provide protection from import duties and may be a lower-cost alternative that makes it possible for the product to compete with local offerings. Some retailers subcontract with manufacturers in Mexico and China to produce many of the products—especially clothing—sold in its department stores.

INTERNATIONAL DIRECT INVESTMENT

Another strategy for entering global markets is international direct investment in foreign firms, production, and marketing facilities. With so many Canadians coming from different parts of the world, it is not surprising that foreign direct investment inflows and outflows—the total of Canadian investments abroad and foreign investments in Canada—are important to our economic growth. Canadian firms invested $445.1 billion in other countries in 2004. The two areas to which most of this investment went are the United States at $193.9 billion and the European Union at $91.2 billion. Total foreign investment into Canada for the same period amounted to $365.7 billion. The areas with the largest foreign investment in Canada were the United States at $238.2 billion and the European Union at $91.2 billion.[49]

Although high levels of involvement and high-risk potential are characteristics of investments in foreign countries, firms choosing this method often have a competitive advantage. Direct investment can take several forms. A company can acquire an existing firm in a country where it wants to do business, or it can set up an independent division outside its own borders with responsibility for production and marketing in a country or geographic region. Chinese firms have been seeking to purchase businesses in other countries, mostly in industries involving natural resources such as oil, natural gas, metals, and coal. However, they have been making inroads in consumer products and technology companies as well. For instance, the Lenovo Group, China's largest computer manufacturer, purchased the personal-computer division of IBM.[50]

Companies may also engage in international marketing by forming joint ventures, in which they share the risks, costs, and management of the foreign operation with one or more partners. These partnerships join the investing companies with nationals of the host

assessment check 4

4.1 What are the three basic strategies for entering international markets?

4.2 What is a franchise?

4.3 What is international direct investment?

countries. While some companies choose to open their own facilities overseas, others share with their partners. Service companies often find that joint ventures provide the most efficient way to penetrate a market.

Although joint ventures offer many advantages, foreign investors have encountered problems in several areas throughout the world, especially in developing economies. Lower trade barriers, new technologies, lower transport costs, and vastly improved access to information mean that many more partnerships will be involved in international trade.

FROM MULTINATIONAL CORPORATION TO GLOBAL MARKETER

A **multinational corporation** is a firm with significant operations and marketing activities outside its home country. Examples of multinationals include General Electric, Siemens, and Mitsubishi in heavy electrical equipment, and Timex, Seiko, and Citizen in watches. Since they first became a force in international business in the 1960s, multinationals have evolved in some important ways. First, these companies are no longer exclusively North American based. Today, it is as likely for a multinational to be based in Japan, Germany, or Great Britain as in North America. Second, multinationals no longer think of their foreign operations as mere outsourcing appendages that carry out the design, production, and engineering ideas conceived at home. Instead, they encourage constant exchanges of ideas, capital, and technologies among all the multinational operations.

Multinationals often employ huge foreign workforces relative to their North American staffs. A large percentage of all Ford and IBM personnel are located outside North America. These workforces are no longer seen merely as sources of cheap labour. On the contrary, many multinationals centre technically complex activities in locations throughout the world. Texas Instruments does much of its research, development, design, and manufacturing in East Asia. In fact, it is increasingly common for multinationals to bring product innovations from their foreign facilities back to North America.

Multinationals have become global corporations that reflect the interdependence of world economies, the growth of international competition, and the globalization of world markets. A look at the marketing communications industry, where the majority of firms are owned by multinationals, shows the importance of global marketing strategies to these multinationals.[51]

DEVELOPING AN INTERNATIONAL MARKETING STRATEGY

In developing a marketing mix, international marketers may choose between two alternative approaches: a global marketing strategy or a multi-domestic marketing strategy. A **global marketing strategy** defines a standard marketing mix and implements it with minimal modifications in all foreign markets. This approach brings the advantage of economies of scale to production and marketing activities. Procter & Gamble (P&G) marketers follow a global marketing strategy for Pringles potato chips, its leading export brand. P&G sells one product with a consistent formulation in every country. P&G meets 80 percent of worldwide demand with only six flavours of Pringles and one package design. This standardized approach saves money since it allows large-scale production runs and reinforces the brand's image.

A global marketing perspective can effectively market some goods and services to segments in many nations that share cultures and languages. This approach works especially well for products with strong, universal appeal such as McDonald's, luxury items like Rolex watches, and high-tech brands like Microsoft. Global advertising outlets, such as international editions of popular consumer and business magazines and international transmissions of TV channels such as CNN, MTV, and the CNBC financial network, help marketers deliver a single message to millions of global viewers. International satellite television channels such as StarTV reach 260 million Asian viewers through a host of sports, news, movie, music, and entertainment channels programmed in eight languages.

A global marketing strategy can be highly effective for luxury products that target upscale consumers everywhere. Marketers of diamonds and luxury watches, for instance, typically use advertising

5 Differentiate between a global marketing strategy and a multi-domestic marketing strategy.

multinational corporation Firm with significant operations and marketing activities outside its home country.

global marketing strategy Standardized marketing mix with minimal modifications that a firm uses in all of its domestic and foreign markets.

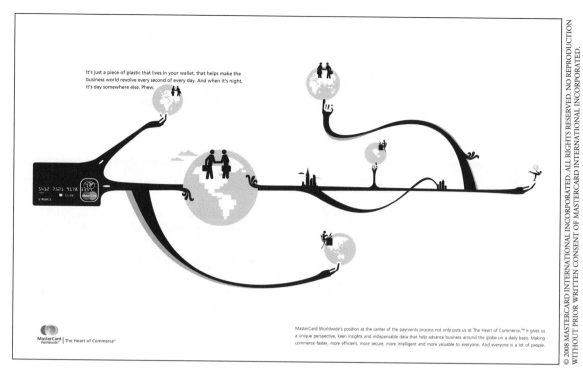

This "The Heart of Commerce" ad for MasterCard Worldwide demonstrates its international product strategy.

with little or no copy—just a picture of a beautiful diamond or watch with the name discreetly displayed on the page.

But a global strategy doesn't always work. After a quick spike in sales of its computers in China, Dell saw just as rapid a decline. The firm discovered that competitors such as Hewlett-Packard and the Chinese firm Lenovo were more successful at selling their computers through retail stores. Dell's well-known practise of building computers to order and shipping them directly to consumers was not succeeding in China. So the firm had to re-evaluate its marketing strategy there to include a retail presence.[52]

A major benefit of a global marketing strategy is its low cost to implement. Most firms, however, find it necessary to practise market segmentation outside their home markets and tailor their marketing mixes to fit the unique needs of customers in specific countries. This **multi-domestic marketing strategy** assumes that differences between market characteristics and competitive situations in certain nations require firms to customize their marketing decisions to effectively reach individual marketplaces. Many marketing experts believe that most products demand multi-domestic marketing strategies to give them realistic global marketing appeal. Cultural, geographic, language, and other differences simply make it difficult to send one message to many countries. Specific situations may allow marketers to standardise some parts of the marketing process but customize others.

multi-domestic marketing strategy Application of market segmentation to foreign markets by tailoring the firm's marketing mix to match specific target markets in each nation.

assessment check 5

5.1 What is a multinational corporation?

5.2 What are two ways in which multinationals have changed since the 1960s?

5.3 What is the difference between a global marketing strategy and a multi-domestic marketing strategy?

⑥ Describe the alternative marketing mix strategies used in global marketing.

INTERNATIONAL PRODUCT AND PROMOTIONAL STRATEGIES

Global marketers can choose from among five strategies for selecting the most appropriate product and promotion strategy for a specific foreign market: straight extension, promotion adaptation, product adaptation, dual adaptation, and product invention. As Figure 6.4 indicates, the strategies centre on whether to extend a domestic product and promotional strategy into international markets or adapt one or both to meet the target market's unique requirements.

Product Strategy

	Same Product	Product Adaptation	New Product

Same Promotion	**Straight Extension**
	Wrigley's gum
	Coca-Cola
	Eastman Kodak
	  cameras and film
		Product Adaptation
		Campbell's soup
			Product Invention
			Nonelectric sewing
			  machines
			Manually operated
			  washing machines

Different Promotion	**Promotion Adaptation** Bicycles/motorcycles Outboard motors	**Dual Adaptation** Coffee Some clothing	

(left axis label: **Promotion Strategy**)

figure 6.4

Alternative International Product and Promotional Strategies

A firm may follow a one-product, one-message straight extension strategy as part of a global marketing strategy. This strategy permits economies of scale in production and marketing. Also, successful implementation creates universal recognition of a product for consumers from country to country. After pursuing a strategy of adapting its dolls to reflect the looks and styles of 40 different nationalities, marketers for Mattel Toys discovered that children around the world just wanted regular Barbies. So Mattel went back to its one-product, one-message strategy. Its subsequent introduction of Rapunzel Barbie, complete with ankle-length blond locks, to 59 countries was the firm's biggest product launch ever.[53]

Other strategies call for product adaptation, promotion adaptation, or both. In Latin America, Nike relies on local soccer stars instead of Michael Jordan to promote its products. David Beckham represents Pepsi in his home country of England. Some marketing research has revealed that consumers around the world are becoming less enamoured of major North American brands, so marketers are taking this into consideration when creating global messages.[54]

Finally, a firm may select product invention to take advantage of unique foreign market opportunities. To match user needs in developing nations, an appliance manufacturer might introduce a hand-powered washing machine even though such products became obsolete in industrialized countries years ago. Although Chapter 11 discusses the idea of branding in greater detail, it is important to note here the importance of a company's recognizable name, image, product, or even slogan around the world.

Marketoid

Almost 90 percent of all companies that export products are located in Quebec, Ontario, Alberta, and British Columbia.

INTERNATIONAL DISTRIBUTION STRATEGY

Distribution is a vital aspect of overseas marketing. Marketers must set up proper channels and anticipate extensive physical distribution problems. Foreign markets may offer poor transportation systems and warehousing facilities—or none at all. Global marketers must adapt promptly and efficiently to these situations to profit from overseas sales.

A distribution decision involves two steps. First, the firm must decide on a method of entering the foreign market. Second, it must determine how to distribute the product within the foreign market through that entry channel. The next auto imports are likely to come from Chinese manufacturer Geely (pronounced *Jeely*). The firm decided to unveil its initial models at the North American Auto Show in Detroit, where dealers and car buffs could catch the first glimpse of the Free Cruiser and Beauty Leopard. Some dealers took the cars seriously—and asked for more information about importing and selling them. "What you're seeing is the first stage," predicts Mike Hanley, a global director for Ernst & Young. "Everybody recognizes that Chinese cars will end up in North America. It's a matter of time."[55]

PRICING STRATEGY

Pricing can critically affect the success of an overall marketing strategy for foreign markets. Considerable competitive, economic, political, and legal constraints often limit pricing decisions. Global marketers can succeed if they thoroughly understand these requirements.

Solving an Ethical Controversy

Fair-Trade Pricing for Coffee Growers: Is It Fair to Everyone?

IF you think your morning cup of coffee is liquid gold, you're right: coffee is the world's second most valuable traded commodity after oil. But until recently, the farmers who grow the coffee—largely in developing nations such as Mexico, Nicaragua, Guatemala, Colombia, Peru, Ethiopia, and Indonesia—saw very little profits. In fact, they spent generations in poverty because of the low prices commanded by their crops. Now the practise of fair trade—paying farmers better prices regardless of world market prices—is taking hold. It is also taking hold in the minds of consumers. No one doubts the benefits to the farmers, who now have a better standard of living with more money to invest in their farms, schools, and health care. But some question whether consumers should bear the burden of artificially higher prices.

Is fair-trade pricing for coffee growers also fair to consumers?

PRO

1. Most consumers are happy to pay a higher price for fair-trade goods because it appeals to their sense of social responsibility. "The whole concept of fair trade goes to the heart of North American values and the sense of right and wrong. Nobody wants to buy something that was made by exploiting someone else," says Ben Cohen of Ben & Jerry's ice cream, which uses fair-trade coffee products in its ice cream. Cohen's firm actually absorbs the full cost of the switch to fair trade.

2. Fair-trade coffee products are usually of superior quality because farmers have the cash to invest in their farms. So the higher price reflects value. Consumers become connoisseurs of coffee from these regions. "They don't just want French roast," explains Paul Rice, head of the nonprofit organization that certifies fair trade. "They want Guatemalan Antiguan, and they know where Antigua is."

CON

1. Prices should reflect true fluctuations in world markets, as in the case of oil. Consumers should not be forced to pay artificially increased prices.

2. Consumers are unlikely to pay more if they don't have to, and they may shift to less expensive brands that are available. "I think [fair trade] will be a minor part of consumer spending," predicts one economic analyst. "Most consumers are looking for good value. I think it's unlikely they're going to pay extra to help foreign workers."

Where do you stand: pro or con?

Sources: "Fair Trade Coffee," Global Exchange, http://www.globalexchange.org, accessed March 24, 2006; Margot Roosevelt, "The Coffee Clash," *Time*, http://www.time.com, accessed March 24, 2006; Jeffrey MacDonald, "How to Brew Justice," Time Inside Business, January 2006, pp. A16–A18; Joyce King, "Java Becomes Star in War on Unfair Trade," *USA Today*, October 21, 2005, http://www.usatoday.com; Terence Chea, "Coffee Ice Cream Brings Fair Trade Label into Frozen Foods," *San Francisco Chronicle*, April 19, 2005, http://www.sfgate.com.

Companies must adapt their pricing strategies to local markets and change them when conditions change. In India, Unilever's partner Hindustan Lever offers "penny packets" of shampoo to lower-income consumers, who typically cannot afford to buy an entire bottle of shampoo. Although local firms follow the same practise, Hindustan Lever wants to develop loyalty among these consumers so that if they move up the income scale, they will be more apt to buy the firm's higher-priced products as well.[56]

An important development in pricing strategy for international marketing has been the emergence of commodity marketing organizations that seek to control prices through collective action. The Organization of Petroleum Exporting Countries (OPEC) is a good example of this kind of collective export organization, and many others exist.[57] Pricing agreements such as fair-trade pricing in the coffee industry, described in the "Solving an Ethical Controversy" feature, have drawn criticism from those who believe that the agreements do not benefit everyone.

COUNTERTRADE

countertrade Form of exporting whereby goods and services are bartered rather than sold for cash.

In a growing number of nations, the only way a marketer can gain access to foreign markets is through **countertrade**—a form of exporting in which a firm barters products rather than selling them for cash. Less-developed nations sometimes impose countertrade requirements when they lack sufficient foreign currency to attain goods and services they want or need from exporting countries. These countries allow sellers to exchange their products only for domestic products as a way to control their balance-of-trade problems.

Countertrade became popular two decades ago, when companies wanted to conduct business in eastern European countries and the former Soviet Union. Those governments did not allow exchanges of hard currency, so this form of barter facilitated trade. PepsiCo made one of the largest countertrades ever when it exchanged $3 billion (U.S.) worth of Pepsi Cola for Russian Stolichnaya vodka, a cargo ship, and tankers from the former Soviet Union.

Barter activity continues to thrive around the globe. Malaysia and Indonesia are bartering palm oil in exchange for 18 Russian jet fighters. Libya is bartering fuel to Zimbabwe in exchange for beef, coffee, and tea. China has set up the Yangpu Oil Barter Exchange, the world's first such barter exchange for oil and gas.[58]

assessment check 6

6.1 What are the five strategies for selecting the most appropriate product and promotion strategy for a specific international market?

6.2 What is countertrade?

CANADA AS A TARGET FOR INTERNATIONAL MARKETERS

Foreign marketers regard Canada as an inviting target. It offers access to the North American markets, high levels of discretionary income, political stability, a generally favourable attitude toward foreign investment, and a relatively well-controlled economy.

Among the best-known industries in which foreign manufacturers have established Canadian production facilities is automobiles. Most of the world's leading auto companies have built assembly plants here. America's big three automakers (Ford, General Motors, and Daimler-Chrysler) and Japan's (Honda, Cami, and Toyota) all have manufacturing plants in Canada. Manufacturing relating to the auto industry accounts for 15 percent of Canada's total manufacturing production. It is critical to the Ontario economy where it accounts $100 billion of output or a third of manufacturing in the province.[59]

Canada is a country rich in natural resources that are in demand worldwide as manufacturing increases in many areas of the world. This makes companies in the natural resource sector attractive for foreign investment. It is also one area of foreign investment that is meeting with some resistance and calls for caution from Canadian business leaders. Business leaders have been warning for years that foreign ownership of resources, telecommunications, and infrastructure-related companies could cause problems for Canada in the future.[60]

All the concern over foreign ownership and foreign companies investing in Canada may be academic, however. Foreign investors continue to purchase Canadian companies, invest in Canadian stocks, and purchase Canadian bonds. Some predict the value of the Canadian dollar may affect these investments in the longer term.[61]

⑦ Explain the attractiveness of Canada as a target market for international marketers.

assessment check 7

7.1 What characteristics of Canada make it an inviting target for international marketers?

7.2 Why is auto manufacturing so important to Canada, particularly Ontario?

NORM BETTS/BLOOMBERG NEWS/LANDOV

Foreign car manufacturers have taken advantage of Canadian consumers' desire for foreign cars by locating many new assembly plants in Canada. This assembly-line worker is employed in Toyota's plant in Cambridge, Ontario.

Strategic Implications

THIS first decade of the new century has marked a new era of truly global marketing, in which the world's marketplaces are accessible to nearly every firm. Marketers in both small, localized firms and giant businesses need to re-evaluate the strengths and weaknesses of their current marketing practises and realign their plans to meet the new demands of this era.

Marketers are the pioneers in bringing new technologies to developing nations. Their successes and failures will determine the direction global marketing will take and the speed with which it will be embraced. Actions of international marketers will influence every component of the marketing environments: competitive, economic, social-cultural, political-legal, and technological.

The greatest competitive advantages will belong to those marketers who capitalize on the similarities of their target markets and adapt to the differences. In some instances, the actions of marketers today help determine the rules and regulations of tomorrow.

Marketers need flexible and broad views of an increasingly complex customer. Goods and services will become more customized as they are introduced in foreign markets—yet some recognizable brands, such as Mattel's Barbie dolls, seem to remain universally popular just as they are. New and better products in developing markets will create and maintain relationships for the future. ◆◆◆

REVIEW OF CHAPTER OBJECTIVES

① Describe the importance of global marketing from the perspectives of the individual firm and the nation.

Global marketing expands a company's market, allows firms to grow, and makes them less dependent on their own country's economy for success. For the nation, global trade provides a source of needed raw materials and other products not available domestically in sufficient amounts, opens up new markets to serve with domestic output, and converts countries and their citizens into partners in the search for high-quality products at the lowest possible prices. Companies find that global marketing and international trade can help them meet customer demand, reduce certain costs, provide information on markets around the world, and increase employment.

② Identify the major components of the environment for global marketing.

The major components of the international environment are competitive, economic, social-cultural, political-legal, and technological. A country's infrastructure also plays an important role in determining how effective marketers will be in manufacturing, promoting, and distributing their goods and services.

③ Outline the basic functions of GATT, WTO, NAFTA, FTAA, and the European Union.

The General Agreement on Tariffs and Trade is an accord that has substantially reduced tariffs. The World Trade Organization oversees GATT agreements, mediates disputes, and tries to reduce trade barriers throughout the world. The North American Free Trade Agreement removes trade restrictions among Canada, Mexico, and the United States. The Free Trade Area of the Americas seeks to create a free trade area covering the entire Western Hemisphere. The European Union is a customs union whose goal is to remove all barriers to free trade among its members.

④ Identify the alternative strategies for entering international markets.

Several strategies are available to marketers, including exporting, importing, franchising, foreign licensing, subcontracting, and direct investment. This progression moves from the least to the most involvement by a firm.

⑤ Differentiate between a global marketing strategy and a multi-domestic marketing strategy.

A global marketing strategy defines a standard marketing mix and implements it with minimal modifications in all foreign markets. A multi-domestic marketing strategy requires firms to customize their marketing decisions to reach individual marketplaces.

⑥ Describe the alternative marketing mix strategies used in global marketing.

Product and promotional strategies include the following: straight extension, promotion adaptation, product adaptation, dual adaptation, and product invention. Marketers may also choose among distribution, pricing, and countertrade strategies.

⑦ Explain the attractiveness of Canada as a target market for international marketers.

Canada is close to the United States and has high levels of discretionary income, political stability, a relatively favourable attitude toward foreign investment, and a relatively well controlled economy.

assessment check answers

1.1 Define *importing* and *exporting*.
Importing involves purchasing foreign goods and services. Exporting refers to marketing domestically produced goods and services abroad.

1.2 What is the largest category of exports from Canada?
The largest category of exports from Canada is machinery and industrial products.

1.3 What must global marketers be able to do effectively to reach international markets?
Global marketers must be able to adapt their goods and services to local preferences.

2.1 What are the three criteria that determine a nation's prospects as a host for international business expansion?
A nation's size, per-capita income, and stage of economic development determine its prospects as a host for international business expansion.

2.2 What are the two major categories of trade barriers?
The two categories of trade barriers are tariffs and nontariffs.

3.1 What is the World Trade Organization (WTO)?
The World Trade Organization (WTO) oversees GATT agreements and mediates disputes. It also continues efforts to reduce trade barriers around the world.

3.2 What countries are parties to the NAFTA accord?
The United States, Canada, and Mexico are parties to NAFTA.

3.3 What is the goal of the European Union (EU)?
The European Union seeks to remove all barriers to free trade among its members and strengthen its position in the world as an economic and political power.

4.1 What are the three basic strategies for entering international markets?
The three basic strategies are importing and exporting, contractual agreements, and international direct investment.

4.2 What is a franchise?
A franchise is a contractual agreement in which a wholesaler or retailer (the franchisee) agrees to meet the operating requirements of a manufacturer or other franchiser.

4.3 What is international direct investment?
International direct investment is direct investment in foreign firms, production, and marketing facilities.

5.1 What is a multinational corporation?
A multinational corporation is a firm with significant operations and marketing activities outside the home country.

5.2 What are two ways in which multinationals have changed since the 1960s?
Two ways these firms have changed are that they are no longer exclusively North American-based, and they no longer think of their foreign operations as mere outsourcing appendages.

5.3 What is the difference between a global marketing strategy and a multi-domestic marketing strategy?
A global marketing strategy defines a marketing mix and implements it with minimal modifications in all foreign markets. A multi-domestic marketing strategy requires that firms customize their marketing decisions to reach individual marketplaces.

6.1 What are the five strategies for selecting the most appropriate product and promotion strategy for a specific international market?
The five strategies are the following: straight extension, promotion adaptation, product adaptation, dual adaptation, and product invention.

6.2 What is countertrade?
Countertrade is a form of exporting in which a firm barters products rather than selling them for cash.

7.1 What characteristics of Canada make it an inviting target for international marketers?
Canada is an inviting target because it offers access to the North American markets, has high levels of discretionary income, has

political stability, has a generally favourable attitude toward foreign investment, and has a relatively well-controlled economy.

7.2 Why is auto manufacturing so important to Canada, particularly Ontario?

Manufacturing relating to the auto industry accounts for 15 percent of Canada's total manufacturing production. It is critical to the Ontario economy where it accounts for $100 billion of output or a third of manufacturing in the province.

MARKETING TERMS YOU NEED TO KNOW

These terms are printed in red in the text. They are defined in the margins of the chapter and in the Glossary that begins on p. G-1. Other important terms are printed in bold black type in the chapter but not included in this list. Their definitions can be found in the Glossary.

exporting 194
importing 194
exchange rate 199
tariff 202
import quotas 204
free trade area 205
General Agreement on Tariffs and Trade (GATT) 205

World Trade Organization (WTO) 205
North American Free Trade Agreement (NAFTA) 206
Free Trade Area of the Americas (FTAA) 206
European Union (EU) 207
franchise 209

foreign licensing 209
multinational corporation 211
global marketing strategy 211
multi-domestic marketing strategy 212
countertrade 214

ASSURANCE OF LEARNING REVIEW

1. What are the benefits to firms that decide to engage in global marketing?
2. Why is a nation's infrastructure an important factor for global marketers to consider?
3. What are the two different classifications of tariff? What is each designed to do?
4. How does an import quota restrict trade?
5. What are two major victories achieved by the Uruguay Round of GATT conferences?
6. Why has the progress of the WTO been slow?
7. What are the three alternatives for first-time exporters to reach foreign customers?
8. Define and describe the different types of contractual agreements that provide flexible alternatives to exporting.
9. In what conditions is a global marketing strategy generally most successful?
10. What type of nation benefits most from countertrade? Why?

PROJECTS AND TEAMWORK EXERCISES

1. Imagine that you and a classmate are marketers for one of the following companies: Apple Computer, Burger King, General Mills, or Mattel Toys. Choose one of the following markets into which your company could expand: Mexico, India, or China. Research the country's infrastructure, social-cultural environment, technological environment, and any trade barriers your firm might encounter. Then present your findings to the class, with a conclusion on whether you think the expansion would be beneficial.
2. Assume that you work for KFC, which already has outlets around the world. With a classmate, identify a country that KFC has not yet reached and write a brief plan for entering that country's market. Then create a print ad for that market (you can write the ad copy in English). It may be helpful to visit KFC's website for some ideas.
3. London is hosting the 2012 Summer Olympics. By yourself or with a classmate, identify a company that might benefit from promoting its goods or services at the London Olympics. In a presentation, describe which strategy you would use: straight extension, product or promotion adaptation, dual adaptation, or product invention. Consider the fact that England is a member of the European Union.
4. Suppose you work for a firm that is getting ready to introduce an MP3 player to the Chinese marketplace. With a classmate, decide which strategies your firm could use most effectively for entering this market. Present your ideas either in writing or to the class.
5. With a classmate, research the Chinese auto manufacturer Geely to find out more about the cars it plans to launch in North America. Then create an ad for the firm, targeting Canadian consumers.

CRITICAL THINKING EXERCISES

1. Few elements in the global marketing environment are more difficult to overcome than the unexpected, such as natural disasters or outbreaks of disease such as the avian flu. Travel may be curtailed or halted by law, by a breakdown in infrastructure, or simply by fear on the part of consumers. Suppose you work for a firm that has resorts on several continents. As a marketer, what kinds of contingency plans might you recommend for your firm in the event of an unexpected disaster?

2. Zippo lighters have been around for decades. But as the number of smokers in Canada continues to decline, Zippo has spent the last half century scouting the world for new markets. Today, Zippo is a status symbol among Chinese consumers, who prefer North American products. To reduce the sale of made-in-China knockoffs, Zippo's ads show Chinese consumers how to identify a real Zippo. In addition, Zippo has worked with government officials to find a safe way to package its lighters for air travel.[62] Both of these examples demonstrate a firm adapting to requirements of a new marketplace. Do you think a global marketing strategy or a multidomestic strategy would work best if Zippo decided to enter other markets? Explain the reasons for your choice.

3. Do you agree with the goals and ideas of the proposed FTAA? Why or why not?

4. Do you agree with countertrade as a legitimate form of conducting business? Why or why not? Describe a countertrade agreement that Microsoft might make in another country.

5. Foreign investment continues to grow in Canada. Do you think this is a positive trend for Canadian businesses and consumers? Why or why not?

ETHICS EXERCISE

Cheap—and illegal—copies of pirated popular movies, video games, and music are often available for sale in Asia within days of their worldwide release. The entertainment industry has so far had little success in stopping the flow of these copies into consumers' hands. Do you think multinational economic communities should be more effective at combating piracy? Why or why not? What actions could they take?

INTERNET EXERCISES

1. **The European Union.** To answer the following questions, you'll need to visit the EU website (http://europa.eu.int). A Google or Yahoo! news search may also be required.

   a. What are the purposes of the EU and the benefits for EU members? From the perspective of a Canadian marketer, what are some of the challenges and opportunities presented by the EU?

   b. Which countries have adopted the euro? Which countries have not adopted the euro? What are the advantages and disadvantages of a single European currency?

   c. Review several recent trade disputes involving the EU. What products and countries are involved? What are the primary issues? How can trade disputes complicate the marketing of Canadian products in Europe?

2. **International promotional strategies.** Visit the websites of two North American companies that do extensive business in international markets (examples include McDonald's, Ford, Boeing, Coca-Cola, and Procter & Gamble). Also, visit the websites of two non-North American companies that have extensive North American operations and sales (examples include Toyota, Unilever, Nestlé, and Philips). Review the material on the websites and perform the following exercises:

   a. Note two or three differences in promotional strategies you found between the companies' products sold in North America and those sold in other countries.

   b. Note two or three similarities among promotional strategies used by companies in different countries.

   c. Based on your findings, did you find any differences between the North American and non-North American companies?

Note: Internet Web addresses change frequently. If you don't find the exact site listed, you may need to access the organization's home page and search from there or use a search engine such as Google.

Case 6.1

Harlequin—Canada's Global Publishing Company

When you hear the name Harlequin you probably think of those sappy paperback novels that are read by the 40-year-old-plus group. You know the ones—the hero and heroine go through several trials and tests but always end up together living happily ever after. The names and locations change, but the storyline is always the same, resulting in a happy ending. The formula has put Harlequin in the ranks of global brands like Coke, Disney, and Nike.

Harlequin Enterprises, a division of TorStar, the group that owns the *Toronto Star* newspaper, started publishing women's fiction—commonly referred to as "chick lit"—in 1949. Today, Harlequin publishes 115 titles a month in 25 different languages. As if those numbers weren't impressive enough, the company sells books in 94 international markets on six continents. Since the company started it has shipped over 5 billion books. Harlequin titles have appeared on *The New York Times* best-seller lists consistently, in one year for 188 weeks. With 96 percent of its sales outside Canada, it is not only a successful international publisher but one of Canada's most successful international companies. Harlequin has been successful for a number of reasons: a good branding strategy, an imaginative distribution strategy, efficient international operations, and a product that hits its target market.

In recent years Harlequin has expanded its product line. The company now produces movies, mostly for television, based on its novels. One of its recent successful expansions is eHarlequin.com. The novels are loaded at regular intervals, usually daily or weekly. One Valentine's Day, a new chapter of a novel was put online every hour as a special feature. These online novels appeal to a younger target market. The Harlequin website allows the young readers to share their thoughts about the books in chat rooms linked to each chapter.

The move to a younger target market continued with the launch of the Red Dress Ink series. Harlequin felt that if it attracted readers in their teens they would continue reading Harlequin. This series carries the traditional Harlequin romance story line as found in the novels and short stories but instead of having every story end in marriage, the stories in this series are about dating. The promotional strategy for the launch was to have a different type of launch in the countries where the line was being published, making the type of promotion relevant to the market. For example, in England, 15-second radio spots were developed. In Italy, where the title of the first novel had to be changed because there was no direct translation, copies of the novel were attached to an issue of *Cosmopolitan* magazine. In the United States, 250 000 copies were hung on the doors of college dorms, and in Canada, book signings took place at bookstores. In the Spanish market, 15-minute television spots based on a talk-show format were produced and ran between such women's programming as soap operas. Throughout Europe, billboards went up to promote the new book.

Recently Harlequin has teamed up with NASCAR, the car racing organization, signing a licensing agreement to publish titles with NASCAR plotlines. What do NASCAR and romance novels have in common? As it turns out 40 percent of NASCAR fans are women so titles like *Full Throttle* and *Speed Bumps* hit the market in an attempt to attract these stock car racing fans.

What's next for the romance novel? You will have to watch their website to find out for sure, but one thing is certain whether you live in Japan, France, Australia, or Canada: you can count on several new Harlequin titles hitting the market each month.

Questions for Critical Thinking

1. How do you think the global reach of the Internet has affected the marketing strategy of Harlequin? Does this make it more or less difficult to devise promotional strategies that cross borders?

2. What should Harlequin do to ensure that cultural traditions and varying reading habits don't negatively affect any of its new lines?

Sources: "Harlequin Buys Stake in Women.com," *Marketing Daily*, July 5, 1999; Andrea Zoe Aster, "How Harlequin Woos Women," *Marketing*, March 31, 2003, p. 8; "eHarlequin Scores with Online Dating Service," *Marketing Daily*, June 13, 2001; "Logging On," *Marketing Daily*, February 19, 2001; Ryan Starr, "True Love Pays," *Canadian Business,* November 11, 2002, p. 22; "Harlequin Drops Book Bombshell," *Marketing Daily*, August 6, 2004; eharlequin.com, accessed October 29, 2007; David Brown, "Some Racey New Romance From Harlequin," *Marketing Daily*, November 3, 2005.

Case 6.2

Hyundai Gets a Second Chance

Second chances are rare in marketing. Once consumers decide a product's quality is substandard, the brand—if not the entire company—is probably doomed. When South Korean automaker Hyundai rolled its first model—the Pony—onto Canadian roads in 1983, consumers were lured by Pony's low price tag. But soon Hyundai owners discovered they were getting what they'd paid for. The cars began to reveal quality-control problems, requiring frequent repairs or part replacements. It wasn't long before the name Hyundai became synonymous with poor quality, and the target of jokes by late-night TV hosts. In an industry that has been dominated by American, Japanese, and German auto giants, how could a family-owned South Korean start-up with a bad reputation return to the ring after being knocked out so soundly?

Upon his father's retirement, Chung Mong Koo took over Hyundai as its chairman. He spent several years studying Toyota's success with its philosophy of *kaizen,* or continuous improvement. Then he established a zero-defect policy for all of Hyundai's factories. And he hammered the message home to every single Hyundai executive, manager, and worker. He visited the factories and inspected the cars himself. Finally, he unleashed the new Hyundais to the world marketplace, with a 10-year warranty. Consumers who were experiencing sticker shock at some of the new models from other manufacturers, and who liked the security of the new warranty, gave the Sonata a try. They found that the car performed exactly as advertised. Industry watchdogs such as *Consumer Reports* and J. D. Power and Associates took a grudging second look. And they liked what they saw. Hyundai rose to second place in J. D. Power and Associates's survey of initial car quality, tied with Honda behind Toyota. *Consumer Reports* named the Sonata as the most reliable car.

Hyundai has raised the bar even higher. The latest Sonata has six air bags—most other manufacturers offer only four as a standard feature—a six-speaker CD and MP3 player, and an advanced antilock braking system—all for a price tag of less than $25 000. Competitors not only are paying attention, they are worried. "Hyundai has quality and prices that have caught customers' attention, not to mention ours," admitted Toyota vice chairman Fujio Cho. In fact, Hyundai has become the fastest-growing major automaker in the world, spending $1.6 billion a year on research and development of new products. "I have an unlimited account," says Lee Hyun Soon, a senior executive in R&D. The firm has also spent billions on new manufacturing facilities around the world, in countries such as the United States and China—both huge markets for trucks and cars. Under the watchful eye of Chung Mong Koo, Hyundai is making the most of its second chance. "We can't allow any defects to damage our cars," he insists. It is a simple marketing philosophy that resonates around the world.

Questions for Critical Thinking

1. How does a focus on quality convey a universal message to all of Hyundai's potential customers?
2. Do you think that Hyundai's pricing strategy will be effective in all markets? Why or why not?
3. What steps might Toyota and Honda have to take to compete effectively with Hyundai?

Sources: Kim Tae-jin, "Alabama Plant Is a Hyundai Success Story," *International Herald Tribune*, February 27, 2006, http://www.iht.com; "Toyota Sees Hyundai as Threat in America," MSNBC, January 10, 2006, http://www.msnbc.msn.com; Cheryl Jensen, "2006 Hyundai Sonata: Filling the Camry's Rearview Mirror," *The New York Times*, November 6, 2005, http://www.nytimes.com; "Hyundai to Set Up $1.3 Billion China Venture," Livedoor, June 22, 2005, http://www.livedoorinc.com; Michael Schuman, "Hyundai Revs Up," *Time Asia*, April 25, 2005, http://www.time .com; hyundaicanada.com, accessed October 29, 2007.

Video Case 6.3

Lonely Planet Brings You the World

The written video case on Lonely Planet appears on page VC-9. The recently filmed Lonely Planet video is designed to expand and highlight the concepts in this chapter and the concepts and questions covered in the written video case.

DEBORAH MCKENZIE

COURTESY OF DEBORAH MCKENZIE

Talking About Global Marketing Management with Deborah McKenzie

Here are highlights of our interview with Deborah McKenzie, Global Marketing Manager. For the complete video interview and transcript, go to http://www.contemporarymarketing2.nelson.com

Q2: What attracted you to the field that you are in?
DM: In the early 90s, I took a "careers" course at IBM and all results led to the marketing profession. I have never looked back.

Q3: What was your first marketing job and how did you get it?
DM: My first job was an integrated marketing communications specialist in IBM Software Group Marketing. I then moved on to a Canadian marketing manager role, then to a North American position, and am currently a global marketing manager delivering marketing programs to IBM's geographies worldwide.

Q4: Briefly describe one of your typical days.
DM: As a global marketing manager I work from a home office. My colleagues are all over the world. I can start my day on conference calls as early as 7:00 A.M., talking to Europe, work with my North American marketing colleagues during the day, and can end up on conference calls talking to Asia until 10:00 P.M. at night. I also juggle my AMA responsibilities, as well as teaching, throughout a typical work day. It's a 12-hour day. But I love my job and my profession!

Q5: What was the biggest challenge/surprise when you entered the field?
DM: Cultural influences. Some creative concepts are acceptable in some countries, and in other countries they can be an insult to the culture. You have to be very careful in this global world!
For example, we had to put together a security presentation dealing with the payment card industry. This involved payment cards such as Visa, American Express, and MasterCard. Presentation needed to comply with the Corporate Governance Webcast regulations. One of the sentences was red-flagged. The sentence read "Are you in payment card purgatory?" This could be viewed as inappropriate and even offensive when interpreted as "Are you in payment card hell?" in some cultures. Because of this, we chose to reword the question to read "Are you in payment card misery?"

Q7: How do you feel CRM has evolved as a marketing practice and what is your experience with it?
DM: CRM allows for a more defined target market selection as you gain a large amount of information about the consumer. As a consumer, I find great privileges in a more tailored approach through great loyalty programs and tracking practices. CRM practices allow relationship-generation campaigns versus demand-generation campaigns. This also facilitates the creation of data models, which are able to predict buyer behaviour.

Q11: What are the important skills that marketing students needs to succeed?
DM: You need the entire package. Don't think if you are in strategy, you only need to "strategize." Ensure you know how to execute tactics (roll up your sleeves) and measure your results!

Ensure you know how to execute tactics (roll up your sleeves) and measure your results!

Q12: What is a good entrance into the industry?
DM: If you know that you want to be a marketer in a large corporation, work for one of their distribution channels partners first. It's an easier way into the large corporation. Once you've proven yourself as a business partner, they'll want to hire you.

Q13: Any last words or advice for future marketing graduates?
DM: Always read! It's the most inexpensive form of education. Whether it's the national newspaper, business and marketing trade magazines, or non-fiction . . . keep on reading!

Spreading Laughs in Unexpected Places

The first audience exposed to The Compass Players (precursor to The Second City) didn't know that they were about to see a revolutionary mix of sketch and improvisational comedy. The Compass Players began the Second City legacy of groundbreaking comedy in a small tavern in 1959. Their first audience had, in fact, not paid a dime for the entertainment they stumbled on. They found a comedy show based on contemporary headlines, rooted in cutting-edge humour, and spawned from improvisation. Soon after, Second City was formed, opening in a converted Chinese laundry. Word of the fearless cast of actors spread across the Midwest. While The Second City developed its technique, it defined a role for itself in the market. It has entertained a continuously growing body of consumers and has identified a market for custom work in the world of business, which is, ironically, a world that is frequently lampooned on their stages.

The Second City was created by artists—young, hip, intelligent actors, who educated themselves on politics, cultural sentiment, and social hierarchy. It was the early 1960s, and as America was entering a decade of cultural change, The Second City developed a voice that challenged the core values of the day. It attracted a body of consumers who were interested in the comedic take on controversial issues such as civil rights, Vietnam, and the Cold War. Bernie Sahlins, Second City's principal founder, said that SC's comedy spoke to this changing cultural climate. Within eight months of opening, Second City had grabbed national attention. Its product, its comedy, began to take shape as a creative innovation worthy of more expansive entrepreneurial ventures.

In the entertainment industry, two features define the consumer perception of The Second City. It's the launch pad for globally recognized comedic talent, and the live theatre venue dedicated to satire and improvisation. As Second City has developed a variety of related business ventures, it has aimed to, in the words of VP Kelly Leonard, "stay true to their core." Its continued focus on the SC style of comedy has distinguished it from competitors. Consumers interested in live comedic theatre have very few alternatives if they also seek satire and improvisation. The Second City legacy is, similarly, exclusive to its business. As tourists come to Chicago looking for a night of entertainment, The Second City is a recognizable brand that has stuck to its roots throughout five decades of expansion.

Capitalizing on Second City's reputation is its communications division. As the modern businessperson faces a workplace in which communication is critical, The Second City has found a key place as teacher, creator, and entertainer.

Tom Yorton, president of Second City Communications, comes from an extensive corporate background. His experience in numerous industries, including high-tech, Internet, retail, automotive, airlines, fitness, restaurants, lodging, financial services, and health care, have helped make him accessible to businesses seeking SC's expertise. Second City Communications performs the most sophisticated business-to-business marketing employed by the organization. Yorton's small team of professionals collaborates with a variety of businesses, including Pepsi and Motorola, designing hilarious and subject-specific performances for their corporate events.

Enriching the buyer–seller relationship with corporate clients is fundamental to the success of SC Communications. While Second City's theatrical casts have always been well versed on topical issues, the SC Communications team must understand the challenges of its client. Throughout the buying process, SC Communications educates itself on its client. It often relays potential script ideas to the clients and gains feedback from the corporate heads of these businesses. Yorton reports that, through quality interactions with companies, SC Communications has let its marketing work for itself.

SC Communications has become the fastest-growing division of the company and established a reputation that leads businesses to seek out SC Communications. Keith Kramer, president of Chicago Faucets, recently hired SC Communications to help in a presentation for a global conglomerate acquiring his company. He is quoted as saying, "I could either inflict death by PowerPoint, or bring in Second City. I chose Second City." Second City's B2B marketing uses the language of business and the efficiency of comedy to show its relevance in today's corporate world.

After all, in high-pressured business, in which thinking quickly on your feet, trusting your instincts, and taking big risks is paramount, it makes for good business to train with the masters of improvisation. SC Communications provides numerous training options to executives looking for techniques in active listening, presentation skills, teamwork, customer service, and creativity. The Second City website hosts a number of "case studies" that detail how it has designed training events based on the specific needs of the client. SC Communications is making impressive strides in video technology to address public relations and training methods for large companies with thousands of employees across the country. The corporate market has come to know Second City and is delighted by its sense of humour and impressed by its sense of business.

The Second City is adept at understanding its consumer base—perhaps because approval of its product has been as clear as the sound of laughter. By commenting on modern culture for nearly 50 years, Second City has become a social influence all its own. Its recognizable characteristics have enabled its jump into the corporate world. No matter what project the varied teams at The Second City are focusing on, its signature skills of improvisation make any material suitable for the stage.

Questions

1. Describe who you think the average audience member at a Second City show might be.
2. What is the consumer perception of Second City?
3. Why do you think that Second City Communications is helpful to businesses?
4. What are some of the techniques that Second City uses to help businesspeople in their work?

Part 2 CBC Video Case

CBC

Visit the website for Contemporary Marketing at **http://www.contemporarymarketing2e.nelson.com** to view the CBC video and video case summary for Part II.

part 3

TARGET MARKET SELECTION

chapter 7

Marketing Research, Decision Support Systems, and Sales Forecasting

CHAPTER OBJECTIVES

1. Describe the development of the marketing research function and its major activities.

2. Explain the steps in the marketing research process.

3. Distinguish between primary and secondary data and identify the sources of each type.

4. Explain the different sampling techniques used by marketing researchers.

5. Identify the methods by which marketing researchers collect primary data.

6. Explain the challenges of conducting marketing research in global markets.

7. Outline the most important uses of computer technology in marketing research.

8. Identify the major types of forecasting methods.

POINTS CARDS OR MARKET RESEARCH

Air Miles, Petro-Points, and Canadian Tire Options are all examples of loyalty programs where customers collect points that they later redeem for a product or service. Are these programs put in place to build customer loyalty or to collect information about customers? The simple answer is both. A properly designed loyalty program should be a tool for collecting and analyzing data on the customers who use them.

Loyalty programs have been around since the early 1980s but in Canada one of the oldest is Air Mile Rewards. Air Mile Rewards was started in the early 1990s by a Toronto-based company, Loyalty Group, with 13 organizations signing on. When companies join together for loyalty programs, as with Air Miles, they share the operations and marketing costs but they also share in the ongoing market research.

Canadians like loyalty programs so there is lots of information to share. Canada has one of the highest participation rates of all countries where these programs are offered. Roughly 72 percent of Canadians collect points in at least one scheme. The highest participation rate is with Air Miles at 63 percent but others such as the one operated by HBC has 43 percent of Canadians joining in. Many people belong to more than one program, and 17 percent of all Canadians belong to four or more plans. Almost one-quarter of all Canadians belong to at least two, and only about 20 percent have no loyalty plan affiliation. The membership in these programs is not uniform across the country. The highest participation is in Atlantic Canada, at almost 80 percent, with Quebec coming in at the lowest rate of 50 percent. Even at 50 percent companies can collect a great deal of information about who their customers are and what their purchasing patterns are.

The people who collect points cover most of the demographic groups. Air Miles boasts 67 percent of Canadian females are members but male consumers are adequately represented at 58 percent. Even programs like the Canadian Tire Options have almost as many men (27 percent) as women (30 percent). Some programs seem to appeal more to one gender than the other, such as the HBC plan, which has 54 percent female participants opposed to only 30 percent male. Participation in these programs covers all age groups as well. Air Miles shows the highest participation in the 55- to 64-year-old group at 72 percent but even the smallest participation rate in the 65+ age group at 54 percent gives a respectable picture of the consumer behaviour of this market segment. Blockerbuster rewards is more heavily used by a younger demographic with 35 percent aged 18 to 24, 20 percent aged 25 to 34, and 18 percent aged 35 to 44 but than drops off to only 9 percent above 45 years old. There is even a smaller spread of usage rates across income levels for most plans. The usage demographics show that companies can get valuable information about the shopping habits of every segment of the market.

Companies participating in these loyalty programs reap other benefits in addition to the valuable research on their customers' spending patterns. Research shows customers who participate in these programs have positive attitudes toward the companies involved. Customers were more likely to feel valued by the company, resulting in their spending more than the customer who did not collect points. By identifying the customers who are high-value or spend the most, companies are able to design their rewards program specifically for these consumers. Research also shows that those customers who redeem points for merchandise or travel are more likely to purchase more than those who don't.

Collecting loyalty points provides everyone involved with advantages: companies get loyal customers and valuable research and consumers get rewarded for purchases they make.

---

connecting with customers

At first glance a loyalty program is a method for rewarding and encouraging repeat purchases. These programs have other benefits for the customers. As they amass more and more points, customers are building an emotional attachment to the companies and the brands the companies sell.[1]

Chapter Overview

COLLECTING and managing information about what customers need and want is a challenging task for any marketer. **Marketing research** is the process of collecting and using information for marketing decision making. Data come from a variety of sources. Some results come from well-planned studies designed to elicit specific information. Other valuable information comes from sales force reports, accounting records, and published reports. Still other data emerge from controlled experiments and computer simulations. Thanks to new database technologies, some data that companies collect are compiled for them through their loyalty programs. Marketing research, by presenting pertinent information in a useful format, aids decision makers in analyzing data and in suggesting possible actions.

This chapter discusses the marketing research function. Marketers use research to understand their customers, target customer segments, and develop long-term customer relationships—all keys to profitability. Information collected through marketing research underlies much of the material on market segmentation discussed in the following chapter. Clearly, the marketing research function is the primary source of the information needed to make effective marketing decisions. The use of technology to mine data and gather business and competitive intelligence is also discussed, as is technology's vast impact on marketing research decision making and planning. This chapter also explains how marketing research techniques are used to make accurate sales forecasts, a critical component of marketing planning. ◆◆◆

marketing research Process of collecting and using information for marketing decision making.

Marketoid

Fifty-two percent of all 9- to 13-year-olds in Canada belong to a loyalty rewards program

---

① Describe the development of the marketing research function and its major activities.

THE MARKETING RESEARCH FUNCTION

Before looking at how marketing research is conducted, we must first examine its historical development, the people and organizations it involves, and the activities it entails. Because an underlying purpose of research is to find out more about consumers, research is clearly central to effective customer satisfaction and customer relationship programs. Media technologies such as the Internet and virtual reality are opening up new channels through which researchers can tap into consumer information.

DEVELOPMENT OF THE MARKETING RESEARCH FUNCTION

More than 125 years have passed since the first organized marketing research project was undertaken in 1879. A second important milestone in the development of marketing research occurred 32 years later, when the first commercial research department was organized at Curtis Publishing, publishers of *The Saturday Evening Post*.

Most early research gathered little more than written testimonials from purchasers of firms' products. Research methods became more sophisticated during the 1930s as the development of statistical techniques led to refinements in sampling procedures and greater accuracy in research findings.

In recent years, advances in computer technology have significantly changed the complexion of marketing research. Besides accelerating the pace and broadening the base of data collection, computers have aided marketers in making informed decisions about problems and opportunities. Simulations, for example, allow marketers to evaluate alternatives by posing "what-if" questions. Marketing researchers at many consumer goods firms simulate product introductions through computer programs to determine whether to risk real-world product launches or even to subject products to test marketing.

WHO CONDUCTS MARKETING RESEARCH?

The size and organizational form of the marketing research function are usually tied to the structure of the company. Some firms organize research units to support different product lines, brands, or geographic areas. Others organize their research functions according to the types of research they need performed, such as sales analysis, new-product development, advertising evaluation, or sales forecasting. The Go Green Box describes how Shell made use of the consumer research it conducted.

Many firms outsource their research needs and thus depend on independent marketing research firms. These independent organizations might specialize in handling just part of a larger study, such as conducting consumer interviews. Firms can also contract out entire research studies.

Marketers usually decide whether to conduct a study internally or through an outside organization based on cost. Another major consideration is the reliability and accuracy of the information collected by an outside organization. Because collecting marketing data is what these outside organizations do full time, the information they gather is often more thorough and accurate than that collected by less experienced in-house staff. Often, an outside marketing research firm can provide technical assistance and expertise not available within the company's marketing department. Interaction with outside suppliers also helps to ensure that a researcher does not conduct a study only to validate a favourite viewpoint or preferred option.

The Market Research and Intelligence Association is a not-for-profit association with chapters across Canada representing all aspects of the research industry.

MARKET RESEARCH AND INTELLIGENCE ASSOCIATION

Go Green

Shell Did the Research

When research found that "92 percent of Canadians say that the more environmentally responsible a company is, the more they are likely to purchase products or services from them," companies like Shell listened. Companies had little choice when 40 percent of survey respondents stated that they would punish those companies that didn't by not buying their products and, even worse, would speak up and let others know that the companies were not acting responsibly.

From Shell's point of view it also makes good corporate sense, giving Shell a competitive edge in the marketplace. Shell has found that by promoting and engaging in good environmental practises it is easier to get permission to drill wells, build gas plants, and sell gas. Their environmental program has four arms: protecting the environment, alternative energy, managing resources, and living up to their commitments.

Under the initiative of protecting the environment, it was the first company to achieve ISO 14001 registration for its oil sands operations, along with registering all of its major plants. Projects under its alternative energy category include developing advanced biofuels and adding wind energy to its portfolio of more eco-friendly choices. Reducing environmental impact is the aim of the category managing resources, which includes biodiversity; climate change—focusing on reducing long-term greenhouse gas emissions; effective land use—to reduce the company's environmental impact on wildlife; sustainable mobility, which looks at ways to keep society mobile without compromising the needs of future generations; and maintaining the quality of water through responsible use.

Living up to its commitments is where Shell puts the money behind what it is preaching. It partners with the Nature Conservancy of Canada in land conservation projects and endows the Shell Environmental Fund, which helps Canadians put environmental ideas into action; in partnership with Environment Canada and Canadian Geographic, it presents the Canadian Environmental Awards.

Shell has proven that it not only did its homework by researching what Canadians thought were important issues, but it also put the resources behind finding solutions.

Sources: http://www.shell.ca, accessed November 26, 2007; Rebecca Harris, "Growing Responsibilities," *Marketing*, August 15, 2005, pp. 15–17; Norma Ramage, "Sustainable Marketing," *Marketing*, March 7, 2005, p. 6.

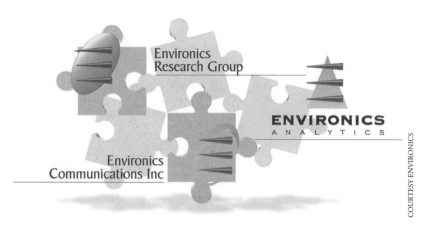

COURTESY ENVIRONICS

Environics is a full-service marketing research firm.

Marketoid

Seventy percent of all 14- to 18-year-olds in Canada belong to a loyalty rewards program.

Marketing research companies range in size from sole proprietorships to national and international firms such as Nielsen. They can be classified as syndicated services, full-service suppliers, or limited-service suppliers, depending on the types of services they offer to clients. Some full-service organizations are also willing to take on limited-service activities.

Syndicated Services

An organization that regularly provides a standardised set of data to all customers is called a **syndicated service**. Companies providing syndicated product research may base their reports on personal interviews, exposure to advertising, or point-of-sale scanner data captured from a retail store. Clients include advertisers, advertising agencies, magazines, newspapers, broadcasters, and cable TV networks.

Another syndicated service provider is J. D. Power and Associates, a global marketing information firm that specializes in surveying customer satisfaction, product quality, and buyer behaviour. Among its customers are companies in the telecommunications, travel and hotel, marine, utilities, health care, building, consumer electronics, automotive, and financial services industries.[2]

Full-Service Research Suppliers

An organization that contracts with clients to conduct complete marketing research projects is called a **full-service research supplier**. Environics Research Group, which has offices across Canada and the United States, is an example of a full-service company.[3] A full-service supplier becomes the client's marketing research arm, performing all the steps in the marketing research process (discussed later in this chapter).

Limited-Service Research Suppliers

A marketing research firm that specializes in a limited number of activities, such as conducting field interviews or performing data processing, is called a **limited-service research supplier**. Working almost exclusively for major movie studios, Nielsen National Research Group specializes in testing promotional materials for and marketing of motion pictures.[4] The firm also prepares studies to help clients develop advertising strategies and to track awareness and interest. Syndicated services can also be considered a type of limited-service research supplier.

Customer Satisfaction Measurement Programs

In their marketing research, firms often focus on tracking the satisfaction levels of current customers. For example, one firm charges a monthly fee to clients and does everything from designing and managing a firm's customer feedback area on its website to moderating online discussion groups and analyzing comments.[5] Some marketers have gained valuable insights by tracking the dissatisfaction that led customers to abandon certain products for those of competitors. Some customer defections are only partial; customers

assessment check 1 ✓

1.1 Identify the different classifications of marketing research suppliers and explain how they differ from one another.

1.2 What research methods can be used to measure customer satisfaction?

COURTESY RESEARCHBYNET

Researchbynet is a limited-service research supplier specializing in online research.

may remain somewhat satisfied with a business but not completely satisfied. Such attitudes could lead them to take their business elsewhere. Studying the underlying causes of customer defections, even partial defections, can be useful for identifying problem areas that need attention.

THE MARKETING RESEARCH PROCESS

As discussed earlier, business executives rely on marketing research to provide the information they need to make effective decisions regarding their firm's current and future activities. The chances of making good decisions improve when the right information is provided at the right time during decision making. To achieve this goal, marketing researchers often follow the six-step process shown in Figure 7.1. In the initial stages, researchers define the problem, conduct exploratory research, and formulate a hypothesis to be tested. Next, they create a design for the research study and collect needed data. Finally, researchers interpret and present the research information. The following sections take a closer look at each step of the marketing research process.

DEFINE THE PROBLEM

A popular anecdote advises that well-defined problems or research questions are half-solved. A well-defined problem permits the researcher to focus on securing the exact information needed for the solution. Clearly defining the question that research needs to answer increases the speed and accuracy of the research process.

Researchers must carefully avoid confusing symptoms of a problem with the problem itself. A symptom merely alerts marketers that a problem exists. For example, suppose that a maker of frozen pizzas sees its market share drop from 8 to 5 percent in six months. The loss of market share is a symptom of a problem the company must solve. To define the problem, the firm must look for the underlying causes of its market share loss.

A logical starting point in identifying the problem might be to evaluate the firm's target market and marketing mix elements. Suppose, for example, a firm has recently changed its promotional strategies. Research might then seek to answer the question "What must we do to improve the effectiveness of our marketing mix?" The firm's marketers might also look at possible environmental changes. Perhaps a new competitor entered the firm's market. Decision makers will need information to help answer the question "What must we do to distinguish our company from the new competitor?"

When Loblaws, the national grocery chain, wanted to find out why people were not eating more healthfully even though research showed that about half of all Canadians were considered overweight or obese, they turned to the research firm Ipsos-Reid to find out. Their research showed that although 87 percent of Canadians were trying to eat more healthfully, 40 percent felt it was too difficult and time consuming to read the nutritional labels on food packages. In response to these findings, Loblaws developed an entire line of food products under its President's Choice brand. This new group of products named PC Blue Menu consists of a line of fresh and frozen products with packaging that shows the health benefits clearly on the front of the package.[6]

CONDUCT EXPLORATORY RESEARCH

Once a firm has defined the question it wants to answer, researchers can begin exploratory research. **Exploratory research** seeks to

② Explain the steps in the marketing research process.

Marketoid

Eighty-three percent of 19- to 24-year-olds in Canada own a loyalty card.

exploratory research Process of discussing a marketing problem with informed sources both within and outside the firm and examining information from secondary sources.

figure 7.1

The Marketing Research Process

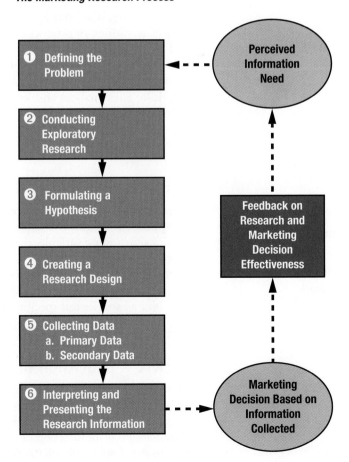

discover the cause of a specific problem by discussing the problem with informed sources both within and outside the firm and by examining data from other information sources. Marketers might talk with their wholesalers, retailers, and customers. They might also ask for input from the sales force or look for overall market clues.

In addition to talking with employees, exploratory research can include evaluation of company records, such as sales and profit analyses, and available competitive data. Marketing researchers often refer to internal data collection as situation analysis. The term *informal investigation* is often used for exploratory interviews with informed persons outside the researchers' firms.

Using Internal Data

Marketoid

Ninety-one percent of Canadians 25 to 29 years old have at least one loyalty or points card.

Marketers can find valuable data in their firm's own internal records. Typical sources of internal data are sales records, financial statements, and marketing cost analyses. Marketers analyze sales performance records to gain an overall view of company efficiency and to find clues to potential problems. Easily prepared from company invoices or a computer database system, this **sales analysis** can provide important details to management. The study typically compares actual and expected sales based on a detailed sales forecast by territory, product, customer, and salesperson. Once the sales quota—the level of expected sales to which actual results are compared—has been established, it is a simple process to compare actual results with expected performance.

Other possible breakdowns for sales analysis separate transactions by customer type, product, sales method (mail, telephone, or personal contact), type of order (cash or credit), and order size. Sales analysis is one of the least expensive and most important sources of marketing information available to a firm.

Accounting data, as summarized in the firm's financial statements, can be another good tool for identifying financial issues that influence marketing. Using ratio analysis, researchers can compare performance in current and previous years against industry benchmarks. These exercises may hint at possible problems, but only more detailed analysis would reveal specific causes of indicated variations.

A third source of internal information is *marketing cost analysis*—evaluation of expenses for tasks such as selling, warehousing, advertising, and delivery to determine the profitability of particular customers, territories, or product lines. Firms often examine the allocation of costs to products, customers, and territories. Marketing decision makers then evaluate the profitability of particular customers and territories on the basis of the sales produced and the costs incurred in generating those sales. Sometimes internal data can produce remarkably detailed customer profiles.

Like sales analysis and financial research, marketing cost analysis is most useful when it provides information linked to other forms of marketing research. A later section of this chapter will address how computer technologies can accomplish these linkages and move information among a firm's units.

FORMULATE A HYPOTHESIS

Marketoid

Canadian Tire money was introduced in 1958 at the company's first gas bar in Toronto.

After defining the problem and conducting an exploratory investigation, the marketer needs to formulate a **hypothesis**—a tentative explanation for some specific event. A hypothesis is a statement about the relationship among variables that carries clear implications for testing this relationship. It sets the stage for more in-depth research by further clarifying what researchers need to test. For example, a restaurant might want to see whether good customer service is related to its increased sales, so its marketers would conduct a survey of customers to test this hypothesis.

Not all studies test specific hypotheses. However, a carefully designed study can benefit from the rigour introduced by developing a hypothesis before beginning data collection and analysis.

CREATE A RESEARCH DESIGN

To test hypotheses and find solutions to marketing problems, a marketer creates a **research design,** a master plan or model for conducting marketing research. In planning a research project, marketers must be sure that the study will measure what they intend to measure. A second important research design consideration is the selection of respondents. Marketing researchers use sampling techniques (discussed later in the chapter) to determine which consumers to include in their studies.

Cadbury Schweppes, the candy and gum manufacturer, trains "sensory panellists" for several months to test gum by, for instance, chewing at a steady rate for set periods of time, usually three minutes. After each chewing session, the testers clear their palates with salted crackers and water and then use computers to record their feedback about flavour and texture.[7]

COLLECT DATA

Marketing researchers gather two kinds of data: secondary data and primary data. **Secondary data** are collected from previously published or compiled sources. Data Statistics Canada collects when they do a census are secondary data when used by companies. **Primary data** refer to information collected for the first time specifically for a marketing research study. An example of primary data is statistics collected by a company from a survey that asks current customers about their preferences for product improvements.

secondary data
Previously published information.

primary data
Information collected specifically for the investigation at hand.

Secondary data offer two important advantages: (1) it is almost always less expensive to gather secondary rather than primary data, and (2) researchers usually spend less time to locate and use secondary data. A research study that requires primary data may take three to four months to complete, while a researcher can often gather secondary data in a matter of days.

Secondary data do have limitations that primary data do not. First, published information can quickly become obsolete. A marketer analyzing the population of various areas may discover that even the most recent census figures are already out of date because of rapid growth and changing demographics. Second, published data collected for an unrelated purpose may not be completely relevant to the marketer's specific needs. For example, census data do not reveal the brand preferences of consumers.

Although research to gather primary data can cost more and take longer, the results can provide richer, more detailed information than secondary data offer. The choice between secondary and primary data is tied to cost, applicability, and effectiveness. Many marketing research projects combine secondary and primary data to fully answer marketing questions. This chapter examines specific methods for collecting both secondary and primary data in later sections.

assessment check 2

2.1 What are the six steps in the marketing research process?

2.2 What is the goal of exploratory research?

INTERPRET AND PRESENT RESEARCH INFORMATION

The final step in the marketing research process is to interpret the findings and present them to decision makers in a format that allows managers to make effective judgments. Possible differences in interpretations of research results may occur between marketing researchers and their audiences due to differing backgrounds, levels of knowledge, and experience. Both oral and written reports should be presented in a manner designed to minimize such misinterpretations.

Marketing researchers and research users must cooperate at every stage in the research process. Too many studies go unused because management considers the results are of little use, once they hear lengthy discussions of research limitations or unfamiliar terminology. Marketing researchers must remember to direct their reports toward management and not to other researchers. They should spell out their conclusions in clear and concise terms that can be put into action. Reports should confine technical details of the research methods to an appendix, if they are included at all. By presenting research results to all key executives at a single sitting, researchers can ensure that everyone will understand the findings. Decision makers can then quickly reach consensus on what the results mean and what actions are to be taken.

Marketoid

Over 70 percent of Via Rail Canada's loyalty program revenue is generated by 30 percent of its members.

MARKETING RESEARCH METHODS

Clearly, data collection is an integral part of the marketing research process. One of the most time-consuming parts of collecting data is determining what method the marketer should use to obtain the data. This section discusses the most commonly used methods by which marketing researchers find both secondary and primary data.

③ Distinguish between primary and secondary data and identify the sources of each type.

SECONDARY DATA COLLECTION

Secondary data come from many sources. The overwhelming quantity of secondary data available at little or no cost challenges researchers to select only data that are relevant to the problem or issue being studied.

Secondary data consist of two types: internal and external data. Internal data, as discussed earlier, include sales records, product performance reviews, sales force activity reports, and marketing cost reports. External data come from a variety of sources, including government records, syndicated research services, and industry publications. Computerized databases provide access to vast amounts of data from both inside and outside an organization. The following sections on government data, private data, and online sources focus on databases and other external data sources available to marketing researchers.

Government Data

All levels of government—federal, provincial, and municipal—provide information, much of it free. The two largest sources of information are provided by two federal government agencies, Statistics Canada (http://www.statcan.ca) and Industry Canada (http://www.ic.gc.ca).

Statistics Canada collects, organizes, and publishes information gained from a census taken every five years, several hundred other annual surveys, and internal government sources of data. The first census was taken in Canada in 1666 when the 3215 residents of New France were asked their age, sex, marital status, and occupation. The first census as a country was completed in 1871, and the basic format has changed little since that time, although the type and number of questions has evolved. In 1971, Statistics Canada became a separate department of the government, devoted entirely to information management.

In early May every five years, surveys are mailed to every home in Canada. Eighty percent receive a survey containing seven questions; the remainder receive a survey with 59 questions. The information is compiled to present a picture of Canada as a whole and broken down into smaller geographic units. Statistics Canada further assists market researchers by providing definitions and codes that are consistent not only for census data but for all surveys it conducts.[8]

Industry Canada's mandate is to assist Canadians and Canadian companies to become more competitive in the world marketplace. In March 1996, Industry Canada launched Strategis, its website, in order to provide business and consumer information in a more efficient electronic format. The site includes millions of electronic documents, thousands of links to related websites, and statistical data relating to Canada and other countries. People visiting the site can obtain information about consumer trends, laws, exporting, investing, financing, and economic statistics.[9]

Provincial and municipal governments also provide information about their areas. Some of the information on their websites comes from Statistics Canada but other information is collected locally. The aim of these government-sponsored websites is to provide relevant information quickly.

Industry Canada's website contains a wealth of data, including company directories, guides on business and the environment, and Industry Canada services. Marketers can use such secondary data to learn about markets and their customers.

Private Data

Many private organizations provide information for marketing decision makers. A trade association may be an excellent source of data on activities in a particular industry. A listing of trade associations is available in many libraries or online and can help marketers track down associations that may have data pertinent to their industry or company. Also, the advertising industry continuously collects data on audiences reached by various media.

Business and trade magazines also publish a wide range of valuable data. Most libraries offer listings of international periodicals that can point researchers in the direction of trade publications that publish industry-specific research. General business magazines can also be good sources. Magazines such as *Marketing, Strategy*, and *Canadian Business* publish information about specific markets, consumer behaviour, environmental trends, retail sales, and new products, along with other topics.

Data security is always an issue for firms collecting data for research. The "Marketing Failure" feature explores how one firm dealt with a security breach of their database.

Because few libraries carry specialized trade journals, the best way to gather data from them is either directly from the publishers or through online periodical databases like ProQuest Direct's *ABI/Inform*, available at many libraries. Increasingly, trade publications maintain web home pages that allow archival searches. Larger libraries can often provide directories and other publications that can help researchers find secondary data. For instance, there are directories available that list market research reports, studies, and surveys that are available either free or for a fee.

Several firms offer information to businesses by subscription. These companies provide global database services with continuing data on consumer attitudes, lifestyles, and buying behaviour in many countries.

Electronic systems that scan UPC bar codes speed purchase transactions, and they also provide data used for inventory control, ordering, and delivery. Scanning technology is widely used by grocers and other retailers, and marketing research companies, such as Nielsen, store this data in commercially available databases. These scanner-based information services track consumer purchases of a wide variety of UPC-coded products. Retailers can use this information to target customers with the right merchandise at the right time.

Newer techniques that rely on radio-frequency identification (RFID) technology are in growing use. Wal-Mart has run successful tests showing that RFID reduced out-of-stocks and cut down dramatically on manual orders and excess inventory.[10] Use of RFID to track individuals' purchases and use of products is, however, controversial because of privacy concerns. Currently, the technology is used for aggregate data.

Nielsen SalesNet uses the Internet to deliver scanner data quickly to clients. Data are processed as soon as they are received from supermarkets and are then forwarded to marketing researchers so they can perform more in-depth analysis. At the same time, Nielsen representatives summarize the data in both graphic and spreadsheet form and post it on the Internet for immediate access by clients.

Marketoid

A survey by Leger Marketing found that 60 percent of Canadians had redeemed an offer from a loyalty program at least once.

Online Sources of Secondary Data

The tools of cyberspace sometimes simplify the hunt for secondary data. Hundreds of databases and other sources of information are available online. A well-designed, Internet-based marketing research project can cost less yet yield faster results than offline research.

The Internet has spurred the growth of research aggregators—companies that acquire, catalogue, reformat, segment, and then resell premium research reports that have already been published. Aggregators put valuable data within reach of marketers who lack the time or the budget to commission custom research. Because Web technology makes their databases easy to search, aggregators are able to compile detailed, specialized reports quickly and cost-effectively.[11]

Internet search tools such as Google and Yahoo! can find specific sites that are rich with information. Discussion groups may also provide information and insights that can help answer some marketing questions. Additionally, a post to a chat room or newsgroup may draw a response that uncovers previously unknown sources of secondary data. One market research firm has software designed to use keywords to scour blogs for useful consumer information on the Internet. "The blogosphere is overflowing with brutally honest opinion," says the firm's CEO. "Our goal is to track those opinions down."[12]

Researchers must, however, carefully evaluate the validity of information they find on the Internet. People without in-depth knowledge of the subject matter may post information in a newsgroup. Similarly, Web pages might contain information that has been gathered using questionable research methods. The phrase *caveat emptor* (let the buyer beware) should guide evaluation of secondary data on the Internet.

assessment check 3

3.1 Distinguish between primary and secondary data.

④ Explain the different sampling techniques used by marketing researchers.

sampling Process of selecting survey respondents or research participants.

probability sample Sample that gives every member of the population a chance of being selected.

SAMPLING TECHNIQUES

Before undertaking a study to gather primary data, researchers must first identify which participants to include in the study. **Sampling** is the process of selecting survey respondents or research participants. It is one of the most important aspects of research design because if a study fails to involve consumers who accurately reflect the target market, the research is likely to yield misleading conclusions.

The total group of people that the researcher wants to study is called the **population** or **universe**. For a political campaign study, the population would be all eligible voters. For research about a new lipstick line, it might be all women in a certain age bracket. The sample is a representative group chosen from this population. Researchers rarely gather information from a study's total population, resulting in a census. Unless the total population is small, the costs of a census are simply too high.

Samples can be classified as either probability samples or nonprobability samples. A **probability sample** is one that gives every member of the population a chance of being selected. Types of probability samples include simple random samples, stratified samples, and cluster samples.

In a **simple random sample,** every member of the relevant universe has an equal opportunity of selection. The weekly lotteries sponsored by provincial lottery organizations, such as British Columbia Lottery Corporation, where every numbered ball has an equal chance of dropping out of the machine, are an example of a simple random sample. In a **stratified sample,** randomly selected subsamples of different groups are represented in the total sample. Stratified samples provide efficient, representative groups that are relatively homogeneous for a certain characteristic for such studies as opinion polls, in which groups of individuals share various divergent viewpoints. In a **cluster sample,** researchers select a sample of subgroups (or clusters) from which they draw respondents. Each cluster reflects the diversity of the whole population being sampled. This cost-efficient type of probability sample is widely used when the entire population cannot be listed or enumerated.

marketing failure — Winners and HomeSense Customer Data Hacked

Background. TJX, based in Framingham, Maryland, is the parent company for Winners and HomeSense Stores in Canada, along with retailers in the United States, United Kingdom, and Ireland. In January 2007, the company made public a major breach in its computer system. The company's news release stated that starting in 2003 but mainly between May and December 2006 customer information, including credit card, debit card, and personal identification, was accessed.

The Challenge. Like all customer information databases, TJX faces the constant possibility that unauthorized users will gain access to its stored data. As one industry expert stated, "The bad guys are smart and getting more organized. They will make use of all of the skills available to them to try to find ways to obtain the information they need to commit fraud." As many as 45 million records—perhaps even twice that number—were stolen from the company. The thief used a data capturing program called a "sniffer" to access customer information passing through the company's computer.

The Strategy. Investigators from the United States, the RCMP, and the privacy commissioners of Canada and the province of Alberta conducted a seven-month investigation. These investigations found that the company's computer security software was outdated and that the company was storing sensitive data longer than required.

The Outcome. Prosecutors said the case was one of the largest attempts ever made to steal personal data. While acknowledging that no system is ever completely secure, TJX has updated its computer security and settled several class-action lawsuits compensating individuals affected by the theft. One outcome from this case may be a change in the law making the retailer responsible for customer information and allowing banks to recover any damages resulting in breaches of security.

Sources: Joseph Pereira, "TJX Ruling Gives Banks a Breakthrough: Burden of Protecting Customer Card Data May Shift to Retailers," *The Wall Street Journal,* October 26, 2007, p. B.3; Joseph Pereira, "TJX's Security System Faulted in Canada Probe," *The Wall Street Journal,* September 26, 2007, p. B.3; TJX website, www.tjx.com, accessed November 19, 2007.

In contrast, a **nonprobability sample** relies on personal judgment somewhere in the selection process. In other words, researchers decide which particular groups to study. Types of nonprobability samples are convenience samples and quota samples. A **convenience sample** is a nonprobability sample selected from among readily available respondents; this sample is often called an *accidental sample* because those included just happen to be in the place where the study is being conducted. Mall intercept surveys and TV call-in opinion polls are good examples. Marketing researchers sometimes use convenience samples in exploratory research but not in definitive studies. A **quota sample** is a nonprobability sample that is divided to maintain the proportion of certain characteristics among different segments or groups as is seen in the population as a whole. In other words, each field worker is assigned a quota that specifies the number and characteristics of the people to contact. It differs from a stratified sample, in which researchers select subsamples by some random process; in a quota sample, they hand-pick participants.

nonprobability sample Sample that involves personal judgment somewhere in the selection process.

assessment check 4

4.1 What is sampling?

4.2 What are the different types of probability samples?

4.3 Identify the types of nonprobability samples.

PRIMARY RESEARCH METHODS

Marketers use a variety of methods for conducting primary research, as Figure 7.2 shows. The principal methods for collecting primary data are observation, surveys and interviews, and controlled experiments. The choice among these methods depends on the issues under study and the decisions that marketers need to make. In some cases, researchers may decide to combine techniques during the research process.

⑤ Identify the methods by which marketing researchers collect primary data.

Observation Method

In observational studies, researchers view the overt actions of subjects being studied. Marketers trying to understand how consumers behave in certain situations find observation to be a useful technique. Observation tactics may be as simple as counting the number of cars passing by a potential site for a fast-food restaurant or checking the licence plates at a shopping centre near a provincial border or near the Canada–U.S. border to determine where shoppers live.

Technological advances provide increasingly sophisticated ways for observing consumer behaviour. The television industry relies on data from people meters, which are electronic remote-control devices that record the TV-viewing habits of individual household members to measure the popularity of TV shows. Traditional people meters require each viewer to press a button each time he or she turns on the TV, changes channels, or leaves the room.

Marketers have long worried that some viewers do not bother to push people meter buttons at appropriate times, skewing research findings. In response, one company recently tested a portable people meter (PPM) that participants keep with them at all times. Throughout the day, the PPM picks up and stores codes embedded in radio and broadcast, cable, and satellite TV programming as well as

figure 7.2

Types of Primary Research

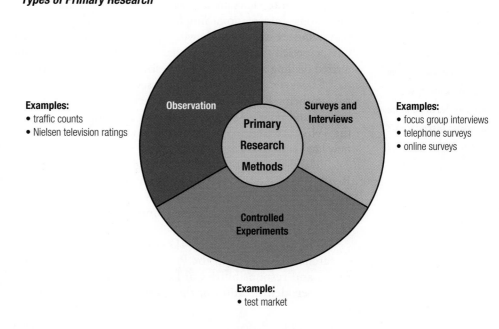

Examples:
• traffic counts
• Nielsen television ratings

Examples:
• focus group interviews
• telephone surveys
• online surveys

Observation

Surveys and Interviews

Primary Research Methods

Controlled Experiments

Example:
• test market

Internet content and cinema advertising. At night, the participant puts the PPM into a docking station, from which the data are uploaded. The PPM even has a built-in motion detector to ensure that it is not abandoned midtest.[13]

Acknowledging the growing prevalence of TiVo and other digital video recording (DVR) technologies in households, Nielsen Media Research, in partnership with DVR market leader TiVo, has begun distributing its well-known television ratings in three versions: live, live plus 24 hours (to count viewers who play back shows within a day of recording them), and live plus seven days (to count those who play back shows within a week). The technology allows broadcasters to track viewing habits in the 7 percent of TV households that now use digital video recording to tailor their viewing. Marketers may soon be able to make media decisions knowing how many people are "timeshifting" shows—and the accompanying advertising—to watch them after the broadcast date.[14]

Videotaping consumers in action is also gaining acceptance as a research technique. Cookware manufacturers may videotape consumers cooking in their own kitchens to evaluate how they use their pots and pans. A toothbrush manufacturer asked a marketing research firm to videotape consumers brushing their teeth and using mouthwash in its quest to develop products that would leave behind the sensation of cleanliness and freshness.

In an effort to understand what makes younger consumers tick, a trend-forecasting firm auditioned and hired a panel of more than 300 "diverse, trend-setting, savvy teens" for its Trendwatch Panel. The teens participate in focus group discussions and respond to research queries on the company's online bulletin board.[15]

Interpretative Research

Another type of primary research is **interpretative research,** a method in which a researcher observes a customer or group of customers in their natural setting and interprets their behaviour based on an understanding of the social and cultural characteristics of that setting. We discuss interpretative research in more detail later.

Survey and Interview Methods

Observation alone cannot supply all the desired information. Researchers must ask questions to get information on attitudes, motives, and opinions. It is also difficult to get exact demographic information—such as income levels—from observation. To discover this information, researchers can use either interviews or questionnaires.

Telephone Interviews

Telephone interviews are a quick and inexpensive method for obtaining a small quantity of relatively impersonal information. Simple, clearly worded questions are easy for interviewers to pose over the phone and are effective at drawing appropriate responses. Telephone surveys have relatively high response rates, especially with repeated calls. To maximize responses and save costs, some researchers use computerized dialling and digitally synthesized voices that interview respondents.

However, phone surveys have several drawbacks. Most important, many people refuse to take part in them. Their reasons include lack of time, negative associations of phone surveys with telemarketing, and poorly designed surveys or questions that are difficult to understand.[16] While changes to the Telecommunications Act exclude marketing research from the national Do Not Call Registry, the new law requires market research firms to maintain their own Do Not Call lists.[17]

Many respondents are hesitant to give personal characteristics about themselves over the telephone. Results may be biased by the omission of typical households where adults are off working during the day. Other households, particularly market segments such as single women and physicians, are likely to have unlisted numbers. While computerized random dialling can give access to unlisted numbers, it maybe restricted in some areas.

The popularity of caller-ID systems to screen unwanted calls is another obstacle for telephone researchers. Included in the Personal Information Protection and Electronic Documents Act are rights and responsibilities of both the market researcher and the respondents. The importance of proper identification of the purpose of the research may reduce the importance of issues like caller-ID.[18]

ETIQUETTE TIPS FOR MARKETING PROFESSIONALS

How to Conduct Phone Surveys

TELEPHONE surveys are a common method of conducting marketing research because they're simple to develop and easy to do. But that doesn't mean they don't require preparation to make the process efficient for you and for participants. Respect their time and input with a few courteous tips.

1. Develop and test your research questions ahead of time. They should be brief, clear, and easy to tabulate. Time your questionnaire before you begin.

2. Prepare your opener by knowing how you'll introduce yourself and your purpose, but if you can, avoid writing or memorizing a script. Try for a natural, conversational greeting and introduction.

3. Explain the purpose of your survey and say how much time it will take. Be brief, upbeat, and polite, and make it clear that you aren't selling anything.

4. If the respondent is reluctant, try gentle persuasion, but say thank you and hang up if the resistance is firm.

5. Ask the respondent to verify his or her name and any other contact information you're collecting.

6. Read each question carefully and in its entirety and record the answer. Listen carefully, stay on topic, and avoid introducing comments that could influence the respondent's answers.

7. Thank the respondent for participating.

8. Organize and evaluate your results.

Sources: "Conducting Your Phone Survey," SurveyGold, http://surveygold .com, accessed March 22, 2006; "How to Conduct a Telephone Survey," eHow, http://www.ehow.com, accessed March 22, 2006; "How to Write a Survey or Questionnaire," eHow, http://www.ehow.com, accessed March 22, 2006; "Is Cold Calling Painful for You?" Unlock the Game, http://www .unlockthegame.com, accessed March 22, 2006.

Other obstacles restrict the usefulness of telephone surveys abroad. In areas where telephone ownership is rare, survey results will be highly biased. Telephone interviewing is also difficult in countries that lack directories, that charge landline telephone customers on a per-minute basis, or where call volumes congest limited phone line capacity.

Personal Interviews

The best means for obtaining detailed information about consumers is usually the personal interview because the interviewer can establish rapport with respondents and explain confusing or vague questions. In addition to contacting respondents at their homes or workplaces, marketing research firms can conduct interviews in rented space in shopping centres, where they gain wide access to potential buyers of the merchandise they are studying. These locations sometimes feature private interviewing space, videotape equipment, and food-preparation facilities for taste tests. As mentioned earlier, interviews conducted in shopping centres are typically called **mall intercepts**. Downtown retail districts and airports provide other valuable locations for marketing researchers.

Focus Groups

Marketers also gather research information through the popular technique of focus group interviews. A **focus group** brings together eight to 12 individuals

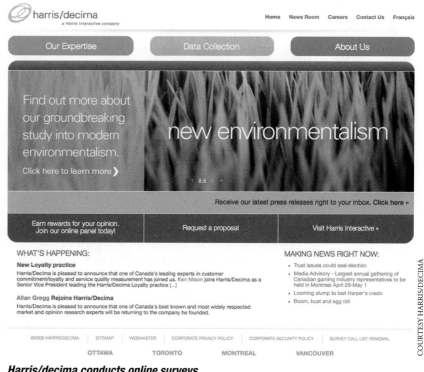

Harris/decima conducts online surveys.

focus group
Simultaneous personal interview of a small group of individuals, which relies on group discussion about a certain topic.

in one location to discuss a subject of interest. Unlike other interview techniques that elicit information through a question-and-answer format, focus groups usually encourage a general discussion of a predetermined topic. Focus groups can provide quick and relatively inexpensive insight into consumer attitudes and motivations.

In a focus group, the leader, or moderator, typically begins by explaining the purpose of the meeting and suggesting an opening topic. The moderator's main purpose, however, is to stimulate interaction among group members to encourage their discussion of numerous points. The moderator may occasionally interject questions as catalysts to direct the group's discussion. The moderator's job is difficult, requiring preparation and group facilitation skills.

Focus group sessions often last one or two hours. Researchers usually record the discussion on tape, and observers frequently watch through a one-way mirror. Some research firms also allow clients to view focus groups in action through videoconferencing systems.

Focus groups are a particularly valuable tool for exploratory research, developing new-product ideas and preliminary testing of alternative marketing strategies. They can also aid in the development of well-structured questionnaires for larger scale research.

Focus groups do have drawbacks. The CEO of an ad agency explains what many think is one of the biggest problems in focus groups—that people are just not honest in front of others. "There's peer pressure in focus groups that gets in the way of finding the truth about real behaviour and intentions," he says. Yahoo's chief marketing officer also voices dissatisfaction with focus groups and prefers "immersion groups" in which the company's product developers meet to talk informally with a handful of users and without professional moderators.[19]

Researchers are finding ways to re-create the focus group environment over the Internet. With experienced moderators who have the technical skills to function fluently online, it is possible to gain valuable qualitative information at a fraction of the cost it takes to run a traditional focus group session.

Nielsen reports that online focus groups can be both cost and time efficient, with immediate results in the form of chat transcripts. The convenience of online conversations tends to improve attendance as well, particularly among those who are otherwise difficult to include such as professionals and people who travel frequently, and the problem of peer pressure is virtually eliminated. Some drawbacks include the lack of access to body language and nonverbal cues, the difficulty of testing any products in which taste or smell is relevant, and the potential for samples to be non-representative because they are limited to those who have Internet access and a certain comfort level with technology.[20]

Mail Surveys

Although personal interviews can provide very detailed information, cost considerations usually prevent an organization from using personal interviews in a large-scale study. A mail survey can be a cost-effective alternative. Mail surveys can provide anonymity that may encourage respondents to give candid answers. They can also help marketers track consumer attitudes through ongoing research and sometimes provide demographic data that may be helpful in market segmentation.

Mail questionnaires do, however, have several limitations. First, response rates are typically much lower than for personal interviews. Second, because researchers must wait for respondents to complete and return questionnaires, mail surveys usually take a considerably longer time to conduct. A third limitation is that questionnaires cannot answer unanticipated questions that occur to respondents as they complete the forms. In addition, complex questions may not be suitable for a mail questionnaire. Finally, unless they gather additional information from non-respondents through other means, researchers must worry about possible bias in the results stemming from differences between respondents and non-respondents.

COURTESY ZINC RESEARCH

In an increasingly competitive business climate, companies turn to organizations like Zinc who provide assistance with research projects.

Researchers try to minimize these limitations by carefully developing and pretesting questionnaires. Researchers can boost response rates by keeping questionnaires short and by offering incentives—typically discount coupons or money.

Fax Surveys

The low response rates and long follow-up times associated with mail surveys have spurred interest in the alternative of faxing survey documents. In some cases, faxes may supplement mail surveys; in others, they may be the primary method for contacting respondents. Because millions of households do not have fax machines, securing a representative sample of respondents is a difficult undertaking in fax surveys of final consumers. As a result, most of these surveys focus on business-related research studies.

Online Surveys and Other Internet-Based Methods

The growing population of Internet users has spurred researchers to conduct online surveys. Using the Web, they are able to speed the survey process, increase sample sizes, ignore geographic boundaries, and dramatically reduce costs. While a standard research project can take up to eight weeks to complete, a thorough online project may take two weeks or less. Less intrusive than telephone surveys, online research allows participants to respond at their leisure. The novelty and ease of answering online may even encourage higher response rates. One online marketing research firm found that among 660 consumers who consistently avoid ads on TV and the Internet, most were actually more likely to participate in online product discussions at product review sites or in blogs and to post comments on websites more often.[21]

Businesses are increasingly including questionnaires on their Web pages to solicit information about consumer demographics, attitudes, and comments and suggestions for improving goods and services or improving marketing messages. Marketers are also experimenting with electronic bulletin boards as an information-gathering device. On a password-protected website, moderators pose questions to selected respondents—usually just 15 to 25—over a predetermined period of time. Respondents have a chance to try out new products and are able to submit feedback at their leisure. Online polling is also increasingly popular. One television station uses online polls to produce unique news stories. "Online polling allows us to poll our market more frequently than we ever could if we were doing traditional telephone surveys," says the station's news director. The station has a pool of about 5000 people recruited on air and online whom it rotates through various polls. The station finds that many people are glad to be included in the polls and that the online method avoids the problem that telephone surveys often face: their samples are skewed toward the elderly simply because they are the only ones home.[22]

The growth of the Internet is creating a need for new research techniques to measure and capture information about website visitors. At present, no industry-wide standards define techniques for measuring web use. Some sites ask users to register before accessing the pages; others merely keep track of the number of "hits," or number of times a visitor accesses a page. Marketers have tried to place a value on a site's "stickiness" (longer-lasting site visits) as a means of measuring effectiveness. Others use "cookies," which are electronic identifiers deposited on viewers' computers, to track click-through behaviour—the paths users take as they move through the site. However, because some consumers change their Internet service providers frequently, and special software is available to detect and remove them, cookies have lost some of their effectiveness.

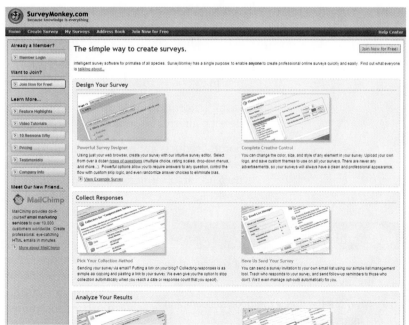

COURTESY SURVEYMONKEY.COM

SurveyMonkey.com provides assistance with all aspects of online surveys.

Researchers help marketers track blog topics with a combination of text analysis technology and human insight. Polaroid recently used this technique to discover that blogging photographers talk about archiving problems and photo longevity, bumping the topic to a priority product development issue for the camera company.[23]

Some software can monitor the overall content that a person is viewing and display banner advertisements likely to be of interest. For example, a search using the keyword *"car"* might call up a banner ad for General Motors or Ford. Profiles of web users from numerous sites are being collected and organized into as many as 800 categories, including sports and hobbies. Researchers can use this information to develop marketing strategies. The popularity of video games has led to the emergence of a new advertising platform, advergames. Sony Pictures's website for the horror film *The Cave* featured a complex advergame with an attention-grabbing storyline, and Unilever promoted its Axe line of men's products with an online dating game called *Mojo Master*. Said Unilever's Axe development manager, "As long as they perceive value in the [game] experience, they don't mind that they're being marketed to."[24]

Experimental Method

The third—and least-used—method for collecting primary data is the **controlled experiment.** A marketing research experiment is a scientific investigation in which a researcher controls or manipulates a test group (or groups) and compares the results with those of a control group that did not receive the experimental controls or manipulations.

The most common use of this method by marketers is **test-marketing,** or introducing a new product in a specific area and then observing its degree of success. Up to this point, a product development team may have gathered feedback from focus groups. Other information may have come from shoppers' evaluations of competing products. Test-marketing is the first stage at which the product performs in a real-life environment.

One woman enjoyed the experience of pilot-testing an Internet-enabled kitchen in her home. The collaborative project paired IBM, Whirlpool, and other marketers in setting up such prototypes as a cook range with both hot and cold modes, a refrigerator with a mobile web tablet that could send shopping orders directly from the kitchen to a grocery delivery service, and an under-cabinet entertainment centre with a flip-down screen that held a VCR, DVD player, television, radio, and Internet access. The women could interact with all the appliances via cell phone. Whirlpool's director for corporate innovation and technology described the results of the experiment by saying, "These guys behaved different while using these products. They ate more home-cooked meals."[25]

Some firms omit test-marketing and move directly from product development to full-scale production. These companies cite three problems with test-marketing:

1. Test-marketing is expensive. A firm can spend more than $1 million depending on the size of the test-market city and the cost of buying media to advertise the product.

2. Competitors quickly learn about the new product. By studying the test market, competitors can develop alternative strategies.

3. Some products are not well suited to test-marketing. Few firms test-market long-lived, durable goods such as cars because of the major financial investments required for their development, the need to establish networks of dealers to distribute the products, and requirements for parts and servicing.

Companies that decide to skip the test-marketing process can choose several other options. A firm may simulate a test-marketing campaign through computer-modelling software. By plugging in data on similar products, it can develop a sales projection for a new product. Another firm may offer an item in just one region or in another country, adjusting promotions and advertising based on local results before going to other geographic regions. Another option may be to limit a product's introduction to only one retail chain to carefully control and evaluate promotions and results.

assessment check 5

5.1 What are the major internal sources of secondary data?

5.2 What are the major methods of collecting primary data?

CONDUCTING INTERNATIONAL MARKETING RESEARCH

As corporations expand globally, they need to gather correspondingly more knowledge about consumers in other countries. Although marketing researchers follow the same basic steps for international studies as for domestic ones, they often face some very different challenges.

Organizations can tap into many secondary sources as they research global markets. One major information source is the government, particularly Industry Canada. Another useful source for Canadian companies is the U.S. government. Both Industry Canada and the U.S. Department of Commerce publish reports that discuss marketing activities in many other countries. Commercial guides for almost every country in the world are compiled by local embassies. Industry Canada provides information on competition, international agreements, and directories of local contacts through its online database or its international trade offices located across the country.[26]

When conducting international research, companies must be prepared to deal with both language issues—communicating their message in the most effective way—and cultural issues, or capturing local citizens' interests while avoiding missteps that could unintentionally offend them. Companies also need to take a good look at a country's business environment, including political and economic conditions, trade regulations affecting research studies and data collection, and the potential for short- and long-term growth. Many marketers recommend using local researchers to investigate foreign markets.

Businesses may need to adjust their data collection methods for primary research in other countries because some methods do not easily transfer across national frontiers. Face-to-face interviewing, for instance, remains the most common method for conducting primary research outside North America.

While mail surveys are a common data collection method in developed countries, they are useless in many other nations because of low literacy rates, unreliable mail service, and a lack of address lists. Telephone interviews may also not be suitable in other countries, especially those where many people do not have phones. Focus groups can be difficult to arrange because of cultural and social factors. In Latin American countries, for example, highly educated consumers make up a sought-after and opinionated minority, but they have little time to devote to lengthy focus group discussions. Middle- to lower-income Latin Americans may not be accustomed to articulating their opinions about products and grow reticent in the presence of others, whereas in some countries where violence and kidnapping are common, affluent consumers are reluctant to attend any meetings with strangers.[27] To help with such difficulties, a growing number of international research firms offer experience in conducting global studies.

6 Explain the challenges of conducting marketing research in global markets.

Nielsen is a global information and media company.

COURTESY THE NIELSEN COMPANY

assessment check 6

6.1 What are some organizations that can serve as sources of international secondary marketing data?

6.2 What is the most common method of primary data collection outside North America?

INTERPRETATIVE RESEARCH

We mentioned earlier that interpretative research is a method that observes a customer or group of customers in their natural settings and then interprets their behaviour based on an understanding of social and cultural characteristics of that setting. Interpretative research has attracted considerable interest in recent years. Developed by social anthropologists as a method for explaining behaviour that operates below the level of conscious thought, interpretative research can provide insights into consumer behaviour and the ways in which consumers interact with brands. The researcher first spends an extensive amount of time studying the culture, and for that reason, the studies are often called *ethnographic* studies. The word *ethnographic* means that a researcher takes a cultural perspective of the population being studied. For that reason, interpretative research is often used to interpret consumer behaviour within a foreign culture, where language, ideals, values, and expectations are all subject to different cultural influences. But ethnographic research is also used domestically by looking at the consumer behaviour of different groups of people.

Interpretative research focuses on understanding the meaning of a product or the consumption experience in a consumer's life. Its methods capture consumers interacting with products in their environment—in other words, capturing what they actually do, not what they say they do. Typically, subjects are filmed in specific situations, such as socializing with friends in a bar for research into beverage consumption, or for extended periods of time for paid participants. Paid participants are followed by a videographer, who records the day-to-day movements and interactions, or they may film themselves. Kimberly-Clark has been conducting research for several years by paying consumers to wear mini video cameras attached to visors and linked to a sound recorder. The Consumer Vision System, as it's called, records consumer behaviour while participants are shopping or doing chores.[28]

Cost is an issue in interpretative research. This type of study takes time and money—a typical ethnographic project can cost about $1250 to $1750 per subject, so for instance to study 10 people's cooking habits would cost about $15 000.[29] Because of its expense, interpretative research is used only when a company needs detailed information about how consumers use its products.

⑦ Outline the most important uses of computer technology in marketing research.

COMPUTER TECHNOLOGY IN MARKETING RESEARCH

In a world of rapid change, the ability to quickly gather and analyze business intelligence can create a substantial strategic advantage. Computer databases provide a wealth of data for marketing research, whether they are maintained outside the company or designed specifically to gather important facts about its customers. Chapter 9 will explore how companies are leveraging internal databases and customer relationship management technology as a means of developing long-term relationships with customers. This section addresses important uses of computer technology related to marketing research: marketing information systems (MISs), marketing decision support systems (MDSSs), data mining, business intelligence, and competitive intelligence.

MARKETING INFORMATION SYSTEMS (MISs)

In the past, many marketing managers complained that their information problems resulted from too much rather than too little information. Reams of data were difficult to use and not always relevant. At times, information was almost impossible to find. Modern technological advances have made constraints like these obsolete.

A **marketing information system (MIS)** is a planned, computer-based system designed to provide decision makers with a continuous flow of information relevant to their areas of responsibility. A component of the organization's overall management information system, a marketing information system deals specifically with marketing data and issues.

A well-constructed MIS serves as a company's nerve centre, continually monitoring the market environment—both inside and outside the organization—and providing instantaneous information. Marketers can store data for later use, classify and analyze that data, and retrieve it easily when needed.

MARKETING DECISION SUPPORT SYSTEMS (MDSSs)

marketing decision support system (MDSS) Marketing information system component that links a decision maker with relevant databases and analysis tools.

A **marketing decision support system (MDSS)** consists of software that helps users quickly obtain and apply information in a way that supports marketing decisions. Taking MIS one step further, it allows managers to explore and connect such varying information as the state of the market, consumer behaviour, sales forecasts, competitors' actions, and environmental changes. MDSSs consist of four main characteristics: they are interactive, investigative, flexible, and accessible. An MDSS can create simulations or models to illustrate the likely results of changes in marketing strategies or market conditions.

While an MIS provides raw data, an MDSS develops this data into information useful for decision making. For example, an MIS might provide a list of product sales from the previous day. A manager could use an MDSS to transform this raw data into graphs illustrating sales trends or reports estimating the impacts of specific decisions, such as raising prices or expanding into new regions.

DATA MINING

Data mining is the process of searching through computerized data files to detect patterns. It focuses on identifying relationships that are not obvious to marketers—in a sense, answering questions that marketing researchers may not even have thought to ask. The data are stored in a huge database called a *data warehouse*. Software for the marketing decision support system is often associated with the data warehouse and is used to mine data. Once marketers identify patterns and connections, they use this intelligence to check the effectiveness of different strategy options.

Data mining is an efficient way to sort through huge amounts of data and to make sense of that data. It helps marketers create customer profiles, pinpoint reasons for customer loyalty or the lack thereof, analyze the potential returns on changes in pricing or promotion, and forecast sales. Data mining also offers considerable advantages in retailing, the hotel industry, banking, utilities, and many other areas and holds the promise of providing answers to many specific strategic questions.

Data mining software also helps Eastman Kodak check out its competitors' patent filings and flags insider trading for government agencies. One company uses data mining to scan warranty claims for common problems in its cargo-vehicle division that get fast attention from the quality improvement team.[30]

BUSINESS INTELLIGENCE

Business intelligence is the process of gathering information and analyzing it to improve business strategy, tactics, and daily operations. Using advanced software tools, marketers gather information from both within and outside the organization. Business intelligence can thus tell the firm how its own sales operation is doing or what its top competitors are up to.

The key is not only gathering the information but also getting it into a form that employees can make sense of and use for decision making and strategizing. Software can help users collect, aggregate, and create reports with outside information available on the Web from such databases as, say, Dun & Bradstreet. Hewlett-Packard used a business intelligence application to identify market opportunities for its image display technology. "You have all these great plans and you can only do a couple," said an HP executive. "You need something that is fast and quick to sort through the potentials." Thanks to its ability to sort through data and answer questions, business intelligence software is expected to grow at about twice the rate of the rest of the business software industry.[31]

COMPETITIVE INTELLIGENCE

Competitive intelligence is a form of business intelligence that focuses on finding information about competitors using published sources, interviews, observations by salespeople and suppliers in the industry, government agencies, public filings such as patent applications, and other secondary sources, including the Internet. Its aim is to uncover the specific advantages a competitor has, such as new-product launches, new features in existing goods or services, or new marketing or promotional strategies. Even a competitor's advertising can provide clues. Marketers use competitive intelligence to make better decisions that strengthen their own competitive strategy in turn.

> *Marketoid*
>
> **A study done by Leger Marketing found that 51 percent of Canadians prefer a loyalty program to give immediate rewards rather than accumulating points.**

> **assessment check 7**
>
> **7.1** Distinguish between an MIS and an MDSS.
>
> **7.2** What is data mining?
>
> **7.3** Describe the process of collecting business and competitive intelligence.

SALES FORECASTING

A basic building block of any marketing plan is a **sales forecast,** an estimate of a firm's revenue for a specified future period. Sales forecasts play major roles in new-product decisions, production scheduling, financial planning, inventory planning and procurement, distribution, and human-resource planning. An inaccurate forecast may lead to incorrect decisions in each of these areas. The accompanying "Solving an Ethical Controversy" feature discusses the possible misuse of sales forecasts.

Marketing research techniques are used to deliver effective sales forecasts. A sales forecast is also an important tool for marketing control because it sets standards against which to measure actual performance. Without such standards, no comparisons can be made.

> ⑧ Identify the major types of forecasting methods.
>
> **sales forecast** Estimate of firm's revenue for a specified future period.

Solving an Ethical Controversy

Did Microsoft Control the Supply of Xbox 360s or Just Forecast Too Low?

ALTHOUGH it was launched with great fanfare, Microsoft's Xbox 360 was so hard to find during its first five weeks on the market that only 600 000 units were sold in that time, about half the number of the first Xbox a few years before. Microsoft expected to meet its six-month sales target of about 5 million units anyway, and it added production capacity at a third Xbox factory. But some critics of its strategy say that the launch was flawed by the shortage and that Microsoft worsened the problem not just by underproducing but also by diverting units to Europe and Japan, where they didn't sell. Shortages of new products are commonplace in the electronics business, but are they deliberate?

Do companies artificially whip up consumer demand for new products by deliberately reducing sales forecasts and then withholding supply?

PRO

1. Product shortages can help a new product succeed by generating "buzz" and mystique that makes it even more desirable.

2. Companies use a high initial price to generate profits for new products. They then lower prices when supply is plentiful later.

CON

1. Companies do not want to alienate customers by deliberately limiting supplies. It merely annoys consumers to hear the marketing pitch for a product they know they won't be able to find.

2. Global product rollouts can be difficult to control. When a company launches a new product worldwide over a short time span, temporary shortages are bound to occur.

Where do you stand: pro or con?

Sources: Nicholas Varchaver, "Xbox vs. PlayStation: Playing Hard to Get," *Fortune,* February 6, 2006, p. 26; Tim Harford, "Xbox Economics," *Slate,* December 21, 2005, http://www.slate.com; Nick Wingfield and Robert A. Guth, "Shortages of Hot Gifts: A Christmas Ritual," *Deseret Morning News,* December 11, 2005, http://deseretnews.com; Todd Bishop, "Questions Surround Xbox 360 Shortage," *Seattle Post-Intelligencer,* November 18, 2005, http://seattlepi.nwsource.com.

Marketoid

Twenty percent of Canadians feel gift cards or cash are a good incentive for loyalty programs.

Planners rely on short-run, intermediate, and long-run sales forecasts. A short-run forecast usually covers a period of up to one year, an intermediate forecast covers one to five years, and a long-run forecast extends beyond five years. Although sales forecasters use an array of techniques to predict the future—ranging from computer simulations to studying trends identified by futurists—their methods fall into two broad categories: qualitative and quantitative forecasting.

Qualitative forecasting techniques rely on subjective data that report opinions rather than exact historical data. **Quantitative forecasting** methods, by contrast, use statistical computations such as trend extensions based on past data, computer simulations, and econometric models. As Table 7.1 shows, each method has benefits and limitations. Consequently, most organizations use a combination of both techniques.

QUALITATIVE FORECASTING TECHNIQUES

Planners apply qualitative forecasting methods when they want judgmental or subjective indicators. Qualitative forecasting techniques include the jury of executive opinion, Delphi technique, sales force composite, and survey of buyer intentions.

Jury of Executive Opinion

The technique called the **jury of executive opinion** combines and averages the outlooks of top executives from such areas as marketing, finance, production, and purchasing. Top managers bring the following capabilities to the process: experience and knowledge about situations that influence sales, open-minded attitudes toward the future, and awareness of the bases for their judgments. This quick

table 7.1   *Benefits and Limitations of Various Forecasting Techniques*

TECHNIQUES	BENEFITS	LIMITATIONS
Qualitative Methods		
Jury of executive opinion	Opinions come from executives in many different departments; quick; inexpensive	Managers may lack background knowledge and experience to make meaningful predictions
Delphi technique	Group of experts can accurately predict long-term events such as technological breakthroughs	Time-consuming; expensive
Sales force composite	Salespeople have expert customer, product, and competitor knowledge; quick; inexpensive	Inaccurate forecasts may result from low estimates of salespeople concerned about their influence on quotas
Survey of buyer intentions	Useful in predicting short-term and intermediate sales for firms that serve only selected customers	Intentions to buy may not result in actual purchases; time-consuming; expensive
Quantitative Methods		
Market test	Provides realistic information on actual purchases rather than on intent to buy	Alerts competition to new-product plans; time-consuming; expensive
Trend analysis	Quick; inexpensive; effective with stable customer demand and environment	Assumes the future will continue the past; ignores environmental changes
Exponential smoothing	Same benefits as trend analysis, but emphasizes more recent data	Same limitations as trend analysis, but not as severe due to emphasis on recent data

and inexpensive method generates good forecasts for sales and new-product development. It works best for short-run forecasting.

Delphi Technique

Like the jury of executive opinion, the **Delphi technique** solicits opinions from several people, but it also gathers input from experts outside the firm, such as academic researchers, rather than relying completely on company executives. It is most appropriately used to predict long-run issues, such as technological breakthroughs, that could affect future sales and the market potential for new products.

The Delphi technique works as follows: a firm selects a panel of experts and sends each a questionnaire relating to a future event. After combining and averaging the answers, the firm develops another questionnaire based on these results and sends it back to the same people. The process continues until it identifies a consensus. Although firms have successfully used Delphi to predict future technological breakthroughs, the method is both expensive and time-consuming.

Sales Force Composite

The **sales force composite** technique develops forecasts based on the belief that organization members closest to the marketplace—those with specialized product, customer, and competitive knowledge—offer the best insights concerning short-term future sales. It typically works from the bottom up. Management consolidates salespeople's estimates first at the district level, then at the regional level, and finally countrywide to obtain an aggregate forecast of sales that reflects all three levels.

The sales force composite approach has some weaknesses, however. Because salespeople recognize the role of their sales forecasts in determining sales quotas for their territories, they are likely to make conservative estimates. Moreover, their narrow perspectives from within their limited geographic territories may prevent them from considering the impact on sales of trends developing in other territories, forthcoming technological innovations, or the major changes in marketing strategies. Consequently, the sales force composite gives the best forecasts in combination with other techniques.

Marketoid

Thirty-one percent of women said they liked travel as a loyalty reward.

Survey of Buyer Intentions

A **survey of buyer intentions** gathers input through mail-in questionnaires, online feedback, telephone polls, and personal interviews to determine the purchasing intentions of a representative group of present and potential customers. This method suits firms that serve limited numbers of customers but often proves impractical for those with millions of customers. Also, buyer surveys gather useful information only when customers willingly reveal their buying intentions. Moreover, customer intentions do not necessarily translate into actual purchases. These surveys may help a firm to predict short-run or intermediate sales, but they employ time-consuming and expensive methods.

QUANTITATIVE FORECASTING TECHNIQUES

Quantitative techniques attempt to eliminate the subjectiveness of the qualitative methods. They include such methods as market tests, trend analysis, and exponential smoothing.

Test Markets

One quantitative technique, the test market, frequently helps planners in assessing consumer responses to new-product offerings. The procedure typically begins by establishing one or more test markets to gauge consumer responses to a new product under actual marketplace conditions. Market tests also permit experimenters to evaluate the effects of different prices, alternative promotional strategies, and other marketing mix variations by comparing results among different test markets.

The primary advantage of market tests is the realism that they provide for the marketer. However, these expensive and time-consuming experiments may also communicate marketing plans to competitors before a firm introduces a product to the total market.

Trend Analysis

Trend analysis develops forecasts for future sales by analyzing the historical relationship between sales and time. It implicitly assumes that the collective causes of past sales will continue to exert similar influences in the future. When historical data are available, planners can quickly and inexpensively complete trend analysis. Software programs can calculate the average annual increment of change for the available sales data. This average increment of change is then projected into the future to come up with the sales forecast. So, if the sales of a firm have been growing $15.3 million on average per year, this amount of sales could be added to last year's sales total to arrive at next year's forecast.

Of course, trend analysis cannot be used if historical data are not available, as in new-product forecasting. Also, trend analysis makes the dangerous assumption that future events will continue in the same manner as the past. Any variations in the determinants of future sales will cause deviations from the forecast. In other words, this method gives reliable forecasts during periods of steady growth and stable demand. If conditions change, predictions based on trend analysis may become worthless. For this reason, forecasters have applied more sophisticated techniques and complex, new forecasting models to anticipate the effects of various possible changes in the future.

assessment check 8

8.1 Describe the jury of executive opinion.

8.2 What is the Delphi technique?

8.3 How does the exponential smoothing technique forecast sales?

Exponential Smoothing

A more sophisticated method of trend analysis, the **exponential smoothing** technique, weighs each year's sales data, giving greater weight to results from the most recent years. Otherwise, the statistical approach used in trend analysis is applied here. For example, last year's sales might receive a 1.5 weight, while sales data from two years ago could get a 1.4 weighting. Exponential smoothing is considered the most commonly used quantitative forecasting technique.

Strategic Implications

MARKETING research can help an organization develop effective marketing strategies. Approximately 75 percent of new products eventually fail to attract enough buyers to remain viable. Why? A major reason is the seller's failure to understand market needs.

Consider, for example, the hundreds of dot-com companies that went under. A characteristic shared by all those failing businesses is that virtually none of them was founded on sound marketing research. Very few used marketing research techniques to evaluate product potential, and even fewer studied consumer responses after the ventures were initiated. While research might not have prevented every dot-com meltdown, it may have helped a few of those businesses survive the waning economy in which they were launched.

Marketing research ideally matches new products to potential customers. Marketers also conduct research to analyze sales of their own and competitors' products, to gauge the performance of existing products, to guide the development of promotional campaigns, and to develop and refine products. All these activities enable marketers to fine-tune their marketing strategies and reach customers more effectively and efficiently.

Marketing researchers have at their disposal a broad range of techniques with which to collect both quantitative and qualitative data on customers, their lifestyles, behaviours, attitudes, and perceptions. Vast amounts of data can be rapidly collected, accessed, interpreted, and applied to improve all aspects of business operations. Because of customer relationship management technology, that information is no longer generalized to profile groups of customers—it can be analyzed to help marketers understand every customer. ◆◆◆

REVIEW OF CHAPTER OBJECTIVES

① **Describe the development of the marketing research function and its major activities.**

Marketing research, or the collection and use of information in marketing decision making, is changing faster than ever before. Today, the most common marketing research activities are (1) determining market potential, market share, and market characteristics and (2) conducting sales analyses and competitive product studies. Most large companies now have internal marketing research departments. However, outside suppliers still remain vital to the research function. Some perform the complete research task, while others specialize in a limited area or provide specific data services.

② **Explain the steps in the marketing research process.**

The marketing research process can be divided into six specific steps: (1) defining the problem, (2) conducting exploratory research, (3) formulating hypotheses, (4) creating a research design, (5) collecting data, and (6) interpreting and presenting the research information. A clearly defined problem focuses on the researcher's search for relevant decision-oriented information. Exploratory research refers to information gained both within and outside the firm. Hypotheses, tentative explanations of specific events, allow researchers to set out specific research designs—that is, the series of decisions that, taken together, make up master plans or models in order to conduct the investigations. The data collection phase of the marketing research process can involve either or both primary (original) and secondary (previously published) data. After the data are collected, researchers must interpret and present them in a way that will be meaningful to management.

③ Distinguish between primary and secondary data and identify the sources of each type.

Primary data can be collected by the firm's own researchers or by independent marketing research companies. Three principal methods of primary data collection are observation, survey and interview, or experiment. Secondary data can be classified as either internal or external. Sources of internal data include sales records, product evaluation, sales force reports, and records of marketing costs. Sources of external data include the government and private sources, such as business magazines. Both external and internal data can also be obtained from computer databases.

④ Explain the different sampling techniques used by marketing researchers.

Samples can be categorized as either probability samples or nonprobability samples. A probability sample is one in which every member of the population has a chance of being selected. Probability samples include simple random samples, in which every item in the relevant universe has an equal opportunity to be selected; stratified samples, which are constructed such that randomly selected subsamples of different groups are represented in the total sample; and cluster samples, in which geographic areas are selected from which respondents are drawn. A nonprobability sample is arbitrary and does not allow application of standard statistical tests. Nonprobability sampling techniques include convenience samples, in which readily available respondents are picked, and quota samples, which are divided so that different segments or groups are represented in the total sample.

⑤ Identify the methods by which marketing researchers collect primary data.

Observation data are gathered by observing consumers via devices such as people meters or videotape. Survey and interview data can be collected through telephone interviews, mail or fax surveys, personal interviews, focus groups, or a variety of online methods. Telephone interviews provide over half of all primary marketing research data. They give the researcher a fast and inexpensive way to get small amounts of information but generally not detailed or personal information. Personal interviews are costly but allow researchers to get detailed information from respondents. Mail surveys are a means of conducting national studies at a reasonable cost; their main disadvantage is potentially inadequate response rates. Focus groups elicit detailed, qualitative information that provides insight not only into behaviour but also into consumer attitudes and perceptions. Online surveys can yield fast responses but face obstacles such as the adequacy of the probability sample. The experimental method creates verifiable statistical data through the use of test and control groups to reveal actual benefits from perceived benefits.

⑥ Explain the challenges of conducting marketing research in global markets.

The major challenge of conducting marketing research in global markets is finding information. Many resources are available to help organizations research global markets. Government resources include Statistics Canada, Industry Canada, small-business development centres, and foreign embassies. Private companies, such as marketing research firms and companies that distribute research from other sources, are another resource. Electronic networks offer online international trade forums, in which marketers can establish global contacts.

⑦ Outline the most important uses of computer technology in marketing research.

Important uses of computer technology in marketing research include (1) a marketing information system (MIS)—a planned, computer-based system designed to provide managers with a continuous flow of information relevant to their specific decision-making needs and areas of responsibility; (2) a marketing decision support system (MDSS)—a marketing information system component that links a decision maker with relevant databases and analysis tools; (3) data mining—the process of searching through consumer information files or data warehouses to detect patterns that guide marketing decision making; (4) business intelligence—the process of gathering information and analyzing it to improve business strategy, tactics, and daily operations; and (5) competitive intelligence—the form of business intelligence that focuses on finding information about competitors using published sources, interviews, observations by salespeople and suppliers in the industry, government agencies, public filings such as patent applications, and other secondary methods, including the Internet.

⑧ Identify the major types of forecasting methods.

There are two categories of forecasting methods. Qualitative methods are more subjective since they are based on opinions rather than exact historical data. They include the jury of executive opinion, the Delphi technique, the sales force composite, and the survey of buyer intentions. Quantitative methods are more factual and numerical measures such as test markets, trend analysis, and exponential smoothing.

assessment check answers

1.1 Identify the different classifications of marketing research suppliers and explain how they differ from one another.

Marketing research suppliers can be classified as syndicated services, which regularly send standardized data sets to all customers; full-service suppliers, which contract to conduct complete marketing research projects; or limited-service suppliers, which specialize in selected activities.

1.2 What research methods can be used to measure customer satisfaction?

Some companies look at feedback from existing customers, for instance, hiring marketing research firms to collect and analyze customer feedback at their websites. Other firms collect feedback about customer defections—why a customer no longer uses a product. Other organizations conduct research through online polls and surveys.

2.1 What are the six steps in the marketing research process?

The marketing research process can be divided into six specific steps: (1) defining the problem, (2) conducting exploratory research, (3) formulating hypotheses, (4) creating a research design, (5) collecting data, and (6) interpreting and presenting the research information.

2.2 What is the goal of exploratory research?

Exploratory research seeks to discover the cause of a specific problem by discussing the problem with informed sources within and outside the firm and examining data from other information sources.

3.1 Distinguish between primary and secondary data.

Primary data are original; secondary data have been previously published.

4.1 What is sampling?

Sampling is the process of selecting representative survey respondents or research participants from the total universe of possible participants.

4.2 What are the different types of probability samples.

Types of probability samples include simple random samples, stratified samples, and cluster samples.

4.3 Identify the types of nonprobability samples.

Nonprobability samples are convenience samples and quota samples.

5.1 What are the major internal sources of secondary data?

Sources of internal data include sales records, product evaluation, sales force reports, and records of marketing costs.

5.2 What are the major methods of collecting primary data?

Three principal methods of primary data collection are observation, survey and interview, and experiment.

6.1 What are some organizations that can serve as sources of international secondary marketing data?

Industry Canada and the U.S. Departments of Commerce offer reports and guides to many countries.

6.2 What is the most common method of primary data collection outside the North America?

Face-to-face interviewing remains the most common method for conducting primary research outside North America.

7.1 Distinguish between an MIS and an MDSS.

A marketing information system (MIS) is a planned, computer-based system designed to provide managers with a continuous flow of information relevant to their specific decision-making needs and areas of responsibility. A marketing decision support system (MDSS) is a marketing information system component that links a decision maker with relevant databases and analysis tools to help answer "what-if" questions.

7.2 What is data mining?

Data mining is the process of searching through huge consumer information files or data warehouses to detect patterns that can help marketers ask the right questions and guide marketing decision making.

7.3 Describe the process of collecting business and competitive intelligence.

Business intelligence is the process of gathering information and analyzing it to improve business strategy, tactics, and daily operations. Competitive intelligence focuses on finding information about competitors using published sources, interviews, observations by salespeople and suppliers in the industry, government agencies, public filings such as patent applications, and other secondary methods including the Internet.

8.1 Describe the jury of executive opinion.

The jury of executive opinion combines and averages the outlooks of top executives from areas such as marketing, finance, production, and purchasing.

8.2 What is the Delphi technique?

The Delphi technique solicits opinions from several people within the firm but also includes input from experts outside the firm such as academic researchers.

8.3 How does the exponential smoothing technique forecast sales?

Exponential smoothing weighs each year's sales data, giving greater weight to results from the most recent years.

MARKETING TERMS YOU NEED TO KNOW

These terms are printed in red in the text. They are defined in the margins of the chapter and in the Glossary that begins on p. G-1. Other important terms are printed in bold black type in the chapter but not included in this list. Their definitions can be found in the Glossary.

marketing research 230

exploratory research 233

secondary data 235

primary data 235

sampling 238

probability sample 238

nonprobability sample 239

interpretative research 240

focus group 242

marketing decision support system (MDSS) 246

sales forecast 247

ASSURANCE OF LEARNING REVIEW

1. Outline the development and current status of the marketing research function.
2. What are the differences between full-service and limited-service research suppliers?
3. List and explain the steps in the marketing research process. Trace a hypothetical study through the stages in this process.
4. Distinguish between primary and secondary data. When should researchers collect each type of data?
5. What is sampling? Explain the differences between probability and nonprobability samples and identify the various types of each.

6. Distinguish among surveys and interview, experiments, and observational methods of primary data collection. Cite examples of each method.
7. Define and give an example of each of the methods of gathering survey data. Under what circumstances should researchers choose a specific approach?
8. Describe the experimental method of collecting primary data and indicate when researchers should use it.
9. Describe business intelligence.
10. Contrast qualitative and quantitative sales forecasting methods.

PROJECTS AND TEAMWORK EXERCISES

1. Nielsen offers data collected by optical scanners from the United Kingdom, France, Germany, Belgium, the Netherlands, Austria, Italy, and Finland. This scanner data tracks sales of UPC-coded products in those nations. In small teams, imagine that you are one of Nielsen's clients. One team might be a retail chain, another an Internet company, and still another a toy manufacturer. Discuss the types of marketing questions these data might help you answer. Share your list with other teams.
2. Set up two class teams to debate the use of the Internet to research new domestic markets. What other research options are available?
3. Today, an ever-increasing percentage of new homes sold in North America are manufactured homes. New manufactured homes are built using higher-quality materials than those used in the past. As a result, the market for manufactured homes has grown to include more affluent buyers. One company tries to appeal to upscale buyers by custom-building its homes according to the customer's specifications. What type of data and information should this company gather through its ongoing market intelligence to predict demand for its products? Would primary or secondary methods work best? Name some specific secondary sources of data the company might study to find useful business intelligence.

4. Discuss some of the challenges Pizza Hut might face in conducting marketing research in potential new international markets. What types of research would you recommend the company use in choosing new countries for expansion?
5. Which sales forecasting technique(s) are most appropriate for each of the following products? Prepare your arguments in pairs or teams:
   a. Post Shredded Wheat breakfast cereal
   b. Handbags
   c. Kinko's copy shops
   d. *Marketing* magazine
6. Assume you are responsible for launching a new family of skincare products for teens, with separate product lines for males and females. You would like to collect primary data from a sampling of each market before you prepare your marketing campaign. Let one team make the case for using a focus group and another team devise a plan supporting the use of an online chat room. Present the class with the benefits of each method and the ways in which each team plans to overcome its method's possible shortcomings. Now take this project one step further by having a classroom discussion on whether a decision support system could enhance the data collected from each method. How could an MDSS make the data more useful?

7. Interpretative research offers marketing researchers many possibilities, including the opportunity to improve product features such as packaging for food or over-the-counter medication that is difficult for seniors or people with disabilities to open. List some other ways in which you think this observation method can help make existing product offerings more appealing or more useful to specific kinds of users. What kind of products would you choose, and how would you test them?

8. Use the Internet to research the details of the national Do Not Call Registry and prepare a report outlining what it does and does not allow marketers to do. Research the effects the registry will have on individuals and businesses. Do you think the public understands the purpose of the registry? Why or why not, and if not, what do you think marketers can do to clarify it?

9. McDonald's conducts extensive marketing research for all its new products, including new menu items for its overseas stores. Due to cultural and other differences and preferences, the company cannot often extrapolate its results from one country to another. For instance, Croque McDo fried ham-and-cheese sandwiches are unlikely to be as popular in North America as they are in France, which invented the *croque monsieur* sandwich on which McDonald's product is based. Can you think of any other kinds of firms that share this limitation on global applications of their research? In contrast, what sorts of questions *could* multinational firms answer on a global basis? Why?

10. Outdoor advertising, including billboards, ads on bus shelters, and shopping mall displays, accounts for only a tiny portion of the billions spent on advertising in a typical year in North America. Nielsen is giving global positioning devices to 700 study participants in order to track how many times they pass by specially coded billboards in a particular city. List some other ways you can think of to research the effectiveness of outdoor advertising and cite the pros and cons of each.

CRITICAL THINKING EXERCISES

1. Some companies are broadening their markets by updating classic products to appeal to younger people's tastes and preferences. For example, Wrigley's has introduced two new Juicy Fruit flavours that it hopes will duplicate the success of Altoids and Mountain Dew in becoming revitalized and popular brands. What primary and secondary market information would you want to have if you were planning to reinvigorate an established brand in each of the following categories? Where and how would you obtain the information?
   a. Household cleaner
   b. Moist packaged cat food
   c. Spray starch
   d. Electrical appliances

2. Marketers sometimes collect primary information by using so-called *mystery shoppers* who visit stores anonymously (as if they were customers) and note such critical factors as store appearance and ambiance, items in stock, and quality of service, including waiting time and courtesy of employees. (The CEO of Staples has gone on mystery shopper trips and sometimes asked his mother to make similar trips.) Prepare a list of data that you would want to obtain from a mystery shopper surveying a chain of gas stations in your area. Devise a format for inputting the information that combines your need to compile the data electronically and the researcher's need to remain undetected while visiting the stores.

3. Select a sales forecasting method (or combination of methods) for each of the following information needs and explain why you chose it.
   a. Prediction of next year's sales based on last year's figures
   b. Prediction of next year's sales based on weighted data from the last five years
   c. Expected sales categorized by district and by region
   d. Estimated product usage for the next year by typical consumers
   e. Probable consumer response to a new product

4. The Internet provides ready access to secondary market information but is also a portal to an almost limitless store of primary information via message boards, chat rooms, e-mail questionnaires, newsgroups, and website registration forms. What are some specific drawbacks of each of these methods for obtaining primary information from customers?

ETHICS EXERCISE

Consumer groups sometimes raise objections to marketers' methods of collecting primary data from customers. They object to such means as product registration forms; certain types of games, contests, or product offers; and "cookies" and demographic questionnaires on company websites. Marketers believe that such tools offer them an easy way to collect market data. Most strictly control the use of such data and never link identifying information with consumers' financial or demographic profiles. However, the possibility of abuse or error always exists.

Research the code of ethics of the Canadian Marketing Association (CMA) and pay particular attention to the guidelines for use of the Internet in marketing research.

1. Check the websites of a few large consumer-products companies. How effectively do you think these sites are at informing visitors about the use of "cookies" on the sites? Do you think marketers could or should improve their protection of site visitors' privacy? If so how?

2. Do you think it violates the code of ethics if marketers compile a mailing list based on information provided on warranty and product registration cards and then use the list to send customers new-product information? Why or why not? Does your opinion change if the company also sends list members special discount offers and private sale notices?

INTERNET EXERCISES

1. **Marketing research tools.** Chapter 7 describes tools used by marketing researchers to collect and analyze data. The following exercises are designed to help you learn more about several of these marketing research tools.

   a. Focus groups: Visit http://www.managementhelp.org/evaluatn/focusgrp.htm, which describes how a focus group should be conducted. Read through the guidelines and prepare a summary you can use during a class discussion of the topic.

   b. Marketing research on the Web: As noted in the chapter, many organizations find it efficient and effective to use the Web when conducting marketing research. Go to http://www.decisionanalyst.com/online.dai and list the advantages of Web-based marketing research.

   c. Statistical tools: SAS and SPSS have products that are widely used by marketing professionals. Both, for instance, offer data-mining packages. Visit either the SAS (http://www.sas.com) or the SPSS (http://www.spss.com) website and learn more about the data mining packages, including actual customer experiences. What other products do SAS or SPSS offer to assist marketing researchers?

2. **Online data sources.** An enormous amount of statistical data is online, and much of it can be obtained for free. To give you an idea of the scope of data available online, go to the main web page of Statistics Canada (http://www.statcan.ca). Click the most recent year and answer the following questions:

   a. Under Latest Indicators, on the home page, what is the current population of Canada? Under Canadian Statistics, what is Canada's population projection for 2011?

   b. What are the five largest metropolitan areas? What are the five fastest-growing metropolitan areas? Which metropolitan areas have the highest percentage of Chinese residents?

   c. What are the average annual earnings for workers with a university certificate, diploma, or degree? Has the gap between the average annual earnings of high school and college graduates narrowed or widened in recent years?

Note: Internet Web addresses change frequently. If you don't find the exact sites listed, you may need to access the organization's home page and search from there or use a search engine such as Google.

Case 7.1

Marketing Research Goes to the Movies

It was bound to happen—Hollywood has discovered the power of the Internet. In the past, studios would test-screen films with random audiences a few months before release, showing them free at malls, say, and then gathering reactions from viewers. Afterward, that information would sometimes send writers, directors, and actors back to work to film revised scenes, new scenes, alternative endings, and even dramatic plot changes. Test screenings have fallen out of favour lately, sometimes because of fear of negative word of mouth about an unfinished picture and sometimes because tight schedules don't allow time for making any changes. And test screenings cost money that studios sometimes don't want to spend on films that are already over budget. But this doesn't mean that writers, directors, and backers don't want audience feedback.

Some films are screened privately, as *Spider-Man* was. But the reactions of friends and colleagues might not reflect unbiased opinion. Aside from industry efforts, movie fans have colonized the Internet, setting up fan sites and message boards for popular films well before they open. *Lord of the Rings* fans opened multiple sites to trade information, rumours, and opinions for more than five years, starting during the production phase and including the three years over which the trilogy of movies was released. Dozens of other films spawned similar sites, though perhaps none as long-lived.

At first, much of the information on sites like SuperHeroHype.com, Aintitcool.com, and DarkHorizons.com came from people in the industry who had access to film sets and inside information. Film companies soon realized they couldn't easily control what reached the public from these sources and put nondisclosure clauses in all their employment contracts. Now, despite their lingering fears that websites will become nothing more than portals to stolen copies of new films, studios are realizing that an important new opportunity exists for give-and-take on the Internet. For instance, when fans of the popular comic-book superhero The Hulk learned that his movie incarnation might not be wearing the character's trademark purple pants in the Ang Lee film, they took to the Internet to vent their frustration and protest. Marvel Studios chief Avi Arad and Lee listened, and The Hulk was properly costumed.

Other filmmakers and studios are responding also. New Line Cinema, for instance, set up its own *Lord of the Rings* website and cooperated with major fan site theonering.net, offering exclusive information and news in exchange for a promise that the site would not host any unauthorized material. The partnership has been a success for fans and studio alike, and *Rings* director Peter Jackson even participated in online chats on the site, which drew 20 million visits a month at its peak.

Of course, some filmmakers' fears about the Internet are well founded. Sometimes copies of films are leaked and downloaded. Negative reviews of new films have appeared on the Internet before release, but whether they alone are responsible for flops like *Gigli* is debatable. So perhaps the lesson for Hollywood is just to make better movies.

In the meantime, the Internet fan base is thriving. One film, *The Yank*, sported a fan site before any film had even been shot. Could there be a better way to build an audience?

Questions for Critical Thinking

1. Do you think filmmakers and film companies should actively cultivate the Internet community? Why or why not? What possible advantages and drawbacks could such a strategy have?

2. Find an upcoming film that has an official website. What features does the site have? Which ones are designed to deliver information to the public and which are designed to capture information? How successful do you think this site will prove to be as a marketing research tool? Why?

3. How can filmmakers control the information that appears on the Internet? Should they take these steps? Why or why not?

Sources: Scott Bowles, "Fans Use Their Muscle to Shape the Movie," *USA Today,* June 20–22, 2003, pp. 1A, 2A; Ty Burr, "Web Buzz Control Is Hollywood's Newest Mission," Boston Globe, July 24, 2003; Tom King, "Hollywood Previews Go Private," *The Wall Street Journal,* April 26, 2002, p. W9.

Case 7.2

Forecasting Pitfalls for SUV Makers

Consumers' thirst for big fuel-guzzling SUVs seemed unquenchable. Then, after holding steady for years, sales of large SUVs suddenly dropped nearly 20 percent recently. One factor behind the slump was soaring gas prices. Uncertainty about how high fuel prices would stay—and for how long—led some car buyers to switch from SUVs to more fuel-efficient family-sized cars and minivans. Some buyers looked for smaller cars, and still others turned to hybrids, creating long waiting lists at hybrid dealers' showrooms. That shift in buying habits hurt General Motors, which is well known for its SUVs and pickup trucks. "Obviously, if we have a serious supply constraint in motor fuels that will hurt vehicles with higher fuel consumption," said GM's vice chairman Bob Lutz. "But we can't predict that."

Perhaps they couldn't. SUV makers had committed to their current level of production two years before the rise in fuel prices, when the price of filling the tank was much less of an issue for consumers. New models of the Chevrolet Tahoe, the Chevrolet Suburban, the GMC Yukon, the Ford Expedition, and the Cadillac Escalade were already rolling out. Chrysler released its big new Aspen, with three rows of seats.

Auto industry executives remained upbeat about SUVs, agreeing with GM's Lutz that "people still love these things." Ford CEO Jim Padilla said, "Big SUVs are alive and well." But one economist admitted that "every time gas prices go up another 20 cents, you know you see some people making a [buying] decision based on that."

Dealers fell back on incentives to boost sales, offering cash back, lower prices, and new technology that cuts eight cylinders back to four at certain speeds to save fuel. Even Nissan, which avoids discounts, was willing to deal in order to keep its big Armada SUV moving off the lot. "I don't know if we can launch the Aspen without incentives, just because it's the nature of the market in that segment," said Chrysler's vice president of global sales and marketing.

Perhaps Detroit has learned something about the difficulties of forecasting sales in a particularly uncertain world of rising fuel costs. GM, which is increasing production of its most profitable SUVs, has plans for a hybrid Tahoe. But where will the price of gas be when it rolls off the assembly line?

Questions for Critical Thinking

1. Should the auto industry base its sales forecasts more heavily on qualitative or quantitative techniques? Why?

2. What forecasting techniques would help auto industry executives more accurately forecast movements in the price of oil? How should they factor these forecasts into their sales projections?

Sources: Michael Ellis, "Fulfilling Demand: GM to Boost Output of Its Large SUVs," *Detroit Free Press,* March 22, 2006, http://www.freep.com; Josee Valcourt, "SUVs Roll Out, Despite Gas Woes," *Detroit News,* January 10, 2006, http://www.detnews.com; "High Gas Prices Changing Auto Market," Fox News, September 26, 2005, http://www.foxnews.com.

Video Case 7.3

Nielsen Media Research Plays the Rating Game

The written video case on Nielsen Media Research appears on page VC-10. The recently filmed Nielsen Media Research video is designed to expand and highlight the concepts in this chapter and the concepts and questions covered in the written video case.

chapter 8

Market Segmentation, Targeting, and Positioning

CHAPTER OBJECTIVES

(1) Identify the essential components of a market.

(2) Outline the role of market segmentation in developing a marketing strategy.

(3) Describe the criteria necessary for effective segmentation.

(4) Explain the geographic, demographic, and psychographic approaches to segmenting consumer markets.

(5) Describe product-related segmentation.

(6) Identify the steps in the market segmentation process.

(7) Discuss four basic strategies for reaching target markets.

(8) Summarise the types of positioning strategies, and explain the reasons for positioning and repositioning products.

PHOTO BY F MICELOTTA/AMERICAN IDOL 2008/ GETTY IMAGES FOR FOX

NEL

AMERICAN IDOL IS A HIT WITH CANADIAN TEENS

Some adults admit to watching *American Idol*. Others don't. But teens and preteens are wild about the reality talent show, and they aren't hiding their obsession. They like *Canadian Idol* too but *American Idol* tops the ratings. Ask a teen, and you'll get a complete rundown of all the *American Idol* winners and runners-up. After several seasons on the air, the show remains a ratings hit. One season premiere brought the highest entertainment ratings in the network's history. Viewer numbers didn't fall off after that either. When slotted head-to-head against other events—like the Olympics, hockey playoffs, or the Grammy Awards show—*Idol* won hands down. This may seem an ironic twist of fate, because the contestants on *American Idol* hope to take home their own Grammy someday.

Idol is the biggest hit with teen girls, despite the producers' decision to raise the age limit of contestants to 28. "To me, the best part of the show is all the singers," explains one teen. "I like to watch them as they try out and see if I can pick the one that's going to make it all the way." Executive producer Ken Warwick points out the social aspect of the show for teens at school. "When they go to school the next day, it's become *the* show to watch, and if they haven't seen it, they've got a problem," he observes. Parents note that there aren't many shows targeted for their teens and preteens—many shows are pitched to younger kids, while shows for adults contain too much sex and violence.

Teens aren't just watching the show on television. They visit the show's website in huge numbers, even between seasons. The site averages 3 million visitors each season, a statistic that includes adults as well as children. Network executives now view the site as a year-round business unit, not just a support structure for the show while it is airing.

Although teens are perhaps the most passionate *Idol* fans, they aren't the only ones. Marketing research reveals that adults who watch reality-talent television have certain characteristics. They tend to be active in sports such as jogging, swimming, and golf. They gravitate toward new cars and cell phone services. And they eat at fast-food restaurants 10 or more times a month. These findings help the network and its advertisers create commercials and other marketing messages that target the right audience.

But *Idol* doesn't exclude its younger viewers from marketing efforts. Parents who are searching for the latest birthday party theme can let their kids host their very own *American Idol* party. Parents can order an entire *Idol* birthday party package—complete with invitations, party favours, decorations, and contestant numbers.

The success of *American Idol* through several seasons illustrates how vital it is for marketers to identify and target a market with their messages. If they hit just the right note, their messages may reach the stars.[1]

---

connecting with customers

Reality shows, like *Canadian Idol* and *American Idol*, have been very successful. This success is a result of the show producers finding the right type of show for each part of the market or each market segment. Along with the entertainment reality shows, there are the romance reality shows *The Bachelor* and the intellectual reality shows *The Apprentice*.[2]

Chapter Overview

EACH of us is unique. We come from different backgrounds, live in different households, and have different interests and goals. You and your best friend may shop at different stores, listen to different music, play different sports, and take different courses in college. Suppose you like country music, but your best friend prefers oldies hits. Marketers for all kinds of music-related products, ranging from CDs to live concerts, want to capture your interest as well as that of your friends. Do you play an instrument or sing, or are you a fan who goes to clubs and downloads music? Marketers look at current customers and potential customers to figure out what their characteristics are, whether they can identify certain subgroups, and how they can best offer products to meet their needs. Your interests and needs, your lifestyle and income, the city

market Group of people with sufficient purchasing power, authority, and willingness to buy.

where you live, and your age all contribute to the likelihood that you will listen to and buy certain types of music. All these factors make up a market. A **market** is composed of people with sufficient purchasing power, authority, and willingness to buy. And marketers must use their expertise to understand the market for a good or service, whether it's a download by the latest *American Idol* winner, a new radio station, or a 12-string guitar.

Many markets include consumers with different lifestyles, backgrounds, and income levels. Nearly everyone buys toothpaste, but that does not mean every consumer has the same lifestyle, background, or income. So it is unusual for a single marketing mix strategy to attract all sectors of a market. By identifying, evaluating, and selecting a target market to pursue, such as consumers who prefer toothpaste made with all-natural ingredients or those who want an extra-whitening formula, marketers are able

to develop more efficient and effective marketing strategies. On the other hand, some products—such as luxury sports cars or fly fishing supplies—are intended for a more specific market. In either case, the target market for a product is the specific segment of consumers most likely to purchase a particular product.

Marketing now takes place on a global basis more than ever, incorporating many target markets. To identify those markets, marketers must determine useful ways for segmenting different populations and communicating with them successfully. This chapter discusses useful ways to accomplish this objective, explaining the steps of the market segmentation process and surveying strategies for reaching target markets. Finally, it looks at the role of positioning in developing a marketing strategy. ◆◆◆

 Marketoid

In 2005, Canada's music industry reported revenues of roughly $942 million.

---

① Identify the essential components of a market.

consumer products Products bought by ultimate consumers for personal use.

TYPES OF MARKETS

Products are usually classified as either consumer products or business products. **Consumer products** are bought by ultimate consumers for personal use, such as cell phones or fashion magazines. **Business products** are goods and services purchased for use either directly or indirectly in the production of other goods and services for resale. Most goods and services purchased by individual consumers, such as DVDs, or restaurant meals, are considered consumer products. Rubber and raw cotton are examples of items generally purchased by manufacturers and are, therefore, classified as business products. Goodyear buys rubber to manufacture tires; textile manufacturers convert raw cotton into cloth.

However, in many cases, a single product can serve different uses. Tires purchased for the family car constitute consumer products. But tires purchased by General Motors to be mounted on its Chevy Tahoe are business products because they become part of another product destined for resale. Or a product that was once a business product might be modified for consumer use, and vice versa. A line of professional cookware sold to restaurants—a business product—could be adapted by its

assessment check 1

1.1 Define target market.

1.2 Distinguish between a consumer product and a business product.

manufacturer to become a line of cookware for home use—a consumer product. If you want to determine the classification of an item, just think about who is going to buy the product, who will use it, and how or why the product will be used. The bottle of mouthwash you buy at the supermarket is a consumer product, but if a large hotel chain purchases large quantities of the same mouthwash from a wholesaler, it becomes a business product.

> **business products** Goods and services purchased for use either directly or indirectly in the production of other goods and services for resale.

THE ROLE OF MARKET SEGMENTATION

> **2** Outline the role of market segmentation in developing a marketing strategy.

There are 6.5 billion people in the world today, roughly 33 million of whom live in Canada.[3] In today's business world, there are too many variables in consumer needs, preferences, and purchasing power to attract all consumers with a single marketing mix. That's not to say that firms must actually change products to meet the needs of different market segments—although they often do—but they must attempt to identify the factors that affect purchase decisions and then group consumers according to the presence or absence of these factors. Finally, they adjust marketing strategies to meet the needs of each group.

Consider motor vehicles. Unlike a century ago, when Henry Ford pronounced that customers could order any colour of car they liked—as long as it was black—today there is a make, model, and colour for every taste and budget. But auto manufacturers need to adjust their messages for different markets. And savvy marketers are looking toward markets that show growth, such as the Chinese population, which is the largest ethnic group in the country, and the aging baby boomers, whose need for goods and services are changing.[4]

> **market segmentation** Division of the total market into smaller, relatively homogeneous groups.

The division of the total market into smaller, relatively homogeneous groups is called **market segmentation.** Both profit-oriented and not-for-profit organizations practise market segmentation.

CRITERIA FOR EFFECTIVE SEGMENTATION

> **3** Describe the criteria necessary for effective segmentation.

Segmentation doesn't automatically guarantee success in the marketing arena; instead, it is a tool for marketers to use. Its effectiveness depends on the following four basic requirements.

First, the market segment must present measurable purchasing power and size. With jobs, incomes, and decision-making power, female consumers represent a hefty amount of purchasing power. Women make up half the potential market for many new electronic products. In fact, research shows that 70 percent of all consumer electronic purchases are influenced by women.[5]

Companies such as Canadian Tire, Rona, and Home Depot recognize the importance of women to their success. Armed with research showing that women initiate more than 80 percent of home improvement projects—especially large ones such as remodelling a kitchen or adding a bathroom—these companies have refocused their marketing efforts to target women. They have made their stores more comfortable for browsing, with wider aisles, clear signs to direct shoppers, and more salespeople who can answer their questions. The companies also stock more appliances and home decor items, from paints to laminate floors to Jacuzzi tubs. Such efforts have rebuilt these companies' reputations and competitiveness in the home improvements retail market.[6]

Second, marketers must find a way to promote effectively and to serve the market segment. Because women now wield such purchasing power in the technology market, marketers need to find different ways to appeal to them. Some companies have taken this advice to heart. Research in Motion, who manufactures the BlackBerry, has created ads featuring working mums.

Third, marketers must then identify segments that are sufficiently large to give them good profit potential. Since women—who make up about half of the Canadian population—are influencing 70 percent of all electronic purchases as we saw earlier, there is plenty of profit potential for the electronics

TD VISA serves the Chinese-Canadian market.

262   PART 3 Target Market Selection

2.1 Define market segmentation.

2.2 Describe the role of market segmentation.

assessment check 3

3.1 Identify the four criteria for effective
    segmentation.

industry.[7] One industry expert explained women purchase electronics differently from men. While men want bigger, better, and faster, women want technology that will enhance their lives. Electronic retailers will have to develop marketing strategies that take in the differences in order to capture these female electronic shoppers.[8]

And fourth, the firm must aim for segments that match its marketing capabilities. Targeting a large number of small markets can be an expensive, complex, and inefficient strategy, so smaller firms may decide to stick with a particular niche, or target market. To compete for women's business, an electronic retailer could install a supervised play area for children while their mothers shop. It could create showrooms made to look like real living rooms and family rooms with the latest entertainment equipment installed, so women could see how the products would look in their own homes.

④ Explain the geographic, demographic, and psychographic approaches to segmenting consumer markets.

SEGMENTING CONSUMER MARKETS

Market segmentation attempts to isolate the traits that distinguish a certain group of consumers from the overall market. An understanding of the group's characteristics—such as age, gender, geographic location, income, and buying patterns—plays a vital role in developing a successful marketing strategy. In most cases, marketers seek to pinpoint a number of factors affecting buying behaviour in the target segment. Marketers in the travel industry consider employment trends, changes in income levels and buying patterns, age, lifestyle, and other factors when promoting their goods and services. To boost flagging attendance at its theme parks, Disney World has been advertising to adults who are empty nesters and groups of friends instead of focusing entirely on families with young children. Marketers rarely identify totally homogeneous segments, in which all potential customers are alike; they always encounter some differences among members of a target group. But they must be careful to ensure that their segments accurately reflect consumers.

In the next sections, we discuss the four common bases for segmenting consumer markets: geographic segmentation, demographic segmentation, psychographic segmentation, and product-related segmentation. These segmentation approaches can give important guidance for marketing strategies, provided they identify significant differences in buying behaviour.

GEOGRAPHIC SEGMENTATION

geographic segmentation Division of an overall market into homogeneous groups based on their locations.

Marketers have long practised **geographic segmentation**—dividing an overall market into homogeneous groups on the basis of their locations. Geographic location does not ensure that all consumers in a location will make the same buying decisions, but this segmentation approach does help identify some general patterns. Campbell Soup uses this approach for some of its products, as described in the "Marketing Success" feature.

The roughly 33 million people living in Canada are not scattered evenly across the country. Instead, they are concentrated in major metropolitan areas. Toronto is the largest city, with a population of 5.4 million. Montreal is the second largest with 3.6 million, and third place goes to Vancouver at 2.2 million.[9] Figure 8.1 shows populations of the 10 largest cities in Canada.

The provinces with the most residents are Ontario (12.8 million), Quebec (7.7 million), British Columbia (4.3 million), Alberta (3.4 million), and Manitoba (1.1 million). By contrast, Prince Edward Island has a population of only 138 000, 32 000 of whom live in Charlottetown.[10]

A look at the worldwide population distribution illustrates why so many firms are pursuing customers around the globe. China has the most citizens, with 1.3 billion people, and India is second with 1.1 billion. The United States is third with about 300 million, and Indonesia is fourth with 248 million. Japan is a distant tenth with 127 million.[11] As in Canada, much of the world's population lives in urban environments. The two largest cities in the world are Shanghai, China, with 14.6 million, and Bombay,

India, with 12.6 million. The two largest metropolitan areas are Tokyo, Japan, with almost 37 million and New York, with nearly 19 million.[12]

Population size alone, however, may not be reason enough for a business to expand into a specific country. Businesses also need to look at a wide variety of economic variables. Some businesses may decide to combine their marketing efforts for countries that share similar population and product-use patterns instead of treating each country as an independent segment. This grouping is taking place with greater frequency throughout the European Union as the currency and trade laws of the member nations are becoming more unified.

While population numbers indicate the overall size of a market, other geographic indicators such as job growth can also give useful guidance to marketers depending on the type of products they sell. Automobile manufacturers might segment geographic regions by household income because it is an important factor in the purchase of a new car.

Geographic areas also vary in population migration patterns. The most recent census data indicate that 68 percent of the population lives in 33 metropolitan areas across the country. These 33 metropolitan areas accounted for 90 percent of the population growth. The largest growth was in Alberta at 10.6 percent and Ontario at 6.6 percent. The fastest growing cities in Canada are Barrie, Ontario, and Calgary, Alberta, which in one year showed growth rates of 19.2 percent and 13.4 percent respectively.[13]

The move from urban to suburban areas after World War II created a need to redefine the urban marketplace. This trend radically changed cities' traditional patterns of retailing and led to the decline in many downtown shopping areas—although recent trends have been toward the revitalization of downtown areas. Subsequently, traditional city boundaries became almost meaningless for marketing purposes.

COURTESY OF CHEIL WORLDWIDE, SAMSUNG, AND CBC

Sports fans are an increasingly important market for consumer electronics.

marketing success ⋯⋯ Campbell's Segments Its Soups

Background. Your supermarket no doubt has at least one shelf filled with Campbell's Soups. Whether you want classic chicken noodle or something trendier, you have plenty of recipes from which to choose. But if you visit a supermarket in a different part of the country, you might see different selections. That's because Campbell's has figured out how to target the populations of diverse markets.

The Challenge. Not everyone in Canada wants tomato or chicken and rice soup for lunch. Some prefer New England clam chowder, while others crave French Canadian pea or bean with bacon. Still others are watching carbs or calories and want their soup to be low in either or both. And some consumers follow a low-salt diet, so they want their tomato or chicken soup to be a low-sodium concoction. Campbell's has figured out not only who wants what but also what their ethnic background is and where they live.

The Strategy. Campbell's has identified a range of market segments, including ethnic and regional components. In addition to serving these markets in Canada, Campbell's has operations in

countries such as Mexico, France, and Ireland, where it offers products created specifically for the tastes of those consumers. People who want Mexican flavours can enjoy tortilla soup; French consumers prefer *Liebig*, which is soup packaged in cartons. For consumers who are health conscious, Campbell's has created its Healthy Request line of soups, including bean and vegetable, herbed chicken noodle, and vegetable beef with barley.

The Outcome. By segmenting consumers, Campbell's has been able to serve up exactly what each segment wants in its soup bowls. The firm continues to create new recipes, and it has recently been recognized with the Blood Pressure Canada Certificate of Excellence for its sodium-reduction efforts and industry leadership.

Sources: Campbell's website, http://www.campbellsoupcompany.com, accessed April 11, 2006; "Mining for Drivers of Consumer Behavior," Manifold Data Mining, April 11, 2006, http://www.manifolddatamining.com; Tom Zind, "Stirring up the Pot," *Prepared Foods,* May 2005, http://www.findarticles.com; William A. Roberts, "Soup's On; Sides, Too," *Prepared Foods,* May 2005, http://www.findarticles.com; Campbell's http://campbellsoup.ca, accessed December 16, 2007.

figure 8.1

Canada's 10 Largest Cities

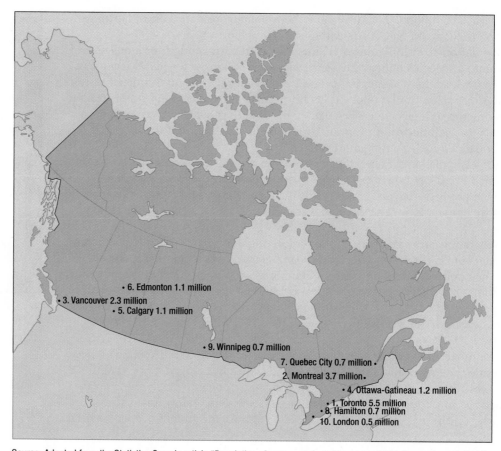

- 6. Edmonton 1.1 million
- 3. Vancouver 2.3 million
- 5. Calgary 1.1 million
- 9. Winnipeg 0.7 million
- 7. Quebec City 0.7 million
- 2. Montreal 3.7 million
- 4. Ottawa-Gatineau 1.2 million
- 1. Toronto 5.5 million
- 8. Hamilton 0.7 million
- 10. London 0.5 million

Source: Adapted from the Statistics Canada article "Population of census metropolitan areas (2001 Census boundaries)," available at http://www40.statcan.ca/l01/cst01/demo05a.htm, accessed June 24, 2008.

In an effort to respond to these changes, the government has classified urban data into the following categories:

1. A **census metropolitan area (CMA)** is the largest classification. A CMA is a geographic area surrounding an urban core with a population of at least 100 000. Once Statistics Canada classifies an area as a CMA, it will always count as a CMA even if the population drops below 100 000. As of the 2006 census, there were 33 CMAs across the country, including six new ones—Brantford, Guelph, Peterborough, Barrie, Moncton, and Kelowna. CMAs are further divided into census subdivisions if certain conditions are present.

2. A **census agglomeration (CA)** is virtually the same as a CMA except it is smaller. The population of a CA is between 10 000 and 99 999.

In defining CMAs and CAs, Statistics Canada has kept in mind that many companies use both Canadian and American statistics to compare markets. Although the methods used by both countries are not identical, they are similar enough that markets from both countries can be compared.[14]

USING GEOGRAPHIC SEGMENTATION

Demand for some categories of goods and services can vary according to geographic region, and marketers need to be aware of how these regions differ. Marketers of major brands are particularly interested in defining their **core regions**, the locations where they get 40 to 80 percent of their sales.

Residence location within a geographic area is an important segmentation variable. City dwellers often rely on public transportation and may get along fine without automobiles, whereas those who live in the suburbs or rural areas depend on their own cars and trucks. Also, those who live in the suburbs spend more on lawn and garden care products than do people in the city.

Climate is another important segmentation factor. Consumers who live in chilly areas, for example, eat more soup than people who live in warmer southern climates. But here's a surprise—they also eat a great deal of ice cream!

Geographic segmentation provides useful distinctions when regional preferences or needs exist. A consumer might not want to invest in a snow blower or flood insurance but may *have* to because of the location of his or her home. But it's important for marketers not to stop at geographic location as a segmentation method because distinctions among consumers also exist within a geographic location. Consider those who relocate from one region to another for work or family reasons. They may bring with them their preferences from other parts of the country. Using several segmentation variables is probably a much better strategy for targeting a specific market.

GEOGRAPHIC INFORMATION SYSTEMS (GISs)

Super Bowl Sunday is more than a sporting event—it is also the single biggest sales day of the year for pizza. On that day alone hundreds of thousands of pizzas are delivered across the country. For companies in the pizza business it is important that they have a delivery system that is as streamlined and efficient as possible. Delivery companies traditionally plan their routes by using statistical databases, maps, and reports. These sources provide valuable information

COURTESY GARAGA, INC.

Geographic segmentation is illustrated by the buying habits of suburban homeowners.

but not in a format that is quick and easy to use. So some delivery companies have invested in geographic information systems. Once used mainly by the military, **geographic information systems (GISs)** are computer systems that assemble, store, manipulate, and display data by their location. GISs simplify the job of analyzing marketing information by relating data to their locations. The result is a geographic map overlaid with digital data about consumers in a particular area. A growing number of companies benefit from using a GIS to locate new outlets, assign sales territories, plan distribution centres—and map out the most efficient delivery routes. Although the earliest geographic information systems were prohibitively expensive for all but the largest companies, recent technological advances have made GIS software available at a much lower cost, increasing usage among smaller firms.

DEMOGRAPHIC SEGMENTATION

The most common method of market segmentation defines consumer groups according to demographic variables such as gender, age, income, occupation, education, household size, and stage in the family life cycle. This approach is also called *socioeconomic segmentation*. Marketers review vast quantities of available data to complete a plan for demographic segmentation. One of the primary sources for demographic data in Canada is Statistics Canada. Marketers can obtain many of the census statistics online at http://www.statcan.ca.

The following discussion considers the most commonly used demographic variables. Keep in mind, however, that while demographic segmentation is helpful, it can also lead to stereotyping—a preconception about a group of people—which can alienate a potential market or cause marketers to miss a potential market altogether. The idea is to use segmentation as a starting point, not as an end point.

Market segmentation often falls along gender lines. Car companies consider young women's preferences in the design of their cars.

SEGMENTING BY GENDER

Gender is an obvious variable that helps define the markets for certain products. But segmenting by gender can be tricky. In some cases, the segmenting is obvious—lipstick for women, facial shaving products for men. But in recent years, the lines have increasingly blurred. Men sometimes wear earrings and use skin-care products, once both the province of women. Women purchase power tools and pickup trucks, once considered traditionally male purchases. So marketers of cars and trucks, power tools, jewellery, and skin-care products have had to change the way they segment their markets. Dell recently increased its advertising in women's magazines. The magazines featured Dell's laser printer, plasma TV, and notebook computer in their "must-have" gift sections.[15] Nivea, well-known for its skin-care products for women and babies, created an entire line of men's skin-care products called Nivea for Men.

Some companies successfully market the same—or similar—products to both men and women. Sony developed a campaign for its flat screen TV aimed at both genders. Calling its brand "The World's First Television for Men and Women," Sony created ads with the tagline "Coveted by Men, Admired by Women."[16]

As the balance of purchasing power in many families has shifted toward women, marketers have learned that working women who regularly use the Internet make most of the decisions about retail items (such as clothing), health care goods and services, and fitness products. Decisions about vacations, financial investments, and home improvement products are often shared equally. In the category of consumer electronics, women edge ahead of men by about 10 percent.[17] Marketers who understand these trends can develop more effective strategies and messages for consumers.

SEGMENTING BY AGE

Age is another variable that marketers use to segment their markets. As with gender, age seems to be an easy distinction to make—baby food for babies, retirement communities for seniors. But also like gender, the distinctions become blurred as consumers' roles and needs change and as age distribution shifts and projected changes in each group take place. Baby aspirin is no longer marketed just to parents for their infants; now it is also marketed to adults to help prevent heart disease.

The Cohort Effect

Marketers can learn from a sociological concept called the **cohort effect**, the tendency of members of a generation to be influenced and bound together by significant events occurring during their key formative years, roughly age 17 to 22. These events help define the core values of the age group that eventually shapes consumer preferences and behaviour. For seniors, who are discussed later in this section, the events would be the Great Depression and World War II because many were in this age bracket at that time. For older baby boomers, it would be the Vietnam War and the civil rights movement. Marketers have already labelled people who were in the 17-to-22 age bracket at the time of the September 11, 2001, terrorist attacks the **9/11 Generation**. Clearly, this group's previous priorities and values changed, and those changes will become more evident as time passes.

The significance of the cohort effect for marketers lies in understanding the general characteristics of each group as it responds to its defining life events. The social and economic influences that each group experiences help form their long-term beliefs and goals in life—and can have a lasting effect on their buying habits and the product choices they make. For marketers to be effective in reaching their targeted age segments, they need to understand some basic characteristics of each age group. We highlight a few of the distinguishing characteristics next and briefly discuss how some marketers are providing products to meet each age segment's wants and needs.

School-Age Children

School-age children—and those who are even younger—exert considerable influence over family purchases, as marketers are keenly aware, particularly in the area of food. Research shows that the eating habits of children under the age of 12 are influenced by television advertising. With the obesity rates of children increasing, industry experts are calling for the food industry to aim their advertising at nutritious food and drinks.[18]

Tweens and Teens

Tweens—also called *preteens*—and teens are a rapidly growing market. According to recent research, the average disposal income of a teen is $131 per week. Multiply that by 52, and you have over $6000 per year. Teens make 54 visits to the mall a year and make a purchase 50 percent of the time. Shopping has been described as the number one hobby for teens.[19]

Teens are spending this money on clothes, technology, food, and entertainment. For example, 55 percent own a cell phone, 79 percent own a portable CD player, and 80 percent download music from the Internet at least once a month.[20]

This group, commonly referred to as Generation Y, isn't as cynical about advertising as their older counterpart—Generation X. They are, however, marketing savvy. A significant number of them are anti-brand, believing that price matters but quality is more important.[21] In fact, "they like being marketed to. They like that someone's paying attention to them," says the publisher of one teen magazine.[22]

Marketing to this group can be challenging but also lucrative. This is the second-largest group of consumers in Canada and they know what they want. Research shows that friends are important, products have short life cycles, and diversity is embraced.

Generation X

The group born between 1966 and 1981—who are now between ages 25 and 40—are often referred to as **Generation X**. This group faced some economic and career challenges as they began their adult lives and started families: housing costs were high and debt associated with college loans and credit cards was soaring. But their financial squeeze should ease as they enter their prime earning years.

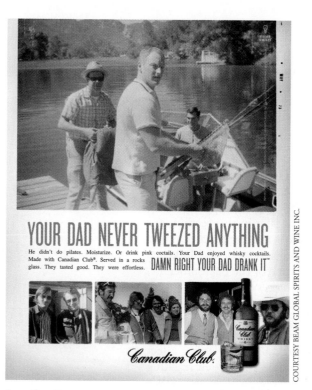

YOUR DAD NEVER TWEEZED ANYTHING

He didn't do pilates. Moisturize. Or drink pink coctails. Your Dad enjoyed whisky cocktails. Made with Canadian Club®. Served in a rocks glass. They tasted good. They were effortless. **DAMN RIGHT YOUR DAD DRANK IT™**

Canadian Club.

COURTESY BEAM GLOBAL SPIRITS AND WINE INC.

Canadian Club: appealing to baby boomers' nostalgia for past family gatherings

This group is very family oriented—not defining themselves by their careers as much as previous generations—well educated, and optimistic. Because they grew up with television, this generation of consumers is far more technologically savvy than their elders.[23] Marketers who understand these traits can appeal to this group of consumers, particularly if they ask Gen Xers directly what they want or need, especially in new technology products.

Baby Boomers

Baby boomers—people born between 1947 and 1965—are a popular segment to target because of their numbers. Almost one in every three Canadians was born in this period. This group has been described as rebellious and spoiled, when in fact only about 25 percent of the boomers fit that description.[24]

Baby boomers will see their disposable income increase in the next few years as their mortgages are paid off and their children leave home, which is why businesses are trying to woo this group. Different subgroups within this generation complicate segmentation and targeting strategies. Some boomers put off having children until their 40s, while others their age have already become grandparents. Boomer grandparents are healthier and more physically active than their own grandparents were, and they expect to take an active role in their grandchildren's lives. When buying toys, for instance, they often purchase items that focus on a shared experience—games they can play with their grandchildren or craft sets they can assemble together. Boomers are buying more than toys for their grandchildren, they are the largest group purchasing building and auto supplies, and personal health care products.[25]

Seniors

Marketers also recognize a trend dubbed the greying of the population. By 2026, 36 percent of the Canadian population will be over 55. As Canadians have continued to live longer, the median age of the Canadian population has dramatically increased.

The current median age is now 39.5 years, up from 25.4 years in 1996. The average life expectancy in Canada has increased for both genders to age 77 for men, and to age 82 for women. Explanations for these increases in life spans include better medicines and healthier lifestyles.[26]

In Canada, the senior group spends $35 billion a year. They like luxury—expensive homes, clothes, and cars—and, although not all seniors fit into this group, those that have the money spend it. Some refer to these prosperous consumers as WOOFs—Well-Off Older Folks.

One thing is for sure: the seniors of today fit into more market segments than ever before, and it would be a mistake for marketers to consider them all alike.[27] Traditionally, one way marketers have targeted seniors is through the senior discount, whether it's for a cup of coffee at McDonald's or a pass at the ski slopes. But with more seniors living longer and collecting these discounts, some companies are rolling them back. However, not all marketers agree with this cost-cutting approach because seniors do make up such a large group of potentially loyal customers.

SEGMENTING BY ETHNIC GROUP

According to Statistics Canada, the ethnic makeup of our population is changing. Other than the two largest ethnic groups, English and French, there are slightly fewer than 4 million people from different ethnic backgrounds in Canada. Because of comparatively high immigration and birth rates among some of these ethnic groups, Statistics Canada projects somewhere between 6.3 million and 8.5 million, or 19 percent to 23 percent, of the population will be made up of ethnic groups other than English and French by 2017.[28]

The three largest groups, Chinese, South Asians, and Blacks, account for 75 percent of those indicating an ethnic category on the Statistics Canada census; however, the South Asian group may catch up to the Chinese in numbers by 2017. From a marketer's perspective, it is important to understand the spending patterns of these groups.[29]

French and English

Many companies today realize there are major differences between the French- and English-speaking markets in Canada, besides language, but these markets have not always been treated differently. For many years, companies ran their English ads in Quebec in direct translations.[30]

The father of made-in-Quebec marketing, Jacques Bouchard, spent 30 years studying the French-Canadian consumer. He explains the differences between the French and English consumers using a six-element model based on roots.

- Root number one, Rural Root, refers to the 77 percent of Quebecers who feel the need to be closer to nature; the number in the rest of Canada is 58 percent. Quebecers like to keep their options open; the province has the highest number of fishermen and hunters; and they crave a simple life but describe their lives as hectic. Sixty-six percent feel the need to sustain their traditions, and although they don't consider themselves as smart shoppers they have a high coupon usage rate. Compared to the rest of Canada, they have a higher concern for quality and are less likely to own power tools.

- The Minority Root describes Quebecers in relation to other parts of the world. They live for the moment, having the lowest savings rate in the country, generally are more tolerant and understanding than the rest of Canada, have a matriarchal family structure, and love to gossip.

- The North American Root explains how they enjoy an American lifestyle—love to shop, describe their homes as "lived in," are more likely to have a swimming pool, prefer the United States to the rest of Canada, and are more likely to be offended by advertising.

- The Catholic Root looks at the influence of religion. Religion has declined in importance in Quebec, but Quebecers feel closer to people of the same religious, national, or ethnic backgrounds.

- The Latin Root is reflected in the importance of enjoying life. Quebec has the lowest birth rate of any province but Quebecers love children. They enjoy looking young, have a need to be creative, and seek love and tenderness.

- The French Root is evident in their feeling of connection with a region. They are more likely to shop with a list, feel people should be allowed to do their own thing, place less emphasis on family togetherness than on individuals, are more likely to use bath products and perfumes, and are aware of brands with an image.[31]

Marketers from various organizations have attempted to reach the Quebec market. Ads made specifically for the Quebec market, like those produced by Ontario Tourism and MasterCard, seem to work best. However, companies that are designing promotions aimed

figure 8.2

Canadian Visible Minority Populations

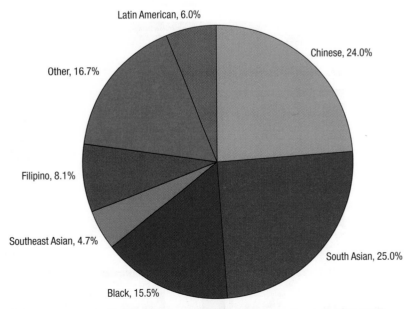

Source: Adapted from the Statistics Canada website article "Visible minority groups, 2006 counts, for Canada, provinces and territories - 20% sample data," available at http://www12.statcan.ca, accessed 30 June 2008.

at international markets, like the recent Dove "Real Beauty" campaign, have also been very successful in this market.[32]

Chinese Canadians

The largest ethnic group in Canada, the Chinese, is not a homogeneous segment. While it is true that most Chinese Canadians live in Toronto, Vancouver, and Montreal, they did not all come from the same areas of the world, nor are their shopping habits similar.

When Hong Kong was repatriated, a large number of fairly wealthy immigrants arrived in Canada; since then, arrivals from Hong Kong have slowed while those arriving from mainland China, Taiwan, and Southeast Asia are on the increase. People from each of these environments bring different values with them based on their home country and, in some cases, a different language. Hong Kong, for example, is heavily influenced by its past connection to Britain, and people from Hong Kong place higher importance on recognition and status. Physical comforts and luxuries are important to consumers from mainland China. The only democratic Chinese country is Taiwan, where national identity plays an important role. The values that all Chinese cultures share include a trust in family, hard work, thrift, and a tendency to save and invest in both tangible and liquid assets.[33]

Chinese consumers spend $30 billion annually, but have been described as culturally stubborn, spending within their own community; they are likely to get information about products and services from ethnic media. One company, T&T supermarkets, a Taiwan–based food chain, has 16 big-box stores across Canada aimed at the Chinese market. Seventy percent of the products T&T sells are imported from Asia. The company president explained that this high level of imports was mainly due to Canadian companies not understanding the Chinese consumer. Canadian companies have been slow to develop trilingual labels (Chinese/English/French), produce Chinese-language promotional material, and support events within the Chinese community.[34]

Other Ethnic Groups

Ethnic backgrounds in Canada are more diverse than just Chinese and French, and the number of ethnic groups represented is growing. So is their spending. It is estimated that $42 billion of the total $316 billion spent on retail goods and services came from ethnic markets. South Asians are the second-largest group in Canada but they are the largest ethnic group in Ontario. Their countries of origin include India, Pakistan, and Bangladesh. The majority of their purchases are in food, recreation, and clothing. They particularly like brand-name goods and are likely to shop around for a good deal. One ethnic group that little is known about is the Black population. Representing 2 percent of the population, they arrived in Canada mostly from the Caribbean. They tend to shop at stores that either employ Black people or have operations in the Caribbean. The Hispanic/Latino group in Canada comes from Spanish-speaking countries such as Mexico or Italy and Portugal and is not nearly as large as in the United States but we know more about them. They spend about $5 billion a year on products such as home entertainment equipment and expensive cars. They are brand loyal and like to shop at Canadian-owned companies. Whatever ethnic influences motivate the shopping habits of Canadians, one thing is for sure: they will become more important in the future if projected immigration rates are realized.[35]

The "Solving an Ethical Controversy" box discusses whether the collection of racial data is even appropriate or is an invasion of privacy.

Many firms have launched French websites in an attempt to reach the Quebec market.

COURTESY OF INDIGO BOOKS AND MUSIC INC.

SEGMENTING BY FAMILY LIFE CYCLE STAGES

Still another form of demographic segmentation employs the stages of the **family life cycle**—the process of family formation

Solving an Ethical Controversy

What Kind of Information Should Marketers Collect?

A critical part of a marketer's job is to collect information about existing and potential customers. But at what point does this information gathering cross the line to become an invasion of people's privacy? The debate over whether universities and colleges, governments, and other organizations should be allowed to collect racial and ethnic data on individuals has reached a heated level.

In Canada, there are laws regulating the type of information that can be collected about individuals and how this information is used. However, some researchers argue that without such information, it is more difficult to prove discrimination in hiring or workplace promotions by companies, governments, or other organizations.

Is the collection of racial and ethnic data an invasion of an individual's privacy?

PRO

1. Collecting such data serves no positive purpose in most cases and may in fact lead to stereotyping or prejudiced behaviour on the part of organizations that receive the data.

2. Racial and ethnic data do not necessarily provide an accurate picture of a person. There are so many different factors affecting how people behave that racial and ethnic data alone do not provide enough information, even for people with the same racial or ethnic background.

CON

1. People can always opt not to offer racial or ethnic data to organizations.

2. Such data can help not-for-profit and for-profit organizations serve their customers better. A firm that has some information on the ethnic background of its customers may be able to provide sales representatives who speak a certain language or products that better suit customers' tastes.

Where do you stand: pro or con?

Sources: "Racial Privacy Initiative," http://www.racialprivacy.org, accessed February 9, 2004; "Racial Privacy Initiative Defeated," MSNBC, October 7, 2003, http://www.msnbc.com; Robert Tomsho, "Some Seek Ban on Collection of Ethnic Data," Wall Street Journal, June 30, 2003, pp. B1, B4; Michael S. Victoroff, MD, "Medically, Race Means Nothing," *Managed Care Magazine*, April 2002, http://www.managedcaremag.com.

---

and dissolution. The underlying theme of this segmentation approach is that life stage, not age per se, is the primary determinant of many consumer purchases. As people move from one life stage to another, they become potential consumers for different types of goods and services.

An unmarried person setting up an apartment for the first time is likely to be a good prospect for inexpensive furniture and small home appliances. This consumer probably must budget carefully, ruling out expenditures on luxury items. On the other hand, a young single person who is still living at home will probably have more money to spend on products such as a car, entertainment, and clothing. As couples marry, their consumer profiles change. Couples without children are frequent buyers of personalized gifts, power tools, furniture, and homes. Eating out and travel may also be part of their lifestyles.

The birth of a first child changes any couple's consumer profile considerably; parents must buy cribs, changing tables, baby clothes, baby food, car seats, and similar products. Parents usually spend less on the children who follow the first because they have already bought many essential items for the first child. Today, the average woman gives birth to fewer children than she did a century ago and usually waits until she is older to have them. Although the average age for Canadian women to have their first child is 28, many women wait longer, often into their 30s and 40s.[36] This means that, if they work outside the home, older women are likely to be more established financially, with more money to spend. However, if a woman chooses to stay at home after the birth of a child, income can drop dramatically.

Families typically spend the most during the years their children are growing—on everything from housing, food, and clothing, to braces and college. Thus, they often look to obtain value wherever they can. Marketers can create satisfied and loyal customers among this group by giving them the best value possible.

Marketoid

Of the sales of recordings by Canadian artists, roughly 57 percent came from Ontario and 32 percent from Quebec.

Your walls are your canvas. Your life is your inspiration. And your paint is Benjamin Moore.

Discover the paint that best captures your personality, style and taste at your local Benjamin Moore® retailer.

The backdrop to your life.
benjaminmoore.ca

COURTESY OF BENJAMIN MOORE

This ad targets families with young children—an example of segmenting by family life cycle stage.

Once the children are grown and on their own—or at least off to university or college—married couples enter the empty nest stage. Empty nesters may have the disposable incomes necessary to purchase premium products once university or college tuitions and mortgages are paid off. They may travel more, eat out more often, redecorate the house, or go back to school themselves. They may treat themselves to a new and more luxurious car or buy a vacation home. In later years, empty nesters may decide to sell their homes and become customers for retirement or assisted living communities. They may require home-care services or more health care products as well. However, many retirees will continue to work a couple of days a week. "Keeping mentally active, keeping in touch with people and to earn money" were the reasons given to continue working.[37]

One trend noted by researchers in the past decade is an increase in the number of grown children who have returned home to live with their parents. Called boomerangs, some of these grown children bring along families of their own. Another trend is the growing number of grandparents who care for grandchildren on a regular basis—making them customers all over again for baby and child products such as toys, food, and safety devices.

SEGMENTING BY HOUSEHOLD TYPE

According to Statistics Canada, from 1981 to 2006, the average size of households in Canada declined from 2.9 to 2.5 people.[38] There are several reasons for the trend toward smaller households: lower fertility rates (including the decision to have fewer children or no children at all), young people's tendency to postpone marriage, the frequency of divorce, and the ability and desire of many people to live alone.

Today's households represent a wide range of diversity. They include households with a married couple and their children; households that are blended through divorce or loss of a spouse and remarriage; those headed by a single parent, same-sex parents, or grandparents; couples without children; groups of friends; and single-person households.

Couples without children may be young or old. If they are seniors, their children may have already grown and are living on their own. The percentage of couples with no children under the age 25 living at home has increased steadily for the last 10 years. Couples living common-law (living together but not married) has also seen a significant increase, reaching 15.5 percent by 2006. This trend is strongest in Quebec, where common-law relationships represent 25 percent of all common-law families in Canada.[39] Couples who are younger and do not have children are considered attractive to marketers because they often have high levels of income to spend. These couples typically eat out often, take expensive vacations, and buy luxury cars.

The 2001 census was the first time data on same-sex partnerships was collected. In the 2006 census same-sex couples represented only 0.6 percent of all couples with 54 percent of these being male; however, female same-sex couples were more likely to have children living with them.[40] While the controversy over same-sex marriage rages on, same-sex couples in Canada have the same legal, social, and financial benefits as opposite-sex couples.

People live alone for a variety of reasons—sometimes by choice and sometimes by necessity such as divorce or widowhood. In response, marketers have modified their messages and their products to meet the needs of single-person households. Food industry manufacturers are downsizing products, offering more single-serve foods ranging from soup to macaroni and cheese.

Regardless of the type of household, households are often used to collect information about trends in society as can be seen by the ongoing study of households and the environment discussed in the Go Green box.

SEGMENTING BY INCOME AND EXPENDITURE PATTERNS

Part of the earlier definition of *market* described people with purchasing power. Not surprisingly, then, a common basis for segmenting the consumer market is income. Marketers often target geographic areas known for the high incomes of their residents. Or they might consider age or household type when determining potential buying power.

Engel's Laws

How do expenditure patterns vary with income? Over a century ago, Ernst Engel, a German statistician, published what became known as **Engel's laws**—three general statements based on his studies of the impact of household income changes on consumer spending behaviour. According to Engel, as household income increases, the following will take place:

1. A smaller percentage of expenditures go for food.

2. The percentage spent on housing, household operations and clothing remains constant.

3. The percentage spent on other items (such as recreation and education) increases.

Go Green

Households and the Environment

Environmental trends are so important in today's society that Statistics Canada, Environment Canada, and Health Canada have joined forces to collect information about how Canadian households are adapting to environmentally friendly products and practises. The results of the studies are available on the Statistics Canada website under EnviroStats.

As part of this initiative, Statistics Canada performed the Households and the Environment Survey (HES). Over 28 000 households across Canada were asked questions relating to household activities that would have both positive and negative impacts on the environment. Topics covered included water (its quality, consumption, and conservation), energy use, pesticides and fertilisers, recycling habits, transportation decisions, and gas-powered equipment. The results were compared to similar studies conducted in the early 1990s.

With regard to water, the survey found almost 30 percent of households drank bottled water. The usage rates of bottled water were highest in Kitchener at 46 percent and St. Catharines-Niagara at 41 percent. The survey also found that 60 percent of Canadian households had water-saving showerheads, up from 42 percent in 1994, and 41 percent had a water-saving toilet, up from 15 percent in 1994.

The energy use part of the survey found that Canadians are purchasing more environmentally friendly devices. The number of households using at least one compact fluorescent light increased from 19 percent in 1994 to 59 percent. British Columbia and Ontario had the highest usage rates at almost 66 percent, and Quebec came in on the lower end at 50 percent. Households with programmable thermostats increased from 16 percent in 1994 to 42 percent. The highest rate at 52 percent was Ontario, with the Maritime Provinces having the lowest rate. Another interesting statistic uncovered in the study is that 16 percent of the households that had programmable thermostats had not programmed them.

The study also highlighted areas where improvements were still needed, such as pesticide use and transportation. Pesticide use was down only slightly, even though some areas have enacted laws to control their use, and the majority of Canadians are still commuting to work alone in a private vehicle.

Sources: "Household and the Environment Survey," http://www.statcan.ca, July 11, 2007, accessed December 12, 2007; EnviroStats, Winter 2007, http://www.statcan.ca, accessed December 30, 2007.

Rolex targets people with significant disposable incomes.

© MARK SYKES/ALAMY

Are Engel's laws still valid? Recent studies say yes, with a few exceptions. Researchers note a steady decline in the percentage of total income spent on food and beverages as income increases. Although high-income families spend greater absolute amounts on food items, their purchases represent declining percentages of their total expenditures compared with low-income families. The second law remains partly accurate. However, the percentage of fixed expenditures for housing and household operations has increased over the past 30 years, and the percentage spent on clothing rises with increased income because of choice. The third law remains true, with the exception of personal-care costs, which appear to decline as a percentage of increased income.[41]

Engel's laws can help marketers target markets at all income levels. Regardless of the economic environment, consumers still buy luxury goods and services. One reason is that some companies now offer their luxury products at different price levels. Mercedes-Benz has its lower-priced C-class models, while the jewellery store Birks sells a $100 sterling silver heart pendant with chain. Both of these firms continue to offer their higher-priced items as well but have chosen to broaden their market by serving other consumers.

DEMOGRAPHIC SEGMENTATION ABROAD

Marketers often face a difficult task in obtaining the data necessary for demographic segmentation abroad. Many countries do not have scheduled census programs. Germany skipped counting from 1970 to 1987, and France conducts a census about every seven years. By contrast, Japan conducts a census every five years; however, the mid-decade assessments are not as complete as the end-of-decade counts.

Also, some foreign data include demographic divisions not found in the Canadian census. Not all countries collect information on religious affiliation, for instance. On the other hand, some of the standard segmentation data for Canadian markets are not available abroad. Many nations do not collect income data. Great Britain, Japan, Spain, France, and Italy are examples. Similarly, family life cycle data are difficult to apply in global demographic segmentation efforts. Ireland acknowledges only three marital statuses—single, married, and widowed—while Latin-American nations and Sweden count their unmarried cohabitants.

One source of global demographic information is the Industry Canada website. Industry Canada provides a searchable online database of population statistics for many countries.

PSYCHOGRAPHIC SEGMENTATION

Marketers have traditionally referred to geographic and demographic characteristics as the primary bases for dividing consumers into homogeneous market segments. Still, they have long recognized the need for fuller, more lifelike portraits of consumers in developing their marketing programs. As a result, psychographic segmentation can be a useful tool for gaining sharper insight into consumer purchasing behaviour.

WHAT IS PSYCHOGRAPHIC SEGMENTATION?

Psychographic segmentation divides a population into groups that have similar psychological characteristics, values, and lifestyles. Lifestyle refers to a person's mode of living; it describes how an individual operates on a daily basis. Consumers' lifestyles are composites of their individual psychological profiles, including their needs, motives, perceptions, and attitudes. A lifestyle also bears the mark of many other influences, such as family, job, social activities, and culture.

The most common method for developing psychographic profiles of a population is to conduct a large-scale survey that asks consumers to agree or disagree with a collection of several hundred AIO statements. These **AIO statements** describe various activities, interests, and opinions. The resulting data allow researchers to develop lifestyle profiles. Marketers can then develop a separate marketing strategy that closely fits the psychographic makeup for each lifestyle segment.

Marketing researchers have conducted psychographic studies on hundreds of goods and services such as beer and air travel. Schick used this approach to assess consumer behaviour and attitudes of women toward their shavers and other products in order to learn about women's shaving needs and to determine how women perceive Schick's products.[42] Many businesses turn to psychographic research in an effort to learn what consumers in various demographic and geographic segments want and need.

Psychographic Segmentation

VALS™

A quarter century ago, the research and consulting firm SRI International developed a psychographic segmentation system called VALS™. Today VALS is owned and managed by SRI Consulting Business Intelligence (SRIC-BI), an SRI spin-off. VALS originally stood for "values and lifestyles" because it categorized consumers by their social values—how they felt about issues such as legalization of marijuana or abortion rights. A decade later, SRIC-BI revised the system to link it more closely with consumer buying behaviour. The revised VALS system categorizes consumers by psychological characteristics that correlate with purchase behaviour. It is based on two key concepts: resources and self-motivation. **VALS** divides consumers into eight psychographic categories: Actualizers, Thinkers, Achievers, Experiencers, Believers, Strivers, Makers, and Survivors. Figure 8.3 details the profiles for these categories and their relationships.

The VALS framework in the figure displays differences in resources as vertical distances, and primary motivation is represented horizontally. The resource dimension measures income, education, self-confidence, health, eagerness to buy, and energy level. Primary motivations divide consumers into three groups: principle-motivated consumers who have a set of ideas and morals—principles—that they live by; achievement-motivated consumers who are influenced by symbols of success; and action-motivated consumers who seek physical activity, variety, and adventure.

SRIC-BI has created several specialized segmentation systems based on this approach. JapanVALS™ was developed to help companies understand Japanese consumers, and U.K. VALS™ segments consumers in the United Kingdom. GeoVALS™ estimates the percentage of each VALS type by U.S. zip code or block group. SRI-BI used the VALS segmentation information in conjunction with consulting projects and on a subscriber basis. Product, service, and media data are available by VALS types from companies' databases.

Other tools available include Canada's Social Value Tribes, developed by Michael Adams and Environics Research Group Ltd. Environics crunches the numbers on hundreds of personal variables that include political views, religious affiliations, and social attitudes and comes up with 12 psychographic categories within three tribes that reflect Canadian social values. Depending on your own variables, you might be a "thrill-seeking materialist" or an "aimless dependent," both fitting into the Gen X Tribe. Information about each group's fundamental motivation and key values is available.[43]

psychographic segmentation
Division of a population into groups that have similar psychological characteristics, values, and lifestyles.

<figure>
figure 8.3

The VALS™ Framework

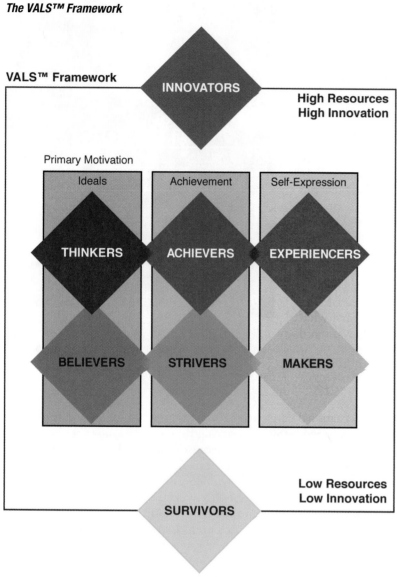

Source: SRI Consulting Business Intelligence, www.sric-bi.com/VALS/
</figure>

PSYCHOGRAPHIC SEGMENTATION OF GLOBAL MARKETS

As JapanVALS suggests, psychographic profiles can cross national boundaries. RoperASW, a marketing research firm, recently surveyed 7000 people in 35 countries. From the resulting data, Roper identified six psychographic consumer segments that exist in all 35 nations, although to varying degrees:

- *Strivers*, the largest segment, value professional and material goals more than the other groups. One-third of the Asian population and one-fourth of Russians are strivers. They are slightly more likely to be men than women.

- *Devouts* value duty and tradition. While this segment comprises 22 percent of all adults, they are most common in Africa, the Middle East, and developing Asia. They are least common in Western Europe and developed Asian countries. Worldwide, they are more likely to be female.

- *Altruists* emphasize social issues and societal well-being. Comprising 18 percent of all adults, this group shows a median age of 44 and a slightly higher percentage of women. Altruists are most common in Latin America and Russia, with a significant number of young Chinese adults.[44]

- *Intimates* value family and personal relationships. They are divided almost equally between males and females. One American or European in four would be categorized as intimates, but only 7 percent of consumers in developing Asia fall into this category.

- *Fun seekers*, as you might guess from their name, focus on personal enjoyment and pleasurable experiences. They make up 12 percent of the world's population, with a male–female ratio of 54 to 46. Many live in developed Asia.

- *Creatives*, the smallest segment, account for just 10 percent of the global population. This group seeks education, technology, and knowledge, and their male–female ratio is roughly equal. Many creatives live in Western Europe and Latin America, although 17 percent of China's young adult market can be identified as such.[45]

Roper researchers note that some principles and core beliefs—such as protecting the family—apply to more than one psychographic segment.

USING PSYCHOGRAPHIC SEGMENTATION

No one suggests that psychographic segmentation is an exact science, but it does help marketers quantify aspects of consumers' personalities and

assessment check 4

4.1 Under what circumstances are marketers most likely to use geographic segmentation?

4.2 What is demographic segmentation?

4.3 What are the major categories of demographic segmentation?

4.4 What is psychographic segmentation?

4.5 Name the eight categories of VALS.

lifestyles to create goods and services for a target market. Psychographic profile systems like those of Roper and SRIC-B1 can paint useful pictures of the overall psychological motivations of consumers. These profiles produce much richer descriptions of potential target markets than other techniques can achieve. The enhanced detail aids in matching a company's image and product offerings with the types of consumers who use its products.

Identifying which psychographic segments are most prevalent in certain markets helps marketers plan and promote more effectively. Often, segments overlap. Consumers who are most likely to be the first to buy new tech products could live in Vancouver or Halifax, they could just as easily be status oriented as action oriented, and they might be creatives or fun seekers. What they do have in common is the tendency to be the first on their block to purchase the latest tech devices.[46]

Psychographic segmentation is a good supplement to segmentation by demographic or geographic variables. For example, marketers may have access to each consumer type's media preferences in network television, cable television, radio format, magazines, and newspapers. Psychographic studies may then refine the picture of segment characteristics to give a more elaborate lifestyle profile of the consumers in the firm's target market. A psychographic study could help marketers of goods and services across the country predict what kinds of products consumers in those cities would be drawn to and eliminate those that are not attractive.

With its focus on cozy moments, this Sunbeam ad appeals to intimates.

PRODUCT-RELATED SEGMENTATION

⑤ Describe product-related segmentation.

product-related segmentation Division of a population into homogeneous groups based on their relationships to the product.

Product-related segmentation involves dividing a consumer population into homogeneous groups based on their relationships to the product. This segmentation approach can take several forms:

1. segmenting based on the benefits that people seek when they buy a product

2. segmenting based on usage rates for a product

3. segmenting according to consumers' brand loyalty toward a product

SEGMENTING BY BENEFITS SOUGHT

This approach focuses on the attributes that people seek and the benefits they expect to receive from a good or service. It groups consumers into segments based on what they want a product to do for them.

Consumers who quaff Starbucks premium coffees are not just looking for a dose of caffeine. They are willing to pay extra to savour a pleasant experience, one that makes them feel pampered and appreciated. Women who work out at Curves want to look their best and feel healthy. Pet owners who feed their cats and dogs Science Diet believe that they are giving their animals a great-tasting, healthy pet food.

Even if a business offers only one product line, however, marketers must remember to consider product benefits. Two people may buy the same product for very different reasons. A box of baking soda could end up serving as a refrigerator freshener, a toothpaste substitute, an antacid, or a deodorizer for a cat's litter box.

SEGMENTING BY USAGE RATES

Marketers may also segment a total market by grouping people according to the amounts of a product that they buy and use. Markets can be divided into heavy-user, moderate-user, and light-user segments.

The **80/20 principle** holds that a big percentage of a product's revenues—maybe 80 percent—comes from a relatively small, loyal percentage of total customers—perhaps 20 percent. The 80/20 principle is sometimes referred to as Pareto's Principle. Although the percentages need not exactly equal these figures, the general principle often holds true: relatively few heavy users of a product can account for much of its consumption.

Depending on their goals, marketers may target heavy, moderate, or light users as well as non-users. A company may attempt to lure heavy users of another product away from their regular brands to try a new brand. Non-users and light users may be attractive prospects because other companies are ignoring them. Usage rates can also be linked to other segmentation methods such as demographic and psychographic segmentation.

SEGMENTING BY BRAND LOYALTY

A third product-related segmentation method groups consumers according to the strength of the brand loyalty they feel toward a product. A classic example of brand loyalty segmentation is a frequent-purchase program—it might be frequent flyer, frequent stay, or frequent purchase of shoes or gasoline. Other companies attempt to segment their market by developing brand loyalty over a period of time, through consumers' stages of life. Children whose parents dress them in Baby Gap clothes may grow up to wear Gap Kids and Gap clothing.

Consumers may develop loyalty to seemingly similar brands but for different reasons. One study showed that retailers like Wal-Mart and Zellers have loyal customers whose definition of value is different. Wal-Mart shoppers prefer to do all of their household shopping at one store—which also happens to offer low prices. Zellers shoppers, who desire low prices as well, are more focused on the store's stylish furniture and home decor offerings from well-known designer Alfred Sung. Convenience and price are important to the Wal-Mart–exclusive shopper, whereas style and selection appear to hold more weight with the Zellers shopper.[47]

USING MULTIPLE SEGMENTATION BASES

Segmentation is a tool that can help marketers increase their accuracy in reaching the right markets. Like other marketing tools, segmentation is probably best used in a flexible manner—for instance, combining geographic and demographic segmentation techniques or dovetailing product-related segmentation with segmentation by income and expenditure patterns. The important point to keep in mind is that segmentation is a tool to help marketers get to know their potential customers better and ultimately satisfy their needs with the appropriate goods and services.

assessment check 5

5.1 List the three approaches to product-related segmentation.

5.2 What is the 80/20 principle?

---

⑥ **Identify the steps in the market segmentation process.**

THE MARKET SEGMENTATION PROCESS

To this point, the chapter has discussed various bases on which companies segment markets. But how do marketers decide which segmentation base—or bases—to use? Firms may use a management-driven method, in which segments are predefined by managers based on their observation of the behavioural and demographic characteristics of likely users. Or they may use a market-driven method, in which segments are defined by asking customers which attributes are important. Then marketers follow a four-stage process.

DEVELOP A RELEVANT PROFILE FOR EACH SEGMENT

After identifying promising segments, marketers should understand the customers in each one. This in-depth analysis of customers helps managers accurately match buyers' needs with the firm's marketing offers. The process must identify characteristics that both explain the similarities among customers within each segment and account for differences among segments.

The task at this stage is to develop a profile of the typical customer in each segment. Such a profile might include information about lifestyle patterns, attitudes toward product attributes and brands, product-use habits, geographic locations, and demographic characteristics.

FORECAST MARKET POTENTIAL

In the second stage, market segmentation and market opportunity analysis combine to produce a forecast of market potential within each segment. Market potential sets the upper limit on the demand that competing firms can expect from a segment. Multiplying by market share determines a single firm's maximum sales potential. This step should define a preliminary go or no-go decision from management because the total sales potential in each segment must justify resources devoted to further analysis. For example, if electronics firms are trying to determine whether to market a new product to teens, they need to determine what the demand for it would be and the disposable income of that group.

FORECAST PROBABLE MARKET SHARE

Once market potential has been estimated, a firm must forecast its probable market share. Competitors' positions in targeted segments must be analyzed, and a specific marketing strategy must be designed to reach these segments. These two activities may be performed simultaneously. Moreover, by settling on a marketing strategy and tactics, a firm determines the expected level of resources it must commit—that is, the costs it will incur to tap the potential demand in each segment.

Apple's iPod took the marketplace by storm, and some believe the iPod is poised to increase Apple's market share of desktop computer sales as loyal iPod users drop their PCs in favour of Mac computers. Researchers predict that as consumers abandon obsolete PCs, instead of upgrading to a new PC, they will switch to a Mac. Because the iPod is already well established, instead of causing a brief downturn in PC sales, a long-term shift toward Apple's Macs and related products might occur.[48]

SELECT SPECIFIC MARKET SEGMENTS

The information, analysis, and forecasts accumulated throughout the entire market segmentation decision process allow management to assess the potential for achieving company goals and to justify committing resources in developing one or more segments. Demand forecasts, together with cost projections, determine the profits and the return on investment (ROI) that the company can expect from each segment. Marketing strategy and tactics must be designed to reinforce the firm's image, yet keep within its unique organizational capabilities.

At this point in the analysis, marketers weigh more than monetary costs and benefits; they also consider many difficult-to-measure but critical organizational and environmental factors. The firm may lack experienced personnel to launch a successful attack on an attractive market segment. Similarly, a firm with a dominant market position may face possible legal problems with the Competition Bureau if it increases its market concentration or is seen to be engaging in anti-competitive acts.[49] This assessment of both financial and nonfinancial factors is a difficult but vital step in the decision process.

assessment check 6

6.1 Identify the four stages of the process of market segmentation.

6.2 Why is forecasting important to market segmentation?

STRATEGIES FOR REACHING TARGET MARKETS

⑦ Discuss four basic strategies for reaching target markets.

Marketers spend a lot of time and effort developing strategies that will best match their firm's product offerings to the needs of particular target markets. An appropriate match is vital to the firm's marketing success. Marketers have identified four basic strategies for achieving consumer satisfaction: undifferentiated marketing, differentiated marketing, concentrated marketing, and micromarketing.

UNDIFFERENTIATED MARKETING

undifferentiated marketing Strategy that focuses on producing a single product and marketing it to all customers; also called *mass marketing*.

A firm may produce only one product or product line and promote it to all customers with a single marketing mix; such a firm is said to practise **undifferentiated marketing,** sometimes called *mass marketing*. Undifferentiated marketing was much more common in the past than it is today.

While undifferentiated marketing is efficient from a production viewpoint, the strategy also brings inherent dangers. In the past, consumers often preferred to identify themselves with a mass-marketed brand because of a higher perceived quality and a sense of status associated with the brand. But this is no longer the case.[50] A firm that attempts to satisfy everyone in the market with one standard product may suffer if competitors offer specialized alternatives to smaller segments of the total market and better satisfy individual segments. In fact, firms that implement strategies of differentiated marketing, concentrated marketing, or micromarketing may capture enough small segments of the market to defeat another competitor's strategy of undifferentiated marketing.

DIFFERENTIATED MARKETING

differentiated marketing Strategy that focuses on producing several products and pricing, promoting, and distributing them with different marketing mixes designed to satisfy smaller segments.

Firms that promote numerous products with differing marketing mixes designed to satisfy smaller segments are said to practise **differentiated marketing.** By providing increased satisfaction for each of many target markets, a company can produce more sales by following a differentiated marketing strategy than undifferentiated marketing would generate. A marketer of a variety of meat products might practise a differentiated strategy. In order to increase sales, it might introduce a new snack food for children to take to school for lunch. In general, however, differentiated marketing also raises costs. Production costs usually rise because additional products and variations require shorter production runs and increased setup times. Inventory costs rise because more products require added storage space and increased efforts for record keeping. Promotional costs also rise because each segment demands a unique promotional mix.

Despite higher marketing costs, however, an organization may be forced to practise differentiated marketing to remain competitive. The travel industry now recognises the need to target smaller groups of travellers with specialized interests. One company, for instance, may target seniors with trips that focus on history, hiking, golfing, cooking, or other special interests.

CONCENTRATED MARKETING

concentrated marketing Focusing marketing efforts on satisfying a single market segment; also called *niche marketing*.

Rather than trying to market its products separately to several segments, a firm may opt for a concentrated marketing strategy. With **concentrated marketing** (also known as **niche marketing**), a firm focuses its efforts on profitably satisfying only one market segment. This approach can appeal to a small firm that lacks the financial resources of its competitors and to a company that offers highly specialised goods and services. American Express, a large firm with many financial products, introduced a new credit card designed for a very specific market, women in the luxury market who shop at Holt Renfrew.[51]

Sears, Zellers, and Wal-Mart all sell skateboards, but West 49 is aimed straight at tweens and teens. This chain of skateboard shops is located in malls, because tweens don't drive. They make the stores cool places for kids to hang out. The stores have Nintendo games available for free to encourage kids to visit the stores even if they aren't going to buy a new board that day. They employ salespeople who are aged 16 to 19 and who really enjoy skateboarding, so the tweens feel comfortable asking questions. The salespeople are kept up to date on the latest changes through training and websites, which really isn't required because of their passion for the sport.[52]

MICROMARKETING

micromarketing Targeting potential customers at very narrow, basic levels, such as by postal code, specific occupation, or lifestyle— possibly even individuals themselves.

The fourth targeting strategy, still more narrowly focused than concentrated marketing, is **micromarketing,** which involves targeting potential customers at a very basic level, such as by postal code, specific occupation, or lifestyle. Ultimately, micromarketing can target even individuals themselves. The salesperson at your favourite clothing boutique may contact you when certain merchandise that she thinks you will like arrives at the store. The Internet allows marketers to make micromarketing even more effective. By tracking specific demographic and personal information, marketers can send e-mail directly to individual consumers who are most likely to buy their products. If you purchase a book via Chapters.Indigo.ca, the company will offer to send you e-mail notices about other books that may be of interest.

But micromarketing, like niche marketing, can become too much of a good thing if companies spend too much time, effort, and marketing dollars to unearth a market that is too small and specialised to be profitable. In addition, micromarketing may cause a company to lose sight of other larger markets.

SELECTING AND EXECUTING A STRATEGY

Although most organizations adopt some form of differentiated marketing, no single best choice suits all firms. Any of the alternatives may prove most effective in a particular situation. The basic determinants of a market-specific strategy are (1) company resources, (2) product homogeneity, (3) stage in the product life cycle, and (4) competitors' strategies.

A firm with limited resources may have to choose a concentrated marketing strategy. Small firms may be forced to select small target markets because of limitations in their sales force and advertising budgets. On the other hand, an undifferentiated marketing strategy suits a firm selling items perceived by consumers as relatively homogeneous. Marketers of grain, for example, sell standardised grades of generic products rather than individual brand names. Some petroleum companies implement undifferentiated marketing to distribute their gasoline to the mass market.

The firm's strategy may also change as its product progresses through the stages of the life cycle. During the early stages, undifferentiated marketing might effectively support the firm's effort to build initial demand for the item. In the later stages, however, competitive pressures may force modifications in products and in the development of marketing strategies aimed at segments of the total market.

The strategies of competitors also affect the choice of a segmentation approach. A firm may encounter obstacles to undifferentiated marketing if its competitors actively cultivate smaller segments. In such instances, competition usually forces each firm to adopt a differentiated marketing strategy.

Having chosen a strategy for reaching their firm's target market, marketers must then decide how best to position the product. The concept of **positioning** seeks to put a product in a certain position, or place, in the minds of prospective buyers. Marketers use a positioning strategy to distinguish their firm's offerings from those of competitors and to create promotions that communicate the desired position.

To achieve this goal of positioning, marketers follow a number of positioning strategies. Possible approaches include positioning a product according to the following categories:

1. *Attributes*—Kraft Foods: "Good food in every bite"

2. *Price/quality*—Omega watches: "We measure the 100th of a second that separates winning from taking part"

3. *Competitors*—Avis, the car rental company, proclaims, "We try harder."

4. *Application*—Whirlpool wants to "Wash your world clean."

positioning Placing a product at a certain point or location within a market in the minds of prospective buyers.

assessment check 7

7.1 Explain the difference between undifferentiated and differentiated marketing strategies.

7.2 What are the benefits of concentrated marketing?

Indulgence

Treat yourself to train travel at its best! Relax in a spacious seat and enjoy attentive service, delicious meals and special treats.

For information on *VIA 1*™ class, VIA's first class service on board southern Ontario and Québec trains, contact VIA Rail Canada at 1 888 VIA-RAIL (1 888 842-7245). ☏ TTY 1 800 268-9503 (hearing impaired) or visit viarail.ca.

™Trademark owned by VIA Rail Canada Inc.   A MORE HUMAN WAY TO TRAVEL   VIA Rail Canada™

COURTESY VIA RAIL CANADA

VIA Rail positions itself against its competitors by promoting luxury travel.

⑧ Summarise the types of positioning strategies, and explain the reasons for positioning and repositioning products.

5. *Product user*—Yellow Pages invites you to "Let your fingers do the walking."

6. *Product class*—The diamond industry claims, "A diamond is forever."

Whatever strategy they choose, marketers want to emphasize a product's unique advantages and to differentiate it from competitors' options. A **positioning map** provides a valuable tool in helping managers position products by graphically illustrating consumers' perceptions of competing products within an industry. Marketers can create a competitive positioning map from information solicited from consumers or from their accumulated knowledge about a market. A positioning map might present two different characteristics—price and perceived quality—and show how consumers view a product and its major competitors based on these traits. The hypothetical positioning map in Figure 8.4 compares selected retailers based on possible perceptions of the prices and quality of their offerings.

figure 8.4

Hypothetical Positioning Map for Selected Retailers

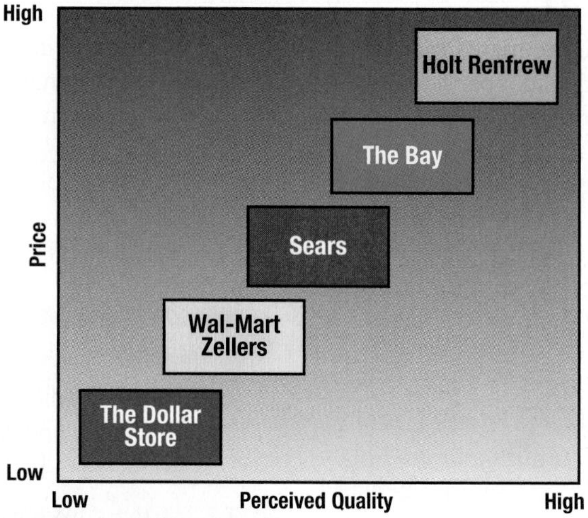

Sometimes changes in the competitive environment force marketers to **reposition** a product—changing the position it holds in the minds of prospective buyers relative to the positions of competing products. Repositioning may even be necessary for already successful products or firms in order to gain greater market share. Fast-food restaurants such as McDonald's and Burger King have repositioned themselves several times over the years in response to shifts in consumer preferences. They have changed ingredients and menu items, and created new marketing campaigns to appeal to different segments of the population. McDonald's current campaign carries the tagline "I'm lovin' it" in an appeal to young urban consumers.

assessment check 8 ✓

8.1 What are the four determinants of a market-specific strategy?

8.2 What is the role of positioning in a marketing strategy?

Strategic Implications

To remain competitive, today's marketers must accurately identify potential customers. They can use a variety of methods to accomplish this, including segmenting markets by gender and segmenting by geographic location. The trick is to figure out the best combination of methods for segmentation to identify the most lucrative, long-lasting potential markets. Marketers must also remain flexible, responding to markets as they change—for instance, following a generation as it ages or reaching out to new generations by revamping or repositioning products.

The greatest competitive advantage will belong to firms that can pinpoint and serve markets without segmenting them to the point where they are too small or specialized to garner profits. Marketers who can reach and communicate with the right customers have a greater chance of attracting and keeping those customers than marketers who are searching for the wrong customers in the wrong place. ◆◆◆

REVIEW OF CHAPTER OBJECTIVES

① Identify the essential components of a market.

A market consists of people and organizations with the necessary purchasing power, willingness, and authority to buy. Consumer products are purchased by the ultimate consumer for personal use. Business products are purchased for use directly or indirectly in the production of other goods and services. Certain products may fall into both categories.

② Outline the role of market segmentation in developing a marketing strategy.

Market segmentation is the process of dividing a total market into several homogeneous groups. It is used in identifying a target market for a good or service. Segmentation is the key to deciding a marketing strategy.

③ Describe the criteria necessary for effective segmentation.

Effective segmentation depends on these four basic requirements: (1) The segment must have measurable purchasing power and size; (2) marketers can find a way to promote to and serve the market; (3) marketers must identify segments large enough for profit potential; and (4) the firm can target a number of segments that match its marketing capabilities.

④ Explain the geographic, demographic, and psychographic approaches to segmenting consumer markets.

Geographic segmentation divides the overall market into homogeneous groups according to population locations. Demographic segmentation classifies the market into groups based on characteristics such as age, gender, and income level. Psychographic segmentation uses behavioural profiles developed from analyses of consumers' activities, opinions, interests, and lifestyles to identify market segments.

⑤ Describe product-related segmentation.

Product-related segmentation can take three basic forms: segmenting based on the benefits that people seek when they buy a product; segmenting based on usage rates for a product; and segmenting according to consumers' brand loyalty toward a product.

⑥ Identify the steps in the market segmentation process.

Market segmentation is the division of markets into relatively homogeneous groups. Segmentation follows a four-step sequence: (1) developing user profiles; (2) forecasting the overall market potential; (3) estimating market share; and (4) selecting specific market segments.

⑦ Discuss four basic strategies for reaching target markets.

Four strategies are (1) undifferentiated marketing, which uses a single marketing mix; (2) differentiated marketing, which produces numerous products, each with its own mix; (3) concentrated marketing, which directs all the firm's marketing resources toward a small segment; and (4) micromarketing, which targets potential customers at basic levels, such as postal code or occupation.

⑧ Summarise the types of positioning strategies, and explain the reasons for positioning and repositioning products.

Positioning strategies include positioning a good or service according to attributes, price/quality, competitors, application, product user, and product class.

Positioning helps create a memorable impression of a product in a consumer's mind and is used to differentiate a product from competitors' products. Changes in the competitive environment may require repositioning to maintain or even grab more of the market share.

assessment check answers

1.1   Define target market.

A target market is the specific segment of consumers most likely to purchase a particular product.

1.2   Distinguish between a consumer product and a business product.

A consumer product is purchased by the ultimate buyer for personal use. A business product is purchased for use directly or indirectly in the production of other goods and services.

2.1   Define market segmentation.

Market segmentation is the process of dividing a total market into several homogeneous groups.

2.2   Describe the role of market segmentation.

The role of market segmentation is to identify the factors that affect purchase decisions and then group consumers according to the presence or absence of these factors.

3.1   Identify the four criteria for effective segmentation.

The four criteria for effective segmentation are as follows: (1) the market segment must present measurable purchasing power and size, (2) marketers must find a way to promote effectively and to serve the market segment, (3) marketers must identify segments that are sufficiently large to give them good profit potential, and (4) the firm must aim for segments that match its marketing capabilities.

4.1   Under what circumstances are marketers most likely to use geographic segmentation?

Marketers usually use geographic segmentation when regional preferences exist and when demand for categories of goods and services varies according to geographic region.

4.2   What is demographic segmentation?

Demographic segmentation defines consumer groups according to demographic variables such as gender, age, income, occupation, household, and family life cycle.

4.3   What are the major categories of demographic segmentation?

The major categories of demographic segmentation are gender, age, ethnic group, family life cycle, household type, income, and expenditure patterns.

4.4   What is psychographic segmentation?

Psychographic segmentation divides a population into groups that have similar psychological characteristics, values, and lifestyles.

4.5   Name the eight categories of VALS.

The eight categories are the following: innovators, thinkers, achievers, experiencers, believers, strivers, makers, and survivors.

5.1   List the three approaches to product-related segmentation.

The three approaches are segmenting by benefits sought, segmenting by usage rates, and segmenting by brand loyalty.

5.2   What is the 80/20 principle?

The 80/20 principle states that a big percentage (80 percent) of a product's revenues comes from a relatively small number (20 percent) of loyal customers.

6.1   Identify the four stages of the process of market segmentation.

The four stages are developing user profiles, forecasting the overall market potential, estimating market share, and selecting specific market segments.

6.2   Why is forecasting important to market segmentation?

Forecasting is important because it can define a preliminary go or no-go decision based on sales potential. It can help a firm avoid a disastrous move or point out opportunities.

7.1   Explain the difference between undifferentiated and differentiated marketing strategies.

Undifferentiated marketing promotes a single product line to all customers with a single marketing mix. Differentiated marketing promotes numerous products with different marketing mixes designed to satisfy smaller segments.

7.2   What are the benefits of concentrated marketing?

Concentrated marketing can allow a firm to focus on a single market segment, which is especially appealing to smaller firms and those that offer highly specialized goods and services.

8.1   What are the four determinants of a market-specific strategy?

The four determinants are company resources, product homogeneity, stage in the product life cycle, and competitors' strategies.

8.2   What is the role of positioning in a marketing strategy?

Positioning places a product in a certain position in the minds of prospective buyers so that marketers can create messages that distinguish their offerings from those of competitors.

MARKETING TERMS YOU NEED TO KNOW

These terms are printed in red in the text. They are defined in the margins of the chapter and in the Glossary that begins on p. G-1. Other important terms are printed in bold black type in the chapter but not included in this list. Their definitions can be found in the Glossary.

market 260	geographic segmentation 262	differentiated marketing 280
consumer products 260	psychographic segmentation 275	concentrated marketing 280
business products 261	product-related segmentation 277	micromarketing 280
market segmentation 261	undifferentiated marketing 280	positioning 281

ASSURANCE OF LEARNING REVIEW

1. What is the difference between a market and a target market?
2. What are census metropolitan areas? Why do marketers try to identify these regions?
3. What is the cohort effect? What event—or events—do you consider significant enough to have influenced and bound together your generation?
4. What are the two largest racial/ethnic minority groups in Canada? Why is it important for marketers to understand these and other ethnic/racial groups?
5. Describe the three changes that will take place as a household income increases, according to Engel. Do Engel's laws still hold true?

6. Identify and describe the six psychographic segments that exist in all nations studied by VALS researchers.
7. Identify a branded product to which you are loyal, and explain why you are loyal to the product. What factors might cause your loyalty to change?
8. Choose another branded product. Create a relevant profile for the marketing segment that product serves.
9. Describe a situation in which you think micromarketing would be especially successful.
10. Under what circumstances might marketers decide to reposition a product?

PROJECTS AND TEAMWORK EXERCISES

1. On your own or with a partner, choose a product that could serve both business and consumer markets. Create an advertisement that shows how the product can serve businesses.
2. Choose your favourite activity—it may be a sport, an artistic pursuit, a volunteer opportunity. Identify the best basis for segmenting the market for this activity. Next, identify your target market. Finally, write a brief plan outlining your strategy for reaching your target market.
3. Find an advertisement that uses product-related segmentation as part of its strategy for reaching consumers. Present the ad to the class, identifying specific aspects of the ad, such as segmenting by benefits sought, segmenting by usage rates, or segmenting by brand loyalty.
4. With a partner, identify a product that you are familiar with that is either niche marketed or micromarketed. How might the

firm's marketers widen the audience for the product? Present your ideas and discuss them in class.
5. On your own or with a classmate, select one of the following products. Visit the firm's website to see how the product is positioned. Present your findings to the class, detailing how—and why—the product is positioned the way it is.
   a. Slim-Fast bars and shakes
   b. McDonald's chicken nuggets
   c. Kleenex
   d. Sheraton Hotels
   e. Roots clothing
   f. Porsche automobiles
6. Now discuss how you might reposition your product—and why. Create an ad illustrating your product's new positioning strategy.

CRITICAL THINKING EXERCISES

1. Create a profile of yourself as part of a market segment. Include such factors as where you live, your age and gender, and psychographic characteristics.
2. Select one of the following products and explain how you would use segmentation by income and expenditure patterns to determine your targeted market.
   a. Disney theme parks   c. Stouffer's Lean Cuisine
   b. Sony Cyber-shot camera   d. Porsche Boxster

3. How do you think the Internet has affected differentiated marketing techniques?
4. Think of a product that reminds you of your childhood—a particular candy, a toy or game, a television show or movie, or a brand of clothing. Describe how you would reposition that product for today's marketplace. Would you try to appeal to children or a different market segment?

ETHICS EXERCISE

Marketers are making a new pitch to men—at the risk of political incorrectness. Marketers for firms such as Unilever and Wendy's have been frustrated at not being able to reach young male consumers with their messages. After searching for clues about what this crowd likes, these firms have created marketing campaigns designed to grab their attention—perhaps at the expense of other consumers. A spokesperson from one ad agency says

that means advertising built on "bad boy" attitudes, lowbrow humour, and sex.[53]

1. What are some of the pitfalls of this kind of segmentation?
2. Do you think these ads will be successful in the long run? Why or why not?
3. Should marketers be concerned about offending one market segment when trying to reach another? Why or why not?

INTERNET EXERCISES

1. **Geographic segmentation.** As discussed in the chapter, Statistics Canada is an important source of data used by marketers to make decisions concerning geographic segmentation of their products. Visit the Statistics Canada website (http://www.statcan.ca). Click on "Community Profiles." Search for a city in your province and answer the following questions:
   a. What is the current population and the population change shown?
   b. How many private dwellings are there?
   c. What is the median age of the population?
2. **How companies segment their markets.** Visit the websites of Ford Motor Company (http://www.ford.com) and Procter & Gamble (http://www.pg.com). How does each company segment its markets (such as geographic, product-related, or demographic)? Does the company use more than one method of product segmentation?
3. **Segmenting by brand loyalty.** Visit the Guinness Brewing Company's web store (http://www.guinnesswebstore .com). Prepare a brief report on how Guinness uses its web store to build brand loyalty. Pick another company you have heard of and visit its website. How does this company use its website to enhance brand loyalty?

Note: Internet Web addresses change frequently. If you don't find the exact sites listed, you may need to access the organization's or company's home page and search from there or use a search engine such as Google.

Case 8.1

"I Am Canadian"

In 2000, Molson Breweries launched their famous "I am Canadian" commercial, or the "Rant" ad. The ad defined Canada so well it has been used by politicians to promote the country—but it was designed to sell beer. It seems an appropriate statement about Canada because Canadians drink a lot of beer. In fact, beer is the most popular alcoholic beverage in the country. In 2005, Canadians spent $16.8 billion on alcoholic beverages, and beer accounted for over 50 percent of those sales, with wine coming in at 25 percent and spirits (vodka, scotch, etc.) at 24 percent. This was the first year when wine sales exceeded spirit sales. These figures alone don't tell the whole story about the Canadian beer market or consumer tastes in beer. The rest of the story includes two major breweries, several dominant brands, differing consumption rates, microbreweries, and imported beers.

Consumers across the nation spent an average of $638.60 per person on alcoholic beverages annually, but per-person sales were highest in Newfoundland and Labrador and lowest in Manitoba. Research indicates that 33 percent of consumers do not drink beer at all. Females are not likely to be beer drinkers, and males over the age of 45 are not likely beer drinkers, either. This research would indicate that the majority of beer drinkers are young males. The two provinces with the highest total beer sales are, not surprisingly, Ontario and Quebec, with total annual sales of $3.2 billion and $2.3 billion respectively.

The two dominant beer brands are Molson Canadian (the Rant) and Labatt's Blue, each holding roughly 12 percent market share. Labatt and Molson have been the major players in the Canadian beer market for many years; however, both are now owned by foreign companies, Labatt by the Belgian company Interbrew, and Molson by the American beer giant Coors. Canadians are usually loyal to a particular brand (74 percent) as opposed to Americans, who showed only 65 percent brand loyalty. Consumers will switch brands if there is a promotional giveaway or an ad that catches their interest. The highest brand-switching rates occur on the east coast and in Ontario, where roughly 40 percent will change brands for a giveaway like a T-shirt; in Quebec, 70 percent of beer buyers indicate no promotion incentive would cause them to try a different brand.

Most brands appeal to certain predictable segments of the population, like younger drinkers. Some brands, however, don't follow a pattern and cross into different market segments. One of these brands is Labatt 50. Labatt 50 is popular with older and younger drinkers in Quebec and Ontario. Quebecers like the brand because they think it is a Quebec beer, mainly because ads in the past have focused on French-Canadian themes. Ontario 50 drinkers think it is an Ontario beer so they have remained loyal. The ads for English Canada focused on high-energy, colourful themes that always included some upbeat music. The package size is also different in the two markets—jumbo size in Quebec, and regular size for the rest of the country. Labatt 50 appeals to the cool counterculture group mainly in the Toronto market. This group started taking it to parties because few others drank it so they would be assured that they could drink the beer they brought.

Another trend is emerging in the beer market mainly due to the aging boomer segment. These folks can't drink as much beer as when they were younger and have turned to premium beers. This accounts for the rapid rise of microbreweries, like Creemore, and to the 34.7 percent increase in imported beer sales.

Based on all the research for this market, it would be safe to say that beer companies are in for even more changes in the years to come. The factors contributing to these changes will be the aging boomer market and the fickle younger market. Want to bet on a sure thing? It's pretty certain that the majority of future beer drinkers will still be male.

Questions for Critical Thinking

1. If Labatt were to expand its target market for Labatt 50, which segment or segments of the market might the firm include?
2. How you would describe the positioning strategies of Molson and Labatt for their different beer brands?

Sources: "Control and Sale of Alcoholic Beverages," http://www.statcan.ca, accessed December 28, 2007; Ryan Bigge, "One Beer, Two Solitudes," *Marketing,* May 5, 2003, p. 12; Lesley Daw, "Joe vs. Stanley in Beer Share Battle," *Marketing,* June 5, 2000, p. 2; Dave Scholz and Jean-Marc Leger, "The Fickle Beer Consumer," *Marketing,* May 10, 2004, p. 22; David Menzies, "Crying in His Creemore," *Marketing,* May 23, 2005, p. 11.

Case 8.2

Beauty at Every Age

Unilever, which describes itself as a multi-local, multinational company, is big. They have operations in over 80 countries and are a force in markets from soup to soap since 1872. With brands like Sunlight Soap, Knorr food products, Hellmann's mayonnaise, Axe grooming products for men—and many more—Unilever covers many segments. Having so many different products to market would present a challenge for most companies, but Unilever has found success by "putting a positive social message" into its promotional material and creating meaningful experiences for its customers. The results are impressive—not only has the company won many prestigious awards but sales, market share, and ROI have increased.

One product line, Dove, has been particularly successful. The company did a global study on how women viewed themselves. The results showed that only 2 percent of women internationally viewed themselves as beautiful—in Canada it was only 1 percent. This study and its overwhelming results were the driving force behind the "Real Beauty" Campaign, which aimed to get women of all ages to rethink their definitions of beauty while at the same time reposition the Dove product line as "an agent of change" in today's society. The campaign included different tactics for each age category and product within the line but the central theme was the same: we need to change the stereotypes of what is beauty and get women, of all ages, feeling better about themselves.

For women over 50, Unilever's global study showed that 91 percent of these women thought it was time for society to think more positively about aging. Not surprisingly, companies are listening to this age group because these are the boomers and there are a lot of them. The result was a new Dove product line—pro-age. The pro-age line includes products for the hair, face care, cleaners, and lotions. The products in this line were designed to meet the changing needs of women as they get older. For example, the hair products give extra fullness and thickness.

Unilever's commitment to reducing the influence of stereotypes and promoting its products can be seen in its "Real Beauty" campaign. For a number of years, Dove had used real women, not models, in ads. These women, in all shapes, sizes, cultural backgrounds, and ages, are portrayed in the ads without any altering or retouching of photos. For the pro-age line, the women, all age appropriate, appear without any clothes. The "Real Beauty" campaign also includes some less traditional marketing techniques, such as developing a play where older women talk to their bodies; for younger women, it's the Dove Self-Esteem Fund. The Self-Esteem fund aims to change the attitudes about beauty of 5 million younger women by 2010.

The success of these initiatives has been overwhelming. In a two-year period Dove sales in Canada increased 18 percent in the first year and another 12 percent the following year. These numbers are pretty impressive considering that Dove was already the number one cleansing product in the world.

Questions for Critical Thinking

1. Unilever segments by age and product. Can you think of other ways in which Unilever might segment its market?
2. What type of strategy would likely be best for reaching Dove's target market? Why?

Sources: http://www.unilever.ca, accessed December 29, 2007; Rebecca Harris, "Dove at First Sight," *Marketing,* December 10, 2007, pp. 22–28.

Video Case 8.3

Harley-Davidson Rules the Road by Understanding Its Customers

The written case on Harley-Davidson appears on page VC-11. The recently filmed Harley-Davidson video is designed to expand and highlight the concepts in this chapter and the concepts and questions covered in the written video.

chapter **9**

Relationship Marketing and Customer Relationship Management (CRM)

CHAPTER OBJECTIVES

1. Contrast transaction-based marketing with relationship marketing.

2. Identify and explain the four basic elements of relationship marketing as well as the importance of internal marketing.

3. Identify the three levels of the relationship marketing continuum.

4. Explain how firms can enhance customer satisfaction and how they build buyer–seller relationships.

5. Explain customer relationship management (CRM) and the role of technology in building customer relationships.

6. Describe the buyer–seller relationship in business-to-business marketing, and identify the four types of business partnerships.

7. Describe how business-to-business marketing incorporates national account selling, electronic data interchange and web services, vendor-managed inventories (VMI), CPFaR, managing the supply chain, and creating alliances.

8. Identify and evaluate the most common measurement and evaluation techniques within a relationship marketing program.

COURTESY OF BEST BUY CANADA LTD.

BEST BUY BETS ON CUSTOMERS

Personal computing technology is becoming more and more sophisticated. Most consumers need more and more assistance to make their way through the retail maze. They must decide not only what to buy but how to install and network the equipment. And then there's maintenance and service. With all these complications, where can customers turn for help?

Best Buy has an answer. The $30-billion consumer electronics retailer has carefully studied its customers, their needs and habits, its own sales figures, census data, and the layout and appearance of its 900-plus stores, and it has formulated an innovative strategy for retaining its nearly 20 percent share of the Canadian and U.S. markets. In the past, says Brad Anderson, Best Buy's CEO, "we were treating every customer as though they were the same." But its research showed that the company was earning nearly half its sales from 10 percent of its customers. So Best Buy set out to court these big spenders with a new "centricity" approach that customizes the layouts of its stores and the services they offer for five separate categories of customers, which bear people's names.

"Barry" stores cater to the young-professional tech enthusiast with upscale TVs and home theatre systems. "Buzz" stores appeal to young gadget lovers and boast game consoles and a big selection of DVDs and CDs set amid inviting-looking black leather chairs. "Jill" stores try to soften the warehouse style of Best Buy's stores because research showed that female shoppers strongly disliked it. Personal shopping assistants at "Jill" stores are available to walk female customers through the purchase decision. "Ray" stores are pitched at the budget-conscious family man and emphasize flexible financing options, while "Mr. Storefront" locations are specialized for the small-business owner.

The centricity concept, backed by extensive sales and demographic research to identify the best personality for each individual store location, has been overwhelmingly successful. So Best Buy has accelerated its transformation to bring more of its stores into the centricity model sooner. "Barry" stores predominate, but some stores target more than one of the five profiles, such as "Jill and Barry" stores, and a few are designed to appeal to all five at once. Best Buy is even exploring three additional profiles—"Carrie," the young single woman, and "Helen and Charlie," the empty nesters.

The company typically spends hundreds of thousands of dollars per store to redo lighting and fixtures in its physical centricity transformation. But its biggest per-store investments are on training employees in specialized selling and customer relationship techniques and in financial measures that help them gauge for themselves the effectiveness of in-store marketing strategies.

And the customer-centric focus doesn't stop at the stores. The company's inventory and supply system is being revamped to add flexibility that allows stores to stock different goods for their own local markets. The service arm of Best Buy has also been beefed up with the purchase and expansion of the Geek Squad, a 24-hour computer service and support team. The Geek Squad boasts nearly 10 000 members who staff Best Buy's in-store service counters and make emergency house calls for fees that range up to about $300 for troubleshooting and repair.

Best Buy's competition is paying attention. Costco has formed a partnership with a company that installs flat-screen TVs and surround-sound systems, Circuit City is testing a variation on Best Buy's "centricity" concept in its stores, and Dell is offering higher levels of customer service than ever—for a fee.

The decision by Best Buy's management team to focus on something the discount stores, like Wal-Mart, and direct-to-customer models, like Dell, didn't offer—personalized customer service—was a good one.

connecting with customers

Best Buy did its homework, and its customers are pleased. One store visitor said, "They have the help when you need the help. Over the last few years, it's become the place to go." What has been good for the customer has also been for Best Buy's bottom line. Sales in the converted stores are nearly double other stores in the chain.[1]

Chapter Overview

AS Best Buy's success demonstrates, marketing revolves around relationships with customers and with all the business processes involved in identifying and satisfying them. The shift from **transaction-based marketing,** which focuses on short-term, one-time exchanges, to customer-focused relationship marketing is one of the most important trends in marketing today. Companies know that they cannot prosper simply by identifying and attracting new customers; to succeed, they must build loyal, mutually beneficial relationships with both new and existing customers, suppliers, distributors, and employees. This strategy benefits the bottom line because retaining customers costs much less than acquiring new ones. Building and managing long-term relationships between buyers and sellers are the hallmarks of relationship marketing. **Relationship marketing** is the development, growth, and maintenance of cost-effective, high-value relationships with individual customers, suppliers, distributors, retailers, and other partners for mutual benefit over time.

Relationship marketing is based on promises: the promise of low prices, the promise of high quality, the promise of prompt delivery, the promise of superior service. A network of promises—within the organization, between the organization and its supply chain, and between buyer and seller—determines whether a relationship will grow. A firm is responsible for ensuring it keeps or exceeds the agreements it makes, with the ultimate goal of achieving customer satisfaction.

This chapter examines the reasons organizations are moving toward relationship marketing and customer relationship management, explores the impact this move has on producers of goods and services and their customers, and looks at ways to evaluate customer relationship programs. ◆◆◆

transaction-based marketing Buyer and seller exchanges characterized by limited communications and little or no ongoing relationship between the parties.

relationship marketing Development, growth, and maintenance of long-term, cost-effective relationships with individual customers, suppliers, employees, and other partners for mutual benefit.

① Contrast transaction-based marketing with relationship marketing.

THE SHIFT FROM TRANSACTION-BASED MARKETING TO RELATIONSHIP MARKETING

Since the Industrial Revolution, most manufacturers have run production-oriented operations. They have focused on making products and then promoting them to customers in the hope of selling enough to cover costs and earn profits. The emphasis has been on individual sales or transactions. In transaction-based marketing, buyer and seller exchanges are characterized by limited communications and little or no ongoing relationships. The primary goal is to entice a buyer to make a purchase through such inducements as low price, convenience, or packaging. The goal is simple and short term: sell.

Some marketing exchanges remain largely transaction based. In residential real estate sales, for example, the primary goal of the agent is to make a sale and collect a commission. While the agent may seek to maintain the appearance of an ongoing buyer–seller relationship, in most cases, the possibility of future transactions is limited. The best an agent can hope for is to represent the seller again in a subsequent real estate deal that may be several years down the line or, more likely, to gain positive referrals to other buyers and sellers.

Today, many organizations have embraced an alternative approach. Relationship marketing views customers as equal partners in buyer–seller transactions. By motivating customers to enter a long-term relationship in which they repeat purchases or buy multiple brands from the firm, marketers obtain a clearer understanding of customer needs over time. This process leads to improved products or customer service, which pays off through increased sales and lower marketing costs. In addition, marketers have discovered that it is less expensive to retain satisfied customers than it is to attract new ones or to repair damaged relationships.

The move from transactions to relationships is reflected in the changing nature of the interactions between customers and sellers. In transaction-based marketing, exchanges with customers are generally sporadic and in some instances disrupted by conflict. As interactions become relationship oriented, however, conflict changes to cooperation, and infrequent contacts between buyers and sellers become ongoing exchanges.

As Figure 9.1 illustrates, relationship marketing emphasizes cooperation rather than conflict between all the parties involved. This ongoing collaborative exchange creates value for both parties and builds customer loyalty. Customer relationship management goes a step further and integrates the customer's needs into all aspects of the firm's operations and its relationships with suppliers, distributors, and strategic partners. It combines people, processes, and technology with the long-term goal of maximizing customer value through mutually satisfying interactions and transactions.

Twenty-first-century marketers now understand they must do more than simply create products and then sell them. With so many goods and services to choose from, customers look for added value from their marketing relationships. Owners of GM cars enrolled in the OnStar program, for instance, now get not only the vehicle with their purchase but also the benefits of OnStar's free Vehicle Diagnostics feature, now standard on all GM vehicles. Vehicle Diagnostics operates through OnStar's cellular-based system to perform checkups remotely and let customers know the status of their engine and transmission, air bags, and anti-lock brakes, as well as when to come in for an oil change or a recall. Says GM North America's vice president of vehicle sales, service, and marketing, "OnStar is not a program, it's a philosophy."[2]

In general, the differences between the narrow focus of transaction marketing and the much broader view of relationship marketing can be summarized as follows:

Relationship marketing:

- focuses on the long term rather than the short term

- emphasizes retaining customers over making a sale

- ranks customer service as a high priority

- encourages frequent customer contact

- fosters customer commitment with the firm

- bases customer interactions on cooperation and trust

- commits all employees to provide high-quality products

As a result, the buyer–seller bonds developed in a relationship marketing partnership last longer and cover a much wider scope than those developed in transaction marketing.

figure 9.1

Forms of Buyer–Seller Interactions on a Continuum from Conflict to Integration

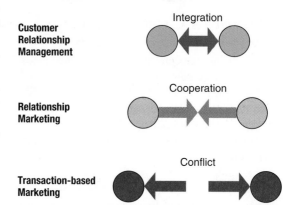

Source: From BOONE/KURTZ. *Contemporary Marketing*, 13th edition. © 2008 South-Western, a part of Cengage Learning, Inc. Reproduced by permission. www.cengage.com/permissions

assessment check 1

1.1 What are the major differences between transaction-based marketing and relationship marketing?

ELEMENTS OF RELATIONSHIP MARKETING

To build long-term customer relationships, marketers need to place customers at the centre of their efforts. When a company integrates customer service and quality with marketing, the result is a relationship marketing orientation.

But how do firms achieve these long-term relationships? They build them with four basic elements.

1. They gather information about their customers. Database technology, discussed later in this chapter, helps a company identify current and potential customers with selected demographic, purchase, and lifestyle characteristics.

② Identify and explain the four basic elements of relationship marketing as well as the importance of internal marketing.

Go Green

Toyota's Customer One Program

"Customer One" is Toyota's all-encompassing initiative to create the best customer satisfaction for both employees and customers. Global surveys have shown that Toyota scored tops in customer satisfaction, but it has yet to reach that point with the Canadian market. In an effort to improve the company's Canadian ratings, the "Customer One" program was introduced, involving everyone connected to Toyota, including other companies, employees, and dealerships. The program covers product development, such as hybrid cars; process improvements, such as reduction of manufacturing times and the elimination of waste; and social responsibility through the Learning Ground program.

Toyota was the first to mass-produce a hybrid car, the Prius, in 1997. It has continued to work on hybrid technology and now has several hybrid models on the road, including the top-selling North American family car, the Camry. Toyota uses that same philosophy in its manufacturing plants. In 2000, it set a goal to reduce waste in the manufacturing process to 10 kilograms per vehicle. This target was reached and the company now has production waste below 7 kilograms per vehicle.

Toyota Earth Day Scholarship Program and Toyota Evergreen Learning Grounds are two ways the company and its dealerships promote the environment in communities across Canada. The scholarship program rewards graduating high school students for their environmental work in their communities. The Learning Ground program is designed to transform schoolyards into natural learning environments by providing expert assistance, funds, and information packages to participating schools. The Learning Ground program has involved over 250 000 students and in one year alone implemented the program in 132 schools.

Toyota has accomplished a great deal in its attempt to improve its impact on the environment but it is not finished. It has an ongoing commitment that "starts with design and development, continues through manufacture, distribution and sales, even when the vehicles are in the hands of their customers and does not end until the vehicle is retired in an eco-friendly manner."

Sources: Mary Dickie, "The Greener Machine: Yoichi Tomihara Incorporates the Toyota Way Into His Drive for Environmental and Sales Supremacy," *Strategy*, December 2007, p. 17; http://www.toyota.ca, accessed January 4, 2008.

2. They analyze the data they have collected and use it to modify their marketing mix to deliver differentiated messages and customized marketing programs to individual consumers.

3. Through relationship marketing, they monitor their interactions with customers. They can assess the customer's level of satisfaction or dissatisfaction with their service. Marketers can also calculate the cost of attracting one new customer and figure out how much profit that customer will generate during the relationship. Information is fed back, and they are then able to seek ways to add value to the buyer–seller transaction so that the relationship will continue.

4. With customer relationship management (CRM) software, they use intimate knowledge of customers and customer preferences to orient every part of the organization, including both its internal and external partners, toward building a unique company differentiation that is based on strong, unbreakable bonds with customers. Sophisticated technology and the Internet help make that happen.

One company that demonstrates relationship marketing and shows how successful it can be is Toyota Canada, as discussed in the "Go Green" Box.

INTERNAL MARKETING

The concepts of customer satisfaction and relationship marketing are usually discussed in terms of **external customers**—people or organizations that buy or use a firm's goods or services. But marketing in organizations concerned with customer satisfaction and long-term relationships must also address **internal customers**—employees or departments within the organization whose success depends on the work of other employees or departments. A person processing an order for a new piece of equipment is the internal customer of the salesperson who completed the sale, just as the person who bought the product is the salesperson's external customer. Although the order processor might never directly encounter an external customer, his or her performance can have a direct impact on the overall value the firm is able to deliver.

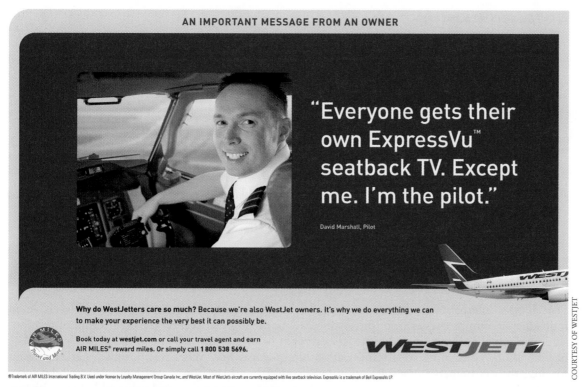

AN IMPORTANT MESSAGE FROM AN OWNER

"Everyone gets their own ExpressVu™ seatback TV. Except me. I'm the pilot."

David Marshall, Pilot

Why do WestJetters care so much? Because we're also WestJet owners. It's why we do everything we can to make your experience the very best it can possibly be.

Book today at westjet.com or call your travel agent and earn AIR MILES® reward miles. Or simply call 1 800 538 5696.

WESTJET

®Trademark of AIR MILES International Trading B.V. Used under license by Loyalty Management Group Canada Inc. and WestJet. Most of WestJet's aircraft are currently equipped with live seatback television. ExpressVu is a trademark of Bell ExpressVu LP.

COURTESY OF WESTJET

WestJet ranks as one of Canada's most admired corporate cultures.

Internal marketing involves managerial actions that enable all members of an organization to understand, accept, and fulfill their respective roles in implementing a marketing strategy. Good internal customer satisfaction helps organizations attract, select, and retain outstanding employees who appreciate and value their role in the delivery of superior service to external customers. With time to market growing ever shorter, Procter & Gamble, for instance, has to make sure that collaboration and the sharing of information among its more than 100 000 employees—and between them and suppliers, distributors, and retailers—is as quick and easy as possible. The company recently adopted a five-product package of Microsoft software that includes instant messaging, a document-sharing program, and a conference service in order to maximize these internal communications.[3]

Employee knowledge and involvement are important goals of internal marketing. Companies that excel at satisfying customers typically place a priority on keeping employees informed about corporate goals, strategies, and customer needs. Employees must also have the necessary tools to address customer requests and problems in a timely manner. Company-wide computer networks aid the flow of communications between departments and functions. Several companies—like Procter & Gamble—also include key suppliers on their networks to speed and ease communication of all aspects of business from product design to inventory control.

Employee satisfaction is another critical objective of internal marketing. Employees can seldom, if ever, satisfy customers when they themselves are unhappy. Dissatisfied employees are likely to spread negative word-of-mouth messages to relatives, friends, and acquaintances, and these reports can affect purchasing behaviour. Satisfied employees buy their employer's products, tell friends and families how good the customer service is, and ultimately send a powerful message to customers. One recommended strategy for offering consistently good service is to attract good employees, hire good employees, and retain good employees.[4]

WestJet, known for its customer service, relies on its employees, also referred to as WestJetters, to turn its corporate values of being the fun and friendly airline into its core marketing strategy. WestJet has been able to communicate its focus on employees and their contribution to customer satisfaction to the flying public. It has accomplished this not only through its marketing communications but by establishing a "Guest Experience Committee," composed of employees, that reviews every aspect of WestJet's operations.[5]

Marketoid

In 2005 online sales increased 38.4 percent to $39.2 billion.

assessment check 2

2.1 What are the four basic elements of relationship marketing?

2.2 Why is internal marketing important to a firm?

table 9.1   *Three Levels of Relationship Marketing*

CHARACTERISTIC	LEVEL 1	LEVEL 2	LEVEL 3
Primary bond	Financial	Social	Structural
Degree of customization	Low	Medium	Medium to high
Potential for sustained competitive advantage	Low	Moderate	High
Examples	Car dealer's no-interest financing plan	Harley-Davidson's Harley Owners Group (HOG)	Chapter's member program of discounts and special offers

Source: Reprinted with the permission of The Free Press, a Division of Simon & Schuster Adult Publishing Group, from MARKETING SERVICES: Competing Through Quality by Leonard L. Berry and A. Parasuraman. Copyright © 1991 by The Free Press. All Rights Reserved.

(3) Identify the three levels of the relationship marketing continuum.

THE RELATIONSHIP MARKETING CONTINUUM

Like all other interpersonal relationships, buyer–seller relationships function at a variety of levels. As an individual or firm progresses from the lowest level to the highest level on the continuum of relationship marketing, as shown in Table 9.1, the strength of commitment between the parties grows. The likelihood of a continuing, long-term relationship grows as well. Whenever possible, marketers want to move their customers along this continuum, converting them from Level 1 purchasers, who focus mainly on price, to Level 3 customers, who receive specialized services and value-added benefits that may not be available from another firm.

FIRST LEVEL: FOCUS ON PRICE

Interactions at the first level of relationship marketing are the most superficial and the least likely to lead to a long-term relationship. In the most prevalent examples of this first level, relationship marketing efforts rely on pricing and other financial incentives to motivate customers to enter into buying relationships with a seller. North American automakers have used extensive discounts and sales incentives to attract customers, for instance. In one recent month the industry—led by GM, Ford, and Chrysler—spent nearly $3 billion on incentives. DaimlerChrysler offered five-year no-interest financing on select vehicles, and Chrysler also offered cash back and reduced interest rates, or a bonus on leased cars. Ford matched customers' down payments.[6]

Although these programs can be attractive to users, they may not create long-term buyer relationships. Because the programs are not customized to the needs of individual buyers, they are easily duplicated by competitors. The lesson is that it takes more than a low price or other financial incentives to create a long-term relationship between buyer and seller.

SECOND LEVEL: SOCIAL INTERACTIONS

As buyers and sellers reach the second level of relationship marketing, their interactions develop on a social level—one that features deeper and less superficial links than the financially motivated first level. Sellers have begun to learn that social relationships with buyers can be very effective marketing tools. Customer service and communication are key factors at this stage.

Social interaction can take many forms. The owner of a local shoe store or dry cleaner might chat with customers about local events. An art gallery may host a reception for artists and customers. The service department of an auto dealership might call a customer after a repair to see whether the customer is satisfied or has any questions. An investment firm might send holiday cards to all its customers. MySpace.com, the hugely popular social networking site, is all

The first level of relationship marketing.

BRAND X PICTURES/©2008 JUPITERIMAGES CORPORATION

about social interaction. "The secret to our success is our one-to-one relationship with our users," says Chris DeWolfe, co-founder and CEO of the service. "All the site's features have stemmed from users' requests." Despite the recent acquisition of MySpace by News Corp., DeWolfe says, "We don't plan to change that at all."[7]

THIRD LEVEL: INTERDEPENDENT PARTNERSHIP

At the third level of relationship marketing, relationships are transformed into structural changes that ensure buyer and seller are true business partners. As buyer and seller work more closely together, they develop a dependence on one another that continues to grow over time. Chapters maintains a "member program" that rewards members with a 10 percent discount on nearly every item in the store and a 5 percent discount for online purchases, plus member-only special offers and discounts, for a membership fee of $25 a year. Both the store and the customer benefit from the program—the store develops a loyal customer who makes repeat purchases, and the customer gets discounts and other offers that offset the membership fee.[8]

> **assessment check 3**
>
> **3.1** Identify the three levels of the marketing relationship.
>
> **3.2** Which level is the most complicated? Why?

ENHANCING CUSTOMER SATISFACTION

④ Explain how firms can enhance customer satisfaction and how they build buyer–seller relationships.

Marketers monitor customer satisfaction through various methods of marketing research. As part of an ongoing relationship with customers, marketers must continually measure and improve how well they meet customer needs. As Figure 9.2 shows, three major steps are involved in this process: understanding customer needs, obtaining customer feedback, and instituting an ongoing program to ensure customer satisfaction. The research methods available to institute an ongoing customer satisfaction program are discussed in the Chapter 7.

UNDERSTANDING CUSTOMER NEEDS

Knowledge of what customers need, want, and expect is a central concern of companies focused on building long-term relationships. This information is also a vital first step in setting up a system to measure **customer satisfaction**. Marketers must carefully monitor the characteristics of their product that really matter to customers. They also must remain constantly alert to new elements that might affect satisfaction.

Satisfaction can be measured in terms of the gaps between what customers xpect and what they perceive they have received. Such gaps can produce favourable or unfavourable impressions. Goods or services may be better or worse than expected. If they are better, marketers can use the opportunity to create loyal customers.

If goods or services are worse than expected, a company may start to lose customers. A recent survey found that Dell's customer satisfaction rating fell more than 6 percent, a big drop for the company that used to head the list of top performers on customer service. In one year there were 23 percent more complaints about Dell, and another 5 percent the following year. In the past, dependable customer support has allowed Dell to increase its market share in the consumer market, helped by low prices and a convenient direct-to-customer sales model. But some observers predict that unhappy customers will spread the word. In the meantime, Dell is improving its service by shortening wait times to speak with a technician, offering remote assistance that lets its technicians access the customer's PC software and fix it, and providing one-year service-desk memberships through which Dell users can customize the level of support they want. However, all these options come with a fee or only with the purchase of a higher-end computer. Even "free shipping" now means shipping to the nearest post office for pickup by the customer.[9]

figure 9.2

Three Steps to Measure Customer Satisfaction

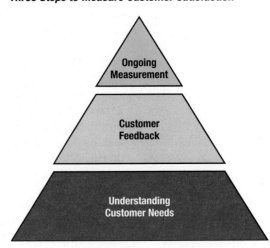

What if there is such a thing as **too much golf** when you retire?

To explore this and other unexpected questions, talk to an RBC advisor today.

You know there's more to retirement than golf, travel and long walks on the beach. But what exactly does "more" mean to you? To help you answer that, an RBC advisor can take you through our unique discovery and planning process. It all starts by asking you a few unexpected questions that get right to the heart of what's really important to you. All to help you set the right course for your retirement. So for a conversation about finances that's more than just about finances, make an appointment today.

Call now to have an RBC mobile financial planner come to your home.
📞 1-866-335-4055   🖥 rbc.com/yourfuture

vancouver 2010   RBC PREMIER NATIONAL PARTNER   F🏌RST > FOR YOU

COURTESY RBC

Investment advice and financial planning services are provided by Royal Mutual Funds Inc. Royal Mutual Funds Inc. is licensed as a financial services firm in the province of Quebec. ®Registered trademarks of Royal Bank of Canada. Used under license. ©Royal Bank of Canada 2007. "© 2005, VANOC. Under license.

RBC: Assuring customers they get more than they expect.

To avoid unfavourable gaps, marketers need to keep in touch with the needs of current and potential customers. They must look beyond traditional performance measures and explore the factors that determine purchasing behaviour to formulate customer-based missions, goals, and performance standards.

OBTAINING CUSTOMER FEEDBACK AND ENSURING CUSTOMER SATISFACTION

The second step in measuring customer satisfaction is to compile feedback from customers regarding current performance. Increasingly, marketers try to improve customers' access to their companies by including toll-free 800 numbers or website addresses in their advertising. Most firms rely on reactive methods of collecting feedback. Rather than solicit complaints, they might, for example, monitor blogs or other online discussion groups to track customers' comments and attitudes about the value received. Some companies hire mystery shoppers, who visit or call businesses posing as customers, to evaluate the service they receive. Their unbiased appraisals are usually conducted semiannually or quarterly to monitor employees, diagnose problem areas in customer service, and measure the impact of employee training.

Some companies are using websites to obtain customers' feedback, allowing them to accurately identify and respond to customers' needs. Recently, Dell launched ideastorm.com, where ideas are submitted for improvements to products or services. Once the ideas submitted are considered by the company, the website is used to survey customers in order to determine the demand for idea.[10]

Any method that makes it easier for customers to complain actually benefits a firm. Customer complaints offer firms the opportunity to overcome problems and prove their commitment to service. People often have greater loyalty to a company after a conflict has been resolved than if they had never complained at all.

Many organizations also use proactive methods to assess customer satisfaction, including visiting, calling, or mailing out surveys to clients to find out their level of satisfaction. Companies are also paying more and more attention to the millions of bloggers on the Internet. One cell phone company benefited from blog watching, which helped inspire a new promotion aimed at teenagers. The company used special technology to identify the demographics of online groups by comparing their speech patterns and discussion topics. The company found that teen cell phone users resented the fact that incoming calls were charged to their allowable minutes, leading the cell phone company to offer unlimited "call me" minutes in its next promotion.[11]

assessment check 4

4.1   How is customer satisfaction measured?

4.2   Identify ways that marketers may obtain customer feedback.

BUILDING BUYER–SELLER RELATIONSHIPS

Marketers of consumer goods and services have discovered that they must do more than simply create products and then sell them. With a dizzying array of products to choose from, many customers are seeking ways to simplify both their business and personal lives, and relationships provide a way to do this.

One reason consumers form continuing relationships is their desire to reduce choices. Through relationships, they can simplify information gathering and the entire buying process as well as decrease the risk of dissatisfaction. They find comfort in brands that have become familiar through their ongoing relationships with companies. Such relationships may lead to more efficient decision making by customers and higher levels of customer satisfaction.

A key benefit to consumers in long-term buyer–seller relationships is the perceived positive value they receive. Relationships add value because of increased opportunities for frequent customers to save money through discounts, rebates, and similar offers; via special recognition from the relationship programs; and through convenience in shopping.

Marketers should also understand why consumers end relationships. Computerized technologies and the Internet have made consumers better informed than ever before by giving them unprecedented abilities to compare prices, merchandise, and customer service. If they perceive that a competitor's product or customer service is better, customers may switch loyalties. Many consumers dislike feeling that they are locked into a relationship with one company, and that is reason enough for them to try a competing item next time they buy. Some customers simply become bored with their current providers and decide to sample the competition.

HOW MARKETERS KEEP CUSTOMERS

One of the major forces driving the push from transaction-based marketing to relationship marketing is the realization that retaining customers is far more profitable than losing them. A recent study found that marketers, on average,

LIFE'S BRIGHTER *under the sun*

ADVERTISING: ACLC INC. PHOTOGRAPHY: GEORGE SIMHONI - WESTSIDE STUDIO MODEL: MAGDALENA ALEXANDER / KING TALENT

Sun Life: Adding value by providing a wide range of products and services.

- have a 60 to 70 percent chance of selling again to the same customer

- have a 20 to 40 percent chance of winning back an ex-customer

- have only a 5 to 20 percent chance of converting a prospect into a customer[12]

Also, customers usually enable a firm to generate more profits with each additional year of the relationship. A good example of this is the Hudson's Bay Company's rewards program, one of the largest in Canada. The millions of members earn points for every purchase made at any one of the Hbc group of stores, including the Bay, Zellers, Home Outfitters, Designer Depot, or Shop.hbc.com. Customers who spend more are rewarded with extra points. The program allows customers to combine their rewards points card with an Hbc credit card or Hbc MasterCard.[13]

Programs like the Hudson's Bay Company's are an example of **frequency marketing.** These programs reward top customers with cash, rebates, merchandise, or other premiums. Buyers who purchase an item more often earn higher rewards. Frequency marketing focuses on a company's best customers with the goal of increasing their motivation to buy even more of the same or other products from the seller.

Many different types of companies use frequency programs, from fast-food restaurants, retail stores, and telecommunications companies to travel firms. Popular programs include airline frequent-flyer programs, such as Air Canada's Aeroplan, and retail programs, such as Staples Card.

The Internet is proving a fertile medium for frequency-marketing initiatives. Borrowing from the airlines' frequent-flyer model, one American casino has created a web-based program to reward frequent gamblers. About 80 percent of the customers who visit the casino each day are members of the Total Rewards program. Loyalty cards are swiped in the casino to monitor time spent at slot machines or card tables and to total up the sums gambled. A website allows members to view their points and learn how to earn more benefits as they gamble their way up to platinum or diamond status. The program also identifies which so-called high rollers yield the highest profits.[14]

In addition to frequency programs, companies use **affinity marketing** to retain customers. Each of us holds certain things dear. Some feel strongly about their college or university, while for others it's

frequency marketing
Frequent buyer or user marketing programs that reward customers with cash, rebates, merchandise, or other premiums.

affinity marketing
Marketing effort sponsored by an organization that solicits responses from individuals who share common interests and activities.

a sports team or not-for-profit organization. These examples, along with an almost unending variety of others, are subjects of affinity programs. An affinity program is a marketing effort sponsored by an organization that solicits involvement by individuals who share common interests and activities. With affinity programs, organizations create extra value for members and encourage stronger relationships.

Affinity credit cards are a popular form of this marketing technique. The sponsor's name appears prominently in promotional materials, on the card itself, and on monthly statements. For example, the Bank of Montreal offers so many affinity cards, their website has them grouped by category such as Arts and Culture and Pets and Animal Welfare.[15]

Not all affinity programs involve credit cards. One public television station thanks members who contribute more than $40 annually with a card that entitles them to discounts at participating restaurants, museums, theatres, hotels, and car rental companies.[16]

DATABASE MARKETING

database marketing
Use of software to analyze marketing information, identifying and targeting messages toward specific groups of potential customers.

The use of information technology to analyze data about customers and their transactions is referred to as **database marketing.** The results form the basis of new advertising or promotions targeted to carefully identified groups of customers. Database marketing is a particularly effective tool for building relationships because it allows sellers to sort through huge quantities of data from multiple sources on the buying habits or preferences of thousands or even millions of customers. Companies can then track buying patterns, develop customer relationship profiles, customize their offerings and sales promotions, and even personalize customer service to suit the needs of targeted groups of customers. Properly used, databases can help companies in several ways, including these:

- identifying their most profitable customers

- calculating the lifetime value of each customer's business

- creating a meaningful dialogue that builds relationships and encourages genuine brand loyalty

- improving customer retention and referral rates

- reducing marketing and promotion costs

- boosting sales volume per customer or targeted customer group

Where do organizations find all the data that fill these vast marketing databases? Everywhere! Credit card applications, software registration, and product warranties all provide vital statistics of individual customers. Point-of-sale register scanners, customer opinion surveys, and sweepstakes entry forms may offer not just details of name and address but information on preferred brands and shopping habits. Websites offer free access in return for personal data, allowing companies to amass increasingly rich marketing information.

Maserati, the Italian luxury car manufacturer, uses database marketing in Canada. Masersati found that Canada is one of its hottest growth markets, particularly for its Quattroporte, a four-door sedan model. The problem the company encountered was the perception that customers could not afford the car. A direct marketing firm helped Maserati identify potential customers based on household income, current car ownership, and proximity to other Maserati owners. The aim was to get these customers into the dealers. The campaign was successful with sales increases of more than 100 percent a year.[17]

New technologies such as radio frequency identification (RFID) allow retailers to identify shipping pallets and cargo containers, but most observers anticipate that in the near future RFID will be cost effective enough to permit tagging of individual store items, allowing retailers to gather information about the purchaser as well as managing inventory and deterring theft, but raising privacy concerns.[18]

Interactive television promises to deliver even more valuable data—information on real consumer behaviour and attitudes toward brands. Linked to digital television, sophisticated set-top boxes already collect vast amounts of data on television viewer behaviour, organized in incredible detail. As the technology makes its way into more homes, marketers receive firsthand knowledge of the kind of programming and products their targeted customers want. In addition, rather than using television to

Solving an Ethical Controversy

Too Much Data, Not Enough Protection?

ONE leading e-mail marketer was accused of making unauthorized use of personal data it "mined" from other unsuspecting firms, including 6 million e-mail addresses of consumers who were then sent unwanted electronic advertising messages. The case, called the largest deliberate breach of Internet privacy so far discovered, was settled with a $1.1-million fine and an agreement that the company would change its practices.

In another case, the theft of data from Polo Ralph Lauren forced banks and credit card companies to inform about 180 000 MasterCard holders that their credit card information might have been exposed to criminals and to admit that other cards might be at risk.

Are marketers doing enough to protect the information they collect about customers?

PRO

1. Marketers are doing the best they can. There are no uniform privacy laws to guide companies about how to protect data.

2. Companies realize the importance of their databases, but there is little a company can do against a determined thief.

CON

1. Companies are collecting more data than they have the resources to protect. They need to take a hard look at what data they actually need and develop policies to limit data collection.

2. Organizations need to spend more resources to secure valuable customer data. If they can't, the government should regulate how much data can be gathered and the uses companies can make of it.

Where do you stand: pro or con?

Sources: Christopher Wolf, "Dazed and Confused: Data Law Disarray," *BusinessWeek*, April 3, 2006, http://www.businessweek.com; Roy Mark, "Data-Breach Disclosure Bill Passes House Panel," Internetnews.com, March 30, 2006, http://www.internet-news.com; Michael Gormley, "Firm to Pay $1.1M to Settle E-Mail Case," Associated Press, March 12, 2006, http://news.yahoo.com; "Polo Ralph Lauren Customers' Data Stolen," Associated Press, April 14, 2005, http://story.news.yahoo.com.

advertise to the masses, they can talk directly to the viewers most interested in their products. At a click of a button, viewers can skip ads, but they also can click to a full-length infomercial on any brand that captures their interest.[19]

As database marketing has become more complex, a variety of software tools and services enables marketers to target consumers more and more narrowly while enriching their communications to selected groups. After all, a huge collection of data isn't valuable unless it can be turned into information that is useful to a firm's marketers. **Application service providers (ASPs)** assist marketers by providing software when it is needed to capture, manipulate, and analyze masses of consumer data. One type of software collects data on product specifications and details, which marketers can use to isolate products that best meet a customer's needs. This feature would be particularly important in selling business products that are expensive and require high involvement in making a purchase decision. One company provides such database services to non-profit organizations that are trying to cultivate a wider base of members and supporters. The company supplies software and online services designed to help groups such as Easter Seals, Mothers Against Drunk Driving, the Avon Foundation, museums, and other organizations identify and communicate with contributors. HCI Direct, a large direct marketing company selling hosiery products in Canada, the United States, and the United Kingdom, has about 2 million active customers worldwide. It works with an ASP to build a database that allows HCI to conduct offline and one-to-one communication with current and prospective customers.[20]

Firms can also use database marketing to rebuild customer relationships that may have lapsed. One telecommunications service provides voice, e-mail, and chat capabilities for its corporate clients to help them customize sales and marketing programs to gain new customers and win lost customers back.[21]

With the ability to gather almost unlimited amounts of customer information comes the responsibility for safeguarding it and protecting customers from unauthorized use. The "Solving an Ethical Controversy" feature provides some insight into the debate over how much protection is enough.

WE ARE
CLOSE TO YOU
YOU CAN
DEPEND ON US

LFS Laurentian Financial Services is pleased to announce its new corporate brand name. From now, we will be known as "Desjardins Financial Security Independent Network."

With more than 1,000 financial associates in 34 financial centres, we are committed to assuring you a better quality of life, and helping you achieve a perfect balance between financial security and financial freedom. Our expertise in life and health insurance, retirement planning and asset management will provide you with the peace of mind you and your family deserve.

We are associated with Desjardins Financial Security, the fourth largest insurer in Canada that supports more than five million Canadians throughout life's stages. From our large combination of insurance and savings products, we enable you to design the safety net you need to protect your quality of life and help you achieve your financial goals.

Support and guidance... that's what we're all about!

We are close to you
Contact us for more information

1-877-438-7656

desjardinsfinancialsecurity.com/partner

® Registered trademark owned by Desjardins Financial Security

Desjardins
Financial Security®
Independent Network

Life, health, retirement

COURTESY DESJARDINS FINANCIAL SECURITY

Desjardins: Offering support for one-to-one marketing.

CUSTOMERS AS ADVOCATES

Recent relationship marketing efforts are focusing on turning customers from passive partners into active proponents of a product. **Grassroots marketing** involves connecting directly with existing and potential customers through non-mainstream channels. The grassroots approach relies on marketing strategies that are unconventional, nontraditional, not by the book, and extremely flexible. Grassroots marketing is sometimes characterized by a relatively small budget and lots of legwork, but its hallmark is the ability to develop long-lasting, individual relationships with loyal customers.

With **viral marketing**, firms let satisfied customers get the word about products out to other consumers—like a spreading virus. In the mid-1990s, Hotmail's founders added a simple line of text at the end of every e-mail sent, offering recipients their own free Hotmail accounts. The result brought 8.7 million users in 18 months, and online viral marketing was born. Video clips are a popular tactic for viral marketing efforts on the Internet, according to a recent survey, and the most popular means of encouraging recipients to spread the news are encouraging them to forward an e-mail and including an easy way to refer others to a website, such as a "tell a friend" box to click.[22] Burger King has found viral marketing especially useful in reversing sales declines because it is an effective way to reach the food chain's core target market, young men.[23]

Buzz marketing gathers volunteers to try products and then relies on them to talk about their experiences with their friends and colleagues. "Influencers," or early adopters of products, are ideal carriers of buzz marketing messages because their credibility makes their choices valuable among their peers. They are often recruited online through chat rooms, blogs, and instant messaging. Word of mouth, the idea behind buzz marketing, isn't new, but technology has made many more applications possible. Vespa used buzz marketing to introduce its scooters to people who talked about their "cool factor," and Ford lent its Focus cars to drivers for six months, hoping they would make personal recommendations to others.[24] Techniques in this area are still evolving; marketing professionals are developing rules and standards for transparency in buzz marketing efforts that they hope will prevent fraud and preserve the value of buzz marketing.[25]

⑤ Explain customer relationship management (CRM) and the role of technology in building customer relationships.

customer relationship management (CRM) Combination of strategies and tools that drives relationship programs, reorienting the entire organization to a concentrated focus on satisfying customers.

CUSTOMER RELATIONSHIP MANAGEMENT

Emerging from—and closely linked to—relationship marketing, **customer relationship management (CRM)** is the combination of strategies and technologies that empowers relationship programs, reorienting the entire organization to a concentrated focus on satisfying customers. Made possible by technological advances, it leverages technology as a means to manage customer relationships and to integrate all stakeholders into a company's product design and development, manufacturing, marketing, sales, and customer service processes.

CRM represents a shift in thinking for everyone involved with a firm—from the CEO down—and encompassing all other key stakeholders, including suppliers, dealers, and other partners. All recognize that solid customer relations are fostered by similarly strong relationships with other major stakeholders. Since CRM goes well beyond traditional sales, marketing, or customer service functions, it requires a top-down commitment and must permeate every aspect of a firm's business. Technology makes that possible by allowing firms—regardless of size and no matter how far-flung their operations—to manage activities across functions, from location to location, and among their internal and external partners.

BENEFITS OF CRM

CRM software systems are capable of making sense of the vast amounts of customer data that technology allows firms to collect. An electrical connector's manufacturer was looking for a way to track pending sales to forecast revenue more accurately. With CRM software from a German firm, the company has been able to improve its forecasts dramatically and also set up more efficient workflows, such as identifying sales prospects with preset criteria and routing them to the appropriate area for follow-up.[26]

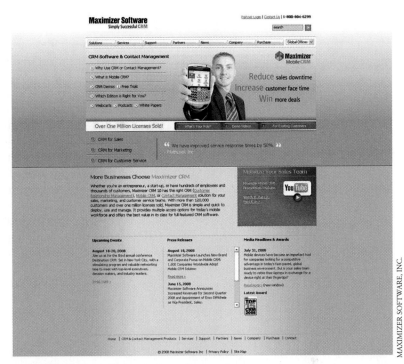

Another key benefit of customer relationship management systems is that they simplify complex business processes while keeping the best interests of customers at heart. CRM software also helped a medical supply company track customer feedback about its medical devices. Thanks to improved technology, the company seamlessly integrated the software into its existing systems.[27]

Selecting the right CRM software system can be critical to the success of a firm's entire CRM program. CRM can be used at three different levels—individual, server-based, and Internet-based—or combination of them. Most business applications are server-based

Maximizer software: Simplifying CRM systems.

(designed for several people to use) or Internet-based (with almost unlimited flexibility and value but some loss of privacy).[28] A firm may choose to buy a system from a company or rent hosted CRM applications through websites. Purchasing a customized system can cost a firm millions of dollars and take months to implement, while hosted solutions—rented through a website—are cheaper and quicker to get up and running. But purchasing a system allows a firm to expand and customize, whereas hosted systems are more limited. Experienced marketers also warn that it is easy to get mired in a system that is complicated for staff to use.

Software solutions are just one component of a successful CRM initiative. The most effective companies approach customer relationship management as a complete business strategy, in which people, processes, and technology are all organized around delivering superior value to customers. Successful CRM systems share the following qualities:

- They are results driven. The firm must decide on specific goals and benefits before attempting to implement a CRM strategy.

- They communicate effectively across functions. Effective customer relationship management depends on cross-disciplinary teams, such as sales and customer service, that work together to solve customer problems.

- They are streamlined. A concentrated focus on the customers allows firms to weed out wasteful business practices.

- They provide a complete and up-to-date picture of the customer that is easily shared within the company.

- They help identify new markets and sales opportunities.

- They reduce response time and increase customer retention.

- They constantly seek improvement. By tracking and measuring results, firms can continuously improve relationships with customers.[29]

Once the groundwork has been laid, technology leads firms toward a clearer understanding of each customer and his or her needs.

PROBLEMS WITH CRM

CRM is not a magic wand. The strategy needs to be thought out in advance, everyone in the firm must be committed to it, and everyone must understand how to use it. If no one can put the system to work, it is an expensive mistake.

Experts explain that failures with CRM often result from failure to organize—or reorganize—the company's people and business processes to take advantage of the benefits the CRM system can offer. Such planning failures can be prevented by mapping out the organization's existing structure and ensuring that CRM's information flows will be directed to the right employees, who will be trained to use them.[30] Other problems arise when data are not input to the CRM program accurately and on a regular basis. A number of human workflow processes need to be made automatic in order for a CRM system to yield the information it was designed to produce.[31] As one CRM specialist says, "Just reorganizing a company around a new customer focus doesn't mean that a company is doing CRM. Even applying new technologies to enable that customer focus isn't necessarily CRM. CRM is not only changing that focus but changing the business processes around that focus to support a new customer focus, and it's applying technologies to automate those new business processes."[32]

ETIQUTTE TIPS FOR MARKETING PROFESSIONALS

How to Deal with Rude People

NEARLY 70 percent of respondents to a recent poll said that rudeness is on the rise, spurred by gadgets such as PDAs and cell phones that encourage users to focus on themselves rather than on the people around them. Other factors blamed are the demand for instant gratification, the hurried pace of modern life, and a general decline of formality and rules for behaviour. How can you best deal with others who are rude? Here are some tips.

In the office:

- Set the example by always exhibiting thoughtful behaviour.
- If someone is rude, control your first reaction, which might be anger or annoyance, and look for some good in the individual, or in the skills or abilities he or she brings to the workplace.
- Remember that everyone has a bad day once in a while.
- Let the person know, politely and quietly, that rudeness in your firm is counterproductive.
- Ask specific questions about the person's behaviour to try to find out the reason for it. It might be a situation you can deal with or change.

In the retail environment:

- Ask polite questions to understand what will best satisfy the customer.

- Immediately and calmly take whatever steps you are authorized to in order to correct the situation that prompted the customer complaint. Refer the problem to a manager if you must.
- After ensuring that you've done everything you can, thank the customer for bringing the situation to your attention.

On the road:

- On your way to the office or a meeting, avoid rush-hour traffic, where aggressive or reckless driving most often occurs.
- Allow plenty of time to get to your destination so you won't be tempted to invite rude behaviour with your own anxiety.

Finally:

- Remember that other people's rudeness is not your fault. Don't let their behaviour influence yours.

Sources: Peter Murphy, "How to Quickly and Easily Deal with Rude People," Ezine Articles, http://ezinearticles.com, accessed April 4, 2006; Loretta Chao, "As Workloads Increase, So Does Office Rudeness," *The Wall Street Journal*, January 23, 2006, accessed at http://www.collegejournal.com; Donna Cassata, "Poll Shows Rudeness Growing within U.S.," *Morning News*, October 15, 2005, p. 1B.

RETRIEVING LOST CUSTOMERS

Customers defect from an organization's goods and services for a variety of reasons. They might be bored, they might move away from the region, they might not need the product anymore, or they might have tried—and preferred—competing products. Figure 9.3 illustrates the yearly defection rates for some industries. An increasingly important part of an effective CRM strategy is **customer winback**, the process of rejuvenating lost relationships with customers.

In many cases, a relationship gone sour can be sweetened again with the right approach. After the poor customer service ratings, Dell announced plans to open two large new customer service centres to help speed response time and improve the quality of help provided. Survey respondents had indicated that their problems were not with Dell's computers, but with the company's service time and service quality.[33] A good rule for service providers is to anticipate where problems will arise and figure out in advance how to prevent them in the first place. The second part of this strategy is to accept that mistakes will occur in even the best system and to have a high-quality recovery effort in place that employees are empowered to enact.[34]

Sometimes firms may need to change some of their strategies to win back customers or make them more profitable to a seller. To attract baby boom women to its new anti-aging cosmetics line, Cover Girl is reintroducing modelling superstar Christie Brinkley, now in her early 50s, who promoted the Cover Girl line for nearly 20 years until 1996. "The Advanced Radiance line is about advanced makeup that delivers beautiful radiance," said the vice president for global cosmetics at Procter & Gamble, which makes Cover Girl products.[35]

One of the easiest ways to lose a customer, or to damage any business relationship, is rudeness. But good manners are a two-way street. The "Etiquette Tips for Marketing Professionals" feature gives some suggestions for salvaging relationships when other people are rude to you.

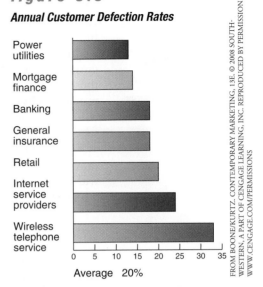

figure 9.3
Annual Customer Defection Rates

Average 20%

Source: Data from Andrew Greenyer, "The Danger of Defection," *CRM Today*, February 17, 2007, http://www.crmtoday.com.

FROM BOONE/KURTZ, CONTEMPORARY MARKETING, 13E. © 2008 SOUTH-WESTERN, A PART OF CENGAGE LEARNING, INC. REPRODUCED BY PERMISSION. WWW.CENGAGE.COM/PERMISSIONS

assessment check 5

5.1 Define *customer relationship management*.

5.2 What are the two major types of CRM systems?

5.3 Describe two steps a firm can take to rejuvenate a lost relationship.

BUYER–SELLER RELATIONSHIPS IN BUSINESS-TO-BUSINESS MARKETS

⑥ Describe the buyer–seller relationship in business-to-business marketing, and identify the four types of business partnerships.

Customer relationship management and relationship marketing are not limited to consumer goods and services. Building strong buyer–seller relationships is a critical component of business-to-business marketing as well.

Business-to-business marketing involves an organization's purchase of goods and services to support company operations or the production of other products. Buyer–seller relationships between companies involve working together to provide advantages that benefit both parties. These advantages might include lower prices for supplies, quicker delivery of inventory, improved quality and reliability, customized product features, and more favourable financing terms.

A **partnership** is an affiliation of two or more companies that help each other achieve common goals. Partnerships cover a wide spectrum of relationships from informal cooperative purchasing arrangements to formal production and marketing agreements. In business-to-business markets, partnerships form the basis of relationship marketing.

A variety of common goals motivates firms to form partnerships. Companies may want to protect or improve their positions in existing markets, gain access to new domestic or international markets, or quickly enter new markets. Expansion of a product line—to fill in gaps, broaden the product line, or differentiate the product—is another key reason for joining forces. Other motives include sharing resources, reducing costs, warding off threats of future competition, raising or creating barriers to entry, and learning new skills.

partnership Affiliation of two or more companies that help each other achieve common goals.

Marketoid

In 2005, e-commerce sales increased more than 38 percent over 2004. This was the fourth year in a row that e-commerce sales increased at this rate.

CHOOSING BUSINESS PARTNERS

How does an organization decide which companies to select as partners? The first priority is to locate firms that can add value to the relationship—whether through financial resources, contacts, extra manufacturing capacity, technical know-how, or distribution capabilities. The greater the value added, the greater the desirability of the partnership. In many cases, the attributes of each partner complement those of the other; each firm brings something to the relationship that the other party needs but cannot provide on its own. Other partnerships join firms with similar skills and resources to reduce costs.

Organizations must share similar values and goals for a partnership to succeed in the long run. Fast-food companies such as McDonald's and Burger King have often partnered with movie companies such as Disney. The fast-food company would run promotions featuring characters from recently released movies. Since the fast-food companies and the movies target the same group of customers—families with young children—the campaigns succeeded in generating excitement for two distinct products in a single promotion.[36]

TYPES OF PARTNERSHIPS

Companies form four key types of partnerships in business-to-business markets: buyer, seller, internal, and lateral partnerships. This section briefly examines each category.

In a **buyer partnership,** a firm purchases goods and services from one or more providers. Strong buyer partnerships can influence strategic decisions. An airline purchased spa products from an international spa and beauty product firm, to give away on its red-eye flights between the west and east coasts. The kits contain eye masks, ear plugs, moisturizer, lip balm, and a spa promotional offer. The airline recently ranked first in an airline quality survey. "They've always moved in a different direction," said an aviation industry watcher. "That's why they've stayed alive. This is another out-of-the-box marketing play. It cost them almost nothing, and it gets people to think."[37]

When a company assumes the buyer position in a relationship, it has a unique set of needs and requirements that vendors must meet to make the relationship successful. While buyers want sellers to provide fair prices, quick delivery, and high quality levels, a lasting relationship often requires more effort. To induce a buyer to form a long-term partnership, a supplier must also be responsive to the

marketing failure   The Perils of Big Partners

Background. LookSmart is an online media company that offers consumers, advertisers, and publishers the ability to find, save, and share articles. The company was happy to count Microsoft among its early customers, in a relationship that accounted for a whopping 70 percent of LookSmart's revenue. Buoyed by the profitable partnership, the company had been growing rapidly and holding its own against rivals Google and Yahoo!. Revenue increased 50 percent a year, and LookSmart's share price tripled in 12 months.

The Marketing Problem. LookSmart's dependence on Microsoft proved to be a mistake. When the software giant suddenly decided not to renew its licence for the Web directory that LookSmart markets, the company's stock fell 52 percent in one day.

The Outcome. Revenues are down by more than half, and the company is still struggling to recover from the loss of its giant customer. LookSmart has not had a profitable quarter since losing Microsoft's

business. A new CEO was brought in. He promptly fired the company's senior managers and has been looking for ways to diversify the business and create long-term growth.

Lessons Learned. The new CEO has promised never again to rely on one customer for such a large portion of the company's business. "It is critical that we are organized in a way that lets us move quickly and have leaders who can set a tone of performance, speed, and urgency," he said. "I believe we have accomplished this and we will be in better shape to realize the company's goals."

Sources: LookSmart website, http://www.looksmart.com, accessed April 27, 2006; "Interchange Corporation Chooses LookSmart's Furl to Power Local.com's Page Saving and Archiving System," Business Wire, accessed at http://www.findarticles.com, December 13, 2005; Kurt Badenhausen, "Your Big Best Friend—or Not," Forbes, October 31, 2005, pp. 182–84; Matt Hicks, "LookSmart Hits More Financial Snags," eWeek, accessed at http://www.findarticles.com, January 2005.

purchaser's unique needs. Buyer relationships can be particularly risky when the seller is small and the buyer is very large, as LookSmart found in its partnership with Microsoft (see the "Marketing Failure" feature).

Seller partnerships set up long-term exchanges of goods and services in return for cash or other consideration. Sellers, too, have specific needs as partners in ongoing relationships. Most prefer to develop long-term relationships with their partners. Sellers also want prompt payment.

The importance of **internal partnerships** is widely recognized in business today. The classic definition of the word *customer* as the buyer of a good or service is now more carefully defined in terms of external customers. However, customers within an organization also have their own needs. Internal partnerships are the foundation of an organization and its ability to meet its commitments to external entities. If the purchasing department selects a parts vendor that fails to ship on the dates required by manufacturing, production will halt, and products will not be delivered to customers as promised. As a result, external customers will likely seek other more reliable suppliers. Without building and maintaining internal partnerships, an organization will have difficulty meeting the needs of its external partnerships.

Lateral partnerships include strategic alliances with other companies or with not-for-profit organizations and research alliances between for-profit firms and colleges and universities. The relationship focuses on external entities—such as customers of the partner firm—and involves no direct buyer–seller interactions. Strategic alliances are discussed in a later section of this chapter.

COBRANDING AND COMARKETING

Two other types of business marketing relationships include cobranding and comarketing. **Cobranding** joins together two strong brand names, perhaps owned by two different companies, to sell a product. The automotive world is packed with cobranded vehicles. A car buyer can pick up the Columbia Edition of the Jeep Liberty and wear home a new Columbia ski jacket in the bargain. Ford teamed with Harley-Davidson for the Harley-Davidson F-150 pickup truck that sounded like a motorcycle. Stella McCartney by Adidas is the newest cobranded sportswear collection, using style and practicality to achieve marketing success neither brand might have done so well or so quickly on its own. Companies like Canadian Tire and MasterCard have cobranded credit cards with loyalty programs such as Canadian Tire Money and Air Miles.[38]

In a **comarketing** effort, two organizations join to sell their products in an allied marketing campaign. The governments of the Yukon, Nunavut, and Northwest Territories joined together in a $5-million promotional campaign. Using the Canada Winter Games taking place in Whitehorse, the promotional campaign aimed to promote tourism and economic development across all three areas.[39]

cobranding Cooperative arrangement in which two or more businesses team up to closely link their names on a single product.

comarketing Cooperative arrangement in which two businesses jointly market each other's products.

assessment check 6

6.1 What are the four key types of business marketing partnerships?

6.2 Distinguish between cobranding and comarketing.

IMPROVING BUYER–SELLER RELATIONSHIPS IN BUSINESS-TO-BUSINESS MARKETS

(7) Describe how business-to-business marketing incorporates national account selling, electronic data interchange and web services, vendor-managed inventories (VMI), CPFaR, managing the supply chain, and creating alliances.

Organizations that know how to find and nurture partner relationships, whether through informal deals or contracted partnerships, can enhance revenues and increase profits. Partnering often leads to lower prices, better products, and improved distribution, resulting in higher levels of customer satisfaction. Partners who know each other's needs and expectations are more likely to satisfy them and forge stronger long-term bonds. Often, partnerships can be cemented through personal relationships, no matter where firms are located.

In the past, business relationships were conducted primarily in person, over the phone, or by mail. Today, businesses are using the latest electronic, computer, and communications technology to link up. E-mail, the Internet, and other telecommunications services allow businesses to communicate anytime and anyplace.

A comarketing effort: Tabi, GE, and Canadian Living *magazine.*

NATIONAL ACCOUNT SELLING

Some relationships are more important than others due to the large investments at stake. Large manufacturers such as Procter & Gamble or Clorox pay special attention to the needs of major retailers such as Wal-Mart. Manufacturers use a technique called **national account selling** to serve their largest, most profitable customers. The large collection of supplier offices in north-western Arkansas—near Wal-Mart's home office—suggests how national account selling might be implemented. These offices are usually called teams or support teams.

The advantages of national account selling are many. By assembling a team of individuals to serve just one account, the seller demonstrates the depth of its commitment to the customer. The buyer–seller relationship is strengthened as both collaborate on business projects. Finally, cooperative buyer–seller efforts can bring about dramatic improvements in both efficiency and effectiveness for both partners. These improvements find their way to the bottom line in the form of decreased costs and increased profits.

BUSINESS-TO-BUSINESS DATABASES

As noted earlier, databases are indispensable tools in relationship marketing. They are also essential in building business-to-business relationships. Using information generated from sales reports, scanners, and many other sources, sellers can create databases that help guide their own efforts and those of buyers who resell products to final users.

ELECTRONIC DATA INTERCHANGE AND WEB SERVICES

electronic data interchange (EDI)
Computer-to-computer exchanges of invoices, orders, and other business documents.

Technology has transformed the ways in which companies control their inventories and replenish stock. Gone are the days when a retailer would notice stocks were running low, call the vendor, check prices, and reorder. Today's **electronic data interchanges (EDIs)** automate the entire process. EDI involves computer-to-computer exchanges of invoices, orders, and other business documents. It allows firms to reduce costs and improve efficiency and competitiveness. Retailers such as Wal-Mart and The Home Depot require vendors to use EDI as a core **quick-response merchandising** tool. Quick-response merchandising is a just-in-time strategy that reduces the time merchandise is held in inventory, resulting in substantial cost savings. An added advantage of EDI is that it opens new channels for gathering marketing information that is helpful in developing long-term business-to-business relationships.

Web services provide a way for companies to communicate even if they are not running the same or compatible software, hardware, databases, or network platforms. Companies in a customer–supplier relationship, or a partnership such as airlines and car rental firms, may have difficulty getting their computer systems to work together or exchange data easily. Web services are platform-independent information exchange systems that use the Internet to allow interaction between the firms. They are usually simple, self-contained applications that can handle functions from the simple to the complex.[40]

VENDOR-MANAGED INVENTORY

vendor-managed inventory (VMI)
Inventory management system in which the seller—based on an existing agreement with a buyer—determines how much of a product is needed.

The proliferation of electronic communication technologies and the constant pressure on suppliers to improve response time have led to another way for buyers and sellers to do business. **Vendor-managed inventory (VMI)** has replaced buyer-managed inventory in many instances. It is an inventory management system in which the seller—based on an existing agreement with the buyer—determines how much of a product a buyer needs and automatically ships new supplies to that buyer. The entertainment division of Mosaic, a sales and marketing company, provides vendor-managed inventory services to its motion picture studio clients, handling in-store merchandising and restocking of DVDs in outlets such as Wal-Mart and Best Buy.[41]

Some firms have modified VMI to an approach called **collaborative planning, forecasting, and replenishment (CPFaR).** This approach is a planning and forecasting technique involving collaborative efforts by both purchasers and vendors. One wholesale hardware cooperative owned by independent retailers relies on its 50 trading partners to use computer-assisted ordering. At the company's 12 distribution centres, inventory has been reduced, while service levels have climbed above 97 percent. Shorter lead times, more accurate forecasting, and faster reactions to marketplace trends are other benefits realized from its CPFaR program.[42]

MANAGING THE SUPPLY CHAIN

Good relationships between businesses require careful management of the **supply chain,** sometimes called the *value chain*, which is the entire sequence of suppliers that contribute to the creation and delivery of a product. This process affects both upstream relationships between the company and its suppliers and downstream relationships with the product's end users. The supply chain is discussed in greater detail in Chapter 12.

supply chain Sequence of suppliers that contribute to the creation and delivery of a good or service.

Effective supply-chain management can provide an important competitive advantage for a business marketer that results in:

- increased innovation

- decreased costs

- improved conflict resolution within the chain

- improved communication and involvement among members of the chain

By coordinating operations with the other companies in the chain, boosting quality, and improving its operating systems, a firm can improve speed and efficiency. Because companies spend considerable resources on goods and services from outside suppliers, cooperative relationships can pay off in many ways.

BUSINESS-TO-BUSINESS ALLIANCES

Strategic alliances are the ultimate expression of relationship marketing. A strategic alliance is a partnership formed to create a competitive advantage. These more formal long-term partnership arrangements improve each partner's supply chain relationships and enhance flexibility in operating in today's complex and rapidly changing marketplace. The size and location of strategic partners are not important. Strategic alliances include businesses of all sizes, of all kinds, and in many locations; it is what each partner can offer the other that is important.

Companies can structure strategic alliances in two ways. Alliance partners can establish a new business unit in which each takes an ownership position. In such a joint venture, one partner might own 40 percent, while the other owns 60 percent. Alternatively, the partners may decide to form a cooperative relationship that is less formal and does not involve ownership—for example, a joint new-product design team. The cooperative alliance

Effective supply-chain management can provide an important competitive advantage for a business marketer.

COLORBLIND IMAGES/BLEND IMAGES/@2008 JUPITERIMAGES CORPORATION can operate more flexibly and can change more easily as market forces or other conditions dictate. In either arrangement, the partners agree in advance on the skills and resources that each will bring into the alliance to achieve their mutual objectives and gain a competitive advantage. Resources typically include patents, product lines, brand equity, product and market knowledge, company and brand image, and reputation for product quality, innovation, or customer service. Relationships with customers and suppliers are also desirable resources, as are a convenient manufacturing facility, economies of scale and scope, information technology, and a large sales force. Skills that alliance partners can contribute include marketing skills such as innovation and product development, manufacturing skills including low-cost or flexible manufacturing, and planning and research and development expertise.

Companies form many types of strategic alliances. Some create horizontal alliances between firms at the same level in the supply chain; others define vertical links between firms at adjacent stages. The firms may serve the same or different industries. Alliances can involve cooperation among rivals who are market leaders or between a market leader and a follower. IBM helped the All England Lawn Tennis and Croquet Club improve the way the press and photographers sent copy and photographs from the Wimbledon matches to their editors' sports desks, using onsite workstations equipped to allow instant transfers of words and pictures from courtside. To design and implement the wireless networking facilities it needed, IBM formed a strategic alliance with Cisco Systems.[43]

(8) Identify and evaluate the most common measurement and evaluation techniques within a relationship marketing program.

EVALUATING CUSTOMER RELATIONSHIP PROGRAMS

One of the most important measures of relationship marketing programs, whether in consumer or business-to-business markets, is the lifetime value of a customer. This concept can be defined as the revenues and intangible benefits such as referrals and customer feedback that a customer brings to the seller over an average lifetime, less the amount the company must spend to acquire, market to, and service the customer. Long-term customers are usually more valuable assets than new ones because they buy more, cost less to serve, refer other customers, and provide valuable feedback. The "average lifetime" of a customer relationship depends on industry and product characteristics. Customer lifetime for a consumer product such as microwave pizza may be very short, while that for an automobile or computer will last longer.

For a simple example of a lifetime value calculation, assume that a Chinese takeout restaurant determines that its average customer buys dinner twice a month at an average cost of $25 per order over a lifetime of five years. That business translates this calculation to revenues of $600 per year and $3000 for five years. The restaurant can calculate and subtract its average costs for food, labour, and overhead to arrive at the per-customer profit. This figure serves as a baseline against which to measure strategies to increase the restaurant's sales volume, customer retention, or customer referral rate.

Another approach is to calculate the payback from a customer relationship, or the length of time it takes to break even on customer acquisition costs. Assume that an Internet service provider spends $75 per new customer on direct mail and enrolment incentives. Based on average revenues per subscriber, the company takes about three months to recover that $75. If an average customer stays with the service 32 months and generates $800 in revenues, the rate of return is nearly 11 times the original investment. Once the customer stays past the payback period, the provider should make a profit on that business.

In addition to lifetime value analysis and payback, companies use many other techniques to evaluate relationship programs, including the following:

- tracking rebate requests, coupon redemption, credit card purchases, and product registrations

- monitoring complaints and returned merchandise and analyzing why customers leave

- reviewing reply cards, comment forms, and surveys

- monitoring click-through behaviour on websites to identify why customers stay and why they leave

These tools give the organization information about customer priorities so that managers can make changes to their systems, if necessary, and set appropriate, measurable goals for relationship programs.

A hotel chain may set a goal of improving the rate of repeat visits from 44 to 52 percent. A mail-order company may want to reduce time from 48 to 24 hours to process and mail orders. If a customer survey reveals late flight arrivals as the number one complaint of an airline's passengers, the airline might set an objective of increasing the number of on-time arrivals from 87 to 93 percent.

Companies large and small are able to implement technology to help measure the value of customers and the return on investment from expenditures on developing customer relationships. They can choose from among a growing number of software products, many of which are tailored to specific industries or flexible enough to suit companies of varying sizes.

assessment check 8

8.1 Define the term *lifetime value of a customer*.

8.2 Why are customer complaints valuable to evaluating customer relationship programs?

Strategic Implications

A FOCUS on relationship marketing helps companies create better ways to communicate with customers and develop long-term relationships. This focus challenges managers to develop strategies that closely integrate customer service, quality, and marketing functions. By leveraging technology—both through database marketing and through customer relationship management applications—companies can compare the costs of acquiring and maintaining customer relationships with the profits received from these customers. This information allows managers to evaluate the potential returns from investing in relationship marketing programs.

Relationships include doing business with consumers as well as partners, such as vendors, suppliers, and other companies. Partners can structure relationships in many different ways to improve performance, and these choices vary for consumer and business markets. In all marketing relationships, it is important to build shared trust. For long-term customer satisfaction and success, marketers must make—and keep—promises. ◆◆◆

REVIEW OF CHAPTER OBJECTIVES

① **Contrast transaction-based marketing with relationship marketing.**

Transaction-based marketing refers to buyer–seller exchanges characterized by limited communications and little or no ongoing relationships between the parties. Relationship marketing is the development and maintenance of long-term, cost-effective relationships with individual customers, suppliers, employees, and other partners for mutual benefit.

② **Identify and explain the four basic elements of relationship marketing as well as the importance of internal marketing.**

The four basic elements are database technology, database marketing, monitoring relationships, and customer relationship management (CRM). Database technology helps identify current and potential customers. Database marketing analyzes the information provided by the database. Through relationship marketing, a firm monitors each relationship. With CRM, the firm orients every part of the organization toward building a unique company with an unbreakable bond with customers. Internal marketing involves activities within the company designed to assist all employees understand, accept, and fulfill their roles in the marketing strategy.

③   **Identify the three levels of the relationship marketing continuum.**

The three levels of the relationship marketing continuum are (1) focus on price, (2) social interaction, and (3) interdependent partnership. At the first level, marketers use financial incentives to attract customers. At the second level, marketers engage in social interaction with buyers. At the third level, buyers and sellers become true business partners.

④   **Explain how firms can enhance customer satisfaction and how they build buyer–seller relationships.**

Marketers monitor customer satisfaction through various methods of marketing research. They look to understand what customers want—including what they expect—from goods or services. They also obtain customer feedback through means such as toll-free numbers and websites. Then they use this information to improve. Firms build buyer–seller relationships through frequency marketing programs, affinity marketing, database marketing, and one-to-one marketing.

⑤   **Explain customer relationship management (CRM) and the role of technology in building customer relationships.**

Customer relationship management is the combination of strategies and technologies that empowers relationship programs, reorienting the entire organization to a concentrated focus on satisfying customers. Made possible by technological advances, it leverages technology as a means to manage customer relationships and to integrate all stakeholders into a company's product design and development, manufacturing, marketing, sales, and customer service processes. CRM allows firms to manage vast amounts of data from several sources to improve overall customer satisfaction. The most effective companies approach CRM as a complete business strategy in which people, processes, and technology are all organized around delivering superior value to customers. A recent outgrowth of CRM is virtual relationships, in which buyers and sellers rarely, if ever, meet face to face.

⑥   **Describe the buyer–seller relationship in business-to-business marketing, and identify the four types of business partnerships.**

By developing buyer–seller relationships, companies work together for their mutual benefit. Advantages may include lower prices for supplies, faster delivery of inventory, improved quality or reliability, customized product features, or more favourable financing terms. The four different types of business partnerships are buyer, seller, internal, and lateral. Regardless of the type of partnership, partners usually share similar values and goals that help the alliance endure over time. Two other types of business marketing relationships include cobranding and comarketing.

⑦   **Describe how business-to-business marketing incorporates national account selling, electronic data interchange and web services, vendor-managed inventories (VMI), CPFaR, managing the supply chain, and creating alliances.**

National account selling assists firms form a strong commitment with key buyers, resulting in improvements in efficiency and effectiveness for both parties. The use of electronic data interchanges allows firms to reduce costs and improve efficiency and competitiveness. Web services are software applications that allow firms with different technology platforms to communicate and exchange information over the Internet. Vendor-managed inventory (VMI) is a system in which sellers can automatically restock to previously requested levels. The collaborative planning, forecasting, and replenishment (CPFaR) approach bases plans and forecasts on collaborative seller–vendor efforts. Managing the supply chain provides increased innovation, decreased costs, conflict resolution, and improved communications. Strategic alliances can help both partners gain a competitive advantage in the marketplace.

⑧ **Identify and evaluate the most common measurement and evaluation techniques within a relationship marketing program.**

The effectiveness of relationship marketing programs can be measured using several methods. In the lifetime value of a customer, the revenues and intangible benefits that a customer brings to the seller over an average lifetime, less the amount the company must spend to acquire, market to, and service the customer, are calculated. With this method, a company may determine its costs to service each customer and develop ways to increase profitability. The payback method calculates how long it takes to break even on customer acquisition costs. Other measurements include tracking rebates, coupons, and credit card purchases; monitoring complaints and returns; and reviewing reply cards, comment forms, and surveys. These tools give the organization information about customer priorities so managers can make changes to their systems and set measurable goals.

assessment check answers

1.1 What are the major differences between transaction-based marketing and relationship marketing?

Transaction-based marketing refers to buyer–seller exchanges involving limited communications and little or no ongoing relationships between the parties. Relationship marketing is the development and maintenance of long-term, cost-effective relationships with individual customers, suppliers, employees, and other partners for mutual benefit.

2.1 What are the four basic elements of relationship marketing?

The four basic elements are database technology, database marketing, monitoring relationships, and customer relationship management (CRM).

2.2 Why is internal marketing important to a firm?

Internal marketing enables all members of the organization to understand, accept, and fulfil their respective roles in implementing a marketing strategy.

3.1 Identify the three levels of the marketing relationship.

The three levels of the relationship marketing continuum are (1) focus on price, (2) social interaction, and (3) interdependent partnership.

3.2 Which level is the most complicated? Why?

The third level is most complex because the strength of commitment between the parties grows.

4.1 How is customer satisfaction measured?

Marketers monitor customer satisfaction through various methods of marketing research.

4.2 Identify ways that marketers may obtain customer feedback.

Marketers can include a toll-free phone number or website address in their advertising; monitor online discussion groups, and blogs; and hire mystery shoppers.

5.1 Define *customer relationship management*.

Customer relationship management is the combination of strategies and technologies that empowers relationship programs, reorienting the entire organization to a concentrated focus on satisfying customers.

5.2 What are the two major types of CRM systems?

The two major types of CRM systems are purchased and customized.

5.3 Describe two steps a firm can take to rejuvenate a lost relationship.

Marketers can rejuvenate a lost relationship by changing the product mix if necessary or changing some of their processes.

6.1 What are the four key types of business marketing partnerships?

The four key types of business partnerships are buyer, seller, internal, and lateral.

6.2 Distinguish between cobranding and comarketing.

Cobranding joins two strong brand names, perhaps owned by two different companies, to sell a product. In a comarketing effort, two organizations join to sell their products in an allied marketing campaign.

7.1 Name four technologies businesses can use to improve buyer–seller relationships in B2B markets.

The use of electronic data interchanges allows firms to reduce costs and improve efficiency and competitiveness. Web services provide a way for companies to communicate even if they are not running the same or compatible software, hardware, databases, or network platforms. Vendor-managed inventory (VMI) is a system in which sellers can automatically restock to previously requested levels. The collaborative planning, forecasting, and replenishment (CPFaR) approach bases plans and forecasts on collaborative seller–vendor efforts.

7.2 What are the benefits of effective supply chain management?

Managing the supply chain provides increased innovation, decreased costs, conflict resolution, and improved communications.

8.1 Define the term *lifetime value of a customer*.

In the lifetime value of a customer, the revenues and intangible benefits that a customer brings to the seller over an average lifetime, less the amount the company must spend to acquire, market to, and service the customer, are calculated.

8.2 Why are customer complaints valuable to evaluating customer relationship programs?

Customer complaints give the organization information about customer priorities so that managers can make changes to their systems if necessary and set appropriate, measurable goals for relationship programs.

MARKETING TERMS YOU NEED TO KNOW

These terms are printed in red in the text. They are defined in the margins of the chapter and in the Glossary that begins on p. G-1. Other important terms are printed in bold black type in the chapter but not included in this list. Their definitions can be found in the Glossary.

transaction-based marketing 290
relationship marketing 290
frequency marketing 297
affinity marketing 297
database marketing 298

customer relationship management (CRM) 300
partnership 303
cobranding 305
comarketing 305

electronic data interchange (EDI) 306
vendor-managed inventory (VMI) 306
supply chain 307

ASSURANCE OF LEARNING REVIEW

1. Describe the benefits of relationship marketing. How does database technology help firms build relationships with customers?
2. What types of factors might the firm monitor in its relationships?
3. What is an affinity marketing program?
4. What is an application service provider (ASP)? How does it work?
5. Distinguish among grassroots marketing, viral marketing, and buzz marketing.
6. Describe at least four qualities of a successful CRM system.
7. Explain how marketers can turn customers into advocates.
8. Describe each of the four types of business partnerships.
9. Give an example of cobranding and comarketing.
10. Why is it important for a firm to manage the relationships along its supply chain?
11. What is the most important factor in a strategic alliance?
12. Explain how a firm goes about evaluating the lifetime value of a customer.

PROJECT AND TEAMWORK EXERCISES

1. With a teammate, choose one of the following companies. Create a plan to attract customers at the first level of the relationship marketing continuum—price—and move them to the next level with social interactions. Present your plan to the class.
   a. amusement or theme park
   b. health spa
   c. manufacturer of surfboards or snowmobiles
   d. manufacturer of cell phones
2. With a teammate, select a business with which you are familiar and design a frequency marketing program for the firm. Now design a grassroots, viral marketing, or buzz marketing campaign for the company you selected. Present your campaign to the class.
3. A hotel chain's database has information on guests that includes demographics, number of visits, and room preferences. Describe how the chain can use this information to develop several relationship marketing programs. How can it use a more general database to identify potential customers and to personalize its communications with them?
4. Select a local business enterprise. Find out as much as you can about its customer base, marketing strategies, and internal functions. Consider whether a customer relationship management focus would help the enterprise's competitive position. Argue your position in class.
5. Suppose you and a classmate were hired by a local independent bookstore to help its owner win back customers lost to a large bookstore chain. Design a plan to win back the store's

lost customers and rebuild those relationships. Present your plan in class.

6. Choose a company that makes great stuff—something you really like, whether it is designer handbags, electronics equipment, the tastiest ice cream flavours, or the best jeans. Now come up with a partner for your firm that you think would make a terrific strategic alliance. Write a plan for your alliance, explaining why you made the choice, what you want the two firms to accomplish, and why you think the alliance will be successful.

7. With a teammate, interview a local business owner to find out what methods he or she uses to evaluate customer relationships. You might discover that the businessperson uses very systematic techniques or perhaps just talks to customers. Either way, you will learn something valuable. Discuss your findings in class.

CRITICAL THINKING EXERCISES

1. Suppose you were asked to be a marketing consultant for a restaurant that specializes in a cultural cuisine, such as Italian or Chinese. The owner is concerned about employee satisfaction. When you visit the restaurant, what clues would you look for to determine employee satisfaction? What questions might you ask employees?

2. What types of social interaction might be appropriate—and effective—for a local bank to engage in with its customers?

3. What steps might a music retailer take to win back its lost customers?

4. Explain why a large firm like General Mills might use national account selling to strengthen its relationship with a chain of supermarkets in Calgary.

5. Why is it important for a company to calculate the lifetime value of a customer?

ETHICS EXERCISE

Suppose you work for a firm that sells home appliances such as refrigerators, microwaves, and clothes washers and dryers. Your company has been slowly losing customers, but no one seems to know why. Employee morale is sliding as well. You believe that the company is run by honest, dedicated owners who want to please their customers. One day, you overhear an employee quietly advising a potential customer to shop at another store. You realize that your firm's biggest problem may be lack of employee satisfaction—which is leading to external customer loss.

1. Would you approach the employee to discuss the problem?

2. Would you ask the employee why he or she is turning customers away?

3. What steps do you think your employer could take to turn the situation around?

INTERNET EXERCISES

1. **Loyalty marketing programs.** Airlines, hotel chains, and rental car companies were among the first to introduce loyalty marketing programs designed to reward frequent customers. Customer loyalty programs have since expanded to a wide variety of other companies. Visit the following websites and review their customer loyalty programs. In what ways do these companies attempt to reward frequent customers?
   a. Amazon.com (http://www.amazon.com)
   b. Staples (http://www.staples.ca)
   c. Indigo Books & Music Inc. (http://www.chapters .indigo.ca)

2. **Relationship marketing.** Review the material on relationship marketing in the chapter and then visit the three websites that follow. Identify five ways in which the brand's marketers have applied the principles of relationship marketing.
   a. Swiffer (http://www.swiffer.com)
   b. Snapple (http://www.snapple.com)
   c. Armor All (http://www.armorall.com)

Note: Internet web addresses change frequently. If you don't find the exact sites listed, you may need to access the organization's home page and search from there or use a search engine such as Google.

Case 9.1

Hilton Is OnQ with Customers

Information is power. It can help marketers understand their customers, meet their needs, and even anticipate future needs. It can help firms communicate better with suppliers and partners. And it can help organizations manage their customer relationships. Technology like Hilton Hotels' OnQ system is designed to provide marketers with the information they need to gain an edge over the competition and create loyal customers.

Hilton Hotels is a big company. The firm owns several well-known, branded hotel chains in addition to the Hilton brand—Hampton Inn, Homewood Suites by Hilton, Embassy Suites, Hilton Garden Inn, and Doubletree. Some of these hotels cater to business travellers, others to leisure travellers. In all, there are over 2000 hotels, many of which are franchises. Communication among all these enterprises is key to creating a unified marketing message. OnQ is technology that integrates several major business functions—property management, reservations, customer relationship management (CRM), and back-office systems such as accounting and purchasing. "We believe having consistent technology across all brands and key customer touch points is the essential ingredient necessary to establish guest satisfaction and loyalty within our family of hotel brands," explains Tim Harvey, Hilton's chief information officer.

OnQ is so sophisticated it is actually simple. The system creates a database of information about customers that is consistent throughout the organization, which includes over 200 000 employees at call centres and hotels. It also supports the HHonors loyalty program—a frequency marketing program that has millions of customer members. Because all the data are compiled and streamlined in a single program, staffers such as customer service representatives or front-desk personnel can retrieve the information they need rapidly to help customers on the spot. It also individualizes the experience for customers. "CRM for us means the customer really matters," says a company representative. "We want people in our organization to realize that what is important is to treat customers consistently, one customer at a time, 365 days a year, no matter where we touch them. We want to enable our employees to delight guests." So a business customer who happens to be travelling with his or her family during the weekend gets the same treatment in either circumstance—at any one of the Hilton hotels.

OnQ also helps Hilton marketers tailor marketing messages to certain segments of their guest population. The company emphasizes that the true purpose of OnQ is to serve customers but they also use it for marketing and selling other company programs.

Finally, there is the issue of promises made, promises kept, and trust. OnQ helps Hilton make and keep its promises to customers, building trust over the long term.

Questions for Critical Thinking

1. How might OnQ promote internal marketing throughout the Hilton organization?
2. Identify three specific ways Hilton staff could use OnQ to enhance customer service and enhance customer satisfaction.

Sources: "Hilton Hotels Corp. Takes Lead with OnQ," *Hotels Magazine,* August 2003, http://www.hotelsmag.com; Esther Shein, "Hilton Hotels CIO Talks OnQ," *CIO Update,* July 15, 2003, http://www.cioupdate.com; Reid A. Paul, "Hilton Is OnQ," *Hospitality Technology Magazine,* June 2003, http://www.htmagazine.com; Martin Schneider, "Eight Brands, One Customer," *Destination CRM,* May 9, 2003, http://www.destinationcrm.com.

Case 9.2

The True Cost of Customer Service

Few people believe that airline travel will ever return to the "good old days" when amenities were free and plentiful. Blankets, pillows, meals, and timely arrival with your baggage and a smile seem to have been left permanently on the tarmac. Or have they?

Some analysts believe that the threat of bankruptcy, among other factors, is inducing airlines to improve customer service, often in simple ways that won't hurt the bottom line. "A bankrupt airline is anxious not to lose customers, especially business travellers," said one expert, "and may be wary of cutting service below competitors' levels for fear of confirming passenger suspicions that the company is not long for this world." United Airlines, for instance, scored 64 of a possible 100 in a study of customer satisfaction the year before it filed for bankruptcy protection. One recent passenger, who had abandoned the airline for past rudeness of its employees, said that a cheap fare persuaded her to try again. "It was like flying on a different airline," she said. "The flight attendants were friendly and the service was efficient."

Contrary to what you might think, customer satisfaction may actually improve just before a bankruptcy filing. Companies suffering during hard times often try harder to increase business, including better service or offering deep discounts or other promotions. Some evidence of this extra effort is United's on-time arrival guarantee and promise of 500 free award miles if it doesn't come through. Another troubled airline, Delta, began a service recovery program called First Point of Contact that "focuses on empowering our front-line customer service employees to resolve customer concerns at the first point of contact," according to the company's executive vice president and chief of customer service. The program retrained everyone from phone agents to flight attendants.

Some skeptics, however, point to other recent surveys that give the airline industry failing grades for customer service, with a surge in customer complaints and record-high lost-baggage claims. One industry watcher says that dramatic industry layoffs, combined with a return to pre-9/11 levels of air travel, have created the situation. Employees, he claims, are frustrated by reduced pay and benefits and by having to pick up the slack created by fewer workers. And the extras that some airlines are bringing back come with a twist—a fee, ranging from $2 for a snack on Air Canada to $75 for exit-row seats on Virgin Atlantic. Some airlines charge $5 to $30 for curbside baggage checking, for not booking your flight online, or for requesting anything other than a computer-generated ticket. "I always thought when you paid for your ticket, handling your luggage, your beverage, and all the other service was included in the price of the ticket," said one passenger. "Now they are telling me everything is extra. I'm disappointed."

Some airlines are defending the new fees by claiming that customers have made it clear they value low-price tickets above all else. The fees are structured so that the additional services or conveniences are paid for only by those who want them. Other carriers claim that customer service was always a priority whether bankruptcy loomed or not. As long as airlines continue to compete on price and try to balance low-cost operations with bankruptcy threats, however, it looks like good customer service remains in the eye of the beholder.

Questions for Critical Thinking

1. Do you think airlines have improved customer service efforts? Why or why not?
2. What advantage do good customer relationships have for airlines on the brink of bankruptcy? Are they worth the cost and effort?
3. Do you think passengers will consider amenities that they pay for to fall under the category of "customer service"? Why or why not? How might their perception affect the airlines' customer service efforts and track record?

Sources: Dawn Gilbertson, "Airline Report Shows Low Marks in Service," *Arizona Republic,* April 4, 2006, http://www.azcentral.com; Leslie Miller, "Service on Airlines Gets a Little More Expensive," *CRM Buyer,* April 4, 2006, http://www.crmbuyer.com; "'Service' in the Skies," *USA Today,* March 24, 2006, http://www.usatoday.com; Joel J. Smith, "Airline: $15 for Legroom," *Detroit News,* March 14, 2006, http://www.detnews.com; Christopher Elliott, "When Fliers Benefit from Airline Bankruptcy," *The New York Times,* January 17, 2006, http://www.nytimes.com; "Air Canada Flyers to Pay Only for Selected Services," *Marketing Daily,* October 30, 2006, http://www.aircanada.com, accessed January 3, 2008.

Video Case 9.3

The Little Guys Home Electronics:
Big on Customer Relationships

The written video case on The Little Guys appears on page VC-12. The recently filmed *The Little Guys* video is designed to expand and highlight the concepts in this chapter and the concepts and questions covered in the written video case.

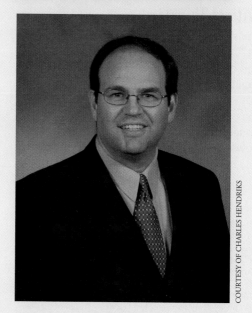

CHARLES HENDRICKS

COURTESY OF CHARLES HENDRICKS

One of the key skills required in marketing is communication skills and the need to present findings and ideas in a compelling manner.

Talking About Marketing with Charles Hendricks

Here are highlights of our interview with Charles Hendricks, a veteran marketer. For the complete video interview and transcript, go to http://www.contemporarymarketing2.nelson.com

Q1: Could you please tell us about your academic work/background?
CH: My extracurricular involvement in university was just as important as my academic work. While I graduated with a business degree and a major in marketing, I was attractive to Procter & Gamble due to my extensive involvement in student government and other extracurricular activities that demonstrated that I had the skill set to be successful in a management capacity. While in university, I had established a student-run bus/transportation service that competed with government-run services, led the largest student services survey, "tackled" the university administration and successfully ran for, and held, public office—all while achieving good grades.

Q2: What attracted you to the field that you are in?
CH: More than anything, I knew that I wanted a dynamic job and a dynamic career—one where I would be working with people and utilizing my personal skills in the areas of presentation and communication skills. Most definitely, I wanted to work in the business field. The only discipline that appealed to me was marketing—the one that would allow me to lead business teams in planning and delivering business growth by looking at product development, sales, promotion planning, pricing, etc. To me, marketing was the most exciting and most dynamic discipline.

Q3: What was your first marketing job and how did you get it?
CH: I was successful in landing a job at Procter & Gamble via their on-campus recruiting efforts. My first job was in sales and business development where I worked with external customers, helping them in their marketing efforts. Most importantly, I engaged in discussions with retailers, helping them to develop their advertising plans and planning for the merchandising of P&G brands. I touched all elements of marketing, including pricing and promotional planning and even worked with customers in understanding product category productivity and shelving analysis. Later, I progressed into various other roles and functions while managing businesses in several regions in Canada. I enjoyed all elements on people and business management and even got involved in management recruiting efforts of the company.

Q6: What was the biggest challenge/surprise when you entered the field?
CH: One comes to learn very quickly that everyone has their own ideas about what's right and wrong and about what will work and what won't work. Coupled with the difficulty of having to prove your ideas internally comes the challenge of proving your ideas externally with customers. The marketing discipline requires analysis and creative recommendations based on findings. Different people will draw different conclusions from the analysis, which will lead to the development of competing ideas. Managers need to present their plans and secure agreement to proceed. One of the key skills required in marketing is communication skills and the need to present findings and ideas in a compelling manner.

Q10: What are the important skills that marketing students needs to succeed?
CH: I believe that marketing students need to be academically sound—with a thorough understanding of the key elements of marketing theory and their practical application. Separate from the academic components of marketing, students must be able to demonstrate an ability to set and achieve goals and to work well with others in team environments. Creativity, strong communication skills, and presentation skills round out some key skill sets required to succeed.

A Legacy of Laughter Opens Doors to the Future

When the hit show *Whose Line Is It Anyway?* spun prime-time television on its head with completely improvised material, viewers wondered where its talented cast of actors had come from. Two of its cast members, Ryan Stiles and Colin Mochrie, began their careers at The Second City. A similar curiosity surrounds such stars as Mike Myers, who travelled through live comedy venues at a young age before being cast by *Saturday Night Live (SNL)*. Myers has called The Second City his "college," as he began with the troupe after his senior year of high school. SC alumni are behind a long list of entertainment success stories, including *The Simpsons, The Daily Show*, and The Blues Brothers. Many prolific careers began at The Second City, including such stars as *Saturday Night Live*'s former head writer Tina Fey and the iconic Bill Murray. The Second City continues to use its legacy of great talent to capture the hearts of its target market. All of SC's business ventures, big and small, are related to the captivating underlying character of The Second City.

As tourists walk into The Second City theatre, a long list of alumni, including every actor who played in a new revue, occupies a few giant placards at the entrance. Inside, giant photos of the actors in full character adorn the walls. Whether the consumer grew up in the 1960s, when Mike Nichols and Elaine May were becoming a famous comic duo, or more recently when *SNL*'s Amy Poehler became a sensation, there are clearly a number of famous faces for anyone to recognize.

Second City's Communication Division has made strategic casting decisions to fit its target market of successful businesspeople. Fred Willard of *Best in Show* and *Everybody Loves Raymond*, a successful SC alum, appears prominently in SC's online and print brochures. His career may be most recognizable to the 50- and 60-year-olds leading some of America's most powerful businesses today, but he's also a cult favourite of young businesspeople making their way up the corporate ladder. Colin Mochrie of *Whose Line Is It Anyway?* and Fred Willard are just two SC actors who have reached great heights in the entertainment industry and continue to directly provide marketing and creative input for their comedic home. SC Communications knows the importance of bringing talented personalities right to the customer's door.

Second City theatres market to two important market segments with different approaches. For the tourist market they establish a presence in hotels with marketing materials and concierge contacts. For local residents they stay visible with entertainment listings and public-relations efforts providing reminders that SC still offers fresh, affordable comedy with a local flavour. The Second City Touring Company markets to a larger geographical area and uses several strategies to reach its market segments, which are primarily college venues and performing arts centres. For the college market, the marketing approach stresses the show's cutting-edge social commentary. For the performing arts centres, it stresses the troupe's consistent and successful track record.

Developing a cohesive entertainment business means marketing to, and producing for, a variety of voices and demographics. The Second City has developed an Outreach and Diversity division that has gained an exciting amount of interest from a number of minority communities. By producing such ensembles as Stir-Friday Night, BrownCo, and GayCo, and by offering apprenticeships for participating high school students, The Second City has fostered mutually rewarding bonds with various communities. Archived footage of a diverse range of famous Second City alumni plays a key role in some of the training and workshop programs offered by The Second City Training Center.

SC uses a differentiated marketing strategy, designed to attract various market segments. Throughout the company's continued expansion, its main focus has always remained its comedy. Since its origin, Second City has been positioned, by virtue of its talent, at the top of the comedy theatre market. Second City has continued to take advantage of its status by investing in the newest entertainment medium: the Internet.

The benefits of technology, including self-broadcasting websites such as YouTube.com, have opened up the entertainment market to anyone capable of speaking into a microphone or turning on a computer. Second City is prepared to work within the technology/entertainment boom. Kelly Leonard, SC's vice president, recently reported on alliances being formed with media content distribution agencies. "We have realized for some time that this is a major area for The Second City, as we have a tremendous inventory of short form content and the set process for creating a steady stream of this content. These new media forms will serve two or three purposes: exposing us to a youth market, becoming a marketing tool, and eventually [being] a source of income for us." The Second City has begun to use its website to market to this youth market segment by producing podcasts and posting interviews and video clips. SC expects to continue to target the plugged-in youth market, which presents significant growth opportunities.

Customer relationship management is an intrinsic part of The Second City, which was created to challenge, surprise, and delight the audience. These original goals of Second City comedy remain integrated throughout all its business ventures. SC doesn't have to use software systems to tally customer feedback. Laughter can be just as accurate a barometer of customer satisfaction. Second City simply listens to its audience, its corporate partner, its community, and its stars. Speaking on behalf of the stage that launched their careers, Second City's talented alumni make the strongest marketing call. Having alumni such as Hollywood actor Alan Arkin being quoted, saying "The Second City saved my life, quite literally," means that The Second City is as much a marketing success for its actors as it is for its audience.

Questions

1. Where and when did you first hear of The Second City? What first impression did this create?

2. How does the Second City approach its market segmentations?

3. What market segment do you think The Second City has neglected to target?

4. How is The Second City vulnerable in using its celebrity alumni as a major marketing tool?

Part 3 CBC Video Case

CBC

Visit the website for Contemporary Marketing at http://www.contemporarymarketing2e.nelson.com to view the CBC video and video case summary for Part III.

PRODUCT DECISIONS

chapter 10

Product and Service Strategies

CHAPTER OBJECTIVES

1. Define product and distinguish between goods and services and how they relate to the goods–services continuum.

2. Explain the importance of the service sector in today's marketplace.

3. List the classifications of consumer goods and services and briefly describe each category.

4. Describe each of the types of business goods and services.

5. Explain how quality is used by marketers as a product strategy.

6. Explain why firms develop lines of related products.

7. Describe the way marketers typically measure product mixes and make product mix decisions.

8. Explain the concept of the product life cycle and identify the different stages.

9. Describe how a firm can extend a product's life cycle, and explain why certain products may be deleted.

SATELLITE: THE NEW SOUND OF RADIO

Just when it seemed the life of broadcast radio was dwindling—local stations gobbled up by programming giants and music buffs tuning into iPods instead of their favourite stations—a new sound hit the air waves. Satellite radio is bringing listeners back, and here's why: the signal is strong and clear, and you won't lose it when you're driving in your car. You have your choice of talk, sports, entertainment, and music programs. You get to hear controversial celebrities and you won't be bothered by irritating commercials. The catch is that you have to pay for all these benefits. You buy a satellite radio for as little as $30, then you subscribe to one of the two providers currently available: Sirius or XM. Rates for the providers are very similar: both have $14.99 monthly plans and $164.89 yearly fees. But if you're a radio buff, the cost is likely to be well worth it. And if you're not, satellite might turn you into one.

It's easy to think of Sirius Satellite Radio and XM Canada as the Coke and Pepsi of radio. The technologies are identical and the philosophies are similar, so competition between the two providers is head-to-head and intense. Gaining an advantage at this stage is vital, because satellite radio has moved past the introductory stage in its life cycle and is now beginning to grow. Whoever wins the most fans now could win the long-term game. So, curious consumers might be asking, how do they compare?

In both cases, you need a receiver to get a satellite signal. Before even making this purchase, however, you'll have to decide which provider you want to subscribe to. To operate, a Sirius radio must have a Sirius subscription, and an XM radio requires an XM subscription. Once subscribed, you can purchase anything ranging from a simple car radio to a tabletop radio for your home or office. To find out more about the offerings from a firm, you can visit its website, which gives you information about everything from subscription rates to what's on tonight. Each service provider carries different stations. If you want news and talk, both stations have a variety of world, national, and local news, as well as political commentators. And Sirius has Howard Stern.

Sirius is banking on Stern, the former "shock jock" of FM radio. In his move to Sirius, Stern commanded $500 million in cash and stock over a five-year period, but the firm believes that the cost will be well worth it in new subscribers, advertising revenues, and publicity. One industry expert is skeptical of the gamble. "If every single one of Howard Stern's listeners came over, that's more than 10 million subscribers. If that's the only growth for Sirius, that's not a success. It's not Howard Stern radio, it's Sirius radio." Other industry experts believe that this type of original content, provided by Stern and others such as Ellen DeGeneres and rock star Tommy Lee (shown in photo) sets satellite radio apart from broadcast radio.

Both Sirius and XM Canada are using similar promotional techniques such as newspaper advertising. The objective of both is to make Canadians aware of the benefits of satellite radio over conventional radio.

Satellite radio still faces some major challenges, such as persuading radio listeners to pay for the service and competing against providers of on-demand and iTunes content. And as more competitors enter the arena, Sirius and XM will have to find ways to distinguish themselves from the others. But right now they have a chance to make the most of this new medium—and they are going to do everything they can to get you to tune in.

connecting with customers

Satellite radio, whether Sirius or XM Canada, provides customers with the opportunity to choose the type of radio stations they want to listen to, sports, music, or talk shows. The service allows the customer to listen to the radio, in a car, at home, or on a portable device. It is even easy for a customer to sign up for the high-quality, commercial-free service through websites or retail outlets.[1]

Chapter Overview

W E'VE discussed how marketers conduct research to determine unfilled needs in their markets, how customers behave during the purchasing process, and how firms expand their horizons overseas. Now our attention shifts to a company's marketing mix, the blend of four elements of a marketing strategy—product, distribution, promotion, and price—to satisfy the target market. This chapter focuses on how firms select and develop the goods and services they offer, starting with planning which products to offer. The other variables of the marketing mix—distribution channels, promotional plans, and pricing decisions—must accommodate the product strategy selected.

Marketers develop strategies to promote both tangible goods and intangible services. Any such strategy begins with investigation, analysis, and selection of a particular target market, and it continues with the creation of a marketing mix designed to satisfy that segment. Both tangible goods and intangible services intend to satisfy consumer wants and needs, but the marketing efforts supporting them may be vastly different. Sirius and XM sell both types of products—they offer subscriptions to radio service, and they sell the radios that subscribers need to hear the service. This is the case with many companies, as you'll see in this chapter.

This chapter examines both the similarities and the differences in marketing goods and services. It then presents basic concepts—product classifications, development of product lines, and the product life cycle—that marketers apply in developing successful products. Finally, the chapter discusses product deletion and product mix decisions. ◆◆◆

---

① Define product and distinguish between goods and services and how they relate to the goods–services continuum.

Marketoid

In 2006, regular radio advertising revenue increased 5.3 percent to $1.4 billion.

WHAT IS A PRODUCT?

At first, you might think of a product as an object you hold in your hand, such as a baseball or a toothbrush. You might also think of the car you drive as a product. But this doesn't take into account the idea of a service as a product. Nor does it consider the idea of what the product is used for. So a television is more than a box with a screen and a remote control. It's really a means of providing entertainment—your favourite movies, news programs, or reality shows. Marketers acknowledge this broader conception of product; they realize that people buy *want satisfaction* rather than objects. Want satisfaction can apply to the purchase of products or even the giving of gifts, as described in the "Etiquette Tips for Marketing Professionals" feature.

You might feel a need for a television to satisfy a want for entertainment. You might not know a lot about how the device itself works, but you understand the results. If you are entertained by watching TV, then your wants are satisfied. If, however, the television is working just fine but you don't like the programming offered, you may need to satisfy your desire for entertainment by changing your cable service or purchasing satellite service. Each of those services is a product.

Marketers think of a product as a compilation of package design and labelling, brand name, price, availability, warranty, reputation, image, and customer-service activities that add value for the customer. Consequently, a **product** is a bundle of physical, service, and symbolic attributes designed to satisfy a customer's wants and needs.

assessment check 1a

1.1 Define the term product.

1.2 Why is the understanding of want satisfaction so important to marketers?

product Bundle of physical, service, and symbolic attributes designed to satisfy a customer's wants and needs.

WHAT ARE GOODS AND SERVICES?

Services are intangible products. A general definition identifies **services** as intangible tasks that satisfy the needs of consumer and business users. But you can't hold a service in your hand the way you can **goods,** which are tangible products that customers can see, hear, smell, taste, or touch like the television

ETIQUETTE TIPS FOR MARKETING PROFESSIONALS

Giving the Right Gift

WHEN holidays and other special occasions roll around, you want to do the right thing for your co-workers, your boss, and your staff (if you are a manager). While it may have seemed easy to choose gifts for your parents, siblings, and friends when you were growing up, giving gifts at work is a completely different matter. To whom should you give a gift? How much should you spend? What should you give? When and where do you present it to the person? Here are a few suggestions for giving the right gift—to the right person:

1. *Check your firm's gift-giving rules.* Many companies have their own rules or guidelines about gift giving, which will answer many of your questions. Ask someone in the human resources department.
2. *Ask a co-worker who has been at the firm longer than you have.* Someone who has worked there longer and been through a few holiday seasons can give you good pointers.
3. *If you are still uncertain about whether to give and to whom, ask your boss.* Then follow his or her guidelines.
4. *If there is a dollar limit, follow it.* Don't think you have to spend more on your boss just to impress him or her. If you want to spend more for a co-worker who is a close friend, arrange to exchange gifts outside the office. If the limit is too high for you, ask a few co-workers if they want to chip in for group gifts.
5. *Give something consumable.* Gifts of food—homemade cookies or chocolates from the specialty shop around the corner—are appreciated by everyone, and they don't collect dust on someone's shelf. Gift cards are welcome, too. However, avoid gifts of alcohol.
6. *Give something appropriate to your industry or useful on the job.* A dish or basket to collect paper clips on a desk, a good pen, a cell phone case, a travel mug or water bottle—something as simple as these items can make a person's job easier.
7. *Be equitable.* If everyone in the office is exchanging gifts, try to do cookies or gift cards for everyone (unless someone has an allergy or other condition that requires a different gift).
8. *Remember, it really is the thought that counts.* Office gifts are a way to say thank you to co-workers for their support, to a boss who has given you an opportunity, and to support staff who went the extra mile to meet that project deadline.

Sources: Donna L. Mataldo, "Gift-Giving Guidelines for the Office," About. com, http://couponing.about.com, accessed May 1, 2006; Amy Keyishan, "Office Gift-Giving Etiquette," *Ladies' Home Journal,* http://www.lhj.com, accessed May 1, 2006; Marshall Loeb, "Office Gift-Giving Etiquette: Santa's Rules Change at Work," Career Journal.com, December 8, 2005, http://www.careerjournal.com.

---

just described. Most service providers cannot transport or store their products; customers simultaneously buy and consume these products, like haircuts, car repairs, and visits to the dentist. One way to distinguish services from goods is the **goods–services continuum**, as shown in Figure 10.1.

This spectrum helps marketers visualize the differences and similarities between goods and services.[2] A car is a pure good, but the dealer may also offer repair and maintenance services or include the services in the price of a lease. The car falls at the pure good extreme of the continuum because the repair and maintenance services are an adjunct to the purchase. A dinner at an exclusive restaurant is a mix of goods and services. It combines the physical goods of gourmet food with the intangible services of attentive wait staff, elegant surroundings, and often a visit to your table by the chef, who inquires about your satisfaction with the meal. At the other extreme, a dentist provides pure service—cleaning teeth, filling cavities, taking X-rays. The dentist's office may also sell items such as electric toothbrushes or night guards, but it's the service that is primary in patients' minds.

You can begin to see the diversity of services. Services can be distinguished from goods in several ways:

1. *Services are intangible.* Services do not have physical features that buyers can see, hear, smell, taste, or touch prior to purchase. Service firms essentially ask their customers to buy a promise—that the haircut be stylish, that the insurance will cover injuries, that the lawn will be mowed.

service Intangible task that satisfies the needs of consumer and business users.

good Tangible products that customers can see, hear, smell, taste, or touch.

figure 10.1

The Goods–Services Continuum

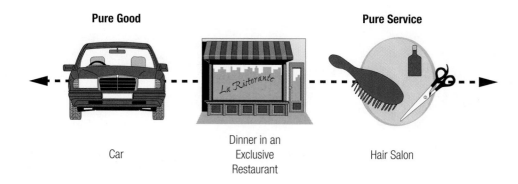

Pure Good

Car

Dinner in an Exclusive Restaurant

Pure Service

Hair Salon

2. *Services are inseparable from the service providers.* Consumer perceptions of a service provider become their perceptions of the service itself. The name of a doctor, lawyer, or hair stylist is synonymous with the service they provide. A bad haircut can deter customers, while a good one will attract more to the salon. A house-cleaning service such as Merry Maids depends on its workers to leave each house spotless, because its reputation is built on this service.

3. *Services are perishable.* Providers cannot maintain inventories of their services. A day spa can't stockpile facials or pedicures. A travel agent can't keep quantities of vacations on a shelf. For this reason, some service providers, such as airlines and hotels, may raise their prices during times of peak demand—such as during spring break from school—and reduce them when demand declines.

assessment check 1b

1.3 Describe the goods–services continuum.

1.4 List the six characteristics that distinguish services from goods.

4. *Companies cannot easily standardize services.* However, many firms are trying to change this. Most fast-food chains promise that you'll get your meal within a certain number of minutes and that it will taste the way you expect it to. A hotel chain may have the same amenities at each location—a pool, fitness room, free breakfast, or movies.

5. *Buyers often play important roles in the creation and distribution of services.* Service transactions frequently require interaction between buyer and seller at the production and distribution stages. While some restaurant chains are attempting to standardize to meet customers' expectations, others are striving to customize, involving consumers in decisions about how food is prepared or presented—which is a service in itself.

6. *Service standards show wide variations.* An upscale steakhouse and your school cafeteria are both restaurants. Their customers, however, experience considerably different cuisine, physical surroundings, service standards, and prices.

Keep in mind that a product often blurs the distinction between services and goods. Avis is a service that provides rental cars, which are goods. Lenscrafters provides eye examinations—services from optometrists—while also selling eyeglasses and contact lenses (goods).

Discover how the values of our past can provide
peace of mind today.

At The Co-operators, we insure people today the same way we did in 1945… with care.

When you need expert insurance and financial advice, you can rely on Sandy Alfonsi-Torosantucci of Assurance Rolan Belliveau Insurance Limited. As your

Co-operators agent, Sandy can show you a wide range of insurance products and financial plans. And she looks forward to working with you to make sure you get the

right coverage – designed to fit your needs. Personal service and friendly advice is just a phone call away. So, give Sandy a call today and give yourself peace of mind.

THE CO-OPERATORS GROUP, GUELPH, ONTARIO

The Co-operators Group: The promise of peace of mind.

IMPORTANCE OF THE SERVICE SECTOR

(2) Explain the importance of the service sector in today's marketplace.

You would live a very different life without service firms to fill many needs. You could not place a phone call, log on to the Internet, flip a switch for electricity, or even take a university course if organizations did not provide such services. During an average day, you probably use many services without much thought, but these products play an integral role in your life.

The service sector makes a crucial contribution to the Canadian economy by providing both products and jobs. Several of Canada's largest companies are pure services, such as the Royal Bank of Canada and Manulife Financial Corporation. Other large companies, Research In Motion Ltd., for example, while not entirely a service firm, provide services in conjunction with the goods they sell.[3]

The Canadian service sector now makes up roughly 70 percent of the economy and is growing faster than the goods-producing sector. In the years from 1997 to 2004, Canada's gross domestic product (GDP) grew at a rate of 3.6 percent a year. During this same period, goods-producing industries grew at 3.0 percent; the service sector's growth was 3.9 percent. In 2004, goods-producing industries grew at a faster rate than services, 3.4 percent for goods and 2.8 percent for services. In the previous three years services grew faster than goods.[4]

Services also play a crucial role in the international competitiveness of Canadian firms. However, as with manufacturing, economists are beginning to worry about the offshoring of service jobs such as customer-service call centres being moved to developing nations such as India. While Canadian firms have been slower than their U.S. counterparts to send jobs offshore, the trend is increasing. In another emerging trend, firms are beginning to engage in **homeshoring**, which essentially entails hiring contract workers to do jobs from their homes. Not only do firms save on office space, furnishings, and supplies, most also save on health care and other benefits.[5]

Observers cite several reasons for the growing importance of services, including consumer desire for speed and convenience and technological advances that allow firms to fulfill this demand. Services that involve wireless communications, data backup and storage, and even meal preparation for busy families are on the rise. Consumers are also looking to advisors to help plan for a financially secure future and insurance to protect their homes and families.

Most service firms emphasize marketing as a significant activity for two reasons. First, the growth potential of service transactions represents a vast marketing opportunity. Second, the environment for services is changing. For instance, increased competition is forcing traditional service industries to differentiate themselves from their competitors. Providing superior service is one way to develop long-term customer relationships and compete more effectively. As we discussed earlier, relationship marketing is just one of the ways service firms can develop and solidify their customer relationships.

> ### assessment check 2
>
> **2.1** Identify two reasons that services are important to the Canadian economy and business environment.
>
> **2.2** Why do service firms emphasize marketing?

Professional services: An important part of the service sector.

③ List the classifications of consumer goods and services and briefly describe each category.

CLASSIFYING GOODS AND SERVICES FOR CONSUMER AND BUSINESS MARKETS

A firm's choices for marketing a good or service depend largely on the offering itself and on the nature of the target market. Product strategies differ for consumer and business markets. Consumer products (sometimes called **B2C products**) are those destined for use by ultimate consumers, while business products or **B2B products** (also called *industrial* or *organizational products*) contribute directly or indirectly to the output of other products for resale. Marketers further subdivide these two major categories into more specific categories, as discussed in this section.

Some products fall into both categories. A case in point is prescription drugs. Traditionally, pharmaceutical companies marketed prescription drugs to doctors, who then made the purchase decision for their patients by writing the prescription. Thus the medications could be classified as a business product. However, many drug companies now advertise their products in consumer-oriented media, including magazines and television. Even though it is not legal to show these ads on Canadian television, Canadian cable and satellite television services provide access to American channels so Canadian consumers see these ads. A recent report revealed that of the $19.1 billion spent promoting drugs in one year, $2.7 billion was spent on advertising aimed at consumers, with the rest aimed at doctors.[6]

COURTESY OF BCAA PET INSURANCE

An unsought product.

TYPES OF CONSUMER PRODUCTS

The most widely used product classification system focuses on the buyer's perception of a need for the product and his or her buying behaviour. However, **unsought products** are marketed to consumers who may not yet recognize any need for them. Examples of unsought products are long-term-care insurance and funeral services.

However, relatively few products fall into the unsought category. Most consumers recognize their own needs for various types of consumer purchases and actively seek them, so customer buying behaviour variations are the key to distinguishing the various categories. The most common classification scheme for sought products divides consumer goods and services into three groups based on customers' buying behaviour: convenience, shopping, and specialty. Figure 10.2 illustrates samples of these three categories, together with the unsought classification.

Convenience Products

Convenience products refer to goods and services that consumers want to purchase frequently, immediately, and with minimal effort. Milk, bread, and soft drinks are convenience products. Convenience services include 24-hour quick-stop stores, walk-in hair salons, copy shops, and dry cleaners.

Marketers further subdivide the convenience category into impulse items, staples, or emergency items. **Impulse goods and services** are purchased on the spur of the moment, such as a visit to a car wash or a pack of gum tossed in at the register. Some marketers have even come up with ways to make impulse shopping on the Internet attractive. Flowers Canada.com, a site that provides flowers, gift baskets, and plants, promotes same-day delivery on its website. Consumers can order such items as roses for a birthday or a "get well soon" arrangement and it will be delivered the same day anywhere in Canada.[7]

Staples are convenience goods and services that consumers constantly replenish to maintain a ready inventory; gasoline, toothpaste, and dry cleaning are good examples. Marketers spend many hours and dollars creating messages for consumers about these products, partly because there are so many competitors.

Emergency goods and services are bought in response to unexpected and urgent needs. A snow shovel purchased during a snowstorm and an emergency visit to a vet with a sick pet are examples. Depending on your viewpoint, the products offered by Flowers Canada.com's last-minute gifts could also fall into this category!

Since consumers devote little effort to purchase decisions about convenience products, marketers must strive to make these exchanges as simple as possible. Store location can boost a convenience product's visibility. Marketers compete vigorously for prime locations, which can make all the difference between a consumer choosing one gas station, vending machine, or dry cleaner over another.

In addition, location *within* a store can make the difference between success and failure of a product, which is why manufacturers fight so hard for the right spot on supermarket shelves. Typically, the larger and more powerful grocery manufacturers such as Sara Lee, Kellogg, and General Mills get the most visible spots. Kraft Foods has eight or 10 special displays in many supermarkets. Brands like Miracle Whip, Ritz crackers, Philadelphia cream cheese, Kool-Aid, and Oreo cookies all belong to Kraft—and enjoy prime shelf space. But visibility to consumers comes at a price, often through a practise called **slotting allowances**, or slotting fees, money paid by producers to retailers to guarantee display of their merchandise. According to retailers, the purpose of slotting allowances is to cover their losses if a product doesn't sell. The practise of slotting fees has been investigated and it was discovered that these fees are far from uniform; they vary greatly across product categories, in both whether fees are charged and, if they are, how large the fees will be.[8]

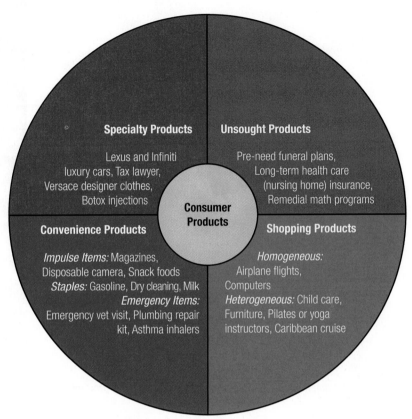

figure 10.2

Classification of Consumer Products

Shopping Products

In contrast to the purchase of convenience items, consumers buy **shopping products** only after comparing competing offerings on such characteristics as price, quality, style, and colour. Shopping products typically cost more than convenience purchases. This category includes tangible items such as clothing, furniture, and appliances as well as services such as child care, home renovations, auto repairs, and insurance. The purchaser of a shopping product lacks complete information prior to the buying trip and gathers information during the buying process.

Several important features distinguish shopping products: physical attributes, service attributes such as warranties and after-sale service terms, prices, styling, and places of purchase. A store's name and reputation have considerable influence on people's buying behaviour. The personal selling efforts of salespeople also provide important promotional support.

Buyers and marketers treat some shopping products, such as refrigerators and washing machines, as relatively *homogeneous* products. To the consumer, one brand seems largely the same as another. Marketers may try to differentiate homogeneous products from competing products in several ways. They may emphasize price and value, or they may attempt to educate buyers about less obvious features that contribute to a product's quality, appeal, and uniqueness.

Other shopping products seem *heterogeneous* because of basic differences among them. Examples include furniture, physical-fitness training, vacations, and clothing. Differences in features often separate competing heterogeneous shopping products in the minds of consumers. Perceptions of style, colour, and fit can all affect consumer choices.

Specialty Products

Specialty products offer unique characteristics that cause buyers to prize those particular brands. They typically carry high prices, and many represent well-known brands. Examples of specialty goods include Hermès scarves, Gucci leather goods, Ritz-Carlton resorts, Tiffany jewellery, and Hummer automobiles. Specialty services include professional services such as financial, legal, and medical services.

convenience products
Goods and services that consumers want to purchase frequently, immediately, and with minimal effort.

shopping products
Products that consumers purchase after comparing competing offerings.

specialty products
Products that offer unique characteristics that cause buyers to prize those particular brands.

COURTESY CADBURY ADAMS CANADA INC.

COURTESY WOLVERINE CANADA

Examples of a convenience (impulse) product and a shopping product.

Purchasers of specialty goods and services know exactly what they want—and they are willing to pay accordingly. These buyers begin shopping with complete information, and they refuse to accept substitutes. Because consumers are willing to exert considerable effort to obtain specialty products, producers can distribute them through relatively few retail locations. In fact, some firms intentionally limit the range of retailers that carry their products to add to their cachet. Both highly personalized service by sales associates and image advertising help marketers promote specialty items. Because these products are available in so few retail outlets, advertisements frequently list their locations or give toll-free telephone numbers that provide customers with this information.

In recent years some makers of specialty products have broadened their market by selling some of their goods through company-owned discount outlets. But these stores nearly always carry items from previous years' inventory. The stores attract consumers who want to own specialty items but who cannot or do not wish to pay their high prices.

CLASSIFYING CONSUMER SERVICES

Like tangible goods, services are also classified based on the convenience, shopping, and specialty products categories. But added insights can be gained by examining several factors that are unique to classifying services. Service firms may serve consumer markets, business markets, or both. A firm offering architectural services may design either residential or commercial buildings or both. A cleaning service may clean houses, offices, or both. In addition, services can be classified as equipment-based or people-based. A car wash is an equipment-based service, whereas a law office is people-based. Marketers may ask themselves any of these five questions to help classify certain services:

1. What is the nature of the service?

2. What type of relationship does the service organization have with its customers?

3. How much flexibility is there for customization and judgment on the part of the service provider?

4. Do demand and supply for the service fluctuate?

5. How is the service delivered?[9]

A marketer attempting to classify the activities of a boarding kennel would answer these questions in one way; a marketer evaluating a lawn care service would come up with different answers. For example, customers would bring their pets to the kennel to receive service, while the lawn care staff would travel to customers' homes to provide service. Workers at the kennel are likely to have closer interpersonal relationships with pet owners—and their pets—than lawn care workers, who might not meet their customers at all. A marketer assessing demand for the services of a ski resort or a food concession at the beach is likely to find fluctuations by season. And a dentist has flexibility in making decisions about a patient's care, whereas a delivery service must arrive with a package at the correct destination, on time.

APPLYING THE CONSUMER PRODUCTS CLASSIFICATION SYSTEM

The three-way classification system of convenience, shopping, and specialty goods and services helps to guide marketers in developing a successful marketing strategy. Buyer behaviour patterns differ for the three types of purchases. For example, classifying a new food item as a convenience product leads to insights about marketing needs in branding, promotion, pricing, and distribution decisions. Table 10.1 summarizes the impact of this classification system on the development of an effective marketing mix.

The classification system, however, also poses a few problems. The major obstacle in implementing this system results from the suggestion that all goods and services must fit within one of the three categories. Some fit neatly into one category, but others share characteristics of more than one category. For example, how would you classify the purchase of a new automobile? Before classifying the expensive good, which is handled by a few exclusive dealers in the area as a specialty product, consider other characteristics. New car buyers often shop extensively among competing models and dealers before deciding on the best deal. And there is a wide range of models, features, and prices to consider. At one end of the spectrum is a basic Ford that could be purchased for less than $20 000. At the other end is what people are calling European super cars such as the Porsche Carrera GT, costing $500 000 or more. The Porsche is fast, powerful, and hard to find—which boosts its value.

So it's a good idea to think of the categorization process as a continuum representing degrees of effort expended by consumers. At one end of the continuum, they casually pick up convenience items; at the other end, they search extensively for specialty products. Shopping products fall between these extremes. In addition, car dealers may offer services, both during and after the sale, that play a big role in the purchase decision. On this continuum, the new car purchase might appear between the categories of shopping and specialty products but closer to specialty products.

A second problem with the classification system emerges because consumers differ in their buying patterns. One person may walk into a hair salon and request a haircut without an appointment, while another may check references and compare prices before selecting a stylist. But the first consumer's impulse purchase of a haircut does not make hair styling services a convenience item. Marketers classify goods and services by considering the purchase patterns of the majority of buyers.

Jewellery: A specialty product.

INGVALD KALDHUSSATER/SHUTTERSTOCK

assessment check 3

3.1 What are the three major classifications of consumer products?

3.2 Identify five factors marketers should consider in classifying consumer services.

table 10.1   *Marketing Impact of the Consumer Products Classification System*

	CONVENIENCE PRODUCTS	SHOPPING PRODUCTS	SPECIALTY PRODUCTS
Consumer Factors			
Planning time involved in purchase	Very little	Considerable	Extensive
Purchase frequency	Frequent	Less frequent	Infrequent
Importance of convenient location	Critical	Important	Unimportant
Comparison of price and quality	Very little	Considerable	Very little
Marketing Mix Factors			
Price	Low	Relatively high	High
Importance of seller's image	Unimportant	Very important	Important
Distribution channel length	Long	Relatively short	Very short
Number of sales outlets	Many	Few	Very few; often one per market area
Promotion	Advertising and promotion by producer	Personal selling and advertising by both producer and retailer	Personal selling and advertising by both producer and retailer

④ Describe each of the types of business goods and services.

TYPES OF BUSINESS PRODUCTS

Business buyers are professional customers. Their job duties require rational, cost-effective purchase decisions. For instance, General Mills applies much of the same purchase decision process to buying flour that Pillsbury does.

The classification system for business products emphasizes product uses rather than customer buying behaviour. B2B products generally fall into one of six categories for product uses: installations, accessory equipment, component parts and materials, raw materials, supplies, and business services.[10] Figure 10.3 illustrates the six types of business products.

Installations

The specialty products of the business market are called **installations**. This classification includes major capital investments for new factories and heavy machinery and for telecommunications systems. Purchases of new Bombardier airplanes by Air Canada or Air Inuit are considered installations.

Since installations last for long periods of time and their purchases involve large sums of money, they represent major decisions for organizations. Negotiations often extend over several months and involve numerous decision makers. Vendors often provide technical expertise along with tangible goods. Representatives who sell custom-made equipment work closely with buying firms' engineers and production personnel to design the most satisfactory products possible.

Price typically does not dominate purchase decisions for installations. A purchasing firm buys such a product for its efficiency and performance over its useful life. The firm also wants to minimize breakdowns. Downtime is expensive because the firm must pay employees while they wait for repairs on the machine. Installations are major investments often designed specifically for the purchasers.

Training of the buyer's workforce to operate the equipment correctly, along with significant after-sale service, is usually involved. As a result, marketers of these systems typically focus their promotional efforts on employing highly trained sales representatives, often with technical backgrounds. Advertising, if the firm uses it at all, emphasizes company reputation and directs potential buyers to contact local sales representatives.

Most installations are marketed directly from manufacturers to users. Even a one-time sale may require continuing contacts for regular product servicing. Some manufacturers prefer to lease extremely expensive installations to customers rather than sell the items outright, and they assign personnel directly to the lessees' sites to operate or maintain the equipment.

Accessory Equipment

Only a few decision makers may participate in a purchase of **accessory equipment**—capital items that typically cost less and last for shorter periods than installations. Although quality and service exert important influences on purchases of accessory equipment, price may significantly affect these decisions. Accessory equipment includes products such as power tools, computers, PDAs, and cell phones. Although these products are considered capital investments and buyers depreciate their costs over several years, their useful lives generally are much shorter than those of installations.

Marketing these products requires continuous representation and dealing with the widespread geographic dispersion of purchasers. To cope with these market characteristics, a wholesaler—often called an industrial distributor—might be used to contact potential customers in its own geographic area. Customers usually do not require technical assistance, and a manufacturer of accessory equipment often can distribute its products effectively through wholesalers. Advertising is an important component in the marketing mix for accessory equipment.

Component Parts and Materials

Whereas business buyers use installations and accessory equipment in the process of producing their own final products, **component parts and materials** represent finished business products of one producer that become part of the final products of another producer. Some materials, such as flour, undergo further processing before becoming part of the finished product. Textiles, paper pulp, and chemicals are also examples of component parts and materials. Bose supplies its luxury sound systems to auto manufacturers such as Audi, Infiniti, Cadillac, and Ferrari. Marketers for the auto manufacturers believe that Bose systems are a good match between premium sound and their luxury vehicles, comparing the high performance of the Bose sound systems to the high performance of their cars.[11]

Purchasers of component parts and materials need regular, continuous supplies of uniform-quality products. They generally contract to purchase these items for set periods of time. Marketers commonly emphasize direct sales, and satisfied customers often become regular buyers. Wholesalers sometimes supply fill-in purchases and handle sales to smaller purchasers.

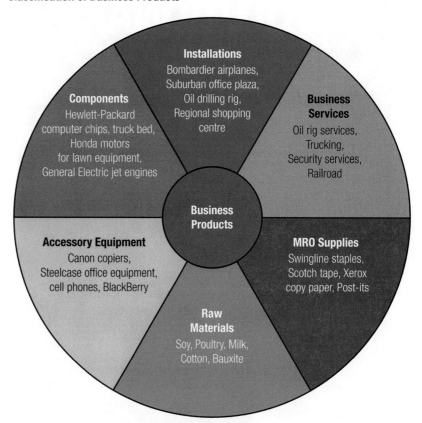

figure 10.3

Classification of Business Products

Installations
Bombardier airplanes, Suburban office plaza, Oil drilling rig, Regional shopping centre

Business Services
Oil rig services, Trucking, Security services, Railroad

Components
Hewlett-Packard computer chips, truck bed, Honda motors for lawn equipment, General Electric jet engines

Business Products

MRO Supplies
Swingline staples, Scotch tape, Xerox copy paper, Post-its

Accessory Equipment
Canon copiers, Steelcase office equipment, cell phones, BlackBerry

Raw Materials
Soy, Poultry, Milk, Cotton, Bauxite

Installation product.

THE CANADIAN PRESS (LARRY MACDOUGAL)

Accessory equipment.

Raw Materials

Farm products, such as beef, cotton, eggs, milk, poultry, and soybeans, and natural resources, such as coal, copper, iron ore, and lumber, constitute **raw materials**. These products resemble component parts and materials in that they become part of the buyers' final products. Cargill supplies many of the raw materials for finished food products—dry corn ingredients, flour, food starch, oils and shortenings, soy protein and sweeteners, and beef and pork. Food manufacturers then take and turn these materials into finished products, including cake and barbecued ribs.[12]

Most raw materials carry grades determined according to set criteria, assuring purchasers of the receipt of standardized products of uniform quality. As with component parts and materials, vendors commonly market raw materials directly to buying organizations, typically according to contractual terms. Wholesalers are increasingly involved in purchasing raw materials from foreign suppliers.

Price is seldom a deciding factor in a raw materials purchase since the costs are often set at central markets, determining virtually identical transactions among competing sellers. Purchasers buy raw materials from the firms they consider best able to deliver the required quantities and qualities.

Supplies

If installations represent the specialty products of the business market, operating supplies are its convenience products. **Supplies** constitute the regular expenses that a firm incurs in its daily operations. These expenses do not become part of the buyer's final products.

Supplies are also called **MRO items** because they fall into three categories: (1) maintenance items, such as brooms, filters, and light bulbs; (2) repair items, such as nuts and bolts used in repairing equipment; and (3) operating supplies, such as fax paper, Post-it Notes, and pencils. Staples sells all kinds of supplies to small, medium, and large businesses. Companies can purchase everything from paper and labels to filing cabinets, lighting, computers, and copiers. The firm also offers print services and the production of custom artwork.[13]

A purchasing manager regularly buys operating supplies as a routine job duty. Wholesalers often facilitate sales of supplies due to the low unit prices, the small order size, and the large number of potential buyers. Since supplies are relatively standardized, heavy price competition frequently keeps costs under control. However, a business buyer spends little time making decisions about these products. Exchanges of products frequently demand simple telephone, Web, or EDI (electronic data interchange) orders or regular purchases from a sales representative of a local wholesaler.

Business Services

business services
Intangible products that firms buy to facilitate their production and operating processes.

The **business services** category includes the intangible products that firms buy to facilitate their production and operating processes. Examples of business services are financial services, leasing and rental services that supply equipment and vehicles, insurance, security, legal advice, and consulting. As mentioned earlier, many service providers sell the same services to both consumers and organizational buyers—telephone, gas, and electric, for example—although service firms may maintain separate marketing groups for the two customer segments.

Organizations also purchase many adjunct services that assist their operations but are not essentially a part of the final product. Companies like Chapters/Indigo that receive orders by phone or over the

Internet count on Canada Post to deliver their books, music, and gifts. Although Canada Post's services are not part of Chapters' products, they are essential to the firm's operations.

Price may strongly influence purchase decisions for business services. The buying firm must decide whether to purchase a service or provide that service internally. This decision may depend on how frequently the firm needs the service and the specialized knowledge required to provide it.

Purchase decision processes vary considerably for different types of business services. A firm may purchase window-cleaning services through a routine and straightforward process similar to that for buying operating supplies. By contrast, a purchase decision for highly specialized environmental engineering advice requires complex analysis and perhaps lengthy negotiations similar to those for purchases of installations. This variability of the marketing mix for business services and other business products is outlined in Table 10.2.

The purchase of the right business services can make a difference in a firm's competitiveness. The Regus Group provides businesses with facilities for meetings and conferences in 350 cities across 60 countries. Not only are these facilities staffed by experts available for assistance, but they are also equipped with every electronic medium and amenity a business could possibly need. Regus offers expertise as well as lower prices than hotels, where many firms routinely conduct conferences and other meetings.[14]

Canada Revenue Agency supplies businesses with services designed just for them.

QUALITY AS A PRODUCT STRATEGY

No matter how a product is classified, nothing is more frustrating to a customer than having a new item break after just a few uses or having it not live up to expectations. The cell phone that hisses static at you unless you stand still or the seam that rips out of your new jacket aren't life-altering experiences, but they do leave an impression of poor quality that likely will lead you to make different purchases in the future. Then there's the issue of service quality—the department store that seems to have no salespeople or the computer help line that leaves you on hold for 20 minutes.

assessment check 4

4.1 What are the six main classifications of business products?

4.2 What are the three categories of supplies?

(5) Explain how quality is used by marketers as a product strategy.

table 10.2   **Marketing Impact of the Business Products Classification System**

FACTOR	INSTALLATIONS	ACCESSORY EQUIPMENT	COMPONENT PARTS AND MATERIALS	RAW MATERIALS	SUPPLIES	BUSINESS SERVICES
Organizational Factors						
Planning time	Extensive	Less extensive	Less extensive	Varies	Very little	Varies
Purchase frequency	Infrequent	More frequent	Frequent	Infrequent	Frequent	Varies
Comparison of price and quality	Quality very important	Quality and price important	Quality important	Quality important	Price important	Varies
Marketing Mix Factors						
Price	High	Relatively high	Low to high	Low to high	Low	Varies
Distribution channel length	Very short	Relatively short	Short	Short	Long	Varies
Promotion method	Personal selling by producer	Advertising	Personal selling	Personal selling	Advertising by producer	Varies

total quality management (TQM) Continuous effort to improve products and work processes with the goal of achieving customer satisfaction and world-class performance.

Quality is a key component to a firm's success in a competitive marketplace. The efforts to create and market high-quality goods and services have been referred to as **total quality management (TQM)**. TQM expects all of a firm's employees to continually improve products and work processes with the goal of achieving customer satisfaction and world-class performance. This means that engineers design products that work, marketers develop products that people want, and salespeople deliver on their promises. Managers are responsible for communicating the goals of total quality management to all staff members and for encouraging workers to improve themselves and take pride in their work. Of course, achieving maximum quality is easier said than done, and the process is never complete.

WORLDWIDE QUALITY PROGRAMS

Although the movement began in the 1920s as an attempt to improve product quality by improving the manufacturing process, it was during the 1980s that the quality revolution picked up speed in corporations. The campaign to improve quality found leadership in large manufacturing firms such as Ford, Xerox, and Motorola that had lost market share to Japanese competitors. Smaller companies that supplied parts to large firms then began to recognize quality as a requirement for success. Some companies today are using a process called Sigma Six, in which cross-functional teams work at improving the quality of their products and services by eliminating virtually all defects. Today, commitment to quality has spread to service industries, not-for-profit organizations, government agencies, and educational institutions.

In order to assist Canadian companies improve quality and to advance the quality movement in Canada, an independent, not-for-profit organization was developed to work in partnership with the Canadian government. The National Quality Institute (NQI) provides advice on change management, facilitates organizational assessments, organizes events to promote quality, offers educational certification programs, and presents the annual Canada Awards for Excellence.[15] In the United States, the Malcolm Baldrige National Quality Award was established in 1987 to recognize excellence in management.

The quality movement is also strong in European countries. The European Union's **ISO 9002** (formerly ISO 9000) standards define international criteria for quality management and quality assurance. These standards were originally developed by the International Organization for Standardization in Switzerland to ensure consistent quality among products manufactured and sold throughout the nations of the European Union (EU). The standards now include criteria for systems of management as well. Many European companies require suppliers to complete ISO certification, which is a rigorous 14-month process, as a condition of doing business with them. The Canadian member body of ISO is the Standards Council of Canada.[16]

BENCHMARKING

Firms often rely on an important tool called **benchmarking** to set performance standards. The purpose of benchmarking is to achieve superior performance that results in a competitive advantage in the marketplace. A typical benchmarking process involves three main activities: identifying manufacturing or business processes that need improvement, comparing internal processes to those of industry leaders, and implementing changes for quality improvement.

Benchmarking requires two types of analyses: internal and external. Before a company can compare itself with another, it must first analyze its own activities to determine strengths and weaknesses. This assessment establishes a baseline for comparison. External analysis involves gathering information about the benchmark partner to find out why the partner is perceived as the industry's best. A comparison of the results of the analysis provides an objective basis for making improvements. Large firms that have engaged in benchmarking include 3M, DuPont, General Mills, Kraft Foods, and Sun Microsystems. These firms conduct formal, complex programs, but smaller firms may decide to use benchmarking as well.[17]

QUALITY OF SERVICES

As a consumer, your perception of the quality of the service you have purchased is usually determined during the **service encounter**—the point at which the customer and service provider interact. Employees such as cashiers and customer-service representatives have a powerful impact on their customers' decision to return or not. You might pass the word to your friends about the friendly staff at a local breakfast eatery, the slow cashiers at a local supermarket, or the huge scoops of ice cream you got at the nearby ice cream stand. Those words form powerful marketing messages about the services you received.

Service quality refers to the expected and perceived quality of a service offering, and it has a huge effect on the competitiveness of a company. The findings of a survey conducted by the research firm Leger Marketing reinforce the importance of service quality. The survey results showed that the most important criteria contributing to consumer's opinions in the eight industries sectors tested, including government service, courier, financial, and retail, was the quality of service. Service quality tested higher than honest dealings and products that meet the needs of customers.[18]

Service quality is determined by five variables:

1. *Tangibles*, or physical evidence. A tidy office and clean uniform are examples.

2. *Reliability*, or consistency of performance and dependability.

3. *Responsiveness*, or the willingness and readiness of employees to provide service. A salesperson who asks, "How may I help you?" is an example.

4. *Assurances,* or the confidence communicated by the service provider. "Relax, it's FedEx," say ads for the delivery firm.

5. *Empathy,* or the service provider's efforts to understand the customer's needs and then individualize the service. "Managing the economy that means most: yours," says American Express to reassure its customers.

If a gap exists between the level of service that customers expect and the level they think they have received, it can be favourable or unfavourable. If you get a larger steak than you expected or your plane arrives ahead of schedule, the gap is favourable, and you are likely to try that service again. But if your steak is tiny, cold, and overcooked or your plane is two hours late, the gap is unfavourable, and you will probably find another restaurant or mode of transportation next time. Some wine and liquor stores have found a way to capitalize on the dissatisfaction that many consumers feel with the service they have received when shopping. Instead of conveying a snobbish attitude that intimidates customers—and often turns them away from the store—some shops are going out of their way to make customers feel comfortable and welcome. They create handwritten signs, offer a basket of bargain wines, and arrange the store to facilitate browsing and shopping. They also train their staff to smile and offer friendly assistance.[19]

Providing assurance and empathy as a means of enhancing service quality

COURTESY OF TD BANK FINANCIAL GROUP

assessment check 5

5.1 What is TQM?

5.2 What are the five variables of service quality?

DEVELOPMENT OF PRODUCT LINES

⑥ Explain why firms develop lines of related products.

product line Series of related products offered by one company.

Few firms today market only one product. A typical firm offers its customers a **product line**—that is, a series of related products. Designer Ralph Lauren has a range of product lines, beginning with men's and women's clothing (Polo), moving on to home furnishings (Ralph Lauren Home), and adding its new Rugby brand. Each line encompasses a variety of products. For example, Polo offers clothing such as polo shirts and slacks; accessories such as sunglasses; and fragrances such as Polo Black for men. Ralph Lauren Home offers sheets and pillowcases, comforters and blankets, and towels.[20]

The motivations for marketing complete product lines rather than concentrating on a single product include the desire to grow, enhancing the company's position in the market, optimal use

Sleep tight and don't let the plaque, gingivitis, stains, bad breath, sensitivity, tartar and cavities bite.

Protect your mouth with new Crest Pro-Health Night.® It's the only all-in-one toothpaste that protects all these areas dentists check most, even at night. For a clean mouth.

Recognized for cavities, gingivitis, sensitivity and whitening

*Fights cavities, tartar, gingivitis and plaque. Builds protection against sensitivity.

Healthy Looking, Beautiful Smiles for Life.

COURTESY CREST CANADA/PROCTER & GAMBLE

Crest expands its toothpaste line with specialty products.

of company resources, and exploiting the product life cycle. An example of a company that enhanced its position in the market by developing a product line is described in the "Go Green" box. The following subsections examine each of the first three reasons. The final reason, exploiting the stages of the product life cycle, is discussed in the main section that focuses on strategic implications of the product life cycle concept.

DESIRE TO GROW

A company limits its growth when it concentrates on a single product, even though the company may have started that way, as retailer Roots did with its single negative heel shoe. Now the company sells a complete line of casual wear for men and women, not to mention hats and watches along with fragrances and home furnishings. The company has grown to 110 stores in Canada and the United States, with 30 more in Asia, in addition to its online retailing. The company customizes its products for films, television shows, musical groups, and sports teams.[21]

ENHANCING THE COMPANY'S POSITION IN THE MARKET

A company with a line of products often makes itself more important to both consumers and marketing intermediaries than a firm with only one product. A shopper who purchases a hat for outdoor

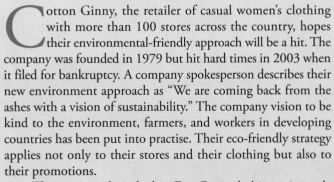

Go Green

Cotton Ginny Launches Eco-Ganic Clothing

Cotton Ginny, the retailer of casual women's clothing with more than 100 stores across the country, hopes their environmental-friendly approach will be a hit. The company was founded in 1979 but hit hard times in 2003 when it filed for bankruptcy. A company spokesperson describes their new environment approach as "We are coming back from the ashes with a vision of sustainability." The company vision to be kind to the environment, farmers, and workers in developing countries has been put into practise. Their eco-friendly strategy applies not only to their stores and their clothing but also to their promotions.

The company launched its Eco-Ganic clothing using only 100 percent organically grown cotton. The product line includes T-shirts, fleece clothing, and baby outfits. Part of the promotion included educating consumers that cotton is one of the most chemically treated crops on the planet. But cotton is not the only fibre used. Other lines of clothes will be made from bamboo, soy, or corn. At the moment, only about 40 percent of the clothing

sold by the company is organic but the aim is to have all of it made from eco-friendly fabrics within two years.

To go along with the clothing, the company is moving to make its stores and promotions eco-friendly as well. The new stores are loft-like with an earthy focus. As for promoting the line, the company does use some traditional approaches, such as advertising in fashion magazines, but it also uses some guerrilla approaches. One Earth Day, April 22, the company sent a street team out to catch people in environmentally friendly acts, such as cycling or using coffee mugs. Those spotted received free T-shirts or discount coupons.

The eco-friendly corporate strategy seems to be working for Cotton Ginny as it moves to have all its stores converted and all its clothing made with organic fibres.

Sources: Cotton Ginny site, http://www.cottonginny.ca, accessed January 23, 2008; "Cotton Ginny Launches Eco-Ganic Clothing Line," http://thegreenpages.ca; Karen Mazurkewich and Annette Bourdeau, "A Green Rebirth: How Cotton Ginny's Laurie Dubrovac Rejuvenated a Dead Brand," *Strategy*, May 2007, p. 22.

activities often buys related clothes. For instance, Tilley Endurables offers a wide range of products, allowing consumers to completely outfit themselves for outdoor activities or travel. They can purchase hats, pants, shorts, dresses, socks, and even towels. The company sells its products in company stores in Toronto, Montreal, and Vancouver, through its mail-order catalogue, and on the Internet. In addition, many other stores throughout Canada, the United States, and England carry Tilley clothes. The company started making hats, advertising them in sailing magazines and selling them at boating shows. Few would know about Tilley products if the company had not expanded beyond its original hat.[22] Business buyers often expect a firm that manufactures a particular product to offer related items as well.

OPTIMAL USE OF COMPANY RESOURCES

By spreading the costs of its operations over a series of products, a firm may reduce the average production and marketing costs of each product. The Calgary Stampede is a good example, once the site of a single 10-day event. Today the Stampede Development Park is the location of year-round events promoting tourism, economic development, education, and entertainment.[23]

> **assessment check 6** ✓
>
> **6.1** List the four reasons for developing a product line.

THE PRODUCT MIX

A company's **product mix** is the assortment of product lines and individual product offerings that the company sells. The right blend of product lines and individual products allows a firm to maximize sales opportunities within the limitations of its resources. Marketers typically measure product mixes according to width, length, and depth.

(7) Describe the way marketers typically measure product mixes and make product mix decisions.

PRODUCT MIX WIDTH

The *width* of a product mix refers to the number of product lines the firm offers. As Table 10.3 shows, Johnson & Johnson offers a broad line of retail consumer products in the Canadian market, as well as business-to-business products to the medical community. Consumers can purchase over-the-counter medications, nutritional products, dental care products, and first-aid products, among others. Health care professionals can obtain prescription drugs, medical and diagnostic devices, and wound treatments. LifeScan, one of Johnson & Johnson's subsidiaries, offers the OneTouch Ultra 2 Blood Glucose Monitoring System, which is designed to simplify blood-sugar testing for people with diabetes. In conjunction with the testing system, LifeScan provides Simple Start educational materials, which teach patients how to use the device and also offer tips on managing diabetes that include understanding portion control and monitoring carbohydrate intake.[24]

table 10.3   *Johnson & Johnson's Mix of Health Care Products*

ALLERGY, COLDS, FLU	NUTRITIONALS	SKIN AND HAIR CARE	DENTAL CARE	MEDICAL DEVICES AND DIAGNOSTICS
Motrin pain reliever	Lactaid digestive aid	Aveeno lotions	REACH dental floss	VITROS chemistry immunodiagnostics
Tylenol pain reliever	Splenda sweetener	Clean & Clear facial cleansers and toners	STIM-U-DENT plaque remover	Diabetes management products
Simply Sleep	Viactiv calcium supplement	Johnson's Baby Shampoo	REACH toothbrushes	Orthopedic joint replacement products
		Neutrogena soaps and shampoos		MAMMOTOME Breast Biopsy System

Source: Information from Johnson & Johnson website, http://www.jnj.com, accessed May 1, 2006.

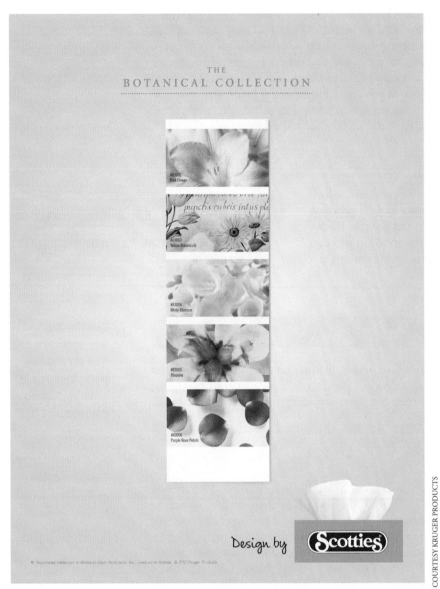

THE
BOTANICAL COLLECTION

Design by **Scotties**

COURTESY KRUGER PRODUCTS

Scotties creates depth in its product mix with variations on its packages to match room colours.

PRODUCT MIX LENGTH

The *length* of a product mix refers to the number of different products a firm sells. Table 10.3 identifies some of the hundreds of health care products offered by Johnson & Johnson. Some of J&J's most recognizable brands are Band-Aid, Motrin, Tylenol, and Neutrogena.

PRODUCT MIX DEPTH

Depth refers to variations in each product that the firm markets in its mix. Johnson & Johnson's Band-Aid brand bandages come in a variety of shapes and sizes, including Finger-Care Tough Strips, Flexible Fabric for elbows and knees, and Advance Healing Blister bandages.

PRODUCT MIX DECISIONS

Establishing and managing the product mix have become increasingly important marketing tasks. Adding depth, length, and width to the product mix requires careful thinking and planning—otherwise a firm can end up with too many products, including some that don't sell well. To evaluate a firm's product mix, marketers look at the effectiveness of its depth, length, and width. Has the firm ignored a viable consumer segment? It may improve performance by increasing product line depth to offer a product variation that will attract the new segment. Can the firm achieve economies in its sales and distribution efforts by adding complementary product lines to the mix? If so, a wider product mix may seem appropriate. Does the firm gain equal contributions from all products in its portfolio? If not, it may decide to lengthen or shorten the product mix to increase revenues. Decorating diva Debbie Travis, whose product mix includes television programs, books, and how-to videos, announced a new offering. Partnering with Canadian Tire, Debbie Travis first launched a line of paint followed by a storage organization line, kitchen and bathroom items, and furniture. In keeping with the theme of her television programs and books, the aim of the new line is to make decorating "simple, stylish and affordable."[25]

Another way to add to the mix is to purchase product lines from other companies. Or a firm can acquire entire companies through mergers or acquisitions. Molson Inc., founded in 1786 by John Molson, purchased Creemore Springs Brewery in order to expand its product line into the premier or boutique beer market.[26]

A firm should assess its current product mix for another important reason: to determine the feasibility of a line extension. A **line extension** adds individual offerings that appeal to different market segments while remaining closely related to the existing product line. Recognizing that winter sports enthusiasts want to enjoy their favourite tunes while on the slopes, Burton Snowboards and Motorola developed Burton Audex Snowboard Jackets, which use Motorola's Bluetooth technology to give wireless connectivity to wearers for their cell phones and iPods—without having to pull the devices out of their pockets. The Audex has a microphone embedded in the collar, a mini caller ID sewn into the sleeve, and a control pane that lets users receive or make phone calls and manage music on their iPods.[27]

The marketing environment also plays a role in a marketer's evaluation of a firm's product mix. In the case of Burton and Motorola, the social-cultural environment had shifted so that consumers were looking for more ways to use their communications and music devices.

Careful evaluation of a firm's current product mix can also help marketers in making decisions about brand management and new-product introductions. Chapter 11 examines the importance of branding, brand management, and the development and introduction of new products.

assessment check 7

7.1 Define product mix.

7.2 How do marketers typically measure product mixes?

THE PRODUCT LIFE CYCLE

⑧ Explain the concept of the product life cycle and identify the different stages.

Products, like people, pass through stages as they age. Successful products progress through four basic stages: introduction, growth, maturity, and decline. This progression, known as the **product life cycle**, is shown in Figure 10.4.

The product life cycle concept applies to products or product categories within an industry, not to individual brands. For instance, video camera cell phones are currently in the introductory stage but rapidly moving to the growth stage. Digital cameras are now in the growth stage, while traditional film cameras are in decline. There is no set schedule or time frame for a particular stage of the life cycle. Some products pass through certain stages rapidly, while others move more slowly. DVD players shot through the introductory stage, while the Segway human transporter seems to be stuck in the introductory stage.

product life cycle
Progression of a product through introduction, growth, maturity, and decline stages.

INTRODUCTORY STAGE

During the **introductory stage** of the product life cycle, a firm works to stimulate demand for the new market entry. Products in this stage might bring new technology to a product category. Since the product is unknown to the public, promotional campaigns stress information about its features. Additional promotions try to induce distribution channel members to carry the product. In this phase, the public becomes acquainted with the item's merits and begins to accept it. Entrepreneurs such as Roger Shiffman thrive on the introductory stage of their products' life cycles, as described in the "Marketing Success" feature.

A recent product whose introductory stage has been successful is the CD burner, which plays and creates a new CD—although it won't burn over an existing CD.[28] Other successful new products include Stouffer's Bistro frozen meals from Nestlé, which are frozen food products including Flatbread and Bristro Crustini.[29] Both of these food products are designed for busy consumers.

Technical problems and financial losses are common during the introductory stage as companies fine-tune product design and spend money on advertising. Many users remember early problems with the Internet—jammed portals, order fulfilling glitches, dotcoms that went bust. But DVD players and camera phones have experienced few of these setbacks. Although the photos taken by camera phones lack the clarity

Marketoid

In 2006, Canadians listened to their radios on average for 18.6 hours a week.

figure 10.4

Stages in the Product Life Cycle

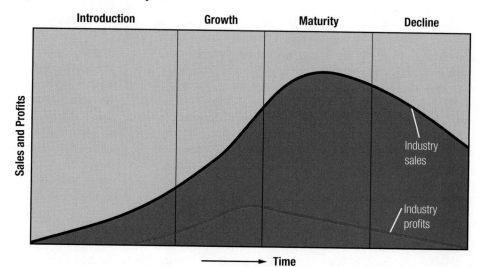

of full-featured cameras, new models will eventually catch up. And consumers don't seem to mind this, perhaps because they are still enjoying taking pictures with their phones. But another problem has cropped up—the issue of privacy. Camera phones are already so widespread that they have been banned from fitness centres, schools, and similar venues because officials fear that someone might post photos from the locker room or other private areas on the Internet.

GROWTH STAGE

Sales volume rises rapidly during the **growth stage** as new customers make initial purchases and early buyers repurchase the product, such as DVD players and camera phones. The growth stage usually begins when a firm starts to realize substantial profits from its investment. Word-of-mouth reports, mass advertising, and lowered prices all encourage hesitant buyers to make trial purchases of products. In the case of big-screen TVs, both the plasma and LCD versions, low prices have not been a factor— many cost several thousand dollars. Big-screen simply means anything larger than 40 inches—which, by today's standards, may seem small. As sales volume rises, competitors enter the marketplace, creating new challenges for marketers. As companies with competing technologies vie for dominance, the TVs themselves get bigger and bigger. Recently, L. G. Philips LCD announced its new 100-inch LCD, to compete against Samsung's 102-inch plasma, which was upstaged by Panasonic's 103-inch plasma.[30]

However, the growth stage may also bring new challenges for marketers. Inevitably, success attracts competitors, who rush into the market with similar offerings. An item that built enviable market share during the introductory stage may suddenly lose sales to competitive products. To compete effectively, a firm may need to make improvements and changes to a product during this stage. Additional spending on promotion and distribution may also be necessary.

MATURITY STAGE

Sales of a product category continue to grow during the early part of the **maturity stage,** but eventually, they reach a plateau as the backlog of potential customers dwindles. By this time, many competitors have entered the market, and the firm's profits begin to decline as competition intensifies.

At this stage in the product life cycle, differences between competing products diminish as competitors discover the product and promotional characteristics most desired by customers. Available supplies exceed industry demand for the first time. Companies can increase their sales

Marketoid

Radio listening is lowest in the teenage group, who spend only 7.6 hours a week listening to the radio.

marketing success   Is iZ the Next Big Thing?

Background. Maybe you remember Furby, the endearing electronic furball that chatted with you like a friend. Its inventor, Roger Shiffman, left Hasbro—in fact, left toys altogether—several years ago to pursue a relaxing retirement. But he's back with a new company and a new gadget. The company is called Zizzle and the gadget is call iZ.

The Challenge. For several years after Shiffman's successful launch of Furby, the toy industry in general was flagging. And Shiffman didn't quite settle into retirement. Instead, he formed a new company. "We need a shake-up in toys," observes Avi Arad, CEO of Marvel Studios.

The Strategy. As Shiffman grew restless in retirement, he decided the marketplace needed a new toy. Instead of relying on focus groups, surveys, and other marketing research, he followed his instinct for good toys. He hired Jeff Breslow, president of design firm

Big Monster Toys, to develop the new toy. "I want another Furby," he told Breslow.

The Outcome. The result of this assignment was iZ—a posable, animatronic creature that plays catchy beats when you poke its belly. It emits musical leads and rhythms when its ears are twisted, and its antennae produce all kinds of sound effects, including giggles and burps. iZ will also receive and play music from just about any source, including CD players and iPods. Kids like iZ because it allows them to create new sounds and songs every time they play with it. So do adults. "It's certainly unique," reports John Sullivan, senior vice president at Toys R Us. "We have yet to carry something that appeals to so broad a range of people."

Sources: Zizzle website, http://www.zizzle.com, accessed May 1, 2006; Wendy Cole, "Toyland's Savior?" *Time Inside Business,* September 2005, p. A19; "A Happy Tune for Zizzle's iZ?" *BusinessWeek,* August 23, 2005, http://www.businessweek.com.

and market shares only at the expense of competitors, so the competitive environment becomes increasingly important. Cell phones are now in the maturity stage—and they are so commonplace that their use in public is considered disruptive by some, as described in the "Solving an Ethical Controversy" feature.

In the maturity stage, heavy promotional outlays emphasize any differences that still separate competing products, and brand competition intensifies. Some firms try to differentiate their products by focusing on attributes such as quality, reliability, and service. Others focus on redesign or other ways of extending the product life cycle.

As competition intensifies, competitors tend to cut prices to attract new buyers. Although a price cut may seem the easiest method for boosting purchases, it is also one of the simplest moves for competitors to duplicate. Reduced prices decrease revenues for all firms in the industry, unless the lower prices stimulate enough new purchases to offset the loss in revenue on each unit sold.

DECLINE STAGE

In the **decline stage** of a product's life, innovations or shifts in consumer preferences bring about an absolute decline in industry sales. Dial telephones became touch-tone phones, which evolved to portable phones, which are now being replaced by conventional cell phones, which in turn are being replaced by camera phones.

AFTER 70 YEARS, WE HIT A GROWTH SPURT.

All the way to 8" tall. Which places the Zippo MPL™ head and shoulders above the competition. With an adjustable flame, metal construction and low fuel indicator, it makes lighting candles, fireplaces and grills a snap. And our lifetime guarantee ensures we'll also outlive the competition. To see what's up with a Zippo MPL, visit zippo.com   **Zippo** FOR REAL

Using promotion—and product extensions—to extend the maturity stage of the product life cycle.

YOU'LL NOTICE THE MOST VIBRANT FALL COLOURS
THIS YEAR ARE RED AND WHITE.

─── HARVEST PORK AND APPLE BAKE ───

2 cups	uncooked broad egg noodles
I cup	baby carrots, quartered lengthwise
2 tbsp	canola oil
I lb	pork tenderloin, cut into ¾" medallions
2 cups	sliced mushrooms
½ cup	chopped onion
I can	(10 oz/284 mL) CAMPBELL'S® Condensed Low Fat Cream of Celery Soup
½ cup	apple juice
I tbsp	chopped fresh thyme
¼ tsp	ground cinnamon
⅛ tsp	ground black pepper
I	red apple, unpeeled, cut into wedges

Prep Time: 10 mins.   Serves: 4   Cook Time: 50 mins.

1. Cook noodles by package directions, omitting salt and oil and adding carrots for last 2 min of cook time. Drain.

2. Heat I tbsp (15 mL) oil at medium-high in skillet. Cook pork until browned and cooked through – about 4 min per side; remove pork. Reduce heat to medium. Add mushrooms and onion and cook about 5 min in remaining oil.

3. Mix soup, juice, thyme, cinnamon and pepper in shallow 2 qt (2L) baking dish. Stir in noodle and mushroom mixtures. Layer in pork and apples.

4. Bake at 350°F (180°C) for 30 min.

For more great tasting and nutritious recipe ideas like this one, visit us online at **cookwithcampbells.ca**

NUTRITION SCOOP™

PER SERVING: 550 calories, IIg fat, 2g saturated fat, 0.2g trans fat, 450mg sodium, 55g carbohydrates, 4g fibre, 30g protein, 4% RDI calcium.

Full serving of Vegetables   Source of Fibre   Very High in Protein

Rediscover.

Campbell's
M'm! M'm! Good!®

COURTESY CAMPBELL COMPANY OF CANADA

Products in the maturity stage like Campbell's Soup increase sales by providing new uses for their products.

assessment check 8

8.1 Identify the four stages of the product life cycle.

8.2 During which stage or stages are products likely to attract the most new customers?

⑨ Describe how a firm can extend a product's life cycle, and explain why certain products may be deleted.

Some manufacturers refuse to give up in the decline stage. Zippo lighters have been around for more than 70 years; the company reports that it has made more than 350 million lighters to date. While the firm dominates the market for refillable lighters, the market itself has been on the decline. But in recent years, collectors have started to rejuvenate the market—as tobacco collectibles become hotter in the market, Zippo lighters have increased again in popularity. Vintage Zippos are particularly sought after.[31] Although this secondary market doesn't bring revenue directly to Zippo, it does shine a new light on the old firm. Meanwhile, Zippo itself has launched new products, including its Zippo Multi-Purpose Lighter made to do nonsmoking chores like lighting candles, fireplaces, grills, and camping lanterns. The firm has hosted concerts aimed at aging baby boomers who recall holding their Zippos aloft to encourage rock groups to play encores. And Zippo is licensing products that focus on its brand image as the flame that never goes out—such as tiki torches and patio heaters.[32] The next section of this chapter discusses more specific strategies for extending the life cycle of a product.

As sales fall, profits for the product category decline, sometimes actually becoming negative. This downward trend forces firms to cut prices further in a bid for the dwindling market. Companies gradually drop the declining items from their product lines and search for alternatives.

The traditional product life cycle differs from fad cycles. Fashions and fads profoundly influence marketing strategies. Fashions are currently popular products that tend to follow recurring life cycles. For example, bell-bottom pants that were popular in the 1960s and 1970s have returned as flares or boot-cut pants. In contrast, fads are products with abbreviated life cycles. Most fads experience short-lived popularity and then quickly fade, although some maintain residual markets among certain segments. Beanie Babies and power beads are examples of fads.

EXTENDING THE PRODUCT LIFE CYCLE

Marketers usually try to extend each stage of the life cycles for their products as long as possible. Product life cycles can stretch indefinitely as a result of decisions designed to increase the frequency of use by current customers, increase the number of users for the product, find new uses, or change package sizes, labels, or product quality.

INCREASING FREQUENCY OF USE

During the maturity stage, the sales curve for a product category reaches a maximum point if the competitors exhaust the supply of potential customers who previously had not made purchases. However, if current customers buy more frequently than they formerly did, total sales will rise even though no new buyers enter the market.

For instance, consumers buy some products during certain seasons of the year. Marketers can boost purchase frequency by persuading these people to try the product year round. For decades, most people used sunscreen only during warm and sunny seasons of the year. With greater warnings about the risks of sun damage and skin cancer, however, companies now advertise the benefits of using sunscreen year round. In a similar move, candy and chocolate companies release special products for different holidays, including Halloween and Easter.

INCREASING THE NUMBER OF USERS

A second strategy for extending the product life cycle seeks to increase the overall market size by attracting new customers who previously have not used the product. Marketers may find their products in different stages of the life cycle in different countries. This difference can help firms extend product growth. Items that have reached the maturity stage in Canada may still be in the introductory stage somewhere else.

In recent years, the Walt Disney Company has spent time and money on advertising its theme parks to attract adults in addition to young families. Television commercials portray empty nesters taking off to Disney World for a second honeymoon once their children are grown. Dance studios are reaching out to all kinds of people who just want to stay in shape—not just aspiring ballerinas or competitive ballroom dancers. One industry expert reports that dancing for exercise is a growing trend in many regions. Dance studios are responding by offering beginner and novice classes to customers who want to get fit, lose weight, and learn a few moves.[33]

Cadbury increases frequency of use for its candy by offering different sizes.

FINDING NEW USES

Finding new uses for a product is an excellent strategy for extending a product's life cycle. New applications for mature products include oatmeal as a cholesterol reducer, antacids as a calcium supplement, and aspirin for promoting heart health.

Marketers sometimes conduct contests or surveys to identify new uses for their products—often, consumers are the ones who have come up with the new ideas. The WD-40 company conducted one such survey to find the top 2000 uses for its oil, which had always been used for cleaning metal parts and lubricating squeaky door hinges. The firm discovered one person sprays it on a snow shovel to keep snow from sticking and another used it to extricate a python stuck in the exhaust pipe of a public bus.[34] Duct tape is another product with many uses—its maker, 3M, even includes a Duct Tape Workshop on its website, where consumers can learn how to make such items as a Duct Tape wallet.[35]

CHANGING PACKAGE SIZES, LABELS, OR PRODUCT QUALITY

Many firms try to extend their product life cycles by introducing physical changes in their offerings. Alternatively, new labels or changes in product size can lengthen a product's life cycle. Food marketers have brought out small packages designed to appeal to one-person households and extra-large containers for customers who want to buy in bulk. Other firms offer their products in convenient packages for use away from home or for use at the office. Kraft recently introduced its 100-calorie Snack Packs, which contain just the right portion of Oreos, Chips Ahoy cookies, and Nabisco crackers. After selling more than $100 million of these snack packs in the first year, the firm added more choices, including 100-calorie Snack Packs of Ritz Chips and Wheat Thins Multigrain Chips.[36]

PRODUCT DELETION DECISIONS

To avoid wasting resources promoting unpromising products, marketers must sometimes prune product lines and eliminate marginal products. Marketers typically face this decision during the late maturity and early decline stages of the product life cycle. Periodic reviews of weak products should justify either eliminating or retaining them.

A firm may continue to carry an unprofitable item to provide a complete line for its customers. For example, while most grocery stores lose money on bulky, low-unit-value items such as salt, they continue to carry these items to meet shopper demand.

Shortages of raw materials sometimes prompt companies to discontinue production and marketing of previously profitable items. A firm may even drop a profitable item that fails to fit into its existing product line or fails to fit the direction in which the firm wants to grow. Some of these products return to the market carrying the names of other firms that purchase these "orphan brands" from the original manufacturers.

assessment check 9

9.1 Describe the four strategies for extending a product's life cycle.

9.2 Under what circumstances do firms decide to delete a product from their line?

Strategic Implications

MARKETERS who want their businesses to succeed will continue to develop new goods and services to attract and satisfy customers. They will engage in continuous improvement activities, focusing on quality and customer service. And they will continually evaluate their company's mix of products.

Marketers everywhere are constantly developing new and better products that fit their firm's overall strategy. Technological innovations are one area in which new products quickly replace old ones. Marketers are sometimes faced with the dilemma of lagging sales for formerly popular products. They must come up with ways to extend the lives of certain products to extend their firm's profitability and sometimes must recognize and delete those that no longer meet expectations. ◆◆◆

REVIEW OF CHAPTER OBJECTIVES

① **Define product and distinguish between goods and services and how they relate to the goods–services continuum.**

Marketers define a product as the bundle of physical, service, and symbolic attributes designed to satisfy customers' wants and needs. Goods are tangible products that customers can see, hear, smell, taste, or touch. Services are intangible tasks that satisfy the needs of customers. Goods represent one end of a continuum, and services represent the other.

(2) **Explain the importance of the service sector in today's marketplace.**

The service sector makes a crucial contribution to the Canadian economy by means of products and jobs. The service sector now makes up roughly 70 percent of the economy. Services have grown because of consumers' desire for speed, convenience, and technological advances.

(3) **List the classifications of consumer goods and services and briefly describe each category.**

Consumer products—both goods and services—are classified as convenience products (frequently purchased items), shopping products (products purchased after comparison), and specialty products (those that offer unique characteristics that consumers prize).

(4) **Describe each of the types of business goods and services.**

Business products are classified as installations (major capital investments), accessory equipment (capital items that cost less and last for shorter periods than installations), component parts and materials (finished business products of one producer that become part of the final products of another producer), raw materials (natural resources such as lumber, beef, or cotton), supplies (the regular expenses that a firm incurs in daily operations), and business services (the intangible products that firms buy to facilitate their production and operating processes).

(5) **Explain how quality is used by marketers as a product strategy.**

Many companies use total quality management (TQM) in an effort to encourage all employees to participate in producing the best goods and services possible. Companies may also participate in ISO 9002 certification or benchmarking to evaluate and improve quality. Consumers often evaluate service quality on the basis of tangibles, reliability, responsiveness, assurance, and empathy, so marketers of service firms strive to excel in all of these areas.

(6) **Explain why firms develop lines of related products.**

Companies usually produce several related products rather than individual ones to achieve the objectives of growth, optimal use of company resources, increased company importance in the market, and to make optimal use of the product life cycle.

(7) **Describe the way marketers typically measure product mixes and make product mix decisions.**

Marketers must decide the right width, length, and depth of product lines. Width is the number of product lines. Length is the number of products a company sells. Depth refers to the number of variations of a product available in a product line. Marketers evaluate the effectiveness of all three elements of the product mix. They may purchase product lines from other companies or extend the product line if necessary. Firms may also acquire entire companies and their product lines through mergers and acquisitions.

(8) **Explain the concept of the product life cycle and identify the different stages.**

The product life cycle outlines the stages that a product goes through during its "life," including introduction, growth, maturity, and decline.

(9) **Describe how a firm can extend a product's life cycle, and explain why certain products may be deleted.**

Marketers can extend the product life cycle by increasing frequency of use or number of users, finding new uses for the product, or changing package size, label, or quality. If none of these is successful, or if the product no longer fits a firm's line, the firm may decide to delete a product from its line.

assessment check answers

1.1 Define the term *product*.

A product is a bundle of physical, service, and symbolic attributes designed to satisfy a customer's wants and needs.

1.2 Why is the understanding of want satisfaction so important to marketers?

The understanding of want satisfaction is important to marketers because it helps them understand why people purchase certain goods and services.

1.3 Describe the goods–services continuum.

The goods–services continuum is a spectrum that helps marketers visualize the differences and similarities between goods and services.

1.4 List the six characteristics that distinguish services from goods.

The six characteristics distinguishing services from goods are the following: (1) services are intangible, (2) services are inseparable from the service providers, (3) services are perishable, (4) companies cannot easily standardize services, (5) buyers often play important roles in the creation and distribution of services, (6) service standards show wide variations.

2.1 Identify two reasons why services are important to the Canadian economy and business environment.

The service sector makes an important contribution to the economy with products and jobs. Services also play a vital role in the international competitiveness of Canadian firms.

2.2 Why do service firms emphasize marketing?

The growth of potential service transactions represents a vast marketing opportunity, and the environment for services is changing—so marketers need to find new ways to reach customers.

3.1 What are the three major classifications of consumer products?

The three major classifications are convenience products, shopping products, and specialty products.

3.2 Identify five factors marketers should consider in classifying consumer services.

The five factors are the following: (1) the nature of the service, (2) the relationship between the service organization and its customers, (3) flexibility for customization, (4) fluctuation of supply and demand, and (5) the way the service is delivered.

4.1 What are the six main classifications of business products?

The six main classifications of business products are the following: (1) installations, (2) accessory equipment, (3) component parts and materials, (4) raw materials, (5) supplies, and (6) business services.

4.2 What are the three categories of supplies?

The three categories of supplies are maintenance items, repair items, and operating supplies.

5.1 What is TQM?

TQM stands for total quality management, a process that expects all of a firm's employees to continually improve its products and work processes.

5.2 What are the five variables of service quality?

The five variables of service quality are tangibles, reliability, responsiveness, assurances, and empathy.

6.1 List the four reasons for developing a product line.

The four reasons firms want to develop product lines are the following: (1) a desire to grow, (2) enhancing the company's position in the market, (3) optimal use of company resources, and (4) exploiting the stages of the product life cycle.

7.1 Define product mix.

The product mix is a company's assortment of product lines and individual product offerings.

7.2 How do marketers typically measure product mixes?

The product mix is measured by width, length, and depth.

8.1 Identify the four stages of the product life cycle.

The four stages are introduction, growth, maturity, and decline.

8.2 During which stage or stages are products likely to attract the most new customers?

Products usually attract the most new customers during the introductory and growth stages.

9.1 Describe the four strategies for extending a product's life cycle.

The four strategies are increasing frequency of use, increasing the number of users, finding new users, and changing packaging or quality.

9.2 Under what circumstances do firms decide to delete a product from their line?

Firms may decide to delete a product if none of the strategies for extending a product's life work, if raw materials become unavailable, or if the product no longer fits the existing or future product line.

MARKETING TERMS YOU NEED TO KNOW

These terms are printed in red in the text. They are defined in the margins of the chapter and in the Glossary that begins on p. G-1. Other important terms are printed in bold black type in the chapter but not included in this list. Their definitions can be found in the Glossary.

product 324	shopping product 329	product line 337
service 325	specialty product 329	product life cycle 341
good 325	business services 334	
convenience products 329	total quality management (TQM) 336	

ASSURANCE OF LEARNING REVIEW

1. Give an example of a product that blurs the distinction between goods and services, and explain why it does.
2. What are the differences between consumer products and B2B products?
3. What are unsought products? Give an example of an unsought product, and explain how it might be marketed.
4. What important features distinguish shopping products from one another?
5. How does marketing for installations and accessory equipment differ?
6. How do firms use benchmarking?
7. Describe briefly how Roots has achieved each of the objectives for developing a product line.
8. What is a line extension? Describe how **one** of the following might create a line extension:
   a. Kleenex tissues
   b. Kraft Ritz crackers
   c. Renuzit air fresheners
   d. Twinings tea
9. What types of challenges do marketers face with products that are in the introductory stage? What steps can they take to overcome these hurdles?
10. Provide an example of a product whose life cycle was extended by increasing its frequency of use, finding new users, finding new uses, or changing the packaging. Your product may have undergone a combination of these.

PROJECTS AND TEAMWORK EXERCISES

1. On your own or with a classmate, choose one of the following goods. Then create a marketing strategy for developing services to support your good.
   a. Purina cat or dog food
   b. Lean Cuisine frozen meals
   c. Ikea furniture
2. The next time you go grocery shopping—by yourself or with your roommate—keep a list of all the convenience products you buy. When you get home, make a table showing which of these products are impulse, staple, and emergency goods.
3. Consider a customer-service experience you have had in the last month or so. Was it positive or negative? Describe
your experience to the class and then discuss how the firm might improve the quality of its customer service—even if it is already positive.
4. With a classmate, choose a firm that interests you. Visit the firm's website and measure its product mix. Then create a chart like the one for Johnson & Johnson in Table 10.3, identifying the company's major product lines, along with a few specific examples.
5. With the same classmate, create a plan for further extending one of the firm's product lines. Describe the strategy you would recommend for extending the line as well as new products that might be included.

CRITICAL THINKING EXERCISES

1. Draw a line representing the goods–services continuum. Then place each of the following along the continuum. Briefly explain your decision.
   a. Google
   b. eBay
   c. Starbucks coffee
   d. L'Oréal shampoo
2. Think of a shopping product you purchased in the last six months. Describe your decision process, including the features you used in comparing it to competitors. Have you been satisfied with your purchase? Why or why not? Would you make the purchase again, or go to a competitor?
3. Why is the service encounter so important to a firm's relationships with its customers? When is a service gap favourable? When is it unfavourable?
4. Why is it important for even a small company to develop a line of products?
5. Choose one of the following products, and describe your strategy for taking it to the next stage in its product life cycle. For products in the maturity or decline stage, describe a strategy for extending their life cycle.
   a. Camera phone (growth)
   b. SUV (maturity)
   c. Day spa (growth)
   d. Answering machine (maturity)
   e. VCR (decline)
6. Describe a fad that has come and gone during your lifetime, such as Beanie Babies. Did you take part in the fad? Why or why not? How long did it last? Why do you think it faded?

ETHICS EXERCISE

Suppose you work for a firm that is planning to delete a certain item or service from its product line. Yet the firm is still selling the product, despite the fact that within months there will be no replacement parts or customer service in place to handle
any problems that consumers might have with it. Would you continue to market the product without telling customers about its upcoming deletion, or would you inform them and suggest an alternative? Explain your decision.

1. **Product classifications.** Visit the website of each of the following companies. Review their product offerings and classify each as being a convenience, shopping, or specialty product.
   a. Gillette (http://www.gillette.com)
   b. Procter & Gamble (http://www.pg.com)
   c. Unilever (http://www.unilever.com)
2. **Managing the product life cycle.** Dozens of products have been around for many, many years. The firms behind these products seem adept at managing and extending the product life cycle. Visit each of the websites listed. Prepare a report on

how the company behind each of these products has managed the product life cycle.
   a. Arm and Hammer: http://www.armandhammer.com
   b. Band Aid: http://www.bandaid.com
   c. Clorox: http://www.clorox.com

Note: Internet Web addresses change frequently. If you don't find the exact sites listed, you may need to access the organization's home page and search from there or use a search engine such as Google.

Case 10.1

The Canadian Word for Coffee—Tims

What could be more Canadian than hockey? How about a coffee and doughnut? Even more Canadian would be a coffee and doughnut shop started by and named after a hockey player. Tim Hortons is so Canadian that terms like "double, double" (coffee with double cream and double sugar) and Tims (coffee) are part of everyday language across the country. If that wasn't enough of a sign that Tim Hortons is doing it right, they have even been named Marketer of the Year by *Marketing* magazine. The reasons they are so successful are easy—quality products and an efficient operation.

In 1964, an NHL player, Tim Horton, opened a coffee shop in Hamilton, Ontario. The original store sold only beverages and doughnuts but it was a place for the average person to meet friends. In 1965, Ron Joyce left the Hamilton police department to run the store, and in 1967, he became a full partner in the company. Tragedy struck in 1974, when Tim Horton, then playing for the Buffalo Sabres, was killed in a car accident returning home after a game in Toronto. Shortly after the accident, Joyce bought Horton's share of the business to become sole owner of the 40-store chain. It was at this time that the company decided to focus all its efforts on providing an always-fresh product and outstanding service. Another important milestone in the company's history occurred in 1995, when it merged with Wendy's International Inc., a company based in the United States. Today it operates as a separate entity from Wendy's and has more than 2700 stores in Canada and more than 300 in the United States.

Not only has the company grown but the number of items on the menu has as well. In 1976, new items started appearing on the menu board beginning with Timbits, a bite-sized doughnut hole. Other closely related products followed, including muffins, cakes, pies, croissants, soups, sandwiches, bagels, beef stew, and chili. When customers asked for Tims coffee to enjoy at home, the company responded by producing cans and pouches of their famous coffee for home brewing. While product development was important

to the success of the company, two things were kept in mind: the ever-changing tastes of their customers and the stores' ability to deliver a quality product and service. Recent additions to the menu are breakfast sandwiches, a chicken fajita wrap, and several new soups.

Throughout all the expansion, new stores, and additional menu items, the company has stayed true to its customer. The marketing team describes the company as "unpretentious, friendly, honest, caring and dependable," which is also how it describes its customers. The team reinforces this image in everything it does from its "true story" commercials, community involvement, and sponsorship programs to its Children's Foundation. It advertises on TV, radio, billboards, and newspapers but is best known for its TV ads. The true stories ads show a dog picking up coffee and doughnuts for its owner and a college student in Scotland being sent coffee from home. The Timbit sports program sponsors children's team. In addition to sponsoring children's sport teams, it also supports several programs connected with professional teams in the National Hockey League, curling, the Canadian Football League, Bob Izumi's Real Fishing Show, and the Canadian Cycling Association.

What's next for Tim Hortons? According to the company, it is going to continue to expand in both Canada and the United States.

Questions for Critical Thinking
1. At what stage of the product life cycle is Tim Hortons? What steps can be taken to manage the product portfolio?
2. How important do you think product and service quality are as a product strategy for Tim Hortons?

Sources: Rebecca Harris, "Down-Home Smarts," *Marketing*, February 7, 2005, pp. 15–19; Tim Hortons website, www.timhortons.com, accessed January 22, 2008; "Tim Hortons Is Marketing's Marketer of the Year," *Marketing Daily*, February 4, 2005; Rebecca Harris, "A Cup of Canadiana: Tim Hortons, Oakville, Ont.," *Marketing*, December 13, 2004.

Case 10.2

Pampering Pets: Lavishing Our Friends with Love

Sometimes an industry can sprout an entirely new arm—or leg or tail. That's the case with the pet-care industry, which until recently consisted of the basics: food, collars, leashes, litter, and a few toys. Today, pet owners have a choice of goods and services that rival those of humans. Not surprising when you consider that the average Canadian household spends more than $300 a year on their pets.

You can find companies such dog day care centres where pampered pooches may receive fitness sessions, play time, ice cream breaks, story time, and, of course, walks. Depending on the services selected, owners may pay $135 a day, per dog, if their pets stay overnight as well. The array of services and the price resemble nothing else so much as a spa—and that's the general idea of the kennel's owners. In other words, pet owners want luxury for their animal companions, and they are willing to pay for it.

PetSmart, one of the leading pet supply firms, reports that services have become a significant part of its business. Several years ago, the retail chain opened PetsHotels. One popular—if unusual—service at the hotels is that travelling owners can phone their dogs.

It's not just hotels for pets that are catering to animals; human hotels are getting into the act, as well. For years, certain hotels and inns have allowed pets to stay with their owners. But some have added layers of luxury. At some Holiday Inns room service is available where guests can order pet food, leashes, pet toys, grooming, or walking services. Many of these hotels are registered with Pets Can Stay, a travel agency, marketing body, and certification program for pet welcoming establishments.

In addition to services, today's Fido or FiFi can have all the gimmicks, gadgets, and gewgaws he or she wants. You'd expect a firm like PetSmart to offer a variety of pet items, but clothing stores are also providing pet products. Tabi, the women's clothing store, also carries a line of sweaters for dogs. Pet owners can even outfit their animals in the latest in designer wear at specialty stores like Mona's Dog Boutique located in the trendy fashion district in Toronto. Stores like Mona's carry everything from a $20 T-shirt to a $70 winter coat.

Not surprisingly, pet food has come a long way from the original cans of mystery meat. Gourmet foods from a wide range of makers have already hit the shelves. Food giant Nestlé Purina recently launched Beneful Prepared Meals, a line of entrées in such lip-smacking flavours as roasted chicken with pasta. The Canadian government has even got into the act by developing the "Guide for the Labelling and Advertising of Pet Food" in order to address consumer concerns about the lack of uniformity and monitoring of pet food.

What's behind the demand for all these new pet products? One industry expert attributes it to empty nesters, people whose children are grown and gone. "The house is suddenly quiet and because the pet is replacing the children, you tend to humanize them a little bit," he explains. The owner of the designer clothing store says her clients range from empty nester to gay couples and single women. Whoever the customers are, one thing is for sure: the products are designed for the consumers buying them, not necessarily the consumers using them. Pets may not know the difference between a can of regular dog food and gourmet turkey medley, but their owners do.

Questions for Critical Thinking

1. How does PetSmart benefit by offering goods *and* services to pet owners? Describe how the firm might offer both in the same location. Visit PetSmart's website at http://www.petsmart.com and create a chart illustrating the mix of some of the firm's pet-care products.
2. Suppose you were a marketer for a firm that makes gourmet pet food. Describe how you would market the firm's gourmet pet dinners to extend their product life cycle. (Be sure to use what you know about why consumers buy these products.)

Sources: Jim Salter, "Gourmet Offerings Cater to Pampered Pooch," Associated Press, April 26, 2006, http://news.yahoo.com; Kim Campbell Thornton, "New Products for Pampered Pets," MSNBC, March 29, 2006, http://www.msnbc.msn.com; Deborah Yao, "Pet Boarding Industry Finds Pampering Pays," Associated Press, February 27, 2006, http://news.yahoo.com; Christopher Elliott, "Diamonds in the Ruff," *U.S. News & World Report,* March 28, 2005, pp. 68, 70; Michelle Halpern, "Heavy Petting," *Marketing,* March 21, 2005, pp. 14–16; Industry Canada site, http://www.competitionbureau.gc.ca, accessed January 23, 2008; Annette Bourdeau, "Purina's Pet-Generated Media," Strategy, January 2007, p. 25.

Video Case 10.3

Wild Oats Natural Marketplace: Offering Products at their Peak

The written case on Wild Oats appears on page VC-13. The recently filmed Wild Oats video is designed to expand and highlight the concepts in this chapter and the concepts and questions covered in the written video case.

chapter 11

Developing and Managing Brand and Product Categories

CHAPTER OBJECTIVES

① Explain the benefits of category and brand management.

② Identify the different types of brands.

③ Explain the strategic value of brand equity.

④ Discuss how companies develop strong identities for their products and brands.

⑤ Identify and briefly describe each of the new-product development strategies.

⑥ Describe the consumer adoption process.

⑦ List the stages in the new-product development process.

⑧ Explain the relationship between product safety and product liability.

CONQUERING FLOORS WITH P&G'S SWIFFER

Who wants to spend time thinking about cleaning? Consumer goods giant Procter & Gamble does—so that you don't have to. The firm markets branded products in nearly 50 categories, including Tide laundry detergent, Pampers diapers, and Crest toothpaste. Its recent push to create a new cleaning tool that would be unique in its product category resulted in a triumph of design. The Swiffer is a simple electrostatic sweeper for hardwood floors with a rectangular head and a long swivelling pole for hard-to-reach nooks and crannies. Although the Swiffer is not a glamorous product, it has proven wildly successful among consumers. Its name has even entered the lexicon of pop culture, as users talk about how they "Swiffer" their floors.

And, in what is probably a first for a household cleaning product, the Swiffer appeared on the cover of *Rolling Stone*. The vice president for research and development at P&G's home-care division says, "If you would have bet me that one of P&G's brands would have been on the cover of *Rolling Stone* with Jessica Simpson, I would have lost that bet." Already one of the company's most profitable items, the Swiffer is now also the centrepiece of a whole new brand.

The Swiffer relies on a phenomenon called *entrainment*, which means that instead of simply pushing dirt around the floor as many conventional cleaning devices do, its disposable wet or dry cloths immediately capture it. Add to this obvious competitive advantage P&G's decision to package the product partially disassembled so that its box could be sold on a supermarket shelf in the well-travelled cleaning products aisle, and a spectacularly successful product was born.

The Swiffer now has a 87 percent share of the market for quick household cleaning tools and earns about $750 million a year for P&G. Following up on the Swiffer's success, P&G's design teams tackled other household cleaning problems and soon came up with the Swiffer WetJet Power Mop and the Swiffer Duster.

In order to develop this extensive line of floor products, P&G undertook an extensive research process. The process began with P&G teams interviewing consumers in their homes, taking pictures, and asking them about their household cleaning problems and preferences. The product development team then produced prototypes of products based on the information customers provided. The teams returned to the homes of consumers with the prototypes to demonstrate to the same consumers. The prototype trials were so successful that some consumers were reluctant to give the prototypes back.

The product development team was not finished. The prototype products still had long months of design tinkering ahead, while the team looked for the best ways to make the new products into something "Swifferesque." They experimented with different materials and designs. After several iterations and tests, the design team arrived at a model that worked, and all that remained was to choose the colours. To let consumers know about the new products, distinctive packaging was designed. Follow-up tests with consumers proved the new products were a hit, and product launches followed. With people continually looking for ways to simplify household chores, P&G is cleaning up with its innovative products.[1]

> ## *connecting with customers*
>
> P&G has successfully connected with their customers by providing them with cleaning products that make their lives easier. This is evident in the fact that the Swiffer holds a 87 percent share of the market for quick household cleaning tools.

Chapter Overview

BRANDS play a huge role in our lives. We try certain brands for all kinds of reasons: on recommendations from friends, because we want to associate ourselves with the images certain brands possess, or because we remember colourful advertisements. We develop loyalty to certain brands and product lines for varying reasons as well—the quality of a product, price, and habit are a few examples. This chapter examines the way companies make decisions about developing and managing the products and product lines that they hope will become consumer necessities. Developing and marketing a product and product line and building a desired brand image are costly propositions. To protect its investment and maximize the return on it, a specialized marketer called a *category manager*, who is responsible for an entire product line, must carefully nurture both existing and new products.

This chapter focuses on two critical elements of product planning and strategy. First, it looks at how firms build and maintain identity and competitive advantage for their products through branding. Second, it focuses on the new-product planning and development process. Effective new-product planning and meeting the profit responsibility that a category manager has for a product line require careful preparation. The wants and desires of consumers change constantly, and successful marketers manage to keep up with—or stay just ahead of—those changes. ◆◆◆

---

(1) **Explain the benefits of category and brand management.**

Marketoid

Canadian women still do more housework than men but the number of men who do housework is increasing.

brand Name, term, sign, symbol, design, or some combination that identifies the products of one firm while differentiating them from the competition's.

MANAGING BRANDS FOR COMPETITIVE ADVANTAGE

Think of the last time you went shopping for groceries. As you moved through the store, chances are your recognition of various brand names influenced many of your purchasing decisions. Perhaps you chose Colgate toothpaste over competitive offerings or loaded Heinz ketchup into your cart instead of the store brand. Walking through the snack food aisle, you might have reached for Doritos or Lay's potato chips without much thought.

Marketers recognize the powerful influence that products and product lines have on customer behaviour, and they work to create strong identities for their products and protect them. Branding is the process of creating that identity. A **brand** is a name, term, sign, symbol, design, or some combination that identifies the products of one firm while differentiating these products from competitors' offerings. Canada's best managed brands as determined by Interbrand are illustrated in Table 11.1.

As you read this chapter, consider how many brands you are aware of—both those you are loyal to and those you have never tried or have tried and abandoned. Table 11.2 shows some selected brands, brand names, and brand marks. Satisfied buyers respond to branding by making repeat purchases of the same product because they identify the item with the name of its producer. One buyer might derive satisfaction from an ice cream cone with the brand name Chapman; another might derive the same satisfaction from one with the name Breyers.

BRAND LOYALTY

Brands achieve widely varying consumer familiarity and acceptance. A snowboarder might insist on a Burton snowboard, but the same consumer might show little loyalty to particular brands in another product category such as soap. Marketers measure brand loyalty in three stages: brand recognition, brand preference, and brand insistence.

table 11.1   *Canada's Best Managed Brands*

CANADA	VALUE (MILLIONS)
1 BlackBerry	5,607.7
2 Royal Bank of Canada	4,141.1
3 TD Canada Trust	3,779.6
4 Shoppers Drug Mart	3,137.5
5 Petro-Canada	3,132.6
6 Manulife	2,559.9
7 Bell	2,537.0
8 Scotiabank	1,870.4
9 Canadian Tire	1,828.5
10 Tim Hortons	1,604.6

Source: Interbrand/Report on Business, "Competing in the Global Brand Economy: Best Canadian Brands 2008," June 2008, Interbrand Corporation website, http://www.interbrand.com/images/studies/BestCanadianBrands2008.pdf (accessed September 22, 2008). Reproduced with permission of Interbrand.

table 11.2   *Selected Brands, Brand Names, and Brand Marks*

BRAND TYPE	
Private brand	Sam's Choice (Wal-Mart) or President's Choice beverage
Family brand	RAID insect sprays or Campbell soups
Individual brand	Purex or Clorox
Brand name	Life or Cheetos
Brand mark	Colonel Sanders for KFC or Mr. Peanut for Planters

Brand recognition is a company's first objective for newly introduced products. Marketers begin the promotion of new items by trying to make them familiar to the public. Advertising offers one effective way for increasing consumer awareness of a brand. Glad is a familiar brand in Canada, and it drew on customers' recognition of its popular sandwich bags and plastic wraps when it introduced a new plastic food wrap that seals around items with just the press of a finger.

Other tactics for creating brand recognition include offering free samples or discount coupons for purchases. Once consumers have used a product, seen it advertised, or noticed it in stores, it moves from the unknown to the known category, which increases the probability that some of those consumers will purchase it.

At the second level of brand loyalty, **brand preference,** buyers rely on previous experiences with the product when choosing it, if available, over competitors' products. You may prefer Nike shoes or Roots clothes to other brands and buy their new lines as soon as they are offered. If so, those products have established brand preference.

Brand insistence, the ultimate stage in brand loyalty, leads consumers to refuse alternatives and to search extensively for the desired merchandise. A product at this stage has achieved a monopoly position with its consumers. Although many firms try to establish brand insistence with all consumers, few achieve this ambitious goal. Companies that offer specialty or luxury goods and services, such as Tiffany diamonds or Lexus automobiles, are more apt to achieve this status than those that offer mass-marketed goods and services.

One problem facing many brand names is the persistence of counterfeiting. See the accompanying "Solving an Ethical Controversy" feature for some questions about how far to carry the fight against fakes.

brand recognition
Consumer awareness and identification of a brand.

brand preference
Consumer reliance on previous experiences with a product to choose that product again.

brand insistence
Consumer refusal of alternatives and extensive search for desired merchandise.

assessment check 1

1.1 What is a brand?

1.2 Differentiate between brand recognition, brand preference, and brand insistence.

Solving an Ethical Controversy

Counterfeiters: Is It Worth the Fight to Stop Them?

MILLIONS of counterfeit goods are produced every year. It's estimated that about 10 percent of all perfumes and toiletries and 12 percent of toys and sporting goods on the market are fakes and that criminal organizations, which are behind many of the world's counterfeiting operations, are making billions on sales of phony branded products every year. Shoes, perfumes, watches, appliances, stereos, car parts, food, prescription drugs, alcohol, sportswear, designer clothing, toys, cosmetics, and even champagne are frequent targets of counterfeiters, as are CDs, cassettes, videotapes, and DVDs.

It has been estimated that the jobs, taxes, and sales lost to counterfeiters every year amount to billions, and most large companies are spending millions annually in the fight against fakes. But no one sees an end to counterfeiting. Not all countries have signed on to copyright protection treaties, and continuing attempts to get them to police illegal operations have met with limited success. Also, technologies of various kinds are making it easier all the time to produce and market bogus branded goods.

Should companies continue to invest more and more in trying to prevent counterfeiting of their brands?

PRO

1. Counterfeit drugs, for example, can be tainted and therefore dangerous, and other counterfeit goods are often shoddy and unreliable.

2. These knock-offs carrying well-respected brand names are often poor imitations of the real item, and their presence in the marketplace is likely to cause irreparable harm to the overall image of the legitimate products carrying the brand.

CON

1. Counterfeiters will always find an easy market for bargain-priced goods and so will never give up.
2. The effort of fighting counterfeiters is very hard for foreign firms, unless they can secure the cooperation of local authorities in stamping out this problem.

Where do you stand: pro or con?

Sources: Sarah McBride, "The Hunt for Movie Pirates," *The Wall Street Journal,* April 12, 2004, pp. B1, B3; Erwin Lemuel G. Oliva, "Canon Seeks Alliance with Vendors vs. Counterfeit Goods," *Inquirer News Service,* http://news.inq7.net/index.index.php, April 20, 2004; "How Can I Protect Myself from Counterfeit Goods?" BBC News, http://www.bbc.co.uk, accessed April 17, 2004; "Psst. Wanna Real Rolex?" *The Economist,* http://www.economist.com, January 22, 2004; Michael Wilson, "2 Chinatown Stores Raided in Counterfeit-Goods Sweep," *The New York Times,* http://www.nytimes.com, December 3, 2003; Timothy W. Maier, "Counterfeit Goods Pose Real Threat," Insight, http://www.insight mag.com, October 30, 2003; Matthew Benjamin, "A World of Fakes," *U.S. News & World Report,* July 14, 2003, pp. 46–47.

---

(2) **Identify the different types of brands.**

TYPES OF BRANDS

Companies that practise branding classify brands in many ways: private, manufacturer's or national, family, and individual brands. In making branding decisions, firms weigh the benefits and disadvantages of each type of brand.

generic products
Products characterized by plain labels, no advertising, and the absence of brand names.

Some firms, however, sell their goods without any efforts at branding. These items are called **generic products.** They are characterized by plain labels, little or no advertising, and no brand names. Common categories of generic products include food and household staples. These no-name products were first sold in Europe at prices as much as 30 percent below those of branded products. This product strategy was introduced in North America three decades ago. The market shares for generic products increase during economic downturns but subside when the economy improves. However, many consumers request generic substitutions for certain brand-name prescriptions at the pharmacy whenever they are available.

Manufacturers' Brands versus Private Brands

manufacturer's brand
Brand name owned by a manufacturer or other producer.

Manufacturers' brands, also called *national brands*, define the image that most people form when they think of a brand. A **manufacturer's brand** refers to a brand name owned by a manufacturer or other producer. Well-known manufacturers' brands include Hewlett-Packard, Sony, Pepsi Cola, Dell, and Heinz. In contrast, many large wholesalers and retailers place their own brands on the merchandise they market. The brands offered by wholesalers and retailers are usually called **private brands** (or private labels). Although some manufacturers refuse to produce private label goods, most regard such production as a way to reach additional market segments. Wal-Mart offers many private label products at its stores, including its Old Roy dog food.

The growth of private brands has paralleled that of chain stores. Manufacturers not only sell their well-known brands to stores but also put the store's own label on similar products. Such leading manufacturers as Westinghouse and Heinz generate ever-increasing percentages of their total incomes by producing goods for sale under retailers' private labels. Private brands are popular in the grocery business, where it is estimated that more than 30 percent of all merchandise on the shelves is private labels. They also make up about 16 percent of all global retail sales and are especially popular in western European countries such as Germany and the United Kingdom.[2]

Hardware retailers, such as Home Hardware, Canadian Tire, and Rona, have all introduced their own private brand lines of tools and household products. Hardware retailers have made the move in order to differentiate themselves in the industry. One product category where private brands have not been as popular is beauty care products.[3] Staples, the office supply retailer, sells more than 1,000 products under its own brand name. But the firm also invests heavily in product design, development, and packaging, as a product manufacturer would. And it filed for more than 25 patents in a recent year.[4]

Captive Brands

The nation's major retailers—for example, Canadian Tire— have come up with a spin-off of the private label idea. So-called **captive brands** are national brands that are sold exclusively by a retail chain. Captive brands typically provide better profit margins than private labels. One of Canadian Tire's captive brands is the Debbie Travis line of paints and other home decor products. Canadian Tire is hoping to not only increase its decor business but also attract younger shoppers into their stores.[5]

Family and Individual Brands

A **family brand** is a single brand name that identifies several related products. For example, KitchenAid markets a complete line of appliances under the KitchenAid name, and Johnson & Johnson offers a line of baby powder, lotions, plastic pants, and baby shampoo under its name. All Heinz products, from their tomato ketchup to their vegetable soup, carry the Heinz brand.

Alternatively, a manufacturer may choose to market a product as an **individual brand**, which uniquely identifies the item itself, rather than promoting it under the name of the company or under an umbrella name covering similar items. Unilever, for example, markets Knorr, Bertolli, Lipton, and Slim-Fast food products; Pond's and Sunsilk beauty products; and Lifebuoy and Dove soaps. PepsiCo's Quaker Oats unit markets Aunt Jemima breakfast products and Gatorade beverages. Individual brands cost more than family brands to market because the firm must develop a new promotional campaign to introduce each new product to its target market. Distinctive brands are extremely effective aids in implementing market segmentation strategies.

On the other hand, a promotional outlay for a family brand can benefit all items in the line. Family brands also help marketers introduce new products to both customers and retailers. Since supermarkets stock thousands of items, they hesitate to add new products unless they are confident they will be in demand.

YOUR VACATION MIGHT END, BUT THE MEMORIES CAN LAST A LIFETIME.

Once you discover the beauty of Ontario Parks you'll come back again and again. Preserve memories from your visits with HP Vivera inks. With each photo you print using HP Vivera inks, you'll get bright, vivid, true-to-life colours that resist fading. Exceptional ink purity means excellent photos and prints, every time. Your memories will last a lifetime – trust them to HP Vivera inks.

Find out more at hp.ca/parks or visit your local retailer.

WHAT DO YOU HAVE TO SAY?

Return your empty HP cartridge for recycling now. It's free. It's easy. Visit hp.ca/recycle

© 2007 Hewlett-Packard Development Company, L.P. Simulated images.

Manufacturer's brand: Hewlett-Packard.

family brand Single brand name that identifies several related products.

Marketoid

In the past 20 years the total average workday for people between the ages of 25 and 54 has increased by 30 minutes per day.

And you thought we only made cars.

Sure, Honda is best known for its automobiles. But we are, first and foremost, an engineering company. As well as the world's largest engine manufacturer. Today, we build some of the most dependable motorcycles, personal watercraft, lawnmowers, marine engines, generators, snowblowers, tillers and all-terrain vehicles out there. And, yes. We also manufacture those world-renowned cars.

From our low-emission automobiles to our clean and quiet marine engines, every Honda is designed to balance the thrill of fun and performance with society's need for fuel efficiency and cleaner air. Ultimately, it's the kind of thinking that improves the quality of life. And, certainly, the adventuresome quality of your weekends. Get things going at honda.com.

HONDA
The power of dreams.

Products marketed by Honda using a family brand.

Family brands should identify products of similar quality, or the firm risks harming its overall product image. If Rolls-Royce marketers were to place the Rolls name on a low-end car or a line of discounted clothing, they would severely tarnish the image of the luxury car line. Conversely, Lexus, Infiniti, and Porsche put their names on luxury sport-utility vehicles to capitalize on their reputations and to enhance the acceptance of the new models in a competitive market.

Individual brand names should, however, distinguish dissimilar products. Kimberly-Clark markets two different types of diapers under its Huggies and Pull-Ups names. Procter & Gamble offers shaving products under its Gillette name; laundry detergent under Cheer, Tide, and other brands; and dishwasher detergent under Cascade.

> **assessment check 2** ✓
>
> **2.1** Identify the different types of brands.
>
> **2.2** How are generic products different from branded products?

---

(3) Explain the strategic value of brand equity.

BRAND EQUITY

As individuals, we often like to say that our strongest asset is our reputation. The same is true of organizations. A brand can go a long way toward making or breaking a company's reputation. A strong brand identity backed by superior quality offers important strategic advantages for a firm. First, it increases the likelihood that consumers will recognize the firm's product or product line when they make purchase decisions. Second, a strong brand identity can contribute to buyers' perceptions of product quality. Branding can also reinforce customer loyalty and repeat purchases. A consumer who tries a brand and likes it will probably look for that brand on future store visits. All these benefits contribute to a valuable form of competitive advantage called *brand equity*.

brand equity Added value that a respected, well-known brand name gives to a product in the marketplace.

Brand equity refers to the added value that a certain brand name gives to a product in the marketplace. Brands with high equity confer financial advantages on a firm because they often command comparatively large market shares and consumers may pay little attention to differences in prices. Studies have also linked brand equity to high profits and stock returns. Service companies are also aware of the value of brand equity. Bell Canada, the company that once held a monopoly position in the telephone market, has withstood the onslaught of many competitors and expanded into other markets. One reason Bell Canada was able to accomplish this is a brand name that has long stood for quality and dependability, as the "Marketing Success" feature discusses.

In global operations, high brand equity often facilitates expansion into new markets. Currently, Coca-Cola is the most valuable—and most recognized—brand in the world.[6] Similarly, Disney's brand equity allows it to market its goods and services in Europe and Japan—and now China. What makes a global brand powerful? According to Interbrand Corp., which measures brand equity in dollar values, a strong brand is one that has the power to increase a company's sales and earnings. A global brand is generally defined as one where at least 20 percent of total sales are generated outside its home country, as Coca-Cola does. Interbrand's top 10 global brands include Microsoft, Disney, McDonald's, and IBM.[7]

The global advertising agency Young & Rubicam (Y&R) developed another brand equity system called the Brand Asset Valuator. Y&R interviewed more than 500 000 consumers in 44 countries and collected information on over 35 000 brands to help create this measurement system. According to Y&R, a firm builds brand equity sequentially on five dimensions of brand personality. These five dimensions are differentiation, energy, relevance, esteem, and knowledge:

- *Differentiation* refers to a brand's ability to stand apart from competitors. Brands such as Porsche stand out in consumers' minds as a symbol of unique product characteristics.

- *Energy* refers to how adaptive and dynamic a brand is. Brands that work for more than one product category are adaptive and dynamic. Campbell's soup and Rogers are examples.

- *Relevance* refers to the real and perceived appropriateness of the brand to a big consumer segment. A large number of consumers must feel a need for the benefits offered by the brand. A brand with high relevance is Hallmark.

- *Esteem* is a combination of perceived quality and consumer perceptions about the growing or declining popularity of a brand. A rise in perceived quality or in public opinion about a brand enhances a brand's esteem. But negative impressions reduce esteem. Brands with high esteem include Starbucks and Honda.

- *Knowledge* refers to the extent of customers' awareness of the brand and understanding of what a good or service stands for. Knowledge implies that customers feel an intimate relationship with a brand. Examples include Jell-O and Band-Aid.[8]

Marketoid

The increase in working hours over the last 20 years means Canadians are working an extra nine days each year.

marketing success   Bell Builds on its Brand

Background. Founded in 1880, Bell Canada started out with the rights to develop the telephone industry in Canada. Even at this early date the company had the foresight to realize that in order for communications companies to be effective they needed to reach a large number of people. Bell held a monopoly position in the market for many years but when the industry was deregulated, along came competitors. As it had throughout its history, Bell embraced the advances that were occurring in the industry to build on its brand and expand into new markets.

The Challenge. Over the last number of years Bell Canada has faced challenges on a number of fronts because of increased competition resulting from deregulation and new technologies. In order to respond to these challenges, Bell needed to find a way to build on its existing strong brand image.

The Strategy. In order for Bell to reinvent its brand image to convey the connectivity of its services and to build a national branding campaign, the company needed to completely rethink its communication strategy. It turned to the ad agency Cossette. The creative team at

Cossette came up with two comedic beavers, Frank and Gordon in English Canada and the same pair named Jules and Bertrand in Quebec. Three spots were developed: "Waiting Room," in which the beavers are waiting to audition to be the spokespersons for Bell; "Audition," in which the beavers are convincing the ad director why they are perfect for the job; and "The Gig," in which the beavers get the job.

The Outcome. The beavers were launched during the Super Bowl, costing Bell about $650 000. Since the launch, the beavers have grown in popularity. One industry expert explains that the beaver branding wins in two ways. First, Bell has the same branding across the country. Second, they were able to build a brand that works across all their divisions, each with different consumers.

Sources: Paul-Mark Rendon, "The Frank and Gordon Show," *Marketing,* February 6, 2006, p. 27; Bell Canada Enterprises site, http://www.bce.ca; "Telephone Deregulation Likely to Bring Intense Marketing War," *Marketing,* December 14, 2006; Karen Mazurkewich, "Winner Jim Little's Big Coup—Likely the Biggest Campaign of 2006 was also the Most Loved—and Hated," *Strategy,* March 2007, p. 48.

Sometimes a brand requires a makeover. After running into customer complaints about shoddy design in its lower-priced C-class SUVs, Mercedes dropped to 14th place in the J. D. Power quality survey. The low finish spurred the company to start a broad quality-improvement effort, streamlining its manufacturing processes, buying better component parts, and simplifying overcomplicated passenger comfort features, including eliminating 600 electronic functions that weren't being used. Although Mercedes has since climbed back to fifth in the quality survey, the company plans to do more to regain its reputation for durability and dependability.[9]

THE ROLE OF CATEGORY AND BRAND MANAGEMENT

category management
Product management system in which a category manager—with profit and loss responsibility—oversees a product line.

Because of the tangible and intangible value associated with strong brand equity, marketing organizations invest considerable resources and effort in developing and maintaining these dimensions of brand personality. Traditionally, companies assigned the task of managing a brand's marketing strategies to a **brand manager**. Today, because they sell about 80 percent of their products to national retail chains, major consumer goods companies have adopted a strategy called **category management**. In this strategy a manufacturer's *category manager* maximizes sales for the retailer by overseeing an entire product line, often tracking sales history with data from the retail checkout point and aggregating it with sales data for the entire category (obtained from third-party vendors) and qualitative data such as customer surveys.[10]

Unlike traditional product managers, category managers have profit responsibility for their product group and also help the retailer's category buyer maximize sales for the whole category, not just the particular manufacturer's product. These managers are assisted by associates usually called *analysts.* Part of the shift to category management was initiated by large retailers, which realized they could benefit from the marketing muscle of large grocery and household goods producers such as Kraft and Procter & Gamble. As a result, producers began to focus their attention on in-store merchandising instead of mass-market advertising. Some manufacturers that are too small to dedicate a category manager to each retail chain assign a category manager to each major channel, such as grocery, convenience, drugstore, and so on.[11]

Some of the steps companies follow in the category management process include defining the category based on the target market's needs, identifying the role of the retailer in that category (such as a preferred provider or a convenience provider), finding opportunities for growth, setting performance targets and establishing a means to measure progress (such as a category scorecard), and creating a marketing strategy (such as building traffic, enhancing image, or defending turf). An important next step is choosing the marketing mix by selecting the category product assortment and choosing price, promotion, and supply chain strategies. Finally, the category manager is ready to roll out the plan and review performance on a regular basis.[12]

Hershey's vending division offers category management services to its institutional customers, providing reduced inventory costs, improved warehouse efficiency, and increased sales.[13] Manufacturers of frozen breakfast items have improved sales for Kellogg and General Mills with category management strategies.[14]

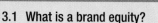

assessment check 3

3.1 What is a brand equity?

3.2 What are the five dimensions of brand personality?

3.3 How does category management help retailers?

---

(4) Discuss how companies develop strong identities for their products and brands.

PRODUCT IDENTIFICATION

Organizations identify their products in the marketplace with brand names, symbols, and distinctive packaging. Almost every product that is distinguishable from another gives buyers some means of identifying it. Sunkist Growers, for instance, stamps its oranges with the name Sunkist. Iams stamps a paw print on all of its pet food packages. For nearly 100 years, Prudential Insurance Co. has used the Rock of Gibraltar as its symbol. Choosing how to identify the firm's output represents a major strategic decision for marketers. Produce growers will soon have another option to choose from, other than paper stickers. A new technology employs laser tattoos to mark fruits and vegetables with their names, identification numbers, and country of origin. The tattoos are visible and edible, good news for consumers who are tired of peeling tiny stickers from their apples and tomatoes. The numbers on the produce stickers provide valuable information in the form of price look-up (PLUS) codes, which operate similarly to traditional bar codes by identifying the product to the retailer's computer system and then retrieving the price for grocery checkout. But the stickers have their drawbacks. "If they are sticky enough to stay on the fruit through the whole distribution and sales network," said the general manager of one onion grower, "they are so sticky that the customer can't get them off." The laser tattoos will include the four- or five-digit PLUS number and avoid the sticky labels.[15]

BRAND NAMES AND BRAND MARKS

A name plays a central role in establishing brand and product identity. The American Marketing Association defines a **brand name** as the part of the brand consisting of words or letters that form a name that identifies and distinguishes the firm's offerings from those of its competitors. The brand name is, therefore, the part of the brand that people can vocalize. Firms can also identify their brands by brand marks. A **brand mark** is a symbol or pictorial design that distinguishes a product such as Mr. Peanut for Planters nuts.

Effective brand names are easy to pronounce, recognize, and remember. Short names, such as Nike, Ford, and Bounty, meet these requirements. Marketers try to overcome problems with easily mispronounced brand names by teaching consumers the correct pronunciations. For example, early advertisements for the Korean carmaker Hyundai explained that the name rhymes with *Sunday*. Sensitivity to clear communication doesn't end with the choice of brand name; marketers should also be aware of how well they get their point across in interpersonal communications. The "Etiquette Tips for Marketing Professionals" feature provides some tips for avoiding technical jargon in business.

A brand name should also give buyers the correct connotation of the product's image. The name Lunchables for Kraft's prepackaged lunches suggests a convenient meal that can be eaten anywhere. Nissan's X-Terra connotes youth and extreme sports to promote the off-road SUV.

A brand name must also qualify for legal protection. The Trade-marks Act states that registered trademarks should not contain names or surnames unless the name is viewed in the mind of the consumer as that product, such as McDonald's. Clearly descriptive words such as sweet for baked goods cannot become registered trademarks.[16]

Marketers feel increasingly hard-pressed to coin effective brand names, as multitudes of competitors rush to stake out brand names for their own products. Some companies register names before they have products to fit the names to prevent competitors from using them. When choosing names, experts give this advice: Stay away from cute names, make sure customers will understand it, and be sure it is easy to pronounce and remember. In addition they advise not to be too creative or not to copy others but remember that a good name is unique, powerful, and one-of-a-kind.[17]

When a class of products becomes generally known by the original brand name of a specific offering, the brand name may become a descriptive generic name. If this occurs, the original owner may lose exclusive claim to the brand name. The generic names nylon, aspirin, escalator, kerosene, and zipper started as brand names. Other generic names that were once brand names include cola, yo-yo, linoleum, and shredded wheat.

Marketers must distinguish between brand names that have become legally generic terms and those that seem generic only in many consumers' eyes. Consumers often adopt legal brand names as descriptive names. Jell-O, for instance, is a brand name owned exclusively by General Foods, but many consumers casually apply it as a descriptive name for gelatine desserts. Similarly, many people use the term Kleenex to refer to facial tissues. English and Australian consumers use the brand name Hoover as a verb for vacuuming. Xerox is such a well-known brand name that people frequently—though

Minute Maid and Coke brand marks on one product.

"THE COCA-COLA COMPANY, USED WITH PERMISSION.

brand name Part of a brand consisting of words or letters that form a name that identifies and distinguishes a firm's offerings from those of its competitors.

ETIQUETTE TIPS FOR MARKETING PROFESSIONALS

Avoiding Technical Jargon

IF you're like most people, you become annoyed with technical jargon when you aren't sure what it means. Worse yet, jargon can have negative effects on a business conversation if it clouds the meaning of a message. On the other hand, jargon serves as useful shorthand in a conversation between two people who clearly understand what is being said. In general, it's best to use common sense—and err on the side of clarity. Here are a few tips on when—and when *not*—to use technical jargon.

When to use technical jargon:

1. Use an abbreviation without explanation if you are certain everyone with whom you are communicating knows it. Use a term such as *CAD*, for instance, which stands for computer-aided design, only if you are communicating with people who work in that field and already know what computer-aided design is.
2. Use a technical term such as *category management*, if necessary, but surround it with conventional terms that reflect its meaning, to help listeners unfamiliar with it.

3. Keep technical terms to a minimum so that the necessary ones have impact.

When *not* to use technical jargon:

1. Avoid technical jargon when you are communicating with an audience outside your industry, including customers. Instead of referring to an *output device* on a computer, simply say *printer*.
2. Eliminate jargon when speaking or writing to someone from another country or someone whose first language is not English.
3. Stay away from acronyms specific to your organization when you're communicating with someone outside it. Exceptions can be made for terms such as IBM because they are so well known.

Sources: Nancy Halligan, "Technical Writing," http://www.technical-writing-course.com, accessed April 19, 2006; Michael Bernhardt, "Seven Sins to Avoid with Your Next Public Speaking Engagement," http://www.refresher.com/!sevensins.html, accessed April 19, 2006; Joe Fleischer, "You Don't Need a Hero," *Call Center Magazine*, October 1, 2005, http://www.callcentermagazine.com.

---

incorrectly—use it as a verb to mean photocopying. To protect its valuable trademark, Xerox Corp. has created advertisements explaining that Xerox is a brand name and registered trademark and should not be used as a verb.

TRADEMARKS

Businesses invest considerable resources in developing and promoting brands and brand identities. The high value of brand equity encourages firms to take steps in protecting the expenditures they invest in their brands.

trademark Brand for which the owner claims exclusive legal protection.

A **trademark** is a brand for which the owner claims exclusive legal protection. A trademark should not be confused with a trade name, which identifies a company. The Coca-Cola Company is a trade name, but Coke is a trademark of the company's product. Some trade names duplicate companies' brand names. For example, Kodiak is the men's work boot brand name of the Kodiak Corporation.

Marketoid

The workday has become longer for both men and women. In the years since 1986 it has increased by 0.6 hours for men and 0.7 hours for women.

Protecting Trademarks

Trademark protection confers the exclusive legal right to use a brand name, brand mark, and any slogan or product name abbreviation. It designates the origin or source of a good or service. Frequently, trademark protection is applied to words or phrases, such as *Bud* for Budweiser.

Firms can also receive trademark protection for packaging elements and product features such as shape, design, and typeface. In Canada, the Trade-marks Act allows companies to register Distinguishing Guises, which identify the shape of the product, packaging, or wrapping. The act gives companies the right to take legal action for trademark infringement even if other products using its brand are not particularly similar or easily confused in the minds of consumers. The infringing company does not even have to know that it is diluting another's trademark. The Trade-marks Office, the government agency responsible for registering trademarks, will not police or monitor a trademark to ensure no one else is infringing on it.[18]

The Internet may be the next battlefield for trademark infringement cases. Some companies are attempting to protect their trademarks by filing infringement cases against companies using similar Internet addresses.

Trade Dress

Visual cues used in branding create an overall look sometimes referred to as **trade dress**. These visual components may be related to colour selections, sizes, package and label shapes, and similar factors. For example, McDonald's golden arches, Merrill Lynch's bull, and the yellow of Shell's seashell are all part of these products' trade dress. A combination of visual cues may also constitute trade dress. Consider a Mexican food product that uses the colours of the Mexican flag: green, white, and red. Trade dress disputes have led to numerous courtroom battles.

Mr. Clean: Trademark of the famous household cleaner.

DEVELOPING GLOBAL BRAND NAMES AND TRADEMARKS

Cultural and language variations make brand-name selection a difficult undertaking for international marketers; an excellent brand name or symbol in one country may prove disastrous in another. An advertising campaign for E-Z washing machines failed in the United Kingdom because the British pronounce z as "zed." A firm marketing a product in several countries must also decide whether to use a single brand name for universal promotions or tailor names to individual countries. Most languages contain *o* and *k* sounds, so *okay* has become an international word. Most languages also have a short *a,* so Coca-Cola works as an effective brand abroad.

PACKAGING

A firm's product strategy must also address questions about packaging. Like its brand name, a product's package can powerfully influence buyers' purchase decisions.

Marketers are applying increasingly scientific methods to their packaging decisions. Rather than experimenting with physical models or drawings, more and more package designers work with special computer graphics programs that create three-dimensional images of packages in thousands of colours, shapes, and typefaces. Another software program helps marketers design effective packaging by simulating the displays shoppers see when they walk down supermarket aisles. Companies conduct marketing research to evaluate current packages and to test alternative package designs. The environmental impact of packaging is becoming increasingly important to marketers as discussed in the Go Green Box.

A package serves three major objectives: (1) protection against damage, spoilage, and pilferage; (2) assistance in marketing the product; and (3) cost effectiveness. Let's briefly consider each of these objectives.

Protection against Damage, Spoilage, and Pilferage

The original objective of packaging was to offer physical protection for the merchandise. Products typically pass through several stages of handling between manufacturing and customer purchases, and

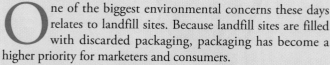

Go Green

Eco-Friendly Packages

One of the biggest environmental concerns these days relates to landfill sites. Because landfill sites are filled with discarded packaging, packaging has become a higher priority for marketers and consumers.

Two recent studies reflect the change in consumer attitudes toward packaging. *Marketing* magazine along with Ipsos Reid surveyed 1000 Canadians asking questions on what makes a product green. Brandspark International polled 10 000 Canadians as part of their Best New Products award program in order to determine product appeal and repurchase intent.

The results of the *Marketing* and Ipsos Reid study showed that although 71 percent of respondents indicated they were purchasing more environmentally friendly products over the past year, only 57 percent would pay more for these products. When asked what information would make it easier for a consumer to purchase environmentally friendly products, 73 percent wanted more information on packages and labels. Advertising campaigns (36 percent), websites (16 percent), and word of mouth (23 percent) were the sources consumers went to for more environmental information.

In the BrandSpark International research, more consumers commented on packaging than in previous years, particularly what they perceived as excessive packaging. The winner in the gum category was Excel 60-pack, which consumers liked because they felt it was more environmentally friendly. Representatives from Wrigley Canada, makers of Excel gum, admitted that the aim of the new package design was not so much to be environmentally friendly but rather to provide more gum per package to consumers.

The BrandSpark research also showed the growing importance of packaging from the company's point of view. Companies stated that the increase in recycling costs has prompted them to look for lighter packages that are easier and more cost effective to recycle, while at the same time communicating the products benefits and value.

If these trends in packaging continue, consumers can look forward to more innovation in packaging.

Sources: BrandSpark site, http://www.brandspark.ca, accessed February 8, 2008; Rebecca Harris, "Gotta Be Good," *Marketing*, February 26, 2007, pp. 26–27; Rebecca Harris, "Green Thinking," *Marketing*, June 11, 2007, pp. 18–24.

a package must protect its contents from damage. Furthermore, packages of perishable products must protect the contents against spoilage in transit and in storage until purchased by the consumer.

Fears of product tampering have forced many firms to improve package designs. Over-the-counter medicines are sold in tamper-resistant packages covered with warnings informing consumers not to purchase merchandise without protective seals intact. Many grocery items and light-sensitive products are packaged in tamper-resistant containers as well. Products such as spaghetti sauce and jams, packaged in glass jars, often come with vacuum-depressed buttons in the lids that pop up the first time the lids are opened.

Many packages offer important safeguards for retailers against pilferage. Shoplifting and employee theft cost retailers millions of dollars each year. To limit this activity, many packages feature oversized cardboard backings too large to fit into a shoplifter's pocket or purse. Efficient packaging that protects against damage, spoilage, and theft is especially important for international marketers, who must contend with varying climatic conditions and the added time and stress involved in overseas shipping.

Assistance in Marketing the Product

The proliferation of new products, changes in consumer lifestyles and buying habits, and marketers' emphasis on targeting smaller market segments have increased the importance of packaging as a promotional tool. Many firms are addressing consumers' concerns about protecting the environment by designing packages made of biodegradable and recyclable materials. To demonstrate serious concern regarding environmental protection, Procter & Gamble, Coors, McDonald's, BP Chemical, and other firms have created ads that describe their efforts in developing environmentally sound packaging.

In a grocery store where thousands of different items compete for notice, a product must capture the shopper's attention. Marketers combine colours, sizes, shapes, graphics, and typefaces to establish distinctive trade dress that sets their products apart from the products of competitors. Packaging can help establish a common identity for a group of items sold under the same brand name. Like the brand name, a package should evoke the product's image and communicate its value.

Packages can also enhance convenience for the buyers. Pump dispensers, for example, facilitate the use of products ranging from mustard to insect repellent. Squeezable bottles of honey and ketchup make the products easier to use and store. Packaging provides key benefits for convenience foods such as meals and snacks packaged in microwavable containers, juice drinks in aseptic packages, and frozen entrees and vegetables packaged in single-serving portions.

Pfizer Inc. found that a change in product packaging actually induced a change in user behaviour. Sales of its Listerine mouthwash grew by more than 10 percent when the company introduced a built-in hand grip and larger cap for the club-store-sized bottle of its popular product. It seems that the grip makes lifting the big bottle easier, and the wider mouth encourages users to swish more of the product around in their mouths, finishing the bottles more quickly than before and sending them back to the store for more.[19]

Some firms increase consumer utility with packages designed for reuse. Empty peanut butter and jelly jars have long doubled as drinking glasses. Parents can buy bubble bath in animal-shaped plastic bottles suitable for bathtub play. Packaging is a major component in Avon's overall marketing strategy. The firm's decorative, reusable bottles have even become collectibles.

Cost-Effective Packaging

Although packaging must perform a number of functions for the producer, marketers, and consumers, it must do so at a reasonable cost. Sometimes changes in the packaging can make packages both cheaper and better for the environment. Compact disc manufacturers, for instance, once packaged music CDs in two containers, a disc-sized plastic box inside a long cardboard box that fit into the record bins in stores. Consumers protested against the waste of the long boxes, and the recording industry finally agreed to eliminate the cardboard outer packaging altogether. Now CDs come in just the plastic cases, with plastic shrink-wrapping.

Labelling

Labels were once a separate element that was applied to a package; today, they are an integral part of a typical package. Labels perform both promotional and informational functions. A **label** carries an item's brand name or symbol, the name and address of the manufacturer or distributor, information about the product's composition and size, and recommended uses. The right label can play an important role in attracting consumer attention and encouraging purchases.

A number of regulations control package labelling in Canada, some at the federal level and others at the provincial level. The federal government has enacted the Competition Act, the Hazardous Products Act, the Food and Drugs Act, the Consumer Packaging and Labelling Act, and the Textile Labelling Act. The Competition Act, which is administered by the Competition Bureau, regulates false or misleading information.[20]

The Hazardous Products Act is administered by Health Canada. This act protects consumers by regulating the sale, advertising, or importing of potentially dangerous materials. It covers general aspects of labelling but has sections that relate to specific types of products, such as asbestos. The law contains special provisions for some types of packaging, such as glass containers for carbonated drinks; however, most soft drink companies have now switched to plastic bottles.[21]

The Food and Drugs Act regulates the information required on the labels of food, drugs, cosmetics, and medical devices. Consumer textile articles are dealt with under the Textile Labelling Act. The Consumer Packaging and Labelling Act specifically relates to labels for food products ensuring that accurate information describes ingredients and quantities in both French and English.[22]

The **Universal Product Code (UPC)** designation is another important aspect of a label or package. Introduced in 1974 as a method for cutting expenses in the supermarket industry, UPCs are numerical bar codes printed on packages. Optical scanner systems read these codes, and computer systems recognize items and print their prices on cash register receipts. Although UPC scanners are costly, they permit both considerable labour savings over manual pricing and improved inventory control. The Universal Product Code is also a major asset for marketing research. However, many consumers feel frustrated when only a UPC is placed on a package without an additional price tag because they do not always know how much an item costs if the price labels are missing from the shelf.

Nestle-promoting a new package design.

Radio-frequency identification (RFID) tags—electronic chips that carry encoded product identification—may replace some of the functions of UPC codes, such as price identification and inventory tracking. But consumer privacy concerns about the amount of information RFID tracking can accumulate may limit their use to aggregate packaging such as pallets, rather than units sized for individual sale.[23]

BRAND EXTENSIONS

Some brands become so popular that marketers may decide to use them on unrelated products in pursuit of instant recognition for the new offerings. The strategy of attaching a popular brand name to a new product in an unrelated product category is known as **brand extension.** This practise should not be confused with line extensions, which refers to new sizes, styles, or related products. A brand extension, in contrast, carries over from one product nothing but the brand name. In establishing brand extensions, marketers hope to gain access to new customers and markets by building on the equity already established in their existing brands.

brand extension Strategy of attaching a popular brand name to a new product in an unrelated product category.

Working with a handful of trendy designers, Mattel has extended its Barbie fashion doll brand into a line of high-end designer clothing and accessories for women from their teens through their 30s. "It's not Mattel's usual target audience," admits the company's senior vice president of global consumer marketing and entertainment. "Our target market is the fashionista." Barbie-themed jeans, shirts, handbags, and jewellery under the label Barbie Luxe are being designed by the likes of Anna Sui, Anya Hindmarch, Judith Lieber, Nickel, Not Rational, and Paper Denim & Cloth. The company hopes to revise the Barbie brand by tapping into the doll's grown-up fans.[24]

Häagen-Dazs introduces a new product.

Now available in two sizes:

Fully committed.   Let's keep this casual.

PURE PLEASURE.™   Häagen-Dazs New *Miniature Bars*   NOW SMALLER.

COURTESY OF NESTLÉ OF CANADA

BRAND LICENSING

A growing number of firms have authorized other companies to use their brand names. Even colleges and police services have licensed their logos and trademarks. This practice, known as **brand licensing**, expands a firm's exposure in the marketplace, much as a brand extension does. The brand name's owner also receives an extra source of income in the form of royalties from licensees, typically 4 to 8 percent of wholesale revenues.

Brand experts note several potential problems with licensing, however. Brand names do not transfer well to all products. Harley-Davidson, for instance, did not do well with its cake-decorating kits.[25] In addition, if a licensee produces a poor-quality product or an item is ethically incompatible with the original brand, the arrangement could damage the reputation of the brand.

Overextension is another problem. Pierre Cardin was a high-end couture brand that extended into cologne, wine, and bicycles. "It just got nuts," says one industry expert. "Their logo was on everything—at every sort of price point and at every channel distribution."[26]

NEW-PRODUCT PLANNING

As its offerings enter the maturity and decline stages of the product life cycle, a firm must add new items to continue to prosper. Regular additions of new products to the firm's line help protect it from product obsolescence.

New products are the lifeblood of any business, and survival depends on a steady flow of new entries. Some new products may implement major technological breakthroughs. Other new products simply extend existing product lines. In other words, a new product is one that either the company or the customer has not handled before. Only about 10 percent of new-product introductions bring truly new capabilities to consumers.

assessment check 4

4.1 Distinguish between a brand name and a trademark.

4.2 What are the three purposes of packaging?

4.3 Describe brand extension and brand licensing.

PRODUCT DEVELOPMENT STRATEGIES

A firm's strategy for new-product development varies according to its existing product mix and the match between current offerings and the firm's overall marketing objectives. The current market positions of products also affect product development strategy. Figure 11.1 identifies four alternative development strategies as market penetration, market development, product development, and product diversification.

⑤ Identify and briefly describe each of the new-product development strategies.

A **market penetration strategy** seeks to increase sales of existing products in existing markets. Firms can attempt to extend their penetration of markets in several ways. They may modify products, improve product quality, or promote new and different ways to use products. Packaged goods marketers often pursue this strategy to boost market share for mature products in mature markets. Product positioning often plays a major role in such a strategy.

Product positioning refers to consumers' perceptions of a product's attributes, uses, quality, and advantages and disadvantages relative to competing brands. Marketers often conduct marketing research studies to analyze consumer preferences and to construct product positioning maps that plot their products' positions in relation to those of competitors' offerings.

Method is an upstart marketer of brightly coloured household cleaning products in innovative packages. The company has positioned itself as a purveyor of environmentally friendly products, such as a patented non-aerosol air freshener in six scents, sold in bottles that resemble vases, sculptures, bowling pins, and figure eights. To further clinch its position, Method, which has 45 employees compared with Procter & Gamble's 140 000, uses recyclable packaging materials and keeps its products biodegradable by avoiding bleach and chlorine.[27]

A **market development strategy** concentrates on finding new markets for existing products. Market segmentation, discussed in Chapter 8, provides useful support for such an effort. The banks have succeeded in developing a new market by targeting Chinese residents, particularly in Toronto and Vancouver, with special media promotions, including television and newspaper ads, aimed at them.

The strategy of **product development** refers to the introduction of new products into identifiable or established markets. Companies introduce many new products each year but not all are successful. In a recent study, consumers were asked what makes them purchase new products. The three most popular reasons were these: it offers better quality, provides better value for money, and is longer lasting and more durable. Some recent new product successes include Dempster's Ancient Grain bread and Mr. Clean Extra Power Magic Eraser.[28]

Firms may also choose to introduce new products into markets in which they have already established positions to try to increase overall market share. These new offerings are called *flanker brands*. The fragrance industry uses this strategy extensively when it develops scents that are related to their most popular products. The flanker scents are related in both their smell and their names. The food industry uses this strategy extensively when it develops offerings that are related to their most popular products. The flanker products are related in both their nature and their names. Coke, for example, routinely introduces new varieties such as Coke Zero.[29]

Finally, a **product diversification strategy** focuses on developing entirely new products for new markets. Some firms look for new target markets that complement their existing markets; others look in completely new directions. Cisco Systems, the networking company, is entering the consumer electronics market with radios, telephones, and home theatre equipment

figure 11.1

Alternative Product Development Strategies

	Old Product	**New Product**
Old Market	Market Penetration	Product Development
New Market	Market Development	Product Diversification

What's your favourite season?
Spring? Summer? Italy?

THE NEW VISA INFINITE™ CARD. *Now you can experience exclusive benefits and the highest purchasing power in the Visa card portfolio. So whether you're checking in to your hotel in Florence or enjoying dinner at your local trattoria, the Visa Infinite card is designed to exceed your expectations. Learn more at visainfinite.ca*
Expect the exceptional.

Established companies introduce new products.

assessment check 5 ✓

5.1 Distinguish between market penetration and market development strategies.

5.2 What is product development?

5.3 What is product diversification?

⑥ Describe the consumer adoption process.

adoption process Stages that consumers go through in learning about a new product, trying it, and deciding whether to purchase it again.

consumer innovators People who purchase new products almost as soon as the products reach the market.

that will all tap into its expertise in developing computer routers and mine its relationship with portals such as Yahoo! and Google. Cisco's purchase of the big set-top box maker Scientific-Atlanta will give it another advantage in the consumer electronics market.[30]

In selecting a new-product strategy, marketers should keep in mind an additional potential problem: **cannibalization**. Any firm wants to avoid investing resources in a new-product introduction that will adversely affect sales of existing products. A product that takes sales from another offering in the same product line is said to cannibalize that line. A company can accept some loss of sales from existing products if the new offering will generate sufficient additional sales to warrant its investment in its development and market introduction.

THE CONSUMER ADOPTION PROCESS

In the **adoption process,** consumers go through a series of stages from first learning about the new product to trying it and deciding whether to purchase it regularly or to reject it. These stages in the consumer adoption process can be classified as follows:

1. *Awareness.* Individuals first learn of the new product, but they lack full information about it.

2. *Interest.* Potential buyers begin to seek information about it.

3. *Evaluation.* They consider the likely benefits of the product.

4. *Trial.* They make trial purchases to determine its usefulness.

5. *Adoption/Rejection.* If the trial purchase produces satisfactory results, they decide to use the product regularly.

Marketers must understand the adoption process to move potential consumers to the adoption stage. Once marketers recognize a large number of consumers at the interest stage, they can take steps to stimulate sales by moving these buyers through the evaluation and trial stages. Schick, for example, gave away 200 000 new Quattro for Women razors in major cities. The razors were packed in kits with calendar/planners and were sampled outside high-traffic office buildings as part of a six-month campaign in 10 markets. Other samples were handed out at spas, gyms, stadiums, and concert halls. Customers could also request a sample at a special website that racked up 4 million hits and ended up exhausting its supply within a month. "Short of sampling at home in the shower, we look to find unconventional ways to reach high-performance women," said the company's senior brand manager. "We're not just sampling the product, we're delivering the brand message."[31]

ADOPTER CATEGORIES

First buyers of new products, the so-called **consumer innovators,** are people who purchase new products almost as soon as these products reach the market. Later adopters wait for additional information and rely on the experiences of initial buyers before making trial purchases. Consumer innovators welcome innovations in each product area. Some computer users, for instance, rush to install new software immediately after each update becomes available. Some physicians pioneered the uses of new pharmaceutical products for their AIDS patients.

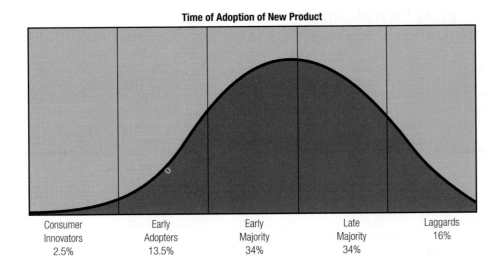

figure 11.2

Categories of Adopters Based on Relative Times of Adoption

A number of studies about the adoption of new products have identified five categories of purchasers based on relative times of adoption. These categories, shown in Figure 11.2, are consumer innovators, early adopters, early majority, late majority, and laggards.

While the adoption process focuses on individuals and the steps they go through in making the ultimate decision of whether to become repeat purchasers of the new product or to reject it as a failure to satisfy their needs, the **diffusion process** focuses on all members of a community or social system. The focus here is on the speed at which an innovative product is accepted or rejected by all members of the community.

Figure 11.2 shows the diffusion process as following a normal distribution from a small group of early purchasers (called *innovators*) to the final group of consumers (called *laggards*) to make trial purchases of the new product. A few people adopt at first, and then the number of adopters increases rapidly as the value of the product becomes apparent. The adoption rate finally diminishes as the number of potential consumers who have not adopted, or purchased, the product diminishes. Typically, innovators make up the first 2.5 percent of buyers who adopt the new product; laggards are the last 16 percent to do so. Figure 11.2 excludes those who never adopt the product.

diffusion process
Process by which new goods or services are accepted in the marketplace.

IDENTIFYING EARLY ADOPTERS

It's no surprise that identifying consumers or organizations that are most likely to try a new product can be vital to a product's success. By reaching these buyers early in the product's development or introduction, marketers can treat these adopters as a test market, evaluating the product and discovering suggestions for modifications. Since early purchasers often act as opinion leaders from whom others seek advice, their attitudes toward new products quickly spread to others. Acceptance or rejection of the innovation by these purchasers can help forecast its expected success. New-car models are multiplying, for instance, and many are sporting a dizzying variety of options such as ports to accommodate—and integrate—the driver's iPod, wireless phone, and laptop. Improved stability controls, collision warnings, and "smart engines" that save fuel are also available. Toyota Motor's president says the auto is "going through a technological revolution that is the most profound in the last 100 years," and one marketing researcher says of the new models hitting showrooms, "the all-purpose family car is a dying breed." Advances in design, manufacturing, and materials are bringing customization to the driving experience, and automakers will be anxiously watching early adopters to gauge the rest of the market.[32]

A large number of studies have established the general characteristics of first adopters. These pioneers tend to be younger, have higher social status, are better educated, and enjoy higher incomes than other consumers. They are more mobile than later adopters and change both their jobs and addresses more often. They also rely more heavily than later adopters on impersonal information sources; more hesitant buyers depend primarily on company-generated promotional information and word-of-mouth communications.

Rate of Adoption Determinants

Frisbees progressed from the product introduction stage to the market maturity stage in a period of six months. By contrast, it took 13 years to convince corn farmers to use hybrid seed corn, an innovation capable of doubling crop yields. Five characteristics of a product innovation influence its adoption rate:

1. *Relative advantage.* An innovation that appears far superior to previous ideas offers a greater relative advantage—reflected in lower price, physical improvements, or ease of use—and increases the product's adoption rate.

2. *Compatibility.* An innovation consistent with the values and experiences of potential adopters attracts new buyers at a relatively rapid rate. Consumers already comfortable with the miniaturization of communications technology are likely to be attracted to camera phones, for instance, and the video iPod with its 2.5-inch screen.

3. *Complexity.* The relative difficulty of understanding the innovation influences the speed of acceptance. In most cases, consumers move slowly in adopting new products that they find difficult to understand or use. Farmers' cautious acceptance of hybrid seed corn illustrates how long an adoption can take.

4. *Possibility of trial use.* An initial free or discounted trial of a good or service means that adopters can reduce their risk of financial or social loss when they try the product. A coupon for a free item or a free night's stay at a hotel can accelerate the rate of adoption.

5. *Observability.* If potential buyers can observe an innovation's superiority in a tangible form, the adoption rate increases. In-store demonstrations or even advertisements that focus on the superiority of a product can encourage buyers to adopt a product.

Marketers who want to accelerate the rate of adoption can manipulate these five characteristics at least to some extent. An informative promotional message about a new allergy drug could help consumers overcome their hesitation in adopting this complex product. Effective product design can emphasize an item's advantages over the competition. Everyone likes to receive something for free, so giving away small samples of a new product lets consumers try it at little or no risk. In-home demonstrations or trial home placements of items such as furniture or carpeting can achieve similar results. Marketers must also make positive attempts in ensuring the innovation's compatibility with adopters' value systems.

ORGANIZING FOR NEW-PRODUCT DEVELOPMENT

A firm needs to be organized in such a way that its personnel can stimulate and coordinate new-product development. Some companies contract with independent design firms to develop new products. Many assign product-innovation functions to one or more of the following entities: new-product committees, new-product departments, product managers, and venture teams.

New-Product Committees

The most common organizational arrangement for activities in developing a new product is to centre these functions in a new-product committee. This group typically brings together experts in such areas as marketing, finance, manufacturing, engineering, research, and accounting. Committee members spend less time conceiving and developing their own new-product ideas than reviewing and approving new-product plans that arise elsewhere in the organization. The committee might review ideas from the engineering and design staff or perhaps from marketers and salespeople who are in constant contact with customers.

Since members of a new-product committee hold important jobs in the firm's functional areas, their support for any new-product plan likely foreshadows approval for further development. However, new-product committees in large companies tend to reach decisions slowly and maintain conservative views. Sometimes members compromise so they can return to their regular responsibilities.

New-Product Departments

Many companies establish separate, formally organized departments to generate and refine new-product ideas. The departmental structure overcomes the limitations of the new-product committee system and encourages innovation as a permanent full-time activity. The new-product department is responsible for all phases of a development project within the firm, including screening decisions, developing product specifications, and coordinating product testing. The head of the department wields substantial authority and typically reports to the chief executive officer, chief operating officer, or a top marketing executive.

Product Managers

A **product manager** is another term for a brand manager, a function mentioned earlier in the chapter. This marketer supports the marketing strategies of an individual product or product line. Procter & Gamble, for instance, assigned its first product manager in 1927, when it made one person responsible for Camay soap.

Product managers set prices, develop advertising and sales promotion programs, and work with sales representatives in the field. In a company that markets many products, product managers fulfill key functions in the marketing department. They provide individual attention for each product and support and coordinate efforts of the firm's sales force, marketing research department, and advertising department. Product managers often lead new-product development programs, including creation of new-product ideas and recommendations for improving existing products.

However, as mentioned earlier in the chapter, many companies such as Procter & Gamble and General Mills have either modified the product manager structure or done away with it altogether in favour of a category management structure. Category managers have profit and loss responsibility, which is not characteristic of the product management system. This change has largely come about because of customer preference, but it can also benefit a manufacturer by avoiding duplication of some jobs and competition among the company's own brands and its managers.

Venture Teams

A **venture team** gathers a group of specialists from different areas of an organization to work together in developing new products. The venture team must meet criteria for return on investment, uniqueness of product, serving a well-defined need, compatibility of the product with existing technology, and strength of patent protection. Although the organization sets up the venture team as a temporary entity, its flexible life span may extend over a number of years. When purchases confirm the commercial potential of a new product, an existing division may take responsibility for that product, or it may serve as the nucleus of a new business unit or of an entirely new company.

Some marketing organizations differentiate between venture teams and task forces. A new-product task force assembles an interdisciplinary group working on temporary assignment through their functional departments. Its basic activities centre on coordinating and integrating the work of the firm's functional departments on a specific project.

Unlike a new-product committee, a venture team does not disband after every project. Team members accept project assignments as major responsibilities, and the team exercises the authority it needs to both plan and implement a course of action. To stimulate product innovation, the venture team typically communicates directly with top management, but it functions as an entity separate from the basic organization.

> **assessment check 6**
>
> 6.1 Who are consumer innovators?
>
> 6.2 What characteristics of a product innovation can influence its adoption rate?
>
> 6.3 What is the role of a venture team in new-product development?

THE NEW-PRODUCT DEVELOPMENT PROCESS

⑦ List the stages in the new-product development process.

Once a firm is organized for new-product development, it can establish procedures for moving new-product ideas to the marketplace. Developing a new product is often time-consuming, risky, and expensive. Usually, firms must generate dozens of new-product ideas to produce even one successful product. In fact, the failure rate of new products averages 80 percent. Products fail for a number of reasons, including inadequate market assessments, lack of market orientation, poor screening and project evaluation, product defects, and inadequate launch efforts. And these blunders cost a bundle: firms

figure 11.3

Steps in the New-Product Development Process

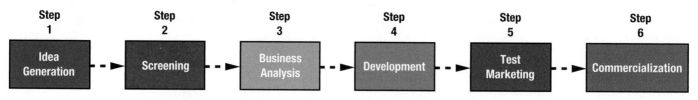

invest nearly half of the total resources devoted to product innovation on products that become commercial failures.

A new product is more likely to become successful if the firm follows a six-step development process shown in Figure 11.3: (1) idea generation, (2) screening, (3) business analysis, (4) development, (5) test marketing, and (6) commercialization. Of course, each step requires decisions about whether to proceed further or abandon the project. And each step involves a greater financial investment.

Traditionally, most companies have developed new products through phased development, which follows the six-step process in an orderly sequence. Responsibility for each phase passes first from product planners to designers and engineers, to manufacturers, and finally to marketers. The phased development method can work well for firms that dominate mature markets and can develop variations on existing products. But with rapid changes in technology and markets, many companies feel pressured to speed up the development process.

This time pressure has encouraged many firms to implement accelerated product development programs. These programs generally consist of teams with design, manufacturing, marketing, and sales personnel who carry out development projects from idea generation to commercialization. This method can reduce the time needed to develop products because team members work on the six steps concurrently rather than in sequence.

Whether a firm pursues phased development or parallel product development, all phases can benefit from planning tools and scheduling methods such as the program evaluation and review technique (PERT) and the critical path method (CPM). These techniques, originally developed by the U.S. Navy, map out the sequence of each step in a process and show the time allotments for each activity. Detailed PERT and CPM flowcharts help marketers to coordinate all activities entailed in the development and introduction of new products.

Method, discussed earlier as an example of positioning, kept its time-to-market cycle to months instead of years by using one name for all its products and outsourcing its manufacturing. The tiny organization is based on innovating, and innovating fast.[33]

IDEA GENERATION

New-product development begins with ideas from many sources: suggestions from customers, the sales force, research-and-development specialists, competing products, suppliers, retailers, and independent inventors. Marissa Mayer is Google's director of consumer Web products, but her function is to champion innovation, encouraging the company's intensely creative employees to produce a constant flow of new ideas.[34] Ray Ozzie, the creator of Lotus Notes, has been hired by Microsoft to integrate its entire product line to tap into the power of the Internet. "Ray really starts with the customer," says one Microsoft executive. "He looks at things 'outside in,' as he says, not technology-out."[35]

SCREENING

Screening separates ideas with commercial potential from those that cannot meet company objectives. Some organizations maintain checklists of development standards in determining whether a project should be abandoned or considered further. These checklists typically include factors such as product uniqueness, availability of raw materials, and the proposed product's compatibility with current product offerings, existing facilities, and present capabilities. The screening stage may also allow for open discussions of new-product ideas among different parts of the organization.

BUSINESS ANALYSIS

A product idea that survives the initial screening must then pass a thorough business analysis. This stage consists of assessing the new product's potential market, growth rate, and likely competitive strengths. Marketers must evaluate the compatibility of the proposed product with organizational resources.

Concept testing subjects the product idea to additional study prior to its actual development. This important aspect of a new product's business analysis represents a marketing research project that attempts to measure consumer attitudes and perceptions about the new-product idea. Focus groups and in-store polling can contribute effectively to concept testing. The Wrigley Science Institute is a multimillion-dollar effort by Wrigley, makers of chewing gum, to test "emerging research" that suggests that chewing gum might actually be good for you. The institute consists of an international advisory panel of independent scientists and researchers who will look at the potential benefits of gum for stress management, weight management, and alertness and concentration. The company's senior director of corporate relations explained, "We're doing this to learn more about our business and the products that we sell, as well as a brand-new science. But clearly, at the end of the day it has to deliver value. If you can get people to think about chewing gum in a new way, it's good for the category. And we're the category leader."[36]

The screening and business analysis stages generate extremely important information for new-product development because they (1) define the proposed product's target market and customers' needs and wants and (2) determine the product's financial and technical requirements. Firms that are willing to invest money and time during these stages tend to be more successful at generating viable ideas and creating successful products.

Marketoid

The proportion of Canadians aged 25 to 54 who did housework daily rose from 72 percent in 1986 to 79 percent in 2005.

DEVELOPMENT

Financial outlays increase substantially as a firm converts an idea into a visible product. The conversion process is the joint responsibility of the firm's development engineers, who turn the original concept into a product, and of its marketers, who provide feedback on consumer reactions to the product design, package, colour, and other physical features. Many firms implement computer-aided design systems to streamline the development stage, and prototypes may go through numerous changes before the original mock-up becomes a final product.

TEST MARKETING

As discussed in Chapter 7, many firms test-market their new-product offerings to gauge consumer reaction. After a company has developed a prototype, it may decide to test-market it to measure consumer reactions under normal competitive conditions. Test marketing's purpose is to verify that the product will perform well in a real-life environment. If the product does well, the company can proceed to commercialization. If it flops, the company can decide to fine-tune certain features and reintroduce it or pull the plug on the project altogether. Industries that rely heavily on test marketing are snack foods and movies. Of course, even if a product tests well and reaches the commercialization stage, it may still take awhile to catch on with the general public.

Introducing
2X Concentrated Ultra Tide
Twice the stain-fighting power in every drop.*

RATED Tide ULTRA CLEAN

*vs. non-concentrated Tide®

A new standard of **clean.**
Visit www.tide.ca

Makeovers are not just the stuff of reality TV. Products get image makeovers, too.

assessment check 7

7.1 Where do ideas for new products come from?

7.2 What is concept testing?

7.3 What happens in the commercialization stage?

COMMERCIALIZATION

When a new-product idea reaches the commercialization stage, it is ready for full-scale marketing. Commercialization of a major new product can expose the firm to substantial expenses. It must establish marketing strategies, fund outlays for production facilities, and acquaint the sales force, marketing intermediaries, and potential customers with the new product. The marketing team at Method, for instance, brainstormed to determine which competitive advantages of its new air-freshener line to promote, considering environmentally friendly, long-lasting, non-staining, effective, safe, economical and non-aerosol before settling on "non-aerosol," "concentrated," and "effective."[37]

(8) Explain the relationship between product safety and product liability.

PRODUCT SAFETY AND LIABILITY

A product can fulfill its mission of satisfying consumer needs only if it ensures safe operation. Manufacturers must design their products to protect users from harm. Products that lead to injuries, either directly or indirectly, can have disastrous consequences for their makers. **Product liability** refers to the responsibility of manufacturers and marketers for injuries and damages caused by their products. Chapter 3 discussed some of the major consumer protection laws that affect product safety. Product safety is controlled by laws that are administered by different government agencies as well as voluntary standards. The laws covering product safety include the Hazardous Products Act, the Motor Vehicle Safety Act, and many acts and regulations under the Canadian Food Inspection Agency. These laws cover many areas of product safety such as regulating and even banning certain products, requiring packaging that is not injurious to children, and ensuring food safety. In addition to the laws relating to product safety, two standards organizations operate in Canada: the National Standards System and the Standards Council of Canada. Standards are technical specifications or other criteria that companies adhere to either voluntarily or because they are required to by law.

Regulatory activities and the increased number of liability claims have prompted companies to sponsor voluntary improvements in safety standards. Safety planning is now a vital element of product strategy, and many companies now publicize the safety planning and testing that go into the development of their products. Volvo, for example, is well known for the safety features it designs into its automobiles, and consumers recognize that fact when they decide to purchase a Volvo.

assessment check 8

8.1 What role do the various product safety acts play in protecting consumers?

8.2 What role do standards play in protecting the safety of consumers?

Strategic Implications

MARKETERS who want to see their products reach the marketplace successfully have a number of options for developing them, branding them, and developing a strong brand identity among consumers and business customers. The key is to integrate all the options so that they are compatible with a firm's overall business and marketing strategy and ultimately the firm's mission. As marketers consider ideas for new products, they need to be careful not to send their companies in so many different directions as to dilute the identities of their brands, making it nearly impossible to keep track of what their companies do well. Category management can help companies develop a consistent product mix with strong branding, while at the same time meeting the needs of customers. Looking for ways to extend a brand without diluting it or compromising brand equity is also an important marketing strategy. Finally, marketers must continue to work to produce high-quality products that are also safe for all users. ◆◆◆

REVIEW OF CHAPTER OBJECTIVES

① Explain the benefits of category and brand management.

Category management is beneficial to a business because it gives direct responsibility for creating profitable product lines to category managers and their product group. Consumers respond to branding by making repeat purchases of favoured goods and services. Therefore, managing brands and categories of brands or product lines well can result in a direct response from consumers, increasing profits and revenues for companies and creating consumer satisfaction. Brand and category managers can also enhance relationships with business customers such as retailers.

② Identify the different types of brands.

A generic product is an item characterized by a plain label, no advertising, and no brand name. A manufacturer's brand is a brand name owned by a manufacturer or other producer. Private brands are brand names placed on products marketed by a wholesaler or retailer. A family brand is a brand name that identifies several related products. An individual brand is a unique brand name that identifies a specific offering within a firm's product line to avoid grouping it under a family brand.

③ Explain the strategic value of brand equity.

Brand equity provides a competitive advantage for a firm because consumers are more likely to buy a product that carries a respected, well-known brand name. Brand equity also smoothes the path for global expansion.

④ Discuss how companies develop strong identities for their products and brands.

Effective brands communicate to a buyer an idea of the product's image. Trademarks, brand names, slogans, and brand icons create an association that satisfies the customer's expectation of the benefits that using or having the product will yield.

⑤ Identify and briefly describe each of the new-product development strategies.

The success of a new product can result from four product development strategies: (1) market penetration, in which a company seeks to increase sales of an existing product in an existing market; (2) market development, which concentrates on finding new markets for existing products; (3) product development, which is the introduction of new products into identifiable or established markets; and (4) product diversification, which focuses on developing entirely new products for new markets.

⑥ Describe the consumer adoption process.

In the adoption process, consumers go through a series of stages from learning about the new product to trying it and deciding whether to purchase it again. The stages are called awareness, interest, evaluation, trial, and adoption/rejection.

⑦ List the stages in the new product development process.

The stages in the six-step process are (1) idea generation, (2) screening, (3) business analysis, (4) development, (5) test marketing, and (6) commercialization. These steps may be performed sequentially or, in some cases, concurrently.

⑧ Explain the relationship between product safety and product liability.

Product safety refers to the goal of manufacturers to create products that can be operated safely and will protect consumers from harm. Product liability is the responsibility of marketers and manufacturers for injuries and damages caused by their products. There are major consumer protection laws in place to protect consumers from faulty products.

assessment check answers

1.1 What is a brand?

A brand is a name, term, sign, symbol, design, or some combination that identifies the products of one firm while differentiating these products from competitors' offerings.

1.2 Differentiate between brand recognition, brand preference, and brand insistence.

Brand recognition is a company's first objective for newly introduced products and aims to make these items familiar to the public. Brand preference means buyers rely on previous experiences with the product when choosing it over competitors' products. Brand insistence leads consumers to refuse alternatives and to search extensively for the desired merchandise.

2.1 Identify the different types of brands.

The different types of brands are manufacturer's (or national) brands, private brands, captive brands, family brands, and individual brands.

2.2 How are generic products different from branded products?

Generic products are characterized by plain labels, little or no advertising, and no brand names.

3.1 What is brand equity?

Brand equity refers to the added value that a certain brand name gives to a product in the marketplace.

3.2 What are the five dimensions of brand personality?

The five dimensions of brand personality are differentiation, energy, relevance, esteem, and knowledge.

3.3 How does category management help retailers?

Category management helps retailers by providing a person—a category manager—to oversee an entire product line and maximize sales for that retailer. It teams the consumer-goods producer's marketing expertise with the retailer's in-store merchandising efforts to track and identify new opportunities for growth.

4.1 Distinguish between a brand name and a trademark.

A brand name is the part of the brand consisting of words or letters that forms a name distinguishing a firm's offerings from competitors. A trademark is a brand for which the owner claims exclusive legal protection.

4.2 What are the three purposes of packaging?

A package serves three major objectives: (1) protection against damage, spoilage, and pilferage; (2) assistance in marketing the product; and (3) cost effectiveness.

4.3 Describe brand extension and brand licensing.

Brand extension is the strategy of attaching a popular brand name to a new product in an unrelated product category. Brand licensing is the strategy of authorizing other companies to use a brand name.

5.1 Distinguish between market penetration and market development strategies.

In a market penetration strategy, a company seeks to increase sales of an existing product in an existing market. In a market development strategy, the company concentrates on finding new markets for existing products.

5.2 What is product development?

Product development refers to the introduction of new products into identifiable or established markets.

5.3 What is product diversification?

A product diversification strategy focuses on developing entirely new products for new markets.

6.1 Who are consumer innovators?

Consumer innovators are the first buyers of new products—people who purchase new products almost as soon as these products reach the market.

6.2 What characteristics of a product innovation can influence its adoption rate?

Five characteristics of a product innovation influence its adoption rate: relative advantage, compatibility, complexity, possibility of trial use, and observability.

6.3 What is the role of a venture team in new-product development?

A venture team gathers a group of specialists from different areas of an organization to work together in developing new products.

7.1 Where do ideas for new products come from?

New-product development begins with ideas from many sources: suggestions from customers, the sales force, research-and-development specialists, assessments of competing products, suppliers, retailers, and independent inventors.

7.2 What is concept testing?

Concept testing subjects the product idea to additional study prior to its actual development.

7.3 What happens in the commercialization stage?

When a new-product idea reaches the commercialization stage, it is ready for full-scale marketing.

8.1 What role do the various product safety acts play in protecting consumers?

The various safety acts regulate the safety of consumer products such as food and automobiles.

8.2 What role do standards play in protecting the safety of consumers?

Standards are technical specifications or other criteria that companies adhere to either voluntarily or because they are required to by law.

MARKETING TERMS YOU NEED TO KNOW

These terms are printed in red in the text. They are defined in the margins of the chapter and in the Glossary that begins on p. G-1. Other important terms are printed in bold black type in the chapter but not included in this list. Their definitions can be found in the Glossary.

brand 354	manufacturer's brand 356	trademark 362
brand recognition 355	family brand 357	brand extension 366
brand preference 355	brand equity 358	adoption process 368
brand insistence 355	category management 360	consumer innovators 368
generic products 356	brand name 361	diffusion process 369

ASSURANCE OF LEARNING REVIEW

1. What are the three stages marketers use to measure brand loyalty?
2. Identify and briefly describe the different types of brands.
3. Why is brand equity so important to companies?
4. What are the characteristics of an effective brand name?
5. What role does packaging play in helping create brand loyalty and brand equity?
6. What is category management and what role does it play in the success of a product line?
7. Describe the different product development strategies.
8. What are the five stages of the consumer adoption process?
9. Describe the different ways companies can organize to develop new products.
10. List the six steps in the new-product development process.

PROJECTS AND TEAMWORK EXERCISES

1. Locate an advertisement for a product that illustrates an especially effective brand name, brand mark, packaging, and overall trade dress. Explain to the class why you think this product has a strong brand identity.
2. With a classmate, go shopping in the grocery store for a product that you think could benefit from updated or new package design. Then sketch out a new package design for the product, identifying and explaining your changes as well as your reasons for the changes. Bring the old package and your new package design to class to share with your classmates.
3. What category of consumer adopter best describes you? Do you follow the same adoption pattern for all products, or are you an early adopter for some and a laggard for others? Create a graph or chart showing your own consumer adoption patterns for different products.
4. With a classmate, choose a firm that interests you and together generate some ideas for new products that might be appropriate for the company. Test your ideas out on each other and then on your classmates. Which ideas make it past the first stage? Which don't? Why?
5. Consider the steps in the new-product development process. Do you think this process accounts for products that come into being by chance or accident? Why or why not? Defend your answer.
6. With a classmate, visit a couple of supermarkets and look for generic products. How many did you find and in what product categories? Are there any products you think could be successfully marketed as generics that are not now? Why do you think they would be successful?
7. Which product labels do you read? Over the next several days, keep a brief record of the labels you check while shopping. Do you read nutritional information when buying food products? Do you check care labels on clothes before you buy them? Do you read the directions or warnings on a product you haven't used before? Make notes about what influenced your decision to read or not read the product labels. Did you feel they provided enough information, too little, or too much?
8. Some brands achieve customer loyalty by retaining an air of exclusivity and privilege, even though that often comes along with high price tags. Louis Vuitton, the maker of luxury leather goods, is one such firm. "You buy into the dream of Louis Vuitton," says one loyal customer. "We're part of a sect, and the more they put their prices up, the more we come back. They pull the wool over our eyes, but we love it." What kind of brand loyalty is this, and how does Vuitton achieve it?
9. Visit a grocery store, look at print ads, or view television advertising to develop a list of all the different brands of bottled water. How do the producers of bottled water turn this commodity item into a branded product? How does each differentiate its brand from all the others?
10. As the owner of a huge food business, Philip Morris is more than just a cigarette maker. Eager to make a new start in the wake of damaging lawsuits brought by smokers, the company changed its name to Altria. What associations do you think this name is intended to convey? Do you think it will help improve the company's image? Why or why not?

CRITICAL THINKING EXERCISES

1. With smoking bans in effect in many places, Zippo Manufacturing, maker of the well-known lighters, is looking for ways to license its brand name to makers of products such as grills, torches, space heaters, and fireplaces. Do you think this is a good strategy for Zippo? Why or why not? Identify another well-known product that you think would profit from a licensing strategy. What kind of companies would make good licensing partners for this firm? Do you think the strategy would be successful? Why or why not?

2. General Mills and several other major food makers have begun producing organic foods. But they have deliberately kept their brand names off the packaging of these new products, thinking that the kind of customer who goes out of his or her way to buy organic products is unlikely to trust multinational brands. Other companies, however, such as Heinz and PepsiCo are betting that their brand names will prove to be persuasive in the $11-billion organic foods market. Which strategy do you think is more likely to be successful? Why?

3. After the terrorist attacks of 9/11, an ad hoc task force of DDB Worldwide advertising professionals in 17 countries set out to discover what people abroad thought of the United States. In the course of their research, they developed the concept of "America as a Brand," urged U.S. corporations with overseas operations to help "restore" positive impressions of Brand America around the world, and urged the United States to launch Al Hurra as an alternative to the popular Al Jazeera network. Do you think foreigners' perception of a country and its culture can be viewed in marketing terms? Why or why not?

4. Brand names contribute enormously to consumers' perception of a brand. One writer has argued that alphanumeric brand names, such as the Toyota RAV4, Jaguar's X-Type sedan, the Xbox game console, and the GTI from Volkswagen, can translate more easily overseas than "real" names like Golf, Jetta, Escalade, and Eclipse. What other advantages and disadvantages can you think of for each type of brand name? Do you think one type is preferable to the other? Why?

ETHICS EXERCISE

As mentioned in the chapter, some analysts predict that bar codes may soon be replaced by a wireless technology called *radio frequency identification (RFID)*. RFID is a system of installing tags containing tiny computer chips on, say, supermarket items. These chips automatically radio the location of the item to a computer network where inventory data are stored, letting store managers know not only where the item is at all times but also when and where it was made and its colour and size. Proponents of the idea believe RFID will cut costs and simplify inventory tracking and reordering. It may also allow marketers to respond quickly to shifts in demand, avoid under- and overstocking, and reduce spoilage by automatically removing outdated perishables from the shelves. Privacy advocates, however, think the chips provide too much product-preference information that might be identified with individual consumers. In the meantime, Wal-Mart is asking its top suppliers to begin using the new technology on products stocked by the giant retailer.

1. Do you think RFID poses a threat to consumer privacy? Why or why not?

2. Do you think the technology's possible benefits to marketers outweigh the potential privacy concerns? Are there also potential benefits to consumers, and if so, what are they?

3. How can marketers reassure consumers about privacy concerns if RFID comes into widespread use?

INTERNET EXERCISES

1. Patents. Visit the website of Industry Canada (http://www.ic.gc.ca). Review the patent application procedure. Note how much it costs to apply for a patent, how the patent application is evaluated, the benefits of a patent, and the length of time a patent is valid. Prepare a brief report to your class on the patent application process.

2. Packaging. Companies use packaging to help market their products. Visit each of the following websites and prepare a brief report on how each company has used packaging as part of its brand management strategy.

a. H. J. Heinz: http://www.heinz.com
b. Campbell Soup: http://www.campbellsoup.com
c. General Mills (Yoplait Yogurt): http://www.yoplait.com

Note: Internet Web addresses change frequently. If you don't find the exact sites listed, you may need to access the organization's or company's home page and search from there or use a search engine such as Google.

Case 11.1

What Will Become of the Box?

Did you eat breakfast this morning? If you're like many consumers today, you probably answered no. Or even if you had breakfast, it's less and less likely that you sat down at your kitchen table and ate a leisurely bowl of cereal. About half of all North Americans now either skip the day's first meal or eat it on the run, opting for yogurt, pastry, a nutrition bar, or a sandwich consumed on the way to work or school.

Nutritionists may cringe but it's cereal manufacturers who are really worried. The market for cold cereal is in a state of near stagnation, and efforts to revive the category have to overcome not just a simple preference for plain or frosted flakes but an enormous shift in lifestyles and eating habits that seems to have passed this mature food category by.

Cereal makers have tried various methods to increase demand in this market. They've introduced new products and new flavours, added fruit, promoted cereal as a weight-loss option, and launched expensive ad campaigns. Quaker even used a *CSI*-themed ad to promote one of their new cereals. Kellogg included toning ball and exercise instructional DVDs in their Special K cereal. The exercise giveaways were supported with television ads and radio spots. Still, many of the top brands are losing money, and overall sales growth has stalled. There's no question that quicker and more convenient substitutes are growing faster than traditional dry cereals.

Many industry experts offer ideas for reviving interest in a bowl of cereal and milk. They suggest promoting cereal as a healthy meal or snack for any time of the day, not just breakfast. (That might even include a vegetable-based product to serve with tomato juice instead of milk.) Kellogg has already introduced Vive, a mixture of flakes, granola clusters, cinnamon, and soy. Its target market is 35- to 45-year-olds who eat soy-based products in an effort to reduce the risk of cancer and heart disease. Kellogg has also teamed up with Tetley to promote green tea. Aimed at the female head of the household who is health conscious and younger than black tea drinkers, the green tea promotion educates these consumers on the benefits of green tea. Industry experts urge cereal makers to team up with dairy farmer groups to produce ads similar to the successful milk campaigns. But perhaps the most interesting suggestion is to simply reinvent the whole concept of cereal by repackaging it.

Suggestions for thinking outside the cereal box range from bagging individual servings in zippered plastic bags to using metallized bag linings, as potato chip makers have long done. Other packaging options include cereals in sleeves like the kind crackers come in, a milk-and-cereal combination with a long shelf life and vacuum-packed cereal in containers like the ones that juice brands use. Currently being tested is a canister with a three-way spout that allows consumers to mix and match different options, such as three different brands or three different flavours or textures of the same brand.

Of course cereal bars are already growing in popularity and, ironically, are among the many breakfast options competing with the more than 100 current varieties of traditional cereal products. Realistically, says one Kellogg's executive, there is no "single silver bullet that will solve the issue we face today." So, what are you having for breakfast tomorrow?

Questions for Critical Thinking

1. One industry consultant argues that cereal companies should be focusing on new-product innovations instead of on ways to repackage the same old products. Do you agree? Why or why not? Support your answer with evidence from the case or from your reading of the chapter.

2. How can cereal manufacturers reposition their brands in light of today's hectic lifestyles and even changes in eating habits (like carb avoidance as advocated by the Atkins diet)? What would it take for you to perceive dry cereal as a convenient and healthy food? How do you think companies like Kellogg's could use your answer to persuade the general public?

Sources: *William* A. Roberts Jr., "A Cereal Star," *Prepared Foods,* http:// www .preparedfoods.com, November 25, 2003; "The U.S. Market for Food Bars: Cereal, Snacks, Sports, Meal Replacement," report of Global Information, Inc., http://www .the-infoshop.com, September 2003; Sonia Reyes, "What Will Become of the Box?" *Brandweek,* January 27, 2003, pp. 24–28; "Cereal Bars: Major Markets Outlook to 2006," Food Info Net, http://www.foodinfonet.com, January 15, 2003; Astrid Van Den Broeck, "Kellogg Markets 'Tasty' Soy Cereal," *Marketing,* April 23, 2001, p. 3; Michelle Warren, "QTG Gets Breakfast Ready," *Marketing,* May 12, 2003, p. 2; James Careless, "Cereal Killer," *Marketing,* May 14, 2001, p. 24; Paul Brent, "Time to Get Active?" *Marketing,* October 9, 2006, pp. 31–32; Sarah Dobson, "Kellogg Wants Customers to 'Have a Ball,'" *Marketing,* January 9, 2006; Sarah Dobson, "Quaker Ad Features Sleuths Tackling Cereal Mystery," *Marketing,* March 22, 2006.

Case 11.2

Worm Poop—New Product?

Since when is worm poop a new product? Since Tom Szaky developed a poop-based plant food. Tom Szaky, born in Hungary and raised in Toronto, was a student at Princeton University when he became an "eco-capitalist." So why is worm poop so successful? Worm poop, it seems, hit the market at the right time, meets the needs of customers, is priced right, and has a very persistent founder.

While at Princeton, Szaky went to Montreal to visit friends attending McGill. The McGill friends were growing the healthiest marijuana plant Szaky had ever seen, because it was fed a steady diet of worm poop. The red wigglers were fed organic waste such as coffee grinds, banana peels, or whatever was left over from meals.

When Szaky returned to Princeton, he and some friends invested $20 000 in worms. They made a deal with the Princeton cafeteria to remove their organic waste to feed the worms, bottled the resulting fertilizer in recycled plastic soda bottles, and sold it to local gardeners. They realized that they needed to grow in order to make the business viable. Szaky entered every business plan contest he could find and won $1 million from a contest sponsored by a venture capital firm. Szaky eventually turned down the venture capital offer but the win got their worm poop enough attention that other investors came forward. The company Terracycle Inc. was born.

Szaky took a permanent leave from Princeton to open a plant in Trenton, New Jersey, in an abandoned warehouse. Everything needed to open an office and plant was second-hand, including desks, phones, computers—even the large tubs used in manufacturing the fertilizer were retrieved from a landfill site. The manufacturing process was easy enough: you take worm poop, brew it into a tea, and put the liquid in used soda bottles.

In order to get the 20 000 used soda bottles they needed daily, they went to schools and charities. They paid school children a few cents for each bottle—the students benefited by using the money earned to pay for school trips and sports equipment. Another win for the company was the fact that the school children felt good about supporting the environment. The remainder of the bottles the entrepreneurs needed came from recycling companies.

Szaky admits that he is no tree hugger; rather, he wants to make money, a lot of money, selling worm poop. In order to achieve his goals, he hires young people who would have difficulty finding other jobs to work in the plants, but he also hires experts. The company has expert researchers and expert marketers on staff. They also know their customers. They determined that people would buy eco-friendly products if they were priced right, so they priced their products below their competitors'.

Terracycle's marketing strategy consists almost entirely of public relations. The founders have appeared on several television programs, and many articles about them have appeared in business and environmental magazines. Some of the publicity has come from an unwanted source, a lawsuit from the largest producer of fertilizer, Miracle-Gro. Miracle-Gro sued Terracycle for false advertising and trade-dress infringement. Once again, Terracycle's defence was unconventional. They knew that lawsuits were expensive so they set up a website—suedbyscotts.com—to let the world know what was happening. The lawsuit was settled out of court when Terracycle agreed to change the colours of its packaging and its advertising.

Terracycle's unconventional marketing strategy is working for the company. Its sales have been increasing by 300 percent a year, it has won awards for its products, and its products are being sold in Wal-Mart and Home Depot.

Questions for Critical Thinking

1. What aspects of the new product development process did Terracycle follow and which ones didn't they follow?
2. Are there other product strategies the company could use? What are they? Why do you think they could be important to the firm?

Sources: Jack Neff, "When the Worm Poop Hits the Fan—Market It," *Advertising Age,* April 23, 2007, pp. 4–5; Fayazuddin A. Shirazi, "Brand Battle," *Chief Executive,* September 2007, p. 16; Cindy Rovins, "Getting into the Big Box by Thinking Outside the Bin," *In Business,* January/February 2007, pp. 14–16; Christopher Shulgan, "The Worm Wrangler," *Maclean's,* June 4, 2007, pp. 34–35; Gwendolyn Bounds, "A Growing Dispute: Fertilizer Start-up Uses Web as Defense," *The Wall Street Journal,* May 22, 2007, p. B1; Kate Calder, "Edgar & Ellen's Worm Poop Promo Brings the Green Movement Down to Kids," *KidScreen,* June 2007, p. 53.

Video Case 11.3

Rebranding at JPMorgan Chase

The written video case on JPMorgan Chase appears on page VC-13. The recently filmed JPMorgan Chase video is designed to expand and highlight the concepts in this chapter and the concepts and questions covered in the written video case.

marketer's minute highlights

GRACE MISTRY

COURTESY OF GRACE MISTRY

Talking About Marketing with Grace Mistry

Here are highlights of our interview with Grace Mistry of BMO Bank of Montreal. For the complete video interview and transcript, go to http://www.contemporarymarketing2.nelson.com

Q2: What attracted you to the field that you are in? What was your first marketing job and how did you get it?

GM: A combination of circumstances led me to the marketing profession. After having worked the summer after my second year at university for *WeddingBells* magazine in Toronto, I was approached by them the following year to take on a maternity leave contract as retail services manager. I decided to complete my final credits between U of T and Ryerson and get my feet wet in the working world and full-time hours. There I got a taste for how editorial and advertising came together to create a bi-annual publication and what it took to put together industry events (i.e., bridal shows). After the contract ended, I took on a marketing manager role in a start-up high-tech company and spent four years as a marketing generalist looking after the creation of everything from brochures, the company newsletter and website, managing tradeshows, etc.

Q4: What do you like/dislike about your job?

GM: What keeps me in marketing is the fact that the discipline marries business strategy with creativity so there's never a dull day. Pet peeves include meetings for the sake of meetings where there's no clear agenda or when objectives are unknown, which makes for an unproductive use of time. Also, everyone wants to be a marketer and has a friendly suggestion about new ways to spin products, what a new program should look like or a promotional idea, and it can be difficult to manage expectations. Regularly communicating with key stakeholders your marketing plans is how to deal with this.

What keeps me in marketing is the fact that the discipline marries business strategy with creativity so there's never a dull day.

Q5: What was the biggest challenge/surprise when you entered the field?

GM: How diverse marketing is. While there are varying definitions for the discipline, I'm not sure that any one of them provides a glance into all the facets that make it marketing. For example, my first full-time job included product marketing, event marketing, marketing communications, and e-marketing.

Q6: What is your biggest accomplishment?

GM: In my professional career it would have to be the recipient of BMO Bank of Montreal's top employee honours, 2005 Annual Best of the Best, in recognition for high degree of effort developing and executing seasonal mass advertising marketing campaigns that outperformed business projections and delivered exceptional return on investment. In my volunteer work it would be successfully leading a 17-person board of directors as President of the Toronto Chapter of the American Marketing Association to deliver on the strategic plan in fiscal 2007.

Q7: What is your biggest mistake and what did you learn from it?

GM: Don't be afraid to try new things and have them fail. You can only be wiser from the experience. That's why it's called a "test-and-learn".

Q8: Could you please give us a few key presentation tips?

GM: Be prepared. Be prepared. Be prepared. Knowing the subject that you're going to present on will allow you to feel more comfortable delivering it no matter who the crowd is (e.g., your peers, executives, students). Also, be mindful of the audience's knowledge/interest on the subject and tailor your comments accordingly (i.e., don't waste executives' time with details, give them the broad strokes—they tend to favour a one-page handout versus lots of slides). Don't prepare an hour's worth of material if you've only got 15 minutes. Be focused and to the point. The focus should be on you delivering the message not the slides or handouts, they're just supplemental.

Q9: What are the important skills that marketing students needs to succeed?
GM: Everyone wants/needs a job, but where you can choose to take on challenging work (puts you outside your comfort zone), do it so you can enrich your experience as a person/ marketer. Informally seek guidance from people you admire (whether they are marketers or not) and be willing to give back to them too. Don't stop learning; it's critical to growing as a person and professional marketer. For example, AMA Toronto offers monthly events on hot and emerging topics to keep you on your toes. Visit **http://amatoronto.org** for details.

Comedy's the Name of the Game in This Mix

On a Friday night at The Second City, the audience line stretches past the box office, down the spiral staircase, and even out onto the streets of Chicago, Detroit, or Toronto. Patrons are shown a seat by the host and generally order a round of drinks for their party. The stage lights come up, and over a backdrop of rock music the cast of The Second City bursts onto the stage. Tonight, the first scene of the show is filled with a lightning-paced musical montage. Comedic bits and melodic vignettes preview the characters about to entertain the night's audience. After the scripted show, the crowd is treated to Second City's signature art form—improvisation. These unscripted scenes are based on single word suggestions from the audience and result in quick and hilarious character dialogues. Whether on the Mainstage in Chicago or starting up a new show in Denver, improvisers at The Second City excel in off-the-cuff comedy. It's easy for a customer to forget that the "product" of The Second City is an artistic creation formed as part of a business model.

The Second City has made significant product decisions to build its brand into an attractive mix of related services. Positioning these services in the market has kept SC competitive in the theatre and entertainment industries. To maintain brand equity throughout expansion, SC has stayed true to its roots. Company co-founder Bernie Sahlins relates Second City's success to its dedication to the stage: "I think that's why SC has survived, because it comes from the theatre. . . As long as it holds on to that, it's going to do well." With multiple stages, national touring companies, a booming corporate comedy division, and a growing Training Center, the SC product is offered to a number of audiences. Rooted in stage comedy, the Second City brand remains recognizable. Whether in the theatre, the classroom, or the corporate staff room, Second City must continue producing an impressive cast of performers.

CEO Andrew Alexander has produced more than 200 Second City revues since joining the company in 1974. He has played a strong role in SC's care and growth, which has included finding, cultivating, and producing great talent. He says that SC "looks for individuals that are intelligent, have a point of view, and the potential to become a good actor . . . and a comedic sensibility doesn't hurt." This general welcoming of talent has brought hundreds of performers of all ages to Second City's door. Because The Second City offers an intangible service to its consumers, standardizing the product throughout the organization is a challenge. To meet this challenge and widen its product line, Second City has created an instructional division with Training Centers in six cities.

Since opening its first Training Center in 1985, The Second City has attracted a wide range of aspiring actors, comedy enthusiasts, and casual hobbyists. Vice president Kelly Leonard notes that the reputation of the Second City brand has attracted most of the Training Center's student body. It also markets toward the less theatrically inclined, those who wish to "take a different direction in their life—branch out, get better at communicating." Aptly, Second City offers a versatile program. The Training Center has classes on the techniques of acting, writing, music, directing, and, of course, improvisation. Classes are often taught by the same performers who create shows for the Second City stage. This fosters a recognizable community for Second City participants, wherein famous alumni and acclaimed productions are benchmarked for study or revue. The life cycle of the Second City performer in training can start in kindergarten and continue on with SC's extensive list of offerings. With around 2000 students enrolled at any given time, the top management at SC must create a cohesive curriculum rooted in the fundamentals of the brand.

For Kelly Leonard, "Second City's culture is built upon improvisation. We 'yes, and' to ideas. We are always creating." The Second City mantra of "yes, and" is a technique of accepting and building off ideas presented in scenes. The creative power of "yes, and" is strung throughout all aspects of The Second City. The new product development process for The Second City has especially benefited from this radical approach to generating ideas. The Second City Theatricals Division, headed by Leonard, produces plays and sketch comedy for performing arts centres and private events. Leonard saw a unique opportunity to extend the product onto Norwegian Cruise Lines, exclusively producing shows for the exotic travelling company. The operation has become a lucrative new product line for Second City.

Today, a number of Second City ensembles perform on ships and stages around the world. The process of hiring and cultivating performers is paramount to producing quality talent. As television and the Internet create competitive alternatives for consumers, The Second City must position its brand as a reliable source of stage comedy. "I think that as the entertainment universe becomes more loud or more crowded, we will strengthen our position through simple quality. More, decidedly, does not mean better. We have to be rock solid and stay true to the brand," says Kelly Leonard. With SC producer Beth Kligerman and a number of other creative personnel, Leonard oversees the selection process for talent at The Second City. Selecting the best graduates of the Training Center and occasionally a talented walk-in, SC consistently makes quality a fundamental product strategy.

Across the nation, prominent marquees display The Second City's stacked logo above the entrance of each theatre. SC adopted this "splotched" style logo during its 25th anniversary year. This "graffiti on the wall" look for the logo signifies its subversive style. Hints to that character are found not only on Second City marquees, but in the nature of its service as well. "In The Second City, culture, authority, and the norm are to be disturbed—creativity and originality are to be celebrated," says Kelly Leonard.

The Second City manages its brand in the same way its performers hit the stage: with a dedication to the core product and an eager sense to accept and build on ideas. This commitment has allowed The Second City to develop an impressive product mix.

Questions

1. Given Second City's welcoming of new ideas, what sort of new product planning do you think The Second City could do? How would you relate it to Second City's focus on the theatre?

2. How does Second City's Training Center function as a separate product line for the business? How does it benefit the company in multiple ways?

3. How would you define the Second City product (specialty, unsought, convenient, or shopping)? Why? How is this reflected in its brand?

4. What advantages might the Second City product have to the traditional life cycles of a product? What disadvantages?

Part 4 CBC Video Case

CBC

Visit the website for Contemporary Marketing at http://www.contemporarymarketing2e.nelson.com to view the CBC video and video case summary for Part 4.

DISTRIBUTION DECISIONS

chapter 12

Marketing Channels and Supply Chain Management

CHAPTER OBJECTIVES

1. Describe the types of marketing channels and the roles they play in marketing strategy.

2. Outline the major channel strategy decisions.

3. Describe the concepts of channel management, conflict, and cooperation.

4. Identify and describe the different vertical marketing systems.

5. Explain the roles of logistics and supply-chain management in an overall distribution strategy.

6. Identify the major components of a physical distribution system.

7. Compare the major modes of transportation.

8. Discuss the role of transportation intermediaries, combined transportation modes, and warehousing in improving physical distribution.

ZAPPOS.COM: SHOES TO YOUR DOOR

Wandering through a maze of shoe stores at the mall, searching for the perfect pair, can be frustrating. One store carries your size, but the styles are frumpy. Another has better styles but the wrong colours. A third store has brands you've never heard of and don't want to try. The last shop had the shoes you're looking for—but they sold the last pair yesterday. The people who work at Zappos.com know all about this experience—they've had it themselves. In fact, founder Nick Swinmurn got the inspiration for his firm while on an unsuccessful quest for shoes. The Internet was still a fairly new way to sell consumer goods in 1999, but he thought he could make it work.

Shoes are a $40-billion market in Canada and the United States. In 1999 when Zappos was founded, $2 billion of those sales came from mail order. Brick-and-mortar retailers estimated that they were losing about one of every three sales because they didn't have the right size or colour in stock. Swinmurn realized the huge opportunity that lay in front of him. If he could offer one of the largest selections of shoes available and deliver them to consumers' homes as quickly as possible, his firm could fill consumers' needs for shoes in a way no other company had yet been able to.

From the beginning, service and selection have been Zappos.com's mantra. The call centre is open round the clock and is staffed by about 200 workers who take and fulfill orders. "We believe that the most important key to our success will be our service-oriented culture, and we spend a lot of time and effort working on ways to constantly improve our culture," says the company's website. Every new employee undergoes four weeks of customer service training before starting a job. Because the warehouse is open 24/7, a customer who orders shoes as late as 11 p.m. can still get next-day delivery in the United States. Delivery within Canada ranges from 5 to 10 days. Regular shipping and return shipping are free to newcomers in the United States. Customers in Canada pay a $10 delivery charge regardless of order size. This strategy has helped the firm grow as it has added new products such as handbags to its lineup. "If customers know that they're going to get the best service from Zappos and they're going to get it overnight, then anytime we're going to add a product category, our customers will be loyal to us," says CEO Tony Hsieh.

Service and selection are the perfect fit at Zappos. The firm now carries more than 500 name brands, in 90 000 styles, with about 2 million pairs in stock at its main warehouse ready for shipment. Unlike other online retailers, Zappos doesn't accept back orders if shoes are out of stock. Instead, the firm offers an alternative so that customers are never kept waiting for a pair of shoes. The warehouse location is strategic—it's right near the UPS air hub at the Louisville International Airport. "We can get shoes to [customers in] California faster than you could from California," quips Craig Adkins, director of warehouse operations. "We have a very good relationship with UPS. They leave their trailers here, and we fill them up."

To succeed over the long run, Zappos must build and maintain strong relationships with its vendors—the manufacturers and wholesalers that supply the shoes and handbags. Open and frequent communication is the basis of these relationships. Zappos set up an extranet with its vendors so that they can see which brands and models of shoes are selling and how profitable they are. Zappos also hosts a vendor appreciation party to kick off the big shoe trade show each year. "I can see my business from their point of view," explains Tom Austin, a territory manager for Clarks shoes. "[Zappos] just says, 'I don't want to run out of shoes, you take care of us.' You can't believe how pleasant [Zappos] is to work with."[1]

connecting with customers

Zappos connects with its customers by offering unequalled selection, combined with outstanding service. It sells more than 500 brands of shoes in 90 000 styles. Customers who order from Zappos are nearly always assured they can find what they want, can place their order 24/7, and can receive delivery overnight in the United States and in about 5 to 10 days in Canada. The company's reputation for selection and service has allowed it to add product lines, such as handbags, to continue to meet its customers' needs.

Chapter Overview

DISTRIBUTION—moving goods and services from producers to customers—is the second marketing mix variable and an important marketing concern. Although a sleek design and stylish photo might motivate

distribution Movement of goods and services from producers to customers.

consumers to purchase a pair of high-end shoes from Zappos, these strategies are useless if customers don't receive those shoes when they want them— and Zappos knows this. A distribution strategy has two critical components: (1) marketing channels and (2) logistics and supply-chain management.

A **marketing channel**—also called a **distribution channel**—is an organized system of marketing institutions and their interrelationships that enhances the physical flow and ownership of goods and services from producer to consumer or business

marketing (distribution) channel System of marketing institutions that enhances the physical flow of goods and services, along with ownership title, from producer to consumer or business user.

user. The choice of marketing channels should support the firm's overall marketing strategy. By contrast, **logistics** refers to the process of coordinating the flow of information, goods, and services among members of the marketing channel. **Supply-chain management** is the control of activities of purchasing, processing, and delivery through which raw materials are transformed into products and made available to final consumers. Efficient logistical systems support customer service, enhancing customer relationships—an important goal of any marketing strategy.

A key aspect of logistics is physical distribution, which covers a broad range of activities aimed at efficient

logistics Process of coordinating the flow of information, goods, and services among members of the distribution channel.

supply-chain management Control of the activities of purchasing, processing, and delivery through which raw materials are transformed into products and made available to final consumers.

movement of finished goods from the end of the production line to the consumer. Although some marketers use the terms *transportation* and *physical distribution* interchangeably, these terms do not carry the same meaning. **Physical distribution** extends beyond transportation to include such important decision areas as customer service, inventory control, materials handling, protective packaging, order processing, transportation, warehouse site selection, and warehousing.

physical distribution Broad range of activities aimed at efficient movement of finished goods from the end of the production line to the consumer.

Well-planned marketing channels and effective logistics and supply-chain management provide ultimate users with convenient ways for obtaining the goods and services they desire. This chapter discusses the activities, decisions, and marketing intermediaries involved in managing marketing channels and logistics. Chapter 13 looks at other players in the marketing channel: retailers, direct marketers, and wholesalers. ◆◆◆

① Describe the types of marketing channels and the roles they play in marketing strategy.

THE ROLE OF MARKETING CHANNELS IN MARKETING STRATEGY

A firm's distribution channels play a key role in its overall marketing strategy because these channels provide the means by which the firm makes the goods and services available to ultimate users. Channels perform four important functions. First, they facilitate the exchange process by reducing the number of marketplace contacts necessary to make a sale. Suppose you want to buy a digital camera. You've had an Olympus camera in the past and been satisfied with it, so when you see an ad for the Stylus 600 you are interested. You visit the Olympus website, where you find out that the camera has such features as Bright Capture Technology and an all-weather LCD screen. Then you discover that Olympus also has a digital photo printer, making it convenient to print out individual pictures at home. The site locates a nearby dealer for you, where you can go to see the actual camera and printer. The dealer forms part of the channel that brings you, a potential buyer, and Olympus, the seller, together to complete the exchange process. It's important to keep in mind that all channel members benefit when they work together; when they begin to disagree or—worse yet—compete directly with each other, everyone loses.

Distributors adjust for discrepancies in the market's assortment of goods and services via a process known as *sorting,* the second channel function. A single producer tends to maximize the quantity it makes of a limited line of goods, while a single buyer needs a limited quantity of a wide selection of merchandise. Sorting alleviates such discrepancies by channelling products to suit both the buyer's and the producer's needs.

The third function of marketing channels involves standardizing exchange transactions by setting expectations for products, and it involves the transfer process itself. Channel members tend to standardize payment terms, delivery schedules, prices, and purchase lots among other conditions. Standardization helps make the transactions efficient and fair for all members of the channel.

The final marketing channel function is to facilitate searches by both buyers and sellers. Buyers search for specific goods and services to fill their needs, while sellers attempt to learn what buyers want. Channels bring buyers and sellers together to complete the exchange process.

Hundreds of distribution channels exist today, and no single channel best serves the needs of every company. Instead of searching for the best channel for all products, a marketing manager must analyze alternative channels in light of consumer needs to determine the most appropriate channel or channels for the firm's goods and services.

Costco is an important channel member, bringing many quality brands to Canadian consumers.

Marketers must remain flexible because channels may change over time. Today's ideal channel may prove inappropriate in a few years. Or the way a company uses that channel may change. Two decades ago, Michael Dell came up with a revolutionary way to sell computers—by the telephone, directly to consumers. Later, Dell added Internet sales to its operations. Although Dell is still one of the world's largest PC manufacturers, its sales via phone and the Internet have begun to slide as more consumers seem to prefer to visit retail stores to try out new gadgets and features. The shift has caused Dell to re-examine the way it sells computers.[2]

The following sections examine the diverse types of channels available to marketers. They look at the decisions marketers must make to develop an effective distribution strategy that supports their firm's marketing objectives.

TYPES OF MARKETING CHANNELS

The first step in selecting a marketing channel is determining which type of channel will best meet both the seller's objectives and the distribution needs of customers. Figure 12.1 depicts the major channels available to marketers of consumer and business goods and services.

Most channel options involve at least one **marketing intermediary**. A marketing intermediary (or *middleman*) is an organization that operates between producers and consumers or business users. Retailers and wholesalers are both marketing intermediaries. A retail store owned and operated by

figure 12.1

Alternative Marketing Channels

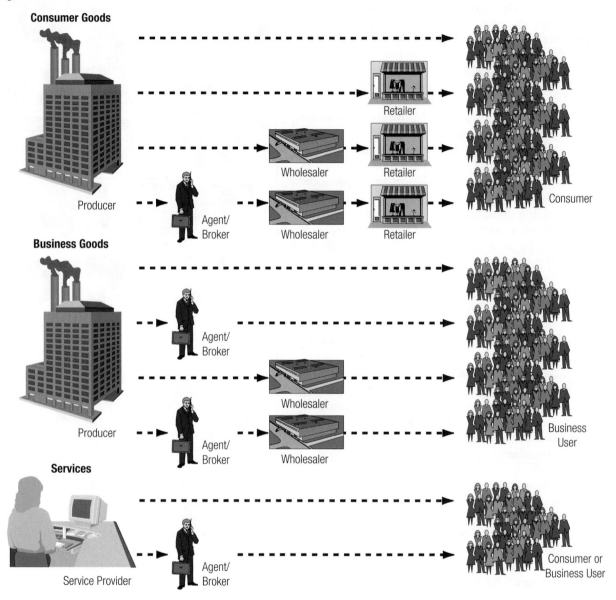

someone other than the manufacturer of the products it sells is one type of marketing intermediary. A **wholesaler** is an intermediary that takes title to the goods it handles and then distributes these goods to retailers, other distributors, or sometimes end consumers. Although some analysts believed that the Internet would ultimately render many intermediaries obsolete, that hasn't happened. In fact, most online sales are handled through websites operated by channel intermediaries. Virtually all major retailers have staked their claims in cyberspace by setting up **electronic storefronts,** websites where they offer items for sale to consumers. Wal-Mart's electronic storefront, Walmart.com, has expanded its online offerings substantially over the past few years. It also began offering more upscale merchandise recently on Walmart.com, including cashmere scarves, 18-carat white gold rings, and 60-inch plasma televisions. This online strategy is part of the retailer's overall effort to lure more affluent shoppers and better compete with firms such as Target. Walmart.com is also a testing ground for merchandise the company might decide to carry in its regular stores.[3]

A short marketing channel involves few intermediaries. By contrast, a long marketing channel involves many intermediaries working in succession to move goods from producers to consumers. Business products usually move through short channels due to geographic concentrations and comparatively

Marketoid

More than 8.4 million Canadians aged 16 and over made at least one online purchase in 2007.

few business purchasers. Service firms market primarily through short channels because they sell intangible products and need to maintain personal relationships within their channels. Haircuts, manicures, and dental cleanings are all provided through short channels. Not-for-profit organizations also tend to work with short, simple, and direct channels. Any marketing intermediaries in such channels usually act as agents, such as independent ticket agencies or fundraising specialists.

DIRECT SELLING

The simplest and shortest marketing channel is a direct channel. A **direct channel** carries goods directly from a producer to the business purchaser or ultimate user. This channel forms part of **direct selling**, a marketing strategy in which a producer establishes direct sales contact with its product's final users. Direct selling is an important option for goods that require extensive demonstrations in convincing customers to buy.

Direct selling plays a significant role in business-to-business marketing. Most major installations, accessory equipment, and even component parts and raw materials are sold through direct contacts between producing firms and final buyers. Firms such as Xerox that market items to other businesses often develop and maintain large sales forces to call on potential customers. Rob Galarneau, co-owner of Swarm Enterprises, purchased an iGen3 digital production press from Xerox. Valued at about $1 million, he expects the press will solidify his company's position as the most digitally advanced print shop in Edmonton and that it will quickly triple his digital print business revenue.[4]

Direct selling is also important in consumer goods markets. Direct sellers such as Avon Canada, Pampered Chef, and Tupperware Canada sidestep competition in store aisles by developing networks of independent representatives who sell their products directly to consumers. Many of these companies practise a direct selling strategy called the *party plan,* originally popularized by Tupperware. A seller attends a gathering at a host customer's home to demonstrate products and take orders. Beijo Bags is one such business. Launched several years ago by entrepreneur Susan Handley, the bags are sold at home-based parties across Canada and the United States by independent sales reps who are mostly stay-at-home mums—and customers themselves. In just three years, Beijo Bags hit $10 million in sales.[5]

The Internet provides another direct selling channel for both B2B and B2C purchases. Consumers who want to sport designer handbags—but don't want to pay full price for them—can rent them from shouldercandy.com and receive them usually within three business days. For those who like to change bags often but can't or won't pay the hundreds or thousands of dollars for Prada's, Gucci's, or Louis Vuitton's latest, the site may be a real bargain.[6]

Direct mail can be an important part of direct selling—or it can encourage a potential customer to contact an intermediary such as a retailer. Either way, it is a vital communication piece for many marketers, as described in the "Etiquette Tips for Marketing Professionals" feature.

CHANNELS USING MARKETING INTERMEDIARIES

Although direct channels allow simple and straightforward marketing, they are not practical in every case. Some products serve markets in different areas of the country or world or have large numbers of potential end users. Other categories of goods rely heavily on repeat purchases. The producers of these goods may find more efficient, less expensive, and less time-consuming alternatives to direct channels by using marketing intermediaries. This section considers five channels that involve marketing intermediaries.

Producer to Wholesaler to Retailer to Consumer

The traditional channel for consumer goods proceeds from producer to wholesaler to retailer to user. This method carries goods between literally thousands of small producers with limited lines and local retailers. A firm with limited financial resources will rely on the services of a wholesaler that serves as an immediate source of funds and then markets to hundreds of retailers. On the other hand, a small retailer can draw on a wholesaler's specialized distribution skills. In addition, many manufacturers hire their own field sales representatives to service retail accounts with marketing information. Wholesalers may then handle the actual sales transactions.

electronic storefront
Online store where customers can view and order merchandise much like window shopping at traditional retail establishments.

direct channel
Marketing channel that moves goods directly from a producer to the business purchaser or ultimate user.

ETIQUETTE TIPS FOR MARKETING PROFESSIONALS

Preparing an Effective Direct-Mail Piece

A S a marketer, communicating with your customers—or potential customers—is probably your most important responsibility. Preparing a direct-mail piece can be a particular challenge because it must catch a consumer's eye, keep his or her interest, create a desire for a product, and call for action (such as a phone call or visit to a store). And with consumers' time always a concern, direct marketers need to target the most likely prospects and avoid wasting others' time. Here are a few tips for creating an effective marketing message through direct mail—one that can truly serve customers' needs:

1. Know what your objectives are and communicate them clearly to avoid wasting prospective customers' time and your money. Do you want the consumer to make an immediate purchase or call your organization for more information?
2. Know your target audience and their needs. Sending mail to people who do not buy your type of product only creates an annoyance—junk mail.
3. Write a clear headline directed to your target audience. Your offer should be featured prominently in the headline

or near the beginning of the piece so consumers can quickly determine the intent of your mailing. Be sure the offer is easy to read and understand.
4. In a few sentences—or with a brief list—describe how consumers will benefit from the offer.
5. Provide all the necessary contact information—fax number, e-mail address, website address, phone number, mailing address for customer convenience. Potential customers should have a variety of ways to reach you or your company so that they can choose which method best suits them.
6. Create a clean, clear, eye-catching design for your piece. Make sure all illustrations support the text. Clutter only works against you by confusing potential customers.

Sources: "Direct Mail Buyer's Guide," BuyerZone.com, http://www.buyerzone.com, accessed May 19, 2006; "Preparing an Effective Direct Mail Piece," BlueGrass, http://www.bgmailing.com, accessed May 19, 2006; Joanna L. Krotz, "Sending the Right Message: How to Match a Direct Mailer to Your Marketing," Microsoft, http://www.microsoft.com/smallbusiness, accessed May 19, 2006.

Producer to Wholesaler to Business User

Similar characteristics in the organizational market often attract marketing intermediaries to operate between producers and business purchasers. The term *industrial distributor* commonly refers to intermediaries in the business market that take title to the goods.

Producer to Agent to Wholesaler to Retailer to Consumer

In markets served by many small companies, a unique intermediary—the agent—performs the basic function of bringing buyer and seller together. An agent may or may not take possession of the goods but never takes title. The agent merely represents a producer by seeking a market for its products or a wholesaler (which does take title to the goods) by locating a supply source.

Producer to Agent to Wholesaler to Business User

Like agents, brokers are independent intermediaries who may or may not take possession of goods but never take title to these goods. Agents and brokers also serve the business market when small producers attempt to market their offerings through large wholesalers. Such an intermediary, often called a **manufacturers' representative**, provides an independent sales force to contact wholesale buyers. A kitchen equipment manufacturer may have its own manufacturers' representatives to market its goods, for example.

Producer to Agent to Business User

For products sold in small units, only merchant wholesalers can economically cover the markets. A merchant wholesaler is an independently owned wholesaler that takes title to the goods. By maintaining regional inventories, this wholesaler achieves transportation economies, stockpiling goods and making small shipments over short distances. For a product with large unit sales, however, and for which transportation accounts for a small percentage of the total cost, the producer-agent-business user channel is usually employed. The agent in effect becomes the producer's sales force, but bulk shipments of the product reduce the intermediary's inventory management function.

Many manufacturers rely on industrial distributors such as Acklands-Grainger to get their products to final customers in business-to-business markets.

H.F. (HERB) MACKENZIE.

DUAL DISTRIBUTION

Dual distribution refers to movement of products through more than one channel to reach the firm's target market. Sears Canada, for instance, has a three-pronged distribution system, selling through stores, catalogues, and the Internet. Marketers usually adopt a dual distribution strategy either to maximize their firm's coverage in the marketplace or to increase the cost effectiveness of the firm's marketing effort. For instance, automobile parts manufacturers promote products through both direct sales forces and independent salespeople. The cost-effectiveness goal, on the other hand, might lead a manufacturer to assign its own sales force to sell in high-potential territories while relying on manufacturers' representatives (independent, commissioned salespeople) in lower volume areas.

dual distribution
Network that moves products to a firm's target market through more than one marketing channel.

REVERSE CHANNELS

While the traditional concept of marketing channels involves the movement of goods and services from producer to consumer or business user, marketers should not ignore **reverse channels**—channels designed to return goods to their producers. Reverse channels have gained increased importance with rising prices for raw materials, increasing availability of recycling facilities, and passage of additional antipollution and conservation laws. Purchase a new set of tires, and you'll probably pay a recycling charge for disposing of the old tires. The intent is to halt the growing litter problem of illegal tire dumps. Automotive batteries contain potentially toxic materials, including 8 kilograms of lead and nearly 4 litres of sulphuric acid. Despite this, every element in a spent battery can be reclaimed, recycled, and reused in new batteries. Environmentally friendly consumers can turn in their old batteries at the time they purchase new ones. To help in this effort, the Canadian Automobile Association (CAA) holds an annual CAA Great Battery Roundup during which consumers can drop off their dead batteries.[7]

Some reverse channels move through the facilities of traditional marketing intermediaries. In provinces that require bottle deposits, retailers and local bottlers may perform these functions in

Marketoid

In one recent year, the average Canadian recycled 112 kilograms of material; the highest recycling rates were in Nova Scotia.

the consumer beverage industry. For other products, provincial governments establish redemption centres, develop systems for rechannelling products for recycling, and create specialized organizations to handle disposal and recycling. Staples collects empty printer cartridges at its stores, and some Nike retail outlets collect worn-out sneakers for recycling. Other reverse channel participants include community groups that organize cleanup days and develop recycling and waste disposal systems. Timberland actually gives its employees paid time off to participate in programs that involve cleaning up parks, schools, and other public places.

Reverse channels also handle product recalls and repairs. An appliance manufacturer might send recall notices to the buyers of a washing machine. An auto manufacturer might send notices to car owners advising them of a potential problem and offering to repair it at no cost through local dealerships.

assessment check 1

1.1 Distinguish between a marketing channel and logistics.

1.2 What are the different types of marketing channels?

1.3 What four functions do marketing channels perform?

---

② Outline the major channel strategy decisions.

CHANNEL STRATEGY DECISIONS

Marketers face several strategic decisions in choosing channels and marketing intermediaries for their products. Selecting a specific channel is the most basic of these decisions. Marketers must also resolve questions about the level of distribution intensity, assess the desirability of vertical marketing systems, and evaluate the performance of current intermediaries.

SELECTION OF A MARKETING CHANNEL

Consider the following questions: What characteristics of a franchised dealer network make it the best channel option for a company? Why do operating supplies often go through both agents and merchant wholesalers before reaching their actual users? Why would a firm market a single product through multiple channels? Marketers must answer many such questions in choosing marketing channels.

A variety of factors affect the selection of a marketing channel. Some channel decisions are dictated by the marketplace in which the company operates. In other cases, the product itself may be a key variable in picking a marketing channel. Finally, the marketing organization may base its selection of channels on its size and competitive factors. Individual firms in a single industry may choose different channels as part of their overall strategy to gain a competitive edge. Book publishers, for instance, may sell through bookstores, directly to consumers on their own websites, or through nontraditional outlets, including specialty retailers such as craft stores or home improvement stores.[8]

Market Factors

Channel structure reflects a product's intended markets, either for consumers or business users. Business purchasers usually prefer to deal directly with manufacturers (except for routine supplies or small accessory items), but most consumers make their purchases from retailers. Marketers often sell products that serve both business users and consumers through more than one channel.

Other market factors also affect channel choice, including the market's needs, its geographic location, and its average order size. To serve a concentrated market with a small number of buyers, a direct channel offers a feasible alternative. But in serving a geographically dispersed potential market in which customers purchase small amounts in individual transactions—the conditions that characterize the consumer-goods market—distribution through marketing intermediaries makes sense.

Product Factors

Product characteristics also guide the choice of an optimal marketing channel strategy. Perishable goods, such as fresh fruit and vegetables, milk, and fruit juice, move through short channels. Trendy or seasonal fashions, such as swimsuits and ski wear, are also examples.

Vending machines represent another short channel. Typically, you can buy a bag of M&Ms, Miss Vickie's potato chips, or a Coke from a vending machine. But how about underwear or a beer? If you're a guest at Tokyo's Shibuya Excel Hotel, you can do just that. In addition, you can get a serving of dried squid or a package of batteries. The vending machine, manufactured by Sanyo Electric, is so large that it is really an automated convenience store. "This is four vending machines in one," boasts Misao Awane of Sanyo. "It holds 200 different products, at three different temperatures."[9]

Complex products such as custom-made installations and computer equipment are often sold directly to ultimate buyers. In general, relatively standardized items that are also nonperishable pass through comparatively long channels. Products with low unit costs, such as cans of dog food, bars of soap, and packages of gum, typically travel through long channels. Perishable items such as fresh flowers, meat, and produce require much shorter channels.

Perishable goods—such as fresh fruit—move through short channels, sometimes directly from the grower to the consumer.

MICHAEL ROBERTSON

Organizational and Competitive Factors

Companies with strong financial, management, and marketing resources feel less need for help from intermediaries. A large, financially strong manufacturer can hire its own sales force, warehouse its own goods, and extend credit to retailers or consumers. But a small firm with fewer resources may do better with the aid of intermediaries. Entrepreneur Cheryl Tallman knew she had a unique product—a kit for freezing fresh baby food—but her talent lay in selling, not manufacturing and distribution. So she created partnerships with a manufacturer and a distributor while she concentrated on marketing her Fresh Baby kits to baby boutiques and other retailers. "If we'd tried to develop competencies in all this other stuff, we'd be distracting our attention from what we're really good at," explains Tallman.[10]

A firm with a broad product line, such as Unilever Canada or Dell Canada, can usually market its products directly to retailers or business users since its own sales force can offer a variety of products. High sales volume spreads selling costs over a large number of items, generating adequate returns from direct sales. Single-product firms often view direct selling as unaffordable.

The manufacturer's desire for control over marketing its products also influences channel selection. Some manufacturers choose to sell their products only at their own stores. Manufacturers of specialty or luxury goods such as scarves from Hermès and watches from Rolex strictly limit the number of retailers that can carry their products, as explained in Chapter 8.

Businesses that explore new marketing channels must be careful to avoid upsetting their channel intermediaries. In the past decade, conflicts frequently arose as companies began to establish an Internet presence in addition to traditional outlets. Today, firms look for new ways to handle both without damaging relationships. Still, some firms feel compelled to develop new marketing channels to remedy inadequate promotion of their products by independent marketing intermediaries. In recent years, insurance giant Allstate has been moving away from its reliance on proprietary agents to sell its products and toward direct retail channels such as the Internet. Allstate has made this move in order to compete more effectively with lower-cost providers such as Geico.[11] Movie studios have begun to release films to DVD or to on-demand TV service either more quickly or simultaneously with their movie releases, as described in the "Marketing Success" feature.

Table 12.1 summarizes the factors that affect the selection of a marketing channel. The table also examines the effect of each factor on the channel's overall length.

table 12.1 *Factors Influencing Marketing Channel Strategies*

	CHARACTERISTICS OF SHORT CHANNELS	CHARACTERISTICS OF LONG CHANNELS
Market factors	Business users	Consumers
	Geographically concentrated	Geographically dispersed
	Extensive technical knowledge and regular servicing required	Little technical knowledge and regular servicing not required
	Large orders	Small orders
Product factors	Perishable	Durable
	Complex	Standardized
	Expensive	Inexpensive
Organizational factors	Manufacturer has adequate resources to perform channel functions	Manufacturer lacks adequate resources to perform channel functions
	Broad product line	Limited product line
	Channel control important	Channel control not important
Competitive factors	Manufacturer feels satisfied with marketing intermediaries' performance in promoting products	Manufacturer feels dissatisfied with marketing intermediaries' performance in promoting products

DETERMINING DISTRIBUTION INTENSITY

Another key channel strategy decision is the intensity of distribution. *Distribution intensity* refers to the number of intermediaries through which a manufacturer distributes its goods in a particular market. Optimal distribution intensity should ensure adequate market coverage for a product. Adequate market coverage varies depending on the goals of the individual firm, the type of product, and the consumer segments in its target market. In general, however, distribution intensity varies along a continuum with three general categories: intensive distribution, selective distribution, and exclusive distribution.

marketing success   Skipping the Box Office Rush

Background. Movie buffs used to have to wait many months after seeing their favourite film on the big screen before being able to view it at home. But in recent years, movie marketers have recognized that the lag time between a theatre release and a release of DVD or on-demand service may represent a lost opportunity.

The Challenge. With the popularity of home theatres, on-demand service, and constant entertainment innovations, the movie industry has struggled to find ways to keep its audience interested—at a profit. If studios released movies simultaneously to theatres and DVD or on-demand channels, would they lose money?

The Strategy. Studios have already begun to shrink the time between a theatre debut and the DVD release. Now some companies are pushing the strategy further. "So much great film has fallen by the wayside," explains Jonathan Sehring, president of IFC Entertainment, which has a film production and distribution unit. "The studios

are collapsing the window between the theatrical release and the DVD. We're taking that one step further." IFC announced plans to launch six films intended for simultaneous release to independent theatres and on-demand service provided by cable companies.

The Outcome. Committed to this modified way of distributing new movies, IFC has said that it would make more and more movies available this way, including some films from other distributors. Some industry experts are skeptical that the big studios may be slower to react. But producer Steve Tisch disagrees. "I think the industry will resist and resist some more, and then slowly embrace it."

Sources: Jennifer Whitehead, "Winterbottom Film to Get Simultaneous Cinema, DVD, and Online Release," *Digital Bulletin,* February 13, 2006, http://www.brandrepublic.com; Sharon Waxman, "Missed It in the Theater Today? See It on DVD Tonight," *The New York Times,* January 23, 2006, http://www.nytimes.com; Xeni Jardin, "Thinking outside the Box Office," *Wired,* December 2005, http://www.wired.com.

Intensive Distribution

An **intensive distribution** strategy seeks to distribute a product through all available channels in a trade area. Because Campbell Soup practises intensive distribution for many of its products, you can pick up a can from its microwavable line just about anywhere—the supermarket, the drugstore, and even Staples. Usually, an intensive distribution strategy suits items with wide appeal across broad groups of consumers.

intensive distribution
Distribution of a product through all available channels.

Selective Distribution

In another market coverage strategy, **selective distribution,** a firm chooses only a limited number of retailers in a market area to handle its line. Italian design firm Versace sells its merchandise only through a limited number of select boutiques worldwide. By limiting the number of retailers, marketers can reduce total marketing costs while establishing strong working relationships within the channel. Moreover, selected retailers often agree to comply with the company's strict rules for advertising, pricing, and displaying its products. **Cooperative advertising**, in which the manufacturer pays a percentage of the retailer's advertising expenditures and the retailer prominently displays the firm's products, can be utilized for mutual benefit, and marginal retailers can be avoided. Where service is important, the manufacturer usually provides training and assistance to the dealers it chooses.

selective distribution
Distribution of a product through a limited number of channels.

Exclusive Distribution

When a producer grants exclusive rights to a wholesaler or retailer to sell its products in a specific geographic region, it practises **exclusive distribution.** The automobile industry provides a good example of exclusive distribution. A city with a population of 40 000 may have a single Ford dealer. Exclusive distribution agreements also govern marketing for some major appliance and apparel brands.

exclusive distribution
Distribution of a product through a single wholesaler or retailer in a specific geographic region.

Marketers may sacrifice some market coverage by implementing a policy of exclusive distribution. However, they often develop and maintain an image of quality and prestige for the product. If it's harder to find a Free People silk dress, the item seems more valuable. In addition, exclusive distribution limits marketing costs since the firm deals with a smaller number of accounts. In exclusive distribution, producers and retailers cooperate closely in decisions concerning advertising and promotion, inventory carried by the retailers, and prices.

Legal Problems of Exclusive Distribution

Exclusive distribution presents potential legal problems in three main areas: exclusive dealing, market restriction, and tied selling. Although none of these practices is illegal per se, all may break the law if they reduce competition or tend to create monopolies.

As part of an exclusive distribution strategy, marketers may try to enforce an **exclusive dealing agreement**, a practice that prohibits a marketing intermediary (a wholesaler or, more typically, a retailer) from handling competing products. Producers of high-priced shopping goods, specialty goods, and accessory equipment often require such agreements to assure total concentration on their own product lines. Such contracts violate the Competition Act only if the producer's or dealer's sales volumes represent a substantial percentage of total sales in the market area. While exclusive distribution is legal for companies first entering a market, such agreements violate the Competition Act if used by firms with a sizable market share seeking to bar competitors from the market.

Producers may also try to set up **closed sales territories**, a practice sometimes referred to as *market restriction,* to restrict their distributors to certain geographic regions. Although the distributors gain protection from rival dealers in their exclusive territories, they sacrifice any opportunities in opening new facilities or marketing the manufacturers' products outside their assigned territories. Again, the legality of a system of market restriction depends on whether the restriction decreases competition.

The legality of closed sales territories also depends on whether the system imposes horizontal or vertical restrictions. Horizontal territorial restrictions result from agreements between retailers or wholesalers to avoid competition among sellers of products from the same producer. Such agreements consistently have been declared illegal. Vertical territorial restrictions—those between producers and wholesalers or retailers—are more likely to meet legal criteria. Such agreements likely satisfy the law in cases where manufacturers occupy relatively small market shares. In such instances, the restrictions may actually increase competition among competing brands; the wholesaler or retailer faces no competition from other dealers carrying the manufacturer's brand, so it can concentrate on effectively competing with other brands.

COURTESY OF KRUPS, GROUPE SEB

Krups uses a selective distribution strategy to reach customers across Canada.

The third legal question of exclusive distribution involves **tying agreements**, which allow channel members to become exclusive dealers only if they also carry products other than those that they want to sell. In the apparel industry, for example, an agreement might require a dealer to carry a comparatively unpopular line of clothing to get desirable, fast-moving items. Tying agreements are reviewable under the Competition Act and not an offence. These practices are, therefore, not prohibited unless an order has been obtained after a review by the Competition Tribunal. Prohibiting such practices is more likely to happen when they reduce competition or create monopolies that keep competitors out of major markets. Recently the Coca-Cola Company entered into an agreement with the European Union—which is governed by the European Commission—to refrain from making tying agreements between its most popular brands—such as Coke, Diet Coke, and Sprite—and its lesser-known products.[12]

WHO SHOULD PERFORM CHANNEL FUNCTIONS?

A fundamental marketing principle governs channel decisions. A member of the channel must perform certain central marketing functions. Responsibilities of the different members may vary, however. Although independent wholesalers perform many functions for manufacturers, retailers, and other wholesaler clients, other channel members could fulfill these roles instead. A manufacturer might bypass its wholesalers by establishing regional warehouses, maintaining field sales forces, serving as sources of information for retail customers, or arranging details of financing. For years, auto manufacturers have operated credit units that offer new-car financing.

An independent intermediary earns a profit in exchange for providing services to manufacturers and retailers. This profit margin is low, however, ranging from 1 percent for food wholesalers to 5 percent for durable goods wholesalers. Manufacturers and retailers could retain these costs, or they could market directly and reduce retail prices—but only if they could perform the channel functions and match the efficiency of the independent intermediaries.

To grow profitably in a competitive environment, an intermediary must provide better service at lower costs than manufacturers or retailers can provide for themselves. In this case, consolidation of channel functions can represent a strategic opportunity for a company.

assessment check 2

2.1 Identify four major factors in selecting a marketing channel.

2.2 Describe the three general categories of distribution intensity.

(3) Describe the concepts of channel management, conflict, and cooperation.

CHANNEL MANAGEMENT AND LEADERSHIP

Distribution strategy does not end with the choice of a channel. Manufacturers must also focus on channel management by developing and maintaining relationships with the intermediaries in their marketing channels. Positive channel relationships encourage channel members to remember their partners' goods and market them. Manufacturers also must carefully manage the incentives offered to induce channel members to promote their products. This effort includes weighing decisions about pricing, promotion, and other support efforts that the manufacturer performs.

Increasingly, marketers are managing channels in partnership with other channel members. Effective cooperation allows all channel members to achieve goals that they could not achieve on their own. Keys to successful management of channel relationships include the development of high levels of coordination, commitment, and trust between channel members.

Not all channel members wield equal power in the distribution chain, however. The dominant member of a marketing channel is called the **channel captain.** This firm's power to control a channel may result from its control over some type of reward or punishment to other channel members, such as granting an exclusive sales territory or taking away a dealership. Power might also result from contractual arrangements, specialized expert knowledge, or agreement among channel members about their mutual best interests.

In the grocery industry, consumer goods manufacturers, such as Procter & Gamble and Kraft Foods, once were considered channel captains. Today, however, the power has shifted to the retail giants, such as Loblaws, Sobeys, Provigo, and Safeway. Manufacturers who want to get their products on the shelves and properly marketed have to pay slotting fees, described in Chapter 10, to do so. Partnering among retailers—including grocery chains—is a growing trend, as firms are recognizing that they can compete more effectively as channel captains if they join forces. Several grocery retailers might form a so-called *value network* to achieve dominance.[13]

Another strategy is the building of supercentres like Wal-Mart's. Wal-Mart's grocery sales have reached about $80 billion through its supercentres, making it the largest seller of supermarket goods in the United States. It is also one of the largest resellers of supermarket goods in Canada, where it has recently invested hundreds of millions of dollars opening new stores, most of which were supercentres.[14]

channel captain
Dominant and controlling member of a marketing channel.

CHANNEL CONFLICT

Marketing channels work smoothly only when members cooperate in well-organized efforts to achieve maximum operating efficiencies. Yet channel members often perform as separate, independent, and even competing forces. Two types of conflict—horizontal and vertical—may hinder the normal functioning of a marketing channel.

Horizontal Conflict

Horizontal conflict sometimes results from disagreements among channel members at the same level, such as two or more wholesalers or two or more retailers, or among marketing intermediaries of the same type, such as two competing discount stores or several retail florists. More often, horizontal conflict causes sparks between different types of marketing intermediaries that handle the same manufacturers' products. This sometimes results when a marketing intermediary adds new products that it has not previously sold to its product assortment. When the sixth book in the Harry Potter series, *Harry Potter and the Half-Blood Prince,* was launched, many independent bookstores expected to capitalize on the publicity surrounding the launch. Leishman Books in Ottawa, for example, hired extra staff and brought cupcakes and juice in preparation for the midnight launch. However, much of its anticipated sales were taken by the 24-hour Shoppers Drug Mart located next door. Shoppers Drug Mart sold the book at a 40 percent discount. John Winter, a Toronto retail analyst, stated that he has never seen this before, but he was not surprised. Items such as this draw traffic to stores and they are good items to use as promotional items.[15]

Vertical Conflict

Vertical relationships may result in frequent and severe conflict. Channel members at different levels find many reasons for disputes, such as when

Canadian Tire reduces vertical channel conflict when customers who visit CanadianTire.ca can sometimes download a coupon that can be redeemed only at Canadian Tire stores.

retailers develop private brands to compete with producers' brands or when producers establish their own retail stores or create mail-order operations that compete with retailers. Producers may annoy wholesalers and retailers when they attempt to bypass these intermediaries and sell directly to consumers. A few years ago, Tupperware—traditionally sold only by independent consultants at in-home parties—tried selling its products through retail stores. The move led to a precipitous drop in party bookings and sales. Tupperware abandoned this strategy, but by then three-quarters of the sales force had dropped out. Tupperware has since created new incentive programs to try to recruit new and former consultants.[16]

Recently, the European Union imposed a tax of nearly 45 percent on imports of Chinese-made colour televisions in an effort to stop Chinese manufacturers from "dumping" thousands of televisions on the market at below-market prices. The practice had caused conflict between European retailers, who could sell many of the lower-priced televisions, and European manufacturers, who could not compete with the Chinese imports. The EU has also investigated Chinese and Vietnamese dumping of leather shoes.[17]

The Grey Market

grey goods Goods produced for sale in one market and then diverted to another market.

Another type of channel conflict results from activities in the grey market. Sometimes, Canadian manufacturers license their technology and brands abroad, then find themselves in competition in the Canadian market against versions of their own brands produced by overseas affiliates. In other instances, foreign manufacturers provide exclusive distribution rights to Canadian resellers who then find they have competition from other resellers who buy the products from foreign distributors. These **grey goods**, goods produced for sale in one market and then diverted to another market, enter Canadian channels through the actions of unauthorized foreign distributors. While licensing agreements usually prohibit foreign licensees from selling in Canada, and exclusive distribution agreements prohibit manufacturers from selling to non-authorized Canadian resellers, no such rules inhibit their distributors.

Quebec-based Euro-Excellence is a reseller of quality confectionery products, including Swiss-made Toblerone and Belgian-made Cote d'Or chocolate bars. These bars are manufactured by Kraft in Europe, and Kraft Canada has the exclusive Canadian distribution rights. However, Euro-Excellence buys them from a European distributor and then sells them in Canada.[18] In this instance, the grey goods were legitimate products. However, the grey market is frequently used to sell counterfeit products. A Montreal medical-device distributor, Alexander Vega, has been sued by Johnson & Johnson for selling counterfeit One-Touch diabetes test strips that were imported from China. Vega claimed that he was assured they were genuine Johnson & Johnson test strips that had been bought by the Chinese company for resale. Toronto lawyer Lorne Lipkus claims that almost every time a Canadian company is caught selling counterfeit products, its defence claim is that it thought the products were simply grey market goods.[19]

ACHIEVING CHANNEL COOPERATION

The basic antidote to channel conflict is effective cooperation among channel members. Cooperation is best achieved when all channel members regard themselves as equal components of the same organization. The channel captain is primarily responsible for providing the leadership necessary to achieve this kind of cooperation.

Samsung Electronics is committed to achieving channel cooperation to have its products reach as many homes and offices worldwide as possible. The firm believes that one way to achieve this coordination is to train its partners thoroughly in marketing its products. One training session focused on the launch of health-conscious air-conditioning products and gathered together partners from the United Arab Emirates, Qatar, Bahrain, Oman, Yemen, and Kuwait. "Samsung always believed in providing world-class training to its partner community, as they are the key interface between the company and its customers, and play a vital role in helping customers make the right decisions," said S. Y. Kim, general manager of the home appliances division at Samsung.[20]

assessment check 3 ✓

3.1   What is a channel captain? What is its role in channel cooperation?

3.2   Identify and describe the three types of channel conflict.

VERTICAL MARKETING SYSTEMS

④ Identify and describe the different vertical marketing systems.

Efforts to reduce channel conflict and improve the effectiveness of distribution have led to the development of vertical marketing systems. A **vertical marketing system (VMS)** is a planned channel system designed to improve distribution efficiency and cost effectiveness by integrating various functions throughout the distribution chain.

A vertical marketing system can achieve this goal through either forward or backward integration. In **forward integration**, a firm attempts to control downstream distribution. For example, a manufacturer might set up a retail chain to sell its products. **Backward integration** occurs when a manufacturer attempts to gain greater control over inputs in its production process. A manufacturer might acquire the supplier of a raw material the manufacturer uses in the production of its products. Backward integration can also extend the control of retailers and wholesalers over producers that supply them.

A VMS offers several benefits. First, it improves chances for controlling and coordinating the steps in the distribution or production process. It may lead to the development of economies of scale that ultimately saves money. A VMS may also let a manufacturer expand into profitable new businesses. However, a VMS also involves some costs. A manufacturer assumes increased risk when it takes control of an entire distribution chain. Manufacturers may also discover that they lose some flexibility in responding to market changes.

Marketers have developed three categories of VMSs: corporate systems, administered systems, and contractual systems. These categories are outlined in the sections that follow.

vertical marketing system (VMS) Planned channel system designed to improve distribution efficiency and cost effectiveness by integrating various functions throughout the distribution chain.

CORPORATE AND ADMINISTERED SYSTEMS

When a single owner runs organizations at each stage of the marketing channel, it operates a **corporate marketing system.** Roots, for example, sells its branded products through 225 Roots stores, more than half of them in Canada. An **administered marketing system** achieves channel coordination when a dominant channel member exercises its power. Even though Goodyear sells its tires through independently owned and operated dealerships, it controls the stock that these dealerships carry. Other examples of channel captains leading administered channels include McKesson Canada, Shoppers Drug Mart, and Costco.

corporate marketing system VMS in which a single owner operates the entire marketing channel.

administered marketing system VMS that achieves channel coordination when a dominant channel member exercises its power.

CONTRACTUAL SYSTEMS

Instead of common ownership of intermediaries within a corporate VMS or the exercising of power within an administered system, a **contractual marketing system** coordinates distribution through formal agreements among channel members. In practice, three types of agreements set up these systems: wholesaler-sponsored voluntary chains, retail cooperatives, and franchises.

contractual marketing system VMS that coordinates channel activities through formal agreements among participants.

Wholesaler-Sponsored Voluntary Chain

Sometimes an independent wholesaler will try to preserve a market by strengthening its retail customers through a wholesaler-sponsored voluntary chain. The wholesaler adopts a formal agreement with its retailers to use a common name and standardized facilities and to purchase the wholesaler's goods. The wholesaler may even develop a line of private brands to be stocked by the retailers. This practice often helps smaller retailers compete with rival chains—and strengthens the wholesaler's position as well.

IGA (Independent Grocers' Alliance) Food Stores is a good example of a voluntary chain. True Value Hardware, with over 300 member stores across Canada, is another. Because a single advertisement promotes all the retailers in the trading area, a common store name and similar inventories allow the retailers to save on advertising costs.

table 12.2   **Entrepreneur.com's Top 20 Franchise 500 Rankings**

RANK	FRANCHISE NAME/DESCRIPTION	STARTUP COSTS
1	7-Eleven Inc., Convenience store	Varies
2	Subway, Submarine sandwiches and salads	$80K–310K
3	Dunkin' Donuts, Coffee, doughnuts, baked goods	Varies
4	Pizza Hut, Pizza	$1.1M–1.7M
5	McDonald's, Hamburgers, chicken, salads	$950K–1.8M
6	Sonic Drive In Restaurants, Drive-in restaurant	$820K–2.3M
7	KFC Corp., Chicken	$1.1M–1.7M
8	InterContinental Hotels Group, Hotels	Varies
9	Domino's Pizza LLC, Pizza, breadsticks, buffalo wings	$118.5K–460.3K
10	RE/MAX Int'l. Inc., Real estate	$35K–200K
11	UPS Store, The/Mail Boxes Etc., Postal, business and communications services	$170.8K–279.4K
12	Ace Hardware Corp., Hardware and home improvement store	$400K–1.1M
13	Jani-King, Commercial cleaning	$11.3K–34.1K+
14	Jiffy Lube Int'l. Inc., Fast oil change	$214K–273K
15	Arby's, Sandwiches, chicken, salads	$336.5K–2.4M
16	Baskin-Robbins USA Co., Ice cream, frozen yogurt, frozen beverages	$156.9K–560.4K
17	Circle K, Convenience store	$648K
18	Kumon Math & Reading Centers, Supplemental education	$30.96K–129.4K
19	Great Clips Inc., Hair salon	$110K–202K
20	Bonus Building Care, Commercial cleaning	$8.8K–14.7K

Wee Piggies & Paws has more than 70 Mom-Preneurs and is a Canadian franchise success.

COURTESY WWW.WEEPIGGIES.COM

Retail Cooperative

In a second type of contractual VMS, a group of retailers establishes a shared wholesaling operation to help them compete with chains. This is known as a **retail cooperative**. The retailers purchase ownership shares in the wholesaling operation and agree to buy a minimum percentage of their inventories from this operation. The members typically adopt a common store name and develop common private brands. Ace Hardware is an example of a retail cooperative.

Franchise

A third type of contractual vertical marketing system is the franchise, in which a wholesaler or dealer (the franchisee) agrees to meet the operating requirements of a manufacturer or other franchiser. Franchising is a huge and growing industry. There are more than 85 000 franchise units (franchisees) in Canada, controlled by about 950 franchisors. Total annual sales exceed $70 billion. After the United States, Canada is the world's most developed franchise market.[21] Table 12.2 shows the 20 fastest growing franchises in the United States. Most of these now operate in Canada as well. Other important franchise operations in Canada include Tim Hortons, Canadian Tire, M&M Meat Shops, and Rona Inc.

Franchise owners pay anywhere from several thousand to more than a million dollars to purchase and set up a franchise. Typically, they also pay a royalty on sales to the franchising company. In exchange for these initial and ongoing fees, the franchise owner receives the right to use the company's brand name as well as services such as training, marketing, advertising, and volume discounts. Major franchise chains justify the steep price of entry since it allows new businesses to sell winning brands. But if the brand enters a slump or the corporation behind the franchise makes poor strategic decisions, franchisees are often hurt.

assessment check 4

4.1 What are vertical marketing systems (VMSs)? Identify the major types.

4.2 Identify the three types of contractual marketing systems.

LOGISTICS AND SUPPLY CHAIN MANAGEMENT

⑤ Explain the roles of logistics and supply-chain management in an overall distribution strategy.

Pier 1 Imports purchases its eclectic mix of items from 600 vendors in 55 countries, and more than 80 percent comes from small companies. If high-demand items or seasonal products are late into its warehouses or are shipped in insufficient quantities, the company misses opportunities to deliver popular shopping choices to its 1200 retail stores and could lose ground to competitors such as Pottery Barn and Crate & Barrel. The situation facing Pier 1 illustrates the importance of logistics. Careful coordination of Pier 1's supplier network, shipping processes, and inventory control is the key to its continuing success. In addition, the store's buyers develop relationships with suppliers in 55 countries, including Mexico and China.[22]

Effective logistics requires proper supply-chain management, the control of activities of purchasing, processing, and delivery through which raw materials are transformed into products and made available to final consumers. The supply chain, also known as the *value chain,* is the complete sequence of suppliers and activities that contribute to the creation and delivery of goods and services. The supply chain begins with the raw-material inputs for the manufacturing process of a product and then proceeds to the actual production activities. The final link in the supply chain is the movement of finished products through the marketing channel to customers. Each link of the chain benefits the consumers as raw materials move through manufacturing to distribution. The chain encompasses all activities that enhance the value of the finished goods, including design, quality manufacturing, customer service, and delivery. Customer satisfaction results directly from the perceived value of a purchase to its buyer.

To manage the supply chain, businesses must look for ways to maximize customer value in each activity they perform. Supply-chain management takes place in two directions: upstream and downstream, as illustrated in Figure 12.2. **Upstream management** involves managing raw materials, inbound logistics, and warehouse and storage facilities. **Downstream management** involves managing finished product storage, outbound logistics, marketing and sales, and customer service.

Companies choose a variety of methods for managing the supply chain. They can include regular person-to-person meetings and high-tech systems such as radio frequency identification. Pharmaceutical manufacturers, for example, have special needs to ensure temperature-sensitive items are maintained within a specific temperature range to protect product integrity. Special radio frequency-enabled temperature data loggers allow shippers to track temperature changes as product moves through the supply chain and to reroute, recall, or reschedule replacement shipments when temperatures vary from an acceptable range.[23]

Logistical management plays a major role in giving customers what they need when they need it and thus is central in the supply chain. Another important component of this chain, *value-added service,* adds some improved or supplemental service that customers do not normally receive or expect. The following sections examine methods for streamlining and managing logistics and the supply chain as part of an overall distribution strategy.

RADIO FREQUENCY IDENTIFICATION (RFID)

One tool that marketers are using to help manage logistics is **radio frequency identification (RFID)** technology. With RFID, a tiny chip with identification information that can be read from a distance by a radio frequency scanner is placed on an item. These chips are already widely used in tollway pass transmitters, allowing drivers to zip through toll booths without stopping

radio frequency identification (RFID) Technology that uses a tiny chip with identification information that can be read from a distance by a scanner using radio waves.

figure 12.2

The Supply Chain of a Manufacturing Company

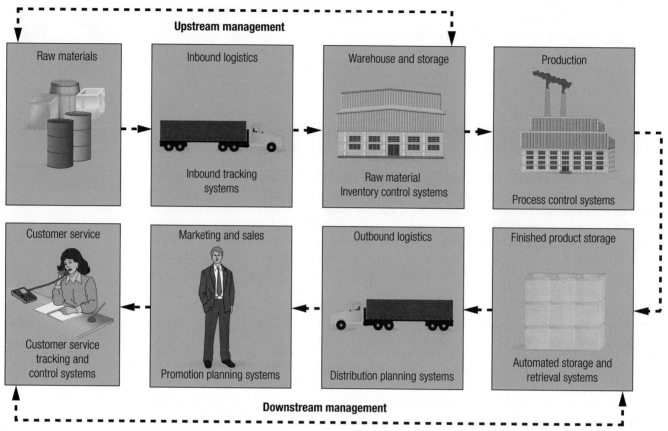

Source: Adapted from STAIR/REYNOLDS. Principles of Information Systems, Seventh Edition, 7E. © 2006 South-Western, a part of Cengage Learning, Inc. Reproduced by permission. www.cengage.com/permissions

or rolling down their windows. They are also embedded in employee ID cards that workers use to open office doors without keys. But businesses such as retail giant Wal-Mart, manufacturer Procter & Gamble, credit-card firms MasterCard and American Express, and German retailer Metro AG are eagerly putting the technology to wider use; they say it will speed deliveries, make consumer bar codes obsolete, and provide marketers with valuable information about consumer preferences. Wal-Mart is pushing its biggest suppliers to attach RFID tags to pallets and cases of products such as Coca-Cola and Dove soap, saying that the technology will vastly improve its ability to track inventory and keep the right amount of products in stock.

Kimberly-Clark, maker of such household staples as Kleenex and Huggies, is another large firm that has embraced RFID technology for supply-chain management, tagging more than 144 of the products in its current line. In addition, the company has built a 5000-square-foot warehouse for the purpose of experimenting with and testing uses for RFID. "RFID should give us visibility into our whole supply chain," muses CEO Terry Assink. "From our supplier's supplier all the way to the shelf—not the pantry, mind you, but the store shelf. Think about that."[24]

Some privacy groups have expressed concern about the data obtained from RFID tags, but one survey revealed that 58 percent of respondents would not mind the technology if they were assured that it would be disabled before they left the store with a purchased product. That's not much different from a clerk mechanically removing the big plastic tag from an item of clothing. But analysts encourage businesses to adopt specific codes of conduct surrounding the use of RFID technology—for their own good as well as for the protection of consumers. "Without clarification about how RFID works," warns Forrester Research staffer Christine Overby, "consumers will base their opinion on the Big Brother stories currently making the headlines."[25]

Solving an Ethical Controversy

RFID: Do You Want Chips in Your Wallet or on Your Shopping Cart?

MUCH has been written in recent years concerning the use—and potential for abuse—of RFID technology. The number of business applications continues to grow. Wal-Mart started the controversy several years ago when it announced that it expected its major supply partners to use the technology to identify all cases and pallets delivered to its distribution centres. A Canadian RFID pilot project, which included Loblaw Companies, Maple Leaf Foods, General Mills Canada, Unilever Canada, and others, showed that retailers would be the immediate beneficiaries from the adoption of RFID technology. Manufacturers, depending on the sophistication of their supply chain, would see varied results. What about consumers? Rollin Ford, Wal-Mart executive vice president and CIO, says, "On a daily basis, more than 24 million people shop our stores. If 100 000 extra trips are avoided by having items in stock, we will save customers $22.8 million a year in gas savings and reduce greenhouse gases by 80 209 metric tons." While this sounds impressive at an aggregate level, unless consumers see personal advantages of RFID technology, their skepticism and distrust will be likely to grow. Consumer concern most likely will continue to increase as the technology moves from identifying cases and pallets, to identifying individual products on store shelves, shopping carts, and even people once they become a common item embedded in credit and debit cards.

Should retailers continue to adopt RFID technology throughout their in-store operations?

PRO

1. Consumers will benefit from fewer out-of-stock occurrences, particularly during store sales and promotions; better product quality and freshness, including assur-

ance that products are authentic and not counterfeit; quicker and better targeted product recalls; and automatic warranty activations. Identifying product inventory and exact store locations will also be enhanced.

2. Putting RFID tags on store assets, such as shopping carts, will identify how these assets are used in-store. Retailers will be able to identify when too many carts are outside the store and where they are located, and when specific types of carts are not in sufficient supply, such as scooters and kid-friendly carts. When a large number of carts are in use within the store, management can decide in advance whether additional checkouts should be opened to better serve customers.

CON

1. Retailers will be able to track shopping carts and tell how long they spend in each store area and, at the checkout, there will even be the potential to tie purchase information to specific customer information if customers use store loyalty cards. That is, customers may participate in very exact marketing research, without their knowledge or permission.

2. As use continues to expand and the technology continues to develop, retailers will be able to identify when particular customers are in the store and target them with specific in-store promotions. Consumers' privacy will be compromised.

Where do you stand: pro or con?

Sources: NCR Corporation, "RFID Solutions," http://www.ncr.com/solutions/rfid_solutions/index.jsp?lang=EN, accessed December 2, 2007; Jeremy N. Smith, "Retail RFID Gets Real," *World Trade*, April 2007, p. 74; "Wal-Mart Expands Commitment to RFID," Material Handling Management, May 2007, p. 8; George H. Condon, "Are We There Yet . . . With RFID?" *Canadian Grocer*, August 2007, pp. 46–48.

ENTERPRISE RESOURCE PLANNING

Software is an important aspect of logistics management and the supply chain. An **enterprise resource planning (ERP) system** is an integrated software system that consolidates data from among the firm's units. Roughly two-thirds of ERP system users are manufacturers concerned with production issues such as sequencing and scheduling. Dow Corning is one such firm. The company adopted several programs from German software giant SAP AG to help it streamline processes and reduce costs globally. In addition, Dow uses SAP's software in its human resources department—also on a global basis.[26]

As valuable as it is, ERP and its related software aren't always perfect. For example, ERP failures were blamed for Hershey's inability to fulfill all its candy orders during one Halloween period, when a

Schenker Logistics and BAX Global have combined to provide global logistics solutions throughout North America and the world.

fall-off in sales was blamed on a combination of shipping delays, inability to fill orders, and partial shipments while candy stockpiled in warehouses. Several major retailers were forced to shift their purchases to other candy vendors.

LOGISTICAL COST CONTROL

In addition to enhancing their products by providing value-added services to customers, many firms are focusing on logistics for another important reason: to cut costs. Distribution functions currently represent almost half of a typical firm's total marketing costs. To reduce logistical costs, businesses are re-examining each link of their supply chains to identify activities that do not add value for customers. By eliminating, reducing, or redesigning these activities, they can often cut costs and boost efficiency. As just described, new technologies such as RFID can save businesses millions—or even billions—of dollars.

Because of increased security requirements in recent years, businesses involved in importing and exporting have faced a major rise in logistical costs. U.S. Customs and Border Protection has initiated a voluntary program for transportation carriers that requires them to ensure the integrity of their own security practices. Carriers that participate in the Customs-Trade Partnership Against Terrorism (C-TPAT) program are eligible to receive expedited service at major border crossings. They also help ensure their access to the United States in the event of another high-security alert, when only security-approved carriers will be allowed to cross the border.[27]

Third-Party Logistics

Some companies try to cut costs and offer value-added services by outsourcing some or all of their logistics functions to specialist firms. **Third-party (contract) logistics firms** (3PL firms) specialize in handling logistical activities for their clients. Third-party logistics is a huge industry, estimated at $333 billion worldwide, $115 billion of which takes place in North America alone.[28] PBB Global Logistics is a leading North American third-party international logistics provider headquartered in Fort Erie, Ontario. With 85 strategic locations across North America and a global network of logistics service providers, it provides a host of services, including customs brokerage, international freight forwarding, transportation, trade and regulatory services, and warehousing and distribution.

Through outsourcing alliances, producers and logistical service suppliers cooperate in developing innovative, customized systems that speed goods through carefully constructed manufacturing and distribution pipelines. Although many companies have long outsourced transportation and warehousing functions, today's alliance partners use similar methods to combine their operations.

assessment check 5

5.1 What is upstream management? What is downstream management?

5.2 Identify three methods for managing logistics.

---

⑥ Identify the major components of a physical distribution system.

PHYSICAL DISTRIBUTION

A firm's physical distribution system is an organized group of components linked according to a plan for achieving specific distribution objectives. It contains the following elements:

1. *Customer service.* What level of customer service the distribution activities should support.

2. *Transportation.* How the firm should ship its products.

3. *Inventory control.* How much inventory the firm should maintain at each location.

4. *Protective packaging and materials handling.* How the firm can package and efficiently handle goods in the factory, warehouse, and transport terminals.

5. *Order processing.* How the firm should handle orders.

6. *Warehousing.* Where the distribution system will locate stocks of goods and the number of warehouses the firm should maintain.

All these components function in interrelated ways. Decisions made in one area affect efficiency in others. The physical distribution manager must balance each component so that the system avoids stressing any single aspect to the detriment of overall functioning. A firm might decide to reduce transportation costs by shipping its products by less costly—but slow—water transportation. But slow deliveries would likely force the firm to maintain higher inventory levels, raising those costs. This mismatch between system elements often leads to increased production costs. So balancing the components is crucial.

The general shift from a manufacturing economy to a service economy in Canada has affected physical distribution in two key ways. First, customers require more flexible—yet reliable—transportation service. Second, the number of smaller shipments is growing much faster than the number of large shipments. Although traditional, high-volume shipments will continue to grow, they will represent a lower percentage of the transportation industry's revenues and volume.[29]

THE PROBLEM OF SUBOPTIMIZATION

Logistics managers seek to establish a specified level of customer service while minimizing the costs of physically moving and storing goods. Marketers must first decide on their priorities for customer service and then figure out how to fulfill those goals by moving goods at the best cost. Meshing together all the physical distribution elements is a huge challenge that firms don't always meet.

Suboptimization results when the managers of individual physical distribution functions attempt to minimize costs, but the impact of one task on the others leads to less than optimal results. Imagine a hockey team composed of record-holding players. Unfortunately, despite the individual talents of the players, the team fails to win a game. This is an example of suboptimization. The same thing can happen at a company when each logistics activity is judged by its own accomplishments instead of the way it contributes to the overall goals of the firm. Suboptimization often happens when a firm introduces a new product that may not fit easily into its current physical distribution system.

Effective management of the physical distribution function requires some cost trade-offs. By accepting relatively high costs in some functional areas to cut costs in others, managers can minimize their firm's total physical distribution costs. Of course, any reduction in logistical costs should support progress toward the goal of maintaining customer-service standards.

CUSTOMER-SERVICE STANDARDS

Customer-service standards state the goals and define acceptable performance for the quality of service that a firm expects to deliver to its customers. Internet retailers such as 1-800-FLOWERS.ca and Occasionally Gifted thrive because of their ability to ship within hours of receiving an order. A pizza parlour might set a standard to deliver customers' pizzas hot and fresh to their homes within 30 minutes of their order. An auto repair shop might set a standard to complete all oil changes in a half hour.

Designers of a physical distribution system begin by establishing acceptable levels of customer service. These designers then assemble physical distribution components in a way that will achieve this standard at the lowest possible total cost. This overall cost breaks down into five components: (1) transportation, (2) warehousing, (3) customer service/order processing, (4) administrative costs, and (5) inventory control.

TRANSPORTATION

The transportation industry has been largely deregulated. Deregulation has been particularly important for motor carriers, railroads, and air carriers. Many transporters are now free to develop unique solutions to shippers' needs. The trucking industry now operates far more efficiently than it did under government regulation; many carriers have reduced empty mileage by two-thirds.

H.F. (HERB) MACKENZIE

Trucking companies, such as Midland Transport, move about 90 percent of all consumer goods within Canada and about two-thirds, by value, of our trade with the United States.

Typically adding 10 percent to the cost of a product, transportation and delivery expenses represent the largest category of logistics-related costs for most firms. Also, for many items—particularly perishable ones such as fresh fish or produce—transportation makes a central contribution to satisfactory customer service.

Many logistics managers have found that the key to controlling their shipping costs is careful management of relationships with shipping firms. Freight carriers use two basic rates: class and commodity rates. A class rate is a standard rate for a specific commodity moving between any pair of destinations. A carrier may charge a lower commodity rate, sometimes called a *special rate,* to a favoured shipper as a reward for either regular business or a large-quantity shipment. Railroads and inland water carriers frequently reward customers in this way.

In addition, the railroad and motor carrier industries sometimes supplement this rate structure with negotiated, or contract, rates. In other words, the two parties finalize terms of rates, services, and other variables in a contract.

Classes of Carriers

Freight carriers are classified as common, contract, and private carriers. **Common carriers**, often considered the backbone of the transportation industry, provide transportation services as for-hire carriers to the general public. The government still regulates their rates and services, and they cannot conduct their operations without permission from the appropriate regulatory authority. Common carriers move freight via all modes of transport. FedEx is a major common carrier serving businesses and consumers. One way the firm remains competitive is by developing new methods for enhancing customer service. Recently, FedEx introduced a service called Insight, which essentially reverses the package-tracking process—instead of following a package from shipment to delivery, customers can go online to find out what is going to be delivered to them that day. One FedEx customer that has benefited greatly from this new service is a firm that conducts testing of bone marrow samples. Time is essential for the delivery of these samples. Now the firm can find out exactly how many completed test kits will be arriving in the lab each day.[30]

Contract carriers are for-hire transporters that do not offer their services to the general public. Instead, they establish contracts with individual customers and operate exclusively for particular industries, such as the motor freight industry. These carriers operate under much looser regulations than common carriers.

Private carriers do not offer services for hire. These carriers provide transportation services solely for internally generated freight. As a result, they observe no rate or service regulations. Many large retailers operate their own private fleets in Canada.

assessment check 6

6.1 What are the six major elements of physical distribution?

6.2 What is suboptimization?

Major Transportation Modes

Logistics managers choose among five major transportation alternatives: railroads, motor carriers, water carriers, pipelines, and air freight. Each mode has its own unique characteristics. Logistics managers select the best options for their situations by matching the situation features to their specific transportation needs.

Railroads

Railroads continue to control the largest share of the freight business as measured by tonne-kilometres. The term *tonne-kilometre* indicates shipping activity required to move one tonne of freight one kilometre. Rail shipments quickly rack up tonne-kilometres because this mode provides the most efficient way for moving bulky commodities over long distances. Rail carriers generally transport huge quantities of coal, chemicals, grain, nonmetallic minerals, lumber and wood products, and automobiles. The railroads have improved their service standards through a number of innovative concepts, such as unit trains, run-through trains, **intermodal operations,** and double-stack container trains. Unit trains carry much of the coal, grain, and other high-volume commodities shipped, running back and forth between single loading points (such as a mine) and single destinations (such as a power plant) to deliver a single commodity. Run-through trains bypass intermediate terminals to speed up schedules. They work similar to unit trains, but a run-through train may carry a variety of commodities.

In piggyback operations, one of the intermodal operations, highway trailers and containers, ride on railroad flatcars, thus combining the long-haul capacity of the train with the door-to-door flexibility of the truck. A double-stack container train pulls special rail cars equipped with bathtub-shaped wells so they can carry two containers stacked on top of one another. By nearly doubling train capacity and slashing costs, this system offers enormous advantages to rail customers. Canada's two major railways, Canadian Pacific Railway (CP) and Canadian National Railway (CN), are both focused on lowering fuel consumption and smog-causing emissions. These environmental improvements are starting to be noticed by customers. Mike LoVecchio, senior manager, media relations for CP, says, "Double-stacked intermodal freight trains can replace more than 200 trucks on our highways."[31]

intermodal operations Combination of transport modes such as rail and highway carriers (piggyback), air and highway carriers (birdyback), and water and highway carriers (fishyback) to improve customer service and achieve cost advantages.

Marketoid

In 2007, railways loaded 284.5 million tonnes of freight. Only 4.5 million tonnes included manufactured products.

Motor Carriers

Trucks transport about 90 percent of all consumer goods products within Canada and about two-thirds, by value, of our trade with the United States. Canadian for-hire truckers haul more than 600 million tonnes of freight annually, and in one recent year, they transported more than 225 billion tonne-kilometres of freight.[32] Trucking offers some important advantages over the other transportation modes, including relatively fast shipments and consistent service for both large and small shipments. Motor carriers concentrate on shipping manufactured products, while railroads typically haul bulk shipments of raw materials. Motor carriers, therefore, receive greater revenue per ton shipped, making road transportation one of the most expensive shipping methods.

Technology has also improved the efficiency of trucking. Many trucking firms now track their fleets via satellite communications systems,

CANADIAN PACIFIC

CP hauls double-stacked containers—originating from the Port of Vancouver—through the Rogers Pass to the urban centres of the east.

and in-truck computer systems allow drivers and dispatchers to make last-minute changes in scheduling and delivery. The Internet is also adding new features to motor carrier services.

Water Carriers

Two basic types of transport methods move products over water: inland or barge lines and ocean-going, deepwater ships. Barge lines efficiently transport bulky, low unit value commodities such as grain, gravel, lumber, sand, and steel. Montreal-based Canada Steamship Lines operates a fleet of 15 self-unloading bulk carriers on the Great Lakes–St. Lawrence Waterway system.[33]

Ocean-going ships carry a growing stream of containerized freight between ports around the world. Inbound container freight ballooned 25 percent in 2006 at Vancouver, Canada's largest port.[34] In total, Canadian ports handle more than 450 million tonnes of goods annually. Approximately half of Canadian international trade, by value, is carried by marine transportation.[35] New supertankers from global companies such as Maersk Sealand are the size of three football fields, almost doubling the capacity of other vessels. At full capacity, the ships can cut the cost of shipping a container across the Pacific by a fifth. Shippers that transport goods via water carriers incur very low costs compared with the rates for other transportation modes. Standardized modular shipping containers maximize savings by limiting loading, unloading, and other handling.

Ships often carry large refrigerated containers, called reefers, for transporting everything from fresh produce to medical supplies. These containers, along with their non-refrigerated counterparts, improve shipping efficiency because they can easily be removed from a ship and attached to trucks or trains. Although shipping by water has traditionally been less expensive than other modes of transportation, costs for this mode have increased dramatically because of tightened international security measures.

Pipelines

Although the pipeline industry ranks third after railroads and motor carriers in tonne-kilometres transported, many people scarcely recognize its existence. Oil pipelines carry two types of commodities: crude (unprocessed) oil and refined products, such as gasoline, jet fuel, and kerosene. In addition, one so-called *slurry pipeline* carries coal in suspension after it has been ground up into a powder and mixed with water. TransCanada Pipelines has a network of more than 59 000 kilometres of pipeline and transports most of Western Canada's natural gas to markets in Canada and the United States.[36] Enbridge delivers more than 2 million barrels per day of crude oil and liquids through its 13 500-kilometre system, the world's longest system.[37]

Although pipelines offer low maintenance and dependable methods of transportation, a number of characteristics limit their applications. They have fewer locations than water carriers, and they can accommodate shipments of only a small number of products. Finally, pipelines represent a relatively slow method of transportation; liquids travel through this method at an average speed of only five to six kilometres per hour.

Air Freight

Although the air freight industry grew steadily for many years, recently that growth has levelled off—at least in

Pipe and valves at Enbridge's Edmonton terminal.

COURTESY ENBRIDGE

certain market sectors, such as overnight delivery service. The reason is simple: cost-conscious businesses are thinking twice about paying a premium for overnight delivery and are instead relying on less-expensive, guaranteed ground deliveries. FedEx recently announced that it expected to carry more domestic ground shipments than air shipments in one year—for the first time in the company's history. One industry watcher predicts this trend will continue for several years with surface transportation representing an ever-larger share of FedEx's shipping mix.[38] Purolator Courier remains Canada's largest domestic air shipper, handling more than 1.1 million pieces, pick-up and delivery, each day. Purolator handles more than 180 000 kilograms of air freight each night.[39]

Comparing the Five Modes of Transport

Table 12.3 compares the five transportation modes on several operating characteristics. Although all shippers judge reliability, speed, and cost in choosing the most appropriate transportation methods, they assign varying importance to specific criteria when shipping different goods. For example, while motor carriers rank highest in availability in different locations, shippers of petroleum products frequently choose the lowest ranked alternative, pipelines, for their low cost.

Examples of types of goods most often handled by the different transports include the following:

- *Railroads.* Lumber, iron, steel, coal, automobiles, grain, chemicals

- *Motor carriers.* Clothing, furniture, fixtures, lumber, plastic, food, leather, machinery

- *Water carriers.* Fuel, oil, coal, chemicals, minerals, petroleum products

- *Pipelines.* Oil, diesel fuel, jet fuel, kerosene, natural gas

- *Air freight.* Flowers, technical instruments, machinery, high-priced specialty products, direct-to-consumer e-commerce goods

assessment check 7

7.1 Identify the five major modes of transport.

7.2 Which mode of transport is currently being replaced by ground delivery, and why?

Freight Forwarders and Supplemental Carriers

Freight forwarders act as transportation intermediaries, consolidating shipments to gain lower rates for their customers. The transport rates on less-than-truckload (LTL) and less-than-carload (LCL) shipments often double the per-unit rates on truckload (TL) and carload (CL) shipments. Freight forwarders charge less than the highest rates but more than the lowest rates. They profit by consolidating shipments from multiple customers until they can ship at TL and CL rates. The customers gain two advantages from these services: lower costs on small shipments and faster delivery service than they could achieve with their own LTL and LCL shipments.

In addition to the transportation options reviewed so far, a logistics manager can ship products via a number of auxiliary, or supplemental, carriers that specialize in small shipments. These carriers include Purolator Courier, Canpar, United Parcel Service (UPS), FedEx, DHL International, Canada Post, and bus freight services.

⑧ Discuss the role of transportation intermediaries, combined transportation modes, and warehousing in improving physical distribution.

table 12.3 *Comparison of Transport Modes*

MODE	SPEED	DEPENDABILITY IN MEETING SCHEDULES	FREQUENCY OF SHIPMENTS	AVAILABILITY IN DIFFERENT LOCATIONS	FLEXIBILITY IN HANDLING	COST
Rail	Average	Average	Low	Low	High	Average
Water	Very slow	Average	Very low	Limited	Very high	Very low
Truck	Fast	High	High	Very extensive	Average	High
Pipeline	Slow	High	High	Very limited	Very low	Low
Air	Very fast	High	Average	Average	Low	Very high

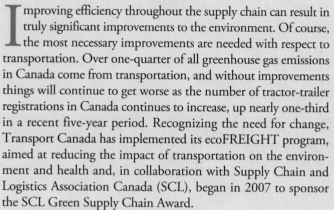

Go Green

Greening the Supply Chain

Improving efficiency throughout the supply chain can result in truly significant improvements to the environment. Of course, the most necessary improvements are needed with respect to transportation. Over one-quarter of all greenhouse gas emissions in Canada come from transportation, and without improvements things will continue to get worse as the number of tractor-trailer registrations in Canada continues to increase, up nearly one-third in a recent five-year period. Recognizing the need for change, Transport Canada has implemented its ecoFREIGHT program, aimed at reducing the impact of transportation on the environment and health and, in collaboration with Supply Chain and Logistics Association Canada (SCL), began in 2007 to sponsor the SCL Green Supply Chain Award.

What can be done to improve the efficiency of transportation? Well, obviously, using less transportation, better modes of transportation, and improved transportation equipment are a good start. One way to use less transportation is to improve packaging so that more product can be shipped in a single shipment. In 2003, Hewlett-Packard used 396 grams of packaging per camera and could fit only 200 on a pallet. Recently, the packaging has been reduced to 164 grams, and 720 units can now be shipped on a single pallet. Using better modes of transportation could involve using more ocean rather than air transportation, for example, as Hewlett-Packard encourages with its Green Cargo program. Alternatively, shippers could make greater use of piggyback, one intermodal method of

transportation, rather than simply using truck transportation. As noted earlier in this chapter, a single double-stacked intermodal freight train can replace more than 200 trucks on the road. According to New Brunswick Southern Railway research, a 20-car freight train emits less than half of the CO_2 that would be emitted by 20 loaded transport trucks. Improved transportation equipment could use more efficient tires, aerodynamic mirrors, synthetic lubricants, or new technology engines or fuels. Montreal-based Railpower Technologies recycles older locomotives, replacing their engines with smaller diesel motors and a battery pack. The hybrid locomotives that they produce use up to 70 percent less fuel and emit up to 90 percent less smog-precursor oxides into the atmosphere. Whether they decide to go with less or better, companies that have started to implement actions to "green" their supply chain will have an advantage as government regulation and consumer concern continue to increase.

Sources: Transport Canada News Release H153/07, "Transport Canada Sponsors First Annual SCL Green Supply Chain Award," August 13, 2007; "What Impact Transportation Has on the Environment," *Truck News,* June 2007, p. 6; Nicolas Van Praet, "A Green Company Struggles to Get out of the Red," *Financial Post Business,* March 2007, p. 17; David Shipley, "The Resurgence of Rail Transportation; As CN Rail Prepares to Convene Its Shareholder Meeting in Moncton, the Company Says Rail Is Enjoying a Renaissance," *New Brunswick Telegraph Journal* (Saint John), April 21, 2007, pp. C1–2; Robert J. Bowman, "The Greening of the Supply Chain," SupplyChainBrain.com, November 1, 2006, http://www.supplychainbrain.com.

Intermodal Coordination

Transportation companies emphasize specific modes and serve certain kinds of customers, but they sometimes combine their services to give shippers the service and cost advantages of each. *Piggyback* service, mentioned in the section on rail transport, is the most widely used form of intermodal coordination. *Birdyback* service, another form of intermodal coordination, sends motor carriers to pick up a shipment locally and deliver that shipment to local destinations; an air carrier takes it between airports near those locations. *Fishyback* service sets up a similar intermodal coordination system between motor carriers and water carriers.

Intermodal transportation generally gives shippers faster service and lower rates than either mode could match individually because each method carries freight in its most efficient way. However, intermodal arrangements require close coordination between all transportation providers.

Recognizing this need, multimodal transportation companies have formed to offer combined activities within single operations. Piggyback service generally joins two separate companies—a railroad and a trucking company. A multimodal firm provides intermodal service through its own internal transportation resources. Shippers benefit because the single service assumes responsibility from origin to destination. This unification prevents disputes over which carrier delayed or damaged a shipment.

H.F. (HERB) MACKENZIE

Sobeys operates 22 distribution centres—such as this one in Stellarton, Nova Scotia—that serve more than 1300 stores owned or franchised across Canada.

WAREHOUSING

Products flow through two types of warehouses: storage and distribution warehouses. A storage warehouse holds goods for moderate to long periods in an attempt to balance supply and demand for producers and purchasers. For example, Toronto-based Atlas Cold Storage operates 52 controlled atmosphere—also called *cold storage*—warehouses from Newfoundland to British Columbia, and throughout much of the United States.[40] It stores a variety of perishable products, including fruits, vegetables, fish, and many other items. By contrast, a distribution warehouse assembles and redistributes goods, keeping them moving as much as possible. Many distribution warehouses or centres physically store goods for less than 24 hours before shipping them to customers.

Logistics managers have attempted to save on transportation costs by developing central distribution centres. A manufacturer might send a single, large, consolidated shipment to a break-bulk centre—a central distribution centre that breaks down large shipments into several smaller ones and delivers them to individual customers in the area. Many Internet retailers use break-bulk distribution centres.

Wal-Mart operates an enormous distribution network of approximately 160 distribution centres around the world. The firm plans to open even more centres. By increasing the number of centres in strategic locations, Wal-Mart can reduce its transportation distances and costs significantly. In addition, Wal-Mart is rapidly building distribution centres in most of the countries where it operates stores. Each centre represents a full supply-chain system that includes all logistics—a large centre may have as many as a hundred docking centres. China, which already has 56 Wal-Mart stores, has several distribution centres—with more to come. These centres, as well as the stores, employ tens of thousands of local workers.[41]

Automated Warehouse Technology

Logistics managers can cut distribution costs and improve customer service dramatically by automating their warehouse systems. Although automation technology represents an expensive investment, it can provide major labour savings for high-volume distributors such as grocery chains. A computerized system might store orders, choose the correct number of cases, and move those cases in the desired sequence to loading docks. This kind of warehouse system reduces labour costs, worker injuries, pilferage, fires, and breakage.

Warehouse Locations

Every company must make a major logistics decision when it determines the number and locations of its storage facilities. Two categories of costs influence this choice: (1) warehousing and materials handling costs and (2) delivery costs from warehouses to customers. Large facilities offer economies of scale in facilities and materials handling systems; per-unit costs for these systems decrease as volume increases. Delivery costs, on the other hand, rise as the distance from warehouse to customer increases. As just mentioned, Wal-Mart continues to work to increase the number of warehouse locations to reduce distance and cost.

Warehouse location also affects customer service. Businesses must place their storage and distribution facilities in locations from which they can meet customer demands for product availability and delivery times. They must also consider population and employment trends. For example, because of Moncton's central location in the Atlantic region, many firms have established distribution centres in the area. Pratt & Whitney Canada, a designer and manufacturer of aircraft engines, has opened a distribution centre in Amsterdam, Holland, to serve its customers in Europe, Africa, and the Middle East, and another in Singapore to serve its customers in the Pacific Rim Region.[42]

INVENTORY CONTROL SYSTEMS

Inventory control captures a large share of a logistics manager's attention because companies need to maintain enough inventory to meet customer demand without incurring unneeded costs for carrying excess inventory. Some firms attempt to keep inventory levels under control by implementing just-in-time (JIT) production. Others are beginning to use RFID technology, discussed earlier in this chapter.

Companies such as Costco have shifted responsibility—and costs—for inventory control from retailers back to individual manufacturers. Costco gives Kimberly-Clark access to individual store sales data. Kimberly-Clark uses the information to track inventory levels of its diapers and other products and replenishes stocks as needed.[43] Vendor-managed inventory (VMI) systems like this are based on the assumption that suppliers are in the best position to spot understocks or surpluses, cutting costs along the supply chain that can be translated into lower prices at the checkout.

ORDER PROCESSING

Like inventory control, order processing directly affects the firm's ability to meet its customer service standards. A company may have to compensate for inefficiencies in its order processing system by shipping products via costly transportation modes or by maintaining large inventories at many expensive field warehouses.

Order processing typically consists of four major activities: (1) conducting a credit check; (2) keeping a record of the sale, which involves tasks such as crediting a sales representative's commission account; (3) making appropriate accounting entries; and (4) locating orders, shipping them, and adjusting inventory records. A stockout occurs when an order for an item is not available for shipment. A firm's order processing system must advise affected customers of a stockout and offer a choice of alternative actions.

As in other areas of physical distribution, technological innovations improve efficiency in order processing. Many firms are streamlining their order processing procedures by using e-mail and the Internet, often their least costly fulfillment channel.

Marketoid

Vancouver is Canada's largest port, handling more than $53 billion in goods annually and generating nearly 70 000 jobs with $4 billion GDP and $8.9 billion in economic output.

PROTECTIVE PACKAGING AND MATERIALS HANDLING

Logistics managers arrange and control activities for moving products within plants, warehouses, and transportation terminals, which together compose the **materials handling system**. Two important concepts influence many materials handling choices: unitizing and containerization.

Unitizing combines as many packages as possible into each load that moves within or outside a facility. Logistics managers prefer to handle materials on pallets (platforms, generally made of wood, on which goods are transported). Unitizing systems often lash materials in place with steel bands or shrink packaging. A shrink package surrounds a batch of materials with a sheet of plastic that shrinks after heating, securely holding individual pieces together. Unitizing promotes efficient materials handling because each package requires minimal labour to move. Securing the materials together also minimizes damage and pilferage.

Logistics managers extend the same concept through **containerization**—combining several unitized loads. A container of oil rig parts, for example, can be loaded in Alberta and trucked or shipped by rail to Vancouver, and then loaded on a ship headed to Saudi Arabia.

assessment check 8

8.1   What are the benefits of intermodal transportation?

8.2   Identify the two types of warehouses and explain their function.

In addition to the benefits outlined for unitizing, containerization also markedly reduces the time required to load and unload ships. Containers limit in-transit damage to freight because individual packages pass through few handling systems en route to purchasers.

Strategic Implications

SEVERAL factors, including the burgeoning e-commerce environment, are driving changes in channel development, logistics, and supply-chain management. As the Internet continues to revolutionize the ways manufacturers deliver goods to ultimate consumers, marketers must find ways to promote cooperation between existing dealer, retailer, and distributor networks while harnessing the power of the Web as an alternative channel. This system demands not only delivery of goods and services faster and more efficiently than ever before but also superior service to Web-based customers.

In addition, increased product proliferation—grocery stores typically stock almost 50 000 different items—demands logistics systems that can manage multiple brands delivered through multiple channels. And those channels must be finely tuned to identify and rapidly rectify problems such as retail shortfalls or costly overstocks. The trend toward leaner retailing, in which the burden of merchandise tracking and inventory control is switching from retailers to manufacturers, means that to be effective, logistics and supply-chain systems must result in cost savings. ◆◆◆

REVIEW OF CHAPTER OBJECTIVES

① **Describe the types of marketing channels and the roles they play in marketing strategy.**

Marketing (distribution) channels are the systems of marketing institutions that enhance the physical flow of goods and services, along with ownership title, from producer to consumer or business user. In other words, they help bridge the gap between producer or manufacturer and business customer or consumer. Types of channels include direct selling, selling through intermediaries, dual distribution, and reverse channels. Channels perform four functions: facilitating the exchange process, sorting, standardizing exchange processes, and facilitating searches by buyers and sellers.

② **Outline the major channel strategy decisions.**

Decisions include selecting a marketing channel and determining distribution intensity. Selection of a marketing channel may be based on market factors, product factors, organizational factors, or competitive factors. Distribution may be intensive, selective, or exclusive.

③ **Describe the concepts of channel management, conflict, and cooperation.**

Manufacturers must practise channel management by developing and maintaining relationships with the intermediaries in their marketing channels. The channel captain is the dominant member of the channel. Horizontal and vertical conflict can arise when there is disagreement among channel members. Cooperation is best achieved when all channel members regard themselves as equal components of the same organization.

④ **Identify and describe the different vertical marketing systems.**

A vertical marketing system (VMS) is a planned channel system designed to improve distribution efficiency and cost effectiveness by integrating various functions throughout the distribution chain. This may be achieved by forward integration or backward integration. Options include a corporate marketing system, operated by a single owner; an administered marketing system, run by a dominant channel member; and a contractual marketing system, based on formal agreements among channel members.

⑤ Explain the roles of logistics and supply-chain management in an overall distribution strategy.

Effective logistics requires proper supply-chain management. The supply chain begins with raw materials, proceeds through actual production, and then continues with the movement of finished products through the marketing channel to customers. Supply-chain management takes place in two directions: upstream and downstream. Tools that marketers use to streamline and manage logistics include radio frequency identification (RFID), enterprise resource planning (ERP), and logistical cost control.

⑥ Identify the major components of a physical distribution system.

Physical distribution involves a broad range of activities concerned with efficient movement of finished goods from the end of the production line to the consumer. As a system, physical distribution consists of six elements: (1) customer service, (2) transportation, (3) inventory control, (4) materials handling and protective packaging, (5) order processing, and (6) warehousing. These elements are interrelated and must be balanced to create a smoothly functioning distribution system and to avoid suboptimization.

⑦ Compare the major modes of transportation.

Railroads rank high on flexibility in handling products; average on speed, dependability in meeting schedules, and cost; and low on frequency of shipments. Motor carriers are relatively high in cost but rank high on speed, dependability, shipment frequency, and availability in different locations. Water carriers balance their slow speed, low shipment frequency, and limited availability with lower costs. The special nature of pipelines makes them rank relatively low on availability, flexibility, and speed, but they are also low in cost. Air transportation is high in cost but offers very fast and dependable delivery schedules.

⑧ Discuss the role of transportation intermediaries, combined transportation modes, and warehousing in improving physical distribution.

Transportation intermediaries facilitate movement of goods in a variety of ways, including piggyback, birdyback, and fishyback services—all forms of intermodal coordination. Methods such as unitization and containerization facilitate intermodal transfers.

assessment check answers

1.1 Distinguish between a marketing channel and logistics.
A marketing channel is an organized system of marketing institutions and their interrelationships designed to enhance the flow and ownership of goods and services from producer to user. Logistics is the actual process of coordinating the flow of information, goods, and services among members of the marketing channel.

1.2 What are the different types of marketing channels?
The different types of marketing channels are direct selling, selling through intermediaries, dual distribution, and reverse channels.

1.3 What four functions do marketing channels perform?
The four functions of marketing channels are (1) facilitating the exchange process by reducing the number of marketplace contacts necessary for a sale; (2) sorting; (3) standardizing exchange transactions; and (4) facilitating searches by buyers and sellers.

2.1 Identify four major factors in selecting a marketing channel.
The four major factors in selecting a marketing channel are market, product, organizational, and competitive.

2.2 Describe the three general categories of distribution intensity.
Intensive distribution seeks to distribute a product through all available channels in a trade area. Selective distribution chooses a limited number of retailers in a market area. Exclusive distribution grants exclusive rights to a wholesaler or retailer to sell a manufacturer's products.

3.1 What is a channel captain? What is its role in channel cooperation?
A channel captain is the dominant member of the marketing channel. Its role in channel cooperation is to provide the necessary leadership.

3.2 Identify and describe the three types of channel conflict.
Horizontal conflict results from disagreements among channel members at the same level. Vertical conflict occurs when channel members at different levels disagree. The grey market causes conflict because it involves competition in the Canadian market of

brands produced by overseas affiliates, which are often lower priced than the same goods manufactured in Canada.

4.1 What are vertical marketing systems (VMSs)? Identify the major types.

Vertical marketing systems are planned channel systems designed to improve the effectiveness of distribution, including efficiency and cost. The three major types are corporate, administered, and contractual.

4.2 Identify the three types of contractual marketing systems.

The three types of contractual systems are wholesale-sponsored voluntary chains, retail cooperatives, and franchises.

5.1 What is upstream management? What is downstream management?

Upstream management involves managing raw materials, inbound logistics, and warehouse and storage facilities. Downstream management involves managing finished product storage, outbound logistics, marketing and sales, and customer service.

5.2 Identify three methods for managing logistics.

Methods for managing logistics include RFID technology, enterprise resource planning (ERP) systems, and logistical cost control.

6.1 What are the six major elements of physical distribution?

The major elements of physical distribution are customer service, transportation, inventory control, materials handling and protective packaging, order processing, and warehousing.

6.2 What is suboptimization?

Suboptimization occurs when managers of individual functions try to reduce costs but create less than optimal results.

7.1 Identify the five major modes of transport.

The five major modes of transport are railroads, motor carriers, water carriers, pipelines, and air freight.

7.2 Which mode of transport is currently being replaced by ground delivery, and why?

Air transport is in many cases being replaced by ground delivery because of cost.

8.1 What are the benefits of intermodal transportation?

Intermodal transportation usually provides shippers faster service and lower rates than a single mode could offer.

8.2 Identify the two types of warehouses and explain their function.

The two types of warehouses are storage and distribution. Storage warehouses hold goods for moderate to long periods of time in order to balance supply and demand. Distribution warehouses assemble and redistribute goods as quickly as possible.

MARKETING TERMS YOU NEED TO KNOW

These terms are printed in red in the text. They are defined in the margins of the chapter and in the Glossary that begins on p. G-1. Other important terms are printed in bold black type in the chapter but not included in this list. Their definitions can be found in the Glossary.

distribution 390
marketing (distribution) channel 390
logistics 390
supply-chain management 390
physical distribution 390
electronic storefronts 392
direct channel 393

dual distribution 395
intensive distribution 399
selective distribution 399
exclusive distribution 399
channel captain 401
grey goods 402
vertical marketing system (VMS) 403

corporate marketing system 403
administered marketing system 403
contractual marketing system 403
radio frequency identification (RFID) 405
enterprise resource planning (ERP) system 407
intermodal operations 411

ASSURANCE OF LEARNING REVIEW

1. What is a marketing intermediary? What is the intermediary's role?
2. Why would marketers use a dual distribution strategy?
3. Describe the three levels of distribution intensity. Give an example of a product in each level.
4. Compare and contrast the two types of channel conflict.
5. What are the benefits of owning a franchise? What are the drawbacks?
6. List some ways companies are streamlining their supply chains.
7. What is suboptimization? How can effective management of the physical distribution function avoid or overcome this problem?

8. Which mode of transport would probably be selected for the following goods?
   a. natural gas
   b. lumber
   c. fresh flowers
   d. crude oil and refined oil
   e. clothing made in Canada
   f. a diamond ring
   g. grain

9. Which two categories of costs influence the choice of how many storage facilities a firm might have and where they are located?

10. Describe the two concepts that influence materials handling choices.

PROJECTS AND TEAMWORK EXERCISES

1. Imagine a vending machine that would charge more for soft drinks during hot weather. The Coca-Cola Company has tested such a device. What is your opinion of a temperature-sensitive vending machine? Would your opinion change if there were no nearby alternatives—say, a convenience store or another vending machine? How do you think customers would react? With a partner, poll your classmates or your dorm or eating facility to find out.

2. The traditional channel for consumer goods runs from producer to wholesaler to retailer to user. With a classmate, select a product from the following list (or choose one of your own) and create a chart that traces its distribution system. You may go online to the firm's website for additional information.
   a. a kayak from the Mountain Equipment Co-op website or catalogue
   b. a meal at Swiss Chalet
   c. a CD or DVD from Best Buy

3. On your own or with a classmate, identify, draw, and explain a reverse channel with which you are personally familiar. What purpose does this reverse channel serve to businesses? To the community? To consumers?

4. On your own or with a classmate, choose one of the franchises listed in Table 12.2 and visit the website of that company. Based on what you can learn about its contractual marketing system as well as other information about its products, logistics, supply-chain management, and physical distribution system, would you be interested in purchasing a franchise from this company? Why or why not? Present your findings in class.

5. For the franchise you selected, create a chart outlining the physical distribution objectives.

CRITICAL THINKING EXERCISES

1. Movielink is a joint venture of five Hollywood studios that offers movies over the Internet. Recently, the company signed a deal with Twentieth Century Fox, which means that all the major studios are now offering consumers the option to download certain films—ones to which the studios have Internet distribution rights.[44] How do you think this new arrangement will affect the way movies are distributed to the public in the future?

2. Auto dealerships often have exclusive distribution rights in their local markets. How might this affect the purchase choices consumers make? What problems might a dealership encounter with this type of distribution?

3. The new Airbus 380, the largest passenger jet in existence, has the capacity to carry 550 travellers. It also contains 32 000 major parts. The cockpit is built in France, the front and aft fuselages in Germany, the engines in the United Kingdom and the United States, and the tailcone in Spain. New factories were built to handle the scale and complexity of the Airbus. Some of the parts are so large that there aren't aircraft big enough to transport them. These are just a few of the challenges faced by Airbus.[45] Describe steps that Airbus can take to achieve and maintain channel cooperation during the first years of this venture.

4. At one time, Toro, a U.S. manufacturer of snow blowers and lawn mowers, sold its products through a selective network of authorized dealers. These dealers often carried considerable inventory of equipment. They invested in spare parts inventory and provided considerable after-sale service to consumers who purchased Toro equipment from them. However, in a move to increase its distribution intensity, Toro began to sell its products through national mass merchandisers such as Canadian Tire. What would you expect the reaction to be from Toro authorized dealers? Why? What could Toro do to reduce the negative consequences of dealer reactions?

5. After a trip to Mexico, where you were inspired by the craftsmanship of a number of artisans you met there, you've decided to establish an import business for home furnishings, accessories, and some toys. What type (or types) of transportation would you use to get the goods to Canada, and why?

McDonald's has been the focus of criticism for many years—from nutrition experts, consumer health groups, and the like. Critics point to the high fat and calorie content of McDonald's burgers, fries, and shakes, claiming that they contribute to obesity and other health problems. McDonald's has responded in a number of ways—by adding salads to its menu, including fruit and other more healthful choices in children's meals, and offering lower-fat, lower-calorie sandwich items. Still, there are always critics willing to take a shot at the company's menu.

So McDonald's is trying a new tactic: opening up the supply chain to the media's view. The company invited Reuters reporters to tour one meat-processing plant to see exactly how its burgers are made. Reporters learned that each box of burger patties has a tracking number that can be traced back to the meat packer that supplied the beef. In the future, McDonald's plans to add a feature to its website that allows consumers to track the source of each ingredient in popular food items such as the Egg McMuffin. By providing this information, McDonald's marketers hope that consumers will focus on the quality of the food they are purchasing.[46]

1. Do you think that opening up the supply chain is an ethical strategy by McDonald's? Why or why not?
2. Do you think the strategy will work, or do you think it might backfire? Explain your answer.

1. **Packaging.** Companies use packaging to assist in the marketing of their products. Visit each of the following websites and prepare a brief report on how each company has used packaging as part of its brand management strategy.
   a. H.J. Heinz: http://www.heinz.com
   b. Campbell Soup: http://www.campbellsoup.ca
   c. Yoplait yogurt: http://www.yoplait.ca
2. **Vendor-managed inventory.** Visit the following website to learn more about vendor-managed inventory (http://www.vendormanagedinventory.com). Review the definition of vendor-managed inventory, how a vendor-managed inventory program should be set up, the benefits of vendor-managed inventory, and some of the problems with a vendor-managed inventory system. Prepare a brief oral report on the subject that you can present to your class.

Note: Internet Web addresses change frequently. If you don't find the exact sites listed, you may need to access the organization's home page and search from there or use a search engine such as Google.

Case 12.1

Heavy Metal at Hyundai

Shipping is a major mode of transportation in the physical distribution of many products, including oil, cars, electronics, and bathroom tiles. Shipping is a complex industry with few players willing to take on the risks associated with building expensive new ships, handling potential environmental disasters, and negotiating through a complicated array of international regulations. Despite these risks, shipbuilding itself is enjoying a recent boom. The upturn is due to the phase-out of single-hull ships (replaced by new, double-hull vessels), the upswing of China's economy that fuels more trade between Asia and North America, and the increasing demand for oil from developing countries.

The largest player in the global shipbuilding industry is Korea's Hyundai Heavy Industries, followed by Daewoo and Samsung. Not surprisingly, the world's largest shipyard also belongs to Hyundai. Built more than three decades ago, the yard now runs so efficiently that it can turn out a new $80-million vessel every four days of operation. Despite the firm's current prowess, Hyundai engineers continue to develop plans for even larger, more complex ships. On the drawing board is a supervessel that could carry as many as 10 000 steel containers—or 30 million pairs of sneakers.

Why doesn't the firm feel comfortable with its first-place position? China has been outspoken about its intent to become the leading shipbuilder in the world by 2015. China already puts pressure on leaders in other industries, including North American manufacturers of numerous products. With its large workforce and lower wages, China is poised to take on just about any industry it wants. So Hyundai executives continually develop new strategies for improving or enhancing their products as they develop new ones. As the old ore carriers and oil tankers are phased out of the shipping market in general, Hyundai looks for ways to build the enormous container ships. But—just like an auto manufacturer—marketers also seek ways to "load" them with expensive features. "We obviously want the more value-added-type vessel—[liquid natural gas] carriers, more complicated container vessels, ice-glass carriers," explains Han Dae Yoon, chief marketing officer of Hyundai's shipbuilding division. "Shipbuilders have to be selective." By focusing on the higher end of the market—letting Chinese shipbuilders take contracts for simple tankers and bulk carriers—Hyundai keeps itself out front. "Now the South Koreans are moving more toward the Lexus end in order to have an edge over the Chinese," notes Peter E. Bartholomew of Industrial Research and Consulting.

China's exploding economy has also created another potential challenge for Hyundai—a shortage of some building materials such as steel, which can make up 20 percent of the material on one ship. This shortage caused the price of steel plate to jump 70 percent in one year, contributing to a $30-million loss by the firm in one quarter. But Hyundai is still ahead of its competition, perhaps because its leaders take nothing for granted. Even with Hyundai's nine dry docks booked solidly with contracts for 102 ships worth a total of more than $8 billion, no one at Hyundai rests. "When you are being chased,

you have to do something that the chaser cannot do," says Han Dae Yoon. That means building bigger, better ships—faster.

Questions for Critical Thinking

1. With what types of intermediaries do you think Hyundai must maintain relationships?
2. Describe ways in which Hyundai can manage its supply chain effectively.
3. What role does Hyundai play in the global marketplace?

Souces: James Brooke, "Korean Shipbuilders See China's Shadow," *Seoul Times*, May 20, 2006, http://theseoultimes.com; Moon Ihlwan, "Korea's Shipbuilding Industry Sails Ahead," *BusinessWeek*, May 12, 2006, http://www.businessweek.com; Hyundai Heavy Industries website, http://english.hhi.co.kr, accessed May 8, 2006.

Case 12.2

BAX to the Future: How a Logistics Firm Has Survived and Grown

Wars in Afghanistan and Iraq, and terrorists' actions and threats around the world, have resulted in tightened security in many countries. This is having a huge impact on the supply chain of many industries. Today's marketplace conditions are complicated and volatile, which means that global companies must find new ways to manage all aspects of their supply channels, including their physical distribution systems. That's where BAX Global comes in. With revenues of nearly $3 billion and nearly 500 offices in 133 countries, BAX offers a wide range of supply-chain services to its customers and can manage any size or weight of shipment between virtually any two places in the world.

BAX provides other businesses with all the traditional services associated with logistics management, including transportation, storage, documentation, order assembly, packaging, and distribution. However, the company goes much further than that. BAX marketers work with their business customers to figure out how BAX can help its customers reduce costs and time, increase efficiency, and create and monitor ways to measure performance. For physical distribution, BAX operates a huge fleet of planes and trucks with real-time tracking, so customers have access at all times to the status of their products.

All of this does not come easily in the current marketing environment. When recent security measures were implemented in several countries, this created more demands on logistics firms to keep goods flowing so that compliance with import/export regulations didn't completely shut down manufacturing operations. BAX Global figured out a way to help. "Security used to be a paragraph at the bottom of a [contract proposal]," explains Jerry Levy, vice president of marketing for BAX Global. "Now companies, especially electronics companies, want a full disclosure of your security knowledge and procedures, along with security requirements, in any country where they do business. They say they want expedited deliveries to keep inventory levels low, but on the other side they

want flawless compliance of security procedures." That's not easy. In addition, as more and more firms expand into markets in developing countries, they are looking toward firms like BAX to provide services to make up for a lack of infrastructure in those countries. "People want financial, purchasing, order fulfillment, warehousing, and sales support, not just transport services," says Levy.

So BAX gives customers what they want by building security procedures right into the entire operational schedule. "That way, it doesn't cost more for clients," says Pete Cheviot, director of corporate security for BAX Global. BAX's program includes security measures both for its customers' products and against terrorism. With its DIRECTSHIP program, customers can reduce supply-chain time by skipping distribution centres and shipping directly to customers. BAX's electronic documentation capability provides preclearance. "A pre-alert process is integrated into the operation," explains Levy. This means that any potential problems can be handled en route, and customers have access to information about their shipments at all times through MyBAX, the firm's extranet. BAX considers itself a strategic partner to its customers and strives for nothing less than 100 percent customer satisfaction. That makes for a powerful supply-chain strategy.

Questions for Critical Thinking

1. As a third-party logistics firm, how does BAX Global help its customers achieve their own goals?
2. BAX Global has set its customer service standards at 100 percent. Describe additional steps the firm might take to achieve this.

Sources: BAX Global website, http://www.baxworld.com, accessed December 1, 2007; "BAX Global," *Inbound Logistics*, http://www.inboundlogistics.com, accessed April 17, 2004; "BAX Forwarder Network Enhances Its Wholesale Airport-to-Airport Services with Online Shipping Tools," *PR Newswire*, February 9, 2004, http://www.prnewswire.com; "Fast Forwarding," *Fortune*, September 1, 2003, pp. S2–S5.

Video Case 12.3

American Apparel: Supply Fits Demand

The written case on American Apparel appears on page VC-14. The recently filmed American Apparel video is designed to expand and highlight the concepts in this chapter and the concepts and questions covered in the written video case.

chapter 13

Retailers, Wholesalers, and Direct Marketers

CANADA'S NATIONAL SPORTS / LIFESTYLE RETAILER

CHAPTER OBJECTIVES

① Explain the wheel of retailing.

② Discuss how retailers select target markets.

③ Show how the elements of the marketing mix apply to retailing strategy.

④ Explain the concepts of retail convergence and scrambled merchandising.

⑤ Identify the functions performed by wholesaling intermediaries.

⑥ Outline the major types of independent wholesaling intermediaries and the appropriate situations for using each.

⑦ Compare the basic types of direct marketing and nonstore retailing.

⑧ Describe how much the Internet has altered the wholesaling, retailing, and direct marketing environments.

FORZANI: FOCUSED GROWTH

Forzani's Locker Room was established in Calgary in 1974 by John Forzani and three of his Calgary Stampeder teammates. Today, the Forzani Group operates 479 corporate and franchised stores from coast to coast in Canada. Corporate stores operate under four banners: Sport Chek, Sport Mart, Coast Mountain Sports, and National Sports; franchised stores operate under 10 banners: Sports Experts, Econosports, Intersport, RnR, Tech Shop, Pegasus, Hockey Experts, Fitness Source, Atmosphere, and Nevada Bob's Golf. Revenue exceeded $1.26 billion in 2007. Nearly 40 percent of sales came from franchised operations.

Managing a portfolio of retail concepts is challenging. The competitive landscape and consumer tastes are continually changing. As a consequence, smart retailers like the Forzani Group are always making adjustments to their store operations—adjusting merchandise strategy as consumer demand changes, and updating and improving retail image. Many of Forzani's flagship Sport Chek stores, for example, have brighter lighting, lighter in-store colours, and better signage. Inventory has been reduced to allow products to be better seen by consumers, and the products have been displayed in a "boutique" format. Visuals, graphics, and life-sized mannequins enhance the store image. These changes, along with retail technology improvements and staff training, are positioning the Forzani Group for continued strong growth.[1]

> ## connecting with customers
>
> The Forzani Group connects with its customers by catering to their diverse needs, considering geography, demographics, lifestyles, and budgets. Sport Chek and Sports Experts are the "big box" retailers: 40 000 or more private- and manufacturer-branded products; National Sports is a family and team sporting goods store; Sport Mart provides value to price-conscious consumers; Coast Mountain Sports and Atmosphere focus on the outdoor experience; Econosports is an opening price point banner; RnR is an urban-lifestyle retailer that caters to walkers and hikers; Tech Shop caters to runners; Nevada Bob's targets golfers; Hockey Experts is a hockey store; and Intersport takes advantage of Forzani's purchasing power and offers service at prices that most specialty stores simply cannot match.

Chapter Overview

IN exploring how today's retailing sector operates, this chapter introduces many examples that explain the combination of activities involved in selling goods to ultimate consumers, as the Forzani Group does in its efforts to attract people who are interested in enjoying many sports and leisure activities across Canada. Then the chapter looks at nonstore retailing. Direct marketing, a channel consisting of direct communication to consumers or business users, is a major form of nonstore retailing. It includes not just direct mail and telemarketing but direct-response advertising, infomercials, and Internet marketing. A less pervasive but growing aspect of nonstore retailing is automatic merchandising. The chapter concludes with a discussion on the role of wholesalers and other intermediaries who deliver goods from the manufacturer into the hands of retailers or other intermediaries. ◆◆◆

----

① **Explain the wheel of retailing.**

retailing Activities involved in selling merchandise to ultimate consumers.

Marketoid

Canadian annual retail sales exceed $400 billion, but wholesale sales exceed $500 billion.

RETAILING

Retailers are the marketing intermediaries who are in direct contact with ultimate consumers. **Retailing** describes the activities involved in selling merchandise to these consumers. In a very real sense, retailers represent the distribution channel to most consumers since a typical shopper has little contact with manufacturers and virtually no contact with wholesaling intermediaries. Retailers determine locations, store hours, number of sales personnel, store layouts, merchandise selections, and return policies—factors that often influence the consumers' images of the offerings more strongly than consumers' images of the products themselves. Both large and small retailers perform the major channel activities: creating time, place, and ownership utilities.

Retailers act as both customers and marketers in their channels. They sell products to ultimate consumers, and at the same time, they buy from wholesalers and manufacturers. Because of their critical location in the marketing channel, retailers often perform a vital feedback role. They obtain information from customers and transmit that information to manufacturers and other channel members.

EVOLUTION OF RETAILING

The development of retailing illustrates the marketing concept in operation. Early retailing in North America can be traced to the establishment of trading posts, such as the Hudson's Bay Company, and to pack peddlers who carried their wares to outlying settlements. The first type of retail institution, the general store, stocked a wide range of merchandise that met the needs of an isolated community or rural area. Supermarkets appeared in the early 1930s in response to consumers' desire for lower prices. In the 1950s, discount stores delivered lower prices in exchange for reduced services. The emergence of convenience food stores in the 1960s satisfied consumer demand for fast service, convenient locations, and expanded hours of operation. The development of off-price retailers in the 1980s and 1990s reflected consumer demand for brand-name merchandise at prices considerably lower than those of traditional retailers. In recent years, Internet-enabled retailing has increased in influence and importance.

wheel of retailing Hypothesis that each new type of retailer gains a competitive foothold by offering lower prices than current outlets charge; the result of reducing or eliminating services.

A key concept, known as the **wheel of retailing,** attempts to explain the patterns of change in retailing. According to the wheel of retailing, a new type of retailer gains a competitive foothold by offering customers lower prices than current outlets charge and maintains profits by reducing or eliminating services. Once established, however, the innovator begins to add more services, and its prices gradually rise. It then becomes vulnerable to new low-price retailers that enter with minimum services—and so the wheel turns, as illustrated in Figure 13.1. The Canadian retail graveyard is littered with former giants such as Eaton's, Woolco, Kmart, and catalogue retailer Consumers Distributing.

Many major developments in the history of retailing appear to fit the wheel's pattern. Early department stores, chain stores, supermarkets, discount stores, hypermarkets, and catalogue retailers all emphasized limited service and low prices. Most of these retailers gradually increased prices as they added services.

Some exceptions disrupt this pattern, however. Suburban shopping centres, convenience food stores, and vending machines never built their appeals around low prices. Still, the wheel pattern has been a good indicator enough times in the past to make it an accurate indicator of future retailing developments.

assessment check 1

1.1 What is retailing?

1.2 Explain the wheel-of-retailing concept.

RETAILING STRATEGY

Like manufacturers and wholesalers, a retailer develops a marketing strategy based on the firm's goals and strategic plans. The organization monitors environmental influences and assesses its own strengths and weaknesses in identifying marketing opportunities and constraints. A retailer bases its key decisions on two fundamental steps in the marketing strategy process: (1) selecting a target market and (2) developing a retailing mix to satisfy the chosen market. The retailing mix specifies merchandise strategy, customer-service standards, pricing guidelines, target market analysis, promotion goals, location/distribution decisions, and store atmosphere choices. The combination of these elements projects a desired retail image. Retail image communicates the store's identity to consumers. As Figure 13.2 points out, components of retailing strategy must work together to create a consistent image that appeals to the store's target market.

Canadian Tire is one retailer that takes great care to manage its retail image. The company recently tested a new store format called Concept 20/20. These stores have wider aisles and a greater selection of products for female consumers: ready-to-assemble furniture, and more housewares, home decor products, and gardening items. Same-store sales increased by less than 1 percent in traditional Canadian Tire stores in 2006, but by 8 percent in Concept 20/20 stores. As a result, the company has a five-year plan to spend $1.75 billion to upgrade its store network.[2]

figure 13.1
Wheel of Retailing

New form of retail outlet appears with ...
- Low level of service
- Low profit margins
- Low prices to consumers

1.

Over time ...
- Level of service increases
- Profit margins increase
- Prices to consumers increase

2.

More time ...
- Level of service continues to increase
- Profit margins continue to increase
- Prices to consumers continue to increase

3.

SELECTING A TARGET MARKET

A retailer starts to define its strategy by selecting a target market. Factors that influence the retailer's selection are the size and profit potential of the market and the level of competition for its business. Retailers pore over demographic, geographic, and psychographic profiles to segment markets. In the end, most retailers identify their target markets by certain demographics.

A study by MasterCard and Environics Research found that 22 percent of Canadian women were 35 to 54 years old and living at home with no children. This segment of consumers, underserved and having considerable discretionary income, is now being increasingly targeted by Canadian retailers. Liz Claiborne Canada has opened stores under its Yzza banner and Reitmans has opened a new chain called Cassis, both targeting the over-40s style-conscious woman.[3]

Deep-discount retailers, such as Dollarama and Buck-or-Two, originally targeted lower-income bargain hunters. They had less glamorous, but high-traffic, locations. Low-price merchandise was crammed into narrow, cluttered aisles. Customers were attracted by many cents-off basics, such as

② Discuss how retailers select target markets.

Marketoid

Dollarama Group dominates the dollar store business in Canada, with more than 500 locations and sales of approximately $1 billion.

figure 13.2

Components of Retail Strategy

shampoo, cereal, and laundry detergent, and sometimes picked up higher-margin goods as they approached the checkout. Increasingly, these retailers are appearing in more upscale locations, including shopping malls. They are improving the attractiveness of their stores and their product assortment to target more upper-middle-class consumers who are increasingly shopping for the bargains they offer.

After identifying a target market, a retailer must then develop marketing strategies to attract these chosen customers to its stores or website. The following sections discuss tactics for implementing different strategies.

MERCHANDISING STRATEGY

A retailer's merchandising strategy guides decisions regarding the items it will offer. A retailer must decide on general merchandise categories, product lines, specific items within lines, and the depth and width of its assortments. At Claire's Stores, a chain of accessories stores catering to teen girls, CEOs and sisters Marla and Bonnie Schaefer introduced a higher-margin product mix after inheriting the business from their father. Focusing more on jewellery, they have introduced a new line of pieces selected by Mariah Carey as well as a Mary-Kate and Ashley brand of cosmetics.[4]

To develop a successful merchandise mix, a retailer must weigh several priorities. First, it must consider the preferences and needs of its previously defined target market, keeping in mind that the competitive environment influences these choices. The retailer must also consider the overall profitability of each product line and product category.

assessment check 2

2.1 How does a retailer develop a marketing strategy?

2.2 How do retailers select target markets?

③ Show how the elements of the marketing mix apply to retailing strategy.

Category Management

As mentioned in Chapter 11, a popular merchandising strategy is *category management,* in which a category manager oversees an entire product line for both vendors and retailers and is responsible for the profitability of the product group. Category management seeks to improve the retailer's product category performance through more coordinated buying, merchandising, and pricing. Rather than focusing on the performance of individual brands, such as Flex shampoo or Kleenex tissue, category management evaluates performance according to each product category. Laundry detergent, skin-care products, and paper goods, for example, are each viewed as individual profit centres, and different category managers supervise each group. Those that underperform are at risk of being dropped from inventory, regardless of the strength of individual brands. To improve their profitability, for example, some department stores have narrowed their traditionally broad product categories to eliminate high-overhead, low-profit lines such as toys, appliances, and furniture.

The Battle for Shelf Space

As discussed in Chapter 12, large-scale retailers are increasingly taking on the role of channel captain within many distribution networks. Some have assumed traditional wholesaling functions, while others dictate product design and specifications to manufacturers. The result is a shift in power from the manufacturers of top-selling brands to the retailer that makes them available to customers.

Adding to the pressure is the increase in the number of new products and variations on existing products. To identify the varying items within a product line, retailers refer to a specific product offering as a **stockkeeping unit (SKU).** Within the skin-care category, for example, each facial cream, body moisturizer, and sunscreen in each of a variety of sizes and formulations is a separate SKU. The proliferation of new SKUs has resulted in a fierce battle for space on store shelves.

Increasingly, major retailers, such as Sears Canada and Loblaws, make demands in return for providing shelf space. They may, for example, seek pricing and promotional concessions from manufacturers as conditions for selling their products. Retailers also routinely require that manufacturers participate in their electronic data interchange (EDI) and quick-response systems. Manufacturers unable to comply may find themselves unable to penetrate the marketplace.

stockkeeping unit (SKU) Offering within a product line such as a specific size of liquid detergent.

Go Green

Buying Green—Get Bamboozled

Canadian retailers are slowly adding "green" products to their shelves and, not surprisingly, sales are slowly increasing. Two major problems that many green products face are price, and persuading customers that they perform at least as well as their conventional alternatives.

Some of the latest green products are manufactured wholly or in part from bamboo, and while they may not always solve the first problem, price, they frequently outperform existing products. Bamboo is the fastest-growing plant in the world—some species as fast as 1.5 metres per day. Bamboo forests release 35 percent more oxygen into the atmosphere than equivalent forests. The "woody" plant combines strength with versatility, making it possible to manufacture flooring, tile, countertops, kitchen cabinets, bathroom vanities, and, once it is pulped and spun, one of the world's softest yarns. From this yarn, manufacturers are making everything from diapers to suits, panties to sweaters, T-shirts to boxer briefs, bath towels to bedroom linens.

Bamboo products are beginning to appear at many Canadian retailers, large and small. You can find bamboo in OhSoSoft towels and linens at Beddazzle Bedroom and Bathroom Studio in Tecumseh, Ontario; the Ology line of clothing at Cotton Ginny; sweaters at Laura Canada; the oqoqo line at Lululemon; and in the Retro Curves halter babydoll at La Senza. Canadian designers Arnold Brandt (men's wear) and Linda Lundström (women's wear) are now using bamboo in some fabrics. Even babies—who have had a bum wrap for centuries—now have bamboo diapers. Bamboo is especially suited for diapers: it is 60 percent more absorbent than cotton and dries 20 percent more quickly. It is hypoallergenic and naturally antibacterial, and its tiny micro-holes promote ventilation, helping it repel bad odour longer. Manufactured in Scotland and imported into Canada by Montreal-based Bummis, which holds North American distribution rights, Bamboozle diapers are now available from several Canadian retail stores. A diapering kit composed of diapers and covers retails for $160, considerably less than the estimated $2500 to $3000 it would cost to keep a baby in disposable diapers.

Sources: Stephanie Whittaker, "Women of the Cloth: The Bottom Line for Bummis Is More Than Just Dollars and Cents," *The Gazette* (Montreal), April 16, 2007, p. B.1; Karen Hall, "Bamboo Comfort; Strong as Steel, Soft as Cashmere," *Windsor Star*, August 18, 2007; p. H1; Shelley Boettcher, "Bamboo: The Latest Eco-darling," *Calgary Herald*, March 16, 2007, p. C.11; Donna Nebenzahl, "Bamboo Fashioned into Floors, Beds, and Clothes," *Edmonton Journal*, November 24, 2007, p. I.10.

Slotting allowances, described in Chapter 10, are just one of the range of nonrefundable fees grocery retailers receive from manufacturers to secure shelf space for new products. A manufacturer can pay a retailer as much as $40 000 per item just to get its new products displayed on store shelves.[5] Other fees include failure fees (imposed if a new product does not meet sales projections), annual renewal fees (a "pay to stay" inducement for retailers to continue carrying brands), trade allowances, discounts on high-volume purchases, survey fees for research done by the retailers, and even fees to allow salespeople to present new items.

CUSTOMER-SERVICE STRATEGY

Some stores build their retailing strategy around heightened customer services for shoppers. Gift wrapping, alterations, return privileges, product demonstrations, bridal registries, consultants, interior design services, delivery and installation, and perhaps even electronic shopping via store websites are all examples of services that add value to the shopping experience. A retailer's customer-service strategy must specify which services the firm will offer and whether it will charge customers for these services. Those decisions depend on several conditions: store size, type, and location; merchandise assortment; services offered by competitors; customer expectations; and financial resources. Many retailers now support websites where consumers can check product inventory at specific locations and then get driving directions to those locations. Williams-Sonoma stores in Toronto and Calgary regularly provide consumers with cooking classes where they can see and use the latest kitchenware products.

The basic objective of all customer services focuses on attracting and retaining target customers, thus increasing sales and profits. Some services—such as convenient restrooms, lounges, and complimentary coffee—enhance shoppers' comfort. Other services are intended to attract customers by making shopping easier and faster than it would be without the services. Some retailers, for example, offer child-care services for customers. Canadian Tire offers an online gift registry—Celebration Station—for

Marketoid

Restaurant workers average $317 weekly in Canada; retail salespeople average $482.

Home Depot's decision to revamp its stores and improve customer service led to its best sales growth in years.

AP PHOTO/CHUCK BURTON

all occasions. Couples who register can design their own personal wedding website (celebrationsites.ca) where they can provide personal information, pictures, and details of their wedding. Canadian Tire builds loyalty among customers who value this free service.[6]

A customer-service strategy can also support efforts in building demand for a line of merchandise. Despite the trend toward renovation, redecorating, and do-it-yourself home projects, Home Depot was experiencing slowing sales until its recent decision to revamp its own stores, improve customer service, and upgrade its marketing efforts. Home Depot is now seeing its best growth in years, assuring its customers with its familiar slogan, "You can do it; we can help."

PRICING STRATEGY

Prices reflect a retailer's marketing objectives and policies. They also play a major role in consumer perceptions of a retailer. Consumers realize, for example, that when they enter a Gucci boutique in Milan, New York, or Tokyo, they will find such expensive products as $275 snakeskin belts and $900 handbags. Customers at any of Dollar Giant's locations across Canada expect a totally different type of merchandise; the company's motto is "Nothing over a dollar."

Markups and Markdowns

The amount that a retailer adds to a product's cost to set the final selling price is the **markup.** The amount of the markup typically results from two marketing decisions:

1. *The services performed by the retailer.* Other things being equal, stores that offer more services charge larger markups to cover their costs.

2. *The inventory turnover rate.* Other things being equal, stores with a higher turnover rate can cover their costs and earn a profit while charging a smaller markup.

markup Amount that a retailer adds to the cost of a product to determine its selling price.

A retailer's markup exerts an important influence on its image among present and potential customers. In addition, the markup affects the retailer's ability to attract shoppers. An excessive markup may drive away customers; an inadequate markup may not generate sufficient income to cover costs and return a profit. Retailers typically state markups as percentages of either the selling prices or the costs of the products.

Marketers determine markups based partly on their judgments of the amounts that consumers will pay for a given product. When buyers refuse to pay a product's stated price, however, or when improvements in other items or fashion changes reduce the appeal of current merchandise, a retailer must take a **markdown.** The amount by which a retailer reduces the original selling price—the discount typically advertised for a sale item—is the markdown. Markdowns are sometimes used to evaluate merchandisers. For example, a department store might base its evaluations of buyers partly on the average markdown percentages for the product lines for which they are responsible.

markdown Amount by which a retailer reduces the original selling price of a product.

The formulas for calculating markups and markdowns are provided in the "Financial Analysis in Marketing" appendix at the end of the text.

LOCATION/DISTRIBUTION STRATEGY

Retail experts often cite location as a potential determining factor in the success or failure of a retail business. A retailer may choose to locate at an isolated site, in a central business district, or in a planned shopping centre. The location decision depends on many factors, including the type of merchandise, the retailer's financial resources, characteristics of the target market, and site availability.

In recent years, many localities have become saturated with stores. As a result, some retailers have re-evaluated their location strategies. A chain may close individual stores that do not meet sales

Solving an Ethical Controversy

Are Gift Cards Truly a Gift?

GIFT cards are popular in Canada, now the second most popular gift after clothing. In 2006, Canadians, on average, purchased 4.8 gift cards having an average value of $67. During the Christmas season, gift cards accounted for $1.26 billion sales, but three months later, 40 percent were still not redeemed. Retail cards made up 75 percent of purchases. Unfortunately, most can be redeemed only at the issuing store. In some Canadian provinces, gift cards are allowed to be sold with an expiry date, and issuers are allowed to charge an "inactivity" on unused balances after a specified period of time. Manitoba has banned the sale of cards with expiry dates and inactivity fees. Ontario has done the same but has complicated the issue for consumers—loopholes exempt cards for specific services, such as restaurant meals, spas, etc. Also exempted are shopping mall cards that can be used at more than one store within a mall, although this issue is being examined. Bruce Cran, president of the Canadian Consumers' Association, says, "We've always said you shouldn't touch them with a 40-foot pole."

Should any gift card issuers be allowed to reduce the value of their cards with handling fees, inactivity fees, and other charges?

PRO

1. The cards provide value and convenience that buyers should be willing to pay for, so the fees cover those costs.
2. The fees are minimal in comparison to the face value on most cards, so they are acceptable.

CON

1. Gift cards are already limited in that they can't be redeemed for cash or if the issuer becomes bankrupt and can't be replaced if lost or stolen, so reducing their value places further restrictions on their use.
2. The user should get the full face value that the gift giver intended for the card. It's unfair to assess a fee that wouldn't ordinarily be charged with a direct purchase.

Where do you stand: pro or con?

Sources: Rosann Semchuk, "Canadians Redefining the Gift Card Experience," *Calgary Herald,* April 26, 2007, p. B.7; Dana Flavelle, "Unredeemed Gift Cards a Present for Retailers: One-quarter Never Used, According to U.S. Survey," *Toronto Star,* November 14, 2007, p. B.1; Karen Howlett, "New Gift-card Rules Riddled with Loopholes, Critics Say," *Globe and Mail,* December 7, 2007, p. A.4.

and profit goals. Other retailers have experimented with nontraditional location strategies. GoodLife Fitness saw an opportunity when Loblaws rolled out its Real Canadian Superstore concept. These stores had high traffic and ample parking and attracted women aged 35 to 50 with high household incomes. The companies decided to experiment by opening a GoodLife Fitness club within a Real Canadian Superstore location. Real Canadian Superstore strengthened its position as a one-stop-shop for customers, and GoodLife Fitness benefited from increased visibility, credibility, and access to Canada's fastest-growing fitness segment. There are now 53 GoodLife Fitness locations within Real Canadian Superstores.[7]

Locations in Planned Shopping Centres

Over the past several decades, retail trade has shifted away from traditional downtown retailing districts and toward suburban shopping centres. A **planned shopping centre** is a group of retail stores designed, coordinated, and marketed to shoppers in a geographic trade area. Together, the stores provide a single convenient location for shoppers as well as free parking. They facilitate shopping by maintaining uniform hours of operation, including evening and weekend hours.

planned shopping centre Group of retail stores planned, coordinated, and marketed as a unit.

There are five main types of planned shopping centres. The smallest, the *neighbourhood shopping centre,* is likely to consist of a group of smaller stores, such as a drugstore, a dry cleaner, a card and gift shop, and perhaps a hair-styling salon. This kind of centre provides convenient shopping for 5000 to 50 000 shoppers who live within a few minutes' commute. It contains 5 to 15 stores, and the product mix is usually confined to convenience items and some limited shopping goods.

A *community shopping centre* serves 20 000 to 100 000 people in a trade area extending a few kilometres from its location. It contains anywhere from 10 to 30 retail stores, with a branch of a local department store or some other large store as the primary tenant. In addition to the stores found in a neighbourhood centre, a community centre probably encompasses more stores featuring shopping goods, some professional offices, a branch bank, and perhaps a movie theatre or supermarket. Community shopping centres typically offer ample parking, and tenants often share some promotion costs. With the advent of stand-alone big-box retailers, some community shopping centres have declined in popularity. Some department stores are also moving away from the strategy of locating in shopping centres and opting for freestanding stores, such as the recently opened Sears Canada store in Charlottetown's Royalty Power Centre. Sears Canada also opened 48 Sears Home stores across Canada. These stores range in size from 35 000 to 60 000 square feet and carry an extensive assortment of mattresses and box springs, appliances, and furniture.[8]

A *regional shopping centre* is a large facility with at least 400 000 square feet of shopping space. Its marketing appeal usually emphasizes major department stores with the power to draw customers, supplemented by as many as 200 smaller stores. A successful regional centre needs a location within 30 minutes' driving time of at least 250 000 people. A regional centre—or a super-regional centre such as the West Edmonton Mall—provides a wide assortment of convenience, shopping, and specialty goods, plus many professional and personal service facilities.

A *power centre,* usually located near a regional or super-regional mall, brings together several huge specialty stores, such as Rona, Designer Depot, Costco, Canadian Tire, Michaels, or Pier 1 Imports, as stand-alone stores in a single trading area. Restaurants such as East Side Mario's and Swiss Chalet may also be included. Power centres are gaining in popularity in Canada today because they add value through product selection, competitive prices, and ample parking.

Recently, a fifth type of planned centre has emerged, known as a *lifestyle centre.* This retailing format seeks to offer a combination of shopping, movie theatres, stages for concerts and live entertainment, decorative fountains and park benches in greenways, and restaurants and bistros in an attractive outdoor environment. At around 300 000 to 1 million square feet, the centres are large, but they seek to offer the intimacy and easy access of neighbourhood village retailing with a fashionable cachet. Convenience, safety, and pleasant ambiance are also part of the appeal. Canada's first lifestyle centre, The Village at Park Royal located in West Vancouver, has old-fashioned gas lamps and a lighthouse. Each store differs in design and colour, and the main street has many sculptures and plantings, along with a pond and stepping stones where children can play. There are no big anchor stores but rather a mix of just the right upscale tenants—Lululemon Athletica, Danier Leather, Urban Barn, and Kiss & Makeup, for instance. Restaurants are also much more prominent in lifestyle centres than in enclosed malls.[9]

Retail analysts say the decline of shopping malls and the rising market for luxury goods is fuelling the rapid growth of lifestyle centres. "Developers want to take shopping centres closer and closer to where the affluent, professional people live," says one retail expert. "Lifestyle centres are a means to that end." Another explains the lifestyle centre's appeal by saying, "This format creates a sort of shopping/leisure destination that's an extension of [a consumer's] personal lifestyle."[10] Others, however, see the entertainment aspects of these malls as the biggest drawing card. The Lac Mirabel complex is planned to open north of Montreal in 2009. It promises to have Canada's largest indoor aquarium, which will house over 20 000 animal species, a butterfly and hummingbird sanctuary, high-tech amusement rides, a 70 000-square-foot "Kidtropolis" educational facility, a 3000-person convention centre, and a 6000-seat performance centre. It is expected to attract 25 to 30 million visitors per year.[11]

PROMOTIONAL STRATEGY

To establish store images that entice more shoppers, retailers use a variety of promotional techniques. Through its promotional strategy, a retailer seeks to communicate to consumers information about its stores—locations, merchandise selections, hours of operation, and prices. If merchandise selection changes frequently to follow fashion trends, advertising is typically used to promote current styles effectively. In addition, promotions help retailers attract shoppers and build customer loyalty.

Innovative promotions can pay off in unexpected ways. IKEA China used the interiors of the elevators in 20 Beijing apartment buildings to demonstrate to residents how small apartments can be inexpensively transformed into comfortable living spaces. The elevators were covered with floor-to-ceiling posters picturing ingeniously styled and decorated apartments, and the elevator operators gave out IKEA catalogues to their passengers. "It's a strategic decision to go where the competition isn't," said IKEA's worldwide marketing communications manager.[12]

National retail chains often purchase advertising space in newspapers, on radio, and on television. Other retailers are experimenting with promoting over the Internet or using Bluetooth's wireless technology to send marketing messages to customers' cell phones. Like many retail chains, Canadian Tire promotes its stores through advertising circulars in local newspapers, in print advertisements, through broadcast media, and on its website. Sometimes a well-chosen location aids promotion. Recognizing that movies and pizza go together, Pizza Hut has opened kiosks in movie rental stores where customers get a direct phone line to the nearest Pizza Hut location.

Retailers also try to combine advertising with in-store merchandising techniques that influence decisions at the point of purchase. At H&M's trendy clothing stores, for instance, chic new fashions arrive almost daily, and because nothing is overstocked, styles sell out before they need to be marked down. This "fast fashion" strategy encourages customers to stop in more often, sometimes weekly or even every day to browse the new arrivals.[13]

A friendly, well-trained, and knowledgeable salesperson plays a vital role in conveying the store's image to consumers and in persuading shoppers to buy. To serve as a source of information, a salesperson must possess extensive knowledge regarding credit policies, discounts, special sales, delivery terms, layaways, and returns. To increase store sales, the salesperson must persuade customers that the store sells what those customers need. To this end, salespeople should receive training in selling up and suggestion selling.

Good customer service begins the minute a prospective customer walks in the door. The "Etiquette Tips for Marketing Professionals" feature lists some suggestions about how to treat your own customers.

By *selling up,* salespeople try to persuade customers to buy higher-priced items than originally intended. For example, an automobile salesperson might convince a customer to buy a more expensive model than the car that the buyer had initially considered. Of course, the practice of selling up must always respect the constraints of a customer's real needs. If a salesperson sells customers something that they really do not need, the potential for repeat sales dramatically diminishes.

Another technique, *suggestion selling,* seeks to broaden a customer's original purchase by adding related items, special promotional products, or holiday or seasonal merchandise. Here, too, the salesperson tries to help a customer recognize true needs rather than unwanted merchandise. Beauty advisers in upscale department stores are masters of suggestion selling.

Just as knowledgeable and helpful sales personnel can both boost sales and set retailers apart from competitors, poor service influences customers' attitudes toward a retailer. Increasing customer complaints about unfriendly, inattentive, and uninformed salespeople have prompted many retailers to intensify their attention to training and motivating salespeople. Older training methods are giving way to online learning in many firms. Nike, for instance, logged a 2 percent increase in sales after training 10 000 sales associates worldwide, using an online learning system.[14]

STORE ATMOSPHERICS

While store location, merchandise selection, customer service, pricing, and promotional activities all contribute to a store's consumer awareness, stores also project their personalities through **atmospherics**—physical characteristics and amenities that attract customers and satisfy their shopping needs. Atmospherics include both a store's exterior and interior decor.

A store's exterior appearance, including architectural design, window displays, signs, and entryways, helps to identify the retailer and attract its target market shoppers. The Canadian Tire red triangle and green maple leaf is an exterior element that readily identifies this retailer. Other retailers design eye-catching exterior elements aimed at getting customers' attention.

ETIQUETTE TIPS FOR MARKETING PROFESSIONALS

Providing the Personal Touch to Retail Transactions

THE retail business is all about the customer, and that means treating people well from the minute they enter your store. What's the best way to greet them? "May I help you?" often invites a "No, just looking" response, and that may waste your best chance to develop a customer relationship.

Here are some tips for greeting shoppers and treating them well.

1. Let customers know right away that they're welcome to the store, and make them feel relaxed and comfortable.
2. Remember that ignoring customers isn't just bad service, it's rude.
3. Try starting with "Hi! How are you today?" or "Good to see you! What's new?"
4. Follow with some reference to the merchandise the customer is looking at or moving toward, or mention an item you're promoting just now. "Have you seen these yet? They just arrived" is a good follow-up to your initial greeting.
5. Be enthusiastic but not insincere, and pleasant rather than forceful.
6. Make sure you have enough employees on hand to greet everyone who enters the store, and train your staff to do it promptly and well.
7. Once you strike up a conversation, listen to the customer carefully and let him or her express needs and concerns.
8. Ensure that you and your staff know the merchandise thoroughly so you can answer questions and offer suggestions.
9. Avoid hovering or crowding the customer just for the sake of making a sale to someone who then might not feel comfortable enough to return another day.
10. Thank your customers when they leave, and always invite them back.

Sources: "Retail Customer Service Tips," American Marketing Association, http://www.marketingpower.com, accessed May 5, 2006; Anne M. Obarski, "Strive for a Positive 5," Retail Industry, http://retailindustry.about.com, accessed May 5, 2006; "Greeting the Customer," Retail Smarts, http://www.retailsmarts.servenet.com, February 10, 2006.

Consumers readily recognize Tim Hortons, Chapters, and Future Shop locations by their building designs. Many of the more than 100 Canadian locations of East Side Mario's attract customers with their signature giant tomatoes on their buildings.

Atmospherics, which includes the interior décor of a store, help attract customers and satisfy their shopping needs.

The interior decor of a store should also complement the retailer's image, respond to customers' interests, and, most important, induce shoppers to buy. Interior atmospheric elements include store layout, merchandise presentation, lighting, colour, sounds, scents, and cleanliness. When Paul D. House, chief executive, president, and chairman of Tim Hortons joined the company, there were about 200 outlets. He described them as male-dominated, smoky, coffee and doughnut shops, attractive only to a small group of customers. The company improved its product offering, but more important, it consciously decided to improve its atmospherics to appeal particularly to women. Tim Hortons was among the first Canadian food outlets to isolate smoking, and then to ban it outright. Much of the interior visual appearance was improved, and the bar stool counters, a common store feature, were replaced with family-friendly tables. As a result, Tim Hortons customers now cross all income groups and ages at today's 3078 locations. According to House, "The wonderful thing in the parking lot is that you'll see Mercedes-Benzes and you'll see pickup trucks. It cuts across the whole social fabric . . ."[15] The company's locations have become a friendly, inviting place for all types of people to enjoy a beverage, snack, or meal, and to socialize.

When designing the interior and exterior of a store, the fact that many people shop for reasons other than just purchasing needed products must be taken into account. Other common reasons for shopping include escaping the routine of daily life, avoiding weather extremes, fulfilling fantasies, and socializing with family and friends. Retailers expand beyond interior design to create welcoming and entertaining environments that draw shoppers. The Canadian Tire Concept 20/20 stores' new atmospherics, including design, product displays, open plan layout, lighting, and other features have resulted in customers spending an average of 40 percent more browsing time per shopping trip.[16]

assessment check 3

3.1   What is an SKU?

3.2   What are the two components of a markup?

3.3   What are store atmospherics?

TYPES OF RETAILERS

Because new types of retailers continue to evolve in response to changes in consumer demand, a universal classification system for retailers has yet to be devised. Certain differences do, however, define several categories of retailers: (1) forms of ownership, (2) shopping effort expended by customers, (3) services provided to customers, (4) product lines, and (5) location of retail transactions.

As Figure 13.3 points out, most retailing operations fit in different categories. A 7-Eleven outlet may be classified as a convenience store (category 2) with self-service (category 3) and a relatively broad product line (category 4). It is both a store-type retailer (category 5) and a member of a chain (category 1).

CLASSIFICATION OF RETAILERS BY FORM OF OWNERSHIP

Perhaps the easiest method for categorizing retailers is by ownership structure, distinguishing between chain stores and independent retailers. In addition, independent retailers may join wholesaler-sponsored voluntary chains, band together to form retail cooperatives, or enter into franchise agreements with manufacturers, wholesalers, or service-provider organizations. Each type of ownership has its own unique advantages and strategies.

figure 13.3

Bases for Categorizing Retailers

Chain Stores

Chain stores are groups of retail outlets that operate under central ownership and management and handle the same product lines. Chains have a major advantage over independent retailers in economies of scale. Volume purchases allow chains to pay lower prices than their independent rivals must pay. Since a chain may encompass hundreds of retail stores, it can afford extensive advertising, sales training, and sophisticated computerized systems for merchandise ordering, inventory management, forecasting, and accounting. Also, the large sales volume and wide geographic reach of a chain may enable it to advertise in a variety of media.

Independent Retailers

The Canadian retailing structure supports a large number of small stores, many medium-size stores, and a small number of large stores. Approximately 70 percent of the more than 227 000 retail locations in Canada earn less than $500 000 in annual sales. Two-thirds of Canadian retailers employ four or fewer employees.[17] Most of these retail locations are independent retailers.

Independent retailers compete with chains in a number of ways. The traditional advantage of independent stores is friendly, personalized service. Cooperatives offer another strategy for independents. For instance, cooperatives such as Ace Hardware and Pharmasave help independents compete with chains by providing volume buying power as well as advertising and marketing programs.

Marketoid

UFA Co-operative—a retailer cooperative with about 110 000 members— operates more than 35 farm and ranch supply stores, and more than 120 petroleum locations.

CLASSIFICATION BY SHOPPING EFFORT

Another classification system is based on the reasons consumers shop at particular retail outlets. This approach categorizes stores as convenience, shopping, or specialty retailers.

Convenience retailers focus their marketing appeals on accessible locations, long store hours, rapid checkout service, and adequate parking facilities. Local food stores, gasoline stations, and dry cleaners fit this category. GreenStop, Canada's new chain of alternative-fuel stations—offering biodiesel and other ethanol blends—features convenience stores that sell solar-roasted coffee and organic veggie wraps instead of candy bars and cigarettes.[18] Shopping stores typically include furniture stores, appliance retailers, clothing outlets, and sporting goods stores. Consumers usually compare prices, assortments, and quality levels at competing outlets before making purchase decisions. Consequently, managers of shopping stores attempt to differentiate their outlets through advertising, in-store displays, well-trained and knowledgeable salespeople, and appropriate merchandise assortments.

Specialty retailers combine carefully defined product lines, services, and reputations in attempts to convince consumers to expend considerable effort to shop at their stores. Examples include Edie Hats (Vancouver), The Camera Store (Calgary), Woodlands Gallery (Winnipeg), and Aerobics First (Halifax). Many specialty retailers, such as Gap, La Senza, and Running Room, have locations across Canada.

CLASSIFICATION BY SERVICES PROVIDED

Another category differentiates retailers by the services they provide to customers. This classification system consists of three retail types: self-service, limited-service, or full-service retailers.

When customers visit a self-service retailer, they generally expect to find, evaluate, and choose what it is they wish to buy. Self-service is used by stores that sell convenience products, or fast-moving, branded shopping products. Convenience stores, supermarkets, and discount operations such as Giant Tiger, Winners, and Costco may be considered self-service retailers. Limited-service retailers provide a higher level of sales assistance, resulting in increased operating costs and higher prices for customers. Sears Canada and Best Buy are limited-service retailers that sell many shopping products about which customers frequently have questions or want information. Full-service retailers provide knowledgeable salespeople to help customers with all stages of the consumer decision process. Their operating costs are even higher and are reflected in the prices of their products and their product assortment, which often includes many specialty products. Full-service retailers such as Holt Renfrew focus on fashion-oriented merchandise, backed by a complete array of customer services.

H.F. (HERB) MACKENZIE

Globally, 7-Eleven has more than 34 800 franchised or licensed convenience store locations in 17 countries.

CLASSIFICATION BY PRODUCT LINES

Product lines also define a set of retail categories and the marketing strategies appropriate for firms within those categories. Grouping retailers by product lines produces three major categories: specialty stores, limited-line retailers, and general merchandise retailers.

Specialty Stores

A *specialty store* typically handles only part of a single product line. However, it stocks this portion in considerable depth or variety. Specialty stores include a wide range of retail outlets: examples include fish markets, grocery stores, men's and women's shoe stores, and bakeries. Although some specialty stores are chain outlets, most are independent small-scale operations. They represent perhaps the greatest concentration of independent retailers who develop expertise in one product area and provide narrow lines of products for their local markets.

Specialty stores should not be confused with specialty products. Specialty stores typically carry convenience and shopping goods. The label *specialty* reflects the practice of handling a specific, narrow line of merchandise. For example, Lady Foot Locker is a specialty store that offers a wide selection of name-brand athletic footwear, apparel, and accessories made specifically for women.

Limited-Line Retailers

Customers find a large assortment of products within one product line or a few related lines in a **limited-line store**. This type of retail operation typically develops in areas with a large enough population to sufficiently support it. Examples of limited-line stores are Golf Town (golf clothing and equipment) and The Brick (furniture). These retailers cater to the needs of people who want to select from complete lines in purchasing particular products.

A unique type of limited-line retailer is known as a **category killer**. These stores offer huge selections and low prices in single product lines. Stores within this category—for example, Best Buy, Toys "R" Us, and Home Depot—are among the most successful retailers in the nation. Category killers at

marketing success   Pete's Frootique Wins One Customer at a Time

Background. Pete Luckett left school to work in a greengrocers operation in Nottingham, England, where he learned how to chat, banter, dazzle, and wow customers. At 21, Pete got his own stall, but four years later he wanted change. Pete came to North America and eventually settled in Saint John, New Brunswick, where he tried farming. In 1982, he left farming and opened Pete's Frootique in the Saint John Market. In 1992, he sold this business and moved to Nova Scotia. He reopened Pete's Frootique in Bedford and followed with a second location in Halifax in 2004. Today Pete owns a farm again. When it comes to produce, Pete grows it, buys it, cooks it, and sells it—both wholesale and retail.

The Challenge. In the $14-billion Canadian grocery market, where large retail chains control 80 percent market share, independent grocers such as Pete's Frootique need to differentiate themselves to succeed. They have neither the scope nor scale of their larger competitors. Competing on price is not possible, especially when Pete's spends $15 000 to $20 000 weekly just to transport fresh produce from Toronto.

The Strategy. Pete's has turned grocery shopping into an experiential event. The focus is on creating one customer at a time and

building business through word of mouth; Pete's spends virtually nothing for advertising. Three piano players rotate between his two stores. Mothers with children are given free raisins. Staff engage customers and freely sample produce for them. Pete's has a passion for variety and freshness and keeping customers smiling. And it all takes place in a boutique environment within the larger store: PiccaLily Circus (flower shop), British Butcher, Fish Monger, Tast'a Gouda, Go Go (ready-to-serve), and more.

The Outcome. Pete's has won the Canadian Independent Grocer of the Year Award (three times) and the Atlantic Canada Entrepreneur of the Year Award (twice). In addition, Pete received a Gemini Award for *The Food Hunter* television series, and an honorary doctorate from Saint Mary's University in Halifax. Pete won't talk about sales but does admit Pete's is now a multimillion-dollar wholesale and retail business.

Sources: Kathleen Martin, "Froot Flavoured," *Marketing*, April 3, 2006; William Hanley, "Robin Hood of Fresh Food Retailing," *National Post*, June 24, 2006, p. FW4; Pete's Frootique website, http://www.petesfrootique.com, accessed October 13, 2007.

first took business away from general merchandise discounters, which were not able to compete in selection or price. Recently, however, expanded merchandise and aggressive cost cutting by warehouse clubs and by Wal-Mart have turned the tables. Competition from Internet companies that are able to offer unlimited selection and speedy delivery have also taken customers away. While they still remain a powerful force in retailing, category killers are not invulnerable.[19]

General Merchandise Retailers

General merchandise retailers, which carry a wide variety of product lines that are all stocked in some depth, distinguish themselves from limited-line and specialty retailers by the large number of product lines they carry. The general store described earlier in this chapter is a primitive form of a general merchandise retailer. This category includes variety stores, department stores, and mass merchandisers such as discount stores, off-price retailers, and hypermarkets.

Variety Stores

A retail outlet that offers an extensive range and assortment of low-price merchandise is called a *variety store*. Less popular today than they once were, many of these stores have evolved into or given way to other types of retailers such as discount stores or hybrid combinations of drugstores and variety stores, such as Herbie's Drug & Food Warehouse. The country's variety stores now account for less than 1 percent of all retail sales. However, variety stores remain popular in other parts of the world. Many retail outlets in Spain and Mexico are family-owned variety stores.

Department Stores

In essence, a **department store** is a series of limited-line and specialty stores under one roof. By definition, this large retailer handles a variety of merchandise, including men's, women's, and children's clothing and accessories; household linens and dry goods; home furnishings; and furniture. It serves as a one-stop shopping destination for almost all personal and household products. The Bay and Sears Canada are classic examples.

Department stores built their reputations by offering wide varieties of services, such as charge accounts, delivery, gift wrapping, and liberal return privileges. As a result, they incur relatively high operating costs, averaging about 45 to 60 percent of sales.

Department stores have faced intense competition over the past several years. Relatively high operating costs have left them vulnerable to competition from specialty stores, discount stores, and Internet retailers. In addition, department stores' traditional locations in downtown business districts have suffered from problems associated with limited parking, traffic congestion, and population migration to the suburbs.

The Bay, however, is fighting back. Since its takeover in 2006 by Jerry Zucker, internal processes have been streamlined and decision making has become more decentralized. End-of-season inventory has been reduced. Store aisles are cleaner and more attractive. According to Ron Telpner, chair and CEO of the BrainStorm Group, the staff are easier to recognize and more communicative. There is a new boutique-style approach to merchandising, and a new in-house brand, Baia, is targeted at the up-market consumer. According to Telpner, the Bay's new strategy is to become everything that specialty stores represent with regard to core competencies and retail execution, but under a single roof.[20]

Mass Merchandisers

Mass merchandising has made major inroads into department store sales by emphasizing lower prices for well-known brand-name products, high product turnover, and limited services. A **mass merchandiser** often stocks a wider line of items than a department store but usually without the same depth of assortment within each line. Discount houses, off-price retailers, hypermarkets, and catalogue retailers are all examples of mass merchandisers.

Discount Houses

A **discount house** charges low prices and offers fewer services. Early discount stores sold mostly appliances. Today, they offer soft goods, drugs, food, gasoline, and furniture.

By eliminating many of the free services provided by traditional retailers, these operations can keep their markups 10 to 25 percent below those of their competitors. Some of the early discounters have since added services, stocked well-known name brands, and boosted their prices. In fact, many now resemble department stores.

A discount format that is gaining strength is the *warehouse club.* Costco and Wal-Mart's Sam's Club are the largest warehouse clubs in Canada. These no-frills, cash-and-carry outlets offer consumers access to name-brand products at deeply discounted prices. Selection at warehouse clubs includes everything from gourmet popcorn to fax machines to peanut butter to luggage and sunglasses sold in vast warehouse-like settings. Attracting business away from almost every retailing segment, warehouse clubs now even offer fresh food and gasoline. Customers must be members to shop at warehouse clubs.

Off-Price Retailers

Another version of a discount house is an *off-price retailer.* This kind of store stocks only designer labels or well-known brand-name clothing at prices equal to or below regular wholesale prices and then passes the cost savings along to buyers. While many off-price retailers are located in outlets in downtown areas or in freestanding buildings, a growing number are concentrating in *outlet malls*—shopping centres that house only off-price retailers.

Inventory at off-price stores changes frequently as buyers take advantage of special price offers from manufacturers selling excess merchandise. Off-price retailers such as Winners, Designer Depot, Home Sense, and Home Outfitters also keep their prices below those of traditional retailers by offering fewer services. Off-price retailing has been well received by today's shoppers.

Hypermarkets and Supercentres

Another innovation in discount retailing is the creation of **hypermarkets**—giant one-stop shopping facilities that offer wide selections of grocery and general merchandise products at discount prices, typically filling up 200 000 or more square feet of selling space (about a third larger than most supercentres). Store size determines the major difference between hypermarkets and supercentres. Hypermarkets typically fill up 200 000 or more square feet of selling space, about a third larger than most **supercentres**. With regard to merchandise strategy, hypermarkets generally carry a larger proportion of food items than supercentres, including fresh meat, fish, and produce. Carrefour added 103 new hypermarket stores in 2006, bringing its worldwide total to 1040 locations.[21] Despite great success in Europe, hypermarkets have had limited success in the United States, and even less success in Canada, where they can be found only in Quebec. However, most consumers would find it difficult to distinguish a hypermarket from a Wal-Mart supercentre store.

CLASSIFICATION OF RETAIL TRANSACTIONS BY LOCATION

Although most retail transactions occur in stores, nonstore retailing serves as an important marketing channel for many products. In addition, both consumer and business-to-business marketers rely on nonstore retailing to generate orders or requests for more information that may result in future orders.

Direct marketing is a broad concept that includes direct mail, direct selling, direct response retailing, telemarketing, Internet retailing, and automatic merchandising. The last sections of this chapter will consider each type of nonstore retailing.

Scrambled merchandising is practiced by many retailers around the world. This Irish business offers gas and solid fuel; hardware and fancy goods; and funeral director services.

④ Explain the concepts of retail convergence and scrambled merchandising.

retail convergence
A situation in which similar merchandise is available from multiple retail outlets, resulting in the blurring of distinctions between type of retailer and merchandise offered.

scrambled merchandising
Retailing practice of combining dissimilar product lines to boost sales volume.

RETAIL CONVERGENCE AND SCRAMBLED MERCHANDISING

Many traditional differences no longer distinguish familiar types of retailers, rendering any set of classifications less useful. **Retail convergence,** whereby similar merchandise is available from multiple retail outlets distinguished by price more than any other factor, is blurring distinctions between types of retailers and the merchandise mix they offer. A few years ago, a customer looking for a fashionable coffeepot might have headed straight for Williams-Sonoma or Starbucks. Today, she's just as likely to pick one up at Canadian Tire or Wal-Mart, where she can check out new spring fashions or stock up on paper goods.

Scrambled merchandising—in which a retailer combines dissimilar product lines in an attempt to boost sales volume—has also muddied the waters. Drugstores, such as the newly renovated Shoppers Drug Mart stores, not only fill prescriptions but offer cameras, cards, magazines, small appliances, home decor accessories, and even fresh and prepared foods. Speaking for Loblaw, spokesperson Geoff Wilson says, "We are still very much a food retailer first—that is our heritage. But we ... see the opportunity in leveraging the food traffic to sell general merchandise, and the vehicle associated with selling general merchandise is the Real Canadian Superstores." The company is allocating as much as 75 percent of its new square footage to general merchandise such as clothing, housewares, and toys.[22]

assessment check 4

4.1 How do we classify retailers by form of ownership?

4.2 Categorize retailers by shopping effort and by services provided.

4.3 List several ways to classify retailers by product line.

⑤ Identify the functions performed by wholesaling intermediaries.

wholesaler Channel intermediary that takes title to goods it handles and then distributes these goods to retailers, other distributors, or B2B customers.

wholesaling intermediary
Comprehensive term that describes wholesalers as well as agents and brokers.

WHOLESALING INTERMEDIARIES

Recall from Chapter 12 that several distribution channels involve marketing intermediaries called **wholesalers.** These firms take title to the goods they handle and sell those products primarily to retailers or to other wholesalers or business users. They sell to ultimate consumers only in insignificant quantities if at all. **Wholesaling intermediaries,** a broader category, include not only wholesalers but also agents and brokers, who perform important wholesaling activities without taking title to the goods.

FUNCTIONS OF WHOLESALING INTERMEDIARIES

As specialists in certain marketing functions, as opposed to production or manufacturing functions, wholesaling intermediaries can perform these functions more efficiently than producers or consumers. The importance of these activities results from the utility they create, the services they provide, and the cost reductions they allow.

Creating Utility

Wholesaling intermediaries create three types of utility for consumers. They enhance time utility by making products available for sale when consumers want to purchase them. They create place utility by helping to deliver goods and services for purchase at convenient locations. They create ownership (or possession) utility when a smooth exchange of title to the products from producers or intermediaries to final purchasers is complete. Possession utility can also result from transactions in which actual title does not pass to purchasers, as in rental-car services.

Providing Services

Table 13.1 lists a number of services provided by wholesaling intermediaries. The list clearly indicates the marketing utilities—time, place, and possession utility—that wholesaling intermediaries create

table 13.1 *Wholesaling Services for Customers and Producer-Suppliers*

SERVICE	BENEFICIARIES OF SERVICE	
	Customers	Producer-Suppliers
Buying Anticipates customer demands and applies knowledge of alternative sources of supply; acts as purchasing agent for customers.	Yes	No
Selling Provides a sales force to call on customers, creating a low-cost method for servicing smaller retailers and business users.	No	Yes
Storing Maintains warehouse facilities at lower costs than most individual producers or retailers could achieve. Reduces risk and cost of maintaining inventory for producers.	Yes	Yes
Transporting Customers receive prompt delivery in response to their demands, reducing their inventory investments. Wholesalers also break bulk by purchasing in economical carload or truckload lots, then reselling in smaller quantities, thereby reducing overall transportation costs.	Yes	Yes
Providing Marketing Information Offers important marketing research input for producers through regular contacts with retail and business buyers. Provides customers with information about new products, technical information about product lines, reports on competitors' activities and industry trends, and advisory information concerning pricing changes, legal changes, and so forth.	Yes	Yes
Financing Grants credit that might be unavailable for purchases directly from manufacturers. Provides financing assistance to producers by purchasing products in advance of sale and by promptly paying bills.	Yes	Yes
Risk Taking Evaluates credit risks of numerous, distant retail customers and small-business users. Extends credit to customers that qualify. By transporting and stocking products in inventory, the wholesaler assumes risk of spoilage, theft, or obsolescence.	Yes	Yes

or enhance. These services also reflect the basic marketing functions of buying, selling, storing, transporting, providing market information, financing, and risk taking.

Of course, many types of wholesaling intermediaries provide varying services, and not all of them perform every service listed in the table. Producer-suppliers rely on wholesaling intermediaries for distribution and selection of firms that offer the desired combinations of services. In general, however, the critical marketing functions listed in the table form the basis for any evaluation of a marketing intermediary's efficiency. The risk-taking function affects each service of the intermediary.

Dominion Citrus Limited, based in Markham, Ontario, supplies fresh produce, Mediterranean food products, maple syrup, and premium juices to retailers, food service companies, and other food distribution businesses. It procures, processes, packs, sorts, grades, warehouses,

Dominion Citrus is a wholesaler that offers a suite of integrated services aimed at providing value-added solutions to its customers.

© DENIS PEPIN/SHUTTERSTOCK

and distributes to over 400 customers, mainly in Ontario and Quebec, but also in the United States and Europe.[23]

Lowering Costs by Limiting Contacts

When an intermediary represents numerous producers, it often cuts the costs of buying and selling. The transaction economies are illustrated in Figure 13.4, which shows five manufacturers marketing their outputs to four different customers. Without an intermediary, these exchanges create a total of 20 transactions. Adding a wholesaling intermediary reduces the number of transactions to nine.

Tenaquip Industrial Distribution buys from hundreds of manufacturers and sells to over 10 000 customers. It has more than 200 000 square feet of warehouse space and over $10 million of inventory. Tenaquip sells more than 450 000 products, from adhesives to bug zappers, from 13 locations across Canada. The company maintains all its catalogues online. Customers are guaranteed all in-stock items will be shipped the same day they are ordered if the order is received by 4 p.m.[24]

(6) Outline the major types of independent wholesaling intermediaries and the appropriate situations for using each.

TYPES OF WHOLESALING INTERMEDIARIES

Various types of wholesaling intermediaries operate in different distribution channels. Some provide wide ranges of services or handle broad lines of goods, while others specialize in individual services, goods, or industries. Figure 13.5 classifies wholesaling intermediaries by two characteristics: ownership and title flows (whether title passes from manufacturer to wholesaling intermediary). The three basic ownership structures are these: (1) manufacturer-owned facilities, (2) independent wholesaling intermediaries, and (3) retailer-owned cooperatives and buying offices. The two types of independent wholesaling intermediaries are merchant wholesalers, which take title of the goods, and agents and brokers, which do not.

Manufacturer-Owned Facilities

Several reasons lead manufacturers to distribute their goods directly through company-owned facilities. Some perishable goods need rigid control of distribution to avoid spoilage; other goods require complex installation or servicing. Some goods need aggressive promotion. Goods with high-unit values allow profitable sales by manufacturers directly to ultimate purchasers. Manufacturer-owned facilities include sales branches, sales offices, trade fairs, and merchandise marts.

A *sales branch* carries inventory and processes orders for customers from available stock. Branches provide a storage function like independent wholesalers and serve as offices for sales representatives in their territories. They are prevalent in marketing channels for chemicals, commercial machinery and equipment, motor vehicles, and petroleum products.

A *sales office,* in contrast, does not carry inventory, but it does serve as a regional office for a manufacturer's sales personnel. Locations close to the firm's customers help limit selling costs and support active customer service. For example, many Ontario manufacturers have established sales offices in eastern and western Canada.

A *trade fair* (or trade exhibition) is a periodic show at which manufacturers in a particular industry display their wares for visiting retail and wholesale buyers. For example, the Canadian Giftware & Tableware Association holds a trade fair in January and August of each year in Toronto where more than 1100 exhibitors display their products to

figure 13.5

Transaction Economies through Wholesaling Intermediaries

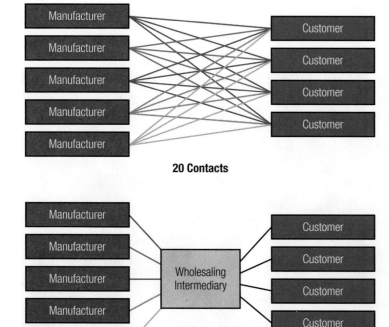

20 Contacts

9 Contacts

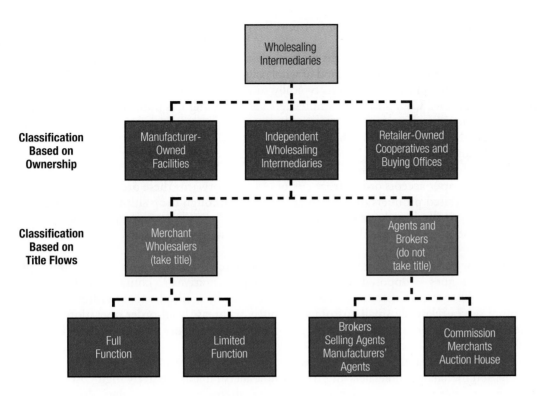

figure 13.6

Major Types of Wholesaling Intermediaries

25 000 or more retail buyers. Smaller gift fairs are held regularly in Halifax, Calgary, Vancouver, and many other Canadian cities.

A *merchandise mart* provides space for permanent showrooms and exhibits, which manufacturers rent to market their goods. One of the world's largest merchandise marts is Chicago's Merchandise Mart Center, a 7-million-square-foot complex that hosts more than 30 seasonal buying markets each year. Many large merchandise marts are located in the United States, but they attract exhibitors from Canada and around the world.

Independent Wholesaling Intermediaries

Many wholesaling intermediaries are independently owned. These firms fall into two major categories: merchant wholesalers and agents and brokers.

Merchant Wholesalers

A **merchant wholesaler** takes title to the goods it handles. Merchant wholesalers account for roughly 60 percent of all sales at the wholesale level. Further classifications divide these wholesalers into full-function or limited-function wholesalers, as indicated in Figure 13.6. Tenaquip, mentioned in the previous section, is a merchant wholesaler.

A full-function merchant wholesaler provides a complete assortment of services for retailers and business purchasers. Such a wholesaler stores merchandise in a convenient location, allowing customers to make purchases on short notice and minimizing inventory requirements. The firm typically maintains a sales force that calls on retailers, makes deliveries, and extends credit to qualified buyers. Full-function wholesalers are common in the drug, grocery, and hardware industries. In the business-goods market, full-function merchant wholesalers (often called *industrial distributors*) sell machinery, inexpensive accessory equipment, and supplies.

A **rack jobber** is a full-function merchant wholesaler that markets specialized lines of merchandise to retailers. A rack jobber supplies the racks, stocks the merchandise, prices the goods, and makes regular visits to refill shelves.

Limited-function merchant wholesalers fit into four categories: cash-and-carry wholesalers, truck wholesalers, drop shippers, and mail-order wholesalers. Limited-function wholesalers serve the food, coal, lumber, cosmetics, jewellery, sporting goods, and general merchandise industries.

A *cash-and-carry wholesaler* performs most wholesaling functions except for financing and delivery. Although feasible for small stores, this kind of wholesaling generally is unworkable for large-scale grocery stores. Today, cash-and-carry operations typically function as departments within regular full-service wholesale operations. Cash-and-carry wholesalers are becoming less popular in Canada but are still commonplace in many European countries.

A **truck wholesaler**, or **truck jobber**, markets perishable food items such as bread, tobacco, potato chips, candy, and dairy products. Truck wholesalers make regular deliveries to retailers, perform sales and collection functions, and promote product lines.

A **drop shipper** accepts orders from customers and forwards these orders to producers, which then ship the desired products directly to customers. Although drop shippers take title to goods, they never physically handle or even see the merchandise. These intermediaries often operate in industries selling bulky goods that customers buy in large lots. Coal and lumber would be examples.

A **mail-order wholesaler** is a limited-function merchant wholesaler that distributes physical or online catalogues as opposed to sending sales representatives to contact retail, business, and institutional customers. Customers then make purchases by mail, phone, or online. Such a wholesaler often serves relatively small customers in outlying areas. Mail-order operations mainly exist in the hardware, cosmetics, jewellery, sporting goods, and specialty food lines as well as in general merchandise.

Table 13.2 compares the various types of merchant wholesalers and the services they provide. Full-function merchant wholesalers and truck wholesalers rank as relatively high-cost intermediaries due to the number of services they perform, while cash-and-carry wholesalers, drop shippers, and mail-order wholesalers provide fewer services and set lower prices since they incur lower operating costs.

Agents and Brokers

A second group of independent wholesaling intermediaries, agents and brokers, may or may not take possession of the goods they handle, but they never take title. They normally perform fewer services than merchant wholesalers, working mainly to bring together buyers and sellers. Agents and brokers fall into five categories: commission merchants, auction houses, brokers, selling agents, and manufacturers' representatives (reps).

Commission merchants, who predominate in the markets for agricultural products, take possession when producers ship goods such as grain, produce, and livestock to central markets for sale. Commission merchants act as producers' agents and receive agreed-upon fees when they make sales. Since customers inspect the products and prices fluctuate, commission merchants receive considerable latitude in marketing decisions. The owners of the goods may specify minimum prices, but the commission

table 13.2 *Comparison of the Types of Merchant Wholesalers and Their Services*

		LIMITED-FUNCTION WHOLESALER			
SERVICE	Full-Function	Cash-and-Carry	Truck	Drop Shipper	Mail-Order
Anticipates customer needs	Yes	Yes	Yes	No	Yes
Carries inventory	Yes	Yes	Yes	No	Yes
Delivers	Yes	No	Yes	No	No
Provides market information	Yes	Rarely	Yes	Yes	No
Provides credit	Yes	No	No	Yes	Sometimes
Assumes ownership risk by taking title	Yes	Yes	Yes	Yes	Yes

merchants sell these goods at the best possible prices. The commission merchants then deduct their fees from the sales proceeds.

An auction house gathers buyers and sellers in one location and allows potential buyers to inspect merchandise before submitting competing purchase offers. Auction house commissions typically reflect specified percentages of the sales prices of the auctioned items. Auctions are common in the distribution of tobacco, used cars, artwork, livestock, furs, and fruit. The Internet has led to a new type of auction house that connects customers and sellers in the online world. A well-known example is eBay, which auctions a wide variety of products in all price ranges.

Brokers work mainly to bring together buyers and sellers. A broker represents either the buyer or the seller, but not both, in a given transaction, and the broker receives a fee from the client when the transaction is completed. Intermediaries that specialize in arranging buying and selling transactions between domestic producers and foreign buyers are called *export brokers.* Brokers operate in industries characterized by large numbers of small suppliers and purchasers, such as real estate, frozen foods, and used machinery. Since they provide one-time services for sellers or buyers, they cannot serve as effective channels for manufacturers seeking regular, continuing service. A firm that seeks to develop a more permanent channel might choose instead to use a selling agent or manufacturers' agent.

broker Agent wholesaling intermediary who does not take title to or possession of goods in the course of its primary function, which is to bring together buyers and sellers.

A **selling agent** typically exerts full authority over pricing decisions and promotional outlays, and it often provides financial assistance for the manufacturer. Selling agents act as independent marketing departments because they can assume responsibility for the total marketing programs of client firms' product lines. Selling agents mainly operate in the coal, lumber, and textiles industries. For a small, poorly financed, production-oriented firm, such an intermediary might prove the ideal marketing channel.

While a manufacturer may deal with only one selling agent, a firm that hires **manufacturers' representatives** often delegates marketing tasks to many of these agents. Such an independent salesperson may work for a number of firms that produce related, noncompeting products. Manufacturers' reps are paid on a commission basis, such as 6 percent of sales. Unlike selling agents, who may contract for exclusive rights to market a product, manufacturers' agents operate in specific territories. They may develop new sales territories or represent relatively small firms and those firms with unrelated lines. Uponor Canada—with a head office and warehouse in Regina, Saskatchewan, and a manufacturing plant in Saint John, New Brunswick—sells radiant floor heating systems, polyethylene plumbing systems, and fire protection systems. It uses a national network of manufacturers' representatives to sell its products to wholesale distributors across Canada.[25]

manufacturers' representative Agent wholesaling intermediary who represents manufacturers of related but noncompeting products and who receives a commission on each sale.

The importance of selling agents in many markets has declined because manufacturers want better control of their marketing programs than these intermediaries allow. In contrast, the volume of sales by manufacturers' agents has more than doubled and now accounts for 37 percent of all sales by agents and brokers. Table 13.3 compares the major types of agents and brokers on the basis of the services they perform.

assessment check 6

6.1 What is the difference between a merchant wholesaler and a rack jobber?

6.2 Differentiate between agents and brokers.

table 13.3   *Services Provided by Agents and Brokers*

SERVICE	Commission Merchant	Auction House	Broker	Manufacturers' Agent	Selling Agent
Anticipates customer needs	Yes	Sometimes	Sometimes	Yes	Yes
Carries inventory	Yes	Yes	No	No	No
Delivers	Yes	No	No	Sometimes	No
Provides market information	Yes	Yes	Yes	Yes	Yes
Provides credit	Sometimes	No	No	No	Sometimes
Assumes ownership risk by taking title	No	No	No	No	No

RETAILER-OWNED COOPERATIVES AND BUYING OFFICES

Retailers may assume numerous wholesaling functions in an attempt to reduce costs or provide special services. Independent retailers sometimes band together to form buying groups that can achieve cost savings through quantity purchases. Other groups of retailers establish retailer-owned wholesale facilities by forming cooperative chains. Large chain retailers often establish centralized buying offices to negotiate large-scale purchases directly with manufacturers.

---

⑦ Compare the basic types of direct marketing and non-store retailing.

direct marketing Direct communications, other than personal sales contacts, between buyer and seller, designed to generate sales, information requests, or store or website visits.

DIRECT MARKETING AND OTHER NONSTORE RETAILING

Although most retail transactions occur in stores, nonstore retailing is an important marketing channel for many products. Both consumer and business-to-business marketers rely on nonstore retailing to generate leads or requests for more information that may result in future orders.

Direct marketing is a broad concept that includes direct mail, direct selling, direct-response retailing, telemarketing, Internet retailing, and automatic merchandising. Direct and interactive marketing expenditures amount to hundreds of billions of dollars in yearly purchases across North America. The last sections of this chapter consider each type of nonstore retailing.

DIRECT MAIL

Direct mail is a major component of direct marketing. It comes in many forms, ranging from sales letters, postcards, brochures, booklets, catalogues, and house organs (periodicals published by organizations to cover internal issues), to video and audio cassettes. Both not-for-profit and profit-seeking organizations make extensive use of this distribution channel.

Direct mail offers several advantages such as the ability to select a narrow target market, achieve intensive coverage, send messages quickly, choose from various formats, provide complete information, and personalize each mailing piece. Response rates are measurable and higher than other types of advertising. In addition, direct mailings stand alone and do not compete for attention with magazine articles and television programs. On the other hand, the per-reader cost of direct mail is high, effectiveness depends on the quality of the mailing list, and some consumers object strongly to direct mail, considering it "junk mail."

Direct-mail marketing relies heavily on database technology in managing lists of names and in segmenting these lists according to the objectives of the campaign. Recipients get targeted materials, often personalized with their names within the ad's content.

Catalogues are a popular form of direct mail, with more than 10 000 different consumer specialty mail-order catalogues—and thousands more for business-to-business sales—finding their way to almost every home and business in Canada and the United States. In a typical year, mail-order catalogues generate billions of dollars in consumer and business markets. Catalogues can be a company's only or primary sales method. L.L. Bean and Spiegel are well-known examples. Brick-and-mortar retailers such as Canadian Tire, Tilley Endurables, and IKEA Canada also distribute catalogues. All these companies now accept orders over their websites or by telephone, making it virtually impossible to tell what impact catalogues have on sales. However, this does not cause concern for Cass Hall, marketing manager at IKEA Canada, who says, "We've always looked at it as a broader shopping tool. Traditionally it's been to drive people into the store and help plan their visit. More and more it's a branding tool for us."[26]

New technologies are changing catalogue marketing. Today's catalogues can be updated quickly, providing consumers with the latest information and prices. Online catalogues allow marketers to display products in three-dimensional views and can include video sequences of product demonstrations.

DIRECT SELLING

Through direct selling, manufacturers completely bypass retailers and wholesalers. Instead, they set up their own channels to sell their products directly to consumers. Avon, Regal, Nu Skin, Shaklee, and party-plan marketers such as Tupperware are all direct sellers. This channel was discussed in detail in Chapter 12.

DIRECT-RESPONSE RETAILING

Customers of a direct-response retailer can order merchandise by mail or telephone, by visiting a mail-order desk in a retail store, or by computer or fax machine. The retailer then ships the merchandise to the customer's home or to a local retail store for pickup.

Many direct-response retailers rely on direct mail, such as catalogues, to create telephone and mail-order sales and to promote in-store purchases of products featured in the catalogues. Additionally, some firms, such as Lillian Vernon, make almost all their sales through catalogue orders. Mail-order sales have grown at about twice the rate of retail store sales in recent years.

Avon is known and respected for direct selling through its many independent sales representatives across Canada and throughout the world.

Direct-response retailers are increasingly reaching buyers through the Internet and through unique catalogues. Although catalogues may run into the thousands, with some industry experts estimating that there are 10 000 at any given time, some of which are niche catalogues selling specialty products such as art supplies or boating products, about 500 are from well-established marketers. Canadian Tire, which has served Canadian consumers for more than 80 years, has built much of its business through catalogue sales. The company now has retail locations across Canada but still generates considerable revenue from its catalogues, which are sent to approximately 9 million Canadian households each year.[27]

Direct-response retailing also includes home shopping, which runs promotions on cable television networks to sell merchandise through telephone orders. One form of home shopping has existed for years—*infomercials* that run for at least 30 minutes. Such products as Veg-O-Matic vegetable slicers have been featured on these commercials. More recently, TV networks such as The Shopping Channel (TSC) have successfully focused exclusively on providing shopping opportunities. Programming ranges from extended commercials to call-in shows to game-show formats. Shoppers call a toll-free number to buy featured products, and the retailer ships orders directly to their homes.

TELEMARKETING

Telemarketing refers to direct marketing conducted entirely by telephone. It is the most frequently used form of direct marketing. It provides marketers with a high return on their expenditures, an immediate response, and the opportunity for personalized two-way conversations. Telemarketing is discussed in further detail in Chapter 16.

assessment check 7

7.1 What is direct marketing?

7.2 What is direct mail?

INTERNET RETAILING

⑧ Describe how much the Internet has altered the wholesaling, retailing, and direct marketing environments.

Internet-based retailers sell directly to customers via virtual storefronts on the Web. They usually maintain little or no inventory, ordering directly from vendors to fill customer orders received via their websites. In recent years, conventional retailers have anxiously watched the rise—and then the demise—of many poorly planned, financed, and marketed Internet-based retailers. During the dot-com bust, 130 e-tailers failed. Even early successes like Ezshop, an online home furnishings retailer, eventually ran aground. Traditional retailers, using the Web to support brick-and-mortar stores—the so-called brick-and-click retailers—have had much better staying power. Sears Canada, Future Shop, and Canadian Tire, for example, have succeeded in extending their expertise to the Web. Office Depot has been successful because of its brand name, its low-cost buying strategies, and its extensive distribution network—customers can pick up purchases they initiate on the Web at their nearest Office Depot outlet.[28]

COURTESY OF AVON CANADA

H. F. (HERB) MACKENZIE

Vending machines are common throughout Canada, but are a very popular form of merchandising in Japan.

AUTOMATIC MERCHANDISING

The world's first vending machines dispensed holy water for five-drachma coins in Egyptian temples around 215 B.C. This retailing method has grown rapidly ever since; today, approximately 6000 North American vending machine operators sell more than $7 billion in convenience goods annually.[29]

Although vending machines have traditionally been limited to snacks and soft drinks, Japanese consumers use automatic merchandising for everything from fresh sushi to new underwear. Recently, Canadian marketers have begun to realize the potential of this underused marketing tool. Some of the newer vending machines can monitor inventory and transmit data back to the vending operator so stockouts can be better managed and malfunctions can be repaired more quickly. Some vending machines can sense the presence of people and can be programmed to talk to them. As technological advances and credit-card payments make it easier to sell high-cost items, vending machines will be used to distribute many additional products to consumers. Even iPods are now being sold from vending machines at some of North America's busiest airports.[30]

> ## assessment check 8
>
> 8.1 Describe Internet-based retailers.
>
> 8.2 Explain how the Internet has enhanced retailers' functions.

Strategic Implications

AS the Internet revolution steadily becomes a way of life—both for consumers and for the businesses marketing goods and services to them—technology will continue to transform the ways in which retailers, wholesalers, and direct marketers connect with customers.

In the retail sector, the unstoppable march toward lower and lower prices has forced retailers from Sears Canada to dollar stores to re-evaluate everything from their logistics and supply networks to their profit margins. Many have used the power of the Internet to strengthen such factors as store image, the merchandising mix, customer service, and the development of long-term relationships with customers.

Though manufacturers first anticipated that Internet technology would enable them to bypass such intermediaries as wholesalers and agents, bringing them closer to the customer, the reality is quite different. Successful wholesalers have been able to establish themselves as essential links in the supply, distribution, and customer-service network. By leveraging technology, they have been able to carve out new roles, providing such expert services as warehousing or fulfillment to multiple retail clients.

The Internet has empowered direct marketers by facilitating ever more sophisticated database segmentation. Traditional catalogue and direct mail marketers have integrated Internet sites, Web advertising, and e-mailing programs into a cohesive targeting, distribution, and repeat-buying strategy. ◆◆◆

REVIEW OF CHAPTER OBJECTIVES

① **Explain the wheel of retailing.**

The wheel of retailing is the hypothesis that each new type of retailer gains a competitive foothold by offering lower prices than current suppliers and maintains profits by reducing or eliminating services. Once established, the innovator begins to add more services, and its prices gradually rise, making it vulnerable to new low-price retailers. This turns the wheel again.

② **Discuss how retailers select target markets.**

A retailer starts to define its strategy by selecting a target market. The target market dictates, among other things, the product mix, pricing strategy, and location strategy. Retailers deal with consumer behaviour at the most complicated level, and a clear understanding of the target market is critical. Strategies for selecting target markets include merchandising, customer services, pricing, location/distribution, and promotional strategies.

③ **Show how the elements of the marketing mix apply to retailing strategy.**

A retailer must first identify a target market and then develop a product strategy. Next, it must establish a customer-service strategy. Retail pricing strategy involves decisions on markups and markdowns. Location is often the determining factor in a retailer's success or failure. A retailer's promotional strategy and store atmosphere play important roles in establishing a store's image.

④ **Explain the concepts of retail convergence and scrambled merchandising.**

Retail convergence is the coming together of shoppers, goods, and prices, resulting in the blurring of distinctions between types of retailers and the merchandise mix they offer. Similar selections are available from multiple sources and are differentiated mainly by price. Scrambled merchandising refers to retailers' practice of carrying dissimilar product lines in an attempt to generate additional sales volume. Retail convergence and scrambled merchandising have made it increasingly difficult to classify retailers.

⑤ **Identify the functions performed by wholesaling intermediaries.**

The functions of wholesaling intermediaries include creating utility, providing services, and lowering costs by limiting contacts.

⑥ **Outline the major types of independent wholesaling intermediaries and the appropriate situations for using each.**

Independent wholesaling intermediaries can be divided into two categories: merchant wholesalers and agents and brokers. The two major types of merchant wholesalers are full-function merchant wholesalers, such as rack jobbers, and limited-function merchant wholesalers, including cash-and-carry wholesalers, truck wholesalers, drop shippers, and mail-order wholesalers. Full-function wholesalers are common in the drug, grocery, and hardware industries.

Limited-function wholesalers are sometimes used in the food, coal, lumber, cosmetics, jewellery, sporting goods, and general merchandise industries. Agents and brokers do not take title to the products they sell; this category includes commission merchants, auction houses, brokers, selling agents, and manufacturers' reps. Companies seeking to develop new sales territories, firms with unrelated lines, and smaller firms use manufacturers' reps. Commission merchants are common in the marketing of agricultural products. Auction houses are used to sell tobacco, used cars, livestock, furs, and fruit. Brokers are prevalent in the real estate, frozen foods, and used machinery industries.

Compare the basic types of direct marketing and nonstore retailing.

Direct marketing is a distribution channel consisting of direct communication to a consumer or business recipient. It generates orders and sales leads that may result in future orders. Because direct marketing responds to fragmented media markets and audiences, growth of customized products, and shrinking network broadcast audiences, marketers consider it an important part of their planning efforts. While most Canadian retail sales take place in stores, such nonstore retailing activities as direct mail, direct selling, direct-response retailing, telemarketing, Internet retailing, and automatic merchandising are important in marketing many types of goods and services.

⑧ **Describe how much the Internet has altered the wholesaling, retailing, and direct marketing environments.**

The Internet has affected everything from how supply networks operate to how relationships are formed with customers. Successful wholesalers have carved out a niche as a source of expertise offering faster, more efficient, Web-enabled distribution and fulfillment. The Internet has allowed retailers to enhance their merchandising mix and their customer service by, among other things, giving them access to much broader selections of goods. Direct marketers have merged their traditional catalogue or direct mail programs with an Internet interface that allows for faster, more efficient, and more frequent contact with customers and prospects.

assessment check answers

1.1 What is retailing?
Retailing describes the activities involved in selling merchandise to ultimate consumers.

1.2 Explain the wheel-of-retailing concept.
The wheel of retailing is the hypothesis that each new type of retailer gains a competitive foothold by offering lower prices than current suppliers and maintains profits by reducing or eliminating services.

2.1 How does a retailer develop a marketing strategy?
A retailer develops a marketing strategy based on its goals and strategic plans.

2.2 How do retailers select target markets?
Strategies for selecting target markets include merchandising, customer services, pricing, location/distribution, and promotional strategies.

3.1 What is an SKU?
An SKU or stock-keeping unit is a specific product offering within a product line.

3.2 What are the two components of a markup?
A markup consists of the product's cost and an amount added by the retailer to determine its selling price.

3.3 What are store atmospherics?
Store atmospherics are physical characteristics and amenities that attract customers and satisfy their shopping needs.

4.1 How do we classify retailers by form of ownership?
There are two types of retailers by form of ownership: chain stores and independent retailers.

4.2 Categorize retailers by shopping effort and by services provided.
Convenience retailers and specialty retailers are classified by shopping effort; self-service, self-selection, and full-service describe retailers in terms of services provided.

4.3 List several ways to classify retailers by product line.
Retailers classified by product line include specialty stores, limited-line retailers, and general-merchandise retailers. General-merchandise retailers include variety stores, department stores, and mass merchandisers.

5.1 What is a wholesaler? How does it differ from a wholesaling intermediary?
A wholesaler is a channel intermediary that takes title to goods it handles and then distributes these goods to retailers, other distributors, or B2B customers. A wholesaling intermediary can be a wholesaler, an agent, or a broker and perform wholesaling activities without taking title to the goods.

5.2 How do wholesaling intermediaries help sellers lower costs?
Wholesaling intermediaries lower the number of transactions between manufacturers and retail outlets, thus lowering distribution costs.

6.1 What is the difference between a merchant wholesaler and a rack jobber?
A merchant wholesaler takes title to the goods it handles. A rack jobber is a full-function merchant wholesaler that markets specialized lines of merchandise to retailers.

6.2 Differentiate between agents and brokers.

Agents and brokers may or may not take possession of the goods they handle but they never take title. Brokers work mainly to bring together buyers and sellers. A selling agent typically exerts full authority over pricing decisions and promotional outlays and often provides financial assistance for the manufacturer.

7.1 What is direct marketing?

Direct marketing is a distribution channel consisting of direct communication to a consumer or business recipient. It generates orders and sales leads that may result in future orders.

7.2 What is direct mail?

Direct mail is a form of direct marketing that includes sales letters, postcards, brochures, booklets, catalogues, house organs, and video and audio cassettes.

8.1 Describe Internet-based retailers.

Internet-based retailers sell directly to customers via virtual storefronts on the Web. They usually maintain little or no inventory, ordering directly from vendors to fill customers' orders.

8.2 Explain how the Internet has enhanced retailers' functions.

The Internet has allowed retailers to enhance their merchandising mix and their customer service by, among other things, giving them access to much broader selections of goods. Direct marketers have merged their traditional catalogue or direct-mail programs with an Internet interface that allows for faster, more efficient, and more frequent contact with customers and prospects.

MARKETING TERMS YOU NEED TO KNOW

These terms are printed in red in the text. They are defined in the margins of the chapter and in the Glossary that begins on p. G-1. Other important terms are printed in bold black type in the chapter but not included in this list. Their definitions can be found in the Glossary.

retailing 426
wheel of retailing 426
stockkeeping unit (SKU) 428
markup 430
markdown 430

planned shopping centre 431
retail convergence 440
scrambled merchandising 440
wholesaler 440
wholesaling intermediary 440

broker 445
manufacturers' representatives 445
direct marketing 446

ASSURANCE OF LEARNING REVIEW

1. Find some examples of retailers that demonstrate the concept of the wheel of retailing. Explain the stages they went through and are in currently.
2. How do retailers identify target markets? Explain the major strategies by which retailers reach their target markets.
3. Explain the importance of a retailer's location to its strategy.
4. What is retail convergence?
5. Define *scrambled merchandising*. Why has this practice become so common in retailing?
6. What is a wholesaling intermediary? Describe the activities it performs.
7. Distinguish among the different types of manufacturer-owned wholesaling intermediaries. What conditions might suit each one?
8. Differentiate between direct selling and direct-response retailing. Cite examples of both.
9. In what ways has the Internet changed direct-response retailing?
10. Define *automatic merchandising* and explain its role in Canadian retailing today and in the future.

PROJECTS AND TEAMWORK EXERCISES

1. Research and then classify each of the following retailers:
   a. Future Shop
   b. Bonnie Togs
   c. Danier Leather
   d. DeBoer's
   e. Zellers
2. Visit a local Wal-Mart store and observe such aspects as product placement, shelf placement, inventory levels on shelves, traffic patterns, customer service, and checkout efficiency. Discuss what makes Wal-Mart the world's most successful retailer.
3. Winners has become known for trendy clothes and stylish housewares, all readily available in spacious stores at reasonable prices. Visit a local Winners store or the company's website and compare its product selection to a hardware store and/or a department store. Make a list of each store's advantages and disadvantages, including convenience, location,

selection, service, and general prices. Do any of their product lines overlap? How are they different from each other?

4. In pairs, match each industry with the most appropriate type of wholesaling intermediary.

_____ hardware	a. drop shipper
_____ perishable foods	b. truck wholesaler
_____ lumber	c. auction house
_____ wheat	d. full-function merchant
_____ used cars	wholesaler
	e. commission merchant

5. In teams, develop a retailing strategy for an Internet retailer. Identify a target market and then suggest a mix of merchandise, promotion, service, and pricing strategies that would help a retailer to reach that market via the Internet. What issues must Internet retailers address that do not affect traditional store retailers?

6. With a classmate, visit two or three retail stores that compete with one another in your area and compare their customer-service strategies. (You might wish to visit each store more than once to avoid making a snap judgment.) Select at least five criteria and use them to assess each store. How do you think each store sees its customer-service strategy as fitting into its overall retailing strategy? Present your findings in detail to the class.

7. Visit a department store and compare at least two departments' pricing strategies based on the number of markdowns you find and the size of the discount. What, if anything, can you conclude about the success of each department's retailing strategy?

8. Think of a large purchase you make on a nonroutine basis, such as a new winter coat or expensive clothing for a special occasion. Where will you shop for such items? Will you travel out of your way? Will you go to the nearest shopping centre? Will you look on the Internet? Once you have made your decision, describe any strategies used by the retailer that led you to this decision. What would make you change your mind about where to shop for this item?

9. Outlet malls are a growing segment of the retail market. Visit a local outlet mall or research one on the Internet. What types of stores are located there? How do the product selection and price compare with typical stores?

10. Addition Elle is a national chain of stores that feature clothing for plus-size women. Recommend an appropriate retailing strategy for this type of retailer.

CRITICAL-THINKING EXERCISES

1. Talbots made its name as a retailer of classic sportswear for women, but it has recently expanded its target market to include men and children. Men, however, typically don't enjoy shopping for clothes, and children shop with their parents. Visit http://talbots.com and assess how well Talbots is reaching men through its website. Do you think Talbots' target market is still women who shop for the men in their lives? Why or why not? How can Talbots widen its appeal on the Internet?

2. Several major retailers have begun to test the extreme markdown strategy that lies behind popular "dollar" stores such as Great Canadian Dollar Store or Dollar Giant. Wal-Mart and A&P, for example, are opening sections in selected stores that feature items from snacks to beauty supplies priced at $1. Is this experiment simply a test of pricing strategy? What else might motivate these retailers to offer such deep discounts?

3. When A and B Sound, a company with 21 music stores that controlled 20 percent of recorded music sales in Western Canada, filed for court protection from its creditors, it was only one symptom of the general decline of the retail music store. Industry analysts blame everything from music downloading programs to changes in consumers' tastes. Most, however, feel that music stores will somehow remain viable. What are some changes that these retailers could make in their merchandising, customer service, pricing, location, and other strategies to try to reinvent their business?

4. McDonald's has traditionally relied on a cookie-cutter approach to its restaurant design. One store looked essentially like every other—until recently. The chain has decided to loosen its corporate design mandate to fit within special markets and to update its image with customers. Research McDonald's makeover efforts. What types of changes has the company made and where? How have changes in atmospherics helped the chain with customers? Have the changes you researched modified your perception of McDonald's at all? If so, how?

As the largest company in the world, with 1.5 million employees worldwide and $320 billion (U.S.) in sales in a recent year, many people would argue that Wal-Mart has become too big and powerful. It has twice as many stores in Mexico as it does in Canada, and it is the largest private-sector employer in that country. It imports so much from China that, if it were a country, Wal-Mart would be China's eighth-largest trading partner, ahead of Britain and Russia. Wal-Mart is currently opening a new store approximately every 42 hours. Some observers believe Wal-Mart is also responsible for the low inflation rates and high productivity gains of recent years in Canada and the United States, accounting for as much as 12 percent of total productivity gains since the late 1990s. However, its unbeatable buying power and efficiency have forced many local stores to close when Wal-Mart opens a new store in their area.

1. Some economists fear what might happen to the economy if Wal-Mart has a bad year (so far it has had more than four decades of nonstop growth). Should retailers have that much influence on the economy? Why or why not?

2. Wal-Mart is selective about what it sells, refusing, for instance, to carry music or computer games with mature ratings, magazines with content that it considers too adult, or a popular morning-after pill. Because of its sheer size, these decisions can become influential in the culture. Do you think this is a positive or negative effect of the growth of this retailer? Why?

1. **Retailing strategy.** Visit the website of electronics retailer Best Buy (http://www.bestbuy.ca). The website is classified as a shopping site, or online store. Review the material in the chapter on retailing strategy and store atmospherics. Answer the following questions.
   a. How does the design and layout of the Best Buy Web store appeal to the company's target market(s)?
   b. How would you describe the atmospherics created by the online store? If you can visit a brick-and-mortar store, compare the store's atmospherics to the Web store.
   c. In what ways does Best Buy use its online store to enhance its brick-and-mortar stores?

2. **Retailing statistics.** Statistics Canada reports regularly on Canadian retail sales. Visit the website listed below and access the most recent retail sales reports. Its daily reports include everything from nonstore retail sales to trends in retailing sales from traditional retail establishments. Be prepared to consider and report on the following questions:
   a. What trends can you identify in Canadian retail sales?
   b. By how much have retail sales grown over the past month or past year?
   c. Which categories are growing the most quickly? Which categories are growing the most slowly?
   d. Can you identify any seasonal patterns in retail sales?
   e. What have you found that is interesting and more recent than what is provided in your text?

3. http://statscan.com

Note: Internet Web addresses change frequently. If you don't find the exact sites listed, you may need to access the organization's or company's home page and search from there or use a search engine such as Google.

Case 13.1

Costco Challenges Mighty Wal-Mart

Costco Wholesale Corp., the big national warehouse club with locations across Canada and the United States, is highly profitable. The company is worth about $42 billion (U.S.), which makes it only about 20 percent the size of Wal-Mart, but it ranks as one of the larger company's biggest competitors.

Sam's Club, the warehouse arm of Wal-Mart, was founded the same year as Costco (1983) and has more than 600 stores in Canada, the United States, Mexico, Puerto Rico, and China. However, the average Costco store earns nearly twice as much revenue as the average Sam's Club ($112 million compared to $63 million (U.S.)).

Costco has carved out its market by appealing not so much to bargain hunters with moderate budgets but to more sophisticated urban shoppers who look for the "new luxury." They appreciate bargains on expensive name brands and "treasure hunt" items, but they also don't mind buying money-saving private-label commodities such as paper towels, detergent, and vitamins in bulk from stacked pallets in the store's cavernous, no-frills environment. Small-business owners make up a large portion of Costco customers. "We understood that small-business owners, as a rule, are the wealthiest people in a community," says Chairman Jeff Brotman. "So they would not only spend significant money on their businesses, they'd spend a lot on themselves if you gave them quality and value . . . You couldn't entice a wholesale customer with 20-pound tins of mayonnaise; you had to romance him with consumer goods." Costco's customers pay a small annual fee for a membership card that allows them to shop there; the annual renewal rate is an impressive 86 percent.

Costco doesn't offer unlimited choices. But by stocking fewer items and reducing the number of sizes, brands, and colours it carries, the company streamlines its distribution process and turns over inventory faster. Thanks to its large volume and its ability to attract affluent customers (who return to the store an average of 11.4 times a year), Costco is able to offer prestigious brands like Titleist, Cuisinart, and Levi's, labels that wouldn't ordinarily want to annoy their full-price retail customers by striking a deal with a discounter.

Costco sees itself as an innovator in retailing. Among the goods and services it offered before Sam's Club did were the sale of fresh meat and produce and of its own premium private-label brand (Kirkland Signature). Costco also started selling gasoline before Sam's Club did and is now one of the largest independent gasoline retailers in some regions. Costco has 61 stores in Canada, and Sam's has recently opened six here with more to come.

The two firms also differ in their employment practices. Wal-Mart pays a competitive wage among retailers but Costco generally pays higher wages. Wal-Mart offers its health plan to fewer than half its workers; Costco covers over 80 percent of its workers and pays 92 percent of their health care costs. Wal-Mart's employee turnover rate is 21 percent a year; Costco's is 6 percent, the lowest in the retailing industry. Some business analysts want Costco to cut its employment costs to increase profits, but Costco has consistently high productivity, and its labour and overhead costs are less than 10 percent of sales (Sam's Club's costs are 17 percent). Says Costco's CEO Jim Sinegal, "Paying your employees well is not only the right thing to do but it makes for good business."

Questions for Critical Thinking

1. Sam's Club is adding more upscale merchandise, including pricey jewellery. Do you think it can successfully capture many of the "new luxury" buyers in Costco's target market? Why or why not?

2. From the case or from your own experience, how would you characterize Costco's merchandising strategy? Its customer-service strategy? Its pricing and location/distribution strategies? Its atmospherics?

Sources: Stanley Holmes and Wendy Zellner, "The Costco Way," *BusinessWeek*, April 12, 2004, pp. 76–77; Christine Frey, "Costco's Love of Labor: Employees' Well-being Key to Its Success," *Seattle Post-Intelligencer*, May 29, 2004, http://seattlepi.nwsource.com; John Helyar, "The Only Company Wal-Mart Fears," *Fortune*, November 24, 2003, pp. 158–66; Kate Berry, "No Frills Fills: Discounter Costco Gaining Larger Share of Gas Market," *Los Angeles Business Journal*, April 7, 2003, accessed at http://www.findarticles.com; Sam's Club Canada home page, http://www.samsclubcanada.ca, accessed April 28, 2005.

Case 13.2

Let's Have a Party—Bring Your Wallet

D irect selling is an important marketing channel (discussed in Chapter 12) and provides opportunity for people interested in exploring personal selling (to be discussed in Chapter 16). It is an important form of nonstore retailing; sales have been increasing between 10 and 20 percent per year over the past decade and are now nearly $2 billion annually in Canada, where there are more than 60 direct selling companies. They employ more than 600 000 independent salespeople—called representatives, distributors, dealers, or consultants.

One direct selling company that has been particularly successful in recent years is The Pampered Chef. It has been operating in the United States since 1980 and in Canada since 1996. Sales in Canada have now exceeded $50 million annually. While the company accepts orders directly through its website, most products are sold through in-home cooking demonstrations, referred to as Cooking Shows. Basically, this is a "party plan"—a salesperson makes a demonstration of some of the more than 200 available products at the home of a "party host." Often, the party host has been a participant at a previous Cooking Show where the salesperson has asked for volunteers to host a future Cooking Show.

Guests at the parties receive a small gift for their attendance, while hosts receive a larger gift for hosting the party. Salespeople take orders at the party and collect payment immediately or when the product is delivered to the purchaser. More than 1 million Cooking Shows are held annually in North America.

Pampered Chef Consultants have a lot of personal freedom. In recent years, they have even been able to have their personal websites, but the company does have a number of restrictions to ensure its image in the marketplace is protected. As independent business owners, some work a few hours per week, or a few days per month. Others, such as Terri Newberry, work six hours per day, four or five days and several evenings per week. Some sell to supplement their own or family income; some treat this as their primary source of income and achieve considerable success. Terri Newberry, for example, started as a Pampered Chef Consultant in 1993. She earned just over $500 her first month, $1000 her fourth month, and progressed to just under $10 000 per month by 2005. In Canada, there are seven levels of salespeople from consultant to senior executive director. Salespeople can earn more than just their commission. Depending on their sales level, they can earn free products, jewellery, and even vacation cruises. In 2006, 3300 Pampered Chef salespeople stayed at the Four Seasons in Palm Beach, Florida, and then cruised aboard Royal Caribbean's *Navigator of the Seas* and *Enchantment of the Seas*.

Why is The Pampered Chef so successful? Certainly a lot of credit goes to its independent sales force, and the party plan method of retailing. But it could not do this without a selection of quality products and a company philosophy that promotes honesty and fairness for its salespeople and customers. The Pampered Chef is a member of the Direct Sellers Association (DSA), as are approximately 70 percent of all direct selling companies in Canada. All member companies must rededicate annually to abide by the DSA code of ethics, which provides appropriate business practices with respect to product sales, consumer care, and recruitment and sales force relations. Come to the party—fill your wallet.

Questions for Critical Thinking

1. Why is the party plan such a successful method of nonstore retailing? How can companies such as The Pampered Chef continue to maintain their strong growth in the future?

2. Would you ever consider becoming a Pampered Chef Consultant? Why or why not? What factors in the marketing environment would provide future opportunities for you as a Pampered Chef consultant? What factors do you see as potential future threats? Explain.

Sources: Direct Sellers Association website, http://www.dsa.ca; The Pampered Chef website, http://www.pamperedchef.com; The Pampered Chef–Canada website, http://www.pamperedchef.com/index.jsp?localeString=en_ca; The Pampered Chef blog, http://mlmblog.typepad.com/pampered_chef/2006/06/home_is_where_t.html; Paul Burnham Finney, "When Top Salespeople Get to Ride the Waves," *International Herald Tribune*, May 8, 2006, http://www.iht.com/articles/2006/05/08/business/cruise.php; all websites accessed December 10, 2007.

Video Case 13.3

BP Connects with Drivers

The written case on The BP appears on page VC-15. The recently filmed BP video is designed to expand and highlight the concepts in this chapter and the concepts and questions covered in the written video case.

marketer's minute highlights

AMANDA HEROLD

COURTESY OF AMANDA HEROLD

I spend a lot of time communicating . . .

Talking About Marketing with Amanda Herold

Here are highlights of our interview with Amanda Herold of Bell Canada. For the complete video interview and transcript, go to **http://www.contemporarymarketing2.nelson.com**

Q4: Briefly describe one of your typical days.

AH: In my current position, I attend and host many meetings (mostly teleconferences) to align the strategy, implementation of my products, as well as share results. For example, I'll discuss recent marketing strategies with my manager. Then I'll meet with an agency about a banner they are developing and give my feedback on the storyboards, and in the same meeting, receive a quote for updating an existing online demo and ask for a quote on developing posters.

I'll come up with a few potential slogans for the banner, pitch them to some colleagues and my manager. After I pick the most appropriate slogan and images, I'll e-mail Marcom to translate my slogan to French and ensure my images align with branding. I host a weekly team touchpoint where I'll discuss these findings with my team and reach out to them if I will need their help implementing or otherwise. They also share their findings, such as page traffic results, and sometimes they also reach out to me to strategically promote their services. I spend a lot of time communicating.

Q5: What do you like/dislike about your job?

AH: I like the technology industry, specifically Internet, because it is fast-paced, so we are always exploring new ideas. We are also in the Web 2.0 age, so there are a lot of new and interesting promotional opportunities for social marketing and e-marketing. E-marketing in an Internet company is also unique, because some of our services, for example e-mail, also feed into our promotional tactics. I work for a big company, which allows me to learn about many different areas of marketing and business. My company has a fairly informal culture as well, which I enjoy.

In terms of dislikes, I'd say since my area is extremely fast-paced, it is a challenge to keep ahead of the quick shifts in strategy; sometimes my priorities change daily. Occasionally, one of my planned promotions can become obsolete before I get to implement it! Also there are the typical challenges faced with promoting via technology—the odd server issue, strange computer anomalies, etc.

Q6: What was the biggest challenge/surprise when you entered the field?

AH: My biggest initial challenge was grasping a macro perspective of who specifically to contact for my projects and who would also require my assistance for projects.

Q7: What is your biggest accomplishment?

AH: One of my favourite projects was a contest I ran to promote a specific online tool. I doubled traffic to the tool page, from approx 60k to approx 120k. My AD and VP were really happy, and I was quite proud. It was a lot of work, but a success!

Q9: Could you please give us a few key presentation tips?

AH: If time allows, practice anything you are going to present; this will give you added confidence. Smile. Make eye-contact. Focus on your audience and gauge their response to what you're saying.

Know your material inside-out, but if someone asks you a question, don't be afraid to admit you don't know the answer. Just say "Good question, I'll find that out for you", write it down, and remember to follow-up quickly with the person and/or group. In some cases, you may need to redirect them as well.

Q10: What are the important skills that marketing students needs to succeed?
AH: I would cite openness to change, flexibility, curiousness, analytical skills, creativity, and time management. Interpersonal skills help too; these can be learned.

Q11: What is a good entrance into the industry?
AH: Internships can be useful, if you take on fulfilling tasks. Connections are another entrance. Working experience in entry level non-marketing positions can help as well because you gain a good knowledge of how a company works from the ground up. Even if you are just starting out, often companies like to promote from within.

Q12: Any last words or advice for future marketing graduates?
AH: Take as much from your classes as you can. Try to lead at least one school project, even if it is outside your comfort zone. Look for opportunities to collaborate with your professors and peers. When you graduate and you're looking for a job, use your connections and be persistent. Try to gain some practical marketing experience, either through consulting or volunteering. Pick a field you enjoy because it will help you naturally excel and stay curious. Good luck and have fun!

Laughter Coming Your Way

The Second City uses a variety of marketing channels to distribute its product. Whether at the local theatre, on the high seas, or for a corporate conference, The Second City provides a direct service to its customer. Strategic distribution is essential for making the SC product conveniently available. By using a variety of channels, The Second City increases its accessibility and its utility as a company. Its distribution aids, fashions, and facilitates its product marketing. A tourist who witnesses Second City's flair for off-the-cuff humour may be inclined to hire its communications division for a business event. So Second City's distribution and marketing departments function as reciprocally related partners.

The Second City operates five different theatres across North America in Chicago, Toronto, Detroit, Denver, and Las Vegas. These locations were chosen largely because they access SC's largest market, the tourist population. Decorated in photos of famous alumni and Second City memorabilia, they project their legacy as a comedic fixture of the entertainment industry. By distributing Second City's product across the continent, they allow a greater number of consumers to experience it. But The Second City is a small enough company that distribution across the continent presents managerial challenges. To meet the localized needs of its theatres, SC uses different ownership practices for different locations. SC Detroit, for instance, is marketed vertically as the company's only franchise. The Las Vegas theatre is a partnership designed to attract tourists off the glitzy, yet beaten path. Second City Denver is a community-based endeavour working closely with the Denver Center for the Performing Arts. The first two locations, Chicago and Toronto, are the only Second City theatres fully owned by three shareholders who work closely within theatre operations.

Lou Carbone, Second City's chief financial officer, says that SC does not have plans to open another theatre in the near future. SC's current focus is on finding more innovative ways to dually distribute its comedy far and wide with multiple product lines and services. Second City Theatricals performs classic and new material for a variety of performing arts centres and private events. It often produces shows for youth or traditional theatre-going audiences to distribute the brand as a specialized product line. It recently joined forces with the Steppenwolf Theater, in which an SC Theatricals production will be represented by the highly acclaimed Chicago venue. SC Theatricals also spawned SC's partnership with Norwegian Cruise Lines. The Second City is exclusively distributed to its target tourist market with full-time companies performing on four NCL ships.

Since the mid-1990s The Second City has produced shows in such locations as Scotland, Vienna, Saudi Arabia, Tokyo, and Hong Kong. These international endeavours are often contractual marketing agreements with organizations that temporarily house a Second City touring company. In the United States, Second City's national touring company focuses on the nation's college campuses and performing arts centres. By distributing internationally, The Second City acquires unique promotion and global awareness. In the United States, its touring companies attract the textbook-reading, socially conscious college population looking for an entertaining study break.

The Second City similarly distributes its brand to the youth and technically adept market through the Internet. Second City Chicago's musical director, Ruby Streak, hosts a weekly podcast called *We'll Be Right Back. Second City Radio,* which was broadcast from Chicago's WCKG-FM and featured current cast and alumni of The Second City, is also offered on the Second City website. Video clips from a variety of former SC productions are showcased next to interviews of famous SC alumni. Secondcity.com also features volumes of Second City Television for purchase. *SCTV* was the company's most acclaimed television distribution venture. Launching a variety of impressive careers and securing the brand name throughout the continent, *SCTV* distribution continues as a company commodity nearly 20 years after production ended.

For Second City Communications, however, the product is customized and sold directly to the buyer. SC Communications offers services in the form of learning and development, event support, entertainment, or video production. Over the last 15 years, SC Communications has worked with more than 400 Fortune 1000 companies. Whether answering Wal-Mart's call to develop an Emmyesque event celebration, or celebrating a lucrative year for Acura with the help of alumnus Martin Short, SC Communications distributes its product directly by addressing the needs of the client. It links the communicative power of improvisation with the corporate need for agility, teamwork, and innovation. Its marketing channel is selected by designing the products (and services) to be competitive in the industry. As a result, SC Communications is routinely sought out by businesses for consultation. "People pay us because we're good," SC Communication's website declares. It has marketed its product/service throughout the business channel. It has become Second City's most lucrative division and has blazed a trail in an important new market.

Customers of The Second City may see a show only once in their lifetime. They may routinely check out podcasts on the website, see a couple of touring company shows in college, or call on Second City Communications to spice up an otherwise stale sales conference for their company. By selecting a variety of distribution channels, The Second City makes its product available to a broad spectrum of consumers. They have excelled as a convenient, unique service provider in the entertainment industry.

Questions

1. Why might The Second City not look to develop more fixed stages in the near future?
2. What is The Second City's location/distribution strategy? How do atmospherics play a role in the company?
3. Name three marketing channels that The Second City has selected. How and why does it distribute its product in this way?
4. How has Second City Theatricals developed an innovative approach to distribution and marketing?

Part 5 CBC Video Case

Visit the website for Contemporary Marketing at **http://www.contemporarymarketing2e.nelson.com** to view the CBC video and video case summary for Part 5.

part 6

PROMOTIONAL DECISIONS

chapter 14

Integrated Marketing Communications

CHAPTER OBJECTIVES

① Explain how integrated marketing communications relates to the development of an optimal promotional mix.

② Describe the communication process and how it relates to the AIDA concept.

③ Explain how the promotional mix relates to the objectives of promotion.

④ Identify the different elements of the promotional mix and explain how marketers develop an optimal promotional mix.

⑤ Describe the role of sponsorships and direct marketing in integrated marketing communications.

⑥ Discuss the factors that influence the effectiveness of a promotional mix.

⑦ Contrast pushing and pulling strategies.

⑧ Explain how marketers budget for and measure the effectiveness of promotion.

⑨ Discuss the value of marketing communications.

GILLETTE FUSES ITS MARKETING COMMUNICATIONS

Razor burn and shaving nicks may soon be history. They will be if Gillette marketers can spread the word to consumers about the firm's new five-blade Fusion razor. To reach potential customers, Gillette is making sure you'll see the Fusion just about everywhere you go. Naturally, you'll find one if you happen to be in the shaving aisle at the supermarket or drugstore. But you might also notice a display at the checkout in a sporting-goods store. If you happened to be at a recent Super Bowl, you could have received a free shave before the game. If you weren't there but were glued to the TV for the game, you were exposed to the Fusion commercials dubbed "The Miracle of Shaving." If you stay up to watch David Letterman—and you're a Ben Roethlisberger fan—you could have watched the late-night talk show host shave the Steelers quarterback's beard on TV. Say you don't watch football but like to head to a NASCAR track; you'll be greeted by Fusion promotions, too. All these strategic placements and information sources are provided in addition to the obvious advertising venues—magazines such as *Sports Illustrated* and *Men's Health*. And if you want to learn more about the Fusion before you shop, you can visit its interactive Web page at Gillettefusion.com.

Gillette, which is owned by Procter & Gamble, is engaged in a well-planned marketing campaign to communicate the message about Fusion through a variety of media and methods, even if the choices seem a little unusual. But the campaign makes sense. "We just want trial," explains marketing director for blades and razors for Gillette. "We're trying to put the product wherever men shop." Gillette marketers believe that if men try the Fusion, which is packed with new shaving technology, they will become loyal users.

The firm wants to develop demand for its new razor in every way possible. In a highly competitive market, this means differentiating the Fusion from competing products such as Schick's Quattro razor. In addition to the five blades—no other razor has that many—Gillette designers placed the blades closer together, which reduces skin irritation. The Fusion blades have a smoother coating than others, with a strip containing vitamin E and skin-soothing aloe. In addition, the design is high-tech. "The razor does have a futuristic feel and look to it, so we wanted the ads to convey that, too," says a representative of the agency that created the Fusion ads.

Although the Fusion may seem to be a luxury grooming purchase—at an initial purchase price of $17 for a kit containing the razor and two replaceable blade cartridges and another $18 for four more replacements—Gillette is emphasizing the value of the purchase over time. For a man who shaves every day, the Fusion should cost less than other products.

Gillette tested the Fusion against its own Mach3 and Schick's Quattro on 9000 men, and the feedback was positive. "[Participants] preferred Fusion by a 2-to-1 margin over its rivals," claims the president of Gillette's blades and razors division. By developing demand for the Fusion, Gillette marketers hope also to increase demand for its companion products, such as shaving cream and aftershave. In fact, the firm is so confident of Fusion's success that it is launching new related grooming products. "Fusion will get so much attention that it will drive a lot of men to try these grooming products," predicts one consultant. Gillette has reason to feel confident about the success of Fusion as it holds more than 66 percent of the global razor and blade market.[1]

connecting with customers

Gillette connects with customers by providing innovate new products that meet customers' needs. It ensures its products meet the shaving needs of men by testing them on customers. After producing products that meet the shaving needs of their customers, Gillette distributes and promotes the products where men are sure to get the message.

Chapter Overview

TWO of the four components of the marketing mix—product and distribution strategies—were discussed in previous chapters. The three chapters in Part 6 analyze the third marketing mix variable—promotion. **Promotion** is the function of informing, persuading, and influencing the consumer's purchase decision.

This chapter introduces the concept of integrated marketing communications, briefly describes the elements of a firm's promotional mix—personal and non-personal promotion—and explains the characteristics that determine the success of the mix. Next, we identify the objectives of promotion and describe the importance of developing promotional budgets and measuring the effectiveness of promotion. Finally, we discuss the importance of the business, economic, and social aspects of promotion. Chapter 15 covers advertising, public relations, and other non-personal selling elements of the promotional mix, including sponsorships and guerrilla advertising. Chapter 16 completes this part of the book by focusing on personal selling and sales promotion.

Throughout *Contemporary Marketing,* special emphasis has been given to new information that shows how technology is changing the way marketers approach *communication,* the transmission of a message from a sender to a receiver. Consumers receive **marketing communications**—messages that deal with buyer–seller relationships—from a variety of media, including television, radio, magazines, direct mail, the Internet, and cell phones. Marketers can broadcast an ad on the Web to mass markets or design a customized appeal targeted to a small market segment. Each message the customer receives from any source represents the brand, company, or organization. A company needs to coordinate all these messages for maximum total impact and to reduce the likelihood the consumer will completely tune them out.

To prevent this loss of attention, marketers are turning to **integrated marketing communications (IMC),** which coordinates all promotional activities—media advertising, direct mail, personal selling, sales promotion, public relations, and sponsorships—to produce a unified, customer-focused promotional message. As you saw in the opening story, Gillette uses IMC to get the message out about its Fusion razor. IMC is a broader concept than marketing communications and promotional strategy. It uses database technology to refine the marketer's understanding of the target audience, segment this audience, and select the best type of media for each segment.

This chapter shows that IMC involves not only the marketer but also all other organizational units that interact with the consumer. Marketing managers set the goals and objectives of the firm's promotional strategy in accordance with overall organizational objectives and marketing goals. Based on these objectives, the various elements of the promotional strategy—personal selling, advertising, sales promotion, direct marketing, publicity, and public relations—are formulated into an integrated communications plan. This plan becomes a central part of the firm's total marketing strategy to reach its selected market segments. The feedback mechanism, including marketing research and field reports, completes the system by identifying any deviations from the plan and suggesting improvements. ◆◆◆

promotion
Communications link between buyers and sellers. Function of informing, persuading, and influencing a consumer's purchase decision. p. 61

marketing communications
Messages that deal with buyer–seller relationships.

integrated marketing communications (IMC) Coordination of all promotional activities to produce a unified, customer-focused promotional message.

INTEGRATED MARKETING COMMUNICATIONS

Stop and think for a moment about all the marketing messages you receive in a single day. You click on the television for the morning news, and you see plenty of commercials. Listen to the car radio on the way to work or school, and you can sing along with the jingles. You get catalogues, coupons, and fliers in the mail. People even leave promotional fliers under your car's windshield wiper while it sits in the parking lot. When you go online, you're deluged with banner and pop-up ads and even marketing related e-mail. Marketers know that you are receiving many types of communication. They know they need to compete for your attention. So they look for ways to reach you in a coordinated manner through integrated marketing communications.

Successful marketers use the marketing concept and relationship marketing to develop customer-oriented marketing programs. The customer is at the heart of integrated marketing communications. An IMC strategy begins not with the organization's goods and services but with consumer wants or needs and then works in reverse to the product, brand, or organization. It sends receiver-focused rather than product-focused messages.

Rather than separating the parts of the promotional mix and viewing them as isolated components, IMC looks at these elements from the consumer's viewpoint: as information about the brand, company, or organization. Even though the messages come from different sources—sales presentations, word of mouth, TV, radio, newspapers, billboards, direct mail, coupons, public relations, and online services—consumers may perceive them as "advertising" or a "sales pitch." IMC broadens promotion to include all the ways a customer has contact with an organization, adding to traditional media and direct mail such sources as package design, store displays, sales literature, and online and interactive media. Unless the organization takes an integrated approach to present a unified, consistent message, it may send conflicting information that confuses consumers.

Conflicting messages that could confuse or mislead consumers came to light in a study conducted by TerraChoice described in the "Go Green" feature.

Today's business environment is characterized by many diverse markets and media, creating both opportunities and challenges. The success of any IMC program depends on identifying the members of an audience and understanding what they want. Without accurate, current information about existing and potential customers, their purchase histories, needs, and wants, marketers may send the wrong message. But they cannot succeed simply by improving the quality of the messages or by sending more of them. IMC must not only deliver messages to intended audiences but also gather responses from them. Databases and interactive marketing are important IMC tools that help marketers collect information from customers and segment markets according to demographics and preferences. Marketers can then design specialized communications programs to meet the needs of each segment.

Young male consumers can be hard to pin down. But marketers for companies such as Old Spice and Panasonic have tailored new marketing messages to the lifestyle of this segment. Instead

① Explain how integrated marketing communications relates to the development of an optimal promotional mix.

Marketoid

National advertising and related services industries saw their operating revenues increase by 12.6 percent in 2005.

Marketoid

Firms in the advertising industry in Canada earned $5.6 billion in operating revenues in 2005.

Joint integrated marketing promotion.

Go Green

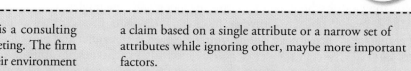

"Greenwashing"

TerraChoice Environmental Marketing is a consulting firm specializing in environmental marketing. The firm helps companies who want to develop their environment programs by advising on strategy development, communication programs, purchasing, ecolabelling, and product development. Its environmental marketing recommendations are based on established criteria produced by such organizations as the International Organization for Standardization (ISO), U.S. Environmental Protection Agency, and the Canadian Consumer Affairs Branch.

As part of a recent research project into environmental claims companies were making about their products, TerraChoice coined a new term—Greenwash—the act of misleading consumers about the environmental practices of a company or the environmental benefits of a product. Their research looked at over a thousand products and all but one were guilty of making false or misleading claims relating to how environmentally friendly the products were. TerraChoice identified six categories or "Six Sins of Greenwashing":

1. Sin of the Hidden Trade-off—found in 57 percent of the products. This sin occurs when a product makes a claim based on a single attribute or a narrow set of attributes while ignoring other, maybe more important factors.
2. Sin of No Proof—found in 26 percent of the tested products. If there was no supporting information or reliable third-party certification, this sin was committed.
3. Sin of Vagueness—found in 11 percent of the products. A claim that is poorly defined or so broad as to be meaningless falls into this group.
4. Sin of Irrelevance—found in 4 percent of the products. A sin that falls under this heading is making a true statement, but it is unimportant or not helpful.
5. Sin of Lesser of Two Evils—found in 1 percent of the products. These claims, while true, would distract the purchaser from a greater environmental issue.
6. Sin of Fibbing—found in 1 percent of the products. This claim is totally false.

Source: TerraChoice website, http://www.terrachoice.com, accessed February 18, 2008.

Some connections simply can't be made on the internet.

GIRLS NEED GUIDES. For more information or to enroll your daughter, call 1-800-565-8111 or visit us at girlguides.ca

COURTESY GIRL GUIDES OF CANADA

Girl Guides of Canada promote the benefits of their organization to both girls and their mothers.

of trying to get these consumers to come to them, marketers are taking their message to young men. In some cases, it means hitting the late-night party circuit—because that's where the guys are. Panasonic now puts its television ads on late-night television, because that's when young men watch TV. Old Spice has introduced a line of scents for 18- to 24-year-olds called After Hours, with print ads showing a neon sign that reads, "A good night's sleep just means you had a really boring night."[2]

The increase in media options provides more ways to give consumers product information; however, it can also create information overload. Marketers have to spread available dollars across fragmented media markets and a wider range of promotional activities to achieve their communication goals. Mass media such as TV ads, while still useful, are no longer the mainstays of marketing campaigns. In fact, more media dollars have been spent on newspaper than television advertising in recent years. Newspaper ads are likely to be directed at a more focused target market.[3] Audiences are also more fragmented. So to reach desired groups, organizations are turning to niche marketing by advertising in special-interest magazines, by purchasing time on cable TV channels, by reaching out through telecommunications media such as cell phones or the Internet, and by sponsoring events and activities. Without an IMC program, marketers frequently encounter problems within their own organizations because separate departments have authority and responsibility for planning and implementing specific promotional mix elements.

The coordination of an IMC program often produces a competitive advantage based on synergy and interdependence among the various elements of the promotional mix. With an IMC strategy, marketers can create a unified personality for the product or brand by choosing the right elements from the promotional mix to send the message. At the same time, they can develop more narrowly focused plans to reach specific market segments and choose the best form of communication to send a particular message to a specific target audience. IMC provides a more effective way to reach and serve target markets than less coordinated strategies. Establishing an effective IMC program requires teamwork.

IMPORTANCE OF TEAMWORK

IMC requires a big-picture view of promotion planning, a total strategy that includes all marketing activities, not just promotion. Successful implementation of IMC requires that everyone involved in every aspect of promotion—public relations, advertising, personal selling, and sales promotion—functions as part of a team. The team members must present a consistent, coordinated promotional effort at every point of customer contact with the organization. This way, they save time, money, and effort. They avoid duplication of efforts, increasing marketing effectiveness and reducing costs. Ultimately, it means that the result—the IMC program—is greater than the sum of its parts.

Teamwork involves both in-house resources and outside vendors. It involves marketing personnel; members of the sales force who deal with wholesalers, retailers, and organizational buyers; and customer-service representatives. A firm gains nothing from a terrific advertisement featuring a great product, an informational website, and a toll-free number if unhelpful salespeople frustrate customers when they answer the phones. The company must train its representatives to send a single positive message to consumers and also to solicit information for the firm's customer database.

IMC also challenges the traditional role of the advertising agency. A single agency may no longer fulfill all a client's communications requirements, including traditional advertising and sales promotions, interactive marketing, database development, direct marketing, and public relations. To best serve client needs, an agency must often assemble a team with members from other companies.

ROLE OF DATABASES IN EFFECTIVE IMC PROGRAMS

With the explosive growth of the Internet, marketers have the power to gather more information faster and to organize it more easily than ever before. By sharing this detailed knowledge appropriately among all relevant parties, a company can lay the foundation for a successful IMC program.

The move from mass marketing to a customer-specific marketing strategy—a characteristic of online marketing—requires not only a means of identifying and communicating with the firm's target market but also information regarding important characteristics of each prospective customer. As discussed in Chapter 9, organizations can compile different kinds of data into complete databases with customer information, including names and addresses, demographic data, lifestyle considerations, brand preferences, and buying behaviour. This information provides critical guidance in

Indigo uses a website and promotional contests in an IMC campaign.

designing an effective IMC strategy that achieves organizational goals and finds new opportunities for increased sales and profits. This increased ability to acquire huge amounts of data poses a new challenge: how to sift through it efficiently so that it becomes useful information. Newer technology allows researchers to do exactly that—working with millions of sets of data to make very specific analyses.[4]

Direct sampling is another method frequently used to quickly obtain customer opinions regarding a particular firm's goods and services. If you've ever received a free sample of bath soap, aspirin, or even a newspaper in your mailbox, you've been the recipient of direct sampling. In an effort to attract interest in a new microwaveable cheese omelette, the maker used sampling along with in-store point of sale material and coupons.[5]

---

assessment check 1 ✓

1.1 Define *promotion*.

1.2 What is the difference between marketing communications and integrated marketing communications (IMC)?

---

② Describe the communication process and how it relates to the AIDA concept.

THE COMMUNICATION PROCESS

When you have a conversation with someone, do you wonder whether the person understood your message? Do you worry that you might not have heard the person correctly? Marketers have the same concerns—when they send a message to an intended audience or market, they want to make sure it gets through clearly and persuasively. That is why the communication process is so important to marketing. The top portion of Table 14.1 shows a general model of the communication process and its application to promotional strategy.

The **sender** acts as the source in the communication system as he or she seeks to convey a **message** (a communication of information, advice, or a request) to a receiver. An effective message accomplishes three tasks:

1. It gains the receiver's attention.

2. It achieves understanding by both receiver and sender.

3. It stimulates the receiver's needs and suggests an appropriate method of satisfying them.

Table 14.1 also provides several examples of promotional messages. Although the types of promotion may vary from a highly personalized sales presentation to such non-personal promotions as television advertising and dollar-off coupons, each goes through every stage in the communications process.

The three tasks just listed are related to the **AIDA concept** (attention-interest-desire-action), the steps consumers take in reaching a purchase decision. First, the promotional message must gain the potential consumer's attention. It then seeks to arouse interest in the good or service. At the next stage, it stimulates desire by convincing the would-be buyer of the product's ability to satisfy his or her needs. Finally, the sales presentation, advertisement, or sales promotion technique attempts to produce action in the form of a purchase or a more favourable attitude that may lead to future purchases.

AIDA concept Steps through which an individual reaches a purchase decision: attention, interest, desire, and action.

The message must be **encoded,** or translated into understandable terms, and transmitted through a communications channel. **Decoding** is the receiver's interpretation of the message. The receiver's response, known as **feedback,** completes the system. Throughout the process, **noise** (in such forms as ineffective promotional appeals, inappropriate advertising media, or poor radio or television reception) can interfere with the transmission of the message and reduce its effectiveness.

The marketer is the message sender in Table 14.1. He or she encodes the message in the form of sales presentations, advertising, displays, or publicity releases. The **channel** for delivering the message may be a salesperson, a public relations announcement, a website, or one of the numerous advertising media. Decoding is often the most troublesome step in marketing communications because consumers do not always interpret promotional messages in the same way that senders do. Since receivers usually decode messages according to their own frames of reference or experi-

table 14.1 **Relating Promotion to the Communication Process**

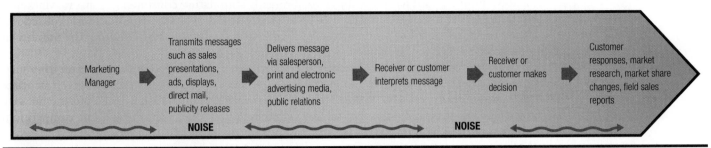

Type of Promotion	Sender	Encoding by Sender	Channel	Decoding by Receiver	Response	Feedback
Personal selling	IBM e-solutions networking system	Sales presentation on new applications of system	IBM sales representative	Office manager and employees discuss sales presentation and those of competing suppliers.	Order is placed for IBM e-solutions system installation.	Customer asks about a second system for subsidiary company.
Dollar-off coupon (sales promotion)	Kellogg's Special K cereal	Coupons prepared by Kellogg's marketing department and advertising agency	Coupon insert in weekend newspaper	Newspaper reader sees coupon for Special K cereal and saves it.	Special K is purchased by consumer using coupon.	Kellogg researchers see increase in market share.
Television advertising	Paramount Canada's Wonderland	Advertisement developed by Wonderland's advertising agency featuring the new park rides	Network television ads air during program with high percentages of viewers under 20 years old	Teens and young adults see ad and decide to try out the park.	Wonderland tickets are purchased.	Customers purchase season ticket packages for Wonderland.

ences, a sender must carefully encode a message in a way that matches the frame of reference of the target audience. Consumers today are bombarded daily by hundreds of sales messages through many media channels. This communications traffic can create confusion as noise in the channel increases. Since the typical shopper will choose to process only a few messages, ignored messages waste communications budgets.

The AIDA concept is also vital to online marketers. It is not enough to say a website has effective content or high response rates. Marketers must know just how many "eyeballs" are looking at the site, how often they come to view a message, and what they are examining. Most important, they must find out what consumers do besides just look. The bottom line is that if nobody is responding to a website, it might as well not exist. Experts advise attracting users' attention by including people in advertisements and other communications in addition to new content and formats. Marketers associated with the FIFA World Cup soccer tournament know that as many as 38 billion viewers watch the tournament during June and July. Yahoo! set up a World Cup website, whose traffic was measured by comScore Networks, providing important marketing information to firms involved with the tournament. Europeans visited the site most often, followed by those from the Asia Pacific area and Latin America. Africans, Middle Easterners, and North Americans visited the site the least often. By using this and other information, marketers can tailor their messages to interested consumers. "Major brands can reach consumers worldwide in a very cost effective manner, as long as they utilize the capabilities of online advertising to adapt their message to the local user," notes Bob Ivins, managing director for comScore in Europe.[6]

Feedback, the receiver's response to the message, provides a way for marketers to evaluate the effectiveness of the message and tailor their responses accordingly. Feedback may take the form of attitude changes, purchases, or nonpurchases. In some instances, organizations use promotion to create favourable attitudes toward their goods or services in the hope of future purchases. Other promotional communications have the objective of directly stimulating consumer purchases. Marketers using infomercials that urge the viewer to call a toll-free number to place orders for music collections, the latest fitness fad, or other products can easily measure their success by counting the number of calls they receive that result in orders.

Even nonpurchases may serve as feedback to the sender. Failure to purchase may result from ineffective communication in which the receivers do not believe or, don't remember it, or even associate it with another firm's products. Alternatively, receivers may remember it correctly, but the message may have failed to persuade them that the firm's products are better than those of the competition. So marketers need to be keenly aware of the reasons that messages fail.

Noise represents interference at some stage in the communication process. It may result from disruptions such as transmissions of competing promotional messages over the same communications channel, misinterpretation of a sales presentation or advertising message, receipt of the promotional message by the wrong person, or random events such as people conversing or leaving the room during a television commercial. Noise can also result from distractions within an advertising message itself. Buzzwords and jargon can create a linguistic jungle for consumers who are just trying to find out more about a product. One investment firm sent a notice to its customers reading, "Please ensure that all registered holders complete and sign the enclosed Form of Renunciation. Due to a temporary issue, we are currently unable to pre-populate all holders' names and addresses." Most recipients probably scratched their heads and asked, "What?" Worse, they may have ignored the message or tossed the letter in the trash.[7]

Noise can be especially problematic in international communications. One problem is that there may be too many competing messages. Italian television channels, for instance, broadcast all advertisements during a single half-hour slot each night. Or technology may be poor, and language translations inaccurate. Nonverbal cues, such as body language and tone of voice, are important parts of the communication process, and cultural differences may lead to noise and misunderstandings. For example, in North America, the round o sign made with the thumb and first finger means "okay." However, in Mediterranean countries, it means "zero" or "the worst." A Tunisian interprets this same sign as "I'll kill you," and to a Japanese consumer it means "money." It's easy to see how misunderstanding could arise from this single gesture.

Perhaps the most misunderstood language for North American marketers is English. With 74 English-speaking nations, local terms can confuse anyone trying to communicate globally. The following examples illustrate how easy it can be for marketers to make mistakes in English-language promotional messages:

- *Police:* bobby (Britain), garda (Ireland), police wallah (South Asia)

- *Porch:* stoep (South Africa), gallery (Caribbean)

- *Bar:* pub (Britain), hotel (Australia), boozer (Australia, Britain, New Zealand)

- *Bathroom:* loo (Britain), dunny (Australia)

- *Ghost or monster:* duppy (Caribbean), taniwha (New Zealand)

- *Barbecue:* braai (South Africa), barbie (Australia)

- *Truck:* lorry (Britain and Australia)

- *Soccer:* football (the rest of the world)

Faulty communications can be especially risky on a global level, where noise can lead to some interesting misinterpretations. Here are three recent international examples:

- *On a sign in a Bucharest hotel lobby:* The lift is being fixed for the next day. During that time, we regret that you will be unbearable.

- *From a Japanese information booklet about using a hotel air conditioner:* Cooles and Heates: If you want just condition of warm in your room, please control yourself.

Marketoid

The largest growth in advertising revenues was fuelled by a 25 percent increase in both Alberta and British Columbia.

ETIQUETTE TIPS FOR MARKETING PROFESSIONALS

Cultural Considerations in Marketing Messages

Integrated marketing communications requires some skilled decision making—but what about creating an IMC campaign for a diverse audience? Differences in language, social and cultural values, and lifestyle among consumers can create challenges for marketers who want to reach and attract consumers of different backgrounds. Before you become overwhelmed by the possibilities, consider a few questions you might ask to help you learn more about certain groups of consumers in order to serve them and develop a strong relationship:

1. Find out how your group views work—would they accept less pay for a job with less stress? Do they place more emphasis on how much they earn? This may affect the types of goods and services they want or need.
2. What type of relationship does this group generally have toward your category of products—is it something they value or something they can do without? For example,

new Canadians are brand conscious but are not brand loyal.
3. On what products does this group spend the most money? Research shows that ethnic Canadians have higher levels of home ownership and therefore are purchasers of furniture, appliances, and household goods.
4. How does the group of consumers like to pay for purchases? New Canadians are price conscious and prefer spending cash rather than using credit cards.

Sources: "Multicultural Snapshot," Allied Media, http://www.allied-media.com, accessed June 12, 2006; "Selling Ethnicity Inc.," *Time*, http://www.time.com, accessed June 12, 2006; "The Psychology of Consumers," *Consumer Psychologist*, http://www.consumerpsychologist.com, accessed June 12, 2006; "How Minorities Are Becoming Markets of Consequence," *Brand Central Station*, January 13, 2006; Don Miller, "The Problem," *Marketing*, January 16, 2006, p. 20; Paul-Mark Rendon, "Ethnic Understanding," *Marketing*, April 17, 2006, p. 10.

• *In an Acapulco hotel:* The manager has personally passed all the water served here.

Marketers involved in IMC on an international level—or in Canada, where diverse audiences are involved—can benefit from some of the suggestions offered in the "Etiquette Tips for Marketing Professionals" feature.

assessment check 2

2.1 What are the three tasks accomplished by an effective message?

2.2 Identify the four steps of the AIDA concept.

2.3 What is noise?

OBJECTIVES OF PROMOTION

③ Explain how the promotional mix relates to the objectives of promotion.

What specific tasks should promotion accomplish? The answers to this question seem to vary as much as the sources consulted. Generally, however, marketers identify the following objectives of promotion:

1. Provide information to consumers and others.
2. Increase demand.
3. Differentiate a product.
4. Accentuate a product's value.
5. Stabilize sales.

It should be noted that marketers would not be trying to achieve all objectives at once.

PROVIDE INFORMATION

The traditional function of promotion was to inform the market about the availability of a particular good or service. In fact, marketers still direct much of their current promotional efforts at providing product information to potential customers. An advertisement for a musical performance typically provides information about the performer, time, and place. A commercial for a theme park offers information about rides, location, and admission price. Information can also help differentiate a product from its competitors by focusing on its features or benefits.

In addition to traditional print and broadcast advertising, marketers often distribute a number of high-tech, low-cost tools to give consumers product information. DVDs are currently used to promote products such as cosmetics, automobiles, and exercise equipment, providing virtual demonstrations of the products. Consumers still regard the promotional DVD as a novelty, so they are less likely to consider them junk mail and throw them out. Many companies also send disks containing software that provides information about or sampling of a good or service. Music companies and Internet service providers such as AOL are regular users of this promotional technique.

INCREASE DEMAND

Most promotions pursue the objective of increasing demand for a product. Some promotions are aimed at increasing **primary demand,** the desire for a general product category such as HDTVs. Millions of dollars are spent each year to promote tourism across the country. Funded by different levels of government, tourism-related companies such as airlines, local hotels, restaurants and tourist attractions, this type of promotion has the objective of increasing the number of visitors to an area. These visitors will spend their vacation money in more than one place.[8]

Primary-demand promotions are also typical for firms holding exclusive patents on significant product improvements and for marketers who decide to expand overseas, creating new markets for their products in other parts of the world. When Procter & Gamble first introduced its Pampers disposable diapers in Hungary, most parents were using overpants with paper inserts to diaper their babies. So early Pampers television ads focused on generating interest in the novel product.

More promotions, however, are aimed at increasing **selective demand,** the desire for a specific brand. Movie studios have been looking for ways to get consumers to watch their films. So they've launched integrated campaigns that include Internet, video podcast, and cell phone marketing efforts. Warner Bros. filmed 27 behind-the-scenes production "diaries" during the filming of *Superman Returns* and posted links to the videos on its website, iTunes, and the Superman fan site BlueTights Network. The response was "beyond our wildest expectations," says one marketer. Fans conducted nearly 60 million downloads from the iTunes link alone.[9]

GLOBE NEWSWIRE/ASSOCIATED PRESS

PERF: Offering product information and benefits to consumers

DIFFERENTIATE THE PRODUCT

A frequent objective of the firm's promotional efforts is **product differentiation.** Homogeneous demand for many products results when consumers regard the firm's output as virtually identical to its competitors' products. In these cases, the individual firm has almost no control over marketing variables such as

TWO GLASSES TODAY. BECAUSE THEY'LL NEED IT TOMORROW.

There's no telling what your child might grow up to be. As a parent, you want to do all you can to prepare them for the future. And that includes giving them plenty of milk. Canada's Food Guide to Healthy Eating recommends kids get at least two servings of milk, chocolate milk or milk products every single day. Milk, with calcium, protein, and 13 other essential vitamins and nutrients that help your child build a strong, healthy body.
www.dairygoodness.ca

COURTESY DAIRY FARMERS OF CANADA

Dairy Farmers of Canada use promotion to tell consumers about the benefits of drinking milk.

Safe, like cotton balls covered in bubble wrap.

The all-new 2007 CR-V has been completely redesigned with class-leading safety features like the impact-reducing ACE™ body structure, six airbags, active head restraints and Vehicle Stability Assist with Traction Control. Combine this with the 166-horsepower, 2.4-litre i-VTEC® engine, plus available Real Time™ 4-wheel drive, and the CR-V gives you unmatched driving confidence in a small SUV. It's also why the CR-V received the Top Safety Pick from the IIHS. Find out more at honda.ca.

HONDA

AGENCY: GRIP LIMITED/PHOTOGRAPHER: TERRY COLLIER, COURTESY HONDA CANADA

Honda: Differentiating its SUV by how safe it is

price. A differentiated demand schedule, in contrast, permits more flexibility in marketing strategy, such as price changes. It may seem difficult to differentiate among the many brands and styles of running shoes, but Reebok is attempting to do just that with a recent campaign. The theme of the campaign is "I am what I am," which is an effort to convey the message that Reebok is inclusive of many types of athletes. Nike's "Just Do It" campaign gives off an aura of exclusivity—only hard-core athletes need apply—while Reebok seeks to celebrate the athlete in everyone. Even so, the firm has gathered a stellar lineup to speak for its products, including NBA players Allen Iverson and Yao Ming and rappers Jay-Z and 50 Cent. "Every other sporting goods commercial is about buying the shoe to become something you're not," says tennis ace Andy Roddick, who is featured in some of the ads. "This is about being yourself."[10]

ACCENTUATE THE PRODUCT'S VALUE

Promotion can explain the greater ownership utility of a product to buyers, thereby accentuating its value and justifying a higher price in the marketplace. This objective benefits both consumer and business products. A firm's promotional messages must build brand image and equity and at the same time deliver a call to action. Advertising typically offers reasons a good or service fits into the consumer's lifestyle. Today, consumers everywhere value their time; the challenge for marketers is to demonstrate how their products will make their lives better.

Marketers must choose their words wisely when creating messages that accentuate their product's value. One expert advises staying away from five words: *quality, value, service, caring,* and *integrity*. These overused words are vague and tend to fall on deaf ears.[11]

STABILIZE SALES

Sales of most goods and services fluctuate throughout the year. Sales fluctuations may result from cyclical, seasonal, or irregular demand. Ice cream, ski trips, and swimming pools have obvious fluctuations, as do snow shovels and lawn mowers. Sales of bottled water and flashlights might spike before a storm, while vacation rentals might be cancelled in the path of the same oncoming bad weather. Stabilizing these variations is often an objective of promotional strategy. Although it may seem less obvious than ice cream, coffee sales follow a seasonal pattern, rising during the colder months and dropping when the weather turns warm. To stimulate summer sales of coffee, Tim Hortons created the Iced Cappuccino, promoting it as creamy and cool.[12]

assessment check 3

3.1 What are the objectives of promotion?

3.2 Why is product differentiation important to marketers?

---

4 Identify the different elements of the promotional mix and explain how marketers develop an optimal promotional mix.

promotional mix
Subset of the marketing mix in which marketers attempt to achieve the optimal blending of the elements of personal and non-personal selling to achieve promotional objectives.

ELEMENTS OF THE PROMOTIONAL MIX

Like the marketing mix, the promotional mix requires a carefully designed blend of variables to satisfy the needs of a company's customers and achieve organizational objectives. The **promotional mix** works like a subset of the marketing mix, with its product, distribution, promotion, and pricing elements. With the promotional mix, the marketers attempt to create an optimal blend of various elements to achieve promotional objectives. The components of the promotional mix are personal selling and non-personal selling, including advertising, sales promotion, direct marketing, public relations, and guerrilla marketing.

Personal selling, advertising, and sales promotion usually account for the bulk of a firm's promotional expenditures. However, direct marketing, guerrilla marketing, sponsorships, and public relations also contribute to integrated marketing communications. Later sections of this chapter examine the use of guerrilla marketing, sponsorships, and direct marketing, and Chapters 15 and 16 present detailed discussions of the other elements. This section defines the elements and reviews their advantages and disadvantages.

PERSONAL SELLING

Personal selling is the oldest form of promotion, dating back as far as the beginning of trading and commerce. Traders vastly expanded both market sizes and product varieties as they led horses and camels along the Silk Road from China to Europe roughly between 300 B.C.E. and A.D. 1600, conducting personal selling at both ends. Personal selling may be defined as a seller's promotional presentation conducted on a person-to-person basis with the buyer. This direct form of promotion may be conducted face to face, over the telephone, through videoconferencing, or through interactive computer links between the buyer and seller.

Careers in personal sales many include real estate, insurance, financial investment, or sales of tractors, cars, or vacuum cleaners; individuals may work in retail or wholesaling; they may be regional managers or in the field. In other words, the range of jobs, as well as the products they represent, is huge.

NON-PERSONAL SELLING

Non-personal selling includes advertising, product placement, sales promotion, direct marketing, guerrilla marketing, publicity, and public relations. Advertising and sales promotion are usually regarded as the most important forms of non-personal selling. About one-third of marketing dollars spent on non-personal selling activities are allocated for media advertising; the other two-thirds fund trade and consumer sales promotions.

Advertising

Advertising is any paid, non-personal communication through various media about a business, not-for-profit organization, product, or idea by a sponsor identified in a message that is intended to inform, persuade, or remind members of a particular audience. It is a major promotional mix component for thousands of organizations. Mass consumption and geographically dispersed markets make advertising particularly appropriate for marketing goods and services aimed at large audiences likely to respond to the same promotional messages.

Advertising primarily involves mass media, such as newspapers, television, radio, magazines, movie screens, and billboards, but also includes electronic and computerized forms of promotion such as Web commercials, CDs and DVDs, and television monitors in supermarkets. The rich potential of the Internet as an advertising channel to reach millions of people one at a time has attracted the attention of companies large and small, local and international. As consumers become increasingly savvy—and tune out messages that don't interest them—marketers are finding new ways to grab their attention. In fact, some forms of advertising seem to be everywhere, as the accompanying "Solving an Ethical Controversy" feature suggests.

Product Placement

Product placement is a form of non-personal selling in which the marketer pays a motion picture or television program owner a fee to display his or her product prominently in the film or show. The practice gained attention more than two decades ago in the movie *E.T.: The Extra-Terrestrial* when Elliott, the boy who befriends E.T., lays out a trail of Reese's Pieces for the

Marketoid

Fifty-eight percent of Canadian advertising revenues were generated in Ontario, with another 24 percent coming from Quebec.

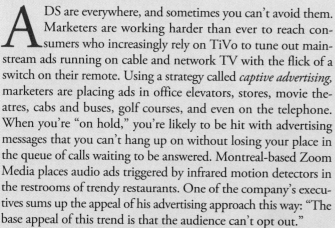

Solving an Ethical Controversy

Captive Advertising

ADS are everywhere, and sometimes you can't avoid them. Marketers are working harder than ever to reach consumers who increasingly rely on TiVo to tune out mainstream ads running on cable and network TV with the flick of a switch on their remote. Using a strategy called *captive advertising*, marketers are placing ads in office elevators, stores, movie theatres, cabs and buses, golf courses, and even on the telephone. When you're "on hold," you're likely to be hit with advertising messages that you can't hang up on without losing your place in the queue of calls waiting to be answered. Montreal-based Zoom Media places audio ads triggered by infrared motion detectors in the restrooms of trendy restaurants. One of the company's executives sums up the appeal of his advertising approach this way: "The base appeal of this trend is that the audience can't opt out."

A recent class-action suit was brought against Loews Cineplex Entertainment Group, alleging that the company gives false start times for films because it screens the ads first.

University campuses used to be one place where captive advertising was not allowed. Over the last several years, this tradition has been changing. For example, the University of British Columbia allows Coke and Telus to advertise on campus. Even though UBC thoroughly checks out the signage and positions on campus before approving any advertising deals, the university still is allowing them on campus. On-campus advertising often does not work if students feel marketers have bought the access to campuses.

Should captive advertising be regulated?

PRO

1. It is becoming intrusive and annoying.
2. In cases like the showing of ads before a feature film, the practice is actually deceptive.

CON

1. Research shows the ads are effective.
2. Most consumers don't really mind them.

Where do you stand: pro or con?

Sources: American Indoor Advertising, "Advertising to a Captive Audience," http://www.indoorads.com/, accessed May 15, 2004; Chester Dawson, "Coming Soon: More Big-Screen Ads," *BusinessWeek*, July 14, 2003, p. 44; Michele Orecklin, "Captive Marketing: There's No Escape," *Time special* "Inside Business" section, June 2003; "A Silly Lawsuit on Cinema Ads," editorial, *Advertising Age*, March 3, 2003, p. 22; Wayne Friedman, "Cinema-Ad Lawsuit Could Chill Business," *Advertising Age*, February 24, 2003, p. 4; Eric Ahlberg, "Big Brands On Campus," *Marketing*, February 26, 2007, p. 32.

extraterrestrial to follow, to draw the alien from his hiding place. Product sales for Reese's Pieces candies went through the roof. (Interestingly, this was not the moviemaker's first choice of candy; Mars turned down the opportunity to have its M&Ms appear in the film.) Today, hundreds of products appear in movies and on television shows, and the fees charged to marketers for these placements have soared.

Some firms have moved to the next generation of product placement, seeking new places for their merchandise. One popular venue for product placement is video games. Not only do these placements generate recognition and awareness, but they can also result in an immediate sale. Video game players who are engaged in the online game Everquest II can click an icon for Pizza Hut and have their pizza delivered within 30 minutes. This capability represents a huge opportunity for both game publishers and advertisers. Advertisers reach precisely the market they have targeted, and game publishers stand to gain from placement fees. "Game publishers have to recognize that there are millions, if not billions, of dollars in advertising money coming their way in the next few years," predicts one industry expert who places in-game ads for clients.[13]

sales promotion
Marketing activities other than personal selling, advertising, guerrilla marketing, and public relations that stimulate consumer purchasing and dealer effectiveness.

Sales Promotion

Sales promotion consists of marketing activities other than personal selling, advertising, guerrilla marketing, and public relations that stimulate consumer purchasing and dealer effectiveness. This broad category includes displays, trade shows, coupons, contests, samples, premiums, product demonstrations, and various nonrecurring, irregular selling efforts. Sales promotion provides a short-term incentive, usually in combination with other forms of promotion, to emphasize, assist, supplement, or otherwise support the objectives of the promotional program. Restaurants, including those that serve fast food, often place certain items on the menu at a lower price "for a limited time only." Advertisements may contain coupons for free or discounted items for a specified period of time. Or companies may conduct sweepstakes for prizes such as new cars or vacations, which may even be completely unrelated to the products the companies are selling.

Movie promotional tie-ins are a classic example. Although this is still a popular—and profitable—type of promotion, some companies are discovering they aren't getting the return on their investment that they had hoped for. If the movie flops, it may be bad news for the product as well. So marketers are tweaking the process to get more out of it. Some movie studios are looking to nontraditional partners—firms that haven't been traditionally involved in tie-ins—to create a different image. Disney/Pixar enlisted 17 promotional partners for its release of *Cars*, most of which produce goods or services that are not necessarily geared for children. Organizations included Hertz and Mack Trucks. In addition, *Cars* producers announced that they were looking for marketing partners willing to deliver messages about childhood obesity.[14]

Benjamin Moore includes a toll free phone number and website address in their ads.

Sales promotion geared to marketing intermediaries is called **trade promotion.** Companies spend about as much on trade promotion as on advertising and consumer-oriented sales promotion combined. Trade promotion strategies include offering free merchandise, buyback allowances, and merchandise allowances along with sponsorship of sales contests to encourage wholesalers and retailers to sell more of certain products or product lines.

Direct Marketing

Another element in a firm's integrated promotional mix is direct marketing, the use of direct communication to a consumer or business recipient designed to generate a response in the form of an order (direct order), a request for further information (lead generation), or a visit to a place of business to purchase specific goods or services (traffic generation). While many people equate direct marketing with direct mail, this promotional category also includes telephone marketing (telemarketing), direct-response advertising and infomercials on television and radio, direct-response print advertising, and electronic media. Direct marketing is such an important element of the promotional mix that it is discussed in depth later in this chapter.

Public Relations and Publicity

Public relations refer to a firm's communications and relationships with its various publics. These publics include customers, suppliers, stockholders, employees, the government, and the general public. Public relations programs can conduct either formal or informal contacts. The critical point is that every organization, whether or not it has a formally organized program, must be concerned about its public relations.

public relations Firm's communications and relationships with its various publics.

Publicity is the marketing-oriented aspect of public relations. It can be defined as non-personal stimulation of demand for a good, service, person, cause, or organization through unpaid placement of significant news about it in a published medium or through a favourable presentation of it on the radio or television. Compared with personal selling, advertising, and even sales promotion, expenditures for public relations are usually low in most firms. Since companies do not pay for publicity, they have less control over the publication by the press or electronic media of good or bad company news. But this often means that consumers find this type of news source more believable than if the information were disseminated directly by the company.

Of course, bad publicity can damage a company's reputation and diminish brand equity. During the recent spikes in gasoline prices, oil companies became the target of criticism and charges of price gouging. In an attempt to convince frustrated customers the price hikes were legitimate, Petro-Canada produced videos for its own website and YouTube in which employees explain gasoline pricing.[15]

Every year, surveys identify which industries consumers feel serve them best and which are the worst—the publicity can affect each, for better or worse. Organizations that are enjoying good publicity generally try to make the most of it. Those who have suffered from bad publicity try to turn the situation around. Bill Gates—both admired and criticized, largely because of the power and wealth he has accumulated—announced his retirement from day-to-day operations of Microsoft in order to devote his energy full-time to his charitable organization, the Bill & Melinda Gates Foundation. Many believe that the move will improve his public image.

Guerrilla Marketing

Guerrilla marketing uses unconventional, innovative, and low-cost techniques to attract consumers' attention. It is a relatively new approach used by marketers whose firms are underfunded for a full marketing program. Many of these firms can't afford the huge costs involved in the orthodox media of print and broadcasting, so they need to find an innovative, low-cost way to reach their market. But some large companies, such as PepsiCo and Toyota, engage in guerrilla marketing as well.

guerrilla marketing Unconventional, innovative, and low-cost marketing techniques designed to get consumers' attention in unusual ways.

As mentioned in Chapter 9, *buzz marketing* can be part of guerrilla marketing. This type of marketing works well to reach college students and other young adults. Marketing firms may hire students to mingle among their own classmates and friends, creating buzz about a product. Often called *campus ambassadors,* they may wear logo-bearing T-shirts or caps, leave Post-it notes with marketing messages around campus, and chat about the good or service with friends during class breaks or over meals. Vancity, the Vancouver-based credit union, used this technique to promote its Enviro Visa card. The credit union purchased 45 bikes, put its logos on them, and then gave them to people to use for three weeks. After the three weeks, they were to be passed on to someone else to use to encourage alternative transportation methods.[16]

Viral marketing, also mentioned in Chapter 9, is another form of guerrilla marketing that has rapidly caught on with large and small firms. Unilever Canada successfully used viral marketing in its "Real Beauty" campaign, using a video named "Real Beauty School." The video directs young women to the company's website to take part in self-esteem activities.[17]

The results of guerrilla marketing can be funny and outrageous—even offensive to some people. But they almost always get consumers' attention. Some guerrilla marketers stencil their company and product names anywhere graffiti might appear. Street artists are hired to plaster company and product logos on blank walls or billboards. Ethical issues of cluttering public spaces aside, the messages do seem to draw interest.

ADVANTAGES AND DISADVANTAGES OF TYPES OF PROMOTION

As Table 14.2 indicates, each type of promotion has both advantages and shortcomings. Although personal selling entails a relatively high per-contact cost, it involves less wasted effort than do non-personal forms of promotion such as advertising. Personal selling often provides more flexible promotion than the other forms because the salesperson can tailor the sales message to meet the unique needs—or objections—of each potential customer.

table 14.2 **Comparison of the Six Promotional Mix Elements**

	PERSONAL SELLING	ADVERTISING	SALES PROMOTION	DIRECT MARKETING	PUBLIC RELATIONS	GUERRILLA MARKETING
Advantages	Permits measurement of effectiveness Elicits an immediate response Tailors the message to fit the customer	Reaches a large group of potential consumers for a relatively low price per exposure Allows strict control over the final message Can be adapted to either mass audiences or specific audience segments	Produces an immediate consumer response Attracts attention and creates product awareness Allows easy measurement of results Provides short-term sales increases	Generates an immediate response Covers a wide audience with targeted advertising Allows complete, customized, personal message Produces measurable results	Creates a positive attitude toward a product or company Enhances credibility of a product or company	Is low cost Attracts attention because it is innovative Is less cluttered with competitors trying the same thing
Disadvantages	Relies almost exclusively upon the ability of the salesperson Involves high cost per contact	Does not permit totally accurate measurement of results Usually cannot close sales	Is non-personal in nature Is difficult to differentiate from competitors' efforts	Suffers from image problem Involves a high cost per reader Depends on quality and accuracy of mailing lists May annoy consumers	May not permit accurate measurement of effect on sales Involves much effort directed toward non-marketing-oriented goals	May not reach as many people If the tactics are too outrageous, they may offend some people

The major advantages of advertising come from its ability to create instant awareness of a good, service, or idea; build brand equity; and deliver the marketer's message to mass audiences for a relatively low cost per contact. Major disadvantages include the difficulty in measuring advertising effectiveness and high media costs. Sales promotions, by contrast, can be more accurately monitored and measured than advertising, produce immediate consumer responses, and provide short-term sales increases. Direct marketing gives potential customers an action-oriented choice, permits narrow audience segmentation and customization of communications, and produces measurable results. Public relations efforts such as publicity frequently offer substantially higher credibility than other promotional techniques. Guerrilla marketing efforts can be innovative—and highly effective—at a low cost to marketers with limited funds, as long as the tactics are not too outrageous, but it is more difficult to reach people. The marketer must determine the appropriate blend of these promotional mix elements to effectively market the firm's goods and services.

assessment check 4

4.1 Differentiate between personal and non-personal selling.

4.2 What are the six major categories of non-personal selling?

SPONSORSHIPS

One of the most significant trends in promotion offers marketers the ability to integrate several elements of the promotional mix. Commercial sponsorships of an event or activity apply personal selling, advertising, sales promotion, and public relations in achieving specific promotional goals. These sponsorships, which link events with sponsors and with media ranging from TV and radio to print and the Internet, have become a $28-billion worldwide business. Sponsorship spending is growing more rapidly than spending for both advertising and sales promotion.[18]

Sponsorship occurs when an organization provides money or in-kind resources to an event or activity in exchange for a direct association with that event or activity. The sponsor purchases two things: (1) access to the activity's audience and (2) the image associated with the activity. Sponsorships typically involve advertising, direct mail and sales promotion, publicity in the form of media coverage of the event, and personal selling at the event itself. They also involve relationship marketing, bringing together the event, its participants, the sponsoring firms, and their channel members and major customers. Marketers underwrite varying levels of sponsorships, depending on the amount their companies wish to spend and the types of events.

Commercial sponsorship is not a new phenomenon. Aristocrats in ancient Rome sponsored gladiator competitions and chariot races featuring teams that were often supported financially by competing businesses. More than 2000 years ago, wealthy Athenians underwrote drama, musical, and sporting festivals. Craft guilds in 14th-century England sponsored plays (occasionally insisting that the playwrights insert "plugs" for their lines of work in the scripts).

Today's sponsorships, although they include both commercial and not-for-profit events, are most prevalent in sports—the Olympics, the Tour de France bicycle race, and thousands of smaller events as well. Local firms may sponsor soccer, hockey, and baseball teams, while giants such as the beer companies sponsor events such as the NASCAR racing series.[19] Firms try to associate themselves with sporting events that match the image of their brand. Avon, whose products mostly focus on women, sponsors the annual Avon Walk for Breast Cancer, whose proceeds go to research, treatment, and care.[20] Tim Hortons is a major sponsor of activities from their children's summer camps to Tim Bits Hockey. It includes national sports teams—the National Hockey League, the Canadian Football League, Canadian Curling Association, and the Canadian Cycling Association—in its sponsorship activities.[21]

Companies may also sponsor concerts or art exhibits, reading and child-care programs, programs that support small businesses and create new jobs, and humanitarian programs such as the Make-a-Wish Foundation and Habitat for Humanity.

(5) Describe the role of sponsorships and direct marketing in integrated marketing communications.

sponsorship
Relationship in which an organization provides funds or in-kind resources to an event or activity in exchange for a direct association with that event or activity.

WALK US THROUGH THIS

Help us retire the red ribbon.

SANTA MARGHERITA is proud to support the **National AIDS Walk For Life.**

From Aug. 19 - Sept. 15

50¢ from the sale of **Santa Margherita Pinot Grigio** will go to support the **National AIDS Walk For Life.**

Available in

VINTAGES
FINE WINE & PREMIUM SPIRITS

REPRESENTED BY SAVERIO SCHIRALLI AGENCIES LIMITED

Join the **National AIDS Walk for Life**

September 16-23 in over 50 locations across Canada, or to make a personal donation, contact www.aidswalkforlife.ca / www.marcheactionSIDA.ca

PUBLIC IMAGE DESIGN

Winery Santa Margherita sponsors the AIDS Walk for Life event.

HOW SPONSORSHIP DIFFERS FROM ADVERTISING

Even though sponsorship spending and traditional advertising spending represent forms of non-personal selling, they are different in many ways. These differences include potential cost effectiveness, the sponsor's degree of control versus that of advertising, the nature of the message, and audience reaction.

Escalating costs of traditional advertising media have made commercial sponsorships a cost-effective alternative. Except for the really large events—which often have multiple sponsors—most are less expensive than an advertising campaign that relies on television, print, and other advertising. In addition, sponsors often gain the benefit of media coverage anyway, as the events they are associated with are covered by the news. And in the case of naming rights of such venues as sports arenas, the name serves as a perpetual advertisement. Examples include the Air Canada Centre in Toronto, the Scotiabank Place in Ottawa, and the Bell Centre in Montreal.

Marketers have considerable control over the quantity and quality of market coverage when they advertise. Sponsors have little control of sponsored events beyond matching the audiences to profiles of their own target markets. Instead, event organizers control the coverage, which typically focuses on the event—not the sponsor. By contrast, a traditional advertisement allows the marketer to create an individual message containing an introduction, a theme, and a conclusion.

Audiences react differently to sponsorship as a communications medium than to other media. The sponsor's investment provides a recognizable benefit to the sponsored activity that the audience can appreciate. As a result, sponsorship is often viewed more positively than traditional advertising. Some marketers have tried to take advantage of this fact by practising **ambush marketing,** in which a firm that is not an official sponsor tries to link itself to a major international event, such as the Olympics or a concert tour by a musical group. While it might be tempting to assume that smaller firms with limited marketing budgets would be most likely to engage in ambush marketing, this is not always the case. A recent Lufthansa advertisement featured soccer players, airplanes, and a soccer ball along with the airline's logo. But Emirates airline—not Lufthansa—was an official airline sponsor of the FIFA World Cup soccer tournament.[22] While creating a vague advertisement is not illegal, some ambush practices clearly are. If a non-sponsor used the Olympic rings in an advertisement, the ad would be an illegal use of a trademark.

To assess the results of sponsorships, marketers use some of the same techniques by which they measure advertising effectiveness. However, the differences between the two promotional alternatives often necessitate some unique research techniques as well. A few corporate sponsors attempt to link expenditures to sales. Other sponsors measure improved brand awareness and image as effectiveness indicators; they conduct traditional surveys before and after the events to secure this information. Still other sponsors measure the impact of their event marketing in public relations terms.

Marketoid

Advertising revenues from government sources rose by 1.8 percent in 2005, standing at 8.3 percent of the country's total.

DIRECT MARKETING

Few promotional mix elements are growing as fast as direct marketing. In fact, a study by the Institute of Communication Agencies and Canada Post shows that direct marketing now accounts for roughly 17 percent of advertising budgets.[23] Both business-to-consumer and business-to-business marketers rely on this promotional mix element to generate orders or sales leads (requests for more information) that may result in future orders. Direct marketing also helps increase store traffic—visits to the store or office to evaluate and perhaps purchase the advertised goods or services.

Direct marketing opens new international markets of unprecedented size. Electronic marketing channels have become the focus of direct marketers, and Web marketing is international marketing. Consumers in Europe and Japan are proving to be responsive to direct marketing. But most global marketing systems remain undeveloped, and many are almost dormant.

Direct marketing communications pursue goals beyond creating product awareness. Marketers want direct marketing to persuade people to place an order, request more information, visit a store, call a toll-free number, or respond to an e-mail message. In other words, successful direct marketing should prompt consumers to take action. Since direct marketing is interactive, marketers can tailor individual responses to meet consumers' needs. They can also measure the effectiveness of their efforts more easily than with advertising and other forms of promotion. Direct marketing is a very powerful tool that helps organizations win new customers and enhance relationships with existing ones.

The growth of direct marketing parallels the move toward integrated marketing communications in many ways. Both respond to fragmented media markets and audiences, growth in customized products, shrinking network broadcast audiences, and the increasing use of databases to target specific markets. Lifestyles also play a role because today's busy consumers want convenience and shopping options that save them time.

Databases are an important part of direct marketing. Using the latest technology to create sophisticated databases, a company can select a narrow market segment and find good prospects within that segment based on desired characteristics. Marketers can cut costs and improve returns on dollars spent by identifying customers who are most likely to respond to messages and by eliminating others from their lists who are not likely to respond. In fact, mining information about customers is a trend boosted by the growth of e-commerce.

DIRECT MARKETING COMMUNICATIONS CHANNELS

Direct marketing uses many different media forms: direct mailing, such as brochures and catalogues; telecommunications initiated by companies or customers; television and radio through special offers, infomercials, or shopping channels; the Internet via e-mail and electronic messaging; print media such as newspapers and magazines; and specialized channels such as electronic kiosks. Each works best for certain purposes, although marketers often combine two or more media in one direct marketing program. As long as it complies with current "do not call" regulations, a company might start with telemarketing to screen potential customers and then follow up by sending more material by direct mail to those who are interested.

DIRECT MAIL

As the amount of information about consumer lifestyles, buying habits, and wants continues to mount, direct mail has become a viable channel for identifying a firm's best prospects. Marketers gather information from internal and external databases, surveys, personalized coupons, and rebates that require responses. **Direct mail** is a critical tool in creating effective direct-marketing campaigns. It comes in many forms, ranging from sales letters, postcards, brochures, booklets, catalogues, and *house organs* (periodicals issued by organizations), to DVDs, videotapes, and audiocassettes.

Direct mail offers advantages such as the ability to select a narrow target market, achieve intensive coverage, send messages quickly, choose from various formats, provide complete information, and personalize each mailing piece. Response rates are measurable and higher than other types of advertising. In addition, direct mailings stand alone and do not compete for attention with magazine ads or radio and TV commercials. On the other hand, the per-reader cost of direct mail is high, effectiveness depends on the quality of the mailing list, and some consumers object strongly to what they consider junk mail.

One organization that has been very successful with its direct mail program is Tourism BC with its BC Escapes program. Tourism BC's primary objective was to get people interested in British Columbia as a vacation destination. By including on the direct piece a list of questions, such as timing of the visit and whether it was a single, couple, or young family travelling, it was able to achieve some added advantages. It could customize the vacation information sent out, such as including activities for children if it was a young family replying. Tourism BC also saw its response rate increase to roughly 23 percent of those receiving the original direct mail piece and an increase in the number who requested future direct mail material.[24]

CATALOGUES

Catalogues have been part of the Canadian marketing scene since as long ago as 1884, when Timothy Eaton used them to reach customers who could not shop at his Yonge Street store in Toronto. For many families, particularly those living in rural areas, the Eaton's catalogue was their only means of obtaining everything from dry goods to hardware. These early catalogues are even being reproduced today as memorabilia. Catalogues from stores such as Eaton's (until they closed), Sears, and Canadian Tire have been around so long that they have become a tradition in many households. References to children thumbing through the Sears Wish Book trying to decide what toys they wanted for Christmas or choosing their first bike from the Canadian Tire catalogue have been referred to as being as Canadian as references to the Mounties or maple syrup.[25]

From a customer's point of view, the advantages of catalogue shopping include convenience, time saving, availability, amount of information, special interest, and less sales pressure. Catalogue shopping can be done at any time without relying on store hours or needing to consider the time it takes to drive to the malls, parking, or dealing with crowds.

From a company's point of view, the advantages of catalogue selling include the ability to target niche markets and being able to display a large number of products. Companies may experience lower overheads, lower costs per sale, and better inventory control. However, catalogues are expensive and time-consuming to produce.

TELEMARKETING

Although its use has been limited by recently enacted legislation, telemarketing remains a frequently used form of direct marketing.[26] It provides marketers with a high return on their expenditures, an immediate response, and the opportunity for personalized two-way conversations. In addition to business-to-consumer direct marketing, business-to-business telemarketing is another form of direct customer contact.

Telemarketing refers to direct marketing conducted entirely by telephone, and it can be classified as either outbound or inbound contacts. Outbound telemarketing involves a sales force that uses only the telephone to contact customers, reducing the cost of making personal visits. The customer initiates inbound telemarketing, typically by dialling a toll-free number that firms provide for customers to use at their convenience to obtain information and/or make purchases.

New predictive dialler devices improve telemarketing's efficiency and reduce costs by automating the dialling process to skip busy signals and answering machines. When the dialler reaches a human voice, it instantaneously puts the call through to a salesperson. This technology is often combined with a print advertising campaign that features a toll-free number for inbound telemarketing.

Because recipients of both consumer and business-to-business telemarketing calls often find them annoying, the federal government has passed legislation relating to telemarketing activities. The legislation is administered by Bell Canada. The Canadian Marketing Association provides a Do Not Contact Service and it will continue to provide the service for unwanted mail. Not all unwanted calls will be stopped by this legislation; survey research firms, registered charities, political parties, and companies

Marketoid

Advertising revenue from foreign sources increased 6.2 percent in 2005, accounting for 9.2 percent of all revenue.

that already have a relationship with the consumer will be exempt from these new rules. Companies conducting telemarketing activities will be required to update their call list every 30 days and those not complying could face fines of between $1500 and $15 000.[27]

DIRECT MARKETING VIA BROADCAST CHANNELS

Broadcast direct marketing can take three basic forms: brief direct-response ads on television or radio, home shopping channels, and infomercials. Direct-response spots typically run 30, 60, or 90 seconds and include product descriptions and toll-free telephone numbers for ordering. Often shown on cable television and independent stations and tied to special-interest programs, broadcast direct marketing usually encourages viewers to respond immediately by offering them a special price or a gift if they call within a few minutes of an ad's airing. Radio direct-response ads also provide product descriptions and addresses or phone numbers to contact the sellers. However, radio often proves expensive compared with other direct marketing media, and listeners may not pay close enough attention to catch the number or may not be able to write it down because they are driving a car, which accounts for a major portion of radio listening time.

Home shopping channels such as Shop TV Canada and The Shopping Channel represent another type of television direct marketing. Broadcasting around the clock, these channels offer consumers a variety of products, including jewellery, clothing, skin care, home furnishings, computers, cameras, kitchen appliances, and toys. In essence, home shopping channels function like on-air catalogues. The channels also have websites that consumers can browse through to make purchases. In both cases, customers place orders via toll-free telephone numbers and pay for their purchases by credit card.

Infomercials are 30-minute or longer product commercials that resemble regular television programs. Because of their length, infomercials do not get lost as easily as 30-second commercials can, and they permit marketers to present their products in more detail. But they are usually shown at odd hours, and people often watch only portions of them. Think of how many times you have channel-surfed past an infomercial for Bow-flex, Proactiv skin care, or Ronco's rotisserie. Infomercials provide toll-free telephone numbers so that viewers can order products or request more information. Although infomercials incur higher production costs than prime-time 30-second ads on national network TV, they generally air on less expensive cable channels and in late-night time slots on broadcast stations.

ELECTRONIC DIRECT MARKETING CHANNELS

Anyone who has ever visited the Web is abundantly aware of the growing number of commercial advertisements that now clutter their computer screen. Web advertising is a recurring theme throughout this text, corresponding to its importance as a component of the promotional mix. By 2008, Canadian companies will be spending $800 million on Web advertising, a 20 percent increase in three years. Worldwide Internet advertising is expected to account for 7 percent of all advertising by 2008.[28]

Web advertising, however, is only one component of electronic direct marketing. E-mail direct marketers have found that traditional practices used in print and broadcast media are easily adapted to electronic messaging. You may be receiving periodic e-mail notices from retailers from whom you've made past purchases, telling you about new products or special offers. Anti-virus program makers routinely provide new downloads with the latest protection via the Web and notify you by e-mail. Experts agree that the basic rules for online direct marketing mirror those of traditional practices. Any successful offline direct marketing campaign can be applied to e-mail promotions. Electronic media deliver data instantly to direct marketers and help them track customer buying cycles quickly. As a result, they can place customer acquisition programs online for less than the cost of traditional programs.

OTHER DIRECT MARKETING CHANNELS

Print media such as newspapers and magazines do not support direct marketing as effectively as do Web marketing and telemarketing. However, print media and other traditional direct marketing channels are still critical to the success of all electronic media channels. Magazine ads with toll-free

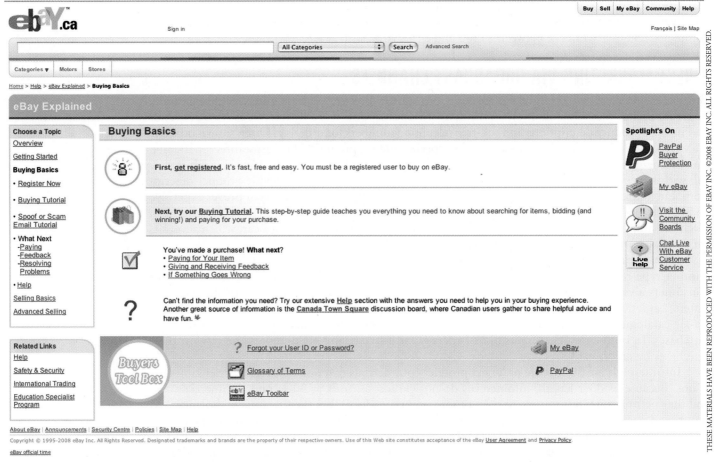

eBay was founded in September 1995. Today, the eBay community includes more than 100 million registered members worldwide. It is the most popular shopping destination on the Internet.

assessment check 5

5.1 Define sponsorship.

5.2 How is sponsorship different from advertising?

5.3 Define direct mail.

5.4 What are the benefits of electronic direct marketing?

telephone numbers enhance inbound telemarketing campaigns. Companies can place ads in magazines or newspapers, include reader-response cards, or place special inserts targeted for certain market segments within the publications. Newspapers are becoming savvy about the Internet, producing online versions of their content—which naturally include online, interactive ads.[29]

Kiosks provide another outlet for electronic sales. Kiosks are used by a wide variety of organizations, including B.C. Olympic Games, Rogers Sportsnet, and Motorola. The kiosks are being used for everything from taking a virtual visit to British Columbia to allowing college students to participate in sports pools from their campus or the local hockey rink. Motorola Inc. teamed up with Eastman Kodak Co. to ensure their new camera phones will work with Kodak service kiosks.[30]

⑥ Discuss the factors that influence the effectiveness of a promotional mix.

DEVELOPING AN OPTIMAL PROMOTIONAL MIX

By blending advertising, personal selling, sales promotion, and public relations to achieve marketing objectives, marketers create a promotional mix. Since quantitative measures are not available to determine the effectiveness of each mix component in a given market segment, the choice of an effective mix of promotional elements presents one of the marketer's most difficult tasks. Several factors influence the effectiveness of a promotional mix: (1) the nature of the market, (2) the nature of the product, (3) the stage in the product life cycle, (4) the price, and (5) the funds available for promotion.

NATURE OF THE MARKET

The marketer's target audience has a major impact on the choice of a promotion method. When a market includes a limited number of buyers, personal selling may prove a highly effective technique. However, markets characterized by large numbers of potential customers scattered over sizable geographic areas may make the cost of contact by personal salespeople prohibitive. In such instances, extensive use of advertising often makes sense. The type of customer also affects the promotional mix. Personal selling works better in a target market made up of industrial purchasers or retail and wholesale buyers than in a target market consisting of ultimate consumers. Similarly, pharmaceutical firms use large sales forces to sell prescription drugs directly to physicians and hospitals, but they also advertise to promote over-the-counter medications for the consumer market. So the drug firm must switch its promotional strategy from personal selling to consumer advertising based on the market it is targeting.

The car manufacturers have responded to changes in the market. With increasing gas prices and the focus on more environmentally friendly products, most car companies have recently introduced new technology along with new vehicles. Even the Hummer, the vehicle that no one could accuse of being environmentally friendly, is going green with a new engine that can run on gas or ethanol. Car manufacturers are now talking sustainability through biofuels, clean diesel, and plug-in hybrids rather than horsepower. New technology alone is not the only change that consumers see in this market. New smaller models are also showing up in cars such as Ford's Verve and Chevrolet's Volt.[31]

NATURE OF THE PRODUCT

A second important factor in determining an effective promotional mix is the product itself. Highly standardized products with minimal servicing requirements usually depend less on personal selling than do custom products with technically complex features or requirements for frequent maintenance. Marketers of consumer products are more likely to rely heavily on advertising than are business products. For example, soft drinks lend themselves more readily to advertising than do large pieces of business machinery.

Promotional mixes vary within each product category. In the B2B market, for example, installations typically rely more heavily on personal selling than does marketing of operating supplies. In contrast, the promotional mix for a convenience product is likely to involve more emphasis on manufacturer advertising and less on personal selling. However, personal selling plays an important role in the promotion of shopping products, and both personal and non-personal selling are important in the promotion of specialty items. A personal-selling emphasis is also likely to prove more effective than other alternatives in promotions for products involving trade-ins.

Promotion focusing on the nature of the product.

Inspiration is everywhere.

THE SCOTTIES® DESIGN CHALLENGE

Create the next Scotties box design for a chance to win* a $25,000 room makeover by celebrity designer Kimberley Seldon, and have your winning design produced.

Visit scotties.ca for details.

Scotties
Nice touch.

COURTESY KRUGER PRODUCTS

Scotties: Promoting a mature product.

STAGE IN THE PRODUCT LIFE CYCLE

The promotional mix must also be tailored to the product's stage in the product life cycle. In the introductory stage, both non-personal and personal selling are used to acquaint marketing intermediaries and final consumers with the merits of the new product. Heavy emphasis on personal selling helps inform the marketplace of the merits of the new good or service. Salespeople contact marketing intermediaries to secure interest in and commitment to handling the newly introduced item. Trade shows are frequently used to inform and educate prospective dealers and ultimate consumers about its merits over current competitive offerings. Advertising and sales promotion are also used during this stage to create awareness, answer questions, and stimulate initial purchases.

As the product moves into the growth and maturity stages, advertising gains relative importance in persuading consumers to make purchases. Marketers continue to direct personal-selling efforts at marketing intermediaries in an attempt to expand distribution. As more competitors enter the marketplace, advertising begins to stress product differences to persuade consumers to purchase the firm's brand. In the maturity and early decline stages, firms frequently reduce advertising and sales promotion expenditures as market saturation is reached and newer products with their own competitive strengths begin to enter the market. However, some firms use marketing to

marketing success   Beer Grows Up

Background. Beer advertisements used to feature kegs or parties. Beer was considered the lower-end beverage, hardly in the same class with fine wine, gourmet food, or affluent consumers.

The Challenge. As the consumer population ages, and as micro-breweries develop a loyal following, the larger brewers—such as Molson Coors, Anheuser-Busch, and Labatts—are faced with the challenge of coming up with new products and new marketing efforts to attract older, more affluent consumers.

The Strategy. Anheuser-Busch has launched a whole new campaign emphasizing the finer aspects of beer, including the art of brewing and blending flavours, as well as its suitability at more formal gatherings or with upscale foods. Molson Coors, in an attempt to keep its traditional markets, such as hockey fans, designed a new interactive website incorporating never-before-seen television-type ads into live hockey Web feeds. Molson and Labatt have both purchased smaller breweries. Molson purchased the premium brewery Creemore. Labatt

purchased the discount brewery Lakeport, famous for the dollar-a-beer pricing strategy. Labatt used a marketing campaign, "Refuse to be Labelled," in which promotional material showed all the different shapes the company's bottles have taken over the years.

The Outcome. Some industry watchers worry that Budweiser and Labatt may lose its base of fans, but others see the effort to change the image of beer as a necessity. Molson Coors, on the other hands, sees its interactive website as a success when it became the number one beer site in Canada with 200 000 visitors and over 812 000 full video views.

Sources: Clarke Canfield, "Craft Beer Industry Enjoys Resurgence," *Sacramento Bee*, March 27, 2006, http://www.sacbee.com; "Tastes Great, Less Filling, and Perfect with Cheese: Beer Tries to Brew Up a New Image," *Knowledge*, January 25, 2006, http://knowledge.wharton.upenn.edu; Parija Bhatnagar, "What, No Keg? Beer Gets a Makeover," *CNN Money.com, January 20, 2006,* http://money.cnn.com; "Lakeport Deal Could Change Canadian Beer Market," *Marketing*, February 2, 2007; "Media Innovation Awards," *Marketing*, November 26, 2007; Ryan Bigge, "One Beer, Two Solitudes," *Marketing*, May 5, 2003, p. 12.

breathe new life into mature products to attract new customers and keep existing ones (see the "Marketing Success" feature).

PRICE

The price of an item is the fourth factor that affects the choice of a promotional mix. Advertising dominates the promotional mixes for low-unit-value products due to the high per-contact costs in personal selling. These costs make the sales call an unprofitable tool in promoting most lower-value goods and services. Advertising, in contrast, permits a low promotional expenditure per sales unit because it reaches mass audiences. For low-value consumer goods, such as chewing gum, soft drinks, and snack foods, advertising is the most feasible means of promotion. Even shopping products can be sold at least partly on the basis of price. On the other hand, consumers of high-priced items such as luxury cars expect lots of well-presented information from qualified salespeople. High-tech direct marketing promotions such as video presentations on a notebook computer or via cell phone, fancy brochures, and personal selling by informed, professional salespeople appeal to these potential customers.

FUNDS AVAILABLE FOR PROMOTION

A real barrier in implementing any promotional strategy is the size of the promotional budget. A single 30-second television commercial during the Super Bowl telecast costs an advertiser $2.5 million. While millions of viewers may see the commercial, making the cost per contact relatively low, such an expenditure exceeds the entire promotional budgets of thousands of firms, a dilemma that at least partially explains how guerrilla marketing got its start. And if a company wants to hire a celebrity to advertise its goods and services, the fee can run into the millions of dollars a year. Table 14.3 summarizes the factors that influence the determination of an appropriate promotional mix.

assessment check 6

6.1 What are the five factors that affect the choice of a promotional mix?

6.2 Why is the choice of a mix a difficult task for marketers?

---

table 14.3   *Factors Influencing Choice of Promotional Mix*

	EMPHASIS	
	PERSONAL SELLING	**ADVERTISING**
Nature of the market		
Number of buyers	Limited number	Large number
Geographic concentration	Concentrated	Dispersed
Type of customer	Business purchaser	Ultimate consumer
Nature of the product		
Complexity	Custom-made, complex	Standardized
Service requirements	Considerable	Minimal
Type of good or service	Business	Consumer
Use of trade-ins	Trade-ins common	Trade-ins uncommon
Stage in the product life cycle	Often emphasized at every stage; heavy emphasis in the introductory and early growth stages in acquainting marketing intermediaries and potential consumers with the new good or service	Often emphasized at every stage; heavy emphasis in the latter part of the growth stage, as well as the maturity and early decline stages, to persuade consumers to select specific brands
Price	High unit value	Low unit value

⑦ **Contrast pushing and pulling strategies.**

pulling strategy
Promotional effort by the seller to stimulate final-user demand, which then exerts pressure on the distribution channel.

pushing strategy
Promotional effort by the seller directed to members of the marketing channel rather than final users.

PULLING AND PUSHING PROMOTIONAL STRATEGIES

Marketers may implement essentially two promotional alternatives: a pulling strategy or a pushing strategy. A **pulling strategy** is a promotional effort by the seller to stimulate final-user demand, which then exerts pressure on the distribution channel. When marketing intermediaries stock a large number of competing products and exhibit little interest in any one of them, a firm may have to implement a pulling strategy to motivate them to handle its product. In such instances, this strategy is implemented with the objective of building consumer demand so that consumers will request the product from retail stores. Advertising and sales promotion often contribute to a company's pulling strategy.

In contrast, a **pushing strategy** relies more heavily on personal selling. Here the objective is promoting the product to the members of the marketing channel rather than to final users. To achieve this goal, marketers employ cooperative advertising allowances to channel members, trade discounts, personal selling efforts by salespeople, and other dealer supports. Such a strategy is designed to gain marketing success for the firm's products by motivating representatives of wholesalers and/or retailers to spend extra time and effort promoting the products to customers. About half of manufacturers' promotional budgets are allocated for cash incentives used to encourage retailers to stock their products.

Timing also affects the choice of promotional strategies. The relative importance of advertising and selling changes during the various phases of the purchase process. Prior to the actual sale, advertising usually is more important than personal selling. However, one of the primary advantages of a successful advertising program is the support it gives the salesperson who approaches the prospective buyer for the first time. Selling activities are more important than advertising at the time of purchase. Personal selling provides the actual mechanism for closing most sales. In the post-purchase period, advertising regains primacy in the promotional effort. It affirms the customer's decision to buy a particular good or service and reminds him or her of the product's favourable qualities by reducing any cognitive dissonance that might occur.

The promotional strategies used by auto marketers illustrate this timing factor. Car, truck, and SUV makers spend heavily on consumer advertising to create awareness before consumers begin the purchase process. At the time of their purchase decisions, however, the personal-selling skills of dealer salespeople provide the most important tools for closing sales. Finally, advertising is used frequently to maintain post-purchase satisfaction by citing awards such as *Motor Trend*'s Car of the Year and results of J. D. Power's customer-satisfaction surveys to affirm buyer decisions.

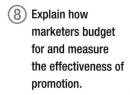

assessment check 7

7.1 What is a pulling strategy?

7.2 What is a pushing strategy?

⑧ **Explain how marketers budget for and measure the effectiveness of promotion.**

BUDGETING FOR PROMOTIONAL STRATEGY

Promotional budgets may differ not only in amount but also in composition. Business-to-business marketers generally invest larger proportions of their budgets in personal selling than in advertising, while the reverse is usually true of most producers of consumer goods. Research shows that more advertising dollars go to television advertising than other media, closely followed by newspaper and then magazines, radio, Internet, and outdoor with a much lesser amount going to cinema.[32] Global media spending figures are shown in Table 14.4.

Evidence suggests that sales initially lag behind promotional expenses for structural reasons—funds spent filling up retail shelves, boosting low initial production, and supplying buyer information. This fact produces a threshold effect in which few sales may result from substantial initial investments in promotion. A second phase might produce sales proportionate to promotional expenditures—the most predictable range. Finally, promotion reaches the area of diminishing returns where an increase in promotional spending fails to produce a corresponding increase in sales.

For example, an initial expenditure of $40 000 may result in sales of 100 000 units for a consumer goods manufacturer. An additional $10 000 expenditure during the second phase may generate sales of 30 000 more units, and another $10 000 may produce sales of an additional 35 000 units.

The cumulative effect of the expenditures and repeat sales will have generated increasing returns from the promotional outlays. However, as the advertising budget moves from $60 000 to $70 000, the marginal productivity of the additional expenditure may fall to 28 000 units. At some later point, the return may actually become zero or negative as competition intensifies, markets become saturated, and marketers employ less expensive advertising media.

The ideal method of allocating promotional funds would increase the budget until the cost of each additional increment equals the additional incremental revenue received. In other words, the most effective allocation procedure increases promotional expenditures until each dollar of promotional expense is matched by an additional dollar of profit. This procedure—referred to as marginal analysis—maximizes the input's productivity. The difficulty arises in identifying the optimal point, which requires a precise balance between marginal expenses for promotion and the resulting marginal receipts. In addition, as marketing communications become more integrated, it becomes harder to identify exact amounts that companies spend on individual elements of promotion.[33]

Traditional methods used for creating a promotional budget include the percentage-of-sales and fixed-sum-per-unit methods, along with techniques for meeting the competition and achieving task objectives. Each method is briefly examined in Table 14.5.

The **percentage-of-sales method** is perhaps the most common way of establishing promotional budgets. The percentage can be based on sales either from some past period (such as the previous year) or forecasted for a future period (the current year). While this plan is appealingly simple, it does not effectively support the achievement of basic promotional objectives. Arbitrary percentage allocations can't provide needed flexibility. In addition, sales should depend on promotional allocation rather than vice versa.

The **fixed-sum-per-unit method** differs from budgeting based on a percentage of sales in only one respect: it allocates a predetermined amount to each sales or production unit. This amount can also reflect either historical or forecasted figures. Producers of high-value consumer durable goods, such as automobiles, often use this budgeting method.

Another traditional budgeting approach, **meeting competition,** simply matches competitors' outlays, either in absolute amounts or relative to the firms' market shares. But this method doesn't help a company gain a competitive edge. A budget that is appropriate for one company may not be appropriate for another.

table 14.4 *Global Media Expenditure 2007 by Medium*

	$ (U.S. MILLION)	%
Newspaper	124 047	27.8
Magazines	54 393	12.2
Television	168 359	37.7
Radio	36 472	8.2
Cinema	1984	0.4
Outdoor	25 126	5.6
Internet	35 999	8.1

Source: ZenithOptimedia website, http://www.zenithoptimedia.com, accessed February 15, 2008.

table 14.5 *Promotional Budget Determination*

METHOD	DESCRIPTION	EXAMPLE
Percentage-of-sales method	Promotional budget is set as a specified percentage of either past or forecasted sales.	"Last year we spent $10 500 on promotion and had sales of $420 000. Next year we expect sales to grow to $480 000, and we are allocating $12 000 for promotion."
Fixed-sum-per-unit method	Promotional budget is set as a predetermined dollar amount for each unit sold or produced.	"Our forecast calls for sales of 14 000 units, and we allocate promotion at the rate of $65 per unit."
Meeting competition method	Promotional budget is set to match competitor's promotional outlays on either an absolute or relative basis.	"Promotional outlays average 4 percent of sales in our industry."
Task-objective method	Once marketers determine their specific promotional objectives, the amount (and type) of promotional spending needed to achieve them is determined.	"By the end of next year, we want 75 percent of the area high school students to be aware of our new, highly automated fast-food prototype outlet. How many promotional dollars will it take, and how should they be spent?"

The **task-objective method** develops a promotional budget based on a sound evaluation of the firm's promotional objectives. The method has two steps:

1. The firm's marketers must define realistic communication goals that they want the promotional mix to achieve. Say that a firm wants to achieve a 25 percent increase in brand awareness. This step quantifies the objectives that promotion should attain. These objectives in turn become integral parts of the promotional plan.

2. Then the company's marketers determine the amount and type of promotional activity required for each objective that they have set. Combined, these units become the firm's promotional budget.

A crucial assumption underlies the task-objective approach: marketers can measure the productivity of each promotional dollar. That assumption explains why the objectives must be carefully chosen, quantified, and accomplished through promotional efforts. Budgeters should usually avoid general marketing objectives such as "We want to achieve a 5 percent increase in sales." A sale is a culmination of the effects of all elements of the marketing mix. A more appropriate promotional objective might be "We want to achieve an 8 percent response rate from a targeted direct mail advertisement."

Promotional budgeting always requires difficult decisions. Still, recent research studies and the spread of computer-based models have made it a more manageable problem than it used to be.

MEASURING THE EFFECTIVENESS OF PROMOTION

It is widely recognized that part of a firm's promotional effort is ineffective. John Wanamaker, a leading 19th-century retailer, expressed the problem this way: "Half the money I spend on advertising is wasted; the trouble is I don't know which half."

Evaluating the effectiveness of a promotion today is a far different exercise in marketing research than it was even a few decades ago. For years, marketers depended on store audits conducted by large organizations like Nielsen. Other research groups conducted warehouse withdrawal surveys of shipments to retail customers. These studies were designed to determine whether sales had risen as a direct result of a particular promotional campaign. During the 1980s, the introduction of scanners and automated checkout lanes completely changed marketing research. For the first time, retailers and manufacturers had a tool to obtain sales data quickly and efficiently. The problem was that the collected data were used for little else other than determining how much of which product was bought at what price and at what time.

By the 1990s, marketing research entered another evolutionary period with the advent of the Internet. Now marketing researchers can delve into each customer's purchase behaviour, lifestyle, preferences, opinions, and buying habits. All this information can also be obtained in a matter of seconds. The next section explains the impact of electronic technologies on measuring promotional effectiveness. However, marketers today still depend on two basic measurement tools: direct sales results tests and indirect evaluations.

Most marketers would prefer to use a **direct sales results test** to measure the effectiveness of promotion. Such an approach would reveal the specific impact on sales revenues for each dollar of promotional spending. This type of technique has always eluded marketers, however, due to their inability to control other variables operating in the marketplace. A firm may receive $20 million in additional sales orders following a new $1.5-million advertising campaign, but the market success may really have resulted from the products benefiting from more intensive distribution as more stores decide to carry them or price increases for competing products rather than from the advertising outlays.

Marketers often encounter difficulty isolating the effects of promotion from those of other market elements and outside environmental variables. **Indirect evaluation** helps researchers concentrate on quantifiable indicators of effectiveness, such as recall (how much members of the target market remember about specific products or advertisements) and readership (size and composition of a message's audience). The basic problem with indirect measurement is the difficulty in relating these variables to sales. Will the fact that many people read an ad lead directly to increased sales?

Marketers need to ask the right questions and understand what they are measuring. Promotion to build sales volume produces measurable results in the form of short-term returns, but brand-building programs and efforts to generate or enhance consumers' perceptions of value in a product, brand, or organization cannot be measured over the short term.

MEASURING ONLINE PROMOTIONS

The latest challenge facing marketers is how to measure the effectiveness of electronic media. Early attempts at measuring online promotional effectiveness involved counting hits (user requests for a file) and visits (pages downloaded or read in one session). But it takes more than counting "eyeballs" to measure online promotional success. What matters is not how many times a website is visited but how many people actually buy something. Traditional numbers that work for other media forms are not necessarily relevant indicators of effectiveness for a website. For one thing, the Web combines both advertising and direct marketing. Web pages effectively integrate advertising and other content, such as product information, that may often prove to be the page's main—and most effective—feature. For another consideration, consumers generally choose the advertisements they want to see on the Net, whereas traditional broadcast or print media automatically expose consumers to ads.

One way that marketers measure performance is by incorporating some form of direct response into their promotions. This technique also helps them to compare different promotions for effectiveness and rely on facts rather than opinions. Consumers may say they will try a product when responding to a survey question yet not actually buy it. A firm may send out three different direct mail offers in the same promotion and compare response rates from the groups of recipients receiving each alternative. An offer to send for a sample may generate a 75 percent response rate, coupons might show a 50 percent redemption rate, and rebates might appeal to only 10 percent of the targeted group.

The two major techniques for setting Internet advertising rates are cost per impression and cost per response (click-throughs). **Cost per impression** is a measurement technique that relates the cost of an ad to every thousand people who view it. In other words, anyone who sees the page containing the banner or other form of ad creates one impression. This measure assumes that the site's principal purpose is to display the advertising message. **Cost per response (click-throughs)** is a direct marketing technique that relates the cost of an ad to the number of people who click it. However, not everyone who clicks on an ad makes a purchase. So the **conversion rate** measurement was developed, which is the percentage of website visitors who actually make a purchase. All three rating techniques have merit. Site publishers point out that click-through rates are influenced by the creativity of the ad's message. Advertisers, on the other hand, point out that the Web ad has value to those who click it for additional information.

Marketoid

Global ad expenditure is expected to grow 6.7 percent in 2008.

assessment check 8

8.1 What is the most common way of establishing a promotional budget?

8.2 What is the task-objective budgeting method? Describe its two steps.

8.3 What is the direct sales results test?

8.4 What is indirect evaluation?

THE VALUE OF MARKETING COMMUNICATIONS

⑨ Discuss the value of marketing communications.

The nature of marketing communications is changing as new formats transform the traditional idea of an advertisement or sales promotion. Sales messages are now placed subtly, or not so subtly, in movies and television shows, blurring the lines between promotion and entertainment and changing the traditional definition of advertising. Messages show up at the beach in the form of skywriting, in restrooms, on stadium turnstiles, buses, and even police cars.

Despite new tactics by advertisers, promotion has often been the target of criticism. Some people complain that it offers nothing of value to society and simply wastes resources. Others criticize promotion's role in encouraging consumers to buy unnecessary products that they cannot afford. Many ads seem to insult people's intelligence or offend their sensibilities, and they criticize the ethics—or lack thereof—displayed by advertisers and salespeople.

New forms of promotion are considered even more insidious because marketers are designing promotions that bear little resemblance to paid advertisements. Many of these complaints cite issues that constitute real problems. Some salespeople use unethical sales tactics. Some product advertising hides its promotional nature or targets consumer groups that can least afford the advertised goods or services. Many television commercials contribute to the growing problem of cultural pollution. One area that has sparked both criticism and debate is promotion aimed at children.

While promotion can certainly be criticized on many counts, it also plays a crucial role in modern society. This point is best understood by examining the social, business, and economic importance of promotion.

SHARE A LITTLE MAGIC · SHARE A LITTLE MAGIC · SHARE A LITTLE MAGIC · SHARE A LITTLE MAGIC ·

Big Brothers Big Sisters

Share a little magic with a young person.
Volunteer to be a mentor today.

www.sharealittlemagic.ca

Promotional message addressing an important social concern: mentoring young people.

SOCIAL IMPORTANCE

We live in a diverse society characterized by consumer segments with differing needs, wants, and aspirations. What one group finds tasteless may be quite appealing to another. But diversity is one of the benefits of living in our society because it offers us many choices and opportunities. Promotional strategy faces an averaging problem that escapes many of its critics. The one generally accepted standard in a market society is freedom of choice for the consumer. Consumer buying decisions eventually determine acceptable practices in the marketplace, which is why consumers who criticize beer ads may also agree that it is acceptable for them to appear.

Promotion has also become an important factor in campaigns aimed at achieving social objectives. Advertising agencies often donate their time and expertise in creating **public service announcements (PSAs)** aimed at promoting such important causes as stopping drug abuse. Good examples of such messages are provided by the Big Brothers/Big Sisters Agencies and MADD. Big Brothers and Big Sisters organizations provide a wide variety of mentoring programs and their ads are designed to encourage individuals to volunteer to be a mentor. The MADD ads are designed to educate and inspire all people, especially teens, about the dangers of driving under the influence of alcohol or other drugs and how impaired driving can affect innocent people's lives. Ads like these reinforce how socially acceptable it is to contribute time to good causes (and in the case of MADD ads, how unacceptable it is to drink and drive.)[34]

Promotion performs an informative and educational task crucial to the functioning of modern society. As with everything else in life, what is important is how promotion is used rather than whether it is used.

BUSINESS IMPORTANCE

Promotional strategy has become increasingly important to both large and small business enterprises. The well-documented, long-term increase in funds spent on promotion certainly attests to management's faith in the ability of promotional efforts to encourage attitude changes, brand loyalty, and additional sales. It is difficult to conceive of an enterprise that would not attempt to promote its good or service in some manner. Most modern institutions simply cannot survive in the long run without promotion. Business must communicate with its publics.

Nonbusiness enterprises also recognize the importance of promotional efforts. The Canadian government is the leading advertiser in Canada, promoting many concepts and programs. The advertising budget for Ontario alone is said to be above $50 million a year for such programs as the Ontario Lottery and Gaming Corporation and the Liquor Control Board of Ontario.[35] Religious organizations have acknowledged the importance of promotional channels to make their viewpoints known to the public at large.

ECONOMIC IMPORTANCE

Promotion has assumed a degree of economic importance if for no other reason than because it provides employment for millions of people. More important, however, effective promotion has allowed society to derive benefits not otherwise available. For example, the criticism that promotion costs too much isolates an individual expense item and fails to consider its possible beneficial effects on other categories of expenditures.

Marketoid

Between 2007 and 2010, Internet "adspend" is expected to grow 69 percent.

Promotional strategies increase the number of units sold and permit economies of scale in the production process, thereby lowering the production costs for each unit of output. Lower unit costs allow lower consumer prices, which in turn make products available to more people. Similarly, researchers have found that advertising subsidizes the information contents of newspapers and the broadcast media. In short, promotion pays for many of the enjoyable entertainment and educational opportunities in contemporary life as it lowers product costs.

assessment check 9

9.1 Identify the three areas in which promotion exerts influence.

Strategic Implications

WITH the incredible proliferation of promotional messages in the media, today's marketers—who are also consumers themselves—must find new ways to reach customers without overloading them with unnecessary or unwanted communications. Guerrilla marketing has emerged as an effective strategy for large and small companies, but ambush marketing has raised ethical concerns. Product placement has gained in popularity, in movies, television shows, and video games.

In addition, it is difficult to overstate the impact of the Internet on the promotional mix for future marketers—small and large companies alike. Even individual entrepreneurs have found the Internet to be a lucrative launch pad for their enterprises. But even though cyberspace marketing has been effective in business-to-business transactions and, to a lesser extent, for some types of consumer purchases, a major source of Internet revenues is advertising.

Integrating marketing communications into an overall consumer-focused strategy that meets a company's promotional and business objectives has become more and more critical in the busy global marketplace. Chapter 15 will examine specific ways marketers can use advertising and public relations to convey their messages; then Chapter 16 will discuss personal selling, sales force management, and sales promotion in the same manner. ◆◆◆

REVIEW OF CHAPTER OBJECTIVES

① **Explain how integrated marketing communications relates to the development of an optimal promotional mix.**

Integrated marketing communications (IMC) refers to the coordination of all promotional activities to produce a unified, customer-focused promotional message. Developing an optimal promotional mix involves selecting the personal and non-personal selling strategies that will work best to deliver the overall marketing message as defined by IMC.

② **Describe the communication process and how it relates to the AIDA concept.**

In the communication process, a message is encoded and transmitted through a communications channel; then it is decoded, or interpreted by the receiver; finally, the receiver provides feedback, which completes the system. The AIDA concept (attention-interest-desire-action) explains the steps through which a person reaches a purchase decision after being exposed to a promotional message. The marketer sends the promotional message, and the consumer receives and responds to it via the communication process.

③ **Explain how the promotional mix relates to the objectives of promotion.**

The objectives of promotion are to provide information, stimulate demand, differentiate a product, accentuate the value of a product, and stabilize sales. The promotional mix, which is the blend of numerous variables intended to satisfy the target market, must fulfill the overall objectives of promotion.

④ **Identify the different elements of the promotional mix and explain how marketers develop an optimal promotional mix.**

The different elements of the promotional mix are personal selling and non-personal selling (advertising, product placement, sales promotion, direct marketing, and public relations). Guerrilla marketing is frequently used by marketers with limited funds and firms attempting to attract attention for new-product offerings with innovative promotional approaches. Marketers develop the optimal mix by considering the nature of the market, the nature of the product, the stage in the product life cycle, price, and funds available for promotion.

⑤ **Describe the role of sponsorships and direct marketing in integrated marketing communications.**

Sponsorship, which occurs when an organization provides money or in-kind resources to an event or activity in exchange for a direct association with the event or activity, has become a hot trend in promotion. The sponsor purchases access to an activity's audience and the image associated with the activity, both of which contribute to the overall promotional message being delivered by a firm. Direct marketing involves direct communication between a seller and a B2B or final customer. It includes such promotional methods as telemarketing, direct mail, direct-response advertising and infomercials on TV and radio, direct-response print advertising, and electronic media.

⑥ **Discuss the factors that influence the effectiveness of a promotional mix.**

Marketers face the challenge of determining the best mix of components for an overall promotional strategy. Several factors influence the effectiveness of the promotional mix: (1) the nature of the market; (2) the nature of the product: (3) the stage in the product life cycle; (4) price; and (5) the funds available for promotion.

⑦ **Contrast pushing and pulling strategies.**

In a pulling strategy, marketers attempt to stimulate final-user demand, which then exerts pressure on the distribution channel. In a pushing strategy, marketers attempt to promote the product to channel members rather than final users. To do this, they rely heavily on personal selling.

⑧ **Explain how marketers budget for and measure the effectiveness of promotion.**

Marketers may choose among several methods for determining promotional budgets, including percentage-of-sales, fixed-sum-per-unit, meeting competition, or task-objective, which is considered the most flexible and most effective. Today, marketers use either direct sales results tests or indirect evaluation to measure effectiveness. Both methods have their benefits and drawbacks because of the difficulty of controlling variables.

⑨ **Discuss the value of marketing communications.**

Despite a number of valid criticisms, marketing communications provide socially important messages, are important to businesses, and contain economic importance. As with every communication in society, it is important to consider how promotion is used rather than whether it is used at all.

 assessment check answers

1.1 Define *promotion*.
Promotion is the function of informing, persuading, and influencing the consumer's purchase decision.

1.2 What is the difference between marketing communications and integrated marketing communications (IMC)?
Marketing communications are messages that deal with buyer-seller relationships, from a variety of media. IMC coordinates all promotional activities to produce a unified, customer-focused promotional message.

2.1 What are the three tasks accomplished by an effective message?
An effective message gains the receiver's attention; it achieves understanding by both receiver and sender; and it stimulates the receiver's needs and suggests an appropriate method of satisfying them.

2.2 Identify the four steps of the AIDA concept.

The four steps of the AIDA concept are attention, interest, desire, and action.

2.3 What is noise?

Noise represents interference at some stage in the communication process.

3.1 What are the objectives of promotion?

The objectives of promotion are to provide information to consumers and others, to increase demand, to differentiate a product, to accentuate a product's value, and to stabilize sales.

3.2 Why is product differentiation important to marketers?

Product differentiation, distinguishing a good or service from its competitors, is important to marketers because they need to create a distinct image in consumers' minds. If they can do so, they can then exert more control over variables such as price.

4.1 Differentiate between personal selling and non-personal selling.

Personal selling involves a promotional presentation conducted on a person-to-person basis with a buyer. Non-personal selling involves communication with a buyer in any way other than on a person-to-person basis.

4.2 What are the six major categories of non-personal selling?

The six major categories of non-personal selling are advertising, product placement, sales promotion, direct marketing, public relations, and guerrilla marketing.

5.1 Define sponsorship.

Sponsorship occurs when an organization pays money or in-kind resources to an event or activity in exchange for a direct association with that event or activity.

5.2 How is sponsorship different from advertising?

Although sponsorship generates brand awareness, the sponsor has little control over the message or even the coverage, unlike advertising.

5.3 Define direct mail.

Direct mail is communications in the form of letters, postcards, brochures, and catalogues containing marketing messages and sent directly to a customer or potential customer.

5.4 What are the benefits of electronic direct marketing?

Electronic media deliver data instantly to direct marketers and help them track customer buying cycles quickly.

6.1 What are the five factors that affect the choice of a promotional mix?

The five factors affecting the choice of a promotional mix are the nature of the market, the nature of the product, the stage in the product life cycle, price, and the funds available for promotion.

6.2 Why is the choice of a mix a difficult task for marketers?

The choice of a mix is difficult because no quantitative measures are available to determine the effectiveness of each component in a given market segment.

7.1 What is a pulling strategy?

A pulling strategy is a promotional effort by the seller to stimulate final-user demand.

7.2 What is a pushing strategy?

A pushing strategy is an effort to promote a product to the members of the marketing channel.

8.1 What is the most common way of establishing a promotional budget?

The most common method of establishing a promotional budget is the percentage-of-sales method.

8.2 What is the task-objective budgeting method? Describe its two steps.

The task-objective method develops a promotional budget based on an evaluation of the firm's promotional objectives. Its two steps are defining realistic communication goals and determining the amount and type of promotional activity required for each objective set.

8.3 What is the direct sales results test?

The direct sales results test reveals the specific impact on sales revenues for each dollar of promotional spending.

8.4 What is indirect evaluation?

Indirect evaluation helps researchers concentrate on quantifiable indicators of effectiveness.

9.1 Identify the three areas in which promotion exerts influence.

The three areas in which promotion exerts influence are society, business, and the economy.

MARKETING TERMS YOU NEED TO KNOW

These terms are printed in red in the text. They are defined in the margins of the chapter and in the Glossary that begins on p. G-1. Other important terms are printed in bold black type in the chapter but not included in this list. Their definitions can be found in the Glossary.

marketing communications 464
integrated marketing communications
  (IMC) 464
AIDA concept 468

promotional mix 474
sales promotion 476
public relations 477
guerrilla marketing 477

sponsorship 479
pulling strategy 488
pushing strategy 488

1. What is the role of integrated marketing communications (IMC) in a firm's overall marketing strategy? When executed well, what are its benefits?
2. Describe the five stages of communication.
3. What is the difference between primary demand and selective demand?
4. Differentiate between advertising and product placement. Which do you think is more effective, and why?
5. What are the benefits and drawbacks of publicity?
6. Why is sponsorship such an important part of a firm's IMC?
7. For each of the following goods and services, indicate which direct marketing channel or channels you think would be best:
   a. vacation time share
   b. denim jacket
   c. custom-made bracelet
   d. lawn care service
   e. magazine subscription
8. How does the nature of the market for a firm's goods or services affect the choice of a promotion method?
9. What is the difference between a pushing strategy and a pulling strategy?
10. What are two major ways of setting Internet advertising rates, and how do they work?

PROJECTS AND TEAMWORK EXERCISES

1. On your own or with a friend, select a print advertisement that catches your attention and analyze it according to the AIDA concept (attention-interest-desire-action). Identify features of the ad that catch your attention, pique your interest, make you desire the product, and spur you toward a purchase. Present your findings to the class.
2. With a classmate, locate up to five print ads that illustrate each of the five objectives of promotion (an ad might fulfill more than one objective). Present the ads to the class, identifying the objectives fulfilled in each.
3. With a classmate, choose a good or service that you feel could benefit from guerrilla marketing. Imagine that you have a limited promotional budget and come up with a plan for a guerrilla approach. Outline several ideas and explain how you plan to carry them out. Present your plan to the class.
4. Evaluate two or three pieces of direct mail that you have received lately. Which items caught your attention and at least made you save the mailing? Which items did you toss in the trash without even opening or considering beyond an initial glance? Why?
5. Watch a television show and see how many products you can find placed within the show. Present your findings to the class.

CRITICAL THINKING EXERCISES

1. Choose one of the following products and discuss what you think the objective(s) of promotion should be for the product:
   a. beef
   b. Kraft Macaroni & Cheese
   c. Toyota Prius
   d. cell phone service
2. Identify a corporate sponsorship for a cause or program in your area, or find a local company that sponsors a local charity or other organization. What do you think the sponsor is gaining from its actions? (Be specific.) What does the sponsored organization receive? Do you think this sponsorship is good for your community? Explain.
3. What are some of the advantages and disadvantages of using a celebrity spokesperson to promote a good or service? How might this affect a firm's public relations efforts?
4. Take a careful look at a direct mail catalogue that you have received recently. Who is the audience for the products? Did the firm target you correctly or not? What is the response the firm is seeking?
5. Describe a public service announcement that you have seen recently. Do you believe that the announcement will help the organization achieve its goals? Why or why not?

ETHICS EXERCISE

Pop-up ads, those unsolicited messages that sometimes pop onto your computer screen and block the site or information you're looking for until you close or respond to them, are inexpensive to produce and cost nearly nothing to send. But they are so annoying to some computer users that dozens of special programs have been written to block them from appearing on the screen during Internet use.

1. Do you think that because they are unsolicited, pop-up ads are also intrusive? Are they an invasion of privacy? Explain your reasoning.
2. Do you consider the use of pop-up ads to be unethical? Why or why not?

INTERNET EXERCISES

1. **Integrated marketing communication.** Promotional mix, guerrilla marketing, and sponsorships are all aspects of integrated marketing communication. Review the appropriate chapter material and then complete the following exercises.
   a. Visit two prominent shopping websites, including one that has brick-and-mortar stores in addition to its online store. Write a brief report comparing and contrasting the promotional mix used by each retailer.
   b. Guerrilla Marketing International (http://www.gmarketing.com/) is an excellent source of information on guerrilla marketing. Visit its website and research how e-mail can fit into a guerrilla marketing campaign. Bring the material to class so you can participate in a group discussion on the subject.
   c. Many companies sponsor a variety of events. Visit Tim Hortons', website (http://www.timhortons.com) and prepare a report on how Tim Hortons uses sponsorships as part of its integrated marketing communication strategy.

2. **AIDA.** Visit the websites of at least two online retailers—such as Mountain Equipment Co-op (http://www.mec.ca), Chapters Indigo (http://www.chapters.indigo.ca), or one of your favourites. Write a brief report explaining how the companies have succeeded in applying the AIDA (attention-interest-desire-action) concept discussed in the chapter.

Note: Internet Web addresses change frequently. If you don't find the exact sites listed, you may need to access the organization's or company's home page and search from there or use a search engine such as Google.

Case 14.1

GoodLife Fitness Clubs

Even good companies get it wrong sometimes. GoodLife Fitness Clubs seemed to be doing everything right—the company had a business formula that worked great, expansion programs that were going well, community involvement, and lots of awards to prove it. So how come the Competition Bureau went after it?

In 1979, David Patchell-Evans, Patch to his friends, opened a 2000-square-foot fitness club in London, Ontario. Today the company owns and operates 90 clubs in Alberta, Manitoba, Ontario, Quebec, New Brunswick, and Nova Scotia. The company employs 2500 people and has 200 000 members who work out either in the women's-only clubs or the larger co-ed facilities. It has even opened clubs in grocery stores with child-care centres. This makes GoodLife the largest privately owned group of fitness clubs in the world. The company's culture and core values are described as caring, trust, integrity, happiness, peak attitude, passion, and personal fitness.

After graduating with a degree in physical education from the University of Western Ontario, Patch wanted to share with others his knowledge of physical fitness and his commitment to good spiritual and emotional health. GoodLife's hiring requirements mirror the qualifications of the owner: a university degree in physical fitness or kinesiology and a desire to improve the quality of life for others.

GoodLife takes its caring philosophy into the communities where it is located. The company's Community Relations Department supports over 3000 charitable initiatives each year, including its own GoodLife Kids Foundation. Other charities supported include the Canadian Breast Cancer Society, Firefighter Combat Challenge Teams, the Canadian Diabetes Association, the Heart and Stroke Foundation, and the Terry Fox Foundation. On a personal level, Patch, the parent of an autistic child, has made a personal pledge to help parents and children dealing with autism. He has funded a research project to investigate why the incidence of autism is so high in Canada—one in every 250 children born or about 3000 cases annually. All community and charity events are handled through the company's public relations and community relations departments.

Concerns about GoodLife's marketing practices came to the attention of the Competition Bureau, Canada's law enforcement agency that polices competitive pricing, consumer packaging and labelling, and precious metals. The bureau determined that GoodLife's billboard and newspaper ads and its storefront signage were misleading, in that they failed to disclose additional mandatory fees. This meant the price of memberships was actually higher than consumers were led to believe from the ads.

When GoodLife heard the concerns of the Competition Bureau, the company took immediate corrective action. In addition to changing its advertising, it entered into a 10-year consent agreement to publish corrective notices in newspapers in Ontario and Quebec and on its website; pay an administrative penalty of $75 000; and administer a new corporate compliance policy to cover its marketing practices and to ensure all future promotional material is not false or misleading. The voluntary agreement satisfied the Competition Bureau and the matter did not need to proceed to litigation.

The company may have got its advertising wrong but the adverse public relations stemming from the incident does not seem to have harmed the company's reputation too badly. As Patch goes on the international speaker circuit promoting his book, *Living the Good Life*, he will no doubt be asked about this one blemish in what otherwise appears to be the perfect community-minded company.

Questions for Critical Thinking

1. What elements does GoodLife include in its marketing program? Is it effective? Would you change any part of it?
2. In your view did GoodLife handle the Competition Bureau complaint properly? Is there anything you would have done differently? What should the company do to reduce the effect of any bad publicity arising from the complaint?

Sources: Industry Canada, "Competition Bureau Reaches Settlement with GoodLife Fitness Clubs in Advertising Case," http://www.strategis.ic.gc, February 9, 2005; GoodLife Fitness Clubs, http://www.goodlifefitness.com; "GoodLife Fined for Misleading Ads," *Marketing Daily*, February 10, 2005.

Case 14.2

Scotiabank—You are Richer Than You Think

The Scotiabank is one of Canada's oldest and largest companies. It has a very diverse customer base and a large variety of products. It spends $21.1 million on traditional advertising, about half what its competitors the Royal Bank Financial Group and TD Canada Trust spend. In order to get its message out to its target market, it spent $42 million on sponsorships and donations in Canada and throughout the world. It focuses its sponsorship initiatives on educational programs, health care, social services, and arts and culture, some traditional programs—some not so traditional. Its two objectives are to increase brand awareness and to differentiate its brand from others.

One of its more recent sponsorship deals is with *Hockey Night in Canada*'s pre-game show. This is not Scotiabank's first relationship with hockey. It already had partnerships with the Calgary Flames, Edmonton Oilers, and Ottawa Senators, including the naming of the Ottawa arena known as Scotiabank Place. Adding to these sponsorships, Scotiabank became the official bank for the National Hockey League and the National Hockey League Players' Association. In order to support the younger hockey players, Scotiabank has a contest in which minor hockey teams can enter a contest to appear on the pre-game show.

Scotiabank realizes that not everyone is a hockey fan, however. In order to reach other sport fans and cultures, it sponsors the Cricket World Cup, which takes place in the Caribbean.

To reach a different group of customers, Scotiabank joined with Cineplex movie theatres, and theatres in major centres such as Vancouver, Toronto, Montreal, Calgary, and Edmonton have been renamed Scotiabank Theatres. A loyalty program, Scene cards, was developed along with this initiative. Customer collect points they can redeem for free movies or popcorn. This program has been very successful for Scotiabank mainly because of the number of cinema-goers it connects with. When Cineplex Entertainment purchased Famous Players in 2005, it became overwhelmingly the largest movie theatre company in Canada, representing 90 percent of the country's box office revenues. In addition to movies, the theatres hold non-movie events such as *Metropolitan Opera: Live in HD*. This event has attracted a sold-out crowd of upscale 50- to 60-year-olds. Scotia's wealth management division gave away tickets to the event as part of its relationship-building program.

The Scotiabank Giller Prize supports Canadian fiction writers by providing the winning author with a monetary prize of $40 000, and runners-up receive $2500. More important in some respects is that being recognized as a Giller Prize contender means increased book sales.

Cavalcade of Lights, Nuit Blanche, AIDS Walk for Life, Toronto Waterfront Marathon, the Rat Race for United Way, Buskerfest, and Cities: John Hartman round out the list of sponsored events. The Cavalcade of Lights takes place in December in Nathan

Phillips Square in heart of Toronto, providing fireworks, concerts and skating parties on Saturday nights. Nuit Blanche is an overnight arts and culture event that includes art exhibitions, theatre performances, and other unique programs. The Toronto Waterfront Marathon and the Rat Race for United Way are both running events but attract very different participants. The serious marathon attracts roughly 10 000 runners from 30 different countries and from across Canada. On the other hand, the Rat Race event attracts rat-costumed runners running toward the Big Cheese party at the end of the race.

From *Hockey Night in Canada* pre-game shows and other international sporting events to movie theatres and cultural events, Scotiabank covers a wide range of demographics in its diverse sponsorship program.

Questions for Critical Thinking

1. Identify the different customer groups that would be attracted to each of the sponsorship events. Suggest other types of promotion that would also attract these groups.
2. What are the benefits and drawbacks for each of the sponsored events?
3. If you were hired by Scotiabank to change its integrated marketing communications program, what changes would you make?

Sources: Scotiabank website, http://www.scotiabank.com, accessed February 19, 2008; Chris Daniels, "Movie Mogul," *Marketing*, January 28, 2008, pp. 32–35; Chris Powell, "Canada's Top Marketers 2007: Scotiabank," *Marketing*, November 26, 2007; pp. 18–29; Rebecca Harris, "Skin Deep," *Marketing*, January 29, 2007, pp. 18–19.

Video Case 14.3

The Toledo Mud Hens: Family Fun = A Winning Strategy

The written video case on The Toledo Mud Hens appears on page VC-16. The recently filmed Toledo Mud Hens video is designed to expand and highlight the concepts in this chapter and the concepts and questions covered in the written video case.

Advertising and Public Relations

CHAPTER OBJECTIVES

1. Identify the three major advertising objectives and the two basic categories of advertising.

2. List the major advertising strategies.

3. Describe the process of creating an advertisement.

4. Identify the major types of advertising appeals and discuss their uses.

5. List and compare the major advertising media.

6. Outline the organization of the advertising function and the role of an advertising agency.

7. Explain the roles of cross promotion, public relations, publicity, and ethics in an organization's promotional strategy.

8. Explain how marketers assess promotional effectiveness.

CELEBRITY ENDORSEMENTS

Marketers invest considerable money and effort into lining up celebrity spokespeople for their companies. The reason is clear: to borrow for their brands some of the glamour and goodwill attached to sports, film, and TV stars. Regardless of the objectives of the advertising or public relations, celebrity endorsements work with several advertising strategies and for different media.

Wayne Gretzky is a celebrity who has moved from the hockey arena to the arena of products and causes. He likes to build relationships with the companies he works with, thereby combining advertising with publicity and public relations. In order to do this, he established his own production company, Take 99 Productions, and often blends his product endorsements with other causes he supports, such as minor hockey or charities.

Nike uses celebrity endorsements in order to differentiate its product. Although Nike has been very successful in achieving this objective, it has had some surprises along the way. Executives at Nike, one of the first companies to use sports celebrities to endorse its products, were horrified by a Masters Golf Tournament snafu. The collar of the shirt worn by the winner, Tiger Woods, visibly wilted in the hot, humid air. But the sports apparel and equipment giant's chagrin over a limp collar was nothing compared to the dismay many a marketer has felt when a highly paid spokesperson's reputation becomes tarnished or his or her impact otherwise diminishes.

Some celebrity ads are created for selective markets and are not successful in others. Quebec is the strongest market for Pepsi in North America, and Pepsi has been successful with its ads in that market featuring comedian Claude Meunier. These ads have been airing for over 16 years, a relationship not matched by many celebrity endorsers. Ads featuring Meunier have continued for so long because they work. One reason for this successful partnership is Claude himself. He not only stars in the ads but often writes his own material, such as one that ran over Christmas featuring Claude dressed as a blue Santa. One of the ads in this series was recognized by the industry, winning the Grand Prix Cassie award for advertising effectiveness.

Bad publicity or retirement can reduce a spokesperson's visibility or portray unwanted associations and thus reduce the effectiveness of the celebrity endorser and the ad. Nike is coping with the retirement of NBA star Michael Jordan by building "Team Jordan," which includes several stars from other basketball teams. The concept of the team was developed when Jordan signed with Nike, and part of its purpose is to expand endorsements beyond athletic wear and into casual clothing.

Some advertisers are not afraid of the "bad boy" image that some athletes cultivate. And if the endorsement gets too uncomfortable for the firm, most endorsement contracts include a morals clause that allows the marketer to end the relationship if the spokesperson is convicted of a crime, for instance. Many observers believe such clauses will be getting tougher in the future. Some companies have worked around the issue of celebrities behaving badly by using cartoon characters or celebrities who have died. Other companies will sponsor film festivals hoping to get a photo of a celebrity wearing or using their product.

Celebrity endorsements can be used for many situations in advertising and public relations. They have been used for more than just testimonial ads, have been tested in different media, and have been successful with publicity and public relations campaigns. So whether the company is Nike using sports figures to promote sporting products or Ford using a sports figure to promote a line of vehicles, celebrity endorsements have achieved the objectives of advertisers.[1]

connecting with customers

Companies feel that building relationships with celebrities builds relationships with their customers. Customers identify with the well-known celebrities. Customers feel if their favourite movie, television, and sport celebrities endorse a product it must be good and they should try it. Regardless of the type or objective of advertising or whether the celebrities endorse a product relating to their field, celebrity endorsements work.

Chapter Overview

FROM the last chapter, you already know that the non-personal elements of promotion include advertising and public relations. Thousands of organizations rely on non-personal selling in developing their promotional mixes and integrated marketing communications strategies. Advertising is the most visible form of non-personal promotion, and marketers often use it together with sales promotion (discussed in the next chapter) to create effective promotional campaigns. Television is probably the most obvious medium for

Marketoid

The most reported organic class in Canada consists of field crops and hay.

non-personal selling dollars. But movie theatre advertising has become important in North America, where even universities are now using it to promote their programs to prospective students.[2]

Marketers seeking excitement for new-product launches have recently paid millions for celebrities to promote their products. Catherine Zeta-Jones was recently paid $20 million to promote one product, while Angelina Jolie earned more than $12 million from a luxury apparel company, and Nicole Kidman's contract with Chanel No. 5 perfume is worth $12 million.[3]

This chapter begins with a discussion of the types of advertising and explains how advertising is used to achieve a firm's objectives. It then considers alternative advertising strategies and the process of creating an advertisement. Next we provide a detailed look at various advertising media channels: television, radio, print advertising, direct mail, and outdoor and interactive media. The chapter then focuses on the importance of public relations, publicity, and cross promotions. Alternative methods of measuring the effectiveness of both online and offline non-personal selling are examined. We conclude the chapter by exploring current ethical issues relating to non-personal selling. ◆◆◆

---

① **Identify the three major advertising objectives and the two basic categories of advertising.**

advertising Paid, non-personal communication through various media about a business firm, not-for-profit organization, product, or idea by a sponsor identified in a message that is intended to inform or persuade members of a particular audience.

Marketoid

Almost half of the 2462 farming operations in Canada that reported themselves as organic were in Saskatchewan.

ADVERTISING

Twenty-first-century advertising is closely related to integrated marketing communications (IMC) in many respects. While IMC involves a message dealing with buyer–seller relationships, **advertising** consists of paid non-personal communication through various media with the purpose of informing or persuading members of a particular audience. Advertising is used by marketers to reach target markets with messages designed to appeal to business firms, not-for-profit organizations, or ultimate consumers.

North American companies are among the world's leading advertisers. General Motors, Procter & Gamble, Unilever, L'Oréal, and Ford Motor Co. are five of the top advertisers in the world, each spending more than $2 billion annually—an average of almost $6 million a day.[4]

Advertising spending varies among industries as well as companies. The cosmetics industry is widely known for pouring dollars into advertising, as is the auto manufacturing industry. In a recent survey 49 percent of companies said they would be increasing the amount they spend on advertising, and another 36 percent said their spending would remain the same.[5]

As previous chapters have discussed, the emergence of the marketing concept, with its emphasis on a companywide consumer orientation, boosted the importance of integrated marketing communications. This change in turn expanded the role of advertising. Today, a typical consumer is exposed to hundreds of advertising messages each day. Advertising provides an efficient, inexpensive, and fast method of reaching the ever-elusive, increasingly segmented consumer market.

TYPES OF ADVERTISING

Advertisements fall into two broad categories: product advertising and institutional advertising. **Product advertising** is non-personal selling of a particular good or service. This is the type of advertising the average person usually thinks of when talking about most promotional activities.

Institutional advertising, in contrast, promotes a concept, an idea, a philosophy, or the goodwill of an industry, company, organization, person, geographic location, or government agency. This term has a broader meaning than *corporate advertising,* which is typically limited to non-product advertising sponsored by a specific profit-seeking firm. Institutional advertising is often closely related to the public relations function of the enterprise.

OBJECTIVES OF ADVERTISING

Marketers use advertising messages to accomplish three primary objectives: to inform, to persuade, and to remind. These objectives may be used individually or, more typically, in conjunction with each other. For example, an ad for a not-for-profit agency may inform the public of the existence of the organization and at the same time persuade the audience to make a donation, join the organization, or attend a function.

Informative advertising seeks to develop initial demand for a good, service, organization, person, place, idea, or cause. The promotion of any new market entry tends to pursue this objective because marketing success at this stage often depends simply on announcing availability. Therefore, informative advertising is common in the introductory stage of the product life cycle, such as for hybrid cars or camera cell phones.

Persuasive advertising attempts to increase demand for an existing good, service, organization, person, place, idea, or cause. Persuasive advertising is a competitive type of promotion suited to the growth stage and the early part of the maturity stage of the product life cycle. 7Up's recent campaign announces that its original variety is "100% natural," now that an artificial preservative has been removed from the soft drink's formula.[6]

Reminder advertising strives to reinforce previous promotional activity by keeping the name of a good, service, organization, person, place, idea, or cause before the public. It is common in the latter part of the maturity stage and throughout the decline stage of the product life cycle. Procter & Gamble, for instance, seeks to remind consumers, particularly women, about the stain-fighting qualities of its Tide detergent by focusing on the emotional commitment many people have to clothing.[7]

Figure 15.1 illustrates the relationship between advertising objectives and the stages of the product life cycle. Informative advertising tends to work best during the early stages, while reminder advertising is effective later on. Persuasive advertising, if done well, can be effective through the entire life cycle.

Traditionally, marketers stated their advertising objectives as direct sales goals. A more current and realistic standard, however, views advertising as a way to achieve communications objectives, including informing, persuading, and reminding potential customers of the product. Advertising attempts to condition consumers to adopt favourable viewpoints toward a promotional message. The goal of an ad is to improve the likelihood that a customer will buy a particular good or service, now or sometime in the future. In this sense, advertising illustrates the close relationship between marketing communications and promotional strategy.

To get the best value for a firm's advertising investment, marketers must first determine what that firm's advertising objectives are. Effective

COURTESY HOMEGROWN ONTARIO/© RICK MILLER/CORBIS

Home-grown Ontario: institutional advertising.

product advertising
Nonpersonal selling of a particular good or service.

figure 15.1

Advertising Objectives in Relation to Stage in the Product Life Cycle

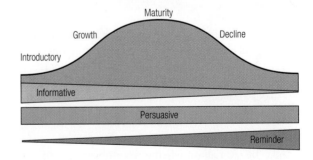

assessment check 1

1.1 What are the goals of institutional advertising?

1.2 At what stage in the product life cycle are informative ads used?

1.3 What is reminder advertising?

institutional advertising Promotion of a concept, idea, philosophy, or goodwill of an industry, company, organization, person, geographic location, or government agency.

informative advertising Promotion that seeks to develop initial demand for a good, service, organization, person, place, idea, or cause.

persuasive advertising Promotion that attempts to increase demand for an existing good, service, organization, person, place, idea, or cause.

reminder advertising Advertising that reinforces previous promotional activity by keeping the name of a good, service, organization, person, place, idea, or cause before the public.

advertising can enhance consumer perceptions of quality in a good or service, leading to increased customer loyalty, repeat purchases, and protection against price wars. In addition, perceptions of superiority pay off in the firm's ability to raise prices without losing market share.

Some basic do's and don'ts apply to advertising in general and can help ensure that messages are presented in ways that are effective, not offensive. The "Etiquette Tips for Marketing Professionals" feature outlines a few of these rules.

ADVERTISING STRATEGIES

If the primary function of marketing is to bring buyers and sellers together, then advertising is the means to an end. Effective advertising strategies accomplish at least one of three tasks: informing, persuading, or reminding consumers. The secret to success in choosing the best strategy is developing a message that best positions a firm's product in the audience's mind. Among the advertising strategies available for use by marketers are comparative advertising and celebrity advertising as well as plans about global and interactive ads. Channel-oriented decisions such as retail and cooperative advertising can also be devised.

Marketers often combine several of these advertising strategies to ensure that the advertisement accomplishes set objectives. As markets become more segmented, the need for personalized advertising increases. The next sections describe strategies that contemporary marketers may use to reach their target markets. Grocery stores used environmental issues as part of their advertising strategies as described in the "Go Green" feature.

COMPARATIVE ADVERTISING

Firms whose products are not the leaders in their markets often favour **comparative advertising,** a promotional strategy that emphasizes advertising messages with direct or indirect comparisons to dominant

---

ETIQUETTE TIPS FOR MARKETING PROFESSIONALS

Advertising Do's and Don'ts

AS advertising expands its reach to interactive media such as computer games and even cell phones, it will undergo many changes. Some basics, however, never change, including the rules of composing effective advertising messages. Here are a few fundamental do's and don'ts, including some special reminders about advertising in new media.

Do

1. Be clear about whether your objective is to inform, to persuade, or to remind.
2. Keep your message short and simple.
3. Choose visuals and graphics that attract attention in a positive way and that show the product, if illustrated, accurately in all details.
4. Disclose all relevant information about the good or service in the ad.
5. For product placements, make sure the brand is relevant to the context, such as a car added to a video racing game.

Don't

1. Don't advertise sales or specials unless you've really lowered prices, and don't increase prices just to later be able to afford a "free" giveaway.
2. Don't make claims about the product that you can't substantiate.
3. Don't even think about running tasteless ads. Check a humorous message with a wide variety of readers or viewers before you run with it.
4. Don't waste resources on ads that aren't well targeted.
5. Don't send spam. Ever.

Sources: Farid Aziz, "Online Advertising Mistakes—3 Don'ts for Newbies," *AF Work,* http://www.allfreelancework.com, accessed November 6, 2006; "Newspaper Advertising Do's and Don'ts," Workforce Planning for Wisconsin State Government, http://workforceplanning.wi.gov, accessed May 31, 2006; "Advertising Do's and Don'ts," Business Infosource, Government of Saskatchewan, http://www.cbsc.org, April 1, 2006; Fran Kennish, "In-Game Advertising Dos and Don'ts," iMedia Connection, March 3, 2006, http://www.imediaconnection.com; "Super Don'ts," *USA Today,* February 3, 2006, http://www.usatoday.com.

brands in the industry. By contrast, advertising by market leaders seldom acknowledges competing products even exist, and when they do, they usually do not point out any benefits of the competing brand.

Wireless telecommunications carriers have been battling it out in media advertising, promoting their calling plans and inviting comparison to competitors. Some offer "in" calling, free text messaging, no roaming charges, or extended hours at reduced rates to compete against similar offers from other companies.

A generation ago, comparative advertising was not the norm; in fact it was frowned on. But some industry experts now encourage comparative advertising, believing such ads keep marketers competitive and consumers better informed about their choices. Comparative advertising has its drawbacks, as it draws attention to competitive products and it may cause confusion regarding the message marketers are trying to get out to the consumer. Generally speaking, when there is competition through advertising, prices tend to go down because people can shop around. This benefit has proved increasingly true for online consumers, who now use shopping bots to help find the best prices on goods and services.

CELEBRITY TESTIMONIALS

A popular technique for increasing advertising readership in a cluttered promotional environment and improving overall effectiveness of a marketing message involves the use of celebrity spokespeople. About one of every five ads currently includes celebrities. This type of advertising is also popular in foreign countries. In Japan, 80 percent of all ads use celebrities, both local and international stars. North American celebrities featured in Japanese ads include actors Harrison Ford for Kirin Beer, Jodie Foster for Keri Cosmetics and Latte Coffee, and Paul Newman for Evance watch stores. Japanese consumers view foreign stars as images more than actual people, which helps marketers to sell products. They also associate stars with quality.

Both the number of celebrity ads and the dollars spent on those ads have increased in recent years. Professional athletes are among the highest-paid product endorsers, raking in millions each year. They appear in advertisements for a wide variety of products, many having little or nothing to do with sports.

> **②** List the major advertising strategies.

> **comparative advertising** Advertising strategy that emphasizes messages with direct or indirect promotional comparisons between competing brands.

> *Marketoid*
>
> **In 2006, the sale of certified organic products accounted for less than 1 percent of the $46.5 billion Canadians spent in grocery stores.**

Go Green

The End of Plastic Bags?

Grocery stores are using advertising and public relations to promote themselves and get an environmental message across at the same time. Metro Inc., A&P, and Loblaws have all launched campaigns to sell reusable grocery bags to replace plastic ones. Their message was loud and clear: keep the plastic grocery bags out of the landfill sites.

As part of a brand makeover for Loblaws, Galen Weston, the executive chairman of the company, promotes the 99-cent reusable grocery bags in a television commercial. His pitch: buy a reusable bag and reduce the number of plastic grocery bags hitting the landfills by a billion a year. Weston is hoping that consumers will see the connection between value and values particularly with the concept of respect for the environment getting so much press. Loblaws took respect for the environment one step further when it opened the first "bagless" store where customers are either forced to bring their own bags or purchase reusable ones.

Loblaws is not the only grocery chain jumping on the reusable grocery bag bandwagon. Metro Inc. has joined in at both its Metro stores and its A&P chain. First launched in the Metro chain, the bags sell for a dollar. The launch was accompanied by point-of-purchase print material and radio spots. The original sales forecast was for 500 000 in the first month but sales exceeded this, selling between 650 000 and 700 000. A follow-up campaign reminded shoppers to use the bags. The A&P chain launched its reusable bag program with a contest for children up to Grade 6 to design the artwork for the bag. The winning design was announced on Earth Day.

Promotes the company, promotes environmental awareness, and reduces operating costs—no wonder these programs have been successful.

Sources: Kristin Laird, "A&P Begins Reusable Bag Design Contest," *Marketing*, April 3, 2008; David Brown, "Canada's Top Marketers 2007: Loblaw Companies," *Marketing*, November 26, 2007, pp. 18–29; Rebecca Harris, "Heir Apparent," *Marketing*, August 13, 2007, pp. 9–12; Danny Kucharsky, "Green Grocer," *Marketing*, February 20, 2006, p. 5.

Nike has signed English soccer star Wayne Rooney for more than $9 million, while Suzuki endorses not only sports gear from several Japanese firms but also the services of a brokerage firm, Sato Pharmaceuticals, NTT Communications, and Shin Nippon Oil.[8] But actors, singers, and other media stars top the list of most powerful celebrities. Those who make the most money and attract the most attention include George Lucas, Steven Spielberg, Madonna, Elton John, and Johnny Depp, along with sports icons Tiger Woods and Shaquille O'Neal. But topping the list is talk show host Oprah Winfrey.[9]

One advantage of associations with big-name personalities is improved product recognition in a promotional environment filled with hundreds of competing 15- and 30-second commercials. Advertisers use the term *clutter* to describe this situation. As e-marketing continues to soar, one inevitable result has been the increase in advertising clutter as companies rush to market their goods and services online. But marketers need to remember that an effective online site must have meaningful content and helpful service.

Another advantage to using celebrities occurs when marketers are trying to reach consumers of another culture. Advertisements shown in the Quebec market often use a local celebrity. Both Pepsi and Goodyear have used this approach successfully. Goodyear used the TV and radio personality J. P. Collier for more than 12 years, showing him in a racing car. Pepsi used the comedian Claude Meunier, who wrote his own material for the spots. Research conducted by Pepsi throughout the years showed the importance of understanding the market. Ads in which Meunier was less involved in the creative were less effective in communicating the Pepsi message.[10]

A celebrity testimonial generally succeeds when the celebrity is a credible source of information for the product being promoted. The most effective ads of this type establish relevant links between the celebrities and the advertised goods or services, such as the models and actresses who endorse Revlon cosmetics. Michelle Wie, already the world's highest-paid female golfer when she was still only 15, has signed deals with Nike and Sony that are reported to be worth about $10 million a year and is represented by the William Morris agency, which has represented far more Hollywood clients than sports figures.[11]

However, a celebrity who endorses too many products may create marketplace confusion. Customers may remember the celebrity but not the product or brand; worse, they might connect the celebrity to a competing brand. Another problem can arise if a celebrity is involved in a scandal or has legal problems, as marketers do not want their products associated with a negative image.

Some advertisers try to avoid such problems by using cartoon characters as endorsers. Some advertisers may actually prefer cartoon characters because the characters can never say anything negative about the product, they do exactly what the marketers want them to do, and they cannot get involved in scandals. The only drawback is high licensing fees; popular animated characters often cost more than live celebrities. Companies may create their own cartoon characters or "talking" animals, which

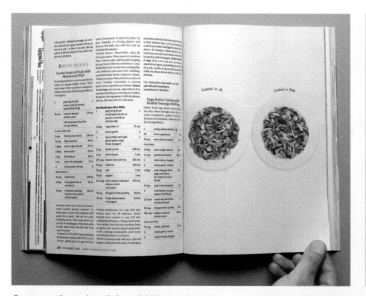
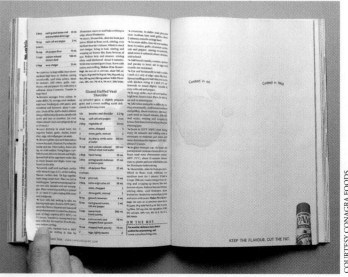

Comparative advertising: PAM cooking oil spray compared with traditional cooking oil.

eventually become celebrities in their own right as a result of many appearances in advertisements, as is the case with the Keebler elves and the Geico gecko.

In recent years, marketers have begun to consider celebrities as marketing partners rather than pretty or famous faces who can sell goods and services. Tiger Woods has been active in developing Nike's golf gear and apparel. Former supermodel Claudia Schiffer not only agreed to endorse a signature line of Palm-Pilots, but she also assisted in positioning the handheld computers in the electronics market by selecting fashionable colours and her own favourite software programs.

Celebrity seen in computer ads.

SCOTT GRIES/GETTY IMAGES

RETAIL ADVERTISING

Most consumers are confronted daily with **retail advertising**, which includes all advertising by retail stores that sell goods or services directly to the consuming public. While this activity accounts for a sizable portion of total annual advertising expenditures, retail advertising varies widely in its effectiveness. One study showed that consumers often respond with suspicion to retail price advertisements. Source, message, and shopping experience seem to affect consumer attitudes toward these advertisements.

An advertiser once quipped that the two most powerful words to use in an ad are "New" and "Free"—and these terms are often capitalized on in retail ads. Although "Free" may be featured only in discussions of customer services, the next best term—"Sale"—is often the centrepiece of retail promotions. And "New" typically describes new lines of products being offered. However, many retail stores continue to view advertising as a secondary activity, although that is changing. Local independent retailers rarely use advertising agencies, perhaps because of the expense. Instead, store managers may accept responsibility for advertising in addition to their other duties. Management can begin to correct this problem by assigning one individual the sole responsibility and authority for developing an effective retail advertising program.

A retailer often shares advertising costs with a manufacturer or wholesaler in a technique called **cooperative advertising**. For example, an apparel marketer may pay a percentage of the cost of a retail store's newspaper advertisement featuring its product lines. Cooperative advertising campaigns originated to take advantage of the media's practice of offering lower rates to local advertisers than to national ones. Later, cooperative advertising became part of programs to improve dealer relations. The retailer likes the chance to secure advertising that it might not be able to afford otherwise. Cooperative advertising can strengthen vertical links in the marketing channel, as when a manufacturer and retailer coordinate their resources. It can also involve firms at the same level of the supply chain. In a horizontal arrangement, a group of retailers—for example, all the Ford dealers in Edmonton—might pool their resources.

cooperative advertising
Strategy in which a retailer shares advertising costs with a manufacturer or wholesaler.

INTERACTIVE ADVERTISING

Millions of advertising messages float across idle—and active—computer screens in homes and offices around the country every day. Net surfers play games that are embedded with ads from the site sponsors. Companies offer free e-mail service to people willing to receive ads with their personal messages. Video screens on grocery carts display ads for shoppers to see as they wheel down the aisles of grocery stores.

Since marketers realize that two-way communications provide more effective methods for achieving promotional objectives, they are interested in interactive media. **Interactive advertising** involves two-way promotional messages transmitted through communication channels that induce message recipients to participate actively in the promotional effort. Achieving this involvement is the difficult task facing contemporary marketers. Although interactive advertising has become nearly synonymous with e-commerce and the Web, it also includes other formats such as kiosks in shopping malls or text messages on cell phones. Multimedia technology, the Internet, and commercial online services are changing the nature of advertising from a one-way, passive communication technique to more effective, two-way marketing communications. Interactive advertising creates dialogue between marketers and individual shoppers, providing more materials at the user's request. The advertiser's challenge is to gain and hold consumer interest in an environment where these individuals control what they want to see.

Interactive advertising changes the balance between marketers and consumers. Unlike the traditional role of advertising—providing brief, entertaining, attention-catching messages—interactive media provide information to help consumers throughout the purchase and consumption processes. In a sense, it becomes closer to personal selling as consumers receive immediate responses to questions or requests for more information about goods and services. Interactive advertising provides consumers with more information in less time to help them make necessary comparisons between available products.

Successful interactive advertising adds value by offering the viewer more than just product-related information. An ad on the Web can do more than promote a brand; it can create a company store, provide customer service, and offer additional content. Many marketers at companies both large and small are hoping that such ads will soon be so finely targeted that they can cut through increasing "advertising clutter" and reach only consumers who are ready to hear their message.

Most firms deliver their interactive advertising messages through proprietary online services and through the Web. In fact, online ad spending is expected to reach the $1-billion mark shortly. Currently it has surpassed consumer magazines with annual spending increases of 42.5 percent and roughly 30 percent in the last two years.[12]

assessment check 2

2.1   What is comparative advertising?

2.2   What makes a successful celebrity testimonial?

2.3   What is cooperative advertising?

③ Describe the process of creating an advertisement.

CREATING AN ADVERTISEMENT

Marketers spend billions a year on advertising campaigns in Canada alone. With so much money at stake, they must create effective, memorable ads that increase sales and enhance their organizations' images. They cannot afford to waste resources on mediocre messages that fail to capture consumers' attention, communicate their sales message effectively, or lead to a purchase, donation, or other positive action for the organization.

Research helps marketers create better ads by pinpointing goals that an ad needs to accomplish, such as educating consumers about product features, enhancing brand loyalty, or improving consumer perception of the brand. These objectives should guide the design of the ad. Marketers can also discover what appeals to consumers and can test ads with potential buyers before committing funds for a campaign.

Marketers sometimes face specific challenges as they develop advertising objectives for services. They must find a creative way to fill out the intangible images of most services and successfully convey the benefits that consumers receive. The "You've always got time" message of Tim Hortons, along with a picture of a steaming cup of coffee, is an example of how creative advertising can make the intangible nature of services tangible.

TRANSLATING ADVERTISING OBJECTIVES INTO ADVERTISING PLANS

Once a company defines its objectives for an advertising campaign, it can develop its advertising plan. Marketing research assists managers in making strategic decisions that guide choices in technical areas such as budgeting, copywriting, scheduling, and media selection. Post-tests, which are discussed in greater detail later in the chapter, measure the effectiveness of advertising and form the basis for feedback concerning possible adjustments. The elements of advertising planning are shown in Figure 15.2. Experienced marketers know the importance of following even the most basic steps in the process, such as market analysis.

As Chapter 8 explained, positioning involves developing a marketing strategy that aims to achieve a desired position in a prospective buyer's mind. Marketers use a positioning strategy that distinguishes their good or service from those of competitors. Effective advertising then communicates the desired position by emphasizing certain product characteristics, such as performance attributes, price/quality, competitors' shortcomings, applications, user needs, and product classes.

ADVERTISING MESSAGES

The strategy for creating a message starts with the benefits a product offers to potential customers and moves to the creative concept phase, in which marketers strive to bring an appropriate message to consumers using both visual and verbal components. Marketers work to create an ad with meaningful, believable, and distinctive appeals—one that stands out from the clutter and is more likely to escape zapping by the television remote control.

Usually, ads are created not individually but as part of specific campaigns. An **advertising campaign** is a series of different but related ads that use a single theme and appear in different media within a specified time period. Examples of advertising campaigns include the series of Fido ads featuring different dogs, one of which has a dog sitting beside a Mafioso who likes a new service, and the McDonald's "I'm Lovin It" ads.[13]

In developing a creative strategy, advertisers must decide how to communicate their marketing message. They must balance message characteristics, such as the tone of the appeal, the extent of information provided and the conclusion to which it leads the consumer, the side of the story the ad tells, and its emphasis on verbal or visual primary elements.

assessment check 3

3.1 What is an advertising campaign?

3.2 What are an advertisement's three main goals?

ADVERTISING APPEALS

Should the tone of the advertisement focus on a practical appeal such as price or gas mileage, or should it evoke an emotional response by appealing to, say, fear, humour, sex, guilt, or fantasy? This is another critical decision in the creation of memorable ads that possess the strengths needed to accomplish promotional objectives. Recent research suggests that skeptical consumers might actually be more responsive to consumer-product ads that appeal to their emotions than to ads that deliver information. Nonskeptics were found to respond better to informational advertising.[14]

Fear Appeals

In recent years, marketers have relied increasingly on fear appeals. Ads for insurance, autos, health care products, and even certain foods imply that incorrect buying decisions could lead to illness, injury, or other bad consequences. Even ads for business services imply that if a company doesn't purchase the advertised services, its competitors will move ahead or valuable information may be lost.

Fear appeals can backfire, however. Viewers are likely to practise selective perception and tune out statements they perceive as too strong or not credible. Some consumer researchers believe that viewer or reader backlash will eventually occur due to the amount of advertising based on fear appeals.

Humour in Advertising Messages

A humorous ad seeks to create a positive mood related to a product. Humour can improve audience awareness and recall and enhance the consumer's favourable image of the brand. After all, if the ad makes the consumer feel good, then the product may do the same. But advertising professionals differ in their opinions of the effectiveness of humorous ads. Some believe that humour distracts attention from brand and product features; consumers remember the humour but not the product. Humorous ads, because they are so memorable, may lose their effectiveness sooner than ads with other kinds of appeals. In addition, humour can be tricky because what one group of consumers finds funny may not be funny at all to another group. Men and women sometimes

figure 15.2
Elements of the Advertising Planning Process

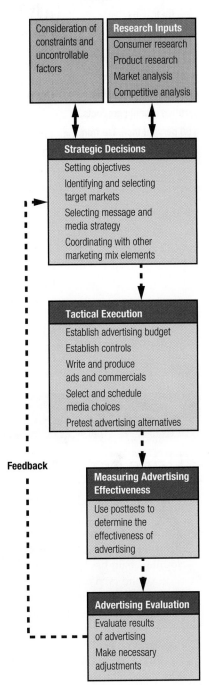

advertising campaign
Series of different but related ads that use a single theme and appear in different media within a specified time period.

have a different sense of humour, as do people of different ages. This distinction may become even greater across cultures.

Ads Based on Sex

Ads with sex-based appeals have what is called "stopping power" because they attract the reader's or viewer's attention. Research indicates, however, that sexual content in an ad boosts recall of the ad's content only if the appeal is appropriate to the type of product advertised.[15] Some advertisers have begun to tone down their appeals based on sex. The "Solving an Ethical Controversy" feature examines the pros and cons of using sex to sell.

DEVELOPING AND PREPARING ADS

The final step in the advertising process—the development and preparation of an advertisement—should flow logically from the promotional theme selected. This process should create an ad that becomes a complementary part of the marketing mix with a carefully determined role in the total marketing strategy. Preparation of an advertisement should emphasize features like its creativity, its continuity with past advertisements, and possibly its association with other company products.

What immediate tasks should an advertisement accomplish? Regardless of the chosen target, an advertisement should (1) gain attention and interest, (2) inform and/or persuade, and (3) eventually lead to a purchase or other desired action. It should gain attention in a productive way; that is, it should instill some recall of the good or service. Otherwise, it will not lead to buying action.

Gaining attention and generating interest—cutting through the clutter—can be formidable tasks. "People are tired of commercials that look like commercials," according to the creative director of giant ad agency Saatchi & Saatchi. "People are looking for things that are real," a desire that has led some marketers to create ads that reflect the popularity of reality television, such as a Toyota spot that looks like a home movie or Anheuser-Busch ads meant to look like mini-documentaries.[16] Stimulating buying

Solving an Ethical Controversy

Using Sex to Sell

ADS that rely on sex appeal are nothing new, nor is the fact that the products advertised, such as toothpaste and vacation packages, sometimes have little connection with the provocative copy and images that promote them. One retail clothing chain has become widely successful using sexually provocative and even explicit advertising, featuring amateur models who are often company employees. The company's founder promotes a freewheeling atmosphere, publicizing its policy of free massages at work and his own "loving" relationships with employees and colleagues.

While few firms go so far, and the reaction to these promotions hasn't all been positive, there's no doubt that sexual appeals for all kinds of products are in wide use and are often effective.

Should marketers use sex to sell products?

PRO

1. There is so much sexuality elsewhere in the culture today that marketers have to keep pushing the barriers just to get noticed.

2. It attracts attention, so it is a legitimate means to sell products. In short, it works.

CON

1. Explicit or provocative ads are demeaning to both men and women and help lower the standards of what is acceptable in our culture.

2. When sex is irrelevant to the good or service, relying on sexual marketing is counterproductive. It can confuse the message.

Where do you stand: pro or con?

Sources: "Bush Signs Broadcast Decency Law," *The New York Times*, June 15, 2006, http://www.nytimes.com; Kathleen Wereszynski, "Girl Culture Begets Backlash," *Fox News*, May 31, 2006, http://www.foxnews.com; Beth Potter, "Sex! Now Wanna Buy the Toaster?" *Denver Post*, May 9, 2006, http://www.denverpost .com; Dan Glaister, "Nice and Sleazy," *The Guardian*, January 10, 2006, http:// www.guardian.co.uk; Susan Aschoff, "It's Grrrl Power vs. Abercrombie & Fitch," *St. Petersburg (FL) Times*, November 5, 2005, http://www.sptimes.com; Stuart Eskenazi, "Hot Retailer Aims to Recharge Buzz, and Business, on the Ave.," *Seattle Times*, October 22, 2005, http://seattletimes.nwsource.com.

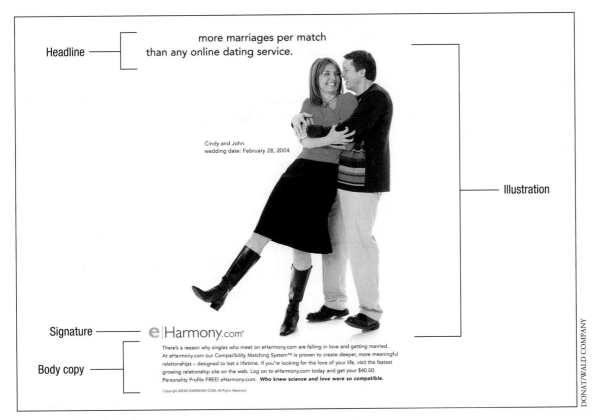

Headline — more marriages per match than any online dating service.

Cindy and John
wedding date: February 28, 2004

Illustration

Signature — e|Harmony.com®

Body copy —

There's a reason why singles who meet on eHarmony.com are falling in love and getting married. At eHarmony.com our Compatibility Matching System™ is proven to create deeper, more meaningful relationships – designed to last a lifetime. If you're looking for the love of your life, visit the fastest growing relationship site on the web. Log on to eHarmony.com today and get your $40.00 Personality Profile FREE! eHarmony.com. **Who knew science and love were so compatible.**

Copyright ©2004 EHARMONY.COM. All Rights Reserved.

DONAT/WALD COMPANY

Elements of a typical ad.

action is often difficult because an advertisement cannot actually close a sale. Nevertheless, if an ad gains attention and informs or persuades, it probably represents a worthwhile investment of marketing resources. Too many advertisers fail to suggest how audience members can purchase their products if they desire to do so. Creative design should eliminate this shortcoming.

The eHarmony.com ad shows the four major elements of this print advertisement: headline, illustration, body copy, and signature. *Headlines* and *illustrations* (photographs, drawings, or other artwork) should work together to generate interest and attention. *Body copy* informs, persuades, and stimulates buying action. The *signature,* which may include the company name, address, phone number, Web address, slogan, trademark, or simply a product photo, names the sponsoring organization. An ad may also have one or more subheads—headings subordinate to the main headline that either link the main headline to the body copy or subdivide sections of the body copy.

After advertisers conceive an idea for an ad that gains attention, informs and persuades, and stimulates purchases, their next step involves refining the thought sketch into a rough layout. Continued refinements of the rough layout eventually produce the final version of the advertisement design that is ready to be executed, printed, or recorded.

The creation of each advertisement in a campaign requires an evolutionary process that begins with an idea and ultimately results in a finished ad that is ready for distribution through print or electronic media. The idea itself must first be converted into a thought sketch, which is a tangible summary of the intended message.

Advances in technology allow advertisers to create novel, eye-catching advertisements. Innovative computer software packages now allow artists to merge multiple images to create a single image with a natural, seamless appearance. Computer-generated images appeal to younger, computer-literate consumers.

CREATING INTERACTIVE ADS

Web surfers want engaging, lively content that takes advantage of the medium's capabilities and goes beyond what they find elsewhere. The Web's major advantages make it possible for advertisers to provide that, offering speed, information, two-way communications, self-directed entertainment, and personal choice. Web ads are also vibrant in their visual appeal, such as the World Wide Fund for Nature ad that shows a roll of toilet paper unwinding to the floor.[17]

Web ads have grown from information-based home pages to innovative, interactive channels for transmitting messages to cyberaudiences, including banners, pop-ups, keyword ads, advertorials, and interstitials. *Advergames* are either online games created by marketers to promote their products to targeted audiences in an interactive way or ads or product placements inserted into online video games. Automakers are using these product placements to reach younger audiences—those who may not watch their TV commercials as often. Cadillac inserts its cars into a Microsoft Xbox game, and Toyota pays for its Scion to be featured—and "purchased"—in the fictitious world of Whyville.net, an interactive community for 8- to 15-year-old computer users.[18]

Banners, advertisements on a web page that link to an advertiser's site, are the most common type of advertising on the Web. They can be free of charge or cost thousands of dollars per month depending on the amount of hits the site receives. Online advertisers often describe their Internet ads in terms of richness, referring to the degree to which new technologies—such as streaming video, 3-D animation, JavaScript, and interactive capabilities—are implemented in the banners.

Banners have evolved into a more target-specific technique for Internet advertising with the advent of *missiles:* messages that appear on the screen at exactly the right moment. When a customer visits the site of Company A's competitor, a missile can be programmed to appear on the customer's monitor that allows the customer to click a direct link to Company A's site. However, many people feel the use of such missiles is a questionable practice.

Keyword ads are an outcropping of banner ads. Used in search engines, keyword ads appear on the results page of a search and are specific to the term being searched. Advertisers pay search engines to target their ads and display only the banners when users search for relevant keywords, allowing marketers to target specific audiences. For example, if a user searched the term *digital camera*, keyword ads might appear for electronic boutiques or camera shops that sell digital cameras. Google and Yahoo! have long earned revenue from such ads; Microsoft is ready to join them with its new adCenter, which will be able to accurately target ads to receptive audiences.[19]

Banner designs that have also evolved into larger advertising squares that closely resemble advertisements in the telephone book's Yellow Pages are called *advertorials*. Advertisers quickly expanded on these advertorials with *interstitials*—ads that appear between web pages of related content. Interstitials appear in a separate browser window while the user waits for a web page to download.[20]

Then there are pop-ups, which are little advertising windows that appear in front of the top window of a user's computer screen, and pop-unders, which appear under the top window. Some industry observers believe that pop-ups may be on the decline, partly because several lawsuits have been filed charging deceptive business practices and computer tampering.[21] Indeed, many users complain that interstitials, like pop-ups and missiles, are intrusive and unwanted. Interstitials are more likely to contain large graphics and streaming presentations than banner ads and therefore are more difficult to ignore than typical banner ads. But despite complaints, some studies show that users are more likely to click interstitials than banners.

Perhaps the most intrusive form of online advertising is *adware,* which allows ads to be shown on users' screens through the use of software downloaded to their computers without their consent or through trickery. Such software can be difficult to remove, and some legislators and industry experts believe that reputable marketers should avoid dealing with Internet marketing firms that promote the use of adware.[22]

assessment check 4

4.1 What are some common emotional appeals used in advertising?

4.2 What are the main types of interactive ads?

⑤ List and compare the major advertising media.

MEDIA SELECTION

One of the most important decisions in developing an advertising strategy is the selection of appropriate media to carry a firm's message to its audience. The media selected must be capable of accomplishing the communications objectives of informing, persuading, and reminding potential customers of the good, service, person, or idea being advertised.

table 15.1 *Comparison of Advertising Media Alternatives*

MEDIA OUTLET	ADVANTAGES	DISADVANTAGES
Broadcast		
Network television	Extensive coverage; repetition; flexibility; prestige	High cost; brief message; limited segmentation
Cable television	Same strengths as network TV; less market coverage since not every viewer is a cable subscriber	Same disadvantages as network TV, although cable TV ads are considerably more targeted to specific viewer segments
Radio	Immediacy; low cost; flexibility; targeted audience; mobility; captive audience	Brief message; highly fragmented audience
Print		
Newspapers	Tailored to individual communities; ability to refer back to ads	Limited life
Direct mail	Selectivity; intense coverage; speed; flexibility; opportunity to convey complete information; personalization	High cost; consumer resistance; dependence on effective mailing list
Magazines	Selectivity; quality image reproduction; long life; prestige	Lack of flexibility
Outdoor	Quick, visual communication of simple ideas; link to local goods and services; repetition	Brief exposure; environmental concerns
Electronic		
Internet	Two-way communications; flexibility; link to self-directed entertainment	Poor image reproduction; limited scheduling options; difficult to measure effectiveness

Source: Reprinted with permission from the March 8 issue of Advertising Age Fact Pack 2008 Edition. Copyright © Crain Communications Inc. 2008.

Research identifies the ad's target market to determine its size and characteristics. Advertisers then match the target characteristics with the media best able to reach that particular audience. The objective of media selection is to achieve adequate media coverage without advertising beyond the identifiable limits of the potential market. Finally, cost comparisons between alternatives should determine the best possible media purchase.

Table 15.1 compares the major advertising media advantages and disadvantages. *Broadcast media* include television (network and cable) and radio. Newspapers, magazines, outdoor (out of home) advertising, and direct mail represent the major types of print media. Electronic media include the Internet and kiosks.

TELEVISION

Canadian companies spend roughly $3.3 billion on television advertising annually.[23] The attractiveness of television advertising is that marketers can reach local and national markets. Whereas most newspaper advertising revenues come from local advertisers, the greatest share of television advertising revenues comes from organizations that advertise nationally. The newest trend in television advertising is virtual ads—banner-type logos and brief messages that are superimposed onto television coverage of sporting events so that they seem to be a part of the arena's signage but cannot be seen by anyone attending the game. Then there are streaming headlines run by some news stations, which are paid for by corporate sponsors whose names and logos appear within the news stream.

Other trends in television advertising is the abbreviated spot—a 15- or 30-second ad—that costs less to make and buy and is too quick for most viewers to zap with their remote control—and single-advertiser shows. Sometimes called *ad takeovers,* these single-advertiser spots allow for longer commercials and effectively block competitors from buying time on the same show. Marketers also hope that with takeovers they are "putting so many ads in that you can't possibly TiVo out every last one."[24]

In fact, TiVo is unveiling a new way for advertisers to get their messages across, through small logos called *billboards* that pop up over television commercials as viewers fast-forward through them. These billboards offer contests, giveaways, and links to more ads. If the user selects an ad, TiVo downloads contact information directly to the advertiser, with the viewer's permission. TiVo already gathers collective information about viewers' habits and sells it to networks and marketers. Far from becoming "the weapon of mass destruction" of advertising, as one observer called it, TiVo is now viewed as the "first generation of the TV advertising of the future," according to one industry expert.[25] The "Marketing Success" feature discusses another way television advertisers are trying to "TiVo-proof" their messages.

A recent study does show that TiVo or DVRs are having an impact on purchasing patterns. The purchase of new packaged goods products were 5 percent lower and roughly 20 percent of all brands tested were lower in DVRs homes. Sales of packaged food products were the most affected. The study also showed that diversifying media selection reduced or eliminated the effect of DVRs.[26]

In the past decade, ad spending for television has changed significantly mainly due to changes in the industry. The number of specialty channels has increased and the number of homes subscribing to cable, satellite, or the new digital services has also increased. Twenty-five percent of the total advertising dollars spent on television are now going to pay television and specialty channels.[27]

Television advertising offers the advantages of mass coverage, powerful impact on viewers, repetition of messages, flexibility, and prestige. Its disadvantages include loss of control of the promotional message to the telecaster (which can influence its impact), high costs, and some public distrust. Compared with other media, television can suffer from lack of selectivity because specific TV programs may not reach consumers in a precisely defined target market without a significant degree of wasted coverage. However, the growing specialization of cable TV channels can help to resolve the problem.

Finally, some types of products are actually banned from television advertising. Tobacco goods, such as cigarettes, cigars, and smokeless tobacco, fall into this category.

RADIO

Radio advertising has always been a popular media choice for up-to-the-minute newscasts and for targeting advertising messages to local audiences. But in recent years, radio has become one of the fastest-growing media alternatives. As more and more people find they have less and less time, radio

marketing success   HDTV and Super Bowl Advertising

Background. Although technology is creating many new opportunities for advertisers, it also threatens to close some tried-and-true avenues for pushing marketing messages. Television shows can be downloaded from the Internet without their advertising, and digital video recorders and cable video-on-demand allow viewers to skip past commercials even more easily than they did with homemade VHS recordings.

The Challenge. Getting viewers to sit still for advertising is the challenge facing today's top advertisers. With the cost of creating commercials rising and the sheer number of marketing messages creating a sea of clutter, the stakes are climbing ever higher to beat the ease of zapping past commercials.

The Strategy. High-spending marketers such as FedEx, Bayer, Anheuser-Busch, VISA, MasterCard, and McDonald's are investing millions in two strategies. More households have at least one high-definition-capable TV, so marketers are creating high-definition ads. The aim is to ensure viewers a "seamless transition" from ad to programming and to capture attention with the highest-quality images. "When you're watching a high-def broadcast, and you see a [standard] commercial come on, it looks like someone put a sheet over your television," says one producer of TV commercials. But high-def ads look great on both kinds of receivers, making them worth the expense for marketers determined to get the word out.

The second strategy is to place ads in programming that goes beyond mere entertainment. Live events such as the Academy Awards, the Olympics, and especially the Super Bowl are the kind of "TiVo-proof" pop-culture moments that still draw huge audiences eager to participate in real time.

The Outcome. Award shows and big sports contests have become a tremendous opportunity for creating memorable advertising that viewers actually want to watch. "The Super Bowl is a huge rocket shot of creativity," says one media buying firm. Some ads created for the Super Bowl broadcast have gone on to have long lives on the Internet, where millions of people play them again and again. What more could an advertiser want?

Sources: Laura Petrecca, "Advertisers Jump on Board Live TV," *USA Today,* January 26, 2006, p. 1B; Paul R. LaMonica, "SB XL Ads: A Druid, Fabio and the King," *CNN Money.com,* January 22, 2006, http://money.cnn.com; Laura Petrecca, "More Super Bowl Marketers Shoot High-Def Ads," *USA Today,* January 13, 2006, p. 1B; Theresa Howard, "Ad Sales Boom for Super Bowl, Olympics," *USA Today,* January 6, 2006, http://www.usatoday.com.

provides immediate information and entertainment at work, at play, and in the car. In addition, as e-commerce continues to push the growth in global business, more people are travelling abroad to seek out new markets. For these travellers, radio, because many radio stations are airing over the Internet, is a means of staying in touch with home—wherever that may be. Marketers frequently use radio advertising to reach local audiences. But in recent years, it has been playing an increasingly important role as a national—and even global—listening favourite. Thousands of online listeners use the Internet to beam in on radio stations from almost every city—tuning in on an easy-listening station in London, a top-40 Hong Kong broadcaster, or a chat show from Toronto. Other listeners equip their vehicles with satellite radio to maintain contact with hometown or destination stations during long trips.

Satellite radio providers offer much higher-quality digital signals than regular radio stations, with many more available channels that are mostly free of government regulations and are generally commercial-free. XM Radio, the first such service to be licensed, began airing commercials on a few of its nearly 200 music, sports, and talk channels. XM and its chief competitor, Sirius Satellite Radio, charge an annual fee; listeners must have a special receiver to decode the signals. By contrast, terrestrial radio stations that combine digital and analog signals to beam multiple types of content called HD radio are both ad- and subscription-free for the moment.[28]

Advertisers like the ability to reach people while they drive because they are a captive audience. With an increase in commuters, this market is growing. Stations can adapt to local preferences by changing format, such as going from country and western to an all-news or rock-and-talk station. The variety of stations allows advertisers to easily target audiences and tailor their messages to those listeners. Other benefits include low cost, flexibility, and mobility. Disadvantages include fragmentation (reaching most people in a market may require ads placed on 10 or more stations), the temporary nature of messages (unlike print ads, radio and TV ads are instantaneous and must be rebroadcast to reach consumers a second time), and a lack of research information as compared with television.

While most radio listening is done at home, in cars, or with headset-equipped portables, technology has given birth to Net radio. Web-cast radio allows customers to widen their listening times and choices through their computers. The potential for selling on this new channel is great. A listener can simply "click here to purchase the song you're hearing." Other goods are easily adapted to click-and-sell possibilities.

NEWSPAPERS

Newspaper advertising continues to dominate local markets, accounting for $3.7 billion of annual advertising expenditures in Canada.[29] In addition to retail advertisements, classified advertising is an important part of newspaper revenues.

Newspapers' primary advantages start with flexibility because advertising can vary from one locality to the next. Newspapers also allow intensive coverage for ads. Readers control their exposure to the advertising message, unlike television or radio advertising messages, and can refer back to newspaper ads.

Newspaper advertising does have some disadvantages: hasty reading (the typical reader spends about 28 minutes reading the newspaper),[30] and relatively poor reproduction quality, although that is changing as technology improves.

Newspapers have also begun to struggle to "get through the noise" of other advertisers. To retain big advertisers, some companies have launched annual, semiannual, or monthly magazines featuring a single topic such as fashion or business. These magazines provide advertisers with higher reproduction qualities for their ads and take advantage of the finely tuned distribution capabilities of the newspapers. Another way newspapers are moving ahead is through the Internet. After years of avoiding the Internet, most papers have an online version.[31]

MAGAZINES

Advertisers divide magazines into two broad categories: consumer magazines and business magazines. These categories are also subdivided into monthly and weekly publications. An annual study on magazine readerships indicates that 72 percent of Canadians read magazines.[32] The primary advantages of magazine advertising include the following: selectivity in reaching precise target markets, quality reproduction, long life, the prestige associated with some magazines, and the extra services that many

Serving Creemore and surrounding area for over 50 years as your local Ford Dealer.

New & Used
Sales, Leasing & Service

Service Department open 6 days a week

2 locations to serve you
Collingwood   **Stayner**
371 Hume St   247 King St
(705) 445-4300   (705) 428-2920
1-800-661-4301   1-800-463-2920
www.hannamotors.com

COURTESY OF HANNA MOTOR SALES CO. LTD.

Newspapers offer intensive coverage in local markets.

publications offer. The primary disadvantage is that magazines lack the flexibility of newspapers, radio, and television.

Media buyers study circulation numbers and demographic information for various publications before choosing optimal placement opportunities and in negotiating rates. The same advertising categories have claimed the title for big spenders for several years running. Automotive, retail, and movies and media advertising have held their first, second, and third places, respectively, each year and have continued to show strong growth percentages. Advertisers seeking to promote their products to target markets can reach them by advertising in the appropriate magazines.

DIRECT MAIL

As discussed in Chapter 13, direct mail advertising consists of sales letters, postcards, leaflets, folders, booklets, catalogues, and house organs (periodicals published by organizations to cover internal issues). Its advantages come from direct mail's ability to segment large numbers of prospective customers into narrow market niches, speed, flexibility, detailed information, and personalization. Disadvantages of direct mail include high cost per reader, dependence on the quality of mailing lists, and some consumers' resistance to it.

The advantages of direct mail explain its widespread use. Data are available on previous purchase patterns and preferred payment methods, as well as household characteristics such as number of children or seniors.

The downside to direct mail is clutter, otherwise known as *junk mail.* So much advertising material is stuffed into people's mailboxes every day that the task of grabbing consumers' attention and evoking some interest is daunting to direct mail advertisers. Three of every five respondents to a survey about "things most likely to get on consumers' nerves" rated junk mail at the top—above telemarketing, credit card fees, and the fine print on billing statements.

OUTDOOR ADVERTISING

Outdoor advertising, perhaps the oldest and simplest media business around, attracts $25.2 billion in advertising globally each year.[33] Traditional outdoor advertising takes the form of billboards, painted bulletins or displays (such as those that appear on the walls of buildings), and electronic spectaculars (large, illuminated, and sometimes animated signs and displays). Transit advertising includes ads placed both inside and outside buses, subway trains and stations, and commuter trains. Some firms place ads on the roofs of taxicabs, on bus stop shelters and benches, on entertainment and sporting event turnstiles, in public restrooms, and even on parking meters. A section of highway might be cleaned up by a local real estate company or restaurant, with a sign implanted where passersby can easily see it. All these are forms of outdoor advertising.

This form of advertising has the advantages of immediate communication of quick and simple ideas, repeated exposure to a message, and strong promotion for locally available products. Outdoor advertising is particularly effective along metropolitan streets and in other high-traffic areas.

But outdoor advertising, just like every other type, is subject to clutter. It also suffers from the brevity of exposure to its messages by passing motorists. Driver concerns about rush-hour safety and limited time also combine to limit the length of exposure to outdoor messages. As a result, most of these ads use striking, simple illustrations, short selling points, and humour to attract people interested in products like such as vacations, local entertainment, and lodging.

A third problem involves public concern over aesthetics. Many areas of the country, for example, regulate the placement of outdoor advertising near major highways. Critics have even labelled billboard advertising as "pollution on a stick."

New technologies are helping to revive outdoor advertising. Technology livens up the billboards themselves with animation, large sculptures, and laser images. Canada has two organizations to assist companies with outdoor advertising. The Canadian Outdoor Measurement Bureau (COMB) provides information relating to traffic patterns and audience data. The Outdoor Advertising Association of Canada (OAAC) is made up of companies in the industry.[34]

The website for Marketing *magazine advertises upcoming events.*

INTERACTIVE MEDIA

Interactive media—especially the Internet—are growing up. Keyword ads dominate online advertising, helping online revenues grow for several consecutive years to a new record of about $1 billion annually.[35] "Interactive advertising continues to experience tremendous growth as marketers experience its overall effectiveness in building brands and delivering online and offline sales," said one industry expert.[36] Not surprisingly, interactive advertising budgets are being beefed up at a growing number of companies.

Ads are coming to cell phones as well, as video and broadcast capabilities explode. About 90 percent of consumer marketers plan to dive into cell phone advertising, and revenues from such advertising are expected to grow in the next few years. To counter consumer resistance, some experts advise offering opt-in features and incentives, such as credits toward the phone bill.[37] Some marketers even envision capitalizing on global positioning systems in some phones to beam ads to users in the vicinity of certain retail stores. However, laws in many areas prevent wireless carriers giving out information about a customer's location without permission or to sell phone numbers to telemarketers, making the use of incentives more likely.[38] Virgin Mobile USA already offers SugarMama, the first ad-supported cell phone service. The program is aimed at teenagers, who can earn up to 75 free minutes a month by watching 30-second commercials on their computers or text messages on their phones—and answering questions about the ads (from Pepsi, Microsoft's Xbox, and Truth, an antismoking campaign) to prove they paid attention.[39]

OTHER ADVERTISING MEDIA

As consumers filter out appeals from traditional as well as Internet ads, marketers need new ways to catch their attention. In addition to the major media, firms use a vast number of other vehicles to communicate their messages. Canadian companies are spending millions on movie theatre commercials. The trend began as theatre owners realized that a lag of 20 minutes between the time patrons enter the theatre until the film actually starts could not be filled with upcoming previews, and they began to fill the time with ads. Cineplex Media, the company that manages the advertising side of Cineplex Entertainment, sells ad space not only on the big screen but everywhere in the theatres.[40]

Magazine ad promoting the American Marketing Association and the Marketing Hall of Legends.

Ads also appear on T-shirts, inlaid in-store flooring, in printed programs of live theatre productions, and as previews on movie DVDs. Directory advertising includes the familiar Yellow Pages in telephone books, along with thousands of business directories. Some firms pay to have their advertising messages placed on hot-air balloons, blimps, banners behind airplanes, and on scoreboards at sporting events. Johnson & Johnson and Yahoo!, among others, pay to have their logos and company messages placed on cars. Regular people literally drive the advertiser's message home. The drivers are chosen based on their driving habits, routes, occupations, and living and working locations and are paid a monthly fee for the use of the outside of their vehicles as advertising space.

MEDIA SCHEDULING

Once advertisers have selected the media that best match their advertising objectives and promotional budget, attention shifts to **media scheduling**—setting the timing and sequence for a series of advertisements. A variety of factors influences this decision as well. Sales patterns, repurchase cycles, and competitors' activities are the most important variables.

Seasonal sales patterns are common in many industries. An airline might reduce advertising during peak travel periods and boost its media schedule during low travel months. *Repurchase cycles* may also play a role in media scheduling—products with shorter repurchase cycles will more likely require consistent media schedules throughout the year. Competitors' activities may influence advertising in two ways, one by avoiding scheduling media during periods of heavy advertising by competitors and the other by matching competitors' advertising schedules.

Advertisers use the concept of reach, frequency, and gross rating points to measure the effectiveness of media scheduling plans. *Reach* refers to the number of different people or households exposed to an advertisement at least once during a certain period, typically four weeks. *Frequency* refers to the number of times an individual is exposed to an advertisement during a certain period. By multiplying reach times frequency, advertisers quantitatively describe the total weight of a media effort, which is called *gross rating point (GRP = frequent × reach)*.

Recently, marketers have questioned the effectiveness of reach and frequency to measure ad success online. The theory behind frequency is that the average advertising viewer needs a minimum of three exposures to a message to understand it and connect it to a specific brand. For Web surfers, the "wear-out" is much quicker—hence, the greater importance of building customer relationships through advertisements.

A media schedule is typically created in the following way. Say an auto manufacturer wants to advertise a new model designed primarily to appeal to professional consumers in their 30s. The model would be introduced in November with a direct mail piece offering test drives. Outdoor, newspaper, and magazine advertising would support the direct mail campaign but also follow through the winter and into the spring and summer. The newspaper ads might actually be cooperative, for both the manufacturer and local dealers. Early television commercials might air during a holiday television special in mid-December, and then one or more expensively produced, highly creative spots would be first aired during the Super Bowl in late January. Another television commercial—along with new print ads—might be scheduled for fall clearance sales as the manufacturer gets ready to introduce next year's models. This example illustrates how marketers might plan their advertising year for just one product. While this example illustrates a media schedule for a larger company with a significant advertising budget, smaller companies with smaller budgets are less likely to use television unless they decide to use a local channel.

assessment check 5

5.1 What types of products are banned from advertising on television?

5.2 What are some advantages radio offers to advertisers? What about newspapers?

5.3 Define *media scheduling* and identify the most important factors influencing the scheduling decision.

(6) Outline the organization of the advertising function and the role of an advertising agency.

ORGANIZATION OF THE ADVERTISING FUNCTION

Although the ultimate responsibility for advertising decision making often rests with top marketing management, organizational arrangements for the advertising function vary among companies. A producer of a technical industrial product may operate with a one-person department within the company, who works primarily to write copy for submission to trade publications. A consumer goods company, on the other hand, may staff a large department with advertising specialists.

The advertising function is usually organized as a staff department reporting to the vice president (or director) of marketing. The director of advertising is an executive position with the responsibility for the functional activity of advertising. This position requires not only a skilled and experienced advertiser but also an individual who communicates effectively within the organization. The success of a firm's promotional strategy depends on the advertising director's willingness and ability to communicate both vertically and horizontally. The major tasks typically organized under advertising include advertising research, design, copywriting, media analysis, and in some cases, sales and trade promotion.

ADVERTISING AGENCIES

Most large companies in industries characterized by sizable advertising expenditures hire an independent **advertising agency,** a firm whose marketing specialists assist businesses in planning and preparing advertisements. Advertising is a huge global industry. Ranked by worldwide revenue, Japan's Dentsu is the world's largest advertising agency, followed by New York City–based McCann-Erickson Worldwide.[41]

Most large advertisers cite several reasons for relying on agencies for at least some portion of their advertising. Agencies typically employ highly qualified specialists who provide a degree of creativity and objectivity that is difficult to sustain in a corporate advertising department. Some agencies also manage to reduce the cost of advertising by allowing the advertiser to avoid many of the fixed expenses associated with maintaining an internal advertising department.

Figure 15.3 shows a hypothetical organization chart for a large advertising agency. Although job titles may vary among agencies, the major functions may be classified as creative services; account services; marketing services, including media services, marketing research, and sales promotion; and finance and management. Whatever organization structure is selected, an agency often stands or falls on its relationships with its clients. The fast pace and pressure of ad agencies are legendary, but good communication remains paramount to maintaining that relationship.

advertising agency
Firm whose marketing specialists assist advertisers in planning and preparing advertisements.

assessment check 6

6.1 What is the role of an advertising agency?

6.2 What are some advantages of using an agency?

figure 15.3

***Advertising Agency
Organizational Chart***

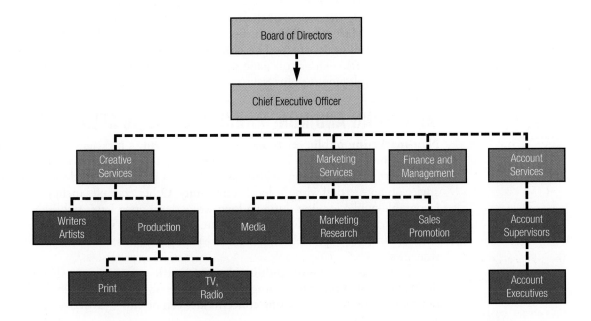

⑦ Explain the roles of cross promotion, public relations, publicity, and ethics in an organization's promotional strategy.

PUBLIC RELATIONS

In Chapter 14, we defined public relations as the firm's communications and relationships with its various publics, including customers, employees, stockholders, suppliers, government agencies, and the society in which it operates. Organizational public relations efforts date back to 1889, when George Westinghouse hired two people to publicize the advantages of alternating-current electricity and to refute arguments originally championed by Thomas Edison for direct-current systems.

Public relations is an efficient, indirect communications channel through which a firm can promote products, although it serves broader objectives than those of other components of promotional strategy. It is concerned with the prestige and image of all parts of the organization. Today, public relations plays a larger role than ever within the promotional mix, and it may emphasize more marketing-oriented information. In addition to its traditional activities, such as surveying public attitudes and creating a good corporate image, PR also supports advertising in promoting the organization's goods and services.

Public relations is in a period of major growth as a result of increased public pressure on industries regarding corporate ethical conduct and environmental and international issues. International expenditures on public relations are growing more rapidly than those for advertising and sales promotion. Many top executives are becoming more involved in public relations as well. The public expects top managers to take greater responsibility for company actions than they have accepted in the past. Those who refuse are widely criticized and censured.

The PR department is the link between the firm and the media. It provides press releases and holds news conferences to announce new products, the formation of strategic alliances, management changes, financial results, or similar developments. The PR department may issue its own publications as well, including newsletters, brochures, and reports.

A PR plan begins much like an advertising plan, with research to define the role and scope of the firm's overall public relations and current challenges. Next come strategic decisions on short-term and long-term goals and markets, analysis of product features, and choices of messages and media channels—or other PR strategies such as speaking engagements or contests—for each market. Plan execution involves developing messages highlighting the benefits that the firm brings to each market. The final step is to measure results.

The Internet has actually changed some PR planning, as PR representatives now have more direct access to the public instead of having their messages filtered through journalists and the news media. This direct access gives them greater control over their messages, as Wal-Mart is discovering. Working with its public relations firm, the world's largest retailer has begun distributing information, news, and topic suggestions to sympathetic bloggers, who spread the word on the Internet. Critics of the company's image-boosting strategy say that some bloggers are misrepresenting the source of the information by posting it word-for-word as their own. Nevertheless, Wal-Mart, which says it discourages its correspondents from cutting and pasting, insists it is simply telling its story. The company also continues to rely on more conventional public relations outlets such as full-page newspaper ads to set the record straight about its sometimes criticized employment policies.[42]

MARKETING AND NON-MARKETING PUBLIC RELATIONS

Non-marketing public relations refers to a company's messages about general management issues. When a company makes a decision that affects any of its publics, input from public relations specialists can help smooth its dealings with those publics. A company that decides to close a plant would need advice on how to deal with the local community. Other examples include a company's attempts to gain favourable public opinion during a long strike or an open letter published in a newspaper discussing an issue that affects an industry or a community. Although some companies organize their public relations departments separately from their marketing divisions, PR activities invariably affect promotional strategies.

In contrast, **marketing public relations (MPR)** refers to narrowly focused public relations activities that directly support marketing goals. MPR involves an organization's relationships with consumers or other groups about marketing concerns and can be either proactive or reactive.

With proactive MPR, the marketer takes the initiative and seeks out opportunities for promoting the firm's products, often including distribution of press releases and feature articles. For example, companies send press releases about new products to newspapers, television stations, and relevant consumer, business, and trade publications. It is a powerful marketing tool since it adds news coverage that reinforces direct promotion activities.

Reactive MPR responds to an external situation that has potential negative consequences for the organization. When the formula of Bausch & Lomb's ReNu with MoistureLoc contact lens solution was implicated as a possible cause of serious eye infections, the company immediately and voluntarily pulled the product from store shelves, and its CEO appeared on television to announce the recall and reassure the public that the company's other eye-care products were safe. The company's quick action undoubtedly contributed to minimizing its losses despite the fact that a complete product recall had to be done.[43]

PUBLICITY

The aspect of public relations that is most directly related to promoting a firm's products is **publicity:** non-personal stimulation of demand for a good, service, place, idea, person, or organization by unpaid placement of significant news regarding the product in a print or broadcast medium. It has been said that if advertising is the hammer, publicity is the nail. It creates credibility for the advertising to follow. Firms generate publicity by creating special events, holding press conferences, and preparing news releases and media kits. Lululemon, the Canadian retailer of yoga clothing, has used this approach effectively. For example, when it opened its new store in Vancouver, it had a contest to give away free yoga outfits to the first 30 people who arrived at the store naked.[44]

While publicity generates minimal costs compared with other forms of promotion, it does not deliver its message entirely for free. Publicity-related expenses include the costs of employing marketing personnel assigned to create and submit publicity releases, printing and mailing costs, and related expenses.

Firms often pursue publicity to promote their images or viewpoints. Other publicity efforts involve organizational activities such as plant expansions, mergers and acquisitions, management changes, and research breakthroughs. A significant amount of publicity, however, provides information about goods and services, particularly new products.

Because many consumers consider news stories to be more credible than advertisements as sources of information, publicity releases are often sent to media editors for possible inclusion in news stories. The media audiences perceive the news as coming from the communications media, not the sponsors. The information in a publicity release about a new good or service can provide valuable assistance for a television, newspaper, or magazine writer, leading to eventual broadcast or publication. Publicity releases sometimes fill voids in publications, and at other times, they become part of regular features. In either case, they offer firms valuable supplements to paid advertising messages.

publicity Non-personal stimulation of demand for a good, service, place, idea, person, or organization by unpaid placement of significant news regarding the product in a print or broadcast medium.

CROSS PROMOTION

In recent years, marketers have begun to combine their promotional efforts for related products using a technique called **cross promotion,** in which marketing partners share the cost of a promotional campaign that meets their mutual needs—an important benefit in an environment of rising media costs. Relationship marketing strategies like comarketing and cobranding, discussed in Chapter 9, are forms of cross promotion. Marketers realize that these joint efforts between established brands provide greater benefits in return for both organizations; investments of time and money on such promotions will become increasingly important to many partners' growth prospects.

One cell company helps promote artists such as Coldplay, Gwen Stefani, and Alicia Keys by featuring their songs as exclusive cell phone ringtones. "When we pick the right artists and package it, we sell more ringtones than we would have otherwise," says the company's vice

cross promotion Promotional technique in which marketing partners share the cost of a promotional campaign that meets their mutual needs.

assessment check 7

7.1 Distinguish between marketing public relations and nonmarketing public relations.

7.2 What is publicity?

7.3 What are the advantages of cross promotion?

president of consumer data services. "Customers see it as a value-add and the artist sees it as a value-add." All proceeds from the Peter Gabriel song recorded by Alicia Keys were donated to a group providing AIDS medicines to children and families in Africa. A company spokesperson says, "We think this will expand the appeal of ringtones and help out a great cause."[45]

⑧ Explain how marketers assess promotional effectiveness.

MEASURING PROMOTIONAL EFFECTIVENESS

Each element of the promotional mix represents a major expenditure for a firm. Although promotional prices vary widely, advertisers typically pay a fee based on cost to deliver the message to viewers, listeners, or readers—the so-called *cost per thousand (CPM)*. Billboards are the cheapest way to spend advertising dollars, with television and some newspapers the most expensive. So while price is an important factor in media selection, it is by no means the only one—or all ads would appear on billboards!

Because promotion represents such a major expenditure for many firms, they need to determine whether their campaigns accomplish appropriate promotional objectives. Companies want their advertising agencies and in-house marketing personnel to demonstrate how promotional programs contribute to increased sales and profits. Marketers are well aware of the number of advertising messages and sales promotions that consumers encounter daily, and they know that these people practise selective perception and simply screen out many messages.

By measuring promotional effectiveness, organizations can evaluate different strategies, prevent mistakes before spending money on specific programs, and improve their promotional programs. As the earlier discussion of promotional planning explained, any evaluation program starts with objectives and goals; otherwise, marketers have no yardstick against which to measure effectiveness. However, determining whether an advertising message has achieved its intended objective is one of the most difficult undertakings in marketing. Sales promotions and direct marketing are somewhat easier to evaluate because they evoke measurable consumer responses. Like advertising, public relations is also difficult to assess on purely objective terms.

The **post office** at your finger tips.

Visit canadapost.ca today to:

- Find a postal code
- Find a rate
- Ship from home
- Track a package
- Find a post office

- Change your address
- Buy stamps and mailing supplies
- Put your mail temporarily on hold
- Redirect mail to a temporary residence
- Receive, pay and store your bills in an online mailbox

Visit canadapost.ca today!

CANADA POST   POSTES CANADA
From anywhere... to anyone

COURTESY OF CANADA POST

Magazine ad in which Canada Post promotes online services.

MEASURING ADVERTISING EFFECTIVENESS

Measures to evaluate the effectiveness of advertising, while difficult and costly, are essential parts of any marketing plan. Without an assessment strategy, marketers will not know whether their advertising achieves the objectives of the marketing plan or whether the dollars in the advertising budget are well spent. To answer these questions, marketers can conduct two types of research. **Media research** assesses how well a particular medium delivers the advertiser's message, where and when to place the advertisement, and the size of the audience. Buyers of broadcast time base their purchases on estimated Nielsen rating points, and the networks have to make good if ratings do not reach promised levels. Buyers of print advertising space pay fees based on circulation. Circulation figures are independently certified by specialized research firms.

The other major category, **message research**, tests consumer reactions to an advertisement's creative message. Pretesting and post-testing, the two methods for performing message research, are discussed in the following sections.

Pretesting

To assess an advertisement's likely effectiveness before it actually appears in the chosen medium, marketers often conduct **pretesting.**

The obvious advantage of this technique is the opportunity to evaluate ads when they are being developed. Marketers can conduct a number of different pretests, beginning during the concept phase in the campaign's earliest stages, when they have only rough copy of the ad, and continuing until the ad layout and design are almost completed.

Pretesting employs a variety of evaluation methods. For example, focus groups can discuss their reactions to mock-ups of ads using different themes, headlines, or illustrations. CopyTest is an Internet-based advertising pretesting system developed by Decision Analyst that predicts the effectiveness of advertising pieces, including television storyboards, finished television and radio commercials, and magazine, newspaper, and billboard ads.[46]

To screen potential radio and television advertisements, marketers often recruit consumers to sit in a studio and indicate their preferences by pressing two buttons, one for a positive reaction to the commercial and the other for a negative reaction. Sometimes proposed ad copy is printed on a postcard that also offers a free product; the number of cards returned represents an indication of the copy's effectiveness. *Blind product tests* are also frequently used. In these tests, people are asked to select unidentified products on the basis of available advertising copy.

Mechanical devices offer yet another method of assessing how people read advertising copy. One mechanical test uses a hidden camera to photograph eye movements of readers. The results help advertisers determine headline placement and copy length. Another mechanical approach measures the galvanic skin response—changes in the electrical resistance of the skin produced by emotional reactions.

Smart car promotion showing their award and ecoAUTO Rebate program.

Post-testing

Post-testing assesses advertising copy after it has appeared in the appropriate medium. Pretesting generally is a more desirable measurement method than post-testing because it can save the cost of placing ineffective ads. However, post-testing can help in planning future advertisements and in adjusting current advertising programs.

One of the most popular post-test methods is a readership test, also called a recognition test. In this test people are interviewed who have read selected magazines to determine whether they observed various ads in them. A copy of the magazine is used as an interview aid, and each interviewer starts at a different point in the magazine and asks aided and unaided questions relating to the ads. For larger ads, respondents are asked about specifics, such as headlines and copy.

Unaided recall tests are another method of post-testing the effectiveness of advertisements. Respondents do not see copies of the magazine after their initial reading but are asked to recall the ads from memory. A research company conducts telephone interviews the day after a commercial has aired on television to test brand recognition and the advertisement's effectiveness. Another similar test measures ad awareness by telephone polling that asks each consumer to name the advertisement that first comes to mind of all the ads he or she has seen, heard, or read in the previous 30 days.

Inquiry tests are another popular form of post-test. Advertisements sometimes offer gifts—generally product samples—to people who respond to them. The number of inquiries relative to the advertisement's cost forms a measure of its effectiveness.

Split runs allow advertisers to test two or more ads at the same time. Although advertisers traditionally place different versions in newspapers and magazines, split runs on cable television systems frequently test the effectiveness of TV ads. With this method, advertisers divide the cable TV audience or a publication's subscribers in two: half view advertisement A and the other half view advertisement B. The relative effectiveness of the alternatives is then determined through inquiries or recall and recognition tests.

Marketoid

Canada has 916 certified organic farms growing fruits and vegetables.

"Noted %" indicates the percentage of readers interviewed who saw any part of the advertisement; 63% noted this ad.

"Read Some %" indicates the percentage of readers interviewed who read any amount of the body copy; 52% read some of the ad.

And you thought we only made cars.

Sure, Honda is best known for its automobiles. But we are, first and foremost, an engineering company. As well as the world's largest engine manufacturer. Today, we build some of the most dependable motorcycles, personal watercraft, lawnmowers, marine engines, generators, snowblowers, tillers and all-terrain vehicles out there. And, yes. We also manufacture those world-renowned cars.

From our low-emission automobiles to our clean and quiet marine engines, every Honda is designed to balance the thrill of fun and performance with society's need for fuel efficiency and cleaner air. Ultimately, it's the kind of thinking that improves the quality of life. And, certainly, the adventuresome quality of your weekends. Get things going at honda.com.

HONDA
The power of dreams.

"Associated %" indicates the percentage of readers interviewed who saw any part of the ad that indicates the brand or advertiser; 62% associated this ad with Honda.

"Read Most %" indicates the percentage of readers interviewed who read more than half of the body copy; 20% read most of the ad.

Magazine Advertisement with Starch Scores - one method of measuring recall

Regardless of the exact method they choose, marketers must realize that pretesting and post-testing are expensive efforts. As a result, they must plan to use these techniques as effectively as possible.

MEASURING PUBLIC RELATIONS EFFECTIVENESS

As with other forms of marketing communications, organizations must measure PR results based on their objectives both for the PR program as a whole and for specific activities. In the next step, marketers must decide what they want to measure. This choice includes determining whether the message was heard by the target audience and whether it had the desired influence on public opinion.

The simplest and least costly level of assessment measures outputs of the PR program: whether the target audience received, paid attention to, understood, and retained the messages directed to them. To make this judgment, the staff could count the number of media placements and gauge the extent of media coverage. They could count attendees at any press conference, evaluate the quality of brochures and other materials, and pursue similar activities. Formal techniques include tracking publicity placements, analyzing how favourably their contents portrayed the company, and conducting public opinion polls.

To analyze PR effectiveness more deeply, a firm could conduct focus groups, interviews with opinion leaders, and more detailed and extensive opinion polls. The highest level of effectiveness measurement looks at outcomes: did the PR program change people's opinions, attitudes, and behaviour? PR professionals measure these outcomes through before-and-after polls (similar to pretesting and post-testing) and more advanced techniques like psychographic analysis (discussed in Chapter 8).

EVALUATING INTERACTIVE MEDIA

Marketers employ several methods to measure how many users view Web advertisements: *hits* (user requests for a file), *impressions* (the number of times a viewer sees an ad), and *click-throughs* (when the user clicks the ad to get more information). *View-through* rates measure responses over time. However, some of these measures can be misleading. Because each page, graphic, or multimedia file equals one hit, simple interactions can easily inflate the hit count, making it less accurate. To increase effectiveness, advertisers must give viewers who do click through their site something good to see. Successful Web campaigns use demonstrations, promotions, coupons, and interactive features.

Internet marketers price ad banners based on cost per thousand (CPM). Websites that sell advertising typically guarantee a certain number of impressions—the number of times an ad banner is downloaded and presumably seen by visitors. Marketers then set a rate based on that guarantee times the CPM rate.

assessment check 8

8.1 What is CPM?

8.2 Distinguish between media research and message research.

8.3 Describe several research techniques used in post-testing.

ETHICS IN NON-PERSONAL SELLING

Chapter 3 introduced the topic of marketing ethics and noted that promotion is the element in the marketing mix that raises the most ethical questions. People actively debate the question of whether marketing communications contribute to better lives. The final section of this chapter takes a closer look at ethical concerns in advertising and public relations.

ADVERTISING ETHICS

Even though advertising to children and beer ads are legal, these types of promotions continue to be debated as important ethical issues. One area of controversy is advertising aimed at children. When it comes to influencing parents' purchase decisions, nothing beats influencing kids. By promoting goods and services directly to children, firms can sell not only to them but to the rest of the household, too. But many parents and consumer advocates question the ethics of promoting directly to children. Their argument: at a time when kids need to learn how to consume thoughtfully, they are being inundated with promotional messages teaching the opposite. To woo younger consumers, especially teens and those in their 20s, advertisers attempt to make these messages appear as different from advertisements as possible; they design ads that seem more like entertainment.

Alcoholic beverage advertising on television is another controversial area. Beer marketers advertise heavily on television and spend far more on advertising in print and outdoor media than do marketers of hard-liquor brands. While all areas of Canada have some restrictions on advertising of alcoholic beverages, some want much stricter regulation of all forms of such advertising on television and other media. Some areas of the country run ads promoting responsible drinking and the dangers of drinking and driving in an effort to show the other side of the drinking issue. Critics decry advertisements with messages implying that drinking the right beer will improve a person's social life or help to win a sports contest. The Northwest Territories and Nunavut have the tightest restrictions on alcohol ads.

In cyberspace ads, it is often difficult to separate advertising from editorial content since many sites resemble magazine and newspaper ads or television infomercials. Another ethical issue surrounding advertising online is the use of **cookies**, small text files that are automatically downloaded to a user's computer whenever a site is visited. Each time the user returns to that site, the site's server accesses the cookie and gathers information: What site was visited last? How long did the user stay? What was the next site visited? Marketers claim that this device helps them determine consumer preferences and argue that cookies are stored in the user's PC, not the company's website. The problem is that cookies can and do collect personal information without the user's knowledge.

Marketoid

In British Columbia 80 percent of the certified organic farms grew fruit, vegetables, or greenhouse products.

DECEPTIVE ADVERTISING

Deceptive advertising refers to exaggerated claims of a product's superiority or the use of subjective or vague statements that may not be literally true. While there are a few laws in Canada dealing with deceptive advertising, the Competition Act does regulate deceptive ads relating to pricing.

Exaggeration in ads is not new. Consumers seem to accept advertisers' tendencies to stretch the truth in their efforts to distinguish their products and get consumers to buy. This inclination may provide one reason that advertising does not encourage purchase behaviour as successfully as sales promotions do. A tendency toward exaggeration does raise some ethical questions, though: Where is the line between claims that attract attention and those that provide implied guarantees? To what degree do advertisers deliberately make misleading statements?

Advertising Standards Canada (ASC) is the self-regulatory body for the advertising industry. The 170 members of this organization promote the integrity and viability of advertising, hoping that effective self-control will reduce the number of laws enacted to control abuse. To date they have been effective in doing so. They administer the Canadian Code of Advertising Standards, which includes those aspects covered in the Competition Act, as well as other issues such as those relating to advertising to children. This group also investigates any complaints relating to the industry but they have no authority to enforce their decisions.[47]

General boasts of product superiority are considered so self-praising or exaggerated that the average consumer would not rely on them to make a buying decision. A quantifiable statement, on the other hand, implies a certain level of performance. For example, tests can establish the validity of a claim that a brand of long-life light bulbs outlasts three regular light bulbs.

ETHICS IN PUBLIC RELATIONS

Several public relations issues open organizations to criticism. Various PR firms perform services for the tobacco industry; publicity campaigns defend unsafe products. Also, marketers must weigh ethics before they respond to negative publicity. For example, do firms admit to problems or product deficiencies, or do they try to cover them up?

Strategic Implications

GREATER portions of corporate ad budgets will migrate to the Web in the near future. This trend means that marketers must be increasingly aware of the benefits and pitfalls of Internet advertising. But they should not forget the benefits of other types of advertising as well.

Promotion industry experts agree that e-commerce broadens marketers' job tasks, though many promotional objectives still remain the same. Today, advertisers need 75 different ways to market their products in 75 countries in the world and innumerable market segments. In years to come, advertisers also agree that channels will become more homogeneous while markets become more fragmented. ◆◆◆

REVIEW OF CHAPTER OBJECTIVES

① **Identify the three major advertising objectives and the two basic categories of advertising.**

The three major objectives of advertising are to inform, to persuade, and to remind. The two major categories of advertising are product advertising and institutional advertising. Product advertising involves the non-personal selling of a good or service. Institutional advertising is the non-personal promotion of a concept, idea, or philosophy of a company or organization.

② **List the major advertising strategies.**

The major strategies are comparative advertising, which makes extensive use of messages with direct comparisons between competing brands; celebrity, which uses famous spokespeople to boost an advertising message; retail, which includes all advertising by retail stores selling products directly to consumers; and interactive, which encourages two-way communication either via the Internet or kiosks.

③ **Describe the process of creating an advertisement.**

An advertisement evolves from pinpointing goals, such as educating consumers, enhancing brand loyalty, or improving a product's image. From those goals, marketers move to the next stages: creating a plan, developing a message, developing and preparing the ad, and selecting the appropriate medium (or media). Advertisements often appeal to consumers' emotions with messages focusing on fear, humour, or sex.

④ **Identify the major types of advertising appeals and discuss their uses.**

Advertisers often focus on making emotional appeals to the reader's or viewer's fear, humour, sex, guilt, or fantasy. While these can be effective, marketers need to recognize that fear appeals can backfire, people's sense of humour can differ according to gender, age, and other factors, and use of sexual imagery must not overstep the bounds of taste.

⑤ **List and compare the major advertising media.**

The major media include broadcast (television and radio), newspapers and magazines, direct mail, outdoor, and interactive. Each medium has benefits and drawbacks. Newspapers are flexible and dominate local markets. Magazines can target niche markets. Interactive media encourage two-way communication. Outdoor advertising in a high-traffic location reaches many people every day; television and radio reach even more. Direct mail allows effective segmentation.

⑥ **Outline the organization of the advertising function and the role of an advertising agency.**

Within a firm, the advertising department is usually a group that reports to a marketing executive. Advertising departments generally include research, art and design, copywriting, and media analysis. Outside advertising agencies assist and support firms. These specialists are usually organized by creative services, account services, marketing services, and finance.

⑦ **Explain the roles of cross promotion, public relations, publicity, and ethics in an organization's promotional strategy.**

Cross promotions, illustrated by tie-ins between popular movies and fast-food restaurants, permit the marketing partners to share the cost of a promotional campaign that meets their mutual needs. Public relations consists of the firm's communications and relationships with its various publics, including customers, employees, stockholders, suppliers, government, and the society in which it operates. Publicity is the dissemination of newsworthy information about a product or organization. This information activity is frequently used in new-product introductions. Although publicity is welcomed by firms, negative publicity is easily created when a company enters a grey ethical area with the use of its promotional efforts. Therefore, marketers should be careful to construct ethically sound promotional campaigns, avoiding such practices as exaggeration and deceit.

⑧ **Explain how marketers assess promotional effectiveness.**

The effectiveness of advertising can be measured by both pretesting and post-testing. Pretesting is the assessment of an ad's effectiveness before it is actually used. It includes such methods as sales conviction tests and blind product tests. Post-testing is the assessment of the ad's effectiveness after it has been used. Commonly used post-tests include readership tests, unaided recall tests, inquiry tests, and split runs.

assessment check answers

1.1 What are the goals of institutional advertising?

Institutional advertising promotes a concept, an idea, a philosophy, or the goodwill of an industry, company, organization, person, geographic location, or government agency.

1.2 At what stage in the product life cycle are informative ads used?

Informative ads are common in the introductory stage of the product life cycle.

1.3 What is reminder advertising?

Reminder advertising strives to reinforce previous promotional activity by keeping the name of a good, service, organization, person, place, idea, or cause before the public.

2.1 What is comparative advertising?

Comparative advertising makes extensive use of messages with direct comparisons between competing brands.

2.2 What makes a successful celebrity testimonial?

Successful celebrity ads feature figures who are credible sources of information for the product being promoted.

2.3 What is cooperative advertising?

In cooperative advertising a manufacturer or wholesaler shares advertising costs with a retailer.

3.1 What is an advertising campaign?

An advertising campaign is a series of different but related ads that use a single theme and appear in different media within a specified time period.

3.2 What are an advertisement's three main goals?

Advertising's three main goals are to educate consumers about product features, enhance brand loyalty, and improve consumer perception of the brand.

4.1 What are some common emotional appeals used in advertising?

Advertisers often focus on making emotional appeals to fear, humour, sex, guilt, or fantasy.

4.2 What are the main types of interactive ads?

Interactive ads include Internet banners, pop-ups, keyword ads, advertorials, advergames, and interstitials.

5.1 What types of products are banned from advertising on television?

Tobacco goods such as cigarettes, cigars, and smokeless tobacco are banned from television advertising.

5.2 What are some advantages radio offers to advertisers? What about newspapers?

Radio ads allow marketers to target a captive audience and also offer low cost, flexibility, and mobility. Newspaper ads are flexible and provide intensive coverage of the market. Readers can also refer back to newspaper ads.

5.3 Define *media scheduling* and identify the most important factors influencing the scheduling decision.

Media scheduling sets the timing and sequence for a series of advertisements. Sales patterns, repurchase cycles, and competitors' activities are the most important variables in the scheduling decision.

6.1 What is the role of an advertising agency?

An advertising agency's role is to help businesses plan and prepare advertisements.

6.2 What are some advantages of using an agency?

Advantages of using an ad agency are the availability of highly qualified specialists who provide creativity and objectivity, and sometimes cost savings.

7.1 Distinguish between marketing public relations and non-marketing public relations.

Marketing public relations refers to narrowly focused public relations activities that directly support marketing goals. Non-marketing public relations refers to a company's messages about general issues.

7.2 What is publicity?

Publicity is non-personal stimulation of demand for a good, service, place, idea, person, or organization by unpaid placement of significant news regarding the product in a print or broadcast medium.

7.3 What are the advantages of cross promotion?

Cross promotion divides the cost of a promotional campaign that meets the mutual needs of marketing partners and provides greater benefits for both in return.

8.1 What is CPM?

CPM is cost per thousand, a fee based on cost to deliver the advertisers' message to viewers, listeners, or readers.

8.2 Distinguish between media research and message research.

Media research assesses how well a particular medium delivers the advertiser's message, where and when to place the ad, and the size of the audience. Message research tests consumer reactions to an advertisement's creative message.

8.3 Describe several research techniques used in post-testing.

Commonly used post-tests include readership tests, unaided recall tests, inquiry tests, and split runs.

MARKETING TERMS YOU NEED TO KNOW

These terms are printed in red in the text. They are defined in the margins of the chapter and in the Glossary that begins on p. G-1. Other important terms are printed in bold black type in the chapter but not included in this list. Their definitions can be found in the Glossary.

advertising 502
product advertising 503
institutional advertising 504
informative advertising 504

persuasive advertising 504
reminder advertising 504
comparative advertising 505
cooperative advertising 507

advertising campaign 509
advertising agency 519
publicity 521
cross promotion 521

ASSURANCE OF LEARNING REVIEW

1. Identify and define the two broad categories of advertising. Give an example of each.
2. Describe each of the four major advertising strategies.
3. What variables might marketers consider in creating an advertising message for a firm that offers financial services, including retirement accounts, credit cards, and other investments?
4. What are the advantages and disadvantages of the types of emotional appeals in advertising?
5. Identify and describe the different advertising media. Give an example of one type of product that could best be advertised in each.
6. How is advertising through interactive media different from advertising in traditional media? Describe how you think a chain of golf resorts could use interactive advertising effectively.
7. What is the role of an advertising agency?
8. How can firms use marketing public relations (MPR) to their advantage?
9. Describe the ways in which marketers assess promotional effectiveness.
10. Identify the major ethical issues affecting advertising, sales promotion, and public relations.

PROJECTS AND TEAMWORK EXERCISES

1. With a classmate, review a number of advertising messages across several media and identify two effective messages and two you think are ineffective. Describe why you think each is effective or ineffective. Bring at least two of the ads to class to discuss with classmates.
2. Choose a magazine that interests you and analyze the advertisements in one issue. Describe whom you think the magazine's readers are by reviewing the ads.
3. With a classmate, find an example of cross promotion. If possible, bring it to class to discuss its effectiveness. Then create your own plan for cross promoting two products that you think would be good candidates for cross promotion.
4. Access the Internet and surf around to some sites that interest you. How many banner ads or pop-ups do you see? Do you like to view these ads, or do you find them intrusive? Which are most appealing? Which are least?
5. Select two different advertisers' television or print ads for the same product category (cars or soft drinks, for instance) and decide what emotion each appeals to. Which ad is more effective and why?
6. Which kind of appeal do you think would be most effective in advertising each of the following? Why?
   a. whitening toothpaste
   b. wireless Internet access
   c. diamond jewellery
   d. anti-litter campaign
   e. anti-cavity toothpaste
   f. discount shoe store
7. Do outdoor ads and pop-up ads have any characteristics in common? What are they?
8. Research suggests that advertising appeals based on sex are successful only when they are appropriate to the type of product being advertised. With a classmate, discuss whether each of you agrees or disagrees with this observation. Prepare to present your reasoning to the class.
9. List as many advertisements as you can remember seeing, reading, or hearing in the last week. Narrow your list down to five or six ads you can recall with some detail and accuracy. What was memorable about each of these ads?
10. Think back to any good or bad publicity you have heard about a company or its products recently. If it was good publicity, how was it generated and what media were used? If it was bad publicity, where did you find out about it and how did the firm try to control or eliminate the situation?

CRITICAL THINKING EXERCISES

1. Design a print ad, with rough-draft copy and an image (or a description of an image), for an electronics store you visit frequently. Be sure to include the elements of a typical ad and identify the appeal you chose.

2. One writer says that children exposed to exaggeration in ads grow into teens who are healthily skeptical of advertising claims. Find several print ads aimed at children, and identify what you think might be exaggeration in these ads. Select one ad that you think children would be influenced by, and rewrite the ad without the exaggeration.

3. Comparative advertising, in which marketers directly compare the advertised product with a competitor's, is controversial. The advertising industry is self-regulating on this issue, and disputes between companies regarding incorrect or misleading comparative ads are likely to result in lawsuits. Consequently, since the law provides few specific guidelines, advertisers who use comparative ads are responsible for monitoring the honesty and fairness of their messages. What do you think advertisers' criteria for fairness should be? Locate two or three comparative ads and compare the advertisers' criteria to your own. Which set of guidelines is stricter, yours or the advertisers'? Use the ads to illustrate a presentation to your class.

4. Some marketers believe that marketing in schools—through advertisements on book covers, product placement in lesson plans, and ads in educational videos and other programs—is acceptable only if the ads are designed to help schools financially by giving them supplies they cannot afford or helping them get money to buy these items. Others feel advertising has no place in schools at all. But the majority expect it to increase in the future. Find out about advertiser participation in the schools in your area. Do you agree that it has a benefit? Why or why not? Interview a few high school students you know and find out what they think. Prepare a brief report about your findings.

ETHICS EXERCISE

Major League Baseball recently cancelled plans to plant a temporary Spider-Man logo on first, second, and third bases to promote the film *Spider-Man 2* after sports fans voiced strong objections. Shocked by this sacrilege and convinced that, once advertising moved from signage to the field of play, the uniforms of players, coaches, and umpires would be covered with more brand images than a NASCAR race car, tradition-oriented fans cried foul. They wrote letters; they called sports-talk radio programs. Their vocal media complaints proved successful, and baseball commissioner Bud Selig announced that the Spider-Man logo "proposal" had been rejected. But one sports marketing executive predicted that "marketers will always push the envelope, and I think somebody will try something like this again." New York Yankee pitching great Whitey Ford said of the proposed ads, "With the salaries they're paying now, they have to make money . . . Today, television calls the shots."

1. Do you think marketing at sporting events and stadiums will become more aggressive if salaries for top players continue to climb? If the alternative is to charge higher ticket prices, which is preferable in the short term? In the long term? Why?

2. Some fans and sportswriters were outraged at the proposal to market a movie by using the bases, even though the plan was quickly cancelled. Do you think advertisers should "test the waters" first for certain types of ads? Why or why not? If yes, what sort of feedback mechanism would you suggest marketers use?

INTERNET EXERCISES

1. **Public relations.** Complete the following exercises to learn more about public relations and apply what you learned in the chapter.
   a. Visit http://aboutpublicrelations.net/toolkit.htm. Prepare a brief report on how to use photos and graphics for public relations.
   b. Read the summary in the *Occupational Outlook Handbook* (http://www.bls.gov/oco/ocos086.htm) for public relations specialists. What is the nature of the work? Who employs public relations specialists? How much do they earn? What is the job outlook for public relations specialists?
   c. A couple of years ago, many retailers came under criticism for selling clothing produced in factories where workers were poorly paid, often abused, and subjected to hazardous working conditions. In response, retailers instituted new standards for vendors. Some retailers went even further. Visit the website of The Gap Stores (http://www.gap.com). Click on About Gap Inc. and then Social Responsibility. Read about the company's annual social audit and its other efforts to protect garment workers. Explain how these efforts are examples of the effective use of public relations and publicity as described in the chapter.

2. **Advertising.** Visit the Marketing magazine website (http://www.marketingmag.ca) to access information on advertising in Canada. Complete the following:
   a. Who received the latest marketing awards?
   b. Who received the latest digital marketing awards
   c. Who received the latest marketing innovation awards?

Note: Internet Web addresses change frequently. If you don't find the exact sites listed, you may need to access the organization's or company's home page and search from there or use a search engine such as Google.

Case 15.1

Lululemon

Lululemon founder Chip Wilson moved from businesses related to surfing and snowboards into yoga. His first idea was to open a store that could be a community hub for healthy living aimed at busy professional women juggling jobs and families. He opened Kitsilano in November 2000 in the beach area of Vancouver. He quickly found that his vision was too broad and that one store could not carry everything from diet to exercise.

After taking his first yoga class, he realized that the cotton clothing being worn was inappropriate and he set out to change it. His passion for the technical aspects of athletic fabrics came to the fore and he started experimenting. In order to pay the bills, his design studio was used as a yoga studio at night. This concept became the foundation for all future Lululemon stores.

What makes Lululemon different from all other athletic clothing stores out there? The major difference is the way it markets its stores and products. Lululemon does very little traditional marketing, spending less than $50 000 a year on measured media (TV, radio, magazines, newspaper, and outdoor advertising). Not bad for a company that can boast sales of $1400 per square foot, making it one of the most successful athletic clothing retailers in Canada.

Lululemon products include tops and bottoms for both men and women, along with yoga accessories and other gear. That does not seem so different from everyone else. What makes its yoga attire different is fabric, design, and the design process. The clothes come in one of four specially designed fabrics. Fabric content ranges from all-natural fibres to 1 percent polyester but all have unique features to allow users to feel more comfortable while working out. These features include quick drying, light weight, and shape retention. Features built into the garments include flat seaming to avoid irritation, special panels and gussets to ensure the clothing stays in place, and even thumb holes on the sleeves for those cooler days.

Lululemon has made its design process part of its promotional strategy. Twice a year, groups of certified instructors in each community where a store is located meet with representatives of the company's design team. In exchange for their feedback on new designs, they receive a store discount. Individuals who embody the Lululemon culture are designated as ambassadors. Ambassadors are provided product for a year in exchange for their input into the design of new clothing and are featured in communication material such as posters, the website, and postcards. An added bonus to these two programs is that people involved in the programs will promote Lululemon products to others in their fitness activities.

Another part of the Lululemon promotional strategy is its stores. There are Lululemon retail stores in Canada, the United States, Japan, and Australia. Each store is designed specifically for its community and each runs its own promotions. These promotions could include painting graffiti across the store front or plastering the windows with a slogan. Each store has a community coordinator whose job it is to organize events in order to create brand awareness. Stores promote local yoga studios and some even have free yoga classes. The store employees are referred to as educators, and a large portion of the promotional budget goes into training them.

The future for Lululemon: more stores, of course. The company plans further expansion into existing markets with a goal to open 350 stores a year. Industry experts wonder whether its grassroots marketing program will work in other markets but the company does not seemed concerned.

Questions for Critical Thinking

1. Do you think Lululemon's grassroots marketing program is as effective as television commercials?
2. What effects will its expansion program into other countries have on its marketing program?

Sources: Lululemon website, http://www.lululemon.com, accessed April 15, 2008; Eve Lazarus; "The Tao of Lululemon," *Marketing*, April 14, 2008, pp. 22–27.

Case 15.2

Mobile Media

With the advent of PVRs allowing television viewers to bypass the commercials, companies are looking for new ways to get their messages out. Luckily, advances in other areas of technology are providing some new options. Along with this new technology comes a whole set of terms; SMS, QR codes, on-deck, and off-deck are all terms associated with mobile media or ads appearing on electronic devices such as PDAs and cell phones.

One reason marketers are looking to these new technologies are the number of people they can reach. The statistics tell the story: 54 percent—over 17 million—of the Canadian population now subscribe to a cell service. Two-thirds or 64 percent of Canadian households have at least one cell phone, and in Quebec, which has the lowest usage rate, there are still 51 percent with cell phones. The numbers are equally impressive when you look at other demographics; 74 percent of 18- to 34-year-olds have them, 72 percent of 35- to 54-year-olds have them, and 48 percent of those over 55 have them. This means that marketers can reach a large proportion of the population using this technology.

While the majority of cell phone owners use their phones for voice calls while on the go, research shows that 25 percent of cell phone users also have access to a SMS or Short Message Service. 20th Century Fox Home Entertainment used this service to launch the DVD for its movie *Mr. & Mrs. Smith*. Fox was able to attract its target market of females aged 15 to 35 because this group is high wireless users. The campaign turned cell phones into spy gadgets that customers used to complete missions delivered to them by text messaging. Those who successfully completed the missions could win prizes.

Having the ability to search the Web from cell phones is another emerging technology. Shoppers would have the ability to search for information while they were shopping for a particular product. This is where the concept of on-deck and off-deck come into play. On-deck means the website is listed on the menu of the cell phone. This feature is controlled by the wireless carrier. If a website is off-deck, the customer must type in the Web address to access it.

The biggest impact for marketers might come from mobile video. In this technology, which is much like television, marketers would be able to broadcast their messages directly to cell phones.

There are still some obstacles to overcome before this method becomes viable. Video capability has not yet been streamlined across carriers, so content would be carrier specific. There are other difficulties relating to mobile video, including the fact that even though 25 percent of cell phones have video capabilities, only 2 percent of people use them.

Some marketers are looking to cell phones to provide immediate two-way communication with shoppers in retailer outlets. Shoppers seeing a product they are interested in would be prompted to text in a code allowing them to receive a coupon reducing the price at the cash register. This process would allow retailers to build a database of customers interested in certain products and who are motivated by the lower prices. The problems with this new technology are again related to the technology itself. Mobile coupons require two-dimensional code or QR code. QR code is expensive for retailers to install and requires the retail outlet to install 2-D scanners.

With all these new technologies being developed that marketers could use to get their messages out to customers in a more targeted manner, there is one certainty: cell phones of the future will have more functions than just voice communication.

Questions for Critical Thinking

1. Advertising messages follow consumers as they work, shop, commute, vacation, recuperate, and even visit public restrooms. Marketers are enthusiastic about innovative advertising, but does it work? Do you think wildly unusual advertising is effective? Why or why not?
2. What else can marketers do to break through advertising clutter? Are they merely creating even more clutter by advertising on everything, including police cars, sports team uniforms, park benches, and cell phones?

Sources: Chris Powell, "Screen Captures," *Marketing*, March 12, 2007, pp. 23–24; Chris Daniels, "I Want My PDA," *Marketing*, October 15, 2007, pp. 48–49; Chris Daniels, "Beyond Text," *Marketing*, May 28, 2007, pp. 28–29; Edward Sattaur, "Mission Accomplished," *Marketing*, May 15, 2006, p. 20; Chris Daniels, "Measuring Mobile," *Marketing*, October 15, 2007, p. 52; Chris Daniels, "The Code Breakers," *Marketing*, April 30, 2007, p. 8; "Mobile in Motion: Wireless That Works," *Marketing*, Working Knowledge Supplement, March 14, 2007.

Video Case 15.3

BP: Beyond Petroleum

The written video case on BP appears on page VC-17. The recently filmed BP video is designed to expand and highlight the concepts in this chapter and the concepts and questions covered in the written video case.

chapter 16

Personal Selling and Sales Promotion

CHAPTER OBJECTIVES

1. Describe the role of today's salesperson.

2. Describe the four sales channels.

3. Describe the major trends in personal selling.

4. Identify and briefly describe the three basic sales tasks.

5. Outline the seven steps in the sales process.

6. Identify the seven basic functions of a sales manager.

7. Explain the role of ethical behaviour in personal selling.

8. Describe the role of sales promotion in the promotional mix, and identify the different types of sales promotion.

SELLING FOOD EQUIPMENT SOLUTIONS

TFI Food Equipment Solutions (TFI) is a Canadian industrial distributor with approximately $20 million sales revenue. Sales come mainly from two major product lines—Taylor and Henny Penny. These manufacturers produce equipment used in food service operations in institutions, stores, and restaurants and account for nearly 90 percent of TFI sales. The two product lines complement each other very well. Taylor is focused on ice cream and beverage equipment. Henny Penny produces fryers, rotisseries, blast chillers/freezers, heated food display units, etc.

To service its customers, TFI employs two types of salespeople. Ten salespeople service the single-outlet market. Single-outlet customers include many smaller, independent convenience, variety, and grocery stores. Salespeople each have a protected territory that is part of the five provinces where TFI has been appointed to represent Taylor and Henny Penny—Ontario, and the four Atlantic provinces (New Brunswick, Nova Scotia, Prince Edward Island, and Newfoundland and Labrador). The busiest period for sales to single-outlet customers is just prior to the summer, when demand for ice cream and beverages peaks. These salespeople get company vehicles, and their out-of-pocket expenses are reimbursed by TFI. They are not paid a salary, but earn commissions of 12 to 18 percent of sales revenue, depending on what is sold and the final price that they negotiate for each sale. Salespeople are expected to sell $400 000 (usually between 35 and 50 sales) of equipment annually, although some sell considerably more.

TFI also employs three national account salespeople. Judi Saliba and Vico Singh sell to accounts such as 7-Eleven, Burger King, Esso, Harvey's, KFC, Mac's Convenience Stores, McDonald's, Milestone's Grill & Bar, Wendy's, and other large multi-outlet businesses. Bill Moyer specializes in servicing the supermarket chains: Loblaws, Sobeys, and Wal-Mart, among others. Because the selling tasks are different—relationship management and providing service are even more important—these salespeople receive a high salary component—ranging between $50 000 and $70 000—and a smaller commission (1 to 4 percent) since the sales revenue from these accounts is so much greater. These accounts contribute approximately 43 percent of total company sales revenue, while the single-outlet customers contribute approximately 31 percent. The balance of sales revenue comes from parts and service sales.

Alex Pettes, recently appointed president, is always looking for additional products to sell as he is motivated to grow the company. He has recently secured the rights to sell two new products nationally in Canada. One product is an automatic French fry vending machine that produces hot French fries in just 45 seconds, "coin to cup." These machines, priced at approximately $20 000, cook fries without oil, are self-cleaning, and can be customized to accept coins, tokens, cards, etc. The Revolver system is the second product. It is a single-portion blending machine that sells for approximately $2200. It is described as a "blend in cup" beverage system, and it can be used to make malts, milkshakes, iced cappuccino, and a host of other popular drinks. The key to selling both products is to show customers how they can increase their business and make a profit; that is, TFI, and the TFI salespeople, succeed by showing customers how they can succeed.[1]

Chapter Overview

TFI Food Equipment Solutions illustrates the importance of fitting the selling techniques of salespeople to match the needs of customers. Successful salespeople must be able to add value for their customers. In exploring personal selling strategies, this chapter gives special attention to the relationship-building opportunities that the selling situation presents.

Personal selling is the process of a seller's person-to-person promotional presentation to a buyer. The sales process is essentially interpersonal, and it is basic to any enterprise. Accounting, engineering, human resource management, production, and other organizational activities produce no benefits unless a seller matches the needs of a client or customer. The fact

personal selling
Interpersonal influence process involving a seller's promotional presentation conducted on a person-to-person basis with the buyer.

that almost 10 percent of the Canadian labour force is employed in sales positions testifies to the importance of selling. While the average firm's advertising expenses may represent from 1 to 3 percent of total sales, personal selling expenses are likely to equal 10 to 15 percent. This makes personal selling the single largest marketing expense in many firms.

Personal selling is a primary component of a firm's promotional mix when one or more of several well-defined factors are present:

1. Customers are geographically concentrated.

2. Individual orders account for large amounts of revenue.

3. The firm markets goods and services that are expensive, are technically complex, or require special handling.

4. Trade-ins are involved.

5. Products move through short channels.

6. The firm markets to relatively few potential customers.

Table 16.1 summarizes the factors that influence the importance of personal selling in the overall promotional mix based on four variables: consumer, product, price, and marketing channels.

This chapter also explores *sales promotion,* which includes all those marketing activities other than personal selling, advertising, and publicity that enhance consumer purchasing and dealer effectiveness. Often overlooked in promotional discussions of high-profile advertising, the typical firm allocates more promotional dollars for sales promotion than for advertising. ◆◆◆

① Describe the role of today's salesperson.

THE EVOLUTION OF PERSONAL SELLING

Selling has been a standard business activity for thousands of years. As long ago as 2000 B.C., the Code of Hammurabi protected the rights of the Babylonian salesman, who was referred to as a *peddler.* Throughout Canadian history, selling has been a major factor in economic growth. Early peddlers travelled with their goods from town to town and farm to farm, helping expand trade among early settlers. Today, professional salespeople are problem solvers who focus on satisfying the needs of customers before, during, and after sales are made. Armed with knowledge about their firm's goods or services, those of competitors, and their customers' business needs, salespeople pursue a common goal of creating mutually beneficial long-term relationships with customers.

Personal selling is a vital, vibrant, dynamic process. As domestic and foreign competition increases emphasis on productivity, personal selling is taking on a more prominent role in the marketing mix. Salespeople must communicate the advantages of their firms' goods and services over those of competitors. They must be able to do the following:

Marketoid

A total of 1 690 538 new vehicles were sold in 2007 in Canada.

table 16.1   *Factors Affecting the Importance of Personal Selling in the Promotional Mix*

VARIABLE	CONDITIONS THAT FAVOUR PERSONAL SELLING	CONDITIONS THAT FAVOUR ADVERTISING
Customer	Geographically concentrated	Geographically dispersed
	Relatively low numbers	Relatively high numbers
Product	Expensive	Inexpensive
	Technically complex	Simple to understand
	Custom-made	Standardized
	Special handling requirements	No special handling requirements
	Transactions frequently involve trade-ins	Transactions seldom involve trade-ins
Price	Relatively high	Relatively low
Channels	Relatively short	Relatively long

- Focus on customers' needs and problems, and offer solutions. Follow through with phone calls and other communications.

- Develop knowledge about the industry in general as well as their own firms' goods and services and those of the competition, including any technical expertise required.

- Go the extra mile. This means making an extra effort to fulfill customers' needs—beyond their expectations.[2]

H. F. (HERB) MACKENZIE

Château des Charmes—one of Canada's leading family-owned wineries—adds value for its customers through counter sales. Visitors to the winery can sample its quality products and speak with well-informed and knowledgeable counter sales staff.

Relationship marketing affects all aspects of an organization's marketing function, including personal selling. This means that marketers in both internal and external relationships must develop different sales skills. Instead of working alone, many salespeople now unite their efforts in sales teams. The customer-focused firm wants its salespeople to form long-lasting relationships with buyers by providing high levels of customer service rather than going for quick sales. Even the way salespeople perform their jobs is constantly changing. Growing numbers of companies have integrated communications and computer technologies into the sales routine. These trends are covered in more detail later in the chapter.

Personal selling is an attractive career choice today. About three of every five marketing graduates choose a sales position as their first marketing job, in part because they see attractive salaries and career advancement potential. A recent survey of 1000 Canadian employers identified sales representative as the position most difficult to fill.[3] Company executives usually recognize a good salesperson as a hard worker who can solve problems, communicate clearly, and be consistent. In fact, many corporations are headed by executives who began their careers in sales.

assessment check 1

1.1 What is personal selling?

1.2 What is the main focus of today's salespeople?

② Describe the four sales channels.

THE FOUR SALES CHANNELS

Personal selling occurs through several types of communication channels: over-the-counter selling (including online selling), field selling, telemarketing, and inside selling. Each of these channels includes both business-to-business and direct-to-customer selling. Although telemarketing and online selling are lower-cost alternatives, their lack of personal interaction with existing or prospective customers often makes them less effective than personalized, one-to-one field selling and over-the-counter channels. In fact, many organizations use a number of different channels. TD Waterhouse uses advertising, a toll-free number, and a website address to encourage prospective customers to talk with its professional investment advisors.

OVER-THE-COUNTER SELLING

over-the-counter selling Personal selling conducted in retail and some wholesale locations in which customers come to the seller's place of business.

The most frequently used sales channel, **over-the-counter selling,** typically describes selling in retail and some wholesale locations. Most over-the-counter sales are direct-to-customer, although business customers are frequently served by wholesalers with over-the-counter sales reps. Customers typically visit the seller's location on their own initiative to purchase desired items. Some visit their favourite stores because they enjoy shopping. Others respond to many kinds of appeals, including direct mail, personal letters of invitation from store personnel, and advertisements for sales, special events, and new-product introductions.

Marketers are getting increasingly creative in their approach to over-the-counter selling. Sony of Canada holds an annual "Ladies Night"—a special event to engage and inform women on the latest consumer electronics technologies. National marketing manager J. D. Revilla says, "Women account for 70 percent of the buying decisions made about consumer electronics products, according to recent research. Women are also making up an increasingly larger percentage of early adopters of new technology."[4]

Electronics giant Best Buy continues to outsell its competitors; with 700 stores, the firm's sales hover around $34 billion (U.S.). Perhaps Best Buy's success is because of the training its salespeople receive. The training focuses on the firm's mantra: CARE Plus. *C* stands for contact with the customer. *A* means asking questions to learn what the customer needs. *R* represents making recommendations to the customer. *E* stands for encouragement, praising the customer for a wise purchase.

Local retailers often know their customers by name. They also know their customers' likes and dislikes. The owner of a bookstore in your hometown might call you when a new book by your favourite author arrives. Taking a page from this type of selling, Amazon.ca creates personalized messages for its customers as well— even though its salespeople have never met their customers in person. Amazon's software can send you reminders for gift purchases, recommend related purchases, or even stop you from making the same purchase twice. The site also welcomes you by name when you log on.

Regardless of a retailer's innovation, a few things remain the same in over-the-counter selling. One survey reveals the things that customers *don't* want to hear salespeople say:

- "That's not my department."
- "If it's not on the rack [or shelf], we don't have it."

Companies such as Acklands-Grainger—Canada's largest industrial distributor—rely on field selling, inside selling, telemarketing, and over-the-counter selling, all part of a comprehensive selling strategy.

H.F. (HERB) MACKENZIE

- "That's the policy."
- "I'm new here."
- "I'm closing" or "I'm on a break."
- "The computer is down."[5]

While these quotes may seem humorous, they also ring true—you've probably heard them yourself. Each conveys the message that the salesperson is not willing or able to serve the customer—exactly the opposite of what every retailer wants to convey.

FIELD SELLING

Field selling involves making sales calls on prospective and existing customers at their businesses or homes. Some situations involve considerable creative effort, such as the sales of major computer installations. Often, the salesperson must convince customers first that they need the good or service and then that they need the particular brand the salesperson is selling. Field sales of large industrial installations such as Boeing's 787 Dreamliner also often require considerable technical expertise.

Because field salespeople earn better than average incomes and often have high travel expenses, field selling is considerably more expensive than other selling options. In fairly routine field selling situations, such as calling on established customers in industries such as food, textiles, or wholesaling, the salesperson basically acts as an order taker who processes regular customers' orders. These salespeople may make six to eight sales calls in a single day. More complex field selling situations may involve weeks of preparation, formal presentations, and many hours of servicing customers following sales. These salespeople may make only one or two sales calls per day. Field selling is a lifestyle that many people enjoy. For some, positive aspects include travel, making and growing personal and professional relationships, helping customers solve buying problems, and financial recognition for superior performance. However, there are negative aspects to many sales jobs: travel delays, impact on family life, and pressure to meet sales objectives.

Taking their cue from the successes of businesses such as Avon, Mary Kay Cosmetics, and Tupperware, thousands of smaller businesses now rely on field selling in customers' homes. Often called **network marketing,** this type of personal selling relies on lists of family members and friends of the salesperson or "party host" who organizes a gathering of potential customers for an in-home demonstration of products. Rags Land, which sells children's clothing, is one such company. Rags Land customers enjoy sitting in a friend's living room and picking out clothes while their children play together; they don't have to find parking spaces or worry about losing a child at the mall. The costs of this type of field selling are minimal compared with those of traditional firms. "From a purely business standpoint, it's a very appealing way to do business because there is robust cash flow and low overhead," explains Amy Robinson, spokesperson for the Direct Selling Association.

TELEMARKETING

Telemarketing, a channel in which the selling process is conducted by phone, serves two general purposes—sales and service—and two general markets—business-to-business and direct-to-customer. Both inbound and outbound telemarketing are forms of direct marketing.

Outbound telemarketing involves a sales force that relies on the telephone to contact customers, reducing the substantial costs of personal visits to customers' homes or businesses. Technologies such as predictive diallers, autodialling, and random-digit dialling increase chances that telemarketers will reach customers at home. *Predictive diallers* weed out busy signals and answering machines, nearly doubling the number of calls made per hour. *Autodialling* allows telemarketers to dial numbers continually; when a customer answers the phone, the call is automatically routed to a sales representative. *Random-digit dialling* allows telemarketers to reach unlisted numbers and block caller-ID.

A major drawback of telemarketing is that most consumers dislike the practice. After the United States implemented a national Do Not Call Registry in 2003, pressure increased to create a similar registry in Canada, resulting in 2007 in the Canadian Radio-television and Telecommunications Commission announcing rules for a Canadian Do Not Call List, which was implemented in 2008.

field selling Sales presentations made at prospective customers' locations on a face-to-face basis.

Marketoid

Toronto-based Sun Life Financial, in a strategic alliance with Aditya Birla Group, has an insurance sales group of more than 85 000 people in 256 cities in India.

telemarketing Promotional presentation involving the use of the telephone on an outbound basis by salespeople or on an inbound basis by customers who initiate calls to obtain information and place orders.

H.F. (HERB) MACKENZIE

Telemarketing positions in Canada require greater technical knowledge and better sales process skills, resulting in higher salaries.

Telemarketers that call numbers registered on the list will face fines of $1500 for individuals, and up to $15 000 for corporations. However, political parties, registered charities, marketing researchers and pollsters, newspapers, and businesses that have had business dealings with the phone call recipient within the previous 18 months are exempted and can override the list.[6] Unethical, or at least questionable, marketers have found ways around the U.S. law. More than 3 million complaints were registered there in 2006, resulting in fewer than 30 lawsuits initiated by the Federal Trade Commission.[7] Hopefully the Canadian experience will be better, but Canadians can still expect to see a considerable increase in the amount of junk mail they receive from marketers who no longer call. Anticipating long-term growth in direct marketing, Montreal-based Transcontinental Inc., Canada's largest commercial printer, has acquired PLM Group Ltd., Canada's fourth-largest printer, but the leader in producing direct marketing flyers and catalogues.[8]

Marketoid

The call-centre industry employs 1.6 million people in India, and indirectly supports another 6 million people—approximately 10 times the size of the industry in Canada.

Inbound telemarketing typically involves a toll-free number that customers can call to obtain information, make reservations, and purchase goods and services. When a customer calls a toll-free number, the caller can be identified and routed to the person with whom he or she has done business previously, creating a human touch not possible before. This form of selling provides maximum convenience for customers who initiate the sales process. Many large catalogue merchants such as Pottery Barn, L. L. Bean, and Lands' End keep their inbound telemarketing lines open 24 hours a day, 7 days a week.

Some firms are taking dramatic steps to incorporate inbound telemarketing into their overall marketing strategy. The majority of call-centre positions in Canada are inbound positions, and these are beginning to require greater technical knowledge and better sales process skills, resulting in higher salaries.[9] As the industry continues to mature, Canadian call centres will need to focus more on these types of telemarketing positions as companies will continue to outsource inexpensive, low-tech telemarketing jobs overseas. India, for example, has become the call-centre capital of the world. Call centre revenues in India were $39.6 billion (U.S.) in 2007, up a third from the year before.[10] However, even India is beginning to outsource its call-centre services as wages there have been increasing.[11] It is now possible that a Canadian subsidiary of a U.S. company can outsource its call-centre services to a firm in India, and when customers have a problem, they will be talking to a telemarketer in Vietnam who has been contracted by the Indian firm. That's globalization.

INSIDE SELLING

inside selling Selling by phone, mail, and electronic commerce.

The role of many of today's telemarketers is a combination of field selling techniques applied through inbound and outbound telemarketing channels with a strong customer orientation, called **inside selling**. Inside sales reps perform two primary jobs: they turn opportunities into actual sales, and they support technicians and purchasers with current solutions. Inside sales reps do far more than read a canned script to unwilling prospects. Their role goes beyond taking orders to solving problems, providing customer service, and selling. A successful inside sales force relies on close working relationships with field sales representatives to solidify customer relationships.

This is one of the reasons that Canadian companies are now paying higher salaries to inside salespeople. Many currently make $35 000 or more

assessment check 2

2.1 What is over-the-counter selling?

2.2 What is field selling?

2.3 Distinguish between inbound and outbound telemarketing.

annually, and incentive plans can increase their compensation by as much as 40 to 50 percent. Jim Domanski of Ottawa-based Teleconcepts Consulting reports knowing one inside salesperson compensated entirely by commission who has earned over $200 000 in one year.[12]

INTEGRATING THE VARIOUS SELLING CHANNELS

Figure 16.1 illustrates how firms are likely to blend alternative sales channels—from over-the-counter selling and field selling to telemarketing and inside selling—to create a successful cost-effective sales organization. Existing customers whose business problems require complex solutions are likely to be best served by the traditional field sales force. Other current customers who need answers but not the same attention as the first group can be served by inside sales reps who call on them as needed. Over-the-counter sales reps serve existing customers by supplying information and advice and completing sales transactions. Telemarketers may be used to strengthen communication with customers or to re-establish relationships with customers that may have lapsed over a few months.

figure 16.1

Alternative Sales Channels for Serving Customers

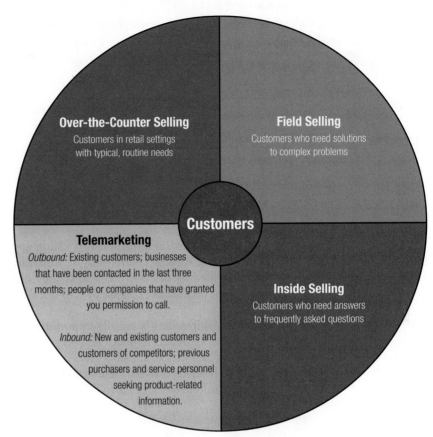

Over-the-Counter Selling
Customers in retail settings with typical, routine needs

Field Selling
Customers who need solutions to complex problems

Customers

Telemarketing
Outbound: Existing customers; businesses that have been contacted in the last three months; people or companies that have granted you permission to call.

Inbound: New and existing customers and customers of competitors; previous purchasers and service personnel seeking product-related information.

Inside Selling
Customers who need answers to frequently asked questions

TRENDS IN PERSONAL SELLING

③ Describe the major trends in personal selling.

In today's complex marketing environment, effective personal selling requires different strategies from those used by salespeople in the past. As pointed out in the discussion of *buying centres* in Chapter 5, rather than selling one on one, in B2B settings it is now customary to sell to teams of corporate representatives who make up the client firm's decision-making units. In business-to-business sales situations involving technical products, customers expect salespeople to answer technical questions—or bring along someone who can. They also want representatives who understand technical jargon and can communicate using sophisticated technological tools. Patience is also a requirement because the B2B sales cycle, from initial contact to closing, may take months or even years. To address all these concerns, companies rely on three major personal selling approaches: relationship selling, consultative selling, and team selling. Regardless of the approach, however, experts agree on a few basic guidelines for conducting successful personal selling.

RELATIONSHIP SELLING

Most firms now emphasize **relationship selling,** a technique for building a mutually beneficial partnership with a customer through regular contacts over an extended period. Such buyer–seller bonds become increasingly important as companies cut back on the number of suppliers and look for companies that provide high levels of customer service and satisfaction. Salespeople must also find ways to distinguish themselves and their products from competitors. To create strong, long-lasting relationships with customers, salespeople must meet buyers' expectations. Table 16.2 summarizes the results of several surveys that indicate what buyers expect of professional salespeople.

relationship selling
Regular contacts between sales representatives and customers over an extended period to establish a sustained seller–buyer relationship.

table 16.2   *What Buyers Expect from Salespeople*

Buyers prefer to do business with salespeople who

- Orchestrate events and bring to bear whatever resources are necessary to satisfy the customer
- Provide counselling to the customer based on in-depth knowledge of the product, the market, and the customer's needs
- Solve problems proficiently to ensure satisfactory customer service over extended time periods
- Demonstrate high ethical standards and communicate honestly at all times
- Willingly advocate the customer's cause within the selling organization
- Create imaginative arrangements to meet buyers' needs
- Arrive well-prepared for sales calls

The success of tomorrow's marketers depends on the relationships they build today in both the business-to-consumer and business-to-business markets. Merrill Lynch recently refocused its i.e., 10 000-plus brokers on a relationship selling approach. The company redirected its brokers to concentrate only on wealthy clients with $1 million or more to invest. Investors with more modest assets are now handled by call centres. The change not only has cut costs but positions Merrill Lynch for faster growth, because brokers are able to offer more sophisticated advice to fewer but more profitable clients.[13]

Relationship selling is equally important in business-to-business sales, if not more so. Firms may invest millions of dollars in goods and services from a single firm, so creating relationships is vital. The Dubai-based Emirates airline now gives building specifications to Boeing and Airbus, not the other way around. But Emirates rewards these firms by ordering more new planes than any other carrier.[14] Boeing's most successful salesperson, Larry Dickenson, is profiled in the "Marketing Success" feature.

marketing success   Star Salesman Lifts Boeing's Profits

Background. A jet is an expensive and complex purchase for an airline. So manufacturers such as Boeing must do everything they can to make the purchase process as smooth and attractive as possible. One sale can mean billions of dollars, and it can all rest on the shoulders of a salesperson such as Boeing's Larry Dickenson.

The Challenge. Asia and the Pacific region are the world's fastest-growing markets for aircraft. Airlines based there are also the largest buyers of the new, longer-range wide-body jets. Boeing wanted to grab the biggest portion of the market, which also meant dealing with foreign government officials, regulations, and agencies. So the firm turned to Larry Dickenson, who already had 20 years of experience in commercial jet sales in Asia.

The Strategy. "I'm just a jet salesman. We have good products, and we try to demonstrate [their] value," says Dickenson. But selling jets is a lot more complicated than that. Dickenson plans each sales call right down to the last detail, including the wording of press releases. He devises creative solutions for pricing, financing, leasing, training, and service. He also hosts events designed to bring people together in a relaxed setting where they can talk—such as golf tournaments.

Golf is popular among Asian businesspeople, so every November Dickenson hosts a lavish tournament in Hawaii for about 100 invited guests. "When you play four hours of golf a day, you get to know your team," he explains.

The Outcome. In a recent year, Dickenson landed $26 billion in Asian sales for Boeing. He orchestrated the sale of 115 Boeing 787 Dreamliners to Qantas, totalling about $10 billion. And he sold an order for sixteen 777 wide-body jetliners to Cathay Pacific Airways. Experts estimate that Boeing now controls about 60 percent of the Asian market for wide-body jets. But Dickenson won't rest on his laurels. He is always watching his competition, particularly John Leahy of Airbus. "I'm always nervous when John is in Asia," he says. Boeing predicts that China alone will need about 2600 new aircraft over the next 20 years—and Larry Dickenson plans to be the person to sell them.

Sources: James Wallace, "Aerospace Notebook: Boeing Doubles up on Retreats," *Seattle Post-Intelligencer*, June 7, 2006, http://seattlepi.nwsource.com; Brad Wong, "Boeing: Need for Planes Keeps Growing," *Seattle Post-Intelligencer*, April 15, 2006, http://seattlepi.nwsource.com; Stanley Holmes, "Boeing's Jet Propellant," *BusinessWeek*, December 26, 2005, p. 40.

CONSULTATIVE SELLING

Field representatives and inside sales reps require sales methods that satisfy today's cost-conscious, knowledgeable buyers. One such method, **consultative selling,** involves meeting customer needs by listening to customers, understanding—and caring about—their problems, paying attention to details, and following through after the sale. It works hand in hand with relationship selling in building customer loyalty. Xerox has turned itself around by employing consultative selling. "About five years ago we really started shifting to the consultative selling model," recalls Keith Stock, vice president of education and learning for North America. "We've become very focused on the customer[s] and helping them solve their business problems, rather than just placing another piece of equipment. We identify opportunities at the customer site and turn that into sales for Xerox."[15]

As rapid technological changes drive business at an unprecedented pace, selling has become more complex, often changing the role of salespeople. Zeks Compressed Air Solutions sells its products through authorized distributors in Canada and the United States. Every Zeks sales representative has a background in engineering. With the job title Application Engineer, they bring technical proficiency to the sales situation. The change in title has helped the company overcome resistance to sales calls, since the expertise offered brings extra value to the customer–seller relationship.

Online companies have instituted consultative selling models to create long-term customers. Particularly for complicated, high-priced products that require installation or specialized service, Web sellers must be able to quickly communicate the benefits and features of their products. They accomplish this through consultative selling.

Sometimes consultative selling takes place outside the workplace—in restaurants or on golf courses, as described in the "Etiquette Tips for Marketing Professionals" feature. Regardless of the venue, however, it is important for salespeople to maintain a professional attitude and demeanour.

consultative selling
Meeting customer needs by listening to customers, understanding their problems, paying attention to details, and following through after the sale.

ETIQUETTE TIPS FOR MARKETING PROFESSIONALS

Good Golfing Manners

IF horse racing is the sport of kings, golf is the sport of businesspeople. Many business and marketing discussions take place on the golf course and in the clubhouse. That's why so many managers with their eyes on the prize, whether it is an important deal or a top company position, take golf lessons. In addition to improving their swing and their knowledge of the rules, golfers must learn a fairly strict code of etiquette that not only affects the game but may also determine the business outcome of a golf outing. Here are a few tips:

1. Arrive well before your tee time in order to greet others, get ready, and warm up.
2. Check your scorecard for any local course rules. Be sure to abide by all the rules—there is no referee to check up on you.
3. Do not swing your golf club until you know that other players are standing at a safe distance. Also make sure you stand at a safe distance from other players who are getting ready to swing.

4. Maintain a reasonable pace when you are playing. Be prepared to take your shot when it is your turn. Always leave the green when your group has finished putting.
5. Take care of the course. Replace any divots and ball marks you create. Obey cart rules. Rake sand traps after hitting.
6. Be quiet on the course. Never talk during someone else's swing. Do not yell after a shot—whether it's good or bad.
7. In general, be courteous to everyone you encounter—in your group, on the course, and in the clubhouse. Not only is this good sportsmanship, it is also an indicator of your temperament and it may influence a business decision later.

Sources: Brent Kelley, "Golf Etiquette Is about More Than Just Manners," *Your Guide to Golf*, http://golf.about.com, accessed June 26, 2006; "Guidelines from the Rules of Golf," USGA, Bill Purdin, "The 10 Commandments of Golf Etiquette," *Legendinc*, http://www.legendinc.com, accessed June 26, 2006.

Think you don't have the opportunity
to talk to all of your customers one-on-one?

(Psst – you already do.)

STATEMENT ENCLOSED

PAUL SMITH
2701 RIVERSIDE DRIVE
OTTAWA ON K1A 0B1

The monthly statements and invoices you're already sending through the mail can be powerful customer relationship tools. They're the perfect opportunity to improve customer loyalty, enhance your brand and boost revenues by cross- or up-selling products or services.

Visit canadapost.ca/takethetest to evaluate how well your current statements and invoices are working for you and enter to win $25,000 towards their redesign. Now that's something to talk about.

Put your invoices to the test for your chance to win **$25,000!**

Visit www.canadapost.ca/takethetest

COURTESY CANADA POST

Canada Post promotes mail as a powerful tool to help companies cross- or up-sell products or services.

Similar to consultative selling, **cross-selling**—offering many goods or services to the same customer—is another technique that capitalizes on a firm's strengths. It costs a bank five times more to acquire a new customer than to cross-sell to an existing one. Moreover, research shows that the more a customer buys from an institution, the less likely that person is to leave. So a customer who opens a chequing account at a local bank may follow with a safety deposit box, a mortgage loan, and a guaranteed line of credit.

TEAM SELLING

One of the latest developments in the evolution of personal selling is **team selling,** in which the salesperson joins with specialists from other functional areas of the firm to complete the selling process. Teams can be formal and ongoing or created for a specific short-term selling situation. Although some salespeople have hesitated to embrace the idea of team selling, preferring to work alone, a growing number believe that team selling brings better results. Customers often prefer the team approach, which makes them feel well served. Another advantage of team selling is the formation of relationships between companies rather than between individuals.

In sales situations that call for detailed knowledge of new, complex, and ever-changing technologies, team selling offers a distinct competitive edge in meeting customers' needs. In most computer software B2B departments, a third of the sales force is made up of technically trained, non-marketing experts such as engineers or programmers. A salesperson continues to play the lead role in most sales situations, but technical experts bring added value to the sales process. Some companies establish permanent sales-and-tech teams that conduct all sales presentations together; others have a pool of engineers or other professionals who are on call for different client visits.

team selling Selling situation in which several sales associates or other members of the organization are recruited to assist the lead sales representative in reaching all those who influence the purchase decision.

Some resourceful entrepreneurs have begun building a **virtual sales team**—a network of strategic partners, trade associations, suppliers, and others who are qualified and willing to recommend a firm's goods or services. McMahon Worldwide is a small but powerful sales and management company founded a decade ago by Tim McMahon. The firm offers its customers strategies and software for creating their own virtual sales forces—products such as SalesConference.Net, a fully collaborative training and consulting program. MacMahon and his partner Jonathan Narducci practise their own advice by conducting many virtual sessions with clients.[16]

④ Identify and briefly describe the three basic sales tasks.

SALES TASKS

Today's salesperson is more concerned with establishing long-term buyer–seller relationships and helping customers select the correct products for meeting their needs than with simply selling whatever is available. Where repeat purchases are common, the salesperson must be certain that the buyer's purchases are in his or her best interest; otherwise, no future relationship will be possible. The seller's interests are tied to the buyer's in a mutually beneficial relationship.

While all sales activities assist the customer in some manner, they are not all alike. Three basic sales tasks can be identified: (1) order processing, (2) creative selling, and (3) missionary sales. Most of today's salespeople are not limited to performing tasks in a single category. Instead, they often perform all three tasks to some extent. A sales engineer for a computer firm may be doing 50 percent missionary sales, 45 percent creative selling, and 5 percent order processing. Most sales positions are classified on the basis of the primary selling task performed.

assessment check 3 ✓

3.1 Identify the three major personal selling approaches.

3.2 Distinguish between relationship selling and consultative selling.

Then there's the philosophy that *everyone* in the organization, regardless of what his or her job description is, should be engaged in selling. Philip Orsino is CEO of Mississauga-based Masonite International, a global building products company with 14 000 employees and operations in 17 countries. He attributes a selling culture as one of the keys to his company's success: "I think the culture's all about being enthusiastic about your products and being a great sales organization. It's this whole view of everybody coming to work to sell and make doors. And you notice I always put the word 'sell' first."[17]

ORDER PROCESSING

Order processing, which can involve both field selling and telemarketing, is most often typified by selling at the wholesale and retail levels. For instance, a Pepsi-Cola route salesperson who performs this task must take the following steps:

1. *Identify customer needs.* The route salesperson determines that a store has only seven cases left in stock when it normally carries an inventory of 40 cases.

2. *Point out the need to the customer.* The route salesperson informs the store manager of the inventory situation.

3. *Complete (write up) the order.* The store manager acknowledges the need for more of the product. The driver unloads 33 cases, and the manager signs the delivery slip.

Modern devices allow salespeople to increase their efficiency and spend more time on important sales activities.

Order processing is part of most selling positions. It becomes the primary task in situations where needs can be readily identified and are acknowledged by the customer. Even in such instances, however, salespeople whose primary responsibility involves order processing will devote some time persuading their wholesale or retail customers to carry more complete inventories of their firms' merchandise or to handle additional product lines. They also are likely to try to motivate purchasers to feature some of their firms' products, increase the amount of shelf space devoted to these items, and improve product location in the stores.

order processing Selling, mostly at the wholesale and retail levels, that involves identifying customer needs, pointing them out to customers, and completing orders.

Technology now streamlines order-processing tasks. In the past, salespeople would write up an order on the customer's premises but spend much time later, after the sales visit, completing the order and transmitting it to headquarters. Today, many companies have automated order processing. With portable computers and state-of-the-art software, the salesperson can place an order on the spot, directly to headquarters, and thus free up valuable time and energy. Computers have even eliminated the need for some of the traditional face-to-face contacts for routine reorders.

CREATIVE SELLING

When a considerable amount of decision making is involved in purchasing a good or service, an effective salesperson uses **creative selling** techniques to solicit an order. In contrast to the order-processing task, which deals mainly with maintaining existing business, creative selling generally is used to develop new business either by adding new customers or by introducing new goods and services. New products or upgrades to more expensive items often require creative selling. The salesperson must first identify the customer's problems and needs and then propose a solution in the form of the good or service being offered. Creative selling techniques are used in over-the-counter selling, field selling, inside selling, and telemarketing (when attempting to expand an existing business relationship).

creative selling Personal selling that involves situations in which a considerable degree of analytical decision making on the buyer's part results in the need for skillful proposals of solutions for the customer's needs.

Sometimes creative selling can rejuvenate an old product. Newell Rubbermaid's Phoenix program is designed to train young, entry-level salespeople to do whatever it takes to sell Rubbermaid products. They may be found stocking shelves, demonstrating new products, or organizing in-store scavenger hunts. Phoenix program trainees are energetic and enthusiastic—and they have helped turn the company around. As employees progress in their careers, they take part in additional training seminars that teach advanced selling skills, product and channel marketing, negotiating skills, and leadership skills.[18]

MISSIONARY SELLING

missionary selling
Indirect type of selling in which specialized salespeople promote the firm's goodwill among indirect customers, often by assisting customers in product use.

Missionary selling is an indirect approach to sales. Salespeople sell the firm's goodwill and provide their customers with information and technical or operational assistance. A cosmetics company salesperson may call on retailers to check on special promotions and overall product movement, even though a wholesaler takes orders and delivers merchandise. Large pharmaceutical companies are the most aggressive of missionary sales operations. Through extensive gift-giving, wining and dining, free seminars, and other **sales incentives**, teams of sales reps typically court doctors (the indirect customer) in the hope of persuading them to prescribe a particular brand to patients. They also provide physicians with glossy product literature. Here, the doctor is clearly the decision maker, even though the transaction is not complete until the patient hands the prescription over to a pharmacist.

Missionary sales may involve both field selling and telemarketing. Many aspects of team selling can also be seen as missionary sales, as when technical support salespeople help design, install, and maintain equipment; when they train customers' employees; and when they provide information or operational assistance.

assessment check 4

4.1 What are the three major tasks performed by salespeople?

4.2 What are the three steps of order processing?

(5) Outline the seven steps in the sales process.

THE SALES PROCESS

If you have worked in a retail store, or if you've sold magazine subscriptions or candy to raise money for your school or sports team, you will recognize many of the activities involved in the following list of steps in the sales process. Personal selling encompasses the following sequence of activities: (1) prospecting and qualifying, (2) approach, (3) presentation, (4) demonstration, (5) handling buyer concerns, (6) closing, and (7) follow-up.

As Figure 16.2 indicates, these steps follow the AIDA concept (attention-interest-desire-action). Once a sales prospect has been qualified, an attempt is made to secure his or her attention. The presentation and demonstration steps are designed to generate interest and desire. Successful handling of buyer resistance should arouse further desire. Action occurs at the close of the sale.

Salespeople modify the steps in this process to match their customers' buying processes. A neighbour who eagerly looks forward to the Girl Guide cookie sale each year needs no presentation—except for details about new types of cookie offerings. But the same neighbour would expect a demonstration from an auto dealer when looking for a new car or might appreciate a presentation of dinner specials by the waiter prior to ordering a meal at a restaurant.

figure 16.2

The AIDA Concept and the Personal Selling Process

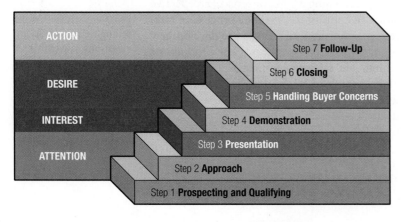

PROSPECTING AND QUALIFYING

Prospecting, the process of identifying potential customers, may involve hours, days, or weeks of effort, but it is a necessary step. Leads about prospects come from many sources: the Internet, computerized databases, trade show exhibits, previous customers, friends and neighbours, other vendors, non-sales employees in the firm, suppliers, and social and professional contacts. Although a firm may emphasize personal selling as the primary component of its overall promotional strategy, direct mail and advertising campaigns are also effective in identifying prospective customers.

As a salesperson, before you begin your prospecting effort, you must be clear about what your firm is selling. But don't limit your thoughts to a narrow definition of the product offerings. Customers are generally looking for solutions to problems, or ways to make their lives better or businesses more successful. In addition, you need to be well informed about the goods and services of the industry in general. Find out how other goods are marketed and packaged. Try out a service yourself. Understand how the industry operates so you will understand what your prospective customers need and want—and how you can serve them.[19]

Qualifying—determining that the prospect really is a potential customer—is another important sales task. Not all prospects are qualified to make purchase decisions. Even though an employee in a firm might like your products, he or she might not be authorized to make the purchase. A consumer who test-drives a Porsche might fall in love with it—but not be able to afford the purchase price. Qualifying can be a two-way street. As a sales representative, you might determine that a certain prospect is qualified to make a purchase. But the prospect must agree in order for the process to go forward. If either you or the prospect determine at the outset that there's no chance for a purchase, then it's best to move on.

APPROACH

Once you have identified a qualified prospect, you need to collect all available, relevant information and plan an **approach**—your initial contact with the prospective customer. If your firm already has a relationship with the customer or has permission to contact the person, you may use telemarketing. But, before you do so, gather as much information as you can.

Information gathering makes **precall planning** possible. As mentioned earlier, educate yourself about the industry in general, as well as goods and services offered by competitors. Read any marketing research that is available. Go to trade shows—you can learn a lot about many companies and their products at one location, usually in one day. Also learn as much as you can about the firm you are planning to approach—browse the company's website, find online news articles and press releases about the company, talk with other people in the industry. Know its product offerings well. If possible, buy at least one of the firm's products and use it yourself. Identify ways you can help the firm do whatever it does better. Without invading an individual customer's privacy, see if there is anything you have in common—perhaps you grew up in the same town, or you both like to play golf.[20] All of this planning will help you make an effective approach.

As you plan your approach, try to answer the following questions:

- Whom am I approaching and what are their jobs within the company?

- What is their level of knowledge? Are they already informed about the idea I am going to present?

- What do they want or need? Should I speak in technical terms or provide general information?

- What do they need to hear? Do they need to know more about specific products or how those products can serve them? Do they need to know how the product works? Do they need to know about cost and availability?

If you are a retail salesperson, you can ask a shopper questions to learn more about his or her needs and preferences. Say you work at a large sporting-goods store. You might ask a young male shopper whether he works out at home, what equipment he already has, what his fitness goals are. The answers to these questions should lead you in the direction of a sale.

PRESENTATION

In your **presentation**, you convey your marketing message to the potential customer. You will describe the product's major features, point out its strengths, and cite other customers' successes with the product. One popular form of presentation is a features-benefits framework wherein you talk about the good or service in terms that are meaningful to the buyer. If you work for a car dealership, you might point out safety features such as side airbags and built-in car seats to a young couple. You probably wouldn't provide them with engine specifications.

No matter what your size, ADP can help you succeed.

Whether your company has one employee or thousands, ADP offers the widest range of cost-effective, easy-to-use solutions that fit your needs. In fact, over 50,000 companies in Canada trust ADP to manage their HR, payroll and time & labour management with unparalleled service and compliance expertise. Find out how ADP can help your company and discover why only ADP can say we're the business behind business.

PAYROLL • HUMAN RESOURCES • BENEFITS • TIME & LABOUR MANAGEMENT • PENSION COMPREHENSIVE OUTSOURCING • PROFESSIONAL SERVICES • OCCUPATIONAL HEALTH AND SAFETY

1-866-228-9675 www.adp.ca

ADP
The business
behind business™

COURTESY OF ADP

Making effective presentations is an important skill when selling products, services, or ideas.

Your presentation should be well organized, clear, and concise. If appropriate, you might use visual sales support materials such as a chart, a brochure, a CD, or even streaming video from your laptop. If this is your first presentation to a potential customer, it will likely be more detailed than a routine call to give an existing customer some updates. Regardless of the situation, though, be attuned to your audience's response so you can modify your presentation—even on the spur of the moment—to meet their needs.

Many presentations now use computer-based multimedia, which can offer everything from interactivity to current pricing information. CNN Headline News salespeople previously used ordinary PowerPoint presentations to sell ads to cable operators. But when the company decided to change the look and feel of its 24-hour cable news network, the sales presentation material changed as well to include audio, video, and high-tech graphics.

However, technology must be used efficiently to be effective. For example, a company's website can be an excellent selling tool if it is easy for salespeople to present and buyers to use. Experts recommend that a site offer obvious links to products directly from the home page. A salesperson can actually use the site during a presentation by showing a potential customer how to use it to learn about and purchase products.[21]

In a **cold calling** situation, the approach and presentation often take place at the same time. Cold calling means phoning or visiting the customer without a prior appointment—and making a sales pitch on the spot. Cold calling requires nerve, skill, and creativity—but salespeople who are successful at it still point to the importance of preparation. Steven J. Schwartz, a Canadian sales trainer and coach, says that with good call planning, strategic message scripting, and effective message delivery, telephone cold calls can be turned into hot calls.[22]

DEMONSTRATION

One of the most important advantages of personal selling is the opportunity to demonstrate a product. During a **demonstration**, the buyer gets a chance to try the product or at least see how it works. A demonstration might involve a test-drive of the latest hybrid car or an in-store cooking class using pots and pans that are for sale.

Many firms use new technologies to make their demonstrations more outstanding than those of their competitors. Multimedia interactive demonstrations are now common. Visitors to the Black & Decker website can click on video demonstrations of such products as the Alligator Lopper (an electric branch clipper) and the Grass Hog String Trimmer and Edger.[23]

The key to an outstanding demonstration—one that gains the customer's attention, keeps his or her interest, is convincing, and stays in the customer's memory—is planning. But planning should also include time and space for improvisation. During your demonstration, you should be prepared to stop and answer questions, redemonstrate a certain feature, or even let the customer try the product firsthand.

HANDLING BUYER CONCERNS

Buyer concerns—previously called *objections*—are expressions of sales resistance. It is common for a prospect to raise several concerns during a sales presentation. It is better if you view them as concerns—an indication that you have not provided all of the information needed to make a decision—rather than as objections—something that you must overcome. There are five types of concerns. They may be expressed as questions or statements as illustrated in Table 16.3.

The Canadian Professional Sales Association offers a seminar, "The Persuasive Communicator: Motivating People to Buy," which is designed to help you handle buyer concerns without being aggressive or obtrusive. Use a buyer concern as an opportunity to reassure your buyer about

table 16.3   ***Common Buyer Concerns***

CONCERN RELATED TO:	QUESTION	STATEMENT
Product	What makes this product unique?	I don't see why this product is better than the one I have.
Price	Is this the best price you can offer?	Your price is certainly not within my budget.
Source	Will you be with this company next year if I have a problem?	I am very satisfied with my current supplier.
Time	Why would I want to buy more hockey equipment in May?	May is a poor month to buy hockey equipment.
Need	Why do I need a new cell phone?	I already have a cell phone that meets my needs.

price, features, durability, availability, and the like. If the concern involves price, you might be able to suggest a less-expensive model or a payment plan. If the concern involves a comparison to competitive products, point out the obvious—and not so obvious—benefits of your own. If the concern involves a question about availability, a few clicks on your laptop should be able to show how many items are in stock and when they can be shipped. A favoured method used by George Hutchison, chairman and CEO of Equisure Financial Network Inc. in North Bay, Ontario, to overcome buyer concerns is the "feel-felt-found" technique. When a major concern is raised, he will often say, "I know how you feel. Others have felt the same way. However, we've found that..." This method demonstrates empathy and reassures the person that other people have successfully overcome the same concern.[24]

CLOSING

The moment of truth in selling is the **closing**—the point at which the salesperson asks the prospect for an order. If your presentation has been effective and you have handled all buyer concerns, a closing would be the natural conclusion to the meeting. But you may still find it difficult to close the sale. Closing does not have to be thought of as a hard sell. Instead, a salesperson can ask low-pressure questions such as "Would you like to give this a try?" "Can I answer any more questions for you?" or "May I have your approval to proceed?"

Other methods of closing include the following:

1. Addressing the prospect's major concern about a purchase and then offering a convincing argument. ("If I can show you how the new heating system will reduce your energy costs by 25 percent, would you be willing to let us install it?")

2. Posing choices for the prospect in which either alternative represents a sale. (Would you prefer the pink sweater or the green one?)

3. Advising the prospect that a product is about to be discontinued or will go up in price soon. (But be completely honest about this—you don't want a customer to learn later that this was not true.)

4. Remaining silent so the prospect can make a decision on his or her own.

5. Offering an extra inducement designed to motivate a favourable buyer response, such as a quantity discount, an extended service contract, or a low-interest payment plan.

Even if the meeting or phone call ends without a sale, the effort is not over. "Never, ever forget the power of a simple, handwritten thank-you note. It's become a lost art in our fast-moving, high-tech society," says one sales expert.[25] You can use a written note or an e-mail to keep communication open, letting the buyer know that you are ready and waiting to be of service.

FOLLOW-UP

The word *close* can be misleading because the point at which the prospect accepts the seller's offer is where much of the real work of selling begins. In today's competitive environment, the most successful salespeople make sure that today's customers will also be tomorrow's.

It is not enough to close the sale and move on. Relationship selling involves reinforcing the purchase decision and making sure the company delivers the highest-quality merchandise. As a salesperson, you must also ensure that customer service needs are met and that satisfaction results from all of a customer's dealings with your company. Otherwise, some other company may get the next order.

These post-sale activities, which often determine whether a person will become a repeat customer, constitute the sales **follow-up**. Some sales experts believe in a wide array of follow-up techniques, ranging from expensive information folders to holiday cards to online greetings. Others recommend phone calls at regular intervals. Some prefer automatic e-mail reminders when it is time to renew or reorder.[26] At the very least, however, you should try to contact customers to find out whether they are satisfied with their purchases. This step allows you to psychologically reinforce the customer's original decision to buy. It also gives you an opportunity to correct any problems and ensure the next sale. Follow-up helps strengthen the bond you are trying to build with customers in relationship selling. You have probably experienced follow-up as a customer—if your auto dealership called to see if you were satisfied with recent service, or if your doctor phoned to find out if you were feeling better.

assessment check 5

5.1 Identify the seven steps of the sales process.

5.2 Why is follow-up important to the sales effort?

---

6 Identify the seven basic functions of a sales manager.

MANAGING THE SALES EFFORT

The overall direction and control of the personal selling effort are in the hands of sales managers. In a typical geographic sales structure, a district or divisional sales manager might report to a regional or zone manager. This manager in turn reports to a national sales manager or vice president of sales.

The sales manager's job requires a unique blend of administrative and sales skills depending on the specific level in the sales hierarchy. Sales skills are particularly important for first-level sales managers because they are involved daily in the continuing process of training and directly leading the sales force. But as people rise in the sales management hierarchy, they require more managerial skills and fewer sales skills to perform well. Ann Livermore, executive vice president of Hewlett-Packard, is passionate about her job. While her company has traditionally maintained an engineering focus, she has recently steered it toward a sales focus by hiring upper-level managers and executives with sales backgrounds. "There's a new energy about closing deals—about hating to lose," she says. "It's easier for an engineer to analytically describe why you lost a deal. But sales managers are much more emotional about it. There's a different hunger. With a truly great sales executive, you can almost see the blood on their teeth."[27]

Sales force management links individual salespeople to general management. The sales manager performs seven basic managerial functions: (1) recruitment and selection, (2) training, (3) organization, (4) supervision, (5) motivation, (6) compensation, and (7) evaluation and control. Sales managers perform these tasks in a demanding and complex environment. They must manage an increasingly diverse sales force that includes more women and minorities. Women account for almost half of Canadian professional salespeople, and their numbers are growing at a faster rate than that for men. Visible minorities are expected to account for 24 percent of the Canadian population by 2016.[28] As the workforce composition continues to change, an even more diverse blend of people will be needed to fill a growing number of sales positions. In fact, employment opportunities for sales and related fields are expected to increase faster than the average for all occupations through the next decade.[29]

RECRUITMENT AND SELECTION

Recruiting and selecting successful salespeople are among the sales manager's greatest challenges. After all, these people will collectively determine just how successful the sales manager is. New salespeople—like you—might come from colleges and universities, trade and business schools, other companies, and even the firm's current non-sales staff. A successful sales career offers satisfaction in all the following five areas that a person generally considers when deciding on a profession:

Go Green

Wind Power: Catch the Wind

Renewable energy is one of the hottest growth industries in Canada today. Across the country, 784 megawatts (MW) of wind power capacity was added in 2006, more than the cumulative installed wind power that existed at the end of 2005. Predictions are that capacity will increase tenfold by 2015, making Canada one of the five or six largest markets for wind power in the world. As a result, companies across Canada are beginning to manufacture and sell a variety of wind power systems for both commercial and residential customers. Some provincial governments are beginning to encourage investment through programs that rebate sales tax. In Ontario, homeowners that generate their own power can participate in an arrangement called "net metering." When they produce more electricity than they need, the excess goes to the grid for credit against future consumption if there are periods when the homeowners cannot produce as much electricity as they needs.

As more small businesses and homeowners look to alternative energy sources, opportunities for salespeople, and sales managers, will grow. Niagara Windpower began operations approximately 10 years ago and now has 10 commission-based salespeople selling throughout the Niagara Peninsula. Recently hired director of sales and marketing Ted Manning says, "I enjoy designing systems and processes, and creating order. This company is just beginning to grow, and it really needs someone with the ability to plan and organize." At this stage, Ted will have lots to do. He will need to plan sales and marketing strategy, decide how to organize the sales force, plan account management strategies, and forecast sales. As well, Ted will be involved in recruitment and selection, training, motivation, compensation, and evaluation decisions. It's quite a challenge, but Ted has always been excited by a challenge.

Source: Personal interview, Ted Manning, February 23, 2007; Niagara Windpower website, http://www.niagarawindpower.com, accessed October 1, 2007; Adrienne Selko, "Wind Power Doubles in Canada," *Industry Week*, http://www.industryweek.com/ReadArticle.aspx?ArticleID=13788, accessed October 1, 2007.

---

1. *Opportunity for advancement.* Studies have shown that successful sales representatives advance rapidly in most companies.

2. *Potential for high earnings.* Salespeople have the opportunity to earn among the highest salaries in many organizations.

3. *Personal satisfaction.* A salesperson derives satisfaction from achieving success in a competitive environment and from helping customers satisfy their wants and needs.

4. *Job security.* Selling provides a high degree of job security because there is always a need for good salespeople.

5. *Independence and variety.* Salespeople often work independently, calling on customers in their territory. They have the freedom to make important decisions about meeting their customers' needs and frequently report that no two workdays are the same.

Careful selection of salespeople is important for two reasons. First, a company invests a substantial amount of time and money in the selection process. Second, hiring mistakes can damage relationships with customers and overall performance, and are also costly to correct. Most larger firms use a seven-step process in selecting sales personnel: application screening, initial interview, in-depth interview, testing, reference checks, physical examination, and hiring decision. An application screening is typically followed by an initial interview. If the applicant looks promising, an in-depth interview is conducted. During the interview, a sales manager looks for the person's enthusiasm, organizational skills, ambition, persuasiveness, ability to follow instructions, and sociability.

Next, the company may administer aptitude, interest, and knowledge tests. One testing approach gaining in popularity is the assessment centre. This technique, which uses situational exercises, group discussions, and various job simulations, allows the sales manager to measure a candidate's skills, knowledge, and ability. Assessment centres enable managers to see what potential salespeople can do rather than what they say they can do. Before hiring a candidate, the firm checks references, reviews company policies, and may request a physical examination.

TRAINING

To shape new sales recruits into an efficient sales organization, managers must conduct an effective training program. The principal methods used in sales training are on-the-job training, individual instruction, in-house classes, and external seminars.

Popular training techniques include instructional videos or DVDs, lectures, role-playing exercises, and interactive computer programs. Simulations can help salespeople improve their selling techniques. Many firms supplement their training by enrolling salespeople in executive development programs at local colleges and by hiring specialists to teach customized training programs. In other instances, sales reps attend courses and workshops developed by outside companies. Salespeople can earn the Certified Sales Professional (CSP) designation after successfully completing training through the Canadian Professional Sales Association. This training program focuses on consultative selling, an approach particularly appropriate for business-to-business sales, but also for financial services sales, or anywhere that understanding customer needs is especially important.

Best Buy is committed to training. Several years ago, its sales managers realized that customers were leaving their stores without buying anything because salespeople didn't know how to explain the electronics they were supposed to sell. If a customer asked which speakers worked well with which plasma screen, the sales staff couldn't always reply. So every new salesperson now receives four hours of classroom training the first day on the job, supplemented by 12 hours of Web-based training. Then the new hire shadows an experienced salesperson on the job until a supervisor says he or she is ready to navigate alone. Salespeople continue to receive product training so that they become adept at selling. Overall, the training focuses on everything from product features to customer interaction.[30]

Still, ongoing sales training is also important for veteran salespeople. Sales managers often conduct this type of training informally, travelling with field reps and then offering constructive criticism or suggestions. Sales meetings, classes, and workshops are other ways to reinforce training. Mentoring is also a key tool in training salespeople. Best Buy's shadowing technique is a form of mentoring.

The Canadian Professional Sales Association offers a certification program for sales professionals who wish to earn the designation of Certified Sales Professional (CSP).

ORGANIZATION

Sales managers are responsible for the organization of the field sales force. General organizational alignments, which are usually made by top marketing management, may be based on geography, products, types of customers, or some combination of these factors. Figure 16.3 presents a streamlined organizational chart illustrating each of these alignments.

A product sales organization is likely to have a specialized sales force for each major category of the firm's products. This approach is common among industrial product companies that market large numbers of highly technical, complex products that are sold through different marketing channels.

Firms that market similar products throughout large territories often use geographic specialization. Multinational corporations may have different sales divisions in different countries. A geographic organization may also be combined with one of the other organizational methods. However, many companies are moving away from using territorial sales reps as they adopt customer-focused sales forces. For example, a single territory that contains two major customers might be redefined so the same sales rep covers both customers. Customer-oriented organizations use different sales force strategies for each major type of customer served. Some firms assign separate sales forces for their consumer and organizational customers. Others have sales forces for specific industries, such as financial services, educational, and automotive. Sales forces can also be organized by customer size, with a separate sales force assigned to large, medium, and small accounts.

A growing trend among firms using a customer-oriented organizational structure is the **national accounts organization**. This structure strengthens a firm's relationship with its largest customers by assigning senior sales personnel to major accounts in each market. Organizing by national accounts helps sales representatives develop cooperation among departments to meet special needs of the firm's most important customers. An example of national account selling is the relationship between Wal-Mart and its major vendors. Wal-Mart Canada is such an important account that many of its suppliers, including Procter & Gamble, have dedicated several salespeople who are responsible solely for this one account. Other examples of companies that have national accounts programs in Canada include Bell Mobility, Cadbury Trebor Allan, Elizabeth Arden, McCain Foods, and Pepsi-Cola.

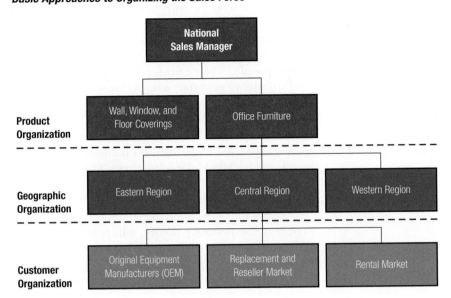

figure 16.3

Basic Approaches to Organizing the Sales Force

As companies expand their market coverage across national borders, they may use a variant of national account sales teams. These global account teams may be staffed by local sales representatives in the countries in which a company is operating. In other instances, the firm selects highly trained sales executives from its domestic operations. In either case, specialized training is critical to the success of a company's global sales force.

The individual sales manager also has the task of organizing the sales territories within his or her area of responsibility. Factors such as sales potential, strengths and weaknesses of available personnel, and workloads are considered in territory allocation decisions.

SUPERVISION

Sales managers have differing opinions about the supervision of a sales force. Individuals and situations vary, so it is impossible to write a recipe for the exact amount of supervision needed in all cases. However, a concept known as **span of control** helps provide some general guidelines. Span of control refers to the number of sales representatives who report to first-level sales managers. The optimal span of control is affected by such factors as complexity of work activities, ability of the individual sales manager, degree of interdependence among individual salespeople, and the extent of training each salesperson receives. A 6-to-1 ratio has been suggested as the optimal span of control for first-level sales managers supervising technical or industrial salespeople. In contrast, a 10-to-1 ratio is recommended if sales representatives are calling on wholesale and retail accounts.

MOTIVATION

What motivates salespeople to perform their best? The sales manager is responsible for finding the answer to this question. The sales process involves problem solving, which sometimes includes frustration—particularly when a sale is delayed or falls through. Information sharing, recognition, bonuses, incentives, and benefits can all be used to help defray frustration and motivate sales staff. Developing an enthusiastic sales staff who are happy at their jobs is the goal of the sales manager. Motivation is an important part of the company's success; according to research by the Forum Corporation, firms that score high on "motivational climate" surveys also score high on sales performance.[31]

Creating a positive, motivating environment doesn't necessarily mean instituting complex or expensive incentive programs. Monetary reward—cash—is often considered king. But sometimes simple recognition—a thank-you, a dinner, a year-end award—can go a long way. It is important for the sales manager to figure out what types of incentives will be most effective with his or her particular group of employees. Some firms go all out, dangling luxury items such as computers, digital cameras, or trips in front of the sales force as rewards. A Caribbean cruise, a trip to Disney World, or a weekend at a luxury spa could be the carrot that works, particularly if family members are included. In a recent three-year period, Maritz Canada, part of Maritz Inc., the world's largest performance improvement company, executed 350 group travel programs that included more than 95 000 people.[32] Some firms purchase gift cards from retailers such as Future Shop or Canadian Tire to distribute to sales staff who perform well. Paul Gallant, a vice president at Carlson Marketing Group in Toronto, says, "Overall, people want to pick what they want to pick… Gifts cards and certificates have been on top for quite some time."[33]

But not all incentive programs are effective at motivating employees. A program with targets that are set too high, that isn't publicized, or that allows only certain sales personnel to participate can actually backfire. So it is important for sales management to plan carefully for an incentive program to succeed.

Sales managers can also gain insight into the subject of motivation by studying the various theories of motivation developed over the years. One theory that has been applied effectively to sales force motivation is **expectancy theory**, which states that motivation depends on the expectations an individual has of his or her ability to perform the job and on how performance relates to attaining rewards that the individual values.

Sales managers can apply the expectancy theory of motivation by following a five-step process:

1. Let each salesperson know in detail what is expected with regard to selling goals, service standards, and other areas of performance. Rather than setting goals just once a year, many firms do so on a semiannual, quarterly, or even monthly basis.

2. Make the work valuable by assessing the needs, values, and abilities of each salesperson and then assigning appropriate tasks.

3. Make the work achievable. As leaders, sales managers must inspire self-confidence in their salespeople and offer training and coaching to reassure them.

4. Provide immediate and specific feedback, guiding those who need improvement and giving positive feedback to those who do well.

5. Offer rewards that each salesperson values, whether it is an incentive as described previously, opportunity for advancement, or a bonus.

COMPENSATION

Money is an important part of any person's job, and the salesperson is no exception. So deciding how best to compensate the sales force can be a critical factor in motivation. Sales compensation can be based on a commission, a straight salary, or a combination of both. Bonuses based on end-of-year results are another popular form of compensation. The increasing popularity of team selling has also forced companies to set up reward programs to recognize performance of business units and teams. Today, about one in four firms rewards business-unit performance.

A **commission** is a payment tied directly to the sales or profits that a salesperson achieves. A salesperson might receive a 5 percent commission on all sales up to a specified quota, and a 7 percent commission on sales beyond that point. This approach to sales compensation is increasingly popular. But while commissions reinforce selling incentives, they may cause some sales force members to overlook non-selling activities, such as completing sales reports, delivering promotion materials, and servicing existing accounts. In addition, salespeople who operate entirely on commission may become too aggressive in their approach to potential customers, a practice that could backfire.

A **salary** is a fixed payment made periodically to an employee. A firm that bases compensation on salaries rather than commissions might pay a salesperson a set amount weekly, bi-monthly, or monthly. A company must balance benefits and disadvantages in paying predetermined salaries to compensate managers and sales personnel. A straight salary plan gives management more control over how sales personnel allocate their efforts, but it reduces the incentive to find new markets and land new accounts.

table 16.4 *Salary, Bonus, and Commission as a Percentage of Total Compensation*

JOB TITLE	BASE SALARY %	BONUS %	COMMISSION %
Junior Salesperson	84	7	9
Intermediate Salesperson	71	11	18
Senior Salesperson	51	10	40
Key Account Salesperson	82	9	9
Customer Service	91	4	5

Source: Adapted from Brett Ruffell, "The 2006 Salary Report," *Contact*, December 2006, pp. 18–24. The Canadian Professional Sales Association, Toronto, Ont., http://www.cpsa.com/PDFFolder/Contact/2006_Dec/Feature.pdf.

Many firms have found that it's best to develop compensation programs that combine features of both salary and commission plans. A new salesperson often receives a base salary while in training, even if he or she moves to full commission later on. If the salesperson does a lot of driving as part of the job, he or she may receive a vehicle. If the person works from home, there might be an allowance toward setting up an office there.

Total compensation packages vary according to industry, with the finance, insurance, and real estate industries coming out on top, followed closely by general services. Compensation also varies according to years of experience in sales. In 2006, the compensation range for junior salespeople in Canada was $31 500 to $52 400 per year, for intermediate salespeople it was $36 900 to $86 600, and for senior salespeople it was $57 500 to $117 200 per year.[34] Table 16.4 shows the percentages for salary, bonus, and commission reported for several sales-related jobs.

EVALUATION AND CONTROL

Perhaps the most difficult tasks required of sales managers are evaluation and control. Sales managers are responsible for setting standards and choosing the best methods for measuring sales performance. Sales volume, profitability, and changes in market share are the usual means of evaluating sales effectiveness. They typically involve the use of **sales quotas**—specified sales or profit targets that the firm expects salespeople to achieve. A particular sales representative might be expected to generate sales of $720 000 in his or her territory during a given year. In many cases, the quota is tied to the compensation system. The sales quota issue is discussed in the "Solving an Ethical Controversy" feature. Databases help sales managers to quickly divide revenues by salesperson, by account, and by geographic area.

In today's marketing environment, other measures such as customer satisfaction, profit contribution, share of product-category sales, and customer retention are also coming into play. This is the result of three factors:

1. A long-term orientation that results from emphasis on building customer relationships.

2. The fact that evaluations based on sales volume alone may lead to overselling and inventory problems that may damage customer relationships.

3. The need to encourage sales representatives to develop new accounts, provide customer service, and emphasize new products. Sales quotas tend to put focus on short-term selling goals rather than long-term relationships.

The sales manager must follow a formal system that includes a consistent series of decisions. This way, the manager can make fair and accurate evaluations. The system helps the sales manager answer three general questions:

1. *Where does each salesperson's performance rank relative to predetermined standards?* This comparison takes into consideration any uncontrollable variables on sales performance, such as a natural disaster or unforeseen change in the industry. Each adjusted rank is stated as a percentage of the standard.

Solving an Ethical Controversy

Sales Quotas—Are They Fair?

MOST firms that rely on personal selling set quotas for their salespeople to meet during a certain period of time. A sales quota is a target level of sales that the salesperson is expected to achieve. While managers often argue that quotas are the best way to set goals and measure performance, critics point out that they may not always be fair to the salesperson or even the firm's customers.

Are sales quotas good for salespeople, customers, and the firms they are designed to promote?

PRO

1. Realistic quotas act as goals for salespeople and can be positive motivators.
2. Sales quotas that are tied to compensation plans attract and retain the most qualified sales staff, and they provide focus on the firm's overall marketing strategy and performance.

CON

1. Sales quotas can cause salespeople to focus on new accounts at the expense of servicing existing accounts—with the result that existing customers may grow frustrated and choose a competitor instead.
2. When a salesperson meets or exceeds a quota one year, the quota is often increased by managers the following year. This practice only creates frustration among salespeople—not productivity.

Where do you stand: pro or con?

Sources: "Dictionary of Marketing Terms," American Marketing Association, http://www.marketingpower.com, accessed June 26, 2006; Donna Siegel, "Setting Sales Quotas for Your Sales Team," Sales MBA, http://www.salesmba.com, accessed June 26, 2006; Paul Dorf, "Sales Compensation: One Size Does Not Fit All," *Marketing Times,* Spring 2006, http://www.emcmarketing.com; Jeffrey Moses, "Setting Sales Quotas without Sacrificing Customer Service," National Federation of Independent Business, March 30, 2006, http://www.nfib.com.

---

2. *What are the salesperson's strong points?* The manager might list areas of the salesperson's performance in which he or she has performed above the standard. Or strong points could be placed in such categories as technical ability, processes, and end results.

3. *What are the salesperson's weak points?* No one likes to hear criticism, but when it is offered constructively, it can be motivation to improve performance. The manager and employee should establish specific objectives for improvement and set a timetable for judging the employee's improvement.

In completing the evaluation summary, the sales manager follows a set procedure so that all employees are treated equally:

- Each aspect of sales performance for which a standard exists should be measured separately. This helps prevent the so-called *halo effect,* in which the rating given on one factor influences those on other performance variables.

- Each salesperson should be judged on the basis of actual sales performance rather than potential ability. This is why rankings are important in the evaluation.

- Sales managers must judge each salesperson on the basis of sales performance for the entire period under consideration, rather than for a few particular incidents.

- The evaluation should be reviewed by a third party—such as the manager's boss or a human resources manager—for completeness and objectivity.

Once the evaluation is complete, both manager and salesperson should focus on positive action—whether it is a drive toward new goals or correcting a negative situation. An evaluation should be motivation for improved performance.

assessment check 6

6.1 What are the seven basic functions performed by a sales manager?

6.2 Define *span of control.*

6.3 What are the three main questions a sales manager must address as part of a salesperson's evaluation?

ETHICAL ISSUES IN SALES

Promotional activities can raise ethical questions, and personal selling is no exception. A difficult economy or highly competitive environment may tempt some salespeople—particularly those new to the business—to behave in ways that they might later regret. They might use the company car for personal errands or pad an expense report. They might give expensive gifts to customers. But today's experienced, highly professional salespeople know that long-term success requires a strong code of ethics. They also know that a single breach of ethics could have a devastating effect on their careers.

Some people believe that ethical problems are inevitable because of the very nature of the sales function. And in the wake of corporate scandals in which top executives have benefited at the expense of customers, employees, and shareholders, ethical managers are working harder than ever to dispel the notion that many salespersons cannot be trusted. So they reinforce ethics codes that may already be in place and strengthen ethics training. The Canadian Professional Sales Association (CPSA) offers an accreditation program for salespeople who wish to become a Certified Sales Professional (CSP). Salespeople who become a CSP must agree to abide by the CPSA Sales Institute Code of Ethics (Figure 16.4).

Sales managers and top executives can do a lot to foster a corporate culture that encourages honesty and ethical behaviour. Here are some characteristics of such a culture:

- *Employees understand what is expected of them.* A written code of ethics—which should be reviewed by all employees—in addition to ethics training helps educate employees in how to conduct ethical business.

- *Open communication.* Employees who feel comfortable talking with their supervisors are more apt to ask questions if they are uncertain about situations or decisions and to report any violations they come across.

figure 16.4

CPSA Sales Institute Code of Ethics

The CPSA Sales Institute Code of Ethics is the set of principles and standards that a certified sales professional will strive to adhere to with customers, organizations, competitors, communities, and colleagues.

The Certified Sales Professional pledges and commits to uphold these standards in all activities:

I will:

1. Maintain honesty and integrity in all relationships with customers, prospective customers, and colleagues and continually work to earn their trust and respect.

2. Accurately represent my products or services to the best of my ability in a manner that places my customer or prospective customer and my company in a position that benefits both.

3. Respect and protect the proprietary and confidential information entrusted to me by my company and my customers and not engage in activities that may conflict with the best interest of my customers or my company.

4. Continually upgrade my knowledge of my products/services, skills, and my industry.

5. Use the time and resources available to me only for legitimate business purposes. I will only participate in activities that are ethical and legal, and when in doubt, I will seek counsel.

6. Respect my competitors and their products and services by representing them in a manner which is honest, truthful, and based on accurate information that has been substantiated.

7. Endeavour to engage in business and selling practices which contribute to a positive relationship with the community.

8. Assist and counsel my fellow sales professionals where possible in the performance of their duties.

9. Abide by and encourage others to adhere to this Code of Ethics.

As a certified sales professional, I understand that the reputation and professionalism of all salespeople depends on me as well as others engaged in the sales profession, and I will adhere to these standards to strengthen the reputation and integrity for which we will strive. I understand that failure to consistently act according to this Code of Ethics may result in the loss of the privilege of using my professional sales designation.

Source: http://www.cpsa.com/SalesCertification/Gui/Html/CodeofEthics.asp. Reprinted with permission.

- *Managers lead by example.* Workers naturally emulate the ethical behaviour of managers. A sales manager who is honest with customers, doesn't accept inappropriate gifts, and leaves the company car at home during a vacation is likely to be imitated by his or her sales staff.

- Regardless of corporate culture, every salesperson is responsible for his or her own behaviour and relationship with customers. If, as a new salesperson, you find yourself uncertain about a decision, ask yourself these questions. The answers should help you make an ethical decision.

assessment check 7

7.1 Why is it important for salespeople to maintain ethical behaviour?

7.2 What are the characteristics of companies that foster corporate cultures that encourage ethical behaviour?

1. Does my decision affect anyone other than myself and the bottom line?

2. Is my success based on making the sale or creating a loyal customer?

3. Is my service of a customer based on ethical behaviour?

4. What price will I pay for this decision?[35]

---

⑧ Describe the role of sales promotion in the promotional mix, and identify the different types of sales promotions.

sales promotion
Marketing activities other than personal selling, advertising, and publicity that enhance consumer purchasing and dealer effectiveness.

SALES PROMOTION

Sales promotion includes those marketing activities other than personal selling, advertising, and publicity designed to enhance consumer purchasing and dealer effectiveness. Sales promotion can be traced back as far as the ruins of Pompeii and Ephesus. In Canada, companies have been giving away trinkets and premiums for more than 100 years.

Sales promotion techniques were originally intended as short-term incentives aimed at producing an immediate response—a purchase. Today, however, marketers recognize sales promotion as an integral part of the overall marketing plan, and the focus has shifted from short-term goals to long-term objectives of building brand equity and maintaining continuing purchases. A frequent-flyer program enables an airline to build a base of loyal customers. A frequent-stay program allows a hotel chain to attract regular guests.

Both retailers and manufacturers use sales promotions to offer consumers extra incentives to buy. These promotions are likely to stress price advantages, giveaways, or special offerings. The general objectives of sales promotion are to speed up the sales process and increase sales volume. Promotions can also help build loyalty. Through a consumer promotion, a marketer encourages consumers to try the product, use more of it, and buy it again. The firm also hopes to foster sales of related items and increase impulse purchases. Skype, a Web telephone company, announced that its Canadian and U.S. customers could make free calls to conventional landline and mobile phones for a limited period of time. The promotion was designed to attract more users and put pressure on competitor Vonage.[36]

Experts warn that creating a loyalty program is more important to companies than ever before because consumers have so many more choices among products than in the past. According to one study, the number of shoppers who identified themselves as "longtime loyal customers" dropped from 84 percent to 77 percent in just one year.[37] This means that marketers must find ways to build loyalty among customers.

Because sales promotion is so important to a marketing effort, an entire promotion industry exists to offer expert assistance in its use and to design unique promotions, just as an entire advertising industry offers similar services for advertisers. These companies, like advertising agencies, provide other firms with assistance in promoting their goods and services.

Sales promotions often produce their best results when combined with other marketing activities. Ads create awareness, while sales promotions lead to trial or purchase. After a presentation, a salesperson may offer a potential customer a discount coupon for the good or service. Promotions encourage immediate action because they impose limited time frames. Discount coupons and rebates usually have expiration dates. In addition, sales promotions produce measurable results, making it relatively easy for marketers to evaluate their effectiveness. If more people buy shoes during a buy-one-get-one-free promotion at a shoe store, its owners know the promotion was successful.

It is important to understand what sales promotions can and cannot do. They can encourage interest in both new and mature products, help introduce new products, encourage trial and repeat purchases, increase usage rates, neutralize competition, and reinforce advertising and personal selling efforts. On the other hand, sales promotions cannot overcome poor brand images, product deficiencies, or poor training for salespeople. While sales promotions increase volume in the short term, they may not lead to sales and profit growth in the long run.

Sales promotion techniques may serve all members of a marketing channel. In addition, manufacturers may use trade promotion methods to promote their products to resellers. Sales promotion techniques include the following consumer-oriented promotions: samples, bonus packs, premiums, coupons, refunds, contests, sweepstakes, and specialty advertising. Trade-oriented promotions include trade allowances, point-of-purchase advertising, trade shows, dealer incentives, contests, and training programs.

CONSUMER-ORIENTED SALES PROMOTIONS

In the promotion industry, marketers use all types of sales promotions, including games, contests, sweepstakes, and coupons to persuade new and existing customers to try their products. Consumer-oriented sales promotions encourage repurchases by rewarding current users, boosting sales of complementary products, and increasing impulse purchases. These promotions also attract consumer attention in the midst of advertising clutter. Figure 16.5 illustrates the objectives of popular sales promotion alternatives and identifies their strengths and weaknesses.

It's important for marketers to use sales promotions selectively because, if they are overused, consumers begin to expect price discounts at all times, which ultimately diminishes brand equity. The following sections describe the various forms of consumer-oriented sales promotions.

Marketoid

Canadian Tire distributes more than $100 million in branded coupons each year and claims a redemption rate of approximately 90 percent.

Coupons and Refunds

Coupons, the most widely used form of sales promotion, offer discounts on the purchase price of goods and services. In 2006, Canadian consumers received 3.6 billion coupons with an average value of $2.02 and redeemed 100 million of them for savings of $134 million.[38] When consumers redeem the coupons at retail outlets, the retailers receive the face value of the coupon plus a handling fee from the manufacturer. A recent Nielsen survey of nearly 10 000 Canadians found that 83 percent had used at least one coupon within the previous year.[39] Marketers spent nearly as much money distributing the coupons as consumers saved. Still, coupons continue to be a popular form of sales promotion.

Free-standing inserts (FSIs) in certain magazines and weekend newspapers account for nearly 58 percent of all coupons distributed in Canada. Magazines, newspapers, package inserts, the Internet, and direct mail are the standard methods of distributing coupons. Tesco, Britain's largest retailer, maintains a database of 12 million members who belong to its Clubcard loyalty program. This allowed Tesco to target first-time purchasers of baby diapers and to send them coupons for baby wipes, toys, and beer. Baby wipes and toys seem logical choices, but why beer? According to analysis done by Tesco, new fathers were less likely to spend time at the pub and more likely to spend time at home.[40]

Refunds, or rebates, offer cash back to consumers who send in proof of purchasing one or more products. Refunds help packaged goods companies to increase purchase rates, promote multiple purchases, and reward product users. Although many consumers find the refund forms too bothersome to complete, plenty still take the time and energy to do so.

Coupons are commonly used to induce customers to try new products.

figure 16.5

Most Popular Sales Promotion Alternatives

KIND OF PROMOTION	OBJECTIVES	STRENGTHS	WEAKNESSES
Coupons	Stimulate trial or brand switching	Attract price-sensitive customers who might not otherwise buy. Encourage retailer support	Not all retailers accept coupons. Have often been counterfeited or redeemed by some retailers without consumer purchases
Refunds (or rebates)	Encourage customers to buy	Help halt sales declines or reduce inventories if new products are about to enter the market	May reduce perceived value of the product. Easy for competition to match
Samples	Stimulate trial of new products	Low customer risk creates awareness and trial	My be very costly for the company
Bonus Packs	Encourage customers to buy and minimize brand switching	Reward loyal customers for continued purchase	Customers will not need to repurchase for a longer period
Premiums	Stimulate trial or create goodwill	Customers like free merchandise and may induce trial of complementary product	My be costly for the company
Contests	Encourage consumers to buy and channel members to increase inventories	A predetermined number of winners, hence cost is usually predictable. May create excitement	Require careful thought to be creative and to avoid costly legal responsibilities
Sweepstakes	Encourage customers to buy and minimize brand switching	A predetermined number of winners, hence cost is usually predictable. Consumers like them because little effort is required	Sales may decline following the promotion
Specialty Advertising	Encourage customer loyalty	Create awareness and help to reinforce previous and future advertising messages. Good customer acceptance	May be very costly for company and may become less effective if competition offers a better promotional item

SAMPLES, BONUS PACKS, AND PREMIUMS

Marketers are increasingly adopting the "try it, you'll like it" approach as an effective means of getting consumers to try and then purchase their goods and services. **Sampling** refers to the free distribution of a product in an attempt to obtain future sales. Samples may be distributed door-to-door, by mail, via demonstrations in stores or at events, or by including them in packages with other products.

Sampling produces a higher response rate than most other promotions. A recent survey showed that 92 percent of consumers preferred receiving free samples rather than coupons. With sampling, keters can target potential customers and be certain that the product reaches them. A Unilever sampling program for Axe Snake Peel targeted 300 000 males aged 18 to 24. Ski and snowboard festivals were chosen as venues to reach this demographic at the time of year that the program was implemented. Samples were distributed at the Telus Ski and Snowboard festival at Whistler, B.C., the Telus Spin event at Mt. Tremblant, Quebec, and the Coors Triple Challenge at Blue Mountain in Ontario.[41] Sampling provides an especially useful way to promote new or unusual products because it gives the consumer a direct product experience. A survey of 10 000 Canadians found sampling was very effective for creating awareness of new products in grocery stores (61 percent) and was the most effective method for introducing new products to the first of the new adopters (89 percent).[42]

A major disadvantage of sampling is the high cost involved. Not only must the marketer give away small quantities of a product that might otherwise have generated revenues through regular sales, but the market is also in effect closed for the time it takes consumers to use up the samples. In addition, the marketer may encounter problems in distributing the samples. Hellmann's marketers annoyed consumers instead of pleasing them when the firm distributed sample packets of Italian and French salad dressing in home-delivered newspapers. Many of the packets burst when the papers hit the driveways.

A **bonus pack** is a specially packaged item that gives the purchaser a larger quantity at the regular price. For instance, Camay soap has offered three bars for the price of two, and Salon Selectives often increases the size of its shampoos and conditioners for the same price as regular sizes.

Premiums are items given free or at reduced cost with purchases of other products. For example, Pantene frequently attaches a purse-size bottle of hairspray to the sides of its other hair-care products. Premiums have proven effective in motivating consumers to try new products or different brands. A premium should have some relationship with the product or brand it accompanies, though. A home improvement centre might offer free nail aprons to its customers, for example.

GNC attracts customers into its store with a price promotion for loyal customers who are Gold Card Members.

Contests and Sweepstakes

Firms often sponsor contests and sweepstakes to introduce new goods and services and to attract additional customers. **Contests** require entrants to complete a task such as solving a puzzle or answering questions in a trivia quiz, and they may also require proofs of purchase. **Sweepstakes,** on the other hand, choose winners by chance, so no product purchase is necessary. They are more popular with consumers than contests because they do not take as much effort for consumers to enter. Marketers like them, too, because they are inexpensive to run and the number of winners is predetermined. With some contests, the sponsors cannot predict the number of people who will correctly complete the puzzles or gather the right number of symbols from scratch-off cards.

Marketers are increasingly turning to the Internet for contests and sweepstakes, because of its relatively low cost and its ability to provide data immediately. Interactivity is also a key part of the online experience—as consumers become more engaged in the contest or sweepstakes event, they also build a relationship with the firm's products. Best Buy blends both online and offline sweepstakes to promote its back-to-school sales. Its Tech 101 sweepstakes awarded MP3 players, dorm refrigerators, and notebooks to winners. Best Buy reported that its website received more than 1 million hits during the promotion, and 300 000 consumers signed up for company e-mails.[43] With the recent rash of court rulings and legal restrictions, the use of contests requires careful administration. A firm contemplating this promotional technique might consider the services of online promotion specialists such as Web-Stakes or NetStakes.

Specialty Advertising

The origin of specialty advertising has been traced to the Middle Ages, when artisans gave wooden pegs bearing their names to prospects, who drove them into the walls at home to serve as convenient

Marketoid

Only 65 percent of shoppers between 18 and 24 years old indicated that they redeem coupons; however, 76 percent of shoppers who earn more than $75 000 reported coupon use.

hangers for armour. Corporations began putting their names on a variety of products in the late 1800s, as newspapers and print shops explored new methods to earn additional revenues from their expensive printing presses. Today, almost everyone has promotional products that they regularly use. A recent study of 800 air travellers found that 71 percent had a promotional product with them, and 81 percent of them could recall the advertiser's name.[44]

specialty advertising
Sales promotion technique that places the advertiser's name, address, and advertising message on useful articles that are then distributed to target consumers.

Specialty advertising is a sales promotion technique that places the advertiser's name, address, and advertising message on useful articles that are then distributed to target consumers. In Canada, this industry employs more than 25 000 people and generates sales in excess of $2.1 billion.[45] Wearable products, including T-shirts and baseball caps, are the most popular products, accounting for 37 percent of specialty advertising sales.[46] Writing instruments, glassware, and calendars are other popular forms.

Advertising specialties help to reinforce previous or future advertising and sales messages. Consumers like these giveaways, which generate stronger responses to direct mail, resulting in three times the dollar volume of sales compared with direct mail alone. Companies use this form of promotion to highlight store openings and new products, motivate salespeople, increase visits to trade show booths, and remind customers about their products.

TRADE-ORIENTED PROMOTIONS

trade promotion Sales promotion that appeals to marketing intermediaries rather than to consumers.

Sales promotion techniques can also contribute effectively to campaigns aimed at retailers and wholesalers. **Trade promotion** is sales promotion that appeals to marketing intermediaries rather than to final consumers. Marketers use trade promotions in push strategies by encouraging resellers to stock new products, continue to carry existing ones, and promote both effectively to consumers. The typical firm actually spends half its promotional budget on trade promotion—as much money as it spends on advertising and consumer-oriented sales promotions combined. Successful trade promotions offer financial incentives. They require careful timing and attention to costs and are easy to implement by retailers. These promotions should bring quick results and improve retail sales.

Trade Allowances

Among the most common trade promotion methods are **trade allowances**—special financial incentives offered to wholesalers and retailers that purchase or promote specific products. These offers take various forms. A buying allowance gives retailers a discount on goods. They include off-invoice allowances through which retailers deduct specified amounts from their invoices or receive free goods, such as one free case for every 10 ordered, when they order certain quantities. When a manufacturer offers a promotional allowance, it agrees to pay the reseller a certain amount to cover the costs of special promotional displays or extensive advertising that features the manufacturer's product. The goal is to increase sales to consumers by encouraging resellers to promote their products effectively.

As mentioned in previous chapters, some retailers require vendors to pay a special slotting allowance before they agree to take on new products. These fees guarantee slots, or shelf space, for newly introduced items in the stores. This practice is common in large supermarket chains. Retailers defend these fees as essential to cover the added costs of carrying the products, such as redesigning display space and shelves, setting up and administering control systems, managing inventory, and taking the risks inherent in stocking new products. The fees can be sizable, from several hundred dollars per store to many thousands of dollars for a retail chain and millions of dollars for nationally distributed products.

Point-of-Purchase Advertising

point-of-purchase (POP) advertising
Display or other promotion located near the site of the actual buying decision.

A display or other promotion located near the site of the actual buying decision is known as **point-of-purchase (POP) advertising**. This method of sales promotion capitalizes on the fact that buyers make many purchase decisions within the store, so it encourages retailers to improve on-site merchandising. Product suppliers assist the retailer by creating special displays designed to stimulate sales of the item being promoted. An unpopular POP display is the cigarette "powerwall." Tobacco companies spend an estimated $300 million on POP displays in Canada, although tobacco powerwalls are now illegal in many Canadian provinces.[47]

Free-standing POP promotions often appear at the ends of shopping aisles. On a typical trip to the supermarket, you might see a POP display for Disney videos, Coppertone sunscreen, or Pepsi's new reduced-calorie drink. Retailers such as Rona, Staples, and Canadian Tire all use POP advertising displays frequently. Electronic kiosks, which allow consumers to place orders for items not available in the store, have begun to transform the POP display industry, as creators of these displays look for ways to involve consumers more actively as well as entertain them.

Trade Shows

To influence resellers and other members of the distribution channel, many marketers participate in **trade shows.** These shows are often organized by industry trade associations; frequently, they are part of these associations' annual meetings or conventions. Vendors who serve the industries display and demonstrate their products for members. Every year, over 4300 different shows in Canada and the United States draw more than 1.3 million exhibitors and 85 million attendees.

Smart merchandisers recognize that many consumers make point-of-purchase buying decisions, so they strategically place complementary products near frequently purchased items. Placing sponges and spatulas near dish detergents is one example.

Industries that hold trade shows include manufacturers of sporting goods, medical equipment, electronics, automobiles, clothing, and home furnishings. Service industries include hair styling, health care, travel, and restaurant franchises. The Canadian Gift & Tableware Association holds Canada's largest trade show in Toronto each January and August, where 1100 exhibitors attract more than 25 000 retail buyers.[48]

Because of the expense involved in trade shows, a company must assess the value of these shows on several criteria, such as direct sales, any increase in product awareness, image building, and any contribution to the firm's marketing communications efforts. Trade shows give especially effective opportunities to introduce new products and to generate sales leads. Some types of shows reach ultimate consumers as well as channel members. Home, recreation, and automobile shows, for instance, allow businesses to display and demonstrate home improvement, recreation, and other consumer products to entire communities.

Dealer Incentives, Contests, and Training Programs

Manufacturers run dealer incentive programs and contests to reward retailers and their salespeople who increase sales and, more generally, to promote specific products. These channel members receive incentives for performing promotion-related tasks and can win contests by reaching sales goals. Manufacturers may offer major prizes to resellers such as trips to exotic places. **Push money** (which retailers commonly refer to as *spiffs*) is another incentive that gives retail salespeople cash rewards for every unit of a product they sell. This benefit increases the likelihood that the salesperson will try to convince a customer to buy the product rather than a competing brand.

For more expensive and highly complex products, manufacturers often provide specialized training for retail salespeople. This background helps sales personnel explain features, competitive advantages, and other information to consumers. Training can be provided in several ways: a manufacturer's sales representative can conduct training sessions during regular sales calls, or the firm can distribute sales literature and DVDs.

assessment check 8

8.1 Define sales promotion.

8.2 Identify at least four types of consumer-oriented sales promotions.

8.3 Identify at least three types of trade-oriented sales promotions.

Strategic Implications

TODAY'S salespeople are a new breed. Richly nourished in a tradition of sales, their roles are strengthened even further through technology. However, as many companies are discovering, nothing can replace the power of personal selling in generating sales and in building strong, loyal customer relationships.

Salespeople today are a critical link in developing relationships between the customer and the company. They communicate customer needs and wants to co-workers in various units within an organization, enabling a cooperative, company-wide effort in improving product offerings and in better satisfying individuals within the target market. For salespeople, the greatest benefit of electronic technologies is the ability to share knowledge when it is needed with those who need to know, including customers, suppliers, and employees.

Because buyers are now more sophisticated, demanding more rapid and lower-cost transactions, salespeople must be quick and creative as they find solutions to their customers' problems. Product life cycles are accelerating, and customers who demand more are apt to switch from one product to another. Recognizing the long-term impact of keeping satisfied buyers—those who make repeat and cross-purchases and provide referrals—versus dissatisfied buyers, organizations are increasingly training their sales forces to provide superior customer service and rewarding them for increasing satisfaction levels.

The traditional skills of a salesperson included persuasion, selling ability, and product knowledge. But today's sales professional is more likely to possess communication skills, problem-solving skills, and knowledge of products, customers, industries, and applications. Earlier generations of salesperson tended to be self-driven; today's sales professional is more likely to be a team player as well as a customer advocate who serves his or her buyers by solving problems.

The modern professional salesperson is greatly assisted by the judicious use of both consumer- and trade-oriented sales promotions. Often overlooked in promotional discussions of high-profile advertising, the typical firm allocates more promotional dollars for sales promotion than for advertising. The proven effectiveness of sales promotion makes it a widely used promotional mix component for most B2C and B2B marketers. ◆◆◆

REVIEW OF CHAPTER OBJECTIVES

① **Describe the role of today's salesperson.**

Today's salesperson seeks to form long-lasting relationships with customers by providing high levels of customer service rather than going for the quick sale. Firms have begun to integrate their computer and communications technologies into the sales function, so people involved in personal selling have an expanded role.

② **Describe the four sales channels.**

Over-the-counter selling involves providing product information and arranging for completion of the sales transaction when customers come to the seller's location. Field selling involves making personal sales calls to customers. Under certain circumstances, telemarketing is used to provide product information and answer questions from customers who call. Inside selling relies on phone, mail, and e-commerce to provide sales and product services for customers on a continuing basis.

③ **Describe the major trends in personal selling.**

Companies are turning to relationship selling, consultative selling, and team selling. Relationship selling occurs when a salesperson builds a mutually beneficial relationship with a customer on a regular basis over an extended period. Consultative selling involves meeting customer needs by listening to customers, understanding and caring about their problems, paying attention to the details, and following through after the sale. Team selling occurs when the salesperson joins with specialists from other functional areas of the firm to complete the selling process.

④ Identify and briefly describe the three basic sales tasks.

Order processing is the routine handling of an order. It characterizes a sales setting in which the need is made known to and is acknowledged by the customer. Creative selling is persuasion aimed at making the prospect see the value of the good or service being presented. Missionary selling is indirect selling, such as making goodwill calls and providing technical or operational assistance.

⑤ Outline the seven steps in the sales process.

The basic steps in the sales process are prospecting and qualifying, approach, presentation, demonstration, handling objections, closing, and follow-up.

⑥ Identify the seven basic functions of a sales manager.

A sales manager links the sales force to other aspects of the internal and external environments. The manager's functions are recruitment and selection, training, organization, supervision, motivation, compensation, and evaluation and control.

⑦ Explain the role of ethical behaviour in personal selling.

Ethical behaviour is vital to building positive, long-term relationships with customers. Although some people believe that ethical problems are inevitable, employers can do much to foster a corporate culture that encourages honesty and ethical behaviour. In addition, each salesperson is responsible for his or her own behaviour and relationship with customers.

⑧ Describe the role of sales promotion in the promotional mix, and identify the different types of sales promotions.

Sales promotion includes activities other than personal selling, advertising, and publicity designed to enhance consumer purchasing and dealer effectiveness. Sales promotion is an integral part of the overall marketing plan, intended to increase sales and build brand equity. Promotions often produce their best results when combined with other marketing activities. Consumer-oriented sales promotions include coupons, refunds, samples, bonus packs, premiums, contests and sweepstakes, and specialty advertising. Trade-oriented promotions include trade allowances, point-of-purchase (POP) advertising, trade shows, and dealer incentives, contests, and training programs.

 assessment check answers ✓

1.1 What is personal selling?
Personal selling is the process of a seller's person-to-person promotional presentation to a buyer.

1.2 What is the main focus of today's salespeople?
The main focus of today's salespeople is to build long-lasting relationships with customers.

2.1 What is over-the-counter selling?
Over-the-counter selling describes selling in retail and some wholesale locations. Most of these transactions take place directly with customers.

2.2 What is field selling?
Field selling involves making sales calls on prospective and existing customers at their businesses or homes.

2.3 Distinguish between outbound and inbound telemarketing.
Outbound telemarketing takes place when a salesperson phones customers; inbound telemarketing takes place when customers call the firm.

3.1 Identify the three major personal selling approaches.
The three major personal selling approaches are relationship selling, consultative selling, and team selling.

3.2 Distinguish between relationship selling and consultative selling.
Relationship selling is a technique for building a mutually beneficial partnership with a customer. Consultative selling involves meeting

customer needs by listening to, understanding, and paying attention to their problems, then following up after a sale.

4.1 What are the three major tasks performed by salespeople?
The three major tasks are order processing, creative selling, and team selling.

4.2 What are the three steps of order processing?
The three steps of order processing are identifying customer needs, pointing out the need to the customer, and completing the order.

5.1 Identify the seven steps of the sales process.
The seven steps of the sales process are prospecting and qualifying, approach, presentation, demonstration, handling objections, closing, and follow-up.

5.2 Why is follow-up important to the sales effort?
Follow-up allows the salesperson to reinforce the customer's purchase decision, strengthen the bond, and correct any problems.

6.1 What are the seven basic functions performed by a sales manager?
The seven basic functions of a sales manager are recruitment and selection, training, organization, supervision, motivation, compensation, and evaluation and control.

6.2 Define *span of control*.
Span of control refers to the number of sales representatives who report to first-level sales managers.

6.3 What are the three main questions a sales manager must address as part of a salesperson's evaluation?
The three main questions a sales manager must address are these: Where does each salesperson's performance rank relative to predetermined standards? What are the salesperson's strong points? What are the salesperson's weak points?

7.1 Why is it important for salespeople to maintain ethical behaviour?
Salespeople need to maintain ethical behaviour because it is vital to their firm's relationships with customers and because they are representing their company. A breach of ethics could also be detrimental to an individual's career.

7.2 What are the characteristics of companies that foster corporate cultures that encourage ethical behaviour?
Characteristics of corporations fostering ethical behaviour include the following: employees who understand what is expected of them, open communication, and managers who lead by example.

8.1 Define *sales promotion*.
Sales promotion includes marketing activities other than personal selling, advertising, and publicity designed to enhance consumer purchasing and dealer effectiveness.

8.2 Identify at least four types of consumer-oriented sales promotions.
Consumer-oriented sales promotions include coupons, refunds, samples, bonus packs, premiums, contests, sweepstakes, and specialty advertising.

8.3 Identify at least three types of trade-oriented sales promotions.
Trade-oriented sales promotions include trade allowances, POP advertising, trade shows, dealer incentives, contests, and training programs.

MARKETING TERMS YOU NEED TO KNOW

These terms are printed in red in the text. They are defined in the margins of the chapter and in the Glossary that begins on p. G-1. Other important terms are printed in bold black type in the chapter but not included in this list. Their definitions can be found in the Glossary.

personal selling 536
over-the-counter selling 538
field selling 539
telemarketing 539
inside selling 540

relationship selling 541
consultative selling 543
team selling 544
order processing 545
creative selling 545

missionary selling 546
sales promotion 558
specialty advertising 562
trade promotion 562
point-of-purchase (POP) advertising 562

ASSURANCE OF LEARNING REVIEW

1. How does each of the following factors affect the decision to emphasize personal selling or non-personal advertising and/or sales promotion?
   a. geographic market concentration
   b. length of marketing channels
   c. degree of product technical complexity
2. Which of the four sales channels is each of the following salespeople most likely to use?
   a. salesperson in a Blockbuster Video store
   b. Coldwell Banker real estate sales agent
   c. route driver for Frito Lay Canada snack foods (sells and delivers to local food retailers)
   d. technical support for Dell
3. What is team selling? Describe a situation in which you think it would be effective.
4. Why is it important for a salesperson to understand order processing regardless of the type of selling he or she is engaged in?
5. What is the role of a sales incentive?

6. Suppose you are hired as a salesperson for a firm that offers time management software for students. What would be your first step in the sales process? Where might you find some leads?

7. What is expectancy theory? How do sales managers use it?

8. What is the role of sales promotion in the marketing effort?

9. What are the benefits of sampling? What are the drawbacks?

10. What is trade promotion? What are its objectives?

PROJECTS AND TEAMWORK EXERCISES

1. Cross-selling can be an effective way for a firm to expand. On your own or with a classmate, locate an advertisement for a firm that you believe could benefit from cross-selling. List ways it could offer multiple goods or services to the same customer. Then create a new ad illustrating the multiple offerings.

2. With a partner, choose one of the following sales situations. Then take turns coming up with creative ways to close the deal—one of you plays the customer and the other plays the salesperson. Present your closing scenarios to the class.

   a. You are a new sales associate at a car dealership, and a potential customer has just test-driven one of your newest models. You have handled all the customer's concerns and settled on a price. You don't want the customer to leave without agreeing to purchase the car.

   b. You operate a lawn care business and have visited several homeowners in a new development. Three of them have already agreed to give your service a try. You are meeting with the fourth and want to close that sale, too.

3. As sales representatives for a cooperative of organic farmers, you and a classmate are invited to make a sales presentation to a national supermarket chain. List the most important messages you wish to relate and then role-play the sales presentation.

4. On your own or with a classmate, go online and research a firm such as Kraft, General Mills, Ford, or Burger King to find out what kinds of consumer-oriented promotions the company is conducting for its various brands or individual products. Which promotions seem the most appealing to you as a consumer? Why? Present your findings to the class.

5. With a classmate, design a specialty advertising item for one of the following companies or its products, or choose one of your own. Present your design sketches to the class.

   a. Canada's Wonderland (Toronto), La Ronde (Montreal), Calaway Park (Calgary), or Playland (Vancouver)

   b. Tim Hortons

   c. Porsche

   d. Telus or Fido wireless

   e. The Green Beanery (**www.greenbeanery.ca**)

   f. Apple iPod

CRITICAL THINKING EXERCISES

1. In the run-up to the implementation of Canada's Do Not Contact registry, Canadians witnessed an increase in door-to-door selling. As a marketer, do you think this type of selling is effective? Why or why not?

2. Montreal-based Van Houtte Inc. operates the largest coffee services network in North America and serves more than 74 000 workplaces. You will find their coffee served in car dealerships, doctors' offices, real estate offices, and in many other types of offices across Canada. Getting equipment and supplies into these offices requires personal selling to office managers, administrative support people, doctors, and even company owners. What role does relationship selling play in this situation? What kind of training should these salespeople receive?

3. Imagine that you want to sell your parents on the idea of you taking a trip, buying a car, attending graduate school—something that is important to you. Outline your approach and presentation as a salesperson would.

4. Why is the recruitment and selection stage of the hiring process one of a sales manager's greatest challenges?

5. InterContinental Hotels Group, which has seven brands including Holiday Inn, began offering its Priority Club members free nights at "any hotel, anywhere"—including those of competitors—as part of a sales promotion.[49] Do you think this would be a successful promotion? Why or why not?

ETHICS EXERCISE

You have been hired by a discount sporting-goods retailer in an over-the-counter sales position. You have completed a training course that includes learning about the products, assisting customers, and cross-selling. You have made several good friends in the training course and sometimes get together after work to go running, play golf, or have dinner. You've noticed that one of your friends has really taken the training course to heart and has adopted a very aggressive attitude toward customers in the store, pushing them to buy just about anything, whether they need it or not. Your friend even boasted about selling a boogie board to the father of a boy who didn't know how to swim.

1. Do you agree with your friend's actions? Why or why not?

2. Should you discuss the situation with your friend? Should you discuss it with your supervisor? Explain your response.

INTERNET EXERCISES

1. **Sales careers**. Visit the website for the Canadian Professional Sales Association (http:// www.cpsa.com). The CPSA provides sales certification where salespeople who qualify can earn the designation of Certified Sales Professional, or CSP. What are the requirements to earn this designation? What are the benefits for salespeople who become CSPs? Click on the link for students and see how students could benefit from a student membership in the CPSA.

2. **Using the Internet.** The chapter discussed how many marketers are using the Internet to support personal selling and enhance sales promotion activities. Review the chapter material and then complete the following exercises.
   a. Many companies now use the Internet to demonstrate their products. Visit http://na.blackberry.com/eng/devices/features/ and view the product information. Make a list of your observations and bring your list to class to participate in a class discussion on the subject.

   b. RedFlagDeals.com is Canada's largest bargain shopping community, offering price information, free stuff, and coupons. Visit http://www.redflagdeals.com. Write a brief report summarizing what you learned and your impressions of online coupons.
   c. An increasing number of Canadian websites feature information on contests and sweepstakes. Visit http://www.sweepstakes.ca, http://www.canadas-weepstakes.com, and http://www.contest-canada.com. Evaluate each of these websites. What kinds of products or prizes are available? Which do you believe is the best? Why? What is your overall assessment of online sweepstakes and contests?

Note: Internet Web addresses change frequently. If you don't find the exact sites listed, you may need to access the organization's home page and search from there or use a search engine such as Google.

Case 16.1

The Independent Sales Force

The sales rep used to be a company man. He lived, breathed, and retired a loyal employee. Then came the company woman, the sales rep who often outsold her male colleagues. Today, there is a whole new emphasis on independent sales forces, either as a company's only method to reach its customers face to face, or as a means to supplement a company sales force in regions where sales volumes do not justify having a company salesperson. These salespeople are professional reps who sell goods and services for a variety of companies, rather than working for just one company as an employee.

Some consumer goods companies have hired independent salespeople for decades. Avon, Tupperware, and Mary Kay are just three of the many firms that have always relied on independent contractors who sell their products directly to consumers. Hiring independent contractors, who develop one-to-one relationships with consumers, has been a successful strategy for all these companies. But this type of direct selling is beginning to expand in new directions as well. Some firms are now experimenting with the use of independent sales forces. Unilever has unveiled plans to start a direct-sales firm marketing cosmetics in South Africa. Hallmark's Binney and Smith unit is launching a direct-sales firm called Big Yellow Box by Crayola.

In B2B markets, independent sales contractors have been popular for decades. They are frequently referred to as manufac-

turers' representatives or manufacturers' agents. In some industries, they have been and continue to be extremely popular. The Canadian sports equipment industry, for example, is made up of roughly 210 manufacturing plants that employ only 10 500 people. Because they are relatively small, with average sales less than $6 million, most of them rely heavily on an independent sales force to sell their products to retailers, sports teams, and other customers across Canada and internationally. In fact, it is estimated that exports account for 58 percent of industry sales. Woods Canada is an example of such a company. It employs approximately 40 people and has a proud history of manufacturing rugged, durable, and dependable outdoor equipment and clothing products for over 120 years in Canada. It uses an independent sales force to sell its products in parts of Canada and in the United States.

There are some downsides to hiring an independent sales force. Management of the sales force becomes one step removed. Firms have less control over impressions created by salespeople as they meet new customers for the first time. But professional reps often have worked their territories and industries for years and can provide access to customers based on relationships they have already built. In an age when marketing relationships are paramount, the independent sales force is finding new ways to create value for firms and their customers.

Questions for Critical Thinking

1. Discuss how independent salespeople can build relationships with the firms they represent as well as the customers to whom they sell products.
2. What steps might companies take to motivate their independent sales forces?

Sources: "Corporate America's New Sales Force," *Fortune,* August 11, 2003, pp. S2–S20; Kimberly Weisul, "Do You Dare Outsource Sales?" BusinessWeek Online, June 18, 2001, http://www.businessweek.com; Industry Canada, http://strategis.ic.gc.ca/epic/internet/insg-as.nsf/en/sg03364e.html.

Case 16.2

Sears Ties Up with Ty Pennington

He's tall and skinny, with hair that sticks straight up on its own. His raspy voice sounds like sandpaper—especially when bellowing through a bullhorn. He never sits still. In fact, he never *stands* still. But audiences—particularly women—love him. That's what Sears is banking on, having signed TV host and designer Ty Pennington for a new line of bedding, bath, and tabletop products to be sold online (**www.sears.ca**) and in its stores.

Ty sells. The former carpenter and host of *Trading Spaces* is now a superstar of home design and furnishings as the host of ABC's *Extreme Makeover: Home Edition*, which is sponsored by Sears. The weekly show features a total makeover—often including complete demolition—of one deserving family's home, with soup-to-nuts design, craftsmanship, furnishing, and decorating. Ty leads the team through the project while the family has been whisked off to vacation somewhere glamorous and far away. Sears supplies almost all of the appliances, fixtures, furniture, bedding, and accessories for each project, and the company has received hundreds of e-mails from viewers complimenting the firm on its goodwill. But Ty is the face of the show and the new face of Sears. Marketing experts applaud the relationship as a good fit.

Pennington's popularity—along with the popularity of other home-improvement show hosts, including Martha Stewart—has most likely contributed to an 18 percent increase in such projects during the last five years. This trend gives Sears a double boost—consumers watch the TV show that features its products, then shop at Sears for everything from tools to appliances to Pennington's own line. Ty Pennington Style actually features seven different lines, with varying designs and colour palettes. But each line includes bedding, rugs, pillows, bath towels and shower curtains, lamps,

dishware, and flatware, along with accessories such as candle-holders and placemats. All are priced affordably compared with higher-end department stores; accessories start at $6, while entire bedding sets can be purchased for $120 to $200. And all bear Ty's name.

While experts agree that a celebrity name alone doesn't sell a product—it has to be what the customer wants—someone as popular as Pennington can attract customers to the store. Consumers are influenced by a celebrity's credibility and integrity—Pennington's association with *Extreme Makeover: Home Edition* reinforces those qualities in consumers' minds. They believe he knows how to do these projects himself, and they trust his sense of design. They also appreciate his—and Sears's—contributions to the community. Pennington is just as complimentary of Sears. "Designing for Sears is very cool," he says, "because they understand today's families have to create modern, casual living spaces." Sears has confidence that whatever Pennington sells, its customers will buy.

Questions for Critical Thinking

1. How might Sears use its relationship with Ty Pennington as a motivator for its retail sales force?
2. Describe a sales promotion that Sears might create for Ty Pennington Style.

Sources: "Ty Pennington Style," Sears, http://www.sears.com, accessed June 26, 2006; "Retailing Today," International Council of Shopping Centers, http://www.icsc.org, accessed June 26, 2006; Holly M. Sanders, "Tiger Woods You Believe, But Trust Trump? Uh-Uh," *New York Post,* April 25, 2006, http://www.nypost.com; Susan Chandler, "Is Sears Trading Faces?" *Chicago Tribune,* March 2, 2006, sec. 3, pp. 1, 4.

Video Case 16.3

Harley-Davidson: Selling the Thrill

The written video case on Harley-Davidson appears on page VC-18. The recently filmed Harley-Davidson video is designed to expand and highlight the concepts in this chapter and the concepts and questions covered in the written video case.

DOMENIC VIVOLO

COURTESY OF DOMENIC VIVOLO

Talking About Marketing with Domenic Vivolo

Here are highlights of our interview with Domenic Vivolo of Astral Media. For the complete video interview and transcript, go to http://www.contemporarymarketing2 .nelson.com

Q2: What attracted you to the field that you are in?

DV: Initially I was interested in the creative side of marketing: the advertising and promotional elements of the marketing mix. However as years passed and I gained greater experience, the strategic side of marketing became more important and interesting. In consumer-centric companies, marketing is the hub or centre of all business activities since the department represents the consumer within the company. All other departments get their direction from marketing's strategic plan. By listening to consumers and reading the market trends, marketers can create new products that meet consumer needs and wants while creatively coming up with successful business models that deliver a return on the company's investments. Creativity becomes more than simply copy writing or art designs.

Q5: What do you like/dislike about your job?

DV: Likes: Creating (new products, services, actual creative, etc.), industry (entertaining people—movies, television, and live events), coaching and training staff members and watching them succeed. A person needs to love the product that they work on as well as the industry that they participate in.

Dislike: At times your job can become frustrating: the speed at which things get done, the lack of resources to accomplish a task, the repetitiveness of procedures. However, these are all realities that one faces in their career and it is how one copes with these constraints that will determine the degree of success one will achieve. If one is unable to master or control them, the person will not be effective or as successful as they can be.

In consumer-centric companies, marketing is the hub or centre of all business activities

Q9: Could you please give us a few key presentation tips?

DV: In marketing, you are constantly communicating to and co-coordinating the actions of other departments. You will find that you will be conducting a number of presentations throughout the year. The key tips to giving an effective presentation are:

1. Be prepared (make sure you know your material and ensure you are prepared for the questions that will be asked).
2. Do not read from your slides (your audience can read and it makes for a boring presentation).
3. Do not put everything on your slides (the slides are there to help guide you through the presentation; they are not to be a full document).
4. Keep your slides simple so you do not distract your audience (do not over-create your slides with extensive and bright colours or fancy transitions and fonts).
5. Make eye contact (this will engage the audience and help them better understand what you are saying).

Q12: Any last words or advice for future marketing graduates?

DV: Be patient and strive to constantly learn. Don't chase a title change or an increase in salary. Money and title will come as you become successful. If you move too quickly, you increase your chances for failure and a string of failures will set you back. Constant growth will make you successful. Look for ways to grow as a marketer, a manager, a leader, and a person. You should keep the end goal in mind but it is the journey to get there that is important.

Promoting Awareness through Humour

With its eyes and ears on the nation's front page, The Second City has hilariously relayed political tensions, economic fluctuations, and cultural trends back to its audience, its consumers. The nature of The Second City product has set the stage for its broad mix of promotional activities. Across its many business ventures, its product is distributed in a mix of personal and non-personal selling. The value of The Second City is promoted with the support of its strong topical, entertaining, and consumer-oriented brand.

Each of Second City's theatres frequently updates its shows to respond to current events. When new revues are being produced, their titles function as brief, humorous advertisements. Gripping titles like *Piñata Full of Bees* and *Holy War, Batman* appeal to tourists and locals alike looking for entertainment with an edge. Captivating pictures of the cast are placed with hotel concierges, convention bureaus, and other visitors and tourist-related publications. The Second City has experimented with radio and TV spots but had little success. Its theatres perpetuate word-of-mouth promotion by maintaining creative relevance as satirists. As with its improvisational technique used on stages, promotional decisions are sometimes made best as quick reactions to a given situation. When the local market began taking Second City's presence for granted, it noticed a difference in sales. SC responded by promoting a differentiated product of more eclectic off-night revues to attract the local crowd. As an innovative entertainment company, its promotional opportunities are nearly limitless. It has, however, avoided sponsorship, which allows it free rein to satirize anyone and everyone. "Second City does not presently allow for corporate sponsorship, for fear that we, as satirists, would put ourselves in a potentially vulnerable position," explains vice president Kelly Leonard. Alternatively, The Second City has been able to play with some guerrilla marketing, such as chalk-writing announcements of new shows on the sidewalks of Chicago.

For Second City's Touring Companies, promotional decisions target the college and performing arts centre markets. East Coast Entertainment, a talent-booking agency focusing on the college market, sells on Second City's behalf at conferences and through continued networking. Predominantly, Second City uses phone sales to book shows around the nation. Over the summer, when the college market is less active, SC touring companies promote themselves locally to stabilize sales. They provide regional showcases and develop new material with a variety of unique performances.

For the Second City Training Center, promotional efforts are based on relationship selling. Celebrity testimonials throughout SC's evolution have garnered consistent interest from the ever-growing market of aspiring actors. This consumer base seeks out The Second City for services and training. The Training Center focuses promotional efforts on regular consumers looking to broaden their creative horizons. It offers a wide range of classes for all age levels and interests. It uses an informative group e-mail list that unifies its student body and fosters a mutually beneficial relationship. It offers discounted shows to students, welcomes student feedback, and posts job openings.

Second City's website embodies its total advertising campaign. Each division of the company is represented by its own electronic promotion. Each theatre has interactive advertisements that lead consumers to newspaper reviews and cast biographies. The website is entirely inclusive. A customer who visits to purchase tickets will also notice the myriad of classes offered by the theatre. Second City has also integrated its marketing with each city in which it operates. A customer who is in town can peruse SC's website for information on local restaurants, hotels, museums, and music venues. Most of SC's retail advertising is offered through the website. Bernie Sahlins, co-founder of the company, published *Days and Nights at the Second City,* which details his experience with the influential theatre company. Books like his, and a number of others on the art and history of improvisation, promote the brand to those already invested in or curious about the company. Other merchandise, such as apparel, is attractive to tourists. A company advertisement then returns home with the consumer wearing a Second City T-shirt or baseball cap.

The Second City Communications Division has been creating virtual comedy shorts to promote the theatre and its services through the Internet. One such video introduces the "Yes, and" principle by presenting a mock business meeting. When communication between employees has broken down, the practice of accepting each other's ideas and building on them enables the group to function as a team. Teamwork is a guiding practice for The Second City. Its focus on collaboration has given each division the autonomy to communicate its own promotional messages while still remaining a part of the team of Second City product offerings.

Second City Communications promotes its services through personal selling. It conducts business by creatively approaching the specific, complex problems of the client. Case studies on SC's website describe how it has succeeded in addressing consumer needs. As a consultant, SC must listen to its customers and build customer loyalty. Success from the Communications division has eliminated the first few steps of a traditional sales process. Clients come to SC's door without much prospecting or approach. SC Communications specializes in presenting and demonstrating its product throughout the production process by fashioning the product to meet customer expectations. Tom Yorton, president of Second City Communications, and his team routinely communicate with clients before and after the sales process. They also partner with an outside publicist to design high-quality print and media promotional materials.

SC Theatricals' exclusive deal with Norwegian Cruise Lines has its cast presenting a series of comedic revues at sea. It also offers customized corporate workshops that capitalize on SC's expertise in the business market and promote the brand to a captive target audience.

The promotional mix supporting The Second City brand simultaneously grows the divisions of the company. By integrating its marketing communications, The Second City promotes its product from a variety of positions . . . and spreads laughter in its wake.

Questions

1. How does the nature of Second City's product function as a promotional tool for the company?

2. Do you think Second City allocates a relatively large amount of funds for promotion? Why or not why? How does this relate to Second City's stage in the product life cycle?

3. Which advertising strategy do you think is most advantageous to The Second City? Does it change for different divisions?

4. What challenges does The Second City find when attempting a sponsorship arrangement? What can you determine from this about the nature of The Second City's promotional strategy?

Part 6 CBC Video Case

Visit the website for Contemporary Marketing at http://www.contemporarymarketing2e.nelson.com to view the CBC video and video case summary for Part 6.

PRICING DECISIONS

chapter 17

Price Concepts

CHAPTER OBJECTIVES

1. Outline the legal constraints on pricing.

2. Identify the major categories of pricing objectives.

3. Explain price elasticity and its determinants.

4. List the practical problems involved in applying price theory concepts to actual pricing decisions.

5. Explain the major cost-plus approaches to price setting.

6. List the chief advantages and shortcomings of using breakeven analysis in pricing decisions.

7. Explain the use of yield management in pricing decisions.

8. Identify the major pricing challenges facing online and international marketers.

PRICING A HOME: A "LOT" TO CONSIDER

For most people, buying a home is the largest purchase they will make during their lifetime. For many first-time home buyers, the decision comes after years of saving and searching, while they try to find a home they like at a price they can afford. The Toronto Real Estate Board reported two records for 2007: 93 193 homes were sold in the Greater Toronto Area (GTA), and the average price was $376 236.

Have you ever considered who determines the actual price for which a home is listed for sale? This is one of the value-added services that real estate agents provide for their clients. They advise sellers what they should expect to get for their home, and how to prepare their home for resale so that they get the best price. When they work with buyers, they advise what homes are available that meet the buyer's specific needs, and help ensure that the buyer pays a fair price when they make a purchase decision.

Most buyers and sellers use the services of a real estate agent or broker. Cristina Lopes and Louise Ruggiero, who have more than 35 years of combined real estate experience, market themselves as "Real Estate Divas" (see www.realestatedivas.ca). They are two Internet-savvy professionals who recognize that nearly 80 percent of buyers now use the Internet to look for a new home, compared with only about 2 percent a decade ago. They sell for Sutton Group—Security Real Estate Inc., a brokerage with more than four decades of experience in the Toronto area.

The two real estate divas recently had a most interesting pricing decision—how to establish a listing price for Toronto's smallest house. The little detached bungalow, sandwiched between two regular-sized homes, is only 300 square feet in area. However, it has a bedroom, kitchen, living room, and full bathroom, along with a patio, a basement suitable for storage, and a space for parking at the rear. It was built in 1912 by contractor Arthur Weeden and has since been home to a number of families, including immigrant families from Brazil, Hungary, and Italy. One family who lived there reportedly had three children. It was sold for only $45 000 in 1994, a low price that resulted from a now-solved encroachment issue. In April 2007, it was sold for $139 000. In early 2008, it is on the market again, listed for $173 000.

When deciding the listing price, Cristina and Louise used comparative market analysis to determine what prices similar homes recently sold for in the area. They also considered the price that the home sold for in 2007, and the improvements that were made to the property, discounted to represent the resale value of those improvements. Finally, they considered real estate appreciation in the area since the last sale of the home. Cristina says, "Even though this is only 300 square feet, it looks more spacious than a condo that's 700 or 800 square feet." Bachelor and one-bedroom condos in Toronto are typically sold for $200 000 or more.

Of course, homes are sold at prices that satisfy both the home seller and home buyer. Supply and demand will determine whether it is a buyer's market or a seller's market, and psychological factors also play a role. There is a lot of interest in Toronto's smallest house. In less than two months, Cristina and Louise have received over 300 telephone and e-mail inquiries, and over 95 000 website hits on this unique property.[1]

connecting with customers

The location of this Sutton Group franchise gives it access to several Toronto neighbourhoods, each with different demographics, including first-time buyers, move-uppers, and empty nesters. Approximately 80 sales staff specialize in the full residential spectrum: detached homes, townhouses, and condos. Many speak two or three languages. Two in-house mortgage brokers are available 24/7. Most important, salespeople such as Cristina and Louise work to gain clients' trust and confidence. For buyers, they carefully establish needs, help with the search process, and keep them informed concerning latest market information. For sellers, they help establish price and make recommendations to get a better price and faster sale. For both, they remain professional, knowledgeable, courteous, and honest.

Chapter Overview

ONE of the first questions shoppers ask is "How much does it cost?" Marketers understand the critical role that price plays in the consumer's decision-making process. For products as varied as lipstick and perfume, automobiles and gasoline, and doughnuts and coffee, marketers must develop strategies that price products to achieve their firms' objectives.

As a starting point for examining pricing strategies, consider the meaning of the term *price*. A **price** is the exchange value of a good or service—in other words, it represents whatever that product can be exchanged for in the marketplace. Price does not necessarily denote money. In earlier

price Exchange value of a good or service.

times, the price of an acre of land might have been 20 bushels of wheat, three head of cattle, or one boat. Even though the barter process continues to be used in some transactions, in the 21st century price typically refers to the amount of funds required to purchase a product.

Prices are both difficult to set and dynamic; they shift in response to a number of variables. A higher than average price can convey an image of prestige, while a lower than average price may connote good value. In other instances, though, a price that is much lower than average may be interpreted as an indicator of inferior quality, and the lower-priced item will certainly be less desirable for some buyers. Real estate

agents, as described in the opening vignette, have a responsibility to get a fair price for the seller, but they must do this while recognizing that the price that is asked is one that will be acceptable to the buyer.

This chapter discusses the process of determining a profitable but justifiable (fair) price. The focus is on management of the pricing function, including pricing strategies, price–quality relationships, and pricing in various sectors of the economy. The chapter also looks at the effects of environmental conditions on price determination, including legal constraints, competitive pressures, and changes in global and online markets. ◆◆◆

---

① **Outline the legal constraints on pricing.**

PRICING AND THE LAW

Pricing decisions are influenced by a variety of legal constraints imposed by federal, provincial, and municipal governments. Included in the price of products are not only the cost of the raw materials, processing and packaging, and profit for the business but also the various taxes that governments require providers to charge. For instance, excise taxes are levied on a variety of products—including cigarettes, alcoholic beverages, and motor fuels. Sales taxes are charged on purchases of most products and services in Canada.

In the global marketplace, prices are directly affected by special types of taxes called *tariffs*. These taxes—levied on the sale of imported goods and services—often make it possible for firms to protect their local markets and still set prices on domestically produced goods well above world market levels. The average tariff on fruits and vegetables around the world is more than 50 percent, although it varies considerably from country to country. Canada and the United States have relatively low tariffs on produce and, due to NAFTA (see Chapter 6), trade virtually duty free with each other and with Mexico.

In some instances, punitive tariffs are levied. Canada and the European Union recently levied a 15 percent penalty tariff on imports of a wide range of consumer products such as clothing, paper products, cigarettes, sweet corn, and oysters from the United States in retaliation for American government subsidies to domestic producers that the World Trade Organization ruled illegal.[2] These tariffs will raise prices in Canadian and EU markets, making these U.S. products less competitive. In still other instances, tariffs are levied to prevent foreign producers from engaging in a practice described in

Chapter 6: *dumping* foreign-produced products in international markets at prices lower than those set in their domestic market.

Not every "regulatory" price increase is a tax, however. Rate increases to cover costly government regulations imposed on the telecommunications industry have been appearing on cell phone bills as system access fees or similarly named costs. But these charges are not taxes, since the companies keep all the income from the fees and apply only some of it to complying with the regulations. In essence, such fees are a source of additional revenues in an industry so price-sensitive that any announced price increase is likely to send some customers fleeing to competitors.[3] In a recent Saskatchewan court ruling, a decision was made to allow a class-action lawsuit to proceed against cell phone companies to recover these fees on behalf of Canadian customers. The suit claims that customers were misled into thinking these fees were a tax or regulatory levy while, in fact, they were not. If the suit is successful, the refund to cell phone customers could be as large as $20 billion.[4]

Almost every person looking for a ticket to a high-demand sporting or concert event has encountered an expensive—and often illegal—form of pricing called *ticket scalping*. Scalpers camp out in ticket lines (or hire someone else to stand in line) to purchase tickets they expect to resell at a higher price. Although some cities have enacted laws prohibiting the practice, it continues to occur in many locations.

Canadian consumers have access to quality fruits and vegetables at reasonable prices as Canada has relatively low tariffs on imported produce.

But the ticket reselling market is both highly fragmented and susceptible to fraud and distorted pricing. In response, buyers and sellers are finding that the Internet is helping to create a market where both buyers and sellers can compare prices and seat locations. Web firms such as StubHub.com and TicketsNow.com act as ticket clearinghouses for this secondary market and have signed deals with several professional sports teams that allow season ticket holders to sell unwanted tickets and for buyers to purchase them with a guarantee.

Pricing is also regulated by the general constraints of the Competition Act legislation, as outlined in Chapter 3. The following sections review some of the most important pricing laws for contemporary marketers.

COMPETITION ACT

Canada has a long history of competition legislation that goes back to the 1889 Act for the Prevention and Suppression of Combines Formed in Restraint of Trade. The Combines Investigation Act was passed in 1923, and the current **Competition Act** has been in effect since 1986. The purpose of the Competition Act is to

- promote the efficiency and adaptability of the Canadian economy

- expand opportunities for Canadian participation in world markets while at the same time recognizing the role of foreign competition in Canada

- ensure that small and medium-sized enterprises have an equitable opportunity to participate in the Canadian economy

- provide consumers with competitive prices and product choices.[5]

The Competition Act tries to balance the interests of businesses and consumers; it tries to foster a fair competitive environment to protect businesses from each other and to protect consumers from unfair business practices. It focuses on a number of pricing-related practices, including *price*

Competition Act The most comprehensive legislation in Canada, designed to help both consumers and businesses by promoting a healthy competitive environment.

discrimination, price fixing (a form of collusion), bid rigging, predatory pricing, false or misleading ordinary selling price representations, and many others.

Price discrimination, which occurs when some customers pay more than others for the same product, dates back to the very beginnings of trade and commerce. Today, however, technology has added to the frequency and complexity of price discrimination, as well as the strategies marketers adopt to get around it. For example, marketers may encourage repeat business by inviting purchasers to become preferred customers, entitling them to average discounts of 10 percent. As long as companies can demonstrate that their price discounts and promotional allowances do not restrict competition, they avoid penalties under the Competition Act. Direct mail marketers frequently send out catalogues of identical goods but with different prices in different editions of the catalogues. Postal code areas that traditionally consist of high spenders get the catalogues with the higher prices, while postal code areas where price-sensitive customers live get the catalogues with the lower prices. Victoria's Secret, Staples, and Simon & Schuster are among the hundreds of companies that employ legal price discrimination strategies.

Firms accused of price discrimination often argue that they set price differentials to meet competitors' prices and that cost differences justify variations in prices. When a firm asserts that it maintains price differentials as good-faith methods of competing with rivals, a logical question arises: What constitutes good-faith pricing behaviour? The answer depends on the particular situation.

A defence based on cost differentials works only if the price differences do not exceed the cost differences resulting from selling to various classes of buyers. Marketers must then be prepared to justify the cost differences. Many authorities consider this provision one of the most confusing areas in the Competition Act. Courts handle most charges brought under the act as individual cases. Therefore, domestic marketers must continually evaluate their pricing actions to avoid potential violations. Price discrimination becomes a more important issue when one company charges different prices to two or more companies that are in competition with each other. This clearly interferes with competition in the marketplace. There have been only three convictions for discriminatory pricing under the Competition Act, all since 1984, with fines ranging from $15 000 to $50 000.[6]

Price fixing is a form of collusion in which sellers get together and collude to set prices higher than they would otherwise be in a free market. Currently, the Competition Bureau is investigating price fixing among oil companies in many parts of Canada. Eleven gas companies and 13 individuals have been charged in Quebec. Three immediately pleaded guilty, and the others face trial beginning in late 2008; if found guilty, they could receive fines up to $10 million or five years in jail for individuals.[7] In investigations by the European Union and the U.S. government, a number of the world's largest airlines were investigated for conspiracy to fix prices, some for freight services and some for passenger fares. Included in the investigations were Air Canada, British Airways, Air France, KLM, SAS, Lufthansa, Korean Air, Cathay Pacific, and Qantas Airways. Among those found guilty, fines have ranged from $61 million (U.S.) to $300 million (U.S.) although investigations are not complete and the guilt of several companies has yet to be determined.[8] In one recent year, the EU levied price-fixing fines of approximately $4 billion.[9]

Bid rigging is another form of collusion, similar to price fixing. It occurs when sellers get together and collude to set prices with respect to one or more requests for competitive proposals. The intent is that one of the sellers will provide the lowest price but, unknown to the customer, one that is higher than it would be in a free market. The winner then agrees to let another competitor "win" another bid, again at an inflated price. Four Toronto-based electrical contractors were fined a total of $2.55 million when it was determined they set prices 10 to 15 percent higher than they should have been

Marketoid

Germany's largest drug maker, Bayer AG, was fined $3.65 million for price fixing involving its rubber and chemicals business in Canada.

A number of health clubs in Canada have been charged with violations under the Competition Act.

H.F. (HERB) MACKENZIE

on several bids.[10] In Japan, a city government cancelled a bid request after one bidding company accidentally faxed information concerning who should win the bid and at what price. The fax asked other bidders to cooperate in the bid rigging.[11]

Predatory pricing occurs when companies set prices below their cost for a sufficiently long period of time to discourage or eliminate competition and then raise their prices or otherwise interfere with competition. Europe's largest drug maker, GlaxoSmithKline, was recently fined $15.5 million for manipulating prices on antibiotics to keep competitors out of the French market.[12]

False or misleading price representations is one form of misleading advertising. A coordinated probe in 16 EU countries found 226 websites that failed to show taxes and fees in published prices, or engaged in other misleading practices. The EU Consumer Protection Commissioner has vowed to shut down or fine those companies that fail to change their ways.[13] Consumer groups have long accused Carrefour, the world's second-largest retailer, of advertising misleading prices. In a recent French court action, it was fined $2.9 million.[14] Misleading price advertising has been common in Canada. Suzy Shier paid a $1-million fine for a second offence, following a previous $300-million fine. Sears Canada was fined $100 000 for misrepresenting savings on tires. Premier Health Club was fined $30 000, and GoodLife Fitness Clubs, which operates more than 90 fitness clubs in Canada, was fined $75 000.[15]

assessment check 1

1.1 What does the Competition Act try to accomplish?

1.2 What is price discrimination? Is it always considered anti-competitive? Explain.

1.3 What is the difference between price fixing and bid rigging?

PRICING OBJECTIVES AND THE MARKETING MIX

(2) Identify the major categories of pricing objectives

The extent to which any or all of the factors of production—natural resources, capital, human resources, and entrepreneurship—are employed depends on the prices those factors command. A firm's prices and the resulting purchases by its customers determine the company's revenue, influencing the profits it earns. Overall organizational objectives and more specific marketing objectives guide the development of pricing objectives, which in turn lead to the development and implementation of more specific pricing policies and procedures.

A firm might, for instance, set a major overall goal of becoming the dominant producer in its domestic market. It might then develop a marketing objective of achieving maximum sales penetration in each region, followed by a related pricing objective of setting prices at levels that maximize sales. These objectives might lead to the adoption of a low-price policy implemented by offering substantial price discounts to channel members.

Price affects and is affected by the other elements of the marketing mix. Product decisions, promotional plans, and distribution choices all affect the price of a good or service. For example, products distributed through complex channels involving several intermediaries must be priced high enough to cover the markups needed to compensate wholesalers and retailers for services they provide. Basic so-called *fighting brands* are intended to capture market share from higher-priced, options-laden competitors by offering relatively low prices to entice customers to give up some options in return for a cost savings.

Pricing objectives vary from firm to firm, and they can be classified into four major groups: (1) profitability objectives, (2) volume objectives, (3) meeting competition objectives, and (4) prestige objectives. Not-for-profit organizations as well as for-profit companies must consider objectives of one kind or another when developing pricing strategies. Table 17.1 outlines the pricing objectives marketers rely on to meet their overall goals.

PROFITABILITY OBJECTIVES

Marketers at for-profit firms must set prices with profits in mind. Even not-for-profit organizations realize the importance of setting prices high enough to cover expenses and provide a financial cushion to cover unforeseen needs and expenses. As the Russian proverb says, "There are two fools in every market: One asks too little, one asks too much." For consumers to pay prices that are either above or

table 17.1 *Pricing Objectives*

OBJECTIVE	PURPOSE	EXAMPLE
Profitability objectives	Profit maximization Target return	Microsoft's initially high price for the Xbox 360
Volume objectives	Sales maximization Market share	Dell's low-priced PCs increase market share and sales of services
Meeting competition objectives	Value pricing	Wal-Mart's lower prices on private house brands
Prestige objectives	Lifestyle Image	High-priced luxury autos such as Lexus and stereo equipment by Bose
Not-for-profit objectives	Profit maximization Cost recovery Market incentives Market suppression	Reduced or zero tolls for high-occupancy vehicles to encourage carpooling

below what they consider to be the going rate, they must be convinced they are receiving fair value for their money.

Economic theory is based on two major assumptions. It assumes, first, that firms will behave rationally and, second, that this rational behaviour will result in an effort to maximize gains and minimize losses. Some marketers estimate profits by looking at historical sales data; others use elaborate calculations based on predicted future sales. It has been said that setting prices is an art, not a science. The talent lies in a marketer's ability to strike a balance between desired profits and the customer's perception of a product's value.

Marketers should evaluate and adjust prices continually to accommodate changes in the environment. The technological environment, for example, forces Internet marketers to respond quickly to competitors' pricing strategies. New search capabilities performed by shopping bots allow customers to compare prices locally, nationally, and globally in a matter of seconds.

Intense price competition—sometimes conducted even when it means forgoing profits altogether—often results when rival manufacturers battle for leadership positions in new-product categories. Passenger airlines have been cutting costs for years in order to compete on pricing. Some amenities, such as in-flight meals, have almost disappeared. Computer technology has allowed airlines to automate many services and put passengers in charge of others, such as making reservations online and checking in at electronic kiosks. Air Canada was first to introduce a "self-tagging" program that allows customers to print their own baggage tags.[16]

Profits are a function of revenue and expenses:

$$\text{Profits} = \text{Revenue} - \text{Expenses}$$

Revenue is determined by the product's selling price and number of units sold:

$$\text{Total Revenue} = \text{Price} \times \text{Quantity Sold}$$

Therefore, a profit-maximizing price rises to the point at which further increases will cause disproportionate decreases in the number of units sold. A 10 percent price increase that results in only an 8 percent cut in volume will add to the firm's revenue. However, a 10 percent price hike that results in an 11 percent sales decline will reduce revenue.

profit maximization Point at which the additional revenue gained by increasing the price of a product equals the increase in total costs.

Economists refer to this approach as **marginal analysis**. They identify **profit maximization** as the point at which the addition to total revenue is just balanced by the increase in total cost. Marketers must resolve a basic problem of how to achieve this delicate balance when they set prices. Relatively few firms actually hit this elusive target. A significantly larger number prefer to direct their effort toward more realistic goals.

Consequently, marketers commonly set **target-return objectives**—short-run or long-run goals usually stated as percentages of sales or investment. The practice has become particularly popular among large firms in which other pressures interfere with profit-maximization objectives. Target-return objectives offer several benefits for marketers in addition to resolving pricing questions. For example, these objectives serve as tools for evaluating performance. They also satisfy desires to generate fair profits as judged by management, stockholders, and the public.

target-return objectives Short-run or long-run pricing objectives of achieving a specified return on either sales or investment.

VOLUME OBJECTIVES

Some economists and business executives argue that pricing behaviour actually seeks to maximize sales within a given profit constraint. In other words, they set a minimum acceptable profit level and then seek to maximize sales (subject to this profit constraint) in the belief that the increased sales are more important in the long-run competitive picture than immediate high profits. As a result, companies should continue to expand sales as long as their total profits do not drop below the minimum return acceptable to management.

Sales maximization can also result from non-price factors such as service and quality. Marketers succeeded in increasing sales for Dr. Scholl's new shoe insert, Dynastep, by advertising heavily in magazines. The ads explained how the Dynastep insert would help relieve leg and back pain. Priced around $14 for two inserts—twice as much as comparable offerings—Dynastep ran over its competitors to become number one in its category.

Another volume-related pricing objective is the **market-share objective**—the goal of controlling a specified minimum share of the market for a firm's good or service. Apple is using this strategy to retain its dominant 83 percent share of the market for digital music downloads, the key to which is the iPod player. Apple recently cut the price of the basic iPod Shuffle model to $89 and introduced a 4 GB iPod Nano at $169, or 25 percent cheaper than the next-higher-capacity model. Because of iPod popularity, several Canadian retailers sell these items for less, making it very difficult for other manufacturers to compete.[17]

Profit Impact of Market Strategies (PIMS) project Research that discovered a strong positive relationship between a firm's market share and product quality and its return on investment.

The PIMS Studies

Market-share objectives may prove critical to the achievement of other organizational objectives. High sales, for example, often mean more profits. The **Profit Impact of Market Strategies (PIMS) project,** an extensive study conducted by the Marketing Science Institute, analyzed more than 2000 firms and revealed that two of the most important factors influencing profitability were product quality and market share. Companies such as clothier Northern Reflections and Best Buy, the electronics giant, have introduced loyalty programs as a means of retaining customers and protecting their market share. Costco now offers an Executive Gold Card Membership for a premium price, but executive members receive 2 percent reward on most purchases as well as additional values on member services. Many executive members get back much more than the additional membership fee they pay, but Costco wins because these members are among the company's most loyal and regular customers.

The relationship between market share and profitability is evident in PIMS data that reveal an average 32 percent return on investment (ROI) for firms with market shares above 40 percent. In contrast, average ROI decreases to 24 percent for firms whose market shares are between 20 and 40 percent. Firms with a minor market share (less than 10 percent) generate average pre-tax investment returns of approximately 13 percent.[18]

The relationship also applies to a firm's individual brands. PIMS researchers compared the top four brands in each market segment

Singapore Airlines competes by offering comfort for business travellers rather than trumpeting the lowest fares.

they studied. Their data revealed that the leading brand typically generates after-tax ROI of 18 percent, considerably higher than the second-ranked brand. Weaker brands, on average, fail to earn adequate returns.

Marketers have developed an underlying explanation of the positive relationship between profitability and market share. Firms with large shares accumulate greater operating experience and lower overall costs relative to competitors with smaller market shares. Accordingly, effective segmentation strategies might focus on obtaining larger shares of smaller markets and on avoiding smaller shares of larger ones. A firm might achieve higher financial returns by becoming a major competitor in several smaller market segments than by remaining a relatively minor player in a larger market.

Meeting Competition Objectives

A third set of pricing objectives seeks simply to meet competitors' prices. In many lines of business, firms set their own prices to match those of established industry price leaders.

Price is a pivotal factor in the ongoing competition between long-distance telephone services and wireless carriers. Some cell phone companies are reviving prepaid calling plans to compete with reduced-rate and unlimited calling plans. These plans allow customers to pay up-front for their minutes at lower costs than before, avoid overage fees, and eliminate long-term contracts.[19]

Pricing objectives tied directly to meeting prices charged by major competitors de-emphasize the price element of the marketing mix and focus more strongly on non-price variables. Pricing is a highly visible component of a firm's marketing mix and an easy and effective tool for obtaining a differential advantage over competitors. It is, however, a tool that other firms can easily duplicate through price reductions of their own. Airline price competition of recent years exemplifies the actions and reactions of competitors in this marketplace. Rather than emphasizing the lowest fares of any carrier, most airlines choose to compete by offering convenient arrival and departure times, enhanced passenger comfort with more room between each row, an attractive frequent-flyer program, and customer-focused alliances with automobile rental, lodging, and other partners. Some airlines even returned to providing passenger meals on long flights, a practice that had been discontinued in a cost-cutting effort. Even when price increases are needed to remain profitable, an announced price hike by one airline will be implemented only if its major competitors match the new price. Because price changes directly affect overall profitability in an industry, many firms attempt to promote stable prices by meeting competitors' prices and competing for market share by focusing on product strategies, promotional decisions, and distribution—the non-price elements of the marketing mix.

Value Pricing

When discounts become normal elements of a competitive marketplace, other marketing mix elements gain importance in purchase decisions. In such instances, overall product value, not just price, determines product choice. In recent years, a new strategy—**value pricing**—has emerged that emphasizes the benefits a product provides in comparison to the price and quality levels of competing offerings. This strategy typically works best for relatively low-priced goods and services.

value pricing Pricing strategy emphasizing benefits derived from a product in comparison to the price and quality levels of competing offerings.

Value-priced products generally cost less than premium brands, but marketers point out that value does not necessarily mean *inexpensive*. The challenge for those who compete on value is to convince customers that low-priced brands offer quality comparable to that of a higher-priced product. An increasing number of alternative products and private-label brands has resulted in a more competitive marketplace in recent years. Consumers are beginning to understand that the lowest price does not always equal the best value. Campers Village, an Alberta-owned and operated company with locations in Calgary and Edmonton, wants to be recognized as the best independent outdoor retailer in Canada. To achieve this, it tries to bring its customers the best products and the best possible value. The company believes that value pricing means much more than a figure on a price tag: "Value pricing means that products are well made, and they function in the environment for which they were created. It means products are durable, and that customers receive authentic advice in their use."[20]

Value pricing is perhaps best seen in the personal computer industry. In the past few years, PC prices have collapsed, reducing the effectiveness of traditional pricing strategies intended to meet competition. In fact, despite rising costs for several standard PC components such as memory chips and LCD screens, PCs priced at under $600 are now the fastest-growing segment of the market. This category now accounts for almost 20 percent of PCs sold in stores. Industry leaders such as Dell, Hewlett-Packard, and Gateway cannot continue to cut prices, so they are adding features such as increased memory and 3-D graphic accelerator cards that increase speed. Dell has even launched a home installation plan to offset tumbling prices in the PC market, and Apple has introduced the Mac Mini for $649.

PRESTIGE OBJECTIVES

The final category of pricing objectives, unrelated to either profitability or sales volume, is prestige objectives. Prestige pricing establishes a relatively high price to develop and maintain an image of quality and exclusiveness that appeals to status-conscious consumers. Such objectives reflect marketers' recognition of the role of price in creating an overall image of the firm and its product offerings.

Prestige objectives affect the price tags of such products as Waterford crystal, Alfa Romeo sports cars, Omega watches, and Tiffany jewellery. When a perfume marketer sets a price of $400 or more per ounce, this choice reflects an emphasis on image far more than the cost of ingredients. Analyses have shown that ingredients account for less than 5 percent of a perfume's cost. Thus, advertisements for Joy that promote the fragrance as the "costliest perfume in the world" use price to promote product prestige. Diamond jewellery also uses prestige pricing to convey an image of quality and timelessness.

In the business world, private jet ownership imparts an image of prestige, power, and high price tags—too high for most business travellers to consider. Recognizing that cost is the primary factor that makes jet

Marketoid

Zoraide shoes are available in only six shoe stores worldwide. All four styles carried by Montreal's Mona Moore boutique are priced at $1692.

---

assessment check 2a

2.1 What are target-return objectives?

2.2 What is value pricing?

2.3 How do prestige objectives affect a seller's pricing strategy?

---

marketing success   Good for the Sole

Background. Corinne Lissoos emigrated from South Africa to Israel in 1985. Four years later, she emigrated to Canada, where Max, her husband, launched a business as a supplier to the auto industry. Corinne very much wanted to become an entrepreneur as well, but she needed to find a promising business idea. She remembered the Naot sandals that Max had discovered in Israel and that he loved so much. She found a business partner, Sandy Galet, and together, they signed a distribution agreement to become the exclusive Canadian distributor for Naot shoes through their company, Solemates.

The Challenge. Getting an exclusive distribution agreement was exciting. However, marketing the shoes effectively was a challenge. The product was relatively unheard of in Canada, and retailers were unwilling to risk putting it on their shelves. The product manufactured at the Kibbutz Naot Mordechai near Kiryat Shmona, Israel, is unique. Each piece of footwear is hand-crafted and designed from the "footprint in the sand concept," providing unmatched support and comfort. A natural cork sole provides shock absorption, and a cushioning layer of latex and a suede footbed conform to the wearer's foot to provide a custom fit. All the materials in the shoes are environmentally friendly. Naot shoes are value priced from $150 to $300. They do not compete with inexpensive imports, nor do they compete with shoes that are positioned as prestige, high-fashion footwear. They are priced to provide exceptional value for customers who want quality, style, and comfort.

The Strategy. At first, Corinne and her partner started to display the shoes in health food stores in midtown Toronto. In 1990 and 1991, they rented a storefront on Eglinton Avenue West, but only for the summer season since the product line consisted entirely of sandals. In 1992, when Naot expanded its product line to include all-year footwear for both men and women, they opened a year-round store, also on Eglinton Avenue West. Eventually, Capezio began to sell the Naot line in its retail chain of shoe stores, and the product gained instant credibility. Soon other retailers were willing to handle the line, and national distribution followed. The growth in distribution grew from the company's limited retail exposure to regional acceptance to national acceptance.

The Outcome. After nearly 15 years, Corinne bought out her partner, and Max joined the company. Solemates now has two locations in Toronto and a location in Montreal that opened in 2006, and is evaluating locations in Vancouver. It also has a 30 000-square-foot warehouse and factory outlet north of Toronto, and a list of 300 retail customers across Canada. For Corinne and Max, there's no business like shoe business.

Source: Solemates, Inc. website, http://www.naotcanada.com, accessed November 30, 2009; "Putting Her Best Foot Forward," *National Post*, October 4, 2007, p. JV2; Sylvia Brooke, "Support Your Feet and Israel Too," *Canadian Jewish News*, March 18, 2004, p. 52.

THE CANADIAN PRESS (BORIS SPREMO)

Winners offers value-priced merchandise every day and continually changes its merchandise assortment to encourage customers to visit often.

ownership prohibitive, companies such as London, Ontario-based OurPLANE have created an alternative—fractional ownership. The company targets firms whose executives travel periodically rather than year round. Instead of buying a previously owned plane, they join executives from other firms in purchasing shares in a new jet.

PRICING OBJECTIVES OF NOT-FOR-PROFIT ORGANIZATIONS

Pricing is also a key element of the marketing mix for not-for-profit organizations. Pricing strategy can help these groups achieve a variety of organizational goals:

1. *Profit maximization.* While not-for-profit organizations by definition do not cite profitability as a primary goal, there are numerous instances in which they do try to maximize their returns on single events or a series of events. A $1000-a-plate political fundraiser is a classic example.

2. *Cost recovery.* Some not-for-profit organizations attempt to recover only the actual cost of operating the unit. Mass transit, and toll roads and bridges are common examples. The amount of recovered costs is often dictated by tradition, competition, or public opinion.

3. *Market incentives.* Other not-for-profit groups follow a lower-than-average pricing policy or offer a free service to encourage increased usage of the good or service. OC Transpo provides public transit services in Ottawa. It has offered free bus service after 9:00 p.m. on Canada Day to encourage use during a period when there would be street closures and when downtown traffic would be congested.

4. *Market suppression.* Price can also discourage consumption. High prices help to accomplish social objectives independent of the costs of providing goods or services. Illustrations include tobacco and alcohol taxes (the so-called sin taxes), parking fines, tolls, and gasoline excise taxes.

METHODS FOR DETERMINING PRICES

Marketers determine prices in two basic ways—by applying the theoretical concepts of supply and demand and by completing cost-oriented analyses. During the first part of the 20th century, most discussions of price determination emphasized the classical concepts of supply and demand. During the last half of the century, however, the emphasis began to shift to a cost-oriented approach. Hindsight reveals certain flaws in both concepts.

Treatments of this subject often overlook another concept of price determination—one based on the impact of custom and tradition. **Customary prices** are retail prices that consumers expect as a result of tradition and social habit. Candy makers have attempted to maintain traditional price levels by greatly reducing overall product size. Similar practices have prevailed in the marketing of soft drinks as bottlers attempt to balance consumer expectations of customary prices with the realities of rising costs.

customary prices Traditional prices that customers expect to pay for certain goods and services.

Wrigley, manufacturer of chewing gum favourites Juicy Fruit, Doublemint, and Big Red, took advantage of the weakness in the industry's customary pricing strategy by introducing a smaller-quantity pack at a lower price. While competitors continued to offer only seven-piece packs for 35 cents, Wrigley priced its five-piece packs at 25 cents. To spur impulse buying, the company prominently displayed the price on the package. The strategy was so successful that within two years of its inception, Wrigley discontinued selling seven-stick gum packs.

Changes in the price of oil on world markets presents another example of supply and demand. Crude oil prices increase as demand increases and decrease as supply increases. The value of Canadian exports soared as the average price for crude oil peaked temporarily near $150 a barrel in mid-2008 as demand far exceeded supply. Canada has the second-largest volume of crude oil reserves in the world, and its supply far exceeds current aggregate Canadian demand. Approximately 99 percent of Canada's excess oil production—which is about two-thirds of the oil it produces—goes to the United States.[21]

Although profits at Canadian refineries have reached record levels, they continue to struggle to produce enough gasoline to meet demand. Recent fires at refineries in both Alberta and Ontario only multiplied the problems, when refineries were temporarily knocked out of service. Adding to the supply problem is the fact that no new refineries have been built in Canada in more than two decades, and oil companies are reluctant to build more out of concerns for returns on their investment.[22]

Higher gas prices have effects on other consumer costs as well. With gas at record highs, hybrid cars are in greater demand than ever before, and some dealers have months-long waiting lists even at premium prices. Consumers are increasingly willing to consider the four-door, full-size family sedan, which is beginning to increase in popularity. While less fuel efficient than compact cars, they offer better fuel economy than minivans and SUVs, along with better handling and braking, and a more comfortable ride. The "Big Three" North American manufacturers each offer a full-size model beginning around $30 000: Chevrolet Impala, Chrysler 300, and Ford Taurus.[23]

Rising energy costs affect the costs of running a laundromat, patrolling the streets in a police cruiser, painting a house with oil-based paint, bringing produce to supermarkets, and even driving to the store

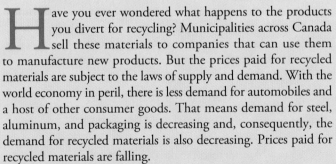

Go Green

The Economics of Green

Have you ever wondered what happens to the products you divert for recycling? Municipalities across Canada sell these materials to companies that can use them to manufacture new products. But the prices paid for recycled materials are subject to the laws of supply and demand. With the world economy in peril, there is less demand for automobiles and a host of other consumer goods. That means demand for steel, aluminum, and packaging is decreasing and, consequently, the demand for recycled materials is also decreasing. Prices paid for recycled materials are falling.

In 2008, Halifax received $1.4 million in revenue from the sale of recycled materials. Near year-end, the price of polyethylene plastic dropped from $700 per tonne to $250 per tonne; paper prices dropped from $130 per tonne to $50 per tonne; aluminum dropped from $100 per tonne to just $10 per tonne. Unless conditions improve, revenue will certainly fall in the future. Toronto has been protected so far because it has negotiated longer-term contracts for the sale of its recycled materials, but these contracts will need to be renegotiated beginning in early 2009.

Fortunately for the environment, efforts to encourage diverting waste are affected little by the prices paid for recycled materials. Municipalities spend millions of dollars each year on landfill sites, and these are getting increasingly difficult to find.

Municipalities must consider new initiatives to increase the diversion of waste through recycling programs. Toronto—where retailers annually hand out 460 million plastic bags—was considering forcing grocery retailers to give a small discount to customers who used their own bags. Opposition eventually led to a compromise: major grocery chains will charge five cents per plastic bag at the checkout. A pilot project by Loblaws found that charging even a nominal fee reduced the number of bags distributed by 55 percent. It is beginning to charge for plastic bags at its locations across Canada. Other retailers will follow suit. Of course, there are other solutions. Leaf Rapids, Manitoba, has simply banned plastic bags completely. Retailers who pass out plastic bags are liable for fines of up to $1000.

The next battle: coffee cups. Toronto city council plans to force coffee shops to give a 20-cent discount to consumers who bring their own mugs.

Source: Daniel Drolet, "Government, Retailers Try to Put Green Revolution in the Bag," *Ottawa Citizen*, August 17, 2007, p. E1; Phoebe Powell, "Recyclable Revenue for Cities Declines; 'We Haven't Seen Prices This Low in a Long Time,'" needs *National Post*, November 26, 2008, p. A5; Jeff Gray and Jennifer Lewington, "Mayor, Supermarkets to Propose Five-Cent Fee for Plastic Bags," *Globe and Mail*, November 26, 2008, p. A15; "Grocers Moving to Contain Plastic Bag Use," *Telegraph Journal* (Saint John), November 28, 2008, p. B7.

to buy it. The alternative-rock band Kill Hannah saw profits from its recent tour get eaten away by the rising cost of hauling its 5000-pound equipment from venue to venue. "You can't raise ticket prices," says the band's bass guitarist, Greg Corner, "but we're spending as much money in gas as a band that's selling out a 3000-seat arena. This tour is really a learning experience."[24]

One price that's often difficult for businesspeople to set is the size of a tip. The "Etiquette Tips for Marketing Professionals" feature offers some guidelines for acknowledging the services of waiters, bellhops, taxi drivers, and others.

PRICE DETERMINATION IN ECONOMIC THEORY

Microeconomics suggests a way of determining prices that assumes a profit-maximization objective. This technique attempts to derive correct equilibrium prices in the marketplace by comparing supply and demand. It also requires more complete analysis than actual business firms typically conduct.

Demand refers to a schedule of the amounts of a firm's product that consumers will purchase at different prices during a specified time period. **Supply** refers to a schedule of the amounts of a good or service that will be offered for sale at different prices during a specified period. These schedules may vary for different types of market structures. Businesses operate and set prices in four types of market structures: pure competition, monopolistic competition, oligopoly, and monopoly.

ETIQUETTE TIPS FOR MARKETING PROFESSIONALS

Tipping Do's and Don'ts

TIPS are part of the price of dining out or using the services of door attendants, taxi drivers, bellhops, porters, valets, maître d's, and others with whom businesspeople come in contact. Tipping is meant to thank anyone who performs a special service for you or who makes your travel more convenient or your meal more enjoyable. Many service providers depend on tips to make ends meet.

But many people are confused by tipping. Who gets a tip and who doesn't? How much is appropriate? What if the service isn't deserving of a tip? Here are a few guidelines to remember about tipping in Canada.

1. If the service is poor, give your server the benefit of the doubt and leave the standard 15 percent tip. But talk to the manager about improving service.
2. Don't make up for high prices by cutting back on the tip. If adding the tip makes the service a stretch for your budget, patronize the service less often or find a cheaper one.
3. Tip hairdressers and manicurists 10 to 20 percent of the total; skycaps and bellhops or door attendants receive $1 per bag (more if the bags are heavy).
4. Tip your taxi, limo, or van driver 15 percent of the total fare, but never less than $1. Add more if the driver helps with your bags. Tip a valet or parking attendant $2 to $5 for returning your car, but not for parking it.

5. Tip the hotel maid daily; different maids take care of your room each day. Leave $1 to $3 on your pillow each time, including the day you check out.
6. Tip the hotel concierge $5 to $10 at the end of your stay if he or she has been helpful with dinner or theatre reservations.
7. Tip for room service as you would for service in a restaurant—15 to 20 percent of the total charge.
8. No tip is required if the maître d' merely seats you in a restaurant. If he or she gets you a special table or a table without a reservation when the restaurant is busy, tip $5 to $10 or more, depending on the average price of a meal.
9. Tip jars at coffee shops, cafeterias, and concessions stands can usually be safely ignored because no extraordinary or personal service is offered.
10. For holiday gifts to those you see regularly, such as doormen, hairdressers, manicurists, and personal trainers, give within your means, or ask the shop owner or manager or your colleagues about what is appropriate. Skip the homemade goodies; cash and gift certificates are still the most widely appreciated gifts.

Sources: James G. Lewis, "Tipping Etiquette," Findalink, http://www.findalink .net, accessed June 16, 2006; "Proper Tipping Etiquette," Essortment, http://msms .essortment.com, accessed June 16, 2006; "Tipping Etiquette," About.com, http:// hotels.about.com, accessed June 16, 2006; Eileen Alt Powell, "Tipping Shouldn't Break Bank," *The Morning News,* December 11, 2005, p. 11D.

Pure competition is a market structure with so many buyers and sellers that no single participant can significantly influence price. Pure competition presupposes other market conditions as well: homogeneous products and ease of entry for sellers due to low start-up costs. The agricultural sector exhibits many characteristics of a purely competitive market, making it the closest actual example.

Monopolistic competition typifies most retailing and features large numbers of buyers and sellers. These diverse parties exchange heterogeneous, relatively well-differentiated products, giving marketers some control over prices.

Relatively few sellers compete in an **oligopoly.** Pricing decisions by each seller are likely to affect the market, but no single seller controls it. High start-up costs form significant barriers to entry for new competitors. Each firm's demand curve in an oligopolistic market displays a unique kink at the current market price. Because of the impact of a single competitor on total industry sales, competitors usually quickly match any attempt by one firm to generate additional sales by reducing prices. Price cutting in such industry structures is likely to reduce total industry revenues. Oligopolies operate in the petroleum refining, automobile, airline, banking, and tobacco industries.

The availability of newer air transportation alternatives, such as WestJet and Porter Airlines, forces established air carriers such as Air Canada to maintain competitive airfares—or risk losing business to the upstarts. Without these competitors, it is very likely that airfares would be higher. But price is more than just the price of the ticket. When Air Canada decided to add a charge for telephone reservations, WestJet's "Guest Experience Committee" recommended against following suit, and management agreed. The committee suggested that while the additional charge would have increased WestJet's revenue and encouraged customers to make reservations via the lower-cost Web-based system, such add-on fees would change the company's image as a lower-cost, higher-service airline.[25]

A **monopoly** is a market structure in which only one seller of a product exists and for which there are no close substitutes. Legislation has nearly eliminated all but temporary monopolies, such as those created through patent protection. Regulated industries, such as utility companies, constitute another form of monopoly. The government allows regulated monopolies in markets in which competition would lead to an uneconomical duplication of services. In return for such a licence, government reserves the right to regulate the monopoly's rate of return.

The four types of market structures are compared in Table 17.2 on the following bases: number of competitors, ease of entry into the industry by new firms, similarity of competing products, degree of control over price by individual firms, and the elasticity or inelasticity of the demand curve facing the individual firm. Elasticity—the degree of consumer responsiveness to changes in price—is discussed in more detail in a later section.

table 17.2 *Distinguishing Features of the Four Market Structures*

	TYPE OF MARKETING STRUCTURE			
CHARACTERISTICS	PURE COMPETITION	MONOPOLISTIC COMPETITION	OLIGOPOLY	MONOPOLY
Number of competitors	Many	Few to many	Few	No direct competitors
Ease of entry into industry	Easy	Somewhat difficult	Difficult	Regulated by government by new firms
Similarity of goods or services offered by competing firms	Similar	Different	Can be either similar or different	No directly competing services
Control over prices by individual firms	None	Some	Some	Considerable
Demand curves facing individual firms	Totally elastic	Can be either elastic or inelastic	Kinked; inelastic below kink; more elastic above	Can be either elastic or inelastic
Examples	2000-hectare ranch	Best Buy stores	Petro-Canada	Liquor Control Board of Ontario

figure 17.1

Determining Price by Relating Marginal Revenue to Marginal Cost

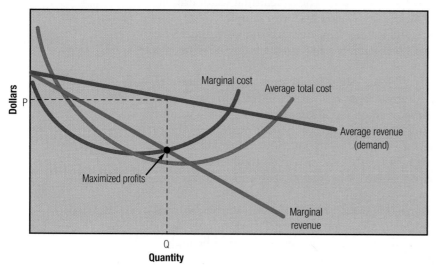

COST AND REVENUE CURVES

Marketers must set a price for a product that generates sufficient revenue to cover the costs of producing and marketing it. A product's total cost is composed of total variable costs and total fixed costs. **Variable costs** change with the level of production (such as raw materials and labour costs), and **fixed costs** remain stable at any production level within a certain range (such as lease payments or insurance costs). **Average total costs** are calculated by dividing the sum of the variable and fixed costs by the number of units produced. Finally, **marginal cost** is the change in total cost that results from producing an additional unit of output.

The demand side of the pricing equation focuses on revenue curves. Average revenue is calculated by dividing total revenue by the quantity associated with these revenues. Average revenue is actually the demand curve facing the firm. Marginal revenue is the change in total revenue that results from selling an additional unit of output. Figure 17.1 shows the relationships of various cost and revenue measures; the firm maximizes its profits when marginal costs equal marginal revenues.

Table 17.3 illustrates why the intersection of the marginal cost and marginal revenue curves is the logical point at which to maximize revenue for the organization. Although the firm can earn a profit at several different prices, the price at which it earns maximum profits is $22. At a price of $24, $66 in profits are earned—$4 less than the $70 profit at the $22 price. If a price of $20 is set to attract additional sales, the marginal costs of the extra sales ($7) are greater than the marginal revenues received ($6), and total profits decline.

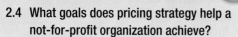

assessment check 2b

2.4 What goals does pricing strategy help a not-for-profit organization achieve?

2.5 What are the two basic ways in which marketers determine prices?

table 17.3   *Price Determination Using Marginal Analysis*

PRICE	NUMBER SOLD	TOTAL REVENUE	MARGINAL REVENUE	TOTAL COSTS	MARGINAL COSTS	PROFITS (TOTAL REVENUE MINUS TOTAL COSTS)
—	—	—	—	—	—	($50)
$34	1	$34	$34	$57	$7	(23)
32	2	64	30	62	5	2
30	3	90	26	66	4	24
28	4	112	22	69	3	43
26	5	130	18	73	4	57
24	6	144	14	78	5	66
22	7	154	10	84	6	70
20	8	160	6	91	7	69
18	9	162	2	100	9	62
16	10	160	(2)	110	11	50

THE CONCEPT OF ELASTICITY IN PRICING STRATEGY

③ Explain price elasticity and its determinants.

Although the intersection of the marginal cost and marginal revenue curves determines the level of output, the impact of changes in price on sales varies greatly. To understand why it fluctuates, it is necessary to understand the concept of elasticity.

Elasticity is the measure of the responsiveness of purchasers and suppliers to price changes. The price elasticity of demand (or elasticity of demand) is the percentage change in the quantity of a good or service demanded divided by the percentage change in its price. A 10 percent increase in the price of eggs that results in a 5 percent decrease in the quantity of eggs demanded yields a price elasticity of demand for eggs of 0.5. The price elasticity of supply of a product is the percentage change in the quantity of a good or service supplied divided by the percentage change in its price. A 10 percent increase in the price of shampoo that results in a 25 percent increase in the quantity supplied yields a price elasticity of supply for shampoo of 2.5.

elasticity Measure of responsiveness of purchasers and suppliers to a change in price.

Consider a case in which a 1 percent change in price causes more than a 1 percent change in the quantity supplied or demanded. Numerically, that means an elasticity measurement greater than 1.0. When the elasticity of demand or supply is greater than 1.0, that demand or supply is said to be elastic. If a 1 percent change in price results in less than a 1 percent change in quantity, a product's elasticity of demand or supply will be less than 1.0. In that case, the demand or supply is called inelastic. For example, the demand for cigarettes is relatively inelastic; research studies have shown that a 10 percent increase in cigarette prices results in only a 4 percent sales decline.

Prices in Zimbabwe are rising at unheard-of rates, the result of hyperinflation that threatens to surpass 1000 percent a year. Toilet paper recently climbed to $417 for a single two-ply sheet, or almost $150 000 a roll—contrast that with a price of about 75 cents in Canada. Although under ordinary inflation, people will continue to buy necessities with relatively inelastic demand such as food, under hyperinflation in Zimbabwe, even staples such as bread, margarine, meat, and tea become unattainable luxuries for the country's 13 million people, many of whom face food shortages and more than 70 percent of whom are unemployed.[26]

Determinants of Elasticity

Why is the elasticity of supply or demand high for some products and low for others? What determines demand elasticity? One major factor influencing the elasticity of demand is the availability of substitutes or complements. If consumers can easily find close substitutes for a good or service, the product's demand tends to be elastic. A product's role as a complement to the use of another product also affects its degree of price elasticity. For example, the relatively inelastic demand for motor oil reflects its role as a complement to a more important product, gasoline. With record high prices of gasoline recently, interest in and demand for energy alternatives has reached a fever pitch, as the "Solving an Ethical Controversy" feature describes.

As increasing numbers of buyers and sellers complete their business transactions online, the elasticity of a product's demand is drastically affected. Take major discounters and other price-competitive box stores, for example. Small businesses and individual do-it-yourselfers shop at Canadian Tire for tools, such as wheelbarrows; parents look for birthday gifts at Wal-Mart; and homeowners go to Future Shop for new refrigerators or stoves. Today, however, the Internet lets consumers contact many more providers directly, often giving them better selections and prices for their efforts with service sites such as Shopbot.ca, PriceGrabber.ca, and Shopzilla.com for consumer goods and electronics; Net-a-Porter.com for high-fashion clothing; and Kayak.com and Expedia.ca for travel bargains. The increased options available to shoppers combine to create a market characterized by demand elasticity.

Elasticity of demand also depends on whether a product is perceived as a necessity or a luxury. The Four Seasons chain of luxury hotels and resorts enjoys such a strong reputation for service, comfort, and exclusiveness that it has become a favourite among affluent individual travellers and business professionals. In other contexts, specialty shops such as Starbucks are considered necessities by some consumers today.

Most people regard high-fashion clothes, such as a $2500 Escada embroidered silk suit as luxuries. If prices for designer outfits increase dramatically, people can respond by purchasing lower-priced substitutes instead. In contrast, dental care is considered a necessity, so price changes have little effect on the frequency of visits to the dentist.

Marketoid

The short-run price elasticity of demand for gasoline is −0.34; the long run price elasticity is −0.84.

Solving an Ethical Controversy

Energy from Ethanol: Hope or Hype?

GASOLINE and petroleum-based products drive the Canadian economy. Demand for the fuel remains strong despite some all-time highs in the price of a litre of gasoline. But with supplies tight and worldwide demand for crude oil increasing, consumers are taking a harder look at corn-based ethanol to help ease the energy crunch. Yet it is not clear how much ethanol can reduce our dependence on foreign oil imports. (Yes, we both export and import crude oil.) That's not stopping some marketers, who point to a future of renewable energy resources and cleaner air. If Brazil can use its sugar cane to become energy independent, they argue, why can't Canada use its abundant corn crop to wean itself from oil, which often comes from unstable—and sometimes hostile—parts of the world? Consumers are left to try to sort fact from fiction.

Is ethanol a viable replacement for petroleum in the market, or are producers overpromising its benefits?

PRO

1. Ethanol is produced from a renewable resource: corn. Existing cars can run on a 10 percent ethanol mixture without any modifications. With minor engine modifications—some experts say about $100 of tinkering—cars could run on 85 percent ethanol power. And corn is domestically produced, creating a reliable supply.
2. Ethanol burns clean, reducing pollution. Governments are beginning to mandate that ethanol be included in gasoline products, and the trend will likely continue.

For example, all gasoline sold in Manitoba must contain 5 percent ethanol, so producers are ensured of some demand for their production. If gas prices continue to rise or the supply is in doubt, then demand for ethanol will continue to surge beyond those minimums.

CON

1. Ethanol production uses considerable amounts of energy. In fact, CIBC World Markets argues that "converting corn from food to fuel has, at best, dubious net energy benefits." At the same time, increased demand for corn drove corn prices up 44 percent between late 2006 and late 2007, contributing to a threatening world food crisis.
2. Ethanol dissolves in water, and current transportation and storage methods are not completely watertight. So new distribution systems would need to be built to handle ethanol. Also, corn is used in many food products and is exported to other countries, so increasing corn-based ethanol could drive up the price of food products and reduce export revenue.

Where do you stand: pro or con?

Sources: "Pumping Ethanol," *Winnipeg Free Press*, January 7, 2008, p. A10; Kerry Benjoe, "Forking It Out to Fill It Up; Gas Hits $1.10," *Leader Post* (Regina), January 4, 2008, p. A1; Gary Norris, "2007 Business Headlines More Ridiculous Than Sublime," *Telegraph-Journal* (Saint John), December 29, 2007, p. C4; Alia McMullen, "Food Crisis Looms, BMO Analyst Warns; China, India Demand; 'It's Going to Hit This Year Hard,' Donald Coxe Says," *National Post*, January 4, 2008, p. FP5.

However, under the continuing influence of higher prices, some products once regarded as necessities may be dismissed as luxuries, leading to decreasing demand. Formerly booming personal computer sales have shown little or no growth in recent years.

Elasticity also depends on the portion of a person's budget that he or she spends on a good or service. People no longer really need matches. They can easily find good substitutes. Nonetheless, the demand for matches remains very inelastic because people spend so little on them that they hardly notice a price change. In contrast, the demand for housing or transportation is not totally inelastic, even though they are necessities, because both consume large parts of a consumer's budget.

Elasticity of demand also responds to consumers' time perspectives. Demand often shows less elasticity in the short run than in the long run. Consider the demand for home air conditioning. In the short run, people pay rising energy prices because they find it difficult to cut back on the quantities they use. Accustomed to living with specific temperature settings and dressing in certain ways, they prefer to pay more during a few months of the year than to explore other possibilities. Over time, though, with global warming becoming a real and present danger, they may find ways to economize. They can better insulate their homes, experiment with alternative cooling systems, or plant shade trees.

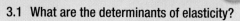

assessment check 3

3.1 What are the determinants of elasticity?

3.2 What is the usual relationship between elasticity and revenue?

Sometimes the usual patterns do not hold true, though. Alcohol and tobacco, which are not necessities but do occupy large shares of some personal budgets, are also subject to inelastic demand.

Elasticity and Revenue

The elasticity of demand exerts an important influence on variations in total revenue as a result of changes in the price of a good or service. Assume, for example, that the Toronto Transit Commission (TTC) officials are considering alternative methods of raising more money for their budget. One possible method for increasing revenues would be to increase fares for commuters. But should the TTC raise or lower the price of a pass? The correct answer depends on the elasticity of demand for its services. A 10 percent decrease in fares should attract more riders, but unless it stimulates more than a 10 percent increase in riders, total revenue will fall. A 10 percent increase in fares will bring in more money per rider, but if more than 10 percent of the riders stop using TTC services, total revenue will fall. A price cut will increase revenue only for a product with elastic demand, and a price increase will raise revenue only for a product with inelastic demand. TTC officials seemed to believe that the demand for its services is inelastic; they recently raised fares as they needed more money to cover operating costs.

One major factor influencing the elasticity of demand is the availability of substitute products. For many consumers, the choice between apples and oranges depends on which is promoted as a weekly special.

④ List the practical problems involved in applying price theory concepts to actual pricing decisions.

PRACTICAL PROBLEMS OF PRICE THEORY

Marketers may thoroughly understand price theory concepts but still encounter difficulty applying them in practice. What practical limitations interfere with setting prices?

First, many firms do not attempt to maximize profits. Economic analysis is subject to the same limitations as the assumptions on which it is based—for example, the proposition that all firms attempt to maximize profits. Second, it is difficult to estimate demand curves. Modern accounting procedures provide managers with a clear understanding of cost structures, so managers can readily comprehend the supply side of the pricing equation. But they find it difficult to estimate demand at various price levels. Demand curves must be based on marketing research estimates that may be less exact than cost figures. Although the demand element can be identified, it is often difficult to measure in real-world settings.

assessment check 4

4.1 List the three reasons why it is difficult to put price theory into practice.

⑤ Explain the major cost-plus approaches to price setting.

PRICE DETERMINATION IN PRACTICE

The practical limitations inherent in price theory have forced practitioners to turn to other techniques. **Cost-plus pricing,** the most popular method, uses a base-cost figure per unit and adds a markup to cover unassigned costs and to provide a profit. The only real difference among the multitude of cost-plus techniques is the relative sophistication of the costing procedures employed. For example, a local apparel shop may set prices by adding a 45 percent markup to the invoice price charged by the supplier. The markup is expected to cover all other expenses and permit the owner to earn a reasonable return on the sale of clothes.

In contrast to this rather simple pricing mechanism, a large manufacturer may employ a complex pricing formula requiring computer calculations. However, this method merely adds a more complicated procedure to the simpler, traditional method for calculating costs. In the end, someone still must make a decision about the markup. The apparel shop and the large manufacturer may figure costs differently, but they are remarkably similar in completing the markup side of the equation.

Cost-plus pricing often works well for a business that keeps its costs low, allowing it to set its prices lower than those of competitors and still make a profit. Wal-Mart keeps costs low by buying most of its inventory directly from manufacturers, using a supply chain that slashes inventory costs by quickly replenishing inventory as items are sold, and relying on wholesalers and other intermediaries only in special instances like localized items. This strategy has played a major role in the discounter becoming the world's largest retailer.

ALTERNATIVE PRICING PROCEDURES

The two most common cost-oriented pricing procedures are the full-cost method and the incremental-cost method. **Full-cost pricing** uses all relevant variable costs in setting a product's price. In addition, it allocates those fixed costs that cannot be directly attributed to the production of the specific item being priced. Under the full-cost method, if job order 515 in a printing plant amounts to 0.000127 percent of the plant's total output, then 0.000127 percent of the firm's overhead expenses are charged to that job. This approach allows the marketer to recover all costs plus the amount added as a profit margin.

The full-cost approach has two basic deficiencies. First, there is no consideration of competition or demand for the item. Perhaps no one wants to pay the price the firm has calculated. Second, any method for allocating overhead (fixed expenses) is arbitrary and may be unrealistic. In manufacturing, overhead allocations often are tied to direct labour hours. In retailing, the area of each profit centre is sometimes the factor used in computations. Regardless of the technique employed, it is difficult to show a cause–effect relationship between the allocated cost and most products.

One way to overcome the arbitrary allocation of fixed expenses is with **incremental-cost pricing**, which attempts to use only those costs directly attributable to a specific output in setting prices. Consider a very small-scale manufacturer with the following income statement:

Sales (10 000 units at $10)		$100 000
Expenses:		
Variable	$50 000	
Fixed	40 000	90 000
Net Profit		$ 10 000

Suppose the firm is offered a contract for an additional 5000 units. Since the peak season is over, these items can be produced at the same average variable cost. Assume that the labour force would otherwise be working on maintenance projects. How low should the firm price its product to get the contract?

Under the full-cost approach, the lowest price would be $9 per unit. This figure is obtained by dividing the $90 000 in expenses by an output of 10 000 units. The incremental approach, on the other hand, could permit any price above $5, which would significantly increase the possibility of securing the additional contract. This price would be composed of the $5 variable cost associated with each unit of production plus some additional per-unit contribution to fixed expenses and overhead. With a $5.10 proposed price ($.10 over the variable cost), for example, the income statement now looks like this:

Sales (10 000 at $10; 5000 at $5.10)		$125 500
Expenses:		
Variable	$75 000	
Fixed	40 000	115 000
Net Profit		$ 10 500

Profits thus increase under the incremental approach.

Admittedly, the illustration is based on two assumptions: (1) the ability to isolate markets such that selling at the lower price will not affect the price received in other markets, and (2) the absence of legal restrictions on the firm. The example, however, does illustrate that profits can sometimes be enhanced by using the incremental approach.

assessment check 5

5.1   What is full-cost pricing?

5.2   What is incremental-cost pricing?

BREAKEVEN ANALYSIS

Breakeven analysis is a means of determining the number of goods or services that must be sold at a given price to generate sufficient revenue to cover total costs. Figure 17.2 graphically depicts this process. The total cost curve includes both fixed and variable segments, and total fixed cost is represented by a horizontal line. Average variable cost is assumed to be constant per unit as it was in the example for incremental pricing.

The breakeven point is the point at which total revenue equals total cost. In the example in Figure 17.2, a selling price of $10 and an average variable cost of $5 result in a per-unit contribution to fixed cost of $5. The breakeven point in units is found by using the following formula, where the per-unit contribution equals the product's price less the variable cost per unit:

$$\text{Breakeven Point (in units)} = \frac{\text{Total Fixed Cost}}{\text{Per-Unit Contribution to Fixed Cost}}$$

$$\text{Breakeven Point (in units)} = \frac{\$40\ 000}{\$5} = 8000 \text{ units}$$

The breakeven point in dollars is found with the following formula:

$$\text{Breakeven Point (in dollars)} = \frac{\text{Total Fixed Cost}}{1 - \text{Variable Cost per Unit Price}}$$

$$\text{Breakeven Point (in dollars)} = \frac{\$40\ 000}{1 - (\$5/\$10)} = \frac{\$40\ 000}{0.5} = \$80\ 000$$

Sometimes breakeven is reached by reducing costs. When Ford Motor Company recently lost millions of dollars, it tried to bring its North American operations back to profitability by slashing costs. Soaring gas prices reduced the popularity of gas-guzzling SUVs, which were a former bright spot in Ford's lineup. So Bill Ford, Jr., announced a 15 percent cutback in production, closing 14 plants and eliminating up to 30 000 factory jobs in North America. The goal was to return quickly to profitability.[27]

Once the breakeven point has been reached, sufficient revenues will have been obtained from sales to cover all fixed costs. Any additional sales will generate per-unit profits equal to the difference between the product's selling price and the variable cost of each unit. As Figure 17.2 reveals, sales of 8001 units (1 unit above the breakeven point) will produce net profits of $5 ($10 sales price less per-unit variable cost of $5). Once all fixed costs have been covered, the per-unit contribution will become the per-unit profit.

Target Returns

Although breakeven analysis indicates the sales level at which the firm will incur neither profits nor losses, most firms' managers include a targeted profit in their analyses. In some instances, management sets a desired dollar return when considering a proposed new product or other marketing action. A retailer may set a desired

breakeven analysis Pricing technique used to determine the number of products that must be sold at a specified price to generate enough revenue to cover total cost.

figure 17.2
Breakeven Chart

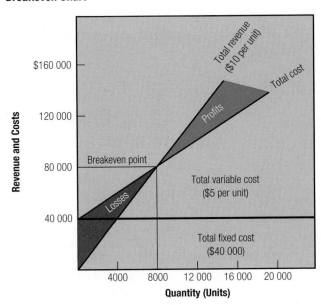

profit of $250 000 in considering whether to expand to a second location. In other instances, the target return may be expressed in percentages, such as a 15 percent return on sales. These target returns can be calculated as follows:

$$\text{Breakeven Point (including specific dollar target return)} = \frac{\text{Total Fixed Cost} + \text{Profit Objective}}{\text{Per-Unit Contribution}}$$

$$\text{Breakeven Point (in units)} = \frac{\$40\ 000 + \$15\ 000}{\$5} = 11\ 000 \text{ units}$$

assessment check 6a

6.1 Give the formula for finding the breakeven point, in units and in dollars.

6.2 What adjustments to the basic breakeven calculation must be made to include target returns?

If the target return is expressed as a percentage of sales, it can be included in the breakeven formula as a variable cost. Suppose the marketer in the preceding example seeks a 10 percent return on sales. The desired return is $1 for each product sold (the $10 per-unit selling price multiplied by the 10 percent return on sales). In this case, the basic breakeven formula will remain unchanged, although the variable cost per unit will be increased to reflect the target return, and the per-unit contribution to fixed cost will be reduced to $4. As a result, the breakeven point will increase from 8000 to 10 000 units:

$$\text{Breakeven Point} = \frac{\$40\ 000}{\$4} = 10\ 000 \text{ units}$$

Evaluation of Breakeven Analysis

Breakeven analysis is an effective tool for marketers in assessing the sales required for covering costs and achieving specified profit levels. It is easily understood by both marketing and non-marketing executives and may help them decide whether required sales levels for a certain price are in fact realistic goals. However, it has its shortcomings.

First, the model assumes that costs can be divided into fixed and variable categories. Some costs, such as salaries and advertising outlays, may be either fixed or variable depending on the particular situation. In addition, the model assumes that per-unit variable costs do not change at different levels of operation. However, these may vary because of quantity discounts, more efficient utilization of the workforce, or other economies resulting from increased levels of production and sales. Finally, the basic breakeven model does not consider demand. It is a cost-based model and does not directly address the crucial question of whether consumers will purchase the product at the specified price and in the quantities required for breaking even or generating profits. The marketer's challenge is to modify the breakeven analysis and the other cost-oriented pricing approaches to incorporate demand analysis. Pricing must be examined from the buyer's perspective. Such decisions cannot be made by considering only cost factors.

assessment check 6b

6.3 What are the advantages of breakeven analysis?

6.4 What are the disadvantages of breakeven analysis?

THE MODIFIED BREAKEVEN CONCEPT

Traditional economic theory considers both costs and demand in determining an equilibrium price. The dual elements of supply and demand are balanced at the point of equilibrium. In actual practice, however, most pricing approaches are largely cost oriented. Since purely cost-oriented approaches to pricing violate the marketing concept, modifications that will add demand analysis to the pricing decision are required.

Consumer research on such issues as degree of price elasticity, consumer price expectations, existence and size of specific market segments, and buyer perceptions of strengths and weaknesses of substitute products is necessary for developing sales estimates at different prices. Because much of the resulting data involves perceptions, attitudes, and future expectations of present and potential customers, such estimates are likely to be less precise than cost estimates.

figure 17.3

Modified Breakeven Chart: Parts A and B

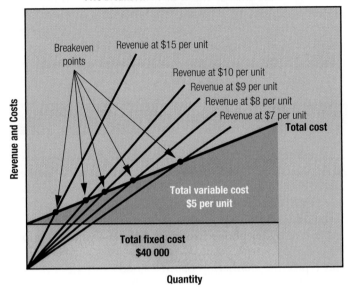

(a)
Five Breakeven Points for Five Different Prices

Breakeven points

Revenue at $15 per unit
Revenue at $10 per unit
Revenue at $9 per unit
Revenue at $8 per unit
Revenue at $7 per unit

Total cost

Total variable cost
$5 per unit

Total fixed cost
$40 000

Revenue and Costs

Quantity

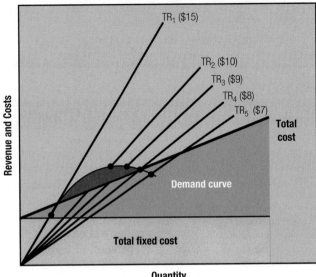

(b)
Superimposing a Demand Curve on the Breakeven Chart

TR_1 ($15)
TR_2 ($10)
TR_3 ($9)
TR_4 ($8)
TR_5 ($7)

Total cost

Demand curve

Total fixed cost

Revenue and Costs

Quantity

The breakeven analysis method illustrated in Figure 7.2 assumes a constant $10 retail price regardless of quantity. But what happens at different retail prices? As Figure 17.3 shows, a more sophisticated approach called **modified breakeven analysis** combines the traditional breakeven analysis model with an evaluation of consumer demand.

Table 17.4 summarizes both the cost and revenue aspects of a number of alternative retail prices. The $5 per unit variable cost and the $40 000 total fixed cost are based on the costs utilized in the basic breakeven model. The expected unit sales for each specified retail price are obtained from marketing research. The table contains the information necessary for calculating the breakeven point for each of the five retail price alternatives. These points are shown in Figure 17.3(a).

The data shown in the first two columns of Table 17.4 represent a demand schedule that indicates the number of units consumers are expected to purchase at each of a series of retail prices. As Figure 17.3(b) shows, these data can be superimposed onto a breakeven chart to identify the range of feasible prices for the marketer to charge.

Figure 17.3 reveals that the range of profitable prices exists from a low of approximately $8 ($TR_4$) to a high of $10 ($TR_2$), with a price of $9 ($TR_3$) generating the greatest projected profits. Changing the retail price produces a new breakeven point. At a relatively high $15 ($TR_1$) retail price, the breakeven

modified breakeven analysis Pricing technique used to evaluate consumer demand by comparing the number of products that must be sold at a variety of prices to cover total cost with estimates of expected sales at the various prices.

table 17.4   Revenue and Cost Data for Modified Breakeven Analysis

| | REVENUES | | | COSTS | | | |
PRICE	QUANTITY DEMANDED	TOTAL REVENUE	TOTAL FIXED COST	TOTAL VARIABLE COST	TOTAL COST	BREAKEVEN POINT (NUMBER OF SALES REQUIRED TO BREAK EVEN)	TOTAL PROFIT (OR LOSS)
$15	2 500	$37 500	$40 000	$12 500	$52 500	4 000	$(15 000)
10	10 000	100 000	40 000	50 000	90 000	8 000	10 000
9	13 000	117 000	40 000	6 000	105 000	10 000	12 000
8	14 000	112 000	40 000	70 000	110 000	13 334	2000
7	15 000	105 000	40 000	75 000	115 000	20 000	(10 000)

point is 4000 units; at a $10 retail price, it is 8000 units; and at the lowest price considered, $7 (TR5), it is 20 000 units.

The contribution of modified breakeven analysis is that it forces the marketer to consider whether the consumer is likely to purchase the number of units required for achieving breakeven at a given price. It demonstrates that a large number of units sold does not necessarily produce added profits, since—other things equal—lower prices are necessary for stimulating additional sales. Consequently, it is important to consider both costs and consumer demand in determining the most appropriate price.

> **assessment check 6c** ✓
>
> **6.5.** What is modified breakeven analysis?

⑦ Explain the use of yield management in pricing decisions.

YIELD MANAGEMENT

yield management
Pricing strategy that allows marketers to vary prices based on such factors as demand, even though the cost of providing those goods or services remains the same; designed to maximize revenues in situations such as airfares, lodging, auto rentals, and theatre tickets, where costs are fixed.

When most of a firm's costs are fixed over a wide range of outputs, the primary determinant of profitability will be the amount of revenue generated by sales. **Yield management** strategies allow marketers to vary prices based on such factors as demand, even though the cost of providing those goods or services remains the same. For example, the Shaw Festival Theatre in Niagara-on-the-Lake, Ontario, offers reduced prices on Tuesday through Friday, and even lower prices on Sunday evening. The Stratford Shakespeare Festival offers rush seats in person or by telephone two hours before scheduled performances, at 50 percent off regular prices.[28]

Similar yield management strategies typify the marketing of such goods and services as the following:

- *Sports teams*—Ottawa Senators and Vancouver Canucks recently began experimenting with a new pricing program: charging more for single-game tickets for games featuring high-profile opponents

- *Lodging*—lower prices off season and higher prices during peak season periods; low-priced weekend rates for most hotels, motels, and bed-and-breakfasts across Canada

- *Auto rental*—lower prices on weekends when business demand is low and higher prices during the week when business demand is higher

- *Airfares*—lower prices on nonrefundable tickets with travel restrictions such as advance-purchase and Saturday-night stay requirements and penalties for flight changes and higher prices on refundable tickets that can be changed without penalty

The following example from the airline industry demonstrates how yield management maximizes revenues in situations where costs are fixed.[29]

Airlines constantly monitor reservations on every flight. Beginning approximately 330 days before the flight, space is allocated between full-fare, discount-fare, and free tickets for frequent flyers who qualify for complimentary tickets. This allocation is monitored and adjusted at regular intervals until the flight departs.

Assume, for example, that Air Canada has scheduled a 180-seat plane as Flight AC123 with an 8 a.m. departure from Ottawa to Winnipeg on October 23. When Flight AC123 leaves its gate, all costs associated with the flight (fuel, crew, and other operating expenses) are fixed. The pricing

EVERY KILOWATT COUNTS FOR BUSINESS

Introducing a new way to manufacture ROA

EXPLORE DEMAND RESPONSE: a powerful solution for managing electricity costs, generating extra revenue, and benefiting the environment. It works by creating a new revenue stream for companies who time-shift their electricity consumption. Visit the OPA online to learn how participating in Demand Response programs can provide your company with a significant financial return on existing assets.

For details visit
www.everykilowattcounts.com/demandresponse

A program offered by

Every Kilowatt Counts **OPA** Ontario Power Authority

™ OPA, Ontario Power Authority, and Every Kilowatt Counts are each official marks of the Ontario Power Authority.

OPA, ONTARIO POWER AUTHORITY, AND EVERY KILOWATT COUNTS ARE EACH OFFICIAL MARKS OF THE ONTARIO POWER AUTHORITY.

Industrial consumers who shift their consumption from peak times to off-peak times are eligible to be paid for the value of the electricity shifted or curtailed.

that maximizes revenues on this flight will also maximize profits. An examination of past sales indicates that Air Canada could sell 40 to 60 one-way, full-fare tickets at $600 per passenger and 100 to 150 one-way restricted-fare tickets at $200 per passenger. Demand for frequent-flyer space should be at least 10 seats.

If Air Canada reserves 60 seats for full-fare passengers and accepts reservations for 110 restricted-fare tickets but sells only 40 full-fare tickets (leaving 20 vacant seats), total revenues will be

$$\text{Revenues} = (40 \times \$600) + (110 \times \$200) = \$46\,000$$

However, if Air Canada's pricing decision makers want to reduce vacancies, they might decide to reduce the number of full-fare tickets to 20 and increase the restricted-fare tickets to 150. If the plane leaves the gate at full capacity, the flight will generate the following total revenues:

$$\text{Revenues} = (20 \times \$600) + (150 \times \$200) = \$42\,000$$

Instead of rigidly maintaining the allocations established nearly a year before the flight, Air Canada will use yield management to maximize the revenue per flight. In this example, the airline initially holds 60 full-fare seats and accepts reservations for up to 110 restricted-fare seats. Thirty days before the October 23 departure, updated computer projections indicate that 40 full-fare seats are likely to be sold. The allocation is now revised to 40 full-fare and 130 restricted-fare tickets. A full flight leaves the gate and revenues are:

$$\text{Revenues} = (40 \times \$600) + (130 \times \$200) = \$50\,000$$

Applying yield management for the Ottawa to Winnipeg flight increases revenues by at least $4000 over the inflexible approach of making advance allocations and failing to adjust them based on passenger reservations and other data.

Marketoid

The cost to fill a fuel-efficient Boeing 777 in Toronto for a one-way flight to London reached $68 948 in June 2008, nearly $200 for each of the plane's 349 seats.

assessment check 7

7.1 Explain the goal of yield management.

GLOBAL ISSUES IN PRICE DETERMINATION

8 Identify the major pricing challenges facing online and international marketers.

It is equally important for a firm engaging in global marketing to use a pricing strategy that reflects its overall marketing strategy. Prices must support the company's broader goals, including product development, advertising and sales, customer support, competitive plans, and financial objectives.

In general, there are five pricing objectives that firms can use to set prices in global marketing. Four of these are the same pricing objectives that we discussed earlier in the chapter: profitability, volume, meeting competition, and prestige. In addition, international marketers work to achieve a fifth objective: price stability.

In the global arena, marketers may choose profitability objectives if their company is a price leader that tends to establish international prices. Profitability objectives also make sense if a firm is a low-cost supplier that can make a good profit on sales.

Volume objectives become especially important in situations where nations lower their trade barriers to expose domestic markets to foreign competition. As the European Union lowered economic barriers between countries, for instance, competition for customers soared. A recent trend has been mergers of European firms to form larger companies that can achieve volume objectives. Luxembourg steel company Arcelor bought big stakes in two Costa Rican firms and one Turkish firm and made a hostile takeover bid for Dofasco, Canada's biggest steel producer. German drug company Merck initiated a hostile bid for rival Schering.[30]

Increased competition in Europe has also spurred firms to work toward the third pricing objective of meeting competitors' prices. The widespread adoption of the euro, the currency of the European Union, has become a driving force in price convergence. "In 2002, the span of prices from the cheapest to the most expensive country was 71 percent," according to the CEO of the marketing research firm ACNielsen Europe. "Today, for identical international brand products, we see that gap reduced to 50 percent. Among Europe's larger markets, stagnating growth and flat consumer demand combined with an increasing competitive retailing industry, are forcing prices down." The company's Euro Price Barometer surveyed the cost of 160 products sold at more than 25 000 grocery stores, supermarkets, and hypermarkets in 15 European countries to find that the introduction of the euro had increased price competition.[31]

COURTESY OF TEKNION

Teknion—a leading Canadian designer, manufacturer, and marketer—has many global pricing challenges as it promotes its products through its showrooms around the world. (This one is in Bangalore, India.)

Prestige is a valid pricing objective in international marketing when products are associated with intangible benefits, such as high quality, exclusiveness, or attractive design. The greater a product's perceived benefits, the higher its price can be. Marketers must be aware, however, that cultural perceptions of quality can differ from one country to the next. Sometimes items that command prestige prices in Canada are considered run-of-the-mill in other nations; sometimes products that are anything but prestigious in Canada seem exotic to overseas consumers. Canadian patrons, for instance, view McDonald's restaurants as affordable fast-food eateries, but in China, they are seen as fashionable and relatively expensive.

The fifth pricing objective, price stability, is desirable in international markets, although it is difficult to achieve. Wars, terrorism, economic downturns, changing governments and political parties, and shifting trade policies can alter prices. A challenge for Wal-Mart in the years ahead will be making substantial inroads in China, where it plans to grow and where local retailers control about 90 percent of the market through price dominance. Wal-Mart will also have to surpass the freshness and quality of the food products offered by the country's many street vendors, who sell everything from live chickens to reptiles with no overhead at prices that are hard to beat. Further hampering Wal-Mart's ability to compete on price may be the expected high costs of training local workers and managers who are not very loyal and dealing with costly problems of piracy and corruption.[32]

Price stability can be especially important for producers of commodities—goods and services that have easily accessible substitutes that other nations can supply quickly. Countries that export international commodities, such as wood, chemicals, and agricultural crops, suffer economically when their prices fluctuate. A nation such as Nicaragua, which exports sugar cane, can find that its balance of payments changes drastically when the international price for sugar shifts. This makes it vulnerable to stiff price competition from other sugar cane producers.

In contrast, countries that export value-oriented products, rather than commodities, tend to enjoy more stable prices. Prices of electronic equipment and automobiles tend to fluctuate far less than prices of crops like sugarcane and bananas.

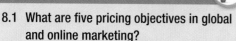

assessment check 8

8.1 What are five pricing objectives in global and online marketing?

8.2 Why is price stability difficult to achieve in online and global marketing?

Strategic Implications

THIS chapter has focused on traditional pricing concepts and methods—principles that are critical to all marketing strategies, especially in e-commerce. Consumers can now compare prices quickly, heightening the already intense competitive pricing environment. The Web allows for prices to be negotiated on the spot, and anything can be auctioned. From airline tickets to automobiles, the Web allows consumers to name their price.

While Internet shopping has not resulted in massive price cutting, it has increased the options available for consumers. Online price comparison engines, known as shopping bots, promise to help consumers find the lowest price for any good or service. Reverse auctions offered by sites such as Priceline.com, which allow customers to submit the highest price they are willing to pay for airline tickets, could conceivably be extended to other types of goods and are already gaining in popularity in business-to-business purchasing.

Electronic delivery of music, books, and other goods and services will only lead to further price reductions. E-business has smoothed out the friction of time, which kept pricing relatively static. The current obsession with time and the ability to measure it will change perceptions and pricing of tangible goods. A growing number of products are not made until they are ordered, and increasingly, their prices are no longer fixed; instead, prices can shift up and down in response to changing market conditions. ◆◆◆

REVIEW OF CHAPTER OBJECTIVES

① Outline the legal constraints on pricing.

A variety of laws affect pricing decisions. The Competition Act of 1986 is the major legislation in Canada that governs pricing and other competitive business practices. Among the pricing-related issues covered by this legislation are price discrimination, price fixing, bid rigging, predatory pricing, and false or misleading ordinary selling price representations. The Competition Act tries to balance the interests of businesses and consumers; it tries to foster a fair competitive environment to protect businesses from each other and to protect consumers from unfair business practices.

② Identify the major categories of pricing objectives.

Pricing objectives should be the natural consequence of overall organizational goals and more specific marketing goals. They can be classified into four major groups: (1) profitability objectives, including profit maximization and target returns; (2) volume objectives, including sales maximization and market share; (3) meeting competition objectives; and (4) prestige objectives.

③ Explain price elasticity and its determinants.

Elasticity is an important element in price determination. The degree of consumer responsiveness to price changes is affected by such factors as (1) availability of substitute or complementary goods, (2) the classification of a good or service as a luxury or a necessity, (3) the portion of a person's budget spent on an item, and (4) the time perspective.

④ List the practical problems involved in applying price theory concepts to actual pricing decisions.

Three problems are present in using price theory in actual practice. First, many firms do not attempt to maximize profits, a basic assumption of price theory. Second, it is difficult to accurately estimate demand curves. Finally, inadequate training of managers and poor communication between economists and managers make it difficult to apply price theory in the real world.

⑤ Explain the major cost-plus approaches to price setting.

Cost-plus pricing uses a base-cost figure per unit and adds a markup to cover unassigned costs and to provide a profit. It is the most commonly used method of setting prices today. There are two primary cost-oriented pricing procedures. Full-cost pricing uses all relevant variable costs in setting a product's price and allocates those fixed costs that cannot be directly attributed to the production of the specific item being priced. Incremental-cost pricing attempts to use only those costs directly attributable to a specific output in setting prices to overcome the arbitrary allocation of fixed expenses. The basic limitation of cost-oriented pricing is that it does not adequately account for product demand.

⑥ **List the chief advantages and shortcomings of using breakeven analysis in pricing decisions.**

Breakeven analysis is a means of determining the number of goods or services that must be sold at a given price to generate revenue sufficient for covering total costs. It is easily understood by managers and may help them decide whether required sales levels for a certain price are realistic goals. Its shortcomings are as follows: First, the model assumes that cost can be divided into fixed and variable categories and ignores the problems of arbitrarily making some allocations. Second, it assumes that per-unit variable costs do not change at different levels of operation, ignoring the possibility of quantity discounts, more efficient utilization of the workforce, and other possible economies. Third, the basic breakeven model does not consider demand. It is a cost-based model and fails to directly address the crucial question of whether consumers will actually purchase the product at the specified price and in the quantities required for breaking even or generating profits.

⑦ **Explain the use of yield management in pricing decisions.**

When most of a firm's costs are fixed over a wide range of outputs, the primary determinant of profitability will be the amount of revenue generated by sales. Yield management pricing strategies are designed to maximize revenues based on such factors as demand in these situations. Examples include airfares, auto rentals, and theatre tickets.

⑧ **Identify the major pricing challenges facing online and international marketers.**

In general, firms can choose from among five pricing objectives to set prices in global marketing. Four of these objectives are the same pricing objectives discussed earlier: profitability, volume, meeting competition, and prestige. The fifth objective is price stability, which is difficult to achieve since wars, border conflicts, terrorism, economic trends, changing governments and political parties, and shifting trade policies can alter prices. The same types of changes can alter pricing in online marketing.

assessment check answers

1.1 What does the Competition Act try to accomplish?
The Competition Act tries to foster a fair competitive environment to protect businesses from each other and to protect consumers from unfair business practices.

1.2 What is price discrimination? Is it always considered anti-competitive? Explain.
Price discrimination occurs when some customers pay more than others for the same product. It is acceptable when discounts are given to meet competition, or can be justified due to cost savings resulting from selling to some customers.

1.3 What is the difference between price fixing and bid rigging?
Both are forms of price collusion and are illegal; however, price fixing occurs when sellers decide to establish prices higher than would exist in a free market whereas bid rigging occurs when the prices relate to one or more competitive bids.

2.1 What are target-return objectives?
Target-return objectives are short-run or long-run goals that are usually stated as percentages of sales or investment.

2.2 What is value pricing?
Value pricing emphasizes the benefits a product provides in comparison to the price and quality levels of competing offerings.

2.3 How do prestige objectives affect a seller's pricing strategy?
Prestige pricing establishes a relatively high price to develop and maintain an image of quality that appeals to status-conscious customers. The seller uses price to create an overall image of the firm.

2.4 What goals does pricing strategy help a not-for-profit organization achieve?
Pricing strategy helps not-for-profit organizations achieve a variety of goals: profit maximization, cost recovery, market incentives, and market suppression.

2.5 What are the two basic ways in which marketers determine prices?
Marketers determine prices by applying the theoretical concepts of supply and demand and by completing cost-oriented analysis.

3.1 What are the determinants of elasticity?
The degree of consumer responsiveness to price changes—elasticity—is affected by such factors as (1) availability of substitute or complementary goods, (2) the classification of a good or service as a luxury or a necessity, (3) the portion of a person's budget spent on an item, and (4) the time perspective.

3.2 What is the usual relationship between elasticity and revenue?

A price cut increases revenue only for a product with elastic demand, and a price increase raises revenue only for a product with inelastic demand.

4.1 List the three reasons why it is difficult to put price theory into practice.

A basic assumption of price theory is that all firms attempt to maximize profits. This does not always happen in practice. A second reason is that demand curves can be extremely difficult to estimate. Finally, managers can be inadequately trained, causing poor communication between economists and managers, which makes it difficult to apply price theory in the real world.

5.1 What is full-cost pricing?

Full-cost pricing uses all relevant variable costs in setting a product's price.

5.2 What is incremental-cost pricing?

Incremental-cost pricing attempts to use only costs directly attributable to a specific output in setting prices to overcome the arbitrary allocation of fixed expenses.

6.1 Give the formula for finding the breakeven point, in units and in dollars.

Breakeven point (in units) = Total fixed cost/Per-unit contribution to fixed cost. Breakeven point (in dollars) = Total fixed cost/(1 − Variable cost per unit price).

6.2 What adjustments to the basic breakeven calculation must be made to include target returns?

Breakeven point (including specific dollar target return) = (Total fixed cost + Profit objective)/Per-unit contribution.

6.3 What are the advantages of breakeven analysis?

Breakeven analysis is easily understood by managers and may help them decide whether required sales levels for a certain price are realistic goals.

6.4 What are the disadvantages of breakeven analysis?

First, the model assumes that cost can be divided into fixed and variable categories and ignores the problems of arbitrarily making some allocations. Second, it assumes that per-unit variable costs do not change at different levels of operation, ignoring the possibility of quantity discounts, more efficient use of the workforce, and other possible economies. Third, the basic breakeven model does not consider demand.

6.5 What is modified breakeven analysis?

The modified breakeven concept combines traditional breakeven analysis with an evaluation of consumer demand. It directly addresses the key question of whether consumers will actually purchase the product at different prices and in what quantities.

7.1 Explain the goal of yield management.

Yield management pricing strategies are designed to maximize revenues in situations in which costs are fixed, such as airfares, auto rentals, and theatre tickets.

8.1 What are five pricing objectives in global and online marketing?

Five pricing objectives in global and online marketing are profitability, volume, meeting competition, prestige, and price stability.

8.2 Why is price stability difficult to achieve in online and global marketing?

Price stability is difficult to achieve because wars, border conflicts, terrorism, economic trends, changing governments and political parties, and shifting trade policies can alter prices.

MARKETING TERMS YOU NEED TO KNOW

These terms are printed in red in the text. They are defined in the margins of the chapter and in the Glossary that begins on p. G-1. Other important terms are printed in bold black type in the chapter but not included in this list. Their definitions can be found in the Glossary.

price 578
Competition Act 579
profit maximization 582
target-return objectives 583

Profit Impact of Market Strategies (PIMS) project 583
value pricing 584
customary prices 586

elasticity 591
breakeven analysis 595
modified breakeven analysis 597
yield management 598

ASSURANCE OF LEARNING REVIEW

1. Distinguish between predatory pricing and price fixing. Why are these pricing-related practices covered by the Competition Act?

2. Give an example of each of the major categories of pricing objectives.

3. What are the major price implications of the PIMS studies? Suggest possible explanations for the relationships the PIMS studies reveal.

4. Identify each factor influencing elasticity and give a specific example of how it affects the degree of elasticity in a good or service.

5. What are the practical problems in applying price theory concepts to actual pricing decisions?
6. Explain the advantages and drawbacks of using incremental-cost pricing rather than full-cost pricing.
7. How can locating the breakeven point assist in price determination?
8. Explain the advantage of modified breakeven analysis over the basic breakeven formula.
9. Explain how the use of yield management can result in greater revenue than other pricing strategies.

PROJECTS AND TEAMWORK EXERCISES

1. In small teams, categorize each of the following as a specific type of pricing objective. Suggest a company or product likely to utilize each pricing objective. Compare your findings.
   a. 5 percent increase in profits over the previous year
   b. prices no more than 6 percent higher than prices quoted by independent dealers
   c. 5 percent increase in market share
   d. 25 percent return on investment (before taxes)
   e. setting the highest prices in the product category to maintain favourable brand image
2. In pairs, discuss the market situations that exist for the following products. Defend your answers and present them to the class.
   a. DVD players   d. remote control car alarms
   b. golf clubs   e. razors
   c. soybeans
3. How are the following prices determined and what do they have in common?
   a. ticket to a local museum   d. printing of business cards
   b. your university tuition   e. lawn mowers
   c. local sales tax rate
4. WebTech Associates of Winnipeg, Manitoba, is considering the possible introduction of a new product proposed by its research and development staff. The firm's marketing director estimates that the product can be marketed at a price of $70. Total fixed cost is $278 000, and average variable cost is calculated at $48.
   a. What is the breakeven point in units for the proposed product?
   b. The firm's president has suggested a target profit return of $214 000 for the proposed product. How many units must be sold to both break even and achieve this target return?
5. The marketing research staff at Regina-based Cyber Specialties has developed the following sales estimates for a proposed new item the firm plans to market through direct mail sales:

Proposed Selling Price	Sales Estimate (units)
$8	55 000
10	22 000
15	14 000
20	5 000
24	2 800

The new product has a total fixed cost of $60 000 and a $7 variable cost per unit.
   a. Which of the proposed selling prices would generate a profit for Cyber Specialties?
   b. The director of marketing for Cyber Specialties also estimates that an additional $0.50 per-unit allocation for extra promotion will produce the following increases in sales estimates: 60 000 units at an $8 unit selling price, 28 000 units at $10, 17 000 units at $15, 6000 units at $20, and 3500 units at $24. Indicate the feasible range of prices if this proposal is implemented and results in the predicted sales increases.
   c. Indicate the feasible price or prices if the $0.50 per-unit additional promotion proposal is not implemented but management insists on a $25 000 target return.
6. Research the price schedule at your local movie theatre multiplex. What price strategy accounts for any price differentials you discover? Why don't matinee prices constitute price discrimination against those who don't qualify for the discounts?
7. Why is it more expensive to buy beer and a hot dog at a Canadian Football League game than it is to buy them at local retail stores?
8. Public funding of national parks has been declining for many years. What would you expect to happen to entry and use fees in this case? Research fees at parks in your province or region to verify your answer and report to the class.
9. How do cell phone companies make money by charging a flat rate per month for a set number of minutes, such as $35 for 300 minutes? Can you think of another plan that would be more profitable? Would it appeal to consumers?
10. Some airline industry executives believe that lower, simpler fares for the major carriers will earn goodwill from customers and send a clear marketing message that they are ready to compete with low-cost rivals. But few big airlines are embracing a new pricing system, frequently opting to launch new no-frills discount airlines to compete with low-cost carriers. Why do you think they are hesitating?

CRITICAL THINKING EXERCISES

1. Prices at amusement parks are expected to rise because operators such as Disney, Paramount, and Six Flags are adding new rides and coping with the rising cost of fuel; they are also copying each other's prices. List as many things as you can think of that parks like these offer patrons in return for their money. Which of these do you think are directly reflected in the price of admission?

2. Musical artists earn only about 9 percent in royalties per CD, using a royalty base of retail price less 25 percent for packaging costs. The rest goes to the producer and to cover recording costs, promotion, copies given away to radio stations and reviewers, and other costs such as videos. What do you think happens to the artist's royalties when a CD is marked down to sell faster? Consider two cases: (1) the marked-down CD sells more copies, and (2) it sells the same number of copies as before.

3. One writer advised consumers to worry not about rising gasoline prices, the cost of which could easily be covered by forgoing one takeout meal a month, but about how high energy prices would affect the rest of the economy. For example, each dollar-a-barrel price increase is equivalent to a $20-million-a-day "tax" on the economy. Explain what this means.

4. One motor vehicle manufacturer recently announced that it will rely less on high-volume strategies such as discounts and rebates to improve its profitability. Another strategy it will employ is to sell fewer cars to rental fleets, which eventually return the cars to the manufacturer for sale at low auction prices. How do these types of sales affect the manufacturer's profitability?

ETHICS EXERCISES

You work for a major bank in your town. The bank has decided it needs new sources of revenue to cover costs for its free chequing account customers. As a result, management implements an automatic courtesy-overdraft fee for people who overdraw their free chequing accounts with a debit card or ATM withdrawal. Under this service, the bank will automatically cover the overdraft and charge the customer a $30 fee—but it won't notify the customer ahead of time. The bank does not plan to advertise this fee to account holders. Managers at the bank maintain that this fee will save customers the embarrassment of having their purchases denied and any returned cheque fees from merchants.[33]

1. You know that the bank advertises its free chequing account service widely in the local media. But the new fees are not advertised, and it bothers you. What course of action would you take?

2. The bank also has a program in which customers can sign up to cover bounced cheques through an automatic savings account transfer. That service is less costly to the account holder, but it doesn't generate as much revenue. A customer has just come to you to open a free chequing account. Do you explain the two options in detail to the customer, or because the courtesy overdraft is a routine feature of free chequing, do you sign the customer up for the "free" account?

INTERNET EXERCISES

1. **Breakeven analysis.** Visit the website listed below to learn more about breakeven analysis and how it can help in pricing decisions. Read the material and prepare a summary you can bring to class to participate in a discussion on the subject. http://www.businessknowhow.com/startup/breakeven.htm

2. **Yield management.** Airlines, hotels, and rental car companies all practise yield management. Complete the following exercises. Relate your experience to the discussion of yield management found in the chapter.

   a. Assume you wish to fly round trip between Calgary and Ottawa. You are flexible with regard to day of travel, time of travel, and departure and arrival airports. Visit the website of WestJet Airlines (http://www.westjet.com) along with a travel site such as Expedia (http://www. expedia.ca) or Orbitz (http://www.orbitz.com). Record and summarize the different fares you find. Why are some fares higher than others?

   b. Now assume you want to stay in a hotel in a popular vacation area, such as Cancun, Mexico, or Whistler, British Columbia. Visiting at least two hotel chains and travel websites, research hotel rates for varying lengths of stay, during different times of the year. Summarize your findings. How much variation did you find in rates for the same hotel?

   c. You would like to rent a car in each of the following cities: Vancouver; Fredericton, New Brunswick; and Windsor, Ontario. Visiting at least two car rental and travel websites, research car rental rates during different times of year, on different days of the week, and for different lengths of time. Record your findings and note any patterns you see.

Note: Internet Web addresses change frequently. If you don't find the exact sites listed, you may need to access the organization's or company's home page and search from there or use a search engine such as Google.

Case 17.1

Value Menus Fill Customer Cravings

Value menus, one of the fast-food industry's most successful pricing strategies, started by accident. Back in 1988, Taco Bell managers were trying to figure out how to increase sales of their new steak and chicken fajitas, which were high-priced by fast-food standards. One day they heard about a Las Vegas franchise that was successfully competing against its local McDonald's by reducing prices, driving up sales volume. Taco Bell jumped at the opportunity, tested the concept, and quickly introduced value menus in all its stores. Sales rebounded by more than 20 percent, and the fast-food landscape was reshaped.

Value menu strategies remained popular with many fast-food chains for years, despite the reduced profitability they brought. Higher volume—especially among young consumers age 18 to 24—and long hours of operation, sometimes around the clock, helped compensate for the crippling price wars between McDonald's, Burger King, Wendy's, KFC, and many others. Then more competition appeared in the form of quick-serve chains whose popularity grew by serving alternatives to burgers. Finally, however, fast-food outlets began to suffer from widespread criticism of their high-calorie meals and from the sameness of their menu offerings. Consumers began to worry about weight gain, diabetes, and high-fat, high-sodium food served in giant portions. Some chains began to decline. McDonald's reported its first quarterly loss as sales dropped and its stock price fell. Some stores did away with their value menus to prop up their profits.

Healthier offerings soon cropped up on fast-food menus, including fresh fruits, salads, and reduced-fat, reduced-calorie offerings. Some were more successful than others, and after a trial period, some fast-food outlets reverted to their old standbys. Wendy's took out its salad bars, and McDonald's dropped the McLean burger. One marketing research executive commented about the public's experiment with healthier fast food, stating that what consumers "say they want and what they actually do are two different things." But both chains, in time, offered packaged salads in their menus for those concerned about calories.

And later, value menus also returned. Wendy's offered a $1.39 value menu, KFC had a $1.39 chicken sandwich, and Burger King's extensive value menu featured a $1.39 Whopper Junior. McDonald's, which has improved both its appearance and its service and made a dramatic profit turnaround, offered a selection of popular food items for $1.39, which it promotes with hip and stylish advertising.

The next phase in fast-food pricing might be tiered pricing. The innovator: Taco Bell again. It now has a selection of value-menu items priced at $1.59 and another selection priced at $1.89.

Questions for Critical Thinking

1. Do you think value pricing and dollar pricing are effective strategies for increasing market share in the fast-food market even if they reduce the profit stores can earn on each meal? Why or why not?
2. Fast-food chains may face renewed challenges to their menu offerings as health concerns about obesity and other ills increase, and as healthier alternatives continue to grow. Do you think pricing strategies can continue to protect the fast-food giants against these threats? Why or why not?

Sources: Melanie Warner, "Salads or No, Cheap Burgers Revive McDonald's," *The New York Times,* April 19, 2006, http://www.nytimes.com; Stuart Morris, "Redefining the Value Menu Will Reinvigorate Sales, Profits for Quick-Service Operations," *Nation's Restaurant News,* February 6, 2006, http://www.findarticles.com; Jyoti Thottam, "Fast-Food Face-Off," *Time,* July 2005, http://www.time.com.

Case 17.2

Cinema Prices: Back to the Future

How much would you pay to see *No Country for Old Men?* This movie won the 2008 Academy Award for Best Picture, and Javier Bardem won an Oscar for Best Supporting Actor. Academy Awards are presented to recognize the best that Hollywood has delivered. Would you expect to pay the same to see Sharon Stone in *Basic Instinct 2?* This movie was dubbed "Basically, It Stinks Too" by organizers of the 2006 Razzie Awards ceremony. Razzies (Golden Raspberry Awards) are presented to recognize the worst that Hollywood has delivered. *Basic Instinct 2* won Razzies for worst movie, worst actress (Sharon Stone), worst prequel or sequel, and worst screenplay. In reality, if the two movies were playing at the same time, you would most likely have your choice of movie, but not your choice of price.

Things may soon change. Box office revenues climbed to $9.7 billion in Canada and the United States in 2007, but attendance was flat compared to 2006, and 12 percent below the modern-day high of 1.6 billion in 2002. The average ticket price in 2007 was $6.82. *Spider-Man 3* grossed $337 million, and *Shrek the Third* grossed $323 million—both sequels and the two highest-grossing movies of the year. In fact, 9 of the 20 highest-grossing movies of 2007 were sequels. Ticket revenue is certainly affected by the number and quality of new releases. In 2006, for example, there were 599 new movie releases, a 30 percent increase over the 474 new movies released in 2004. Movie producers constantly compete for movie viewers, trying to vie for more and better times to release their better movies, frequently changing movie release dates to avoid or go head-to-head against other releases.

In Canada, Ontario accounts for approximately 40 percent of theatre operating revenue. Many cinemas now have a one-price policy. For example, Famous Players Oshawa Centre 8 Cinemas lowered admission price in 2007 to $4.99, regardless of age or day of the week. Other Canadian cinemas that have a one-price policy charge a higher price. At one time it was common to offer special prices for weekend matinees or for less popular weekday evenings. Students and seniors got lower prices for most shows. Some people are predicting that there will be another move to variable pricing, and this time the changes will be even greater. You may not only see higher prices for weekend evenings, you may also see reserved seating at premium prices. Theatres may charge higher prices for shows with popular stars, and lower prices when less popular stars are on the marquee. Movies predicted to be winners might have premium prices; others may have regular, or even lower, prices. Movies may be released at one price, and that price may get reduced the longer the movie remains in theatres. Many venues that offer live theatre—for example, the Shaw Festival at Niagara-on-the Lake, Ontario—have already implemented many of these ideas. Seniors and students get discounted seats.

Higher prices are charged for opening and weekend performances, but preview performances are discounted. Sunday evening performances are even priced lower. At the same time, there are four tiers of prices depending on location within the theatre.

Whatever happens to cinema ticket prices in the future, it is certain that pricing is an issue that many industry people are considering. The competitive marketplace is changing rapidly. It is no longer one theatre competing with another. Today, all theatres are competing with higher-quality DVDs, TiVo, and home stereo systems. Many consumers are considering, too, the cost savings and convenience of staying home, and the safer and more pleasant environment for enjoying their movie experience.

Questions for Critical Thinking

1. Are cinema ticket prices elastic or inelastic? Defend your choice.
2. What are the pros and cons of using yield management to set prices for cinema tickets?

Sources: CNN.com, http://www.cnn.com/interactive/entertainment/0702/slide-show.razzies/frameset.exclude.html, accessed February 11, 2008; David Leonhardt, "Supply, Demand and Movie Tickets," *Globe and Mail,* February 18, 2006, p. R13; CNNMatthews Newswire, "Introducing New Ticket Price of $4.99 at Famous Players Oshawa Centre 8 Cinemas; Experience Multi-million Dollar Movies More Often!" April 5, 2007, p. 1; "2008 Movies Ready to Battle for Box Office; Superheroes and Stupid Spies Are Just Two of the Genres Coming Next Year," *Vancouver Sun,* December 28, 2007, p. D10; Josh Friedman, "Revenues Rise but Movie Attendance Remains Flat," Vancouver Sun, January 5, 2008.

Video Case 17.3

Washburn Guitars: How Much Is the Maya Worth?

The written case on Washburn Guitars appears on page VC-19. The recently filmed Washburn Guitars video is designed to expand and highlight the concepts in this chapter and the concepts and questions covered in the written video case.

chapter 18

Pricing Strategies

CHAPTER OBJECTIVES

1. Compare the alternative pricing strategies and explain when each strategy is most appropriate.

2. Describe how prices are quoted.

3. Identify the various pricing policy decisions that marketers must make.

4. Relate price to consumer perceptions of quality.

5. Contrast competitive bidding and negotiated prices.

6. Explain the importance of transfer pricing.

7. Compare the three alternative global pricing strategies.

8. Relate the concepts of cannibalization, bundle pricing, and bots to online pricing strategies.

LYLE STAFFORD/REUTERS/LANDOV

VANOC: SETTING A PRICE FOR EVERYONE

On October 11, 2007, the Vancouver 2010 Olympic Organizing Committee (VANOC) announced prices for approximately 1.6 million tickets scheduled for sale beginning October 11, 2008—that is, one full year in advance of their for-sale date. But that level of organization and planning is necessary for an event that will involve massive construction projects, millions of volunteers and participants, all taking place while the world watches and waits. Few people can comprehend the scale of such a project. Even the Olympic torch relay leading up to the games will include as many as 12 000 torch bearers who will carry the torch approximately 35 000 kilometres over 100 days—the longest torch relay in one country in the entire history of the Olympic Games. The torch relay event is expected to cost $31 million. The operating budget for the entire 2010 Olympic Winter Games is estimated at $1.63 billion. The largest contributions are expected to come from domestic sponsorships—$760 million; the International Olympic Committee—$400 million (mainly from television revenue); and ticket sales—$232 million.

Prices for the opening and closing ceremonies will range between $175 and $1100. While this may seem high, tickets for the opening ceremonies at Salt Lake City for the 2002 Winter Games went for as much as $1390. Tickets to the men's gold-medal hockey game will go for from $350 to $775, but compared to paying $175 for a regular-season game to see the Vancouver Canucks at GM Place, this does not seem so unreasonable. Ticket prices for men's and ladies' free-skate figure skating finals tickets will cost between $150 and $450; curling finals tickets will range from $65 and $125. Tickets to men's and women's two-person bobsleigh finals will cost between $40 and $85. Tickets to all events preceding event finals will be priced lower, of course. One-half of the total tickets for sale will be priced at $100 or less, with 100 000 priced at only $25. In addition, community groups and social agencies are being consulted as 50 000 tickets will be distributed free to people who would otherwise not be able to attend the Vancouver Olympic Games. VANOC has also organized an online ticket exchange program where ticket holders can buy and sell tickets. People who decide to not attend an event can offer their tickets for sale to people who have been unable to get tickets. This program will help ensure ticket validity and will help reduce the incidence of scalping.

Considerable thought has gone into the ticket pricing strategy for the Vancouver 2010 Winter Olympics. Calgarian Fraser Bullock, former chief operating officer for the 2002 Winter Games in Salt Lake City and a member of the International Olympic Committee's coordinating commission that is overseeing Vancouver's preparations, refers to this as "barbell pricing." It is a common strategy where the best seats to the most popular events are priced high to subsidize prices for less popular events so that almost everyone who wishes can afford to attend. Bullock says, "I think VANOC has done a fantastic job of meeting their fundamental responsibility of making the tickets both affordable and accessible."[1]

connecting with customers

VANOC connects with its customers by generating pre-Olympic interest and buzz. More than two years before the Olympic Games, major sporting events were planned for the Vancouver area: Alpine Skiing World Cup, Ski Jumping World Cup, Four-Continents Figure Skating Championships, Snowboard World Cup, Luge World Cup, Wheelchair Curling Mixed World Championships, Paralympic Alpine Skiing World Cup, and many others. The pre-Olympics torch relay was planned to visit every province and territory of Canada, and to include up to 12 000 torch bearers. Finally, ticket prices were established to be as accessible as possible to most Canadians.

Chapter Overview

FOR most organizations, setting prices is not a one-time decision, nor is it a standard routine. Instead, pricing is a dynamic function of the marketing mix. While about half of all companies change prices once a year or less frequently, one in 10 does so every month. Online companies, which face enormous price pressures, often adjust prices daily. Some even negotiate prices on the spot. As described in the opening vignette, pricing tickets for the 2010 Vancouver Olympic Winter Games requires a very strategic approach as these ticket prices must be established long before they go on sale.

Companies translate pricing objectives into pricing decisions in two major steps. First, someone takes responsibility for making pricing decisions and administering the resulting pricing structure. Second, someone sets the overall pricing structure—that is, basic prices and appropriate discounts for channel members, quantity purchases, and geographic and promotional considerations.

The decision to make price adjustments is directly related to demand. Most businesses slowly change the amounts they charge customers, even when they clearly recognize strong demand. Instead of raising prices, they may choose to scale down customer service or add fees to cover added costs. They may also wait to raise prices until they see what their competitors will do.

Significant price changes in the retail gasoline and airline industries occur in the form of a *step out,* in which one firm will raise prices and then wait to see if others follow suit. If competitors fail to respond by increasing their prices, the company making the step out will usually reduce prices to the original level.

Few businesses want the distinction of being the first to charge higher prices. Since many firms base their prices on manufacturing costs rather than consumer demand, they may wait for increases in their own costs before responding with price changes. These increases generally emerge more slowly

than changes in consumer demand. Finally, since many business executives believe that steady prices help preserve long-term relationships with customers, they are reluctant to raise prices even when strong demand probably justifies the change.

Chapter 17 introduced the concept of price and its role in the economic system and marketing strategy. This chapter examines various pricing strategies and price structures, such as reductions from list prices, and geographic considerations. It then looks at the primary pricing policies, including psychological pricing, price flexibility, product-line pricing, and promotional pricing, as well as price–quality relationships. Competitive and negotiated prices are discussed, and one section focuses entirely on transfer pricing. Finally, the chapter concludes by describing important factors in pricing goods and services for online and global markets. ◆◆◆

---

① Compare the alternative pricing strategies and explain when each strategy is most appropriate.

skimming pricing strategy Pricing strategy involving the use of an initial high price relative to competitive offerings. Price is dropped in incremental steps as supply begins to exceed demand, or when competition catches up.

PRICING STRATEGIES

The specific strategies that firms use to price goods and services grow out of the marketing strategies they formulate to accomplish overall organizational objectives. One firm's marketers may price their products to attract customers across a wide range; another group of marketers may set prices to appeal to a small segment of a larger market; still another group may simply try to match competitors' price tags. In general, firms can choose from three pricing strategies: skimming, penetration, and competitive pricing. The following sections look at these choices in more detail.

SKIMMING PRICING STRATEGY

Derived from the expression "skimming the cream," **skimming pricing strategies** are also known as *market-plus pricing.* They involve the intentional setting of a relatively high price compared with the prices of competing products. Although some firms continue to utilize a skimming strategy throughout most stages of the product life cycle, it is more commonly used as a market entry price for distinctive goods or services with little or no initial competition. As supply begins to exceed demand, or when competition catches up, the initial high price is incrementally dropped.

Such was the case with high-definition, flat-panel TVs, whose average price was approximately $20 000, including installation, when they were introduced in 1999. The resulting sticker shock kept them out of the range of most household budgets. But nearly a decade later, price cuts have brought both LCD and plasma models into the reach of mainstream consumers. Manufacturers such as Sony, Toshiba, Samsung, and LG now offer popular 40- to 42-inch LCD models for between $1200 and $1800. But competition among the higher-end firms is not the sole reason for these price drops. Budget brands such as Maxent, Daytek, Olevia, and Norcent are pressuring the market. These manufacturers offer competing models for around $1000 or less.[2]

A company may practise a skimming strategy in setting a market-entry price when it introduces a distinctive good or service with little or no competition. Or it may use this strategy to market higher-end goods such as HDTVs. British vacuum cleaner manufacturer Dyson has used this practice. Offering entirely new design and engineering, Dyson sells its vacuum cleaners for between $500 and $700, far more than the average vacuum, which goes for around $100. Even iRobot's automated Roomba retails for about $120 to $200 in Canada—and that machine, claims the company, does all the work for you. In fact, the Roomba followed quickly on the heels of the first robotic vacuum for consumers, the Electrolux Trilobite, which sold for $2000. At first, vacuum manufacturers believed they had a premium product with the robotic vacuum. But their hopes were dashed when a robotics company decided it could make one and sell it much more cheaply.[3]

marketing failure   The Joy of Ripping You Off: Priceless!

Background. Companies know that customers are resistant to price increases particularly during a recession but they continually face pressure to increase their bottom lines. One solution is to simply increase hidden charges, those that few customers are knowledgeable about. Among the most egregious are companies in the financial services industry, particularly credit card companies. Within one year, they implemented four rate increases. One Calgary business saw a 28 percent increase in a single month—a hike of more than $1100—without any increase in business volume. Canadian businesses pay among the highest interchange fees in the world: over 2 percent, compared to 1.30 percent in Belgium, 0.90 percent in Sweden, 0.79 percent in Britain, and 0.45 percent in Australia. And Canadians should brace for more. New "premium" cards—including affinity cards—appear regularly. Benefits go to the cardholder, or to the organization that sponsors the affinity card—including colleges and universities, and other not-for-profit organizations—but costs go to the businesses that accept these cards. They are forced to pay "premium" rates. Ultimately, guess who pays? Canadians are also at risk as fee increases are on the horizon for Interac service. Operated as a cooperative venture among banks and other transaction providers, Interac—with its very low fees—has enticed Canadians to become among the heaviest debit card users in the world. Now, application has been made to the Canadian Competition Bureau to restructure Interac fees.

The Marketing Problem. In one recent year, hidden charges for credit card services cost Canadians $4.5 billion. Interac fees, while much lower, have the potential to greatly increase hidden fees that Canadians pay. Canadians make approximately 3.3 billion Interac transactions annually. With increasing pressure to improve financial performance, Canadians will be targeted to pay more for all their financial services. Extra service charges can add millions to a company's coffers. But Canadians are becoming more aware of such hidden fees and are beginning to rebel.

The Outcome. As the issue of hidden fees grows in importance, reactionary groups are increasing pressure on government to take action. The Retail Council of Canada, which represents more than 120 000 Canadian businesses, is lobbying the government to investigate these practices. It also leads a coalition of Canadian businesses that is attempting to intervene in the proposed restructuring of Interac. You can visit its website **at www.stopstickingittous.com**.

Lessons Learned. Companies will need to more carefully consider how to rip off their customers as they look for new and novel ways to do so. Many groups, businesses, and consumers have become sensitized to the issue. Word is spreading, and attempts to lobby government for action are increasing. A word to the wise: with enough greed, you'll eventually get the customer and government attention you deserve.

Dyson's superior engineering and design, combined with new product introductions, allows it to use a skimming pricing strategy.

In some cases, a firm may maintain a skimming strategy throughout most stages of a product's life cycle. The jewellery category is a good example. Although discounters such as Costco and Wal-Mart offer heavier pieces for a few hundred dollars, firms such as Tiffany and Cartier are able to command prices 10 times that amount just for the brand name. Exclusivity justifies the pricing—and the price, once set, rarely falls.

Sometimes maintaining a high price through the product's life cycle works, but sometimes it does not. High prices can drive away otherwise loyal customers. Hockey fans may shift from attending NHL games to junior league hockey games because of ticket, parking, and food prices. Amusement park visitors may shy away from high admission prices and head to the beach instead. If an industry or firm has been known to cut prices at certain points in the past, consumers—and retailers—will expect it. If the price cut doesn't come, consumers must decide whether to pay the higher tab. This has been the case with Sony's PlayStation 3 and Microsoft's Xbox 360. Both firms have traditionally cut prices during the fall, but they did not do so during one recent season. As word leaked out during the summer that there would be no price drop, consumers scrambled to make their purchases early.[4]

Despite the risk of backlash, a skimming strategy does offer benefits. It allows a manufacturer to quickly recover its research and development (R&D) costs. Pharmaceutical companies, which fiercely protect their patents on new drugs, justify high prices because of astronomical R&D costs—an average of 16 cents of every sales dollar, compared with 8 cents for computer makers and 4 cents in the aerospace industry. To protect their brand names from competition from lower-cost generics, drug makers frequently make small changes to their products—such as combining the original product with a complementary prescription drug that treats different aspects of the ailment.

A skimming strategy also permits marketers to control demand in the introductory stages of a product's life cycle and then adjust productive capacity to match changing demand. A low initial price for a new product could lead to fulfillment problems and loss of shopper goodwill if demand outstrips the firm's production capacity. The result is likely to be consumer and retailer complaints and possibly permanent damage to the product's image. Excess demand occasionally leads to quality issues, as the firm strives to satisfy consumer desires for the product with inadequate production facilities.

During the late growth and early maturity stages of its life cycle, a product's price typically falls for two reasons: (1) the pressure of competition and (2) the desire to expand its market. Figure 18.1 shows that 10 percent of the market may buy Product X at $10.00, and another 20 percent could be added to its customer base at a price of $8.75. Successive price declines may expand the firm's market size and meet challenges posed by new competitors.

A skimming strategy has one inherent chief disadvantage: it attracts competition.

figure 18.1

Price Reductions to Increase Market Share

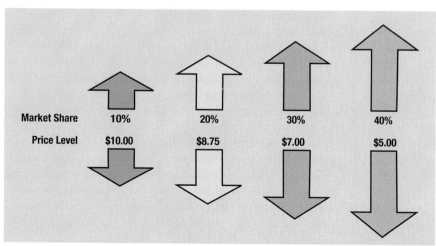

Market Share	10%	20%	30%	40%
Price Level	$10.00	$8.75	$7.00	$5.00

Potential competitors see innovative firms reaping large financial returns and decide to enter the market. This new supply may force the price of the original product even lower than its eventual level under a sequential skimming procedure. However, if patent protection or some other unique proprietary ability allows a firm to exclude competitors from its market, it may extend a skimming strategy.

PENETRATION PRICING STRATEGY

A **penetration pricing strategy** sets a low price as a major marketing weapon. Marketers often price products noticeably lower than competing offerings when they enter new industries characterized by dozens of competing brands. Once the product achieves some market recognition through consumer trial purchases stimulated by its low price, marketers may increase the price to the level of competing products. Marketers of consumer products such as detergents often use this strategy. A penetration pricing strategy may also extend over several stages of the product life cycle as the firm seeks to maintain a reputation as a low-price competitor.

A penetration pricing strategy is sometimes called *market-minus pricing* when it implements the premise that a lower-than-market price will attract buyers and move a brand from an unknown newcomer to at least the brand-recognition stage or even to the brand-preference stage. Since many firms begin penetration pricing with the intention of increasing prices in the future, success depends on generating many trial purchases. Penetration pricing is common among credit card firms, which typically offer low or zero interest rates for a specified introductory period, then raise the rates.

penetration pricing strategy Pricing strategy involving the use of a relatively low entry price compared with competitive offerings, based on the theory that this initial low price will help secure market acceptance.

If competitors view the new product as a threat, marketers attempting to use a penetration strategy often discover that rivals will simply match their prices. Crocs—those soft, rubbery clogs that come in bright colours—may be a fad, but their makers did everything they could to cash in while the weather was hot and the shoes are cool. Crocs got their name because they can wade through water and are tough enough for the garden or the boat. They slip on and off with ease, and fans claim they are the most comfortable shoes they've ever worn. Food service employees, factory workers, and hair stylists love Crocs because they cushion their feet. Some believers have eight or nine pairs and have no intention of stopping there. Crocs, which come in about 20 colours, sell for $30 to $60—a bargain compared with a pair of brand-name running shoes or Birkenstocks, either of which can easily top $100. But Crocs' competitors are never far behind. Similar shoes have appeared on the shelves of Canadian discount retailers and at outdoor markets for as little as $5. Crocs' maker is fighting back with new styles—flip-flops, slides, hiking shoes, even a calf-high boot and Mary Jane shoes.[5]

Retailers may use penetration pricing to lure shoppers to new stores. Strategies might take such forms as zero interest charges for credit purchases at a new furniture store, two-for-one offers for dinner at a new restaurant, or an extremely low price on a single product purchase for first-time customers to get them to come in and shop.

Penetration pricing works best for goods or services characterized by highly elastic demand. Large numbers of highly price-sensitive consumers pay close attention to this type of appeal. The strategy also suits situations in which large-scale operations and long production runs result in low production and marketing costs.

In certain industries, such as insurance, competitive pricing strategies are typical. Here GEICO offers to provide a free car insurance quotation to consumers.

Finally, penetration pricing may be appropriate in market situations in which introduction of a new product will likely attract strong competitors. Such a strategy may allow a new product to reach the mass market quickly and capture a large share prior to entry by competitors. Research shows that about 25 percent of companies use penetration pricing strategies on a regular basis.

Perhaps surprisingly, some auto manufacturers have been using penetration pricing for some new models to attract customers who might not otherwise consider purchasing a vehicle during a given year or who might be looking at a more expensive competitor. Mercedes-Benz Canada launched the second generation of the two-seat Smart car in Canada in December 2007, following its success in Europe. The car uses only 5.4 litres of gasoline per 100 kilometres in combined city and highway driving and its base price is below $15 000. Although skeptics warn that the car is just too small for the North American market, chairman Dieter Zetsche notes that the price of gas is driving its North American introduction. "We may never see cheap gas again," he predicts. He believes that the car is perfect for congested urban areas and that the low sticker price will be attractive to consumers.[6]

Everyday Low Pricing

Closely related to penetration pricing is **everyday low pricing (EDLP),** a strategy devoted to continuous low prices as opposed to relying on short-term, price-cutting tactics such as cents-off coupons, rebates, and special sales. EDLP can take two forms. In the first, retailers such as Wal-Mart and Canadian Tire compete by consistently offering consumers low prices on a broad range of items. Through its EDLP policy, Lowe's Canada offers not only to match any price the consumer sees elsewhere but also to take off an additional 10 percent. Wal-Mart states that it achieves EDLP by negotiating better prices from suppliers and by cutting its own costs. Its executives fly coach and empty their own wastebaskets. "Every penny we save is a penny in our customers' pockets," claims the company website.[7]

The second form of the EDLP pricing strategy involves its use by the manufacturer in dealing with channel members. Manufacturers may seek to set stable wholesale prices that undercut offers that competitors make to retailers, offers that typically rise and fall with the latest trade promotion deals. Many marketers reduce the list prices on a number of products while simultaneously reducing promotion allowances to retailers. While reductions in allowances mean that retailers may not fund such in-store promotions as shelf merchandising and end-aisle displays, the manufacturers hope that stable low prices will stimulate sales instead.

Some retailers oppose EDLP strategies. Grocery stores, for instance, operate on "high-low" strategies that set profitable regular prices to offset losses of frequent specials and promotions. Other retailers believe that EDLP will ultimately benefit both sellers and buyers. Supporters of EDLP in the grocery industry point out that it already succeeds at two of the biggest competitors, Wal-Mart and warehouse clubs such as Costco.

One popular pricing myth is that a low price is a sure sell. Low prices are an easy means of distinguishing the offerings of one marketer from other sellers, but such moves are easy to counter by competitors. Unless overall demand is price elastic, overall price cuts will mean less revenue for all firms in the industry. In addition, low prices may generate an image of questionable quality.

COMPETITIVE PRICING STRATEGY

Although many organizations rely heavily on price as a competitive weapon, even more implement **competitive pricing strategies.** These organizations try to reduce the emphasis on price competition by matching other firms' prices and concentrating their own marketing efforts on the product, distribution, and promotion elements of the marketing mix. As pointed out earlier, while price offers a dramatic means of achieving competitive advantage, it is also the easiest marketing variable for competitors to match. In fact, in industries with relatively homogeneous products, competitors must match each other's price reductions to maintain market share and remain competitive.

Retailers such as The Home Depot and Future Shop both use price-matching strategies, assuring consumers they will meet—and beat—competitors' prices. Grocery chains such as Loblaws, Safeway, Provigo, and Sobeys often compete with seasonal items: watermelon, soft drinks, and hot dogs in the summer; apples, hot chocolate, and turkeys in the winter. As soon as one store lowers the price of an item such as turkey, the rest follow suit.

Marketoid

Wal-Mart's rollback pricing strategy results in an average 10 percent price reduction below EDLP. Rollbacks last an average of 60 days.

competitive pricing strategy Pricing strategy designed to de-emphasize price as a competitive variable by pricing a good or service at the general level of comparable offerings.

When companies continually match each other's prices, prices can really drop, as has been evident periodically in the airline and computer industries. But competitive pricing can be tricky; a price reduction affects not only the first company but also the entire industry as other firms match the price reduction. Unless the lower prices can attract new customers and expand the overall market enough to offset the loss of per-unit revenue, the price cut will leave all competitors with less revenue. Research shows that nearly two-thirds of all firms set prices using competitive pricing as their primary pricing strategy.

What happens when one discounter undercuts another? Although many retailers fear competition from Wal-Mart, one type of store seems well positioned against the powerful chain: the so-called dollar stores. Dollarama and A Buck or Two are two such retailers that have been adding locations across Canada as these stores grow in popularity. Today's equivalent of the five-and-dime variety stores of the 20th century, dollar stores sell inexpensive items ranging from cleaning supplies, paper plates, toothpaste, greeting cards, and other household products—and compete on price and convenience, especially parking and easy access to the goods. Although these stores have yet to threaten Wal-Mart's position—their combined annual sales total just over $20 billion (U.S.) while Wal-Mart's total sales are nearly $320 billion annually—the retail giant is paying attention. As these dollar store chains expand, adding more brand-name products and attracting more price-conscious customers, Wal-Mart is likely to take some competitive action.

Once competitors are routinely matching each other on price, marketers must turn away from price as a marketing strategy, emphasizing other variables to develop areas of distinctive competence and attract customers. Airlines, which are famous for competition based on price, must constantly look for other ways to get people to fly with them.

Allstate Canada encourages prospective customers to get an online quotation.

assessment check 1

1.1 What are the three major pricing strategies?

1.2 What is EDLP?

PRICE QUOTATIONS

 Describe how prices are quoted.

The choice of the best method for quoting prices depends on many industry conditions, including competitive trends, cost structures, and traditional practices, along with the policies of individual firms. This section examines the reasoning and methodology behind price quotation practices.

Most price structures are built around **list prices**—the rates normally quoted to potential buyers. Marketers usually determine list prices by one or a combination of the methods discussed in Chapter 17. The sticker price on a new automobile is a good example: it shows the list price for the basic model and then adds the prices of options. The sticker price on a new Ford Focus lists the car at $19 999. But when options such as a 4-speed automatic transmission, power moonroof, ambient lighting package, audio system upgrade, and luxury package are added, the price can increase to $23 000 or more. This doesn't include any taxes, destination charges, dealer prep charges, or other costs that will be added to the price at the time of purchase.[8]

The price of oil is equally important to consumers—particularly those who drive cars—because it directly affects the list price of gasoline. Factors such as refinery shutdowns, hurricanes, and wars affect the price of oil, and ultimately the price that drivers pay at the pump. Prices may also fluctuate seasonally, as demand for gasoline rises and falls. Demand for gasoline is much higher in Canada during the summer when tourists visit and when Canadians travel longer distances for their vacations. Figure 18.2 illustrates where the money from a litre of gas goes on its journey from the oil field to your gas tank.

figure 18.2

2005 Canadian Average Pump Price

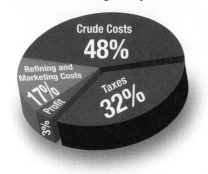

Crude Costs 48%

Refining and Marketing Costs 17%

Profit 3%

Taxes 32%

COURTESY PETRO-CANADA

source: http://petro-canada.ca/en/media/296.aspx

REDUCTIONS FROM LIST PRICE

The amount that a consumer pays for a product—its **market price**—may or may not equal the list price. Discounts and allowances sometimes reduce list prices. A list price often defines a starting point from which discounts set a lower market price. Marketers offer discounts in several classifications: cash, trade, and quantity discounts.

Cash Discounts

Consumers, industrial purchasers, or channel members sometimes receive reductions in price in exchange for prompt payment of bills; these price cuts are known as **cash discounts.** Discount terms usually specify exact time periods, such as 2/10, net 30. This notation means that the customer must pay within 30 days, but payment within 10 days entitles the customer to subtract 2 percent from the amount due. Consumers may receive a cash discount for immediate payment—say, paying with cash instead of a credit card at the gas pump or paying the full cash amount up-front for elective dental services such as braces for teeth. Cash discounts represent a traditional pricing practice in many industries. They fulfill legal requirements provided that all customers can take the same reductions on the same terms.

In recent years, sellers have increasingly attempted to improve their own liquidity positions, reduce their bad-debt losses, and cut collection expenses by moving to a form of *negative cash discount.* Confronted with purchasers who may defer paying their bills as long as possible, a new notice has begun to appear on customer statements:

Due on Receipt. A FINANCE CHARGE of 1.5% per month (18% A.P.R.) is computed on and added to the unpaid balance as of the statement date.

Past-due accounts may be turned over to collection agencies.

Trade Discounts

Payments to channel members for performing marketing functions are known as **trade discounts,** or functional discounts. Services performed by various channel members and the related costs were discussed in Chapters 12 and 13. A manufacturer's list price must incorporate the costs incurred by channel members in performing required marketing functions and expected profit margins for each member.

Trade discounts initially reflected the operating expenses of each category, but they have become more or less customary practices in some industries. In the United States, the Robinson-Patman Act allows trade discounts as long as all buyers in the same category, such as all wholesalers or all retailers, receive the same discount privileges. In Canada, the Competition Act does not recognize trade discounts. Wholesalers and retailers are considered competitors, and they therefore must be treated equally with respect to pricing and related promotional allowances.

Figure 18.3 shows how a chain of trade discounts works. In the first instance, the trade discount is "40 percent, 10 percent off list price" for wholesalers. In other words, the 40 percent discount on the $40 product is the trade discount the retailer receives to cover operating expenses and earn a profit. The wholesaler receives 10 percent of the $24 price to retailers to cover expenses and earn a profit. The manufacturer receives $21.60 from the wholesaler for each order.

In the second example, the manufacturer and retailer decide to bypass the wholesaler. The producer offers a trade discount of 45 percent to the retailer. In this instance, the retailer receives $18 for each product sold at its list price, and the manufacturer

figure 18.3

Chain of Trade Discounts

"40 PERCENT, 10 PERCENT OFF" TRADE DISCOUNT			
List Price	− Retail Trade Discount	− Wholesale Trade Discount	= Manufacturer Proceeds
$40	− $16 ($40 × 40%)	− $2.40 ($24 × 10%)	= $21.60 ($40 − $16 − $2.40)

"45 PERCENT" TRADE DISCOUNT		
List Price	− Retail Trade Discount	= Manufacturer Proceeds
$40	− $18 ($40 × 45%)	= $22 ($40 − $18)

receives the remaining $22. Either the retailer or the manufacturer must assume responsibility for the services previously performed by the wholesaler, or they can share these duties between them.

Quantity Discounts

Price reductions granted for large-volume purchases are known as **quantity discounts.** Sellers justify these discounts on the grounds that large orders reduce selling expenses and may shift some costs for storage, transportation, and financing to buyers. The law allows quantity discounts provided they are applied on the same basis to all customers.

Quantity discounts may specify either cumulative or noncumulative terms. **Cumulative quantity discounts** reduce prices in amounts determined by purchases over stated time periods. Annual purchases of at least $25 000 might entitle a buyer to a 3 percent rebate, and purchases exceeding $50 000 would increase the refund to 5 percent. These reductions are really patronage discounts because they tend to bind customers to a single supply source.

Noncumulative quantity discounts provide one-time reductions in the list price. For example, a firm might offer the following discount schedule for a product priced at $100 per unit:

1 unit	List: $100
2–5 units	List less 10 percent
6–10 units	List less 20 percent
Over 10 units	List less 25 percent

Many businesses have come to expect quantity discounts from suppliers. For example, Toronto manufacturer Action Loose Leaf Inc. offers vinyl binders through its online retail site, Binders By The Box. Customers pay list price when they buy one box, but receive a discount of 20 percent on two boxes, 30 percent on three boxes, 40 percent on four boxes, and 50 percent on five boxes. Without these quantity discounts, customers would either purchase smaller quantities or look for volume discounts from other suppliers.[9]

Allowances

Allowances resemble discounts by specifying deductions from list price. The major categories of allowances are trade-ins and promotional allowances. **Trade-ins** are often used in sales of durable goods such as automobiles. The new product's basic list price remains unchanged, but the seller accepts less money from the customer along with a used product—usually the same kind of product as the buyer purchases.

allowance Specified deduction from list price, including a trade-in or promotional allowance.

Promotional allowances reduce prices as part of attempts to integrate promotional strategies within distribution channels. Manufacturers often return part of the prices that buyers pay in the form of advertising and sales-support allowances for channel members. Automobile manufacturers frequently offer allowances to retail dealers to induce them to lower prices and stimulate sales. In an effort to alert consumers to the difference between a car's sticker price and the price the dealer actually pays to the manufacturer, *Consumer Reports* recently began selling car and truck buyers a breakdown on dealers' wholesale costs. The information reveals undisclosed dealer profits such as manufacturers' holdbacks—amounts as high as 3 percent of the full sticker price—that are refunded to dealers after sales are completed. The breakdown also reveals allowances for the dealers' advertising and other promotional costs. Once they are aware of the dealer's actual cost, car buyers are better able to negotiate a fair purchase price.[10] Dealers dislike the move to reveal their markups, arguing that no other retail sector is forced to give consumers details of their promotional allowances.

Minimum advertised pricing (MAP) occurs when a manufacturer pays a retailer not to advertise a product below a certain price. The music industry came under scrutiny for this policy, which in effect raised prices per CD by $1 to $2 across the board, eliminating most price competition. Under government regulatory pressure, major companies such as Bertelsmann, Sony, and EMI agreed to discontinue MAP allowances.[11]

AP PHOTO/REED SAXON, FILE

Staples has an online rebate centre where customers can find rebate forms, submit rebates online, and check the status of their rebates.

Rebates

In still another way to reduce the price paid by customers, marketers may offer a **rebate**—a refund of a portion of the purchase price. Rebates appear everywhere—on cosmetics packages, appliances, over-the-counter medications, and in automobile promotions—by manufacturers eager to get consumers to try their products or to move products during periods of slow sales. Mattress manufacturer Sealy has successfully used rebates to move consumers up to more expensive models in its product line, offering the biggest rebates for its top-priced mattresses.

Rebates can have their problems. Many consumers complain of the amount of paperwork they have to fill out to get a rebate, particularly on larger items such as computers and kitchen appliances. Others report never receiving the rebate at all. In response to this, Dell has announced that it will phase out rebates and other sales promotions but reduce its regular prices over time. "Customers don't like rebates," explains Ro Parra, senior vice president for Dell's Home and Small Business Group. "They want immediate savings at the time of purchase."[12] OfficeMax has made a similar announcement, citing the same reasons—that customers want savings at the cash register, not later on.[13] However, Staples is continuing with its Easy Rebate program—a promotion that allows consumers to submit their rebates online and track them.[14]

GEOGRAPHIC CONSIDERATIONS

In industries dominated by catalogue and online marketers, geographic considerations weigh heavily on the firm's ability to deliver orders in a cost-effective manner at the right time and place. In other instances, geographic factors affect the marketer's ability to receive additional inventory quickly in response to demand fluctuations. And although geographic considerations strongly influence prices when costs include shipping heavy, bulky, low-unit-value products, they can also affect lightweight, lower-cost products.

Buyers and sellers can handle transportation expenses in several ways: (1) the buyer pays all transportation charges, (2) the seller pays all transportation charges, or (3) the buyer and the seller share the charges. This decision has major effects on a firm's efforts to expand its geographic coverage to distant markets. How can marketers compete with local suppliers in distant markets who are able to avoid the considerable shipping costs that their firms must pay? Sellers can implement several alternatives for handling transportation costs in their pricing policies.

FOB Pricing

FOB (free on board) plant, or **FOB origin,** prices include no shipping charges. The buyer must pay all freight charges to transport the product from the manufacturer's loading dock. The seller pays only to load the merchandise aboard the carrier selected by the buyer. Legal title and responsibility pass to the buyer after the seller's employees load the purchase and get a receipt from the representative of the common carrier. Firms such as Wal-Mart often handle freight charges over the entire supply chain. Because Wal-Mart sources so many products from China, "FOB China" is now becoming common.

FOB (free on board) plant (FOB origin) Price quotation that does not include shipping charges.

Many marketing intermediaries sell only on FOB plant terms to downstream channel members. These distributors believe that their customers have more clout than they do in negotiating with carriers. They prefer to assign transportation costs to the channel members in the best positions to secure the most cost-effective shipping terms.

Sellers may also quote prices as **FOB origin, freight allowed,** or **freight absorbed.** These terms permit buyers to subtract transportation expenses from their bills. The amount such a seller receives for its product varies with the freight charged against the invoice. This alternative is popular among firms with high fixed costs because it helps them to expand their markets considerably by quoting the same prices regardless of shipping expenses.

FOB origin, freight allowed (freight absorbed) Price quotation system that allows the buyer to deduct shipping expenses from the cost of purchases.

Uniform-Delivered Pricing

When a firm quotes the same price, including transportation expenses, to all buyers, it adopts a **uniform-delivered price** policy. This method of handling transportation expenses is the exact opposite of FOB origin pricing. The uniform-delivered system resembles the pricing structure for mail service, so it is sometimes called **postage-stamp pricing.** The price quote includes a transportation charge averaged over all of the firm's customers, meaning that distant customers actually pay a smaller share of shipping costs while nearby customers pay what is known as *phantom freight* (the amount by which the average transportation charge exceeds the actual cost of shipping). Both amazon.ca and chapters.indigo.ca use uniform-delivered pricing for orders over $39.

uniform-delivered price Pricing system for handling transportation costs under which all buyers are quoted the same price, including transportation expenses. Sometimes known as *postage-stamp pricing.*

Zone Pricing

Zone pricing modifies a uniform-delivered pricing system by dividing the overall market into different zones and establishing a single price within each zone. This pricing structure incorporates average transportation costs for shipments within each zone as part of the delivered price of goods sold there; by narrowing distances, it greatly reduces but does not completely eliminate phantom freight. The primary advantage of zone pricing comes from easy administration methods that help a seller to compete in distant markets. Canada Post's parcel rates depend on zone pricing.

zone pricing Pricing system for handling transportation costs under which the market is divided into geographic regions and a different price is set in each region.

Zone pricing helps explain why gasoline can cost more in one suburb than it costs in a neighbourhood just four or five kilometres down the road. One way in which gasoline marketers boost profits is by mapping out areas based on formulas that factor in location, affluence, or simply what the local market will bear. Dealers are then charged different wholesale prices, which are reflected in the prices paid at the pump by customers. Some dealers argue that zone pricing should be prohibited. When drivers shop around for cheaper gas in other zones, stations in high-price zones are unable to compete. Ironically, it is the local dealer, not just the major oil company, which many consumers suspect of price gouging.

Basing-Point Pricing

In **basing-point pricing**, the price of a product includes the list price at the factory plus freight charges from the basing-point city nearest the buyer. The basing point specifies a location from which freight charges are calculated—not necessarily the point from which the goods are actually shipped. In either case, the actual shipping point does not affect the price quotation. For example, a seller might quote a customer a price of $1000 per ton for a shipment of steel from Montreal, but designate the basing point as Hamilton, Ontario. The customer pays for the steel plus a charge equal to the freight that would have resulted had the shipment been made from Hamilton. Such a system seeks to equalize competition between distant marketers since all competitors quote identical transportation rates. This type of pricing was once used for heavy commodity-type items such as steel, lumber, and cement, but few buyers would accept a basing-point system today.

assessment check 2

2.1 What are the three major types of discounts?

2.2 Identify the four alternatives for handling transportation costs in pricing policies.

③ Identify the various pricing policy decisions that marketers must make.

PRICING POLICIES

Pricing policies contribute important information to buyers as they assess the firm's total image. A coherent policy provides an overall framework and consistency that guide day-to-day pricing decisions. Formally, a **pricing policy** is a general guideline that reflects marketing objectives and influences specific pricing decisions.

Decisions concerning price structure generally tend to focus on technical, detailed questions, but decisions concerning pricing policies cover broader issues. Price-structure decisions take the firm's pricing policy as a given, from which they specify applicable discounts. Pricing policies have important strategic effects, particularly in guiding competitive efforts. They form the basis for more practical price-structure decisions.

Firms implement variations of four basic types of pricing policies: psychological pricing, price flexibility, product-line pricing, and promotional pricing. Specific policies deal effectively with various competitive situations; the final choice depends on the environment within which marketers must make their pricing decisions.

PSYCHOLOGICAL PRICING

psychological pricing Pricing policy based on the belief that certain prices or price ranges make a good or service more appealing than others to buyers.

Psychological pricing applies the belief that certain prices or price ranges make products more appealing than others to buyers. No research offers a consistent foundation for such thinking, however, and studies often report mixed findings. Nevertheless, marketers practise several forms of psychological pricing. Prestige pricing, discussed in Chapter 17, sets a relatively high price to convey an image of quality and exclusiveness. Two more psychological pricing techniques include odd pricing and unit pricing.

In **odd pricing,** marketers set prices at odd numbers just under round numbers. Many people assume that a price of $4.95 appeals more strongly to consumers than $5, supposedly because buyers interpret it as $4 plus change. Odd pricing originated as a way to force clerks to make change, thus serving as a cash-control device, and it remains a common feature of contemporary price quotations. One recent survey revealed that consumers believe that a price of $19.95 instead of $20 means that a retailer has worked hard to plan its prices and save the customer every penny possible.[15]

Some producers and retailers practise odd pricing but avoid prices ending in 5, 9, or 0. These marketers believe that customers view price tags of $5.95, $5.99, or $6.00 as regular retail prices, but they think of an amount like $5.97 as a discount price. Wal-Mart avoids using 9s at the end of its prices, and even uses numbers such as 3 or 7.

For some retailers that use a psychological pricing policy, prices regularly end with 9.

Unit pricing states prices in terms of some recognized unit of measurement (such as grams and litres) or a standard numerical count. Unit pricing began to be widely used during the late 1960s to make price comparisons more convenient following complaints by consumer advocates about the difficulty of comparing the true prices of products packaged in different sizes. These advocates thought that posting prices in terms of standard units would help shoppers make better informed purchases. However, unit pricing has not improved consumers' shopping habits as much as supporters originally envisioned. Instead, research shows that unit pricing most often affects purchases only by relatively well-educated consumers with high earnings.

PRICE FLEXIBILITY

Marketing executives must also set company policies that determine whether their firm will permit **price flexibility**—that is, the decision of whether to set one price that applies to every buyer or to permit variable prices for different customers. Generally, one-price policies suit mass-selling marketing programs, whereas variable pricing is more likely to be applied in marketing programs based on individual bargaining. In a large department store, customers do not expect to haggle over prices with retail salespeople. Instead, they expect to pay the amounts shown on the price tags. Generally, customers pay less only when the retailer replaces regular prices with sale prices or offers discounts on damaged merchandise. Variable pricing usually applies to larger purchases such as automobiles, real estate, and hotel room rates. While variable pricing adds some flexibility to selling situations, it may also lead to retaliatory pricing by competitors, and it may stir complaints among customers who find that they paid higher prices than necessary.

One service that is taking off is fractional jet ownership. Fractional jet ownership works something like a time-share—customers buy an ownership stake that includes a certain number of flying hours per year on a private jet. Canada's largest aircraft fractional ownership company, AirSprint, has 20 airplanes. For $500 000 (U.S.), clients can purchase an eighth share in a Pilatus PC12. The share, plus monthly management fees of $4515, and a per-hour flying fee of $905 for fuel and maintenance, buys the client 100 hours of flying time. Although fractional jet ownership isn't cheap, it is a bargain for business travellers and others who want the service of a private jet, but do not want to pay millions of dollars to own one outright.[16] The "Solving an Ethical Controversy" feature raises the issue of whether price flexibility may result in discriminatory pricing.

Nikon offers a range of products and prices to meet everyone's needs.

Marketoid

More consumers are haggling over price; 67 percent have haggled in a recent three-month period. Large retailers are giving sales associates more pricing flexibility for big-ticket items.

PRODUCT-LINE PRICING

Since most firms market multiple product lines, an effective pricing strategy must consider the relationships among all these items instead of viewing each in isolation. **Product-line pricing** is the practice of setting a limited number of prices for a selection of merchandise. For example, a clothier might offer three lines of men's suits—one priced at $395, a second at $650, and the most expensive at $1295. These price points help the retailer to define important product characteristics that differentiate the three product lines and assist the customer in deciding on whether to trade up or trade down.

Retailers practise extensive product-line pricing. In earlier days, five-and-dime variety stores exemplified this technique. It remains popular, however, because it offers advantages to both retailers and customers. Shoppers can choose desired price ranges and then concentrate on other product variables such as colours, styles, and materials. Retailers can purchase and offer specific lines in limited price categories instead of more general assortments with dozens of different prices.

Old Navy, also known for is moderate-priced casual clothing that can outfit an entire family, has recently introduced its most expensive line ever—ruffled leather jackets for $129, silk tops for $29.50, and sweater coats for $34.50. In addition, it is adding special touches to its basics—shell buttons on long-sleeved Henley shirts, and a metallic stamp in place of the old sewn-in label. The firm says it

Solving an Ethical Controversy

Price Discrimination or Variable Pricing?

Early consumer behaviour research indicated that race and family income had an effect on the price paid for consumer durables, but later research brought much of this into question so that it was generally concluded that retailers do not discriminate between buyers on the basis of ethnicity or income. The change in research findings may have resulted from an increased use of a one-price policy implemented by retailers for many consumer products. However, there are still some products for which negotiating price is a common practice, and the opportunity for price discrimination on the basis of personal factors exists. Perhaps the most likely product is cars.

Considerable research on the subject of pricing discrimination was conducted in the 1990s and, while there were some minor inconsistencies, the practice was found to exist consistently. Women paid higher prices than men; blacks paid higher prices than whites. The lowest prices were consistently given to white males. Recently, several car companies have been moving away from variable pricing to a one-price policy because they recognize that many customers do not like the negotiating process. In fact, one suggestion for the higher prices charged to women is that they are not as comfortable negotiating prices or asking for price reductions as males. A one-price system would help to even the playing field for all car purchasers and would go a long way to reducing price discrimination in the purchase of cars. However, since many car purchases involve a trade-in, there would still be the opportunity for salespeople to discriminate among customers with respect to the value they allow on vehicle trade-ins.

Should car dealerships have a one-price policy, or should car prices simply remain negotiable?

PRO

1. A one-price system will make the purchase process fair for all consumers.
2. A one-price system will be more efficient for car dealerships and will ensure that they get a sufficient margin on each sale so they will not have to resort to other means to make money from customers.

CON

1. In a free market, buyers and sellers should be able to negotiate a price with which they are both pleased.
2. While some customers do not enjoy negotiating prices, many other customers do.

Where do you stand: pro or con?

Sources: Gordon L. Wise, Myron K. Cox, and Charles Floto, "Sex and Race Discrimination in the New-Car Showroom: A Fact or Myth?" *The Journal of Consumer Affairs,* Winter 1977, pp. 107–13; ABI/INFORM Global, p. 107; Ian Ayres, "Fair Driving: Gender and Race Discrimination in Retail Car Negotiations," *Harvard Law Review,* February 1991, pp. 817–72; Ian Ayres, "Further Evidence of Discrimination in New Car Negotiations and Estimates of Its Cause," *Michigan Law Review,* October 1995, pp. 109–47.

is increasing quality as well as price in order to compete with more popular clothing firms such as Abercrombie & Fitch.[17]

PROMOTIONAL PRICING

promotional pricing
Pricing policy in which a lower than normal price is used as a temporary ingredient in a firm's marketing strategy.

In **promotional pricing,** a lower than normal price is used as a temporary ingredient in a firm's marketing strategy. To draw people back to its fitness centres following an employee strike, the city of Vancouver offered special admission prices of $2 for adults and $1 for youths, for a limited time.[18] Some promotional pricing arrangements form part of recurrent marketing initiatives, such as a shoe store's annual "buy one pair, get the second pair for one cent" sale. Another firm may introduce a promotional model or brand with a special price to begin competing in a new market.

Managing promotional pricing efforts requires marketing skill. Customers may get hooked on sales and other promotional pricing events. If they know their favourite department store has a one-day sale every month, they are likely to wait to make their purchases on that day. Car shoppers have been offered so many price incentives that it is becoming harder and harder for manufacturers and dealers to take them away. Employee-discount programs have complicated this situation, as auto manufacturers have begun to offer employee discounts to consumers. A Chrysler discount plan, called the Employee Pricing Plus program, essentially offered the same price to consumers as it did to Chrysler employees, during the summer months. Ford and General Motors offered similar plans in an effort to lure consumers their way.[19]

Loss Leaders and Leader Pricing

Retailers rely most heavily on promotional pricing. In one type of technique, stores offer **loss leaders**—goods priced below cost to attract customers who, the retailer hopes, will also buy other, regularly priced merchandise. Loss leaders can form part of an effective marketing program.

Retailers frequently use a variant of loss-leader pricing called **leader pricing.** To earn some return on promotional sales, they offer so-called leader merchandise at prices slightly above cost. Hilio Fashion, the Paris retailer, offered Zimmerli whisper-light boxer briefs at a price of about $60 to get men to visit its store. In Canada, when you can find them, these briefs sell for about $160, suggesting that Hilio used this item as a loss leader.[20] Among the most frequent practitioners of this combination pricing/promotion strategy are supermarkets and mass merchandisers such as Wal-Mart, Zellers, Sobeys, and Loblaws. Retailers sometimes treat private-label products (such as Our Compliments products at Sobeys stores) as leader merchandise since prices of the store brands average 5 to 60 percent less than those of comparable national brands. While store brand items generate lower per-unit revenues than national brands would produce, higher sales volume will probably offset some of the difference, as will related sales of high-margin products such as toiletries and cosmetics.

The personal computer industry provides an excellent example of this trend in pricing. Little more than a decade ago, PCs cost up to $5000. Today, you can get a good-quality notebook computer from makers such as Acer and Dell for around $500. Granted, these machines handle only the basics—e-mail, Web surfing, word processing, and a few other chores. Some experts predict that these prices could drop even lower. As long as these machines deliver reliable computing, they should continue to sell well. Marketers assert that these computers provide consumers with more choices. "Now consumers can buy the computer they want, not just the desktop they can afford," says one industry observer.[21]

Marketers should anticipate two potential pitfalls when making a promotional pricing decision:

1. Some buyers are not attracted by promotional pricing.

2. By maintaining an artificially low price for a period of time, marketers may lead customers to expect it as a customary feature of the product. That is the situation currently faced by North American car manufacturers; sales of their models lag when they do not offer price incentives.

PRICE–QUALITY RELATIONSHIPS

One of the most thoroughly researched aspects of pricing is its relationship to consumer perceptions of product quality. In the absence of other cues, price serves as an important indicator of a product's quality to prospective purchasers. Many buyers interpret high prices as signals of high-quality products. Prestige is also often associated with high prices. In an unusual pairing, designer firm Dolce & Gabbana teamed up with Motorola to offer a high-style design for Motorola's popular Razr cell phone. The gold Razr V31 model comes with special backgrounds, screensavers, MP3 ring tones, animations, and a gold D&G pendant. The two firms are also offering a line of D&G phone accessories, including a gold leather phone case and gold-wired headphones with a gold volume control. Those who want the prestige of owning the new phone will pay between $424.99 and $479.88 for the privilege, depending on the retailer.[22] Despite the appeal of prestige, nearly every consumer loves a good deal. Marketers work hard to convince consumers that they are offering high-quality products at the lowest possible price. Television shopping networks have struggled for many years to convince consumers that their low prices do not reflect the quality of their goods.

loss leader Product offered to consumers at less than cost to attract them to stores in the hope that they will buy other merchandise at regular prices.

Marketoid

Most subcompact cars are sold as loss leaders by dealers. Dealer margins are often $1000 or less, and the cost to sell the car can reach $1200 or more.

assessment check 3

3.1 Define pricing policy.

3.2 Describe the two types of psychological pricing other than prestige pricing.

3.3 What is promotional pricing?

WORK *in* Colour

Q2/06

ORIGINAL HP PRINT CARTRIDGES ARE
MORE RELIABLE.

QualityLogic, one of the world's foremost quality assurance organizations, tested the performance of HP Color LaserJet print cartridges vs. remanufactured brands. The results: HP print cartridges consistently outperformed remanufactured cartridges with 25 percent more client-ready documents.

Nearly one out of every six remanufactured cartridges was dead on arrival or failed prematurely, while dependable HP print cartridges worked every time!

Avoid costly reprints and wasted time – use only original HP colour print cartridges.

Original HP Supplies – Brilliantly Simple

Visit: www.hp.ca/scienceofprinting

COURTESY HEWLETT-PACKARD (CANADA) CO.

HP reminds customers that their replacement components are more reliable than cheaper alternatives.

Go Green

Paying the Price

David Suzuki, Canada's well-known science broadcaster and environmental activist, claims ownership of North America's first Prius, Toyota's initial hybrid car. Suzuki may have been happy contributing to a better environment but, as an early adopter, he undoubtedly paid an economic premium. Now the alternatives available to Canadians are many and, while prices for "green" cars remain high, they are certainly getting more affordable. There are also fuel savings for customers who drive them.

Developed markets continue to look for affordable fuel efficiency, but car manufacturers in China and India are beginning to produce simply affordable cars. China is now the world's third-largest auto producer, and India has entered the race. Both have cars that sell for about $5000 (Cdn). But Tata Motors of India introduced the Nano in 2008, priced at about $2600 (Cdn). It has no airbag, no heater, no radio, no passenger-side mirror, no automatic transmission, no ABS brakes, and only one windshield wiper. Tata claims that his company has not sacrificed safety or emissions standards to keep costs low, but critics argue that the sheer number of cars that will be sold will have a terrible impact on the environment. New Delhi, a city where pollution is already double the safe limit, now registers about 1000 new vehicles daily. The volume of cars, at least, helps maintain highway safety. During peak traffic times, average speed is only 11 kilometres an hour.

The Nano is unlikely to be a threat to the Canadian environment in the near future. Tata's initial market will be India. First export markets will include Southeast Asia, Africa, and South America. The cost to meet regulatory standards for North America would add $5000 to $8000 to the price, exclusive of dealer margins and other distribution costs. The real threat to the Canadian environment comes from Canadian consumers; many continue to choose larger, less fuel-efficient vehicles. Automobile engine power has increased by more than 50 percent in the past decade, negating any improvements due to improved fuel economy. Even the Government of Canada has been trading up. It spent more than $31 million in 2007 to purchase new sport-utility vehicles (SUVs) and leased an additional 85 units. Public Works and Government Services Canada purchased 844 new SUVs in 2007, up from 500 in 2006 and 366 in 2005. A government spokesperson defended the purchases as part of an overall fleet modernization strategy and stated that many uses require the larger vehicles where off-road driving is required, where safety or security are concerned, or where special equipment must be carried. While the price was higher, more than one-third of the purchases had gas-electric hybrid engines. New purchases are all "greener" choices except when law enforcement or security is involved.

Sources: Barbara Righton, "Priced to Move!" *Maclean's,* March 3, 2008, pp. 60–61; Ashling O'Connor, "Price of India-made 'People's Car' Same as DVD Player in a Lexus," *Ottawa Citizen,* January 11, 2008, p. E1; "Let's Adopt the Best Fuel-Economy Rules," *The Gazette* (Montreal), January 21, 2008, p. A18; Glen McGregor, "Government Nearly Doubles SUV Purchases: But One-third of $31M Fleet Upgrade Were Gas-Electric," *Ottawa Citizen,* December 27, 2007, p. A5.

---

④ Relate price to consumer perceptions of quality.

Marketoid

Grand pianos: approximately $6000 from China or Indonesia to more than $200 000 for a Bösendorfer or a Fazioli.

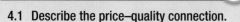

assessment check 4 ✓

4.1 Describe the price–quality connection.

4.2 What are price limits?

The relationship between price and perceived quality provides a widely used tool for contemporary marketers. An ad for the Porsche 911 Turbo, one of the most popular import sports cars in North America, claimed: "Calling it transportation is like calling sex reproduction." Another Porsche 911 ad was voted Advert of the Year 2004 by a panel of 100 marketing decision makers, who described the ad as "a stroke of genius, moving from product presentation towards the history surrounding the product." The ad showed a strong eagle, meant to symbolize the dynamism and precision of the new 911. For this dynamism and precision, Canadians pay more than $60 000. In March 2005, Porsche delivered 2981 vehicles to customers in Canada and the United States, the best sales in the company's history. Included in this figure were 1054 units of the 911, a year-on-year increase of 24 percent.[23]

Probably the best statement of the price–quality connection is the idea of price limits. Consumers define certain limits within which their product–quality perceptions vary directly with price. A potential buyer regards a price below the lower limit as too cheap, and a price above the higher limit seems too expensive. This perception holds true for both national brands and private-label products. Regardless of the price you've paid for a good or service, however, you want it to deliver what

Etiquette Tips for Marketing Professionals

Making Your Complaint—Effectively

WE'VE all been disappointed with a product at some point—either merchandise we bought or a service we tried. Maybe the coffeemaker fizzled out after one pot, or the new clothes iron just didn't get hot enough. Perhaps the hotel lost a reservation or a special restaurant dinner arrived cold. When this happens, we need to make a complaint so that the company knows about the problem and has a chance to correct it.

If you find yourself in this situation, how you handle it can make a difference in how it is resolved. Remember that the mission of a firm is to attract and keep your business—and its employees will likely do their best to help you, especially if you are polite, patient, and persistent. Here are a few tips for expressing your discontent effectively:

1. *Act immediately.* If a product breaks or arrives defective, make the call or visit the store right away. If you wait, you may exceed the return period or warranty. If your restaurant dinner isn't what you expected, speak quietly to the waiter or owner. You could have a new dinner in a matter of minutes.
2. *Focus on the problem, not the person in front of you or on the phone.* Explain the situation as clearly as possible so that the person can take the right corrective steps.

3. *State how you would like the problem to be solved.* Ask for a replacement, a refund, or a rain check. If the seller cannot fulfill your request, listen to the options before making a decision about what to accept. Sometimes it's good to know what your consumer rights are regarding expiration dates, return policies, and so forth in your province.
4. *Be assertive, but polite.* If an employee is unable to help you, ask to speak to a supervisor or someone else who has the authority to make a decision.
5. *Think before you speak.* No matter how frustrated you may become, don't resort to insults or anger. Never raise your voice or lose your cool—if you do, your cause may be lost.
6. *Have a positive attitude.* Generally, people respond better to this than to a sour outlook. If a person has really made an effort to help you, thank him or her. Let the company know an employee has done a good job.

Sources: Mary Mitchell, "Business Etiquette: Avoid These Mistakes," Live and Learn, http://www.uliveandlearn.com, accessed July 21, 2006; "Assertive Communication," University Counseling Service, University of Iowa, http://www.uiowa.edu, accessed July 21, 2006; Denise Anne Taylor, "Business Etiquette," About.com, March 17, 2006, http://www.about.com.

you expect. If it does not, you may need to seek a price adjustment or refund, as described in the "Etiquette Tips for Marketing Professionals" feature.

COMPETITIVE BIDDING AND NEGOTIATED PRICES

(5) Contrast competitive bidding and negotiated prices.

Many government and organizational procurement departments do not pay set prices for their purchases, particularly for large purchases. Instead, they determine the lowest prices available for items that meet specifications through **competitive bidding.** This process consists of inviting potential suppliers to quote prices on proposed purchases or contracts. Detailed specifications describe the good or service that the government agency or business organization wishes to acquire. One of the most important procurement tasks is to develop accurate descriptions of products that the organization seeks to buy. This process generally requires the assistance of the firm's technical personnel, such as engineers, designers, and chemists. In some instances, specifications may be tightly written to favour one or very few suppliers. Recently, the Agence metropolitaine de transport in Quebec awarded a $368-million contract to Bombardier to supply 160 new commuter-train cars. Bombardier was the only bidder, partly due to the tender's Quebec-content expectations.[24]

In some cases, business and government purchasers negotiate contracts with favoured suppliers instead of inviting competitive bids from all interested parties. The terms of such a contract emerge through offers and counteroffers between the buyer and the seller. The Montreal Transit Corp. originally

eBay Canada provides tutorials for customers who wish to buy or sell through its online auctions.

Marketoid

Approximately 6 million Canadians are registered on eBay.

purchased a fleet of 456 low-floor buses without competitive bidding. The buses, which have since proven to be "lemons," must be soon replaced, and MTC officials are in a situation where they may have to negotiate with the original supplier to buy these back as part of a contract for newer replacements.[25] Some provincial and local governments permit their agencies to skip the formal bid process and negotiate purchases under certain dollar limits—say $500 or $1000. This policy seeks to eliminate economic waste that would result from obtaining and processing bids for relatively minor purchases.

NEGOTIATING PRICES ONLINE

Many people see the Internet as one big auction site. Whether it's toys, art, or automobiles, there seems to be an online auction site to serve every person's needs—buyer and seller alike. Auctions are the purest form of negotiated pricing.

Ticket sales are an online auction favourite. Whether it is a Broadway show, a hockey playoff game, or Ozzy Osbourne's OzzFest concert, you can bid for tickets online. Tickets.com catalogues the dates, times, and locations of everything from concerts to museum exhibits. It recently partnered with the Advantix ticketing system to open a sales site for sports venues. In addition, Tickets.com functions as a reseller through its own online auctions. Ticketmaster.ca regularly holds auctions on its site, for everything from premium seats at sporting events to autographed memorabilia and "meet and greet" opportunities with concert performers.

Online auctions also take place at sites such as eBay—The World's Online Marketplace—where consumers can buy and sell items from collectibles, to books and electronic products, to cars. Millions of items are listed on eBay on an average day. Customers often find that it is possible to obtain things through eBay that they might otherwise be unable to obtain. For Christmas 2006, Canadian consumers bought 6470 Wii, most at double their retail price. For Christmas 2007, prices were as high as $750, nearly three times the retail price.[26] But recently, eBay reported that 40 percent of its transactions now take place at fixed prices through the "Buy It Now" option, signalling that perhaps consumers prefer to secure an item by paying a set price for it, or that they do not want to wait up to a week for an auction to close.[27] Transactions on eBay now total about $60 billion (U.S.). The company has recently changed its price strategy, designed to lower the fees it collects but to increase volume. For example, it used to cost $1.20 to list a $25 item and this has been reduced to $1.00. The 5.25 percent closing fee, however, has been increased to 8.75 percent. Sellers can also now include photographs of their products without paying an extra fee.[28]

assessment check 5

5.1   What is competitive bidding?

5.2   Describe the benefits of an auction—to the buyer and to the seller.

⑥ Explain the importance of transfer pricing.

THE TRANSFER PRICING DILEMMA

A pricing problem peculiar to large-scale enterprises is the determination of an internal **transfer price**—the price for moving goods between **profit centres,** which are any part of the organization to which revenue and controllable costs can be assigned, such as a department. As companies expand, they tend to decentralize management and set up profit centres as a control device in the newly decentralized operation.

In a large company, profit centres might secure many needed resources from sellers within their own organization. The pricing problem thus poses several questions: What rate should profit centre A (maintenance department) charge profit centre B (production department) for the cleaning compound used on B's floors? Should the price be the same as it would be if A did the work for an outside party? Should B receive a discount? The answers to these questions depend on the philosophy of the firm involved.

figure 18.4

Transfer Pricing to Escape Taxation

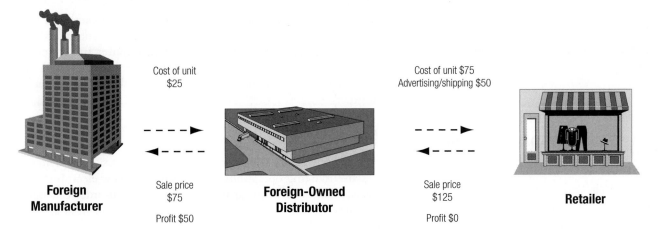

Cost of unit
$25

Cost of unit $75
Advertising/shipping $50

Sale price
$75

Sale price
$125

**Foreign
Manufacturer**

**Foreign-Owned
Distributor**

Retailer

Profit $50

Profit $0

Transfer pricing can be complicated, especially for multinational organizations. The government closely monitors transfer pricing practices because these exchanges offer easy ways for companies to avoid paying taxes on profits. Figure 18.4 shows how this type of pricing manipulation might work. Suppose a South Korean manufacturer of DVD players sells its machines to its Canadian subsidiary for distribution to dealers. Although each unit costs $25 to build, the manufacturer charges its subsidiary $75. In turn, the distributor sells the DVD players to retailers for $125 each. This arrangement gives the South Korean manufacturer a $50 profit on each machine, on which it pays taxes only in South Korea. Meanwhile, the Canadian subsidiary writes off $50 for advertising and shipping costs, leaving it with no profits—and no tax liability.

assessment check 6

6.1 Define transfer price.

6.2 What is a profit centre?

GLOBAL CONSIDERATIONS AND ONLINE PRICING

⑦ Compare the three alternative global pricing strategies.

Throughout this course, we have seen the impact of the Internet on every component of the marketing mix. This chapter has touched on the outer edges of the Internet's influence on pricing practices. Remember that every online marketer is inherently a global marketer who must understand the wide variety of internal and external conditions that affect global pricing strategies. Internal influences include the firm's goals and marketing strategies; the costs of developing, producing, and marketing its output; the nature of the products; and the firm's competitive strengths. External influences include general conditions in international markets, especially those in the firm's target markets; regulatory limitations; trade restrictions; competitors' actions; economic events; and the global status of the industry.

TRADITIONAL GLOBAL PRICING STRATEGIES

In general, a company can implement one of three export pricing strategies: a standard worldwide price, dual pricing, or market-differentiated pricing. Exporters often set standard worldwide prices, regardless of their target markets. This strategy can succeed if foreign marketing costs remain low enough that they do not affect overall costs or if their prices reflect average unit costs. A company that implements a standard pricing program must monitor the international marketplace carefully, however, to make sure that domestic competitors do not undercut its prices.

The dual pricing strategy distinguishes prices for domestic and export sales. Some exporters practise cost-plus pricing to establish dual prices that fully allocate their true domestic and foreign costs to product sales in those markets. These prices ensure that an exporter makes a profit on any product it sells, but final prices may exceed those of competitors. Other companies opt for flexible cost-plus

assessment check 7

7.1 What are the three traditional global pricing strategies?

7.2 Which is the most flexible global pricing strategy?

pricing schemes that allow marketers to grant discounts or change prices according to shifts in the competitive environment or fluctuations in the international exchange rate.

The third strategy, market-differentiated pricing, makes even more flexible arrangements to set prices according to local marketplace conditions. The dynamic global marketplace often requires frequent price changes by exporters who choose this approach. Effective market-differentiated pricing depends on access to quick, accurate market information.

⑧ Relate the concepts of cannibalization, bundle pricing, and bots to online pricing strategies.

CHARACTERISTICS OF ONLINE PRICING

To deal with the influences of the Internet on pricing policies and practices, marketers are applying old strategies in new ways and companies are updating operations to compete with new electronic technologies. Some firms offer online specials that do not appear in their stores or mail-order catalogues. These may take such forms as limited-time discounts, free shipping offers, or coupons that are good only online.

The Cannibalization Dilemma

cannibalization Loss of sales of an existing product due to competition from a new product in the same line.

By pricing the same products differently online, companies run the risk of **cannibalization.** The new twist to an old tactic is that companies are self-inflicting price cuts by creating competition among their own products. During the first decade of e-business, marketers debated whether it was worth taking the risk of alienating customers and channel members by offering lower prices for their products online—which then was an unproven retail outlet. But today, marketers are becoming more savvy about integrating marketing channels, including online sites and affiliated stores—different stores owned by the same company.[29]

Indigo Books and Music Inc. is Canada's largest retail book chain operating under several banners, including Chapters, World's Biggest Bookstore, SmithBooks, and Coles. It also sells books online at chapters.indigo.ca. Customers can visit many retail locations and find bestsellers at 30 percent off and other specials. However, many shoppers know that online selections are better and prices are frequently better. This practice actually gives Indigo Books and Music a chance to compete against Amazon.ca, reaching a wider range of customers.

Use of Shopbots

A second characteristic of online pricing is the use of search programs called **bots** or **shopbots**—derived from the word *robots*—that act as comparison shopping agents. Bots, such as shopbot.ca, search the Web for a specific product and print a list of sites that offer the best prices. In online selling, bots force marketers to keep prices low. However, marketing researchers report that almost four of every five online shoppers will check out several sites before buying, and price is not the only variable they consider when making a purchase decision. Service quality and support information are powerful motivators in the decision process. Also, while price is an important factor with products such as books and DVDs, it is not as important with complex or highly differentiated products, such as real estate or investment banking. Brand image and customer service may outweigh price in these purchase decisions.

BUNDLE PRICING

bundle pricing Offering two or more complementary products and selling them for a single price.

As marketers have watched e-commerce weaken their control over prices, they have modified their use of the price variable in the marketing mix. Whenever possible, they have moved to an approach called **bundle pricing,** where customers acquire a host of goods and services in addition to the tangible products they purchase.

Nowhere is bundle pricing more prevalent than in the telecommunications industry. Consumers are bombarded daily by advertisements for all kinds of Internet, cell phone, and cable or satellite TV packages. Telus and Bell Canada, former telecommunications monopolies, have been competing with discounted bundles of services in several markets, rather than by lowering their home phone rates. The stable pricing in the industry, combined with its own level of customer satisfaction for its VoIP-based telephone technology, has allowed Rogers Communications to actually raise its home phone rates by increasing its "system access fee" by 30 percent.[30] Rogers Communications also competes with bundled services packages of its own. Many marketers believe that bundling for telecom and cable providers is a necessity for retaining customers.[31]

But sometimes consumers resist the practice of bundling, claiming that they are being forced to pay for services they don't want in order to receive the ones they do. This is particularly the case with cable and satellite television packages. Service providers explain that they have spent billions of dollars to expand their networks and technology and would be left with unused capacity if they sold only a few channels at a time. But Charles F. Dolan, chairman of Cablevision Systems Corporation, disagrees, saying that he supports *à la carte* pricing, or giving consumers the option to choose and pay for only the channels they want. This practice, he argues, "will result in a more affordable service for all with more programming options. Consumers should not be obliged directly or indirectly to buy services they do not want."[32]

Customers who buy a bundle of services from Rogers save money.

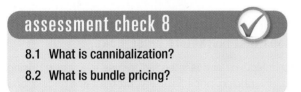

8.1 What is cannibalization?

8.2 What is bundle pricing?

Strategic Implications

PRICE has historically been the marketing variable least likely to be used as a source of competitive advantage. However, using price as part of a marketing program designed to meet a firm's overall organizational objectives can be a powerful strategy.

Technology has forever changed the marketplace, which affects the pricing function. Traditional geographic boundaries that allowed some businesses to operate have been broken by the Internet as well as mass merchandisers who offer a larger selection and lower

prices. A customer in Thunder Bay, Ontario, might want to purchase an individually carved and painted walking cane from Kenya or an ornamental fan from Kyoto. Not a problem—the Web connects buyers and sellers around the globe. Similarly, the cost of shipping an overnight Purolator envelope from Regina to Hamilton is no more than shipping it to a nearby city.

Not only is it possible to escape the boundaries of time and space on the Internet, but price is no longer a constant in the marketing process. With

the increasing number of auction sites and search technologies such as bots, customers now have more power to control the prices of goods and services. Consumers can find the lowest prices on the market, and they can also negotiate prices for many of the products they buy. To succeed, marketers must continue to offer value—fair prices for quality goods and services—and superior customer service. These are the critical success factors in marketing in the new millennium. ◆◆◆

REVIEW OF CHAPTER OBJECTIVES

① Compare the alternative pricing strategies and explain when each is most appropriate.

The alternative pricing strategies are skimming pricing strategy, penetration pricing strategy, and competitive pricing strategy. Skimming pricing is commonly used as a market-entry price for distinctive products with little or no initial competition. Penetration pricing is used when there is a wide array of competing brands. Everyday low pricing (EDLP), a variant of penetration pricing, is used by discounters that attempt to hold the line on prices without having to rely heavily on short-term coupons, rebates, and other price concessions. Competitive pricing is employed when marketers wish to concentrate their competitive efforts on marketing variables other than price.

② Describe how prices are quoted.

Methods for quoting prices depend on such factors as cost structures, traditional practices in the particular industry, and policies of individual firms. Price quotes can involve list prices, market prices, cash discounts, trade discounts, quantity discounts, and allowances such as trade-ins, promotional allowances, and rebates. Shipping costs often figure heavily into the pricing of goods. A number of alternatives for dealing with these costs exist: FOB plant pricing, in which the price includes no shipping charges; FOB origin, freight allowed, or freight absorbed, which allows the buyer to deduct transportation expenses from the bill; uniform-delivered price, in which the same price, including shipping expenses, is charged to all buyers; and zone pricing, in which a set price exists within each region.

③ Identify the various pricing policy decisions that marketers must make.

A pricing policy is a general guideline based on pricing objectives and is intended for use in specific pricing decisions. Pricing policies include psychological pricing, unit pricing, price flexibility, product-line pricing, and promotional pricing.

④ Relate price to consumer perceptions of quality.

The relationship between price and consumer perceptions of quality has been the subject of considerable research. In the absence of other cues, price is an important influence on how the consumer perceives the product's quality. A well-known and accepted concept is that of price limits—limits within which the perception of product quality varies directly with price. The concept of price limits suggests that extremely low prices may be considered too cheap, thus indicating inferior quality.

⑤ Contrast competitive bidding and negotiated prices.

Competitive bidding and negotiated prices are pricing techniques used primarily in the B2B sector and in government and organizational markets. Sometimes prices are negotiated through competitive bidding, in which several buyers quote prices on the same service or good. Buyer specifications describe the item that the government or B2B firm wishes to acquire. Negotiated contracts are another possibility in many procurement situations. The terms of the contract are set through negotiations between buyer and seller.

⑥ Explain the importance of transfer pricing.

A phenomenon in large corporations is transfer pricing, in which a company sets prices for transferring goods or services from one company profit centre to another. The term *profit centre* refers to any part of the organization to which revenue and controllable costs can be assigned. In large companies whose profit centres acquire resources from other parts of the firm, the prices charged by one profit centre to another will directly affect both the cost and profitability of the output of both profit centres.

⑦ Compare the three alternative global pricing strategies.

Companies can choose from three export pricing strategies: a standard worldwide price, dual pricing, or market-differentiated pricing. A standard worldwide price may be possible if foreign marketing costs are so low that they do not affect overall costs or if the price is based on an average unit cost. The dual pricing approach establishes separate domestic and export price strategies. Some exporters use cost-plus pricing methods to establish dual prices that fully allocate their true domestic and foreign costs to their product; others choose flexible cost-plus pricing. Market-differentiated pricing is the most flexible export pricing strategy, since it allows firms to price their products according to marketplace conditions. It requires easy access to quick, accurate market information.

⑧ **Relate the concepts of cannibalization, bundle pricing, and bots to online pricing strategies.**

To deal with the influences of the Internet on pricing policies and practices, marketers are applying old strategies in new ways, and companies are updating operations to compete with new electronic technologies. Cannibalization secures additional sales through lower prices that take sales away from the marketer's other products. Bots, also known as shopbots, act as comparison-shopping agents. Bundle pricing is offering two or more complementary products and selling them for a single price.

assessment check answers

1.1 What are the three major pricing strategies?
The three major pricing strategies are skimming, penetration, and competitive.

1.2 What is EDLP?
EDLP stands for everyday low pricing. It is a variation of penetration pricing often used by discounters.

2.1 What are the three major types of discounts?
The three major types of discounts are cash discounts, trade discounts, and quantity discounts.

2.2 Identify the four alternatives for handling transportation costs in pricing policies.
The four alternatives for handling transportation costs are FOB pricing, uniform-delivered pricing, zone pricing, and basing-point pricing.

3.1 Define *pricing policy*.
A pricing policy is a general guideline that reflects marketing objectives and influences specific pricing decisions.

3.2 Describe the two types of psychological pricing other than prestige pricing.
The two additional types of psychological pricing are odd pricing, in which marketers set prices at odd numbers just under round numbers, and unit pricing, which states prices in terms of a recognized unit of measurement.

3.3 What is promotional pricing?
Promotional pricing is a lower-than-normal price for a set period of time.

4.1 Describe the price–quality connection.
Price serves as an important indicator of a product's quality. However, many marketers now work hard to convince consumers that they are offering high-quality products at the lowest possible price.

4.2 What are price limits?
Price limits indicate certain boundaries within which consumers' product-quality perceptions vary directly with price. A price set lower than expected seems too cheap, and one set above the expected limit is seen as too expensive.

5.1 What is competitive bidding?
Competitive bidding consists of inviting potential suppliers to quote prices on proposed purchases or contracts.

5.2 Describe the benefits of an auction—to the buyer and to the seller.
An auction can provide buyers with opportunities to buy goods and services at very low prices. It can also offer the seller an opportunity to sell to a wider audience (online) perhaps at a higher price than otherwise would be possible, if the item is particularly popular.

6.1 Define transfer price.
A transfer price is the price for moving goods between profit centres.

6.2 What is a profit centre?
A profit centre is any part of the organization to which revenue and controllable costs can be assigned.

7.1 What are the three traditional global pricing strategies?
The three global pricing strategies are standard worldwide pricing, dual pricing, and market-differentiated pricing.

7.2 Which is the most flexible global pricing strategy?
The most flexible global pricing strategy is market-differentiated pricing, which allows firms to set prices according to actual conditions.

8.1 What is cannibalization?
Cannibalization involves cutting prices in one selling channel, which creates direct competition with a firm's own products.

8.2 What is bundle pricing?
Bundle pricing involves combining a number of goods or services together and offering them at a set price.

MARKETING TERMS YOU NEED TO KNOW

These terms are printed in red in the text. They are defined in the margins of the chapter and in the Glossary that begins on p. G-1. Other important terms are printed in bold black type in the chapter but not included in this list. Their definitions can be found in the Glossary.

skimming pricing strategy 610

penetration pricing strategy 613

competitive pricing strategy 614

allowance 617

FOB (free on board) plant (FOB origin) 618

FOB origin, freight allowed (freight absorbed) 619

uniform-delivered pricing 619

zone pricing 619

psychological pricing 620

promotional pricing 622

loss leader 623

cannibalization 628

bundle pricing 628

ASSURANCE OF LEARNING REVIEW

1. Under what circumstances is a skimming pricing strategy most likely to be used? What are its benefits? Drawbacks?
2. Why is competitive pricing risky for marketers?
3. What is the difference between a list price and a market price?
4. What are the benefits and drawbacks to rebates—for both buyers and sellers?
5. How is product-line pricing helpful to both retailers and their customers?
6. What is leader pricing? Why do retailers use it?
7. What is the difference between a competitive bid and a negotiated price?
8. In what ways is transfer pricing somewhat complicated?
9. Describe briefly the three traditional global pricing strategies. Give an example of a firm or product that would be likely to adopt one of the three approaches, and explain why.
10. Although cannibalization generally forces price cuts, in what ways can it actually benefit a firm?

PROJECTS AND TEAMWORK EXERCISES

1. Skimming pricing, penetration pricing, and competitive pricing are the three alternative pricing strategies. Divide your class into three teams. Then assign each team one of the three strategies and ask them to prepare a brief argument discussing the merits of their assigned pricing strategy for the following five products. Ask them to share their findings with the rest of the class. Once all three presentations have been completed, ask the class to vote on the most appropriate strategy for the products.
   a. video game
   b. cell phone with camera feature
   c. monitored burglar, smoke, and fire alarm
   d. special section of the supermarket that stocks locally grown produce
   e. new brand of skin- and hair-care products
2. On your own or with a classmate, figure out how much it will cost to buy and own one of the following cars (or select another model), new, from a dealership. What is the list price? What price do you plan to negotiate?
   a. Toyota Prius
   b. Saturn Vue
   c. Ford Mustang
   d. Volkswagen Beetle
3. Assume that a product sells for $100 per ton and that Hamilton is the basing-point city for calculating transportation charges. Shipping from Hamilton to a potential customer in Brandon, Manitoba, costs $10 per ton. The actual shipping costs of suppliers in three other cities are $8 per ton for Supplier A, $11 per ton for Supplier B, and $10 per ton for Supplier C. Using this information, answer the following questions:
   a. What delivered price would a salesperson for Supplier A quote to the Brandon customer?
   b. What delivered price would a salesperson for Supplier B quote to the Brandon customer?
   c. What delivered price would a salesperson for Supplier C quote to the Brandon customer?
   d. How much would each supplier net (after subtracting actual shipping costs) per ton on the sale?
4. On your own or with a classmate, browse through a local newspaper to find examples of promotional pricing. Tear out a few ads and evaluate them for their effectiveness. Does the promotional pricing make you want to purchase the products being advertised? Why or why not? Present your opinions to the class.

5. As an experiment in the relationship between price and quality, create a survey starting with the following products and adding four more of your own. Interview several consumers—members of your family, residents of your dorm or apartment, or other classmates and friends. Ask them the most they would pay for a quality item. Then ask them the

lowest price they would pay before their perception of the item's quality would drop. Share your findings with the class.
a. 8GB MP3 player
b. laptop computer
c. bag of potato chips (400 grams)
d. leather jacket

CRITICAL-THINKING EXERCISES

1. As a consumer, would you rather shop at a store that features a sale once a month or a store that practises everyday low pricing (EDLP)? Why?
2. Go online and search for some items that offer rebates. What types of products did you find? Do you think rebates are an effective enticement to purchase? Why or why not?
3. Visit your supermarket or flip through your local newspaper and note the prices for different types of products. Which firms seem to use psychological pricing? Do competing firms seem to use the same pricing policies?
4. Are you a bargain hunter, or do you routinely pay full price when you shop? Make a list of the items for which price is a major consideration in your purchase decision. Then make a second list of the products for which price is either secondary or hardly a consideration at all.
5. Frequent-purchase programs are discount offers designed by retailers and service providers to build loyalty among customers. Do these programs always work? What potential drawbacks might they contain?

ETHICS EXERCISE

Cell phone companies are well known for charging penalty fees to subscribers who want to terminate their service contracts early—a practice that has customers and consumer advocate groups grumbling. But in a break with the industry, Verizon Wireless has announced that it will now prorate its termination fee so that customers will only pay an amount that is proportionate to the time left in their contracts. Prior to this plan, Verizon Wireless subscribers would have to pay $175 to cancel their contracts. "The number of complaints on this issue is the single largest that our customers

have," notes CEO Denny Strigl. "It's a legitimate complaint: if they leave in one month or month 23, they pay the same charge."[33]

1. The high termination fee effectively keeps wireless consumers tied to their plans and unable to respond to offers by other firms. Do you think Verizon Wireless is making a good move from a pricing standpoint? From an ethical standpoint? Why or why not?
2. Do you think that other firms will follow Verizon Wireless's lead?

INTERNET EXERCISES

1. **Pricing strategies.** Shopbot.ca (http://www.shopbot.ca) is a so-called shopping bot. Enter a product and Shopbot.ca searches through online retailers and identifies those that sell that particular product along with the price. Visit Shopbot.ca and go shopping for the following products (specify a model). Do the prices of these products vary from online retailer to online retailer? Do some products cost the same regardless of where they are purchased? Prepare a brief report on your findings and what they tell you about the pricing strategies used by various companies.
a. a Nikon digital camera
b. a Bose home theatre system
c. an HP notebook computer

2. **Price markups.** Assume you're in the market for a new car or truck. Visit CarCostCanada (http://www.carcostcanada .com). Pick two or three makes and models that interest you. View a sample price report. Compare the M.S.R.P. price and the dealer invoice price. Are you surprised by the markup? What do you think is a fair markup? What are trading dollars? Summarize your findings and bring your report to class so you can participate in a discussion on pricing.

Note: Internet Web addresses change frequently. If you don't find the exact sites listed, you may need to access the organization's or company's home page and search from there or use a search engine such as Google.

Case 18.1

Air Canada: Everyone Takes a Shot

Trans-Canada Air Lines (TCA), the predecessor of Air Canada, made its inaugural flight in 1937: a 50-minute flight that carried two passengers and mail between Vancouver and Seattle aboard a Lockheed 10A. TCA grew to become Canada's national airline and was renamed Air Canada in 1964. Privatization followed in 1989 and, in 2000, Air Canada acquired Canadian Airlines International. Now, Air Canada's 32 000 employees make it the 14th-largest commercial airline in the world. Its position as Canada's largest airline continues to create problems for it. As a strong market share leader, it is carefully watched by the Canadian government, and the issue that continues to generate the most scrutiny is Air Canada's pricing strategy. Because of the airline's size, the government wants to ensure that its pricing is fair. But what is fair? The Ministry of Transport has sometimes accused Air Canada of charging monopoly prices on some routes and wants it to lower its fares. At the same time, Industry Canada's Competition Bureau has accused Air Canada of predatory pricing and wants it to raise prices on some routes so other airlines can compete.

It has always been difficult for new entrants to compete in the Canadian airline industry. Many have tried; many have failed: Canada 3000 (2001), Roots Air (2001), Jetsgo (2005), CanJet (2006 for scheduled flights), Harmony (2007), and Zoom (2008). Today, there are new contenders hoping to compete with Air Canada. Most notably, Calgary-based WestJet Airlines has been competing for most routes across Canada and has become Canada's second national carrier. In February 2008, WestJet set a record load factor of 82.8 percent—average number of seats filled on its planes—beating both Air Canada's mainline load factor of 79.5 percent and its Jazz load factor of 76.4 percent. It did this despite increasing its capacity by 18 percent. That same month, WestJet celebrated its 12th anniversary and took the initiative by starting a one-day price war that saw the carrier slash its one-way fares on its Toronto-Ottawa-Montreal route to $12. Air Canada countered by reducing its one-way fares to $39 on its Calgary-Edmonton-Vancouver route. WestJet plans to continue its growth strategy as it has begun to focus on U.S. sales through Expedia.com and as it begins to look for interlining deals with a number of international carriers such as British Airways and Cathay Pacific. Being aggressive and having favourable operating costs, WestJet may succeed where many have failed.

Toronto-based Porter Airlines made its inaugural flight in 2006 and initially competed in the heavy Toronto-Ottawa-Montreal corridor. In March 2008, it introduced air service from Toronto to Newark, New Jersey, at an introductory one-way fare of $120. Air Canada's price had been $194, but it immediately countered by lowing its fare to $95, which was then matched by Porter Airlines. After the brief seat sale, Air Canada raised its price to $120, but prices are expected to fluctuate frequently on the route. Air Canada does have the advantage that it offers direct flights from Montreal, Ottawa, and Toronto to Newark, New Jersey, and to New York's LaGuardia airport. Travellers originating from Montreal and Ottawa on Porter Airlines will need to stop over in Toronto as part of their flight. Porter Airlines has plans to expand service to a number of additional U.S. cities in the near future.

Calgary-based Corporate Jet Air is the latest entrant, but has chosen a clear niche strategy. It offers business-class service only with three flights daily between Calgary and Toronto. Customers must pay $16 000 in advance for a package of 10 one-way trips that must be taken within one year. While the price may seem high, it is competitive with Air Canada's executive-class fares, which range between $1510 and $1764. Also, the Corporate Jet Air price includes passenger pick-up and drop-off by limousine service, and check-in time is allowed up to 20 minutes before departure.

While it's debatable whether a third national airline can compete successfully in Canada, the possibility of more niche players cannot be discounted.

Questions for Critical Thinking

1. Explain monopoly pricing and predatory pricing. How is it possible for Air Canada to use both pricing policies at the same time?

2. The Profit Impact of Market Strategies (PIMS) project has found that market share and profitability are positively related. Yet Air Canada, with its high market share, has not been the most profitable airline in the Canadian airline industry. Explain why this may be so.

3. How do you think airline travellers define quality? Do you believe there is a price–quality relationship in Canadian airline travel?

Sources: Scott Deveau, "WestJet Hits Record for Filling Seats," *National Post,* March 6, 2008, p. FP6; Brent Jang, "Upstart Heightens Battle for Business Traveller," *Globe and Mail,* March 6, 2008, p. B3; Brent Jang, "WestJet and Air Canada Battle over Special Prices," *Globe and Mail,* February 29, 2008, p. B6; Scott Deveau, "WestJet Looks to Boost U.S. Ticket Sales; Airline Will Begin Selling Seats on Expedia.com," *Edmonton Journal,* February 14, 2008, p. F3; Brent Jang, "Air Canada, Porter Fight over N.Y. Travellers," *Globe and Mail,"* February 6, 2008, p. B3.

Case 18.2

Can You Squeeze Blood from a Fan?

More than two decades ago, American Airlines began experimenting with a computerized system that continually adjusted seat prices in an attempt to compete with People Express, a discount airline that offered lower prices to air travellers. The idea was to charge lower prices to discretionary and vacation travellers who would help fill seats, and charge higher prices to business and last-minute travellers who had few, if any, alternatives. This system, called yield management, results in variable pricing that is—in a way—the reverse of price skimming. First customers pay less; later customers pay more.

Variable pricing strategies have since spread to professional sports, where they are being increasingly embraced. The Toronto Raptors depend largely on single-game tickets and charge premium prices to see teams that draw larger crowds. The New York Yankees charge about $300 for box seats purchased in advance, but about $400 for ones purchased on game day. In 2007, the Toronto Blue Jays raised season tickets by 10 percent, but single-game tickets went up by less than 1 percent overall; however, some went up, some went down, and some stayed the same. Four early-season Tuesday games were designated "value" games; 35 other games were designated "premium" games. Seven games against the Boston Red Sox and nine games against the New York Yankees were among the premium games.

In hockey, nearly every Canadian team uses variable pricing. The Ottawa Senators, Montreal Canadiens, Calgary Flames, Edmonton Oilers, and Vancouver Canucks all use variable pricing, adjusting prices to reflect such factors as time of season, day of week, opponent, and seat location. Dave Cobb, chief operating officer for the Vancouver Canucks, defends the variable pricing strategy: "We think it's a more effective way of getting the same amount of money because it allows us to maintain all our discount ticket programs that are in place now and also freezes prices on a majority of our games." Only the Toronto Maple Leafs do not use a variable pricing strategy. Why? They don't have to. There are more than 17 000 season-ticket holders in Toronto, and just over 1000 seats available to single-admission ticket holders—at generally the highest prices in the league. Seldom are there any empty seats.

The Ottawa Senators team was an early adopter of variable pricing, experimenting as early as the 2002–03 season. By 2006–07, the Senators offered a discount of 40 percent on seven games, including three exhibition games. Children also received a 40 percent discount for three designated games. When ticket prices were decided, the price to see the Buffalo Sabres—lower-level club seat with taxes and service charges included—was only about $105, the regular price. However, tickets to see the Montreal Canadiens were set at a 10 percent premium, and fans would pay a 40 percent premium to see the Toronto Maple Leafs. However, the Senators have gone beyond variable pricing. In early 2008, the team advertised a special promotion to see the Senators play the Toronto Maple Leafs ($236.05), the Montreal Canadiens ($208.05), or the Pittsburgh Penguins ($188.05). Customers who read the "fine print" found that they had to buy two tickets that were bundled together. Fans who wanted to buy a ticket to one of these games had to also buy a ticket to see the Buffalo Sabres or Florida Panthers for an additional $142.05: total cost $378.10, not including parking, food, or drinks. Both of the less expensive games were also scheduled to be shown for free on television. A spokesperson for the team defended the promotion, which was meant to sell out more games, and to discourage scalpers who would buy tickets only for high-demand games. Fans were not happy.

Questions for Critical Thinking

1. Describe the pricing strategies used by the Toronto Raptors and the Toronto Maple Leafs. Why do the two teams use different pricing strategies?
2. Most professional sports teams today use a variable pricing strategy. What are the benefits and potential drawbacks of using this pricing strategy?
3. The Ottawa Senators have decided to bundle games, forcing some fans to purchase two tickets in a bundle. Do you believe this is a good pricing strategy for the team? Be prepared to defend your choice.

Sources: Hugh Adami, "'One-for-Two Deal' Insults Sens Fans," *Ottawa Citizen*, January 5, 2008, p. C1; Jeff Blair, "Tickets Selling Themselves," *Globe and Mail*, February 8, 2007, p. S3; "Yankee Stadium Tickets Go through the Roof," *Winnipeg Free Press*, December 2, 2006, p. D2; Hugh Adami, "Battle Lines Drawn Once Again: Fans Pay Hefty Price, Too," *Ottawa Citizen*, October 26, 2006, p. B1.Fro.

Video Case 18.3

Whirlpool: Innovation for Every Price Point

The written case on Whirlpool appears on page VC-20. The recently filmed Whirlpool video is designed to expand and highlight the concepts in this chapter and the concepts and questions covered in the written video case.

VICTORIA MCMANUS

COURTESY OF VICTORIA MCMANUS

One of the biggest surprises when I entered the field is how much of it is common sense . . .

Talking About Marketing with Victoria McManus

Here are highlights of our interview with Victoria McManus. For the complete video interview and transcript, go to http://www.contemporarymarketing2.nelson.com

Q1: Could you please tell us about your academic work/background? What was your first marketing job and how did you get it?

VM: I attended my local college, which was Durham College, located in Oshawa Ontario, enrolling in a 3yr Business Administration course majoring in Marketing.

While going to school I supported myself by working evening and weekends at Zellers. Through a job fair at the college I discovered that Zellers was recruiting for a Store Management Training Program. I applied for the position and was accepted. Zellers had an excellent training program that covered every aspect of its retailer business. Once through the training school I was transferred out to the real world as a Group Merchandiser.

One of the most exciting experiences with Zellers was being chosen to be one of the management team to open a brand new concept store. We built it from the ground up, literally. Installed every fixture, hired and trained every staff member, stocked every shelf with merchandise and signed every end. It was a true sense of accomplishment. Corporately all eyes we're on this store which was a great opportunity shine.

I left retail world and found my way into a Direct Marketing position landing a job with the largest lettershop in Canada called Postal Promotions Ltd. During my 7years with the company I was fortunate enough to work with our biggest client on launching the Air Miles campaign. It was probably one of the first campaigns to use Data and Data Mining to speak to each customer individually. Each customer statement had specific coupons and offers based on their previous purchasing habits. No two packages where alike and was a completely automated process driven by barcode and selective insertion technology.

Riviera Concepts was my next step in my career. This was a privately owned Canadian company that manufactured, marketed and distributed prestige fragrance. The privately owned company afforded me the opportunity to move into various positions from Marketing Coordinator working on packaging, art and assisting the Brand Manager to Direct Mail Manager, Key Account manager to my final position as Product Development Manager for which my responsibility was translating the designer's vision into an end product that was cohesive with their Brand image. Canadian product development positions are few and far between.

In 2006 Elizabeth Arden purchased the licenses for many of the fragrances that Riviera Concepts had owned and I was offered the opportunity to move with them. I held a position of Global Marketing Manager reporting to NY and continued to work on the Alfred Sung Brands. In 2007, I moved into the Trade Marketing Manager Position out of the Canadian Sales office and am responsible for all the Canadian Prestige fragrances that Elizabeth Arden carries.

My main responsibilities are to implement and develop strategies for each fragrance brand relative to each Canadian retailer. It's imperative to work closely with the internal Sales team to ensure all retail needs are met, attainable and realistic. This includes developing the forecast, marketing expense budgets, in-store events, preparing and presenting the seasonal promotional programs to retailers and sales staff. Liaise with Global Marketing, Advertising and Public Relations to plan and support the strategies. Provide an open line of communication with retailers including approving national advertising copy. I love the creative aspect of the position which plays out in the launching and advertising of new brands. The position is fiscally driven which results in a lot of number crunching --my least favorite part of the job.

Q2: What was the biggest challenge/surprise when you entered the field?
VM: One of the biggest surprises when I entered the field is how much of it is common sense. It all comes back to who, what, when, where, and why.

Q3: What is your biggest accomplishment?
VM: One of my biggest accomplishments was working on the implementation of a new computer system, JDE Edwards. It was an incredible amount of work and investment of time but well worth it. I was part of a team that reviewed the way we did business in the past and designed how the company needed to do business in the future. I had the opportunity to work with a team of IBM consultants and directors from all departments for which I represented marketing. It elevated my visibility in the company, provided me an understanding of corporate direction from top to bottom and how different aspects of the business affect other areas of the business.

Q4: Could you please give us a few key presentation tips?
VM: When presenting to a group you always have to remember that no one knows your subject better than you do! Don't follow a script word for word. Talk to your slides, talk to your audience. The best speakers/presenters are the ones that stand you in front of you and talk to you. You'll end up listening to them more closely than you would from someone reading to you.
Your presentation should be very visual with commentary to support the visuals.

Q5: What are the important skills that marketing students needs to succeed?
VM: *Attitude*. With a good attitude you can learn anything—and someone will want to teach you!
Listen. Listen closely in meetings. Listen to hallway/water cooler conversations. You'll be surprised what you learn about the business and the customers.
Ask questions. Don't understand something? Ask questions! It goes a long way to helping you stand out and show initiative in the eyes of management.

To Second City, Laughter's Priceless

For an entertainment company based on improvised decision making, Second City's chief financial officer, Lou Carbone, holds a unique responsibility. He operates from the Chicago office as a strategist, a liaison, a treasurer, and, in his own words, "the father figure who may have to say 'no, you can't play with that toy.'" When Second City Communications negotiates a deal with Microsoft or JPMorgan, it turns to Carbone for analysis and guidance. And when Second City Theatricals sees an exciting opportunity in children's theatre, its Lou Carbone measures the financial gain. Lou Carbone and Second City's top management want to make pricing decisions that welcome as many fans as possible. They also want to keep the company adequately funded.

The Second City's ticket prices are set competitively for the live entertainment industry. Intended to attract the general market, tickets are priced at, around, or just below, the traditional theatre rate. Kelly Leonard, Second City's vice president, explains SC's use of a flexible pricing strategy: "We've been sensitive to not underprice ourselves in the marketplace when demand is highest. Therefore, the weekend tickets are significantly more than the weekday prices." This manoeuvre capitalizes on tourist activity at each of SC's main city theatres. In Detroit, Toronto, Las Vegas, and Chicago, the ticket prices fluctuate from $12 to $24, depending on the night. For Second City Los Angeles, which opened with a smaller studio theatre, ticket prices penetrate the industry at a comparatively lower rate of $15 a seat. Conversely, Second City Denver's partnership with the Denver Center for the Performing Arts has set market-plus prices at $28 for a Friday night show. This introduces an evening at The Second City as a prestigious outing for the new Colorado market. SC theatres offer only general-admission seating, so audiences arrive early to get a good seat. This creates more excitement prior to the show and boosts bar sales.

Pricing strategy takes a more complicated, varied approach for Second City Communications. In such negotiations, Lou Carbone brings financial savvy to a company otherwise focused on creating an ideal acting environment. Tom Yorton, president of Second City Communications, collaborates regularly with Carbone. "Thank God for Lou," says Yorton. "The fact is that none of us really have a finance background. He can help educate us to make the place run better. We're an improv theatre, so we make it up as we go along. Finance is one area where you really can't make it up as you go along." SC Communications negotiates with its clients on the assumption that the quality of the product relates directly to the price. Because this division is offering Fortune 1000 clients a product that responds to their need for presentations at specific events or training, it negotiates at an appropriate price for each project and strives to secure long-term relationships. It also offers discounts to nonprofit and educational organizations,

For the Training Center, pricing is designed to make The Second City accessible to a wide variety of consumers. Focusing on volume, SC Training Center sets its price at a competitive, slightly below-market rate. The Training Center student has a variety of incentives. For instance, the SC Training Center produces shows for students in the writing, acting, and improvisation programs. The students enjoy trying their hand at the exciting art form without having to rent the theatre, while Second City acquires a certain percentage of ticket sales. Once a student is involved in the program, ticket prices for Second City's resident shows are discounted. Class prices can be reduced for those involved in internships, and a variety of summer camps and workshops are offered to attract students with limited funds.

Second City also sells a variety of products: DVDs, CDs and books, T-shirts and hats, and beverages from the bar served in the theatre. Each of these items has a different price and a different pricing strategy.

Over the last two years, Lou Carbone has been meeting one on one with department heads to train them in streamlined financial reporting. This practice has also provided The Second City a more consistent strategy for pricing ventures.

No matter which division of Second City is determining price, assessing the cost of production is fundamental. Many innovative ideas, according to Lou Carbone, are challenged by the practical assessment of production costs, travel expenses, labour fees, and unexpected market fluctuations. Forty to 50 percent of all revenue for the Second City goes toward covering labour costs. It employs approximately 325 people in the United States and 50 in Canada. Though it has a relatively small entertainment company, The Second City operates theatres in two countries, as well as a number of touring companies, and offers its product mix of business consultation and training internationally. Its main source of revenue remains, however, its resident stages. Kelly Leonard explains that while this may fluctuate, Second City continues to see its stages as its "financial base." Second City stages are the division of the company most capable of self-sustenance. As new project proposals are generated within the Second City team, its core product of live sketch comedy is often the creative and financial backdrop for the venture. Competitive ticket pricing at the Chicago stages generates consistent sellouts and has given the company a reliable financial resource to nurture each facet of its growing business. SC Toronto, for instance, has been challenged by a struggling economy in that region throughout the last decade. The Second City Chicago has been able to pull from reserves and credit lines to back the operation.

The Second City has evolved from humble financial beginnings to become an iconic fixture of the entertainment industry. It has made pricing decisions that have provided solid returns and have resulted in financial stability. This stability gives Second City the confidence to be innovative and take risks. Exciting project proposals are consistently handed to Lou Carbone and he "has to be the one to pull in the reins." But Carbone says that for a CFO, The Second City is the best place to work. "We're always laughing here," says Carbone, and you can't put a price on that.

Questions

1. Explain The Second City's use of flexible pricing for its resident stages. What are a couple of major factors in determining show ticket prices?
2. Why does Second City Communications use the most negotiating in its pricing?
3. What incentives exist for consumers of SC's Training Centre? How do you think these function in SC's long-term relationship with its students?
4. Which division of The Second City's product mix does the company consider its "financial base"? Why? How has its pricing strategy benefited the whole company?

Part VII CBC Video Case

CBC

Visit the website for Contemporary Marketing at **http://www.contemporarymarketing2e.nelson.com** to view the CBC video and video case summary for Part 7.

Financial Analysis in Marketing

A number of basic concepts from accounting and finance offer invaluable tools to marketers. Understanding the contributions made by these analytic tools can improve the quality of marketing decisions. In addition, marketers are frequently called on to explain and defend their decisions in financial terms. These accounting and financial tools can be used to supply quantitative data to justify decisions made by marketing managers. In this appendix, we describe the major accounting and finance concepts that have marketing implications and explain how they assist in making informed marketing decisions.

FINANCIAL STATEMENTS

All companies prepare a set of financial statements on a regular basis. Two of the most important financial statements are the income statement and balance sheet. The analogy of a motion picture is often used to describe an *income statement,* since it presents a financial record of a company's revenues, expenses, and profits over a period of time, such as a month, quarter, or year. By contrast, the *balance sheet* is a snapshot of what a company owns—called *assets*—and what it owes—called *liabilities*—at a point in time, such as at the end of the month, quarter, or year. The difference between assets and liabilities is referred to as *owner's, partners', or shareholders' equity*—the amount of funds the firm's owners have invested in its formation and continued operations. Of the two financial statements, the income statement contains more marketing-related information.

A sample income statement for Composite Technology is shown in Figure 1. Composite Technology is a B2B producer and marketer. The firm designs and manufactures a variety of composite components for manufacturers of consumer, industrial, and government products. Total sales revenues for 2010 amounted to $675 million. Total expenses, including taxes, for the year were $583.1 million. The year 2010 proved to be profitable for Composite Technology—the firm reported a profit, referred to as net income, of $91.9 million. While total revenue is a fairly straightforward number, several of the expenses shown on the income statement require additional explanation.

For any company that makes its own products (a manufacturer) or simply markets one or more items produced by others (an importer, retailer, or wholesaler), the largest single expense is usually a category called *cost of goods sold.* This reflects the cost, to the firm, of the goods that it markets to its customers. In the case of Composite Technology, the cost of goods sold represents the cost of components and raw materials as well as the cost of designing and manufacturing the composite panels the firm produces and markets to its business customers.

The income statement illustrates how cost of goods sold is calculated. The calculation begins with the value of the firm's inventory at the beginning of 2010. Inventory is the value of raw materials, partially completed products, and finished products held by the firm at the end of a specified time period, say, the end of the year. The cost of materials purchased by Composite Technology buyers during the year and the direct cost of manufacturing the finished products are then added to the beginning inventory figure. The result is cost of goods the firm has available for sale during the year. Once the firm's accountants subtract the value of inventory held by the firm at the end of 2010, they know the cost of goods sold. By simply subtracting cost of goods sold from total sales revenues generated during the year, they determine that Composite achieved gross profits of $270 million in 2010.

figure 1

2010 Income Statement for Composite Technology, Inc.

Composite Technology, Inc.
500 Ridley Road
Somewhere, MB

CT

INCOME STATEMENT
For the Year Ended December 31, 2010
(in $ millions)

Sales	675.0
Cost of Goods Sold	405.0
Gross Income	270.0
Selling, Administrative, and General Expenses	82.1
Research and Development Expenses	25.4
Operating Income	162.5
Depreciation	18.6
Net Interest Expense	2.5
Before Tax Income	141.4
Provision for Income Taxes	49.5
Net Income	91.9

Cost of Goods Sold Calculation	($ millions)
Beginning Inventory	158.0
plus: Raw Materials Purchased	200.7
plus: Direct Manufacturing Expenses	226.3
Total Cost of Goods	585.0
minus: Ending Inventory	(180.0)
Cost of Goods Sold	405.0

Operating expenses are another significant cost for most firms. This broad category includes such marketing outlays as sales compensation and expenses, advertising and other promotions, and other expenses incurred in implementing marketing plans. Accountants typically combine these financial outlays into a single category with the label *Selling, Administrative, and General Expenses.* Other expense items included in the operating expenses section of the income statement are administrative salaries, utilities, and insurance.

Another significant expense for Composite Technology is research and development (R&D). This includes the cost of developing new products and modifying existing ones. Firms such as pharmaceutical, biotechnology, and computer companies spend significant amounts of money each year on R&D. Subtracting selling, administrative, and general expenses and R&D expenses from the gross profit equals the firm's operating income. For 2010, Composite had operating income of $162.5 million.

Depreciation represents the systematic reduction over time in the value of certain company assets, such as production machinery, office furniture, or laptops provided for the firm's sales representatives. Depreciation is an unusual expense in that it does not involve an actual cash expenditure. However, it does reflect the reality that equipment owned by the company is physically wearing out over time from use and/or from technological obsolescence. Also, charging a portion of the total cost of these long-lived items to each of the years in which they are used results in a more accurate determination of the total costs involved in the firm's operation each year.

Net interest expense is the difference between what a firm paid in interest on various loans and what it collected in interest on any investments made during the time period involved. Subtracting depreciation and net interest expense from the firm's operating profit reveals the firm's *before tax income.* Composite had depreciation of $18.6 million and a net interest expense of $2.5 million for the year, so its 2010 taxable income was $141.4 million.

Profit-seeking firms pay taxes calculated as a percentage of their taxable income. Composite paid $49.5 million in taxes in 2010. Subtracting taxes from taxable income gives us the firm's *net income* of $91.9 million.

PERFORMANCE RATIOS

Managers often compute a variety of financial ratios to assess the performance of their firm. These ratios are calculated using data found on both the income statement and the balance sheet. Ratios are then compared with industry standards and with data from previous years. Several ratios are of particular interest to marketers.

A number of commonly used financial ratios focus on *profitability measures.* They are used to assess the firm's ability to generate revenues in excess of expenses and earn an adequate rate of return. Profitability measures include gross profit margin, net profit margin, and return on assets.

Gross Profit Margin

The gross profit margin equals the firm's gross profit divided by its sales revenues. In 2010, Composite had a gross profit margin of

$$\frac{\text{Gross Profit}}{\text{Sales}} = \frac{\$270 \text{ million}}{\$675 \text{ million}} = 40\%$$

The gross profit margin is the percentage of each sales dollar that can be used to pay other expenses and meet the firm's profit objectives. Ideally, businesses would like to see gross profit margins that are equal to or higher than those of other firms in their industry. A declining gross profit margin may indicate that the firm is under some competitive price pressures or that its prices have not been adjusted to account for increases in raw materials or other product costs.

Net Profit Margin

The net profit margin equals net income divided by sales. For 2010, Composite had a net profit margin of

$$\frac{\text{Net Income}}{\text{Sales}} = \frac{\$91.9 \text{ million}}{\$675 \text{ million}} = 13.6\%$$

The net profit margin is the percentage of each sales dollar that the firm earns in profit or retains after all expenses have been paid. Companies—and their shareholders—generally want to see rising, or at least stable, net profit margins.

Return on Assets (ROA)

A third profitability ratio, return on assets, measures the firm's efficiency in generating sales and profits from the total amount invested in the company. For 2010, Composite's ROA is calculated as follows:

$$\frac{\text{Net Income}}{\text{Average Assets}} = \frac{\text{Sales}}{\text{Average Assets}} \times \frac{\text{Net Income}}{\text{Sales}}$$

$$\frac{\$675 \text{ million}}{\$595 \text{ million}} \times \frac{91.9 \text{ million}}{\$675 \text{ million}} = 1.13 \times 13.6\% = 15.4\%$$

The ROA ratio actually consists of two components. The first component, called *asset turnover,* is the amount of sales generated for each dollar invested. The second component is *net profit margin.* Data for total assets are found on the firm's balance sheet.

Assume that Composite began 2010 with $560 million in assets and ended the year with $630 million in assets. Its average assets for the year would be $595 million. As was the case for the other profitability ratios, Composite's ROA should be compared with that of other firms in the industry and with its own previous performance to be meaningful.

Inventory Turnover

Inventory turnover is typically categorized as an *activity ratio* because it evaluates the effectiveness of the firm's resource use. Specifically, it measures the number of times a firm "turns" its inventory each year. The ratio can help answer the question of whether the firm has the appropriate level of inventory. Inventory turnover equals sales divided by average inventory. From the income statement, we see that Composite Technology began 2010 with $158 million in inventory and ended the year with $180 million in inventory. Therefore, the firm's average inventory was $169 million. The firm's inventory turnover ratio equals

$$\frac{\text{Sales}}{\text{Average Inventory}} = \frac{\$675 \text{ million}}{\$169 \text{ million}} = 3.99$$

For 2010, Composite Technology turned its inventory almost four times a year. While a faster inventory turn is usually a sign of greater efficiency, to be really meaningful the inventory turnover ratio must be compared with historical data and appropriate peer firm averages. Different organizations can have very different inventory turnover ratios depending on the types of products they sell. For instance, a supermarket such as Safeway might turn its inventory every two weeks for an annual rate of 26 times per year. By contrast, a large furniture retailer is likely to average only about two turns per year. Again, the determination of a "good" or "inadequate" inventory turnover rate depends on typical rates in the industry and the firm's performance in previous years.

Accounts Receivable Turnover

Another activity ratio that may be of interest to marketers is accounts receivable turnover. This ratio measures the number of times per year a company "turns" its receivables. Dividing accounts receivable turnover into 365 gives us the average age of the company's receivables.

Companies make sales on either a cash or credit basis. Credit sales allow the buyer to obtain a product now and pay for it at a specified later date. In essence, the seller is providing credit to the buyer. Credit sales are common in B2B transactions. It should be noted that sales to buyers using credit cards such as MasterCard and VISA are included as cash sales since the issuer of the credit card, rather than the seller, is providing credit to the buyer. Consequently, most B2C sales are cash sales.

Receivables are uncollected credit sales. Measuring accounts receivable turnover and the average age of receivables are important for firms where credit sales make up a high proportion of total sales. Accounts receivable turnover is defined as

$$\text{Accounts Receivable Turnover} = \frac{\text{Credit Sales}}{\text{Average Accounts Receivable}}$$

Assume that all of Composite Technology's sales are credit sales. Also assume that the firm began 2010 with $50 million in receivables and ended the year with $60 million in receivables (both numbers can be found on the balance sheet). Therefore, it had an average of $55 million in receivables. The firm's receivables turnover and average age equal

$$\frac{\$675 \text{ million}}{\$55 \text{ million}} = 12.3 \text{ times}$$

$$\frac{365}{12.3} = 29.7 \text{ days}$$

Composite turned its receivables slightly more than 12 times per year. The average age of its receivables was slightly less than 30 days. Since Composite expects its customers to pay outstanding invoices within 30 days, these numbers appear appropriate. As with other ratios, however, receivables turnover and average age of receivables should also be compared with peer firms and historical data.

MARKUPS AND MARKDOWNS

In previous chapters, we discussed the importance of pricing decisions for firms. This section expands on our earlier discussion by introducing two important pricing concepts: markups and markdowns. They can help to establish selling prices and evaluate various pricing strategies and are closely tied to a firm's income statement.

Markups

The amount that a marketer adds to a product's cost to set the final selling price is the markup. The amount of the markup typically results from two marketing decisions:

1. The services performed by the marketer. Other things being equal, retailers who offer more services charge larger markups to cover their costs.

2. The inventory turnover rate. Other things being equal, retailers with a higher turnover rate can cover their costs and earn a profit while charging a smaller markup.

A marketer's markup exerts an important influence on its image among present and potential customers. In addition, it affects the retailer's ability to attract shoppers. An excessive markup may drive away customers; an inadequate markup may fail to generate sufficient revenues needed by the retailer to cover costs and earn a profit.

Markups are typically stated as percentages of either the selling prices or the costs of the products. The formulas for calculating markups are as follows:

$$\text{Markup Percentage on Selling Price} = \frac{\text{Amount Added to Cost (Markup)}}{\text{Selling Price}}$$

$$\text{Markup Percentage on Cost} = \frac{\text{Amount Added to Cost (Markup)}}{\text{Cost}}$$

Consider a product with an invoice of 60 cents and a selling price of $1. The total markup (selling price less cost) is 40 cents. The two markup percentages are calculated as follows:

$$\text{Markup Percentage on Selling Price} = \frac{\$0.40}{\$1.00} = 40\%$$

$$\text{Markup Percentage on Cost} = \frac{\$0.40}{\$0.60} = 66.7\%$$

To determine the selling price knowing only the cost and markup percentage on selling price, a marketer applies the following formula:

$$\text{Price} = \frac{\text{Cost in Dollars}}{(100\% - \text{Markup Percentage on Selling Price})}$$

In the previous example, to determine the correct selling price of $1, the marketer would make the following calculation:

$$\text{Price} = \frac{\$0.60}{(100\% - 40\%)} = \$1.00$$

Similarly, you can convert the markup percentage for a specific item based on the selling price to one based on cost and the reverse using these formulas:

$$\text{Markup Percentage on Selling Price} = \frac{\text{Markup Percentage on Cost}}{(100\% + \text{Markup Percentage on Cost})}$$

$$\text{Markup Percentage on Cost} = \frac{\text{Markup Percentage on Selling Price}}{(100\% - \text{Markup Percentage on Selling Price})}$$

Again, data from the previous example give the following conversions:

$$\text{Markup Percentage on Selling Price} = \frac{66.7\%}{(100\% + 66.7\%)} = 40\%$$

$$\text{Markup Percentage on Cost} = \frac{40\%}{(100\% - 40\%)} = 66.7\%$$

Marketers determine markups based partly on their judgments of the amounts that consumers will pay for a given product. When buyers refuse to pay a product's stated price, however, or when improvements in other products or fashion changes reduce the appeal of the current merchandise, a producer or retailer must take a markdown.

Markdowns

A markdown is a price reduction a firm makes on an item. Reasons for markdowns include sales promotions featuring price reductions or a decision that the initial price was too high. Unlike markups, markdowns cannot be determined from the income statement since the price reduction takes place before the sale occurs. The markdown percentage equals dollar markdowns divided by sales. For example, a retailer may decide to reduce the price of an item by $10, from $50 to $40, and sells 1000 units. The markdown percentage equals

$$\frac{(1000 \times \$10)}{(1000 \times \$40)} = \frac{\$10\ 000}{\$40\ 000} = 25\%$$

ASSIGNMENTS

1. Assume that a product has an invoice price of $45 and a selling price of $60. Calculate the markup as a percentage of both the selling price and the cost.

2. A product has an invoice price of $92.50. The seller wants to include a markup on the selling price of 25 percent. Calculate the selling price.

3. Assume a retailer decides to reduce the price of an item by $5, from $15 to $10, and sells 5000 units. Calculate the markdown percentage.

4. Obtain a recent income statement and balance sheet for a business of your choosing whose stock is publicly traded. An easy way to find these is to visit the company's website and click on a link for "Investor Relations." Then look for the company's annual report. Use the relevant data included on the income statement to calculate each of the following ratios:

   a. gross profit margin

   b. net profit margin

   c. inventory turnover

   d. return on assets

   e. price markup

5. This appendix has described how the industry in which a firm operates affects its financial ratios. Solve this critical-thinking exercise by matching the following set of financial ratios to each of the following firms: 3M, Gap, Pfizer, and Wal-Mart. Consider the industry in which each company operates and the way it is likely to affect profits, return on assets, and inventory turnover rates. For example, which of the four would you expect to have the lowest profit margin and which should have the highest profit margin?

FINANCIAL RATIO	FIRM A	FIRM B	FIRM C	FIRM D
Net profit margin	28.4%	3.5%	13.9%	6.5%
Return on assets	20.6%	8.6%	14.6%	10.0%
Inventory turnover	2.1	7.6	3.4	4.9

Video Case Contents

Video Case 1.3

Harley-Davidson Keeps Riders Coming Back

Hog Heaven. That's where Harley-Davidson owners say they are during a ride. "Hogs," as Harley-Davidson motorcycles are affectionately known, represent freedom, adventure, and fun to their devoted owners. Riding one, with its distinctive engine roar and signature teardrop gas tank, is considered a unique experience that symbolizes the best of the American dream. Harley-Davidson bikes have proven to be a surprisingly durable pastime, too: once known as a symbol of rebellion, they now represent a fun indulgence to their owners.

Harley-Davidson, based in Milwaukee, has been manufacturing heavyweight motorcycles for more than a century and has watched them earn an enduring place in America's automotive history—as well as its popular culture. Elvis even rode one. Harley-Davidson knows its customers extremely well. Most are male; only about 11 percent are female. Nearly half have already owned a Harley, and just under a third have already owned a competitor's motorcycle. About 28 percent are first-time bike buyers. The largest group of Harley owners, and the company's target market, consists of 40-something males with a median income of more than $80 000, most of whom have owned a Harley before. The company is adept at using this kind of information about its customers to design its products and accessories and market them successfully.

The only major motorcycle manufacturer based in the United States, Harley-Davidson produces 36 different models and 8 different sport motorcycles. In one recent year its manufacturing plants produced a record number of bikes—350 000—helping fuel the company's steadily climbing annual revenues and earnings. Besides managing its production and distribution to be sure the bikes are ready when and where customers want to purchase them, Harley also makes it easier to own them. It offers its own financing and insurance programs for both dealers and customers.

Among the most successful of Harley's marketing efforts has been its ability to develop long-term relationships with its customers. One result? The number of repeat buyers mentioned earlier. The company uses a number of different relationship-building strategies. First, a full one-year membership in the Harley Owners Group (H.O.G.) comes with every purchase of a new, unregistered Harley-Davidson motorcycle. The company offers associate memberships for H.O.G. family members and passengers, and owner memberships are renewable at a discount. You can even become a member for life, and quite a few owners do. Membership earns owners entry into the members-only part of the company's H.O.G. website, several issues of its *Enthusiast* magazine each year, a subscription to the special member publication called *Hogtales*, a membership manual, toll-free customer service, and a touring handbook for trip planning. Harley-Davidson also organizes and sponsors special events for members, such as Pin

Stops for awarding commemorative pins, Pit Stops for relaxing and socializing with other members at bike races, touring rallies, factory tours and open houses, and parades and charity functions. There are H.O.G. chapters in the United States and 20 other countries, including Australia, Canada, France, Germany, Italy, Japan, the Netherlands, New Zealand, Sweden, South Africa, and the United Kingdom. Links to each chapter on the company's website help connect 1 million members around the world.

Full members in the owner's group can take advantage of the company's online travel service to schedule a Fly & Ride vacation to any of 41 different locations in the United States, Canada, Europe, or Australia, picking up a bike from a local Harley-Davidson dealership on arrival to tour in style or simply renting a bike at selected dealerships. Harley-Davidson has also partnered with the Motorcycle Safety Foundation to sponsor a safe-rider skills program for H.O.G. members, which awards a $50 coupon for those who successfully complete the training.

For H.O.G. members wondering what to spend that $50 on, they can buy items that include a black leather jacket or T-shirt emblazoned with the company's well-known logo, collectible patches, and customized accessories and gear for their bikes. The company has more than 1300 dealerships in 60 countries and satellite stores nearly everywhere. "For Harley-Davidson enthusiasts," says one of the company's repair managers, "the actual motorcycle is only part of the ownership experience; customizing the bike can become an obsession.... A large part of Harley mania is due to the company's ability to provide quality custom components and accessories." In fact, it's said that you will rarely see two bikes that look alike. Harley-Davidson is using every means to build customer satisfaction and fulfill its owners' dreams.

Questions for Critical Thinking

1. How does Harley-Davidson provide customers with form, time, place, and ownership utility for its motorcycles?
2. In what ways does Harley-Davidson practise relationship marketing? Explain.
3. How does Harley-Davidson use the Internet in its marketing?
4. Would you say that Harley-Davidson adopts a consumer orientation in its marketing efforts? Explain your answer.

Sources: Harley-Davidson website, http://www.harley-davidson.com, accessed July 6, 2006; Harley Owners Group website, http://www.hog.com, accessed July 6, 2006; Harley-Davidson Motor Company brochure, http://www.harley-davidson.com; "Hog Heaven: Celebrating 100 Years of the Harley David-son," The Library of Congress, http://www.loc.gov, accessed July 6, 2006; "Lista Storage Units Keep Harley-Davidson Running Fast," *MRO Today*, http://www.mrotoday.com, accessed July 6, 2006.

Video Case 2.3

Timbuk2's Success Is in the Bag

Timbuk2 began like many entrepreneurial businesses—it was started by someone whose need wasn't being met by the marketplace. A San Francisco bike messenger designed a rugged and stylish shoulder bag to carry during his workday. It was so popular with friends and acquaintances that he soon quit his job to start making the custom bags. The new company attracted devoted customers among young professionals both male and female—and fellow bike messengers—but within a few years it was nearly bankrupt.

Backed by private investors and a venture capital firm, Mark Dwight bought Timbuk2 a few years ago and swiftly turned the company around. It now produces more than 30 different products, and its San Francisco factory turns out a bag every 15 minutes. Business has been so good that Timbuk2 recently distributed a total of $1 million in bonuses to its 40 non-management workers to celebrate a banner year with sales of more than $10 million. Production has doubled; more than 1000 specialty retailers in the outdoor, bicycle, and personal computer markets carry Timbuk2 bags nationwide. The company's e-business arm has tripled in size. Most important, the firm now operates with a positive cash flow and is solidly profitable.

When he bought the ailing firm, Dwight knew he would have to bring in experienced managers and impose a carefully thought-out vision for the future. He put together a team of industry veterans and with their help mapped out a detailed five-year plan that included hiring a financial controller and a product developer. The biggest challenge was to streamline production and revamp the company's existing production methods. Instead of stockpiling inventory, the firm's executives decided that Timbuk2 employees would make every bag to order and keep none in stock. Doing so would reduce the costs associated with warehousing items. In addition, they looked at the product lineup to decide which merchandise customers could order as standard designs and which customers would choose to customize. The changes met with some staff resistance, but Dwight credits those changes with keeping the factory from going out of business. He still reviews key performance measures with the entire operational staff in San Francisco every day. "Timbuk2 has the fun-loving culture of a start-up and the operational discipline of a mature company," he says proudly.

Another change Dwight brought to Timbuk2 was the concept of "stretch goals," which are revenue and target profits exceeding those in the company's budget by an aggressive margin but those that management believes can be reached with minimal added investment. "Our stretch goal is designed to inspire *esprit de corps* and exceptional effort," he says. "Since the incremental revenue is achieved with minimal added expense, it turbo-charges our annual profit sharing—and everyone loves that."

Other changes Dwight and his team planned for were significant additions to the product line, which continues to appeal to both men and women. Innovation began with the design and manufacture of a computer bag. Today, one-third of the company's sales come from computer bags, and the Apple Store is its largest single customer.

To keep its costs low, the firm has moved about half its production work to factories in China, but it still employs more than 50 people in sewing jobs in its Mission District location. "Our San Francisco factory is a novelty in the current age of outsourcing and offshoring," says Dwight. "I am committed to keeping [it] open for as long as possible." Although social responsibility is a big part of Timbuk2's overall goals, there's another reason for keeping production close to customers: "Locally produced bags can be customized to customer requests [via Timbuk2's "Build Your Own Bag" website] on a very short lead time," Dwight notes. "That quick response is a unique advantage."

Other elements of Timbuk2's marketing mix are as carefully planned as the company's product line and distribution. For instance, Timbuk2 recently hired a Sausalito marketing firm to manage its branding and marketing activities.

The changes the company instituted have been a resounding success. Its revenues grew 158 percent in a two-year period. That doesn't mean every new idea has worked out well. One big mistake—a short-lived deal to distribute bags in CompUSA stores at lower-than-normal markups—cost the company $50 000 before it was over. But Timbuk2's progress has been on a steady upward track ever since.

Dwight isn't stopping, though. His goals for the future include making Timbuk2 a more environmentally safe operation, so the firm is removing all traces of the dioxin-producing polyvinyl chloride plastic from its bags. This alteration also means changing many of the components in its most popular products to other compatible materials. The company is also planning on making a bigger "footprint" in the retail landscape. It has opened its first retail store, and there's talk of producing lines of apparel and footwear. "I want the Timbuk2 swirl to be as recognizable as the Nike swoosh," says Dwight.

Questions for Critical Thinking

1. What were some of the organizational strengths and weaknesses Mark Dwight inherited with the original Timbuk2, and how did they shape his strategic plans for the firm?
2. Describe how Porter's Five Forces model might apply to the situation facing Timbuk2 today. Be as specific as possible.
3. What are the opportunities and threats facing Timbuk2? How well do you think the company is planning to meet these challenges?
4. What do you think is Timbuk2's product strategy? How effective is it? What suggestions would you make to increase its effectiveness?

Sources: Timbuk2 website, http://www.timbuk2.com, accessed July 26, 2006; Maya Melenchuk, "In the Sack," *San Francisco Bay Guardian,* http://www.sfbg.com, accessed July 26, 2006; "In the Bag: 2005 Fast 50 Winner," *Fast Company,* http://www.fastcompany.com, accessed July 26, 2006; Julie McFadden, "Timbuk2 Goes PVC-Free," OutdoorNewswire, http://www.outdoornewswire.com, July 3, 2006; "Timbuk2 Taps Sausalito Brand Company," *San Francisco Business Times,* February 28, 2006, http://www.bizjournals.com; "Timbuk2 Acquired by Private Equity Investors," Business Wire, October 26, 2005, http://www.findarticles.com; David Worrell, "Go for the Gold," *Entrepreneur,* July 2005, http://www.entrepreneur.com; "Timbuk2: Delivering an Urban Lifestyle," *San Francisco Business Times,* May 4, 2005, http://www.biztimes.com; Andrew Tilin, "Bagging the Right Customers," *Business 2.0,* May 1, 2005, http://money.cnn.com.

Video Case 3.3

Organic Valley Farms: Producing Food That's Good for People and the Earth

Organic Valley's roots are deeply embedded in the welfare of its communities and customers. Organic Valley is a North American organic farming cooperative of more than 750 family farms in 22 states. Its Wisconsin founders laid out its guiding principles: "We think it's a simple truth. The earth's most delicious, most healthful foods are made when farmers work *in harmony with nature.*" That's why Organic Valley's production standards surpass those required by the U.S. Department of Agriculture (USDA) for organic foods, which prohibit the use of antibiotics, synthetic hormones, irradiation, sewage sludge, and genetically modified organisms. Humane treatment of animals is another requirement. All Organic Valley livestock have access to the outdoors, rather than being penned in warehouse-like facilities. Its cows live five to ten times as long as those in conventional dairies, and they produce only 22 kilograms of milk per day rather than the usual 31.

The cooperative's certified organic foods have won awards and attracted customers since its founding in 1988 by seven farmers who wanted to combine the market demand for more healthful food products with their own desire to produce better products at better prices. Organic Valley's current members are all owners in the business, with a voice in its future and a commitment to its environmental stewardship. The group's central mission is to support family farms and help them achieve both economic success and environmental sustainability "into the next generation." One of the benefits that Organic Valley believes it offers customers with its organically produced dairy products, eggs, juice and soybean beverages, meat, and produce is the right to choose high-quality foods produced in healthful, responsible, and humane ways. It also stresses the value of letting consumers know how their food was produced, with what methods and what ingredients.

In fact, Organic Valley sees itself as a partner with its customers, as well as with the member-farmers and employees who play a role in shaping the cooperative's actions. For instance, as farmers continue to join the co-op, at the rate of about 25 to 50 per year, its managers must balance the supply of food it can produce both with consumer demand and with the need to hire people for additional operations. The co-op's governing body is a national board of directors elected every year, which hears members' opinions through regional executive committees to which any member can belong. Marketing is also done centrally by the cooperative's board. In addition to becoming equity owners in a national food brand, co-op members receive support in their production, in planning, in locating feed for their animals (the USDA requires 100 percent organic feed for organic livestock), and in caring for them through veterinary consultations. A quarterly newsletter keeps members informed about the cooperative's plans and reinforces its goals of independence and price stability with a fair return.

Organic Valley is now the largest source of organic milk in the United States, and it is a leader in the $15-billion organic food industry, which is growing more than 20 percent a year. Although organic farms make up only three-tenths of 1 percent of all farms in the United States, Organic Valley sells its products to more than 10 000 stores nationally and is growing faster than the industry as a whole, at a rate of about 25 percent per year. Its sales in a recent year topped $259 million, and it is investing in a new state-of-the-art and environmentally friendly $15-million distribution warehouse in Wisconsin. But George Siemon, its reluctant CEO who is still a farmer at heart and in practice, says, "We wouldn't mind if the growth slowed down. The most important thing to us is to keep our mission. Organic Valley's not looking to conquer the world. We do things our own way, because we care about things other than business success."

The co-op's profit sharing plan pays 45 percent of profits to its farmers, 45 percent to its employees, and 10 percent to the community. This sharing of the organization's success is a key difference between the way the cooperative functions and the way a traditional company distributes its earnings. In the cooperative, everyone is rewarded for success, not just the shareholders. But the cooperative is also eager to share benefits with its local communities—and even with distant ones. Siemon's son spearheaded an impromptu relief effort in the wake of Hurricane Katrina, organizing a group of students and teachers from the Wisconsin high school where he teaches to set up an emergency kitchen using a school bus filled with cooking equipment and co-op support. Other efforts include a national campaign to save family farms by encouraging them to adopt organic methods, an inspirational Web community (at http://www.moomom.com), educational partnerships with organizations that focus on clean water and children's health, and a website where visitors can send instant messages to their elected representatives on topics such as animal cloning and genetically engineered food. After all, as Organic Valley says, "in order to make a difference, companies need to think differently."

Questions for Critical Thinking

1. What types of competition does Organic Valley face? Give an example of each type.
2. How does Organic Valley define its members' rights? What consumer rights does it support? Are these two sets of rights compatible? Why or why not?

3. How does Organic Valley put its ethical standards into action in its product and pricing strategies? Do you think it is doing a good job of this? Why or why not?
4. How do the ethical standards at Organic Valley translate into acts of social responsibility?

Sources: Organic Valley website, http://organicvalley.coop, accessed July 31, 2006; "Organic Valley: The Truest Meaning of Organic," United Buying Clubs, http://www.unitedbuyingclubs.com, accessed July 31, 2006; Gregg Hoffman, "WisBusiness: Cashton Banking on Green Industries," WisBusiness.com, July 26, 2006, http://www.wisbusiness.com; Bryan Welch, "Doing Well by Doing Good," *Mother Earth News,* February 2006, http://www.motherearthnews.com; "Local Growers Try to Cultivate Interest in Organic Farming," *Orlando Business Journal,* January 27, 2006, http://orlando.bizjournals.com; Tom Hundt and Matt Johnson, "Youth Initiative, Organic Valley Help Feed Masses in Hurricane-Torn South," *Vernon County (WI) Broadcaster,* October 5, 2005, http://www.vernonbroadcaster.com.

Video Case 4.3

Nielsen Media Research Watches the TV Watchers

Choosing what to watch on TV was once a simple matter of flipping through a few channels. It's far from simple today. Cable and satellite television have brought us hundreds of channels, often with specialized content and advertising focusing on shopping, sports, music videos, classic movies, cooking, gardening, and many other options. First VCRs and then digital video recording (DVR) technology allowed audiences to "time shift" their viewing, watching shows not when they were broadcast but when viewers wanted or were able to. This freedom came with an added wrinkle—for the first time, consumers could watch commercial broadcasts without commercials, "zapping" through ads to view only the content.

Now podcasts and Webcasts offer portable and customized viewing, and cell phones can receive highly targeted TV programming, such as mini-episodes of popular shows filmed especially for wireless broadcast and never shown on TV at all. It might soon be possible to share your viewing experience in real time, through online communities that your computer will link to automatically when it senses you have tuned in to a specific show.

Viewers are adopting all the media options with enthusiasm, and advertisers want to know exactly what they think. For 70 years they have been paying Nielsen Media Research to find out.

Nielsen provides the only ratings of TV programs' viewership and market share of audience in the United States. These data are the basis for setting television advertising rates, which can exceed $60 billion a year. Advertisers want to spend that money wisely, and they are eager to get a handle on what viewers are watching—why, when, with whom, and how. Nielsen CEO Susan Whiting says of her clients, "Advertisers are asking for more qualitative information. They're asking how engaged the audience is in the programming. They're asking for more frequent measures of the audience and for commercials' ratings."

That's why new consumer behaviours such as time shifting and ad zapping are such a big concern for marketers. Some ads are time sensitive—marketers want them to be seen when the blockbuster film is about to open or when the dealer's lot is full of this year's SUVs. Says one ad buyer, "If you're not watching a show live, you're most likely not watching the commercials or you're watching them too late to matter." But others argue that as many as half of all DVR users do watch commercials and that ads bear fruit even if viewed after the broadcast date by, for instance, reinforcing brand image. Whichever view is correct—and perhaps they both are—consumer behaviour is a topic of intense interest to the advertising industry and to Nielsen Media Research.

So how do people watch TV today? Do they watch the shows that others are discussing at work because they want to feel "in the know"? Do they select personalized programming, such as Spanish-language soap operas or European soccer matches? Is TV a family event, with everyone gathered around the set to watch the new fall lineup and a sitcom together after dinner? Or is a parent TiVo-ing a movie broadcast in the family room while the kids download *SpongeBob SquarePants* episodes to their iPods for viewing on the school bus? Whatever the case, viewers are certainly more fragmented, more demanding, and more mobile than ever before.

Nielsen still collects most of its information about local broadcasts with paper-and-pencil surveys given to randomly selected households, who are asked to record their daily viewing habits as truthfully as possible. More accurate and more sophisticated electronic measures are becoming a bigger and bigger part of Nielsen's arsenal, however.

One way Nielsen is coping with changes in both consumer behaviour and technology is in its tracking of DVR viewing. Only about 8 percent of U.S. homes have a DVR today, but that number is expected to reach 40 percent by 2011. Nielsen hopes to keep ahead of the wave by publishing tracking reports three times a day instead of once. The first report measures how many people watched a show at its broadcast time; the second incorporates the number who recorded the show and watched it within 24 hours. The third report adds the number who played back the show within seven days of its original air date.

Nielsen is exploring ways to measure Internet viewing behaviour as well as viewing choices made on handheld devices such as cell phones and iPods. "The pace of change is incredible," says Whiting. Arbitron, which primarily researches radio audiences, says that fully 15 percent of TV viewing across all age and demographic segments already takes place outside the home.

Questions for Critical Thinking

1. What cultural and social influences do you think are helping change consumer behaviour among TV viewers today? Which ones have changed your behaviour, and how?

2. Do you think TV viewers go through a formal decision process in selecting programming? Why or why not? Which steps in the process do you think are the most important for marketers to know about? Why?

3. What aspects of consumer behaviour can Nielsen Media Research effectively measure? For instance, can the company currently measure attitudes and perceptions? If you answered no, how could the company achieve this goal?

4. Which behavioural influences on viewer behaviour—cultural, social, personal—are most relevant to Nielsen Media Research and its advertising industry clients? Are any influences irrelevant?

Sources: Jason Lee Miller, "Google's Next Rival: Nielsen Media Research," WebProNews.com, June 16, 2006, http://www.webpronews.com; David Lieberman, "Nielsen Media Has Cool Head at the Top," *USA Today,* March 27, 2006, http://www.usatoday.com; Coco Masters, "The Rating Game," *Time Inside Business,* March 2006, p. A18; Brooks Barnes, "New TV Ratings Will Produce Ad-Price Fight," *Wall Street Journal,* December 22, 2005, http://online.wsj.com; John Borland, "Nielsen's Mobile-TV Challenge," CNet News, December 12, 2005, http://news.com.com; Laura Rich, "She Watches Who's Watching What," *New York Times,* June 18, 2005, http://www.nytimes.com.

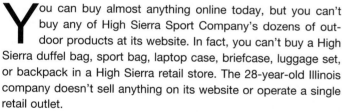

Video Case 5.3

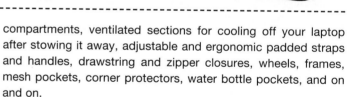

High Sierra Sport Company Excels in B2B

You can buy almost anything online today, but you can't buy any of High Sierra Sport Company's dozens of outdoor products at its website. In fact, you can't buy a High Sierra duffel bag, sport bag, laptop case, briefcase, luggage set, or backpack in a High Sierra retail store. The 28-year-old Illinois company doesn't sell anything on its website or operate a single retail outlet.

You might then be wondering how High Sierra—a privately owned company originally founded as the H. Bernbaum Import & Export Company in 1979—has grown to become the tenth-largest outdoor company in the United States, with a staff of only 40 people and no stores. The answer is that it has developed extraordinary expertise in business-to-business (B2B) sales. It markets its products around the world through more than 1500 retailers and 2250 corporate accounts, including the U.S. Olympic Ski and Snowboarding teams, which it also sponsors.

High Sierra's success is due in large part to its carefully designed product assortment and its smart segmentation of the B2B market. Its high-quality, high-fashion bags and luggage are tailored to outdoor enthusiasts, adventure lovers, athletes, travellers, students, and business professionals. The products offer an array of attractive features: padded interiors, multiple compartments, ventilated sections for cooling off your laptop after stowing it away, adjustable and ergonomic padded straps and handles, drawstring and zipper closures, wheels, frames, mesh pockets, corner protectors, water bottle pockets, and on and on.

With dozens of products to choose from, High Sierra's distributors might have trouble selecting what to offer their retail customers. But the company's product lines are organized into clear functional categories, such as wheeled book bags, business travel, day packs, duffels, wheeled duffels, luggage, lumbar packs, urban messenger bags, and sport and technical bags. The company also characterizes its products by activity—for example, running and cycling, school use, skiing and snowboarding, travel, and messenger—and by "collection," which focuses on the style characteristics of its wide selection. Brand names in this category include A.T. Gear Access, A.T. Gear Ballistic, AT3 Sierra-Lite, Cove Island, Cross-Sport, and RSX.

Trendy styling is important, even though High Sierra's customers aren't the ultimate consumers of its bags. And times have changed. Says the company's national sales manager, "People don't frown on you these days if you're dressed corporate casual and you're carrying a backpack. Ten years ago people would have raised an eyebrow at that." One of the company's newer models, the Sonic Pack, is an attaché with a removable holder for a CD player and a headphone port. The company expects it to be a best seller because of its versatility. "I think we're getting a lot more play on this type of bag because it hits such a broad target of people," says the sales manager.

Business bags are also big sellers to distributors of promotional products. High Sierra does a lot of business with financial services companies, for instance, and recently sold 18 000 units to a financial consulting company promoting a new product line. Insurance firms and food companies are also major customers, along with corporate training programs and trade shows. High Sierra recently won a Microsoft Business Solutions Pinnacle Award for excellence in customer service. Although consumers ultimately drive the company's product decisions—and online retailer eBags .com named it "best of the best" for consumer satisfaction—High Sierra is obviously also doing a very good job of keeping its business customers happy, too.

Questions for Critical Thinking

1. How does High Sierra segment its B2B market? Can you think of any other useful segmentation strategy it could use?

What is it, and what advantage would it offer the company?
2. What kind of market demand does High Sierra face (derived, volatile, joint, inelastic, inventory)? Give examples to support your answer.
3. What advantages and disadvantages would High Sierra have to consider if it wanted to start selling directly to consumers? Why do you think it doesn't do so?
4. Assume you are a buyer for a company looking for a promotional item to use in rewarding your top salespeople. In which stage(s) of the organizational buying process will High Sierra's wide variety of products be most important to you? Why?

Sources: U.S. Ski Team website, http://www.usskiteam.com, accessed August 18, 2006; High Sierra Sport website, http://www.highsierrasport.com, accessed July 6, 2006; "High Sierra Sport Company," Google Finance Company Profile, http://www.google.com/finance, accessed July 6, 2006; "About High Sierra," Luggage.com, http://www.luggage.com, accessed July 6, 2006; "High Sierra Sport Company," Gear Trends, http://www.geartrends.com, accessed July 6, 2006; "High Sierra Sport Company Wins Microsoft Pinnacle Award," Sikich Worldwide press release, April 14, 2006, http://www.icsadvantage.com.

Video Case 6.3

Lonely Planet Brings You the World

Australia-based guidebook publisher Lonely Planet knows all about expanding your horizons around the world—in business as well as in travel. Started in the 1970s by Tony and Maureen Wheeler after the intrepid pair backpacked, penniless, through Asia, the firm has grown enormously. From its first product—a stack of hand-collated sheets about that Asian trip stapled into a yellow cover—Lonely Planet has become the purveyor of 650 different guidebooks in a dozen languages that cover 150 regions and countries, from aboriginal Australia to Zion National Park.

"If people are going somewhere odd," says Tony Wheeler, "the first thing they think of is Lonely Planet." He personally researched the company's new travel guide to East Timor, which has almost no tourist traffic—yet.

Lonely Planet is the world's leading independent publisher of travel guides, with offices in Australia; Oakland, California; and London. It has a staff of approximately 400 and about 150 seasoned authors from more than 20 countries. Its annual gross revenues are about $72 million on sales of more than 6 million books, which are distributed around the world. The company's second title, *Southeast Asia on a Shoestring,* remains one of its most popular, with more than 500 000 copies sold.

Lonely Planet offers curious travellers a wide array of walking, snorkeling, and cycling guides; maps and atlases; phrasebooks,

food guides, and calendars; and a series of travel literature titles, all in addition to hundreds of $12.99 paperback guides with maps, highlights of things to see, language guidance, health and emergency information, and trusted recommendations for sightseeing, entertainment, shopping, dining, and, of course, accommodations. Competition in the market for guidebooks has surged over the years, with California-based Moon Travel Guides and English firm Rough Guides in particular grabbing distinct market shares among the daring and the budget-minded. But Lonely Planet has adapted as it has grown, and its original audience of committed—if frugal—backpackers has been successfully expanded to include families, businesspeople, and serious but savvy travellers of all kinds.

"Our Hawaii book used to be written for people who were picking their own guava and sneaking into the resort pool," says one Lonely Planet writer. "We were getting killed by the competition. So we relaunched it for a more typical two-week American mid-market vacation." The publisher of *Frommer's Travel Guides,* another competitor, sees Wheeler's operation as edging into the upscale market Frommer's targets, and indeed the whole Lonely Planet series was revamped with more focus on "highlights" and "itineraries" and almost none of the original discussions of local history and economics. The once-outspoken guides now take a middle road on questions of local politics as well. For instance, it now publishes a guide to Myanmar (formerly Burma), which has been the object of international sanctions for its repressive government, that tells readers travel itself is a form of communication that can topple barriers.

Yet the guides still don't carry advertising, although the company's website does. And the company donates 5 percent of its profits to charity. It has long held to Tony Wheeler's original advice to travellers—"Just go!" But now it's "go" with a difference. For the long term, the company is embracing an "information model" for its guides. "When Tony washed up on the deserted shores of Bali 30 years ago," says the company's digital-product manager, "it was great to 'just go.' If you just went to Bali now, you might not have a place to stay. We're thinking about every phase of the travel cycle—dream, plan, book, go, come back—and trying to fill each one with Lonely Planet content."

In fact, the company has come a long way from its beginnings, when "we had no idea how independent travel would become and what a huge part of the global economy tourism would become," says Wheeler. Lonely Planet now offers newsletters; a branded phone card; a website that features English, Italian, Spanish, French, and German versions and logs 3 million hits a day; an active online bulletin board called the Thorn Tree; news commentary; blogs; an online shop; and a professional digital travel-image library with more than 100 000 downloadable high-resolution images. Lonely Planet Television is its new television production arm; its "Six Degrees" travel series now airs in more than 30 countries and is available on DVD.

The Lonely Planet website—both English-language and some international versions—offers an array of partnered travel-service offerings including air travel, hotel reservations, travel insurance, rail passes, and expedition bookings. B2B partners include Virgin Atlantic, Eurosport, Sony, Nokia, and AOL. Browsers on the main website can see how Lonely Planet solved some of its corporate challenges such as generating brand awareness and building sales

online through "Lonely Planet Business Solutions," which also offers corporate gifts and incentive and promotional products. The company has also adopted a new automated publishing system to shorten the production cycle of its core product—books.

Looking ahead, however, Wheeler is mindful of the declining road that print encyclopedias have trod. The travel guide of the future, he believes, is "a mobile phone, my handheld computer, and global positioning system all moulded together. You call up Italian restaurants, and find one that looks nice, and then a little arrow points in that direction for 480 metres, and then it phones up for you and books a table." That's quite a distance from a stapled guide to Asia.

Questions for Critical Thinking

1. What elements of the international economic and social-cultural environment can affect Lonely Planet's business, and how?

2. How well do you think Lonely Planet is meeting the technological challenges of the international environment? What do you think it could do that it isn't yet?

3. How could the movement toward economic integration affect Lonely Planet?

4. What kind of international product and promotional strategies does Lonely Planet appear to use?

Sources: Lonely Planet website, http://www.lonelyplanet.com, accessed August 22, 2006; Lonely Planet Images website, http://www.lonelyplanetimages.com, accessed August 22, 2006; Lonely Planet B2B website, http://www.lonelyplanet.biz, accessed August 22, 2006; "Lonely Planet: 'Best of' Eastern Europe," Associated Press, August 21, 2006, http://news.yahoo.com; "Lonely Planet Adopts Typefi Publishing System," PR Web, August 4, 2006, http://www.prweb.com; Tad Friend, "The Parachute Artist," *The New Yorker,* April 18, 2005, http://www.newyorker.com; Chris Brummit, "Lonely Planet Boss Travels the World in Style," *Deseret Morning News,* January 2, 2005, http://deseretnews.com.

Video Case 7.3

Nielsen Media Research Plays the Rating Game

For 70 years, Nielsen Media Research has held a monopoly on collecting data about television viewing in the United States. Its eagerly awaited viewership counts and other statistics are the basis for the advertising rates broadcasters charge to marketers placing commercials on local and national stations every week. The research that Nielsen does has a huge impact in the industry; organizations spend about $60 billion a year on television advertising. In those 70 years, Nielsen has seen viewer habits change dramatically as VCRs, DVDs, iPods, digital video recording (DVR), video on demand, and even cell phones have expanded viewing options.

Though the marketing research firm still relies heavily on television meters and handwritten daily viewing diaries filled out by

thousands of randomly selected consumers each week, the explosion of media technology has forced the company to find new ways to keep up with rapidly changing viewer behaviour. A $2.5-million research effort is under way at Nielsen to find innovative methods to collect data about who watches what, when, and how. And with portable viewing via iPod and cell phone becoming easier all the time, even where we watch is a variable Nielsen wants to capture.

In response to criticism that it has undercounted minority viewers in the past—with corresponding effects on television advertisers' marketing decisions—Nielsen is focusing particular attention in the United States on African Americans and Hispanic Americans, as well as on viewers under 35 and DVR and video-on-demand users. The company plans to offer its clients data on conventional television viewing and also on less traditional methods—Internet use, media viewing in airports and other public places, college dorms, and cell phones and iPods.

The ultimate goal for Nielsen and its advertising clients, of course, is not only to know how many people watch, say, 24 via TiVo three days after the broadcast but also to know how many of them—given the option to skip the ads—watched them instead and how deeply they were "engaged" with the marketing messages. In fact, says one media buyer, "the problem with the way Nielsen has approached the problem is that their focus has been completely on the program. We want to know the truth about who's actually watching the ads we're putting out on television."

"Advertisers need even more information on how you're using television differently," agrees Nielsen's CEO, Susan Whiting. These research efforts will be expensive for the firm. "We are managing a business with increased requirements for quality, technology, [and] speed, and at a time when clients also have more pressure on their budgets," says Whiting. "It's a challenge to balance both things."

One innovation Nielsen is experimenting with is the portable people meter (PPM), a small wearable device now in the testing phase that can pick up audio signals from cell phone viewing. "But for iPods," says Whiting, "we can either measure what you download from your PC—and even how often you're using it at your PC—or put it in a little attachment that would go onto the headset. For cell phones, we would probably use a software application. We have them working in our labs now." In fact, says the company's chief technology officer, when it comes to broadcasting media, "we've never met a device we couldn't measure." Nielsen even anticipates someday having the ability to use the PPM to track actual purchases, by having consumers scan the products they buy.

What might be the result of all Nielsen's television research? Whiting says the future of advertising could hold a lot of experimentation and change: if viewing is measured 365 days a year, the need for programming around the traditional "sweeps" weeks will change. Commercials could be as short as five seconds, product placement in programming could continue to grow, and advertisers might return to one of the oldest sponsorship ideas in the business—supporting an entire show without any interruptions for traditional ads.

Another change could well be in store for Nielsen—competition. TiVo can already tell advertisers what customers are watching, and Google is looking into developing interactive wireless applications that will link your computer and your television, allowing the company not only to track what you're watching but also to send you real-time information, chat, and advertising based on your viewing choices.

Questions for Critical Thinking

1. Nielsen has sister companies that track Internet activity around the world, box office receipts, and the retail sales of audio and video entertainment products and books. Who are the likely clients of these companies, and how would they use its research?

2. Could Nielsen's random sampling return unbiased results? Why or why not? Why do you think the company is dedicating two of its many television indexes to the U.S. national and local Hispanic audience?

3. Much of Nielsen's research is still reported manually by the subjects of its surveys. Do you think this method provides reliable and unbiased results? Why or why not? Why do you think Nielsen has a policy of prohibiting volunteer participants in its television surveys?

4. What are some advantages and disadvantages of the newer methods of automated data collection that both Nielsen and Google are exploring? Are there any privacy questions at issue in these new methods? How would a marketing research company deal with them?

Sources: Jason Lee Miller, "Google's Next Rival: Nielsen Media Research," WebProNews.com, June 16, 2006, http://www.webpronews.com; David Lieberman, "Nielsen Media Has Cool Head at the Top," *USA Today,* March 27, 2006, http://www.usatoday.com; Coco Masters, "The Rating Game," *Time Inside Business,* March 2006, p. A18; Brooks Barnes, "New TV Ratings Will Produce Ad-Price Fight," *Wall Street Journal,* December 22, 2005, http://online.wsj.com; John Borland, "Nielsen's Mobile-TV Challenge," *CNet News,* December 12, 2005, http://news.com; Laura Rich, "She Watches Who's Watching What," *New York Times,* June 18, 2005, http://www.nytimes.com.

Video Case 8.3

Harley-Davidson Rules the Road by Understanding Its Customers

Harley-Davidson grew up along with the U.S. automotive industry. Based in Milwaukee, it is the only major U.S. motorcycle manufacturer. More than 100 years old, the company has a venerable history, making products that tap into America's enduring spirit of individualism, adventure, and fun. From its early days, when inventors strapped crude motors onto bicycles, the firm has evolved and now develops different motorcycles for different customers—producing 36 motorcycle models and 8 sport motorcycles.

Along with its products, Harley-Davidson has developed many sophisticated marketing strategies, most prominent of which is its Harley Owners Group (H.O.G.). Any purchaser of a new, unregistered Harley can join. Another marketing effort focuses on helping owners customize their motorcycles. One reason the company knows which marketing strategies to choose is that it has carefully researched and segmented its market so that it knows exactly who its customers are. For instance, the ratio of male to female Harley owners has been holding nearly steady for years at about 9 to 1, with a slight increase in the number of female owners over the last several years, and almost half of all Harley buyers are repeat purchasers. The target market for Harley-Davidson is males with a median age just over 45 and a median annual income around $80 000. Most of these buyers are previous Harley owners, too. And for those who prefer sport motorcycles, the company's Buell Motorcycle line offers a number of choices.

Harley-Davidson promotes—and actively supports—a feeling of "one big happy family" among owners, particularly with its owners' group. But there are many different kinds of "family" members, and the company can pinpoint them accurately. So although its website features many pictures of men on their bikes, women are shown too. And there's a special owners' membership group called Ladies of Harley (LOH) that women can join. Non-Harley owners who are Harley enthusiasts can buy associate memberships in H.O.G., and devotees can even sign on for lifetime memberships. The company offers H.O.G. members so many different membership benefits and activities to participate in all over the country and the world that it ends up offering something for nearly everyone. If you like long-distance solo rides, you can just head out for the open road with nothing more than a map, free from Harley, to guide you on your way. Or if you're the sociable type, you can join in parades, group rides, parties, rallies, charitable events, and other group activities orchestrated by local H.O.G. chapters in more than 20 countries. There are nearly 1 million H.O.G. members worldwide, and it's easy for them to contact each other on Harley's members-only website (another benefit of membership). If you're not just a social rider but also enjoy volunteering, your local H.O.G. chapter offers plenty of opportunities for leadership and service in your community. As the H.O.G. website says, "Whether you want to simply come along for the ride, take it year by year, or devote the rest of your life to becoming the best H.O.G. member you can be, there's a membership to match your passion."

With so many H.O.G. chapters, each sponsored by a local dealership, Harley-Davidson can maintain accurate demographic information about a large proportion of its members, even though not all Harley owners join H.O.G. Many do, and by encouraging members to make full use of all their benefits, including almost unlimited opportunities to get together for social, educational, and fundraising events and live the Harley lifestyle, the company ensures that owners around the world know that they mean more to the company than just a sale. For customers who want more than a motorcycle off the dealer's lot, there are many options to customize their bikes. The company's broad line of parts and accessories allows riders thousands of options for making their motorcycles truly their own, expressing their individuality and increasing their satisfaction in the Harley experience. In fact, because customization is such a big part of Harley-Davidson's brand, the company recently upgraded its customizing manufacturing operations in the Milwaukee headquarters. For consumers who want to have the Harley look themselves, the company also offers a full line of MotorClothes apparel, including the iconic black leather jacket emblazoned with the company's familiar logo and dozens of other pieces of riding gear. However you want to shape your riding experience, Harley-Davidson is there to help.

Questions for Critical Thinking

1. Does Harley-Davidson's target market meet the criteria for effective segmentation? Explain your answer.
2. Which targeting strategies do you think Harley-Davidson is currently using? Which do you think it should be using? Explain.
3. How well do you think Harley-Davidson applies psychographics to its marketing activities? Give examples.
4. Are there any demographic groups that could be Harley-Davidson customers but are not? If so, how can segmentation help the company's marketers reach them?

Sources: Harley-Davidson website, http://www.harley-davidson.com, accessed July 6, 2006; Harley Owners Group website, http://www.hog.com, accessed July 6, 2006; Harley-Davidson Motor Company brochure, http://www.harley-davidson.com; "Hog Heaven: Celebrating 100 Years of the Harley Davidson," Library of Congress, http://www.loc.gov, accessed July 6, 2006; "Lista Storage Units Keep Harley-Davidson Running Fast," *MRO Today*, http://www.mrotoday.com, accessed July 6, 2006.

Video Case 9.3

The Little Guys Home Electronics: Big on Customer Relationships

When it comes to close relationships, most people probably would not think about their local home electronics store. But if you're a customer of The Little Guys, you just might.

The Little Guys, a family-owned home electronics retailer founded in the 1990s in a Chicago suburb, now earns more than $10 million a year from sales of electronics of all kinds, including amplifiers, CD players, DVD players and recorders, iPod accessories, speakers, and especially plasma and flat-screen TVs and entertainment systems. The brands carried range from Apple to Zenith and include innovators such as Sharp, Sony, Bose, Onkyo, Hitachi, Mitsubishi, and Epson.

But what makes The Little Guys different from its competitors is its deep-seated commitment to customer service. The Little Guys is so eager to make customers feel at home that it even lists the names of its salespeople on the company's website, with photos and brief biographies.

They aren't just ordinary salespeople, either. They are enthusiastic experts in home electronics who are continually trained by the manufacturers whose products they sell. As a result, they can help customers assess their needs, select the right product, answer the most basic or the most technical questions about it, and even help install it and show customers how to get the most from their purchases. In fact, The Little Guys will work with customers who are installing home entertainment centres well before they are ready to buy a plasma TV or other components. For custom jobs, they will even work with the customer's architect and contractor to design and plan everything needed to support the entertainment centre, from wiring during the construction phase to final installation.

The company is proud of its ability to become a partner in the home electronics purchase and installation process. "We've worked with interior designers, architects, and builders," explains the Little Guys website. "We'll meet you at your home or office. If you need custom cabinetry, we work with furniture designers who can create it for you. We can design any audio/video system in any room, including the bathroom." Four full-time installation crews take measurements, connect components, and hook up cable and satellite connections to make sure customers are able to just click the "on" button to begin enjoying their purchase. To keep up to date with technology trends, the company maintains membership in trade associations such as the Custom Electronic Design & Installation Association, Home Theater Specialists of America, and PARA, a nonprofit group that supports personalized, relationship-based shopping coupled with expert technical support.

But what if you're not sure what a home theatre would look like in *your* home? The Little Guys can show you. In its "house within a store," a kitchen, bedroom, and bathroom are all on display to show customers how the latest home electronics equipment can function in just about every room of the house. The display even includes a set of fully equipped home theatre rooms to provide ideas and give customers the opportunity to see state-of-the-art equipment in action in a realistic setting. Browsing is okay, too—the sales staff do not pressure anyone to buy until they are ready.

And if you can't come to the store but live within 160 kilometres, you can fax The Little Guys a sketch of your room and your requirements, or you can fill out a quick questionnaire about your project on the firm's website. Even if you're not sure how much you want to spend, you'll still get a speedy and informative answer. The website also offers a long list of common questions that customers have about what to buy, how it works, and how to use it, with space to ask a new question of your own.

If even that outlet doesn't give you what you're looking for, you can tune in to The Little Guys' weekly one-hour radio show and phone in to chat with staff members about home theatre, high-definition TV, surround sound, whole-house audio, and whatever other product questions you might have.

In a recent consumer behaviour survey of 3000 adults, "helpful and knowledgeable staff" was among the most important factors cited by consumer electronics shoppers, ahead of product availability, financing offers, and rebates. The Little Guys seems to have found an effective way to leverage the power of its own sales staff. Customer relationships are what The Little Guys is all about. "The biggest change in the industry," says co-founder Evie Wexler, "is that five years ago brands drove people to our store. Today, the manufacturers' brands are everywhere, so the brand is now us. It's 'The Little Guys' name that's most important." Maintaining The Little Guys' personal touch has never been a better marketing strategy.

Questions for Critical Thinking

1. How well has The Little Guys achieved each of the four basic elements of long-term customer relationships? Explain your answer.
2. "The single best thing about our store is the people who work here," says The Little Guys website. Why can the company make this claim, and how does it reflect the firm's customer relationships?
3. At which level or levels of the relationship marketing continuum shown in Table 9.1 are The Little Guys' customers? Explain your answer.
4. What does The Little Guys do in order to understand customer needs? What more, if anything, do you think it could do?

Sources: The Little Guys website, http://www.thelittleguys.com, accessed July 27, 2006; Alan Wolf, "Consumers Cutting Back on CE Purchases This Summer," *This Week in Consumer Electronics,* July 17, 2006, http://www.twice.com; Lisa Johnston, "Study: Brand-Name Importance Drops for CE Shoppers," *This Week in Consumer Electronics,* July 3, 2006, http://www.twice.com; Alan Wolf, "Glikes to HTSA: Stay Ahead of the Curve," *This Week in Consumer Electronics,* April 24, 2006, http://www.twice.com.

Video Case 10.3

Wild Oats Natural Marketplace: Offering Products at Their Peak

Think of your local farmers' market or corner produce stand. It's the place where you pick up fresh corn, sweet strawberries, tart raspberries, and crisp lettuce. If you want to make a peach pie, you buy your peaches there, knowing they were plucked from the tree yesterday. If you're planning on a rich, homemade spaghetti sauce, you put half a dozen sun-drenched tomatoes from the stand in your shopping bag. Now imagine an entire grocery store with foods like this: fresh organic produce, dairy products, juices, meat and poultry—even natural tortilla chips and salsa. Add to the list environmentally friendly household and personal products, and you're beginning to get the full flavour of Wild Oats Natural Marketplace.

Wild Oats began its journey with one store in Boulder, Colorado. Today the company operates more than 110 stores in 40 U.S. cities and 24 states and Canada. And all sell natural and organic foods. Wild Oats maintains rigorous criteria for its selection of products, including those under its private label. None of the foods carried by Wild Oats contains hydrogenated oils, artificial colours, flavours, or preservatives. Many are certified organic according to the USDA's National Organic Program, including meat, poultry, seafood, and produce. The seafood is even labelled with its country of origin so that customers know they are purchasing fish from companies that do not engage in controversial seal hunts or related activities. And the eggs are certified to be laid by hens that are humanely treated.

In addition, Wild Oats has a new Choose Local program that showcases products from local growers and producers throughout the country during the summer months. "So many times people don't have a connection to where their food comes from," explains Perry Odak, president and CEO of Wild Oats. "They think milk comes from a grocery store. Through our Local Fest we . . . create a unique, authentic experience for Wild Oats customers—the chance to meet and talk with the people who actually grow and produce the foods we eat."

All of these factors—certified organic foods, environmentally friendly sources, locally grown products—combine to make up the Wild Oats private label. Many supermarket chains have launched their own line of products, reaping the full benefit of offering their own goods, usually at a lower price than national brands, without having to share the profits with outside manufacturers. "Private label can play an important role in merchandising strategy," notes Laura Copeland of Wild Oats. But Wild Oats operates under the strictest standards—every product has to fit certain criteria to bear the Wild Oats label. The firm decided to differentiate its goods based first on quality, then on price.

As part of its strategy, Wild Oats decided to go big. "We started with the large volume [product] categories first," recalls Copeland. "We had a lot to tackle, so we started with the biggest part of the business. The first products we launched were pantry items, the things that people buy on a regular basis." These products included pasta and pasta sauces, and bottled or canned juices. "Over time, we've incorporated more specialty items. And we're always looking for new products, new categories. We now sell more than 1000 private-label products," continues Copeland.

Wild Oats now offers three of its own product lines: Wild Oats Organic, Wild Oats Natural, and Wild Oats Living. Each product line has distinctive qualities. The Organic line is in accordance with the U.S. National Organic Program. The Natural line features products that are not organic but meet Wild Oats's own standards for foods with no high-fructose syrup, no hydrogenated oils, and no synthetic ingredients. The Wild Oats Living line offers environmentally friendly household products, such as cleaners and paper goods. Wild Oats is intent on competing with the big supermarket chains with as many private-label products as possible. "We want to be able to meet our customers' needs across all categories," says Copeland. But the company has to approach this carefully. "The concern about introducing a private-label selection is that consumers will simply switch from the established brand to the private-label brand, cannibalizing sales of the established brand," Copeland explains.

What's next for Wild Oats? Other retailers want to sell Wild Oats products in their stores and on their websites. Wild Oats now offers some of its products through Amazon.com and through online grocer Peapod. "Natural and organic products are available in a limited area of the [United States]," says Copeland. "We're looking to extend our brand beyond our four walls as much as possible."

Questions for Critical Thinking

1. How would you classify most of the consumer goods that are sold by Wild Oats? How does this affect the way they are marketed?

2. What are the benefits to Wild Oats of creating three private-label product lines?

3. Large firms such as Johnson & Johnson and General Mills have product mixes with a huge assortment of product lines and individual offerings. Visit the Wild Oats website at http://www.wildoats.com and sketch out the firm's product mix, showing its width, length, and depth. You don't need to list every product, just a few examples that demonstrate each of the three components in the mix.

4. At what stage would you place the organic foods category in the product life cycle? Based on this answer, describe the approach you think Wild Oats should take toward marketing its Wild Oats Organic line.

Sources: Wild Oats website, http://www.wildoats.com, accessed September 12, 2006; "Wild Oats Urges Customers to 'Choose Local,'" PR Newswire, July 17, 2006, http://biz.yahoo.com; "Food Fest at Wild Oats," *Saugus (MA) Advertiser*, July 13, 2006, http://www.townonline.com; "Wild Oats to Sell Eggs Certified as Humanely Raised," *New Mexico Business Weekly*, June 14, 2006, http://www.bizjournals.com.

Video Case 11.3

Rebranding at JPMorgan Chase

Some brand names and logos are so familiar that they are part of American culture. When we see the logo, we know which brand it represents. Maybe it's the NBC peacock, the Tommy Bahama palm tree, or one of the most recognizable of all, the McDonald's "golden arches." But what about a bank? Marketers at JPMorgan Chase want to make their logo instantly recognizable, too. In a massive campaign to re-create the bank's brand—after the merger of financial institutions JPMorgan and Chase Manhattan—JPMorgan Chase marketers are hard at work. "We want our logo to be as big as the Nike swoosh," says a spokesperson. "Branding is extremely important; it speaks to our reputation and depth of our products."

While the JPMorgan division encompasses all of the firm's subsidiaries and serves governments, large corporations, and institutional investors, the Chase brand is designated for the U.S. consumer and commercial banking businesses that serve small businesses, individuals, consumer and business credit card customers, commercial real estate transactions, and the like. The firm's octagon logo is attached to both the JPMorgan and Chase brands.

How does a financial institution get its brand to stand out the way a fast-food or clothing brand does? As smaller banks and financial firms are folded into the larger entity, fresh signs and advertisements help create awareness of a new identity. The merger of JPMorgan Chase with Bank One a few years ago was a golden opportunity for marketers to create a new bond with business customers and consumers in such places as Illinois and Texas, where JPMorgan Chase branches replaced those of the former Bank One. Now called Chase Bank, the new bank has engaged in an intensive rebranding effort through various media. Radio and TV spots, print ads, billboards, bus signs, and other outdoor advertising—including a presence at the commuter rail stations in downtown Chicago—blanketed the area when the changeover took place. One television commercial featured the Beatles' 1967 hit tune "Hello Goodbye"—with the message that customers could say good-bye to the old and hello to the new. In addition, Chase Bank conducted a sweepstakes whose prizes included up to 1 million mileage points on United Airlines, which is based in Chicago.

Incorporating the Chase name was a major part of the strategy. "Chase is well known," explains Bill Lozito, president of Strategic Name Development. "It opens the door to breaking the emotional bond that consumers may have with Bank One." Although rebranding is often about change, it also helps if some things stay the same. "The same employees are in [Chase Bank], and the employees seem to be well trained and are buying into the change," says Lozito. If familiar faces are behind the counter and at managers' desks—and seem comfortable with the change—then customers can feel relaxed about it as well. But to achieve this positive atmosphere, the vision and values of the new company must be communicated effectively to employees, so that they convey a message of confidence to their customers.

One way to reinforce awareness of the JPMorgan Chase logo is to stamp it on credit cards that are used daily by thousands of customers. The new Chase Freedom Visa has a sky-blue background with the company's octagon prominently printed on it. The card offers consumers the following options: earning cash back for their purchases or points toward rewards. Customers can earn 3 percent cash back on purchases at participating grocery stores, gas stations, and quick service restaurants, or 1 percent for every dollar spent elsewhere. If they prefer a rewards system instead, they can earn points toward hotel stays, car rentals, or airline travel. Once they become established customers, they may switch back and forth between the two programs. The idea is to get consumers to associate the Chase octagon with greater purchasing freedom.

JPMorgan Chase also sponsors events as part of its rebranding effort. The firm has sponsored the JPMorgan Chase Corporate Challenge—a road race in Boston—for more than two decades. The popularity of the 3.5-mile race, which attracts about 12 000 runners from 617 Boston-based companies, supports the rebranding of the firm. Money raised by entry fees and donations goes to a specific beneficiary each year, such as the Boston Arts Festival. Like a road race, rebranding is a true challenge for any firm. The marketplace, like the starting line, is jammed with images. But only a few top competitors cross the finish line in the lead.

Questions for Critical Thinking

1. Describe the brand equity that JPMorgan Chase already has.
2. Using the four dimensions of brand personality on the Brand Asset Valuator, describe the JPMorgan Chase brand.
3. Do you think the JPMorgan Chase octagon will become as recognizable as the Nike swoosh or the McDonald's "golden arches"? Do you think the firm's brand name will have equal success? Why or why not?
4. Describe a new product that JPMorgan Chase might choose to introduce as part of its rebranding effort. Why do you think it would succeed?

Sources: Chase Freedom website, http://www.chasefreedomnow.com, accessed September 19, 2006; JPMorgan Chase website, http://www.jpmorganchase.com, accessed August 14, 2006; "JPMorgan Chase Corporate Challenge," June 15, 2006, http://www.jpmorganchasecc.com; Judy Artunian, "Change of Name Can Come with Risk," *Chicago Tribune*, May 29, 2006, http://www.chicagotribune.com; "Chase Says Hello in Illinois," Chase press release, October 20, 2005, http://investor.shareholder.com/jpmorganchase.

Video Case 12.3

American Apparel: Supply Fits the Demand

American Apparel makes hip T-shirts and other clothing for young urban consumers. Based in Los Angeles, the company was founded in 1997 as a wholesale T-shirt manufacturer by offbeat entrepreneur Dov Charney. The company now operates 131 brick-and-mortar retail stores, as well as a Web store, with sales of more than $250 million a year. American Apparel is not just a patriotic name. Its Los Angeles plant is the largest garment factory in the country, and the clothing truly is designed and made in the United States. With so many manufacturers—particularly in the clothing industry—moving their production overseas, how does a relatively small, independent firm such as American Apparel manage to keep its production profitable in the United States and compete against giants such as The Gap?

Founder Dov Charney and vice president of operations Marty Bailey maintain that the answer to this question lies in vertical integration. "Vertical integration means that all elements of production are carried out under one roof. Design, cutting and sewing, even marketing and photography, all takes place in one building," explains Bailey. Essentially, vertical integration reduces production time. Because everything takes place at one plant, no time is lost shipping materials or components from one facility to another. In addition, all the processes are completed by teams, which Bailey instituted when he joined the firm. A sewing team consists of four to twelve workers, depending on how complicated the garment is. By converting to a team organization, the factory tripled its production output—from 30 000 pieces a day to 90 000.

Meeting demand is critical to success in the ever-changing apparel industry. "Being vertically integrated gives us the ability to respond quickly to changing needs," says Bailey. "If we need to produce more pieces of one colour or style, we can change production immediately. You can only do that if all your production is together."

This flexibility helps American Apparel manage its supply chain while meeting the demand for certain styles, sizes, and colours. The manufacturing process starts with the yarn itself—American Apparel buys raw yarn and knits it into fabric. Knitting machines at the factory are capable of creating smooth jersey or baby ribbed fabric—whatever the design calls for. "Then the fabric is dyed," says Bailey. "We dye as much as we need in the colours we need. If we change colours, or a colour becomes hot, it's easy for us to adjust." If one of the 30 colours available in the unisex T-shirt fades in popularity and another is suddenly a hit, the factory can make fewer of one and more of the other. Or it can quickly add swimsuits, if necessary, or back off on T-shirt dresses. In addition, the factory can modify a style immediately. "We can adjust a pattern this morning and have workers sewing it this afternoon," notes Bailey. "Since our success is based on the design and fit of our garments, this flexibility is important to us."

Just as vital as changes in demand is the flexibility in design to remain ahead of constantly shifting fashion trends. Because both design and production are under one roof, new styles can be created and produced rapidly. "We can develop a product on Monday and have it in stores by Friday," boasts Bailey. This gives American Apparel a competitive edge if a celebrity appears in a certain style one day and consumers are clamouring for it the next. It doesn't take months to design, produce, and ship from a factory overseas. Finally, vertical integration assures quality and the ability to respond to a crisis. "We can see the pieces in real time, as they are produced, instead of waiting for a shipment, examining the quality, and maybe sending it back or waiting for a new shipment," Bailey points out. And if there's a problem with a garment, the factory can usually correct it within hours, instead of weeks.

For the first five years of business, American Apparel sold its garments strictly to wholesalers, who then resold to retailers. In 2002, the company opened its first retail store and now sells directly to consumers through its website. Founder Dov Charney likes the advantage the company stores give his firm. "They allow us to reach the customer directly," he notes. "It's more direct contact than through a website or a third party. Stores also provide immediate feedback. We can see what products sell and what colours and styles people are interested in. Then we can adjust what we make."

American Apparel's young urban image is reinforced by the fact that everything is made by the factory in L.A. "If you have the right product, the right business model, and the ability to serve your customer well, you can be successful," observes Marty Bailey. "I believe we have all of those things."

Questions for Critical Thinking

1. Which types of marketing channels does American Apparel use? What are the benefits of each to the company?
2. In what ways does American Apparel gain an advantage over its competition by being vertically integrated?
3. Although most of American Apparel's processes take place at one facility, what outside components of the supply chain does the firm still have to manage?
4. Suppose American Apparel decided to move its manufacturing operations to Mexico. How would this move affect its physical distribution system?

Sources: American Apparel website, http://www.americanapparel.net, accessed September 13, 2006; Jennifer Ordonez, "California Hustlin'," *Newsweek*, June 18, 2006, http://www.msnbc.msn.com; Stephen Franklin, "More Pay American's Way," *Chicago Tribune*, May 30, 2006, sec. 3, pp. 1, 3.

Video Case 13.3

BP Connects with Drivers

You're staring down a long road. You've got many kilometres to travel before you reach your destination, and your fuel gauge says you're running low on gas. It's after dinnertime and getting late. You're hungry and you could use a decent cup of coffee to keep you awake for the trip ahead. Suddenly you see a welcome sign: BP Connect. You slow down and pull in, sliding next to the pump. After you fill the tank, you head inside the warmly lit shop where other customers are chatting with the clerk, choosing sandwiches and fresh pastries, and filling huge mugs with steaming hot coffee. Now you know you're going to survive the drive.

BP is well known worldwide as a source of fuel. But the firm has been opening its BP Connect convenience stores at a rapid pace. BP Connect stores are different from the average convenience store—they are set up for travellers who want to grab a snack for the road or those who want a break from driving. In fact, the Wild Bean Café located inside each BP Connect convenience store offers gourmet coffee, herbal teas, fountain beverages, fresh-baked breads and pastries, hot specialty soups, custom-made sandwiches, and fresh salads.

This retail strategy comes in response to a changing market—and new opportunities. "Twenty years ago, buying snacks at a gas station was unusual," notes BP spokesperson Polly Flinn. "You didn't buy food from the same guy who worked on your car. In the past 15 years, it's become something to think twice about." BP has done much more than think about it. The firm has developed a strategy to serve consumers who spend more and more time in their cars, who may be on the road during mealtimes, and who want higher-quality food than a bag of chips or a packaged doughnut. "The latest data show more than 60 percent of consumers do not eat breakfast at home any longer," says Flinn. So BP Connect offers an alternative. "Our strategy hinges on the fact that the same kind of people who had to get over buying a Snickers bar at a gas station will now feel comfortable seeing these locations as a place to get a sandwich and a cup of coffee on the go," notes Flinn.

Another important reason for BP's new retailing strategy is the fuel industry itself. Growth in the gasoline industry has been flat or negative for the past few years, while the growth in convenience items—particularly fresh food—has been steady. "The gross margin on food is twice that on convenience [items] and four times what we make on a gallon of gas," Flinn explains. So, as BP invests more in its convenience stores and cafés, these profitable locations begin to offset the ups and downs of the fuel industry. Deciding where to put a BP Connect store is easy—they can fit right in to your local BP gas station. "Our existing BP locations are some of the most convenient corners in the world," Flinn points out. "Right in, right out... The challenge is how to take advantage of these convenient corners and adapt them to consumers' ever-changing tastes."

Those tastes now run more toward fresh gourmet food and beverages and to a more welcoming atmosphere, both of which are served by the Wild Bean Café. The café operates like a store within a store. "This helps create the separation between food and fuel in the customer's mind," says Flinn. "It also creates greater credibility for the Wild Bean brand." Upon finding that consumers wanted to customize their snacks and meals—and save time—BP created a unique system that fulfills both needs. "At Connect, we implemented the New Wild Bean Café Screen that allows customers to create the sandwich they want on a touch screen, order it, and walk away and shop the rest of the store," explains Flinn. "They are controlling their time, rather than having a cashier control their time while they are standing there waiting."

With all of these innovations, BP Connect stores still stock the basics—candy, gum, mints, bottled water, soda, chips, and the like. Every item is placed carefully according to the marketing planogram, a sort of map that illustrates where everything goes. And the stores are kept stocked—Flinn explains that a retailer's nightmare is running out of an item that customers want. But she observes that BP Connect's regular customers tend to make purchases several times a week. "So far, we're pleased with our customer satisfaction and loyalty," says Flinn.

Questions for Critical Thinking

1. Describe the target market for BP Connect and Wild Bean Café stores.
2. How do the elements of the marketing mix apply to BP's retailing strategy (see Figure 13.1)?
3. Using the five different categories discussed in the chapter, how would you classify BP Connect stores as retailers?
4. In what ways does BP Connect represent scrambled merchandising? How does this strategy boost sales?

Sources: BP website, http://www.bp.com, accessed August 22, 2006; "BP Re-Energizes Its Store Brands," *Convenience Store News*, http://www.csnews.com, accessed August 22, 2006; "BP Rebranding in Sunshine State," *CSP Daily News*, May 17, 2006, http://www.cspnet.com.

Video Case 14.3

The Toledo Mud Hens: Family Fun = A Winning Strategy

How does a minor league baseball team set a team attendance record and become the league leader in ticket sales revenue, food and beverage sales, merchandise sales, and corporate sales?

How does a minor league baseball team succeed when the parent major league club controls everything from the ballplayers' compensation to which players stay with the club and for how long? How does the club attract fans when it's difficult to predict or promise which ballplayers the fans will be seeing at the ballpark on a given night?

In the case of the Toledo Mud Hens, the top (Triple-A) minor league affiliate of the Detroit Tigers, they succeed by seeing the club as a marketing, promotion, and sales organization. The Mud Hens marketing team has done a thorough marketing analysis of what draws fans to the ballpark, what interests them, and what keeps them coming back.

The Toledo Mud Hens' Marketing Team's marketing slogans are "Toledo's Family Fun Park" and "The Joy of Mudville." Marketing research reveals that fans come to the ballpark to see baseball, and to see famous or soon-to-be famous baseball players, as well as for the fun, entertainment, and an affordable family outing. They come because they know it will be a special family event, regardless of who is playing, how the team is doing, or what the score that night might be because there is a lot going on at the ballpark in addition to the baseball game.

With a clear receiver-focused marketing campaign target established, the Mud Hens have created their strategy in reverse. What mix of experiences will it take to fulfill the wishes of any fan and any family who attends a game at Fifth Third Field? What will it take to translate that loyalty into advanced or "pre-sale" ticket purchases to make it possible for the Mud Hens to offer more and more value for the family investment?

The Mud Hens sell out 284 corporate suites each year. Group sales to anyone organizing 25 or more people can include a picnic area package. Long concession lines, common at many sporting events, are rare at a Mud Hens game. With the receiver-focused planning aiming at family fan enjoyment at an affordable price, the quality, service, and value of the food service has been a critical ingredient to sales success. Revenue for the food and beverage service equals revenue from ticket sales.

The stadium was also designed with a team store, dubbed The Swamp Shop, to market the large variety of popular Mud Hens merchandise. Here again, long lines, typical at other stadiums, are rare. Also much more emphasis is placed on a myriad of promotions for the fans and family enjoyment. Birthday parties, Boy Scout Sleepovers, High School Baseball, Baseball Camp, Red Hat Ladies, Senior Days, Youth Baseball and Softball Days, Summer Recreation Days, and Home Run Derbies are major promotions throughout the season. Muddy's Knothole Club, tricycle races, musical chairs, fireworks, and many contests during the games provide a kaleidoscope of fun activities before, during, and after the games.

In order to promote this unique family experience to the fans, the Mud Hens marketing team has created an effective Integrated Marketing Communications strategy. The Mud Hens have created an atmosphere that the players love, which boosts team morale and attracts good players. This has turned a long-struggling team into a team that has won two straight league championships and a club that has supplied more that half of the players on the American League Champion Detroit Tigers.

One-third of the tickets sold are season ticket holders, mini plans, and suite sales. Another third of the tickets sold are group sales, and the last third of tickets sold are on an individual sales basis. Two-thirds of the tickets are pre-sold from a week to six months before the games. The Mud Hens average 75 percent of capacity at their ball park throughout the season. Sixty-five percent of all tickets are pre-sold, which greatly benefits the club's cash flow and planning.

Since a high percentage of sales are to loyal, repeat customers, direct mail brochures are a major vehicle in the marketing and sales mix. Currently, 40 percent of the advertising budget is used for direct marketing. Sixty percent of the ad budget mix is for TV, radio, and newspaper advertising to attract individual purchases and keep "top of mind" awareness in the community. Plans are to raise direct marketing gradually to 75 percent as the loyalty of repeat customers trends upwards.

Thirty-five marketing vehicles are now in place to promote and advertise "The Joy of Mudville" at "Toledo's Family Fun Park." The most powerful marketing vehicle is the "pocket schedule," 300 000 of which are distributed annually via retail stores in the Toledo area. The stadium's video boards, LED message centres, and electronic signs also play a prominent role in the marketing strategy.

Direct mail and e-mail for target marketing is particularly effective, especially to repeat customers. Direct mail efforts rely on their large database, which is carefully maintained. CRM (Customer Relations Management) software is used to fully develop and efficiently utilize the database for newsletters and direct messages, as well as to accurately track the campaigns.

Their advertising and PR presence in area newspapers, and on TV and radio, is an important part of the mix to attract new interest to discover "The Joy of Mudville," and show how minor league baseball is significantly different from Major League Baseball. Fifty to sixty games per year are televised in Toledo on the local sports cable station. TV and radio games are also effective marketing tools, generating interest and reminding fans that the team is home, while also generating advertising revenue.

The "Joy of Mudville" at "Toledo's Family Fun Park" message is tightly coordinated through all advertising, PR, and direct sales by the marketing director to promote the large community block party experience that has become a highly important slice of the Toledo quality of family life.

Questions for Critical Thinking

1. In what ways is the Toledo Mud Hens marketing campaign "receiver-focused?"
2. Why does the marketing strategy intend to raise the direct sales mix to 75 percent of the total?
3. Why is it important to increase the number of pre-sold tickets and how does the marketing strategy address this target?
4. Why is the food and beverage sales program playing a significant role in the success of the marketing and sales strategy?

Video Case 15.3

BP: Beyond Petroleum

Nearly a decade ago, two of the world's energy giants merged: British Petroleum and Amoco became BP. Consolidating the two organizations—and the two brands—was a massive undertaking. Getting the message out to the public that this was a new company with a new image was part of the marketing objective. With increasing energy prices, public perception of oil companies in general has had its ups and downs, so BP marketers had their work cut out for them. But the merger offered the perfect opportunity to create a fresh image in consumers' minds.

Instead of focusing on selling products, BP marketers went straight to selling a new perception of the company itself by launching an ad campaign called "BP on the Street." "When you undertake an image campaign, it's critical that you know what you want to do," says BP spokesperson Kathy Leech. "We had two tasks. The first was informative. We had to let people know who BP was. The second was positioning. The goal was to lift BP from the negative aura that surrounds energy companies in the mind of the public. We positioned ourselves as a different kind of energy company."

The tag line of the new campaign was catchy: "Beyond Petroleum." But it also conveyed the message that BP is more than a company that sells fossil fuels. BP is interested in doing more than filling consumers' gas tanks. In fact, BP is willing to face head on some of the tough questions concerning the energy industry. "It is the responsibility of an energy company to provide heat, light, and mobility to people. But you have to recognize that there are environmental costs," says Leech. "And you have a responsibility to mitigate those effects as much as possible." BP was the first large energy company to acknowledge the existence of global warming and to take steps to reduce the impact of its operations on the environment. The firm has invested in new sources of energy such as solar and hydrogen, research in climate change, and energy security—and these programs are featured in the advertising campaign, explaining to consumers why these activities are important to everyone.

If one part of the challenge is to make people aware of the new BP brand as well as its name, another part is to get them to relate to the message. So BP marketers created advertisements featuring real people voicing their concerns about energy issues. "The big issue in any sort of advertising is that people are cynical," admits Kathy Leech. "They are especially cynical about oil companies. By using real people [in the ads], speaking in unscripted situations, we hoped to cut through some of that cynicism."

The ads were originally launched in a few selected cities—Chicago; New York; Washington, D.C.; and London. The idea was to test some local markets and observe how viewers responded to the message. Although consumers liked the underlying principle, the ads were not wildly popular. "The first year, the ads came across as too negative," says Kathy Leech. "Consumers don't like negative advertising." So BP marketers went back to the drawing board and fine-tuned the ads. "The ads are now provocative without being negative," Leech continues. "Also, we are seeking a partnership with consumers. Rather than focusing on what BP is doing, we try to focus on what we can do together." BP has refined its ad campaign further, now targeting an audience that it refers to as opinion holders—those who vote, who follow decisions made by Congress, who may even write to their representatives. "You can't reach everyone," Leech explains. "Instead, we target people who are more informed, who other people go to for their information."

As the "BP on the Street" campaign moved from local advertising outlets to national and eventually international media, targeting its audience became even more important because it allowed BP to better monitor its advertising costs. The cost of advertising rises tremendously as media outlets expand. Despite this expansion, however, BP makes local refinements wherever necessary. Leech notes that American consumers are receptive to British accents, but British consumers don't respond well to American speakers in commercials. German consumers don't care for "person on the street" ads, so BP creates an "expert on the street."

Because of the high cost of an advertising campaign, and because conveying the right message is so crucial, BP marketers track the progress of "BP on the Street" carefully. "We do what is called a key learning summary at the end of each period," says Leech. "We've made adjustments based on what we learn. For example, last year we found that we were presenting too many messages. So we scaled back."

Moving beyond petroleum is essential for an energy firm like BP as it competes in the 21st century. As the firm transforms itself to meet new challenges, it also changes the messages it transmits to the public.

Questions for Critical Thinking

1. What are the objectives of the "BP on the Street" advertising campaign? How would you categorize the campaign?
2. Would celebrity advertising be as effective for "BP on the Street" as the use of average citizens? Why or why not? If BP decided to include a celebrity spokesperson in its campaign, whom would you suggest and why?
3. What kind of appeal do you think would be most effective for the "BP on the Street" advertisements? Why?
4. What role do the "BP on the Street" advertisements play in BP's public relations efforts?

Sources: BP website, http://www.bp.com, accessed August 29, 2006; "Ogilvy Wins BP CO2 Reduction Drive," *Marketing Week*, August 24, 2006, http://www.mad.co.uk; Wendy Melillo and Steve Miller, "Companies Find It's Not Easy Marketing Green," *Brandweek*, July 24, 2006, http://www.brandweek.com.

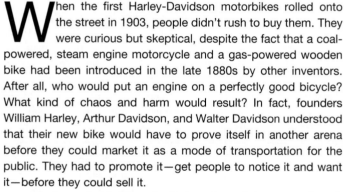

Harley-Davidson: Selling the Thrill

When the first Harley-Davidson motorbikes rolled onto the street in 1903, people didn't rush to buy them. They were curious but skeptical, despite the fact that a coal-powered, steam engine motorcycle and a gas-powered wooden bike had been introduced in the late 1880s by other inventors. After all, who would put an engine on a perfectly good bicycle? What kind of chaos and harm would result? In fact, founders William Harley, Arthur Davidson, and Walter Davidson understood that their new bike would have to prove itself in another arena before they could market it as a mode of transportation for the public. They had to promote it—get people to notice it and want it—before they could sell it.

The team decided to enter their motorcycle in races, where it would be seen by spectators who might be convinced of its quality and desirability. Over the next few years, the Harley-Davidson motorcycle set record after record for speed and for gas mileage—in 1908, a Harley achieved a whopping 188.334 miles per gallon during one race. In 1910, the Harley won seven motorcycle races, and in 1916 a Harley-Davidson Sidecar won the first annual race up Pikes Peak in Colorado. People were taking notice. Meanwhile, William Harley and the Davidsons had offered a distributorship to Chicago businessman C. H. Lange. Consumers in Chicago, who already demonstrated a love for motoracing and auto touring, caught on quickly to the new trend, and soon Lange was asking for more motorcycles to sell. In 1906, the firm's manufacturing operations had to move to larger quarters in Milwaukee. By 1912, there were 200 Harley-Davidson distributorships across the United States.

Rev the engines forward to the 1960s, when Harleys won seven consecutive titles at the Daytona 200. In the 1970s, Harleys won the AMA Grand National Championship four times and broke world records for speed. This visibility on the racetrack through the decades has been a distinctive part of Harley-Davidson's promotional strategy. People like to be part of a winning team.

Harley riders have always had a personal relationship with their motorcycles. They appreciate the high quality, smooth ride, and power of a Harley. They take good care of their bikes. And they like to associate with other Harley riders.

Harley-Davidson has promoted this relationship right from the beginning, through the Harley Owners Group (H.O.G.) and other outreach efforts. H.O.G. boosts dealers' selling efforts by creating a membership in a club of like-minded consumers. Purchasers of new cycles automatically become members for a year, and their families can join as associates at a discount. In addition, Harley-Davidson sponsors special events for customers, including training programs, rallies, factory tours, and parades. Nearly half of the nation's Harley dealers now send their customers localized e-zines that contain announcements of special events, updates on local rides, news items, tips for maintenance, trip planners, and the like. These e-zines are entirely the creation of dealers—not Harley-Davidson's corporate staff—as an effort to stay in close touch with their customers.

The Harley-Davidson Rider's Edge program goes a step further, attracting spectators or motorcycle enthusiasts and turning them into actual riders. These motorcycle training classes, offered by dealerships around the country, are aimed at teaching new and potential customers the basics of riding and maintaining a motorcycle—how to shift, turn, and brake—as well as the purpose of all the dials and knobs on a Harley. The idea is to boost customers' confidence with hands-on experience before they hit the road.

Dealers also hold open houses during the early fall to showcase the year's new models. Consumers can visit a showroom, meet the dealer personally, enjoy games and events, and even test-drive the Harley they've always dreamed about. "We've been doing a lot of things to increase our outreach," says James Ziemer, Harley-Davidson's president and CEO. That means getting more people out on the open road—on Harleys.

Questions for Critical Thinking

1. Describe the role of a salesperson at a Harley-Davidson dealership.
2. Which personal selling approach do Harley-Davidson dealers use? Give an example of how the approach is used.
3. Why is demonstration an important part of the selling process at Harley-Davidson? How does the firm use this technique to its best advantage?
4. How has Harley-Davidson used promotion techniques in its past? What types of sales promotions might a Harley-Davidson dealer use during an open house to encourage consumers to purchase a motorcycle?

Sources: Traci Purdum, "Harley-Davidson Inc: Global Road Trips, Training Programs Prove Profitable," *Industry Week,* July 20, 2006, http://www.industryweek.com; Harley Owners Group website, http://www.hog.com, accessed July 6, 2006; "Hog Heaven," Library of Congress, http://www.loc.gov, accessed July 6, 2006; Ray Schultz, "Harley-Davidson E-Zines Go Their Own Way," *Chief Marketer,* April 12, 2006, http://chiefmarketer.com.

Video Case 17.3

Washburn Guitars: How Much Is the Maya Worth?

What is your most prized possession? It might be a bracelet worn by your grandmother. It might be your car. Perhaps it's your collection of vintage baseball cards or your array of current CDs. If you play a musical instrument, maybe you value your violin or keyboard. If you're a guitar player, it could be a Washburn. Now try to put a price on your prize. Perhaps you inherited it, or someone gave it to you. Maybe you bought it or made it yourself. Assigning a price might be difficult, but that's what marketers do every day. If you're considering a high-end electric guitar like the Washburn Maya, you'd have to think in terms of $1500 or $2700. The Maya isn't cheap—the average electric guitar goes for about $500 to $600. But people who own it—or any other Washburn guitar—say it's well worth the price.

Washburn has been manufacturing high-quality, high-end guitars in the United States since 1883. Based in Illinois, the firm's parent company is now U.S. Music Corporation, which includes a number of different brands such as Randall Amplifiers, Vinci Strings and Accessories, SoundTech Professional Audio, and Oscar Schmidt folk instruments. Still, the firm is best known for its Washburn guitars.

Washburn makes a number of different lines and models of guitars. The Maya series is one of its most recent, used and endorsed by Dan Donegan, the lead guitarist for the rock band Disturbed. Although Donegan's personal guitar isn't for sale—it may end up in the Rock and Roll Hall of Fame someday—guitarists can purchase either the Maya Pro for a list price of $2699 or the Maya Standard, which lists for $1499. The Pro model has a few additional features, including a mahogany neck and abalone finger dots. Donegan, who helped design the line, says he's pleased with the results. "Washburn really went above and beyond to make sure my guitars are to my exact specification," he says. "I really wanted to create a guitar that is somewhat unique but appeals to artists of all musical genres." Washburn benefits from creating signature lines such as the Maya, which is associated with high-profile performers such as Donegan. "Signature models are used to increase the appeal of products in many fields," explains Kevin Lello, vice president of marketing. "Guitar enthusiasts follow the leading guitarists and sometimes choose the same equipment, like the Maya. This strengthens our relationship with Dan and his millions of fans."

Washburn promises that "each guitar represents the finest quality at the best possible price." To achieve this standard, the highest-quality materials must be used while costs are monitored so that consumers may purchase Washburn's products at a reasonable price. "We track quality and costs for everything in our guitar production process, to maximize quality and minimize price... from the man and machine hours to the sandpaper and cleaning supplies," says Gil Vasquez, production manager. Guitar prices vary depending on where they are manufactured. Guitars made in the United States, where Washburn guitars are built, usually command the highest prices because customers believe they are made to the highest standards.

Kevin Lello notes that the Maya series is a "showpiece" for Washburn. The materials used are expensive, as is the handcrafting involved in building the instruments. In addition, the line was designed with the help of Dan Donegan, so the musician receives a royalty on the guitars sold. "We spend a little more in marketing this model as well, with print and Web campaigns," Lello says. But the Maya is not intended to be a high-volume product. Lello observes that although the list price for the Maya Pro is $2699, some retailers discount the price a bit in order to sell it more easily.

While the Maya series is at the upper end of the price range, Washburn also manufactures lower-priced guitars. However, Lello admits that the lower-priced models have hurt the firm's image for high quality. So the firm is trying to turn this around. He believes this is possible because consumers are willing to pay for quality. If they want a $99 guitar, they can purchase one elsewhere. "Demand for good guitars is relatively inelastic," Lello says. Those words are pure music to Washburn.

Questions for Critical Thinking

1. What are the pricing objectives for the Maya series of guitars?
2. Why does Kevin Lello say that the demand for good guitars is relatively inelastic?
3. Would cost-plus pricing be appropriate for the Maya series? Why or why not?
4. What challenges might Washburn face as it markets its products overseas?

Sources: Washburn Guitars website, http://www.washburn.com, accessed August 29, 2006; NexTag Web site, http://www.nextag.com, accessed August 29, 2006; Dan Moran, "U.S. Music Corp.'s Washburn Guitars No Strangers to Fame," Suburban Chicago News, http://www.suburbanchicagonews.com, accessed April 17, 2006; "Washburn Guitars," Answers.com, http://www.answers.com, accessed April 17, 2006; "Disturbed Dan Donegan Signature Series Washburn Guitar at Winter NAMM," All About Jazz, March 3, 2006, http://www.allaboutjazz.com.

Video Case 18.3

Whirlpool: Innovation for Every Price Point

The Whirlpool logo says a lot about the company. It evokes whirling water, constant change, and innovation within a circle that consumers can trust. "Inspired by bold innovations and designs, customers around the globe trust Whirlpool to make their lives easier," says the company website. "More than ever before, our brands are connecting with customers in ways that will last a lifetime." These brands include Whirlpool, KitchenAid, Roper, and Consul, along with others that are distributed to more than 170 countries worldwide. The Michigan-based firm has been innovating since 1911, when Louis, Frederick, and Emory Upton created the Upton Machine Company to produce the first electric, motor-driven wringer washers. Today Whirlpool is a global manufacturer of major home appliances with 68 000 employees and nearly 50 manufacturing and research facilities around the world.

Like many large manufacturers, Whirlpool offers consumers different brands at different prices. By the 1980s, the firm had developed a three-level brand structure in order to give consumers a clear purchasing choice. The KitchenAid brand represents high-end, higher-priced appliances, including its popular stand mixer, coffee mills and grinders, microwave ovens, built-in ovens and cooktops, refrigerators, dishwashers, and washers and dryers. The smaller appliances are sold at retailers known for their cutting-edge design, such as Target, while the larger items—which can run as much as $3800 for a combination microwave and wall oven from the Architect Series—are carried by specialized high-end appliance and electronics retailers such as Chicago-based Abt Electronics, which sells both the large and small KitchenAid products.

The Whirlpool brand, which represents mid-level pricing, is carried by Best Buy, Lowe's, and Sears—a reflection of Whirlpool's relationship with Sears, Roebuck dating back to 1916, when the retailer reported that it was selling Upton washers faster than the manufacturer could make them. Consumers can choose from washers and dryers, refrigerators, microwaves, ovens, dishwashers, trash compactors, and more. They can furnish entire kitchens and laundry rooms with Whirlpool products at mid-level prices, spending as little as $449 for a dishwasher and as much as $2799 for a built-in microwave/oven combination. Whirlpool

believes in innovation that offers choice—there are 46 refrigerator models with a variety of features, including side-by-side design, top or bottom freezers, ice and water dispensers, and Spillguard shelves. All are certified with the Energy Star rating.

Whirlpool refers to its Roper brand as the "workhorse"—simple, sturdy, dependable, and affordable. Consumers can take home a washing machine for as little as $249 and a dishwasher from $229 to $379. Refrigerators top out at $999. Whirlpool can offer such a wide range of products and prices because of its focus on innovation. "Without innovation and differentiation, the fundamental basis for competition was just price," notes president and CEO Jeff Fettig. "But our view was that for us to truly [be able to] execute a differentiated, value-creating strategy, we needed to do something dramatically different. From day one, we took the approach that innovation was not the privilege of a few; it was a right of the masses." This strategy means that whether they are purchasing the most expensive KitchenAid product or the lowest-priced Roper product, consumers get the benefits of innovation in design, construction, and technology.

Innovation is also a factor in appealing to consumers' perception of the price–quality relationship. Consumers who purchase Whirlpool's top-of-the-line KitchenAid appliances believe that they are getting the best products as demonstrated by high-quality design and features. But consumers who purchase Whirlpool's Roper line feel they are getting a good deal because the firm promotes the dependability and durability of these appliances, characteristics that are also achieved through design. Those who select Whirlpool feel that the brand is designed for them, because the brand's slogan is "Inspired by You." So each group of purchasers perceives that the products they are buying provide value and quality. Across all three brands, price increases as the number and complexity of innovative features increase, which consumers view as acceptable and reasonable. With this strategy, consumers have the opportunity to choose which features are important to them and how much they want to pay for an appliance.

As crucial as they are, consumers aren't Whirlpool's only customers. Because Whirlpool is a manufacturer, the firm must also satisfy the needs of its channel members, including retailers such as Target and Sears. Whirlpool provides different types of price breaks to retailers, including volume rebates and discounts if a retailer sends its own truck to pick up goods at the factory rather than having them delivered. Consumer rebates actually benefit retailers as well, because they give consumers an incentive to purchase Whirlpool products. "We're a high innovation company," remarks Fettig. You could say that Whirlpool has been making a stir in the marketplace for a long time.

Questions for Critical Thinking

1. What types of reductions from list price does Whirlpool use? Is this an effective marketing strategy? Why or why not?

2. Describe how Whirlpool uses the product lines in its three brands to promote a positive relationship between price and quality.

3. Do you think consumers would have different price limits across the three Whirlpool brands? Explain your answer.

4. Whirlpool sells its products in many different countries. Which of the three alternative global pricing strategies presented in the chapter do you think would work best for the company? Why?

Sources: Roper website, http://www.roperappliances.com, accessed September 27, 2006; Whirlpool websites, http://www.whirlpoolcorp.com and http://www.whirlpool.com, accessed September 12, 2006; KitchenAid website, http://www.kitchenaid.com, accessed September 12, 2006; "Whirlpool's Future Won't Fade," *BusinessWeek,* May 8, 2006, http://www.businessweek.com.

CHAPTER 1

1. CV Technologies Annual Reports, 2004, 2005, 2006, and 2007; Kali Pearson, "How Cold-fX Got So Hot," *Profit,* November 2005, pp. 47–48; Paul Brent, "It's Bad, But It Works," *Marketing,* December 10, 2007, p. 6; "Maker of Cold-fX Posts Record $6.8M Profit," *Calgary Herald,* February 14, 2008, p. C3.

2. Jefferson Graham, "Amazon Takes on Apple with Copy-protection-free Music," *USA Today,* March 26, 2008, http://news.yahoo.com.

3. Johnnie L. Robertson, "Murdoch's New Groove," *Newsweek,* February 13, 2006, pp. 42–44.

4. Rick Spence, "Four Better—or Four Worse?" *Profit,* March 2007, pp. 19–20.

5. Greg Sandoval, "Podcasting Spurs a Media 'Land Grab,'" Associated Press, July 16, 2005, http://news.yahoo.com.

6. Joseph P. Guiltinan and Gordon W. Paul, *Marketing Management,* 6th ed. (New York: McGraw-Hill, 1996), pp. 3–4.

7. "AMA Adopts New Definition of Marketing," American Marketing Association, http://www.marketingpower.com, accessed March 31, 2008.

8. Statistics Canada, "Study: Canada's Trade with China," *The Daily,* December 14, 2007, http://www.statcan.ca.

9. "Fuji Photo Film to Slash 5000 Jobs, Shift Production to China," Agence France-Presse, January 31, 2006, http://www.afp.com.

10. Kara Aaserud, "The Problem with India," *Profit,* March 2007, pp. 13, 15.

11. Kamal Nath, *India's Century* (New York: McGraw-Hill, 2008), p. 112.

12. "Top 20 Innovative Companies in the World," *Business Week,* August 1, 2005, p. 64.

13. Peter Burrows and Ronald Grover, "Steve Jobs's Magic Kingdom," *Business Week,* January 26, 2006, http://www.businessweek.com.

14. Arnie Williams, "PTC Helps Airbus Megajet Take Off," LookSmart, March 2005, http://www.findarticles.com.

15. Bert Hill, "Analysts See Eye-popping Growth for WiMax Gear," *Ottawa Citizen,* December 12, 2007, p. D6.

16. Daryl-Lynn Carlson, "Recovering from a Miscue: Small Business," *National Post,* March 10, 2008, p. FP10.

17. Kristin Ohlson, "Burst of Energy," *Entrepreneur,* February 2006, pp. 46–47.

18. Timothy McNulty, "Bono's Red Line Will Fight AIDS," *Pittsburgh Post-Gazette,* January 28, 2006, http://www.post-gazette.com.

19. Chris Cobb, "What Are You Drinking? I Dunno, But Madonna Endorsed It," *Gazette* (Montreal), March 15, 2008, p. J6.

20. Sandra O'Loughlin, "Brand Builders," *Brandweek,* March 31, 2003, pp. 16–17.

21. Susan Horsburgh, Ron Arias, and Steve Helling, "eBay's eBoss," *People,* August 4, 2003, pp. 97–98.

22. Stuart Elliott, "At $83,333 a Second, Ads Chase Super Bowl Score," *International Herald Tribune,* February 2, 2006, http://www.iht.com.

23. "Adidas Bets on Beijing Olympics," *International Herald Tribune,* January 30, 2006, http://www.iht.com.

24. Melanie Collison, "Philanthropists Make Dreams," *Edmonton Journal,* February 28, 2008, p. 40.

25. Hollie Shaw, "By Land, Sea and Air," *National Post,* November 30, 2007, p. FP7.

26. Katrina Brooker, "The Pepsi Machine," *Fortune,* February 6, 2006, pp. 68–72.

27. Allison Linn, "Microsoft Plans Launch of Internet Research Lab," TechNewsWorld, January 30, 2006, http://www.technewsworld.com.

28. *Canada Year Book 2007* (Ottawa: Statistics Canada, 2007) p. 297.

29. Rodrique Ngowi, "Cell Phone Use Changes Life in Africa," Yahoo! News, October 16, 2005, http://news.yahoo.com.

30. "E-Tailers Try New Holiday Tricks," *Business Week,* December 12, 2005, http://www.businessweek.com.

31. "Internet Protocol Television," Webopedia, http://webopedia.com, accessed March 23, 2008; Brucey Meyerson, "Interactive TV Poised for a Rollout," *USA Today,* February 14, 2005, http://www.usatoday.com.

32. David Crane, "We're Quickly Losing Our Edge in the Digital World," *Toronto Star,* October 8, 2007, p. B5.

33. Pamela Parker, "Mobile Video in Real Time," ClickZ Network, January 27, 2006, http://www.clickz.com.

34. Ibid.

35. "Where Is Mobile Marketing Headed?" eMarketer, February 3, 2005, http://www.emarketer.com.

36. Adam Plowright, "New TV-phone Worth a Look," *Edmonton Journal,* February 15, 2008, p. D7.

37. Michael Meltzer, "Customer Dialogue Builds Loyalty & Profit," *CRM Today,* http://www.crm2day.com, accessed February 2, 2006.

38. Agent Wildfire website, http://www.agentwildfire.com, accessed March 23, 2008.

39. Tony Martin, "They Blog, Therefore They Are ... Better CEOs," *Globe and Mail,* March 15, 2008, p. B18.

40. Xenon Pharmaceuticals, "Xenon and Takeda Announce Agreement to Develop and Commercialize XEN401 for Pain in Japan and Certain Asian Countries," news release, October 2, 2006, http://www.xenon-pharma.com, accessed March 27, 2008.

41. Jenex Corporation, "The Jenex Corporation Grants Worldwide License to Distribute and Sell Thermapik Device," news release, February 28, 2007, http://www.jenexcorp.com/, accessed March 27, 2008.

42. Imagine Canada, "11th Annual Canadian Business and Community Partnership Awards," http://www.imaginecanada.ca/, accessed March 27, 2008.

43. "Timberland Employees Take a Work Day to Participate in Park Revitalization Project During the Timberland Company's International Day of Community Service?Serv-a-Palooza," press release, October 22, 2005, http://www.nkpr.net/, accessed March 28, 2008.

44. HP Canada, "HP Canada Philanthropy," http://h10084.www1.hp.com/, accessed March 28, 2008.

45. Pfizer Canada, "Community Investment," http://www.pfizer.ca/, accessed March 28, 2008.

CHAPTER 2

1. Marina Strauss, "Loblaw Targets Better Days with More Staff," *Globe and Mail,* May 1, 2008, p. B3; Hollie Shaw, "Price War with Wal-Mart Impacts Loblaw Profit," CanWest News, February 7, 2008, p. 1; Zena Olijnyk, "Lots More Mr. Nice Guy," *Canadian Business,* October 22, 2007, pp. 58–66; Marina Strauss, "Meet Joe, Loblaw's Billion-Dollar Hope," *Globe and Mail,* September 7, 2007, p. B1; Marina Strauss, "A Matter of Taste: Loblaw Seeks the Right Price," *Globe and Mail,* April 27, 2007, p. B18; Jerry Tutunjian, "Loblaw Unveils the Future," *Canadian Grocer,* March 2007, p. 8; "Loblaw Announces Changes That Will Lead to a Leaner and More Responsive Structure," Canada NewsWire, January 22, 2007, p. 1.

2. Jay Greene, "Three-Part Harmony for Microsoft?" *Business Week,* September 12, 2004, http://www.businessweek.com.

3. Cloud Star website, www.cloudstar.com, accessed February 7, 2006; Nichole L. Torres, "Cloud Star Corp.," in Amanda Kooser et al., "Beyond Their Years," *Entrepreneur,* November 2003, pp. 74–85.

4. Laurie Sullivan, "Oracle Seals Siebel Deal," *TechWeb,* January 31, 2006, http://www.techweb.com; Sarah Lacey, "Now, Oracle May Finally Rest," *Business Week,* September 13, 2005, http://www.businessweek.com.

5. "What's Kodak's Strategy?" interview with Brad Stone, *Newsweek,* January 16, 2006, p. 46.

6. Guy Trebay, "Influencers Are Forever," *The New York Times,* June 26, 2005, http://www.nytimes.com.

7. Richard Wright, "Back in Bloom," *Profit,* May 2008, pp. 50–53.

8. Nick Lewis, "Record Store Day Highlights Retailers' Struggle for Survival, *Calgary Herald,* April 19, 2008, p. D1.

9. Justin Ewers, "Maxims in Need of a Makeover," *U.S. News & World Report,* March 27, 2006, pp. EE2–EE6.

10. "iTunes: 1 Billion Served," *Red Herring,* February 23, 2006, http://www.redherring.com; Steve Alexander, "iTunes Trumpets a New Milestone: 1 Billion Downloads Sold," TechNewsWorld, February 23, 2006, http://www.technewsworld.com.

11. Amazon.com press release, "Amazon.com Announces Fourth Quarter Sales Up 42% to $5.7 Billion; 2007 Free Cash Flow More Than Doubles, Surpassing $1 Billion for the First Time," January 30, 2008, www.amazon.com, accessed April 29, 2008.

12. Coastal Contacts website, www.coastalcontacts.com, accessed April 30, 2008; Roger Hardy, "Sandbox Solutions," *Profit,* May 2008, p. 27.

13. Derek F. Abell, "Strategic Windows," *Journal of Marketing,* July 1978, pp. 21–26.

14. "Cars in China: Dream Machines," *The Economist,* June 2, 2005, http://www.economist.com.

15. Tomboy Trades website, www.tomboytrades.com, and Moxie Trades website, www.moxietrades.com, both accessed April 30, 2008; Lisa Wright, "Business Is Booming for 'Pink Boot Lady'; Ever Since an August Story Ran in the Star, Marissa McTasney Has Been Run Off Her Feet," *Toronto Star,* December 31, 2007, p. B3.

16. Rebecca Harris, "Skin Deep," *Marketing,* January 29, 2007, pp. 18–19.

17. Duncan Martell, "HP Charges into Retail Photo Printing Market," Reuters, February 22, 2006, http://news.yahoo.com.

18. Catherine McLean, "Rogers' Next Money Maker: the iPhone," April 30, 2008, www.globeandmail.com.

19. Jason Roberson, "New Marketing Strategy Planned: Higher Sales, New Vehicles Boost Outlook of Mitsubishi," *Detroit Free Press,* January 10, 2006, http://www.freep.com.

20. Nicolas Van Praet, "Hyundai Fires Shot in Canadian Car Pricing Battle," *Star-Phoenix* (Saskatoon), March 27, 2008, p. C12.

21. May Wong, "Lenovo Makes Global Push with Computers," Associated Press, February 23, 2006, http://news.yahoo.com.

22. Ian Austen, "BlackBerry Service to Continue," *The New York Times,* March 4, 2006, http://www.nytimes.com; Anne Broache, "BlackBerry Saved," *The New York Times,* March 3, 2006, http://www.nytimes.com; Stephanie Stoughton, "End to BlackBerry Patent Feud May Finally Be at Hand," *USA Today,* February 19, 2006, http://www.usatoday.com.

23. David Friend, "Media Giants Rethink Newspaper Operations," *Telegraph-Journal* (Saint John), April 19, 2008, p. C5.

24. As mentioned in Jagdish Sheth and Rajendra Sisodia, *Surviving and Thriving in Competitive Markets* (New York: Free Press, 2002).

25. Brent Jang, "Upstart Heightens Battle for Business Traveller," *Globe and Mail,* March 6, 2008, p. B3.

26. Ed Sutherland, "HP to Split Handhelds, Notebooks," Internetnews.com, February 13, 2006, http://www.internetnews.com.

27. Matt Krantz, "Ask Matt: Take a Bite of Apple?" *USA Today,* February 2, 2006, http://www.usatoday.com; Jefferson Graham, "Jobs Has a Knack for Getting His Way," *USA Today, January 25, 2006,* http://www.usatoday.com.

28. Annys Shin, "New CEO's Theme for Six Flags Is Change," *Washington Post,* December 15, 2005, http://www.washingtonpost.com.

APPENDIX NOTES

1. "Corporate Information," Google website, http://www.google.com, accessed June 28, 2006.

2. Travel Alberta, "Strategic Tourism Marketing Plan 2008–2011," available http://www.industry.travelalberta.com/strategicplan, accessed May 4, 2008.

3. Uniboard Canada Inc. website, http://www.uniboard.com, accessed July 4, 2005.

4. Travel Alberta, "Strategic Tourism Marketing Plan 2008–2011."

5. Daren Fonda, "Jim Sinegal, Costco's Discount CEO," *Time,* May 8, 2006, p. 148.

6. Ann Meyer, "Taking on Giants: The Small Shop That Fought Back," *Chicago Tribune,* May 16, 2006, sec. 7, p. 5.

7. Chelsea Emery and Yung Kim, "J. Crew Shares Surge 28 Pct in Market Debut," Reuters, June 28, 2006, http://news.yahoo.com; Anne D'Innocenzio, "J. Crew Prepares to Go Public," Associated Press, June 23, 2006, http://news.yahoo.com; Emily Scardino, "J. Crew Walks Down the Aisle," *DSN Retailing Today,* February 28, 2005, http://www.findarticles.com.

8. Yian Q. Mui, "Retailers Redesign as Boomers Hit 60," *Washington Post,* January 17, 2006, http://www.washingtonpost.com.

9. Brooks Barnes, "Toyota Aims Young, Sponsors Fox Spinoff for Cellphone Screens," *The Wall Street Journal,* April 24, 2006, http://online.wsj.com.

10. Clayton Collins, "Pitches to Tweens Target Parents, Too," *Christian Science Monitor,* April 28, 2006, http://www.csmonitor.com.

11. "Nokia Launches New Online Retail Distribution Channel for N-Gage Games," June 6, 2006, "Nokia and Gameloft Announce Expanded Mobile Gaming Collaboration," May 9, 2006, and "Nokia Simplifies Creation of Online Gaming Communities for Java Technology Games," March 20, 2006, Nokia press releases, http://www.n-gage.com; Grant Gross, "Nokia Slashes N-Gage Price," *PC World,* March 15, 2005, http://www.pcworld.com.

12. Choe Sang-Hun, "Wal-Mart Selling Stores and Leaving South Korea," *The New York Times,* May 23, 2006, http://www.nytimes.com.

13. "How Do I Know I'm Ready for a Second Location," *National Post,* March 10, 2008, p. FP9.

CHAPTER 3

1. AIDS Niagara website, http://www.aidsniagara.com, accessed June 7, 2008; "Canada Finally Poised to Deliver on Promise of Affordable Medicines to Developing Countries?" Canada NewsWire, Ottawa, May 7, 2008; "Prince George, B.C. Airport Guard Resigns over Treatment of HIV/AIDS Group," The Canada Press, Toronto, April 11, 2008; "Rwanda: The Return of Hope," *The Province* (Vancouver), June 1, 2008, p. B2; Carol Sanders, "Experts Gather in Winnipeg for Conference on Ukraine's AIDS Epidemic," The Canada Press, Toronto, April 16, 2008; Jordana Huber, "Activists Angry Judge Wanted Witness with HIV to Don Mask," CanWest News, January 31, 2008; "Books and Arts: Sex and Sensibility; The Business of AIDS," *The Economist,* May 3, 2008, p. 104.

2. Greg Keenan, "How a Stunning Sales Drop Changed It All," http://www.globeandmail.com, June 5, 2008; "GM Canada Sales Plunge 20%," The Canadian Press, http://www.globeandmail.com, June 3, 2008.

3. Susanne Baillie, Dee Van Dyk, and Kali Pearson, "Best Businesses to Go Into Now," *Profit,* December 1, 2002, available ProQuest document 631394561.

4. RenewABILITY Energy website, http://www.renewability.com, accessed June 18, 2008.

5. Vanessa O'Connell, "Why Philip Morris Decided to Make Friends with FDA," *The Wall Street Journal,* November 25, 2003, p. 11.

6. Kees Cools and Alexander Roos, "After a Pause, the Return of Business Alliances," *Christian Science Monitor,* January 30, 2006, http://www.csmonitor.com.

7. Byron Acohido, "Microsoft Rivals File Antitrust Complaint," *USA Today,* February 22, 2006, http://www.usatoday.com; Microsoft Appeals US$1.39-billion European Commission Fine," *National Post,* May 10, 2008, p. FP7.

8. "Synergy Brands to Sell Designer Brand Luxury Goods to Costco through PHS Group," Sys-Con Media, February 1, 2006, http://www.sys-con.com.

9. Green Budget Coalition, http://www.greenbudget.ca/2005_9.html, accessed June 18, 2008.

10. Jim Carlton, "People Favor Solar Power—But Not in Their Neighborhood," *The Wall Street Journal,* February 25, 2004, pp. B1, B4; Green Budget Coalition.

11. Kozo Mizoguchi, "Japanese Make Gasoline from Cattle Dung," Associated Press, March 3, 2006, http://news.yahoo.com; Patrick O'Driscoll, "Utahans Wary of Renewed Interest in Uranium," *USA Today,* January 20, 2006, http://www.usatoday.com; Terence Chea, "California Energy Regulators OK Solar Program," Associated Press, January 12, 2006, http://news.yahoo.com.

12. "Wi-Fi on the Farm," CNN, http://www.cnn.com, accessed October 19, 2005.

13. Kristen Kennedy, "Intel Endorses Wi-MAX with New Line of Chips for Standard," *Computer Reseller News,* http://www.lexis-nexis.com, accessed October 17, 2005.

14. Geoff Kirbyson, "Que Pasa?" *Canadian Business,* March 31, 2008, p. 10. Mart Canada Supercentres to include Tim Hortons," Ottawa, September 13, 2007, p. 1.

15. Canada NewsWire, "Wal-Mart Canada Supercentres to include Tim Hortons," Ottawa, September 13, 2007, p. 1.

16. Nancy Gohring, "Google News Goes Mobile," *PC World,* March 1, 2006, http://www.pcworld.com; "Apple Unveils iPod Home Stereo, Mini-Computer with Intel Chip," Agence France Presse, March 1, 2006, http://www.afp.com.

17. Industry Canada, http://cmcweb.ca/epic/internet/incmc-cmc.nsf/en/h_fe00013e.html, accessed June 18, 2008.

18. National Energy Board, "Our Responsibilities," http://www.neb.gc.ca/clf-nsi/rthnb/whwrndrgvrnnc/rrspnsblt-eng.html, accessed June 18, 2008.

19. Advertising Standards Canada, "Celebrating 50 Years of Advertising Self-Regulation," *Canadian Business,* Advertising Supplement.

20. Erin Pooley, "A Recipe for Change," *Canadian Business,* October 22, 2007, pp. 25–26.

21. Eric Beauchesne, "Canada a Haven from Inflation among Industrial Countries: Annual Rate Fell to 1.4 Percent in March, Report Says," *Vancouver Sun,* April 18, 2008, p. F2.

22. "Canada's Unemployment Rate Falls to Lowest Point Since 1974; September Job Creation Better Than Expected," *Edmonton Journal,* October 6, 2007, p. E3; David Akin, "Canadians Nervous About Economy," *Edmonton Journal,* May 22, 2008, p. A4.

23. Madlen Read, "Oil Prices Rise on Supply Fears," Associated Press, March 3, 2006, http://news.yahoo.com; "Gasoline and Diesel Fuel Update," Energy Information Administration, February 27, 2006, http://tonto.eia.doe.gov; "Q&A: Saudi Oil Attack," BBC News, February 24, 2006, http://news.bbc.co.uk.

24. Crystal Kua, "Reverse Vending," *Honolulu StarBulletin,* July 13, 2005, http://starbulletin.com.

25. Tu Thanh Ha, "Montreal Clothing Plant to Shut, 540 to Lose Jobs," http://www.reporton-business.com, March 3, 2008; "Men's Wearhouse Closing Montreal Plant," The Canadian Press, http://www.reportonbusiness.com, March 3, 2008.

26. Frank Hornig and Wieland Wagner, "China, the US and Battle to Lead a Globalized World," *Der Spiegel,* February 3, 2006, http://service.spiegel.de; Pete Engardio, "Substantial Benefits from China Trade?" *Business Week,* February 8, 2006, http://www.businessweek.com.

27. David J. Lynch, "World Economy Grows, Faces Dangerous Balancing Act," *USA Today,* January 12, 2006, http://www.usatoday.com.

28. Douglas Quan and John Welsh, "Technology Tracks Goods, Now People," *Press-Enterprise* (Riverside, CA), January 20, 2006, http://www.pe.com.

29. "The Emerging Carbohydrate Economy," *Sacramento Bee,* February 26, 2006, http://www.evworld.com.

30. "Research Universities Join Effort to Reduce Costs of Drug Development, Manufacturing," Purdue University, November 3, 2005, http://news.uns.purdue.edu.

31. Valerie Marchant, "The New Face of Work," *Canadian Business,* March 29–April 11, 2004, pp. 37–41.

32. L.S. Sya, "Wi-Fi to March Ahead," RedOrbit, February 5, 2006, http://www.redorbit.com.

33. Bruce Meyerson, "Momentum Grows to Meld Tech Platforms," Associated Press, November 27, 2005, http://news.yahoo.com.

34. Linda Stern, "How to Ride That Aging Baby-Boomer Wave," Reuters, March 4, 2006, http://news.yahoo.com.

35. "Rogers Adds Greek Channel MEGA Cosmos to Its Multicultural Lineup," Canada News-Wire, October 15, 2007, p. 1.

36. Marke Andrews, "Rogers Buys Channel M; The Company Has Long Sought to Have a Multicultural Station in Vancouver," *Vancouver Sun,* July 7, 2007, p. G1.

37. Ethical Consumer website, http://www.ethicalconsumer.org/boycotts/boycottsarchive.htm, accessed June 18, 2008.

38. Martin Mittelstaedt, "Canada First to Label Bisphenol A as Officially Dangerous," http://www.globeandmail.com, April 15, 2008; "Some Retailers Removing BPA Bottles," The Canadian Press, http://www.globeandmail.com, April 15, 2008.

39. Nortel website, "Code of Business Conduct," http://www.nortel.com/corporate/community/ethics/collateral/english_code_2007.pdf, accessed June 18, 2008; Steve Maich, "Selling Ethics at Nortel," Maclean's, January 24, 2005, p. 32.

40. Gordon Keast, "Dancing with the Devil; Why Is a Crown Corporation Investing in Tobacco Stocks When the B.C. Government Is Suing Tobacco Companies?" *Vancouver Sun,* May 15, 2008, p. A17.

41. Rob Linke, "$10B Up in Smoke; Health Smoking-Related Illnesses Have Cost Province More Than $10B in Last 60 Years, Lawyer Says," *Telegraph-Journal* (Saint John), March 24, 2008, p. A1.

42. Alan Stafford, "Privacy in Peril," *PC World,* November 2005, http://www.pcworld.com.

43. Marilynn Marchione, "A Hard Stance against Soft Drinks," *Fort Worth Star-Telegram,* March 5, 2006, http://www.star-telegram.com.

44. Emily Bazar, "Advertisers Catch the School Bus," *USA Today,* December 27, 2005, http://www.usatoday.com; "Junk Food Infiltrating Schools," CBS News, September 7, 2005, http://www.cbsnews.com.

45. John Schmeltzer and Leon Lazaroff, "Kraft Competitors Face Tough Choice," *Chicago Tribune,* January 13, 2005, sec. 3, pp. 1, 8.

46. Bruce Horovitz, "Alcohol Makers on Tricky Path in Marketing to College Crowd," *USA Today,* November 17, 2005, http://www.usatoday.com; Alan Mozes, "Alcohol Merchandise Encourages Underage Drinking," Yahoo! News, May 17, 2005, http://story.news.yahoo.com.

47. Deborah Mendenhall, "Keep Your Credit under Control," *Family Circle,* March 2006, pp. 42–49.

48. Matthew Barton, "SARCAN Now Recycles Electronic Equipment," *Leader Post* (Regina), February 2, 2007, p. A4.

49. inkCanada website, "Statistics | Facts HP Inkjet Printer Cartridge," http://www.inkcanada.ca/2005_09_01_archive.html, accessed June 18, 2008.

50. Theresa Howard, "Being Eco-Friendly Can Pay Economically," *USA Today,* August 15, 2005, http://www.usatoday.com.

51. Statistics Canada, "Study: Organic from Niche to Mainstream," *The Daily,* March 28, 2008.

52. Brian Grow, "The Great Rebate Runaround," *Business Week,* December 5, 2005, pp. 34–

53. Gillian Livingston, "Idea of Storing Nuclear Waste Finds Little Favour in Northern Ontario," Canadian Press NewsWire, Toronto: May 24, 2005.

CHAPTER 4

1. "The Dollars & Sense of Hybrids," *Consumer Reports,* April 2006, http://www.consumerreports.org; Jack Speer, "New Tax Credit Benefits Buyers of Hybrid Cars," **Morning Edition,** National Public Radio, March 10, 2006, **http://www.npr.org**; Chris Birk, "Drivers Devouring Hybrid $$," *(Scranton, PA) Times-Tribune,* March 10, 2006, http://thetimes-tribune.com; *Miguel Llanos, "Consumer Reports Fixes Error on Hybrid Costs," MSNBC, March 9, 2006,* http://www.msnbc.msn.com; "Hybrid Car Buyers to Receive Tax Credits," *USA Today,* December 31, 2005, http://www.usatoday.com.

2. David Baxter, "From Dim Sum to Doughnuts," *Marketing,* June 3, 2002, p. 27; Lou Puim, "How Wal-Mart Learned Diversity," *Marketing,* January 23, 2006, p. 10.

3. Michael Adams, *Fire and Ice* (Toronto: Penguin Canada, 2003); Michael Adams, *Sex in the Snow* (Toronto: Viking, 1997).

4. Adams, *Fire and Ice*; Adams, *Sex in the Snow.*

5. Randall Frost, "Global Packaging: What's the Difference?" Brand channel.com, January 16, 2006, http://www.brandchannel.com.

6. Michael Adams and Jan Kestle, "Neighbourly Rivals," *Marketing,* September 27, 2004, pp. 23–24.

7. Statistics Canada, "Population Projections of Visible Minority Groups, Canada, Provinces and Regions: 2001–2017," Catalogue no. 91-541-XIE.

8. Statistics Canada, "Population Projections of Visible Minority Groups, Canada, Provinces and Regions: 2001–2017."

9. Government of Quebec website, http://www.gouv.qc.ca, accessed July 11, 2005, August 20, 2007.

10. "Cultural Diversity—100,000+ Markets—Percent of Population," *Marketing,* September 23, 2002, http://www.marketingmag.ca, accessed August 20, 2007; "Quebec—Handy Numbers—2007 Edition," http://www.gouv.qc.ca, accessed August 20, 2007.

11. "Quebec—Handy Numbers—2005 Edition."

12. Eric Blais, "The 36 Keys of the Quebecois Revisited," *Marketing,* November 15, 2004, pp. 11–12; Yves Leveille, "What Quebec Wants Now," *Marketing,* June 20, 2005, p. 46; Danny Kucharsky, "Redecorating Quebec's Creative Bedrooms," *Marketing,* February 11, 2002, p. 8.

13. Blais, "The 36 Keys of the Quebecois Revisited"; Leveille, "What Quebec Wants Now"; Kucharsky, "Redecorating Quebec's Creative Bedrooms."

14. "Cultural Diversity—100,000+ Markets—Percent of Population," *Marketing,* September 23, 2002, http://www.marketingmag.ca, accessed August 20, 2007; "Indepth: China: Chinese Immigration," http://www.cbc.ca, accessed July 12, 2005; Statistics Canada, "Population Projections of Visible Minority Groups, Canada, Provinces and Regions: 2001–2017."

15. Don Miller, "Chinese Challenge," *Marketing,* March 13, 2006, p. 24; Rebecca Harris, "Embrace and Prosper," *Marketing,* January 23, 2006, p. 11.

16. Council of Agencies Serving South Asians, "Constructing a Community in Diversity: The South Asian Experience," http://www.cassa.on.ca, accessed July 12, 2005.

17. Chris Daniels, "Shopping Mosaic," *Marketing,* May 17, 2004, pp. 13–15; "Cultural Diversity—100,000+ MarketsPercent of Population"; Eve Lazarus, "Telus Offers Bollywood and Cricket for South Asian Market," *Marketing,* "Marketing Daily," October 31, 2006, http://marketingmag.ca, accessed August 20, 2007.

18. Baxter, "From Dim Sum to Doughnuts"; Jo Marney, "Counting Ethnic Canadians In," *Marketing,* June 4, 2001, p. 24; "Cultural Diversity—100,000+ Markets—Percent of Population."

19. Rebecca A. Clay, "Advertising to Children? Is It Ethical?" *Monitor on Psychology,* February 24, 2006, http://www.apa.org.

20. Trent Edwards, "A Lot Like Lance," *Calgary Herald,* August 11, 2005, http://www.canada.com/calgaryherald.

21. Lesley Young, "Portrait of the New Family," *Marketing,* March 15, 2004, pp. 13–16.

22. Chelsea Emery, "In Terms of Purchasing, It's a Woman's World: Study," Reuters, January 27, 2006, http://news.yahoo.com.

23. Stephanie Thompson, "Hip-Hop Bounces into Toddler Fashions," *Advertising Age,* March 15, 2004, pp. 3, 81; Barbara Lippert, "Her Favorite Things," *Adweek,* March 8, 2004, p. 30; Margaret Hastings, "Empower the Children," *Marketing,* September 26, 2005, p. 16.

24. "Kellogg Pledges Healthier Food, or Fewer Ads to Kids," *Marketing,* June 15, 2007.

25. Gary Levin, "Ad Glut Turns Off Viewers," *USA Today,* October 11, 2005, http://www.usatoday.com.

26. Heather Landy, "Wal-Mart Courts Upscale Shoppers," MiamiHerald.com, March 23, 2006, http://www.miamiherald.com.

27. Eve Lazarus, "Social Shopping," *Marketing,* December 4, 2006, p. 8.

28. These categories were originally suggested in John A. Howard, *Marketing Management: Analysis and Planning* (Homewood, Ill.: Richard D. Irwin, 1963); Henry Assael, "Consumer Behavior and Marketing Action, Kent Publishing Company, 1987, p. 87.

CHAPTER 5

1. The Original Maple Bat Corp. website, http://www.sambat.com, accessed May 10, 2008; Steve Maich, "Big-league Awakening," Macleans.ca, http://www.macleans.ca/topstories/sports/article.jsp?content=20050701_108717_108717, accessed September 4, 2005.

2. Government of Canada website, http://contractscanada.gc.ca/en/how-e.htm, accessed May 9, 2008.

3. Cassandra Kyle, "Hey Ottawa, Let Us in on the Action," *Star-Phoenix* (Saskatoon), October 26, 2007, p. D1.

4. "E-Stats," U.S. Census Bureau, http://www.census.gov/estats, May 11, 2005, accessed March 24, 2006.

5. Nortel website, http://www.nortel.com, accessed May 2, 2006.

6. Allison Enright, "It Takes a Committee to Buy into B-to-B," *Marketing News,* February 15, 2006, pp. 11–13.

7. Jan-Pro website, http://www.jan-pro.com, accessed May 10, 2008.

8. Paulette Thomas, "Manufacturing Your Product," *Startup Journal,* May 16, 2005, http://www.startupjournal.com.

9. "E-Stats," U. S. Census Bureau.

10. Thomas J. Baskind, "Eight Key Steps to Building B2B Major Account Client Alliances," National Business Association, http://www.nationalbusiness.org, accessed March 8, 2006.

11. Marcus Gee, "Looking Beyond America to the Riches of India," *Globe and Mail,* January 16, 2008, p. B10.

12. "RIM Targets Small Firms; Makes Move into Palm's Turf," *Gazette* (Montreal), November 6, 2007, p. B7.

13. Tetra Tech website, http://www.tetratech.com, accessed May 11, 2008.

14. NAICS Association website, http://www.naics.com, accessed May 11, 2008.

15. Akuni Adventures website, http://www.akuni.com, accessed March 8, 2006.

16. Government of Canada, "Satyam Opens a New Development Center in Mississauga," http://investincanada.com/english/view.asp?t=&pid=&x=528&id=66, accessed July 10, 2005.

17. North Hill News website, http://northhillnews.com, accessed May 11, 2008.

18. "Wal-Mart's Children's Miracle Network Campaign Gets Off the Ground in Little Rock," News release, http://walmartstores.com/FactsNews/NewsRoom/8251.aspx, accessed May 11, 2008.

19. Elizabeth Esfahani, "Thinking Locally, Succeeding Globally," *Business 2.0,* December 2005, pp. 96–98.

20. Office Depot website, http://www.officedepot.com, accessed March 10, 2006.

21. Richard Ripley, "Coldwater Fattens up Key Margin," *Journal of Business,* May 5, 2005, p. 1.

22. Karen Mazurkewich, "IT Outsourcing Is Flourishing in India," *Leader Post* (Regina), April 28, 2008, p. D1.

23. Andrea Tan, "Around Asia's Markets: Optimism Returns for Singapore Chip Firm," *International Herald Tribune,* March 7, 2006, http://www.iht.com.

24. "Wal-mart Releases 2008 Annual Report & Proxy to Shareholders," News release, http://www.wal-mart.com, accessed May 12, 2008; "Procter & Gamble Feature," Wal-mart Stores, http://walmartstores.com, accessed March 10, 2006.

25. Xerox website, http://www.xerox.com, accessed March 10, 2006.

26. S. Mitra Kalita, "Hope and Toil at India's Call Centers," *The Washington Post,* December 27, 2005, http://www.washingtonpost.com.

27. Richard J. Newman, "Coming and Going," *U.S. News & World Report,* January 23, 2006, pp. 50–52.

28. Ed Frauenheim, "Report: China's Outsourcing Industry Lags India's," CNet News.com, February 3, 2005, http://www.news.com; Fareed Sakaria, "Does the Future Belong to China?" MSNBC, May 9, 2005, http://www.msnbc.com.

29. Peter Wilson, "Top Russian Outsourcing Company Luxoft Opens Branch Here Offering IT Expertise," *Vancouver Sun,* December 14, 2006, p. C3.

30. Jim Middlemiss, "Law Firms Do the Math; Your Lawyer's Office—Thousands of Miles Away," *National Post,* April 26, 2008, p. FP1.

31. Jim Middlemiss, "Accounting Ripe for Outsourcing," *National Post,* April 26, 2008, p. FP5.

32. Newman, "Coming and Going."

33. Ibid.

34. John W. Miller, "Eastern Europe Becomes Hub for 'Nearshoring' Call-Center Jobs," *The Wall Street Journal,* CareerJournal Europe.com, March 17, 2005, http://www.careerjournaleurope.com.

35. "Signed, Sealed and Procured," CDIT, http://www.cdit.com, accessed March 16, 2006.

36. Chuck MacLean, Purchasing Services, Brock University, personal interview, July 8, 2005.

37. "Flexible Platforms: The Springboard to B2B Success," *Supply Chain Management Review,* http://www.manufacturing.net, accessed March 8, 2006.

38. Office Depot Web site, http://mediarelations.officedepot.com, accessed March 13, 2006; Mike Troy, "Office Depot Shifts Store Expansion to M2 Format," *DSN Retailing Today,* July 24, 2004, accessed at http://www.findarticles.com, March 17, 2006.

39. Chris Daniels, "Closer to You," *Marketing,* September 18, 2006, pp. 22–23.

40. Sumner Lemon, "Chinese Vendors Face Cultural Challenge," *CIO,* May 25, 2005, http://cio-asia.com.

41. Government of Canada, "How the Government of Canada Buys Goods and Services," available http://contractscanada.gc.ca/en/how-e.htm, accessed May 19, 2008.

42. Government of Canada, "What the Government Buys," available http://www.contractscanada.gc.ca/en/what-e.htm, accessed May 19, 2008.

43. MERX website, "About Us," available http://www.merx.com, accessed May 19, 2008.

44. "Interactions with the Pharmaceutical Industry," American College of Physicians, http://ea.acponline.org, accessed March 13, 2006.

45. Greg Burns, "New Doctors Are Allergic to Freebies," *Chicago Tribune,* March 12, 2006, sec. 5, pp. 1, 14.

46. Niagara Public Purchasing Committee website, http://nppc.ca, accessed May 19, 2008.

CHAPTER 6

1. Nokia website, http://www.nokia.com, accessed April 6, 2006; Tom Wright, "Finland Again Ranks First among Global Competitors," *New York Times,* September 29, 2005, http://www.nytimes.com; "Tapping into Good Ideas," *Financial Times,* September 13, 2005, http://www.ft.com; Robert G. Kaiser, "Innovation Gives Finland a Firm Grasp on Its Future," *Washington Post,* July 14, 2005, http://www.washingtonpost.com.

2. Statistics Canada, "Imports, Exports and Trade Balance of Goods on a Balance-of-Payments Basis, By Country or Country Grouping," http://www.statcan.ca, accessed September 8, 2007.

3. Statistics Canada, "Exports of Goods on a Balance-of-Payments Basis By Product," http://www.statcan.ca, accessed September 8, 2007.

4. Nuchhi R. Currier, "World Investment Report 2002: Transnational Corporations and Export Competitiveness," United Nations Chronicle Online Edition, March 2003, http://www.un.org.

5. Statistics Canada, "International Merchandise Trade Annual Review," http://www.statcan.ca, accessed September 8, 2007.

6. Statistics Canada, "Imports, Exports and Trade Balance of Goods on a Balance-of-Payments Basis, By Country or Country Grouping."

7. Jeffrey E. Garten, "Wal-Mart Gives Globalism a Bad Name," *BusinessWeek,* March 8, 2004, p. 24; Ann Zimmerman and Martin Fackler, "Wal-Mart's Foray into Japan Spurs a Retail Upheaval," *Wall Street Journal,* September 19, 2003, pp. A1, A6; Bernard Condon, Michael Freedman, and Naazneen Karmali, "Globetrotter," *Forbes,* April 18, 2005, http://www.forbes.com.

8. "Customer Case Study/Blue Jeans Cable," Paypal website, http://www.paypal.com, accessed March 26, 2006.

9. Statistics Canada, "Employment by Industry," Catalogue no. 71F004XCB; Statistics Canada, "Gross Domestic Product at Basic Prices by Industry," Catalogue no. 15-001-X; http://www.statcan.ca, accessed September 9, 2007.

10. Christine Roy, "The Service Industries and Trade in Services," Statistics Canada, #63F0002XIB, 2001.

11. Statistics Canada, "National Tourism Indicators: Quarterly Estimates Fourth Quarter 2006," Catalogue no. 13-009-XIB; Judy Waytiuk, "Exploring on a Shoestring Budget," *Marketing,* October 23, 2007, pp. 18–19.

12. Statistics Canada, "National Tourism Indicators: Quarterly Estimates Fourth Quarter 2006"; Eve Lazaarus, "Direct Destination," *Marketing,* March 20, 2006, p. 9.

13. Dexter Roberts and David Rocks, "Let a Thousand Brands Bloom," *BusinessWeek,* October 17, 2005, pp. 58–60.

14. Central Intelligence Agency, *World Factbook,* January 10, 2006, http://www.cia.gov.

15. David Cohen, "The Global Reverb of China and India," *BusinessWeek,* February 9, 2006, http://www.businessweek.com.

16. Evan Ramstad and Ken Brown, "China Expands Phone Service Via Internet," *Wall Street Journal,* April 22, 2004, p. B4; Reuters Limited, "Nokia Looks to Dominate Sales in China," Cnet Asia, February 26, 2002, http://www.asia.cnet.com.

17. Philip Bowring, "On Trade, the U.S. and China Need to Go Global," *International Herald Tribune,* March 27, 2006, http://www.iht.com.

18. Colleen Barry, "Euro Currency Begins in Europe," *Mobile Register,* January 1, 2002, p. A11.

19. "Doing Business Abroad," http://www.getcustoms.com, accessed February 19, 2004.

20. Anton Piech, "Speaking in Tongues," *Inc.,* June 2003, p. 50.

21. "Internet Usage Statistics—The Big Picture," Internet World Stats, http://www.internetworldstats.com, accessed December 5, 2005.

22. "European Court Overrules Popular Ban on Genetically Engineered Crops in 164 Regions," Organic Consumers Association, October 5, 2005, http://www.organicconsumers.org.

23. Jan Silva, "Dock Workers Attack EU Building in France," Associated Press, January 16, 2006, http://news.yahoo.com.

24. "ISO 9000 and ISO 14000—in Brief," International Organization for Standardization, http://www.iso.org, accessed March 27, 2006.

25. Canadian Trade Commissioner Service website, http://www.infoexport.gc.ca, accessed November 5, 2007; Team Canada Inc., http://exportsource.ca, accessed November 5, 2007.

26. Free Trade of the Americas, http://www.ftaa-alca.org, November 5, 2007.

27. "Tariffs," http://strategis.ic.gc.ca, accessed September 10, 2007.

28. Canada Gazette website, http://canadagazette.gc.ca, September 10, 2007.

29. Bruce Odessey, "EU Must Cut Farm Tariffs in Trade Talks, United States Insists," Bureau of International Information Programs, U.S. Department of State, December 12, 2005, http://usinfo.state.gov.

30. "WTO Arbitrators Once Again Reject EU's Proposed Banana Import Tariff," *Bridges,* November 2, 2005, http://www.ictsd.org/weekly.

31. Anita Snow, "Cuba to Buy $118 Million in U.S. Food; Total From Trade Round Could Reach $150 Million," Canadian Business Online, http://www.canadianbusiness.com, May 30, 2007, accessed September 12, 2007.

32. Sam Cage, "U.S. Asks WTO to Eye New Airbus Subsidies," ABC News, February 2, 2006, http://abcnews.go.com.

33. Jaksa Kivela, "Doing Business in the People's Republic of China," AllBusiness, May 2005, http://www.allbusiness.com.

34. "WTO Delays Ruling on Canada's Bid for Sanctions on U.S. Exports in Lumber Dispute," *Canadian Business,* June 1, 2005; Michael Tutton, "West Fraser Timber Wins Softwood Case: Panel Tells U.S. to Repay Duties," *Canadian Business,* June 9, 2005.

35. "EU to Act on Asian Shoe Imports," CNN, March 23, 2006, http://www.cnn.com.

36. Eric Wahlgren, "The Outsourcing Dilemma," *Inc.,* April 2004, pp. 41–42; Bruce Nussbaum, "Where Are the Jobs?" *BusinessWeek,* March 22, 2004, pp. 36–48; Stephanie Armour, "Companies Crow about Keeping Jobs in the USA," *USA Today,* March 12, 2004, p. B1; Jesse Drucker, "Global Talk Gets Cheaper," *Wall Street Journal,* March 11, 2004, pp. B1–B2; Scott Thurm, "Lesson in India: Not Every Job Translates Overseas," *Wall Street Journal,* March 3, 2004, pp. A1, A10; Peronet Despeignes, "Poll: Enthusiasm for Free Trade Fades," *USA Today,* February 24, 2004, p. B1; Pete Engardio, "The Future of Outsourcing," *BusinessWeek,* January 30, 2006, pp. 50–58.

37. "Key WTO Members Fail to Plug Gaps in Talks to Promote Doha Round+," TMCnet, March 11, 2006, http://www.tmcnet.com.

38. Steven Chase, "Partners Hold Watershed NAFTA Talks," *Globe and Mail,* March 25, 2006, http://www.theglobeandmail.com.

39. "NAFTA: A Strong Record of Success," Office of the U.S. Trade Representative, March 2006, http://www.ustr.gov.; International Trade Canada, "Overview of the NAFTA," http://www.international.gc.ca, accessed September 13, 2007.

40. Carlos To Echeverria P., "What Is FTAA and What Is Its Current Status?" *Fair Economy,* September 16, 2005, http://www.faireconomy.org. Warren Vieth, "Bush Wins Approval of Trade Pact," *Los Angeles Times,* July 28, 2005, http://www.latimes.com.

41. "European Union Member States," European Union website, http://europa.eu.int, accessed September 13, 2007.

42. "European Union," *World Factbook,* January 10, 2006, http://www.cia.gov.

43. Lara Mills, "Inniskillin Warms to U.S. Icewine Sales," *Marketing,* November 30, 1998, p. 3; Sarah Smith, "Sweet on Icewines," *Marketing,* August 20, 2001, p. 8.

44. "Shaping the Value Chain for Outstanding Performance," PricewaterhouseCoopers survey of 200 leading European businesses.

45. "Grow Your Business," *Entrepreneur,* December 5, 2005, http://www.entrepreneur.com.

46. Ibid.

47. Diana Farrell, "Are You Ready to Go Global?" *Working Knowledge,* Harvard Business School, January 31, 2005, http://hbswk.hbs.edu.

48. "WPT Enterprises, Inc. Announces Results for the First Quarter 2005," http://www.shareholder.com/wpt, accessed March 27, 2006.

49. International Trade Canada, "Opening Doors to the World: Canada's International Market Access Priorities 2006," http://www.international.gc.ca, accessed September 13, 2007.

50. Abe De Ramos, "China's Growing Appetite," *CFO,* November 1, 2005, http://www.cfo.com.

51. "Agency Family Tree 2007," *Marketing,* July 16, 2007, www.marketingmag.ca, accessed September 13, 2007.

52. Louise Lee, Peter Burrows, and Bruce Einhorn, "Dell May Have to Reboot in China," *BusinessWeek,* November 7, 2005, p. 46.

53. Gary Cross, "Japan, the U.S. and the Globalization of Children's Consumer Culture," *Journal of Social History,* Summer 2005, http://www.findarticles.com.

54. Pete Gumber, "Branding America," *Time,* February 20, 2005, http://www.time.com.
55. Daren Fonda, "China's Fast-Moving Vehicles," *Time,* January 16, 2006, pp. 60–61.
56. S. Dinakar, "A Penny a Packet," *Forbes,* November 28, 2005, pp. 186, 188.
57. Robert J. Samuelson, "The Cartel We Love to Hate," *Newsweek,* February 23, 2004, p. 47.
58. "Barter Happenings around the Globe," *BarterNews,* http://www.barternews.com, accessed March 31, 2006.
59. Francine Roy and Clerance Kimanyi, "Canada's Changing Auto Industry," *Canadian Economic Observer,* May 2007, pp. 3.1–3.11.
60. Joe Castaldo, "Is Canada Losing Control?," Canadian Business, May 21, 2007, pp. 24–26; "6 Questions: One-on-one with Deniss Hamilton, President & CEO, ERMS Corp," Canadian Business Online, June 6, 2007, http://www.canadianbusiness.com, accessed September 14, 2007.
61. "Canada's International Investment Position: First Quarter 2007," Statistics Canada, http://www.statcan.ca, accessed September 14, 2007
62. Joe Sharkey, "Change in Rules Ignites Hope for Zippo-Toting Air Travelers," *Ventura County (CA) Star,* August 7, 2005, http://www.venturacountystar.com.

CHAPTER 7

1. David Menzies, "Drink n' Swipe," *Marketing,* September 17, 2007, p. 42; Rebecca Harris, "Kids with Cards," *Marketing,* July 3, 2006, p. 6; Laura Pratt, "Bottom-up Value," *Marketing,* March 7, 2005, p. 17; "Building Loyalty," supplement to *Marketing,* 2006.
2. J. D. Power and Associates website, http://www.jdpower.com, accessed March 17, 2006.
3. Environics Research Group, http://erg.environics.net, accessed July 11, 2008.
4. "Welcome to a New Way of Looking at Nielsen," http://www.nielsenmedia.com, accessed March 17, 2006.
5. Oliver Ryan, "Putting Your Customers to Work," *Fortune,* March 20, 2006, p. 30.
6. Rebecca Harris, "President's Choice Serves Up a Blue Menu," *Marketing Daily,* January 27, 2005.
7. Deborah Ball, "As Chocolate Sags, Cadbury Gambles on a Piece of Gum," *The Wall Street Journal,* January 12, 2006, http://online.wsj.com.
8. Statistics Canada, http://www.statcan.ca, accessed November 17, 2007.
9. Industry Canada, http://strategis.ic.ca, accessed November 17, 2007.
10. Barbara Thau, "Tests Back Wal-Mart's Faith in RFID," *HFN,* November 28, 2005, http://www.hfnmag.com.
11. "Research Distributors," KnowThis.com, http://www.knowthis.com, accessed March 20, 2006.
12. Justin Martin, "Blogging for Dollars," *Fortune,* December 12, 2005, p. S178.
13. "Portable People Meters—A Future-Proof Audience Measurement Solution," Arbitron, http://www.arbitron.com, accessed March 21, 2006; "Wendy's International Selects Arbitron Portable People Meter Radio Ratings Service," Arbitron news release, March 6, 2006.
14. Stuart Elliott, "How to Value Ratings with DVR Delay?" *The New York Times,* February 13, 2006, http://www.nytimes.com.
15. TRU website, http://www.teenresearch.com, accessed March 21, 2006.
16. "Surveys and Non-Response," SuperSurvey Knowledge Base, http://knowledge-base.supersurvey.com, accessed March 21, 2006.
17. Marketing Research and Intelligence Association, http://www.mria-arim.ca/NEWS/DoNotCall.asp, "Support Overwhelming for Do-Not-Call Registry VoxPop Poll Finds," accessed November 24, 2007.
18. "Complying with the Personal Information Protection and Electronic Documents Act," http://www.privcom.gc.ca, accessed November 24, 2007.
19. David Kiley, "Shoot the Focus Group," *BusinessWeek,* November 14, 2005, p. 120.
20. Sonali Desai, "Conducting Multi-Country Focus Group Discussions on the Net," ACNielsen, http://www.acnielsen.com, accessed March 21, 2006.
21. Alex Mindlin, "The Ad-Averse: Finicky and Opinionated," *The New York Times,* October 3, 2005, http://www.nytimes.com.
22. "Online Polling Provides Cost-Effective Local Content," *The Rundown,* August 22, 2005, http://www.tvrundown.com.
23. William M. Bulkeley, "Marketers Scan Blogs for Brand Insights," *The Wall Street Journal,* June 23, 2005, http://online.wsj.com.
24. "Ad Watch Year-End Recap—Part Two," GameDaily, January 9, 2006, http://www.gamedaily.com.
25. Kitty Crider, "Wired Kitchens of Tomorrow Ace Real-Families Test," *Chicago Tribune,* August 7, 2005, p. 6.
26. Industry Canada, http://www.ic.gc.ca, accessed November 24, 2007.
27. Carlos Denton, "Time Differentiates Latino Focus Groups," *Marketing News,* March 15, 2004, p. 52.
28. Todd Wasserman, "Kimberly-Clark Tries Seeing Things from Consumer's POV," *Brandweek,* September 5, 2005, http://www.brandweek.com.
29. Lauren Gibbons Paul, "Ethnography: What Does It Cost?" *CMO,* http://www.cmomagazine.com, accessed March 21, 2006.
30. Brian Bergstein, "Companies Using Tech Analysis on Themselves," Associated Press, August 7, 2005, http://news.yahoo.com.
31. Michael Kahn, "Business Intelligence Software Looks to Future," Reuters Limited, January 15, 2006, http://news.yahoo.com.

CHAPTER 8

1. "American Idol Birthday Party," Amazing Moms.com, http://www.amazingmoms.com, accessed April 12, 2006; "Americanidol.com This Season," March 9, 2006, http://www.americanidol.com; Ann Oldenburg, "Welcome to Idol Nation," *USA Today,* February 13, 2006, http://www.usatoday.com; "American Idol Crushes Grammys in Ratings," MSNBC, February 9, 2006, http://www.msnbc.com; Craig Berman, "American Idol Isn't Kind to Teens," MSNBC, March 30, 3005, http://www.msnbc.com; "Atlanta Ratings Reign for American Idol," Nielsen Media, January 18, 2005, http://www.nielsenmedia.com; "NBC Struggles to Find Olympic Viewers," *Marketing Daily,* February 17, 2006, *Marketing* website, http://www.marketing mag.ca, accessed December 14, 2007; Kerri Tomaino, "Different, Yet the Same," *Marketing,* November 22, 2004, p. 36.
2. Deb Aldridge, "A Healthy Dose of Reality," *Marketing,* May, 10, 2004, p. 24.
3. U.S. Census Bureau, International Database, http://www.census.gov, accessed May 23, 2006; http://www.statscan.ca, accessed December 15, 2007.
4. Statistics Canada, "Population Projections of Visible Minority Groups, Canada, Provinces and Regions; 2001–2017," http://www.statcan.ca, Catalogue no. 91-541-XIE; Rebecca Harris, "The Boomers' Golden Age," *Marketing,* July 12, 2004, p. 14.
5. Rebecca Harris, "Sony Offers Ladies a Night Out," *Marketing Daily,* April 21, 2006.
6. Eve Lazarus, "Mrs. Fix-it," *Marketing,* November 28, 2005, p. 6.
7. Harris, "Sony Offers Ladies a Night Out,"
8. Eve Lazarus, "Aisle Advertising," *Marketing,* May 1, 2006, p. 8.
9. Statistics Canada, "Population of Census Metropolitan Areas (2001 Census boundaries)," http://www40.statcan.ca, accessed December 16, 2007.
10. Statistics Canada, "Population by Year, by Province and Territory," http://www40.statcan.ca, accessed December 16, 2007; "Charlottetown," http:www.city.charlottetown.pe.ca, p. 5, accessed December 16, 2007.
11. International Data Base, U.S. Census Bureau, http://www.census.gov, accessed April 10, 2006.
12. "World City Populations," http://www.world-gazetteer.com, accessed April 10, 2006.
13. "Population and Dwelling Counts," *The Daily,* March 13, 2007, http://www.statcan.ca.
14. "Population and Dwelling Counts," *The Daily,* March 13, 2007, http://www.statcan.ca; Peter Murphy and Henry Puderer, "Census Metropolitan Areas and Census Agglomerations with Census Tracts for the 2001 Census," Statistics Canada publication, catalogue no. 92F0138MIE, no. 2002–1.
15. Pallavi Gogoi, "Meet Jane Geek," *BusinessWeek,* November 23, 2005, http://www.businessweek.com.
16. Michele Gershberg, "Sony Makes Style Pitch to Women for Flat TV," Reuters, September 28, 2005, http://news.yahoo.com.
17. "Household Decision Making Balance of Power," Working Women Online, *Washington Post,* http://www.washingtonpost.com, accessed April 10, 2006.
18. "Report Calls for End to Junk-Food Ads for Kids," *Marketing Daily,* December 7, 2005.
19. Eve Lazarus, "Caboodles Rules," *Marketing,* January 20, 2003, p. 9.
20. "Red Light Web," *Marketing,* September 9, 2002, p. 26.
21. Kelley Lynne Ashton, "Wise to the Game," *Marketing,* August 11, 2003, p. 22.
22. Becky Ebenkamp, "Youth Shall Be Served," *Brandweek,* June 24, 2002, p. 21.
23. Melinda Crowley, "Generation X Speaks Out on Civic Engagement and the Decennial Census," U.S. Census Bureau, http://www.census.gov, accessed May 23, 2006; Kelly Barry, "Young Earners Face Intense Financial Challenge," *USA Today,* January 24, 2006, http://www.usatoday.com.
24. Michael Adams, *Sex in the Snow: Canadian Social Values at the End of the Millennium* (Toronto: Viking, 1997), p. 80.
25. Harris, "The Boomers' Golden Age," Chris Powell, "The Dominant Demo," *Marketing,* June 25, 2007, p. 8.
26. Statistics Canada, http://www.statcan.ca, December 18, 2007.
27. Harris, "The Boomers' Golden Age."
28. Statistics Canada, "Study: Canada's Visible Minority Population in 2017," *The Daily,* March 22, 2005, Statistics Canada website, http://www.statcan.ca, accessed October 22, 2008.
29. Statistics Canada, "Study: Canada's Visible Minority Population in 2017"; Statistics Canada, "Census of Population: Immigration, Birthplace and Birthplace of Parents, Citizenship, Ethnic Origin, Visible Minorities and Aboriginal People," http://www.statcan.ca, January 21, 2003.
30. "The 1940's Landmark Canadian Advertisements," *Marketing,* September 28, 1998.
31. Eric Blais, "The 36 Keys of the Quebecois Revisited," *Marketing,* November 15, 2004, pp. 11–12.
32. Danny Kucharsky, "Quebec, More or Less?," *Marketing,* July 17, 2006, pp. 14–15.
33. Patrick Fong, "Defining the Chinese Market," *Marketing,* June 3, 2002, p. 15; Michael McCullough, "Fireworks Had Died on the Morning of July 1," *Marketing,* September 8, 1997, p. 23.
34. Don Miller, "Chinese Challenge," *Marketing,* March 13, 2006, pp. 24–25.
35. Chris Daniels, "Shopping Mosaic," *Marketing,* May 17, 2004, pp. 13–15.
36. "Births," *The Daily,* July 12, 2005, http://www.statcan.ca, accessed December 18, 2007.
37. Barbara Butrica, Joshua H. Goldwyn, and Richard W. Johnson, "Understanding Expenditure Patterns in Retirement," Urban Institute, January 18, 2005, http://www.urban.org; Rob Gelsbeck, "The New Retirement," *Marketing,* January 16, 2006, p. 4.

38. Statistic Canada, "2001 Census: Marital Status, Common-law Status, Families, Dwellings and Households," http://www.statcan.ca, October 22, 2002; "Household Size, by Province and Territory (2006 Census)," http://www40.statcan.ca, accessed December 19, 2007.

39. "2006 Census: Families, Marital Status, Households and Dwelling Characteristics," *The Daily*, September 12, 2007, http://www.statcan.ca, accessed December 19, 2007; "Selected Trend Data for Canada, 2006, 2001 and 1996 Censuses," http:www12.statcan.ca, accessed December 19, 2007.

40. "2006 Census: Families, Marital Status, Households and Dwelling Characteristics."

41. May Homes and Karen Maser, "Using Median Expenditures: Impact on Household Spending Data," Statistics Canada, Catalogue no. 62F0026MIE.

42. Emily Spensieri, "A Slow, Soft Touch," *Marketing*, June 5, 2006, pp. 15–16.

43. Adams, *Sex in the Snow.*

44. "A Thousand Chinese Desires Bloom," *BusinessWeek*, August 22, 2005, http://www.businessweek.com.

45. Ibid.

46. Mindy Fetterman and Barbara Hansen, "Techies: They're Everywhere," *USA Today*, October 18, 2005, http://www.usatoday.com.

47. Chris Daniels, "Memories of Wal-Mart," *Marketing*, June 13, 2005, p. 9; "The One-Stop Wal-Mart Shoppers vs. The Style-Oriented Target Shoppers," Scarborough Research, September 19, 2005, http://www.scarborough.com.

48. Peter Judge, "iPod Tipped to Boost Apple's Desktop Share," ZDNet UK, March 21, 2005, http://news.zdnet.co.uk.

49. Competition Bureau, http://www.competitionbureau.gc.ca, accessed December 20, 2007.

50. Michel Jensen and Roland van Kralingen, "The End of Traditional Mass Brands," Brandchannel.com, http://www.brandchannel.com, accessed April 12, 2006.

51. Rebecca Harris, "Getting to Know You," *Marketing*, July 3, 2006, pp. 14–15.

52. Michelle Halpern, "Cute, but Scary," *Marketing*, August 9, 2004, pp. 13–15.

53. Theresa Howard, "Ads Take Bite Out of Political Sensitivity," *USA Today*, May 31, 2006, http://www.usatoday.com.

CHAPTER 9

1. Matthew Boyle, "Best Buy's Giant Gamble," CNN Money.com, March 29, 2006, http://money.cnn.com; Nisha Ramachandran, "Best Buy Shapes Up the Big Box," *U.S. News & World Report*, October 17, 2005, pp. 39–41; Don Peppers and Martha Rogers, "Best Buy Counts Customers," CIO, July 1, 2005, http://www.cio.com; "Best Buy's Customer-Centric Model Pays Off," Forbes, June 14, 2005, http://www.forbes.com.

2. Jessica Howell, "OnStar Vehicle Diagnostics," *Road and Travel Magazine*, http://www.roadandtravel.com, accessed April 3, 2006.

3. John Foley, "Selling Soap, Razors—and Collaboration," *InformationWeek*, November 14, 2005, http://www.informationweek.com.

4. Michelle Nichols, "Great Employees Make a Great Business," *BusinessWeek*, March 31, 2006, http://www.businessweek.com.

5. Norma Ramage, "Be Our Guest," *Marketing*, September 10, 2007, p. 6; Norma Ramage, "Taking Ownership," *Marketing*, January 29, 2007, p. 30

6. Jui Chakravorty, "Automakers Extend Deals, Hope Discounts Abate," Reuters, March 3, 2006, http://news.yahoo.com.

7. Carly Mayberry, "MySpace Intent on Staying User-Friendly," Reuters, January 18, 2006, http://news.yahoo.com.

8. chapters.indigo.ca; http://www.chapters.indigo.ca, accessed January 1, 2008.

9. Louise Lee, "Hanging Up on Dell?" *BusinessWeek*, September 30, 2005, http://www.businessweek.com.

10. Rebecca Harris, "Marketing 2.0," *Marketing*, April 30, 2007, pp. 19–24.

11. William M. Bulkeley, "Marketers Scan Blogs for Brand Insights," *Wall Street Journal*, June 25, 2005, http://online.wsj.com.

12. Jill Griffin, "Winning Back 'Lost' Customers," CustomerSat, January 2006, http://www.customersat.com.

13. Hudson Bay Company website; http://www.hbc.com, accessed January 1, 2008.

14. Thomas Hoffman, "Harrah's Bets on Loyalty Program in Caesars Deal," *Computerworld*, June 27, 2005, http://www.computerworld.com.

15. Bank of Montreal website; http://www3.bmo.com, accessed January 1, 2008.

16. WNET New York, http://support.thirteen.org, accessed April 12, 2006.

17. Chris Daniels, "Kings of the Road," *Marketing*, June 25, 2007, pp. 34–35.

18. Randall Frost, "RFID: Beyond the Barcode," Brandchannel.com, January 2, 2006, http://www.brandchannel.com.

19. Matt Stump, "Interactive TV Unchained," *Multichannel News*, October 31, 2005, http://www.multichannel.com.

20. "Donnelly Marketing and Yesmail Chosen by HCI Direct, Inc. to Build Customer Database," CRM Directory.com, February 23, 2006, http://www.crmdirectory.com.

21. "NCO Telecommunications Services," http://www.ncogroup.com, accessed April 3, 2006.

22. "Special Report: Viral Marketing 2006," *Marketing Sherpa*, March 28, 2006, http://www.marketingsherpa.com.

23. Therese Howard, "'Viral' Advertising Spreads through Marketing Plans," *USA Today*, June 23, 2005, http://www.usatoday.com.

24. "Buzz Marketing," CRM.com, http://searchcrm.techtarget.com, accessed April 3, 2006; "What's the Buzz about Buzz Marketing?" Marketing/Wharton, http://knowledge.wharton.upenn.edu, January 12, 2005.

25. Mike Hofman, "Lies, Damn Lies, and Word of Mouth," *Inc.*, April 2006, pp. 25–27.

26. Todd Spangler, "Late Bloomer," *Baseline*, November 8, 2005, http://www.baselinemag.com.

27. Ibid.

28. Michelle Nichols, "A Primer in CRM," *BusinessWeek*, March 17, 2006, http://www.businessweek.com.

29. "Why Is CRM Important," Oracle/Siebel, http://www.siebel.com, accessed April 3, 2006; "Five Benefits of Integrated CRM," Microsoft Dynamics, http://www.microsoft.com, updated November 18, 2005; Kathleen Cholewka, "CRM: The Failures Are Your Fault," *emanager*, January 2002, pp. 23–24.

30. Michael Meltzer, "Getting Started with CRM," *CRM Today*, http://www.crmtoday.com, accessed April 3, 2006.

31. Rashid Khan, "Stop Blaming CRM for Your Customer Service Failures," ContactCenterWorld.com, September 30, 2005, http://www.centerworld.com.

32. Danielle Dunne, "The CRM Backlash," interview with Jill Dyché, *CIO*, http://www.cio.com, accessed April 3, 2006.

33. "Study: Dell Customer Rating Plunges, Apple Leads Pack," IT World.com, August 16, 2005, http://www.itworld.com.

34. "Keeping Customers Happy Keeps Customers," *CRM Buyer*, April 1, 2006, http://www.crmbuyer.com.

35. "Christie Brinkley Returns as Face of CoverGirl," *Promo*, August 23, 2005, http://promomagazine.com.

36. Laura Pratt, "Licence to Shill," *Marketing*, September 10, 2007, pp. 35–37.

37. Adam Goldman, "JetBlue Adds Spa Amenities on Redeyes," Associated Press, April 4, 2006, http://news.yahoo.com.

38. Elliott Ettenberg, "The Church of Harley-Davidson," *Marketing*, July 28, 2003, p. 9; "Automakers Roll Out Concept Cars," *Marketing Daily*, January 10, 2005; Rob Mitchell, "Is Fashion Design a Team Sport?" Brandchannel.com, May 9, 2005, http://www.brandchannel.com; "Building Brand Loyalty: Types of Loyalty Programs," *Marketing*, May 1 2006, pp. 8–11.

39. Matt Semansky, "Outcrop, McDonnell Haynes Partnership to Represent Northern Territories," *Marketing Daily*, June 26, 2006.

40. Eric Puller and Hugh Taylor, "SOA for B2B Commerce," JavaWorld, November 28, 2005, http://www.javaworld.com.

41. "Mosaic Leverages GXS Managed Services to Improve Vendor-Managed Inventory Solutions," Business Wire, September 21, 2005, http://www.businesswire.com.

42. "$2 Billion TruServ Reduces Inventory 41% and Improves Service Level to Above 97% with JDA Portfolio," JDA Software Group, http://www.jda.com, accessed April 4, 2006.

43. "The Perfect Doubles Match: Wimbledon Press Scores with Wireless System from IBM and Cisco," IBM Success Stories, http://www.03.ibm.com, accessed April 4, 2006.

CHAPTER 10

1. Ryan D'Agostino, "Sound Advice," *Money*, February 2006, pp. 139–142; "Is Howard Worth It?" *BusinessWeek*, January 23, 2006, p. 40; Lay Lyman, "Will Stern Push Satellite Radio to Mainstream?" *eCommerce Times*, January 4, 2006, http://www.ecommercetimes.com; Keith Regan, "Sprint Adding Sirius Satellite Radio to Mobile Service," *eCommerce Times*, June 14, 2005, http://www.ecommercetimes.com; David Chilton, "Duelling Signals," *Marketing* January 9, 2006, p. 10; XM Satellite Radio, http://www.xmradio.ca, accessed January 16, 2008; Sirius Satellite Radio, http://www.siriuscanada.ca, accessed January 16, 2008; Future Shop, http://www.futureshop.ca, accessed January 16, 2008

2. Concept first introduced by G. Lynn Shostack, "Breaking Free from Product Marketing," *Journal of Marketing*, April 1977, p. 77; John M. Rathmell, "What Is Meant by Services?" *Journal of Marketing*, October 1980, pp. 32–36.

3. Andrea Jezovit, Marlene Rego, Zena Olijnik, Andy Holloway, and Tom Watson, "The Big 50," *Canadian Business*, May 21, 2007, pp. 28–43.

4. Industry Canada, "Summary of GDP Growth for Goods and Services Producer," http://strategis.ic.gc.ca, accessed January 18, 2008; Industry Canada, "GDP and Growth in Services-Producing Industries," http://strategis.ic.gc.ca, accessed January 18, 2008.

5. Geoffrey York, "Time to Embrace Offshoring: Trade Minister," http://www.vivelecanada.ca, accessed January 20, 2005, p. B1; David Ticcoll, "Offshoring Will Soon Be Making Waves," *Globe and Mail*, February 19, 2004, p. B15; Michelle Conlin, "Call Centers in the Rec Room," *BusinessWeek*, January 23, 2006, http://www.businessweek.com.

6. Anita Manning, "Plugged into Prescription Drugs," *USA Today*, February 14, 2005, http://www.usatoday.com.

7. FlowersCanada.com website, http://www.flowerscanada.com, accessed January 18, 2008.

8. "FTC Releases Grocery Industry Slotting Allowance Report," http://www.ftc.gov, accessed April 24, 2006.

9. Concept introduced by Christopher H. Lovelock, "Classifying Services to Gain Strategic Marketing Insights," *Journal of Marketing*, Summer 1983, p. 10.

10. Michael D. Hutt and Thomas W. Speh, *Business Marketing Management*, eighth edition (Mason, OH: South-Western, 2004).

11. Bose website, http://www.bose.com, accessed April 28, 2006.

12. Cargill site, http://www.cargill.com, accessed January 19, 2008.
13. Staples site, http://www.staples.ca, accessed January 19, 2008.
14. Regus Group website, http://www.regus.com, accessed January 19, 2008.
15. National Quality Institute site, http://wwwnqi.ca, accessed January 19, 2008.
16. International Organization for Standardization website, http://www.iso.org, accessed January 19, 2008.
17. "Improving the Quality Function: Driving Organizational Impact & Efficiency," *Benchmarking Reports,* http://www3.best-in-class.com, accessed May 26, 2006.
18. Angela Kryhul, "The Consumer Connection," *Marketing,* June 5, 2006, pp. 12–13.
19. Dorothy J. Gaiter and John Brecher, "Attention, Wine Shoppers," *SmartMoney,* February 2006, pp. 110–111; Danny Kucharsky, "Guy Mongrain Pitches Good Grocery Wine," *Marketing Daily,* September 18, 2006; Terry Poulton, "Vintage Andy: How Andy Brandt Transformed the LCBO from a Surly Store Chain into the 'Best Retailer of Beverage Alcohol in the World,'" *Strategy,* March 2006, p. 57.
20. "Ralph Lauren Fragrances," Sephora, http://www.sephora.com, accessed April 2006; Rodney Reid, "The New Look of Polo Ralph Lauren," *Viewpoints,* http://www.hs.ttu.edu/viewpoints, accessed April 12, 2006.
21. Roots website, http://www.roots.com, accessed January 20, 2008.
22. Tilley Endurables website, http://www.tilley.com, accessed January 20, 2008.
23. Stampede Park Development site, http://development.calgarystampede.com, accessed January 20, 2008.
24. "New Meter Can Help People with Diabetes," Johnson & Johnson, April 26, 2006, http://www.jnj.com.
25. Canadian Tire site, http://wwwcanadiantire.ca, accessed January 20, 2008.
26. Molson website, http://www.molson.com, accessed January 20, 2008.
27. Bary Alyssa Johnson, "Snowboarders Stay Connected with Wireless Winter Wear," *PC Magazine,* October 28, 2005, http://www.pcmag.com.
28. "Understand CD/DVD Burners," CNet Burner Buying Guide, http://reviews.cnet.com, accessed May 1, 2006.
29. Nestlé site, http://wwwnestle.ca, accessed January 20, 2008.
30. "Big-Screen TVs and What to Watch on Them," *PC World,* April 17, 2006, http://www.pcworld.com.
31. Larry Cantwell, "Tobacco Collectibles are Smokin' at H.S.B.," *St. Louis Post-Dispatch,* September 10, 2005, http://www.stltoday.com.
32. Zippo website, http://www.zippo.com, accessed May 23, 2006; Ellen Neuborne, "Zippo—Inc.com Case Study," *Inc.,* http://www.pf.inc.com/magazine, accessed February 20, 2006.
33. Daniel Yee, "More People Choosing Dance for Exercise," Associated Press, January 26, 2006, http://news.yahoo.com.
34. WD-40 website, http://www.wd40.com, accessed May 23, 2006.
35. 3M website, http://www.3m.com, accessed May 23, 2006.
36. Bruce Horovitz, "In the Newest Snack Packs, Less Is More," *USA Today,* April 23, 2006, http://www.usatoday.com.

CHAPTER 11

1. "Procter & Gamble—Swiffer," Design Continuum, http://www.dcontinuum.com, accessed April 19, 2006; "Swiffer," http://www.pg.com, accessed April 18, 2006; Sarah Lacy, "How P&G Conquered Carpet," BusinessWeek, September 23, 2005, http://www.businessweek.com.
2. Laurie Sullivan, "Retailers Ply Their Own Brands," InformationWeek, April 18, 2006, http://www.informationweek.com.
3. Chris Powell, "Show and Tell," *Marketing,* February 24, 2003, p. 13; Sapna Relan, "Beauty Marks," *Marketing,* June 19, 2006, p. 41.
4. Laurie Sullivan, "Retailers Ply Their Own Brands," *InformationWeek,* April 18, 2006, http://www.informationweek.com.
5. Danny Kucharsky, "Debbie Does Branding," *Marketing,* April 11, 2005, pp. 13–14.
6. Interbrand, "Best Global Brands of 2007," Interbrand website, http://www.interbrand.com, accessed January 26, 2008.
7. Ibid.
8. Young & Rubicam site, http://www.yr.com, accessed January 30, 2008.
9. Alex Taylor III, "Buffing Up a Faded Star," *Fortune,* October 31, 2005, p. 166.
10. "What Is Category Management?" Association for Category Development Professionals, http://www.cpgcatnet.org, accessed February 22, 2006.
11. Ibid.
12. Al Heller, "Consumer-Centric Category Management: A Fresh Spin on Maximizing Performance," *Consumer Insight,* Summer 2005, pp. 6–10.
13. "Category Management," Hershey's Vending Info Center, http://www.hersheys.com, accessed February 22, 2006.
14. "Breakfast of Champions," *Frozen Food Age,* October 2005, http://www.frozenfoodage.com.
15. Elizabeth Levermore, "Light Branding Replaces Labels," *Southland Times* (New Zealand), February 7, 2006, accessed at http://lexis-nexis.com; Julia Moskin, "Tattooed Fruit Is on Way," *New York Times,* July 10, 2005, http://www.nytimes.com; Rachel Yang, "Produce Labels: A Sticky Subject," American Chemical Society, July 5, 2005, http://www.chemistry.org.
16. Industry Canada website, http://strategis.ic.gc.ca, accessed January 30, 2008.
17. Naseem Javed, "The Death of Silly Names," *Marketing,* September 10, 2001, p. 35.
18. Industry Canada website, http://strategis.ic.gc.ca, accessed January 30, 2008.
19. David Goldenberg, "Fresh Breath, Fresher Packaging," CNN Money.com, December 1, 2005, http://money.cnn.com.
20. Competition Bureau, Canada, website, http://www.competitionbureau.gc.ca, accessed January 31, 2008.
21. Health Canada website, http://www.hc-sc.gc.ca, accessed February 1, 2008.
22. Ibid.
23. Stacy Lawrence, "Compliance Lagging for FDA's Bar-Code Mandate," *Baseline,* March 29, 2006, http://www.baselinemag.com.
24. Angela Moore, "Mattel Launches Barbie Clothes for Women," Reuters, October 14, 2005, http://news.yahoo.com.
25. Kenneth Hein, "Living with Your 'Ex': A Brand New World," *Brandweek,* December 5, 2005, pp. 4ff.
26. Constantine von Hoffman, "Overextended," *CMO,* February 2005, http://www.cmomagazine.com.
27. Stephanie Clifford, "Running through the Legs of Goliath," *Inc.,* February 2006, pp. 102–109.
28. Rebecca Harris, "Gotta Be Good," *Marketing,* February 26, 2007, pp. 26–27.
29. Ibid.
30. "Cisco to Pack Retail Shelves," *Red Herring,* January 16, 2006, http://www.redherring.com; Cisco website, http://www.cisco.com, accessed February 2, 2008.
31. Betsy Spethmann, "Schick Revived Quattro with Sampling," *Promo,* December 26, 2005, http://www.promomagazine.com.
32. Lee Walczak and David Welch, "Dream Machines," *BusinessWeek,* January 6, 2006, http://www.businessweek.com.
33. Clifford, "Running through the Legs of Goliath."
34. Ben Elgin, "Managing Google's Idea Factory," *BusinessWeek,* September 26, 2005, http://www.businessweek.com.
35. David Kirkpatrick, "Microsoft's New Brain," CNN Money.com, April 18, 2006, http://money.cnn.com.
36. Dave Carpenter, "Wrigley Looks to Science for Gum Benefits," Associated Press, March 29, 2006, http://news.yahoo.com.
37. Clifford, "Running through the Legs of Goliath."

CHAPTER 12

1. Zappos websites, http://www.zapos.com and http://canada.zappos.com, accessed November 10, 2007; Karla Ward, "High on Heels," Kentucky.com, April 3, 2006, http://kentucky.com; Kimberly Weisul, "A Shine on Their Shoes," *BusinessWeek,* December 5, 2005, pp. 84–85; Brian Moore, "Success Fits Shoe Shipper," *Courier-Journal* (Louisville, KY), February 16, 2005, http://www.courier-journal.com.
2. Louise Lee, "It's Dell vs. the Dell Way," *BusinessWeek,* March 6, 2006, pp. 61–62.
3. Bob Tedeschi, "Where Is Wal-Mart's Fancy Stuff? Try Online," *The New York Times,* http://www.nytimes.com, accessed April 28, 2006.
4. Xerox Canada, "Swarm Installs Edmonton's First Xerox iGen3 to Offer More Flexibility and Higher Digital Print Speeds to Its Customers," Press release, May 16, 2005, http://media.xerox.ca/news/Default.asp?articleID=959, accessed December 3, 2007.
5. Beijo Bags website, http://www.beijobags.com, accessed November 11, 2007; Kimberly L. McCall, "Bags to Riches," *Entrepreneur,* May 2005, http://www.entrepreneur.com.
6. Shoulder Candy website, http://www.shouldercandy.com, accessed September 9, 2008.
7. AAA NewsRoom website, http://www.aaanewsroom.net/Main/Default.asp?CategoryID=4&SubCategoryID=18&ContentID=75, accessed November 11, 2007.
8. Jim Milliott, "Bucking the Odds," *Publishers Weekly,* March 7, 2005, http://www.publishersweekly.com.
9. Ginny Parker, "Vending the Rules," *Time,* May 10, 2006, http://www.time.com.
10. "Key Move: Artful Outsourcing," *Forbes,* March 8, 2006, http://www.forbes.com.
11. Tim Smart, "Allstate Weathers the Storm," *U.S. News & World Report,* January 23, 2006, pp. EE8–EE10.
12. Heba M. Hamouda, "Agreement with Coca-Cola Ends the European Union's Five Year Inquiry into a Potential Abuse of a Dominant Position," Loyola University Chicago School of Law, http://www.luc.edu/law/academics/special/center/antitrust/pdfs/hamouda_cocacola.pdf, accessed November 11, 2007.
13. Allen F. Wysocki, "A Frictionless Marketplace Operating in a World of Extremes," *Choices,* 4th Quarter 2005, pp. 263–91.
14. Wal-Mart website, http://www.walmart.com, accessed June 17, 2006; Dana Flavelle, "Metro Sees Grocery Prices Falling," http://www.thestar.com/Business/article/278822, accessed November 23, 2007; "*Ottawa Citizen*", Foreign Grocers Show Wal-Mart Can Be Beaten," May 20, 2008, p. D.5.
15. Kristin Goff, "Independent Book Stores Cry Foul over Harry Potter Discounting," CanWest News, July 19, 2005, p. 1.
16. Jennifer Barrett, "Can a '50s Icon Do It Again?" *Newsweek,* March 20, 2006, p. E20.
17. "EU Imposes 44.6 pct Anti-Dumping Duty in Imports of China Color TVs," *Forbes,* March 30, 2006, http://www.forbes.com.

18. "Quebec Chocolatier Savours Supreme Court Victory," *National Post,* July 28, 2007, p. FP.6.
19. Tom Blackwell, "Firm Suing Over Fake Diabetes Test Strips; Canadian Denies Knowing They Were Chinese Knock-offs," *National Post,* September 17, 2007, p. A.1.
20. Stuart Wilson, "Samsung Chills Out with Home Appliance Partners," ITP Technology, May 9, 2006, www.itp.net.
21. Industry Canada, "Stat-USA Market Research Reports," http://strategis.ic.gc.ca/epic/internet/inimr-ri.nsf/fr/gr127348f.html, accessed November 24, 2007.
22. Pier 1 Imports website, http://www.pier1.com, accessed May 15, 2006.
23. "Pharmaceutical Firms Look to Logistics Providers, RFID to Manage Shipping of Sensitive Goods," *Manufacturing Business Technology,* September 2007, Vol. 25, No. 9, p. 49.
24. Michael Fitzgerald, "True Believers," *CIO Insight,* December 5, 2005, http://www.cioinsight.com.
25. Mark Long, "RFID Scare Tactics and the Push to Adopt," News Factor Network, January 10, 2006, http://www.newsfactor.com.
26. "MySAP ERP Human Capital management at Dow Corning," SAP, http://www.sap.com, accessed May 15, 2006.
27. Philip Quinn, "Export Firms Facing Rising Costs: Companies Spend More to Expedite Border Clearances," *Vancouver Sun,* October 17, 2006, p. F.11.
28. Thomas A. Foster and Richard Armstrong, "Top 25 Third-Party Logistics Providers: Bigger and Broader," Global Logistics and Supply Chain Strategies, May 1, 2005, http://www.SupplyChainBrain.com, accessed November 24, 2007.
29. "Freight Transportation in a Changing Business Environment," U. S. Department of Transportation, Federal Highway Administration, January 7, 2005, http://ops.fhwa.dot.gov, accessed June 19, 2006.
30. Geoffrey Colvin, "The FedEx Edge," CNN Money.com, March 20, 2006, http://money.cnn.com.
31. Personal correspondence with Mike LoVecchio, Senior Manager, Media Relations, Canadian Pacific Railway, July 4, 2008.
32. Statistics Canada, *Canada Year Book 2007,* Table 30.6, p. 476.
33. Canada Steamship Lines website, http://www.csl.ca, accessed December 1, 2007.
34. Bill Dibenedetto, "Advantage: Vancouver," *Journal of Commerce,* February 19, 2007, p. 1.
35. Statistics Canada, *Canada Year Book 2007,* p. 468.
36. TransCanada Pipelines website, http://www.transcanada.com, accessed December 1, 2007.
37. Enbridge website, http://www.enbridge.com, accessed December 1, 2007.
38. "Logistics Trends: FedEx to handle More Ground Shipments than Air in '05," *Supply & Demand Chain Executive,* May 23, 2005, http://www.sdcexec.com.
39. Purolator Courier website, http://www.purolator.com, accessed December 1, 2007.
40. Atlas Cold Storage website, http://www.atlascold.com, accessed December 1, 2007.
41. "Wal-Mart Reshapes the Retail World," *Forbes,* January 24, 2006, http://moneycentral.msn.com.
42. "New Parts Distribution Centre to Be Opened by Pratt & Whitney Canada in Singapore," *Airline Industry Information,* May 23, 2007, p. 1.
43. Kimberly-Clark website, http://www.kimberly-clark.com, accessed June 20, 2006; "Pampers Out, Huggies In at Some Costcos," *Promo,* June 16, 2005, http://promomagazine.com.
44. Gary Gentile, "Fox to Offer Movies Online via Movielink," Associated Press, November 21, 2005, http://news.yahoo.com.
45. Aida Edemariam, "Wings of Desire," *The Guardian,* February 23, 2006, http://www.guardian.co.uk.
46. McDonald's website, http://www.mcdonalds.com, accessed June 20, 2006; Nichola Groom, "McDonald's Touts Quality in Ad Campaign," Reuters, October 24, 2005, http://news.yahoo.com.

CHAPTER 13

1. The Forzani Group 2007 Annual Report; The Forzani Group website, http://www.forzanigroup.com, accessed December 9, 2007;
2. Canadian Tire 2006 Annual Report; Hollie Shaw, "Camisoles & Cabbages," *National Post,* April 22, 2006, p. FP.1.
3. Angela Kryhul, "A Time for Reinvention," *Marketing,* January 15, 2007, p. 13.
4. Dean Foust, "A Sister Act That's Wowing Them," *BusinessWeek,* March 13, 2006, pp. 84–86.
5. K. Sudhir and Vithala R. Rao, "Are Slotting Allowances Efficiency-Enhancing or Anti-Competitive?" Yale School of Management, http://mba.yale.edu, accessed May 3, 2006.
6. Canadian Tire website, http://www.canadiantire.ca, accessed October 10, 2007.
7. Michelle Magnan, "As Good As It Gets?" *Profit,* March 2007, pp. 44–49.
8. Sears Canada 2006 Annual Report.
9. Eve Lazarus, "Main Street Malls," *Marketing,* April 3, 2006, pp. 11–12.
10. Parija Bhatnagar, "Not a Mall, It's a Lifestyle Center," CNN Money.com, January 12, 2005, http://money.cnn.com.
11. Helga Loverseed, "Quebec Mall Puts West Edmonton on Notice," *Globe and Mail,* October 9, 2007, p. B.9; Hollie Shaw, "Mega-mall for Mirabel?" *National Post,* August 27, 2005, p. FP.1.
12. Emma Hall and Normandy Madden, "IKEA Courts Buyers with Offbeat Ideas," *Advertising Age,* April 12, 2002, p. 10.

13. Rana Foroohar, "A New Fashion Frontier," *Newsweek,* March 20, 2006, accessed at MSNBC, http://www.msnbc.msn.com.
14. Claire Schooley, "Retailers Adopt eLearning to Groom Smarter Store Associates," Forrester Research, http://www.forrester.com, accessed May 4, 2006; "Exclusive Interview with Mr. Frank Russell, CEO and President, Geolearning, Inc.," Distance-Educator.com, February 28, 2005, http://www.distance-educator.com.
15. Ian Austen, "Northern Overexposure," *The New York Times,* September 8, 2007, http://www.nytimes.com/2007/09/08/business/worldbusiness/08doughnuts.html; Paul D. House, Presentation at Brock University, September 14, 2007.
16. Canadian Tire website, http://www.canadiantire.ca, accessed October 10, 2007.
17. Retail Council of Canada, "2005/2006 Federal Pre-Budget Submission Profile of the Retail Industry," http://www.retailcouncil.org/membersonly/submissions/budgets/prebudget_federal05/profile.asp, accessed April 28, 2005.
18. Georgia Flight, "Whole Fuels," *Business 2.0,* December 2005, p. 78.
19. Mike Troy, "A Force Even Category Killers Can't Catch," *DSN Retailing Today,* June 9, 2003, p. 77.
20. Chris Daniels, "The Dawn of a New Bay," *Marketing,* April 30, 2007, pp. 39–42.
21. Carrefour website, http://www.carrefour.com/cdc/group/our-business/our-stores/our-stores-folder/hypermarket.html, accessed October 13, 2007.
22. Hollie Shaw, "Camisoles & Cabbages," *National Post,* April 27, 2006, p. FP.1.
23. Dominion Citrus website, http://www.dominioncitrus.com, accessed October 20, 2007.
24. Tenaquip Industrial Distribution website, http://www.tenaquip.com, accessed October 20, 2007.
25. Craig Shutko, "Uponor Canada Knows What It Takes to Provide Quality," *Leader Post* (Regina), August 30, 2007, p. E.5.
26. Michelle Warren, "Counting on Catalogues," *Marketing,* March 6, 2006, pp. 11–13.
27. Canadian Tire Corporation website, http://www2.canadiantire.ca, accessed October 21, 2007.
28. Office Depot website, http://www.officedepot.com, accessed October 21, 2007.
29. "Sales Size of Establishments for the United States—Vending Machine Operators," *Retail Trade—Subject Series,* U.S. Census Bureau Economic Census, http://www.census.gov, accessed May 4, 2006.
30. Victor Mihailescu, "iPod Vending Stations Are a Great Success," Softpedia, April 10, 2006, http://news.softpedia.com.

CHAPTER 14

1. Cliff Peale, "P&G Angles for Fusion Razor," *(Cincinnati, OH) Enquirer,* February 8, 2006, http://news.enquirer.com; Jenn Abelson, "For Fusion, Gillette Plans a Super Bowl Blitz," *Boston Globe,* January 27, 2006, http://www.boston.com; Claudia Deutsch, "Can a Razor Ever Have Enough Blades?" *The New York Times,* January 27, 2006, http://www.nytimes.com; William C. Symonds, "Gillette's Five-Blade Wonder," *BusinessWeek,* September 15, 2005, http://www.businessweek.com; Rebecca Harris, "Innovation Overload," *Marketing,* October 2, 2006, p. 8; "Gillette and Schick Settle Blade Dispute," *Marketing,* February 21, 2006.
2. Julie Bosman, "If It's after Midnight, Then It's Time to Market to Young Men," *The New York Times,* November 28, 2005, http://www.nytimes.com.
3. Chris Powell, "Spending Shift," *Marketing,* January 15, 2007, p. 10.
4. Michael Fielding, "Global Insights," *Marketing News,* May 15, 2006, pp. 41–42.
5. Rebecca Harris, "Breakfast for Dummies," *Marketing,* January 30, 2006, p. 5.
6. Fiona Torrance, "comScore: World Cup Web Analysis," iMedia Connection, May 31, 2006, http://www.imediaconnection.com.
7. Paul Majendie, "Fanboys and Overdogs Muscling into English Language," Reuters, October 24, 2005, http://news.yahoo.com.
8. Rebecca Harris, "Passport Promotions," *Marketing,* February 12, 2007, p. 6.
9. Laura Petrecca, "Movie Promotions Get Smaller to Reach Bigger Audience," *USA Today,* May 15, 2006, http://www.usatoday.com.
10. Reebok website, http://www.reebok.com, accessed June 6, 2006; Michael McCarthy, "New Theme for Reebok," *USA Today,* February 10, 2005, http://www.usatoday.com.
11. Steve McKee, "Five Words to Never Use in an Ad," *BusinessWeek,* June 7, 2006, http://www.businessweek.com.
12. Tim Hortons website, http://www.timhortons.com, accessed February 10, 2008.
13. Gary Gentile, "Products Placed Liberally in Video Games," Associated Press, May 22, 2005, http://news.yahoo.com.
14. Gail Schiller, "Brave New World for Summer Tie-Ins," Reuters, May 30, 2006, http://news.yahoo.com.
15. Sarah Dobson, "Petro-Canada Pumps Out Straight Talk on Gas Prices," *Marketing,* August 2, 2006.
16. Eve Lazarua, "Fiscally Fun," *Marketing,* July 16, 2007, p. 12.
17. "Canada's Top Marketers 2007," *Marketing,* November 26, 2007, pp. 18–29.
18. "Sponsorship," Cascade Bicycle Club, http://www.cascade.org, accessed May 6, 2006.
19. "Dale Jr. to Race Vintage Earnhardt Paint Scheme on Father's Day," Anheuser-Busch, May 31, 2006, http://www.anheuser-busch.com.
20. Avon Foundation, http://www.avonfoundation.org, accessed June 9, 2006.
21. Tim Hortons website, http://www.timhortons.com, accessed February 12, 2008.

22. Doreen Carvajal, "Can't Tell the Sponsors without a Scorecard," *International Herald Tribune,* May 31, 2006, http://www.iht.com.
23. "Institute of Communication Agencies/Canada Post Survey of Marketing Budgets," Institute of Communications Agencies website, http://www.ica.com, accessed February 12, 2008.
24. Eve Lazarus, "Direct Destination," *Marketing,* March 20, 2006, p. 9.
25. "The Countdown Continues," *Canadian Business,* September 15, 2003.
26. Nik Nanos, "Calling Consumers," *Marketing,* March 26, 2007, p. 13.
27. Canadian Marketing Association website; http://www.the-cma.org, accessed February 13, 2008; Bell Canada website, http://www.bell.ca, accessed February 13, 2008; Nik Nanos, "Calling Consumers," *Marketing,* March 26, 2007, p. 13.
28. Sarah Dobson, "Internet Leads Global Ad Spend Growth," *Marketing,* June 12, 2006.
29. Kevin J. Delaney, "Once-Wary Industry Giants Embrace Internet Advertising," *The Wall Street Journal,* April 17, 2006, http://online.wsj.com.
30. "Cellphones Will Have Direct Link to Google," *Marketing,* January 6, 2006; Matt Semansky, "Sportsnet Forms Interactive Lynk With Fans," *Marketing,* June 19, 2006; Annette Antoniak and Paul Welsh, "Logging for Gold," *Marketing,* May 1, 2006, p. 32.
31. Paul Ferriss, "Green Means Go," *Marketing,* February 11, 2008, pp. 13–16.
32. ZenithOptimedia website, http://www.zenithoptimedia.com, accessed February 15, 2008.
33. Kathleen M. Joyce, "Higher Gear," *Promo,* April 1, 2006, http://promomagazine.com.
34. Mothers Against Drunk Driving website, http://www.madd.ca, accessed February 15, 2008.
35. Chris Daniels, "MBS Keeps Ontario Media," *Marketing,* April 7, 2003, p. 1; David Menzies, "Scratch and Lose," *Marketing,* May 14, 2007, p.14.

CHAPTER 15

1. Gabriel Kahn, "Tiger's New Threads," *The Wall Street Journal,* March 26, 2004, p. B1; "McDonald's Goes Supersize with Yao," *USA Today,* February 13, 2004, p. C23; Rich Thomaselli, "Nike Bets Big on Range of Endorsers," *Advertising Age,* January 5, 2004, p. 8; Stephanie Kang, "Postgame Strategy," *The Wall Street Journal,* November 11, 2003, pp. B1, B5; Harry R. Weber, "LeBron James Replaces Kobe in Sprite Ads," *Marketing News,* September 15, 2003, p. 28; Kenneth Hein, "A Broken Field of Marketing Dreams," *Brandweek,* July 14, 2003, p. 6; Richard O'Brien and Mark Bechtel, "James and the Giant Deal," *Sports Illustrated,* June 2, 2003, p. 23; Astrid Van Den Broek, "Athletic Endorsements With Equity," *Marketing,* March 29, 1999; Lara Mills, "Campaigns With Legs," *Marketing,* May 15, 2000, p. 12; "Nike Co-Founder Phil Knight Resigns as President and CEO," *Marketing Daily,* November 22, 2004; Ron Telpner, "Think Inside the Box," *Marketing,* October 15, 2007, p. 64; Michelle Halpern, "Hollywood's Next Close-up," *Marketing,* June 12, 2006, pp. 11–13.
2. Dorothy Pomerantz, "Coming Distractions," *Forbes,* June 10, 2002, p. 50.
3. "AdWeek Ranks Top Celebrity Advertising Earners," *AdRants,* April 2006, http://www.adrants.com.
4. "Top 25 Global Marketers," *FactPack2006* (special supplement to *Advertising Age*), February 27, 2006, p. 15.
5. Angela Kryhul, "Opportunites Everywhere," *Marketing,* January 15, 2007, pp. 16–19.
6. Theresa Howard, "Food, Beverage Marketers Seek Healthier Images," *USA Today,* April 20, 2006, http://www.usatoday.com.
7. Robert Berner, "Detergent Can Be So Much More," *BusinessWeek,* May 1, 2006, p. 66.
8. Barbara Wall, "Celebrity Cachet Has Firms Banking on What's in a Name," *International Herald Tribune,* May 12, 2006, http://www.iht.com; Eric Engleman, "Ichiro Inc: The M's True Impact Player," *Puget Sound Business Journal,* February 28, 2005, http://seattle.bizjournals.com.
9. "Oprah Tops Powerful Celebs List," CBS News, June 17, 2005, http://www.cbsnews.com.
10. Mills, "Campaigns With Legs."
11. "Golfer Michelle Wie, 15, Turns Pro," CBS News, October 5, 2005, http://www.cbsnews.com; John Hawkins, "Wie to Turn Professional before 16th Birthday," ESPN, September 12, 2005, http://sports.espn.go.com.
12. Chris Powell, "Spending Shift," *Marketing,* January 15, 2007, p. 10.
13. Jeromy Lloyd, Rebecca Harris, Chris Powell, and David Brown, "Picks and Pans," *Marketing,* December 24, 2007, p. 33.
14. "Emotional, Not Factual, Ads Win Skeptical Consumers, Study Shows," *Medical News Today,* August 16, 2005, http://www.medicalnewstoday.com.
15. Terence A. Shimp, *Advertising, Promotion, and Supplemental Aspects of Integrated Marketing Communications,* 6th ed. (Mason, OH: South-Western, 2003), pp. 306–309.
16. Suzanne Vranica and Brian Steinberg, "Ads Reach for 'Reality,'" *The Wall Street Journal,* December 21, 2005, http://online.wsj.com.
17. Sarah Boxer, "Got Wit? Make It Visual in Ads Online," *The New York Times,* October 3, 2005, http://www.nytimes.com.
18. Julie Bosman, "Hey, Kid, You Want to Buy a Toyota Scion?" *The New York Times,* June 14, 2006, p. C2; Yuki Noguchi, "Advertisers Push Deeper into Online Games," *Washington Post,* April 27, 2006, http://www.washingtonpost.com.
19. Allison Linn, "Microsoft Plans Launch of Search Ad System," Associated Press, January 13, 2006, http://news.yahoo.com.
20. "Interstitials," *AdLink,* http://www.adlink.com, accessed May 30, 2006.
21. Brad Stone, "The Web: Are We Nearing the End of Pop-Up Ads?" *Newsweek,* April 17, 2006, http://www.msnbc.msn.com.
22. "Who Is Responsible for Adware?" *The Wall Street Journal,* April 12, 2006, http://online.wsj.com.
23. Powell, "Spending Shift."
24. Jenn Abelson, "And Now, a Few (More) Words from Our (One) Sponsor," *Boston Globe,* October 24, 2005, http://www.boston.com.
25. Gina Piccalo, "TiVo Will No Longer Skip Past Advertisers," *Los Angeles Times,* November 17, 2005, http://www.latimes.com.
26. Jack Neff, "The TIVO Effect," *Marketing,* April 14, 2008, p. 16.
27. Powell, "Spending Shift."
28. Olga Khariff, "Coming Soon to XM: More Commercials," *BusinessWeek,* April 13, 2006, http://www.businessweek.com; "The Battle for America's Ears Has Begun," About.com, http://stereos.about.com, accessed May 30, 2006.
29. Powell, "Spending Shift."
30. "Consumers, Media & U.S. Newspapers," Readership Institute, Media Management Center at Northwestern University, http://www.readership.org, accessed June 16, 2006.
31. Paul Brent, "The Evolving Newspaper," *Marketing,* March 24, 2008, pp. 42–43.
32. Chris Powell, "Generation Yapper," *Marketing,* December 10, 2007, p. 14.
33. Powell, "Spending Shift."
34. Out-Of-Home Data Sources, *Marketing,* September 23, 2002.
35. Powell, "Spending Shift."
36. Anick Jesdanun, "Online Ad Revenues Grow for 3rd Yr. in Row," Associated Press, April 20, 2006, http://news.yahoo.com.
37. David Kiley, "Call It a Sell Phone," *BusinessWeek,* April 3, 2006, p. 55.
38. Matt Richtel, "Marketers Interested in Small Screen," *The New York Times,* January 16, 2006, http://www.nytimes.com.
39. Matt Semansky, "Virgin Mobile Introduces Ad-Supported Cell Service," *Marketing,* May 30, 2006.
40. Chris Daniels, "Movie Mogul," *Marketing,* January 28, 2008, pp. 32–34.
41. "World's Top 10 Core Agency Brands," *FactPack2006,* February 27, 2006, p. 41.
42. Michael Barbaro, "Wal-Mart Enlists Bloggers in P.R. Campaign," *The New York Times,* March 7, 2006, http://www.nytimes.com; Chuck Bartels, "Wal-Mart's CEO on Offensive against Critics," Associated Press, January 13, 2005, http://story.news.yahoo.com.
43. Bill Berkrot, "CDC Report Supports Bausch & Lomb Recall," Reuters, May 19, 2006, http://news.yahoo.com.
44. Eve Lazarus, "The Tao of Lululemon," *Marketing,* April 14, 2008, pp. 22–27.
45. Sue Marek, "Ringing in the New Year," *Wireless Week,* January 1, 2006, http://www.wirelessweek.com.
46. Decision Analyst website, http://www.decisionanalyst.com, accessed May 31, 2006.
47. Advertising Standards Canada website, http://www.adstandards.com, accessed April 14, 2008.

CHAPTER 16

1. Interviews with Alex Pettes, president, TFI Food Solutions, 2007–2008.
2. Barry Farber, "Star Qualities," *Entrepreneur,* May 2006, http://www.entrepreneur.com.
3. Eric Beauchesne, "Canada a World Leader in Skills Shortfall: Two Out of Three Employers Can't Fill Positions," *Edmonton Journal,* February 21, 2006, p. F1.
4. "Popular 'Ladies Night Out' Returns to the Sony Store," Canada News Wire, April 20, 2006. ProQuest document 1087702941, downloaded August 19, 2007.
5. "Annoying Quotes from Sales Clerks Listed," Associated Press, October 25, 2005, http://news.yahoo.com.
6. Tenille Bonoguore, "The End of Unwanted Telemarketing… Almost," *Globe and Mail,* http://www.globeandmail.com, accessed July 3, 2007.
7. Brian Burnsed, "Phonies: Slipping Past the Call Watchdogs," *BusinessWeek,* September 10, 2007, p. 14.
8. Grant Robertson, "More Junk Mail? Printer Hopes So," *Globe and Mail,* August 22, 2007, p. B1.
9. Larry Kusch, "Call Centre Rings Up Jobs," *Winnipeg Free Press,* August 25, 2006, p. B.4; David Shipley, "Ringing in Era of Stability: Employment Province's Call-centre Industry Reaches State of High-tech Maturity," *New Brunswick Telegraph Journal,* June 4, 2007, p. A1.
10. Marcus Gee, "Moving On Up in the Outsourcing World," *Globe and Mail,* September 26, 2007, p. B.12.
11. Ibid.
12. Jim Domanski, personal correspondence, February 21, 2004.
13. Eleanor Laise and William Mauldin, "Hook the Right Broker," Smart Money.com, August 1, 2005, http://www.smartmoney.com.
14. Carol Matlack, "An Airline with a Deafening Roar," *BusinessWeek,* March 27, 2006, p. 46.
15. Chris Taylor, "Changing Gears," *Sales & Marketing Management,* October 2005, p. xx.
16. "MacMahon Worldwide/SalesConference.Net," Groove Networks, http://www.groove.net, accessed June 23, 2006.
17. "Opportunity Knocked," *National Post Business,* November 2003, pp. 34–40.
18. Newell Rubbermaid website, http://newellrubbermaid.com, accessed June 23, 2006.

19. Barry Farber, "Break on Through," *Entrepreneur,* March 2006, http://www.entrepreneur.com.
20. Ibid.; Paul Kaihla, "Firing Up Your Cold Calls," *Business 2.0,* December 2005, pp. 60–65.
21. Kristin Zhivago, "The Tools Your Sellers Need from Your Website," *Revenue Journal,* May 25, 2006, http://www.revenuejournal.com.
22. Steven J. Schwartz, *How to Make Hot Cold Calls,* revised edition (Markham, ON: Fitzhenry and Whiteside, 2005).
23. Black and Decker website, http://blackanddecker.com, accessed June 23, 2006.
24. Rick Kang, "Management by Defiance," *Profit,* June 1999, pp. 63–64.
25. Barry Farber, "Hanging Tough," *Entrepreneur,* April 2006, http://www.entrepreneur.com.
26. Michelle Nichols, "A Hands-On Guide to Staying in Touch," *BusinessWeek,* October 7, 2005, http://www.businessweek.com.
27. "The Livermore Way at HP," *BusinessWeek,* January 30, 2006, http://www.businessweek.com.
28. Harvey Schachter, "The 21st Century CEO," *Profit,* April 1999, pp. 25–34.
29. *Occupational Outlook Handbook.*
30. Lesley Kump, "Teaching the Teachers," *Forbes,* December 12, 2005.
31. Julia Chang, "Ultimate Motivation Guide: Happy Sales Force, Happy Returns," *Sales & Marketing Management,* March 2006, http://www.salesandmarketing.com.
32. Maritz Canada, http://maritzcanada.com, accessed August 19, 2006.
33. Melanie Chambers, "What's Driving Sales?" *Contact,* April 2006, p. 26.
34. Brett Ruffell, "The 2006 Salary Report," *Contact,* December 2006, pp. 18–24.
35. Frank Bucaro, "Sales Ethics: Oxymoron or Opportunity?" *Negotiator Magazine,* http://www.negotiatormagazine.com, accessed June 23, 2006.
36. Eric Auchard, "Skype Launches Free Call Promotion in U.S., Canada," Reuters, May 15, 2006, http://news.yahoo.com.
37. Ken Burke, "Get with the Loyalty Program," *Multichannel Merchant,* May 1, 2006, http://multichannelmerchant.com.
38. "Coupon Fact Sheet for the Year 2006—Coupon Use in Canada," Coupon Industry Association of Canada, http://couponscanada.org/html/couponing_facts.html, accessed September 23, 2007.
39. Ibid.
40. Rebecca Harris, "Getting to Know You," *Marketing,* July 3–10, 2006, pp. 14–15.
41. Mike Mulligan, "Visibility Cloaks," *Marketing,* June 26, 2006, p. 13.
42. Rebecca Harris, "Buzz Boosts Brands," *Marketing,* February 26, 2007, p. 28.
43. Amy Johannes, "Playing the Game," *Promo,* April 1, 2006, http://promomagazine.com.
44. Mark Freed, "Trinkets to Treasure," *Marketing,* May 8, 2006, p. 8.
45. Mario Toneguzzi, "Calgary Promo Show Highlights Evolution of Corporate Gifts; Billion-Dollar Industry No Longer Simply Ball Caps, Pens," *Calgary Herald,* September 11, 2007, p. D1.
46. Ibid.
47. Ben Gelinas, "Teen Girls on Mission to BLAST Tobacco Powerwalls from Stores," *Edmonton Journal,* March 11, 2006, p. B3.
48. Canadian Gift & Tableware Association website, http://www.cgta.org, accessed September 23, 2007.
49. "InterContinental Hotel's Customer Loyalty Program, Priority Club, Now Provides Free Nights at Competitors' Hotels," *Hotel Online,* June 18, 2005, http://hotel-online.com.

CHAPTER 17

1. Personal correspondence from Cristina Lopes and Louise Ruggiero, February 2008; Toronto Real Estate board website, "Hobbit-sized House Fits the Bill," *Ottawa Citizen,* April 16, 2007, p. A3; Claire Sibonney, "Toronto's Tiniest House on the Market Again," *Times–Colonist,* Victoria, B.C., December 22, 2007, p. D8; http://www.torontorealestateboard.com/consumer_info/market_news/mw2007/pdf/mw0712.pdf, accessed February 10, 2008.
2. "Canada and EU Hit U.S. with Retaliatory Tariffs," *International Herald Tribune,* May 2, 2005, http://www.iht.com.
3. Ben Charny, "Net Telephone Fees Have Users Fuming," CNet News, January 27, 2005, http://news.com.com.
4. Neil Scott, "SaskTel to Fight Class-action Suit over Cell Charges," *Vancouver Sun,* September 21, 2007, p. C2.
5. Competition Bureau Canada, "Law & Litigation—About the Acts," http://www.competitionbureau.gc.ca, accessed February 17, 2008.
6. *Competition Law* (North York, ON: CCH Canadian Limited, 1995), p. 4202.
7. "Price-fixing Is Bad No Matter Who Does It," *The Gazette* (Montreal), July 23, 2008, p. A18.
8. "British and Korean Airlines Each Fined $300 Million," *Times-Colonist* (Victoria, B.C.), August 24, 2007, p. D7; "Qantas to Plead Guilty to Price Fixing," *National Post,* November 28, 2007, p. FP18; Huw Jones, "Airlines Charged with Price-fixing; Major European Carriers among Those Affected," *The Gazette* (Montreal), December 22, 2007, p. C5; "Air Canada Included in EC Price-fixing Probe," *Globe and Mail,* December 26, 2007, p. B2.
9. Matthew Newman, "Videotape Makers Fined $110.5 Million for Price-fixing," *Ottawa Citizen,* November 21, 2007, p. D5.
10. Thomas Claridge, "Four Convicted of Rigging Bids," *Globe and Mail,* December 20, 1997, p. B5.
11. "Japan: Errant Fax Reveals Firms' Price-fixing Scam," *Ottawa Citizen,* November 10, 2007, p. A10.
12. "Drug Maker Hit with 'Predatory' Prices Penalty," *Toronto Star,* March 15, 2007, p. C2.
13. "Airline Ticket Advertisers Targeted over False Claims," *Globe and Mail,* November 15, 2007, p. B14.
14. "Retailer Carrefour Fined $2.88 Million for False Ads," *Toronto Star,* June 27, 2007, p. B2.
15. Industry Canada, "Premier Health Club Found Guilty of Misleading Advertising Under the Competition Act," News release, April 19, 2005, http://www.ic.gc.ca/, accessed May 27, 2005; Mitch Moxley, "GoodLife to Pay $75,000 for Misleading Advertising," *National Post,* February 10, 2005, p. FP5.
16. Brent Jang, "Airlines Want to Help You Help Yourself—By Having You Check Your Own Bags," *Globe and Mail,* December 27, 2007, p. A1.
17. Jefferson Graham, "Apple Rolls Out $69 iPods, New Showtime Downloads," *USA Today,* February 8, 2006, http://www.usatoday.com; Apple Canada website, http://www.apple.com/ca, accessed February 17, 2008.
18. Robert D. Buzzell and Frederick D. Wiersema, "Successful Share Building Strategies," *Harvard Business Review,* January-February 1981, pp. 135–44.
19. Ben Patterson, "Prepaid Primer: The What, Why, and How of Prepaid Cell Phones," CNet Networks, April 18, 2006, http://reviews.cnet.com.
20. Campers Village website, http://www.campers-village.com/CVwhatis.html, accessed February 17, 2008.
21. Statistics Canada, *Canada Year Book 2007,* p. 170; "Canada Regains No. 2 Spot for Oil to U.S.," *Calgary Herald,* August 25, 2007, p. C4.
22. "Edmonton Refinery Fire May Spark Gas Price Hike," *Calgary Herald,* March 8, 2007, p. A.1; Ray Turchansky, "Business Leaders Buck Consensus That Price of Oil Headed Higher," *Edmonton Journal,* August 11, 2007, p. F6.
23. Paul Byrne, "The Big Three Focus on Large Family Sedans: The Chevrolet Impala, Chrysler 300 Touring and Ford Taurus," *The Gazette* (Montreal), September 12, 2007, p. E5.
24. Susan Chandler, Kevin Pang, and Robin Jenkins, "The Oil Squeeze," *Chicago Tribune,* April 23, 2006, pp. 1, 20.
25. Norma Ramage, "Be Our Guest," *Marketing,* September 10, 2007, p. 6.
26. "Zimbabwe's Inflation Steams Ahead," BBC News, June 9, 2006, http://news.bbc.co.uk; Michael Wines, "How Bad Is Inflation in Zimbabwe?" The *New York Times,* May 2, 2006, http://www.nytimes.com.
27. Poornima Gupta, "Ford Posts Unexpected Loss," Reuters, July 20, 2006, http://news.yahoo.com.
28. Sue-Ellen Boyes, ed. *Shaw Festival 08,* program brochure; Stratford Shakespeare Festival website, http://www.stratfordfestival.ca/, accessed February 17, 2008.
29. James L. McKenney, *Stouffer Yield Management System,* Harvard Business School Case 9-190-193 (Boston: Harvard Business School, 1994); Anirudh Dhebar and Adam Brandenburger, *American Airlines, Inc.: Revenue Management,* Harvard Business School Case 9-190-029 (Boston: Harvard Business School, 1992).
30. "Europe's Merger Wave," *The Economist,* March 14, 2006, http://www.economist.com; Peter Gumbel, "It's High Time for Mixing Brands," *Time,* December 31, 2005, http://www.time.com.
31. "Breaking News: New ACNielsen Survey Points to Price Convergence in Europe Since the Introduction of the Euro," ACNielsen news release, September 2005, http://www.acnielsen.co.uk.
32. Parija Bhatnaqar, "Wal-Mart's Challenge in China," CNN Money, January 12, 2006, http://money.cnn.com.
33. Kathy Chu, "Rising Bank Fees Hit Consumers," *USA Today,* October 5, 2005, http://www.usatoday.com.

CHAPTER 18

1. Derrick Penner, "Relay to Fire Up Games Spirit; VANOC Hopes to Galvanize Canada by Staging Longest Torch Odyssey in One Country in Olympics History," *Vancouver Sun,* January 29, 2008, p. A1; "Pricing Strategy for Winter Olympics Is Just the Ticket," *The Province* (Vancouver), October 14, 2007, p. A20; Jeff Lee, "2010 Olympic Ticket Prices to Be Unveiled Today; Expect to Pay Top Dollar for Hockey, Curling Seats, Expert Predicts," *Vancouver Sun,* October 11, 2007, p. A3; James Christie, "Subsidized Tickets Part of Olympic Pricing Plan," *Globe and Mail,* October 11, 2007, p. S1.
2. Best Buy website, http://www.bestbuy.ca; Costco website, http://www.costco.ca, and Future Shop website, http://www.futureshop.ca, all accessed January 20, 2008.
3. Electrolux website, http://www.electroluxusa.com, accessed August 24, 2006; iRobot website, http://www.roombavac.com, accessed August 24, 2006; Faye Musselman, "High-End Sales Not Automatic in Robotic Vacs," *Home Furnishing News,* August 29, 2005, http://www.hfnmag.com; Thomas K. Grose, "The Vacuum's Design Moment," *U.S. News & World Report,* May 23, 2005, pp. EE18, EE20; Dyson prices from Future Shop, http://www.futureshop.ca, and iRoomba prices from iRobot Corporation, http://store.irobot.com/home/index.jsp, accessed January 20, 2008.
4. Patrick Klepek, "Microsoft Erases Hopes of Xbox 360 Price Drop," Extreme Tech, June 27, 2006, http://www.extremetech.com.
5. Joanne Viviano, "Crocs Shoes Making Great Strides," Associated Press, June 30, 2006, http://news.yahoo.com.
6. "Daimler to Launch Smart Car in U.S. in 2008," Associated Press, June 29, 2006, http://www.msnbc.com; Smart Canada website, http://www.thesmart.ca, accessed January 20, 2008.

7. Wal-Mart website, http://www.walmartstores.com, accessed July 14, 2006.

8. Ford Canada website, http://www.ford.ca, accessed January 29, 2008.

9. Binders By The Box website, http://www.bindersbythebox.ca, accessed March 16, 2008.

10. "New & Used Car Price Service," *Consumer Reports,* http://www.consumerreports.org, accessed July 17, 2006.

11. "Probe May Delay Change in Digital-Music Prices," CNet News.com, July 30, 2006, http://news.com.com.

12. Ben Ames, "Dell Will Use Fewer Rebates in PC Pricing," *PC World,* July 14, 2006, http://www.pcworld.com.

13. Erica Ogg, "OfficeMax Bids Farewell to Mail-in Rebates," CNet News.com, June 30, 2006, http://news.com.com.

14. "Welcome to Staples Rebate Center," Staples.com, http://www.stapleseasyrebates.com, accessed July 17, 2006.

15. Joel R. Evans and Barry Berman, "Pricing and Small Retailers: Questions to Consider," About.com, http://retailindustry.about.com, accessed July 17, 2006.

16. Felicia Miedema, "The Only Way to Fly," *Driven,* October 2007, pp. 45–51.

17. Amy Merrick, "Can Silk and Leather Tempt Shoppers Back to Old Navy," *The Wall Street Journal,* June 30, 2006, http://online.wsj.com.

18. "Service in the City," *Vancouver Sun,* October 11, 2007, p. B3.

19. Bradford Wernle, "Chrysler Starts Summer Selling Season with Employee-Discount Program," *Auto Week,* June 3, 2006, http://autoweek.com.

20. Jessica Johnson, "Bargain Time in the City of Light," *Globe and Mail,* January 5, 2008, p. T.2.

21. Tom Spring, "Solid $500 Laptops," *PC World,* October 31, 2005, http://www.pcworld.com.

22. "Motorola Razr V31 Dolce & Gabbana," CNet.com, http://inktomi-cnet.com, accessed August 18, 2006; Candace Lombardi, "A Razr for Designer-Label lovers," CNet News.com, June 2, 2006, http://news.com.com.

23. Porsche Cars North America, "Porsche: Sports Cars Push Sales in North America," Press release, April 4, 2005; "Teaser Ad for 911 Campaign Wins 'Advert of 2004,'" Press release, May 17, 2005; available http://www.porsche.com, both accessed November 29, 2008.

24. "Competition Would Have Been Nice," *The Gazette* (Montreal), December 21, 2007, p. A26.

25. Ibid.

26. Dana Flavelle, "Toys Even Santa Can't Find," *Toronto Star,* December 20, 2007, p. B1; Chris Lackner, "Sold-out Toys Spark Online Bid Frenzy: Parents Under Pressure to Deliver," *Calgary Herald,* December 12, 2006, p. A8.

27. eBay website, http://www.ebay.com, accessed July 19, 2006.

28. Richard Blackwell, "EBay Retools the Customer Experience," *Globe and Mail,* January 30, 2008, p. B10.

29. Jamie Birch, "Channel Integration, Cannibalization, and the Affiliate's Brand," ReveNews, May 25, 2006, http://www.revenews.com.

30. Chris Sorensen, "Rogers Bumps Up Phone Fees," *Toronto Star,* January 24, 2008, p. B1.

31. Ed Sutherland, "AT&T Shuffles Broadband Bundle Pricing," Internet News, February 3, 2006, http://www.internetnews.com.

32. Ken Belson, "Chairman of Cable Giant Urges Industry Shift to Flexible Pricing," *The New York Times,* December 2, 2005, http://www.nytimes.com.

33. Bruce Meyerson, "Verizon Wireless to Ease Up on Fees," Associated Press, June 28, 2006, http://news.yahoo.com.

CHAPTER 1

p. 21 Shelly Sanders Greer, "Markham is a Duffer's Dream," *National Post*, May 10, 2008, p. PH17.　**p. 23** Rebecca Harris, "Shopping Habit," *Marketing*, September 18, 2006, p. 6.　**p. 29** Imagine Canada website, http://www.imaginecanada.ca, accessed August 6, 2008.　**p. 32** Statistics Canada, "University Degrees, Diplomas, and Certificates Awarded," *The Daily*, February 7, 2008.　**p. 33** Chris Daniels, "I Want My PDA," *Marketing*, October 15, 2007, pp. 48–49.　**p. 40** Ipsos Canada, "Corporate Social Responsibility (CSR) in Canada: Vital Signs," April 1, 2006, available http://www.ipsos.ca (members only), accessed August 6, 2008.

CHAPTER 2

p. 51 Rachel Naud, "Shedding Some Light: Pets Bring Love, Warmth, and Health into Homes," *Calgary Herald*, May 29, 2008, p. NB1.　**p. 54** John Partridge, "Huge Diamond Pulled from NWT Mine," *Globe and Mail*, July 3, 2008, p. B6.　**p. 60** Statistics Canada, "2006 Census: Ethnic Origin, Visible Minorities, Place of Work and Mode of Transportation," *The Daily*, April 2, 2008.　**p. 62** Statistics Canada, "Road Motor Vehicle Registrations," *The Daily*, February 27, 2008.　**p. 63** Research in Motion, "Research in Motion Reports First Quarter Results," News release, June 25, 2008.

CHAPTER 3

p. 90 Statistics Canada, "Human Activity and the Environment: Climate Change in Canada," *The Daily*, April 22, 2008.　**p. 92** Costco website, http://www.costco.com, "Costco Wholesale Corporation Reports Fourth Quarter and Fiscal Year 2007 Operating Results and September Sales Results," news release, October 10, 2007.　**p. 97** Statistics Canada, "International Merchandise Trade: Annual Review," *The Daily*, April 7, 2008.　**p. 97** Advertising Standards Canada, "Ad Complaints Report 2007," http://adstandards.com, accessed August 7, 2008.　**p. 100** Statistics Canada, *Canada Year Book 2007* (Ottawa, ON: Tr-Graphic, 2007), p. 321.　**p. 107** William Marsden, "Smuggling Guilt to Cost Tobacco Giants $1.1B; Landmark Settlements Stem from 1980s Trade," *National Post*, August 1, 2008, p. A1.　**p. 108** David Hutton, "Protection from Telemarketers Set for Sept. 30," *Globe and Mail*, July 31, 2008, p. A9.　**p. 113** David Fielding, "Everyone's Gone Green," *Report on Business*, September 2007, p. 26.　**p. 114** Statistics Canada, "Study: Organic from Niche to Mainstream," *The Daily*, March 28, 2008.

CHAPTER 4

p. 130 Statistics Canada website, http://www.statcan.ca, accessed Aug 15, 2007.　**p. 136** "Highland Games"; Statistic Canada website http://www42.statcan.ca; accessed August 21, 2007.　**p. 139** "Canada's Population by Age and Sex"; *The Daily,* Thursday, October 26, 2006; Statistics Canada website, http://www.statcan.ca; accessed August 21, 2007.　**p. 145** "Canada's Population by Age and Sex"; *The Daily;* Thursday, October 26, 2006; Statistics Canada website http://statcan.ca; accessed August 21, 2007.　**p. 148** "Births"; *The Daily,* Friday, September 21, 2007; Statistics Canada website http://www.statcan.ca; accessed August 10, 2008.

CHAPTER 5

p. 163 Public Works and Government Services Canada, "What is Crown Assets Distribution?" http://www.tpsgc-pwgsc.gc.ca, accessed August 7, 2008.　**p. 165** Statistics Canada, "North American Industry Classification System (NAICS) 2002 – Canada," http://www.statcan.ca, accessed August 7, 2008.　**p. 170** Health.com, "World's Healthiest Foods," http://eating.health.com, accessed August 7, 2008; Life in Korea website, "Types of Kimchi," http://www.lifeinkorea.com, accessed August 7, 2008.　**p. 171** Jason Kirby, "How Canada's Pop Titan Got Crushed," *Maclean's*, March 17, 2008, p. 39.　**p. 180** See Purchasing Management Association of Canada, "About Us," http://www.pmac.ca, accessed August 8, 2008.　**p. 183** Paul Brent, "Furniture Shopping," *Marketing*, October 23/30, 2006, pp. 20–21.

CHAPTER 6

p. 196 "International Merchandise Trade: Annual Review," *The Daily,* Tuesday, May 8, 2007. Statistics Canada website, http://www.statcan.ca, accessed September 8, 2007; **p. 198** "National Tourism Indicators, Fourth Quarter 2006," catalogue no. 13-009-XIB, March 2007.　**p. 201** "Canadian International Merchandise Trade," *The Daily* August 14, 2007, Statistics Canada website, http://www.statcan.ca, accessed September 6, 2007; **p. 205** "International Merchandise Trade – Annual Review," catalogue no. 65-208-XIE, May 2007.　**p. 207** "Overview of the NAFTA," Foreign Affairs and International Trade Canada website: http:www.international.gc.ca, accessed Sept 13, 2007.　**p. 213** Statistics Canada, A Profile of Canadian Exports 1993 to 2004, catalogue no. 65-506-XIE.

CHAPTER 7

p. 230 Rebecca Harris, "Kids with Cards," *Marketing*, July 3, 2006, p. 6.　**p. 232** Rebecca Harris, "Kids with Cards," *Marketing*, July 3, 2006, p. 6.　**p. 233** Rebecca Harris, "Kids with Cards," *Marketing*, July 3, 2006, p. 6.　**p. 234** Rebecca Harris, "Kids with Cards," *Marketing,* July 3, 2006, p. 6.　**p. 234** "Building Loyalty," *Marketing*, 2006, p. 10.　**p. 235,**" "Building Loyalty," *Marketing,* 2006, p. 11.　**p. 237** "Building Loyalty," *Marketing,* 2006, p. 19.　**p. 240**, "Building Loyalty," *Marketing,* 2006, p. 19.　**p. 247** "Building Loyalty," *Marketing*, 2006, p. 20.　**p. 248** "Building Loyalty," *Marketing,* 2006, p. 22.　**p. 249** "Building Loyalty," *Marketing,* 2006, p. 22.

CHAPTER 8

p. 260 "Sound Recording and Music Publishing," *The Daily,* November 7, 2007, Statistics Canada website, http://www.statcan.ca, accessed December 15, 2007.　**p. 270** "Sound Recording and Music Publishing," *The Daily,* November 7, 2007, Statistics Canada website, http://www.statcan.ca, accessed December 15, 2007.　**p. 271** "Sound Recording and Music Publishing," *The Daily,* November 7, 2007, Statistics Canada website, http://www.statcan.ca, accessed December 15, 2007.　**p. 281** "Sound Recording and Music Publishing," *The Daily,* November 7, 2007, Statistics Canada website, http://www.statcan.ca, accessed December 15, 2007.

CHAPTER 9

p. 293 "Electronic Commerce and Technology," *The Daily,* April 20, 2006, Statistics Canada website http://www.statcan.ca, accessed December 31, 2007.　**p. 304** "Electronic Commerce and Technology," *The Daily,* April 20, 2006, Statistics Canada website http://www.statcan.ca, accessed December 31, 2007.

CHAPTER 10

p. 324 "Private Radio Broadcasting," *The Daily,* August 8, 2007, Statistics Canada website http://www.statcan.ca, accessed January 16, 2008.　**p. 341** "Radio Listening" *The Daily,* June 26, 2007, Statistics Canada website, http://wwwstatcan.ca, accessed January 16, 2008.　**p. 342** "Radio Listening" *The Daily,* June 26, 2007, Statistics Canada website, http://www.statcan.ca, accessed January 16, 2008.

CHAPTER 11

p. 354 "General Social Survey: Paid and Unpaid Work," *The Daily,* July 19, 2006, Statistics Canada website, http://www.statcan.ca, accessed January 26, 2008.　**p. 357** "General Social Survey: Paid and Unpaid Work," *The Daily,* July 19, 2006, Statistics Canada website, http://www.statcan.ca, accessed January 26, 2008.　**p. 359** "General Social Survey: Paid and Unpaid Work," *The Daily,* July 19, 2006, Statistics Canada website, http://www.statcan.ca, accessed January 26, 2008.　**p. 362** "General Social Survey: Paid and Unpaid Work," *The Daily,* July 19, 2006, Statistics Canada website, http://www.statcan.ca, accessed January 26, 2008.　**p. 373** "General Social Survey: Paid and Unpaid Work," *The Daily,* July 19, 2006, Statistics Canada website, http://www.statcan.ca, accessed January 26, 2008.

CHAPTER 12

p. 392 Statistics Canada, "E-commerce: Shopping on the Internet," *The Daily,* November 17, 2008.　**p. 395** Statistics Canada, "Envirostats: Recycling in Canada," *The Daily,* July 13, 2007.　**p. 411** Statistics Canada, "Railway Carloadings," *The Daily,* February 26, 2008.　**p. 412** Statistics Canada, *Canada Year Book 2007*, p. 469.　**p. 416** "TSI and VPA Celebrate Arrival of 1000th Crane in Vancouver," Canada NewsWire, August 31, 2007, p. 1.

CHAPTER 13

p. 426 Statistics Canada, "Study: How the Provinces Fared in Retail Trade," *The Daily,* May 26, 2008, http://www.statcan.ca/Daily/English/080526/d080526a.htm; "Study: The Year in Review for Wholesale Trade," *The Daily,* May 29, 2008, http://www.statcan.ca/Daily/English/080529/d080529c.htm, both accessed September 14, 2008.　**p. 427** Sean Silcoff, "A Loonie Business Plan; Dollarama Has Become a Sector Juggernaut, One Location at a Time," *National Post,* March 22, 2008, p. FP4.　**p. 429** Statistics Canada, "Are Average Wages Higher in Services?" http://www41.statcan.ca/2007/0163/ceb0163_004-eng.htm, accessed September 14, 2008.　**p. 436** UFA website, "About UFA," http://www.ufa.net/aboutUFA/aboutUFA.html, accessed September 14, 2008.　**p. 443** Vancouver 2010 website, "Acklands-Grainger to Help Ensure 'Safety First' at the 2010 Inter Games," News Release, September 8, 2008, http://www.vancouver2010.com, accessed September 14, 2008.

CHAPTER 14

p. 465 "Annual Survey of Advertising and Related Services," *The Daily*, March 27, 2007, Statistics Canada website, http://www.statcan.ca, accessed February 8, 2008. **p. 465** "Annual Survey of Advertising and Related Services," *The Daily*, March 27, 2007, Statistics Canada website, http://www.statcan.ca, accessed February 8, 2008. **p. 470** "Annual Survey of Advertising and Related Services," *The Daily*, March 27, 2007, Statistics Canada website, http://www.statcan.ca, accessed February 8, 2008. **p. 475** "Annual Survey of Advertising and Related Services," *The Daily*, March 27, 2007, Statistics Canada website, http://www.statcan.ca, accessed February 8, 2008. **p. 480** "Annual Survey of Advertising and Related Services," *The Daily*, March 27, 2007, Statistics Canada website, http://www.statcan.ca, accessed February 8, 2008. **p. 482** Annual Survey of Advertising and Related Services," *The Daily*, March 27, 2007, Statistics Canada website, http://www.statcan.ca, accessed February 8, 2008. **p. 491** ZenithOptimedia website; http://www.zenithoptimedia.com, accessed Feb 15, 2008. **p. 492** ZenithOptimedia website; http://www.zenithoptimedia.com, accessed Feb 15, 2008.

CHAPTER 15

p. 502 "Study: Organic from Niche to Mainstream," *The Daily*, March 28, 2008; Statistics Canada website; http://www.statcan.ca, accessed March 29, 2008. **p. 502** "Study: Organic from Niche to Mainstream," *The Daily*, March 28, 2008; Statistics Canada website; http://www.statcan.ca, accessed March 29, 2008. **p. 505** "Study: Organic from Niche to Mainstream," *The Daily*, March 28, 2008; Statistics Canada website; http://www.statcan.ca, accessed March 29, 2008. **p. 510** "Study: Organic from Niche to Mainstream," *The Daily*, March 28, 2008; Statistics Canada website; http://www.statcan.ca, accessed March 29, 2008. **p. 518** "Study: Organic from Niche to Mainstream," *The Daily*, March 28, 2008; Statistics Canada website; http://www.statcan.ca, accessed March 29, 2008. **p. 523** "Study: Organic from Niche to Mainstream," *The Daily*, March 28, 2008; Statistics Canada website; http://www.statcan.ca, accessed March 29, 2008. **p. 525** "Study: Organic from Niche to Mainstream," *The Daily*, March 28, 2008; Statistics Canada website; http://www.statcan.ca, accessed March 29, 2008.

CHAPTER 16

p. 536 Statistics Canada, "Study: New Motor Vehicle Sales, Year in Review," *The Daily*, April 23, 2008. **p. 539** Sun Life Financial website, "History of Sun Life Financial," http://www.sunlife.com/, accessed September 14, 2008. **p. 540** Amrit Dhillon, "Operators in India Sick of Rude Calls; Industry Transformed–But at What Cost?" *The Gazette* (Montreal), February 15, 2008, p. B1; Monica Wolfson, "Call Centre Field Grows, Study Finds," *The Windsor Star*, February 28, 2008, p. A7. **p. 559** Canadian Tire website, "Facts & Stats," http://www2.canadiantire.ca/CTenglish/media/factsStats_ctmoney.html, accessed September 14, 2008. **p. 561** Joann Klimkiewicz, "Look Who's Clipping Coupons," *Edmonton Journal*, September 2, 2006, p. B8FRO.

CHAPTER 17

p. 580 "Bayer Fined $3.65 Million for Price-fixing," *The Globe and Mail*, October 31, 2007, p. B8. **p. 585** Joanne Latimer, "Shoes for Very Discreet Women," *Maclean's*, October 22, 2007, p. 60. **p. 591** Martijn Brons, Peter Nijkamp, Eric Pels, and Piet Rietveld, "A Meta-analysis of the Price Elasticity of Gasoline Demand: A SUR Approach," *Energy Economics*, September 2008, p. 2105. **p. 599** Brent Jang, "$68,000 Fill-ups Herald 'Grim' Era for Airlines," *The Globe and Mail*, June 3, 2008, p. B1.

CHAPTER 18

p. 614 Hollie Shaw, "Wal-Mart Credits Strong Dollar for Deep Price Cuts; Other Merchants Also Wooing Cash-Strapped Consumers," *National Post*, August 16, 2007, p. FP5. **p. 621** Alana Semuels, "Weary Consumers Rediscover Haggling; Practice Makes Comeback on Main Street," *Calgary Herald*, May 10, 2008, p. D2. **p. 623** Mike Karim, "Most Subcompacts Are Loss Leaders for Dealers," *Toronto Star*, August 4, 2007, p. W6. **p. 624** John Terauds, "So You Want to Buy a Grand Piano? Choosing the Right Instrument Can Take Months Then Comes the Careful Adjustment of 12 000 Parts," *Toronto Star*, December 22, 2007, p. E4. **p. 626** eBay website, http://pages.ebay.ca/aboutebay/thecompany/2008.html, accessed September 14, 2008.

glossary

A

accessory equipment Capital items like desktop computers and printers that typically cost less and last for shorter periods of time than installations. p. 332

administered marketing system VMS that achieves channel coordination when a dominant channel member exercises its power. p. 403

adoption process Stages that consumers go through in learning about a new product, trying it, and deciding whether to purchase it again. p. 368

advertising Any paid, non-personal communication through various media about a business firm, not-for-profit organization, product, or idea by a sponsor identified in a message that is intended to inform or persuade members of a particular audience. p. 502

advertising agency Firm whose marketing specialists assist advertisers in planning and preparing advertisements. p. 519

advertising campaign Series of different but related ads that use a single theme and appear in different media within a specified time period. p. 509

affinity marketing Marketing effort sponsored by an organization that solicits responses from individuals who share common interests and activities. p. 297

AIDA concept Steps through which an individual reaches a purchase decision: attention, interest, desire, and action. p. 468

AIO statements Items on lifestyle surveys that describe various activities, interests, and opinions of respondents. p. 275

allowance Specified deduction from list price, including a trade-in or promotional allowance. p. 617

ambush marketing Attempt by a firm that is not an official sponsor of an event or activity to link itself to the event or activity. p. 480

application service providers (ASPs) Outside companies that specialize in providing both the computers and the application support for managing information systems of business clients. p. 299

approach Salesperson's initial contact with a prospective customer. p. 547

Asch phenomenon Impact of groups and group norms on individual behaviour, as described by S. E. Asch. People often conform to majority rule, even when majority rule goes against their beliefs. p. 1

atmospherics Combination of physical characteristics and amenities that contribute to a store's image. p. 433

attitudes Person's enduring favourable or unfavourable evaluations, emotions, or action tendencies toward some object or idea. p. 143

average total costs Costs calculated by dividing the sum of the variable and fixed costs by the number of units produced. p. 590

B

baby boomers People born between the years of 1947 and 1965. p. 268

backward integration Process through which a manufacturer attempts to gain greater control over inputs in its production process, such as raw materials. p. 403

banners Advertisements on a Web page that link to an advertiser's site. p. 512

basing-point pricing System used in some industries during the early 20th century in which the buyer paid the factory price plus freight charges from the basing-point city nearest the buyer. p. 619

benchmarking Method of measuring quality by comparing performance against industry leaders. p. 336

bid rigging A form of collusion, similar to price fixing, which occurs when sellers get together and collude to set prices with respect to one or more competitive proposals. p. 580

bonus pack Specially packaged item that gives the purchaser a larger quantity at the regular price. p. 561

bots (shopbots) Online search programs that act as comparison shopping agents. p. 628

bottom line Business jargon referring to the overall profitability of an organization. p. 28

brand Name, term, sign, symbol, design, or some combination that identifies the products of one firm while differentiating them from the competition's. p. 354

brand equity Added value that a respected, well-known brand name gives to a product in the marketplace. p. 358

brand extension Strategy of attaching a popular brand name to a new product in an unrelated product category. p. 366

brand insistence Consumer refusals of alternatives, resulting in an extensive search for desired merchandise. p. 355

brand licensing Firm's authorization of other companies to use its brand names. p. 366

brand manager Marketer within an organization who is responsible for a single brand. p. 360

brand mark Symbol or pictorial design that distinguishes a product. p. 361

brand name Part of a brand consisting of words or letters that form a name that identifies and distinguishes a firm's offerings from those of its competitors. p. 361

brand preference Consumer reliance on previous experiences with a product to choose that product again. p. 355

brand recognition Consumer awareness and identification of a brand. p. 355

breakeven analysis Pricing technique used to determine the number of products that must be sold at a specified price to generate enough revenue to cover total cost. p. 595

broadband technology Extremely high-speed, always-on Internet connection. p. 35

broker Agent wholesaling intermediary who does not take title to or possession of goods in the course of its primary function, which is to bring together buyers and sellers. p. 445

B2C products *See* consumer products.

bundle pricing Offering two or more complementary products and selling them for a single price. p. 628

business cycle Pattern of differing stages in the level of economic activity of a nation or region. Although the traditional cycle includes the four stages of prosperity, recession, depression, and recovery, most economists believe that future depressions can be prevented through effective economic policies. p. 98

business plan Formal document that outlines a company's objectives, how they will be met, how the business will achieve financing, and how much money the firm expects to earn. p. 74

business products Goods and services purchased for use either directly or indirectly in the production of other goods and services for resale. p. 261

business services Intangible products that firms buy to facilitate their production and operating processes. p. 334

business-to-business (B2B) marketing Organizational sales and purchases of goods and services to support production of other products, for daily company operations, or for resale. p. 160

business-to-business (B2B) product Product that contributes directly or indirectly to the output of other products for resale; also called industrial or organizational product. p. 328

buyer Person who has the formal authority to select a supplier and to implement the procedures for securing a good or service. p. 182

buyer concerns Expressions of sales resistance (previously called *objections*). p. 548

buyer partnership Relationship in which a firm purchases goods or services from one or more providers. p. 304

buyer's market Market in which there are more goods and services than people willing to buy them. p. 25

buying centre Participants involved in an organizational buying decision. p. 181

buzz marketing Marketing that gathers volunteers to try products and then relies on them to talk about their experiences with their friends and colleagues. p. 37

C

cannibalization Loss of sales of an existing product due to competition from a new product in the same line. p. 628

captive brand National brands that are sold exclusively by a retail chain. p. 357

cash discount Price reduction offered to a consumer, business user, or marketing intermediary in return for prompt payment of a bill. p. 616

category captain Vendor who is responsible for dealing with all the suppliers for a project and then presenting the entire package to the buyer. p. 176

category killer Store that offers huge selections and low prices in single product lines. p. 437

category management Product management system in which a category manager—with profit and loss responsibility—oversees a product line. p. 360

cause marketing Identification and marketing of a social issue, cause, or idea to selected target markets. p. 31

census agglomeration (CA) Geographic area with a population between 10 000 and 99 000. p. 264

census metropolitan area (CMA) Geographic area surrounding an urban core with a population of at least 100 000. p. 264

channel Medium through which a message is delivered. p. 390

channel captain Dominant and controlling member of a marketing channel. p. 401

click-throughs *See* cost per response.

closed sales territory Exclusive geographic selling region of a distributor. p. 399

closing Stage of the personal selling process where the salesperson asks the customer to make a purchase decision. p. 549

cluster sample Probability sample in which researchers select a sample of subgroups (or clusters) from which they draw respondents; each cluster reflects the diversity of the whole population being sampled. p. 238

cobranding Cooperative arrangement in which two or more businesses team up to closely link their names on a single product. p. 305

cognitive dissonance Imbalance between beliefs and attitudes that occurs after an action or decision is taken, such as a purchase. p. 149

cohort effect Tendency of members of a generation to be influenced and bound together by events occurring during their key formative years—roughly 17 to 22 years of age. p. 267

cold calling Contacting a prospect without a prior appointment. p. 548

collaborative planning, forecasting, and replenishment (CPFaR) Inventory management technique involving collaborative efforts by both purchasers and vendors. p. 307

comarketing Cooperative arrangement in which two businesses jointly market each other's products. p. 305

commercial market Individuals and firms that acquire products to support, directly or indirectly, production of other goods and services. p. 162

commission Incentive compensation directly related to the sales or profits achieved by a salesperson. p. 554

commission merchant Agent wholesaling intermediary who takes possession of goods shipped to a central market for sale, acts as the producer's agent, and collects an agreed-upon fee at the time of the sale. p. 444

common carriers Businesses that provide transportation services as for-hire carriers to the general public. p. 410

common market Extension of a customs union by seeking to reconcile all government regulations affecting trade. p. 205

comparative advertising Advertising strategy that emphasizes messages with direct or indirect promotional comparisons between competing brands. p. 505

Competition Act The most comprehensive legislation in Canada, designed to help both consumers and businesses by promoting a healthy competitive environment. p. 579

competitive bidding Inviting potential suppliers to quote prices on proposed purchases or contracts. p. 625

competitive environment Interactive process that occurs in the marketplace among marketers of directly competitive products, marketers of products that can be substituted for one another, and marketers competing for the consumer's purchasing power. p. 91

competitive pricing strategy Pricing strategy designed to de-emphasize price as a competitive variable by pricing a good or service at the general level of comparable offerings. p. 614

competitive strategy Methods through which a firm deals with its competitive environment. p. 94

component parts and materials Finished business products of one producer that become part of the final products of another producer. p. 333

concentrated marketing Focusing marketing efforts on satisfying a single market segment; also called *niche marketing*. p. 280

concept testing Method for subjecting a product idea to additional study before actual development by involving consumers through focus groups, surveys, in-store polling, and the like. p. 373

consultative selling Meeting customer needs by listening to customers, understanding their problems, paying attention to details, and following through after the sale. p. 543

consumer behaviour Mental and physical activities of individuals who actually use the purchased goods and services. p. 130

consumer innovators People who purchase new products almost as soon as the products reach the market. p. 368

consumer orientation Business philosophy incorporating the marketing concept that emphasizes first determining unmet consumer needs and then designing a system for satisfying them. p. 25

consumer products Products bought by ultimate consumers for personal use. p. 260

consumer rights In their most basic form, these rights include a person's right to choose goods and services freely, to be informed about these products and services, to be heard, and to be safe. p. 105

consumerism Social force within the environment designed to aid and protect the consumer by exerting legal, moral, and economic pressures on business and government. p. 104

containerization Process of combining several unitized loads into a single, well-protected load for shipment. p. 416

contest Sales promotional technique that requires entrants to complete a task such as solving a puzzle or answering questions on a quiz for the chance to win a prize. p. 561

contract carriers For-hire transporters that do not offer their services to the general public. p. 410

contractual marketing system VMS that coordinates channel activities through formal agreements among participants. p. 403

controlled experiment Scientific investigation in which a researcher manipulates a test group (or groups) and compares the results with those of a control group that did not receive the experimental controls or manipulations. p. 244

convenience products Goods and services that consumers want to purchase frequently, immediately, and with minimal effort. p. 329

convenience retailer Store that appeals to customers on accessible location, long hours, rapid checkout, and adequate parking. p. 436

convenience sample Nonprobability sample selected from among readily available respondents. p. 239

conversion rate The percentage of visitors to a website who make a purchase. p. 491

cookies Controversial techniques for collecting information about online website visitors in which small text files are automatically downloaded to a user's computer to gather such data as length of visit and the site visited next. p. 525

cooperative advertising Agreement under which the manufacturer pays a percentage of the retailer's advertising expenditures and the retailer prominently displays the firm's products. p. 507

core competencies Activities that a company performs well and that customers value and competitors find difficult to duplicate. p. 58

core region Region from which most major brands get 40 to 80 percent of their sales. p. 264

corporate marketing system VMS in which a single owner operates the entire marketing channel. p. 403

cost per impression Measurement technique that relates the cost of an ad to every thousand people who view it. p. 491

cost per response (also called *click-throughs*) Direct marketing technique that relates the cost of an ad to the number of people who click it. p. 491

cost-plus pricing Practice of adding a percentage of specified dollar amount—or markup—to the base cost of a product to cover unassigned costs and to provide a profit. p. 593

countertrade Form of exporting whereby goods and services are bartered rather than sold for cash. p. 214

coupon Sales promotional technique that offers a discount on the purchase price of goods or services. p. 559

creative selling Personal selling that involves situations in which a considerable degree of analytical decision making on the buyer's part results in the need for skillful proposals of solutions for the customer's needs. p. 545

creativity Human activity that produces original ideas or knowledge, frequently by testing combinations of ideas or data to produce unique results. p. 32

critical thinking Process of determining the authenticity, accuracy, and worth of information, knowledge, claims, and arguments. p. 33

cross promotion Promotional technique in which marketing partners share the cost of a promotional campaign that meets their mutual needs. p. 521

cross-selling Selling of multiple, often unrelated goods and services to the same customer based on knowledge of that customer's needs. p. 544

cue Any object in the environment that determines the nature of a consumer's response to a drive. p. 363

culture Values, beliefs, preferences, and tastes handed down from one generation to the next in a society. p. 130

cumulative quantity discount Price discount determined by amounts of purchases over stated time periods. p. 617

customary prices Traditional prices that customers expect to pay for certain goods and services. p. 586

customer behaviour Mental and physical activities that occur during selection and purchase of a product. p. 130

customer relationship management (CRM) Combination of strategies and tools that drives relationship programs, reorienting the entire organization to a concentrated focus on satisfying customers. p. 300

customer satisfaction Extent to which customers are satisfied with their purchases. p. 295

customer winback Process of rejuvenating lost relationships with customers. p. 303

customer-based segmentation Dividing a business-to-business market into homogeneous groups based on buyers' product specifications. p. 165

customer-service standards Statement of goals and acceptable performance for the quality of service that a firm expects to deliver to its customers. p. 409

customs union Establishment of a free trade area plus a uniform tariff for trade with non-member unions. p. 205

D

data mining Process of searching through customer databases to detect patterns that guide marketing decision making. p. 247

database marketing Use of software to analyze marketing information, identifying and targeting messages toward specific groups of potential customers. p. 298

decider Person who chooses a good or service, although another person may have the formal authority to do so. p. 182

decline stage Final stage of the product life cycle, in which a decline in total industry sales occurs. p. 343

decoding Receiver's interpretation of a message. p. 468

Delphi technique Qualitative sales forecasting method that gathers and redistributes several rounds of anonymous forecasts until the participants reach a consensus. p. 249

demand Schedule of the amounts of a firm's product that consumers will purchase at different prices during a specified time period. p. 588

demarketing Process of reducing consumer demand for a good or service to a level that the firm can supply. p. 100

demographic segmentation Division of an overall market into homogeneous groups based on variables such as gender, age, income, occupation, education, sexual orientation, household size, and stage in the family life cycle; also called *socioeconomic segmentation*. p. 266

demonstration Stage in the personal selling process in which the customer has the opportunity to try out or otherwise see how a good or service works before purchase. p. 548

department store Large store that handles a variety of merchandise, including clothing, household goods, appliances, and furniture. p. 438

deregulation movement Opening of markets previously subject to government control. p. 91

derived demand Demand for a resource that results from demand for the goods and services that are produced by that resource. p. 170

differentiated marketing Market strategy that focuses on producing several products and pricing, promoting, and distributing them with different marketing mixes designed to satisfy smaller segments. p. 280

diffusion process Process by which new goods or services are accepted in the marketplace. p. 369

direct channel Marketing channel that moves goods directly from a producer to the business purchaser or ultimate user. p. 393

direct mail Communications in the form of sales letters, postcards, brochures, catalogues, and the like conveying messages directly from the marketer to the customer. p. 446

direct marketing Direct communications, other than personal sales contacts, between buyer and seller, designed to generate sales, information requests, or store or website visits. p. 446

direct sales results test Method for measuring promotional effectiveness based on the specific impact on sales revenues for each dollar of promotional spending. p. 490

direct selling Strategy designed to establish direct sales contact between producer and final user. p. 393

discount house Store that charges low prices but may not offer services such as credit. p. 438

discretionary income Money people have available to spend after buying necessities such as food, clothing, and housing. p. 100

distribution Movement of goods and services from producers to customers. p. 390

distribution strategy Planning that ensures that consumers find their products in the proper quantities at the right times and places. p. 61

downstream management Controlling part of the supply chain that involves finished product storage, outbound logistics, marketing and sales, and customer service. p. 405

drive Any strong stimulus that impels a person to act. p. 145

drop shipper Limited-function merchant wholesaler who accepts orders from customers and forwards these orders to producers, which then ship directly to the customers who place the orders. p. 444

dual distribution Network that moves products to a firm's target market through more than one marketing channel. p. 395

dumping Controversial practice of selling a product in a foreign market at a price lower than what it receives in the producer's domestic market. p. 204

E

ecology The relationship between organisms and their natural environments. p. 113

economic environment Factors that influence consumer buying power and marketing strategies, including stage of the business cycle, inflation, unemployment, income, and resource availability. p. 98

80/20 principle Generally accepted rule that 80 percent of a product's revenues come from 20 percent of its total customers. p. 278

elasticity Measure of responsiveness of purchasers and suppliers to a change in price. p. 591

electronic data interchange (EDI) Computer-to-computer exchanges of invoices, orders, and other business documents. p. 306

electronic storefront Online store where customers can view and order merchandise much like window shopping at traditional retail establishments. p. 392

emergency goods and services Products bought in response to unexpected and urgent needs. p. 328

employee satisfaction Employee's level of satisfaction for his or her company and the extent to which that loyalty or lack of loyalty is communicated to external customers. p. 293

encoding Translating a message into understandable terms. p. 468

end-use application segmentation Segmenting a business-to-business market based on how industrial purchasers will use the product. p. 166

Engel's laws Three general statements based on Engel's studies of the impact of household income changes on consumer spending behaviour: As household income increases, a smaller percentage of expenditures go for food, the percentage spent on housing and household operations and clothing remains constant, and the percentage spent on other items (such as recreation and education) increases. p. 273

enterprise resource planning (ERP) system Software system that consolidates data from among a firm's various business units. p. 407

environmental management Attainment of organizational objectives by predicting and influencing the competitive, political–legal, economic, technological, and social–cultural environments. p. 91

environmental scanning Process of collecting information about the external marketing environment to identify and interpret potential trends. p. 90

ethics Moral standards of behaviour expected by a society. p. 40

European Union (EU) Customs union that is moving in the direction of an economic union by adopting a common currency, removing trade restrictions, and permitting free flow of goods and workers throughout the member nations. p. 207

evaluative criteria Features that a consumer considers in choosing among alternatives. p. 148

event marketing Marketing of sporting, cultural, and charitable activities to selected target markets. p. 32

everyday low pricing (EDLP) Pricing strategy of continuously offering low prices rather than relying on such short-term price cuts as cents-off coupons, rebates, and special sales. p. 614

evoked set Number of alternatives that a consumer actually considers in making a purchase decision. p. 148

exchange control Method used to regulate the privilege of international trade among importing organizations by controlling access to foreign currencies. p. 204

exchange functions Buying and selling functions of marketing. p. 38

exchange process Activity in which two or more parties give something of value to each other to satisfy perceived needs. p. 24

exchange rate Price of one nation's currency in terms of another country's currency. p. 199

exclusive dealing agreement Arrangement between a manufacturer and a marketing intermediary that prohibits the intermediary from handling competing product lines. p. 399

exclusive distribution Distribution of a product through a single wholesaler or retailer in a specific geographic region. p. 399

expectancy theory Theory stating that motivation depends on an individual's expectations of his or her ability to perform a job and how that performance relates to attaining a desired reward. p. 554

exploratory research Process of discussing a marketing problem with informed sources both within and outside the firm and examining information from secondary sources. p. 233

exponential smoothing Quantitative forecasting technique that assigns weights to historical sales data, giving the greatest weight to the most recent data. p. 250

exporting Marketing domestically produced goods and services in foreign countries. p. 194

extended problem solving Situation that involves lengthy external searches and long deliberation; results when brands are difficult to categorize or evaluate. p. 150

external customer People or organizations that buy or use another firm's goods or services. p. 292

F

facilitating functions Functions that assist the marketer in performing the exchange and physical distribution functions. p. 390

false or misleading ordinary selling price representation A form of misleading advertising where consumers are misled with regard to the regular price of a product. p. 581

family brand Single brand name that identifies several related products. p. 357

family life cycle Process of family formation and dissolution. p. 270

feedback Receiver's response to a message. p. 468

field selling Sales presentations made at prospective customers' locations on a face-to-face basis. p. 539

first mover strategy Theory advocating that the company that is first to offer a product in a marketplace will be the long-term market winner. p. 57

fixed costs Costs that remain stable at any production level within a certain range (such as lease payments or insurance costs). p. 590

fixed-sum-per-unit method Method of promotional budgeting in which a predetermined amount is allocated to each sales or production unit. p. 489

FOB (free on board) plant (FOB origin) Price quotation that does not include shipping charges. p. 618

FOB origin, freight allowed (freight absorbed) Price quotation system that allows the buyer to deduct shipping expenses from the cost of purchases. p. 619

focus group Simultaneous personal interview of a small group of individuals, which relies on group discussion about a certain topic. p. 242

follow-up Post-sales activities that often determine whether an individual who has made a recent purchase will become a repeat customer. p. 550

foreign licensing Agreement that grants foreign marketers the right to distribute a firm's merchandise or to use its trademark, patent, or process in a specified geographic area. p. 209

forward integration Process through which a firm attempts to control downstream distribution. p. 403

franchise Contractual arrangement in which a wholesaler or retailer agrees to meet the operating requirements of a manufacturer or other franchiser. p. 209

free trade area Region in which participating nations agree to the free trade of goods among themselves, abolishing tariffs and trade restrictions. p. 205

Free Trade Area of the Americas (FTAA) Proposed free trade area stretching the length of the entire Western hemisphere and designed to extend free trade benefits to additional nations in North, Central, and South America. p. 206

frequency marketing Frequent buyer or user marketing programs that reward customers with cash, rebates, merchandise, or other premiums. p. 297

full-cost pricing Pricing method that uses all relevant variable costs in setting a product's price and also allocates those fixed costs that cannot be directly attributed to the production of the specific item being priced. p. 594

full-service research supplier Marketing research organization that offers all aspects of the marketing research process. p. 232

G

gatekeeper Person who controls the information that all buying centre members will review. p. 181

General Agreement on Tariffs and Trade (GATT) International trade accord that has helped reduce world tariffs. p. 205

general merchandise retailer Store that carries a wide variety of product lines, stocking all of them in some depth. p. 438

Generation X The group born between 1966 and 1981—who are now between ages 25 and 40. p. 267

generic products Products characterized by plain labels, no advertising, and the absence of brand names. p. 356

geographic information systems (GISs) Computer systems that assemble, store, manipulate, and display data by their location. p. 266

geographic segmentation Division of an overall market into homogeneous groups based on their locations. p. 262

global marketing strategy Standardized marketing mix with minimal modifications that a firm uses in all its domestic and foreign markets. p. 211

global sourcing Purchasing goods and services from suppliers worldwide. p. 170

good Tangible product that customers can see, hear, smell, taste, or touch. p. 325

goods–services continuum Spectrum along which goods and services fall according to their attributes, from pure good to pure service. p. 325

grassroots marketing Efforts that connect directly with existing and potential customers through non-mainstream channels. p. 300

green marketing Production, promotion, and reclamation of environmentally sensitive products. p. 113

grey goods Products manufactured abroad under licence from a Canadian firm and then sold in the Canadian market in competition with that firm's own domestic output. p. 402

growth stage Second stage of the product life cycle, which begins when a firm starts to realize substantial profits from its investment in the product. p. 342

guerrilla marketing Unconventional, innovative, and low-cost marketing techniques designed to get consumers' attention in unusual ways. p. 477

H

high-involvement purchase decision Buying decision that evokes high levels of potential social or economic consequence. p. 146

home shopping channel Television direct marketing in which a variety of products are offered and consumers can order them directly by phone or online. p. 483

homeshoring Hiring workers to do jobs from their homes. p. 327

hypermarkets Giant one-stop shopping facilities that offer wide selections of grocery and general merchandise products at discount prices typically filling up 200 000 or more square feet of selling space (about a third larger than most supercentres). p. 439

hypothesis Tentative explanation for some specific event. p. 234

I

import quotas Trade restrictions that limit the number of units of certain goods that can enter a country for resale. p. 204

importing Purchasing foreign goods, services, and raw materials. p. 194

impulse goods and services Products purchased on the spur of the moment. p. 328

inbound telemarketing Sales method in which prospects call a toll-free number to obtain information, make reservations, and purchase goods and services. p. 540

incremental-cost pricing Pricing method that attempts to use only those costs directly attributable to a specific output in setting prices. p. 594

indirect evaluation Method for measuring promotional effectiveness by concentrating on quantifiable indicators of effectiveness such as recall and readership. p. 490

individual brand Single brand that uniquely identifies a product itself. p. 357

industrial products *See* business-to-business (B2B) product.

inelastic demand Demand that, throughout an industry, will not change significantly due to a price change. p. 171

inflation Rising prices caused by some combination of excess consumer demand and increases in the costs of one or more factors of production. p. 99

influencers Typically, technical staff such as engineers who affect the buying decision by supplying information to guide evaluation of alternatives or by setting buying specifications. p. 182

infomercial Paid 30-minute product commercial that resembles a regular television program. p. 483

informative advertising Promotion that seeks to develop initial demand for a good, service, organization, person, place, idea, or cause. p. 503

infrastructure Nation's basic system of transportation networks, communications systems, and energy facilities. p. 199

inside selling Selling by phone, mail, and electronic commerce. p. 540

installations Business products like factories, assembly lines, and huge machinery that are major capital investments. p. 332

institutional advertising Promotion of a concept, idea, philosophy, or goodwill of an industry, company, organization, person, geographic location, or government agency. p. 503

integrated marketing communications (IMC) Coordination of all promotional activities to produce a unified, customer-focused promotional message. p. 464

intensive distribution Distribution of a product through all available channels. p. 399

interactive advertising Two-way promotional messages transmitted through communication channels that induce message recipients to participate actively in the promotional effort. p. 507

interactive marketing Buyer–seller communications in which the customer controls the amount and type of information received from a marketer through such channels as the Internet, CD-ROMs, interactive toll-free telephone numbers, and virtual reality kiosks. p. 34

intermodal operations Combination of transport modes such as rail and highway carriers (piggyback), air and highway carriers (birdyback), and water and highway carriers (fishyback) to improve customer service and achieve cost advantages. p. 411

internal customer Employees or departments within an organization that depend on the work of another employee or department to perform tasks. p. 292

internal marketing Managerial actions that help all members of the organization understand and accept their respective roles in implementing a marketing strategy. p. 293

internal partnership Relationship involving customers within an organization. p. 305

Internet Protocol television (IPTV) Technology that allows a two-way broadcast signal to be sent through a telephone or cable network by way of a broadband connection. p. 35

interpretative research Observational research method developed by social anthropologists in which customers are observed in their natural setting and their behaviour is interpreted based on an understanding of social and cultural characteristics; also known as *ethnography,* or going native. p. 240

introductory stage First stage of the product life cycle, in which a firm works to stimulate the new market entry. p. 341

ISO (International Organization for Standarization) certification Internationally recognized standards that ensure a company's goods and services meet established quality levels and that ensure its operations minimize harm to the environment. p. 201

ISO 9002 International quality standards developed by the International Organization for Standardization in Switzerland to ensure consistent quality among products manufactured and sold throughout the European Union (EU). p. 336

J

joint demand Demand for a product that depends on the demand for another product used in combination with it. p. 170

jury of executive opinion Qualitative sales forecasting method that assesses the sales expectations of various executives. p. 248

just-in-time (JIT)/just-in-time II (JIT II) Inventory practices that seek to boost efficiency by cutting inventories to absolute minimum levels. With JIT II, suppliers' representatives work at the customer's facility. p. 248

L

label Branding component that carries an item's brand name or symbol, the name and address of the manufacturer or distributor, information about the product, and recommended uses. p. 365

lateral partnerships Strategic relationships that extend to external entities but involve no direct buyer–seller interactions. p. 305

leader pricing Variant of loss-leader pricing in which marketers offer prices slightly above cost to avoid violating minimum-markup regulations and earn a minimal return on promotional sales. p. 623

learning Knowledge or skill that is acquired as a result of experience, which changes consumer behaviour. p. 145

lifetime value of a customer Revenues and intangible benefits that a customer brings to an organization over an average lifetime, minus the investment the firm has made to attract and keep the customer. p. 37

limited problem solving Situation in which the consumer invests some small amount of time and energy in searching for and evaluating alternatives. p. 150

limited-line store Retailer that offers a large assortment within a single product line or within a few related product lines. p. 437

limited-service research supplier Marketing research firm that specializes in a limited number of research activities, such as conducting field interviews or performing data processing. p. 232

line extension Development of individual offerings that appeal to different market segments while remaining closely related to the existing product line. p. 340

list price Established price normally quoted to potential buyers. p. 615

logistics Process of coordinating the flow of information, goods, and services among members of the distribution channel. p. 390

loss leader Product offered to consumers at less than cost to attract them to stores in the hope that they will buy other merchandise at regular prices. p. 623

low-involvement purchase decision Routine purchase that poses little risk to the consumer, either socially or economically. p. 146

M

mail-order wholesaler Limited-function merchant wholesaler who distributes catalogues instead of sending sales representatives to contact customers. p. 444

mall intercepts Interviews conducted inside retail shopping centres. p. 241

manufacturer's brand Brand name owned by a manufacturer or other producer. p. 356

manufacturers' representative Agent wholesaling intermediary who represents a number of manufacturers of related but noncompeting products and who receives a commission on each sale. p. 445

marginal analysis Method of analyzing the relationship between costs, sales price, and increased sales volume. p. 582

marginal cost Change in total cost that results from producing an additional unit of output. p. 590

markdown Amount by which a retailer reduces the original selling price of a product. p. 430

market Group of people with sufficient purchasing power, authority, and willingness to buy. p. 260

market development strategy Strategy that concentrates on finding new markets for existing products. p. 367

market penetration strategy Strategy that seeks to increase sales of existing products in existing markets. p. 367

market price Price that a consumer or marketing intermediary actually pays for a product after subtracting any discounts, allowances, or rebates from the list price. p. 616

market segmentation Division of the total market into smaller, relatively homogeneous groups. p. 261

market share/market growth matrix Framework that places SBUs on a chart that plots market share against market growth potential. p. 65

marketing Organizational function and a set of processes for creating, communicating, and delivering value to customers and for managing customer relationships in ways that benefit the organization and its stakeholders. p. 22

marketing (distribution) channel System of marketing institutions that enhances the physical flow of goods and services, along with ownership title, from producer to consumer or business user. p. 390

marketing communications Messages that deal with buyer–seller relationships. p. 464

marketing concept Company-wide consumer orientation with the objective of achieving long-run success. p. 26

marketing decision support system (MDSS) Marketing information system component that links a decision maker with relevant databases and analysis tools. p. 246

marketing ethics Marketers' standards of conduct and moral values. p. 106

marketing information system (MIS) Planned, computer-based system designed to provide managers with a continuous flow of information relevant to their specific decisions and areas of responsibility. p. 246

marketing intermediary (middleman) Wholesaler or retailer that operates between producers and consumers or business users. p. 391

marketing mix Blending of the four strategy elements—product, distribution, promotion, and pricing—to fit the needs and preferences of a specific target market. p. 60

marketing myopia Management's failure to recognize the scope of its business. p. 27

marketing plan Detailed description of the resources and actions needed to achieve stated marketing objectives. p. 74

marketing planning Implementing planning activities devoted to achieving marketing objectives. p. 51

marketing public relations (MPR) Narrowly focused public relations activities that directly support marketing goals. p. 520

marketing research Process of collecting and using information for marketing decision making. p. 230

marketing strategy Overall company-wide program for selecting a particular target market and then satisfying consumers in that market through the marketing mix. p. 55

market-plus pricing The intentional setting of a relatively high price compared with the prices of competing products; also known as *skimming pricing*. p. 610

market-share objective Volume-related pricing objective in which the goal is to achieve control of a portion of the market for a firm's good or service. p. 583

markup Amount that a retailer adds to the cost of a product to determine its selling price. p. 430

mass merchandiser Store that stocks a wider line of goods than a department store, usually without the same depth of assortment within each line. p. 438

materials handling system Set of activities that move production inputs and other goods within plants, warehouses, and transportation terminals. p. 416

maturity stage Third stage of the product life cycle, in which industry sales level out. p. 342

media research Advertising research that assesses how well a particular medium delivers an advertiser's message, where and when to place the advertisement, and the size of the audience. p. 522

media scheduling Setting the timing and sequence for a series of advertisements. p. 518

meeting competition Method of promotional budgeting that simply matches competitors' outlays. p. 489

merchandisers Buyers who are responsible for securing needed business products at the best possible prices. p. 176

merchant wholesaler Independently owned wholesaling intermediary who takes title to the goods that it handles; also known as an industrial distributor in the business-goods market. p. 443

message Communication of information, advice, or a request by the sender to the receiver. p. 468

message research Advertising research that tests consumer reactions to an advertisement's creative message. p. 522

microcultures Smaller groups within a society that have their own distinct characteristics and modes of behaviour, defined by ethnicity, race, region, age, religion, gender, social class, or profession. p. 103

micromarketing Targeting potential customers at very narrow, basic levels, such as by postal code, specific occupation, or lifestyle—possibly even individuals themselves. p. 280

middleman *See* marketing intermediary.

minimum advertised pricing (MAP) Fees paid to retailers that agree not to advertise products below set prices. p. 617

missionary selling Indirect type of selling in which specialized salespeople promote the firm's goodwill among indirect customers, often by assisting customers in product use. p. 546

mobile marketing Marketing messages transmitted via wireless technology. p. 35

modified breakeven analysis Pricing technique used to evaluate consumer demand by comparing the number of products that must be sold at a variety of prices to cover total cost with estimates of expected sales at the various prices. p. 597

modified rebuy Situation in which a purchaser is willing to re-evaluate available options for repurchasing a good or service. p. 180

monopolistic competition Market structure involving a heterogeneous product and product differentiation among competing suppliers, allowing the marketer some degree of control over prices. p. 589

monopoly Market structure in which a single seller dominates trade in a good or service for which buyers can find no close substitutes. p. 589

motive Inner state that directs a person toward the goal of satisfying a need. p. 139

MRO items Business supplies that include maintenance items, repair items, and operating supplies. p. 344

multi-domestic marketing strategy Application of market segmentation to foreign markets by tailoring the firm's marketing mix to match specific target markets in each nation. p. 212

multinational corporation Firm with significant operations and marketing activities outside its home country. p. 211

multiple sourcing Purchasing from several vendors. p. 175

N

national account selling Promotional effort in which a dedicated sales team is assigned to a firm's major customers to provide sales and service needs. p. 306

national accounts organization Organizational arrangement that assigns sales teams to a firm's largest accounts. p. 553

nearsourcing Moving jobs to vendors in countries close to the business's home country. p. 173

need Imbalance between a consumer's actual and desired states. p. 139

network marketing Personal selling that relies on lists of family members and friends of the salesperson who organizes a gathering of potential customers for a demonstration of products. p. 539

new-task buying First-time or unique purchase situation that requires considerable effort by decision makers. p. 180

niche marketing Marketing strategy that focuses on profitably satisfying a single market segment; also called *concentrated marketing*. p. 280

9/11 generation People who were in the 17- to 22 age bracket at the time of the September 11, 2001, terrorist attacks. p. 267

noise Any stimulus that distracts a receiver from receiving a message. p. 468

noncumulative quantity discount Price reduction granted on a one-time-only basis. p. 617

non-marketing public relations Organizational messages about general management issues. p. 520

non-personal selling Promotion that includes advertising, sales promotion, direct marketing, guerrilla marketing, and public relations—all conducted without being face to face with the buyer. p. 474

norms Values, attitudes, and behaviours that a group deems appropriate for its members. p. 135

North American Free Trade Agreement (NAFTA) Accord removing trade barriers among Canada, Mexico, and the United States. p. 165, 206

North American Industrial Classification System (NAICS) Classification used by NAFTA countries to categorize the business marketplace into detailed market segments. p. 165

O

objectives Goals that guide the development of supporting marketing strategy to fulfill a firm's mission. p. 55

odd pricing Pricing policy based on the belief that a price ending with an odd number just under a round number is more appealing—for instance, $9.97 rather than $10. p. 620

offshoring Movement of high-wage jobs from Canada to lower-cost overseas locations. p. 172

oligopoly Market structure, like those in the steel and telecommunications industries, in which relatively few sellers compete, and where high start-up costs form barriers to keep out new competitors. p. 589

one-to-one marketing Customized marketing program designed to build long-term relationships with individual customers. p. 35

opinion leaders Trendsetters who purchase new products before others in a group and then influence others in their purchases. p. 136

order processing Selling, mostly at the wholesale and retail levels, that involves identifying customer needs, pointing them out to customers, and completing orders. p. 545

organization marketing Marketing by mutual-benefit organizations, service organizations, and government organizations intended to influence others to accept their goals, receive their services, or contribute to them in some way. p. 32

organizational product *See* business-to-business (B2B) product.

outbound telemarketing Sales method in which sales representatives place phone calls to prospects and try to conclude the sale over the phone. p. 539

outsourcing Using outside vendors to produce goods and services formerly produced in-house. p. 173

over-the-counter selling Personal selling conducted in retail and some wholesale locations in which customers come to the seller's place of business. p. 538

P

partnership Affiliation of two or more companies that assist each other in the achievement of common goals. p. 303

penetration pricing strategy Pricing strategy involving the use of a relatively low entry price compared with competitive offerings, based on the theory that this initial low price will help secure market acceptance. p. 613

percentage-of-sales method Method of promotional budgeting in which a dollar amount is based on a percentage of past or projected sales. p. 489

perception Meaning that a person attributes to incoming stimuli gathered through the five senses. p. 141

perceptual screen Mental filter or block through which all inputs must pass to be noticed. p. 141

person marketing Marketing efforts designed to cultivate the attention, interest, and preference of a target market toward a person (typically a political candidate or celebrity). p. 29

personal selling Interpersonal influence process involving a seller's promotional presentation conducted on a person-to-person basis with the buyer. p. 536

persuasive advertising Promotion that attempts to increase demand for an existing good, service, organization, person, place, idea, or cause. p. 503

physical distribution Broad range of activities aimed at efficient movement of finished goods from the end of the production line to the consumer. p. 390

physical distribution functions Transportation and distribution of goods and services. p. 39

place marketing Marketing efforts to attract people and organizations to a particular geographic area. p. 30

planned obsolescence Intentional design, manufacture, and marketing of products with limited durability. p. 113

planned shopping centre Group of retail stores planned, coordinated, and marketed as a unit. p. 431

planning Process of anticipating future events and conditions and of determining the best way to achieve organizational goals. p. 50

point-of-purchase (POP) advertising Display or other promotion placed near the site of the actual buying decision. p. 562

political risk assessment (PRA) Units within a firm that evaluate the political risks of the marketplaces in which they operate as well as proposed new marketplaces. p. 201

political-legal environment Component of the marketing environment consisting of laws and interpretations of laws that require firms to operate under competitive conditions and to protect consumer rights. p. 95

population (universe) Total group that researchers want to study. p. 238

Porter's Five Forces Model developed by strategy expert Michael Porter, which identifies five competitive forces that influence planning strategies: the threat of new entrants, the threat of substitute products, rivalry among competitors, the bargaining power of buyers, and the bargaining power of suppliers. p. 56

portfolio analysis Evaluation of a company's products and divisions to determine which are strongest and which are weakest. p. 65

positioning Placing a product at a certain point or location within a market in the minds of prospective buyers. p. 281

positioning map A valuable tool that helps marketers place products in a market by graphically illustrating consumers' perceptions of competing products within an industry. p. 282

postage-stamp pricing System for handling transportation costs under which all buyers are quoted the same price, including transportation expenses; also known as *uniform-delivered price*. p. 619

post-testing Research that assesses advertising effectiveness after it has appeared in a print or broadcast medium. p. 523

predatory pricing A pricing practice in which companies set prices below their cost for a sufficiently long period of time to discourage or eliminate competition and then raise their prices or otherwise interfere with competition. p. 581

precall planning Use of information collected during the prospecting and qualifying stages of the sales process and during previous contacts with the prospect to tailor the approach and presentation to match the customer's needs. p. 547

premium Item given free or at reduced cost with purchases of other products. p. 561

presentation Personal selling function of describing a product's major features and relating them to a customer's problems or needs. p. 547

pretesting Research that evaluates an ad during its development stage. p. 522

price Exchange value of a good or service. p. 578

price discrimination A practice in which some customers pay more than others for the same product. p. 580

price fixing A form of collusion where sellers get together and collude to set prices higher than they would otherwise be in a free market. p. 580

price flexibility Pricing policy permitting variable prices for goods and services. p. 621

pricing policy General guideline that reflects marketing objectives and influences specific pricing decisions. p. 620

pricing strategy Methods of setting profitable and justifiable prices. p. 62

primary demand Desire for a general product category. p. 472

private brand Brand offered by a wholesaler or retailer. p. 356

private carriers Transporters that provide service solely for internally generated freight. p. 410

product Bundle of physical, service, and symbolic attributes designed to satisfy a customer's wants and needs. p. 324

product advertising Non-personal selling of a particular good or service. p. 503

product development Introduction of new products into identifiable or established markets. p. 367

product differentiation When consumers regard a firm's products as different in some way from those of competitors. p. 472

product diversification strategy Developing entirely new products for new markets. p. 367

product liability Responsibility of manufacturers and marketers for injuries and damages caused by their products. p. 374

product life cycle Progression of a product through introduction, growth, maturity, and decline stages. p. 341

product line Series of related products offered by one company. p. 337

product manager Marketer within an organization who is responsible for an individual product or product line; also called a brand manager. p. 371

product mix Assortment of product lines and individual product offerings that a company sells. p. 339

product placement Form of promotion in which a marketer pays a motion picture or television program owner a fee to display a product prominently in the film or show. p. 475

product positioning Consumers' perceptions of a product's attributes, uses, quality, and advantages and disadvantages relative to competing brands. p. 367

product strategy Decisions about what goods or services a firm will offer its customers; also includes decisions about customer service, packaging, brand names, and the like. p. 61

production orientation Business philosophy stressing efficiency in producing a quality product, with the attitude toward marketing that "a good product will sell itself." p. 24

product-line pricing Practice of setting a limited number of prices for a selection of merchandise and marketing different product lines in each of these price levels. p. 621

product-related segmentation Division of a population into homogeneous groups based on their relationships to the product. p. 277

profit centre Any part of an organization to which revenue and controllable costs can be assigned. p. 626

Profit Impact of Market Strategies (PIMS) project Research that discovered a strong positive relationship between a firm's market share and product quality and its return on investment. p. 583

profit maximization Point at which the additional revenue gained by increasing the price of a product equals the increase in total costs. p. 582

promotion Communications link between buyers and sellers. Function of informing, persuading, and influencing a consumer's purchase decision. p. 61

promotional allowance Promotional incentive in which the manufacturer agrees to pay the reseller a certain amount to cover the costs of special promotional displays or extensive advertising. p. 617

promotional mix Subset of the marketing mix in which marketers attempt to achieve the optimal blending of the elements of personal and non-personal selling to achieve promotional objectives. p. 474

promotional pricing Pricing policy in which a lower than normal price is used as a temporary ingredient in a firm's marketing strategy. p. 622

prospecting Personal selling function of identifying potential customers. p. 546

protective tariffs Taxes designed to raise the retail price of an imported product to match or exceed that of a similar domestic tariff. p. 203

psychographic segmentation Division of a population into groups that have similar psychological characteristics, values, and lifestyles. p. 275

psychological pricing Pricing policy based on the belief that certain prices or price ranges make a good or service more appealing than others to buyers. p. 620

public relations Firm's communications and relationships with its various publics. p. 477

public service announcements (PSAs) Advertisements aimed at achieving socially oriented objectives by focusing on causes and charitable organizations that are included in print and electronic media without charge. p. 492

publicity Non-personal stimulation of demand for a good, service, place, idea, person, or organization by unpaid placement of significant news regarding the product in a print or broadcast medium. p. 521

pulling strategy Promotional effort by the seller to stimulate final-user demand, which then exerts pressure on the distribution channel. p. 488

pure competition Market structure characterized by homogeneous products in which there are so many buyers and sellers that none has a significant influence on price. p. 589

push money Financial incentive that gives retail salespeople cash rewards for every unit of a product they sell. p. 563

pushing strategy Promotional effort by the seller directed to members of the marketing channel rather than final users. p. 488

Q

qualifying Determining that a prospect has the needs, income, and purchase authority necessary for being a potential customer. p. 547

qualitative forecasting Use of subjective techniques to forecast sales, such as the jury of executive opinion, Delphi technique, sales force composite, and surveys of buyer intentions. p. 248

quantitative forecasting Use of statistical forecasting techniques such as trend analysis and exponential smoothing. p. 248

quantity discount Price reduction granted for a large-volume purchase. p. 617

quick-response merchandising Just-in-time strategy that reduces the time a retailer must hold merchandise in inventory, resulting in substantial cost savings. p. 306

quota sample Nonprobability sample divided to maintain the proportion of certain characteristics among different segments or groups as the population as a whole. p. 239

R

rack jobber Full-function merchant wholesaler who markets specialized lines of merchandise to retail stores. p. 443

radio frequency identification (RFID) Technology that uses a tiny chip with identification information that can be read from a distance by a scanner using radio waves. p. 405

raw materials Natural resources such as farm products, coal, copper, or lumber, which become part of a final product. p. 334

rebate Refund of a portion of the purchase price, usually granted by the product's manufacturer. p. 618

reciprocity Policy to extend purchasing preference to suppliers that are also customers. p. 180

reference groups People or institutions whose opinions are valued and to whom a person looks for guidance in his or her own behaviour, values, and conduct, such as family, friends, or celebrities. p. 135

refund Cash given back to consumers who send in proof of purchasing one or more products. p. 559

reinforcement Reduction in drive that results from a proper response. p. 145

relationship marketing Development and maintenance of long-term, cost-effective relationships with individual customers, suppliers, employees, and other partners for mutual benefit. p. 26

relationship selling Regular contacts between sales representatives and customers over an extended period to establish a sustained seller–buyer relationship. p. 541

remanufacturing Production to restore worn-out products to like-new condition. p. 185

reminder advertising Advertising that reinforces previous promotional activity by keeping the name of a good, service, organization, person, place, idea, or cause before the public. p. 503

repositioning Changing the position of a product within the minds of prospective buyers relative to the positions of competing products. p. 282

research design Master plan for conducting marketing research. p. 234

resellers Marketing intermediaries that operate in the trade sector. p. 162

response Individual's reaction to a set of cues and drives. p. 145

retail advertising Advertising by stores that sell goods or services directly to the consuming public. p. 507

retail convergence A situation in which similar merchandise is available from multiple retail outlets, resulting in the blurring of distinctions between type of retailer and merchandise offered. p. 440

retail cooperative Group of retailers that establish a shared wholesaling operation to help them compete with chains. p. 404

retailing Activities involved in selling merchandise to ultimate consumers. p. 426

revenue tariffs Taxes designed to raise funds for the importing government. p. 203

reverse channel Channel designed to return goods to their producers. p. 395

role Behaviour that members of a group expect of individuals who hold specific positions within that group. p. 135

routinized response behaviour Rapid consumer problem solving in which no new information is considered; the consumer has already set evaluative criteria and identified available options. p. 150

rule of three Three strongest, most efficient companies in an industry will dominate 70 to 90 percent of the market. p. 63

S

salary Fixed compensation payment made periodically to an employee. p. 554

sales analysis In-depth evaluation of a firm's sales. p. 234

sales force composite Qualitative sales forecasting method based on the combined sales estimates of the firm's salespeople. p. 249

sales forecast Estimate of company revenue for a specified future period. p. 247

sales incentives Programs that reward salespeople for superior performance. p. 546

sales orientation Business assumption that consumers will resist purchasing nonessential goods and services with the attitude toward marketing that only creative advertising and personal selling can overcome consumers' resistance and convince them to buy. p. 2

sales promotion Marketing activities other than personal selling, advertising, guerrilla marketing, and public relations that stimulate consumer purchasing and dealer effectiveness. p. 476, 558

sales quota Level of expected sales for a territory, product, customer, or salesperson against which actual results are compared. p. 555

sampling In marketing research, the process of selecting survey respondents or research participants; in sales promotion, free distribution of a product in an attempt to obtain future sales. p. 238

scrambled merchandising Retailing practice of combining dissimilar product lines to boost sales volume. p. 440

second mover strategy Theory that advocates observing closely the innovations of first movers and then introducing new products that improve on the original offering to gain advantage in the marketplace. p. 57

selective demand Desire for a specific brand within a product category. p. 472

selective distribution Distribution of a product through a limited number of channels. p. 399

self-concept Person's multifaceted picture of himself or herself. p. 146

seller partnership Relationship involving long-term exchanges of goods or services in return for cash or other valuable consideration. p. 146

seller's market Market in which there are more buyers for fewer goods and services. p. 25

selling agent Agent wholesaling intermediary responsible for the entire marketing program of a firm's product line. p. 445

sender Source of the message communicated to the receiver. p. 468

service Intangible activity that satisfies the needs of consumer and business users. p. 325

service encounter Point at which the customer and service provider interact. p. 336

service quality Expected and perceived quality of a service offering. p. 337

shaping Process of applying a series of rewards and reinforcements to permit more complex behaviour to evolve over time. p. 142

shopping products Products that consumers purchase after comparing competing offerings. p. 329

simple random sample Basic type of probability sample in which every individual in the relevant universe has an equal opportunity of being selected. p. 238

skimming pricing strategy Pricing strategy involving the use of a high price relative to competitive offerings. p. 610

slotting allowances Money paid by vendors to retailers to guarantee display of merchandise. p. 329

social responsibility Marketing philosophies, policies, procedures, and actions that have the enhancement of society's welfare as a primary objective. p. 111

social–cultural environment Component of the marketing environment consisting of the relationship between the marketer and society and its culture. p. 104

sole sourcing Purchasing a firm's entire stock of an item from just one vendor. p. 171

span of control The number of representatives who report to first-level sales managers. p. 553

specialty advertising Sales promotion technique that places the advertiser's name, address, and advertising message on useful articles that are then distributed to target consumers. p. 562

specialty products Products that offer unique characteristics that cause buyers to prize those particular brands. p. 329

specialty retailer Store that combines carefully defined product lines, services, and reputation to convince shoppers to spend considerable shopping effort there. p. 436

split runs Methods of testing alternative ads by dividing a cable TV audience or a publication's subscribers in two, using two different ads, and then evaluating the relative effectiveness of each. p. 523

sponsorship Event/sponsor relationship in which an organization provides funds or in-kind resources to an event or activity in exchange for a direct association with that event or activity. p. 479

spreadsheet analysis Grid that organizes information in a standardized, easily understood format. p. 76

staples Convenience goods and services that consumers constantly replenish to maintain a ready inventory. p. 328

status Relative position of any individual member in a group. p. 135

stockkeeping unit (SKU) Offering within a product line such as a specific size of liquid detergent. p. 428

straight rebuy Recurring purchase decision in which a customer repurchases a good or service that has performed satisfactorily in the past. p. 180

strategic alliance Partnership in which two or more companies combine resources and capital to create competitive advantages in a new market. p. 38

strategic business units (SBUs) Key business units within diversified firms. p. 65

strategic planning Process of determining an organization's primary objectives and adopting courses of action that will achieve these objectives. p. 51

strategic window Limited periods during which the key requirements of a market and the particular competencies of a firm best fit together. p. 59

stratified sample Probability sample constructed to represent randomly selected subsamples of different groups within the total sample; each subgroup is relatively homogeneous for a certain characteristic. p. 238

subcontracting Contractual agreements that assign the production of goods or services to local or smaller firms. p. 210

suboptimization Condition that results when individual operations achieve their objectives but interfere with progress toward broader organizational goals. p. 409

subsidy Government financial support of a private industry. p. 204

supercentre Large store, smaller than a hypermarket, that combines groceries with discount store merchandise. p. 439

supplies Regular expenses that a firm incurs in its daily operations. p. 334

supply Schedule of the amounts of a good or service that firms will offer for sale at different prices during a specified time period. p. 588

supply chain Sequence of suppliers that contribute to the creation and delivery of a good or service. p. 307

supply-chain management Control of the activities of purchasing, processing, and delivery through which raw materials are transformed into products and made available to final consumers. p. 390

survey of buyer intentions Qualitative sales forecasting method that samples opinions among groups of present and potential customers concerning their purchase intentions. p. 249

sustainable competitive advantage Superior market position that a firm possesses and can maintain for an extended period of time. p. 56

sweepstakes Sales promotional technique in which prize winners are selected by chance. p. 561

SWOT analysis Analysis that helps planners compare internal organizational strengths and weaknesses with external opportunities and threats. p. 58

syndicated service Organization that provides standardized data on a periodic basis to its subscribers. p. 232

systems integration Centralization of the procurement function within an internal division or as a service of an external supplier. p. 176

T

tactical planning Planning that guides the implementation of activities specified in the strategic plan. p. 51

target market Group of people to whom a firm decides to direct its marketing efforts and ultimately its goods and services. p. 60

target-return objectives Short-run or long-run pricing objectives of achieving a specified return on either sales or investment. p. 583

tariff Tax levied against imported goods. p. 202

task-objective method Development of a promotional budget based on evaluation of the firm's promotional objectives. p. 490

team selling Selling situation in which several sales associates or other members of the organization are recruited to assist the lead sales representative in reaching all those who influence the purchase decision. p. 544

technological environment Applications to marketing of knowledge based on discoveries in science, inventions, and innovations. p. 102

technology Business application of knowledge based on scientific discoveries, inventions, and innovations. p. 33

telemarketing Promotional presentation involving the use of the telephone on an outbound basis by salespeople or on an inbound basis by customers who initiate calls to obtain information and place orders. p. 539

test-marketing Marketing research technique that involves introducing a new product in a specific area and then measuring its degree of success. p. 244

third-party (contract) logistics firm Company that specializes in handling logistics activities for other firms. p. 408

time-based competition Strategy of developing and distributing goods and services more quickly than competitors. p. 94

total quality management (TQM) Continuous effort to improve products and work processes with the goal of achieving customer satisfaction and world-class performance. p. 336

trade allowance Special financial incentive offered to wholesalers and retailers that purchase or promote specific products. p. 562

trade discount Payment to a channel member or buyer for performing marketing functions; also known as a *functional discount*. p. 616

trade dress Visual components that contribute to the overall look of a brand. p. 363

trade industries Retailers or wholesalers that purchase products for resale to others. p. 162

trade promotion Sales promotion that appeals to marketing intermediaries rather than to consumers. p. 562

trade show Product exhibition organized by industry trade associations to showcase goods and services. p. 563

trade-in Credit allowance given for a used item when a customer purchases a new item. p. 617

trademark Brand for which the owner claims exclusive legal protection. p. 362

transaction-based marketing Buyer and seller exchanges characterized by limited communications and little or no ongoing relationships between the parties. p. 290

transfer price Cost assessed when a product is moved from one profit centre in a firm to another. p. 626

trend analysis Quantitative sales forecasting method that estimates future sales through statistical analyses of historical sales patterns. p. 250

truck wholesaler Limited-function merchant wholesaler who markets perishable food items; also called a *truck jobber*. p. 444

tying agreement Arrangement that requires a marketing intermediary to carry items other than those they want to sell. p. 400

U

undifferentiated marketing Market strategy that focuses on producing a single product and marketing it to all customers; also called *mass marketing*. p. 280

unemployment Proportion of people in the economy who are actively seeking work but do not have jobs. p. 100

uniform-delivered pricing Pricing system for handling transportation costs under which all buyers are quoted the same price, including transportation expenses. Sometimes known as *postage-stamp pricing.* p. 619

unit pricing Pricing policy in which prices are stated in terms of a recognized unit of measurement or a standard numerical count. p. 621

Universal Product Code (UPC) Numerical bar code system used to record product and price information. p. 365

unsought products Products marketed to consumers who may not yet recognize a need for them. p. 328

upstream management Controlling part of the supply chain that involves raw materials, inbound logistics, and warehouse and storage facilities. p. 405

user Individual or group that actually uses a business good or service. p. 181

utility Want-satisfying power of a good or service. p. 21

V

VALS™ Segmentation system that divides consumers into eight psychographic categories: actualizers, fulfilleds, believers, achievers, strivers, experiencers, makers, and strugglers. p. 181

value analysis Systematic study of the components of a purchase to determine the most cost-effective approach. p. 181

value pricing Pricing strategy emphasizing benefits derived from a product in comparison to the price and quality levels of competing offerings. p. 584

variable costs Costs that change with the level of production (such as labour and raw materials costs). p. 590

vendor analysis Assessment of supplier performance in areas such as price, back orders, timely delivery, and attention to special requests. p. 181

vendor-managed inventory (VMI) Inventory management system in which the seller—based on an existing agreement with a buyer—determines how much of a product is needed. p. 306

venture team Associates from different areas of an organization who work together in developing new products. p. 371

vertical marketing system (VMS) Planned channel system designed to improve distribution efficiency and cost effectiveness by integrating various functions throughout the distribution chain. p. 403

viral marketing Efforts that allow satisfied customers to spread the word about products to other consumers. p. 300

virtual sales team Network of strategic partners, trade associations, suppliers, and others who recommend a firm's goods or services. p. 544

VoIP Voice-over Internet protocol; the telephone is connected to a personal computer, allowing the user to conduct phone conversations over the Internet, rather than through telephone lines. p. 103

W

wheel of retailing Hypothesis that each new type of retailer gains a competitive foothold by offering lower prices than current suppliers charge; the result of reducing or eliminating services. p. 426

wholesaler Channel intermediary that takes title to goods it handles and then distributes these goods to retailers, other distributors, or B2B customers. p. 440

wholesaling intermediary Comprehensive term that describes wholesalers as well as agents and brokers. p. 440

wireless technology Technology that allows communications connections without wires. p. 35

World Trade Organization (WTO) Organization that replaces GATT, overseeing GATT agreements, making binding decisions in mediating disputes, and reducing trade barriers. p. 205

Y

yield management Pricing strategy that allows marketers to vary prices based on such factors as demand, even though the cost of providing those goods or services remains the same; designed to maximize revenues in situations such as airfares, lodging, auto rentals, and theatre tickets, where costs are fixed. p. 598

Z

zone pricing Pricing system for handling transportation costs under which the market is divided into geographic regions and a different price is set in each region. p. 619